CASSELL DICTIONARY OF Modern Politics

CASSELL DICTIONARY OF
Modern Politics

CIRCA
Research & Reference Information

CASSELL

Cassell Publishers Limited
Villiers House
41/47 Strand
London WC2N 5JE
England

First published 1994

Distributed in the United States
by Sterling Publishing Co., Inc.
387 Park Avenue South, New York, New York 10016-8810

Distributed in Australia
by Capricorn Link (Australia) Pty Ltd
2/13 Carrington Road, Castle Hill, NSW 2154

British Library Cataloguing-in-Publication Data
A catalogue record for this book is available from the British Library

ISBN 0-304-34432-X

Compiled and typeset by CIRCA Research and Reference Information Ltd, Cambridge

Printed and bound in Great Britain by Mackays of Chatham PLC, Chatham, Kent

CONTENTS

INTRODUCTION

This is a dictionary of terms in the broadest sense, whether they are the abbreviations so commonly bandied about, concepts in political science, jargon words, or key events and scandals whose names have become part of the language of international politics. Its coverage is worldwide for the period 1945 to mid-1994, and consequently it includes entries for the countries whose names have entered the language during that period. This is not a biographical dictionary – which would require a separate volume in itself – but the biographical index does provide another route into the web of entries associated with particular individuals.

Within the limits of a single volume, we have tried to include as many current terms as possible, concentrating on those which users are most likely to encounter. Inevitably there will be omissions, for which we apologise. The great majority of terms are in the English language, but we have included a number of foreign words, either where these are generally used for the names of institutions (such as **Bundesbank** or **Knesset**) or where the foreign language term is more familiar than any English translation (such as **force de frappe** or **perestroika**).

Cross-references are indicated by the use of **bold** typeface. Entries for organizations are found under their acronyms. Where the headword or its initial element is a numeral, as in **38th parallel** or **1968**, the entry can be found in the alphabetical sequence (under 'thirty' or 'nineteen' in these examples).

Roger East
Tanya Joseph
Cambridge, July 1994

EDITORS

Roger East is a founder member of CIRCA. He is the editor of *Keesing's Record of World Events,* author of *Revolutions in Eastern Europe* and co-author of *From the Six to the Twelve: The Enlargement of the European Communities.* He has edited or co-edited numerous reference works including *The World Development Directory* and several volumes on political parties.

Tanya Joseph is a regional editor for CIRCA and has written extensively on southern Africa. She has contributed to several books including *The World's News Media* and *Political Parties of Asia and the Pacific,* and is a major contributor to *Political Parties of Africa and the Middle East.*

CONTRIBUTORS

John Coggins is a regional editor for CIRCA. He is a contributor to *Trade Unions of the World* and joint editor of *Political Parties of the Americas and the Caribbean.*

Robert Fraser is consulting editor of *Keesing's Record of World Events* and editor of *Keesing's UK Record.* He is the author of *The World Financial System,* co-author of *Privatization: the UK Experience and International Trends* and editor of *Western European Economic Organizations* and of *The World Trade System.*

D. S. Lewis is a regional editor for CIRCA and has contributed to numerous books. He is the author of *Illusions of Grandeur,* editor of *Korea: Enduring Division,* and joint editor of *Political Parties of Asia and the Pacific* and *Political Parties of the Americas and Caribbean.*

Jolyon Pontin is a regional editor for CIRCA, specializing in the politics of Central and Eastern Europe and the CIS.

D. J. Sagar is a regional editor for CIRCA and has contributed to many books. He is the author of *Major Political Events in Indo-China 1945–1990*, joint editor of *Political Parties of Asia and the Pacific* and a major contributor to *Cambodia: A Matter of Survival*.

Farzana Shaikh is a regional editor for CIRCA. She has written on Indian Islam, is author of *Community and Consensus in Islam: Muslim Representation in Colonial India, 1860–1947* and edited *Islam and Islamic Groups*.

Wendy Slater worked as a CIRCA regional editor before serving as a research analyst for the Radio Free Europe / Radio Liberty Research Institute. She has contributed to several publications as a freelance writer, and is currently studying for a Ph.D. at Cambridge University.

CIRCA Research and Reference Information Ltd specializes in reference works on international politics and current affairs, producing a variety of books, periodicals, ad hoc reports and electronic data. CIRCA is responsible for researching, writing and editing the long-established monthly *Keesing's Record of World Events*, and is also the publisher of the bi-monthly *People in Power* and *Keesing's UK Record*.

THE DICTIONARY

AAM

The Anti-**Apartheid** Movement, a British organization founded in 1959 to raise awareness of apartheid. Sympathetic to the **ANC**, it brought together South African exiles and British activists. It played a key role in campaigns to implement and maintain the sports, cultural and economic boycott of South Africa, including the particularly successful campaign against South African fruit. It also organized demonstrations and street protests in the UK, lobbied parliament and sought to attract media attention to events in South Africa. One of its most successful campaigns was that in 1988 to mark the 70th birthday of the then imprisoned Nelson Mandela, which culminated in a mass rally in London's Hyde Park attended by an estimated 200,000 people. Following the ending of apartheid, AAM decided on 25 June 1994 to transform itself into a solidarity organization for the 11 countries of southern Africa (Angola, **Botswana**, **Lesotho**, Mozambique, **Namibia**, **Swaziland**, **Tanzania**, **Zambia**, **Zimbabwe** and South Africa). The new organization was expected to be launched in October 1994.

ABDULGATE *see* ABSCAM

ABERFAN

A village in South Wales, scene of a coalmining landslip disaster in October 1966. Around 150 children and some of their teachers died when an avalanche of waste, rocks and sludge slid down from a spoil tip and engulfed their primary school. An inquiry report published the following August placed blame for the disaster on the National Coal Board, which was criticized for its total lack of a tipping policy.

ABKHAZIA

The region in northern **Georgia** which has been the site of a civil war since 1992. Although ethnic Abkhaz form only 17.8 per cent of the population of Abkhazia, the Abkhaz legislature declared sovereignty in July 1992, and fighting broke out the following month. Georgian leader Eduard Shevardnadze accused Russia of assisting the Abkhaz rebels in the subsequent civil war. Georgian troops were driven from Abkhazia in August 1993. In February 1994 the legislature declared independence, but without any international recognition.

ABM

Anti-ballistic missile systems, whose development by both the USA and the **Soviet Union** during the 1960s gave new complexity to their nuclear **deterrence** strategies. If one side launched a first strike nuclear missile attack, an effective ABM defence system would bring down some or all of the attacking missiles. This would lend more credibility to the other side's 'second-strike' retaliation capability (also fostered by keeping missiles in hardened silos or on submarines and airborne bombers). If one side had sufficient confidence in its ABM systems, however, it might be more prone to use its own nuclear weapons, undeterred by the fear of mutually assured destruction (**MAD**). Acknowledging this apparent paradox – that ABM systems could fuel the **arms race** and destabilize the deterrence equation – the USA and the Soviet Union devoted much attention in their first round of **SALT** talks (1969–72) to limiting ABM development. The ABM Treaty of May 1972 restricted each side to one land-based ABM system to defend its capital city and one to defend one missile site. One of the few achievements of the bilateral **arms control** process in this period, the ABM Treaty was subsequently threatened by the US Strategic Defence Initiative (**SDI**) which, if successful, would render land-based ABM systems obsolete.

ABORIGINAL RIGHTS

The rights of the native inhabitants of a country. For the Aborigines of Australia, white settlement meant the annexation of tribal lands, discriminatory legislation, the introduction of infectious diseases, the depletion of food crops, and widespread extermination; they now number some 300,000 of a population totalling 17.6 million. Aboriginal land rights campaigners, however, have now successfully challenged the long-established principle of *terra nullius*, whereby white settlers had claimed that the land belonged to no-one before their arrival. On 22 December 1993 the Australian federal Parliament approved legislation recognizing native title to land and thus negating the *terra nullius* principle.

ABORTION ACT

The 1967 basis for the general legalization of abortion in **Great Britain**. Sponsored by the then Liberal MP David Steel, this act, which came into force in April 1968, effectively permitted the termination of pregnancy within 28 weeks, under given conditions and subject to certain safeguards. A major attempt was made through the unsuccessful **Alton Bill** in 1988 to reduce the limit to 18 weeks, while the Human Fertilization and Embryology Act 1990 set a general 24-week limit but provided for a number of exceptions. In the USA abortion legislation depends upon a series of state laws, while the federal position is still generally governed by the 1973 landmark Supreme Court ruling in the **Roe v. Wade** case.

ABRI

The *Angkatan Bersenjata Republik Indonesia*, the Indonesian armed forces.

ABSCAM

The commonly used name for a bribery scandal or 'scam' involving seven members of the US **Congress**, and several state officials from Pennsylvania and New Jersey. Abscam, and the alternative term 'Abdulgate', were both words derived from Abdul Enterprises Ltd, the name of the fictitious company created by the **FBI**, which lay at the centre of the 1978–80 undercover operation. Posing as representatives of Abdul Enterprises, FBI agents gathered evidence against public officials who were prepared to exert improper influence on behalf of the company in return for bribes. The FBI recorded secretly on videotape the behaviour of the congressmen when offered large sums of money. Eight congressmen were originally named when the investigation became public on 2 February 1980, and all were Democrats apart from Richard Kelly (Florida). They included one Senator: Harrison A. Williams Jr of New Jersey. One of the eight, John P. Murtha (Pennsylvania), was not prosecuted and gave evidence against two of his colleagues. Despite attempting to use the defence of 'entrapment', the remaining seven were all convicted, although Kelly's conviction was quashed on appeal in 1982. All resigned their seats in the legislature.

ABU MUSA

The largest of three islands which are the subject of dispute between Iran and the United Arab Emirates (**UAE**). Strategically situated at the entrance to the Persian **Gulf**, the three islands were ruled by the emirate of Sharjah until the creation of the UAE in 1971. The Iranian and UAE governments then concluded an agreement allowing Iran to station troops on Abu Musa, which was administered jointly by Iran and the UAE, with offshore oil revenue shared by the two countries. In April 1992, Iranian troops moved from their base on the island to take control of civilian installations. A year later Iran passed legislation extending Iranian territorial waters, placing Abu Musa well inside them.

ABU NIDAL

Codename of the radical Palestinian leader Sabri Khalil al-Banna, commander of the notorious Revolutionary Council of Fatah (RCF, more commonly known as the Abu Nidal Group). Abu Nidal, perhaps the world's most feared and elusive terrorist, was born in the 1930s in Jaffa. He joined Yassir Arafat's **al-Fatah** in the 1950s, but broke away in 1973 to form his own faction. In his most notorious operation, in 1985, Abu Nidal organized brutal attacks on civilians at Rome and Vienna airports. He has also been accused of involvement in the bombing of Pan Am Flight 103 over **Lockerbie**, Scotland, in 1988, in which 270 people died. Not surprisingly, Abu Nidal's activities have been condemned repeatedly by the mainstream **PLO** factions. He is believed to have been based in Iraq since his expulsion from Syria and Libya in the late 1980s.

ACCT

The *Agence de Coopération Culturelle et Technique,* created in 1970 to co-ordinate action among the francophone countries in the cultural, educational and technological fields, and also responsible for implementing an aid programme. The ACCT plays a role in planning francophone summits (held biennially since 1987), and could become the permanent secretariat of a future francophone commonwealth.

ACHILLE LAURO

An Italian cruise liner hijacked by Palestinian **guerrillas** in October 1985. The liner, travelling from Alexandria to Port Said (both in Egypt), was hijacked by members of the Palestinian Liberation Front (PLF, a constituent member of the **PLO**) who demanded the release of 50 Palestinian prisoners from **Israel**. The guerrillas shot dead a Jewish American passenger, Leon Klinghoffer, before surrendering in Egypt to PLO officials (the PLO having condemned the action and promised to try the hijackers). However, their flight from Egypt to the PLO headquarters in Tunis was intercepted by US fighter planes and the hijackers were taken to Italy where they were tried and convicted in July 1986. Mahmoud Abul Abbas, the PLF leader, was inexplicably released before trial, a move which led to the resignation of the Italian government; he was sentenced in absentia to life imprisonment.

ACID RAIN

A damaging consequence of air pollution, the excessive acidity of rain or snow which can destroy forests, damage crops, upset the chemical balance of lakes and rivers, and corrode buildings. Acid rain contains sulphuric and nitric acid, formed from airborne pollutants which are mainly the emissions of sulphur dioxide and nitrogen oxides from power stations burning **fossil fuel**. Although acid rain is a localized phenomenon, it can be caused by pollutants emitted hundreds of miles away. Accordingly, it has been a focus for efforts to reach international agreements to tackle **transboundary pollution**. The first of these was the 1972 Geneva Convention on Long Range Transport of Air Pollutants signed by 33 countries.

ACLU

The American Civil Liberties Union, one of the most powerful liberal pressure groups in the USA. While generally seeking to protect **civil rights** against the incursion of the state, the ACLU has been particularly active in opposing capital punishment and campaigning to strengthen the rights of accused persons.

ACP

The 68 African, **Caribbean** and Pacific countries, which have a set of special trade, aid and general economic relationships with the European Union (**EU**). The starting point for this was France's desire to maintain trading links with its former colonies. The system was first built up in the 1960s under the **Yaoundé Conventions** (1963 and 1969), and has been developed since then under four successive **Lomé Conventions**. With the expansion of the **EEC** in the 1970s came the inclusion of former British (and then Portuguese) colonies. Separate arrangements outside the ACP structure were made with British **Commonwealth** countries in Asia and with **Latin America**.

In material terms the most important supposed benefits for ACP countries are aid under the European Development Fund (**EDF**), European investment lending, and a scheme known as **Stabex** under which they are compensated for any dramatic fall in their earnings from commodity exports.

ACQUIS COMMUNAUTAIRE

(French, 'the community's attainments') The corpus of existing laws and regulations applied collectively by member states of the European Union (**EU**) at any given time, either generally or in a specific field of activity. New members are required to accept the *acquis communautaire* upon accession, and to arrange its incorporation within their own national laws and regulations, except where they are granted specific **derogations** or transitional arrangements. In preparation for the creation of the European Economic Area (**EEA**) embracing the 12 EU countries and five of the **EFTA** countries from January 1994, the EFTA participants had to pass some 1,500 laws through their national legislatures in order to adopt the *acquis communautaire* in the relevant fields.

ACTION DIRECTE

(French, 'Direct action') A **left-wing** French revolutionary group formed in 1979 and responsible for numerous bombings and assassinations during the 1980s. Two theoretical statements justifying AD's actions issued in 1982 were entitled 'On American Imperialism' and 'For a **communist** Project'. Outlawed on 18 August 1982, AD had links with other European **left-wing** extremist groups, including the German **Rote Armee Fraktion**, the Italian **Brigate Rosse** and the Basque separatists **ETA**; in 1985 it announced plans for joint attacks with the RAF against the 'multinational structures of **NATO**'. AD was severely weakened by the arrest of its leading activists in 1987 and 1989.

ADB

1. The African Development Bank, the Abidjan-based regional bank set up in 1964 to contribute to the economic development and social advancement of member countries. It mobilizes funds to promote private and public capital investment, and provides technical assistance. All African states (except South Africa) are members. Member countries subscribe to the bank's capital stock, according to their population, **GNP**, foreign trade and government revenue. Although membership was initially restricted to African states, since the end of 1982 non-African countries have also been able to join, and thus to increase the ADB's capital. As of early 1994 there were 26 non-African, mainly Arab, members, but African states continue to hold two-thirds of the share capital.

2. The Asian Development Bank, the Manila-based regional development bank for the Asia and the Pacific. Established under the auspices of ESCAP in 1966, the Bank's 56 members comprise 40 'regional' countries of Asia and the Pacific and 16 'non-regional' countries of western Europe and north America. Each member country appoints a governor and an alternate who combine to form the Board of Governors, which in turn selects a 12-member operating Board of Directors. The Bank aims to foster economic growth within the region by administering direct loans or technical assistance to members. In recent years the emphasis has shifted away from the financing of infrastructural projects (an area increasingly dominated by the private sector) towards general 'policy advice' to governments.

ADEN

The Yemeni city and port situated on the Gulf of Aden. Aden was occupied by Great Britain in 1839 to provide a chandling station on the vital route to India. In 1937 the city became a Crown Colony and the Yemeni interior a Protectorate, where tribal leaders retained nominal authority. Aden was amalgamated with the Protectorate in 1963 to form the Federation of South Arabia. The last British troops withdrew in late 1967 and the independent People's Democratic Republic of **Yemen** (South Yemen) was proclaimed with Aden as its capital. With the unification of South and North Yemen in May 1990, Sana'a became the national capital, although Aden remained the country's commercial centre. The union collapsed into civil war in May 1994 and, with Aden under virtual siege from the North, the South seceded.

AFARS AND ISSAS *see* DJIBOUTI

AFFIRMATIVE ACTION

Policies designed to promote the incorporation of minority or disadvantaged groups (e.g. ethnic minorities, women) into political, social and economic institutions, and to promote equality of employment opportunity. The term was first used in the 1960s in the USA, when Presidents John F. Kennedy and Lyndon B. Johnson ordered contractors to 'act affirmatively' to employ workers without discrimination. Affirmative action, which is often regarded as synonymous with positive discrimination, ranges from assessing positively a member of a disadvantaged group to stipulating quotas for the employment of members of such groups, with the aim of correcting historical imbalances which have resulted from discrimination.

AFGHAN WAR

The civil war in Afghanistan, which began in 1978 and in which Soviet troops were heavily involved from December 1979 until February 1989. In the face of an insurrection by **mujaheddin** rebels, Afghanistan's vulnerable pro-Soviet government in 1979 requested, and was thereafter propped up by, the Soviet intervention. This attracted a storm of criticism worldwide; moreover, the operation proved disastrous. The rebels were well armed by the **West** and their **guerrilla** tactics suited Afghanistan's mountainous terrain. The eventual withdrawal of Soviet forces was regarded as a humiliation comparable with the USA's defeat in the **Vietnam War**. Soviet losses in Afghanistan were estimated by the US **State Department** at some 15,000 men; over a million Afghans had lost their lives. The rebels toppled the Afghan government in February 1992, but fighting between rival rebel factions continues and Afghanistan remains unstable.

AFL / CIO

The American Federation of Labor and Congress of Industrial Organizations. An umbrella organization for US trades unions, the AFL/CIO was formed in 1955 by the amalgamation of the AFL, which represented craft unions, and the CIO, which represented unions in industry. Rather than acting for its members in labour negotiations, the AFL / CIO functions as a general pressure group on behalf of US labour. It was influential in the enactment of the 1964 **Civil Rights** Act and the 1965 Voting Rights Act, and also in the introduction of **Medicare**. The political influence of the AFL / CIO has declined in recent years, however, with the overall fall in union membership which in 1990 comprised only 16 per cent of the workforce. In contrast with the UK, where a close relationship still exists between the Labour Party and organized labour, the AFL / CIO no longer has a strong affiliation with the Democratic Party.

AFRICA WATCH *see* HUMAN RIGHTS WATCH

AFRICAN DEVELOPMENT BANK *see* ADB

AFRICAN HUMANISM

A version of **African socialism** expounded by President Kenneth Kaunda of **Zambia**. It was designed to give direction to the newly independent country and was based on Kaunda's view that 'the high valuation of man and respect for human dignity which is a legacy of our tradition should not be lost in the new Africa'.

AFRICAN SOCIALISM

A political ideology developed in the 1950s by African nationalists. Although a relatively nebulous term with no theoretical framework, African socialism generally seeks to combine certain features of African traditional societies with **socialist** concepts. These characteristics include land ownership, the extended family and kinship relationships and the concept of sharing, as well as an emphasis on co-operation rather than competition and on the group rather than the individual. Attempting to achieve socialism in the African context, African socialists tend to reject calls for class struggle, atheism and dictatorship of the proletariat, asserting that socialism can be built on a peasant base. The ideology is most closely associated with Léopold

Senghor of Senegal, Tanzania's Julius Nyerere, who incorporated it into his philosophy of **ujamaa**, and Kenneth Kaunda of Zambia, whose **African Humanism** was greatly influenced by it.

AFRIKANER

(Dutch, 'African') A South African white who speaks Afrikaans – a language derived from Dutch, and who is descended from settlers of Dutch-German-French origin who began to arrive in the Cape in the mid-seventeenth century. Afrikaners, also known as *Boers* (Dutch 'farmers'), constitute about 60 per cent of the white population, but only 8.4 per cent of the total population. Nevertheless, until the recent dismantling of the **apartheid** system, Afrikaners had for half a century controlled the country politically, dominating the National Party which ruled continuously from 1948 until the April 1994 non-racial democratic elections. However, economic power is largely in the hands of English-speaking whites, who regard themselves as more liberal than Afrikaners.

AFRIKANER BROEDERBOND *see* BROEDERBOND

AFTA

The Asean Free Trade Area. In January 1993 the six **ASEAN** countries implemented a Common Effective Preferential Tariff scheme aimed at creating AFTA in 2008. Under the terms of the scheme, intra-regional tariffs on all manufactured (but not agricultural) goods would be reduced to a maximum of 5 per cent by the target date.

AGENDA 21

A 'blueprint for action' adopted at the 1992 **Earth Summit** in Rio, setting out the measures which governments, **UN** organizations, development agencies and other bodies need to take in order to ensure **sustainable development** and the reversal of environmental degradation. Agenda 21 aims to provide a framework within which these objectives may be accomplished, although its recommendations are not binding.

AGENT ORANGE

The notorious herbicide used by the US military machine in Vietnam in the 1960s and 1970s; its active ingredient **245-T** was also used in commercial weedkillers. During the **Vietnam War** some 44 million litres of Agent Orange (in addition to 20 million litres of Agent White and Agent Blue) were sprayed by US forces over 1.7 million hectares of cropland, forests and wooded areas in South Vietnam to defoliate areas of enemy operation. The US **ecocide** in Vietnam had a lasting impact on the country's agricultural development, with vast tracts of land remaining barren in the early 1990s. Agent Orange is also blamed for serious damage to health caused by the presence of **dioxin** contamination. Numerous Vietnamese women have had histories of repeated miscarriage as a result of direct exposure to Agent Orange, while others have given birth to children with dreadful physical or mental afflictions. In the mid-1980s US chemical manufacturers, while denying liability in the matter, agreed to establish a fund for US Vietnam veterans who had claimed health damage from exposure to Agent Orange.

AGR

The Advanced Gas-cooled Reactor, a British-designed type of nuclear reactor which uses for fuel enriched uranium containing 2 per cent of fissile uranium-235. AGRs constituted the second generation of reactors in the UK nuclear energy programme and, being able to operate at higher temperatures, they doubled the capacity of the first-generation **Magnox** reactors. The plan to build AGRs was announced in 1964, but owing to delays from parliamentary and government enquiries and numerous design and costing problems the first AGRs came into operation only in 1976. In subsequent years AGRs were touted as less susceptible to cooling failure than the competing **PWR** design.

AGRARIAN PARTIES

Political parties representing agricultural producers and rural society which emerged from the farmers' associations disillusioned with traditional urban-led parties. Agrarian parties have been influential in North America and Central and **Eastern Europe** during the twentieth century. In the postwar period they have also been influential in **Scandinavia** and Finland where, in the late 1950s and 1960s, the Agrarian Parties founded at the beginning of the century renamed themselves 'Centre Parties' in an attempt to recruit non-rural support.

AID

Assistance in the form of money, **food aid**, goods or training and other services. Foreign aid, which may be in grants or loans on favourable terms, is provided bilaterally by the government of one country to another, sometimes as **tied aid**, or multilaterally through such institutions as regional development banks and the International Development Association (**IDA**). It may be in the form of programme aid in support of a range of activities by the recipient government; it may be more directly project-related; or for disaster relief. The term 'aid' is generally no longer used to include military assistance, and is usually now associated with economic assistance to less developed countries (**LDCs**). Aid also includes actions through non-governmental **NGO** channels, and is a much vaguer term than **ODA**, official development assistance, which can be quantified by donor countries in relation to a **UN** target figure.

AIDS

Acquired Immune Deficiency Syndrome, a fatal disease attacking the human immune system as a result of infection by the human immunodeficiency virus (**HIV**). First identified in the early 1980s, the HIV virus is transmitted in body fluids, primarily by sexual activity but also among intravenous drug users and when infected blood is given in transfusions, notably to haemophiliacs. The World Health Organization (**WHO**) estimated that some 15 million people worldwide were HIV-positive by the end of 1993. Officially declared AIDS cases in mid-1993 stood at over 700,000, with the highest number registered in the USA, but in reality there were known to be at least 2.5 million AIDS cases worldwide, three-quarters of them in Africa, where the disease has spread more rapidly than in any other region. There is as yet no known cure.

AIPAC

The American Israel Public Affairs Committee, **Israel's** official lobbying arm in the USA and as such part of the influential US **Jewish lobby**. The AIPAC is based in Washington DC and concerns itself with legislation and government policy affecting US-Israeli relations.

AIR EXCLUSION ZONE *see* NO-FLY ZONE

AIRBUS INDUSTRIE

The European aircraft consortium, which brings together manufacturers in France, Germany, Spain and the UK. The Airbus project began in the 1960s as a Franco-German initiative. As of 1994 the company produced seven different models (300, 310, 319, 320, 321, 330 and 340) with the French generally manufacturing the front sections of the fuselage, the Germans the bulk of the fuselage, the Spanish the tail and British Aerospace (the UK partner with a 20 per cent stake in the company) the wings; engines are supplied by a variety of producers. In the first half of 1994 Airbus received 69 orders, more than its total in 1993, and with 55 per cent of all orders in the 100-plus seat market it outstripped the US companies Boeing and McDonnell Douglas.

AK-47

An automatic or semi-automatic assault rifle most closely associated with **guerrillas** and terrorist organizations. The weapon, also known by the name of its designer, Mikhail Timofeyevich Kalashnikov, went into production in the **Soviet Union** in 1947. The design specification was passed on to China and to Soviet allies in the **Warsaw Pact** and the weapon itself supplied to pro-Soviet guerrilla groups. Consequently the rifle, capable of firing 600 rounds per minute, is notoriously cheap and widely available – an estimated 50 million have been made.

AKALI DAL

The supreme political organization of the Indian Sikh community, concentrated mainly in the province of Punjab. Founded in December 1920 to promote and preserve Sikh religious practices, it evolved during the 1970s as the chief advocate of Sikh political autonomy and, more recently, of a separate Punjabi state of **Khalistan**. By the early 1980s the party was under the control of militant factions who in June 1984 occupied the **Golden Temple** in Amritsar; hundreds were killed after government troops were ordered to storm the temple. In early 1991 moderate and extremist factions united to form the *Shiromani Akali Dal.*

ALADI

The **Latin American** Integration Association, founded in August 1980 to promote regional integration, development and trade. Replacing the Latin American Free Trade Association (LAFTA), it hoped to overcome problems of economic disparity and uneven development which had dogged LAFTA's 20-year existence. Under ALADI terms member countries were classified according to their stage of development, with poorer countries being given preference. Its members are Bolivia, Ecuador and Paraguay (all classified as less developed), Chile, Colombia, Peru, Uruguay and Venezuela (medium-developed), and Argentina, Brazil and Mexico (more developed).

ALAWI

(Arabic, 'of Ali') An Islamic sub-sect signifying followers of the Caliph Ali, revered by **Shias**, who also share a common ethnic background. Alawis are prominent in Syria, but are also present in Lebanon and Turkey where they are called Alevis. While their total numbers worldwide exceed no more than a few hundred thousand, their historical role has been underlined by frequent attempts to establish an Alawi state, especially in Syria where they form about 10 per cent of a predominantly **Sunni** population. These efforts were rewarded when after a series of coup d'états in the early 1960s, the Alawis gained control of Syria through the **Ba'ath** Party. In 1970 they backed a military coup led by the current President, Lt.-Gen. Hafez al-Assad, which has given them economic and political power ever since.

ALDERMASTON

The site of the UK Atomic Weapons Research Establishment. Between 1958 and 1963 the anti-nuclear campaign group **CND** organized annual four-day marches between London and Aldermaston The first demonstration began in London, while in subsequent years the march ended in a mass rally in Trafalgar Square.

ALFARO VIVE, CARAJO!

(Spanish, 'Alfaro Lives, Dammit!') Ecuadorean **left-wing** nationalist **guerrilla** group named in memory of Gen. Eloy Alfaro, President of Ecuador (in 1895–1901 and 1906–11), an anti-clerical social and economic reformer and leader of the 1895 Liberal Revolution. Founded in the late 1970s, the group only began its armed struggle after the Democratic Left (ID) party, to which it offered support, marginally lost the 1984 presidential election. In 1985–86 the group formed the America Battalion, a short-lived guerrilla version of the **Socialist International**, with the Colombian **M-19**, the Peruvian Tupac Amarú Revolutionary Movement (MRTA) and other unspecified groups from Bolivia, El Salvador, Nicaragua, Panama and Venezuela. In 1986 *Alfaro Vive* split, the bulk disarming in October 1991, and most members joined the ID. One small faction which refused to surrender finally joined 'political and civilian life' in January 1993. Another splinter-group, the Montoneros Free Fatherland, remains active.

AL-FATAH

(Arabic, reversed acronym of the organization's title, *Tahir al-Hatani al Falastani,* 'Movement for the National Liberation of Palestine') The principal mainstream component of the **PLO**, formed by Yassir Arafat and other Palestinian students in 1958. The group's *fedayeen* (**guerrilla**) forces began raids into **Israel** in 1965 (from Jordan and Syria), but went on to play little part in the 1967 or 1973 Arab-Israeli wars. *Al-Fatah* gained virtual control of the PLO's executive committee in 1969 before suffering a serious setback in the early 1970s when its forces were driven from Jordan into Syria and Lebanon. From its southern Lebanese base (known as 'Fatahland'), *Al-Fatah* continued to conduct guerrilla raids into Israel, but by the early 1970s the group encompassed a broad spectrum within its membership, including a majority of 'moderates'. The enforced Palestinian evacuation of Beirut in 1982 weakened *Al-Fatah's* control of the PLO policy line and led to growing support for the **rejectionist** camp.

In the late 1980s and early 1990s *Al-Fatah* played a key role in the organization of the Palestinian **intifada** in the **Israeli-occupied territories**, although the group's secular nationalist approach faced radical opposition in the form of the militant Islamic **Hamas**. At the same time, the group propelled the PLO towards peace negotiations with Israel and the eventual signing of the **Gaza-Jericho First** deal in September 1993.

ALGÉRIE FRANÇAISE

(French, 'French Algeria') The rallying cry during the Algerian war of independence (1954–62) of those who wanted to preserve French rule in Algeria. Its main advocates were **right-wingers** in metropolitan France and European settlers in the French colony of Algeria, the 1 million so-called '**pieds noirs**'. Gen. Charles de Gaulle, propelled back to power in France in 1958 by a government crisis over Algerian policy, announced in September 1959 that he would recognize Algeria's right to self-determination. He won backing in a referendum in January 1961, but enraged the proponents of *Algérie française*, prompting **OAS** terrorism and the generals' coup attempt of April 1961.

AL-JIHAD *see* JIHAD

AL-JIHAD AL-ISLAMI *see* ISLAMIC JIHAD

ALL INDIA MUSLIM LEAGUE

The political organization which spearheaded the movement leading to the creation in August 1947 of the Muslim state of **Pakistan** following the **partition** of India. It was founded in December 1906 by a group of feudal and aristocratic Muslims anxious to protect the political interests of the Muslim minority in British India who, they claimed, were inadequately represented by the dominant nationalist movement, the Indian National Congress. The party's subsequent transformation into a mass movement and its campaign for separate Muslim statehood is generally attributed to Mohammad Ali Jinnah (1876-1948) who was to become Pakistan's first head of state.

ALLIANCE FOR PROGRESS

A US-led economic and social reform initiative for **Latin America** launched by President John F. Kennedy and primarily intended to neutralize the perceived threat to the region posed by the Cuban revolution. Established in Punta del Este, Uruguay, on 17 August 1961 as a 10-year US$20,000 million programme, it was signed by members of the Inter-American Economic and Social Council of the **OAS** with the exception of Cuba, and offered assistance to countries whose ruling conservative elites accepted the need for urgent land and tax reforms. Other associated targets obliged governments to set basic levels for schooling, literacy, home construction and health provision.

In the absence of even mild reforms, especially land redistribution, the objective of the Alliance shifted to the modernization of economies geared to export-led agriculture and commodity markets. This suited large capital, especially US investment, but aggravated the problems of landlessness and unemployment, leading to rural exodus and the exacerbation of urban social problems.

ALLIED RAPID REACTION CORPS

One of the products of **NATO's** re-examination of its role in the 1990s after the end of the **Cold War**. The new mixed-nationality 'corps-sized' formation, made up of units from different European NATO members, based in Germany and under UK command, was agreed in May 1991 and inaugurated in October 1922, and was expected to be operational by the end of 1994.

There would also be a small Immediate Reaction Force, based on NATO's existing Mobile Force. The primary purpose was to ensure that troops were held ready to respond if a member state's security were threatened, but the possibility existed that NATO members would agree to the corps being used for specific 'out-of-area' actions, under the auspices of the **WEU** or, prospectively, the **EU**.

ALLIES

A general term, used in the pre- and immediate post-1945 period for the countries which emerged victorious in the Second World War, defeating the Axis Powers (Italy, Germany and Japan). However, the **Cold War** soon divided the **Soviet Union** from the **Western Allies**, while the differently configured Atlantic Alliance also took shape, with Italy as a founder member of **NATO** and West Germany joining in 1955.

ALPHA 66

A paramilitary group of **anti-Castroites** based in Miami. The group was formed in 1962 after the failed US-sponsored **Bay of Pigs** invasion and was named after its 66 founder members.

ALTON BILL

An attempt to restrict the availability of abortion in the UK. David Alton, a Liberal (and subsequently Liberal Democratic) MP, introduced a bill in the UK House of Commons to limit to 18 weeks the then current 28-week period within which abortions might legally be performed in Great Britain under the 1967 **Abortion Act**. Although the Abortion (Amendment) Bill received a relatively narrow majority on its second reading on 22 January 1988, it failed to complete its remaining stages in parliament.

ALVOR AGREEMENT

The agreement between Portugal and the three main Angolan nationalist organizations (the Popular Movement for the Liberation of Angola, the National Front for the Liberation of Angola and **UNITA**) defining the basic principles of government in the run-up to independence. The agreement, signed at Alvor, Portugal, on 15 January 1975, provided for a ceasefire in the liberation war and for the establishment of a coalition transitional government. It also set the date for independence, and guaranteed the integrity of the **Caprivi Strip** as part of Angola. The agreement was suspended by Portugal in August 1975 after it became clear that fighting between the three nationalist groups had not ended.

AL-ZULFIQAR

(Arabic, 'the sword') An underground Pakistani organization committed to the overthrow of Gen. Zia's military regime and to avenging the 1979 hanging of former Prime Minister Zulfiqar Ali Bhutto. Founded by Bhutto's son Murtaza, the group was directed mainly from Syria, where Murtaza had sought asylum after fleeing Pakistan in 1977. Al-Zulfiqar was implicated in the March 1981 hijacking of a Pakistani airliner to Afghanistan, and several later attacks. Murtaza Bhutto, whose estranged sister Benazir later became Prime Minister, eventually returned to Pakistan in November 1993 after being elected in absentia as a member of the Sind provincial assembly, but still faced terrorist and murder charges.

AMAL

(Arabic, 'hope') A group established in the 1970s as a military and political vehicle for Lebanon's **Shia** community. Amal's founder Musa Sadr 'disappeared' in 1978 during a trip to Libya, and the leadership passed to lawyer Nabi Berri. Amal fought hard against the **Israeli** forces which invaded Lebanon in 1982; it is an indication of the labyrinthine nature of Lebanese politics that in the mid-1980s Amal went on to wage equally intense warfare against the **PLO**. Under Berri's leadership Amal became the mainstream Shia organization in the late 1980s, and lost considerable support to the more militant Iranian-backed **Hezbollah**. With the end of the Lebanese civil war in 1990 Amal comfortably made the transition from militia to political party, and, along with other Shia groups, it controls one of the largest blocs in the legislature.

AMAZON PACT

Officially the Amazon Co-operation Treaty, signed in July 1978 by Bolivia, Brazil, Colombia, Ecuador, Guyana, Peru, **Surinam** and Venezuela, with the primary objective of preserving the delicate ecological balance of the Amazon region. This was to be achieved by the rational use of natural resources, increased scientific and technical co-operation, co-ordination of efforts to fight endemic diseases and the creation of adequate means of transport and communications. Ominously, the treaty safeguards the rights of member countries to exploit their territories economically, provided that this does not infringe those of other signatories.

AMERICAS WATCH *see* HUMAN RIGHTS WATCH

AMF

The Arab Monetary Fund, established in 1976 to provide economic assistance to members of the **Arab League**. Based in Abu Dhabi, it generally provides short- and medium-term loans for countries experiencing balance-of-payments difficulties.

AMIR

(Arabic, 'commander') Traditionally a military title, it currently signifies a princely ruler or head of state of a Muslim country. Its use as a title is common in the **Middle East**, especially in the Gulf states. It is also occasionally adopted by leaders of Muslim religious parties in some parts of Asia.

AMNESTY INTERNATIONAL

The human rights organization founded in 1961 by two London-based lawyers, Peter Benenson and Sean MacBrideKropotkin. Amnesty International, which claims over 1 million members worldwide, was awarded the Nobel Peace Prize in 1978. It campaigns for (i) the release of prisoners of conscience, defined as those imprisoned because of their beliefs, or because of their ethnic origin, colour or gender, and who have neither used nor advocated violence; (ii) the prompt and fair trial of prisoners; (iii) the abolition of 'cruel' punishments, including torture and the death penalty; and (iv) an end to 'disappearances' and extrajudicial executions. Amnesty's main campaign technique is to encourage its members to write directly to officials to protest at particular cases of human rights abuse.

AMOCO CADIZ

A Liberian-registered oil tanker which ran aground off the French coast near Brest on 16 March 1978. The vessel was owned by a branch of the Standard Oil Company of Indiana and was on charter to a subsidiary of Royal-Dutch Shell. Most of the tanker's load of 260,000 tonnes of crude oil was spilt, causing huge environmental damage along the north coast of Brittany and losses to the local economy, including fishing.

AMU

The Arab **Maghreb** Union, a regional organization comprising Algeria, Libya, Mauritania, Morocco and Tunisia. Established in February 1989 with the aim of formulating common policies on defence, economic and international issues, the AMU has largely failed to promote any meaningful co-operation between the five members.

ANARCHISM

A wide-ranging ideology, whose core belief is opposition to the authority of the state. However superficially 'democratic' a state may appear, its role is seen as essentially coercive and it is, therefore, viewed as illegitimate. In its place anarchists advocate self-governing groups of individuals bound together in voluntary and democratic associations. The level of central authority which anarchists are prepared to tolerate for administrative purposes, together with the degree of collectivization envisaged, varies widely between different strands of the ideology.

Although anarchism has tended to be aligned with the **socialist** tradition, in the post-1945 period there has been a significant growth in **right-wing** anarchist theory, particularly in the USA where this has been compatible with individualism, **libertarianism**, and the more recent phenomenon of survivalism. Despite its rich theoretical heritage (which includes nineteenth-century political theorists such as Mikhail Bakunin, Pierre Proudhon and Prince Pyotr Kropotkin) anarchism has persistently been misused to refer to the absence of order. Attempts to apply the doctrine on any scale have been rare, and those which have occurred (such as in the **Ukraine** in 1920 and in Catalonia in 1936) were under wartime conditions and were quickly crushed by **Communist** opponents.

ANC

The African National Congress, South Africa's principal anti-**apartheid** organization, banned between 1960 and 1990 but now the majority party in the coalition government. The ANC's campaign to end apartheid included mass popular protests, an armed struggle against the Pretoria regime, lobbying the international community to impose **sanctions**, and, after the easing of political restrictions, negotiating to establish a democratic constitution.

Founded in 1912 as the South African Native National Congress, the ANC took its present name in 1925. Its Freedom Charter, adopted in June 1955, declares that 'South Africa belongs to all who live in it, black and white', and calls for equal political and social rights for all. Initially the ANC sought to achieve these aims through peaceful means, pursuing various **passive resistance** campaigns. Following the police killing of 69 people at **Sharpeville** in March 1960 and the subsequent banning of the organization, the ANC went underground. In 1961 it abandoned its non-violence policy and established an armed wing, **MK**. The organization suffered a serious setback in 1964 when eight leaders of MK were sentenced to life imprisonment at the end of the **Rivonia trial**. Those sentenced included Nelson Mandela, who became one of the world's most famous political prisoners. On 2 February 1990 the ANC and all other banned organizations were legalized. On 11 February Mandela was unconditionally released. Open negotiations between the ANC and the National Party government began almost immediately. These evolved in December 1991 into substantive multiparty negotiations for the establishment of a democratic constitution. On 26–9 April 1994 one of the principal aims of the ANC was fulfilled when for the first time all South Africans were able to cast their votes in a general election. This resulted in a clear parliamentary majority for the ANC and in the election of Mandela as President.

ANDEAN PACT

A regional economic and social integration alliance. The founding document, the Cartagena Agreement, was signed on 26 May 1969 by Bolivia, Chile, Colombia, Ecuador and Peru; Venezuela joined in 1974. It provided for the gradual establishment of a common external tariff and the removal of all domestic tariffs, with preferential treatment for the less developed Ecuador and Bolivia. Chile left the alliance in 1976 following an amendment to the original agreement regulating foreign investment in member countries. This was modified in 1987 to make the pact's aims more realistic but agreement on a common customs tariff has yet to be finalized. Peru suspended its membership following the 1992 **autogolpe**, but applied to re-join in April 1994.

ANGKAR

(Cambodian, 'the organization'). The name by which the **communist** Party of Cambodia (the **Khmers Rouges**) was known to the Cambodian people during the first two years of its rule (1975–7). Only in September 1977 did Pol Pot reveal that the Party had controlled the country since April 1975 and that he was its general secretary.

ANGLO-IRISH AGREEMENT

An agreement between the UK and Irish governments in November 1985 on the issue of **Northern Ireland**. Under its terms the two governments affirmed that any change in the status of Northern Ireland would come about only with the consent of the majority of the people of Northern

Ireland. The agreement, the most important political initiative since the collapse of the **Sunningdale Agreement**, established an Anglo-Irish Intergovernmental Conference (AIIC) which has met at frequent intervals in the following years to deal with political matters, with security and related matters, with legal matters and with the promotion of co-operation across the border between Ireland and Northern Ireland.

ANGRY BRIGADE

A small radical group in the UK in existence in 1968–71, which carried out several bombings in January–June 1971, directing its protests mainly against new industrial relations legislation, consumerism, and militarism. The Angry Brigade's name, and its association with **anarchism**, student protest and youth culture, encouraged an exaggerated view of its threat to the establishment, compounded by the simultaneous emergence of **Baader-Meinhof** in West Germany. Six people were arrested in London in August 1971, and four of them received 10-year sentences in December 1972 for conspiracy to cause explosions, after a protracted and high-profile Old Bailey trial.

ANGUILLA *see* OPERATION SHEEPSKIN

ANTARCTIC TREATY

An agreement signed in December 1959 to promote peaceful international scientific co-operation in Antarctica. The signatories to the treaty were Argentina, Australia, Belgium, Chile, France, Japan, New Zealand, Norway, South Africa, the former **Soviet Union**, the UK and the USA. There were 26 subsequent accessions, including 10 consultative members. Current territorial claimants to Antarctica include Argentina, Australia, Chile, France, New Zealand, Norway and the UK. Since the mid-1980s concern over the degradation of Antarctica's natural environment and over the deterioration of the **ozone layer** above the continent has led to calls for Antarctica to be declared a 'world park' that would restrict commercial mining and drilling. However, a protocol to ban mining in Antarctica for 50 years, signed in October 1991, still remains to be enforced.

ANTI-CASTROITES

Groups of Cuban exiles, based mainly in Miami, actively opposed to President Fidel Castro and the political system in Cuba. Their most notorious operation was the abortive **Bay of Pigs** invasion in 1961. These groups include armed organizations like **Alpha 66** which favour military intervention, and groups led by the Cuban-American National Foundation (CANF) which support the US trade embargo, tightened by the **Torricelli Bill**. Others such as *Cambio Cubano* ('Cuban Change') favour dialogue and an end to the blockade. The presence of hundreds of moderates at a special exiles conference hosted by the Cuban government in Havana in April 1994 caused major divisions among anti-Castroites.

ANTI-DEFAMATION LEAGUE OF B'NAI B'RITH

A Jewish group based in New York City and founded in 1913. Part of the US **Jewish lobby**, it monitors instances of **anti-Semitism** and produces numerous publications.

ANTI-MARKETEERS

Conservative MPs and peers, generally **right-wingers**, who opposed the accession of the UK to the **EEC** in 1973. In the event only 15 Conservative MPs (including two Ulster Unionists) voted against the second reading of the European Communities Bill in 1972. Some of the same attitudes were reflected in the opposition of certain Conservative backbenchers to the **Maastricht** Treaty of European Union in 1992–3 and to subsequent developments within the **EU**. The term anti-marketeer, which was also used more loosely for Labour MPs who campaigned for a 'no' vote in the 1975 referendum on renegotiated terms for the UK's membership of the Community, implies a greater degree of hostility to the EC/EU than the phrase **Eurosceptic**, but the differentiation between the two is somewhat blurred.

ANTI-NAZI LEAGUE

A **left-wing** organization in the UK formed in the 1970s to oppose the activities of militant **right-wing** and racist parties and organizations. The League lost its prominence in the 1980s, but was revived in January 1992 to counteract the growth of the British National Party.

ANTI-SEMITISM

Hostility towards Jews. Endemic to most parts of Europe throughout the medieval and modern periods, anti-Semitism frequently manifested itself in institutionalized discrimination against Jews and popular outbursts of violent hostility (pogroms). In the late nineteenth century racial – as opposed to religious-cultural – anti-Semitism was developed by racial theorists and social Darwinists. This found its most complete expression in the Nazi **Holocaust**. Since 1945, although widely discredited, both cultural and racial anti-Semitism have continued to exist, the latter being a common characteristic of **fascist** and **neo-Nazi** parties currently in existence in countries throughout Europe. Institutionalized anti-Semitism was evident in the **Communist** regimes of the **Soviet Union** and **Eastern Europe**. Anti-Semitism has also been used as a slur against critics of **Zionism** and **Israeli** policies in the **Middle East**.

ANZUS

The security pact between Australia, New Zealand, and the USA, signed in San Francisco on 1 September 1951 and in force since 29 April 1952. The ANZUS Pact, or Pacific Security Treaty, was designed to offer US support for Australia and New Zealand against the possibility of a resurgent Japan. Article 4 of the treaty states that an attack on any of the signatories is considered to be a 'common danger'. On 12 August 1986, however, the USA declared its security guarantee for New Zealand to be in abeyance, because of New Zealand's 1985 ban on nuclear ships in its territorial waters. Thus, although Australia still has close relations with the other two signatories, the ANZUS Pact is no longer operational.

AOTEOROA

(Maori, 'land of the long white cloud') The name for New Zealand used by the indigenous Maori population, who currently constitute around 10 per cent of the country's inhabitants. In recent years, as the campaign for Maori rights has become more vociferous and effective, the term has been increasingly widely adopted.

AOUZOU STRIP

The northern border area of Chad, claimed by Libya in a long-standing territorial dispute. The 44,500 sq mile (114,000 sq km) strip is thought to contain uranium and oil deposits and was annexed by Libya in June 1973. In February 1994, the **ICJ** ruled in favour of Chad; Libyan troops were reported to have withdrawn by 31 May.

APARTHEID

(Afrikaans, 'apartness' or 'separateness') The policy of 'separate development' in South Africa under which the black population was denied political, economic and social rights. Apartheid was formally instituted after the National Party's election victory in 1948. Under the Population Registration Act (1950) the population was divided into four racial groups (Whites, **Coloureds**, Indians and Africans); Whites enjoyed the best facilities and Africans the worst. Members of each racial group were allocated areas in which to live under the **Group Areas Act** (1950), which evolved into the **bantustans** or homelands policy. The movement of Africans was controlled by the **pass laws**. Separate education and welfare systems were established for each racial group. Other social interaction between racial groups was prohibited through a series of measures including the Separate Amenities Act, Mixed Marriages Act and **Immorality Act**.

The system was enforced by the police and the army, who ruthlessly suppressed opposition. The **ANC** (African National Congress) led the struggle against apartheid; it also successfully lobbied the international community to make South Africa a **pariah state**, subject to a wide range of **sanctions**.

Limited reforms in 1984–5 removed symbols of 'petty apartheid' and created a complicated 'tricameral' electoral system, for Whites, Coloureds and Indians but not Africans. The repeal of the main apartheid legislation began in February 1990, coinciding with the unbanning of the ANC and other principal anti-apartheid organizations and the release from prison of Nelson Mandela, principal leader of the ANC. By June 1991 the last remaining apartheid laws were removed from the statute book, and substantive negotiations for the establishment of a democratic constitution began in December 1991. Non-racial democratic elections on 26–9 April 1994 finally gave Africans their first opportunity to vote in national elections.

APEC

The Asia Pacific Economic Co-operation forum, established in November 1989 to promote multilateral trade in the Asia-Pacific region. To date, the forum has made little concrete progress towards meeting its primary objective. APEC's 17 member states comprise the six **ASEAN** states (Brunei, Indonesia, **Malaysia**, the Philippines, Singapore and Thailand) and Australia, Canada, China, Hong Kong, Japan, South Korea, Mexico, New Zealand, Papua New Guinea, **Taiwan**, and the USA. Originally established as a loose forum, a permanent secretariat was established in Singapore in 1992.

APLA *see* PAC

APO

(German abbreviation for *Ausserparlamentärische opposition*, 'Extra-parliamentary opposition') The protest movement in West Germany in the late 1960s, especially in **1968**. The name APO pointed up the country's lack of parliamentary opposition in 1966–9, when the established parties were all involved in the Christian Democrat-led **grand coalition** government. The APO disintegrated when the October 1969 elections returned a Social Democrat-led government. Some APO members eventually went underground, allying themselves with the **Baader-Meinhof** group, while others joined the **Green** movement.

APOLLO PROJECT

The US-manned lunar exploration project, announced in May 1961 in a climate of Soviet-American confrontation following the **Bay of Pigs** debacle. The Soviet space programme had just recorded its own triumph with the first manned space flight, by Yuri Gagarin, the latest in a series of Soviet successes going back to the launch of **Sputnik** in October 1957. President Kennedy envisaged that a programme to put a man on the moon within the decade would help to restore US prestige.

Apollo relied heavily on the expertise of German rocket pioneers spirited to the USA after the Second World War, and built on the experience gained from the Mercury (1959–63) and Gemini (1964–6) programmes and from the Ranger, Orbiter and Surveyor lunar mapping missions (1962–8). Apollo suffered a setback in January 1967 when three astronauts were killed in ground tests. Apollos 7–10 (October 1968–May 1969) established the technical, navigational and rendezvous ability which made possible the first successful lunar landing, by Neil Armstrong and Buzz Aldrin from Apollo 11 on 20 July 1969. Apollos 12–17 (November 1969–December 1972) included five successful landing missions. The programme, costing US$24,000 million (at the 1962 rate), was cut short thereafter, having been criticized for placing technical achievement above scientific content and for wasting resources which were needed to address pressing social problems.

APOSTLES

An exclusive group at Cambridge University founded in the early nineteenth century. In the early 1930s some members of The Apostles were recruited to work clandestinely for the Soviet intelligence services, most notably Guy Burgess (a senior diplomat who defected in 1951) and Anthony Blunt (a prominent art historian whose activity on behalf of the **Soviet Union** was disclosed in 1979).

APPARATCHIK

A **communist** party official, particularly a functionary of the **CPSU**. The term, although less specific than **nomenklatura**, still evokes the much-resented power and privilege of those who identified with the party machine.

APRIL 19 MOVEMENT *see* M-19

ARAB LEAGUE

The regional organization of Arab states, formed in 1945. As of 1994 the members are Algeria, Bahrain, Comoros, **Djibouti**, Egypt, Iraq, Jordan, Kuwait, Lebanon, Libya, Mauritania, Morocco, Oman, the Palestine Liberation Organization, Qatar, Saudi Arabia, Somalia, Sudan, Syria, Tunisia, the **UAE** and Yemen. The Council, the League's supreme organ, consists of a representative from each member state. The General Secretariat carries out the decisions of the Council and provides financial and administrative services for the personnel of the League. The Secretary-General is appointed by the Council by a two-thirds majority of the member states for a five-year term; the current Secretary-General, Ahmed Esmat Abdel al-Meguid of Egypt, was appointed in 1991.

During the course of its first 25 years the League concentrated mainly on economic, cultural and social programmes. Under the secretary-generalship of Mahmoud Riad (in 1972–9), political activity increased, but internal division, especially concerning the Palestinian question, was common. Egypt was suspended from the Arab League for 10 years after signing the **Camp David agreement** and a peace agreement with **Israel** in 1978–9. Since Egypt's readmission in 1989 the League has dealt with a variety of complex and divisive issues, including the **Middle East peace process**, the aftermath of Iraq's invasion of Kuwait and the **Lockerbie** issue.

ARAB MAGHREB UNION *see* AMU

ARAB MONETARY FUND *see* AMF

ARCTIC TREATY

An agreement signed by representatives from Alaska, Canada, China, Japan, **Scandinavia** and the **Soviet Union** at a meeting in Anchorage on 17–20 September 1990 pledging collaboration on scientific research and environmental protection in the Arctic. The agreement covers joint research into timber harvesting, wildlife management and offshore oil and gas exploration, the monitoring of pollution, the exchange of technical information and the funding of environmental protection programmes. The Anchorage meeting was the third of its kind, and delegates agreed to meet every two years in future.

ARIANE

The expendable three-stage rockets launched by the semi-private French body Arianespace on behalf of the **ESA**. The development of the Ariane programme owed much to the determination of the French government and to the rocketry expertise built up by the French National Space Agency (CNES). The first launch was in December 1979. Ariane's reliability and competitiveness posed a major challenge to the domination of the international satellite launch market by **Intelsat**. Arianespace currently has 35 launches planned up to 1996, including Intelsat satellites, worth an estimated F 15,000 million. The failure of an Ariane-4 rocket in January 1994 was the first in 28 launches from the Kourou space centre in French Guiana.

ARIAS PLAN

A peace plan for **Central America** devised by Costa Rican President Oscar Arias Sánchez, officially called 'Esquipulas II', which won him the 1987 Nobel Peace Prize. An alternative to the **Contadora** plan, it proposed a ceasefire in the region, a suspension of foreign aid to all insurgent forces, a dialogue between governments and opposition parties and the holding of free elections. Initial US support was withdrawn after the plan was redrafted to include Nicaragua in the peace process and by implication criticized the USA's role in the region. The US attempt to pre-empt this final version with its own peace plan failed and the Arias Plan was signed by Central American presidents in August 1987. Its main achievements were the Nicaraguan preliminary ceasefire accord of March 1988, leading to a general election and the demobilization of the US-backed **Contras**, as well as negotiations between governments and insurgents in El Salvador and Guatemala.

ARMALITE

An automatic rifle favoured by paramilitary republican forces in **Northern Ireland**. It was widely used in the republicans' struggle with their Protestant loyalist opponents and against the UK armed forces, but was later largely replaced by the Kalashnikov **AK-47**. The phrase 'the ballot box and the Armalite', coined in 1981, continued to be used to indicate the strategy of aiming to secure eventual victory by violent as well as constitutional means.

ARMENIA

One of the republics which became independent with the collapse of the **Soviet Union**. Modern-day Armenia, in the **Transcaucasus**, has a population of some 3 million, mainly Christians belonging to the historic independent Armenian Church. The current state (ruled by Russia in the nineteenth century, brought under Soviet control in 1920–2 after a brief period of independence, and declared independent again in 1991 following the **August coup**) represents only the eastern 10 per cent of historical Greater Armenia. The other 90 per cent had, by the fifteenth century, all been incorporated into the Ottoman empire, whose genocidal massacres of Armenians in 1894–6 and 1915 left an enduring legacy of anti-Turkish feeling.

The Armenian government has persistently denied direct involvement in the conflict between ethnic Armenians and **Azerbaijan** over **Nagorny Karabakh**. This conflict has, however, left Armenia isolated and impoverished, and has reinforced Armenia's historic reliance on Russia, as well as its poor relations with Turkey.

ARMENIAN SECRET ARMY FOR THE LIBERATION OF ARMENIA *see* ASALA

ARMS CONTROL

A term often paired with disarmament, as in the title of the US Arms Control and Disarmament Agency which was created to handle such issues from 1961 onwards, and applicable to **conventional weapons** as well as to nuclear, chemical and biological warfare. Throughout the **Cold War** the emphasis was on arms control rather than actual disarmament until the **START** and **CFE** agreements of the early 1990s. Arms control efforts related variously to limiting the geographical spread of weapons deployment (the 1959 **Antarctic Treaty**, the 1967 **Latin American** Treaty of **Tlatelolco**, the 1987 Pacific **Rarotonga Treaty**, and the **Outer Space Treaty** and **Seabed Treaty** of 1967 and 1970); preventing the deployment of new weapons and systems (the 1972 **Biological Weapons** Convention, the **ABM** Treaty, the **INF Treaty** and the Geneva negotiations on **chemical weapons**); and controlling the development and proliferation of technology (the 1963 **Partial Test Ban Treaty**, and the 1976 **NPT** agreement).

ARMS FOR HOSTAGES

An aspect of the **Iran-Contra affair**. The secret US sale of arms to Iran in 1985–6, besides providing a source of unauthorized funds for the Nicaraguan **Contra** rebels, was also used as a means of enlisting Iranian government assistance in attempting to secure the release of US hostages, who were being held by pro-Iranian Islamic fundamentalists in Lebanon. The first shipment of arms to Tehran in mid-1985 did result in the release of one US hostage. However, despite further arms deliveries and a visit to Tehran by Oliver North and Robert McFarlane, both senior members of the US **NSC**, no further releases were achieved. The revelation in 1986 of the arms-for-hostages deal was particularly embarrassing for President Ronald Reagan, as he had repeatedly asserted that no such quid pro quo would be countenanced by his administration.

ARMS PROJECT *see* HUMAN RIGHTS WATCH

ARMS RACE

The rapid and competitive build-up of weapons by states which regard themselves as adversaries. An arms race may occur in a regional context (as in the

Middle East or the Asian subcontinent), while at the global level the nuclear arms race between the **superpowers** was a feature of the **Cold War**, marked by periods of particular intensity in weapons development and production. The arms trade, a major export earner for certain countries, is the principal beneficiary of an arms race. Some analysts have also sought to explain the superpower arms race in terms of the power of the **military-industrial complex** in the domestic economy and politics of both superpowers.

ARUBA

A **Caribbean** island off the coast of Venezuela. Along with other islands of the Netherlands Antilles federation, it achieved self-government in 1954; however, 83 per cent of Arubans voted for independence in 1977, concerned that the island's status within the federation had been eroded. In 1986 Aruba seceded from the Netherlands Antilles, and the Netherlands government agreed on full independence in 1996. The date for independence, however, was postponed indefinitely in 1990, amid fears that Netherlands aid would be cut and that independence would bring political instability, as had happened in **Surinam**, another former Netherlands colony.

ARUSHA DECLARATION

The policy document issued by the ruling Tanganyika African National Union (TANU) on 5 February 1967 outlining TANU's policy of socialism and self-reliance. Drafted by Julius Nyerere, it defined **Tanzania** as a socialist state and was incorporated into the Constitution in 1977. It called for rural development to be based upon communal villages, a policy which subsequently became **villagization**. It defined a code of conduct for the ruling elite, including calling on party leaders to renounce their private incomes. It also sought a drastic reduction on foreign investment, to be replaced by 'self-reliance' and hard work.

ARVN

The Army of the Republic of Vietnam, the US-allied South Vietnamese forces defeated during the **Vietnam War**.

ASALA

The Armenian Secret Army for the Liberation of Armenia. A **Marxist-Leninist** terrorist organization, active in the 1970s and 1980s, which sought revenge and recognition for the Turkish pogroms against Armenians in Anatolia in 1915–16. Founded in Beirut in 1975, ASALA targeted Turkish interests abroad, assassinating some 30 diplomats. In 1982–3 it carried out bomb attacks on Ankara and Paris (Orly) airports and in an Istanbul bazaar. In July 1983 the movement split into a relatively moderate Western European branch and a **Middle Eastern** group led by Hagop Hagopian, the movement's original leader. By the late 1980s ASALA had petered out.

ASEAN

Association of South East Asian Nations. A regional co-operative organization established in 1967 with the objective of accelerating the economic progress and stabilization of the **south-east Asia** region. Its members include Indonesia, **Malaysia**, Singapore, Thailand, the Philippines and Brunei (the latter having gained membership in 1984). The organs of ASEAN are its ministerial conference, composed of the foreign ministers of the six member countries and the organization's seven 'dialogue partners' and which meets annually; a standing committee, which meets when necessary between ministerial meetings; and a secretariat, established in 1976. The heads of government of the six have held four summit meetings, most recently in Singapore in January 1992.

While the declaration signed by the member states upon ASEAN's establishment in 1967 emphasized the primacy of economic and social collaboration, during the 1970s and 1980s the organization played a pivotal role in sustaining Vietnam's diplomatic isolation, at the same time encouraging international support for the **Khmer Rouge**-led Coalition Government of Democratic **Kampuchea** (**CGDK**). The signing of a UN-backed Cambodian peace accord in 1991 was a signal for ASEAN to cast off its **Cold War** armour and concentrate instead on its original economic ambitions. Hence, in January 1993 the six implemented a common effective preferential tariff scheme aimed at creating an ASEAN free trade area (**AFTA**) in 2008.

ASIA PACIFIC ECONOMIC CO-OPERATION *see* APEC

ASIA WATCH *see* HUMAN RIGHTS WATCH

ASIAN DEVELOPMENT BANK *see* ADB

ASIO

The Australian Security Intelligence Organization. A federal agency, ASIO was established in March 1948 during a period of concern over the growing influence of the **Soviet Union**, and to counter fears that lax Australian security was endangering nuclear co-operation between the UK and the USA. The Labor government in the 1970s regarded ASIO with great suspicion, claiming that it was involved in clandestine surveillance of government ministers.

ASWAN HIGH DAM

The massive dam across the Nile River at Aswan, Egypt, inaugurated in 1971 at a cost of some US$1,000 million. The commencement of construction of the High Dam in the late 1950s was a triumph for the Egyptian leader Gamal Abdel Nasser and heralded the ascendancy of **Nasserism**. In 1956 the USA withdrew its offer of financial aid for the dam's construction, and in response the Egyptian government without warning nationalized the Suez Canal Company and took over the administration of the canal, prompting the **Suez crisis**. The High Dam was subsequently financed by the **Soviet Union**.

The conclusion of over a century of changes to Egypt's system of irrigation, the High Dam not only provides the means of generating enormous amounts of electrical power, but, for the first time in Egypt's history, allows control of the annual Nile floods. On the debit side, it has led to a gradual decrease in the fertility and hence productivity of Egypt's riverside agricultural lands.

ATOMIC ENERGY COMMISSION

The **UN** body created in 1946 because of the perceived importance of atomic weapons and atomic energy in the postwar world. The aspiration underlying the Commission was that this whole area could become one for co-operative global management rather than competing national interest. At its first meeting the **Baruch Plan** was proposed. However, discussion of this and of the **Soviet** counterproposals reached stalemate and the Commission adjourned indefinitely in 1948.

ATOMS FOR PEACE

A proposal advanced by US President Dwight Eisenhower at the **UN** in 1953. It envisaged not just setting up an agency to foster co-operation in atomic energy – an objective fulfilled by the creation of the **IAEA** in 1957 – but also that countries with nuclear weapons programmes should divert fissionable material to atomic energy. The USA and the **Soviet Union** would thereby place a brake on their **arms race**, and simultaneously give a major boost to the use of atomic power for peaceful purposes.

ATTACHÉS

(French, 'the attached') Loosely organized gangs in Haiti with close links to the army and military police. They first appeared in September 1993, when they began systematically to harass and murder those campaigning for the restoration of democracy and the return of exiled President Jean-Bertrand Aristide, deposed in the September 1991 military coup. They assumed the role of practitioners of terror performed by the **Tontons Macoutes** on behalf of the previous Duvalierist dictatorships. The extreme **right-wing** and pro-military Front for the Advancement and Progress of Haiti (FRAPH), a prime co-ordinator of *attaché* activity, openly calls for a return to **Duvalierism**.

AUGUST COUP

The attempted Soviet **coup d'état** of 19–21 August 1991 by **CPSU** conservatives. Senior figures involved in the coup included Vice-President Gennady Yanayev. On 19 August Soviet President Mikhail Gorbachev was placed under house arrest and a state of emergency was declared. Resistance rallied around Russian President Boris Yeltsin at the seat of parliament, the **White House**, and the coup plotters fled when it became clear that they had failed to win the full backing of the military and the **KGB**. The coup was an attempt to block the imminent signature of a Union treaty granting 'sovereignty' to the 15 constituent republics of the **Soviet Union**. Ironically it precipitated the Union's dissolution and the banning of the CPSU.

AUSSERPARLAMENTÄRISCHE OPPOSITION *see* APO

AUSTRALASIA

A geographical term. Australasia encompasses Australia, New Zealand, Papua New Guinea, and adjacent Pacific islands.

AUTARCHY

A term originally meaning self-government (derived from Greek), which in current usage refers exclusively to the concept of economic self-sufficiency, particularly in the spheres of food, raw materials and production. Autarchy has always been a common component within various brands of fascist ideology, with economic dependency upon other sovereign powers defined as a form of weakness. It has also been adopted by regimes which claim to be **communist**, most notably that of North Korea, where autarchy is an integral aspect of the county's isolationist *Juchist* ideology.

AUTOGOLPE

(Spanish, 'self-coup') A **Latin American** term for a coup by an incumbent president leading to the suspension of the constitution, the closing down of the legislature and the banning of political parties. The term is used most frequently to describe the June 1973 military coup in Uruguay when President Juan María Bordaberry Arocena appeared to be the main actor although in reality power had shifted decisively into the hands of the military. It has most recently been used to described the President Alberto Fujimori's army-backed coup in Peru in April 1992.

AWACS

Airborne Warning and Control Systems aircraft. These aircraft are airborne jamming-resistant radar stations and command and communications centres, and their radar can 'peer' about 300 km over the horizon. The US E-3 Sentry, based on the Boeing 707, is distinctive by the radome dish mounted on top. A similar aircraft based on the Nimrod was originally planned for the British RAF, but insuperable problems caused its cancellation in 1987.

AWAMI LEAGUE

(Bengali, 'People's League') The main opposition party in **Bangladesh**. It was founded in 1949 by **left-wing** Bengali nationalists as the Awami (People's) Muslim League to oppose the **right-wing** orientation of the **All India Muslim League**. Under the leadership of Sheikh Mujibur Rahman, the party led a successful movement for the independence in 1971 of Bangladesh (formerly the province of East Pakistan), from Pakistan. It was the ruling party in Bangladesh from 1971 until Rahman's assassination in August 1975, since when it has been in opposition.

AWB

The South African *Afrikaanse Weerstandsbeweging* or Afrikaner Resistance Movement, a neo-Nazi paramilitary group formed by Eugene Terreblanche in the 1970s. Committed to the preservation of **apartheid**, the AWB is vehemently opposed to allowing political rights to the black population of South Africa. It has called for the right to vote to be restricted to white Christians (thus excluding Jews), and for the abolition of all political parties. It has campaigned for the restoration of the nineteenth century Boer republics. It has been opposed to recent constitutional developments in South Africa, at times violently so. AWB hostility has not been reserved solely for the **ANC** and its allies; it also regards the National Party as having betrayed the Afrikaner **volk**.

AWQAF *see* WAQF

AYACUCHO DECLARATION

A **Latin American** accord committing signatory countries to joint economic and social development via the limitation and use of arms and the nurturing of internal peace. It was signed by Argentina, Bolivia, Colombia, Cuba, Ecuador, Panama, Peru and Venezuela in December 1974 in Lima, Peru, at the 150th anniversary celebrations of the Battle of Ayacucho celebrating the final victory of **South America** over the Spanish.

AYATOLLAH

(Arabic, 'Divine sign') An honorific title for the highest ranking Islamic **Shia** religious authority. The position, awarded currently only to a handful of senior clerics in Iran and Iraq, is believed to be an eighteenth century innovation. By the twentieth century, however, the increase in the numbers of ayatollahs led to the further distinction of the title of 'grand ayatollah'. In recent times the position of ayatollah has been most notably associated with the spiritual leader of Iran's **Islamic revolution**, Ayatollah Ruhollah Khomeini (1902–89). Although never granted the status of 'grand ayatollah', Khomeini's immense popular standing and personal charisma enabled him to adopt the title of 'Imam', signifying, in the Shia canon, the unique exemplar to an age.

AYODHYA MOSQUE

Also known as *Babri masjid*, named after the Moghul emperor, Babar, who built the mosque in the sixteenth century. Located in Ayodhya, in the northern Indian state of Uttar Pradesh, the mosque became a centre of dispute between Hindus and Muslims in the 1980s, when Hindu militant groups claimed the mosque as a site of Hindu worship, alleging that it was the birthplace of the Hindu god Rama. Hindu-Muslim tension over the issue intensified after the pro-Hindu **BJP**, which made huge gains in the June 1991 general election, lent its support to the campaign and was eventually implicated in the destruction of the mosque in December 1992.

AZAD KASHMIR

(Hindi/Urdu, 'free Kashmir') The nominally autonomous area with its own government and parliament, located in the disputed Indian state of Jammu and Kashmir, and which is adjacent to and under the effective political control of **Pakistan**. The predominantly Muslim area, demarcated by an internationally designated ceasefire line agreed in July 1949, derives its name from the self-styled Azad Kashmir movement, a Muslim-led rebellion which erupted in September 1947. Backed by Pathan tribesmen who crossed the border from Pakistan's North West Frontier Province, the rebellion was eventually contained by Indian army units which restricted its advance to the existing ceasefire line in May 1948.

AZANIA

The name given to South Africa by the **PAC** during the 1960s. Derived from a Greco-Persian word dating from the first century AD meaning land of the blacks, the term was used by early cartographers for the coastal area of east Africa. Its use now is associated with anti-**apartheid** organizations with a **black consciousness** tendency such as **AZAPO**.

AZANIAN PEOPLE'S LIBERATION ARMY *see* PAC

AZAPO

The Azanian People's Organization, a South African anti-**apartheid** organization founded in 1978 with the aim of establishing a unitary, democratic, social republic of **Azania**. AZAPO has its roots in the **black consciousness** movement articulated by Steve Biko (who died in police detention in 1977), and its membership is confined to the black population of South Africa (i.e. **Coloureds** and Indians as well as Africans). It refused to participate in

South Africa's first non-racial democratic elections in April 1994.

AZERBAIJAN

One of the republics which became independent with the collapse of the **Soviet Union**. Located in the **Transcaucasus**, Azerbaijan was under Russian control from the eighteenth century. Azeris are a Muslim people who speak a Turkic language; there are approximately 5 million of them in Azerbaijan (which includes **Nakhichevan**, an enclave surrounded by **Armenia** and Iran), and perhaps twice as many in Iran itself.

B-2 *see* STEALTH BOMBER

B-52

The USA's long-range heavy bomber, also known as the Stratofortress, originally designed in 1948 and still in service. The B-52 was intended as a delivery craft for nuclear weapons, but saw significant service as a conventional bomber during the **Vietnam War**. The B-52 has three modified forms, B, G and D, which in one form or another give it a maximum range of 10,000 miles, a bomb load of up to 40,000 pounds, and the capacity (introduced in the 1980s) to launch cruise missiles in mid-flight.

B SPECIALS

The colloquial name given to the Ulster Special Constabulary, a former, controversial, auxiliary police force in **Northern Ireland**. The B Specials (numbering some 8,000 personnel, effectively all Protestant) were established in the early 1920s and were widely seen by the Catholic community as representing an oppressively military and sectarian element of the Royal Ulster Constabulary. They were disbanded in 1970, when their military role was assumed by the Ulster Defence Regiment (UDR) and their police duties by a new RUC reserve force.

BAADER-MEINHOF

An extremist **left-wing** terrorist group active in Germany in the late 1960s and the 1970s, named after leading members Andreas Baader and Ulrike Meinhof. The group, later known as the **Rote Armee Fraktion** (RAF), emerged from the **APO** and the student protests of **1968**. Its underground existence and strategy of violence attracted young radicals, disillusioned with mass protests which had failed to effect fundamental change. Key leaders of the group, including both Baader and Meinhof, were arrested in 1972. During their trial, which opened in Stuttgart on 21 May 1975, Meinhof committed suicide. The remaining three defendants were sentenced on 28 April 1977 to life imprisonment for four murders and 34 attempted murders, and for forming a criminal organization. Baader committed suicide in prison later that year.

BA'ATH

(Arabic, 'renaissance') The movement founded in Syria in the 1940s by Michel Aflaq with the aim of creating a single socialist Arab nation. As an ideology and a political force Ba'athism was central to the formation of the **UAR** in 1958. Although undeniably a major political force in the region, Ba'athism has conspicuously failed to create a single united Arab state. Since the 1970s rival Ba'athist regimes in Syria and Iraq have vied for Arab supremacy.

BABRI MASJID *see* AYODHYA MOSQUE

BABY BOOM

An expression used to describe any great increase in population, but particularly the population rise in the USA and UK between the late 1940s and the early 1960s created by the combination of the ending of the Second World War and the rapid expansion of the economy. Consequently Baby Boomer is used to describe the generation that came of age and joined the workforce in the 1970s. The term itself only gained currency in the 1970s.

BACK TO BASICS

A strategy adopted by the Conservative Party in the UK in late 1993. It sought to restore and reaffirm what the party saw as its fundamental political philosophy. Emphasis was placed not only on a free enterprise economy but also on the basic social value of self-discipline, respect for the law, concern for others, individual responsibility and traditional education. While the cohesion of the family and moral rectitude were also seen as fundamental, the strategy came under some stress as personal, business and sexual scandals rocked the party in early 1994.

BACKBENCHER

A member of the UK House of Commons or House of Lords who is not a member of the government or of the principal opposition team of parliamentary spokespersons. By extension, the term is also used to mean rank-and-file parliamentarians in other countries. The representative body of Conservative backbenchers is the **1922 Committee**.

BAD GODESBERG DECLARATION

The landmark document adopted in 1959 by the West German Social Democratic Party (SPD) at a special congress in Bad Godesberg. Renouncing Marxism, it defined the SPD as a party of 'democratic socialism', expressed support for private property and a free market economy, and accepted existing West German defence commitments. Bad Godesberg helped to broaden the SPD's electoral base and to present it as a potential party of government, and marked the start of the reversal of the party's series of post-war electoral defeats.

BAGHDAD PACT *see* CENTO

BAHAI

A branch of the Babi religious sect founded in the mid-nineteenth century in Persia (now Iran). The Babi sect itself was an offshoot which broke away from the **Twelvers**, the principal strand of **Shia** Islam in Persia. The Bahai faith gradually relinquished its traditional religious trappings in favour of a mixture of syncretism and humanism, and the Bahai have won a wide following in Europe and North America, due largely to their emphasis on world peace. However, they are regarded as heretical by Islam's dominant **Sunni** and Shia sects. In Iran, where the Bahai are not recognized as a religious group, persecution was already prevalent under the Shah's regime, and has been more rigorous since the **Islamic revolution** of 1979. The Bahai were officially banned in 1983, and it is said that at least 10,000 of an estimated Iranian Bahai population of 300,000 have been forced to flee the country.

BAIKONUR

The **Soviet Union's** cosmodrome, or space centre, now part of the former Soviet republic of **Kazakhstan**. Baikonur was the launch site for manned Soviet space flights. Economic problems cast doubt on the future of the cosmodrome, particularly after the collapse of the Soviet Union. In October 1992 Russia and Kazakhstan agreed to coordinate their policies on space research, and in March 1994 they agreed the terms of a 20-year lease on parts of the cosmodrome. The Kazakh government plans to use the remainder of the site for commercial purposes, such as the launch of communications satellites.

BALCEROWICZ PLAN

The economic 'shock therapy' programme of Poland's first post-**communist** Finance Minister, Leszek Balcerowicz, introduced in January 1990. The Balcerowicz plan was widely regarded as eastern Europe's first and most radical market-oriented economic reform package. It abolished price controls and state subsidies but, in an attempt to reduce inflation, it retained wage controls. State spending was to be held down and state-owned enterprises to be privatized. The Balcerowicz plan succeeded in reducing the inflation rate and brought goods into shops, ending the queues of the communist era. However, industrial production declined rapidly and unemployment grew, and the plan proved politically unpopular.

BALKANIZATION

The division of a region (or, often, of one state) into several small and mutually antagonistic states. The original usage refers to the Balkans during the decline and collapse of the Ottoman and Austro-Hungarian empires. The post-**communist** disintegration of **Yugoslavia** has more recently been characterized as Balkanization, as has the collapse of other multi-ethnic states including the **Soviet Union**.

BALKANS

The countries of the Balkan peninsula in south-eastern Europe: Albania, Bulgaria, Greece, Romania, Turkey and the former Yugoslav states of **Bosnia-Hercegovina, Croatia, Macedonia,** and the Federal Republic of **Yugoslavia** (comprising Serbia and **Montenegro**). Arguably **Slovenia** and **Moldova**, on the far western and eastern fringes respectively of the Balkan peninsula, are also Balkan countries.

BALTIC COUNCIL

A grouping formed in March 1989 by the **Baltic states** – then Soviet republics – as a means of promoting co-operation between them. Although relatively little progress was made in 1992–3, the rise of **nationalism** in neighbouring Russia prompted renewed interest in the Baltic Council as a means of institutionalizing political co-operation.

BALTIC STATES

The former Soviet Republics of **Estonia, Latvia, Lithuania,** which border the Baltic Sea. In common usage the phrase should not be construed as referring to other states bordering the Baltic Sea.

BAMBOO CURTAIN

The self-imposed isolation of **communist** China from the rest of the world in order to protect Chinese citizens from contact with the citizens of countries ideologically opposed to China. The phrase is a derivative of **iron curtain**.

BAN THE BOMB!

A slogan used by **CND** and other organizations opposed to nuclear weapons. First coined by members of the World Peace Council in the 1950s, it came into wider usage after being chanted by CND supporters on the first **Aldermaston** march.

BANABANS

The natives of Banaba (**Kiribati**), formerly Ocean Island, who sued the British government in February 1975 for royalties from and compensation for the damage incurred by phosphate mining on Ocean Island. The London Pacific Phosphate Company began mining for phosphate after concluding an agreement in 1900 which offered derisory terms to the Banabans. Although the Banabans' share of phosphate revenues was increased after violent incidents in 1965, they continued to press their case, taking their demands as far as the **UN**. In June 1976 the British High Court found against the Banabans on the royalties case, but ruled that they were owed compensation for damage to the island.

BANANA REPUBLIC

A pejorative term for poor countries ruled by the military or de facto dictatorships. It is most often applied to tropical countries producing in the main fruit and raw materials for export and historically heavily dependent on foreign capital.

BANCO AMBROSIANO *see* CALVI AFFAIR

BAND AID

The charity formed by musicians Bob Geldof and Midge Ure in December 1984 in response to the famine in Ethiopia. The pair wrote the song 'Do They Know It's Christmas?' and arranged for prominent musicians and technicians to donate their services to record the song; it reached Number One in the UK hit record chart on 14 December. All proceeds for the sale of the record went to the charity, which focused on self-help schemes as well as emergency relief. Band Aid also organized **Live Aid** in 1985.

BANDUNG CONFERENCE

The first international conference of Asian-African states, held in April 1955 in the Indonesian town of Bandung. The conference was the precursor of the first meeting of the **non-aligned** states, held in **Yugoslavia** in 1961. Bandung, which had been organized by five signatories to the **Colombo Plan** (Indonesia, India, Burma, **Pakistan** and Ceylon), was attended by delegates from 29 countries, representing half of the world's population. A 10-point Declaration on the Promotion of World Peace and Co-operation, incorporating the principles of the **UN** Charter and the **Five Principles of Co-existence**, was adopted unanimously. The conference is perhaps best remembered for the positive relations projected between India and China.

BANGLADESH

Originally part of British India, then, at the **partition** of the **Indian sub-continent** in 1947, the 'eastern wing' of **Pakistan** known as East Pakistan, separated from its 'western wing' by 950 miles (1,500 km) of Indian territory. It seceded in 1971 to become an independent state within the **Commonwealth** under the new name of Bangladesh.

BANK OF CENTRAL AFRICAN STATES *see* BEAC

BANTUSTANS

The 10 so-called 'homelands' created under the South African **apartheid** system, where Africans (excluded from proper South African citizenship) were deemed to belong. The bantustans were not necessarily contiguous geographical entities, but parcels of territory based on linguistic groups; in all they comprised 13 per cent of South Africa's land area. Bantustans were the only places in which Africans could legally acquire land. Under the Bantu Homelands Citizenship Act (1970) all Africans were allocated as citizens of one or other of the bantustans, even if they lived and worked outside them. Four bantustans were, over the years, declared 'independent sovereign states', but were recognized only by South Africa and each other: Transkei (in 1976); Bophuthatswana (in 1977); Venda (in 1979); and Ciskei (in 1981). Legislative assemblies were created for the other six: Gazankulu, Kangwane, Kwandebele, Kwazulu, Lebowa and Qwaqwa. Under the 1964 **Odendaal Report** 10 bantustans were also established in **Namibia**.

BARCELONA CONVENTION

An international convention concluded in 1976 and effective since 1978 covering the prevention of pollution of the Mediterranean Sea.

BARRE PLAN

An unpopular economic austerity programme unveiled in 1976 by French Prime Minister Raymond Barre, which was intended to curb inflation and increase employment. Barre introduced his plan on 22 September, announcing further measures on 26 April 1977. Despite various austerity and restructuring measures, however, inflation and unemployment continued to grow. The Barre plan was opposed by trades unions, which organized widely observed general strikes in protest.

BARUCH PLAN

One of the first, and potentially most far-reaching, initiatives at the **UN**, put forward in 1946 by the US delegate Bernard Baruch to the newly created but short-lived **Atomic Energy Commission**. It envisaged an international authority with exclusive control over all activities concerned with nuclear weapons, and the abrogation of national sovereignty in this sphere. As the only nuclear-weapons state at that time, the USA would cease production and destroy all stocks. Since the USA already had the research and development experience, however, the **Soviet Union** opposed the plan, which it saw as allowing the US to preserve a crucial technological imbalance.

BASEL CONVENTION

An international agreement imposing restrictions on the cross-border transport and disposal of hazardous wastes, obliging exporters to obtain 'prior informed consent' from the proposed importer, and aiming to reduce the generation of such wastes. Its full name is the Basel Convention on the Control of Transboundary Movements of Hazardous Wastes and their Disposal. Although 116 countries attended the conference where it was adopted, in Basel on 20–22 May 1989, the convention was initially signed by only 34 of them, and many African states and environmental groups objected that it legalized the export of toxic waste to the developing world. The convention was undermined when the **OECD** adopted even less stringent regulations with the intention of protecting the recycling industry in developed countries.

BASIC LAW

1. West Germany's Provisional Constitution of 1949. It was drafted on the authorization of the **Western Allies**, as part of the process of rebuilding Germany's democratic institutions, by a parliamentary council chaired by Konrad Adenauer. Its name reflects a recognition that it was only a temporary arrangement, pending the formation of a unified German state. On Germany's eventual unification in 1990, the Basic Law (or *Grundgesetz*) became the Constitution of the new Federal Republic. It declares Germany to be 'a democratic and social federal state'.

2. The 'mini-constitution' for Hong Kong after 1997. With sovereignty reverting from the UK to China, the colony would become a special administrative region. Partial direct elections to its Legislative Council (Legco) would be phased in gradually. The basic law was drawn up following the Sino-British Joint Declaration of 1984, and the final draft was approved by the Chinese National People's Congress in 1990. Its status was thrown into some uncertainty, however, when the new British Governor, Chris Patten, announced proposals in October 1992 for more rapid democratization. Patten's proposals were openly opposed by the Chinese authorities which saw them as pre-empting the post-1997 situation.

BASQUES

A people of distinctive language, culture and tradition who live in northern provinces of Spain (Vizcaya, Guipúzcoa, Alava, Navarra) and in the Basses-Pyrénées department of France. Numbering slightly over 2 million in Spain, they supported the Republic in the civil war (1936–9) in return for the promise of autonomy. After the victory of Gen. Franco they suffered retribution and the recentralization of government, which generated broad support for the Basque separatist movement **ETA**. After Franco's death in 1975 and the restoration of democracy the situation eased, and in March 1980 a Basque autonomous parliament was elected. They have also demanded their own police force and the inclusion of Navarra in the Basque region. A 1989 pact, in which mainstream Basque parties renounced separatist violence, was not signed by *Herri Batasuna*, ETA's political wing.

BASUTOLAND *see* LESOTHO

BATTLEGROUND STATES

A group of electorally significant US states, control of which tends to determine the outcome of presidential elections. The US president is formally chosen by a 538-member electoral college, representing the 50 states plus three votes for the federal capital district, Washington DC. Each state has a number of electoral college votes corresponding to its combined total of seats in both houses of **Congress**. As the number of seats in the lower chamber of Congress is determined by the population of a state, it follows that larger states have more electoral college votes than smaller ones. The presidential candidate who wins most popular votes within a state gets all of that state's electoral college votes. To secure victory a candidate thus needs to win in any combination of states which have 270 or more electoral college votes. In the 1992 presidential elections, 228 votes could be won in the eight biggest states – the battleground states – California, Florida, Illinois, Michigan, New York, Ohio, Pennsylvania, and Texas.

BAY OF PIGS

The scene of an ill-fated invasion of Cuba by US-armed exiles in 1961. Following the 1959 Cuban revolution in which Fidel Castro came to power, the US government had sponsored the training of exiled **right-**

wing Cubans in preparation for an attempt to oust the Castro regime. President Kennedy, inaugurated in January 1961, inherited this mission and allowed it to proceed. On 14–15 April some 1,400 armed exiles were landed in Cuba at the Bay of Pigs. The operation ran into immediate trouble: it did not spark off the anticipated anti-Castro rising elsewhere in the country, and the Cuban government's military response was much more efficient than had been expected. Devoid of the direct US military support upon which they had been relying, the exiles were comprehensively defeated within 48 hours. The operation was a severe embarrassment for the new US President and served to consolidate Castro's authority within Cuba, to enhance his reputation abroad, and to aggravate the growing tension been Cuba and the USA.

BAY'A

(Arabic, 'a pact', signifying public acclamation of, or swearing allegiance to, a leader) The oath made with a Muslim ruler by his subjects, or on their behalf by the body of religious scholars – the *ulama* – and political chiefs. A traditional feature of Islamic political practice, it is rare in contemporary Muslim states. It remains in use in Saudi Arabia and, most notably, in Morocco where the religious prestige of the current monarch, King Hassan II, is reinforced annually by ritual ceremonies of allegiance.

BCCI

The Bank of Credit and Commerce International, which collapsed spectacularly in July 1991. Founded originally in 1972 by Agha Hassan Abedi, in 1990 BCCI came under the majority control of the family of the ruler of Abu Dhabi. By that time it had some 800,000 depositors with deposits worldwide of some US$20,000 million. In 1991 it became apparent that the bank was insolvent, as a result of suspected massive fraud which also involved the financing of drug trafficking and money-laundering. The Abu Dhabi authorities offered a US$1,700 million compensation settlement, whereby creditors would have received a return of about a third of their deposits over a period of time. A handful of depositors stuck out in the Luxembourg courts for more favourable treatment, and in early 1994 the Abu Dhabi authorities proposed a revised settlement. In the UK a report on the collapse by Lord Justice Bingham expressed serious criticism of the supervisory role played by the Bank of England.

BEAC

Bank of Central African States. The central issuing bank of the six central African countries (Cameroon, Central African Republic, Chad, Congo, Equatorial Guinea and Gabon) within the **franc zone** all of which use a common currency, the **CFA franc**.

BEAGLE CHANNEL

The seaway along the southern coast of Tierra del Fuego and a long-standing area of conflict between Chile and Argentina. Interest in the Beagle Channel islands, occupied by Chile, was revived in 1971 by reports of possible oil deposits in the area. A ruling by the **ICJ** in May 1977, awarding most of the islands to Chile, was rejected by Argentina, and a planned Argentinean invasion of the islands in 1979 was only averted by a Vatican offer to mediate in the dispute. A final joint agreement granted Chile sovereignty over the disputed Picton, Lennox and Nueva islands but only part of offshore waters east of Cape Horn in return for the upholding of its claims to waters east of the Magellan Strait. This was ratified in March 1985, having been approved by referendum in Argentina.

BECHUANALAND *see* BOTSWANA

BEIRA CORRIDOR

Zimbabwe's strategically important link with the sea. The shortest and cheapest route, it runs for 140 miles (200 km) from Mutare in Zimbabwe to the Mozambican Indian Ocean port of Beira. Facilities consist of a railway running parallel to a road, an oil pipeline, and overhead electricity cables. When the white regime in **Rhodesia** declared **UDI** in 1965, the Beira Corridor became a prime target for **guerrilla** attacks by the Zimbabwean liberation movements, providing as it did a lifeline for the white regime through what was then (until Mozambican independence in 1975) its sympathetic Portuguese-run neighbour. After Zimbabwean independence in 1980, the railway and other services were again frequently disrupted, this time by the **MNR**, the Mozambican rebel group, and Zimbabwe committed troops in 1983 to secure the Beira Corridor, as well as the Limpopo Corridor, another vital link. These forces were only withdrawn in April 1993 after the MNR had signed a peace treaty with the Mozambican government.

BEKAA

A valley in southern Lebanon close to the Syrian border, running from Baalbek to Lake Karaoun. The Bekaa has been the scene of numerous armed clashes in Lebanon's recent bloody history, including heavy fighting between **Israeli** and Syrian forces during the former's 1982 invasion of Lebanon. During the course of Lebanon's civil war the Bekaa has served as base for a host of indigenous and foreign armed militias and groups. The continued presence of large numbers of Syrian troops in the Bekaa has been used by some commentators to demonstrate the depth of Syrian hegemony over its western neighbour.

BELARUS *see* BYELARUS

BELAU

A component, also known as Palau, of the UN **Trust Territory** of the Pacific Islands, administered by the USA. Although a compact of free association was signed in 1982 between Belau and the USA, its implementation was delayed by the territory's Constitution, which banned the entry, storage or disposal of nuclear, chemical or biological weapons. Repeated referendums to rescind these clauses were held to achieve this end, but each failed to secure the necessary 75 per cent approval level. Eventually the approval requirement was reduced to a simple majority and the Constitution was duly amended in November 1993.

BELGRANO

An Argentinean battle cruiser, the *General Belgrano*, which was sunk in controversial circumstances on 2 May 1982, ending any hope of a negotiated settlement in the **Falklands War**. Of the 1,093 people aboard, 321 sailors and two civilians were killed in the attack and others later perished at sea. The attack, by the British nuclear submarine HMS *Conqueror*, took place when the *Belgrano* was heading away from the British-imposed 200-mile total **exclusion zone** around the Falklands. The British government claimed that the ship was not steaming to port but to an intermediate point to await further developments, and justified the attack as in keeping with an earlier warning that ships within or outside the zone might be attacked if considered to pose a threat.

BELIZE

A former British crown colony, British Honduras, in **Central America**, which became an independent member of the **Commonwealth** in 1981. Guatemala, which has claimed the territory since 1839, only began seriously pursuing the issue from 1964 when Belize became self-governing. An accord in which Guatemala relinquished claims on Belize was signed in September 1991. However, Guatemala effectively revoked the accord in July 1993, and in April 1994 the issue was brought before the **UN**. This reversal was a blow to Belize, especially in view of the planned reduction of British troops stationed there from 1,500 to 200 by the end of 1994.

BENELUX

The grouping of Belgium, Luxembourg and the Netherlands. The Benelux Economic Union is a customs union established in its current form by a 1958 treaty, but it originally dates back to the Convention of Ouchy in 1932. The three countries aim to promote the free movement of goods, capital and labour and to enforce a common policy in foreign trade. The Benelux countries were founder members of the **EEC**, functioning within it (and now within its development, the **EU**) as a highly cohesive group. Belgium and Luxembourg are also linked by a monetary and customs union, **BLEU**.

BENIN

The country in West Africa which was known as Dahomey prior to November 1975. It had gained independence from France in August 1960, having come under French control in 1863. President Brig.-Gen. Mathieu Kérékou declared the People's Republic of Benin in 1975, and in February 1990 the country was renamed the Republic of Benin, following the government's abandonment of **Marxism-Leninism** and coinciding with democratic reform.

BERLIN AIRLIFT

The 1948–9 operation by the **Western Allies** to supply Berlin when overland links were cut by the occupying Soviet forces. Berlin, the capital of pre-war Germany, lay in the eastern part of Germany which had been liberated by the Red Army in 1945. Berlin itself had been divided into four sectors, administered respectively by the **Soviet Union**, the USA, the UK and France under the **Four-Power Agreement**, and linked to western Germany by road and rail. Reacting to the introduction of the Deutschmark into Allied-occupied zones, which they feared would bring the collapse of the eastern German currency, the Soviets announced on 24 June 1948 that the Allies no longer had jurisdiction in Berlin. The overland links to western Germany were cut. The Western Allies began the airlift on June 26 to sustain the blockaded city, and kept it going until 11 May 1949, when the Soviets agreed to reopen the overland link.

BERLIN WALL

The barrier constructed in 1961 by the East German **communist** regime to encircle the western sectors of Berlin, deep within East Germany, which were administered by the Western powers under the **Four-Power Agreement**. Notwithstanding the 1948–9 **Berlin airlift** crisis, Berlin had remained an open city until 13 August 1961 (the night the Wall went up). Some 3 million inhabitants of the **DDR** (East Germany) had left for the West by 1961, a haemorrhage which threatened the DDR's economic viability, and one immediate purpose of the Wall was to isolate the country from external markets before the implementation of agricultural **collectivization**.

Erected with great speed initially as a fence, the Wall isolated DDR citizens from the West by preventing all access from East to West Berlin except via official border posts such as **Checkpoint Charlie**. A potent symbol of **Cold War** divisions, it was patrolled by armed guards, and escapees were shot on sight. In 1989, however, with the opening of the Hungarian-Austrian border in September, thousands of DDR citizens began flooding into the West once again. On 9 November 1989, demonstrators breached the Berlin Wall itself, setting the scene for German unification a year later.

BERMUDA CONVENTION

The 1946 agreement between the UK and the USA governing each other's access to civil air transport routes across the North Atlantic and the Pacific Ocean and in the Caribbean. This Air Transport Agreement, which also covered fares, was greatly revised in 1966, at a time of considerable expansion of civil air traffic. Both sides accorded each other increased landing and associated rights at this time. A second revision in 1977 (Bermuda Two) extended the agreement to further routes, allowed 'dual designation' of carriers by the two sides on certain routes, provided for the phasing out of the USA's 'fifth freedom' to pick up passengers in London and Hong Kong, and incorporated an existing bilateral agreement on charter services.

BERNE CONVENTION *see* WIPO

BERUFSVERBOT

(German, 'occupational ban') A West German government policy to prevent the employment of radicals in the public service, including the teaching profession. Federal guidelines were issued on 27 January 1972 for vetting the political affiliations of job applicants. The *Berufsverbot* debarred from public service anyone engaged in 'activities against the constitution' or belonging to a **right-wing** or **left-wing** extremist group. In practice the main targets were those suspected of involvement with the **Rote Armee Fraktion**, but the suspicion of investigators could fall on a wide range of leftists, peace activists and anti-nuclear campaigners. In 1985, opponents of the *Berufsverbot* claimed that 6.5 million applicants had been investigated since 1972 and that action had been taken in 7,000 cases. Left-wing *Länder* governments discontinued the practice from 1985.

BESSARABIA

A strip of territory running along the Western bank of the river Dnestr to the Black Sea coast, and bounded to the south by the River Prut and the Danube River delta. Bessarabia is now the main component of the mainly Romanian-speaking Republic of **Moldova**. It was separated from Romania in 1940, when the **Soviet Union** acquired it by threat of force and reconstituted it as the Moldavian Soviet Socialist Republic. There is now growing opposition, however, to the idea of reunification with Romania.

BETANCOURT DOCTRINE

A regional foreign policy initiative sponsored by the government of Venezuelan President Rómulo Betancourt (1959–64). Its guiding general principle was that democratic countries in the hemisphere should deny diplomatic recognition to dictatorships of both the left and the right. The policy was motivated by suspicion that Cuba was supporting Venezuelan **guerrillas** and by a near-fatal attack on Betancourt in June 1960 by an assassin hired by the then de facto ruler of the Dominican Republic, Rafael Trujillo. The **OAS**, traditionally non-interventionist, imposed sanctions on the Dominican Republic and in 1963 expelled Cuba from membership. Subsequent Venezuelan efforts to isolate regimes in Peru, the Dominican Republic, Argentina, Guatemala and Haiti failed to receive the support of other governments in the region.

BEVANITES

UK Labour Party supporters of Aneurin Bevan. Bevan, an MP from 1927 until his death in 1960, was consistently on the left wing of the party, and declined to participate in the wartime coalition government. One of his key achievements in the late 1940s was the establishment of the **NHS**, and he resigned from the government in 1951 over the projected introduction of health service charges as well as rearmament. Throughout much of the 1950s he had support from significant numbers of Labour MPs (notably within the **Tribune Group**) in his charismatic criticism of his party's economic and defence policies.

BEVERIDGE REPORT

The key document laying down the framework for the development of the **welfare state** in the UK. The report, drawn up by the eminent economist Sir William (Lord) Beveridge and published in 1942, recommended principally a universal and compulsory scheme of sickness and unemployment benefits and retirement pensions and the payment of family allowances, as well as a national health service. The coalition government in 1944 accepted the main recommendations, which were then implemented by the post-war Labour government and came into force generally in 1948.

BHARATIYA JANATA PARTY *see* BJP

BHOPAL

The capital of the Indian state of Madhya Pradesh and site in December 1984 of one of the world's worst industrial disasters. The catastrophe, which killed an estimated 4,000 people and blinded thousands more, was caused by an explosion at the US-owned Union Carbide chemical factory, which released the gas methyl isocyanate (MIC). A settlement claim won in February 1989 by the Indian government against Union Carbide worth US$470 million (less than one-fifth of its original claim), was widely regarded as insufficient compensation for victims of the disaster. Criminal proceedings against the company began in India in July 1992 but have since been desultorily pursued.

BIAFRA

The name given to the Eastern Region of Nigeria, with a mainly Ibo population of some 14 million when Lt.-Col. Chukwuemek Ojukwu proclaimed its secession from the Federal Republic of Nigeria in May 1967. There followed two-and-a-half years of terrible civil war, with 100,000 military casualties and up to 2 million other deaths from starvation and disease.

The prospect of an Ibo-led secession arose following the July 1966 coup, in which army officers from northern Nigeria took power, deposed and killed Gen. Johnson Ironsi and installed Gen. Yakubu Gowon as federal head of state. Ojukwu, whom Ironsi had appointed as military governor of the Eastern Region, refused to recognize the new federal government. Widescale massacres of Ibos in the North in September prompted a countrywide return of Ibos to the Eastern Region, and wrecked a compromise worked out in Lagos on a loose federal structure, with Ojukwu subsequently adopting an increasingly hostile stance towards the federal government. Gowon then announced, on 27 May 1967, a plan for the redivision of Nigeria into 12 states (instead of the existing four regions). In so doing he hoped not only to reduce frictions but also to woo away from secession the non-Ibo minorities in Eastern Region, by offering them the prospect of control over a smaller oil-rich state.

Ojukwu responded by proclaiming the Republic of Biafra on 30 May in Enugu. Gowon denounced this 'act of rebellion', and by July there was full-scale fighting. A Biafran campaign for international support won backing from South Africa, **Rhodesia** and Portugal, in the hope that one of black Africa's most powerful countries would be split. France supplied arms to the Biafran rebels, whereas the UK – and the **Soviet Union** – supplied them to the federal forces. In April–May 1968, amid an escalating humanitarian crisis as the war swung against the Biafrans, **Tanzania**, Gabon, **Côte d'Ivoire** and **Zambia** gave belated diplomatic recognition to the rebel republic. Eventually surrendering in July 1970, the Biafrans were then treated with surprising leniency as Gowon adopted a policy of national reconciliation.

BIBLE BELT

A geographically indistinct area of the central and southern USA, many of whose rural and small-town inhabitants are conservative Christians who subscribe to a strict code of received orthodox morality.

BIG BANG

The transformation of the London Stock Exchange in October 1986. This reflected the advent of global stock and bond trading networks and of international round-the-clock trading. In particular it abolished barriers between the different categories of stockbrokers and jobbers, opened up ownership of stockbroking firms to foreign participants, and rapidly led to the closure of the Stock Exchange's trading floor in favour of computerized share transactions. These major changes came only 12 months before **Black Monday**, the global equity market crisis.

BIG BROTHER

The fictional leader of the totalitarian state depicted in George Orwell's political novel **1984**. Big Brother's role shared features common to leadership cults of both right and left. The state's propaganda machine built a **cult of personality**, ascribing to Big Brother semi-divine status as a morally pure, all-knowing, all-powerful being. The term has become synonymous with dictatorship and the **police state**.

BIG FIVE

The original **Big Four** wartime Allies, plus France, which, despite having refused an invitation to be one of five sponsors of the **San Francisco Conference** in April–June 1945, nevertheless participated on an equal footing in the meetings of the sponsoring powers. The Big Five then became the five permanent members of the **UN Security Council**, with veto powers.

BIG FOUR

Originally a term referring to the Second World War alliance of the USA, the **Soviet Union**, the UK and China as represented by Chiang Kai-Shek's nationalist

Kuomintang (**KMT**) government. The term Big Four was also applied to the USA, the Soviet Union, the UK and France, the countries which jointly administered Germany and Austria following the conclusion of the war in 1945.

BIG THREE

The three principal Second World War allies from 1941 to 1945 – the USA, the **Soviet Union** and the UK – whose leaders met to co-ordinate military strategy and to agree upon a structure for the post-war world, notably in Tehran in late 1943, in **Yalta** in February 1945, and in **Potsdam** in July–August 1945.

BIKINI

An atoll in the Marshall Islands, in the South Pacific, used by the USA as an atomic bomb test site. The first test was carried out in 1946; between then and 1962, when testing ended, 66 atomic and hydrogen bombs were exploded on Bikini and neighbouring Enewetak. Some of the inhabitants of Bikini, who had been resettled before the first explosion, returned in 1968 but had to be moved again when tests in 1977 revealed the water and food of the atoll to be too contaminated for consumption.

BILL OF RIGHTS

A widely used collective term for the first 10 amendments to the US Constitution, which were ratified on 15 December 1791. The Bill of Rights guarantees basic political rights including religious freedom, freedom of speech, press and assembly, the rule of law and the right to possess firearms.

BILLYGATE

The generic term for a series of scandals involving Billy Carter, the younger brother of US President Jimmy Carter who held office in 1977–81. One strand of the scandals concerned allegations of financial misconduct; however, an investigation of the Carter family's finances, launched between March and October 1979, found no evidence of misconduct and nothing to support the allegation that loans made to the family's peanut farming business had been diverted into Jimmy Carter's 1976 presidential campaign. The Billygate affair was complicated by the revelation in April 1979 that Billy Carter's trip to Rome and Tripoli in the previous autumn had been paid for by the Libyan government of Col. Moamer al Kadhafi. Allegations that the trip was part of a plan to establish a conduit through which funds could be channelled into the USA were denied, however, and Billy insisted that he had no business links with the Libyan government. Billy Carter made a further visit to Tripoli on 2 September 1979, to attend a celebration of the 10th anniversary of Kadhafi's seizure of power.

BINARY WEAPONS

The product of research to make **chemical weapons** easier to stockpile. In binary weapons two chemicals are kept separate until they reach their target, when they are combined; the chemical reaction then produces a highly lethal agent. The USA launched a major binary weapons programme in 1987, but agreed at the Washington summit in 1990 to halt all production.

BINGHAM REPORT

The September 1978 report of the British inquiry into alleged **sanctions-busting** operations to supply the **UDI** regime in **Rhodesia**. In his report Thomas Bingham QC concluded that there had been some breaches in particular of the oil embargo. It also implied that Prime Minister Harold Wilson had been aware of the continued supply of oil to the Smith regime by Shell, BP and Total. This was denied at the time.

BIODIVERSITY

A contraction of 'biological diversity' – the immense variety of the world's plants, animals and habitats. There are estimated to be 30 million distinct species, some 1.4 million of which have been recorded to date. Present trends indicate, however, that 10 per cent of the world's species may be lost by the year 2000 because of damage to natural habitats from phenomena such as **acid rain** and **deforestation**. Concerns about species loss underlie the 1992

Biological Diversity Convention agreed upon at the **Earth Summit**.

BIO-ETHICS

The moral issues arising from recent and potential medical and scientific developments. These issues relate to such practices as scientifically assisted human reproduction, including surrogacy, **IVF** and artificial insemination; research on human embryos; tissue transfer and organ donation; and genetic engineering. In the UK the 1984 **Warnock Report** established the ethical ground rules for assisted reproduction.

BIOGAS

A gas used for fuel causing virtually no atmospheric pollution, leaving no wastes, and originating from renewable resources. Biogas is produced by fermenting animal dung, crop residues or human sewage in an airtight container, and is rich in methane. The residues of its production may be used as an organic fertilizer.

BIOLOGICAL DIVERSITY, CONVENTION ON

The Convention signed by 154 states at the 1992 **Earth Summit**, which aims to guard against the loss of **biodiversity** by protecting the natural environments of signatory states. It provides for technological transfers and payments to developing countries to compensate them for the extraction of genetic resources, particulary from the tropical rain forests, by pharmaceutical and other biotechnology companies. The US withheld signature until April 1993, when it introduced provisos to protect its biotechnology industry. The Convention formally came into effect in December 1993, having been ratified by 30 of its signatories.

BIOLOGICAL WARFARE

The deliberate dissemination of bacteria, viruses or other harmful biological organisms as an act of war, which is prohibited under the 1925 **Geneva protocol**. Possible targets could be enemy troops, civilian populations, or crops and livestock. Japan, in coming to terms with its militaristic past, faces allegations about biological weapons being used in particular in China in 1937–45; Nazi Germany was also feared to be developing such weapons, and the USA undertook a research programme at that time. The **UN Conference on Disarmament** concluded in 1972 a Biological Weapons Convention prohibiting their possession, which was joined by most countries including both **superpowers**. Iraq became, in the 1990s, the latest country to be accused of developing biological weapons.

BIRMINGHAM SIX

A group of six men – Patrick Hill, Richard McIlkenny, Johnny Walker, William Power, Gerard Hunter and Hugh Callaghan – wrongly imprisoned in the UK for **IRA** activities. Following the IRA bombing of two public houses in Birmingham in November 1974, the six were in August 1975 sentenced to life imprisonment for the murder of the 21 victims. Persistent campaigns for a review of their case eventually bore fruit in March 1991 when all six were freed on appeal and their convictions were overturned as unsafe and unsatisfactory in the light of new evidence. This cast doubt on the reliability of forensic evidence as well as the veracity of police officers involved in the initial interviews. Their release followed that of the **Guildford Four** in October 1989. Within hours of their release Home Secretary Kenneth Baker announced the establishment of a Royal Commission on Criminal Justice, whose report, published on 6 July 1993, recommended the creation of a tribunal to examine alleged miscarriages of justice.

BIS

The Bank for International Settlements, the 'central bankers' bank'. Founded in 1930, it promotes co-operation between central banks and provides additional facilities for international financial operations, as well as a forum for often informal discussions on monetary co-operation in general. There are 33 countries represented in the bank (18 west European, 10 central and east European and five others).

BISHO MASSACRE

The killing of 29 people on Sept. 7, 1992, when troops from the nominally independent Ciskei **bantustan** in South Africa opened fire on a crowd of some 70,000 **ANC** demonstrators. The military ruler of Ciskei, Brig. Joshua Oupa Gqozo, had effectively prohibited the ANC organizing within the bantustan, and the demonstrators were marching towards the Ciskei capital, Bisho, with the aim of forcing his resignation. The Bisho massacre prompted the resumption of talks between the ANC and the South African government, which had been suspended in June 1992 in the wake of the **Boipatong Massacre**.

BISHOPSGATE BOMB

A bomb explosion on 24 April 1993 near Bishopsgate in the City of London, the financial heart of the capital, in which one person was killed and more than 40 injured. The bomb, placed in a truck, was estimate to contain 10 pounds of **semtex** and a tonne of chemical explosive. It caused damage estimated at between £300 million and £400 million (US$450 million–$600 million). The **IRA** later claimed responsibility for the bomb.

BITBURG

A military cemetery in Germany which contains graves of those killed during the Second World War, including graves of SS officers. This SS connection made it highly controversial for US President Ronald Reagan and West German Chancellor Helmut Kohl to include a visit to Bitburg on 5 May 1985 as part of a commemoration – which also included a visit to the Bergen-Belsen concentration camp – of the 40th anniversary of the ending of the war in Europe.

BJP

The *Bharatiya Janata* Party, currently the main opposition group in the Indian parliament. Founded in 1980, the party professes a radical Hindi communalist orientation and is believed to maintain close links with a paramilitary Hindu organization, the **RSS**. The party's performance in general elections in 1989 and 1991 reflected strong support for its Hindu fundamentalist ideology, especially in northern states. However, the BJP's role in heightening Hindu-Muslim tension over the **Ayodhya mosque** dispute and its subsequent implication in the destruction of the mosque triggered a loss of confidence among voters in its northern constituencies.

BLACK BERETS

The elite paramilitary police force formed by the Soviet Interior Ministry in 1987 and also known as OMON. The force had a reputation for ruthlessness, particularly in the **Baltic states**, where three people were killed in an assault by Black Berets on the Latvian Interior Ministry during the crackdown in January 1991.

BLACK CONSCIOUSNESS

A political concept first espoused in South Africa in 1960 by Robert Sobukwe, founder of the **PAC**, and later taken up by Steve Biko and others. Rejecting co-operation with sympathetic whites in the struggle against **apartheid**, the proponents of Black Consciousness argued that the struggle could only be won by blacks – defined initially as Africans, although **Coloureds** and Indians were later invited to join. Black Consciousness was most influential during the **Soweto riots** which began in June 1976, and in October 1977 key Black Consciousness organizations were banned. In present-day South Africa the concept is most closely associated with **AZAPO**.

BLACK ECONOMY

That part of the economy based on illegal or undeclared transactions. In a broader sense it is applied to all transactions not reflected in official statistics, including avoidance of tax by exploiting legal loopholes.

BLACK MONDAY

The first day of the 1987 global equity crisis. Following a week of unsettled conditions on the US stock markets, the **Dow Jones** industrial average index fell on 19 October 1989 by over 500 points, while in London the FTSE-100 index dropped by about 250 points (over 10 per cent). There was a marked knock-on effect in most other major financial centres.

BLACK MUSLIMS

An increasingly significant group among the black population of the USA, particularly since the 1960s, as many converts chose to 'revert' to their 'original' religion as a means of rediscovering a lost collective identity. Islam became inextricably linked with the **civil rights** movement as a means by which many blacks sought to eradicate the legacy of slavery and institutionalized racial discrimination. Most black Muslims subscribe to a belief system considered heretical by orthodox Islam. Allah is identified as black, and the place of the Prophet is taken by Elijah Muhammad. The justification of Elijah's exalted position rests on the fact that he knew Allah personally (in the form of Master Farad Muhammad, founder of the **Nation of Islam**).

BLACK PANTHERS

Those belonging to the Black Panther Party, one of the most radical and influential of all the US **Black Power** movements. The organization was established in Oakland, California, in October 1964 by Huey P. Newton and Bobby Seale. Its programme, as defined by Eldridge Cleaver, one of its most influential writers, included demands for full employment or guaranteed income for the unemployed; better housing; black exemption from military service; improved black education; an end to 'exploitation' by white racist businessmen and to 'police brutality and murder of Black people'; and the release of all black prisoners and their retrial by black juries. The party also proposed a referendum for the black population of the USA on the issue of a separate black state.

Many leading members of the party were imprisoned or were killed in shoot-outs with the police. In 1969 Seale was prosecuted as one of the **Chicago Eight**, although his conviction was later overturned. In February 1971 the party split as a result of differences between Cleaver, who had fled to Algeria in 1968 and who subsequently founded an 'international section', and Newton. In May 1971 Newton announced that the Panthers would abandon the use of violence and would work within the system. Thereafter, the size and influence of the party declined.

BLACK POWER

1. The slogan adopted by black US radicals dismayed that the **civil rights** movement and the 1964 Civil Rights Act had not achieved more fundamental change. After the assassination of Malcolm X in 1965 the Black Power movement became increasingly radical under the influence of Stokely Carmichael (later Kwame Touré), who is credited with coining the term, and of the **Black Panthers**. The movement sought the overthrow of existing political and economic institutions as a prerequisite for the liberation of black Americans. White liberals were alienated by Black Power's implicit rejection of the pacifism of Martin Luther King Jr, and of his goal of integration.

2. A late 1960s movement chiefly among English-speaking anti-colonial black Caribbeans fighting for equal rights and against ruling white and mulatto minorities. It took its inspiration not only from the Black Power movement in the USA but also from the black nationalists of the 1920s and 1930s and from **Rastafarianism** and Haitian **noirisme**. Leading Black Power intellectuals were Walter Rodney, George Beckford, James Millette and Lloyd Best. Violent Black Power protests occurred in Jamaica (1968), Bermuda (1968), Curaçao (1969) and Trinidad (1970), the last triggering an army mutiny so serious for regional stability that US and Venezuelan warships were placed on standby. Black Power gradually merged with a new left movement in the region and had declined by the mid-1970s.

BLACK SASH

The South African liberal women's anti-**apartheid** organization originally formed in 1955 (as the Women's Defence of the Constitution League) in response to the removal of **Coloured** voters from the common voters' role. Black Sash subsequently organized frequent 'vigils' when women would stand silently, wearing black sashes to signify mourning for the violation of human rights. It established a network of advice centres in the **townships**, initially providing advice solely about the **pass laws** but increasingly on other problems. Originally a white women's group, its membership is now open to all races.

BLACK SEA ECONOMIC CO-OPERATION PROJECT

A grouping founded in February 1992 to promote regional economic co-operation between 11 Black Sea states: **Armenia, Azerbaijan**, Bulgaria, Georgia, Greece, **Moldova**, Romania, Russia, Turkey and **Ukraine**. Turkey was the driving force behind the project, seeing a way to extend its trade and influence among post-Soviet republics of the **Transcaucasus** and **Central Asia**.

BLACK SECTIONS

The groups set up at constituency level in the UK Labour Party in the mid-1980s by those who wanted special representation for Black members. Essentially a feature of the Labour Party in London and other urban areas, the establishment of Black Sections caused a major rift in the party. Their supporters argued that Black Sections were the best way to involve Afro-Caribbeans and Asians in mainstream politics. However, opponents regarded them as a form of **apartheid** and the National Executive Committee and the Party Conference repeatedly refused to endorse them. Eventually it was agreed that Black Sections would be dissolved and in 1993 the Black and Asian Socialist Society, a group affiliated to the Labour Party and open to all ethnic minorities, was founded.

BLACK SEPTEMBER

A Palestinian **guerrilla** organization and one of the most notorious terror organizations of the 1970s. Named in commemoration of the Jordanian expulsion of Palestinians in September 1970. The group carried out the 1972 **Munich Olympic massacre** of **Israeli** athletes at the Olympic games.

BLACK WEDNESDAY

The day in September 1992 when sterling, and the Italian lira, withdrew from the exchange rate mechanism (**ERM**) of the European Monetary System (**EMS**). During the first part of September money markets in Western Europe had been very unsettled, and on 16 September sterling came under particularly violent speculative pressure. The UK authorities tried unsuccessfully to defend the pound, introducing large temporary increases in interest rates and spending huge amounts of the official reserves. On the night of 16–17 September, however, it was announced that sterling would no longer be kept within the permitted margins of fluctuation within the ERM, to which the UK had first adhered as recently as October 1990, and that the Italian lira would also float within the ERM.

BLAIR HOUSE ACCORD

The agreement (named after the US President's official guest residence in Washington DC for visiting heads of state and government) reached in November 1992 between the **EC** and the USA that both sides would reduce agricultural export subsidies as part of the **GATT** world trade talks. Although the agreement's textual interpretation became the focus of a bitter dispute between the EC and the USA, it was subsequently incorporated into the final **Uruguay Round** protocol concluded in December 1993.

BLEU

Belgo-Luxembourg Economic Union, a monetary and customs union dating from 1922 which was restored to operation on 1 May 1945 (on the ending of German occupation). In view of the existence of a wider **Benelux** framework for customs union, the main significance of BLEU has been as a somewhat lopsided monetary union.

BLOCK VOTE

The exercise by British trade unions of a determining vote at Labour Party conferences. Traditionally voting strengths within the Labour Party conference have been based on affiliations. In the case of affiliated trade unions this has ensured that votes based on their total membership have together far outweighed those of constituency delegates; moreover, the preponderance of certain large unions has meant that individual general secretaries have often single-handedly determined the outcome of votes on crucial policy matters and the election of the party leader and deputy leader. Reforms agreed in 1992 modified this situation so that the unions' overall voting strength at the annual conference was reduced from about 87 to 70 per cent, while in 1993 **OMOV** (one-member-one-vote) was introduced for the selection of parliamentary candidates, where again trade unions had hitherto in many instances played a decisive role.

BLOODY SUNDAY

A day of serious conflict in the **Bogside** area of Londonderry, **Northern Ireland**, on 30 January 1972. A massive confrontation occurred when a technically illegal **civil rights** march disintegrated into fierce skirmishes with the security forces who had been ordered to make arrests; 13 civilians were killed, but the Widgery tribunal later effectively exonerated the security forces. The incident caused a storm of protest, including an attack on the British embassy in Dublin. It also increased support for the **IRA**, with many locals joining its ranks, while the fundraising activities of **NORAID** and other groups were boosted.

BLUE HELMETS

The colloquial name for **UN** peacekeeping troops. The term derives from the bright blue helmet donned by UN troops in place of their national helmets.

BLUE STREAK

A British rocket which in the 1950s was expected to provide a capability independent of US technological expertise to launch British nuclear warheads against targets in the **Soviet Union**. Its military role was eventually scrapped when, at the 1962 **Nassau conference**, the Macmillan government opted for US-made Polaris submarine delivery systems in tandem with Vulcan bombers rather than ground-based rockets. With an eye to the civilian satellite market, Blue Streak was nevertheless launched 11 times (1964–71), either individually or as the first stage of the Europa rocket, the collaborative effort of the European Launcher Development Organization (ELDO) set up by Belgium, France, West Germany, Italy and the UK in 1964. Due to technical and management problems, the ELDO was finally wound up in 1973 and the Europa project abandoned. Leadership in European rocketry then passed to France with the formation of the **ESA** and the development of the **Ariane** launcher.

B'NAI B'RITH

An international Jewish organization founded in 1843. Although based in Washington DC, the organization has branches in 47 countries and supports programmes designed to promote and preserve Judaism. It also operates as a pressure group in support of **Israel**.

BND

(German acronym for *Bundesnachrichtendienst* – 'Federal Intelligence Service') The BND has its headquarters in Munich, reports to the German Chancellor, and is divided into three main departments dealing with subversion, counterintelligence, and foreign intelligence. When first created in 1956, the BND absorbed the Gehlen Organization, a covert intelligence force which had co-operated with US intelligence agencies after the Second World War.

BOARD OF DEPUTIES OF BRITISH JEWS

An officially recognized representative body of British Jewry, made up of representatives from synagogues and from some secular organizations. It originated in 1760, gaining statutory recognition half a century later. Based in central London, its official title is the London Committee of Deputies of the British Jews.

BOAT PEOPLE

1. The term applied to Vietnamese refugees who fled their homeland by sea following the end of the **Vietnam War** and landed in Hong Kong and various other countries in **south-east Asia**, with the eventual aim of gaining residency in the **West**. The majority of boat people who left during the immediate post-war period were middle-class southerners, but by 1978 they were joined by an increasing number of peasants and urban workers and thousands of Hoa (ethnic Chinese). Most were denied political refugee status (being deemed **economic migrants**) and were forced either to live in camps established at their place of arrival or to return to Vietnam. Improved socio-economic conditions in Vietnam, expansion of legal departures from refugee camps through the **UN's** orderly departure programme and the success of a **UNHCR** information campaign drastically reduced the number of boat people fleeing Vietnam. As a consequence the Hong Kong and other south-east Asian authorities now concern themselves with screening out the remaining 'economic migrants' for **compulsory repatriation**.

2. A term applied to Haitian and Cuban refugees attempting to reach the USA. Given the restrictive US policy on the issuing of visas, many people are tempted to risk crossing the Straits of Florida, often on home-made rafts, and thousands have been drowned. Cuban survivors are not returned and under the 1966 Cuban Adjustment Law obtain legal residence after a year. Such treatment is denied to thousands of Haitians who, since the 1991 military coup, have been deemed **economic migrants** and intercepted by the US Coast Guard, interned and in most cases repatriated to face torture, imprisonment and even death. Under strong domestic pressure from liberal and black lobbies the US adminstration announced in May 1994 that Haitian refugees would not be returned without an asylum hearing.

BODO

A tribal hill people of Mongoloid ethnic origin campaigning for a separate Bodo homeland in the north-eastern Indian state of Assam. In February 1993 Bodo groups, including the militant, outlawed Bodo Security Force, agreed to end their insurgency after the state government signed a peace settlement granting Bodos limited autonomy within the region. Since then there has been renewed violence sparked by Bodo complaints that ethnic Assamese, mainly Muslims, still occupy many of the villages allocated to Bodos.

BODY BAG

Article used by the US military to transport the bodies of personnel killed in action. The term entered the wider vocabulary during the **Vietnam War**, as the rising toll of US casualties became one focus of growing public opposition to the conflict. It has become an emotive term which encapsulates US public fears of foreign military involvement.

BOER *see* AFRIKANER

BOFORS SCANDAL

The scandal involving the armaments companies, Bofors and Nobel Kemi, subsidiaries of Nobel Industries Sweden, which centred on claims – first made in April 1987 – by Swedish members of parliament that they had exported weapons and war materials to Iran and India in contravention of a ban on arms sales to countries at war or to areas of military sensitivity. The controversy intensified after the Indian government requested an investigation into reports that Bofors had paid substantial bribes to high-ranking Indian defence officials and politicians in order to secure a multi-million dollar defence contract in March 1986.

BOGOTAZO

The mass outburst of rioting in the Colombian capital Bogotá in response to the assassination on 9 April 1948 of Jorge Eliécer Gaitán, leader of the opposition Liberal Party. Regarded as a catalyst for two decades of nationwide violence – **La Violencia** – the main outburst was an essentially spontaneous affair by thousands of people who looted the city, many not necessarily to avenge Gaitán but to display their hostility towards a social and economic system dominated by a small, powerful elite.

BOGSIDE

An area of Londonderry in **Northern Ireland** with an almost exclusively Catholic/republican population. Already the scene of violence from 1969, the Bogside on 30 January 1972 (**Bloody Sunday**) saw a massive confrontation with the security forces.

BOHEMIA

Now, with Moravia, the core of the **Czech Republic**. Bohemia had emerged as a kingdom in the tenth century, and Czech **nationalism** later drew on key episodes in Bohemian history, particularly the Hussite wars of the fifteenth century. By the end of the Thirty Years War (1618–48) Bohemia had been absorbed into the Habsburg Empire. A resurgence of Czech nationalism in the late nineteenth and early twentieth centuries coincided with burgeoning economic growth in Bohemia to create a confident, liberal bourgeoisie.

BOIPATONG MASSACRE

A bloody attack on residents of the South African **township** of Boipatong, 40 miles (65 km) south of Johannesburg, on 17 June 1992. At least 45 people were killed. The attackers were later identified as supporters of **Inkatha**, although the organization denied any link with the massacre. Condemning Inkatha, the **ANC** also accused the government's security forces of failing to protect the township dwellers. The incident provoked the withdrawal of the ANC and its allies from the constitutional negotiations forum, **CODESA**. Talks between the ANC and government only resumed in September 1992, after the **Bisho Massacre**.

BOKASSA DIAMONDS AFFAIR

The scandal surrounding the gift of diamonds to French President Valéry Giscard d'Estaing from Jean-Bedel Bokassa, the notorious self-styled Emperor of the Central African Empire (now Republic). Details of the gift were published by the French satirical weekly *Le Canard Enchaîné* in October 1979 following the overthrow of Bokassa. In November 1979 Giscard insisted that the gifts had not been of great value, but the controversy continued to reverberate, particularly after Bokassa himself confirmed in September 1980 that the allegations were true. In March 1981 the **Elysée Palace** confirmed that the diamonds had been received in the period 1973–5 and disclosed that they had been sold in December 1980. The scandal was thought to have been a factor in the defeat of Giscard d'Estaing in the 1981 presidential elections.

BOLOGNA BOMBING

The bombing of Bologna railway station in Italy on 2 August 1980 by **right-wing** terrorists, the culmination of the so-called 'strategy of tension'. The bombing, in which 85 people died, was linked to the clandestine **P-2** masonic lodge, whose Grand Master Licio Gelli was convicted on associated charges in July 1988.

BOMBAY SECURITIES SCANDAL

The multi-million dollar financial fraud involving several Indian state and foreign-owned banks which emerged in May 1992 and caused a dramatic slump on the Bombay stock market. At the heart of the scandal was one of India's leading stockbrokers, Harshad Mehta, who was alleged to have obtained unsecured loans from a number of leading commercial banks. The affair, which generated losses equivalent to nearly US$2,000 million, prompted a host of official and parliamentary inquiries. Although criminal charges have been brought against Mehta and several others implicated in the scandal, trials have yet to be held.

BOPHUTATSWANA *see* BANTUSTAN

BOSNEGER

(Dutch, 'forest blacks') An ethnic group in **Surinam**, called Bush Negroes by English-speaking settlers, representing about 10 per cent of the country's population. They descend from Africans who escaped from slavery in the seventeenth century and settled in the rainforests of the interior. Their long struggle for self-determination and equal rights culminated in 1986, when the Surinamese Liberation Army (Jungle Commando) led by Ronnie Brunswijk began a **guerrilla** campaign against the dictatorship of Lt.-Col. Desiré 'Desi' Bouterse. A peace agreement with a new democratic government was finally achieved on 8 August 1992, although a few small guerrilla groups, organized by individual bosneger clans, are still active.

BOSNIA-HERCEGOVINA

An ethnically diverse **Balkan** republic which has been in a state of civil war since its declaration of independence from **Yugoslavia** in March 1992. Bosnia-Hercegovina was ruled for centuries under the Ottoman Empire until 1878, and then came within the orbit of the Austro-Hungarian Empire. The territory formed the heartland of the Kingdom of Serbs, Croats and Slovenes (Yugoslavia) created in 1919. The brutal civil war in former Yugoslavia has effectively partitioned Bosnia-Hercegovina between Serbs ambitious to create a **Greater Serbia** through **ethnic cleansing**, and Muslims and Croats in a fitful alliance. Some 44 per cent of Bosnia-Hercegovina's pre-war population of 4.2 million were **Bosnian Muslims**, 31 per cent Serbs and 17 per cent Croats.

BOSNIAN MUSLIMS

One of the three main groups which became locked in conflict in the former Yugoslav republic of **Bosnia-Hercegovina** in 1992. The presence of a Muslim community was a legacy of the centuries-long Ottoman Turkish occupation up until 1878. Under Ottoman rule many of the indigenous Croats and Serbs converted to Islam, the religion of their conquerors, but by the mid-twentieth century many Bosnian Muslims no longer adhered strictly to Islam. In 1961, within the Yugoslav state, citizens were given the choice of identifying themselves in census returns as Muslim rather than Croat, Serb or other ethnic identity. A sense of community based on religious affiliation grew stronger, but it was not until the break-up of **Yugoslavia** and the outbreak of the civil war in Bosnia-Hercegovina in 1992, in which Bosnian Muslims became the victims of **ethnic cleansing**, that Muslim **nationalism** became a formidable force.

BOSS

The Bureau of State Security, a now defunct branch of the South African intelligence service. BOSS was established in 1969 by Prime Minister J. B. Vorster under the former head of the Security Police Gen. H. J. van den Bergh. It dominated South African intelligence operations for almost a decade and was used not only against anti-**apartheid** 'subversives' but also against perceived dissident elements in the ruling National Party (NP). Its influence began to wane following South Africa's disastrous invasion of Angola in 1975, an action forced upon the military hierarchy by BOSS, and the organization's failure to predict, or respond effectively to, the 1976 **Soweto riots**. It was eclipsed by military intelligence in 1978 when P. W. Botha became Prime Minister. The organization was later purged and restructured and in 1980 renamed the National Intelligence Service (NIS).

BOTSWANA

A country of 1.5 million inhabitants in southern Africa. Independent since September 1966, it had previously been a British protectorate (known as Bechuanaland) administered as one of the 'High Commission Territories', together with Basutoland (now **Lesotho**) and Swaziland.

BOUGAINVILLE REVOLUTIONARY ARMY *see* BRA

BOUNDARIES COMMISSION

The UK body responsible for defining the boundaries of parliamentary constituencies. These are reviewed periodically to take account of population changes – the process known in the USA as **reapportionment**.

BOURGEOIS NATIONALISM

A Marxist term to describe an inherent feature of **capitalist** systems, in which patriotism is deliberately fostered by the bourgeoisie among the working class in order to divert it from the class struggle. Bourgeois nationalism, according to Marxist theory, leads to imperialism and war.

BOVINE SPONGIFORM ENCEPHALOPATHY *see* BSE

BRA

The Bougainville Revolutionary Army, a **guerrilla** force fighting for independence for the mineral-rich island of Bougainville from the state of Papua New Guinea. Founded in 1988 by Francis Ona, the BRA succeeded in forcing the closure of the island's huge Panguna copper mine in 1989. In March 1990 Papuan troops withdrew from the island and in May the BRA declared an independent Republic of Bougainville, which failed to gain international recognition, however, and was subject to a debilitating Papuan economic blockade. Papuan troops returned in 1992, re-established control over much of the territory and claimed to have defeated the BRA, but guerrilla units continued to operate.

BRADY BILL

US legislation which imposed a five-day waiting period on anyone wishing to buy a handgun, in order that the background of the purchaser could be checked for evidence of a criminal record. The bill was named after Ronald Reagan's press secretary, James S. Brady, who was severely disabled in the 1981 assassination attempt on the President. First proposed in 1986, the measure was bitterly opposed by the gun ownership lobby but was finally approved by **Congress** in November 1993 and signed by President Bill Clinton on 30 November. It notably affected 32 states and the US territory of Puerto Rico, as in the other 18 states comparable or stronger **gun control** legislation had already been enacted. The Brady Bill was the first significant piece of national gun control legislation passed since the banning of the mail order sale of rifles and shotguns in 1968.

BRADY PLAN

A debt reduction plan introduced in March 1989 by the then US Treasury Secretary Nicholas Brady. It represented a major US policy revision on the debt issue, particulary in relation to **Latin America**, and was aimed at encouraging debt-reduction agreements between commercial creditor banks and their **Third-World** debtors. Controversially, support was, and remains, conditional on the adoption of strict **IMF** structural adjustment programmes focused on heavy cuts in public expenditure and the restructuring of economies to attract private investment.

BRANDT COMMISSION

The Independent Commission on International Development Issues, set up in November 1977 and chaired by former West German Chancellor Willy Brandt, which produced in 1980 the influential report *North-South: a programme for survival*. The 18-member commission then continued to meet, up to and after the October 1981 **Cancun** summit, disbanding only in February 1983 after the publication of its final report, *Common Crisis*. The Brandt Commission's basic message was of global interdependence. In this context it stressed that the countries of the developed **North** and the developing **South** must seek common solutions across the spectrum of issues from basic needs to trade, energy, economic recovery, financial stability and security. Its most urgent and specific recommendations were for measures to tackle the world **debt crisis**.

BRD

(German abbreviation of *Bundesrepublik Deutschland* – Federal Republic of Germany or FRG) The official name of Germany. In Germany itself the state is usually designated simply the *Bundesrepublik*. At reunification in October 1990 the BRD incorporated the five **Länder** which had constituted East Germany (the **DDR**). Previously the term BRD had been synonymous with West Germany, which was formed in 1949 from the territory occupied in 1945 by the three **Western Allies**, and which was defined in the 1949 **Basic Law** as a 'democratic and social federal state'.

BRETTON WOODS

The conference held in New Hampshire in July 1944 which laid the basis for the construction of the post-war financial order. In particular it provided for the establishment of the **IMF** and the **World Bank**, and the IMF began operating, with some 30 member states, on 1 March 1947. Although the institutions which emerged from Bretton Woods fell far short of John Maynard Keynes's plans for a genuinely independent world central bank with the power to encroach upon the sovereignty of individual states, they did go some way towards addressing the problems of competitive devaluation, exchange and trade restrictions, and a lack of international reserves which had bedeviled the pre-war world.

BREZHNEV DOCTRINE

The Soviet bloc doctrine named after the then Soviet head of State, Leonid Brezhnev, and set down formally in a statement issued by the **CPSU's** official newspaper **Pravda** in September 1968, underscoring the Soviet claim to a sphere of influence in **Eastern Europe** in the wake of the invasion of **Czechoslovakia** in August of that year. Although the Brezhnev doctrine insisted that each **communist** state might take its 'own separate road to socialism', it added that such states 'must damage neither socialism in their own country, nor the fundamental interests of the socialist countries, nor the worldwide workers' movement'. The doctrine was thus a justification of Soviet intervention to prevent threats to socialism. It hung over the region until 1989, when the so-called **Sinatra doctrine** confirmed its demise.

BRIGATE ROSSE

(Italian, 'Red Brigades') **left-wing** urban **guerrillas**, responsible for a spate of kidnappings and bombings in the 1970s which they carried out with the aim of provoking revolution and civil war. Their most notorious action was the kidnapping and murder of former Prime Minister Aldo **Moro** in 1978. The Red Brigades were formed on 20 October 1970 and described themselves as 'autonomous workers' organizations'. Reacting to the failure of the revolutionary but non-violent groups of the 1960s to achieve change, they prioritized violence, attacking 'the heart of the state' by kidnapping officials. They were almost completely suppressed after having achieved national notoriety by kidnapping a Genoese judge, Mario Sossi in 1974, but from 1976 their influence grew again as the security forces relaxed their grip and as new sympathisers were recruited, disillusioned by the **communist** Party's strategy of co-operation with Christian Democrat-led governments. Their killings increased after Moro's murder, but over the 1980s the Brigades were gradually dismantled, largely owing to the policy of offering reduced sentences to '*pentiti*' ('supergrasses', literally 'repentants') in return for information.

BRILLIANT PEBBLES

Small, space-based missile interceptors forming part of the US strategic weapons system known as the Strategic Defence Initiative (SDI) or '**Star Wars**'. Research into the possible deployment of 'brilliant pebbles' was first mooted in the 1990 US defence budget which called for increased spending on SDI. The thaw in relations between the USA and the former **Soviet Union**, however, brought pressure for cuts in US defence spending, and attention shifted to the idea of a joint superpower ballistic missile defence system with ground- and space-based elements, referred to as **GPALS** ('global protection against limited strikes').

BRITAIN

A term employed loosely to denote either **Great Britain** or the **United Kingdom**. Even in official statements the terms Britain and British are used in such senses, as in 'the British government'.

BRITISH ISLES

The geographical entity comprising the **United Kingdom**, Ireland, and associated islands including the Isle of Man (but not the Channel Islands).

BRIXTON RIOTS

Serious inner-city disturbances in south-east London in 1981. An outbreak of violence on 10–12 April 1981 in the multiracial area of Brixton caused severe damage to property and gave rise to widespread looting. The **Scarman Report**, resulting from a public inquiry into the disorders, made a series of fundamental recommendations both as to the immediate issue and as to more general aspects of the problems facing inner-city areas.

BROADWATER FARM

A council estate in Tottenham, an economically deprived area of north London, and the scene of violent rioting in October 1985 during which a police officer, PC Keith Blakelock, was murdered. The riot followed the death of a local woman, Cynthia Jarrett, when police entered her home. Three young men – Winston Silcott, Mark Braithwaite and Engin Raghip – were subsequently sentenced to life imprisonment for the murder of Blakelock. In November 1991 the Court of Appeal overturned their convictions, finding that police had tampered with confession statements.

BROEDERBOND

(Afrikaans, 'League of Brothers') A secret, elitist South African Afrikaner society. Established in 1918, the *Broederbond* has an enormous influence within the National Party, the ruling party from 1948 until the non-racial democratic elections in April 1994. It was a driving force in the development of Afrikaner **nationalism** and the establishment of **apartheid**. In November 1993 the *Broederbond* opened its membership to all Afrikaans speakers (ending its exclusion of women and non-whites), changed its name to the *Afrikanerbond* (Afrikaner League), and resolved to become more 'transparent', removing restrictions on the identification of members.

BROOKINGS INSTITUTION

An influential US **think tank** based in Washington DC. A generally liberal body, the Brookings Institution brings together a wide range of distinguished figures from the fields of political science, economics, journalism, diplomacy, politics and public service, both formally and informally, and produces its own assessment of contemporary ideas, events and government policies.

BRUGES GROUP

An informal Conservative grouping of '**Eurosceptics**'. The title of the group was a reference to a speech made in the Belgian city of Bruges on 20 September 1988 by the then UK Prime Minister Margaret Thatcher.

BRUNDTLAND REPORT

The influential report of the World Commission on Environment and Development, published in 1988 and focusing on the concept of **sustainable development**. The Commission, chaired by Norwegian Prime Minister Gro Harlem Brundtland, had been set up by the **UN General Assembly** in 1983 with the brief of recommending an agenda for global action for the year 2000 and beyond. Its report, while subscribing to the objective of promoting economic growth, placed greater emphasis on the quality of such growth, and insisted that economic decisions must be integrated with environmental considerations. It also set out goals in terms of basic needs, resource management and technology policies.

BRUSSELS

A shorthand term, often with a pejorative connotation, for the bureaucracy and regulations of the **EU**, which has its main headquarters in the Belgian capital. Brussels is also the headquarters of **NATO** and home of various other European organizations.

BRUSSELS TREATY

The treaty signed in March 1948 creating a military alliance between France, the UK and the **Benelux** countries. In 1954 (at the instigation on the UK following the collapse of plans for a European Defence Community) Germany and Italy joined the Brussels Treaty signatories in what then became the **WEU**. Meanwhile, Western

Europe's military alliance system had already taken on its wider and decisive North Atlantic dimension, with the inclusion of the USA and Canada in the 1949 North Atlantic Treaty on common defence, the basis for the creation of **NATO**.

BSE

Bovine spongiform encephalopathy, commonly known as 'mad cow disease'. Related to scrapie in sheep, it was believed to have developed in cows fed on infected sheep offal. Research began in 1990 on a possible link between BSE and the human degenerative Creutzfeld-Jakob Disease. BSE had first made headlines in the UK in 1988, when farmers were ordered to slaughter all affected cattle, with compensation to farmers concerned. In 1989 the use of all beef offal in human food was banned in the UK. In June 1994 Germany disregarded **EU** agricultural policy rules and imposed a unilateral ban on beef imports from the UK, because of consumer fears about the human health implications of BSE.

BUDDHA SASANA

(Sinhalese, 'Buddhist religion') The basis of the ideology of fundamentalist Sinhalese Buddhist **nationalism** most commonly associated with Solomon Bandaranaike, leader of the Sri Lanka Freedom Party (SLFP) who was assassinated in September 1959. It made distinctive use of Buddhist texts, in particular the Theravada chronicles, in an attempt to present **Sri Lanka** as an island sanctified by the Buddha himself and defended by righteous kings against attacks by evil forces, namely the Tamils.

BUFFER STOCK FINANCING FACILITY

An **IMF** facility introduced in 1969 to help finance IMF members' contributions to approved international commodity buffer stocks of primary products, provided that the member concerned demonstrated a balance of payments need. Between 1969 and the mid-1980s a total of 18 countries made purchases under the facility, to finance buffer stocks of tin, sugar and rubber.

BULGARIAN TURKS

Bulgaria's ethnic Turkish community, which numbers between 500,000 and 1 million out of the total population of 9 million. The Bulgarian Turks were subject to a campaign of forced assimilation under the **Communist** regime which reached crisis point in 1985 with the compulsory changing of Turkish names to **Slavonic** ones. The repressive measures included the phasing-out of Turkish-language teaching and broadcasting; the restriction of Islamic practices and Turkish dress and customs; and restrictions on journalists and foreigners visiting areas with a majority of Turkish inhabitants. Many fled to Turkey to escape the intensified repression in mid-1989. Remarkably, following the general election of October 1990 the ethnic Turkish Movement for Rights and Freedoms supported the coalition government led by the former communist Bulgarian Socialist party, and some 300,000 Bulgarian Turkish refugees began to return. Further controversy was sparked in 1991 with the introduction in some regions of optional Turkish language lessons in schools, to which nationalist Bulgarian parents objected.

BUMIPUTRA

(Malay, 'sons of the soil') A term used to denote the Malays and other indigenous peoples of **Malaysia**, as distinct from citizens of Chinese or Indian descent. The presence of large Chinese and Indian communities in Malaysia is a legacy of the heavy dependence of the tin and rubber industries on immigrant labour during British rule. Their political and economic relationship with the bumiputra has been at the heart of post-independence nation-building. Serious intercommunal rioting broke out in 1969, engendered largely by resentment amongst Malays at the Chinese community's economic dominance. The government's response, known as the New Economic Policy, ultimately failed in its aim to increase the overall economic influence of the bumiputra.

BUNDESBANK

(German, 'federal bank') The central bank of Germany, based in Frankfurt, which acts independently of the federal government and, as an important lever in **Western Europe's** most powerful economy, can influence the pace of European economic and monetary union. The Bundesbank is run by a board of its own directors and the directors of the **Länder** central banks. Its main functions include issuing currency, regulating money circulation and credit supply, setting interest rates and determining the minimum reserve ratio of German banks. Profits from trading are transferred to the government. The Bundesbank was originally created in 1957 in West Germany, extending its role in 1990 to cover the whole of united Germany.

BUREAUCRACY

The system of adminstration of the affairs of state (hence 'bureaucrat' – a functionary of the system). Bureaucracies tend to be highly organized and hierarchical. Although in most cases the bureaucracy is nominally the impartial agent of government, it often behaves as an elite, jealously protective of its own interests, eager to centralise power and unwilling to surrender powers or prerogatives once acquired.

BURKINA FASO

(composite of More, Dioula and Gourmantche, 'land of incorruptible men') The name adopted by Upper Volta on 4 August 1984 on the first anniversary of the coup led by Capt. Thomas Sankara. The name Upper Volta had been retained following independence from France in August 1960.

BURUNDI

A central Africa country which gained independence in July 1962. The majority (80 per cent) of the population are **Hutu**, although the traditionally dominant people are the minority **Tutsi**. In the late nineteenth century Burundi, with **Rwanda**, fell under German control, the two together being known as Ruanda-Urundi. During the First World War, the Germans were driven out by Belgian forces and in 1919 the two territories were mandated to Belgium by the League of Nations, which later administered them as UN **trust territories**.

BUSING

The practice of transporting schoolchildren to schools outside their immediate neighbourhood in order to ensure a racial mix of pupils. The practice was adopted following the dismantling of **segregation** in the US **South**.

BUTCHER OF LYON

The term popularly used to describe former German SS officer Klaus Barbie, who had served as Gestapo commander of the Lyon area in 1942–4 and who was alleged to have been involved in the deportation of Jews and members of the French Resistance. Recruited by US Army intelligence after the war, Barbie had been assisted in emigrating to Bolivia in 1951. He was eventually extradited by the French government and stood trial in Lyon on 11 May–3 July 1987. Although he had already been convicted of war crimes in 1952 and 1954 in absentia (and sentenced to death), the French statute of limitations meant that the convictions were no longer valid, and the 1987 charges related to 'crimes against humanity'. Barbie's refusal to participate in the proceedings on the grounds that his expulsion from Bolivia had been illegal, heightened the impression that the case was being conducted as a show trial. Following his conviction, Barbie, 73, was sentenced to life imprisonment.

BUTSKELLISM

The supposedly shared philosophy behind the policies of the UK Conservative and Labour parties in the 1950s. The term, coined by the *Economist* in the mid-1950s, was used later by **Thatcherite** detractors to deride the blandness of compromise and **consensus politics**. It derives from a combination of the names of R. A. Butler and Hugh Gaitskell (Conservative and Labour Chancellors of the Exchequer in 1950–1 and 1951–5 respectively). Butskellite Conservatism accepted the principle of the **welfare state** and the nationalization of 'the commanding heights of industry' carried out by the Labour government of Clement Attlee in 1945–51. Conversely, a significant element in the attitudes and policies of Gaitskell (leader of his party in 1955–63) was his efforts to eliminate **Clause Four** from the constitution of the Labour Party in the late 1950s.

BUTTER MOUNTAIN

The vast surplus of butter built up in **EC** storage in the 1970s because the farm price support system under the common agricultural policy (**CAP**) gave dairy farmers the incentive to produce more than the market required. The problem was compounded by the fact that New Zealand producers were allowed to export some of their much cheaper butter to the otherwise highly protected EC market for the first five years after the UK joined the EC in 1973. The CAP also created other 'mountains', notably of beef, as well as a 'wine lake'. The issue was eventually tackled in two ways: by measures to dispose of surpluses, including controversial cheap sales to the **Soviet Union**; and by imposing production quotas on farmers.

BYELARUS

One of the successor states of the **Soviet Union**, which declared independence in 1991 following the failed **August coup** attempt. As Byelorussia (meaning white Russia), it had been one of the 15 constituent Soviet republics. Byelarus has a population of some 10.2 million and was a founding member of the **CIS**. Acute economic difficulties have drawn it back into the orbit of the **Russian Federation**; there are nationalist elements in contemporary Byelarus, but the pro-Russian group is very strong. Byelorussia had its roots in historic Russia, and although it became part of the **Lithuanian**-Polish empire in the fifteenth and sixteenth centuries, it came under Russian rule once more in 1795. Briefly independent in 1918, it was divided between Poland and Bolshevik Russia in 1919.

CABINDA ENCLAVE

A resource-rich pocket of land which is part of Angola, although it is bordered by Congo, Zaïre and the sea. Cabinda's rich natural resources include oil, phosphates, coffee, cocoa and timber. The **Alvor Agreement** of 1975 guaranteed its integrity as part of Angola, but this was rejected by the FLEC (the Front for the Liberation of the Enclave of Cabinda), which began a **guerrilla** war against the Luanda government. Although FLEC activity continues, its campaign has been largely ineffective.

CABLE NEWS NETWORK *see* CNN

CABORA BASSA DAM

A hydro-electric dam situated on the Zambezi River in Mozambique. One of Africa's largest hydro-electric constructions, it was completed in 1977. It has a planned total capacity of 2,000 megawatts for distribution throughout the country, although the main market is South Africa. It is owned and will be operated by Portugal until the end of the century when ownership will be transferred to Mozambique; an agreement in 1982 assigned a proportion of revenue to the Maputo government. The dam's transmission lines were frequently the target of the rebel **MNR** during the Mozambican civil war. More than 125 miles (200 km) of power lines were destroyed and Cabora Bassa was reduced to only 1.5 per cent capacity. In January 1994 the Mozambican government, Portugal and South Africa agreed details of a package to rebuild the power lines supplying electricity to South Africa.

CAIRNS GROUP

A trade group founded in 1986 to coincide with the launch of the **Uruguay Round** of **GATT**. Led by Australia and named after the Australian town of Cairns, it is composed of the major agricultural exporting countries which seek to bring about the reform of world agricultural trade through a reduction in subsidies. Its current members are Argentina, Australia, Brazil, Canada, Chile, Colombia, Fiji, Hungary, Indonesia, **Malaysia**, New Zealand, Philippines, Thailand and Uruguay.

CALI CARTEL

The **Latin American** drug cartel based in the city of Cali, in south-west Colombia. Under the leadership of drug baron Rodríguez Orejula, it developed a sophisticated, businesslike organization which facilitated its quiet penetration of the influential social and political circles, in contrast to the violent and high-profile methods of the **Medellín cartel** which took the brunt of armed state action.

CALVI AFFAIR

The scandal surrounding the mysterious death in London in June 1982 of 'God's banker', Roberto Calvi. A member of the **P-2** Masonic lodge, and president of the Italian Banco Ambrosiano (which was closely entwined with the Vatican Bank IOR), Calvi was found hanging under Blackfriars Bridge. A London inquest eventually returned an open verdict but a court in Milan in 1989 decided that Calvi had been murdered. Banco Ambrosiano's collapse and liquidation had far-reaching repercussions, with fraud and corruption trials stretching into the early 1990s.

CAM RANH BAY

A major air-naval base in Vietnam used by the **Soviet Union** from 1979, but originally developed by the United States during the **Vietnam War** at a total cost in excess of US$2,000 million. Following the US withdrawal in 1975, the Soviets pressed for access to Cam Ranh Bay, which, situated midway between Vladivostok and the Indian Ocean, would thus be a base of massive strategic value to the Soviet Far Eastern Fleet. Although the Vietnamese were initially wary of what China's reaction might be, they granted use of the base to the Soviet Union in 1979 in exchange for Soviet diplomatic support and military aid. At its peak in the mid-1980s Cam Ranh served as the Soviet Far Eastern Fleet's main supply and repair base and housed up to 7,000 Soviet servicemen. In the late 1980s the Soviet Union began reducing its air and naval forces at Cam Ranh, a process which was accelerated by the Russian government after the break-up of the Soviet Union in 1991. Russia subsequently failed in its efforts to reach an agreement with Vietnam which would provide for continued use of some of Cam Ranh's facilities.

CAMBRIDGE MAFIA

A media phrase coined because of the number of Cambridge University graduates in the UK Cabinet in the early 1990s – eight out of 22 as of early 1994, whereas Conservative cabinets were traditionally dominated by Oxford men.

CAMELOT

A term widely used to describe the administration of President John F. Kennedy in 1961–3. Kennedy, a Democrat, who was inaugurated in January 1961 at the age of 43, was the youngest elected President in US history, and was 27 years the junior of his (Republican) predecessor, Dwight D. Eisenhower. Camelot, with its connotations of the mythical court of King Arthur, was used as an attempt to encapsulate both the glamour surrounding the new President and First Lady, Jacqueline Kennedy, and the sense of a new dawn which Kennedy's election seemed to herald. It also denoted the image of the new administration summoning the best and the brightest from a new generation to Washington DC and including them within the government. The myth was sealed by Kennedy's assassination in Dallas in November 1963, although in recent years the image has been tarnished by a more sober assessment of Kennedy's record in government.

CAMORRA

The network of groups engaged in organized crime in the Naples region. The Camorra is often grouped together with the Sicilian **Mafia** (*Cosa Nostra*) and the Calabrian **'Ndrangheta**.

CAMP DAVID

The official rural retreat of the US President. Camp David is located in the state of Maryland (near Washington DC) and was named after the son of President Dwight D. Eisenhower.

CAMP DAVID AGREEMENTS

Two framework agreements on **Middle East** peace signed at **Camp David** on 17 September 1978 by **Israeli** Prime Minister Menachem Begin and Egyptian President Anwar el Sadat. With US President Jimmy Carter acting as an intermediary, the Camp David **peace process** had started in November 1977 when Sadat paid a historic visit to **Jerusalem**. The agreements signed by Sadat and Begin at Camp David contained separate provisions for an Israeli-Egyptian peace treaty (eventually signed in March 1979) and an overall Middle East peace settlement. The latter, which dealt in particular with the granting of what was termed 'full autonomy' to the Palestinians of the Israeli-occupied **West Bank** and **Gaza Strip**, proved unworkable. The **PLO** accused Sadat of betraying the Palestinian and Arab cause (a view widely shared in the Arab world), particularly because the agreement did not provide for the genuine self-determination of the Palestinian people in their own land. In the Arab world the price paid by Egypt for Camp David was virtually total political and economic isolation.

CANCUN SUMMIT

A meeting in October 1981 arranged at the instigation of the **Brandt Commission**, and at the invitation of Mexican President José López Portillo, to discuss the progress of **North-South** negotiations. The participants, in what was officially designated an International Meeting on Co-operation and Development, were the leaders of 14 developing countries and eight industrialized countries. Despite subsequent efforts to talk up the 'spirit of Cancun', the summit made no real headway on the issue which continued to stand in the way of substantive North-South dialogue – whether the **UN General Assembly**, with its numerical **Third World** majority, or the **IMF** and **World Bank**, with their voting systems weighted in favour of the industrialized countries, should provide the structure in which to hammer out the shape of a new international economic order.

CANTONIZATION

The division of a country into a large number of units, with the **devolution** of powers from the national level to these units. In Switzerland, a confederation of cantons, the system is seen as a fundamental element in the functioning of democracy. Where cantonization is not a native growth, however, the idea is often seen as synonymous with divide and rule. In relation to plans for **Bosnia-Hercegovina** in 1992–3, the term was used mainly by its opponents to stigmatize the proposals (and the fact that ethnic criteria would determine the units) as a deliberate strategy to render national government powerless.

CAP

The Common Agricultural Policy, a central element in the **EEC** (and thus in the **EC** and now the **EU**) since the 1957 **Rome Treaty**. It is essentially a single internal market for agricultural produce, with an elaborate system for guaranteeing the incomes of farmers by fixing a minimum Community-wide price for their produce. 'Intervention' then involves buying up surpluses to keep prices from falling, although since the introduction of reforms in March 1984 there has been more emphasis on setting quotas to restrict overproduction. According to the principle of Community preference, farmers are protected against competition from overseas by import levies, a particularly controversial matter for the UK in the 1970s because UK consumers were used to cheaper food, particularly from **Commonwealth** countries like New Zealand. The CAP is funded through **FEOGA**, which consumes the lion's share of the Community budget.

CAPE CANAVERAL

The location of the US **NASA** rocket launch centre. It was developed in the 1950s and 1960s on 80,000 acres of sand and swamp adjacent to Cape Canaveral, on Merritt Island, Florida. A $1,000 million construction programme was needed to upgrade it with giant assembly buildings and launch pads to achieve the lunar landing **Apollo Project**. On 29 November 1963, President Lyndon B. Johnson named NASA's launch operations centre and the Cape itself after the late President John F. Kennedy. The centre still bears his name, but continuous lobbying by 4,000 local residents resulted in Cape Kennedy reverting to the name Cape Canaveral on 9 October 1973 by order of the Department of the Interior.

CAPITAL PUNISHMENT

The death penalty imposed by the state. The human rights organization Amnesty

International lists 103 states which apply capital punishment for various crimes. Other states retain capital punishment on their statute books, but do not apply it. A **UN General Assembly** resolution of 1971 stated that, in view of Article 3 of the **Universal Declaration of Human Rights** declaring the right to life, it was desirable to restrict and ultimately abolish capital punishment.

CAPITALISM

An economic system characterized by the profit motive and the control of means of production, distribution, and exchange of goods by private ownership. The principles of capitalism underlie in large part the economies of the industrialized countries of the **West**.

CAPITALIST ROADER

The epithet used to attack Mao Zedong's opponents during the Chinese **Cultural Revolution**. They were accused of following the **capitalist**, rather than the socialist road, and of attempting, with Soviet collusion, to restore capitalism in China. Liu Shaoqui was labelled 'Number One Capitalist Roader', expelled from the Chinese **communist** Party and removed as Chairman of the Republic in October 1968. The epithet was revived in February 1976, when the struggle between moderates and radicals in the party intensified with a campaign against 'unrepentant capitalist roaders', the most prominent of whom was Deng Xiaoping, now China's 'elder statesman' leader.

CAPITOL HILL

Site of the US Capitol, the neo-classical building in Washington DC which houses **Congress**. It has become a synonym for the legislature.

CAPRIVI STRIP

The point at which the north-east corner of **Namibia** extends eastward in a narrow strip of land, sharing borders with four countries: Angola, **Botswana**, **Zambia** and **Zimbabwe**. This cartographical curiosity is the result of an agreement in 1890 between Germany and Great Britain which gave Germany access to the Zambezi, which it believed was navigable to the Indian Ocean on the east of the continent. Following the independence of Angola in 1975 this highly strategic area became increasing militarized, and from the 1970s until Namibian independence in 1990 the lives of the local population were severely disrupted by the deployment of South African forces. South Africa used the Strip as a base for attacks into Angola, in operations to support **UNITA**, as well as for operations into other neighbouring states against **SWAPO**, the Namibian liberation movement.

CARAPINTADAS

(Spanish, 'painted faces') A group within the Argentinean military, largely consisting of non-commissioned officers. The 'painted faces', so-called after their practice of blackening their faces, perpetrated four military uprisings between 1987 and 1990 demanding the broadening of the **Full Stop Law** to ensure the halting of human rights investigations and a total amnesty for security force personnel accused of human rights abuses during the **dirty war**.

CARBON BUDGET

The balance sheet of the exchange of carbon between the atmosphere and the oceans, rocks, flora and fauna. When the carbon budget is in balance, this annual exchange is equal. The burning of **fossil fuels** and **deforestation** have had a substantial effect on the balance of the carbon budget.

CARBON SINK

Any part of the environment which constitutes a reservoir for carbon. Important carbon sinks include forests, **fossil fuels**, limestone and phytoplankton in the ocean. Human activity which releases large amounts of carbon from a carbon sink can have a substantial effect on the **carbon budget**.

CARBON TAX

A tax intended to curb emissions of carbon dioxide from the burning of **fossil fuels** in an attempt to combat the **greenhouse**

effect. The carbon tax was first proposed to **EC** environment ministers in October 1991, but no agreement has been reached. In the USA, the Clinton administration announced plans in the 1994 budget to phase in an energy tax on non-renewable fuels. A May 1993 report by the **IEA**, however, advised that improved energy efficiency in both the developed and the developing world would be more effective than carbon taxes in reducing the emission of **greenhouse gases**.

CARE IN THE COMMUNITY

The policy on mental health care introduced by the UK Conservative government in the 1990s. The National Health Service and Community Care Act of 1990, implemented in England and Wales on 1 April 1993, was designed ostensibly to improve the quality of life and the chances of recovery of some residents of mental institutions, by enabling them to live instead in their own homes. Specialised assistance was to be provided for this, but critics attacked as inadequate the state assistance which was actually made available, and suggested that the expressed objective of reduced institutionalization was merely an excuse for cost-cutting.

CARIBBEAN

A geographical, political and cultural region to the south-east of the USA and east of **Central America**. Comprised mainly of island states, it also includes **Belize**, French Guyana, Guyana and **Surinam** because of their common culture and history. Fifteen states are independent; 12 are self-governing but are to various extents still dependent on the UK (six), France (two), the Netherlands (two) and the USA (two). Languages spoken in the region are English, Spanish, Dutch, French and French Creole. Since the creation of the **West Indies Federation** by the British in 1958, several attempts have been made at Caribbean integration, the most successful so far being **CARICOM**.

CARIBBEAN BASIN INITIATIVE

A US economic assistance scheme set up in 1983. The CBI allowed for tax incentives for US companies investing in beneficiary countries, credit for private companies of the region to import US raw materials and semi-manufactured products, low-interest loans for job creation and free-trade status for around 6,000 Caribbean products. The scheme covered the **Caribbean** and **Central America**, with the exception of Nicaragua whose **Sandinista** government was opposed by the USA. Some countries experienced growth in the manufacturing sector as a result of the CBI, and it temporarily averted complete national bankruptcy in Costa Rica, El Salvador and Honduras. However, it failed to address the roots of economic crisis in the region and by 1988 trade within Central America had fallen to half its 1980 level despite its receipt of the bulk of spending. In addition it undermined **CARICOM**, making many Caribbean states dependent on US policy. Fears were expressed in the Caribbean in 1993 that trade preferences enjoyed under the CBI would be eroded when **NAFTA** came into force.

CARIBBEAN LEGION

A loose **Latin American** alliance of radical nationalists and liberals. The Legion was set up in 1945 by José 'Pepe' Figueres Ferrer, President of Costa Rica in 1953–58 and 1970–74, with the aim of overthrowing dictatorships in Cuba, the Dominican Republic, Nicaragua and Venezuela, and participated in the 1947 uprising in the Dominican Republic. It signed a 'Pact of the Caribbean' in December 1947 with Guatemalan President Juan José Arévalo, who in 1948 supplied the Legion with arms, enabling it to play a major role in the Costa Rican civil war. The organization was officially dissolved the same year but continued to operate in **Central America** until 1955.

CARICOM

The Caribbean Community and Common Market, an alliance of English-speaking **Caribbean** countries promoting economic, political and cultural unity. Founded in 1973 by Barbados, Guyana, Jamaica and Trinidad to succeed the Caribbean Integrated Free Trade Area (CARIFTA), it was later joined by a further nine small countries. Notable achievements were in the health, education and transport sectors, with the foundation of the University of the West Indies and support for the regional LIAT airline and development of inter-island shipping. However, problems included non-compliance by some members with a common external tariff (CET) and other regional tariffs which provoked many divisions until they were restructured in 1992. Members also had conflicting interests arising from their membership of the **Caribbean Basin Initiative** and **OECS**. In March 1994, members agreed to seek early negotiations for **NAFTA** entry. Also pending is the creation of an Association of Caribbean States, encompassing the whole Caribbean Basin region.

CARLOS *see* JACKAL

CARNATION REVOLUTION

The virtually bloodless coup in Portugal on 25 April 1974, also known as the Revolution of the Flowers. A **right-wing** militaristic **Estado Novo** regime had been established in 1932 by António de Oliveira Salazar on his becoming Prime Minister; a new Constitution establishing a corporate state was adopted in 1933. The regime dissipated its fortunes and alienated its younger officer class in a costly battle to maintain its overseas possessions. A secret Armed Forces Movement (*Movimento das Forças Armadas* – MFA), nurtured in Angola in particular, successfully implemented the coup in Lisbon which was masterminded by Capt. Otelo Saraiva de Carvalho. The MFA installed Gen. António Ribeiro de Spínola at the head of a Junta of National Salvation; he became President on May 15, and a largely civilian government was sworn in on the following day. The red carnation became the symbol of the soldiers who had participated in the affair; monarchist sympathizers preferred to wear a white carnation.

CARTAGENA AGREEMENT *see* ANDEAN PACT

CARTER DOCTRINE

The foreign policy doctrine of Jimmy Carter, US President 1977–81, as outlined in his 1980 State of the Union address. Its essence was that 'any attempt by an outside force to gain control of the Persian **Gulf** region will be regarded as an assault on the vital interests of the USA and such an assault will be repelled by any means necessary, including military force'. The doctrine was formulated in response to the Iranian **Islamic revolution** of 1979 and the Soviet intervention in Afghanistan, both of which were perceived as a threat to US oil supplies and strategic interests in the Gulf region.

CASSAÇÕES

(from the Portuguese *cassar*, 'to annul') The revoking of opponents' political rights, a practice of the Brazilian military dictatorship of 1964–85 provided for under the **Institutional Acts**. The procedure was used to silence politicians from the official opposition, journalists, scientists and others. Loss of political rights for an elected politician meant that his or her seat was left unfilled, strengthening the pro-government artificially created ARENA party and effectively neutralizing the Congress. It remained in place throughout the period of **distensaõ** despite the latter's liberal veneer.

CATALYTIC CONVERTER

A device which converts polluting chemicals in the exhaust fumes of petrol-driven vehicles into other substances, less harmful to the environment and human health. Catalytic converters (which currently have up to 90 per cent efficiency) are inserted between the engine and the exhaust. They contain a honeycomb-like structure, coated with platinum, palladium and rhodium. When exhaust fumes pass through the converter, the metals act as catalysts for chemical reactions which convert carbon monoxide and nitrogen oxides into carbon dioxide, water vapour and nitrogen. In the USA, all new cars sold since 1980 have been fitted with catalytic converters. The same measure has been in force in the **EC** since 1993.

CAUCUS

The way in which some US states choose their delegates to the Democratic and Republican party conventions in a presidential election year. The selection process in a caucus is done by a gathering of party activists rather than through a ballot. Caucuses are an alternative to the holding of **primaries**. By tradition, the opening contest of the presidential campaign is the Iowa caucus.

CAUDILLISMO

(Spanish, 'political bossism') A political structure based on patronage. The term originates from the Spanish *caudillo* ('leader') and can refer to a military or a political leader, normally without any particular party allegiance. Gaining power either through charisma, cunning or force a *caudillo* builds up a network of clients who, out of fear or in return for favours granted, will vote for him or his appointed candidate and usually force others to follow suit. Especially prevalent in **Latin American** countries in the turbulent post-independence years, it remains a feature of rural life and continues to undermine the democratic process in many of these countries.

CBI

The Confederation of British Industry, the main employers' organization in the UK. The CBI was formed in 1965 through the merger of the Federation of British Industries, the British Employers' Confederation and the National Association of British Manufacturers. As a pressure group, it ensures that its members' problems and requirements are fully understood within parliament and government as well as, increasingly, within the **EU**. Under both Labour and Conservative governments it was represented on a number of official bodies, although this corporatist function is now less prominent.

CCC

The Commodity Credit Corporation, the main US agency for buying in cereals and other agricultural products under price support schemes. Set up in 1933, it has a major involvement in US **food aid** programmes because of its responsibilities for surplus disposal.

CEB

Christian base communities – **Latin American** Roman Catholic grassroots organizations which apply the message of the gospels in order to transform radically social and political reality. The CEBs were set up following the 1968 Second General Conference of Latin American Bishops in Medellín (Colombia) and the spread of **liberation theology** among Latin American bishops and clergymen. In Nicaragua many CEB priests and lay members actively participated in the 1979 revolution led by **left-wing Sandinistas**. In Guatemala and El Salvador members of CEBs became targets for **death squads**. CEBs are most common in Brazil, where around 10,000 groups are estimated to exist.

CEI

The Central European Initiative, founded in January 1992 to promote regional economic and cultural co-operation, particularly between east and west, and to provide a counterweight to German regional dominance. The CEI's roots lie in a November 1989 agreement between Austria, Hungary, Italy and **Yugoslavia**, leading to the foundation of the **Pentagonale** group (including **Czechoslovakia**) in May 1990. This became the **Hexagonale** group (including Poland) in July 1991. The CEI includes, in addition, **Bosnia-Hercegovina**, **Croatia** and **Slovenia**, while Yugoslavia was expelled from it in early 1992.

CENTO

The Central Treaty Organization, which had been known as the Baghdad Pact until Iraq's withdrawal in 1959. A pro-Western regional defence alliance originally established at the behest of the USA, it was intended to construct a **cordon sanitaire** around the **Soviet Union**. CENTO's members were Iran, **Pakistan**, Turkey and the UK, but there was little or no actual military co-operation between them. The organization was gradually disbanded after the withdrawal of Iran following the assumption of power by the **Islamic revolution** in 1979; Pakistan also withdrew, and Turkey, whose capital, Ankara, acted as the alliance's headquarters, declared CENTO defunct in 1980.

CENTRAL AFRICAN FEDERATION

The shortlived federation of the then British colonies of Northern Rhodesia (**Zambia**), Southern Rhodesia (**Zimbabwe**) and Nyasaland (**Malawi**) established on 1 August 1953 and formally dissolved on 31 December 1963. Also known as the Federation of Rhodesia and Nyasaland, the federation provoked considerable opposition from the black population and galvanized nationalist anti-British sentiment.

CENTRAL AMERICA

A term used to describe the area linking the two great land masses of North and **South America** made up of Spanish-speaking countries: Guatemala, Honduras, El Salvador, Nicaragua, Costa Rica, and Panama. Geographically it also includes Mexico, whose participation in regional initiatives has been spasmodic and equivocal, and **Belize**, where English is the official language and which politically and culturally is considered part of the **Caribbean**. It has been described by successive US administrations as 'our back yard', and **right-wing** forces such as the **contras** in Nicaragua and the military regime in El Salvador have received appreciable US assistance. Central America has also been the main beneficiary of the US-sponsored **Caribbean Basin Initiative**. Notable attempts by the region to follow its own path have been the **Contadora** peace initiative and the Central American Common Market; a regional parliament, Parlacén, has also been established to further integration.

CENTRAL ASIA

The five republics of the former **Soviet Union** east of the Caspian Sea, which became independent states in 1991 as **Kazakhstan**, **Kirgizstan**, **Tajikistan**, **Turkmenistan** and **Uzbekistan**. Central Asians speak a variety of mainly Turkic languages and tend to practise a moderate form of (**Sunni**) Islam. There are considerable Russian minorities in Central Asia.

CENTRAL COMMITTEE

A leading organ in the **CPSU** and similarly in **communist** party structures worldwide, whose full members elected the powerful **politburo** and secretariat (the latter being headed by the **Gensec**). In the Soviet case the central committee, itself elected every five years by the All-Union Party Congress, grew so much that the committee elected in 1986 had 170 candidate members (without voting rights) and 307 full members. According to party statute it met no more than twice a year, and from the mid-1950s to the mid-1960s it was a forum for limited debate, but its meetings came to be regarded under Brezhnev in the 1970s as a ritual presentation of current policy to a gathering of the party elite. The central committee met its demise in 1991 with the banning of the CPSU after the failed **August coup**.

CENTRAL EUROPE

The region comprising Poland, the Czech and Slovak Republics, Hungary and Austria, and arguably also north-eastern Italy and **Slovenia**. The term gained salience following the collapse of **communism** in Europe after **1989**. Many argued that the more widely used term **Eastern Europe** implied that all states in communist Europe east of the **Oder-Neisse line** were equally remote from western Europe. Poles, Czechs, Slovaks and Hungarians in particular preferred the term Central Europe, which allowed them to make a distinction between their own cultural heritage (and therefore suitability for re-entry into 'European' life) and that of states further east. This common perspective also took political form in the **Visegrad Triangle**.

CENTRIST

A political stance aiming to appeal to those who identify neither with **left-wing** nor **right-wing** politics. Centrist views seek to be acceptable to the broadest possible constituency. Centrism is often associated with political stability, consensus and continuity, but has also been claimed by dictatorships in an effort to gain political legitimacy.

CEPAL *see* ECONOMIC COMMISSION

CERES

A 'study, research and education' group on the Marxist left of the French Socialist Party (PS), which was one of the main tendencies forming the PS in 1971 and was influential in drafting key policy statements of the French parliamentary left, the 1972 Common Programme and the 1980 Socialist Project. CERES expounded similar policies to the French **communist** Party, which was then in crisis over whether to form a united front with the PS. CERES eventually lost ground to the 'modernizing' tendency within the PS in the early 1980s.

CERN

(French acronym, European Centre For Nuclear Research) A co-operative agency with 12 member countries, founded in 1952 and located outside Geneva. There, in 1981, a giant underground super proton synchrotron (SPS) accelerator ring became operational, in which anti-protons were collided with protons at near the speed of light to investigate the physics of quarks and gluons, the smallest units of known matter. The discovery in 1983 at an energy of 540GeV of W and Z bosons, messenger particles of the 'weak nuclear force' predicted by theory, was an outstanding innovative achievement.

CFA FRANC

The currency used by west and central African countries in the franc zone. The value of the CFA franc was pegged to the French franc at FF1=50 CFA francs from 1948, giving these countries, almost all of which are former French colonies, a measure of currency stability not enjoyed by most other African countries. The shock of the 50 per cent devaluation effectively forced upon them in January 1994 by the **IMF** and France was thus particularly severe. Countries within the West African Monetary Union (**UMOA**) define the CFA franc as that of the *Communauté financière africaine*, while those countries where the central bank of issue is the Bank of Central African States (**BEAC**) define the CFA franc as that of the *Co-opération financière en Afrique centrale*.

CFCs

Chlorofluorocarbons, a family of chemicals discovered in 1930 which revolutionized the techniques of refrigeration but were later recognized to be **greenhouse gases** which contribute significantly to the **greenhouse effect**. CFCs are stable gases used widely in refrigeration, in aerosol spray cans and in the production of insulating packaging for convenience foods. The chlorine they contain also damage the **ozone layer**. The 1987 **Montreal Protocol** aims to halve the use of CFCs by the end of the century. HCFCs (Hydrochlorofluorocarbons) are less damaging than CFCs, for which they may be substituted in refrigeration and air conditioning, but nevertheless contribute to the depletion of the ozone layer and to the greenhouse effect. The least harmful CFC substitutes at present are HFCs or hydrofluorocarbons. The **EC** plans to end the use of HCFCs by 2014, or before that date if HFCs are deemed sufficiently reliable.

CFE AGREEMENT

The historic agreement on 19 November 1990 in Paris on reducing Conventional Forces in Europe, eliminating more than 60,000 tanks, artillery and other **conventional weapons**. Concluded within the **CSCE** framework by the 34 members of the **NATO** and **Warsaw Pact** alliances, it set limits for each alliance's total weaponry from the Atlantic to the Urals – 20,000 tanks for each side, 30,000 armoured combat vehicles, 20,000 artillery pieces, 2,000 helicopters and 6,800 combat aircraft. Separate agreements limited troop numbers in central Europe and specified prior notification of manoeuvres.

CGDK

The Coalition Government of Democratic **Kampuchea**, the Cambodian resistance movement formed in 1982 and dominated by the **Khmers Rouges**. Faced with defeat on the battlefield, and under increasing pressure from sympathetic **ASEAN** states to present a united front, the three Cambodian rebel factions (the *Khmers Rouges*, the Sihanoukists and the Sonn Sannists) formed the CGDK in 1982 with Prince Norodom Sihanouk as its titular head. For the *Khmers Rouges* the CGDK provided a cloak of respectability to conceal its genocidal past and for the two non-**communist** components it offered membership of a recognized government with the prospect of increased access to foreign assistance, without which they would be unable to match the Chinese-armed *Khmers Rouges*. In February 1990, after years of internal squabbling and little in the way of diplomatic or military co-operation, Sihanouk dissolved the CGDK and announced in its place the formation of a 'National Government of Cambodia'.

CHAEBOL

South Korean term for the huge conglomerates which have provided the basis for South Korea's spectacular economic success since the early 1960s. Although privately owned, the *chaebol* have provided a coherent framework for efficient state **capitalism** whereby successive South Korean governments have been able to maximize resources by intervening to plan, supervise and direct the speed and direction of economic growth.

CHALLENGER DISASTER

The horrifying, globally televised explosion of *Challenger*, one of the US fleet of space shuttles, 72 seconds after take-off on 28 January 1986. All of the seven-member crew were killed, including schoolteacher Christa McAuliffe, the first US civilian to have been included in a space mission.

CHAPPAQUIDDICK

The incident in the early hours of 20 July 1969, when a young woman in a car driven by US Senator Edward Kennedy died, and Kennedy's reputation was clouded thereafter. The accident happened as they were returning from a party; the car plunged off a bridge on Chappaquiddick Island in New England, and Mary Jo Kopechne was drowned. Kennedy did not report the accident until eight hours later. Despite his claims that he had unsuccessfully attempted to rescue Kopechne from the submerged vehicle, his conduct was widely criticized. On July 25 he pleaded guilty to leaving the scene of an accident, and five days later he dropped his plans to run for the US presidency in 1972. While he remained a Senator and contested the Democratic presidential nomination of 1980, the Chappaquiddick incident effectively destroyed any realistic chance of his becoming president.

CHAPULTEPEC ACT

A declaration of solidarity and mutual defence between American nations. It was signed in March 1945 at an Inter-American Conference on the Problems of War and Peace, convened by the Pan-American Union in Mexico City, and formed the basis for later regional organizations, most notably the **Rio Treaty**. Signatory countries were Bolivia, Brazil, Chile, Colombia, Costa Rica, Cuba, Dominican Republic, Ecuador, Guatemala, Haiti, Honduras, Mexico, Nicaragua, Panama, Paraguay, Peru, the USA, Uruguay and Venezuela; Argentina signed a month later.

CHARLOTTETOWN ACCORD

A Canadian constitutional reform package negotiated in mid-1992 to replace the failed **Meech Lake Accord**. The package represented a delicate balancing act: it offered concessions on greater autonomy, as demanded by the French-speaking majority in Quebec and by representatives of the Indian and Inuit communities, but it also included wider reforms designed to appeal to the western provinces – particularly the proposal to create an elected Senate where all of the country's 10 provinces would be equally represented. In an attempt to improve the agreement's chances of approval by each of the country's provincial legislatures – the tortuous process which had resulted in the destruction of the Meech Lake Accord – federal Prime Minister Brian Mulroney called a national referendum on the deal. This referendum, only the third in Canada's history, was held on 26 October 1992 and resulted in the rejection of the Charlottetown Agreement by 54.4 per cent to 44.6 per cent. Its defeat accelerated the rise of separatist sentiments both in Quebec and also in the west.

CHARTER 77

A document drawn up by Czechoslovak dissidents in 1977, which called for the liberalization and democratization of the **communist** regime, and spawned a human rights movement by the same name. Charter 77 served as a focal point for the intellectual opposition in **Czechoslovakia**, and several of its signatories, including Vaclav Havel, emerged as leading political figures in and after the **Velvet Revolution** of 1989. Charter 77 was disbanded in 1992, having 'completed its historical role'.

CHARTER 88

A pressure group in the UK which demands a new constitutional settlement guaranteeing political, civil and human rights. Charter 88 was launched with the publication of a statement, signed by some 240 prominent figures, in the 2 December 1988 issue of the magazine *New Statesman and Society*. Its name referred both to **Czechoslovakia's** dissident **Charter 77**, and the tercentenary of the British 'Glorious Revolution' of 1688. Its signatories claimed that rights were '... being curtailed while the powers of the executive have increased ... and ought to be diminished'.

CHATILA *see* SABRA AND CHATILA

CHATTERING CLASSES

Members of the intelligentsia perceived to set the cultural agenda. The chattering classes' preoccupations, which vary widely from political and moral issues to popular music and fashion, result from the informal conversation said to constitute much of the leisure time of professional people. The media, which employ many members of the chattering classes, often reflect their changing preoccupations.

CHECHENYA

The name adopted by a secessionist republic in southern Russia, with a population of mainly Muslim Chechen-speakers, which broke away from the **Russian Federation** in November 1991. The declaration of secession was made by the parliament of Chechen-Ingushetia, but the Ingushetia region opposed the decision and itself broke away to form the republic of Ingushetia. Gen. Dzhokar Dudayev, who had taken power the month before the secession, has remained in place despite occasional violent clashes with the opposition.

CHECKPOINT CHARLIE

The popular name for the main official crossing point for foreigners between East and West Berlin before the destruction of the **Berlin Wall**. Standing at the junction of Friedrichstrasse and Zimmerstrasse, it was immortalized in scores of espionage novels and films set during the **Cold War** as the place where intelligence agents were exchanged. It was removed on 22 June 1990, as talks on the reunification of Germany progressed. However, there are plans to reconstruct it as a tourist site.

CHEMICAL WEAPONS

Toxic compounds, including nerve gas, produced as weapons of mass destruction; the most recently developed are **binary weapons**. The effects of poison gas horrified troops who encountered it in the First World War, and the 1925 Geneva protocol banned the use of chemical weapons, but not production and stockpiling. Chemical defoliants have been used in the postwar period, notably by the UK in Malaya and by the USA (notoriously, as **Agent Orange**) in the **Vietnam War**. Vietnamese use of **yellow rain** in Cambodia remains an unproven allegation, but the **UN** did confirm that Iraq had used chemical weapons against Iran in 1984. Other countries, including Libya, have been accused of (and have denied) building factories to produce chemical weapons. The two **superpowers** agreed at the Washington summit in 1990 to halt all production, providing fresh impetus for the conclusion of a Chemical Weapons Convention, which was eventually signed in January 1993 after decades of negotiation in the UN Conference on Disarmament. Requiring 65 ratifications if it was to enter into force as scheduled in January 1995, this comprehensive convention banned the use, production and stockpiling of chemical weapons. It set up an International Organization for the Prohibition of Chemical Weapons (IOPCW) to oversee the destruction of all existing stocks. This was to be completed within 10 years – except that Russia and the USA, with huge stocks to destroy, would be allowed a further five years.

CHEQUERS

The official country residence of the UK Prime Minister. The house and estate of Chequers, in Buckinghamshire, north-west of London, was given to the country by Lord and Lady Lee of Fareham in 1917–21.

CHERNOBYL

The site of a Soviet nuclear power plant, in **Ukraine**, where the world's worst ever nuclear power accident occurred on 26 April 1986, during a badly conducted safety test. The explosion, fire and massive irradiation in the No. 4 reactor killed more than 30 people, and an **IAEA** report estimated that 5,300 more would die within 70 years as a direct result of exposure to radiation. Moreover, radioactive material released by the accident laid waste vast areas of adjacent agricultural land (much of it in neighbouring **Byelarus**) and drifted in a cloud across Europe, poisoning farmland as far off as Wales. More than 200 villages around Chernobyl were evacuated, some of them as late as three years after the accident, and much of the contaminated land will remain unusable for over 100 years. The rest of the Chernobyl complex, which had four 1,000 megawatt Soviet RBMK (water-cooled graphite-moderated) reactors and two more under construction, has continued to function after the accident but has became the focus of international pressure for the closure of unsafe nuclear power plants in eastern Europe.

CHETNIK

Originally a Serbian nationalist army of resistance, led by Draza Mihailovic, which occupied parts of eastern and southern **Yugoslavia** during the Second World War. More recently the Chetniks were the militia of the neo-fascist Serbian Radical Party (SRS) led by Vojislav Seselj, allegedly involved in some of the most brutal episodes in the current fighting in **Bosnia-Hercegovina** and **Croatia**. The SRS disbanded the Chetniks in April 1994, by which time the term Chetnik had become synonymous with all Serb irregulars.

CHEVALINE

A British upgrade of the submarine-launched **Polaris** nuclear missile. The Chevaline programme was initiated in 1971, but development was slower and more costly than planned. By the time the missile came into service in 1982, the UK government had already committed itself to buying the US **Trident** II missile as its replacement.

CHICAGO BOYS

A group of **Latin American** economics graduates, mostly from the University of Chicago, under Milton Friedman, whose **Friedmanite** theory of **monetarism** influenced the economic policy of various Latin American military dictatorships in the 1970s, notably that of Chile after the September 1973 coup. Their technical competence and lack of overt party allegiances persuaded the military junta of Gen. Augusto Pinochet Ugarte to let them take charge of an economy weighed down by hyperinflation and a balance of payment crisis. Their April 1976 'Economy Recovery Plan' which included public expenditure cuts, wage freezes, devaluation, privatization and tariff reductions, elicited praise from the world's financial communities, and Chile received huge investment loans. However, by 1982 the Chicago model was in tatters when crippling debt repayments, the bankruptcy of several banks and increasing inflation were added to the social cost of mass unemployment and poverty.

CHICAGO EIGHT

The eight US dissidents who went on trial on 24 September 1969, accused of conspiring to cause a riot at the Democratic convention in Chicago in August 1968, which had been marred by extreme violence as police clashed with thousands of anti-**Vietnam War** protesters. The trial was presided over by US District Court Judge Julius Hoffman, who displayed an extraordinary degree of partiality against the defendants. His obvious bias, together with the tendency of the defendants to mock and disrupt the proceedings of the court, meant that the trial became a cause célèbre. One defendant, Bobby Seale of the **Black Panthers**, was bound and gagged for insisting upon his right to defend himself, and was eventually removed after his case was declared a mistrial. Two defendants were eventually acquitted. The remaining five – Rennie Davis and David Dellinger of the National Mobilization to End the War in Vietnam, Tom Hayden of the Students for a Democratic Society (**SDS**), and Abbie Hoffman and Jerry Rubin of the **Yippies** – were acquitted of conspiracy but convicted of crossing state lines to riot. All were given prison sentences, and were also sentenced to concurrent terms for contempt. Judge Hoffman also handed down prison sentences of up to four years to the defence lawyers for contempt. All of the sentences were later overturned on appeal.

CHILTERN HUNDREDS

The more famous of the two sinecures for which British MPs traditionally apply if they wish to give up their seat. In theory they are not allowed simply to resign, but disqualification from membership of the House of Commons is automatic for the holder of any of certain specified 'offices of profit under the Crown'. The approved procedure for an MP wishing to quit is thus to apply for, and accept, the nominal office of Bailiff of the three Chiltern Hundreds of Stoke, Desborough and Burnham, in Buckinghamshire, or alternatively the nominal office of Steward of the Manor of Northstead.

CHINA *see* FOUR CHINAS; PRC; TAIWAN

CHINA LOBBY

Those within the US political establishment who were strongly committed to the support of Chiang Kai-shek and the Kuomintang (**KMT**), even after their defeat by the **communist** forces of Mao Zedong and their retreat in 1949 to the island of Formosa (later **Taiwan**). The China lobby resisted – successfully until 1971 – the transfer of China's seat in the **UN** from the KMT regime to the communist government of the mainland.

CHINA SYNDROME

The scenario for a potential disaster at a nuclear power station in which the core of the reactor would melt down and fall through the bottom of the plant with such irreversible progress that it would seem to be able to bore right through the earth 'from the USA to China'. In fact, the molten core would first reach the water table and radioactive steam would be released into the atmosphere. A film called *The China Syndrome* popularized the phrase, and a real accident of this kind almost occurred at **Three Mile Island**.

CHITTAGONG AUTONOMISTS

Supporters of an illegal **guerrilla** organization, also known as the *Shanti Bahini* (peace force), seeking autonomy for the minority Chakma tribal people in the Chittagong Hill Tracts of south-east **Bangladesh**. Launched in 1975 under the leadership of Manabendra Larma, the movement triggered violent conflict between native Chakmas (mainly Buddhist, Christian and Hindu) and ethnic (mainly Muslim) Bengalis settled in the area. Allegations of a government-backed campaign of genocide meanwhile prompted thousands of Chakmas to flee to neighbouring India. A peace agreement concluded in November 1992, involving greater autonomy, marked a gradual decline in violence and the return of some refugees from India.

CHOGM

The Commonwealth Heads of Government Meeting – the main policy-making body of the **Commonwealth**. A CHOGM is formally convened every two years. Designed to compensate for the absence of a formal Commonwealth charter or governing structure, it was first assembled in 1935. Since 1965 it has been assisted by the Commonwealth Secretariat, whereas it was previously serviced by the UK Commonwealth Relations Office. In 1989 the CHOGM initiated a high-level appraisal of directions and structure. Major concerns in recent years have included decolonization, economic development and ways of ending **apartheid** in South Africa, over which UK Prime Minister Margaret Thatcher (who with her private secretary allegedly referred privately to CHOGM as 'compulsory handouts to greedy mendicants') was involved in sharp controversies at the 1987 and 1989 CHOGMs.

CHRISTIAN BASE COMMUNITIES
see CEB

CHRISTIAN DEMOCRACY

A term for policies and parties in postwar **Western Europe** and **Latin America** associated with the Christian Church, socially conservative attitudes, and a commitment to liberal democracy and social welfare. Generally right of centre, although often including a minority of **left-wing** intellectuals and trades unionists, Christian Democratic parties support economic intervention by the state. They also defend traditional values, particularly the family, and have a strong historical link with the Church, both Catholic and Protestant. The strongest Christian Democratic movements were those in Germany and Italy, until the Italian Christian Democrat party was fragmented by revelations of institutionalized corruption in the 1990s.

CHRISTIAN DEMOCRAT INTERNATIONAL

An international body established in November 1982, with a secretariat in Brussels, to expand co-operation between parties of a democratic and Christian (Protestant and Catholic) orientation, mainly in Europe and **Latin America**. Its predecessor was the Christian Democrat World Union, founded in July 1961.

CHUNNEL

A familiar contraction of Channel Tunnel. Plans for a tunnel beneath the Channel between England and France, mooted in the nineteenth century, were resurrected in 1957, but abandoned again in 1975 after lengthy studies, even though the French and UK governments had reached an agreement that the chunnel could go ahead. The project was revived in 1981, and after several years of work, various delays and escalating costs a rail tunnel – constructed by Trans-Manche Link, operated by Eurotunnel, and capable of carrying passengers, cars and freight – was inaugurated on 6 May 1994. Controversy remained, however, over high-speed rail links on the English side of the tunnel.

CIA

The Central Intelligence Agency, the USA's federal intelligence gathering agency, often referred to by insiders as The Company. From its headquarters in Langley, Virginia, the CIA co-ordinates **covert operations** in foreign states, as well as gathering a vast range of information about them. It is headed by a Director, currently R. James Woolsey, who holds Cabinet rank.

CIEC

The Conference on International Economic Co-operation, or **North-South** dialogue, conceived by French President Valéry Giscard d'Estaing in 1974 in the wake of the oil crisis. Two CIEC ministerial meetings were held in Paris, in December 1985 and in May–June 1997, in an ultimately unsuccessful effort to reach agreement on the basis for a new international economic order (**NIEO**). The participants were the **G-7** major industrialized countries and the European Commission, for the **North**, and a Group of 19 representing the oil-producing and other developing countries (the **South**). Apart from the plenary sessions, four commissions worked on energy questions, other raw materials, development aid, and international financial problems.

CIS

The Commonwealth of Independent States, formed in December 1991 by 11 of the 15 newly independent republics of the former **Soviet Union – Armenia, Azerbaijan, Byelarus, Moldova**, the **Russian Federation (Russia)**, **Ukraine**, and the five republics of **Central Asia**. The **Baltic States** opted not to join, as did Georgia until December 1993. The CIS was designed to promote inter-republican co-operation in democratic reforms, economic development, environmental improvement and defence and foreign policy. It was widely regarded as a transitional body likely to wither away as the post-Soviet states consolidated their independence. However, it came to be seen by Russia as an effective means of reasserting influence in former Soviet states, and as an umbrella for a peacekeeping role, such as that of Russian troops deployed in Georgia in February 1994 under CIS auspices.

CISKEI *see* BANTUSTAN

CITES

The Convention on International Trade in Endangered Species of Wild Flora and Fauna. The CITES convention came into force in July 1973, banning or restricting trade in over 500 living species and the products derived from them. Some 120 countries subscribe to the convention, which is aimed specifically at protecting species considered to be close to extinction. In 1993 the USA threatened to impose trade sanctions against China and **Taiwan** for failing to act under CITES to stop the commercial trade in rhinoceros horn and tiger bones.

CITIZEN'S CHARTER

A government 'charter' for the improvement in standards of public services in the UK. The basic citizen's charter was an initiative of Prime Minister John Major in 1991. It paved the way for a proliferation of subsidiary charters (numbering nearly 40 by early 1994), covering different aspects of public service. In each case the government or other authority set out standards of services, quality, choice and value for money. In some instances there were guarantees of redress if these standards were not met.

CIVIC FORUM

The Czech coalition of parties formed during the **Velvet Revolution** in November 1989, as the focus of democratic opposition to the **communist** regime. Civic Forum's leaders included the co-signatory of **Charter 77**, Vaclav Havel, then a prominent dissident and subsequently President of postcommunist **Czechoslovakia**. Civic Forum advocated rapid democratization and a transition to the free market. Members of Civic Forum formed a significant part of Czechoslovakia's first postcommunist cabinet, following elections in June 1990 (in which it competed on a joint ticket with the Slovak sister party **Public Against Violence**). Civic Forum split in February 1991 into the radical Civic Democratic Party led by Vaclav Klaus, and the moderate Civic Movement led by Jiri Dienstbier.

CIVIL LIST

Payments by the UK government to meet the official expenses of certain members of the royal family. In early 1993 it was confirmed that Civil List payments were in future to be restricted to the Queen, the Duke of Edinburgh and the Queen Mother.

CIVIL RIGHTS

Those rights which pertain to a person by virtue of citizenship within a given society. The extent, as well as the observance, of civil rights varies between states, although in many cases human rights (those rights which are inalienably attached to a person by virtue of his humanity) are embodied within a code of civil rights. This is particularly true of the USA, where many basic human rights have been enshrined in, and given legal protection by, the **Bill of Rights** and other pieces of legislation. The failure some US states to recognize the civil rights of black citizens led to the development of the **civil rights movement** in the 1950s.

CIVIL RIGHTS MOVEMENT

The movement which began in the 1950s and which struggled to secure civil rights for the black population of the USA. Although amendments to the Constitution had enfranchised blacks and had guaranteed them citizenship, these were not implemented in much of the **South**, where a policy of racial **segregation** remained in operation. The civil rights movement was led by organizations such as the **NAACP**, the Southern Christian Leadership Conference (among whose leaders was Martin Luther King Jr), and **CORE**. It used a campaign of political protest and civil disobedience, including techniques such as the **sit-in** and the **freedom ride**, to challenge segregation and institutionalized racism. The movement also co-ordinated boycotts, encouraged black voter-registration, and presented legal challenges to segregation. This latter tactic produced a series of Supreme Court judgments, beginning in May 1954 with the desegregation of public schools, which outlawed institutionalized discrimination. Civil rights were also extended to the black population through federal legislation such as the Civil Rights Acts of 1957, 1960, 1964 and 1968, and the Voting Rights Act enacted on 6 August 1965.

CIVILIAN PATROLS

Military-directed patrols in Guatemala used by the army to pacify the countryside. Civilian Patrol-type groups first appeared in 1976 but were officially established in 1982–3 in the aftermath of the military's **Scorched Earth** policy, after which they expanded rapidly to comprise more than 900,000 members and became a ubiquitous feature of highland communities. They monitored all rural movement, acted as informers and often terrorized the population as part of the army's counterinsurgency programme against the **URNG guerrillas**. Although they are nominally composed of volunteers, in practice refusal to serve means torture and imprisonment for adult male Indians over 16 years. The continuing operation of the Patrols means that their disarming and disbandment remain major demands of human rights groups and *campesino* ('peasant') associations.

CLARK AMENDMENT

US legislation banning the expenditure of US military funds in Angola, except to gather intelligence, without the express approval of **Congress**. Named after Senator Dick Clark of Iowa, Democratic chairman of the Senate subcommittee on African Affairs, the law came into effect in February 1976. The move stopped further overt aid to **UNITA**, which the US administration had been anxious to continue in order to counter the effects of the support the Popular Movement for the Liberation of Angola (MPLA) was receiving from the **Soviet Union** and Cuba. In his first year in office US President Ronald Reagan called for the repeal of the Clark Amendment on the grounds that it interfered with executive freedom to conduct foreign relations. Although Congress refused to submit in 1981, the Amendment was repealed in July 1985.

CLARK FIELD AIR BASE

One of the two last major US military bases in the Philippines, the other being the **Subic Bay** naval base. The Clark Field base, first leased to the USA in 1947, was closed and handed back to the Philippines in late November 1991. Negotiations over the future of Clark Field, the lease on which had been due to expire in September 1992, began in May 1990, but were affected by the eruption in June 1991 of the **Mount Pinatubo** volcano 10 miles (15 km) from the base. The damage caused by the eruption reduced the value of the base to the USA and facilitated an agreement on its future.

CLASS WAR

The most extreme form of class struggle, a fundamental tenet of Marxism. Marxist theory holds that antagonism between classes is intrinsic to non-**communist** societies and therefore provides the driving force of history; class war is most acute under **capitalism**, when the emergence of the proletariat ignites a war for control of the means of production which will culminate in the victory of the proletariat over the bourgeoisie, and the establishment of **communism**.

Class War is also the name of a contemporary **anarchist** organization in the UK.

CLAUSE FOUR

The statement of the basic tenets of the British Labour Party. The relevant sub-section – Clause Four of the party constitution drawn up in 1918 – reads: 'to secure for the workers by hand or by brain the full fruits of their industry and the most equitable distribution thereof that may be possible upon the basis of the common ownership of the means of production, distribution and exchange, and the best obtainable system of popular administration and control of each industry or service'. While Clause Four has been consistently seen by the left wing of the party as sacrosanct, modernizers from Hugh Gaitskell in 1959 onwards have sought to modify its apparent thorough-going concentration on public ownership and to temper it in practice with a greater acceptance of the mixed economy. By the 1990s the Labour Party had, moreover, generally accepted the reality of successive Conservative governments' privatization programmes, and sought to ensure the effective management of the economy as it had evolved.

CLAUSE 28

Controversial legislation in the UK outlawing any 'promotion' of homosexuality by local authorities. Clause 28, eventually enacted as Section 28 of the Local Government Act 1988, was fiercely contested in parliament and by campaigners for homosexual and other **civil rights**. It prohibits local authorities throughout Great Britain from intentionally promoting homosexuality, or publishing material with the intention of promoting homosexuality, and from promoting the teaching in any of their own schools of the acceptability of homosexuality as a 'pretended family relationship'.

CLEAN AIR LEGISLATION

Legislation passed by individual states to reduce air pollution. In the UK, two Clean Air Acts have been passed, in 1956 and 1968, which restricted the emission of smoke, grit and dust, and established smokeless zones – areas in which the emission of smoke from domestic and industrial users was restricted. Similar legislation was introduced in the USA in 1977 and strengthened in November 1990.

CLIENT STATE

A term synonymous with satellite state, describing a state which is economically dependent and militarily subordinate to a larger allied state. Dependent upon the larger state for its defence, the client state acts as an agent of its patron in foreign affairs. The global reach of the two **superpowers** in the post-1945 era fostered many such relationships.

CLOTURE

A US term for bringing to a close legislative debate on a bill; it is a procedure similar to the British **guillotine**.

CLUB NAVAL PACT

A Uruguayan agreement between the outgoing military **junta** and the Colorado, Broad Front and Civic Union parties, signed on 3 August 1984. The Blancos (or National Party) was the only major party which refused to sign because their chosen candidate was not permitted to stand in the forthcoming November 1984 presidential elections. The agreement gave the military a role in a newly established National Defence Council to advise a future government and allowed for military courts to try civilians during a state of siege. It also provided for the selection of future commanders-in-chief by the president from a list drawn up by the relevant service. The three participating parties defended their actions as the only way of ensuring that elections would take place.

CLUB OF ROME

A non-governmental association of industrialists, policy analysts and scientists, seeking to bring their different perspectives to bear on the problems of the global economy, and emphasising what came to be called sustainable development. The Club of Rome first came to prominence with the publication in 1972 of the **Limits to Growth** report, and was subsequently active in the **NIEO** debate on restructuring the world economy.

CMEA *see* COMECON

CND

The Campaign for Nuclear Disarmament, a British organization which mobilized mass opposition to nuclear weapons in general and the UK's independent nuclear deterrent in particular. Founded in 1958 by a group including Bertrand Russell and Canon John Collins, CND was active in the late 1950s and early 1960s and again in the early 1980s. It organized an annual march to **Aldermaston** for several years and campaigned widely for the adoption of **unilateralism**. However, it faded after the signing of the Partial Test Ban Treaty in 1963. In the early 1980s, under the leadership of Monsignor Bruce Kent, CND was reactivated in response to the planned deployment of US **cruise** missiles in the UK. During this phase CND organized several massive demonstrations and supported the protest at **Greenham Common**, but failed to prevent the deployment of the missiles. It also spawned a European counterpart, **END**. The influence of the organization declined considerably in 1990 with the ending of the **Cold War** and the withdrawal of **cruise** missiles by the USA in return for the destruction of Soviet SS20s.

CNN

Cable News Network, the US national and worldwide cable and satellite television network founded in 1978 by Ted Turner. CNN achieved international prominence during the 1990–1 **Gulf War** through its extensive up-to-the-minute coverage of news and events.

COCOM

The Co-Ordinating Committee for Multilateral Export Controls, embracing all 16 members of **NATO** plus Iceland, set up in 1950 with the objective of preventing the export of sensitive military technology to the former **Soviet Union** and its erstwhile **Warsaw Pact** allies in Eastern Europe. COCOM was formally dismantled in March 1994, the political changes in the former **communist bloc** having rendered it redundant. It was envisaged that it would be replaced by a new scheme open to the former communist states of eastern and central Europe aimed at monitoring the export of **dual-use technology** to the **Third World** and areas of regional conflict.

COD WAR

The general colloquial expression used to dramatize disputes between the UK and Iceland over fishing rights. The 'first cod war' in 1958, over Iceland's extension of its **territorial waters** from six to 12 nautical miles, ended in agreements with the UK, and with West Germany, in 1961. In 1972, however, Iceland announced that it was extending its fishing limits to 50 miles (generally representing the extent of the country's **continental shelf**). This precipitated a 'second cod war' – serious confrontations between British (and West German) fishing vessels and Icelandic gunboats, and direct intervention by the Royal Navy in May 1973. The **ICJ** ruled in July 1974 that Iceland was not entitled to exclude British or West German fishing vessels between the 12-mile and 50-mile limits. A two-year interim fisheries agreement between the UK and Iceland had meanwhile been concluded, in November 1973. Its expiry, and Iceland's declaration of a 200-mile fisheries limit with effect from October 1975, was followed by the 'third cod war'. Royal Navy frigates, sent in late November to protect British trawlers from warp-cutting and other harassment, became involved in confrontations with Icelandic coastguard vessels, and Iceland broke off diplomatic relations with the UK in February 1976, the first such breach between **NATO** member countries. In June 1976 the two sides signed an interim agreement, setting specific limits for a six-month period, after which British trawlers would have only such access rights as Iceland was prepared to allow within its 200-mile zone. Thereafter, with the British long-distance trawler fleets in terminal decline, negotiations on access to Icelandic waters were handed over to the **EC**.

CO-DECISION

A jargon word within the **EU** for the way in which the role of the **European Parliament** is enhanced under Article 113 of the **Maastricht** Treaty, beyond the right to be consulted and the right (under the **Single European Act**) to 'co-operation', but not to the extent of allowing it to initiate legislation. In specified areas Parliament's approval is necessary, as well as that of the **Council of Ministers**, before Community legislation can be adopted. Various suggestions were put forward during 1990 and 1991 as to where this co-decision should apply; the eventual list included legislation on completion of the **single market**, freedom of movement for workers, and new initiatives on the environment, consumer protection, public health, culture, Community transport infrastructure, energy and telecommunications. A special joint Conciliation Commission is invoked if the Parliament and Council cannot agree.

CODESA

The Convention for a Democratic South Africa, a multiparty constitutional negotiation forum which held its inaugural meeting in December 1991. CODESA represented the first substantive talks on South Africa's post-**apartheid** constitution. It brought together representatives of the government and 18 other groups including the **ANC** and **Inkatha**. The CODESA talks collapsed following the withdrawal of the ANC and its allies in the wake of the **Boipatong Massacre** in June 1992. Multiparty talks resumed in March 1993 when 26 groups sent delegates to a multiparty negotiations forum. This unnamed forum was responsible for the Interim Constitution under which the April 1994 non-racial democratic elections were held.

COHABITATION

A peculiarly French expression for the situation which arose in 1986, when the socialist President, François Mitterrand, had to 'cohabit' with a newly elected centre-right government headed by a Gaullist Prime Minister, Jacques Chirac. Despite procedural wrangling, the presidency continued to dominate the executive in these circumstances. While Chirac's government attempted to implement economic liberalization and social and educational reforms, Mitterrand used the president's right to refuse to sign legislation in order to protect what had been achieved by earlier socialist governments in the social field. In 1988 Mitterrand, having won a second seven-year presidential term, called an early general election which resulted in a majority socialist government. However, he had to undertake a second 'cohabitation' from March 1993, this time with Edouard Balladur heading another centre-right coalition.

COHESION FUND

A substantial **EU** fund to subsidize projects in poorer member countries, created as part of the package by which Spain, Portugal, Greece and Ireland were won over to support the 1991 **Maastricht** agreement. The fund was formally established on 16 May 1994. It would provide capital for transport infrastructure projects and environmental measures in member countries whose per capita **GDP** was less than 90 per cent of the Community average. When five former **EFTA** countries joined in the creation of a European Economic Area (**EEA**), effective from 1994, they were also obliged as part of that agreement to contribute to the cohesion fund.

COLD WAR

A phrase in common usage from 1947, describing the protracted period of post-war antagonism between the **communist bloc**, particularly the **Soviet Union**, and the **West**, led by the USA. Sir Winston Churchill's March 1946 speech at Fulton in Missouri, USA, when he warned of the threat of Soviet expansion and of an **iron curtain** falling across Europe, and the subsequent Soviet imposition of communism in East-Central Europe, are usually offered as starting points of the Cold War. The two blocs fought a vigorous propaganda battle in which each sought to discredit its rival and to gain prestige for itself. The balance of terror which followed the Soviet Union's development of the atomic bomb led the blocs to avoid direct military conflict, although there were several dangerous confrontations, including the **Cuban missile crisis**. Much conflict took place by proxy: one bloc funded and trained indigenous military groups to engage opposing forces when it appeared that the rival bloc was likely to extend its sphere of influence, for instance in Afghanistan.

The Cold War forced the two blocs to maintain their readiness for a possible 'hot war'; the expense of the resulting **arms race** eventually helped to bankrupt the Soviet Union. The appointment in 1985 of Mikhail Gorbachev as general secretary of the Communist Party of the Soviet Union marked the beginning of a rapprochement with the West, which was confirmed with the Soviet decision in 1989 not to intervene when the **communist** regimes in eastern Europe were collapsing. The final dissolution in 1991 of the **Warsaw Pact** – the military alliance between the former **communist bloc** countries – provided one of the clearest symbols of the ending of the Cold War.

COLLATERAL DAMAGE

A piece of military jargon widely used during the 1991 **Gulf War** to betoken damage inflicted on non-military targets. Despite the use of **smart weapons**, the US-led air campaign resulted in a widespread loss of civilian life. Little information was released by the allies, but it was acknowledged that some 'collateral damage' had been inflicted.

COLLECTIVE SECURITY

A fundamental notion in international relations, that states may act together to ensure conformity with recognized rules and norms of international behaviour. A basic tenet of the League of Nations after the First World War, it failed to develop effectively in the inter-war era, hampered by the League's restricted mandate and limits on its power to use force against aggression. The Second World War alliance against the German-led Axis coalition again encouraged hopes of postwar co-operation to resist threats to peace, and in the Washington Declaration of 1942 the 26 Allied countries laid the foundations of the **UN**, a determined move in this direction. However, the **Cold War**, which had developed by the early 1950s, and the emergence of rival blocs allied to the USA and the **Soviet Union**, quickly eroded the authority of the UN as an agent of collective security. The **UN Security Council** became locked in stalemate, with its permanent members using their right of veto to prevent action on major issues. The **UN General Assembly** invoked the principle of collective security to override a Security Council veto under the **Uniting for Peace** resolutions to oppose aggression in North Korea and Egypt in 1950 and 1956 respectively.

With the passing of the Cold War there has been a gradual revival of emphasis on collective security, although its precise implementation has been fraught with controversy as in the case of the **Gulf War** against Iraq in January–February 1991. Recent trends suggest that the traditional notion of collective security, as embodied in the UN system, may gradually be redefined, with the widening of what were formerly the Western security alliances (principally **NATO**) to include their former **Warsaw Pact** adversaries, and the enlargement of the security role of newer bodies such as the **CSCE**.

COLLECTIVIZATION

The **communist** land reform, pioneered in the **Soviet Union**, in which agricultural land and property was transferred from peasants and landowners to enormous collective farms (*kolkhoz*). The forced collectivization began in November 1929, on the orders of Stalin, with a ruthless campaign by communist party officials, the secret police and the **Red Army**. At least 5 million *kulaks* or wealthy peasants were killed or banished to Siberia. Many peasants resisted, destroying crops or slaughtering livestock rather than allow their requisition; millions are thought to have died during the consequent famine.

COLOMBO PLAN

The Colombo Plan for Co-operative, Economic and Social Development in Asia and the Pacific. As originally formed in 1950 it covered bilateral aid and technical and other assistance to seven **Commonwealth** countries in south and **south-east Asia**. It rapidly expanded to include other Asian and Pacific countries, and currently includes 20 such countries and four donor countries – Australia, Japan, New Zealand and the USA. Canada and the UK withdrew from participation in 1991–2.

THE COLONELS

The junta of middle-ranking **right-wing** military officers which held power in Greece between 1967 and 1974. Led by Col. Georgios Papadopoulos, the colonels seized power on 21 April 1967, suspending the Constitution and instigating an authoritarian conservative regime characterized by the persecution of **communist** sympathizers. A republic was declared on 1 June 1973, with Papadopoulos becoming the first President. A gradual move towards 'guided democracy' was halted by the bloodless coup staged by Brig.-Gen. Dimitris Ioannides in November 1973, and the reimposition of authoritarian rule. The colonels' regime finally collapsed during the debacle over Turkey's invasion of Cyprus in 1974.

COLONIA DIGNIDAD

(Spanish, 'Dignity Colony') A secretive German community in southern Chile, established after the Second World War. It was a widely suspected that between 1973 and 1990 community members allowed its facilities to be used for the detention and torture of **disappeared** persons by **DINA** military intelligence. Former detainees also made allegations of child abuse and slave labour. The democratically elected government of President Patricio Aylwin Azócar removed the colony's charitable status in 1991 for infringement of its non-profit-making status and tax laws, and ruled that all its land be given to a nearby Methodist church. However, most of the colony was signed over to individual settlers. The call of former detainees and the German government for a complete investigation of the colony remains unanswered.

COLONIALISM

A term associated chiefly, though not exclusively, with the consequences of Western overseas expansion from the sixteenth century. It involved the taking and economic exploitation, though not necessarily the settlement, of African, American, Asian and Australasian territories by Europeans, and was generally supported by a political organization which brought together different cultures, tribes or nationalities under a dominating metropolitan centre.

While frequently the outcome of military conquest, colonialism was justified by an elaborate ideology posited on the assumption that certain territories and people required domination. This idea which was subsequently to evolve as the recognizable creed of imperialism, defined by the attitudes of the dominant metropolis, fuelled a cultural discourse among Western colonial powers which justified their control of foreign territories. Among the Portuguese and Spanish, territorial acquisitions were seen as contributing to a Divine mission; among the French they served to further a *mission civilisatrice*, while among the British they fulfilled the inherent responsibilities of the 'White Man's Burden'. Among later colonial powers, the USA rationalized its foreign territories by appealing to Manifest Destiny.

Today, as a result of the post-war process of **decolonization**, direct or formal colonialism has largely ended. However, some contemporary historians argue that it lingers on in the 'post-colonial' world mainly through prevailing perceptions of the **Third World** in Western literature, academic studies and the media.

COLOUREDS

A term of racial classification used by the **apartheid** authorities in South Africa. It refers to several groups of people, including principally those whose descent is deemed to be mixed in terms of apartheid as well as those of Malayan descent and the original inhabitants of the Cape. The Coloured population remains concentrated in the West Cape province and is predominantly Afrikaans-speaking.

COLUMBUS QUINCENTENARY

The 500th anniversary of Christopher Columbus's first voyage to the Americas. The celebration of the event in October 1992 aroused great controversy on both sides of the Atlantic, since Spain and many governments in **Latin America** insisted on commemorating the 'discovery' of the continent, while the indigenous population protested at what they saw as the celebration of conquest and slavery. It served, however, to stimulate Panamerican indigenous organization and international interest both in the cultures and environments which had flourished before Columbus's arrival in 1492.

COMECON

The informal name for the Council for Mutual Economic Assistance (CMEA), the organization for economic co-operation between **communist** countries. Founded in 1949 as a response to the USA's **Marshall Plan**, its membership encompassed the **Warsaw Pact** countries (excluding Albania) and Cuba, Mongolia and Vietnam. With the collapse of communism in Europe, Comecon was formally disbanded in June 1991, although there were half-hearted efforts to create a successor organization among European ex-members.

COMESA

The Common Market for Eastern and South Africa, a free trade zone and customs union with a system of common external tariffs established under the aegis of the **PTA** in November 1993. As of July 1994 it had 16 members: **Eritrea**, Ethiopia, Kenya, **Lesotho**, Madagascar, **Malawi**, Mauritius, Mozambique, **Namibia**, **Rwanda**, Sudan, Swaziland, **Tanzania**, Uganda, **Zambia** and **Zimbabwe**. Following the successful holding of democratic non-racial elections in April 1994 South Africa was expected to be invited to join.

COMFORT WOMEN

The term used by the armed forces of imperial Japan to refer to women recruited from occupied territories who were forced to serve as unpaid prostitutes for Japanese troops. It was widely estimated that several hundred thousand women were used in this way, particularly between 1937 and 1945. The issue received widespread publicity in the early 1990s, as evidence came to light concerning the scale and level of organization involved in the comfort women programme, and a small number of victims filed compensation claims. In January 1992 Japanese Prime Minister Kiichi Miyazawa visited South Korea – the majority of comfort women were probably taken from Korea, Japan's oldest colony – and gave an unprecedented apology over the matter. Apologies to others of Japan's neighbours were also made, and in August 1993 the outgoing Miyazawa government released the findings of an 18-month inquiry into the issue which went further than ever before in admitting the scale and officially sanctioned nature of the operation.

COMINFORM

The **communist** Information Bureau, established by the communist movement in September 1947 as successor to the Comintern, and effectively devoted to Stalin's aim of consolidating the postwar gains of **communism** in **Eastern Europe**. The Cominform had nine founding members: the communist parties of the **Soviet Union**, France, Italy, Bulgaria, **Czechoslovakia**, Poland, Hungary, Romania, and **Yugoslavia** (which was expelled in June 1948). It was formally abolished in April 1956.

COMMAND ECONOMY

An economy where production and distribution are planned and organized by the state rather than developed under market conditions. This is characteristic of **communist** states but also sometimes occurs to some extent in Western economies, for example for wartime mobilization. Enterprises are set production targets according to the strategic priorities set by the centre, often in the form of a series of **five-year plans**. Historically, there was an over-emphasis on heavy industry and raw material extraction. Critics argue that economic decisions in a command economy tend to be taken on political or bureaucratic grounds – uneconomic enterprises may be supported, for instance, to maintain full employment – and that enterprises tend to respond sluggishly to shifting patterns of consumer demand, producing insufficient quantities of some goods and too much of others. Planned economies existed in the former **Soviet Union** and **Eastern Europe** until the collapse of the communist system; in the **PRC**, planning has been modified by the introduction of market mechanisms.

COMMISSION

The European Commission, which was formally called the Commission of the European Communities (**EC**) until November 1993. Essentially it is the Community body charged with formulating proposals and with managing Community affairs, whereas policy decisions are made by the Council of Ministers. The Commission currently consists of 17 commissioners, having grown from nine in 1967 (when there were six EC member countries, and when the Merger Treaty brought together the **EEC** and **Euratom** Commissions and the High Authority of the **ECSC**). The Commission which takes office in January 1995 will be the first to serve a five-year term, and some changes in the appointment procedure are due from 1996 under the **Maastricht** Treaty. Currently the commissioners are appointed by the **European Council** (and in effect by their national government), but are not supposed to represent national interests, holding instead a community-wide responsibility for a particular area of policy. Their work is supported by the **Brussels**-based **bureaucracy** of 20 directorates-general, with some services also in Luxembourg. The head of the Commission is its President, an office which grew in power and prestige under Jacques Delors, who served two full four-year terms from 1985 with a further two-year extension from January 1993.

COMMITTEE OF 100

A more militant offshoot of **CND** in the UK, formed in 1960 as the Committee of 100 for civil disobedience against nuclear weapons, and headed by Bertrand Russell. It undertook a number of forcible 'sit-downs' outside government buildings and at strategic bases, designed to invite confrontation with the police. It also broadened its scope to include other causes, such as opposition to the visit to London in July 1963 of King Paul and Queen Frederika of Greece. However, it gradually lost its leading role to other more specifically targeted organizations, and disbanded in 1968.

COMMITTEE ON THE PRESENT DANGER

A **right-wing** US pressure group established in the early stages of the administration of US President Jimmy Carter (1977–81) to lobby for increased defence spending.

COMMITTEE OF THE WHOLE

A procedural device whereby an entire legislative assembly transforms itself into a committee presided over by a chair rather than the Speaker. Associated particularly with the UK, the USA, Australia and Canada, the device is often used to consider details of financial or constitutional legislation.

COMMON EUROPEAN HOME

An expression associated particularly with Soviet President Mikhail Gorbachev, which began appearing in Soviet foreign policy rhetoric at the beginning of 1989. Gorbachev himself used it frequently on visits to Western European capitals later that year. The concept of a common home implied ruling out the use of military force by one side against the other; it would also encourage the building of common European institutions such as the **CSCE** in place of the **Cold War** blocs.

COMMON FUND

The main thrust of efforts at **UNCTAD** in the 1970s to stabilize the world market for 18 main primary commodities and minerals crucial to developing countries. The proposal centred on the joint financing of 'buffer stocks', which could buy in when prices were low and sell when they reached agreed ceilings. The Common Fund was part of UNCTAD's Integrated Commodity Programme, its main concrete contribution to the **NIEO** debate. Even in the much reduced form eventually adopted in June 1980, however, the Common Fund proved stillborn, failing to secure the necessary ratifications to enter into effect (particularly from developed countries which were supposed to be the main contributors to the fund's capital).

COMMON MARKET

The popular name for the **EEC**, but also a general term applicable to other organizations which implement free trade and other forms of economic co-operation within a geographical area.

COMMONWEALTH

A voluntary association of 50 independent states which evolved from the British Empire, and has latterly been concerned mainly with decolonization, economic development, and white minority rule in southern Africa. Its origin is generally traced back to the 1931 Statute of Westminster which confirmed the sovereignty of the **'White Commonwealth'** countries, namely Australia, Canada, New Zealand and South Africa, while enabling them to retain the British monarch as queen or head of state. A revised formula agreed in 1949 allowed India, and thus other members, to become republics within the Commonwealth while acknowledging the British monarch as symbolic head of state. Of the Commonwealth's current membership, 16 states, including the UK, have Queen Elizabeth as head of state, five others are national monarchies, and 29 are republics. The organization has no formal charter or governing structure; policy is defined at biennial summits, known as **CHOGMs**, and implemented through the Commonwealth Secretariat, headed by a secretary-general.

COMMONWEALTH FOUNDATION

A London-based body established in 1965 to promote professional co-operation within the **Commonwealth**. Its mandate was extended in 1979 to include co-operation with **NGOs**, and its functions widened to include culture, information, the media, rural development and the interests of people with disabilities and women.

COMMONWEALTH PREFERENCE

A preferential system of trade tariffs between the UK and its **Commonwealth** partners. Opponents of UK entry into the **EC** argued strongly that EC membership would adversely affect Commonwealth countries, and in particular that it would shut out their cheap farm produce. Arrangements announced in 1971 provided for continued special access to UK markets for some Commonwealth countries, in particular New Zealand, and made special arrangements for the gradual introduction of external tariffs and levies on goods from Australia and Canada. **ACP** countries within the Commonwealth were allowed to maintain existing trading arrangements until 1975, pending the entry into force of the **Lomé Convention**.

COMMUNAL VIOLENCE

Violence perpetrated on the basis of differences in race, ethnicity or religion. The term generally has the connotation of mob violence, rather than such clinically implemented genocide as the Nazi extermination of European Jews. It is less often applied in the European context (where the same phenomenon is more often termed ethnic or sectarian violence) than in the **Indian sub-continent**, where the worst explosion was between Hindus and Muslims following **partition** in 1947. Many other parts of Asia, Africa and the **Middle East** decolonized since 1945 have also experienced communal violence, which has recurred with particular intensity when the state is seen to be identified with the interests of a dominant ethnic or religious group, as in Nigeria in 1967–70, **Pakistan** in 1971, **Sri Lanka** since 1983, and **Rwanda** in 1994.

COMMUNISM

The revolutionary ideology which envisages the creation of a free, equal and prosperous society with a minimal state. **Marxism** predicts, and urges, the creation of a communist society by the proletariat, after it has overthrown the bourgeoisie and thereby destroyed a **capitalist** system which it rejects as inherently exploitative and degrading. Marxist ideas on the creation of communist societies have been subject to development and adaptation in the twentieth century in various forms, notably by Lenin, Trotksy, Mao and others.

COMMUNIST

An adherent of the doctrine of **communism**. The term was used in the former **Soviet Union** to denote a member of the ruling party, the **CPSU**, and hence a member of the establishment. In the USA, the anti-Communist hysteria associated with **McCarthyism** reduced the term to a much-feared and highly damaging political weapon.

COMMUNIST BLOC

The coalition of **communist** countries led during the **Cold War** by the **Soviet Union** (hence the synonymous term Soviet bloc), and particularly the **client states** of **Eastern Europe** (hence eastern bloc); the bloc later encompassed Cuba and other pro-Soviet countries outside Europe. Communist bloc states were bound together by security arrangements such as the **Warsaw Pact**, and economic mechanisms such as **Comecon**. Although the **Sino-Soviet split** confirmed China's independence of the bloc, and **Yugoslavia** (after 1948) and Albania (after 1961) were able to evade the Soviet line and have their own foreign policies, other states were kept firmly in line. The 1968 invasion of **Czechoslovakia** after the **Prague Spring** was carried out by troops from five communist bloc countries, and justified in the **Brezhnev doctrine**, although Romania, the only communist bloc state to pursue a relatively independent foreign policy, actually condemned the 1968 invasion. The communist bloc disintegrated after the collapse of communism in eastern Europe in **1989**, although Russia retained enough power to prevent former communist bloc members becoming full members of **NATO**.

COMMUNITY CHARGE

The official name for the controversial 'poll tax' introduced by the UK Conservative government, in Scotland in April 1989 and in England and Wales in April 1990. Local taxes under the previous rates system had been levied according to notional values of homes, but the community charge was based on the number of adults in the household, and for many it represented a considerable increase over the rates. The tax was exceptionally unpopular, provoking nationwide protests including serious rioting in London on 31 March 1990 and demonstrations in normally loyal Conservative areas. Non-payment of the tax was unusually high. The tax was associated closely with Margaret Thatcher's administration and was seen in many ways as her nemesis. Her successor, John Major, took steps to abolish it soon after coming to office; in March 1991 it was announced that it would be replaced by the **Council Tax** in April 1993.

THE COMPANY *see* CIA

COMPASSION FATIGUE

The phenomenon whereby, in the face of almost continuous demands and with its sympathy exhausted, the public feels unable to give to those in need.

COMPENSATORY AND CONTINGENCY FINANCING FACILITY

An **IMF** facility first introduced in 1963, designed to help member countries when their export earnings drop. Compensatory financing has gradually been expanded, and was broadened in 1981 so that it could also help countries whose cereal import costs increase sharply. Countries may also call upon the contingency financing element, when the current account on their balance of payments is hit by fluctuations in certain highly volatile and easily identifiable key variables.

COMPULSORY REPATRIATION

Deportation of refugees to their homeland. In the case of Vietnamese **boat people** in Hong Kong, the Hong Kong authorities carried out the first compulsory repatriation of refugees deemed **economic migrants** in December 1989. Vietnamese and US opposition to the policy meant that the next operation was not carried out until mid-1992, when Vietnam and the UK signed an agreement providing for the blanket return to Vietnam of all so-called economic migrants. Since then compulsory repatriation flights from Hong Kong have occurred at regular intervals.

COMRADES

A term used to describe young black radicals in the mid-1980s in South Africa's **townships**. Loosely affiliated to the **UDF**, the comrades organized grassroots anti-**apartheid** activity through street committees elected to replace the discredited township councils. More controversially, comrades also dispensed justice in so-called 'people's courts' which were established by residents who rejected the state's judicial system. They frequently inflicted punishments on people convicted by the 'people's courts' of crimes ranging from theft to murder, as well as on those who collaborated with the apartheid regime (the offence for which the notorious punishment of **necklacing** was sometimes reserved). Comrades were also frequently involved in violent clashes with supporters of **Inkatha** and other conservative groups. Following the unbanning of the **ANC** in 1990, comrades gradually came under the disciplinary control of that organization.

CONCORDE

The only supersonic aircraft in commercial use. Agreement on this Anglo-French venture was announced in November 1962. The development of the delta-winged airliner cost £1,500 million (US$2,250 million) and the maiden flight of the first prototype took place at Toulouse on 2 March 1968. On that occasion UK Minister of Technology Anthony Wedgwood Benn (now Tony Benn) finally ended speculation as to the spelling of the aircraft's name by announcing that it would have the French final 'e', which he said stood 'for excellence, for England, for Europe and for Entente'. The plane went into commercial use on 21 January 1976. The advantage of Concorde's cruising speed – Mach 2 (1,350 mph/2,150 kph) or twice the speed of sound – is offset commercially by the limited seating capacity (100 passengers) and high running costs.

CONFEDERATION OF BRITISH INDUSTRY *see* CBI

CONGRESS

The bicameral legislature of the USA, a name also adopted for legislatures in other countries. The US Congress consists of a 100-member Senate (upper chamber) elected for six years, with one-third being renewed every two years, and a 435-member House of Representatives (lower chamber) elected for two years. Each state sends two Senators to the upper house, regardless of the size or population of the state. The Senate's powers include the right to ratify foreign treaties, to act as a court of impeachment, and to confirm senior appointments to the judiciary and to the executive. The number of representatives from each state in the House is proportionate to its population.

CONSCIENTIOUS OBJECTOR

A term to describe a person who refuses to be conscripted into the armed forces because of moral objections. When Britain and the USA introduced conscription to raise troops during the First World War conscientious objectors were harshly treated, often forced into overseas service, and sometimes shot for disobeying orders at the front. During the Second World War they were treated a little more sympathetically, with alternative forms of non-military service often being provided. During the **Vietnam War** (the last major conflict to have been fought by a democratic state using conscripted troops) there were many conscientious objectors, some of whom served prison sentences rather than join the armed forces and some of whom became **draft dodgers**.

CONSENSUS POLITICS

The explicit or tacit alignment of the policies of two or more otherwise opposed parties within a legislature or political system. As this course may result in a minimization of confrontation, it may be seen as the converse of the pursuit of **conviction politics**.

CONSERVATISM

A broad ideology which is characterized by opposition to radical change and by defence of the status quo. Conservatism has a rich political heritage, including English theorists such as Edmund Burke and nineteenth century practitioners such as Sir Robert Peel and Benjamin Disraeli. However, its essential pragmatism and distrust of idealistic solutions to social problems have led many to see it as a political approach rather than an ideology in the strictest sense. **Right-wing** in orientation, conservatism tends to advocate adherence to tradition, a hierarchical ordering of society, and respect for religion, the family and the institution of private property.

Although it originated as the ideology of a landed ruling class, in the nineteenth and twentieth centuries conservatism adapted itself to the ascendancy of the bourgeoisie and succeeded in attracting the support of significant sections of the working class. In the 1980s the ideology underwent a revival in Western Europe and the USA as a result of being galvanized by the ideas of the **New Right**.

Conservatism's opponents criticize it for perpetuating political and economic inequalities by duping the underprivileged into accepting the status quo.

CONSTRUCTIVE ENGAGEMENT

The policy adopted by the administration of US President Ronald Reagan towards South Africa. Formulated in 1980–1 by Chester Crocker, the Assistant Secretary of State for African Affairs, the policy was based on the fact that South Africa was extremely important to the economic and strategic interests of the USA and the **West**, and the assumption that South African stability was vital. Crocker also regarded it as vital that the influence of the **Soviet Union** in the region be countered. The Reagan administration therefore pursued a policy of guiding South Africa towards limited reform of **apartheid**. It was hoped that this would defuse political tension but not result in the immediate transfer of power to the black majority. Constructive engagement implied a rejection of **sanctions** as a means of influencing the South African government and was denounced by anti-apartheid activists as tacit acceptance of the apartheid regime.

CONTADORA

An independent **Latin American** initiative for peace in **Central America** set up by Colombia, Mexico, Panama and Venezuela in January 1983. Opposed by the USA, its 21-point 'Document of Objectives', signed on 9 September 1983 by all Central American foreign ministers, included demands for the withdrawal of foreign military presences from the region. Subsequent draft agreements sought to demilitarize the region and reduce the number of foreign advisers and, crucially, recognized the legitimacy of Nicaragua's **Sandinista** government and Nicaragua's sovereignty. The later **Arias Plan** took away the initiative from Contadora but assigned the group a supervisory role. The Contadora group, which with the **Lima Group** formed the **Group of Rio** in 1987, then turned its attention to debt and broad social issues. It was formally dissolved in April 1990.

CONTAINMENT

The US foreign policy geared to restricting the alleged expansionism of the **Soviet Union**. The term featured in the **Long Telegram**, the analysis of Soviet intentions drafted in February 1946 by the US chargé d'affaires in Moscow, George Kennan. In an article signed 'X' in the July 1947 issue of the US periodical *Foreign Affairs*, Kennan wrote: 'Soviet pressure . . . can be contained by the adroit and vigilant application of counterforce at a series of constantly shifting geographical and political points corresponding to the shifts and manoeuvres of Soviet policy.' Containment became linked with the **Truman Doctrine** and the **Marshall Plan**, resulting in targeted US aid, the establishment of military bases worldwide, and a readiness to undertake military intervention. In his 1967 *Memoirs* Kennan denied that he intended containment to imply global and unrestrained application of force by the USA, but rather 'the political containment of a political threat'. He also suggested that it was a specific response, relevant only to the immediate post-1945 period.

CONTIGUOUS ZONE

The offshore area beyond a coastal state's **territorial waters**, within which it could nevertheless enforce rules on such issues as immigration, customs, and environmental protection. A contiguous zone of 12 nautical miles was widely discussed in the early 1960s as an alternative to extending territorial waters from three to 12 miles; by 1982, however, **UNCLOS** had reached consensus on territorial waters up to 12 miles and a contiguous zone extending for a further 12.

CONTINENTAL SHELF

The relatively gradual slope of the seabed offshore before the point where it falls away steeply to the ocean floor. The UK and the USA were among the first countries to claim, in the 1940s, exclusive jurisdiction over the fisheries, mineral and other resources of the continental shelf. This concept had gained eventual acceptance by the time of the agreement at **UNCLOS** in 1982, when the continental shelf was delimited as extending up to 350 nautical miles offshore, depending on local geography, and coastal states were accorded jurisdiction within it, in addition to their rights over a 200-mile **EEZ**.

CONTINUING REVOLUTION

A tenet of Chinese leader Mao Zedong which envisaged the uninterrupted continuation of the proletarian revolution and dictatorship of the proletariat until a truly **communist** society could be established. It was unveiled in *Sixty Articles on Work Methods* – the directive initiating the **Great Leap Forward** – which Mao proclaimed at the end of January 1958. Continuing Revolution is distinct from Leon Trotsky's theory of **permanent revolution**.

CONTINUISMO

(Spanish, 'continuing') The practice often used by dictators in **Latin America** of prolonging presidential terms. As the constitutions in most countries of the region prohibit two consecutive terms, presidents have often resorted to calling referendums to approve the drafting of a new constitution, or have dispensed with the constitution altogether and ruled by decree to remain in power. Notable examples include the Somoza dynasty in Nicaragua (1936–76), Perón in Argentina (1946–55), the Duvaliers in Haiti (1957–86), Pinochet in Chile (1973–90) and Stroessner in Paraguay (1954–89). Alberto Fujimori and Carlos Menem, respectively President of Peru (since 1990) and of Argentina (since 1989), are both currently supervising constitutional amendments in order to achieve a longer period in office.

CONTRAS

(from Spanish, *contra*, 'against') Nicaraguan counter-revolutionary forces financed during the 1980s by the US Reagan administration, in part illegally as revealed by the **Iran-contra affair**. From 1980 to 1991 the 20,000 contras, many of whom were supporters of the dictator Anastasio Somoza ousted in 1979, operated mainly from camps in neighbouring Honduras to destabilize the **left-wing Sandinista** government. They were associated with acts of great brutality and also focused their attacks on economic targets, social infrastructure and organizations identified with the 1979 revolution. The majority demobilized in 1990 under a peace agreement with the new centre-right government of President Violeta Chamorro, but small groups – **re-contras** – remain active.

CONVENTION ON THE RIGHTS OF THE CHILD

A convention adopted by the 44th session of the **UN General Assembly** in November 1989, which seeks to implement the principles contained in the 1959 Declaration on the Rights of the Child. Among its 54 articles are provisions relating to children's rights to survival and development; their protection from economic and political exploitation as well as from sexual abuse; their right to freedom of expression; and the prohibition of conscription for military service for children under 14. A World Summit for Children was held in September 1990, aimed at securing universal ratification of the Convention, and 148 countries had ratified it as of September 1993.

CONVENTIONAL WEAPONS

A broad category, specifically not including **nuclear weapons**, **biological weapons** and **chemical weapons**, and generally treated for **arms control** purposes as not including **ABM** systems.

CONVERGENCE

A jargon word much used in the **EU** for the process by which the economies of member countries are to become more closely comparable in terms of their performance. The third stage of economic and monetary union (**EMU**) may only be embarked upon by those states which have achieved the necessary convergence on four key measures – inflation rates, the control of government deficits, currency stability, and interest rates.

CONVERTIBILITY

The policy which permits one currency to be exchanged freely for others. Key **IMF** objectives include establishing a multilateral system of payments, in respect of current transactions between member countries, and eliminating the foreign exchange restrictions which hamper the growth of world trade. By July 1994 a total of 93 IMF members (out of a total membership of 179) had formally accepted the obligations contained in the relevant sections of Article VIII of the Fund's Articles of Agreement; these included undertakings not to engage in discriminatory currency arrangements or multiple currency practices without IMF approval.

CONVICTION POLITICS

The pursuit of political beliefs with little or no concern for opposing points of view. Depending on the standpoint of the observer, conviction politics (one of the catchphrases of **Thatcherism**) may be seen either as stubbornly dogmatic or as intellectually purist. In either case conviction politics make impossible any approach towards **consensus politics**.

COPARTICIPATION

A Uruguayan system of distribution of government-controlled posts among ruling and opposition parties which was a product of **caudillismo** and compromises between political bosses in the nineteenth century. Under it losing parties obtained a minority of places in government, state-owned companies and committees down to local level. The system reached its peak when the collegiate system of the presidency was introduced in 1952 (under which the ruling party had six seats and the opposition three in the collegiate executive) and was credited with Uruguay's democratic stability until the late 1960s. The Constitution of 1966 restored the presidential system, but coparticipation continues at lower levels.

COPTS

Followers of Coptic Christianity, found mainly in Egypt and Sudan. Copts separated from the Christian mainstream in 451 after proclaiming their Monophysite beliefs according to which Jesus was endowed with one divine nature, rather than two (divine and human) as enunciated by the dominant tradition. Copts have played an important role in public life in Egypt; several have been appointed to important positions in government, the most prominent of whom was the former Deputy Prime Minister and current UN Secretary-General, Boutros Boutros-Ghali. More recently Egyptian Copts who have co-existed for centuries with Muslim communities in Upper Egypt have become the targets of vicious and frequently fatal attacks by militant Egyptian Muslim groups.

CORDILLERA PEOPLE'S LIBERATION ARMY

A **guerrilla** group operating in the Philippines until it signed a ceasefire with the government of President Corazon Aquino on 13 September 1986. The CPLA was formed from a splinter group of the **New People's Army** and was led by a dissident Roman Catholic priest, Fr Conrado Balweg. Although Balweg's group had been active in the Cordillera region of Luzon, the main island of the Philippines, since at least

1980, the CPLA was only officially formed on 29 April 1986. In October 1989 a law granting some autonomy to the Cordillera region was announced.

CORDON SANITAIRE

(French, 'quarantine line') A 'buffer zone', often of neutral territory, separating hostile states from one other, or protecting a state from potential aggressors beyond the cordon. A cordon sanitaire may also be seen as isolating a state and its ideology from foreign corruption by subversive doctrines. Both functions were supposedly performed by the countries of **Eastern Europe** on behalf of the **Soviet Union** during the **Cold War**.

CORE

The Congress of Racial Equality, a key organization in the US **civil rights movement**. Established at Chicago University in 1952 by James Farmer, CORE supported **sit-in** demonstrations and **freedom rides** in its challenge to **segregation** and institutionalized **racism**. In the mid-1960s it endorsed the concept of **Black Power**, and altered its constitution to define itself as 'a mass membership organization for implementing Black Power for Black people'.

COREPER

The Committee of Permanent Representatives of member states of the **EU**, consisting of government officials at ambassadorial level who are responsible for ensuring the continuity of policy between sessions of the **Council of Ministers**.

CO-RESPONSIBILITY LEVY

A tool to help the reform of common agricultural policy (**CAP**) which gained acceptance in the mid-1980s in the **EC** (later the **EU**) despite resistance from farmers. While guaranteed prices remained the core of the CAP, dairy and cereal producers found themselves obliged to pay the levy as a direct contribution to the cost of buying up and storing their surplus production.

CORPORATIST

A form of political and economic state organization, derived from mediaeval guilds, in which society is represented through monopoly associations (corporations), usually based on economic activity, acting as intermediaries between the state and the individual. Under **Fascist** theory, corporatism enables the state to forge class consensus, through enforced mediation between the interests of capital and labour, and provides a form of political representation. A Marxist critique of corporatism charges that it allows the **capitalist** state to deliver the co-operation of workers while depriving them of the right to political opposition. Contemporary political theory describes as neo-corporatist those countries in which a close relationship exists between the state and monopoly associations representing private business.

CORSICAN NATIONAL LIBERATION FRONT *see* FLNC

CORSICANS

The native inhabitants of the French Mediterranean island of Corsica, a small number of whom have resorted to occasional terrorist violence to defend Corsican land, language and culture from perceived encroachment. The threat they identify is twofold, from 'settlers' from metropolitan France and the former French territories of north Africa, and from tourist development. In 1982 Corsica achieved a measure of self-rule, but nationalist and separatist movements persist, in particular the banned **FLNC** and Corsican Movement for Self Determination.

CORTES GENERALES

The Spanish legislature, consisting of a 350-member Congress of Deputies directly elected by proportional representation, and a 255-member Senate of whom 208 are directly elected and the rest are chosen by the assemblies of the 17 autonomous regions. Mainly a rubber-stamping body for the regime of Gen. Francisco Franco in 1939–75, the Cortes became once again a parliament of democratically elected representatives in June 1977.

COSA NOSTRA

(Italian, 'Our business') A widely used term for the Sicilian **Mafia**.

COSVN

Central Office for South Vietnam – the **communist** Party of Vietnam's elusive southern 'nerve centre' which controlled political and military operations in the South during the **Vietnam War**. The infamous US invasion of Cambodia in April–May 1970 failed in its avowed aim of destroying COSVN.

CÔTE D'IVOIRE

The west African country of some 12.9 million people, whose government has expressly requested the discontinuation of the former English language name Ivory Coast. A former French colony, Côte d'Ivoire became independent in 1960.

COUNCIL OF CONSTITUTIONAL GUARDIANS

A body established in 1980 under Article 94 of the 1979 Constitution of the Islamic Republic of Iran. Its primary role is to supervise elections and ensure that all parliamentary legislation is in accordance with the Constitution and Islamic law. Also known as the Council for the Protection of the Constitution, it consists of six qualified religious jurists appointed by the country's spiritual leader (*walih faqih*), and six lay members of the legal profession appointed by the High Council of the Judiciary and approved by the **majlis ash shura**.

COUNCIL OF EUROPE

An intergovernmental organization with its headquarters in Strasbourg, founded on 5 May 1949 by Western European states to promote civil society and human rights. It is chiefly known for the 1950 **European Convention on Human Rights** and for the **European Court of Human Rights** which was set up to implement the Convention. Since the collapse of **communist** regimes in **1989** the Council of Europe has seen itself playing a more prominent role in the integration of **Eastern**, **Central** and **Western Europe** by establishing common standards on economic, legal, scientific, environmental and social issues. At the end of 1993 it had 32 member countries.

COUNCIL OF EUROPEAN UNION *see* EUROPEAN COUNCIL

COUNCIL OF MINISTERS

A term often used for national governments, but also within international organizations, notably for the principal decision-making body in what is now called the European Union (**EU**, formerly the **EC**). Here it consists of ministerial-level representatives of member governments, with the presidency held for six months by each member country in alphabetical rotation. A Council of (Foreign) Ministers meeting usually takes place every month, while ministers responsible for other portfolios have Council of Ministers meetings of varying frequency.

The possibility that one country can veto decisions in the Council of Ministers has blocked a number of initiatives as well as holding up agreements on such matters as the budget or agricultural prices. Decisions are only taken by simple majority vote on minor procedural matters, and the **Luxembourg compromise** of 1966 restricted the proposed introduction of qualified majority voting to instances where no member state invoked its essential national interest. This began to change in the 1970s, with **qualified majority voting** on budgetary issues, and under the **Single European Act**, especially for issues relating to creating the **single market**.

COUNCIL FOR MUTUAL ECONOMIC ASSISTANCE *see* COMECON

COUNCIL FOR THE PROTECTION OF THE CONSTITUTION *see* COUNCIL OF CONSTITUTIONAL GUARDIANS

COUNCIL TAX

A local tax introduced by the UK Conservative government in April 1993 to replace the controversial **community charge** or 'poll tax'. Unlike its predecessor, which was a per capita charge, the new system was a property tax related to the value of people's homes, with a reduction for single adult occupiers.

COUNTERINSURGENCY

A military stratagem adopted by governments against **guerrilla** insurgency. Successful counterinsurgency campaigns include the classic 'Briggs plan' adopted by the British to counter **communist** rebels during the Malayan **Emergency**, and the defeat of the **Huks guerrillas** by the government of the Philippines, both in the early 1950s. The British Malayan campaign (devised by Robert Thompson) became the prototype for early US counterinsurgency efforts during the **Vietnam War**. However, the lessons of Malaya and the Philippines were not applicable to conditions in South Vietnam and, eventually, the USA was forced to bolster counterinsurgency with conventional warfare.

COUP D'ÉTAT

The swift and forcible seizure of power by a small group which can be of any political orientation and is often but not necessarily from the armed forces.

COVERT OPERATIONS

Secret operations conducted by the security agency of a country, often without the knowledge of much of the elected executive. In the USA such activities are the speciality of the Operations Directorate (colloquially known as the 'Department of Dirty Tricks') of the **CIA**.

CPSU

The **communist** Party of the **Soviet Union**, founded in 1918 as the Communist Party (and formerly the Bolshevik Party). CPSU membership had grown to nearly 20 million by the mid-1980s. Its own organs fused with those of the Soviet state, so that the CPSU's leader or **Gensec** was the country's de facto leader. The CPSU was very hierarchical: the **nomenklatura** system ensured that each grade of **bureaucracy** deferred to the one above. Whereas 14 of the 15 Soviet republics each had a republican Communist Party within the CPSU's all-union structure, Russia's party organizations were an integral part of the CPSU itself, until June 1990 when a Russian Communist Party was formed. The CPSU was suspended in 1991 following the **August coup**. The Russian Communist Party thereafter became the dominant party of the left in Russia, although the CPSU was partially reinstated by the courts in December 1992.

CRACK

A highly addictive narcotic which is manufactured by heating cocaine, water and baking powder and breaking the resulting hard substance into small fragments to be inhaled or smoked. Increasing levels of violent crime in the USA in the 1980s have been blamed on the rise of crack addiction, particularly among the urban poor.

CREDIT TRANCHE POLICY

The basic **IMF** policy on the use of the Fund's general resources by member countries. Credit tranche purchases (i.e. borrowings) from the Fund are made available to be drawn in four tranches, or stages. As each successive tranche is drawn, conditions must be met as regards the policies which the member country is required to pursue. The aim is that these policies progressively help to resolve the borrowing country's balance of payment difficulties.

CREEP

The Committee to Re-elect the President. Established in advance of the November 1972 US presidential elections, CREEP worked to achieve the re-election of Richard Nixon by orchestrating a campaign of 'dirty tricks' against his Democratic opponents. Among the activities which it sponsored was the burglary of the Democratic headquarters in June 1972. Despite Nixon's landslide election victory this burglary unleashed the **Watergate** scandal which culminated in Nixon's resignation as President in August 1974, in the face of impeachment proceedings by Congress.

CRIMEA

A peninsula in the Black Sea, which in 1954 was transferred from the Russian Federation to become a republic within **Ukraine**, although 70 per cent of the population of 2.7 million is Russian and 10 per cent is ethnic Tatar. On the south-east tip of the peninsula lies the strategically sensitive port of Sevastopol, the main headquarters of the former Soviet Black Sea Fleet. Since the collapse of the **Soviet Union**, the issues of ownership of the fleet and of pro-Russian sentiment in Crimea have caused tension between Russia and Ukraine. Yuri Meshkov, elected president of the Ukrainian republic of Crimea in January 1994, advocates close links with Russia and has called for a referendum on independence from Ukraine.

CROATIA

A **Balkan** republic which declared independence from **Yugoslavia** in June 1991 and was internationally recognized in January 1992. Catholic Croatia historically formed the eastern bastion of the Austro-Hungarian empire against the Ottomans. From 1918 it was part of the Kingdom of the Serbs, Croats and Slovenes which became **Yugoslavia**, although the German invasion in 1941 fostered the first nominally independent state of Croatia, under the wartime **Ustasa** Nazi puppet regime, responsible for brutal massacres particularly of Serbs. The opening shots of the Yugoslav civil war were fired in Croatia in May 1991, when the Serbs of the **Krajina** rebelled against the prospect of being part of an independent Croatia. With the backing of the Yugoslav National Army, Serbs conquered up to one-third of Croatia, including the town of **Vukovar**. In March 1994 Croatian President Franjo Tudjman appeared to abandon his goal of conquering territory in neighbouring **Bosnia-Hercegovina** and instead agreed on confederation with Bosnia.

CROATIAN SPRING

The brief rise of Croatian reform communism and moderate **nationalism** in 1969–71, under the Tito regime in communist **Yugoslavia**. The Croatian communist party's reformist leadership alienated local Serb conservatives, and in 1971 Josip Broz Tito carried out a purge of the Croatian leadership, including Franjo Tudjman (Croatia's future President) in 1971. In a compromise move prompted in part by the Croatian Spring, Tito introduced a new constitution in 1974 which devolved considerable power to Yugoslavia's republics, encouraging increasingly separate development.

CRONYISM

The practice of appointing friends to government posts. In August 1952 *The New York Times* referred to the sorry reputation of the administration of President Harry S. Truman for 'corruption, cronyism, extravagance, waste and confusion'. From 1946 government in the Philippines was characterised by endemic cronyism, which reached its apogee under Ferdinand Marcos, the dictator ousted by **people power** in 1986.

CROSSMAN DIARIES

The memoirs of a senior UK politician, Richard Crossman, which gave one of the first and most candid accounts of the day-to-day workings of the Cabinet. The *Diaries of a Cabinet Minister* were published in three volumes between 1975 and 1977. Crossman had been a member of the Labour government between 1964 and 1970.

CRS

The *compagnies républicaines de sécurité*, the French mobile police reserve units used as riot squads in many celebrated confrontations, notably with student protestors in the **évènements** of **1968**. The CRS, first established in 1945, are under the authority of the Interior and Administrative Reform Ministry.

CRUISE

US intermediate-range missiles developed in the 1970s and 1980s, designed to fly low over land and read their position from the topography so that, with detailed mapping, they could be guided to their targets. Sea-launched Tomahawk cruise missiles (with non-nuclear warheads) were part of the arsenal of **smart weapons** in the 1991 **Gulf War**. The most famous and controversial cruise missile, however, was the ground-launched version with nuclear warheads, deployed from 1983 in Western Europe but under US sole control. Opposition to cruise was the focus of massive peace campaigns and protests such as that at **Greenham Common**. Introduced (along with **Pershing**) under **NATO's** 1979 **twin-track decision**, the nuclear-armed cruise missiles were removed under the 1987 **INF Treaty**; the last one from Greenham left on 5 March 1991, and the last in Europe was flown out from Comiso in Sicily three weeks later.

CS GAS

A potent tear gas used by police and security forces worldwide for crowd dispersal and riot control. Its chemical name is orthochlorobenzylidene malononitrile; its common name derives from US chemists Ben Carson and Roger Staughton.

CSCE

The Conference on Security and Co-operation in Europe, an intergovernmental organization whose membership had reached 52 by 1994, and which seeks to encompass all recognized states in Europe and the former **Soviet Union**, together with Canada and the USA. The CSCE's main decision-making body is a Council of Foreign Ministers; its permanent Secretariat is based in Prague. Its role includes securing the observance of human rights, and providing a forum for settling disputes among member countries. Some member countries, notably Russia, have latterly advocated its development as the principal organization for managing the responses of European countries on a wide range of continent-wide concerns. Its initial impact, however, was principally in promoting East-West **detente**, bringing together 35 countries including the rival **NATO** and **Warsaw Pact** alliances for the Helsinki CSCE conference which began in July 1973 and culminated in the 1975 **Helsinki Final Act**.

CUBAN MISSILE CRISIS

One of the defining moments of the **Cold War**, when the USA and the **Soviet Union** confronted each other on the brink of military conflict. US hostility towards the Cuban revolution, together with Fidel Castro's open espousal of communism, had helped to bring Cuba into a close relationship with the Soviet Union, and, following the US-sponsored **Bay of Pigs** invasion, Castro successfully requested Soviet weaponry to improve Cuba's defences. Between July and October 1962 the Soviet Union supplied Cuba with jet fighter and bomber aircraft and, more significantly, with nuclear missiles. US aerial reconnaissance on 14 October showed clear evidence of a missile and its launch pad.

Rejecting the advice of those within his administration who advocated an immediate air strike on Cuba, on 22 October US President John Kennedy imposed a naval blockade to prevent the delivery of further Soviet missiles. With a fleet of Soviet vessels already en route to Cuba, for several days a superpower clash seemed imminent. However, on 28 October Soviet Premier Nikita Khrushchev agreed to recall the Soviet convoy and to withdraw the missiles already in place in Cuba, in return for a lifting of the US blockade and a US promise not to invade the island. Khrushchev's demand that US nuclear weapons should be withdrawn from Turkey (which stood in roughly the same proximity to Soviet territory as does Cuba to the USA), was rejected by Kennedy.

Khrushchev later claimed that the incident had achieved its primary objective of securing Cuba from US attack. Nevertheless, it was Kennedy who was widely seen as having emerged victorious from the confrontation. The USA had upheld the **Monroe Doctrine** in unilaterally rejecting the Soviet Union's attempt to establish a military presence in the **Caribbean**. Moreover, Kennedy was seen to have kept his nerve at the height of the crisis and to have forced Khrushchev's compliance with his key demands.

CUITO CUANAVALE

Site of the largest set-piece battle fought in Africa since the Second World War and a turning point in South Africa's military invasion in Angola. Fighting broke out in late 1987 when South African and **UNITA** forces attempted to take the southern Angolan town of Cuito Cuanavale which was being defended by Angolan government forces supported by Cuban troops. By the following May, 3,000 South African troops, half the South African force, had lost their lives as the Angolan and Cuban launched a successful counter-offensive. The enormous South African losses, mainly young white conscripts, placed the Pretoria government under increasing pressure to reassess its role in Angola and negotiate with the Luanda government.

CULT OF PERSONALITY

Devotion to a leader, who is ascribed quasi-divine status by his or her followers and seen as embodying wisdom, goodness and strength. Examples under **communist** dictatorships include Joseph Stalin in the **Soviet Union**, Mao Zedong in China and Kim Il Sung in Korea, although the term is also applicable for instance to Saddam Hussein in Iraq or Mobutu Sese Seko in **Zaïre**. A cult of personality frequently finds expression in an ideology, as with **Stalinism**, **Maoism** or **Mobutuism**. The phenomenon was depicted satirically as **Big Brother** in the novel **1984**.

CULTURAL REVOLUTION

The Great Proletarian Cultural Revolution unleashed in China in 1966 was intended to advance Chairman Mao Zedong's theory of **continuing revolution** and prevent the proletarian revolution from reverting to **capitalism**, but ended in widespread chaos and the purging of some 4.5 million Chinese Communist Party (CCP) members. Prompted by Mao's fear that CCP officials were in danger of becoming a new class, and his conviction that the **Soviet Union** had abandoned socialism, the Cultural Revolution was to dislodge **capitalist roaders** and ensure the establishment of communism by destroying the political and ideological elements of the class structure. The initial phase, driven by the ideological fervour of the **Red Guards**, came to an end in 1969 when the People's Liberation Army intervened to reimpose control. At the height of the Cultural Revolution central government virtually disintegrated as officials at all levels were denounced, humiliated and sent to rural re-education camps. The arrest of the **Gang of Four** in October 1976 marked the end of the Cultural Revolution, which since 1978 has been repudiated by the Chinese leadership. 'Cultural Revolution' was originally a Marxist-Leninist term for a radical transformation in attitudes which should follow the proletarian revolution to create a new socialist culture, and its first implementation was seen in the Soviet Union in the 1920s.

CURRENT-ACCOUNT BALANCE

A calculation of a country's foreign earnings position. The current-account balance is determined by adding net **invisible earnings** to the net (visible) trade balance. The result may be a positive figure (a surplus) or a negative one (a deficit). The term does not cover transactions on capital account.

CZECH REPUBLIC

The **Central European** republic which came into being through the **velvet divorce** of January 1992 when it became separate from **Slovakia**; together they had comprised the former **communist** state of **Czechoslovakia**. The Czech Republic comprises the regions of **Bohemia**, Silesia and Moravia.

CZECHOSLOVAKIA

A country created in the 1918 post-war settlement and dissolved on 31 December 1992. Czechoslovakia bound together two regions of the former Austro-Hungarian empire: the prosperous, industrialized, liberal, Austrian-administered Czech lands of **Bohemia**, Moravia and Silesia, and the poorer, agrarian, Hungarian-administered **Slovakia** and Ruthenia (later ceded to Soviet Ukraine). Czechoslovakia was occupied by Nazi forces in the Second World War and from 1947–8 it was part of the **communist bloc** until the **Velvet Revolution** of 1989. Rising Slovak **nationalism** prompted Czechoslovakia's division into the **Czech Republic** and **Slovakia** on 1 January 1993.

DAC

The Development Assistance Committee, an **OECD** body which co-ordinates the **aid** donor policies of its member countries, holding an annual meeting and producing a report on aid activity.

DAHOMEY *see* Benin

DÁIL ÉIREANN

(Gaelic, 'Assembly of Ireland') The 166-seat lower house of the legislature (**Oireachtas**) of the Republic of Ireland. Members of the *Dáil* (**TDs**) are elected for a five-year term on the basis of proportional representation.

DAKAR CONFERENCE

The meeting in the Senegal capital in July 1987 between senior members of the then banned **ANC** and a 61-member delegation of prominent South Africans, mainly **Afrikaner** intellectuals and members of the business community. A joint communiqué issued at the end of the conference, the Dakar Declaration, expressed broad agreement on the basis of a political solution to ending **apartheid** and accepted the 'historical reality' of the armed struggle while acknowledging that 'not all could support it'. Although the meeting generated no official comment from the South African government, which at the time had a policy of no contact with the ANC, the government-controlled media described the Afrikaners as 'political terrorists'.

DALAI LAMA

The head of Tibet's Buddhist priesthood and spiritual leader of the country. The 14th Dalai Lama, Tenzin Gyatso, was born in Tibet in 1935 and ruled as 'god-king' until 1959, when he fled to India after the failed uprising against Chinese rule. He has since provided a focus for the Tibetan independence movement and was awarded the Nobel Peace Prize in 1989.

D-NOTICES

A system of voluntary self-censorship by the UK press and other media, initiated in 1912. The media generally undertook under these arrangements to abide by directions by the Defence (Press and Broadcasting) Committee, to refrain from referring to certain sensitive areas of information without prior sanction. In August 1993 as part of the 'open government' commitment, the name of the committee was changed to the Defence (Press and Broadcasting) Advisory Committee, and the range of topics now covered by DA-Notices was reduced. Publishers, editors and programme editors were asked to approach the Committee before divulging details of defence plans and operations, conventional weapons, nuclear weapons, government cyphers, security and intelligence services, and the identification of certain sensitive installations.

DATE RAPE

A term first used in *Ms* magazine in 1987 to denote rape perpetuated by an escort on a social date. Mary Koss, a clinical psychologist at the University of Arizona who coined the term, claimed her research showed that some 25 per cent of women had been raped, half of them by an escort on a date, although they themselves might not classify the incident as rape. A controversial term, it is opposed by those who believe its indiscriminate use perpetuates the image of women as passive victims of male aggression. Others see the issue as one of sexual consent and support the use of the term in raising awareness of the prevalence of rape.

DDR

(German abbreviaion of *Deutsche Demokratische Republik* – 'German Democratic Republic', or GDR) East Germany. The DDR comprised the eastern portion of Germany, occupied by Soviet troops after the Second World War. An authoritarian regime imposed one-party rule in the DDR, whose separate statehood was declared on 7 October 1949. The DDR became a **client state** of the **Soviet Union** and a key signatory of the **Warsaw Pact**; every effort was made to isolate the country from the West, for instance the construction of the **Berlin Wall** in 1961. East Germans were nevertheless acutely aware of the relative economic success of the neighbouring Federal Republic of Germany (**BRD**). A popular revolution in November-December 1989 swept the **communists** from power with the acquiescence of Soviet leaders. Free elections on 18 March 1990 gave a mandate for German unification; the wider security implications were resolved in the **two-plus-four talks**, and Germany was unified, and the DDR formally dissolved, on 3 October 1990.

DDT

Dichlorodiphenyltrichloroethane, a pesticide which earned its discoverer the Nobel Prize for Medicine in 1948, but which has been banned in the USA since 1973, and in Europe since 1984, as an environmental hazard. DDT was widely used until the late 1960s to combat insect-borne diseases such as malaria and typhus and to fight crop-destroying pests. The campaign against DDT began with the publication of Rachel Carson's **Silent Spring** in 1962, and gathered force with evidence that it was accumulating in the food chain, eventually reaching humans, and damaging the environment. DDT is still widely used as an insecticide in the developing world, however, particularly against malaria-carrying mosquitoes, since it is effective and cheap to produce.

DEAR LEADER

The term used extensively in North Korea to refer to Kim Jong Il the son and heir apparent of the country's ageing leader Kim Il Sung who was known until his death in July 1994 as the **Great Leader**. Kim emerged as his father's chosen successor in the 1970s, and became the object of a personality cult which is almost as extravagant as that surrounding the Great Leader. Nevertheless, the younger Kim appears to lack his father's status within the armed forces and the ruling **communist** Korean Workers' Party (KWP), and is rumoured to enjoy a lavish, and by some accounts debauched, personal lifestyle. Thus, although he took on many of his father's responsibilities in an effort to achieve a smooth succession, few analysts believe that the Dear Leader's rule will prove as durable as that of his father. Kim Jong Il is alleged to have been responsible for planning numerous acts of hostility against South Korea, including the 1987 bombing of a Korean Airlines passenger aircraft over Burma.

DEATH ON THE ROCK *see* SHOOT TO KILL POLICY

DEATH SQUADS

Right-wing paramilitary groups, normally with intimate ties with security forces, who are used, often with the connivance of governments, to torture and kill those deemed a threat to the state. The term was first coined in the 1960s in Brazil when death squads were used against suspected criminals and formed part of the police force. By the 1970s, governments, especially military regimes, throughout Latin and **Central America** and elsewhere were using death squads primarily in order to fight **guerrillas** and eliminate dissidents. Many squads, especially those in central America, have been financed and trained by the **CIA**.

DEBT-FOR-NATURE SWAPS

Schemes whereby a conservation organization buys up the commercial debt of a developing country on the secondary debt market, in return for which the debtor agrees to implement a conservation programme. Such initiatives began in July 1987 and now cover programmes such as wetland and forest conservation, national parks, protection of endangered species, education and training.

DEBT RESCHEDULING

The process whereby developing countries negotiate new arrangements to pay back their debts more gradually. The first such arrangements date from the mid-1950s. As they became more common, the Hague Club (later the **London Club**) was set up for handling this process among commercial creditors, and the **Paris Club** for official (i.e. government) creditors. The need to reschedule debts became urgent in the wake of the 1973–4 oil price explosion, and again in the latter 1980s, when some countries with huge debts found their payments impossibly crippling, and some extremely poor countries could not meet even interest payments. Debt rescheduling may, but need not, be accompanied by the actual writing off of certain elements of debt incurred in the past.

DECOLONIZATION

The 'withdrawal from empire' by colonial powers, and the achievement of independence by their colonies and other similar territories. The main colonial powers were Belgium, France, the Netherlands, Portugal, Spain, the UK and (especially in the Pacific) the USA. Various former German and Italian colonies and Japanese possessions were also administered as **trust territories** by these colonial powers, or by other countries, under League of Nations and subsequently **UN** mandates.The decolonization process started after the Second World War with the independence of India and **Pakistan**, and accelerated from the early 1960s. The UN set up a Special Committee on the Implementation of the (1960) Declaration on Decolonization, and was also involved with the trust territories through the Trusteeship Council. By early 1994 there were few remaining colonies, principally those of the UK (the Falkland Islands, Gibraltar, Hong Kong, and some **Caribbean** territories), various remaining French overseas territories, and Macao (Portuguese).

DECOMMUNIZATION

The process of reform in former **communist** states, aimed at the dismantling of communist structures and the concurrent reconstruction of the political, economic and social status quo ante through democratization and **privatization**. Some have argued, controversially, that decommunization can be effective and just only if those who prospered under the communist regime, who therefore allegedly have a vested interest in retarding change, are not permitted to remain in positions of authority; and if those deemed responsible for communism's iniquities are formally brought to account by the postcommunist system of justice. Former communist leaders have been tried and imprisoned for alleged abuse of office (as in Bulgaria and Albania); former collaborators with the secret police have been exposed and in some cases dismissed from their state jobs (as in the **lustration** programme in **Czechoslovakia**); and those who shot civilians on state orders have been prosecuted, or face prosecution (such as border guards of the former **DDR**, or former soldiers and policemen involved in violence during the **Hungarian uprising**).

DEEP NORTH

A pejorative term for the Australian state of Queensland, particularly under the rule of State Premier and National Party leader Sir Johannes Bjelke-Petersen. By analogy with the US 'Deep **South**', the term described the institutionalized **racism**, nepotism, **gerrymandering** and corruption endemic to Sir Joh's 19-year reign. He was forced to resign on 1 December 1987 over corruption allegations, which were confirmed in July 1988 by a Commission of Enquiry headed by Tony Fitzgerald.

DEEP THROAT

The pseudonym used by an anonymous informer who provided vital inside information to *Washington Post* journalists Bob Woodward and Carl Bernstein in their investigation of the **Watergate** scandal. The term was originally applied to a particularly penetrative form of fellatio as pioneered by pornographic film star Linda Lovelace in a film of the same name.

DEFCON 3

Defense Condition 3, the highest state of nuclear alert ever actually declared by the USA. The levels of DefCon range from 5, the normal peacetime condition, to 1 – the start of hostilities. During DefCon 3 (most recently used during the **Yom Kippur War** of 1973), nuclear missiles are examined in preparation for launch, and B–52 nuclear bombers fly in holding patterns ready to invade enemy airspace while being refuelled in the air.

DEFORESTATION

The permanent destruction of forested areas as a result of human activity. Trees are cut down for fuel, cut or burned to clear land for arable use, or removed in commercial logging operations; other contributory factors are overgrazing and consequent soil erosion, and damage from airborne pollutants falling as **acid rain**. Deforestation in turn upsets the balance of the **carbon budget** and leads to further soil erosion, as well as reducing **biodiversity** as natural habitats are destroyed, and contributing to **global warming**.

DELORS PLAN

The report presented in April 1989 by a group of **EU** central bank governors headed by **Commission** President Jacques Delors, setting out a three-stage plan for implementing **EMU**. A second set of proposals associated with Delors, dubbed 'Delors II', was presented in February 1992 by the Commission. It envisaged increasing the Community budget by 5 per cent annually from 1993 to 1997, raising more of the money in the form of Community 'own resources' rather than member government contributions, and doubling the **cohesion fund** for spending in the poorer member countries. Delors II was scaled down to a more modest seven-year plan approved by the **European Council** in Edinburgh in December 1992, whereby total expenditure would rise from 66,800 million **ECU** in 1992 to 84,000 million ECU in 1999.

DEMILITARIZED ZONE *see* DMZ

DEMOCRATIC CENTRALISM

The organizational principle of **Leninist** parties and state administrations, envisaging a strong, centralized ruling structure which guarantees popular participation. Democratic centralism stipulates that party bodies are elected democratically, but that majority decisions are binding upon all members; factionalism is, therefore, not permitted. **Maoism** opposes democratic centralism, criticising it for its tendency to degenerate into a bureaucratized hierarchy unwilling to pursue **continuing revolution**.

DEMOCRATIC DEFICIT

In the **EU**, the perception that decision-making lacks democratic legitimacy. The issue was addressed in the **Maastricht** treaty, at the insistence of Germany in particular, by increasing the role of the **European Parliament**, giving it certain new **co-decision** powers, and emphasising the principles of **transparency** and **subsidiarity** in Community decision-making.

DEMOCRATIC PARENTHESIS

A term used to describe a period of political stability in Ecuador between 1948 and 1960. A boom in the traditional export commodities, coffee and cocoa, and in bananas, a new export product, produced unprecedented prosperity which assisted the democratic process and allowed three presidents to serve a full term. Governments invested some of the increased revenue in education, welfare, public works and the development of natural resources, but underlying problems remained. Inability to deal with recession led to a return in 1960 to a dictatorial style of government which plunged the country back into a period of instability and military coups.

DENAZIFICATION

One of the 'four Ds' (together with democratization, disarmament and decartelization) which the victorious Allies of the Second World War agreed at **Potsdam** to implement in the defeated Germany. Denazification meant excluding Nazi activists from the political reconstruction of Germany, and punishing Nazi leaders, a policy which culminated in the **Nuremberg War Crimes Tribunal**.

DEOXYRIBONUCLEIC ACID *see* DNA

DEPENDENCY CULTURE

A term first coined by sociologists in the late 1970s, to describe a condition affecting those members of society who are entirely dependent on welfare benefits and other forms of public assistance. The theory asserts that in time they become habituated to unemployment and lose hope of, or desire for, any other source of income.

DEPENDENCY THEORY

A critique of standard development economics which emerged in the late 1960s. It sought initially to account for the economic and political underdevelopment of **Latin America**, and was later applied to **Third-World** countries in Asia and Africa. Dependency theory puts forward an analysis of economic development in the 'core' **capitalist** countries of Europe, North America and Japan (now often termed the **North**) being achieved by underdeveloping the 'periphery' and creating conditions of economic and political dependence in the Third World or **South**.

DEREGULATION

The removal of governmental and similar regulations on economic and other activities. Such regulations and controls may have built up over a lengthy period of time and may have come to be seen as anachronistic, stultifying and inimical to enterprise. In the UK the Deregulation and Contracting Out Bill was introduced in early 1994 with the aim of doing away with a wide range of existing controls. Also in the UK, the privatization of various public utilities has at the same time been accompanied by the appointment of independent regulators, whose role it is to ensure that the new private-sector successors do not unduly exploit their monopoly or oligopolistic positions. Major deregulation took place in the USA in the 1980s under the Reagan administration.

DERGUE

(Amharic, 'committee') The military ruling body in Ethiopia between 1973 and 1991. The term is most closely associated with the Marxist-Leninist regime of Lt.-Col. Mengistu Haile Mariam who seized power in 1977 and was himself deposed in May 1991.

DEROGATION

A term used in international agreements when a country is exempted – usually temporarily – from having to apply a law or ruling. In the **EU** new member countries sometimes obtain protection for particularly vulnerable industries by getting a derogation in order to avoid applying a common policy regime during a transitional period. Existing members may also seek derogations to delay their introduction of new Community regulations.

DESCAMISADOS

(Spanish, literally 'shirtless'; figuratively 'shabby' or 'wretched') A nickname for working class supporters of populist Argentinean President Juan Domingo Perón Sosa. The term stemmed from an event in October 1945 when Perón, then Secretary for Labour and Social Welfare, was arrested for his radical reforms. Mass demonstrations of trade unionists, in shirtsleeves, brought Buenos Aires to a standstill and eventually secured his release.

DESERT SABRE *see* DESERT STORM

DESERT SHIELD

The code name given to the US-led multinational force, whose establishment was formally announced on 9 November 1990, which was aimed at securing the withdrawal of Iraqi occupation forces from Kuwait. Its active deployment began in January 1991 with the launch of Operation **Desert Storm**, and the total number of forces in the Gulf by the end that month was estimated at 705,000. Of these the US military presence was some 500,000 troops, representing over 34 per cent of the US military's total effective strength, a larger proportion (albeit a smaller absolute number) than had been deployed during the **Vietnam War**; in addition there were troops from Canada, Egypt, France, Morocco, Pakistan, Saudi Arabia, Syria and the UK.

DESERT STORM

The code name given to the air offensive launched by US-led allied forces on the night of 16–17 January 1991 against targets in Iraq and Iraqi-occupied Kuwait. The campaign, which was due to achieve its objectives in a matter of days, went on until 27 February, when the Iraqi forces were defeated. By contrast, the ground war launched on 24 February, codenamed

'Desert Sabre', which was expected to last longer, ended in just four days. Although the war resulted in fewer than 500 casualties on the allied side, Iraqi military casualties were estimated at between 50,000 and 100,000, while Iraqi civilian casualties were thought to have numbered at least 10,000, mostly due to the air war.

DESERTIFICATION

The process by which land deteriorates to desert conditions through the loss of vegetative cover and the impoverishment of the soil. Desertification is largely due to factors such as **deforestation** and overgrazing which result from human activity. It affects at least 20 per cent of the earth's total land area, usually forcing the people who live there to migrate to urban shanty towns. Desertification may be arrested by irrigation, the planting of vegetation, and the erection of barriers against sand dunes. Although action to halt desertification was agreed at the 1992 **Earth Summit**, the June 1994 deadline for signing a UN desertification treaty and completing a plan for Africa was abandoned in late 1993 because of international arguments over debt and aid.

DE-STALINIZATION

The process of revealing and dismantling the **communist bloc's** legacy of **Stalinism**, launched initially by Soviet leader Nikita Khrushchev in his **secret speech** of February 1956 (a second wave began in 1960). Stalin's **cult of personality** was reversed, and in 1961 his body was removed from Vladimir Lenin's tomb. On the policy level, de-Stalinization included (i) rehabilitations of those convicted in the **show trials** of the 1930s to the early 1950s, and the release of many of the millions of inmates of the **gulags**; (ii) limited freedom of expression; (iii) an emphasis on technocracy; and (iv) a more pragmatic approach to **collectivization** in **Eastern Europe**. De-Stalinization was accompanied by rapprochement between the **Soviet Union** and **Yugoslavia**, but tentative moves toward more autonomy for the Soviet Union's **satellite states** were halted by the **Hungarian uprising**. The de-Stalinization programme never questioned the leading role of the communist party, and it was not until 1986 and Mikhail Gorbachev's **glasnost** that the true scale of the Stalinist purges was admitted (an estimated 40 million people had been 'repressed').

DESTAPE

(Spanish, 'uncovering') The traditional and controversial nomination method used by the Institutional Revolutionary Party (PRI) in Mexico to choose its official presidential candidate. From potential candidates, known in the ritual as *taspados* ('covered ones'), the President selects one to be *el destapado* ('uncovered') or *el dedazo* ('designated'). Identification in advance with the chosen candidate can advance a politician's career: given the electoral dominance of the PRI since 1929, *el destapado* is effectively guaranteed office.

DETENTE

The attempt to ease tension between states; particularly the efforts to promote **peaceful coexistence** rather than **Cold War** between the two **superpowers** in the 1970s. This phase of detente ended with the Soviet invasion of Afghanistan in 1979 and the ensuing **Afghan War**.

DETERRENCE

The attempt to prevent an attack from taking place by signalling determination to respond with such force that the attack could gain no advantage. Deterrence may, in theory, be achieved by building alliances or by developing a **collective security** system, but in the postwar world it has been used mainly as the rationale for an individual state to build up its own military strength. Although defensive in posture, the strategy relies in the first instance on credible offensive weapon technology, and, in an atmosphere of mutual mistrust, is likely to stimulate an **arms race**. Nuclear deterrence was the central US strategy of the **Cold War** in different policy guises, from **massive retaliation** through graduated deterrence to **MAD** and then **flexible response**.

DEUXIÈME BUREAU

(French, 'Second Bureau', 'Second Office') The French internal security agency, run by the Ministry of the Interior and Administrative Reform; it has a more aggressive function than its UK counterpart, **MI5**. French external security risks are handled by the **DGSE**.

DEVELOPMENT ASSISTANCE COMMITTEE *see* DAC

DEVOLUTION

The diffusion of powers – constitutional or other – from a central authority to regional or other lower levels. In the UK this term has been used especially to apply to the relationship between the central government on the one hand and Scotland, Wales and **Northern Ireland** on the other. Proposals to devolve large areas of responsibility were, however, decisively defeated in March 1979 in a referendum in Wales and withdrawn after only narrow acceptance in a referendum in Scotland. In Northern Ireland there was a short-lived **power-sharing** experiment with a devolved assembly and executive in 1973–4.

DEW LINE

The Distant Early Warning Line, a chain of ground radar stations north of the Arctic Circle across Canada and Alaska, designed to warn against incoming bomber and missile attack. Agreed in 1954 between Canada and the USA, the Dew Line was built by the USA and was operational for three decades, but was regarded as obsolescent in 1985, when a Canadian-US summit meeting agreed on joint financing of a replacement system.

DGSE

(French acronym for *Direction générale de la sécurité extérieure* – 'General Department for External Security') The French foreign secret service, reporting directly to the Defence Ministry. The DGSE was established in April 1982, replacing the *Service de documentation et contre espionnage extérieure* (SDECE).

DIASPORA

(Greek, 'dispersion') The word used to describe any group of people dispersed, voluntarily or otherwise, throughout the world. The term is often applied to Jewish communities outside the state of **Israel**; the main centre is the USA, with a Jewish population of around 6 million.

DIEN BIEN PHU

The location in western Vietnam of the decisive battle of the First Indo-Chinese War which took place between North Vietnam and France in March–May 1954. The French defeat at Dien Bien Phu destroyed the will of the French to remain in their former colonies in **Indo-China**. It also heralded an increasing US interest in the region.

The First Indo-Chinese War was triggered when the latter attempted to re-occupy the Indo-Chinese colonies it had relinquished at the start of the Second World War. After establishing a puppet regime in southern Vietnam, France began military action against the recently established Democratic Republic of Vietnam (DRV), led by Ho Chi Minh, in late 1946. Under the brilliant command of Gen. Vo Nguyen Giap, the DRV forces (the **Viet Minh**) conducted a classic **guerrilla** war and rarely allowed the French generals to engage in the large-scale battles they craved. Finally, in 1954, Gen. Giap appeared to concede to growing French pressure for a final, 'once-and-for-all' main-force engagement at Dien Bien Phu, a small valley situated near the border with Laos. However, unbeknown to the French (who had some 11,000 soldiers entrenched in the valley), Giap had managed to position some 49,000 well-armed Viet Minh troops in the high ground overlooking the French entrenchments. Giap launched his first assault on 13 March and the French command bunker eventually fell on 8 May, the date on which the world powers convened in Geneva at the start of discussions which would lead in July to the signing of the **Geneva Agreements** providing for an armistice and the partition of Vietnam at the **17th Parallel**.

DIET

The Japanese bicameral legislature. The Diet currently consists of a House of Representatives (lower chamber) composed of 511 members elected for up to four years, and a House of Councillors (upper chamber) comprising 252 members elected for six years with one-third due for re-election every three years. The current system of multi-member constituencies has been an important cause of the rise of **money politics** in postwar Japan, with the political scandals which have accompanied it. Under legislation adopted in early 1994, the number of representatives in the lower house was set to be reduced to 500, of whom 300 would be elected by **single-member constituencies** and 200 would be drawn from party lists on the basis of proportional representation (**PR**).

DIGNITY BATTALIONS

A Panamanian paramilitary force of some 10,000 set up in 1988 as military-sponsored civil defence units. Their nominal role was to assist in the defence of the country in the event of a US intervention. In reality they participated in the harassment of the political opposition and were trained by personnel from the Panamanian Defence Force which was commanded by Gen. Manuel Noriega Morena, the de facto ruler of the country. They were used by Noriega to disrupt the May 1989 general election and put up some resistance to **Operation Just Cause**, the US military invasion in December 1989.

DIKKO AFFAIR

A bizarre diplomatic incident between the UK and Nigeria. UK customs found the Nigerian politician Umaru Dikko drugged in a crate at London's Stansted Airport on 5 July 1984. With him, in other crates, were three Israelis and a Nigerian diplomat, who were later charged with kidnapping and administering drugs. Dikko had been Minister of Transport under the civilian government of President Shehu Shagari, and had fled to London following the coup in December 1983. The new regime expressed a desire for him to return to face corruption charges, but made no formal extradition request. His abduction was apparently the work of Nigerian intelligence agents who had planned to send him home as a secure consignment of diplomatic baggage. The UK government protested at the violation of its sovereignty and the incident led to a period of poor relations between the two countries, exemplified by a series of tit-for-tat diplomatic expulsions.

DINA

The Chilean secret police serving the military **junta** during the 1970s. Close to President Augusto Pinochet Ugarte, it was a powerful component of the repressive state apparatus which also pursued its own lucrative economic agenda, guided by DINA economists who proved the most effective opposition to the **Chicago Boys**. It overreached itself in September 1976 when it carried out the assassination of Orlando Letelier in Washington DC. Powerful friends of Letelier, a Defence Minister before the 1973 coup and a former ambassador to the USA, ensured that relations between the USA and Chile were soured. Although US demands for the extradition of DINA chief Manuel Contreras were refused, the military set up a new secret service, the CNI, in 1977, and DINA was officially disbanded.

DIOXINS

A group of highly toxic chemicals, formed as a byproduct in the manufacture or breakdown of other chemicals, and remaining as a trace in the final product. Dioxins are created in the manufacture of pesticides, and by burning plastics and chemicals containing **PCBs**, but **Greenpeace** contends that the main source of dioxins in the environment is the manufacture of PVC (polyvinylchloride). Dioxins can cause cancer, skin, liver and kidney diseases, and birth defects. They first came to public notice as an environmental hazard in 1976 when an explosion at a chemical plant in **Seveso** in Italy released a cloud of dioxin. Dioxins were also present in **Agent Orange** through the manufacture of **245-T**. The UK 1990 Environmental Protection Act established the limit for dioxin in emissions of gases as 1,000 millionth of a gram per cubic metre.

DIPLOMATIC IMMUNITY *see* VIENNA CONVENTION 1961

DIRECT RULE

The exercise by the **United Kingdom** government of direct responsibility for the government of **Northern Ireland**. Following the breakdown of talks in early 1972 on a solution for the problems of Northern Ireland, the UK government in March of that year took responsibility for all legislative and executive powers, with the new Secretary of State for Northern Ireland being made answerable to the House of Commons. A Northern Ireland Assembly was elected in June 1973, but the short-lived **power-sharing** Northern Ireland Executive collapsed in May 1974 in the face of massive industrial action by Protestant trade unionists opposed to the December 1973 **Sunningdale Agreement**. Under the Northern Ireland Act 1974 (subsequently renewed annually by parliamentary order) direct rule was once more exercised by the Secretary of State. A largely consultative Assembly was set up in 1982, but this was dissolved in June 1986 after it had been boycotted by many of its members in protest at the conclusion of the **Anglo-Irish Agreement** the previous November. Lengthy, but so far inconclusive, discussions have been held in recent years for the establishment of some form of devolved government in Northern Ireland.

DIRTY WAR

A term used to refer to the period of secret repression in Argentina from 1975 to 1983 when the security forces and **death squads** were given free reign to kidnap, torture and kill suspected opponents to the military **junta**. Tens of thousands of people were killed and between 6,000 and 15,000 made up the **disappeared**. A return to democracy in 1983 saw some perpetrators brought to justice. Military pressure on President Raúl Alfonsín Foulkes, however, led to the introduction of a law of **Due Obedience** and the **Full Stop Law** to limit human rights trials. Many perpetrators of the dirty war escaped trial and punishment and others convicted received pardons from President Carlos Menem.

DISAPPEARED

A term for the victims of secret abduction and execution by **death squads** and security forces. The phenomenon first appeared in Guatemala following the 1954 coup, where dissidents were systematically abducted, tortured and killed. These methods were later adopted by other countries, most notably the military regimes of Argentina, Brazil, Chile, El Salvador, Paraguay and Uruguay. The plight of Argentina's disappeared gained international notice through the campaign of the **Mothers of the Plaza de Mayo**. In 1993 documents were found in Paraguay proving that the security forces of Argentina, Chile, Paraguay and Uruguay not only exchanged information about suspected 'subversives' but also co-operated in cross-border abductions and killings. A National Commission on the Disappearance of Persons (Conadep) was set up following Argentina's return to democracy in 1983. During the Argentinean dirty war a total estimated at between 6,000 and 15,000 people disappeared. The figure in Guatemala is thought to be as high as 30,000.

DISPOSABLES

A Colombian term for the most destitute sections of urban society, including vagrants, thieves, prostitutes, street children, drug addicts, the mentally disturbed and homosexuals. Human rights groups estimate that over 2,600 disposables – described by traders and others as a menace and a burden on the community – have been the object of **social cleansing** between 1988 and 1993, mostly murdered by **death squads** made up from members of the security forces and, particularly, the police.

DISTENSÃO

(Portuguese, 'relaxation') A term referring to the easing of repression by the Brazilian military dictatorship of President Ernesto Geisel. The process began in 1974 and was partly influenced by the **Carnation Revolution** in Portugal. Press censorship was gradually lifted, social and political organizations campaigned openly and the Brazilian Democratic Movement Party (PMDB), the only legal opposition party, became more outspoken. However, afraid of the opposition's success, Geisel clamped down again in 1977.

DJIBOUTI

A country of some 421,000 people located in the **Horn of Africa**. Independent since 1977, it was previously a French colony, at which time it was known as the Territory of the Afars and Issas.

DMZ

Demilitarized zone. A neutral belt of land formally separating opposing sides in a conflict. At the close of the **Korean War** in 1953 a provisional boundary was agreed along a DMZ which has since remained the effective boundary between North and South Korea. It followed the length of the 155-mile (170 km) front between the two adversaries, straddling the **38th parallel** in such a way that the central and eastern regions of South Korea gained some 2,300 square miles (6,000 sq km) of North Korean territory (including several significant economic facilities), while in the west, North Korea gained some 800 square miles (2,000 sq km) of territory south of the 1948 border. With no peace treaty having been signed, the DMZ remains one of the most militarily sensitive borders in the world.

DNA

Deoxyribo-nucleic acid, the molecule which forms chromosomes and which contains the blueprint of the genetic make-up of the individual. The double helix structure of the molecule was first determined in 1953 by Francis Crick and James Watson, who, with Maurice Wilkins, were awarded the 1962 Nobel Prize for medicine and physiology for their achievement. Since each act of sexual reproduction produces a unique recombination of DNA, individuals (except for identical twins) may be identified by their DNA, a technique known as DNA fingerprinting or **genetic fingerprinting**. DNA examination procedures are also being perfected to identify genetically inherited diseases and conditions.

DNESTR REPUBLIC

The mainly slav-speaking region which rebelled against Romanian-speaking **Moldova** in 1991–2 and declared its independence in August 1991. The violence first flared up in late 1991 after residents of the region, fearing Moldovan reunification with Romania, supported the Dnestr Republic's independence in a referendum. Hundreds of people died in the spring and summer of 1992, and only the intervention of the Russian 14th Army stationed in Moldova ended the killings. The Russian government denied that the 14th army was supporting the separatist republic.

DOCTORS' PLOT

The conspiracy alleged in January 1953 to exist among a group of Soviet physicians to cause the deaths – under the pretence of illness – of senior **communists**, including Stalin. Many of those accused were Jewish and the incident provoked a wave of anti-Semitism across the **Soviet Union**. The move may have been the first step in a planned purge of leading communists by Stalin. Charges against the doctors of wrecking, terrorism and espionage were dropped after Stalin's death in March 1953.

DOI MOI

(Vietnamese, 'renovation') Vietnamese economic liberalization programme based on the Soviet **perestroika** campaign. Introduced by **communist** Party of Vietnam general secretary and arch-pragmatist Nguyen Van Linh in the south in the mid-1980s, the *doi moi* programme stressed the private marketing of agricultural produce, the dismantling of agricultural co-operatives, the formation of private business in all sectors and foreign investment in indigenous enterprises.

D'OLIVEIRA AFFAIR

A controversy in August and September 1968 which ended by increasing the isolation of South Africa over **apartheid** in sport. Basil D'Oliveira was a South African-born **Coloured** cricketer who had come to England in 1960. He had played many times for England, and distinguished himself in the final international match of the summer of 1968. The MCC (England) team for a winter tour to South Africa was then announced which did not include D'Oliveira, a decision for which sporting reasons were advanced but which was criticized as an attempt to avoid a widely predicted confrontation with the South African authorities. However, on 16 September one of those who had been selected, Tom Cartwright, withdrew because of injury and the selectors chose D'Oliveira to replace him. The South African authorities thereupon declared that the team was unacceptable, with South African Prime Minister J. B. Vorster claiming that it was 'no longer a cricket team but a team of troublemakers for South Africa's **separate development** policies'. On 24 September the tour was cancelled, and there were no further official first-class internationals between England and South Africa until 1994, after the end of the apartheid regime.

DOLLARIZATION

The widespread substitution of the US dollar for another country's currency in general transactions. The dollar, regarded internationally as one of the strongest and most stable currencies, tends to replace weak currencies which are subject to rapid inflation during economic crises. In recent years this has occurred in Russia, where in most daily transactions the rouble and the dollar have become virtually interchangeable.

DOMINO EFFECT

A foreign policy concept devised by US President Dwight D. Eisenhower in April 1954. It posited the danger that Vietnam's fall to **communism** would precipitate a series of communist victories in south-east Asia, a process likened to a falling row of dominoes, which would ultimately threaten the security of the USA. The theory was used to justify US intervention in the **Vietnam War** and, subsequently, US policy towards Nicaragua in the 1980s, although by then it had been largely discredited by events in south-east Asia.

DONBASS RUSSIANS

The Russian-speaking community which forms a majority of the population of the Donbass, a region in eastern **Ukraine** dominated by heavy industry and mining. The region is the potential source of damaging social unrest; the Donbass Russians are increasingly disillusioned with newly independent Ukraine, under whose government the outmoded and uneconomic industries of the Donbass have further decayed. There is growing support for union with Russia.

DOOMSDAY CLOCK

The picture of a clock, the hands of which indicate the time estimated to remain before nuclear war (midnight), which has been printed in every issue of the *Bulletin of Atomic Scientists* since its founding in 1945. Standing at 11.58 at the height of the **Cold War**, the clock was put back to 11.50 in **1989**. The **Worldwatch Institute** watches a similar clock which monitors the possibility of ecological catastrophe.

DOVE

An advocate of a non-belligerent or less aggressive policy, in contrast to **hawk**. The symbolism of the dove of peace helped popularize this term, used in the USA at the time of the **Cuban missile crisis** and, very widely, as the country became split over the **Vietnam War**.

DOW JONES INDEX

The main US stock exchange index. It charts the movement in the average value of selected securities on the New York exchange. Other similar indicators include the FTSE-100 index in the UK, the Nikkei index in Japan and the Hang Seng index in Hong Kong.

DOWNING STREET

The street where the UK Prime Minister's London residence is situated, at Number 10. The term Downing Street is commonly used to denote the Prime Minister's office, and is also employed in the supposedly non-specific attribution of views and comments, as in the expression 'according to Downing Street sources'.

DOWNING STREET DECLARATION

A joint UK-Irish peace declaration on the future of **Northern Ireland** issued in December 1993. Drawn up by the UK Prime Ministers John Major and Albert Reynolds, his Irish counterpart (the **Taoiseach**), at a meeting at Major's **Downing Street** office on 15 December 1993, it reaffirmed the UK government's commitment to a constitutional guarantee for Northern Ireland, emphasized that it was for the people of the island of Ireland alone to exercise their right to self-determination, and contained a UK undertaking to legislate for a united Ireland if that were clearly desired by a majority in the province. The republican **Sinn Féin** was urged to join the constitutional process, but over the following months it press instead for 'clarification' of the declaration.

DRAFT DODGERS

A pejorative term used in the USA to describe those who evade military conscription. It is particularly associated with the **Vietnam War**, and refers not to those objectors who chose imprisonment rather than accept the draft, but rather to those who evaded service by going 'underground' or by leaving the country. It has also been applied to people who avoided the conflict through legitimate means. Among these are President Bill Clinton, who obtained student deferments, and former Vice-President Dan Quayle, who gained exemption by using his family's influence to enter the Indiana National Guard.

DREAD LAW

1974 legislation passed on the **Caribbean** island of Dominica which allowed anyone to shoot on sight 'dreads' or adherents of **Rastafarianism** – who were held responsible for a spate of violence – and which provided for a mandatory prison sentence for anyone wearing dreadlocks and Rastafarian dress. Despite an international outcry the Act remained in force until 1981.

DREAM TICKET

A supposedly ideal combination of candidates for an election. In the UK, the expression became current in 1983, when Neil Kinnock defeated Roy Hattersley to win the leadership of the Labour Party; Hattersley then pledged his support and was elected deputy leader to complete the 'dream ticket'.

DRUG CARTELS *see* CALI CARTEL; MEDELLÍN CARTEL

DRUGS TRADE

The supply of illegal narcotics, primarily marijuana, cocaine and heroin, from the **Caribbean**, **Latin America** and Asia to the USA and other developed countries. The worldwide drugs trade has expanded into new areas with the collapse of regimes in **Eastern Europe** and the **Soviet Union** and the consequent chaos in border and customs regulations. The economies of countries supplying narcotics are largely dependent upon the drugs trade, while the destination countries fear the problems of violent crime and the **black economy** associated with drugs.

DRUKPA

(Dzongkha, 'of the dragon whose roar is as thunder') The Buddhist sect of the same name dominant in Bhutan. In the late 1980s its code became the object of a national culture programme, the *Drigham Namza*, under which all Bhutanese, whatever their ethnic and religious origins, were ordered to wear only 'Bhutanese dress' (the *glos* and *kiras*) in public, and which decreed the official language, Dzongkha, to be the national language, replacing Nepali and various Tibetan dialects spoken by the country's ethnic Tibetan and Nepali minorities. In 1989–90 the measures elicited widespread opposition, mainly among ethnic Nepalese, who protested against Drukpa domination.

DRUSE

The **Shia** Ismaili offshoot and powerful Lebanese minority based in the Chouf mountain area east of Beirut. During the

Lebanese civil war (1975–91) the Druse **militia** – the Progressive Socialist Party (PSP) – fought alongside other Muslim militias and the **PLO** against (Christian) **Phalangists**. PSP head and traditional Druse leader Walid Jumblatt followed government directives and disarmed the militia element of the PSP in 1991.

DUAL-USE TECHNOLOGY

Machinery, electronic equipment or industrial plant which can be used for chemical or **nuclear weapons** production or other military purposes, but is ostensibly intended for non-military use. During the **Cold War** efforts to control Western technology transfer to the **communist bloc** centred on **COCOM**, which was bedevilled by the difficulty of identifying and controlling dual-use technology. In the early 1980s in particular, the USA frequently pressed its allies to support tighter regulations.

DUE OBEDIENCE

An Argentinean legal principle under which officers who violated human rights on the order of their superiors during the **dirty war** were exonerated. The principle was enshrined in the June 1987 'Due Obedience Law' which provided for an amnesty for all officers below the rank of colonel accused of human rights abuses who acted under orders, except for those who committed rape or carried out the abduction of children or the destruction of property. Generals and colonels were also exempted if at the time of committing violations they were not in positions of command.

DUMA

(Russian, 'assembly', 'thought') The name of the parliament of Imperial Russia, which met rarely and had only an advisory function. The name was revived under the 1993 constitution (instigated by President Boris Yeltsin) in the State *Duma* (the lower house of the new Russian parliament or Federal Assembly), whose inaugural session was in January 1994.

DUMBARTON OAKS CONFERENCE

A conference involving the USA, the UK, the **Soviet Union** and China, held in a mansion of that name in Washington DC in August–October 1944, which agreed the basic structure for the **UN**.

DUNKIRK TREATY

A military treaty signed in March 1947 by France and the UK committing each side to support the other militarily in the event of an attack by Germany. One year later, the **Brussels Treaty** extended this commitment to the defence of the **Benelux** countries.

DURAND LINE

The disputed border between Afghanistan and the present state of **Pakistan**, demarcated in 1893 after the second Anglo-Afghan War (1878–80) which ended in a British victory. Both sides subsequently recognized the area between this line and British India as 'free tribal territory' nominally under British control. Its inhabitants were not British subjects and retained their tribal autonomy; this was confirmed by further treaties in 1905, 1921 and 1930. In 1947, 200,000 Pashtun Afghan tribespeople found themselves separated from their compatriots in Afghanistan after the former British territory of the North West Frontier Province acceded to Pakistan. Since then Afghanistan has questioned the border agreements, claiming that they were signed under duress, and has pressed for ethnic Pashtuns to be consolidated as a single unit.

DUVALIERISM

The political climate created in Haiti by the Duvalier family dynasty, beginning with François 'Papa Doc' Duvalier, who became President in 1957 and continuing after his death in 1971 under the presidency of his son, Jean-Claude 'Baby Doc' Duvalier. Often associated with **noirisme**, the Duvaliers mixed fear and patronage to maintain power, and their reign of terror was ruthlessly enforced by the **Tontons Macoutes**, the secret police established by Papa Doc.

Although Baby Doc was a marginally more liberal figure his marriage in 1980 to a mulatto woman was seen as a betrayal of noirisme. He was eventually forced into exile in 1986, and die-hard Duvalierists were constitutionally barred from contesting elections. Nevertheless *Tontons Macoutes* continued to perpetrate terror, and a return to democracy was delayed by the largely Duvalierist military until the election of Fr Jean-Bertrand Aristide as President in December 1990. However, in September 1991 his government was ousted by Gen. Raoul Cédras. Although weaned on Duvalierism, the new regime represented a more independent breed, setting its own agenda and using Duvalierist parties and **attaché** terror gangs to intimidate and kill the opposition. On 31 July 1994 the **UN Security Council** approved a US initiative with the aim of restoring Aristide and removing the last vestiges of Duvalierism.

E-NUMBERS

A codification system used in **EU** member countries for substances added to food during processing. E-numbers cover various preservatives, colourings, emulsifiers and stabilizers, antioxidants, sweeteners, and other miscellaneous additives and are applied to substances which have been tested, pronounced safe and approved by all EU member countries. Concern over food additives has centred on their putative links with symptoms such as hyperactivity in children, asthma, eczema and migraine.

EAEC

The East Asia Economic Caucus, the concept for an all-Asian economic bloc instigated by Malaysian Prime Minister Mahathir Mohamed in late 1990. Mahathir launched the idea as an alternative to the wider pan-Pacific **APEC** grouping, which, he argued, would be dominated by the USA. While the proposal drew fire from Malaysia's **ASEAN** partners, East Asian investors and Western trading partners, it won Mahathir a large amount of international attention.

EAGGF *see* FEOGA

EARLY BIRD

The first commercial geostationary communications satellite, known also as Intelsat 1. Launched in the USA on 6 April 1965, it was positioned over the Atlantic and made available 240 voice circuits and one television channel. It was operated by **Intelsat**.

EARTH DAY

The annual worldwide effort on 22 April by pressure groups to focus public attention on environmental issues. The celebration of Earth Day spread from an event organized by US environmental groups in 1970.

EARTH SUMMIT

The world environmental conference, also known as the **UN** Conference on Environment and Development (UNCED), held in Rio de Janeiro on 3–14 June 1992 and billed as the largest ever gathering of world leaders. Environmentalists criticized the delegates to the Earth Summit for their reluctance to set binding targets for resolving environmental problems, and for failing to address the links between poverty in the developing world and environmental degradation. It was nevertheless a first step towards acknowledging the seriousness of the world's environmental problems and formulating a global response. Its concluding documents included the Rio Declaration, setting out broad principles for future **sustainable development**; the 'blueprint for action' known as **Agenda 21**; the Convention on **Biological Diversity**; the Framework Convention on Climate Change, or **World Climate Convention**; and a non-binding Statement of Forest Principles, aiming to limit destruction of the rainforests. A new UN Sustainable Development Commission was to monitor progress towards the goals agreed at the Summit. In addition, further funding for developing countries to reduce their level of indebtedness was to be co-ordinated by a Global Environment Facility jointly administered by the **World Bank**, the **UNDP** and **UNEP**; in the event, however, the plan to create a permanent funding agency soon became mired in arguments about control of its expenditure.

EARTHWATCH

A global research programme to monitor the environment, predict future trends, and provide policy-makers with vital information on the environment. Earthwatch was initiated by the 1972 UN Conference on the Human Environment in Stockholm. The programme has four sections: the Global Environment Monitoring System (GEMS); the Global Resource Information Database (GRID) which comes within GEMS; the International Register of Potentially Toxic Chemicals (IRPTC) which focuses on waste disposal; and the environmental information system INFOTERRA, which links experts and institutions in 139 countries.

EAST ASIA ECONOMIC CAUCUS *see* EAEC

EAST GERMANY *see* DDR

EAST PAKISTAN *see* BANGLADESH

EAST TIMOR

The disputed eastern half of the island of Timor, situated at the eastern end of the Lesser Sunda island chain in the Indonesian archipelago. Although the western half of the island was incorporated into Indonesia at independence in 1949, East Timor was under Portuguese administration from 1702 until mid-1975 when, during a period of turmoil, Portugal abandoned the island. The territory was occupied by Indonesian armed forces in late 1975 and was subsequently claimed by Indonesia after having been incorporated as its 27th province by an 'act of integration'. The incorporation has not been recognized by a majority of UN member countries and Indonesia's occupation is opposed, both militarily and diplomatically, by **Fretilin**. International human rights organizations have routinely accused the Indonesian government of carrying out flagrant and gross human rights abuses in East Timor.

EASTERN EUROPE

The European region comprising states east of **Central Europe**, extending south to the **Balkan** states of Albania, Bulgaria, Romania and the former **Yugoslavia**, and including the former Soviet republics, except those of **Central Asia** and the **Transcaucasus** (which lie outside Europe's geographical borders). Following the postwar division of Europe along the **iron curtain**, the term Eastern Europe gained a political connotation, being used to denote all **communist** (and more recently postcommunist) states east of the **Oder-Neisse line**. In this usage it excluded two Balkan states, Greece and Turkey, and included, on political rather than geographical criteria, the communist states of Central Europe.

EBRD

The European Bank for Reconstruction and Development, founded in May 1990 by 39 countries (including the USA and the **Soviet Union**), plus the European Commission and the European Investment Bank. The idea of the EBRD was conceived by French President François Mitterrand in late 1989 as a means of promoting postcommunist **Eastern Europe's** transition to a market economy, and it was formally inaugurated in April 1991, when the EBRD announced that its priority was to develop 'an entrepreneurial spirit at grass roots level by helping the establishment of small enterprises'. Economic development in Eastern Europe would be financed through loans, guarantees, equity investment and underwriting. Jacques Attali, the EBRD's first president, resigned in July 1993 after controversy over the £200 million (US$300 million) operating cost of setting up the EBRD, which was reportedly double the amount which had at that stage been disbursed by the EBRD in loans and investments.

EC

The European Communities, more generally referred to as the **EU** since 1 November 1993, the date on which the **Maastricht** Treaty on European Union took effect. The three European Communities were the **EEC**, the **ECSC** and **Euratom**. After the Merger Treaty (signed in 1965 and in force from July 1967) the proper collective term for them was the EC (as indeed it remains in legal terms even since the introduction of 'EU'). However, the acronym EC was much more often expanded as 'European Community' than as the officially correct 'European Communities'. The picture was made more confused in 1993 when, under the Maastricht Treaty, the European Economic Community (EEC) was expressly renamed the European Community.

ECA *see* ECONOMIC COMMISSION

ECE *see* ECONOMIC COMMISSION

ECHO 1

The first US communications satellite. Launched in 1960 by **NASA** as part of the US effort to close the satellite telecommunications lead achieved by the **Soviet Union** with the **Sputnik**, it was an aluminium-coated plastic sphere, 100 feet in diameter when inflated in orbit. It was one of a series of 'passive' communications systems which bounced radio signals from the ground back to earth over intercontinental distances and which predated 'active' satellites bearing multichannel receivers and transmitters.

ECJ

The European Court of Justice, set up under the 1958 **Treaty of Rome** and responsible for ruling on whether **EU** member countries (and institutions) are acting in accordance with Community law. Matters are referred to the ECJ by the EU **Commission** and by individual appellants. It is sometimes confused with a quite separate organization under the **Council of Europe**, namely the **European Court of Human Rights**.

ECLAC *see* ECONOMIC COMMISSION

ECO

The Economic Co-operation Organization, a central Asian regional grouping. First created by Iran, **Pakistan** and Turkey in 1965 as the Regional Co-operation for Development, the defunct grouping was revived as the ECO in 1985. However, it only gained significance in 1992 with the admission of Afghanistan, **Azerbaijan** and the five ex-Soviet Central Asian republics—**Kazakhstan**, **Kirgizstan**, **Tajikistan**, **Turkmenistan** and **Uzbekistan**. The Turkish Republic of Northern Cyprus (**TRNC**), which has recognised only by Turkey, was admitted as a member in 1993. Outwardly, ECO meetings have largely been concerned with matters of economic co-operation and regional tension, such as the Azerbaijan-**Armenia** conflict. However, the organization has, for the most part, served primarily as a forum in which Iran and Turkey have each bid to win recognition as the foremost regional power.

ECOCIDE

Wilful destruction or damage to the environment. Ecocide implies patterns of behaviour which cause a cumulative effect upon the environment and its ecosystems, rather than specific instances of environmental damage. The term was applied in the 1970s to 'ecocidal weapons', herbicides such as **Agent Orange** used by the US military in the **Vietnam War**.

ECO-LABELLING

The European Union's scheme to identify brands of products which are less environmentally damaging than their equivalents. Products are to be assessed on the environmental impact of their whole life-cycle in its various stages from extraction of the raw materials to disposal or recycling. The voluntary labelling scheme aims to increase consumer pressure on manufacturers, but its implementation has been considerably delayed and it has drawn criticism from environmental groups for imposing insufficiently stringent conditions. The first products to go on sale carrying an ecolabel were washing machines in late 1993.

ECOMOG

The **ECOWAS** Monitoring Group, the Nigerian-led peacekeeping force deployed in Liberia by the West African economic grouping in August 1990 following the outbreak of civil war. Initially it was an essentially defensive force, seeking to maintain order and ensure the security of Amos Sawyer whom it backed as interim President. However, in October 1992 after the **NPFL** launched a major offensive on Monrovia, ECOMOG adopted a more aggressive stance, and its forces bombed rebel positions. Under the terms of the July 1993 peace treaty between the warring factions, ECOMOG was expanded to include troops from other African countries. The UN Observer Mission in Liberia (UNOMIL) was charged with supervising the ceasefire and demobilization process.

ECONOMIC CO-OPERATION ORGANIZATION *see* ECO

ECONOMIC MIGRANTS

Non-political refugees. The term has been used by the Hong Kong authorities as a means of classifying Vietnamese **boat people** living in camps in the colony. Those screened out by the authorities as economic migrants were deemed to have fled Vietnam for largely economic reasons (ie to better themselves materially) and were therefore liable to **compulsory repatriation**. A much smaller number were deemed genuine 'political refugees', judged to have fled their homeland because of persecution, and were therefore eligible for resettlement in North America or other third countries.

ECONOMIC AND SOCIAL COMMISSION *see* ECONOMIC COMMISSION

ECONOMIC IMPERIALISM

Also known as informal imperialism, a concept in Marxist and **socialist** theory denoting the exploitation of underdeveloped areas by more advanced economies in order to obtain strategic raw materials and to offload surplus manufactured goods and savings. The developed country must therefore exercise economic and political control over, but need not formally colonize, these foreign markets in order to guarantee their availability.

ECONOMIC COMMISSION

Five regional economic commissions, set up within the **UN** system at various times between March 1947 and August 1973, to promote and report on economic activity and co-operation in their respective regions. Two have since been redesignated as Economic and Social Commissions, respectively the ESCAP (Asia and the Pacific) and the ESCWA (Western Asia); the other three are the ECE (Europe), ECA (Africa) and ECLAC (**Latin America** and the **Caribbean**, also called by its Spanish acronym CEPAL). The commissions report annually to the **ECOSOC** and have secretariats which are integrated with the **UN Secretariat**.

ECONOMIC MIRACLE

The remarkable economic recovery of West Germany after the devastation of the Second World War, and known in German as the *Wirtschaftswunder*. On 20 June 1948 the old Reichsmark was abolished and a new Deutsche mark introduced overnight; wage and price controls and trade restrictions were abolished, and a comprehensive social security scheme was established, thereby setting the conditions for the development of the 'social market economy'. The German economic miracle was stimulated by the economic policies of Ludwig Erhard, and by foreign aid administered through the **Marshall Plan**. West Germany's **GNP**, already restored to pre-war levels by 1950, grew at the fastest rate in Europe through the 1950s and 1960s.

ECONOMIC AND SOCIAL COMMISSION FOR ASIA AND THE PACIFIC *see* ECONOMIC COMMISSION

ECOSOC

The Economic and Social Council, one of the six principal organs of the **United Nations** and established under Chapter X of the UN Charter. It is charged with the supervision of the UN's numerous commissions and expert bodies in the social and economic fields, as well as the co-ordination of the activities of UN specialized agencies. Originally composed of 18 members, it was enlarged in 1965 and 1973 to its present membership of 54.

ECO-TERRORISM

An extremist form of environmental protest which takes the form of terrorist acts carried out against companies or industries thought to be causing unnecessary damage to the environment.

ECOWAS

The Economic Community of West African States, the 16-member economic grouping founded in 1975 with the aim of establishing a **common market** within 15 years. Although some progress has been made in trade liberalization, achievement of this goal remains well behind schedule. In recent years ECOWAS has taken on an increasingly political role, the most obvious example of which is the deployment of a peacekeeping force, **ECOMOG**, in Liberia. In 1993, at their 16th annual meeting, ECOWAS leaders recognized this changed agenda and adopted a revised treaty which enshrined in its constitution the prevention and control of regional conflicts.

ECSC

The European Coal and Steel Community, which brought Italy and the **Benelux** countries into the Franco-German co-operation framework of the 1950 **Schuman Plan**. It was established by the **Six** at a meeting in Paris in April 1951 (i.e. prior to the **EEC**), and the ECSC treaty entered into force on 25 July 1952. The common market in coal and steel was fully operative from 1958. The ECSC High Authority and Council of Ministers were merged into the unified Commission and Council of the three European Communities (**EC**) in 1967.

ECU

The European Currency Unit, the notional monetary unit used in **EU** budgeting, and the benchmark against which the values of member states' currencies are expressed in the **EMS**. It is now also used as the denomination for **Eurocurrency** bonds and even travellers' cheques. The value of the ECU is calculated periodically according to a weighted 'basket' of national currencies. The ECU replaced the European unit of account (EUA) in Community budgeting in 1979.

EEA

The European Economic Area, the world's largest free trade area, which came into existence with effect from January 1994 and embraced five of the seven **EFTA** member countries and the 12 members of the **EU**. A Swiss referendum in December 1992 voted against joining the EEA, which had the effect of keeping out Liechtenstein too, because of its close customs union with Switzerland. The EEA agreement, much delayed, had actually been completed in October 1991 at the end of lengthy negotiations (during most of which it was referred to as the EES, the European Economic Space). It embodied the principles of free movement of goods, services, people and capital, and required the EFTA countries to adopt the EU's **acquis communautaire**, by passing some 1,500 acts into national law, although they would not apply the EU's common agricultural, fisheries or coal and steel policy. The EEA also required new institutions – a ministerial council, courts to arbitrate in disputes, a consultative committee and a joint parliamentary committee. The apparent significance of the achievement of the EEA, however, was much diminished by the expectation that all the non-EU participants except Iceland would become members of the EU proper in January 1995.

EEC

The European Economic Community, a term often loosely used to refer to the whole edifice of European regional integration of which the EEC was the most important element. Strictly speaking, the EEC and **Euratom** were founded under the Treaties of Rome, which were signed in March 1957 by the six member countries of the existing **ECSC** (France, Germany, Italy and the **Benelux** countries) and which came into effect in January 1958. The task of the EEC was to create a **common market**, and to go beyond that in integrating economic policies among its members. After the Merger Treaty (signed in 1965 and in force from July 1967) the proper collective term for the **ECSC**, EEC and **Euratom** was the **EC**, standing for European Communities. The picture was made more confused in 1993 when, under the Maastricht Treaty, the word Economic was deleted from the EEC's name, changing it to the European Community.

EES *see* EEA

EEZ

Exclusive economic zone – the offshore area extending for 200 nautical miles within which a coastal state has control over all economic resources, as established at **UNCLOS** in 1982.

EFTA

The European Free Trade Association, which was set up in 1960 under the Stockholm Convention. Its seven original members were the UK and Denmark (which both left in 1973 to join the **EC**), Portugal (which left for the same reason in 1986), Austria, Switzerland, Norway and Sweden. These were the 'Outer Seven', brought together in what was essentially a British initiative for a less integrationist conception of co-operation than that being pursued by the 'Inner **Six**' countries then setting up the **EEC**. EFTA had achieved by 1969 its main objective, the elimination of internal trade barriers (although not in agricultural trade). Iceland joined in 1970 and Finland and Liechtenstein moved from associate to full membership in 1986 and 1991 respectively. EFTA's main preoccupation in the early 1990s was defining a more structured relationship with the **EC**, a process which led to the creation of the 17-country **EEA** in 1994, but which would become largely irrelevant if four EFTA participants (Austria, Finland, Norway and Sweden) joined the **EU** proper in 1995. Meanwhile, EFTA has been developing arrangements with the countries of **Central Europe** and **Eastern Europe** which offer them a possible staging-post on the road to European integration.

EICHMANN TRIAL

The trial of Adolf Eichmann, a Nazi SS officer, conducted by a court in Jerusalem in 1961. Eichmann, who had escaped from Germany after the war, was captured by **Israeli** intelligence agents in 1960 while living under an assumed identity in Argentina, and was smuggled to Israel. Responsible for having organized the transportation of Jews to Nazi death camps, he was arraigned on 15 criminal charges, including crimes against the Jewish people, crimes against humanity, and war crimes. His trial, which lasted from 11 April to 14 August 1961, was an international spectacle. Eichmann was kept within a bulletproof glass box during the proceedings. He was sentenced to death on 15 December and was hanged shortly before midnight on 31 May 1962.

EISENHOWER DOCTRINE

A foreign policy doctrine formulated by Dwight D. Eisenhower, US President in 1953–61, and proclaimed in the form of a joint resolution passed by **Congress** in 1957. The doctrine authorized the president to assist any **Middle Eastern** country threatened by communism. The policy was aimed particularly at the perceived expansionism of **Nasserist** Egypt which, following the **Suez crisis** of 1956, had become closely aligned with the **Soviet Union**.

EL NIÑO

(Spanish, 'the child') A destructive climatic phenomenon involving a periodic change of direction in the prevailing trade winds and ocean currents flowing from the Americas to Asia across the southern Pacific Ocean. **Global warming** may have reduced its predictability and increased its frequency and duration. Among its effects are thought to be drought-induced bush fires in Australia, storms in California and the Pacific islands, hiatuses in the Indian and East African monsoons, and abnormally warm water along the South American coast which damages the local ecosystem and fishing industry.

ELDO *see* ESA

ELGIN MARBLES

Marble sculptures from the Parthenon in Athens, obtained cheaply from the occupying Turks by the British ambassador Lord Elgin in 1801 and later sold by him to the British Museum. A Greek campaign for their return was spearheaded by Melina Mercouri as Minister of Culture in the 1980s. The Elgin marbles issue is the most celebrated of many disputes about the ownership of cultural treasures removed from their country of origin in wartime, under colonial rule or in circumstances of dubious legality.

ELLICE ISLANDS *see* TUVALU

ÉLYSÉE PALACE

The Paris residence of French Presidents since 1873. The palace was built in 1718 for the Count of Evreux. After the Battle of Waterloo, Napoleon signed his second abdication there on 22 June 1815. The French Council of Ministers now holds its weekly meetings in the Murat salon.

EMERGENCY

The state of emergency imposed in British-administered Malaya in 1948–60 in response to a **communist** insurrection. The revolt, launched by the Communist Party of Malaya, was broken by 1954 following Britain's successful application of **counter-insurgency** measures to isolate the rebels.

EMERGENCY PROVISIONS

Measures whereby the **United Kingdom** government has taken special powers since 1973 to deal with the internal security situation in **Northern Ireland**. The Northern Ireland (Emergency Provisions) Act 1991 brought together various earlier enactments, including the relevant sections of the Prevention of Terrorism (Temporary Provisions) Act 1989. The Emergency Provisions Act is subject to annual renewal by order in Parliament.

EMINENT PERSONS GROUP *see* EPG

EMPTY CHAIR CRISIS

A crisis over institutional authority in the **EC** in 1965. The French instituted a boycott of the **Council of Ministers** in the second half of that year, in a showdown between President de Gaulle and the **Commission**, headed by Dr Walter Hallstein. Hallstein had tried to press forward with EC integration on two fronts, the payment of agricultural levies directly to the Commission, and the use of majority voting rather than unanimity in Council decision-making. The French 'empty chair' tactic forced other member governments to negotiate what became known as thc **Luxembourg compromise**, allowing a member state to veto a Council decision by evoking its essential national interest.

EMS

The European Monetary System, an arrangement for closer monetary co-operation within the **EC**. Put forward by Germany and France in 1978, and operational from March 1979, it was designed as an interim measure, pending decisions on creating an economic and monetary union (as was eventually agreed at **Maastricht** in 1991). The core of the EMS was the **ERM** (Exchange Rate Mechanism), although the UK stayed outside the ERM until 1990, and countries joining the EC were also slow to commit themselves to its monetary disciplines.

EMU

European monetary union within the **EU** framework, which is now embodied in the **Maastricht** treaty. EMU is a long-standing project, dating back to the Werner Report of 1971. Some of its elements were contained within the **EMS** as established in 1979, but a renewed impetus to create a full union came from the **Delors plan** of April 1989. Stage one of a three-stage process, strengthening policies through existing institutions and participation in the EMS, came into effect in July 1990, when remaining constraints on capital movement were lifted for most member countries. Stage two was implemented, according to the timetable agreed at Maastricht in 1991, with the establishment of a European Monetary Institute in Frankfurt on 1

January 1994. The last and most significant step (with a special provision, at UK insistence, for member countries **opting out**) involves transforming this institute into a fully-fledged **European Central Bank**, by July 1998 at the latest, and accepting legally binding policy guidelines, with irrevocably fixed currency rates against a single European currency which is to be established by 1 January 1999.

END

European Nuclear Disarmament, a campaigning organization headquartered in London which demanded the withdrawal from 'Poland to Portugal' of all nuclear weapons, air and submarine bases and of all institutions concerned with research or manufacture of nuclear weapons, although its campaigns tended to focus on the intermediate nuclear forces (INF) issue and the deployment of **cruise** and **Pershing** missiles and Soviet SS20s. It was established in early 1980 by British peace campaigners in **CND** to foster and maintain links with peace groups in both Western and **Eastern Europe**. The influence of the organization declined considerably in 1990 with the ending of the **Cold War** and the subsequent withdrawal and destruction of nuclear weapons in Europe.

ENEMY WITHIN

Clandestine and subversive elements working to undermine the state or other organizations. The controversial use of this term by UK Prime Minister Margaret Thatcher at the time of the 1984–5 **miners' strike** implied the existence of a 'hidden agenda' behind the activities of National Union of Mineworkers' president Arthur Scargill. Critics accused her of somehow equating this 'enemy within' and the 'enemy without' in an effort to reinvoke the **Falklands factor**.

ENERGY CHARTER

An agreement concluded between the countries of Western and **Eastern Europe** and the former **Soviet Union** to ensure access to energy supplies, particularly the vast resources of the former Soviet Union. The charter was signed by representatives of 45 countries in The Hague on 17 December 1991. It offered Western assistance to 'economies in transition', but was criticized for failing to emphasize environmental protection.

ENERGY CRISIS

The severe shortage of non-renewable sources of energy. The term was first used in the 1970s when sudden oil price rises forced a re-evaluation of the use of oil, leading to changes in the automotive industry to make cars more energy-efficient, and an increase in general awareness of the use of finite sources of energy.

ENHANCED STRUCTURAL ADJUSTMENT FACILITY *see* SAF

ENNISKILLEN

Site of an **IRA** bomb explosion in **Northern Ireland** in 1987. The explosion, which aroused particularly strong revulsion, occurred on 8 November 1987, as crowds were gathering for a Remembrance Day Service at Enniskillen, County Fermanagh; 11 people were killed and more than 60 injured. The IRA acknowledged responsibility, but claimed that the bomb had been intended for army personnel rather than civilians and that it had exploded accidentally.

ENOLA GAY

The plane which dropped the atom bomb on **Hiroshima**. A US Army Air Corps B-29 bomber, it was named after the mother of the pilot, Col. Paul W. Tibbets. The bomb, the first nuclear weapon used in warfare (and itself nicknamed **Little Boy**), was dropped on the Japanese city of Hiroshima on 6 August 1945, in the closing days of the Pacific War.

ENOSIS

(Greek, 'oneness') The rallying call of Greek Cypriots seeking union of the island with Greece, arousing fear among the Turkish Cypriot minority and the hostility of Turkey itself. *Enosis* was a key demand in the struggle to end British rule in the

1950s (when the more extreme joined **EOKA**). The Greek government pulled back from demanding immediate *enosis* upon the island's independence in 1960, but it remained very much on the agenda, embittering Greek-Turkish relations while retaining a strong pull for Greeks attracted to the **irredentist** ideal. In 1974, however, the credibility of *enosis* was badly damaged when the Greek **Colonels'** regime tried to advance it by promoting a coup in Cyprus. The immediate result was a Turkish invasion, followed by the fall of the colonels in Greece.

ENTEBBE

A Ugandan city whose airport was the site of a 1976 hijack drama. An Air France airbus, carrying 12 crew and 247 passengers from Tel Aviv to Paris, was hijacked on 27 June 1976 by two West Germans and two Palestinians and flown via Libya to Entebbe. The non-**Israeli** passengers were released there, where six more men joined the hijackers. Israel accused the ruling Amin regime in Uganda of colluding with the hijackers and a crack Israeli commando force flew into Entebbe on 3 July, killed 20 Ugandan soldiers and seven hijackers and rescued all the remaining hostages except three who were killed during the operation.

ENTRYISM

A tactic employed by non-ruling **communist** parties, whereby their members infiltrate other organizations and attempt either to take them over, establishing them as a communist front, or to destroy them. The practice is also known as 'boring from within'. It was abandoned by the **Soviet Union** in the 1950s, but continued to be employed by **Trotskyist** groups elsewhere.

ENVIRONMENTAL AUDIT

An assessment of the true costs of products and services by taking into account the hitherto uncalculated cost of their impact on the environment. Environmental audits are closely linked to the principle of **polluter pays**. In March 1993, the **EC** announced a voluntary scheme for industry, according to which participating companies would carry out a thorough environmental assessment every three years.

ENVIRONMENTAL IMPACT ASSESSMENT

An evaluation of the consequences which any proposed industrial development will have on the environment. An EIA will probably include an **environmental audit**, and will assess the effect of the proposed development on such factors as atmospheric pollution, the fertility of agricultural land, and the topography of an area. EIA techniques were first developed by oil companies in the 1970s to deal with stricter legislation on their activities.

ENVIRONMENTAL PROTECTION AGENCY *see* EPA

ENVIRONMENTALIST

A person who centres his or her political philosophy on the need to preserve the natural environment and to halt or reverse the damage done by industrial development and pollution. Analogous with the term **Green**, environmentalist is less narrowly political and denotes a wider range of views. Environmentalists may come from different political traditions ranging from the radical libertarian to the reformist. The term is also used in philosophy and sociology to indicate a belief that the environment, rather than heredity, is the primary influence on human development.

ENVIRONMENTALLY FRIENDLY

A term for brands of products which have a less harmful impact on the environment than their standard equivalents. Products which may be recycled, which are produced without depleting scarce resources, which do not contain ozone-damaging **CFCs**, or which are energy efficient may be described as environmentally friendly. Government schemes, such as the EU's **eco-labelling**, are designed to help consumers identify such products and are leading to increased **green consumerism**.

EOKA

(Greek, *Ethniki Organosis Kyprion Agoniston*, 'National Organization of Cypriot Fighters') A Greek-Cypriot organization which, from 1955 until the independence of Cyprus in 1960, fought a **guerrilla** campaign against British rule and, unsuccessfully, in favour of **enosis** (union with Greece). EOKA was given covert military support and overt diplomatic encouragement by the Greek government. EOKA also fought against the Turkish Cypriot minority on the island after the British employed auxiliaries from this community to fight the Greek insurgents. In 1967, EOKA assaults on Turkish Cypriot communities brought Greece and Turkey to the brink of war, averted only by **UN** and NATO diplomatic intervention. A successor organization, EOKA B, attracted the support of the Greek regime of the **Colonels** in the early 1970s, and its participation in an ill-considered coup in July 1974, the effect of which was to precipitate an almost immediate Turkish invasion of Cyprus, the establishment of the **TRNC**, and the collapse of the colonels' regime in Greece.

EPA

The Environmental Protection Agency, the US government agency which engages in research on pollution, and undertakes the monitoring of levels of air, water and noise pollution, pesticides and radiation. The EPA reports to government and policy-making bodies on environmental matters, but its recommendations are often in conflict with the demands of industry. It is an executive agency under presidential authority and is headed by a Director appointed by the President and confirmed by the Senate.

EPG

The eminent persons group established at the initiative of the **Commonwealth** in November 1985 to advance the pace of political reform in **apartheid** South Africa. It was headed by the former Australian Prime Minister Malcolm Fraser and the former Nigerian head of state Gen. Olusegun Obasanjo. The group visited South Africa twice during 1986, meeting government ministers and leaders of anti-apartheid organizations, including the **UDF** and **Black Sash**, and the imprisoned **ANC** leader Nelson Mandela. The EPG received a cool reception from the government and on 15 May President P. W. Botha made clear that he would not tolerate 'unsolicited interference' in the country's internal affairs. Any remaining hopes that the initiative would produce significant progress were dashed when on 19 May South African forces attacked alleged ANC targets in Botswana, Zambia and Zimbabwe. In its formal report published in June 1986, the EPG urged the tightening of **sanctions** against South Africa.

EPU *see* EUROPEAN POLITICAL UNION

EQUAL RIGHTS AMENDMENT

A proposed amendment to the US Constitution which would have enshrined within it equal rights for women. The long and ultimately unsuccessful campaign for the ERA, stretching over more than a decade to 1982, was led by the **NOW**. The amendment was passed by 354 votes to 23 in the House of Representatives, and by 84 to 8 in the Senate (on 22 March 1972), but had been ratified by only 35 of the required 38 states by the extended deadline of 30 June 1982, and therefore failed to be adopted.

ERETZ ISRAEL

(Hebrew, 'Land of Israel') The biblical area of **Israel**, including the Israeli-occupied **West Bank**, **Gaza Strip** and **Golan Heights**. Since the acquisition of some of the Arab-held portions of *Eretz Israel* during the 1967 **Six-Day War**, many Israeli politicians have claimed an historic right to sovereignty over them. In pursuance of what they asserted to be an entitlement to 'reclaim' the area for world Jewry, the Israeli government greatly expanded Jewish **settlement** in the **Israeli-occupied territories**, especially the West Bank, after the 1967 War.

ERITREA

A country of some 3.5 million inhabitants in the **Horn of Africa**, and Africa's newest state. A former Italian colony, Eritrea was a British protectorate from 1941 to 1952 when it became federated with Ethiopia under the auspices of the **UN**. In 1962 it was annexed by Ethiopia, provoking a sustained independence struggle which was led by the Eritrean People's Liberation Front (EPLF) from the 1970s. Following the overthrow of the Mengistu regime in Ethiopia in May 1991, in which the EPLF played a major role, Eritrea functioned temporarily as an autonomous region, and attained independence in May 1993.

ERM

The Exchange Rate Mechanism, regarded as the core of the **EMS** (European Monetary System), but badly damaged when the UK and Italy pulled out as a result of **Black Wednesday** in September 1992. The ERM worked by establishing the central rate of exchange for a participating currency against the **ECU**, and requiring the authorities of the country concerned to keep it within a given margin (normally 2.25 per cent) either side of the central rate. Participation in the ERM was not compulsory for countries in the EMS; eight joined at the outset, and others only gradually thereafter, the UK in October 1990.

ESA

The European Space Agency, formed in 1973 as the result of the merger of the European Space Research Organization (ESRO) and the European Launcher Development Organization (ELDO). ESA's convention instructed it to provide for and promote, for exclusively peaceful purposes, co-operation among European states in space research and technology and their space applications. This envisaged the elaboration and implementation of a long-term European space policy linked to a coherent industrial strategy which would encourage member states progressively to integrate national programmes into a common one, particularly the development of and applications of satellites. In the mid-1970s, France was the driving force behind the new **Ariane** rocket programme for which the ESA took responsibility. In 1984 it passed this to Arianespace, a semi-private body dominated by the French National Space Agency (CNES) and French private companies. The current ESA member states are Austria, Belgium, Denmark, France, Germany, Ireland, Italy, Netherlands, Norway, Spain, Sweden, Switzerland and the United Kingdom. Finland is an associate member and Canada is a co-operating state.

ESAF *see* SAF

ESCAP *see* ECONOMIC COMMISSION

ESCWA *see* ECONOMIC COMMISSION

ESF

The European Social Fund, one of the **structural funds** of the **EU** originally established by the 1957 Treaty of Rome. The ESF has grown progressively in significance. ESF money, generally in the form of matching funds to boost what is raised at national or local level, goes mainly to programmes to combat unemployment and to provide training and retraining.

ESTADO NOVO

(Portuguese, 'New State') The fascist regime in Portugal which was established in 1926 and flourished under António de Oliveira Salazar, who became Prime Minister in 1932. Political parties, independent trade unions and strikes were outlawed during this period, and opponents were arbitrarily arrested and tortured by the notorious **PIDE** secret police. An oligarchy of a few powerful families and their business empires in combination with the upper echelons of the armed forces was fostered, and giant corporations were established, protected by tariffs and state controls from foreign competition. By the end of Salazar's rule Portugal was the least developed country in Europe, characterized by high emigration and an insistence on maintaining its overseas possessions in Africa and the **Far East** long after other countries had relinquished theirs. Salazar's death in 1970 ushered in a period of political openness and instability which preceded the 1974 **Carnation Revolution**.

ESTONIA

The smallest of the three **Baltic states**. Once part of the historic Russian empire, Estonia declared independence in 1918, but was effectively annexed by the **Soviet Union** in 1939, becoming one of the 15 Soviet republics; it recovered its independence in August 1991, and was admitted to the **UN** the following month. At least 40 per cent of the population of some 1.6 million are non-Estonian, most of them Russian.

ETA

(Basque, *Euzkadi ta Azkatasuna*, 'Basque Nation and Liberty') The militant Basque separatist organization which fights for the independence of the **Basque** country. ETA defines this as comprising the Spanish provinces of Alava, Guipúzcoa, Vizcaya and Navarra and part of the French department of Basses-Pyrénées. (A referendum in October 1979 approved a regional autonomy statute for Alava, Guipuzcoa and Vizcaya, but this limited measure failed to satisfy ETA.) The organization was formed in 1959 as a splinter from a non-violent Basque autonomy party, and subsequently split into several factions. ETA has carried out bomb attacks, kidnappings and other terrorist activity throughout Spain. Secret talks with the Spanish authorities, which began in January 1987 in Algeria, brought few results, and ETA was weakened by co-operation between the Spanish and French security forces in the late 1980s, the arrests of its leaders in 1992, and public opposition to its tactics.

ETHNIC CLEANSING

A euphemism for the use of terror by one ethnic group to expel another from an ethnically mixed community. The phrase was first widely used in war-torn **Bosnia-Hercegovina** in the summer of 1992, when Bosnian Serbs systematically drove many **Bosnian Muslims** from their homes: their property was often then seized by Serb families. Serb ethnic cleansing was allegedly part of a plan to create an ethnically homogeneous **Greater Serbia** from the ruins of **Yugoslavia**. The Bosnian Serb tactics allegedly included systematic murder and rape, siege and starvation. There were claims that Nazi-style concentration camps had been established, notoriously at **Omarska**. The **UN Security Council** therefore created the nominally UN-protected **safe areas** in May 1993. By the spring of 1993 there were allegations that all three parties in the conflict in Bosnia-Hercegovina had perpetrated ethnic cleansing. These allegations led to the establishment by the Security Council in May 1993 of an international tribunal on war crimes committed in the former Yugoslavia, which began its investigations in November 1993.

EU

The European Union, the most highly developed organization of regional integration in the world, which currently consists of 12 member states: the original **Six** (France, Germany, Italy and the **Benelux** countries), joined in 1973 by Denmark, Ireland and the UK, in 1981 by Portugal and Spain, and in 1986 by Greece.

In general usage the term EU replaced European Community (**EC**) from 1 November 1993, the date on which the **Maastricht** Treaty on European Union took effect. The EC **Council of Ministers** decided on 8 November to call itself the Council of the European Union, or EU Council. Strictly speaking the term EU is a concept which does not have any formal existence in law. It embraces what had been designated since 1967 the European Communities (the **EEC**, the **ECSC** and **Euratom**), other activities incorporated through the **Single European Act**, and also the two 'pillars' of intergovernmental co-operation under the Maastricht treaty, on foreign and security policy and on justice and home affairs.

EUA *see* ECU

EURATOM

The European Atomic Energy Community, part of the **EU** and originally one of the three European Communities, whose institutions were merged from 1967 in the **EC**. **Euratom** first came into existence in 1958, simultaneously with the **EEC**, both these organizations having been established under the Treaties of Rome signed in March 1957. Its stated purpose was to promote the nuclear industry in member countries and to foster co-operation between them.

EUROCOMMUNISM

The attempted synthesis of **communism** and liberal democratic ideas by the communist parties of France, Italy and Spain in the 1970s. In a bid to become more influential in national politics, these parties distanced themselves from the **CPSU**, and advocated a democratic road to socialism, civil liberties, and the right of opposition. The Spanish and Italian parties first issued a joint statement of what came to be regarded as Eurocommunist principles on 12 July 1975; the French and Italian parties followed with a similar statement on 15 November. Under the leadership of Enrico Berlinguer, the Italian Communist Party from 1973 pursued a policy of 'historic compromise' with the other main Italian parties, and won just over one third of the total vote in the 1976 elections. Eurocommunism lost its significance with the collapse of communism in **Eastern Europe** and the **Soviet Union** in the 1980s.

EUROCORPS

A multinational military unit created in Strasbourg in November 1993 under the auspices of the **WEU**, and designed to be 50,000 strong by 1995. It brought together French, German and Belgian troops, to be joined by Spanish and Luxembourgeois contingents. Based on the Franco-German brigade set up in 1989, the Eurocorps was intended to symbolize the shared European outlook of these erstwhile wartime enemies. Its participation in the French Bastille Day ceremonies in Paris in July 1994 was a milestone in Franco-German relations, bringing German troops there for the first time since the Second World War.

EUROCRAT

A common colloquial term for a European **bureaucrat**. Like many other words coined with Euro- as their prefix, it is often used in a hostile tone, to convey the sense that Eurocrats are meddlesome, distant (in **Brussels**) and devoid of common sense.

EUROCURRENCY

Deposits held in banks outside the country in whose currency they are denominated. Eurocurrency consists, more specifically, of Euromarks (held outside Germany), Eurodollars (held outside the USA), Euroyen etc.

EUROCURRENCY BONDS

International bond issues denominated in **ECUs** or in a **Eurocurrency**; also known as Eurobonds.

EURODOLLARS

US dollar deposits outside the USA held (usually in commercial banks) by non-US residents. Eurodollars are a form of **Eurocurrency**.

EUROPA *see* BLUE STREAK

EUROPE OF THE REGIONS

One of the initiatives to develop the **EU** under the **Maastricht** Treaty, designed specifically to help 'close the gap between the EU and its citizens' and to promote the concept of **subsidiarity**. It involves the creation of a 189-member EU Committee of the Regions, which met for the first time in Brussels in March 1994. The Committee has an advisory role on EU social and regional legislation.

EUROPEAN AGRICULTURAL GUIDANCE AND GUARANTEE FUND *see* FEOGA

EUROPEAN BANK FOR RECONSTRUCTION AND DEVELOPMENT *see* EBRD

EUROPEAN CENTRAL BANK

The institution which is to be created, as the cornerstone of monetary union (**EMU**) in the **EU**, under the **Maastricht** Treaty. It is intended to be a supranational body with an independent president, andit is widely expected to be modelled on the German **Bundesbank**. Its creation (to supersede a Frankfurt-based interim European

Monetary Institute) is scheduled to precede the final stage of EMU, not later than July 1998 and possibly earlier if enough member states have made sufficient progress in respect of economic **convergence**.

EUROPEAN COMMISSION *see* COMMISSION

EUROPEAN COMMUNITIES *see* EC; EU

EUROPEAN CONVENTION ON HUMAN RIGHTS

A convention of the **Council of Europe** signed in 1950, with a more practical and less declamatory character than the **UN's** 1948 **Universal Declaration of Human Rights**. Its full title is the European Convention for the Protection of Human Rights and Fundamental Freedoms, and there is a European Commission of Human Rights to examine alleged violations, as well as a European Court of Human Rights, based in Strasbourg, to which individual citizens may take cases. The Convention entered into effect in 1953 after been ratified by 10 member states, although France failed to ratify it until 1974.

EUROPEAN CORPS *see* EUROCORPS

EUROPEAN COUNCIL

The meetings of **EC** heads of state and government and the President of the **Commission**. The European Council (not to be confused with the **Council of Europe**) became a regular forum in 1974, after a series of ad hoc summit meetings had helped to revive the process of integration in the EC. It is now normally held three times a year. In November 1993, after the **Maastricht** Treaty on European Union had come into force and the term **EU** was being adopted widely to describe what had been called the EC, the European Council decided to rename itself the EU Council or the Council of the European Union.

EUROPEAN COURT OF HUMAN RIGHTS

The Strasbourg-based court, not related to the **EU**, which considers cases referred to it either by governments or individuals under the 1953 European Convention for the Protection of Human Rights and Fundamental Freedoms. The Convention was developed under the **Council of Europe**, and countries joining the Council accede separately to this and the various other conventions.

EUROPEAN COURT OF JUSTICE *see* ECJ

EUROPEAN CURRENCY UNIT *see* ECU

EUROPEAN ECONOMIC AREA *see* EEA

EUROPEAN ECONOMIC SPACE *see* EEA

EUROPEAN MONETARY SYSTEM *see* EMS

EUROPEAN MONETARY UNION *see* EMU

EUROPEAN NUCLEAR DISARMAMENT *see* END

EUROPEAN PARLIAMENT

One of the three principal institutions of the **EU**, with the **Council of Ministers** and the European **Commission**. The weakness of the Parliament has given rise to the complaint that the EU suffers a **democratic deficit**, although the **Maastricht** Treaty does increase its role, particularly by giving it powers of **co-decision** with the Council in certain areas and a say in Commission appointments. Previously it was basically only consultative, except that from 1975 it had powers to influence the Community budget. Moreover, it was not until 1979 that it was elected directly, rather than appointed by the parliaments of member states. Elections are held every five years; June 1994 was thus the fourth EP election, and the number of members (MEPs) had by that stage reached 567. The parliament meets in Strasbourg, with committee sessions in Brussels and a secretariat in Luxembourg. It is in the committees that MEPs do their main work, considering Commission proposals en route to the Council of Ministers.

EUROPEAN POLITICAL UNION

One of the two integral parts of the **Maastricht** Treaty as concluded in December 1991 by the **EU** member countries, and sometimes abbreviated as EPU since the other part is **EMU** or economic and monetary union. Both EPU and EMU were the subject of intergovernmental conferences throughout the preceding 12 months. According to the approved text the treaty marked a new stage in 'creating an ever closer union'; it dropped the word 'federal' from its preamble, however, and stressed **subsidiarity**. New areas of EU competence under the treaty include 'union citizenship', and there is an increased role for the **European Parliament**, but the formulation of common foreign and security policies, and co-operation on judicial and home affairs, are defined as separate 'pillars' outside the EU's decision-making machinery.

EUROPEAN SOCIAL CHARTER *see* SOCIAL CHARTER

EUROPEAN SOCIAL FUND *see* ESF

EUROPEAN UNION *see* EU

EUROSCEPTICS

A term increasingly current in the 1990s in the debate about the **Maastricht** Treaty and the future development of the **EU**. It is loosely applied to those who regard closer integration as inimical to national interests. More specifically it refers to those (mostly right-wingers) within the UK Conservative Party who voted against ratification of Maastricht in November 1992, failed to defeat the Major government on that occasion, but thereafter appeared to exercise a growing influence over the party's rhetoric on European issues.

LES ÉVÉNEMENTS

(French, 'the events') The social crisis in France in May **1968** which grew out of student activism and triggered widespread strikes by industrial workers, but ultimately failed to initiate any profound changes. The student demonstrations began on 3 May at Nanterre, thereafter moving to the Sorbonne in Paris. When the authorities closed the university the students took to the streets, engaging in violent battles with the police incited by the brutality of the **CRS**. Members of the French **Communist** Party and the communist-led General Confederation of Workers supported the students by industrial action, gradually bringing France to a standstill. The union leaders, however, successfully deflected discontent into demands for higher wages. President Charles de Gaulle, who at one stage was apparently close to resigning, was assured of military support should he wish to reimpose order by force; on 30 May he assumed sole control of the country, pending early elections in which a **Gaullist** victory marked a conclusive end to the crisis.

EXCHANGE RATE MECHANISM *see* ERM

EXCOMM

Abbreviation of Executive Council of the National Security Council. ExComm formed the core decision-making mechanism of the US government during the 1962 **Cuban missile crisis**, and was responsible for deciding to adopt a naval blockade following the discovery of Soviet missiles on the island.

EXOCET

The French-made air-to-ship (AM-39) and ship-to-ship (MM-38) missiles which became famous when used by Argentina in the 1982 **Falklands War**. The word Exocet came into vogue to convey the impression of a lightning and devastating attack.

EXTENDED FUND FACILITY

An **IMF** facility whereby member countries may borrow money for longer periods and in larger amounts than is generally provided under the **credit tranche policy**. The facility was established in 1974. To use it, a country must present a programme outlining objectives and policies for the whole period of the arrangement (normally three years, but with provision for extension up to four years). Each year it must also present a detailed statement of the policies and measures which it will follow in the next 12-month period.

EXXON VALDEZ

An oil tanker owned by the Exxon Shipping Company, which caused one of the world's worst pollution disasters when it struck a reef off the south Alaskan coast on 24 March 1989. About 40,000 tonnes of the vessel's cargo of crude oil was spilt into the ecologically important Prince William Sound and Gulf of Alaska. The cost of the clean-up was put at between $1,000 million and $2,000 million, and the incident stimulated an upsurge in environmental protest action, not only in North America.

EZLN

(Spanish acronym for *Ejercito Zapatista de Liberación Nacional* – the Zapatista National Liberation Army) A rebel **guerrilla** army some 2,000 strong which provoked upheaval in Mexico in early 1994 with demands for land reform, indigenous rights and political change. The guerrillas appeared abruptly on the scene on 1 January, seizing six municipalities in the poor southern state of Chiapas. Rebel activities quickly spread to the states of Michoacán and Puebla, nearer the capital, Mexico City, on which the guerrillas threatened to march and where they also received appreciable support. The deployment of 12,000 troops failed to crush the rebellion.

The majority of the guerrillas were descendants of the Mayas, and their basic demands for land reform, an end to oppression of the state's indian majority, and recognition of indigenous rights, echoed those made during the Mexican Revolution (1910–17) by Emiliano Zapata, a peasant leader and revolutionary hero. The rebels also demanded clean and fair elections and the resignation of the Institutional Revolutionary Party (PRI) government. Government concessions, intended to contain the situation, included a Special Commission for Peace and Reconciliation in Chiapas, and a pact on fair election practices.

FALANGE

Spain's **right-wing** nationalist party formed in 1937 by Gen. Francisco Franco from the merger of the fascist *Falange Española* with other right-wing, clericalist and monarchist groups. The Falange became the state party, membership of which was a prerequisite for advancement during the Franco era. It was formally abolished on 1 April 1977, but had been largely ineffectual since the passage of a law permitting other political associations on 12 January 1975, some 10 months before Franco's death.

FALASHAS

(Amharic, 'stranger' or 'exile') A name assigned to Ethiopian Jews which they themselves reject. Described by themselves as *Beta Israel* (House of Israel), they claim descent from Menelik I, son of the Queen of Sheba and King Solomon, and have lived for some 2,000 years in Ethiopia, settled mostly in Gondar and Tigre provinces. In 1975 **Israel** recognized the right of the Ethiopian Jews to become Israelis under the **Law of Return**. In the mid-1980s the Israeli government and the **Jewish Agency** organized a secret airlift (**Operation Moses**) of Ethiopian Jews from refugee camps in Sudan, where they had fled to escape famine, to Israel.

FALKLANDS FACTOR

The revival in the political fortunes of the UK Conservative Party, and especially of Prime Minister Margaret Thatcher, which was attributed to the 1982 **Falklands War**. An upsurge of patriotic feeling in the UK was generally considered to have helped the Conservatives win a landslide victory at the general election called by Thatcher in June 1983, a year before the end of the parliamentary term.

FALKLANDS WAR

A conflict between the UK and Argentina in 1982 over the Falkland/Malvinas islands, a British dependency in the South Atlantic which Argentina had long claimed. The Argentine military **junta** launched an invasion of the islands on 2 April 1982, prefaced by the occupation of the British protectorate of South Georgia, largely to restore its domestic standing but also as dramatic gamble to advance its sovereignty claims, since bilateral negotiations had apparently reached stalemate. Efforts to mediate were undertaken variously by **UN**, US and Peruvian diplomats. The UK government, armed with **UN Security Council** resolution 502 demanding an immediate Argentine withdrawal, responded by sending a naval **Task Force** to recapture the Falklands. Notable incidents included the sinking of the **Belgrano** (2 May), the **Exocet** attack on HMS *Sheffield* (4 May), the battles at Goose Green and Mount Longdon (29 May; 11–12 June) and the final capture of Port Stanley (14 June). There were a total of 255 British and 655 Argentinean casualties. The defeat spelled the end of the military dictatorship in Argentina. In the UK, the so-called **Falklands factor** propelled the hitherto unpopular Thatcher government to a landslide victory in the 1983 general election.

FAMILY VALUES

A generic term for a **right-wing** political agenda, used particularly in the USA, which stresses the importance of the nuclear family and the values deemed to be vital to its well-being. Advocated by the Christian right, it also opposes abortion, gay rights, feminism, single parenthood and 'welfare dependency'. Family values formed the basis of the Republican Party's 1992 presidential election campaign, and provided a marked contrast to the liberal social values espoused by the Democratic candidate Bill Clinton, who also was accused of marital infidelity. The defeat of incumbent President George Bush and the election of Clinton provided a severe setback to the political ambitions of advocates of family values.

FAO

The Rome-based Food and Agriculture Organization, one of the largest of the **UN** specialized agencies. Founded in 1945, it aims to combat malnutrition and hunger and to serve as a co-ordinating agency for development programmes relating to food and agriculture, including forestry and fisheries. The organization's supreme policy-making body is the FAO Conference which meets every two years, while interim decisions are taken by the FAO Council composed of representatives from 49 of the 157 member states.

FAR EAST

The Asian countries lying east of the **Indian Subcontinent**, comprising **Indo-China**, **South-East Asia**, the **Four Chinas** and Japan. The term has connotations of the economic dynamism usually associated with these countries. As a geographical description from a Eurocentric standpoint, it is an extension of the terms **Near East** and **Middle East**.

FARC

The Revolutionary Armed Forces of Colombia, **Latin America's** oldest **left-wing guerrilla** force, originally set up under the wing of the **Communist** Party of Colombia in 1949 to protect the self-declared Andean independent Republic of Gaitania. After an army invasion in 1964 it re-formed to become the largest of several guerrilla groups. In the second half of the 1980s the FARC joined the **Simón Bolívar National Guerrilla Co-ordinating Board** (CNGSB), and in March 1989 it announced a willingness to enter peace talks, the latest round of which broke down in March 1992.

FARM BELT

A geographical term to describe the main grain producing area of the USA – in North Dakota, South Dakota, Nebraska, Kansas, Iowa and Missouri – which is part of the **Midwest** region.

FASCISM

A twentieth century ideology, which has been variously interpreted as **right-wing** or **centrist** in orientation. Derived from the Latin *fasces* (the bundles of sticks with an axe protruding carried as a symbol of the authority of Roman magistrates), the term became prominent in the inter-war period following Benito Mussolini's 'March on Rome' in 1922, and the appointment of Adolf Hitler as Chancellor of Germany in 1933. The period also saw fascist movements of varying degrees of success in almost every **capitalist** society. While these varied widely according to national conditions, all manifested fascism's core characteristics. These included **corporatism**, extreme **nationalism** often coupled with **racism**, the leadership principle, militarism, opposition to **communism**, a belief in the organic state as a unifying force for the nation, and a degree of mass mobilization and economic planning not normally associated with right-wing dictatorships. Fascism, known as National Socialism in Germany and the **Falange** in Spain, grew as a response to economic crisis. The ideology contained a significant element of **socialism**, but in practice fascist governments once in power tended to operate in collusion with the interests of capital. Although comprehensively defeated in the Second World War, fascist and **neo-Nazi** fringe movements have continued to operate in most countries in the post-war period and, since the collapse of communism, have proliferated in Russia and **Eastern Europe**.

FAST BREEDER REACTOR

A type of nuclear reactor which produces plutonium from Uranium-238 while generating nuclear power. FBRs have no moderator, such as water as in the **PWR**, to slow down the neutrons generated in the controlled chain reaction which produces **nuclear energy**. Some of these neutrons collide with atoms of uranium-238 (a non-fissile form of Uranium), to form plutonium, a fissile and highly toxic material, which may be extracted by **nuclear reprocessing**.

FAST TRACK PROCEDURE

An accelerated schedule. The US **Congress** may reach a fast track procedure agreement with the administration over how it will handle ratification of an international agreement if the negotiations are completed within a specified time. Congressional acceptance or rejection will then be considered as a whole, sparing the agreement from being unpicked and debated line by line and thus made vulnerable to myriad amendments. As used for example for the agreement concluding the **Uruguay Round** of **GATT**, it can provide a spur for the conclusion of negotiations, although this effect is diluted if Congress seems too easily persuaded to extend the deadline for fast track approval.

FATWA

(Arabic, 'edict') A published opinion or decision regarding religious doctrine. A common feature of Islamic law, it has traditionally been the preserve of a recognized religious authority. Current familiarity with the term dates mainly from February 1989 when Iran's spiritual leader, the late Ayatollah Ruhollah Khomeini, passed a death sentence on the Muslim-born British author, Salman Rushdie, who was judged to have committed apostasy and blasphemy in his novel, **The Satanic Verses**. The controversial ruling, questioned by many Muslims, spawned similar pronouncements by lesser religious figures, most recently against the Bangladeshi author, Taslima Nasreen, who was accused of blasphemy in her novel *Lajja*.

FAVOURITE SON

A US term for a politician who is nominated for President at a party convention by delegates from his own state, but who is not a serious contender. Such nominations tend to occur either for purposes of political bargaining or for reasons of personal publicity.

FBI

The Federal Bureau of Investigation. The FBI is a part of the US Justice Department and is responsible for the investigation of violations of federal law. It is particularly involved in combating inter-state criminal activity, espionage, and domestic threats to national security. It is headed by a Director, the most famous of whom was J. Edgar Hoover who held the post between 1924 and his death in 1972.

FCO

The Foreign and Commonwealth Office, the UK government department responsible for external relations and representation. The Secretary of State for Foreign and Commonwealth Affairs is often popularly referred to simply as the Foreign Secretary. The FCO was created in 1968 through the merger of the original Foreign Office (formed in 1782) and the Commonwealth Office.

FED

The widely used abbreviation for the Federal Reserve Board, one of the most important of the many regulatory commissions which are appointed by, but function independently of, the US government. It consists of seven members, each serving a 14-year term of office, who are appointed by the US president with the approval of the Senate. The Fed and particularly its chair (currently Allan Greenspan) are enormously influential, controlling monetary policy and interest rates and thus effectively functioning as a central bank. It has the reputation of fiscal orthodoxy. It presides over the Federal Reserve System, the central banking structure of the USA, which is also sometimes referred to as the Fed.

FEDERAL REPUBLIC OF GERMANY *see* BRD

FEDERAL REPUBLIC OF YUGOSLAVIA *see* FRY

FEDERALIST

Broadly, an advocate of federal arrangements, either within states (usually to guarantee a high degree of autonomy to their constituent elements) or between states within a supranational organization (usually to promote decision-making and policy implementation on certain issues across the organization as a whole, rather than at individual national level). In the context of the development of the **EU**, from the **Single European Act** to **Maastricht** and beyond, the concept of federalism is anathema to the defenders of national sovereignty; any positive use of 'the f-word' is therefore guaranteed to arouse the wrath of the **Eurosceptics**.

FEDERATED STATES OF MICRONESIA *see* MICRONESIA

FEDERATION OF MALAYA *see* MALAYSIA

FEDERATION OF MALI

The shortlived attempt to unite the French colonies of **Mali** (then French Soudan) and Senegal on a federal basis. The federation was formed in April 1959 and became independent in June 1960 under the presidency of Léopold Senghor of Senegal and with Mali's Modibo Keita as Prime Minister. However, Senegal seceded two months later and the complete failure of the experiment was sealed in September 1960 when the Republic of Mali was proclaimed.

FEDERATION OF RHODESIA AND NYASALAND *see* CENTRAL AFRICAN FEDERATION

FEMINISM

The ideology which advocates the rights of women and their political, social and economic equality with men. The roots of modern feminist thought are conventionally traced back to the late eighteenth century and the works of Mary Wollstonecraft. The first so-called 'wave' of feminism is most often located between the mid-nineteenth and early twentieth centuries and is associated with groups such as the suffragettes demanding votes for women, and those demanding birth control. A second 'wave' has been identified with the **women's lib** movement of the late 1960s and has persisted as a social and political concept since then. Although there are different tendencies within feminism, in broad terms it argues that the rights currently allowed to women are inferior to those of men and that in all social relations their status is either implicitly or explicitly inferior, allowing them to be dominated by men. Feminists argue that biological differences between the sexes do not explain all the observed differences in their social status, roles and behaviour, and that women should not therefore be denied political, social or economic advancement on the basis of their gender. Feminists also advocate that a lower value should not be placed on so-called 'feminine' attributes, such as compassion, as opposed to 'masculine' ones, such as aggression, and that women should not be urged to think that fulfilment is only possible in relation to men.

FEOGA

(French acronym for *Fonds Européen d'Orientation et de Garantie Agricole* – European Agricultural Guidance and Guarantee Fund) The largest fund by far under the **EC** budget, used to finance the common agricultural policy (**CAP**). Most of its money, despite the recent emphasis on reforming the CAP, still goes on price support (the 'guarantee' aspect) rather than on structural policies ('guidance').

FIFTH AMENDMENT

One of the first 10 amendments to the US Constitution which were ratified on 15 December 1791, and which are known collectively as the **Bill of Rights**. The Fifth amendment includes protection against double jeopardy and stipulates that nobody 'shall be compelled in any criminal case to be a witness against himself, nor be deprived of life, liberty, or property without due process of law'. The guarantee against enforced self-incrimination was widely cited by those who were brought before the House Committee on **Un-American Activities**, a stance which became known as 'taking the Fifth'.

FINLANDIZATION

A term used when a major international power casts a long shadow over the affairs and particularly the foreign policy of a small neighbouring state. Finland from 1945 remained an independent state with a pluralist democratic system, but until the collapse of **communism** in Europe its leaders consulted frequently with their Soviet neighbours, and attuned their policies in tacit acknowledgement that they should not cut across vital Soviet interests. For former Soviet republics in the 1990s, Russia's concept of its **near abroad** is a reminder of the delicate balances implied by the notion of Finlandization.

FIRST PAST THE POST

A method of electing a candidate in a **single-member constituency** system in which the winner is the candidate with a **simple plurality**, i.e. the highest vote. It is used for elections to the UK House of Commons and the US **Congress**, but is much criticized by advocates of proportional representation (**PR**).

FIRST WORLD

The most economically developed countries of the world. The term is usually taken to include the **capitalist** democracies of North America, **Western Europe**, Japan, Australia, New Zealand, and, frequently, **Israel** and South Africa.

500 DAYS PLAN

The programme, also known as the Shatalin plan, drawn up in 1990 by radical economists Stanislav Shatalin and Grigory Yavlinsky, to effect a rapid transformation of the Soviet **command economy** to a Western-style market economy within 500 days. The plan envisaged that state monopolies should be divided and privatized, that there should be a drastic reduction in state spending by reducing military expenditure and state support for industry, and that the sovereignty of the **Soviet Union's** republics should be recognized. Although Russian leader Boris Yeltsin adopted elements of the plan in July 1990, and Soviet leader Mikhail Gorbachev expressed support, it was never fully implemented.

FIVE PRINCIPLES OF PEACEFUL CO-EXISTENCE

The five principles (*panch sila*) first set out in an agreement over Tibet signed by India and China on 29 April 1954. Elaborated in the Declaration on World Peace and Co-operation, adopted on 24 April 1955 at the **Bandung conference** which launched the **Non-Aligned Movement**, the five principles cover mutual respect for territorial integrity and sovereignty; mutual non-aggression; mutual non-interference in one another's internal affairs; equality and mutual benefit; and peaceful co-existence.

FIVE-YEAR PLAN

A centrally conceived economic strategy associated especially with the **command economies** of **communist** states, and in many cases seeking the rapid expansion of heavy industry (often using labour freed from the land by **collectivization**). In the **Soviet Union**, where the first five-year plan covered 1928–32, strict production targets were set centrally by **Gosplan**.

FLAG BURNING

A reference to the controversy generated by the issue of the desecration of the US flag. In 1989 the Supreme Court ruled that flag-burning was a form of self-expression and was therefore protected by the **Bill of Rights**. President George Bush favoured amending the Constitution – a process which required two-thirds support of both houses of Congress and ratification by 38 of the 50 states – to provide specific protection for the flag. The Democratic majority in Congress, however, opposed any such tampering with the freedoms enshrined within the Bill of Rights, preferring instead to demonstrate its opposition to the practice by enacting the Flag Protection Act in October 1989. Predictably, the Supreme Court ruled the Act unconstitutional on 11 June 1990. This decision re-ignited the campaign for an amendment to protect the flag, but although such amendments were passed by the House of Representatives (21 June) and the Senate (26 June), both fell short of the requisite two-thirds majority.

FLAGS OF CONVENIENCE

A shipping term used to describe vessels which take advantage of the open registry facilities provided by a small number of countries, notably Liberia, Panama, Cyprus, Bermuda and the Bahamas, and which account for more than one-third of the world's merchant fleet. In return for payment of (relatively small) fees, non-nationals are given the right to fly the flag of these countries and can thus circumvent regulations (including tax and labour restrictions) applicable in their home countries. Developing countries have argued that this practice diverts investment away from those countries which insist on a genuine economic link between themselves and ships on their national registers. They have thus campaigned within **UNCTAD** for the gradual transformation of flags of convenience registries into normal registries. However, these efforts have been opposed by the industrialized countries and the open registry states.

FLANDERS

One of the three regions of Belgium, covering the north of the country and largely Flemish speaking. Regional autonomy for Flanders, **Wallonia** and **Brussels** was confirmed in a process of **devolution** begun in 1970 and crowned by parliamentary approval on 14 July 1993. Flanders has built up an advanced industrial sector, aided by post-1945 investment which transformed a predominantly agricultural economy.

FLEET STREET

A term used to signify the UK national press as a whole, and the influence which it has exerted. Fleet Street in central London was traditionally the location of the head offices of the main national newspapers, but in the 1980s they started moving out of the City of London, and the phrase is no longer logically applicable. The homogeneity implied by the phrase 'Fleet Street' has moreover been broken by the ramifications of new technology, whose introduction by the Times group of newspapers sparked off the lengthy **Wapping dispute** in 1986–7.

FLEXIBLE RESPONSE

The doctrine of **deterrence** which supplanted **MAD** among **NATO** planners, and was formally adopted by the NATO Defence Planning Committee in December 1967. NATO defence would be based on a mixture of **conventional weapons**, theatre **nuclear weapons**, and strategic weapons. It was made explicit that nuclear weapons might be used in response to a Soviet non-nuclear attack in Europe, even before NATO's conventional defences had been defeated, but an aggressor would be uncertain as to the level and timing of any response. NATO commanders were supposed to judge the appropriate level, and be prepared to escalate deliberately, in theory in a carefully controlled process, if one level of defence were proving inadequate. 'Thinking about the unthinkable' use of nuclear weapons was opened up under this doctrine, which was seen by its detractors as a recipe for disastrous instability.

FLN

(French acronym for *Front de libération nationale* – 'National Liberation Front') The dominant political organization in pre- and post-independence Algeria. Founded in 1954 under the leadership of Ahmed Ben Bella and other nationalists to direct the war for independence from French colonial rule, the FLN became the ruling party upon independence in 1962. The advent of multipartyism in the late 1980s revealed the extent of popular dissatisfaction with the **one-party state** socialism of the FLN. After the first round of legislative elections in December 1991 the FLN was running a poor third when the military intervened to halt the advance of the militant Islamic Salvation Front.

FLNC

(French acronym for *Front de libération nationale de la Corse* – 'Corsican National Liberation Front') A clandestine extremist group fighting for self-determination of the island which is currently an integral part of France. Formed in May 1976, it stated among its aims 'the recognition of **Corsica's** national rights' and 'the destruction of all instruments of French **colonialism**', and claimed that tourism and French rule were erasing Corsican individuality. The FLNC carried out numerous bombings from the late 1970s which continued despite measures offering greater self-rule for Corsica in January 1982. It was outlawed in January 1983; although fragmented, it continued to attack 'French' property on Corsica and in mainland France.

FLOWER POWER

A term associated with the youth culture of the 1960s, particularly the hippy movement. It encapsulated the belief in the superiority of 'alternative' values such as love, peace and expanded self-awareness through meditation and drug use.

FLYING PICKET

A mobile group of trade unionists which can be deployed at a range of locations in support of industrial action. In the UK the use of flying pickets became increasingly widespread in the 1970s, and caused considerable disruption of industry. Under the Thatcher government (1979–90) the powers and rights of trade unions were progressively whittled away. The Employment Act 1980 provided that a worker might generally picket only at his or her own place of work (and thus forbade **secondary picketing**); moreover, the code of conduct issued under this Act laid down that the number of members of a picket should not normally exceed six.

FMLN

(Spanish acronym for the Farabundo Martí National Liberation Front) A group of Salvadorean **left-wing guerrillas** now reconstituted as a political party. Founded in 1980 it launched an armed offensive in 1981 and by 1982 controlled a quarter of the country. From 1984 it offered to engage in peace negotiations, but these were rejected by the government until 1989–90. A **UN**-sponsored peace agreement, offering the prospect of electoral and land reform, a significant reduction in the size of the army and an FMLN contribution to national reconstruction, was signed in January 1993. Reorganized into a political party, the FMLN won a quarter of seats in the March

1994 elections but subsequently suffered a damaging split in May when leaders of two moderate factions were suspended for accepting legislative posts.

FOGGY BOTTOM

Colloquialism for the US **State Department**, derived from the area of Washington DC in which the department is located.

FOOD AID

Food rather than money sent abroad on non-commercial terms, for use in emergency relief, for projects where workers were paid in food rather than cash, or for recipient governments to sell cheaply or distribute in other ways. Massive food aid programmes were implemented particularly by the USA in the 1950s and 1960s, under the **PL480** legislation and under the more resounding title **Food for Peace**. American farmers were certainly beneficiaries of this food aid which used up surplus stocks, created by government buying-in to keep up farm incomes, and introduced American cereals in what might later become commercial markets abroad. The programmes were much criticized, however, for discouraging local production in recipient countries and for distorting world trade. The World Food Conference in 1974 set up a **World Food Council** to co-ordinate donors, and the World Food Programme (**WFP**) continues to marshal the flow of multilateral food aid for emergency relief, but (coincidental with the ending of the era of huge cereal surpluses in the **West**) it has become generally acknowledged in the last two decades that there is no developmental role for large food aid programmes.

FOOD FOR PEACE

The new and more resounding name given in 1959 to the US **food aid** programme under **PL480**. The 1959 modification of the programme added a longer-term element to what had been essentially a surplus disposal operation, giving more scope for using food aid to friendly countries for the US foreign policy objective of 'advancing peace in the free world'. The Office of Food for Peace, set up in 1960, was strengthened under President Kennedy as soon as he took office in 1961.

FOOTBALL WAR

The six-day conflict between El Salvador and Honduras in July 1969 which stemmed from the unregulated migration of some 300,000 destitute Salvadorean peasants to the border regions of Honduras. Hondurans resented their presence, while the Salvadoreans claimed they were being persecuted by local Honduran authorities. The catalyst for a full-scale war was the assault by Salvadoreans on a visiting Honduran football team. Salvadorean troops, led personally by President Gen. Fidel Sánchez Hernández, occupied Honduran border villages while Honduran aircraft bombed targets in El Salvador to little effect. The war served the purpose of temporarily rallying popular support for the military in El Salvador at the expense of growing internal political dissent.

FOQUISMO

An insurrectionist theory based on a small nucleus of **guerrillas**. Strongly influenced by the Cuban revolution, it was popularized by the French intellectual Régis Debray, who opposed contemporary **Communist** orthodoxy by claiming that the right conditions for revolution in an underdeveloped country could be achieved by small guerrilla nuclei (*focos*) whose actions would inspire the peasantry to rise up. *Foquismo* was associated with **Guevarism**, named after Cuban revolutionary leader Ernesto 'Che' Guevara whose disastrous Bolivian guerrilla campaign in 1967 finally exposed the theory's flaws, already evident in Guatemala and Nicaragua in the early 1960s. Guerrilla warfare tactics which built on existing conflicts and focused on both the countryside and the urban working class superseded *foquismo* and were successfully used in the **Vietnam War** and by **Sandinistas** in Nicaragua.

FORCE DE FRAPPE

(French, 'striking force') The independent French **nuclear weapons** capability. Viewing the USA as an unreliable defender of European interests, and highly critical of the **special relationship** between the UK and the USA, the French under de Gaulle made something of a fetish of their *force de frappe*; its creation was approved in December 1960. France subsequently resisted the incorporation of its nuclear forces within **NATO**, and refused to sign the 1968 nuclear non-proliferation treaty (**NPT**) until 1992 as a protest against the privileged position accorded to the two **superpowers**.

FOREIGN AID *see* AID

FOREIGN AND COMMONWEALTH OFFICE *see* FCO

FORMOSA *see* TAIWAN

FORTRESS EUROPE

An expression borrowed from military rhetoric, used to dramatize the possibility that the **EU** might retreat behind a wall of economic protectionism if the **GATT Uruguay Round** world trade talks of the 1980s and early 1990s failed. The term was generally used only by opponents of protectionism. It was also used by Japanese and US critics when the EU's **single market** legislation was being drawn up, over the possibility of their being shut out, especially from the financial services sector. However, the **European Council** stated explicitly in December 1988 that **1992** would not mean 'fortress Europe'.

49TH PARALLEL

The line of latitude which delineates much of the land border between the USA and Canada. In the period after the British recognition of US independence in 1783, the land border between Canada and the USA remained a source of dispute, particularly in the area west of the Great Lakes. It was fixed along the 49th parallel by a series of treaties in the nineteenth century.

FOSSIL FUEL

A non-renewable fuel, such as coal, peat, natural gas or oil, which was produced in the earth by geological processes from dead plants and animals and which, when burned, releases water, energy, and carbon dioxide – a **greenhouse gas** and a major factor in **global warming**. The 25 per cent increase in the level of carbon dioxide in the atmosphere which has been monitored as occurring since the Industrial Revolution may be traced to the large-scale burning of fossil fuels. They are also used in the manufacture of substances such as plastics, synthetic fibres and pesticides, which can be pollutants and release greenhouse gases when incinerated.

FOUR CHINAS

A collective term for four Chinese territories: the People's Republic of China (**PRC** – the **communist** mainland), the Republic of China (**Taiwan**), the British colony of Hong Kong, and the Portuguese colony of Macao. The last two will revert to PRC rule by the end of the century (Hong Kong in 1997 and Macao in 1999). Since the **KMT** retreat to Taiwan (then Formosa) in 1949, the Taiwanese government has considered itself to be the true government of mainland China.

FOUR MODERNIZATIONS

The policy, announced by Zhou Enlai on 13 January 1975 to China's National People's Congress, envisaging 'the comprehensive modernization of agriculture, industry, national defence, and science and technology'. This was to be achieved before the end of the century. By 1980, moreover, 'an independent and relatively comprehensive industrial and economic system' was to be in place. The four modernizations were proposed in the context of the ongoing struggle between radicals and moderates in the Chinese leadership after the **Cultural Revolution** in which the pragmatists, such as Zhou and Deng Xiaoping, held that political progress depended upon improved economic performance.

FOUR-POWER AGREEMENT

The September 1971 agreement on Berlin, reached between the USA, the UK, France and the **Soviet Union**, the four powers which had been **Allies** in the Second World War. The final protocol was signed on 3 June 1972. It relaxed the segregation of West Berlin (administered by the **Western**

Allies) from the eastern sector (designated the capital of the **DDR** and under Soviet administration), providing for improved access to West Berlin from the DDR, and stronger ties (but not integration) between West Berlin and the Federal Republic of Germany. The settlement formed part of the West German policy of detente with the East known as **Ostpolitik**.

FOUR TIGERS

The four Asian countries – Hong Kong, South Korea, Singapore and **Taiwan** – whose rapid economic development made them particularly ferocious challengers to the competitiveness of the more established industrialized countries in the 1990s.

FOURONS *see* VOEREN

14 FAMILIES

A reference to the tiny elite that dominates the economy and government in El Salvador, although a symbolic rather than an exact figure. Their influence is the result of draconian late nineteenth century legislation which effectively concentrated land ownership in the hands of an oligarchy of coffee growers, by dispossessing Indian communities and small mestizo farmers and abolishing all communal land tenure. In 1979, the year the **FMLN** began their **guerrilla** war, 0.85 per cent of the landowners held 77.3 per cent of all cultivable land.

FOURTH ESTATE

A term used to indicate the power of the press. The first three 'estates' (traditionally used with reference to France and England) were deemed to be the nobility, the church (clergy) and the commons (citizens), each of which enjoyed and exercised certain rights and powers. By extension, the term fourth estate became employed in the nineteenth century to indicate the countervailing importance of newspapers. The term has tended to drop out of use with the increasing influence of radio and then television.

FOURTH INTERNATIONAL

A **Trotskyist** international organization first established in September 1938 as an alternative to the Third International (the Comintern). After the Second World War, the Fourth International's International Secretariat was formally re-established at the second conference in Paris in 1948 under Michel Pablo. The organization split several times, most seriously in 1951 when the Fourth International-International Committee was established by a British faction. In 1963, the parent body was renamed the Fourth International-United Secretariat. Numerous other Trotskyist organizations have subsequently formed from splits within the Fourth International.

FOURTH WORLD

A term for the world's least developed countries, the poorest of those in the **Third World**. The **UN** defines such countries as those with the lowest per capita **GDP**, literacy levels and manufacturing base. The Fourth World includes countries in Central Africa and in Asia, whose already vulnerable economies could be completely destroyed by natural or man-made disasters.

FPR *see* RPF

FRANC ZONE

The economic grouping which provides for the free movement of currency among its members and gives them a guaranteed French franc exchange rate. Its existence, supported by the **BEAC** and the **UMOA**, has given a measure of stability to African states using the **CFA franc**. Its members are Benin, Burkina, Cameroon, Central African Republic, Chad, Comoros, Congo, Côte d'Ivoire, Gabon, Mali, Niger, Senegal, Togo, and France (including **Mayotte**, St Pierre and Miquelon, and the Overseas Territories and Departments). Equatorial Guinea, which was never part of French Africa, is also a member.

FRANKS REPORT

The official UK report on the circumstances leading up to the 1982 **Falklands War**. Shortly after the end of hostilities, a board of inquiry was set up in July 1982. Its report, published on 18 January 1983, cleared government ministers of blame for the Argentine invasion, but criticized the government's intelligence gathering process; in particular it recommended closer liaison between the intelligence assessment staffs, the Foreign and Commonwealth Office (**FCO**) and the Ministry of Defence, and the transfer of chairmanship of the joint intelligence committee from the FCO to the Cabinet Office.

FREE WORLD

A Western **Cold War** term referring to Western-style democracies with a market economy, and excluding the world's dictatorships, particularly those of the left.

FREEDOM DOCTRINE

A foreign policy doctrine, also known as the Kennedy Doctrine, formulated by US President John F. Kennedy. Articulated at a conference of the **Alliance for Progress** in Punta del Este on 5 July 1961, the essence of the doctrine was an attempt to encourage progress on human rights in **Latin America** by providing US aid to democratic states and support to reformist movements within the continent.

FREEDOM FIGHTERS

A positive term for **guerrillas**, associated particularly with those struggling for national independence from a colonial power. However, their critics and opponents often label them terrorists.

FREEDOM OF INFORMATION ACT

The 1974 legislation passed by the US **Congress** which gives the US public access to a wide range of government-held information, resulting in greater government accountability. In the UK, the government has thus far resisted demands for similar legislation, although soon after becoming Prime Minister John Major committed the Conservative government to a policy of increased openness, resulting for example in the publication of details about **MI6**.

FREEDOM RIDES

The campaigning tactic used in the spring of 1961 by multiracial groups in the USA seeking **civil rights** for blacks, who rode buses into Alabama and Mississippi in an attempt to desegregate public transport facilities. After the activists were brutally attacked by white Southerners, Attorney General Robert Kennedy dispatched 500 federal marshals to Montgomery, Alabama, to preserve order. Nevertheless, the Kennedy administration did not endorse the actions of the freedom riders, nor did it object to their imprisonment. Thus the freedom rides came to be seen not merely as an early battle in the US **civil rights movement**, but also as an indication of the circumspection with which the Kennedy administration approached the civil rights issue.

FRENCH SOUDAN *see* MALI

FRETILIN

(Portuguese abbreviation of *Frente Revolucionaria de Timor Leste*, 'Revolutionary Front of East Timor') The main separatist grouping opposing Indonesian rule in **East Timor**. The group, which has the support of Portugal (the former colonial power in East Timor), suffered a major blow in 1992 when its military commander, Jose 'Xanana' Gusmao, was captured by Indonesian forces.

FRG *see* BRD

FRIEDMANITE

An adherent of the Chicago school of economic theory, which emphasizes the money supply as a main determinant of aggregate demand. The foremost exponent of this **monetarist** school, Milton Friedman (born 1912), was Professor of Economics at the University of Chicago in 1948–83, and Friedmanite theories underlay much free market economic philosophy, notably that of **Thatcherism** in the UK in the 1980s but also such applications as the Chilean and other **Latin American** prescriptions of the **Chicago Boys**.

FRIENDLY FIRE

A term used when wartime casualties are accidentally inflicted by forces on the same side as the victims. Like **collateral damage**, the term was used extensively during the 1990–1 **Gulf War**, particularly in relation to an incident on 26 February 1991, when nine British soldiers were killed in an attack by US warplanes.

FRIENDS OF THE EARTH

An international environmental pressure group with some 800,000 members currently active in 43 countries. Friends of the Earth originated in the USA as an offshoot of the **Sierra Club**. It supports research on environmental issues, lobbies policy makers, and has been most successful in increasing public awareness.

FRONTLINE STATES

An informal grouping of states bordering (or close to) South Africa (Angola, **Botswana**, Mozambique, **Namibia**, **Tanzania**, **Zambia** and **Zimbabwe**). Although united primarily by their attitude to the **apartheid** system in South Africa and their support for the **ANC** and/or **PAC**, leaders of the Frontline States have agreed that given their other mutual interests they should continue meeting despite the holding of non-racial democratic elections in South Africa in April 1994.

FRY

The Federal Republic of **Yugoslavia**, the rump successor state founded in April 1992 and comprising the republics of **Montenegro** and Serbia (including the nominally autonomous provinces of Kosovo and **Vojvodina**). The FRY is widely viewed as an embryonic **Greater Serbia**, and has been placed under **UN** sanctions over its role in the wars in neighbouring **Croatia** and **Bosnia-Hercegovina**, although its leaders consistently deny aiding Serbs in these conflicts.

FTSE-100 INDEX *see* DOW JONES INDEX

FULL STOP LAW

An Argentinian legal measure intended to halt human rights trials. Signed into law in December 1986 by President Raúl Alfonsín Foulkes, it set a deadline of 22 February 1987 for indictments of members of the security forces. Around 1,000 charges were filed by human rights groups by the deadline, resulting in 153 indictments. The law was widely condemned and provoked large demonstrations and protest actions. Belligerent factions of the military, however, thought the Full Stop Law insufficient. Further government concessions in the form of the **Due Obedience** Law did not satisfy them or prevent a series of bombings and killings and four military uprisings between 1987 and 1990 by middle-ranking officers known as the **Carapintadas**.

FUNDAMENTALIST

A currently controversial term which is loosely applied to describe persons or groups professing ideas drawn from a narrow interpretation of religion and which is deemed by some commentators to be intrinsically derogatory. It is generally regarded as antithetical to the modern preference for secular rationality, the adoption of religious tolerance with accompanying tendencies towards relativism, and individualism. Although its current usage has tended most widely to refer to religious extremists in contemporary Muslim societies, the term is being used increasingly to characterize revivalist Christian movements in North America as well the outlook of militant Jewish communities particularly in the **Israeli-occupied territories**. Some Sinhalese nationalist groups like the **JVP** active in the 1980s, and more recently followers of the pro-Hindu Indian political party, the **BJP**, have also been labelled fundamentalist.

FYROM *see* MACEDONIA

G-3

The so-called Group of Three allying Colombia, Mexico and Venezuela since 1987 in the promotion of political and economic co-operation. A G-3 trade pact covering complete access to each country's markets was expected to be concluded in 1994. In 1993, in an effort to extend its political and economic influence in **Central America** and the **Caribbean**, the G-3 signed a framework trade agreement with El Salvador, Guatemala and Honduras and held an historic meeting with **CARICOM** countries and **Surinam**.

Another Group of Three, comprising Brazil, Argentina and Mexico – the three major **Latin American** debtor countries – was launched in New York in September 1987 to co-ordinate an approach to Western creditors.

G-5

Finance ministers of France, Germany, Japan, the UK and the USA, who convene informally to discuss international monetary matters and to establish the agenda for wider formal meetings of the **G-7**.

G-7

The Group of Seven most powerful industrialized countries – Canada, France, Germany, Italy, Japan, the UK and the USA – whose heads of state and government have met for annual summits since the mid-1970s (although Canada was not included in the first such summit, at Rambouillet, France, in November 1975). Also present at all the summits since 1977 has been the president of the European **Commission**. G-7 finance ministers and central bank governors and the heads of the **World Bank** and the **IMF** also meet annually in a process formalized at the Tokyo Economic Summit of May 1986. In recent years G-7 summits have tended increasingly to concentrate on political issues, notably on proposals for a collective strategy for the economic and social reconstruction of the newly independent states which were the former **Soviet Union**. G-7 ministerial meetings, often preceded by consultations shrouded in secrecy, have in turn fuelled speculation of divisions over the co-ordination of economic and fiscal policies.

G-8

The Group of Eight, currently comprising only seven **Latin American** debtor countries. The G-8 was founded in 1987 by Argentina, Brazil, Colombia, Mexico, Peru, Uruguay, Venezuela and Panama to present a joint response on debt to international creditors. Panama was expelled from the group in 1990.

G-10

The Group of 10 leading industrialized countries. Formally established in 1962, the group now has 11 members – Belgium, Canada, France, Germany, Italy, Japan, the Netherlands, Sweden, the UK, the USA and Switzerland, previously an associate member. In 1962 the group agreed to lend funds in their own currencies to the **IMF** under the **GAB**. G-10 ministers and central bank governors meet regularly to discuss international monetary issues.

G-15

The Group of 15 developing countries which came together in 1989 as a result of an initiative from the former Tanzanian leader Julius Nyerere. The group meets annually to further **South-South** consultation and co-operation. Its members are Algeria, Argentina, Brazil, Chile, Egypt, India, Indonesia, Jamaica, **Malaysia**, Mexico, Nigeria, Peru, Senegal, Venezuela and **Zimbabwe**.

G-24

The Group of 24. The term is used within the **IMF** to refer to the group set up to represent the interests of developing countries. Confusingly, 24 was also the number of member countries of the **OECD** (until Mexico joined in 1994) and the term Group of 24 was used for these countries in the early 1990s in respect of an initiative co-ordinated by the **EC** to raise funds to help build market economies in former **communist** countries.

G-77

The Group of 77, a caucus representing developing countries of the **Third World** which emerged during the first meeting of **UNCTAD** in 1964 and was formally consolidated in 1967. The group retained its name despite its a rise in membership from

77 to 130 by 1992. It played a key role in the early years of **North-South** dialogue but gradually lost influence. Negotiations with developed countries in the 1970s often proved acrimonious, as the G-77 frequently criticized **Western** market values and emphasized the need for a new international economic order (**NIEO**) more favourable to developing countries. The group's importance has been further diminished by a trend towards bilateral and regional negotiations.

GAB

The General Arrangements to Borrow of the **IMF**. These arrangements were originally concluded in 1962 by the **G-10** countries to provide additional resources which the Fund could call upon to forestall or cope with a difficulty in the international monetary system. Switzerland, which had become associated with the GAB in 1964, became a formal member in 1983. The GAB arrangements were extended for successive five-year periods. By the early 1990s the total of credit which they made available to the Fund amounted to the equivalent of **SDR** 17,000 million (around $24,000 million).

GABCIKOVO

The site in southern **Slovakia** of a controversial hydro-electric dam on the River Danube, which at that point forms the Hungarian-Slovak border; the Hungarian portion of the dam complex was constructed at Nagymaros. It was originally conceived in 1977 as a joint project between Hungary and **Czechoslovakia**. By 1989 Hungary had pulled out, on economic, ecological and domestic grounds, but Czechoslovakia (and later Slovakia) chose to complete its part of the project, which had become a symbol of national pride. The main loser in Slovakia was the **Magyar** (Hungarian) community, which had historically lived on land due to be partially inundated by dammed water.

GAELTACHT

The Irish-speaking (or Gaelic-speaking) districts of the Republic of Ireland, confined to the west coast, where Gaelic is the first official language, although even there it is spoken by only about a quarter of the population and English (the second official language) is more widely used.

GAIA

The Greek goddess of the Earth, and hence a potent image underpinning the ecological movement. The 'Gaia hypothesis' as expounded in James Lovelock's 1979 book *Gaia: A New Look at Life on Earth* sees all living things as part of a whole rather than as subordinate to humankind. Lovelock states that the Earth is 'a single system made and managed to their own convenience by living organisms', and argues for a biocentric view which respects all living things, including the human race, as parts of a single complex system.

GAL

(Spanish acronym for *Grupo Anti-terrorista de Liberación* – 'Anti-terrorist Liberation Group') The extreme **right-wing** group which murdered a number of **ETA** members and other Basque militants in France and Spain from 1983 onwards. GAL was thought to have links with the clandestine right-wing French **OAS** and to have co-operated with the Spanish police against ETA.

GANG OF FOUR

1. The four radical Chinese leaders whose arrest in October 1976 marked the end of the period of **Cultural Revolution**. They were Zhang Chunqiao, Yao Wenyuan, Wang Hongwen, and Jiang Qing (the wife of Mao Zedong). Their arrests, on charges of plotting to seize power, came after the death of Mao on 9 September 1976. On 16–21 July 1977 a plenary session of the Chinese **Communist** Party central committee expelled them from the party as 'bourgeois careerist conspirators and counter-revolutionary double-dealers'. After their arrest, a campaign against their followers was launched and they were criticized for wrong policies during the cultural revolution and for impeding modernization. Following their conviction in January 1981 Zhang and Jiang received death sentences, later commuted to life imprisonment, while Wang was sentenced to life imprisonment and Yao to 20 years.

2. The term was popularly applied in the UK to the four signatories of the January 1981 **Limehouse Declaration** establishing the forerunner of the Social Democratic Party.

GARIMPEIROS

(Portuguese, 'gold miners') Independent Brazilian river gold prospectors operating illegally in Brazilian and Venezuelan Amazon regions who threaten the environment and indigenous populations. Part of a massive **diaspora** of urban unemployed, their metal extraction methods from the early 1980s, involving the use of mercury and large motorized suction hoses, have resulted in poisoned or dried-up rivers, deforestation and eradication of soil and vegetation. Yanomami Indians have been particular victims of their activity, succumbing to diseases and facing brutality and murder by gold panners. The Venezuelan government bombed illegal *garimpeiro* airstrips in April 1994.

GASTARBEITER

(German, 'Guest worker') An immigrant worker in Germany. During West Germany's **economic miracle** in the 1960s and 1970s the government recruited *gastarbeiter* in large numbers from Turkey and southern European countries. Recruitment from outside the **EC** was halted after 1973. *Gastarbeiter* and their families number over 4 million (over 1.6 million of them Turkish) and although many are now second generation they tend to be poorly integrated into German society and are sometimes victims of **racist** attack by **neo-Nazi** groups. The number of applications for naturalization from *Gastarbeiter* is small, particularly because dual nationality is not permitted. They do not have voting rights, and their children born in Germany do not automatically have German citizenship.

GATT

The General Agreement on Tariffs and Trade – the international organization within the **UN** framework which is supposed to improve the conditions of international trade, through the reduction of tariffs and similar barriers and through the elimination of discriminatory trading practices. GATT was established effective 1 January 1948 after a proposed International Trade Organization had failed to secure the necessary backing. It operates in various ways. It encourages **MFN** (most-favoured-nation) treatment and the elimination of a range of potentially discriminatory measures; it examines trade disputes between member countries; it reviews the trading policies of individual member countries; and it has held a series of major global multilateral trade negotiations such as the **Kennedy Round**, the **Tokyo Round** and the **Uruguay Round**. At the conclusion of the Uruguay Round, in December 1993, the participants agreed to establish a World Trade Organization encompassing GATT itself.

GAULLISM

The political credo of Gen. Charles de Gaulle, which continues to weigh heavily in French conservative domestic and foreign policy. De Gaulle's vision of a strong state, which would embody the unity of the nation rather than mediate between competing interest groups, is reflected in the constitutional structure of the Fifth Republic (inaugurated in 1958), with a powerful president whose mandate depends on direct popular election, and who may have recourse to a referendum to validate a new policy. In external affairs, de Gaulle promoted the idea of a strong and independent France, which would form equal alliances but not depend upon the protection of the USA; hence the independent French nuclear deterrent or **force de frappe** and France's withdrawal from **NATO** military structures in 1966. The Gaullist conception of European integration was to build a confederation of sovereign states, *l'Europe des patries*, in which France's influence would be strong, as a counterbalance to the two **superpowers**. Although de Gaulle himself resigned in April 1969, Gaullist parties remain a feature on the right of the political spectrum; currently the main Gaullist party is the *Rassemblement pour la République* (RPR), formed in December 1976 and led by Jacques Chirac.

GAY PRIDE TRUST

A UK voluntary organization which organizes events to celebrate the pride of homosexual men and women in their sexuality, principally the Lesbian and Gay Pride March and Festival which takes place in London in June of each year. The history of the Trust goes back to 1972 when the first Gay Pride March was held.

GAZA-JERICHO FIRST

The peace agreement signed by **Israel** and the **PLO** in September 1993. The agreement, or declaration of principles (DOP), signed after months of secret negotiations, provided for an Israeli withdrawal from the occupied **Gaza Strip** and the **West Bank** town of Jericho and the handover of the two areas to full Palestinian authority. After months of complex negotiation, Israel finally withdrew from the Gaza-Jericho area in May 1994. It was envisaged that the remainder of the West Bank would be handed over to Palestinian control following elections to a Palestinian authority scheduled for late 1994; 'permanent status' negotiations between Israel and the PLO would be completed by mid-April 1999.

While the world greeted 'Gaza-Jericho First' as a major breakthrough, opposition to it was widespread, ranging from the Israeli right to **Hamas** and other adherents to the so-called **rejectionist** wing of the Palestinian movement. The agreement was also greeted with alarm by Arab states involved in negotiations with Israel, especially Syria which did little to hide its aversion to the agreement.

GAZA STRIP

A 146 square mile (378 sq km) area of land bordering the Mediterranean Sea captured by **Israel** from Egypt during the 1967 **Six Day War**. The capture of the Strip placed an additional 300,000 Palestinians under Israeli administration. During the late 1980s the Palestinian uprising or **intifada** was centred in Gaza and the radical Islamic **Hamas** movement drew most of its support from the area. An agreement signed by the **PLO** and Israel in September 1993 (widely known as **Gaza-Jericho First**) provided for an Israeli withdrawal from Gaza and from the **West Bank** town of Jericho and the handover of the two areas to full Palestinian authority; negotiations on the final status of the **Israeli-occupied territories** would follow. After months of negotiations on the technicalities of the agreement Israeli forces withdrew from all of Gaza (except Jewish **settlements** in the Strip) on 18 May 1994 and a Palestinian administration took control of the area.

GCC

The Gulf Co-operation Council, a regional organization founded in 1981 with the aim of furthering co-operation between the six member states (Bahrain, Kuwait, **Oman**, Qatar, Saudi Arabia and the **UAE**) in economic, cultural and social affairs. In the aftermath of Iraq's 1990-1 invasion of Kuwait, the GCC has placed greater emphasis on defence co-operation. A GCC military committee was established in early 1994 with the aim of, among other things, strengthening the Peninsular Shield Force, the organization's Saudi-based rapid deployment force.

GCHQ

The Government Communications Headquarters, part of the UK intelligence machinery which provides government departments and military commands with signals intelligence. Established in 1946 as the successor to the Government Code and Cipher School, it was officially acknowledged as an intelligence service in 1983, and placed on a statutory basis in 1994. Controversy over GCHQ arose in January 1984 when the Thatcher government announced that employees there were to be forbidden to belong to trade unions; the handful of employees who refused to observe this instruction were eventually dismissed in 1988–9.

GDANSK SHIPYARD

The Lenin shipyard in Gdansk, a Polish seaport on the Baltic coast, which was the site of significant labour unrest in the 1970s and 1980s, and a base for opposition to the **communist** government. A demonstration at the shipyard against price rises in December 1970 prompted a wave of strikes in the Baltic area which led to the replacement of Poland's hardline leader, Wladslaw Gomulka. In August 1980 a strike led by sacked shipyard worker Lech Walesa (the future President) won the right to organize free trade unions in Gdansk, which thus became the birthplace of **Solidarity**.

GDP

Gross domestic product, one of the two common measures of the size of a national economy. GDP is an aggregate measure of economic activity. It represents the value of all goods and services produced domestically. However, it excludes net property income from abroad, which is included in **GNP**. It may be measured in terms either of constant factor cost or of market prices.

GDR *see* DDR

GENERAL AGREEMENT ON TARIFFS AND TRADE *see* GATT

GENERAL ARRANGEMENTS TO BORROW *see* GAB

GENERAL ASSEMBLY *see* UN GENERAL ASSEMBLY

GENERALIZED SYSTEM OF PREFERENCES *see* GSP

GENERATION OF 58

The Venezuelan **left-wing** politicians nurtured on the 1958 popular uprising, many of whom were important leaders in the 1962–9 **guerrilla** war.

GENETIC FINGERPRINTING

The recording of characteristics of the **DNA** of an individual. The use of the procedure for forensic purposes has increased dramatically in recent years. Only a tiny sample of blood, semen or any body tissue is required to establish identification, and genetic fingerprinting evidence has been used extensively. In the USA Timothy Spencer, a serial killer, was the first person to be convicted on the basis of such evidence. He was executed in Virginia on 27 April 1994.

GENEVA AGREEMENTS

A series of declarations adopted on 20 July 1954 with the aim of 'restoring peace in **Indo-China**'. An international conference on Indo-China had opened in Geneva immediately after the French defeat at **Dien Bien Phu** in early May. The main declaration (tacitly adopted, but not signed, by all the attending nations except the USA) temporarily divided Vietnam into two zones, the North being controlled by Ho Chi Minh's government and the South by the Bao Dai regime, but provided that the country be reunited following the holding of nationwide general elections in 1956. Both China and the **Soviet Union** had exerted considerable pressure on the North to accept temporary partition as the only realistic means of removing the French and blocking the entry into Indo-China of the USA. For its part, the USA issued a unilateral declaration in which it agreed to abide by ceasefire agreements signed in respect of Vietnam, Laos and Cambodia on 21 July.

Under the terms of the agreement the **Pathet Lao**, the Laotian **communists**, were provided with 'regroupment areas' in the northeast of the country. The Cambodian communists were not allotted such areas, leading to subsequent accusations among Khmer revolutionaries that they had been betrayed at Geneva by North Vietnam or China.

GENEVA CONVENTIONS

The body of international humanitarian laws adopted in Geneva on 12 August 1949, and endorsed by the **UN**, which are intended to protect and assist war victims. The four conventions relate to the protection of wounded and sick armed forces and medical personnel; the protection of the same category of people at sea, as well as those shipwrecked; the treatment of prisoners of war; and the protection of civilians in time of war. Two additional protocols to the conventions adopted on 8 June 1977 relate to the protection of victims of international armed conflict and victims of civil wars. As at 1 August 1993 there were 181 states party to the Geneva Conventions, 126 party to Protocol I, and 117 party to Protocol II.

GENEVA SUMMIT 1955

A summit meeting in July between the **Soviet Union** and the three main **Western Allies**, and the first real occasion on which the respective leaders (including Bulganin and Khrushchev on the Soviet side) had come together to make declaratory statements about ending the **Cold War** since Stalin's death in March 1953. Substantive discussions between foreign ministers, however, achieved nothing, and the **thaw** ended the following year with the Soviet suppression of the **Hungarian uprising**.

GENEVA SUMMIT 1985

The first of a series of bilateral **superpower** summit meetings in the second half of the 1980s, involving Mikhail Gorbachev on the Soviet side and Ronald Reagan and then George Bush on the US side, and usually their respective foreign and defence ministers and advisers. Although little of substance was agreed at Geneva in November 1985, the meeting marked the beginning of a new phase of **detente**.

GENOCIDE

The deliberate extermination of a whole people, race or nation, often motivated by theories about the superiority of a particular race. The term is most widely used to refer to the Nazi 'final solution' which set out to destroy the Jews in the **Holocaust**. In 1948, the **UN General Assembly** classified genocide as a crime.

GENSEC

Abbreviation of 'general secretary', usually of the **Communist** Party of the **Soviet Union**. In the Soviet system, such was the pre-eminence of the party, and so intertwined were party and state, that the Gensec was the country's de facto leader even when there was a separate head of state.

GEORGIA

One of the republics which became independent with the collapse of the **Soviet Union** in 1991. Located in the **Transcaucasus**, Georgia had been incorporated into the Russian empire in the early nineteenth century, and came under Soviet control after a brief period of independence in 1918–21.

Georgia has been in a state of civil war since its first President, the nationalist Zviad Gamsakhurdia, was ousted in January 1992. Gamsakhurdia committed suicide in December 1993 following a failed bid to return to power. In a second conflict Georgian government troops were defeated in September 1993 by separatist rebels from the northern region of **Abkhazia**. Georgia, which faces a chronic economic crisis and a breakdown of law and order, was forced to seek Russian assistance by joining the **CIS** in December 1993.

GERBIL

The Great Education Reform Bill, the generally pejorative title attributed in the UK to the Education Reform Act 1988. This wide-ranging legislation, relating to England and Wales, in particular introduced the **national curriculum**, provided for the grant-maintained schools which have opted out of local education authority control, devolved budgetary control to individual schools, and established city technology colleges.

GERRYMANDER

The manipulation of electoral constituency boundaries to include or exclude groups of votes according to the interests of a particular party or candidate. The portmanteau word comes from combining the name of Massachusetts Governor Elbridge Gerry (1744–1814) and the word 'salamander', because the 1811 gerrymandered map of Massachusetts was thought to resemble a salamander.

GHANA

The country in West Africa which was the first to become independent from British rule, in March 1957. Formerly known as the Gold Coast, it had been declared a Crown Colony in 1874 after years of informal British rule.

GILBERT ISLANDS *see* KIRIBATI

GLADIO

(Latin, 'sword') A secret Italian anti-**communist** formation set up after the Second World War, which was involved in carrying out terrorist activities to provoke and justify more repressive security measures. A 16-month Italian parliamentary investigation ending on 29 January 1992 alleged that Gladio had been backed by **NATO**, described it as an illegal 'armed band', and claimed that it had been involved in the 'strategy of tension' of the 1970s, when **right-wing** groups such as **P-2** and members of the security forces were engaging in terrorism in order to strengthen support for authoritarian right-wing government. The then Italian President, Francesco Cossiga, admitted on 13 January 1992 that he had been involved in an anti-communist paramilitary force formed in 1948, and said that 'everyone then and now knew about Gladio's activities.'

GLASNOST

(Russian, 'openness') The slogan adopted by Soviet leader Mikhail Gorbachev in 1985 to cover a package of political reforms improving freedom of speech and information. After the **Chernobyl** disaster of April 1986, which was poorly reported, *glasnost* became more radical, featuring a critical reappraisal of the past, including revelations of repression under Stalin; the toleration of press criticism; the publication of long-banned 'subversive' works of literature; and the release of dissidents such as Andrei Sakharov. Glasnost was accompanied by the policy of **perestroika**.

GLASS CEILING

A metaphor for the invisible barriers to personal progress encountered particularly by women and members of ethnic minorities. The term, which implies the existence of ingrained prejudices, is employed to explain why, despite equal opportunities legislation, proportionally very few members of such disadvantaged groups occupy leadership positions. The use of **affirmative action** is advocated as a means of breaking through the glass ceiling.

GLENEAGLES AGREEMENT

The 1977 decision by **Commonwealth** Heads of Government to ban official sporting links with South Africa until the dismantling of **apartheid**. The Agreement, named after the venue of the meeting (the Gleneagles Golf Club in Scotland), was part of the **sanctions** programme launched against the South African apartheid regime.

GLOBAL 2000

The study aiming to predict conditions of life in the years before the millennium, which was commissioned by US President Jimmy Carter in 1977, and the independent environmental centre established as a result of its findings. The study, *The Global Report to the President*, which was completed in 1980, found that pollution, overcrowding, and poverty were likely to grow before the year 2000, in which it followed other studies such as **Limits to Growth**. Carter's successor as US President, Ronald Reagan, took no action on the study; Carter, however, established the independent Global 2000 project in order to implement some of the report's recommendations.

GLOBAL PROTECTION AGAINST LIMITED STRIKES *see* GPALS

GLOBAL WARMING

The progressive gradual rise of the earth's surface temperature thought to be being brought about by the **greenhouse effect** and to be responsible for changes in global climate patterns. Some researchers warn of apocalyptic consequences for human civilization if global warming is not brought under control; its effects seem to include such phenomena as an increase in the frequency and severity of storms, rising sea levels and changes in temperature and rainfall affecting agriculture. A long-term project to determine global temperature by taking underground measurements found a total rise of 0.041° C in average temperature between 1963 and 1990. The second World Climate Conference held in Geneva on 5-7 November 1990 recognized global warming as a reality, despite the continuing scepticism of some scientists. Debates at the **Earth Summit** addressed ways to control as well as respond to global warming, and over 160 countries signed the Framework Convention on Climate Change aimed at reducing emissions of **greenhouse gases**.

GNP

Gross national product, one of the two common measures of the size of a country's economy. GNP is a measure of economic output which includes certain components not covered by **GDP**. It may be measured equally from the supply side or from the demand side. GNP is widely employed as an international basis of comparison. It has also been used as a base for the calculation of the target of 0.7 per cent of income which developed countries were urged to devote to overseas aid, as set out in the report of the **Pearson Commission** in 1969. The corresponding, but not identical, measurement for **communist** countries was **NMP**.

GOLAN HEIGHTS

A strategically important range of hills in south-western Syria and point of Arab-Israeli conflict and dispute. In the **Six-Day War** of 1967, **Israel** captured the Golan Heights from Syria. Previous to this, Syrian forces had been able to use the territory to bombard Israeli **settlements** in the valleys below. In 1981, in the face of strong **UN** condemnation, the Golan Heights were effectively annexed under an Israeli government decree which extended Israeli 'law, jurisdiction and administration' to the territory. Syrian-Israeli peace talks, under way since 1991, have focused on the Golan Heights.

GOLD COAST *see* GHANA

GOLD STANDARD

A monetary convention, now obsolete, whereby a currency's value is denominated in terms of a given weight of gold. From January 1934 until the **Smithsonian agreement** of December 1971 the US dollar's value was defined as being $35 per fine ounce of gold. This value was changed to $38 at the end of 1971, and to $42.22 in 1972. Meanwhile, the dollar's actual convertibility into gold had been suspended, in August 1971. Parities of the currencies of other **IMF** countries, also originally defined in terms of gold or of the US dollar, were gradually delinked from the gold/dollar standard as a result of the monetary turmoil in the 1970s, and there was a switch to defining currencies in terms of the IMF **SDR**, based on the value of a 'basket of currencies'. From the end of 1980 the value of the SDR itself was formally delinked from gold (this link having effectively been discontinued in 1974). Gold thereafter became purely a commodity, whose price fluctuates according to market conditions.

GOLDEN TEMPLE

One of the most sacred Sikh shrines, in Amritsar in the Indian state of Punjab. The temple was the scene of violent clashes in 1984 between members of the militant Sikh **Akali Dal** and Indian troops. Sikh militants were attempting to use the temple as a sanctuary while pursuing an often violent campaign for greater political and religious autonomy for the Punjab, and for constitutional recognition of the Sikh religion as fully distinct from Hinduism. The Indian army stormed the temple on the night of 5–6 June, occupying it until the end of September. Operations were launched simultaneously against 37 other Sikh shrines throughout Punjab. According to official figures, 493 'terrorists' and civilians and 92 soldiers were killed in the ensuing violence; unofficial figures were much higher, suggesting that around 1,000 militants and 250 soldiers died. The Golden Temple itself also sustained considerable damage. The assault sparked protests in other parts of India and desertions by Sikhs from army units. In Punjab itself it unleased further violence and hardened demands for a Sikh homeland, **Khalistan**. The storming of the temple is widely considered to be the motive behind the assassination on 31 October 1984 of Prime Minister Indira Gandhi who had sanctioned the assault. She was killed by two Sikh members of her bodyguard.

GOLDEN TRIANGLE

A roughly triangular area of **south-east Asia**, comprising parts of Burma, Thailand

and Laos, which has long been the source of most of the world's raw opium. The illegal profits to be made from the opium once refined into heroin are immense. For a number of years self-proclaimed Shan nationalist Khun Sa has been the commanding force in the region despite periodic challenges from rival 'drug warlords', the Burmese military and the US Drug Enforcement Administration.

GOLKAR

The *Golongan Karya Pusat* or Functional Group Centre, the ruling political organization in Indonesia since 1971. Technically, Golkar is not a political party but an amalgamation of occupational groups, ranging from farmers to security personnel (traditional political parties being regarded as socially divisive and potentially dangerous under Gen. Suharto's **New Order** regime). However, in reality, Golkar has been used by Suharto and the armed forces as a means of establishing a civilian basis for the regime.

GOP

The widely used abbreviation of Grand Old Party, an informal term referring to the US Republican Party. Originating from the Northern anti-slavery movement, the party was founded in 1854 and its candidate, Abraham Lincoln, won the presidential election of 1860. Between 1860 and 1932 it won 15 of the 19 presidential contests; more recently, it held the **White House** in 1953–61; 1969–77; and 1981–93. Mainstream US politics are dominated by the GOP and the Democratic Party, which was founded in 1800 and tends to be more liberal.

GORBYMANIA

The popular enthusiasm in the **West** for Mikhail Gorbachev, the Soviet leader from 1985 to 1991, who was widely credited with ending the **Cold War**, allowing the overthrow of communism in **Eastern Europe** in 1989, and abolishing dictatorship in the **Soviet Union**. Large crowds turned out to welcome Gorbachev during his visits to the West, particularly in 1989. In 1990 Gorbachev was awarded the **Nobel Prize** for peace. Gorbymania subsided after his resignation in December 1991, and his patent unpopularity in Russia denied him the opportunity to revive his political career.

GOSPLAN

The **Soviet Union's** State Planning Committee established in 1921 'to work out a single state economic plan and methods and means of implementing it'. Gosplan was the driving force behind the **command economy** and the author of the **five-year plans**. Gosplan's early emphasis on balanced economic development gave way to a strong bias toward heavy industry, in accordance with the emerging orthodoxy of **Stalinism**.

GOULASH SOCIALISM

A colloquial term for **communist** Hungary's relatively liberal policies introduced under the **NEM** in the late 1960s, which were designed to secure political stability through economic prosperity. Although goulash socialism featured a relative tolerance of dissent, the leading role of the communist party remained unchallenged.

GOVERNMENT COMMUNICATIONS HEADQUARTERS *see* GCHQ

GPALS

Global Protection Against Limited Strikes, an idea discussed in 1991 as a joint US and Soviet missile defence programme. It envisaged using ground- and space-based elements, as had the highly controversial US **Star Wars** concept. GPALS, however, was intended to reflect the post-**Cold War** common interest of the USA and the (fast disintegrating) **Soviet Union**, in reducing the potency of the nuclear threat from 'renegade' **Third World** countries.

GRAMM-RUDMAN-HOLLINGS

Popular name for the Balanced Budget and Emergency Deficit Control Act, enacted in the USA in 1985 (and amended in 1987). The bill's chief sponsors were senators Phil Gramm, Warren Rudman, and Ernest F.

Hollings. It was passed in response to the frustration of the spiralling federal budget deficit, and provided for a series of targets which would have eliminated the deficit by 1993. In the event of **Congress** and the president being unable to agree upon a budget to meet these targets, automatic cuts were designed to come into operation. Although draconian on paper, the act proved easy to evade and did little to reduce the growing deficit. It was superseded in 1991 by a new budget agreement between president and Congress.

GRAND COALITION

The coalition which governed West Germany (the **BRD**) from December 1966 to October 1969. The Christian Democrats, in government since the creation of the BRD in 1949, formed a coalition for the first (and only) time with what was hitherto the main opposition, Willy Brandt's Social Democratic Party (SPD). This was a major factor in channelling anti-government feeling into the *Ausserparlamentärische opposition* (**APO**), since the only parliamentary opposition was the small centrist Free Democratic Party (FDP).

GRAND JURY

The US investigative mechanism whereby a jury assesses the case against an individual who has been arrested, in order to determine whether there is sufficient evidence to justify the holding of a trial.

GRANMA

The small yacht which carried Fidel Castro, Ernesto 'Che' Guevara and 80 armed **guerrillas** from Mexico to Cuba on 25 November–2 December 1956 and is now an enduring symbol of the Cuban revolution. The yacht itself was restored and is on public display in the grounds of the Museum of the Revolution, in the capital, Havana. *Granma* is also the name of the official newspaper of the Cuban **Communist** Party.

GRAPO

(Spanish acronym of name of October 1 Anti-Fascist Resistance Group) A Spanish **left-wing** urban **guerrilla** group. GRAPO was set up in 1975 as the armed wing of the Marxist-Leninist Organization of Spain (OMLE), a hardline **Stalinist** group opposed to **Eurocommunism**. Its name refers to the killing of four policeman on 1 October 1975, shortly before the end of the Franco era. It subsequently grabbed headlines for dozens of terrorist attacks on military and police personnel and industrialists and for kidnappings, including a Francoist member of the **Cortes generales**. The government claimed in the mid-1980s to have captured all known members, but the group remained sporadically active; two of its leaders were killed during an armed robbery in April 1993.

GRASSY KNOLL

A term which refers to the location of an alleged second gunman in the assassination of President John F. Kennedy in Dallas on 22 November 1963. Whereas the official conclusion was that a single assassin, Lee Harvey Oswald, had fired three shots from the sixth floor of the Texas School Book Depository, to the rear of the President's motorcade, there is strong evidence that shots were also fired from a grassy knoll situated ahead and to the right of the presidential car. Many critics of the findings of the **Warren Commission** have also maintained that a third gunman may have fired from a triple underpass directly ahead of the President's car, thereby setting up a lethal triangular field of fire.

GREAT BRITAIN

The union of England, Wales and Scotland. Great Britain was formed as a result of the 1707 Act of Union when England and Scotland were united, although the crowns of the two countries had already been united in the person of the monarch in 1603, when James VI of Scotland became also James I of England. England and Wales on the one hand and Scotland on the other have separate legal systems, and legislation passed by Parliament may relate to England and Wales, to Scotland or to all three territories, or to the whole of the **United Kingdom**, including **Northern Ireland**. The term **Britain** is frequently used loosely to denote the United Kingdom as the sovereign state.

GREAT LEADER

A term used extensively in North Korea to refer to Kim Il Sung, the President of the Democratic People's Republic of Korea (North Korea) until his death in July 1994. Although he became President in 1970, his real power base was always his position as General Secretary of the ruling Korean Workers' Party (KWP). Like his son and chosen successor, the **Dear Leader**, he was also a member of the party's three-member Presidium. The Great Leader was the author of **Juche**, an individual ideology derived from Marxism-Leninism which emphasizes self-reliance and the dominance of the party. He was also the object of a bizarre personality cult unparalleled within the modern world, whereby his leadership was presented as being infallible and his influence all-embracing.

GREAT LEAP FORWARD

The ill-fated attempt by the Chinese **Communist** Party (CCP), under Mao Zedong, to accelerate industrialization and, thereby, the achievement of socialism. The 1958 policy aimed to increase economic output, principally through the mobilization of labour. 'People's communes' were formed in both the agricultural and industrial sectors, and some 2 million 'backyard furnaces' were established in a largely futile attempt to increase the production of steel. The policy was a disaster and, compounded by the withdrawal of Soviet aid in 1960 because of the **Sino-Soviet split** and poor weather in 1959–61, resulted in the deaths of some 20 million people from starvation. Modernizers in the CCP, including Deng Xiaoping and Zhou Enlai, attempted to rectify the situation by permitting the cultivation of private plots and the development of a limited market in rural areas. The failure of the policy lost Mao much influence within the CCP, but he returned to prominence in 1966 with the unleashing of the **Cultural Revolution**, a phenomenon fuelled partly by his fears that the modernisers' economic policies could lead to the restoration of **capitalism**.

GREAT SATAN

A term to describe the USA coined by the late Iranian leader, Ayatollah Ruhollah Khomeini, when it gained currency following the **Islamic revolution** in February 1979. The USA was seen as the source of evil and the root cause of Iran's disavowal of Islam under the last Iranian Shah (king), Mohammad Reza Pahlavi, and its support for the Shah's 'godless' regime and its opposition to the current Islamic government are regarded by the Iranian clerical establishment as continuing proof of the USA's 'satanic' ends.

GREAT SOCIETY

The phrase used by US President Lyndon B. Johnson to describe the type of caring society which he aimed to create. The 'great society' vision, first outlined in a speech at Ann Arbor, Michigan, on 22 May 1964, was seen as including 'abundance and liberty for all' and demanding the elimination of 'poverty and racial injustice'. Despite the increasing preoccupation with US involvement in the **Vietnam War**, Johnson's period in office did see major steps forward in **civil rights** legislation and welfare provisions.

GREATER SERBIA

The Serb nationalist goal of creating an enlarged republic of Serbia from territory in the former **Yugoslavia**. Serb nationalists nurse a deep-seated sense of injustice as a result of humiliating defeats in their history, most recently at the hands of the Croatian **Ustasa** regime and earlier by the Ottoman Empire. Serb nationalists now identify Croats, **Bosnian Muslims** and Albanians as their historic enemies, and thus argue for the forcible seizure of 'historically Serb' land from **Croatia**, **Bosnia-Hercegovina**, and **Macedonia**.

GREEN

A party, or a party member or supporter, committed to **environmentalist** issues in a political context. The term green was first applied to the environmentalist lobby in Europe in the 1970s, particularly to West German activists who were mainly concerned with anti-nuclear campaigning and drew up '*grune Listen*' (green lists) of pro-environmentalist election candidates. In 1979 the West German greens formed their own national party, which won seats in the federal parliament for the first time in 1983. In the 1989 elections to the European Parliament, Green parties in Belgium, France, West Germany, Italy and the Netherlands all won seats. The term green is also applied as a qualifying adjective to personal behaviour which attempts to minimize the impact of an industrialized society on the environment, as for example, in **green consumerism**.

GREEN BOOK

The three-volume tome expounding the political philosophy of Col. Moamer al Kadhafi, the Libyan 'revolutionary leader'. In the Green Book, published between 1976 and 1979, Kadhafi developed his revolutionary philosophy, the 'Third Universal Theory' – a mix of Islam, Arabism, popular socialism and traditional Bedouin wisdom.

GREEN CARD

The permit issued by the US authorities which grants non-US citizens various rights, chiefly that of being able to engage in legal employment. Green Cards can be very difficult to obtain and are highly sought after, particularly by illegal immigrants.

GREEN CONSUMERISM

The incipient trend among the public in developed countries to purchase **environmentally friendly** brands of products, and to be more conscious of the effects of a consumer society on the environment. Schemes such as **eco-labelling** are government-backed measures to promote green consumerism.

GREEN LINE

The boundary dividing Cyprus between the Greek Cypriot and Turkish-occupied areas since the 1974 Turkish invasion, when the power-sharing arrangement brokered in 1959 between the two ethnic communities completely collapsed. North of the line Turkish Cypriots established the internationally unrecognized **TRNC**; over 40,000 Turkish Cypriots fled there while some 180,000 Greek Cypriots fled south.

GREEN MARCH

The peaceful entry of some 350,000 unarmed Moroccans into the **Western Sahara** in 1975 in an effort to legitimize Moroccan claims on the territory.

GREEN PAPER

A consultative document issued by the UK government. A Green Paper generally sets out policy proposals, often including alternative courses of action, on which representations and expressions of view are invited. As appropriate, such a document may be followed after the end of the consultation period by a **White Paper** containing the government's conclusions and firm decisions on legislative or other similar action.

GREEN POUND

The special fixed (rather than fluctuating) valuation of the pound used in determining the prices paid to UK farmers for their agricultural produce under the **CAP**. Each **EU** member country has a corresponding 'green currency'. A further layer of complexity was created by the introduction of 'monetary compensatory amounts', or MCAs, which were applied to agricultural trade between member states so as to preserve the artificial green currency system. A decision to phase out MCAs was part of the 1984 CAP reform agreement.

GREEN REVOLUTION

An enthusiast's term for the changes in methods of agricultural production in the **Third World** wrought by the application of (mainly Western) research and technology. The heyday of the Green Revolution was the 1960s, when particularly dramatic increases in productivity were achieved, notably in India, with agro-chemicals and high-yielding grains. Critics point, however, to a loss of traditional crops, an emphasis on the cash economy and single-crop production to the detriment of subsistence farming, a cycle of diminishing returns from fertilizer and other inputs, and the vulnerability of Third World farmers as regards the availability and price of machinery and agro-chemicals.

GREENHAM COMMON

The site of a US Air Force base in Berkshire, in the UK. With the news that **cruise** missiles would be deployed at the base, the site became the focus of anti-nuclear protests, and in September 1981 a group of women established a permanent peace camp outside the base. Supported by **CND**, their demonstrations included almost daily breaches in the perimeter fences and the constant harassment of military convoys, although the missiles nevertheless arrived on schedule in 1983. The last missiles were removed on 5 March 1991 as a result of the **INF Treaty** between the **superpowers**; the closure of the camp had been announced in 1990.

GREENHOUSE EFFECT

The progressive, gradual warming of the earth's atmospheric temperature, caused by the insulating effect of carbon dioxide and other **greenhouse gases** as their proportion in the atmosphere has increased. The greenhouse effect occurs because greenhouse gases allow short-wave radiation from the sun to penetrate through to warm the earth, but prevent the resulting long-wave radiation from escaping back into the atmosphere, trapping it beneath an insulating gaseous layer. There is concern that the greenhouse effect may have a devastating impact on human civilization in future through rising sea levels, **desertification** and climatic change. In an effort to combat the greenhouse effect, over 160 governments signed a the **World Climate Convention** at the 1992 **Earth Summit**.

GREENHOUSE GASES

Gases which, because of their properties relating to the transmission or reflection of different types of radiation, may raise the earth's atmospheric temperature and thereby contribute to the **greenhouse effect** and **global warming**. Greenhouse gases include the common gases carbon dioxide and water vapour, and also gases such as methane and **CFCs** which are rarer but whose effect is much greater. The increase in such gases in the atmosphere has come about largely because of human activity such as the burning of fossil fuels, the emission of pollutants into the atmosphere, and **deforestation**.

GREENPEACE

One of the first and best-known environmental pressure groups, whose members, now organized internationally with a headquarters in Amsterdam, engage in non-violent action to disrupt environmentally damaging projects. Greenpeace's undertakings, which are backed by scientific research, have been effective in raising public awareness of environmental issues. The group began in 1971 when a group of Canadian and US activists successfully interrupted planned nuclear tests on Amchitka Island, Alaska. Greenpeace's activities often involve a level of personal danger for their participants, as was demonstrated in the **Rainbow Warrior** affair. Among its successes have been campaigns against whaling, seal culling, and dumping nuclear waste at sea.

GREMIALISMO

(from Spanish, *gremio*, 'guild', 'trade union' or 'professional association') A **right-wing corporatist** movement which emerged in Chile in the late 1960s and opposed the **left-wing** Popular Unity (UP) government of 1970–3; truck owners in particular fomented an atmosphere of instability, leading to the 1973 military coup.

GRENADA INVASION *see* OPERATION URGENT FURY

GREY PANTHERS

A US pressure group organized to promote the interests of the elderly and retired, which has become increasingly powerful since the late 1970s. The name was derived (humorously) from the **Black Panthers**.

GROSVENOR SQUARE

The site of the US embassy in London and the venue of a mass demonstration against the **Vietnam War** on 27 October 1968. Although the actions of the 30,000 protestors did not compare with the revolutionary activity seen on the streets of Paris in **1968**, the demonstration was a strong indication of local popular disapproval of US policy in Vietnam.

GROUP AREAS ACT

One of the cornerstones of **apartheid** which divided South Africa into separate 'group areas' where Whites, **Coloureds** and Indians could live and work. Africans fell outside its scope. Under the Group Areas Act, passed in 1950 and repeatedly amended, Coloureds and Indians were forcibly 'removed' from their homes; 834,000 people were 'removed' between 1960 and 1982. As with other aspects of apartheid, white dominance was evident in the unequal distribution of land. By far the greater part of the land was assigned to the white population, while Coloureds and Indians had only very limited access to agricultural land and were restricted to relatively small urban areas allocated under the Act for residential and business purposes. Under separate legislation beginning with the 1913 Native Land Act, Africans were allocated just 13 per cent of the land which eventually evolved into **bantustans**. The Group Areas Act, the Native Land Act and all other discriminatory land measures were repealed in June 1991.

GROUP OF THREE *see* G-3

GROUP OF FIVE *see* G-5

GROUP OF SEVEN *see* G-7

GROUP OF EIGHT *see* G-8

GROUP OF 10 *see* G-10

GROUP OF 15 *see* G-15

GROUP OF 24 *see* G-24

GROUP OF 77 *see* G-77

GROUP OF RIO

A diplomatic grouping of Spanish-speaking South and Central American countries and Brazil and Mexico. Since its formation at a joint meeting of members of the **Contadora** group and **Lima Group** in Rio de Janeiro, Brazil, on 17–18 December 1986, presidential-level meetings have been held annually to discuss pressing regional issues including foreign debt, drug trafficking and internal conflicts. Panama's membership was suspended in 1988, as was that of Peru following the April 1992 **autogolpe** of President Alberto Fujimori who, nevertheless, was present at the October 1993 summit.

GSP

The generalized system of preferences, formulated by **UNCTAD** in 1970 and introduced by the developed countries in the course of 1972. It involves according non-discriminatory, non-reciprocal tariff preferences to imports from developing countries. In 1993 the USA extended GSP to Russia.

GUAM DOCTRINE *see* NIXON DOCTRINE

GUARDIAN ANGELS

A US volunteer group founded in 1979 to fight crime in New York City. Wearing distinctive red berets, the group provides a high-profile presence on New York's notoriously dangerous subway system as well as on the city's streets. Since its creation it has expanded to 50 cities in 10 countries, and claims a current membership of some 5,000. However, its paramilitary style and harassment of those whom it deems undesirable (such as suspected drug dealers) has led to charges of vigilantism.

GUBU *see* HAUGHEY FACTOR

GUERRILLAS

(Spanish, 'small wars') Small bands of armed insurrectionists carrying out irregular warfare. The term was first used during the Napoleonic Wars in the early nineteenth century to describe the activities of Spanish and Portuguese peasants against the French. It is now most often applied to the armed operations of liberation movements and rebel groups in the **Third**

World. Guerrilla warfare carried out by well trained, motivated guerrillas who enjoy popular support is notoriously difficult to combat, even by large well-equipped armies.

GUEVARISM

A theory of insurrection espoused by Ernesto 'Che' Guevara, most famously in his book *Guerrilla Warfare*. Developed from the experience of the Cuban Revolution and the theory of **foquismo** which sprang from it, it influenced various groups, mostly in **Latin America**, which believed that the Cuban experience could be recreated in any underdeveloped country. Guevara's attempt in 1967 to apply the theory to Bolivian conditions ended in disaster and his murder by the military. Rather than triggering an uprising, as the theory predicted, the nucleus of **guerrillas** received scant support from peasants, suspicious of outsiders, or the local **Communist** Party, jealous of its political role. Although Guevara's death made him a political icon, the theory of Guevarism effectively died with him.

GUIDED DEMOCRACY

Authoritarian and anti-parliamentary system of government introduced by Indonesian President Sukarno in the mid-1950s. With the effective dismantling of the party political system and the introduction of martial law in 1956–7, Sukarno brought to an end a relatively liberal phase of Indonesian politics. Perhaps the most notable aspect of the Guided Democracy period was the extent to which Sukarno's political power was based almost entirely on his populist appeal. His relentless charismatic articulation of a vast array of slogans and concepts (that together came to form the basis of a national–and nationalist–ideology) allowed him to maintain his position at the apex of Indonesia's complex power structure. However, Sukarno's growing support for the **PKI** (the **Communist** Party), and the party's growing influence within **ABRI** (the armed forces), meant that by 1965 the power equilibrium had collapsed; ABRI took control and Sukarno and his Guided Democracy experiment were jettisoned.

GUILDFORD FOUR

A group wrongly imprisoned in the UK for alleged **IRA** activities. Patrick Armstrong, Gerard Conlon, Carole Richardson and Paul Hill were sentenced to life imprisonment in September 1975 for the murder of all or some of the seven victims of the 1974 **IRA** bombing of two public houses in Guildford and one in Woolwich. Campaigns for a review of their case eventually led in October 1989 to their release on appeal, and their convictions were overturned as unsafe and unsatisfactory after new investigations had revealed that misleading evidence had been given at their trial by police officers. Three of these officers were in May 1993 acquitted of conspiring to pervert the course of justice at the 1975 trial. The release of the Guildford Four was followed 15 months later by that of the **Birmingham Six**.

GUILLOTINE

A parliamentary procedure in the UK House of Commons designed to curtail debate. The guillotine takes the form of a 'timetable motion' introduced by the government, laying down a strict schedule for consideration of the different stages of contentious legislation on which the opposition parties have taken, or threaten to take, delaying action. The guillotine procedure does not apply in the House of Lords.

GULAG

(Russian acronym for *Glavnoe Upravlenie Ispravitel'no-trudovykh Lagerei* – Chief Directorate of Labour Camps) The Soviet Union's forced labour camps, established in 1930. Some estimates put the number of camp inmates in the 1940s at over 8 million, of whom 85 per cent were political prisoners. The gulags were often located in the inhospitable arctic or Siberian regions of Russia, and camp conditions were extremely harsh. Although thousands of prisoners falsely accused of political offences were freed in the **de-Stalinization** drive of the mid-1950s, thousands more remained imprisoned until the Gorbachev era. The notoriety of the camps was spread abroad by the work of dissident writer Aleksandr Solzhenitsyn, in particular in *The Gulag Archipelago*.

THE GULF

The Arabian or Persian Gulf, the inlet from the Indian Ocean (through the Gulf of Oman and the Strait of Hormuz) separating Iran and Arabia, and one of the world's crucial shipping lanes, given the existence of vital oilfields in the surrounding land and in the Gulf itself. During the Iran-Iraq War of the 1980s the Gulf was one of the main spheres of battle, with both sides launching attacks on oil tankers and merchant shipping. The Gulf remains a heavily disputed region, with, among other contentious issues, Iran and the **UAE** contesting control of **Abu Musa**.

GULF CONFLICT *see* GULF WAR

GULF CO-OPERATION COUNCIL *see* GCC

GULF CRISIS

A phrase which, in its most common usage, covers the period of confrontation and diplomatic and military manoeuvring between Iraq and a US-led international coalition, which began with the Iraqi invasion of Kuwait on 2 August 1990 and culminated in the 'Gulf conflict' or '(second) **Gulf War**' of January–February 1991.

GULF OF TONGKIN RESOLUTION

The US congressional resolution passed in August 1964 which served as the legal basis for US escalation of its undeclared war against North Vietnam. The resolution, approved with virtually no domestic criticism, authorized US President Lyndon Johnson to 'repel any armed attack against the forces of the USA and to prevent further armed aggression'. The resolution was passed after North Vietnamese patrol boats had allegedly attacked US vessels patrolling in the Gulf of Tongkin, off the North Vietnamese coast. The US government did not reveal that the North Vietnamese attacks on the warships were the direct result of previous clandestine US and South Vietnamese assaults on North Vietnamese targets.

GULF WAR

An alternative name for the protracted and immensely destructive Iran-Iraq war of 1980–90. The same phrase (or the variant 'Gulf conflict') is also used, confusingly, for the major conflict between forces of the US-led coalition (codenamed **Desert Shield**) and Iraqi forces between 16 January and 28 February 1991, in which Iraqi forces were badly defeated and driven out of Kuwait. A careful distinction between the 'first Gulf War' and the 'second Gulf War' is not generally made.

GUN CONTROL

A term used to describe the efforts to place restrictions on the right to buy and carry firearms. In the face of rising rates of murder and violent crime, advocates of gun control in the USA have called for a range of controlling measures, including the imposition of waiting periods and the running of mandatory background checks on those wishing to purchase a gun. Others have called for a revision of the Second Amendment to the US Constitution – which stipulates that 'the right of the people to keep and bear arms shall not be infringed' – on the grounds that the clause was devised by the Founding Fathers as a means of ensuring the existence of 'a well regulated militia', and is now an anachronism. The gun owners' lobby, particularly the powerful **National Rifle Association**, has resisted efforts at gun control, although some restrictions have been imposed in individual states. Bill Clinton has demonstrated a degree of support for gun control unprecedented among US presidents, and in 1993 succeeded in persuading **Congress** to pass the **Brady Bill**, the first significant piece of national gun control legislation enacted since the 1960s.

GYPSIES *see* ROMANIES OF EASTERN EUROPE

H BLOCK

Part of the Maze Prison near in Belfast, **Northern Ireland**, so named because of its H-shaped plan. In the late 1970s and early 1980s a large number of **IRA** prisoners serving sentences for terrorism-related offences staged protests in support of their claim for special political status, by refusing to wear prison clothes and by smearing excrement on the walls of their cells. In late 1980 a group of IRA prisoners went on hunger strike; one of these, Bobby Sands, was elected to the UK House of Commons in April 1981, narrowly defeating his **Unionist** opponent, but died as a result of his hunger strike less than a month later. Two H Block prisoners were elected to the Irish **Dáil** in 1981, although one died shortly after election.

H-BOMB

The hydrogen bomb, the second generation of **nuclear weapons**, whose development, testing and unprecedented menace overshadowed the 1950s. First the USA (on 1 November 1952) and then the **Soviet Union** (in August 1953) tested H-bombs and brought them into their arsenals, giving them (and later the other nuclear powers) a global destructive capacity greatly outweighing even that which they already had with the atom bomb. The H-bomb is a thermonuclear device; its immense power comes from nuclear fusion reactions, which are set off by the heat from an initial nuclear fission.

HABITAT

The **UN** Centre for Human Settlements, which seeks especially to respond to the problems of urban migration in developing countries where about one-third of city dwellers live in slums or shanty towns. By 2025, the UN predicts, urban areas in developing countries will house 46 per cent of the world's population, and another 13 per cent will live in cities in the industrialized countries. Recommendations for the management of human settlements were made at the 1972 UN Conference on the Human Environment in Stockholm, which also led to the establishment of the **Earthwatch** agency.

HAGANAH

(Hebrew, 'defence') The Jewish defence force which operated from 1920 until the creation of **Israel** in 1948 to defend Jewish **settlements** in **Palestine**. Under the British mandate, *Haganah* was banned, and its members frequently clashed with the British as well as the Palestinians. However, *Haganah* generally adopted a policy of moderation and tended to shun the violent terrorist stratagem adopted by **Irgun** and the **Stern Gang**. *Haganah* served as the cornerstone of Israel's armed forces.

HAJ

(Arabic, 'pilgrimage') The canonical pilgrimage to Mecca, Saudi Arabia, which forms one of the five 'pillars' of Islam, the others being *shahadah* (the affirmation of Divine unity); *salah* (daily prayers); *sawm* (fasting in the month of **Ramadan**); and **zakat** (almsgiving). It consists of an elaborate series of rites performed at the Grand Mosque in Mecca and in the immediate environs of the city, at a particular moment of the Islamic year, which, as a lunar calendar, advances some 10 days each year. In recent years the pilgrimage has assumed political significance owing to criticism by radical Muslim regimes of the conservative Saudi government which administers the process.

HALABJA AFFAIR

The incident named after the Kurdish town of Halabja in northern Iraq in which an estimated 6,350 people, mostly civilians, died following a chemical gas attack by the Iraqi army on 17 March 1988. The assault came a day after Iraqi Kurdish forces, with the assistance of Iran, captured the town in an attempt to force the Iraqi government to honour a 1970 agreement granting Kurdish autonomy. Since then Iraqi forces have killed thousands more Iraqi Kurds in what a **UN** report characterized as 'genocide type' operations.

HALLSTEIN DOCTRINE

West Germany's policy in the 1950s and 1960s of severing diplomatic relations with any state which recognized East Germany (the **DDR**), and refusing relations with any **communist** country except for the **Soviet Union**. Named after Walter Hallstein, then State Secretary of the Foreign Ministry, the doctrine was announced on 9 December 1955. It was founded upon the belief that, until the two German states could be united, only the Federal Republic (the **BRD**) enjoyed the democratic legitimacy to represent all Germans. The doctrine was gradually abandoned in the late 1960s, when the new **Ostpolitik** implicitly accepted the DDR as a legitimate entity.

HAMAS

(Arabic, 'zeal'; also the acronym for 'Islamic Resistance Movement') A radical Islamic group operating in **Israeli-occupied territories**. Formally founded in February 1988 by Sheikh Ahmed Ismail Yassin, *Hamas* was arguably the major driving force behind the Palestinian **intifada**, particularly in its heartland, the **Gaza Strip**. The group's avowedly **rejectionist** stance and the success of its armed wing, the *Izz al-Din Qassam* battalions, in striking at Israeli military and civilian targets, have appealed to the sizable minority of Palestinians who opposed the September 1993 **Gaza-Jericho First** peace deal signed by the **PLO** and **Israel**.

HANG SENG INDEX *see* DOW JONES INDEX

HANSARD

The official report of proceedings in the UK Parliament. Originally initiated unofficially in 1803, *Hansard* is now published by Her Majesty's Stationary Office daily during parliamentary sittings, and covers proceedings on the floor of each House of Parliament and (separately) in standing committees. Although widely assumed to be a verbatim account of proceedings, the *Hansard* recorders are given discretion to 'tidy up' Members' spoken English.

HARAMBEE

(Swahili, 'let us pull together') The national slogan adopted by Kenya on independence in 1963 and incorporated in the national coat of arms. One of the main aspects of *harambee* is the concept of self-reliance. At a national level this meant seeking to reduce dependence on foreign aid for development while at a local level it was translated into self-help projects such as water and health schemes.

HARARE DECLARATION

An attempt in 1991 by the heads of government of **Commonwealth** countries to give fresh direction to the organization. The declaration was adopted at the **CHOGM** in Harare, Zimbabwe, on 20 October, following a process of high-level appraisal. It called for the promotion of democracy and the rule of law in member countries. It also underlined a commitment to sustainable economic development and promised to alleviate the debt burdens of the most needy states, but emphasized the need for 'sound economic management' and stressed 'the central role of the market economy'.

HARKIS

Algerian Muslim auxiliary soldiers in the service of the French army during the French occupation of Algeria (1938–62). Some 180,000 Harkis deployed by France subsequently became the targets of the Algerian nationalist movement, the **FLN**. Regarded as collaborators, more than 10,000 were said to have been massacred by their compatriots at independence. There are currently an estimated 800,000 Harkis in France, descendants of former soldiers who arrived after the Algerian war of independence. With the hardening of French anti-immigration opinion in recent years, many Harkis have sought protection by highlighting their special role in support of France.

HARMONIZATION

A bureaucrat's word for making one set of rules compatible with (or identical with) another. The heyday of harmonization in the **EU** (then the **EC**) was the latter part of the 1980s, when hundreds of harmonization directives were adopted, ranging from VAT rates and tax regimes to environmental protection standards, and had to be incorporated in legislation in member countries, in the process of creating the **single market** by **1992**.

HARRODS BOMB

An **IRA** explosion in London during the busy Christmas shopping season in 1984. A car bomb exploded on 17 December outside the Harrods department store in Knightsbridge. Two police officers and three civilians were killed and nearly 100 others were injured. The IRA admitted responsibility, but said that the explosion had been 'unauthorized'.

HAUGHEY FACTOR

A particular distaste, within the Irish political establishment and among middle-class voters, for the supposedly unprincipled ambition of Charles Haughey, who was nevertheless three times **Taoiseach** in 1979–81, 1982 and 1987–92 as leader of *Fianna Fáil*. Haughey's enemies charged in particular that he was the political champion of immoral speculators; they also repeatedly evoked the fact that he had been charged (although acquitted) in 1970 with gun-running for the **IRA**. His style of government was later described by one commentator, in words borrowed from Haughey's own denial of the allegations against him, as grotesque, unbelievable, bizarre and unprecedented (GUBU). Haughey's final resignation, in February 1992, came after it was revealed that he had known about the tapping of journalists' telephones by the security forces.

HAWK

An advocate of a belligerent policy or, more generally (in contrast to **dove**), a supporter of the more aggressive of two policy options. The term was used in the USA at the time of the **Cuban missile crisis** and caught on in popular usage as the country became divided over the **Vietnam War**.

HCFCs *see* CFCs

HDI

The human development index, first published by the **UNDP** in 1990 in its *Human Development Report*. The HDI is a composite indicator of the 'quality of life', taking account of life expectancy, literacy levels and real purchasing power. It has produced some controversial rankings, with the USA coming embarrassingly low on the list among developed countries. Countries such as Colombia, **Sri Lanka** and **Tanzania**, conversely, have an HDI index ranking far ahead of their per capita income ranking.

HEALTH FOR ALL 2000

The slogan encapsulating the aims of the **WHO**, particularly as regards primary health care. Since the creation of the WHO in 1948, the life expectancy and health of the world's population has generally risen. In its report to the 1992 **Earth Summit**, however, WHO said that the health gap between the developed and developing countries was widening and that three-quarters of all deaths worldwide were attributable to diseases relating to the environment and lifestyle.

HEARTS AND MINDS

Phrase widely associated with the gradual depletion of morale and spirit in the USA during the **Vietnam War**. Hence, commentators have asserted that US governments failed to capture the 'hearts and minds of America' and convince the US public of the grounds for military involvement in Vietnam, particularly in the aftermath of the 1968 **Tet offensive**. Prior to the Vietnam War the phrase had been associated with US President Theodore Roosevelt who had summed up his presidential attributes in terms of his ability to 'put into words what is in their hearts and minds but not in their mouths'.

HEBRON MOSQUE MASSACRE

The killing of 29 worshippers in a **West Bank** mosque on 25 February 1994, the worst single attack on Palestinians since **Israel** occupied the area after the **Six-Day War**. The killer, Baruch Goldstein, entered the packed Ibrahimi Mosque during **Ramadan** prayers, and sprayed the congregation with automatic gunfire. Goldstein, an immigrant Jew from New York and member of one of the nearby radical Jewish **settlements**, was eventually overpowered and beaten to death by survivors. The massacre provoked violence throughout the **Israeli-occupied territories** and seriously disrupted the **Middle East peace process**. An Israeli inquiry which ended on 26 June 1994 found that there was no conspiracy behind the killings and, disregarding Palestinian evidence, that no member of the Israeli security forces deserved punishment. The inquiry also ignored Palestinian pleas that it should also consider the presence in the West Bank of thousands of armed and militant Jewish settlers, many of whom bitterly rejected the **Gaza-Jericho First** peace deal signed by the **PLO** and **Israel** in September 1993.

HELSINKI FINAL ACT

The diplomatic agreement at the end of the first **CSCE** conference in Helsinki. The 35 participants, including the members of **NATO** and the **Warsaw Pact** and 13 neutral and non-aligned European countries, effectively accepted the post-1945 status quo in Europe. Four 'baskets' of agreement in the Final Act (also known as the Helsinki Accord) covered, respectively, security and confidence-building; co-operation on economic, scientific and environmental issues; human rights and freedoms; and the holding of follow-up conferences.

HELSINKI WATCH *see* HUMAN RIGHTS WATCH

HERALD OF FREE ENTERPRISE

The British car ferry which overturned and sank off the Belgian coast in 1987 with the loss of 193 lives. Owned by Townsend Thoresen (a subsidiary of the P&O shipping group), the roll-on-roll-off *Herald of Free Enterprise* left the port of Zeebrugge, Belgium, on 6 March 1987 with its bow doors still open, allowing water to rush in and fatally upset the balance of the vessel. The disaster was a contributory factor leading to a tightening of regulations covering the design and operation of passenger ferries and other sea-going vessels.

HEXAGONALE

The six-member grouping of **central European** countries formed in 1991 on the basis of the membership of the **Pentagonale**, which became the Hexagonale on the admission of Poland at the meeting in Dubrovnik on 27 July 1991. The Hexagonale group, whose participating countries were Austria, the then **Czechoslovakia**, Hungary, Italy, Poland and **Yugoslavia**, was modified with the break-up of Yugoslavia, but was the basis of the 1992 **CEI** (Central European Initiative).

HEYSEL STADIUM DISASTER

The death of 39 spectators and the injuring of some 400 others at the final of the 1985 European Cup football competition between Liverpool FC (England) and Juventus (Turin, Italy) in Belgium's Heysel Stadium on 29 May. Most deaths occurred when part of the stadium collapsed as spectators tried to escape charging Liverpool supporters. As punishment, Liverpool FC was banned from playing in European competitions until 1991.

HEZBOLLAH

(Arabic, 'Party of God') The main **fundamentalist**, **Shia** movement in Lebanon. Hezbollah's Iranian-funded **militia** operates in southern Lebanon where, with Syrian consent, it wages a constant and sometimes bloody war against **Israel** and its militia ally, the **South Lebanon Army**. During the 1980s operative affiliates of the group (including **Islamic Jihad** and Islamic Amal) carried out a high-profile kidnapping campaign against Westerners in Lebanon. During the 1991 general election in Lebanon, *Hezbollah* and its Shia ally (and erstwhile enemy) **Amal** emerged with the largest bloc of deputies. Within the confines of its strongholds in the south of the country and the southern slums of Beirut, the party has established an expansive social, political and economic network for its Shia constituency.

HIROSHIMA

The southern Japanese city, with a population of 245,000, which was destroyed on 6 August 1945 by the first atomic bomb used in warfare. The bomb, nicknamed **Little Boy**, was dropped from the US B-29 bomber **Enola Gay**. A second bomb was dropped on Nagasaki on 9 August, although Japan had already decided by then to offer unconditional surrender. It is doubtful whether the destruction of Hiroshima was necessary to force Japan's surrender, given US conventional military superiority, the economic blockade of Japan, and the **Soviet Union's** agreement to enter the Pacific War (which it did on 8 August). The Allies argued, however, that the atomic bomb would enable the war to be ended with minimal Allied casualties and would keep the Soviet Union, with whom relations had begun to deteriorate following the **Yalta** conference, out of the peace settlement in the Pacific. Japan surrendered to the Allies on 14 August, bringing the war to an end. Hiroshima, which suffered appalling casualties and a legacy of radiation damage, remains a symbol of the horror of nuclear war.

HISS CASE

A legal case which typified US anti-**communist** paranoia. Alger Hiss was a former official in the **State Department** and president of the Carnegie Endowment for International Peace. The accusation that he had been a **communist** during the 1930s was made in August 1948 by Whittaker Chambers, who was appearing before the House Committee on **Un-American Activities**, and taken up by young committee member Richard Nixon. Hiss sued Chambers for defamation of character; Chambers, to substantiate his allegation, then accused Hiss of having supplied him with classified State Department documents. Hiss's denial of these allegations led to an indictment for perjury. His first trial resulted in a hung jury, but he was retried and convicted in January 1950 and sentenced to five years' imprisonment.

HIV

Human immunodeficiency virus, the agent responsible for the fatal disease syndrome **AIDS**. First discovered by a French team in 1983 and subsequently confirmed by US researchers in 1984, HIV is transmitted by the exchange of bodily fluids, most commonly through sexual intercourse, by blood transfusion, by contamination of needles among intravenous drug abusers, or from mother to infant during pregnancy and birth. The virus is slow-acting with an incubation period of up to 10 years, and works by damaging the body's defences against other diseases. The number of HIV-positive cases worldwide was estimated by the **WHO** in December 1993 to have exceeded 15 million.

HO CHI MINH TRAIL

A shifting network of concealed tracks developed during the early stages of the **Vietnam War** as a supply route for North Vietnamese and **Viet Cong** forces in South Vietnam and named after North Vietnamese leader Ho Chi Minh. Starting in Hanoi, supplies usually entered Laos through the Mu Gia Pass where they were channelled to a base area near Tchepone before being shifted to different areas depending on their eventual destination. After the extension of the war into Cambodia the trail was extended to the west (the 'Sihanouk trail') to supply forces based in eastern Cambodian sanctuaries. From the start of the war the trail was bombed, but the attacks intensified after 1970 when **B-52** bombers began a series of massive raids. In addition defoliants, including **Agent Orange**, were dropped to destroy the trail's natural camouflage. Ultimately, the efforts of the USA to destroy the trail proved futile and it proved to be a major factor in the South's defeat.

HOJATOLISLAM

(Arabic, 'proof of Islam') A position generally regarded as second only to **Ayatollah** in the **Shia** clerical hierarchy. It emerged in the early nineteenth century as a response to growing numbers of Shia experts qualified to make autonomous religious judgements, and was gradually espoused by those who could claim the largest following. Current familiarity with the term owes much to its adoption by key members of the Iranian government, most notably its President, Hojatolislam Ali Akbar Hashemi Rafsanjani.

HOLOCAUST

A widely used term to describe the policy of industrial genocide pursued by the Nazi regime, particularly between 1942 and 1945. Concentration camps had been established in Germany from 1933 onwards, political opponents had been murdered and there had been a limited experiment in eugenics with the murder of some mental patients. However, it was not until 1942 that death camps such as Auschwitz, Chelmno, Majdanek, and Treblinka were established (most of them in occupied Poland) specifically as extermination centres. In accordance with the extreme racial anti-Semitism of the Nazi ideology, Jews were transported from all over occupied Europe, systematically killed with poison gas, and cremated. Together with murders elsewhere in occupied Europe, this purpose-built infrastructure for genocide accounted for the lives of some 6 million Jews. Large numbers of non-Jews were also killed, including members of racial groups which the Nazis considered inferior (500,000 Gypsies were murdered in the camps, as were many Slavs), homosexuals, and traditional Nazi target groups including **communists** and other 'enemies of the Reich'.

HOLOCAUST DENIAL

The denial that the **Holocaust** ever occurred, or the claim that the number of those killed was far fewer than is generally accepted. Holocaust denial, confined almost exclusively to adherents of **fascism** and neo-fascist ideologies, dismisses the overwhelming historical evidence of the Holocaust. It claims that this evidence is either fabricated or exaggerated; at its most complex, it sees this as a further facet of an alleged international Jewish conspiracy bent upon world domination. Legislation passed in West Germany in 1985 and upheld by the Constitutional Court in 1994, deemed it a crime 'to insult and defame' victims of Nazism, an offence which includes the denial of the Holocaust.

HOLT DROWNING

The disappearance and presumed death of Australian Prime Minister and Liberal Party leader Harold Holt while swimming at Portsea near Melbourne on 17 December 1967. In office since January 1966, Holt had been noted for his pro-US stance, trebling the Australian military commitment in the **Vietnam War** and promising to go 'all the way with LBJ'.

HOMELANDS *see* BANTUSTANS

HORN OF AFRICA

The promontory projecting from the east coast of Africa into the Indian Ocean, comprising Somalia, **Djibouti**, **Eritrea** and Ethiopia. The region is strategically important because it commands the Gulf of Aden and hence the sea route linking the **Middle East** oil fields and the markets of Europe and the **West**. During the **Cold War** both **superpowers** vied for control of the region, with the **Soviet Union** supporting the regime of Lt.-Col. Mengistu Haile Mariam in Ethiopia, while the USA sought close relations with the Somali government of Mohammed Siyad Barre.

HOSTAGE CRISIS

The crisis over the 52 US diplomats who were taken hostage in November 1979 when fundamentalist Islamic students stormed the US embassy in Tehran. The hostages were held for 444 days, and the inability of President Jimmy Carter to secure their release proved a fundamental obstacle to his bid for re-election in November 1980. A bungled attempt to intervene militarily and free the hostages simply added to the image of US impotence. The hostages were finally released on 20 January 1981, although as a final humiliation to Carter the Iranian authorities ensured that they did not leave the country's airspace until after the inauguration of his successor, Ronald Reagan. It was later claimed that, during the election campaign, the Republicans had reached an agreement with the Iranian government to ensure that Carter did not spring an **October Surprise** and gain an eve-of-election boost by securing the release of the hostages. No conclusive evidence was found to support this persistent allegation.

HOT-LINE AGREEMENT

The agreement establishing a direct teletype link between the **Kremlin** and the **White House**, which was concluded on 20 June 1963 following the **Cuban missile crisis**, with the intention of minimizing similar crises in future. The 'hot-line' was first used on 12 December 1971 to avoid possible Sino-Soviet hostilities during the crisis over **Bangladesh**.

HUBBLE SPACE TELESCOPE

An instrument placed into orbit by **NASA** in 1990. Its performance was initially impaired because of a manufacturing error, with the main mirror suffering from spherical aberration, or inability to focus most of the incoming light. A repair mission in December 1993 by the US Endeavour **space shuttle** corrected the optics and replaced gyroscopes, solar arrays and scientific instruments. The extremely high quality of the consequent images in January 1994 surpassed expectations. The telescope is now expected to see with clarity a distance of 10–12,000 million light years, a major advance over the maximum distance of 2,000 million light years from ground-based instruments.

HUD

The US Department of Housing and Urban Development. The HUD was at the centre of a major scandal which came to light in April 1989 when an internal audit showed that former HUD officials and a number of prominent Republicans had received millions of dollars from developers participating in federal housing projects subsidized by the HUD. Numerous prosecutions resulted from the subsequent inquiry, including that of Maryland escrow agent Marilyn Harrell who acknowledged that she had used an estimated $5.5 million in federal funds to buy houses and cars and make mortgage payments for poor people, thereby earning for herself the nickname 'Robin HUD'.

HUDOOD ORDINANCES

A reference to the series of draconian penal laws, *hadd*, based on the Islamic system of punishment which were introduced by Pakistani President Zia ul-Haq under his programme of **Islamization** in 1984. The reforms provoked widespread opposition from women's groups and human rights activists to provisions which made adultery punishable by stoning and penalized theft by ordering the amputation of hands. The laws remain in force despite a commitment by the current government of Prime Minister Benazir Bhutto to seek their repeal.

HUKS

An insurgent movement in the Philippines which developed as a resistance to the Japanese occupation during the Pacific War and which later refused to accept the legitimacy of the government of President Manuel Roxas after independence in 1946. **Counterinsurgency** measures by the government, including the resettlement of landless peasants – who constituted the Huks' principal support – and the capture of the movement's leaders, were largely successful in suppressing the Huks by the early 1950s. In the 1960s, however, the remnants of the Huks became the foundation of the **New People's Army**, the armed wing of the Maoist **Communist** Party of the Philippines—Marxist-Leninist.

HUMAN DEVELOPMENT INDEX *see* HDI

HUMAN GENOME PROJECT

A US project with far-reaching implications for **bio-ethics**, run jointly by the National Institute of Health and the Department of Energy. The purpose of the project is to co-ordinate the work of specially funded laboratories which are concentrating on mapping particular **DNA** sequences, in order ultimately to determine the complete sequence for a human being.

HUMAN RIGHTS WATCH

A US-based international human rights organization, the second largest worldwide after **Amnesty International**. The organization originated in 1978 and has its headquarters in New York. As of July 1994 it had five regional divisions. Human Rights Watch – Helsinki (founded in 1978) monitors and promotes human rights in Europe, taking its name from the **CSCE** conference in Helsinki. The other regional divisions are Human Rights Watch – Americas (founded in 1981); – Asia (1985); – Africa (1988); – **Middle East** (1989). The organization also has four thematic projects: Human Rights Watch – Arms Project (which seeks to prevent the distribution of arms to government and **guerrilla** forces which practice gross abuses of human rights);

Human Rights Watch – Free Expression (which focuses on the connections between restrictions on freedom of expression and global social problems); Human Rights Watch – Prison Project (which investigates prison conditions); and Human Rights Watch – Women's Rights Project (which focuses on violence and systematic discrimination against woman committed or clearly tolerated by governments).

HUMAN SHIELD

A term which became current following Iraq's occupation of Kuwait in August 1990 to describe its use of Western nationals as a defence against possible action by the US-led military coalition (**Desert Shield**). The policy, which was never officially acknowledged by Iraq, followed an Iraqi order issued on 9 August 1990 closing its borders to foreigners trying to leave Iraq or Kuwait and reportedly authorizing the transfer of some 500 Western nationals to sensitive military installations to deter an allied attack. The resulting international outrage forced Iraqi President Saddam Hussein on 6 December to order the release of all foreign hostages held in Iraq and Kuwait.

HUNDRED DAYS

The yardstick against which the early achievement of US presidents is measured. The term originated with President Franklin D. Roosevelt, who was inaugurated on 4 March 1933, in the midst of the severe inter-war depression. Having promised a radical New Deal to reduce unemployment and reflate the economy through an unparalleled degree of federal intervention, Roosevelt unleashed a torrent of legislation during his first hundred days which culminated in the signing of the National Recovery Act on 16 June.

HUNGARIAN DEMOCRATIC FORUM *see* MDF

HUNGARIAN UPRISING

The popular uprising against Soviet domination and domestic dictatorship in 1956. The uprising arguably began with a mass demonstration in Budapest on 22–3 October 1956 against the presence of Soviet troops in the country, prompting four days of fighting in the city. Hungarian workers, students and intellectuals were mobilized and workers' councils were set up all over Hungary. The former **communist** Prime Minister and architect of the **New Course**, Imre Nagy, formed a revolutionary multiparty government on 30 October, and proclaimed Hungary's withdrawal from the **Warsaw Pact**. The **Soviet Union** soon crushed the uprising in a massive attack which began on 4 November, during which tens of thousands of Hungarians were killed, many of them unarmed civilians. Janos Kadar took over as head of a pro-Soviet regime and supervised the **normalization** policy. Nagy was executed on 16 June 1958.

HUTU

A people of central Africa, forming the majority of population of both **Burundi** and **Rwanda**. Ethnically they do not differ from the **Tutsi**, who constitute a minority in both countries, and with whom they share the same language and culture. The difference between them tends to be occupational, similar to the Indian caste system and stems from the pre-colonial and colonial periods when the Tutsi were an elite and the Hutu a peasant class. During the colonial period, the differences between the two groups were exploited by the German occupiers and then the Belgians. Tutsi were given Western-style education and positions in the colonial administration. The Belgian authorities also introduced a system of identity cards which showed the group to which the holder belonged, a system which persists to this day.

In Burundi, this social stratification continued after independence, with Tutsi possessing political, economic and social power until the country's first multiparty elections in June 1993 brought Melchior Ndadaye, a Hutu, to power. Ndadaye, who included both Hutus and Tutsis in his Cabinet, was assassinated in October 1993 by dissident elements in the Tutsi-dominated army reluctant to relinquish power to a democratically elected government. Although the coup failed, it prompted serious violence in which an estimated 150,000, both Hutu and Tutsi, were killed. By mid-

1994 the government expressed optimism that calm had returned.

In Rwanda, the Hutu achieved political and economic power after independence and excluded Tutsi from positions of power. In 1973 Juvénal Habyarimana seized power and although he was initially regarded as a liberalizing force, he soon established a repressive one-party state. In August 1993, following a three-year rebellion by the predominantly Tutsi **RPF**, Habyarimana was forced to agree to the establishment of a power-sharing transitional government, which would include the RPF, and multiparty elections. The transition period had yet to be established when Habyarimana was killed in a plane crash on 6 April 1994. Opponents of the agreement within the ruling classes seized the opportunity to eliminate their opponents and revive the civil war. In the ensuing conflict government troops and the **Interahamwe** militia systematically killed anyone whose loyalty to the regime was doubted, massacring up to 1 million people, both Tutsi and Hutu.

HYANNIS PORT

An exclusive resort on the Cape Cod coast of Massachusetts which is the centre of the **Kennedy Dynasty**. Made famous as a presidential resort during the administration of John F. Kennedy, Hyannis Port also saw a gathering of the Kennedy family and its advisers at times of crisis such as in the aftermath of the **Chappaquiddick** incident.

IAEA

The International Atomic Energy Agency, an autonomous intergovernmental organization within the **UN** system which aims to promote the peaceful uses of nuclear energy. Founded in 1957 and based in Vienna, it currently has 117 members. Since its inception it has acted in close co-operation with the UN in conducting inspections of nuclear installations in countries suspected of developing nuclear weapons. Its most extensive programme of inspection in recent years has been undertaken under the aegis of the UN Special Commission on Iraq (**UNSCOM**) which seeks the elimination of Iraqi weapons of mass destruction under **Gulf War** ceasefire terms imposed by the UN in 1991. Intense controversy arose in 1993–4 over IAEA inspections in North Korea, where the government resisted demands for unfettered access to certain nuclear installations.

IBERIA

The peninsula in south-west Europe, of which Spain comprises four-fifths, with Portugal along the western (Atlantic) coast and Gibraltar at the southern tip. The name is used in some international contexts, such as for Ibero-American summit meetings.

IBRD

The International Bank for Reconstruction and Development, a **UN** specialized agency which is more commonly known as the **World Bank**. Based in Washington DC, it is the largest single source of lending for development, and thus always a focus for argument about **aid** criteria. Its current stated objectives include promoting sustainable economic growth, protecting the environment, and reducing poverty in developing countries. The World Bank was established in 1945 along with the **IMF**, following the **Bretton Woods** conference. Its membership – 177 countries as of early 1994 – is open only to members of the IMF. Voting rights reflect the size of a country's subscription to the capital stock of the Bank, which, in turn, is based on its quota in the IMF (determined according to economic strength). The World Bank Group consists of the IBRD and its three affiliates, the soft-loan **IDA**, the **IFC**, and the Multilateral Investment Guarantee Agency created in 1988.

ICAO

The International Civil Aviation Organization, a **UN** specialized agency which aims to establish international standards and regulations necessary for the safety, security, efficiency and regularity of air transport, and to serve as the medium for co-operation in all fields of civil aviation. Founded in 1947, its membership has risen to 182 countries.

ICBM

Inter-continental ballistic missile. Ballistic missiles classified as ICBMs are those with a range of over 5,500 km (whereas those with a range from 900 to 5,500 km are classified as MRBMs or **IRBMs**). Their introduction, first by the **Soviet Union** in 1957 and rapidly thereafter by the USA, supplanted the reliance on long-range bombers and dramatized the global reach of modern weapons. They could reach their destination in minutes and, being relatively inaccurate, the first ICBMs tended to be targeted on large areas such as major cities. ICBMs are 'strategic delivery vehicles' which were initially developed to carry single nuclear warheads, but were subsequently fitted with **MIRV**s. The **SALT** I agreement in 1972 sought to limit the number and size of ICBMs and submarine-launched **SLBMs**.

ICFTU

The International Confederation of Free Trade Unions. ICFTU was founded in 1949 by unionists in Western countries as a breakaway from the **WFTU** (World Federation of Trade Unions) which they saw as compromised by the domination of **communists**. A criterion for membership is that the union or confederation should be free from the control of any other body, although some ICFTU affiliates are effectively controlled by a political party. ICFTU is based in Belgium, and as of mid-1992 had 154 affiliates in 109 countries representing some 109 million workers. It is predominantly a confederation of national trade union centres, but in some cases (notably Japan) it has affiliated individual unions.

ICJ

The International Court of Justice, based at The Hague and founded in 1946 under a Statute which is an integral part of the **UN** Charter. The ICJ is the principal judicial organ of the UN and is authorized to resolve disputes between UN member states. It is assisted by a governing body composed of 15 judges (including the President), each of a different nationality, who are elected by the **UN General Assembly** and the **UN Security Council** for a nine-year term of office.

ICRC

The International Committee of the Red Cross, founded in Geneva in 1863 as an independent institution of a private character with the aim of helping wounded soldiers on the battlefield. The ICRC now provides protection for both civilian and military victims of war, and in 1990 it was granted observer status at the **UN**. Its executive body, the Assembly, is nationally based, relying exclusively on Swiss citizens, but the organization prides itself on its international mission, and in 1992 it dropped its long-standing policy of employing only Swiss nationals as 'delegates' to deal with sovereign governments. The ICRC and **IFRC** together make up the International Red Cross and Red Crescent Movement.

IDA

The International Development Association, an affiliate of the **IBRD**, established in 1960 as a soft-loan agency for developing countries, especially the poorest among them which are unlikely to attract commercial financing. It provides credits with maturities of up to 40 years, with 10-year grace periods, no interest, and service charges of less than 1 per cent. Apart from transfers from the IBRD, the IDA derives its lending resources from periodic replenishment of donations by the developed and oil-rich countries; the 10th replenishment, approved in January 1993, was to cover the three years from July 1993. The IDA currently has 155 members. The president of the IBRD is also president of the IDA.

IDAF

The International Defence and Aid Fund, the London-based organization which channelled funds to the victims of **apartheid** in South Africa (and **Namibia**). The organization had its origins in a fund to combat **racism** in South Africa founded in 1950 in London by Canon John Collins, Chairman of Christian Action. When the South African government arrested 156 people on charges of treason in 1956, a

Treason Trial Defence Fund was established in London, and Defence and Aid Committees within South Africa sprang up in the early 1960s. However, these committees were soon banned in South Africa, and the organization was forced to operate clandestinely. In 1966 IDAF was formally established with the stated aims of aiding, defending and rehabilitating the victims of apartheid, and supporting their families and dependants. Until its closure in 1991, these aims were fulfilled through the secret channelling of funds (principally from Scandinavian governments and organizations) to former and serving political prisoners and detainees, their families and their defence teams. The third object of IDAF, to 'keep the conscience of the world alive', was carried out by an information department which produced journals, books, films and other audio-visual material on apartheid.

IDB

1. The Inter-American Development Bank, a US-based international development bank founded in 1959 to finance and provide technical aid to projects designed to promote economic and social development in the Americas and the **Caribbean**. Composed of 44 member countries (including 11 from outside the region – Denmark, France, Germany, **Israel**, Italy, Japan, the Netherlands, Portugal, Spain, Sweden, and the UK) its Board of Governors is dominated by the USA, which holds 35 per cent of the votes.

2. The Islamic Development Bank, a specialized institution of the **OIC**, based in Jeddah, Saudi Arabia. It aims to encourage economic development in member countries and among Muslim communities in non-Muslim countries in accordance with **sharia law**. It was formally inaugurated in October 1975 after plans were approved by the OIC Conference of Foreign Ministers in 1973. Its Board of Governors, comprising a representative from each of its 48 member states, is committed to the Islamic principle of **interest-free banking** which is opposed to usury. The Bank's methods of financing include interest-free loans (with a service fee); equity participation in industrial and agricultural projects; leasing operations and instalment sale financing; and profit-sharing operations.

IDF

Israel Defence Forces, the formal name for the Israeli armed forces.

IEA

The International energy Agency, a Paris-based organization founded by the **OECD** in 1974, in response to the oil crisis, for the purpose of promoting co-operation on energy questions among the OECD's 24 member countries and the **EU**. The Agreement on the International Energy Programme, which entered into force in January 1976, commits members to share petroleum in emergencies, to reduce dependence on petroleum imports, to increase the availability of information and to develop relations with petroleum-producing and petroleum-consuming countries.

IFAD

The International Fund for Agricultural Development, a **UN** specialized agency based in Rome, which was founded in 1976 and started operations in 1977. Its principal aim is the funding of rural development programmes, mainly for the poorest **Third World** countries. The decision to create a new organization for this purpose, rather than to entrust this mandate to the existing **FAO**, came about partly because of the desire to involve the oil-rich **OPEC** countries more directly in running and funding a UN development agency. This is reflected in IFAD's tripartite structure, with three categories of member countries (there are currently 21 **OECD** industrialized country members, 12 OPEC members and 111 'category III' developing country members) and equal representation of each category on the Executive Board. Recently the organization has been deeply divided between OECD and OPEC members over each group's respective contributions.

IFC

The International Finance Corporation, an affiliate of the **IBRD**, founded in 1956 to promote private enterprise and assist developing countries in attracting capital for that purpose, both foreign and domestic. The IFC is a source of loans, and also of equity investment capital. It raises most of its resources from capital markets and uses its own funds to mobilize project financing from other investors and lenders through syndications, underwritings and co-financing. It is currently composed of 161 member states and is headed by the president of the IBRD. The function of protecting investments against non-commercial risks was entrusted in 1988 to another IBRD affiliate created for that purpose, the Multilateral Investment Guarantee Agency (MIGA).

IFRC

The International Federation of the Red Cross and Red Crescent Societies; the world federation of the Red Cross and Red Crescent Societies which exist in more than 150 countries. The IFRC is financed by member societies and by voluntary donations. Based in Geneva, it was founded in 1919 as the League of Red Cross Societies. The IFRC and the **ICRC** together make up the International Red Cross and Red Crescent Movement; IFRC member societies are associated with the movement's humanitarian work in peace time, whereas the ICRC is active in time of armed conflict.

ILO

The International Labour Organization, which in 1946 became the first of the **UN** specialized agencies. Based in Geneva, it was originally founded in 1919 with the intention of pursuing social justice as a foundation for world peace by encouraging satisfactory living standards, conditions of work and pay, and employment opportunities. It currently has 169 member states, and has been responsible for the conclusion of 74 international labour conventions. Its supreme deliberative body, the International Labour Organization Conference, meets annually; its executive arm, the Governing Body, is assisted by the International Labour Office which acts as its secretariat.

IMF

The International Monetary Fund, one of the specialized agencies of the **UN**. The IMF was established at the 1944 **Bretton Woods** conference, with the general aim of promoting international monetary co-operation, assisting the growth of international trade, promoting exchange stability, and helping to establish a multilateral system of payments for current transactions. For these purposes it makes available to members resources to give them the opportunity of correcting any balance of payments 'maladjustments' which they may experience. Over the years a wide range of facilities have been introduced to this end. The IMF formally came into being in 1946 and started financial operations in 1947; by mid-1994 membership of the IMF had grown to 179, comprising all major countries of the world except **Taiwan**.

IMMORALITY ACT

the notorious piece of **apartheid** legislation which forbade 'unlawful carnal intercourse' or 'any immoral or indecent act' between a White person and a Black person (i.e. Africans, Indians and **Coloureds**). Under the 1957 Immorality Act (amending a 1927 Act) it was sufficient for the prosecution to prove that one of the accused had attempted, invited or incited the commission of an undefined indecent act. The maximum penalty was seven years hard labour in prison. Between 1950 and 1980 over 11,500 people were convicted under the act. The Immorality Act was repealed along with the Mixed Marriages Act in 1985 as part a limited reform package.

IMO

The International Maritime Organization, a **UN** specialized agency based in London, which aims to ensure maritime safety and the prevention of pollution from ships. The IMO was originally founded in 1959 as the Intergovernmental Maritime Consultative Organization, changing its name and status in 1982. Its governing body is the 32-member Council elected by the IMO Assembly. It had 149 member countries as of April 1994.

IMPORT SUBSTITUTION

The economic phenomenon whereby domestic consumption switches towards domestically produced goods, when cost or other barriers are raised to stem the inflow of imports. The degree to which import substitution is feasible, especially in the short term, has an important influence on government policies. Where there is very little scope for it ('inelasticity of import substitution'), there may not be much effect to be gained from imposing import tariffs or from a sharp devaluation to make import more expensive; consumers may still resort to imports to meet their needs, even though their cost has risen.

IN PLACE OF STRIFE

A document published by the Labour government of the UK on 17 January 1969 setting out its policy for industrial relations, collective bargaining and trade union reform. Among its main proposals were the establishment of a Commission on Industrial Relations, and powers for the government to order a 28-day 'conciliation pause' before strike action was taken and to require compulsory strike ballots. The proposals caused serious dissension within the Labour Party and the trade union movement, and although legislation was introduced it was abandoned by the government in June 1969 after the **TUC** had given a binding undertaking to intervene in serious unconstitutional stoppages.

IN VITRO FERTILIZATION *see* IVF

INAUGURATION

The ceremony involving the administering of the presidential oath of affirmation which marks the moment at which a person formally becomes President. The US presidential oath is as follows: 'I do solemnly swear [or affirm] that I will faithfully execute the office of President of the United States, and will to the best of my ability, preserve, protect and defend the Constitution of the United States.' With presidential elections occurring every four years in early November, it was customary for Presidents to be inaugurated in early March of the following year. Under the 20th amendment to the Constitution, however, ratified on 6 February 1933, it was decided that the presidential and vice presidential terms should end at noon on 20 January. Under normal circumstances the inauguration then takes place, before the **White House**, the official residence of the President, and is attended by the outgoing President and Vice President. The new Vice-President is also sworn into office. The oath of affirmation is followed by an inaugural speech by the new President. It is not stipulated that the inauguration must take place in public. Following the assassination of President John F. Kennedy in Dallas in 1963, Vice President Lyndon Baines Johnson was inaugurated on board the aircraft which was to return him to Washington DC.

INCOMES POLICY

A government-originated policy seeking to ensure non-inflationary growth of incomes within a stable economic framework. The issue of an incomes policy had a particular political importance in the USA and the UK in the 1970s. In the USA, an emergency 90-day wage/price freeze was imposed in August 1971 and was then succeeded by a period of restraint. In the UK the Conservative government introduced a similar 90-day freeze in November 1972, which was likewise followed by a lengthy period of restraint under a price and pay code. The breach of this policy by the National Union of Mineworkers led to industrial action and the imposition of the **three-day week**. The **TUC** in May 1976 agreed new voluntary restraint guidelines with the by now Labour government, and in July 1976 a new **social contract** was agreed by the Labour Party and the TUC. The situation continued to be uneasy, however, and culminated in the 1978–9 **winter of discontent**, as wage demands were sought in excess of the government's 5 per cent guideline.

INDIAN PEACE KEEPING FORCE *see* IPKF

INDIAN SUBCONTINENT

The territory normally designated as South Asia, comprising the independent states of **Bangladesh**, Bhutan, India, the Maldives,

Nepal, **Pakistan** and **Sri Lanka**. Some definitions also include Afghanistan and Burma (**Myanma**).

INDIGENOUS, AFRICAN, AMERICAN AND POPULAR RESISTANCE

An Inter-American organization of indigenous and grassroots organizations. Representing 27 countries, it was founded in 1990 to present an alternative view of the Americas and bring to international attention the plight of the 40 million-strong indigenous population in the lead-up to the **Colombus Quincentenary** in October 1992. They opposed the official government celebrations and denounced the lack of power and land for blacks and the indigenous people, the repression of their culture and the poverty and marginalization they suffered. The recipient of the 1992 Nobel Peace Prize, Rigoberta Menchu, a Guatemalan Quiche indian, was closely associated with the organization.

INDO-CHINA

The term adopted by the French in the nineteenth century for their south-east Asian colonies in Cambodia, Laos and Vietnam. As a political entity, the French Indo-Chinese Union ceased to exist after 1954, but the term has remained in common usage to denote the three countries. Indo-China represents the convergence of Indian and Chinese cultural currents in mainland south-east Asia, so that in a purely geographical sense it might also comprise Burma, peninsular **Malaysia**, Singapore and Thailand.

INDOCUMENTADOS

(Spanish, 'undocumented') A term for illegal workers in the USA from **Latin America** and the **Caribbean**. Drawn mainly from Mexico and **Central America**, their numbers are currently estimated to be growing by 200,000–300,000 per year. They experience considerable public hostility which has grown since the 1970s post-**Vietnam War** recession, when politicians launched electoral promises to save US jobs for 'Americans' – pledges repeated in the May 1994 Californian state elections. Many of the undocumented are non-unionised seasonal workers on low wages and while others are employed on a more permanent basis in the domestic and service sectors; their illegal status makes them vulnerable to poor employment conditions.

INF TREATY

The agreement concluded between the USA and the **Soviet Union** at the Washington summit on 8 December 1987, which came into force in June 1988, requiring that both sides should destroy by 1991 all of their land-based intermediate nuclear forces (INF), most of which were in Europe. This was the first ever agreement going beyond **arms control** to the elimination of a whole category of offensive nuclear weapons. It covered medium-range (1,000–5,500 km) and shorter-range (500–1,000 km) weapons, the most significant being the Soviet SS-20 missiles deployed since 1977, and the US **cruise** and **Pershing** introduced under **NATO's** controversial 1979 **twin-track decision**. The treaty also specified comprehensive procedures for verifying compliance.

INFORMATION SCANDAL

The 1978–9 scandal in South Africa arising from the covert provision of substantial government funds to control part of the English-language press with the aim of promoting the **apartheid** government's image both at home and abroad. Allegations about such funding had been made in the liberal press as early as 1977. In particular there were persistent suggestions that the recently founded *Citizen* had been established by the government. Firm details only emerged, however, in September 1978 when information was leaked to the press which provided proof that the Department of Information under Connie Mulder (hence the popular name for the scandal – 'Muldergate') had misused public funds. The leaks were made in the context of the struggle for the leadership of the ruling National Party (NP), J. B. Vorster having just resigned as Prime Minister ostensibly on health grounds. Mulder had been considered the main contender for the post. It was widely believed that the press had been tipped off by supporters of his rival,

P. W. Botha. With Mulder's reputation seriously damaged, Botha became Prime Minister on 27 September 1978. A subsequent Commission of Inquiry into the scandal accused Mulder of gross inefficiency and misuse of funds. However, it exonerated Vorster, by now State President (then a ceremonial position), who had been implicated by Mulder. Although Mulder resigned from the Cabinet and as NP leader in the Transvaal he refused to play the scapegoat and continued to make allegations against Vorster. He was expelled from the NP in April 1979. Allegations and counter-allegations continued, including claims that two British Labour MPs had been paid to protect South Africa's interest and to spy on anti-apartheid groups in the UK; that enormous sums had been paid to **right-wing** groups in the USA; and that attempts had been made to purchase newspapers around the world. A further Commission of Inquiry (the Erasmus Commission) finally found in July 1979 that Vorster had indeed been aware of the Department of Information's financial operations. Avoiding possible impeachment, Vorster resigned the presidency.

INKATHA

(Zulu, 'mystical coil', a reference to the coil worn by African women to help them carry heavy weights on their heads, conveying the idea of many strands working together lightening the burden) The politically conservative South African organization led by Chief Mangosuthu Buthelezi. Founded in 1976 as a 'cultural movement', it was relaunched in July 1990 as the *Inkatha* Freedom Party. It is a predominantly Zulu organization with a powerbase in Kwazulu-Natal. Although it rejected the **bantustan** policy during the **apartheid** period, it participated in its structures; Buthelezi was, for example, head of the Legislative Assembly of the non-independent Kwazulu bantustan. The organization is very hostile towards the **ANC**. Conflict between its supporters and those of the ANC resulted in violence as early 1986 when it clashed with the pro-ANC **UDF** in Natal. Following the unbanning of the ANC in February 1990 the violence increased and spread from Natal to the **townships** of the Transvaal.

Although *Inkatha* participated in the **CODESA** forum it withdrew from the succeeding pre-election constitutional talks and gave every indication that it would disrupt the country's first democratic polls; violence attributed to *Inkatha* supporters soared. Its main objection to the talks related to the rejection of its demand for a federal constitution which would entrench Buthelezi's position in Kwazulu-Natal. Following a number of significant concessions by the government and ANC, Buthelezi finally agreed on 19 April 1994 to contest the elections on 26–29 April. *Inkatha* won 43 of the 400 National Assembly seats, as well as control of the Kwazulu-Natal provincial assembly, although the results were tainted by allegations of vote rigging. Thanks to the power-sharing mechanism in the Interim Constitution it was given three full and one deputy ministerial posts. It was widely hoped that the appointment of Buthelezi as Minister of Home Affairs would diminish the chances of a resurgence of the conflict between *Inkatha* and the ANC.

INSIDER TRADING

The use of privileged information in the financial markets to secure undue personal benefit. The term applies especially to buying or selling securities with inside knowledge that their price is about to be affected (for example by an imminent takeover bid or by especially favourable or unfavourable financial results). Insider trading became a source of great concern to governments and authorities in the main trading countries in the 1970s and 1980s, and various pieces of legislation were introduced to criminalize it or to intensify countermeasures and to increase penalties for contravention.

INSTITUTIONAL ACTS

Decrees passed by military regimes in **South America** which effectively suspended constitutions. The most notable use of them was in Brazil during the 1964–85 military dictatorship when they legitimized a variety of repressive measures, in particular **cassações** or powers to suspend the political rights of opponents, and abolished direct federal elections and permitted direct intervention at state and municipal levels.

INTELSAT

The International Telecommunications Satellite Consortium. Founded in 1964 after international agreement by 14 signatories, its first significant achievement was the launch of the **Early Bird** satellite. Membership grew to over 100 countries in the 1980s when Intelsat controlled an estimated 95 per cent of international telecommunications traffic. The space segment of the organization is jointly owned, with the number of each government's shares in proportion to national use. Earth tracking stations are owned and operated by individual countries. Its dominant position in the satellite market has been eroded by serious competition in the areas of design, development, construction, launch, operations and maintenance.

INTERAHAMWE

(Kinyarwanda, 'Those Who Stand Together') A militia group in **Rwanda** implicated in the massacre of hundreds of thousands of people in the wake of the death of President Juvénal Habyarimana in April 1994. Trained by the national army and organized as the 'youth wing' of Habyarimana's National Republican Movement for Democracy and Development (MRND), the sole legal political party until 1991, the predominantly **Hutu** *Interahamwe* opposed the 1993 agreement between Habyarimana and the rebel **RPF** which had forced the former to agree to a power-sharing transitional government and multiparty elections. Unwilling to relinquish power to a democratically elected government, after Habyarimana's death the *Interahamwe* operated death squads eliminating all those whose loyalty to the existing regime was doubted.

INTER-AMERICAN DEVELOPMENT BANK *see* IDB

INTER-AMERICAN TREATY ON RECIPROCAL ASSISTANCE *see* RIO TREATY

INTEREST-FREE BANKING

The underlying principle of Islamic banking, based on the Koranic prohibition of usury, or interest on loans (*riba*). It is generally understood to derive from the idea that money is a means of exchange rather than a commodity. Most modern Islamic governments have tended either to circumvent or disregard interest-free banking, either allowing a profit-share arrangement, under which lender and borrower take part of the risk, effectively replacing usury by equity in all financial dealings; or allowing banks to buy a commodity such as a house or a car, and lease it to the 'mortgagee', whose lease payments eventually allow him to take full possession. Among Muslim countries whose governments obliged all banks to follow non-interest practices were Iran in 1984, and Pakistan, through a series of laws culminating in 1985.

INTERGOVERNMENTAL PANEL ON CLIMATE CHANGE *see* IPCC

INTERNATIONAL ATOMIC ENERGY AGENCY *see* IAEA

INTERNATIONAL BANK FOR RECONSTRUCTION AND DEVELOPMENT *see* IBRD

INTERNATIONAL CIVIL AVIATION ORGANIZATION *see* ICAO

INTERNATIONAL COMMITTEE OF THE RED CROSS *see* ICRC

INTERNATIONAL CONFEDERATION OF FREE TRADE UNIONS *see* ICFTU

INTERNATIONAL COURT OF JUSTICE *see* ICJ

INTERNATIONAL DEVELOPMENT ASSOCIATION *see* IDA

INTERNATIONAL ENERGY AGENCY *see* IEA

INTERNATIONAL FEDERATION OF THE RED CROSS *see* IFRC

INTERNATIONAL FINANCE CORPORATION *see* IFC

INTERNATIONAL FUND FOR AGRICULTURAL DEVELOPMENT *see* IFAD

INTERNATIONAL LABOUR ORGANIZATION *see* ILO

INTERNATIONAL MARITIME ORGANIZATION *see* IMO

INTERNATIONAL MONETARY FUND *see* IMF

INTERNATIONAL ORGANIZATION FOR MIGRATION *see* IOM

INTERNATIONAL PLANNED PARENTHOOD FEDERATION *see* IPPF

INTERNATIONAL RED CROSS AND RED CRESCENT MOVEMENT *see* IFRC

INTERNATIONAL TELECOMMUNICATIONS UNION *see* ITU

INTERNATIONAL UNION FOR THE CONSERVATION OF NATURE *see* IUCN

INTERNATIONAL WHALING COMMISSION *see* IWC

INTERNMENT

The policy, pursued in **Northern Ireland** for a number of years in the 1970s, of interning without trial those suspected of belonging to terrorist organizations. It was first introduced by the Northern Ireland government in August 1971 under the Civil Authorities (Special Powers) Acts 1922–43, providing for arrest, interrogation, and in some circumstances indefinite internment. Following the introduction of **direct rule** in March 1972 these arrangements effectively continued. There was continued argument as to the efficacy of the policy, and there ensued a progressive release of internees and detainees between late 1973 and December 1975 (when the last were released); the total number so held over the period 1971–5 was nearly 2,000, of whom just over 100 were **loyalists**.

INTER-PARLIAMENTARY UNION *see* IPU

INTERPOL

The International Criminal Police Organization, established in 1923 and based in Lyon, France. Interpol aims to promote mutual assistance between criminal police authorities in all countries and to support government agencies concerned with combating crime.

INTIFADA

(Arabic, literally 'shaking off', figuratively 'uprising') The Palestinian mass popular uprising in the **Gaza Strip** and **West Bank** which started in December 1987. Incorporating demonstrations, strikes and violent confrontation between Palestinian youths and the Israeli occupying forces, the *intifada* quickly developed into the most serious threat yet to control in the **Israeli-occupied territories**. **Israel** responded with an **iron fist** approach which included beatings, administrative detentions, house demolitions and occasional deportations. As the *intifada* progressed it became increasingly violent, and a large number of Palestinians, and a far smaller number of Israelis, died or were injured in the unrest. The *intifada* was initially organized at grassroots level by the Unified National Command, composed of outposts of the mainstream **PLO** factions. However, particularly in the Gaza Strip, the Islamic fundamentalist **Hamas** came to play a leading role. By the time of the signing of the **Gaza-Jericho First** peace agreement between Israel and the PLO in September 1993, the *intifada* had lost much of its initial impetus.

INVISIBLE EARNINGS

The elements in a country's **current-account balance** which do not relate to visible (merchandise) trade. Invisible earnings include receipts for international transportation, freight, insurance, travel and tourism, and financial and other services; interest, profits and dividends; receipts from certain government transactions; and certain other transfers (including, in the case of the UK, **EU** transactions). Net invisible earnings are calculated by totalling these earnings, and subtracting the payments made in these same categories.

IOANNINA COMPROMISE

A formula on decision-making within the **EU**, devised at a meeting of the EU's **Council of Ministers** in Ioannina, Greece, in March 1994. Negotiations had just been concluded for the enlargement of the EU, with four new members from January 1995, when the UK took a stand against proposals defining the number of votes needed for qualified majority decision-making. In an expanded Council of Ministers, the overall number of votes was to rise from 76 to 90, and the UK eventually accepted that the minimum 'blocking minority' should also rise, from 23 to 27 (i.e. requiring a larger opposing coalition than the current total of two large states and one small state). In return, the compromise formula stated that 23 opposing votes would be enough to hold up a decision for 'a reasonable period', while member states sought consensus.

IOM

The International Organization for Migration, founded (as the Intergovernmental Committee for Migration) in 1951. Its essential purpose is to arrange the organized transfer of migrants, refugees and displaced persons, and it co-ordinates its refugee activities with the **UNHCR** and with governmental and non-governmental organizations.

IPCC

The Intergovernmental Panel on Climate Change, established under the auspices of **UNEP** and the **WMO** to monitor the threat of **global warming**, following a conference in Geneva in November 1988. The IPCC sponsors three expert groups with the briefs of (i) assessing knowledge about climatic change; (ii) monitoring the potential impact of climatic change on agriculture and sea level; and (iii) formulating possible strategies in response to the problem.

IPKF

The Indian Peace Keeping Force controversially stationed in northern **Sri Lanka** from July 1987 to March 1990. Under the terms of an Indo-Sri Lankan agreement signed in July 1987, the IPKF was established to disarm Tamil separatist rebels in northern Sri Lanka in exchange for substantial political reforms for the Tamil-dominated areas in the north and east. However, the main separatist group, the **Tamil Tigers**, rejected the deal and put up resistance to the IPKF, although other Tamil groups collaborated with the Indian forces. The IPKF's protracted withdrawal in 1989–90 was accompanied by heavy fighting in the north and east between the Tamil Tigers and pro-Indian militias. The latter were easily defeated so that upon completion of the IPKF's withdrawal in March 1990 the Tamil Tigers were the dominant military force in the Tamil areas.

IPPF

The International Planned Parenthood Federation. The world's largest voluntary organization in the sphere of family planning and reproductive health, IPPF was founded in Bombay in 1952. It links autonomous national family planning associations in more than 140 countries, and, while it is also supported by financial contributions from private foundations and individuals, the vast majority of its funding comes from more than 20 governments; US funding, which had been severed in 1984 at the Mexico City conference, was resumed by the Clinton administration in 1993.

IPU

The Inter-Parliamentary Union. Established in 1889 and based in Switzerland, the IPU is a non-governmental body which exists to facilitate contacts between members of all parliaments.

IRA

The Irish Republican Army, currently the main militant republican movement in

Northern Ireland. The IRA was originally formed in the early part of the twentieth century to fight for Irish independence, and represented the military wing of **Sinn Féin**. Following the 1969–70 split in *Sinn Féin* the 'Official IRA' was allied with *Sinn Féin*-The Workers' Party (later just Workers' Party) but ceased activity in 1972. The military wing of the party retaining the name *Sinn Féin* was known as the Provisional IRA, although latterly it has generally dropped the prefix 'Provisional'. The IRA has been the main militant republican organization in Northern Ireland, operating also in Ireland and on the mainland of **Great Britain**. Its main targets have been the security forces and 'soft' targets of propaganda value, although its members have also participated in sectarian violence against the Protestant community, particularly where individuals are thought to have connections with the security forces. It has over the years called a number of ceasefires, but even following the **Downing Street Declaration** of December 1993, for which *Sinn Féin* sought 'clarification', it has continued to carry out a number of dramatic attacks. The IRA was proscribed in Northern Ireland in 1974.

IRAN-CONTRA AFFAIR

The foreign policy scandal which dominated the second term of office of US President Ronald Reagan. The affair involved the secret and unauthorized sale of weapons to Iran in 1985–6, and the diversion of the profits to assist the anti-communist **Contra** rebels operating in Nicaragua. There was also an **arms for hostages** dimension to the deal, in that Iranian help was sought in attempting to secure the release of US hostages held by Islamic fundamentalists in Lebanon. The Iran-Contra operation involved senior members of the **NSC**, most notably Robert McFarlane, Admiral John M. Poindexter and Lt.-Col. Oliver North. After it became public in 1986 it was the subject of several investigations including Reagan's own committee of inquiry led by former Republican Senator John Tower; Congressional hearings in 1987; and a six-and-a-half year inquiry by independent counsel (special prosecutor) Lawrence E. Walsh who submitted his final report on the affair on 5 August 1993. Although Walsh succeeded in prosecuting several of the leading figures in the affair, many of the convictions were later overturned on appeal. Also, despite the widespread belief that both Reagan and Vice President George Bush had condoned the operation, insufficient evidence was discovered to pursue a case against them. The trials of other senior figures, most notably former Defence Secretary Caspar Weinberger, were averted when Bush issued a presidential pardon in December 1992, shortly before leaving office.

IRANIAN EMBASSY SIEGE

The 1980 siege and forcible storming of the Iranian embassy in London. The embassy was seized on 30 April 1980 (a year after the **Islamic revolution** in Iran) by a group of Iranian dissidents seeking to draw attention to the plight of the Arab minority in Iran and demanding the release of 91 of their comrades imprisoned in Khuzistan. Of the 26 hostages taken in the embassy, five were released before negotiations failed. After two hostages were shot dead, the building was recaptured in a dramatic operation by the Special Air Service (SAS). The embassy was gutted by fire, and all but one of the six men who had occupied it were killed in the raid.

IRAQGATE

A scandal which centred on the allegation that the administration of US President George Bush funnelled secret assistance to the government of Iraq and then, following the 1990–1 **Gulf War**, sought to conceal the evidence. The conduit through which the $5,500 million in loans was alleged to have been supplied in the late 1980s was the small Atlanta branch of the Italian majority state-owned Banca Nazionale del Lavoro (BNL). While the branch manager of the bank, Christopher Drogoul, pleaded guilty to 60 counts of fraud in 1992, it was believed by many – including the US judge who presided over Drogoul's case – that he had acted on higher authority.

IRBM

Intermediate-range ballistic missile. IRBMs were developed in the 1950s to carry nuclear warheads, and modernized in the late 1970s and 1980s, with the development of the Soviet SS20 and the US **Pershing** II missiles. IRBMs, sometimes known as medium-range or MRBMs, have a range from 550 to 3,500 miles (900 to 5,500 km), ie. less than **ICBMs** but more than the so-called tactical **nuclear weapons**. In **arms control** terms they are classed as intermediate nuclear forces (INF), together with nuclear-armed bomber aircraft and long-range theatre nuclear forces such as **cruise** missiles.

IRGUN

(Hebrew, from *Irgun Zuai Leumi* – National Military Organization) A **right-wing Zionist** underground movement in **Palestine**, founded in 1931. Irgun carried out acts of terrorism and assassination against the British, whom it regarded as illegal occupiers, and Arabs. The group's most infamous operations were the attack on the **King David Hotel** in Jerusalem in 1946, in which more than 90 soldiers and civilians were killed, and the raid on the Arab village of Dayr Yasin in 1947 in which all 254 inhabitants were slaughtered.

After the creation of **Israel** in 1948, the group disbanded, although many of its members went on to become established military and political figures. Irgun's members included two future Israel Prime Ministers, Menachem Begin and Itzhak Shamir, although the latter is usually associated with the more extreme *Lehi* (**Stern Gang**), which he helped form in 1941.

IRIAN JAYA

An Indonesian province and the western portion of the island of New Guinea, adjacent to the state of Papua New Guinea. While Indonesia gained independence in 1949, West New Guinea – as Irian Jaya was then called – remained under Dutch control until 1963, when it was brought under Indonesian administration. Since the early 1970s Indonesian control of Irian Jaya has been contested by the secessionist **OPM**.

IRISH REPUBLICAN ARMY *see* IRA

IRON CURTAIN

The fortified frontier dividing the **Eastern Europe** of the **communist bloc** from the **capitalist** West. Winston Churchill popularized the phrase, using it in a March 1946 speech at Fulton College in Missouri which is often regarded as marking the beginning of the **Cold War**. The collapse of **communism** in Eastern Europe came after work began on 2 May 1989 to dismantle the barrier between Hungary and Austria, precipitating a wave of emigration over the next few months to the West from the **DDR**.

IRON FIST

The **Israeli** policy of 'might, power and beatings' to quell the Palestinian **intifada**. The policy was first proclaimed by the then Defence Minister Itzhak Rabin in early 1988, shortly after the outbreak of the uprising. While the government effectively ignored worldwide criticism of the resulting military brutality against young stone-throwing Palestinians in the **Israeli-occupied territories**, 'iron fist' exacerbated internal divisions within the Israeli political establishment.

IRON LADY

A term, used either as a compliment or in a derogatory manner, to describe the character of Margaret Thatcher during her term of office, first as Conservative Party leader and then as UK Prime Minister in 1979–90. The term was coined by *Red Star*, the **Soviet Union** Defence Ministry newspaper, and was first used on 24 January 1976.

IRON RICE BOWL

A metaphor for the social contract between the Chinese state and its citizens, which entails jobs for life and therefore, in the context of the Chinese system, the social benefits administered through the workplace such as healthcare and housing. The system is one of the key factors militating against China's economic reforms, for it is feared that any radical restructuring of state enterprises to make them more profit-oriented could provoke mass social unrest by breaking the 'iron rice bowl'.

IRREDENTISM

A policy founded on the belief that a particular state has a historic right to sovereignty over specific territory currently outside its borders. It was first used in the late nineteenth century in the phrase *Italia irredenta* – 'unredeemed Italy', to refer to Italian-speaking territory not incorporated in Italy, and often there is a religious or ethnic dimension, as when Hungarian irredentists advocate the return of lands still inhabited by **Magyars** but lost under the terms of the Treaty of Trianon in 1920 to **Czechoslovakia**, Serbia and Romania.

ISLAMIC BANKING *see* INTEREST-FREE BANKING

ISLAMIC COUNCIL OF EUROPE

A London-based organization founded in 1973 as a co-ordinating body for Islamic centres and Muslim groups throughout Europe. Seeking to develop a better understanding of Islam and Muslim culture in the **West**, its autonomous Council acts as a mediating agency between non-Muslim associations and international Muslim organizations, including the **OIC** and the **Muslim World League**.

ISLAMIC DEVELOPMENT BANK *see* IDB

ISLAMIC JIHAD

The clandestine **Sunni** organization which emerged in 1979 in the **Israeli-occupied territories** of the **West Bank** and **Gaza Strip**. Believed to have been founded by a militant wing of the Egyptian **Muslim Brotherhood**, it advocates armed resistance against **Israel** and is said to maintain links with the **al-Jihad** group in Egypt. While primarily opposed to Jewish occupation of **Palestine**, the group is also fiercely critical of most Muslim Arab regimes, although it has generally been supportive of the current Iranian leadership.

An identically named faction also operates in Lebanon where it has been associated with several terrorist attacks against Western targets, including two suicide truck bombings in 1983 in Beirut which killed a total of 300 US and French servicemen. It subsequently gained notoriety when it claimed responsibility for the kidnapping of Western hostages. It maintains close links with the pro-Iranian group, **Hezbollah**, and is a vocal opponent of the pro-Western Muslim governments of Kuwait, Lebanon and Saudi Arabia.

ISLAMIC REVOLUTION

The overthrow of a regime by Islamic **fundamentalists**. The term is most often used to describe the 1979 Iranian revolution. The monarchy of the Shah in Iran was replaced by an Islamic republic in which overall executive authority is exercised by the *wali faqih*, the country's spiritual leader.

ISLAMIC REVOLUTIONARY GUARDS *see* PASDARAN

ISLAMIC SOCIALISM

An ideological position which aims to combine Islamic principles with the broad tenets of Marxism on the assumption that 'true' Islam is progressive and opposed to social and economic oppression. It became particularly fashionable among Arab socialists in the 1950s, especially those associated with regional **Ba'ath** parties, and was subsequently espoused by **left-wing** groups in Iran represented by the **Mujaheddin-i-Khalq**. In the early 1970s it became popular in other parts of the Muslim world, notably in **Pakistan**, where it gained currency as the manifesto of the Pakistan People's Party under its then leader Prime Minister Zulfiqar Ali Bhutto.

ISLAMIST

A Muslim or group of Muslims dedicated to **Islamization** by political means. Many lean towards a radical or militant orientation which favours immediate, and often violent, action against the existing political establishment; others have favoured a moderate approach based on parliamentary politics. While claiming to act in keeping with the fundamental doctrines of their religion (hence their equation with **fundamentalist** groups), Islamists have tended to be selective in their reading of authoritative texts leaving them open to challenge by other Muslims. Prominent Islamist groups include the **Muslim Brotherhood** in Egypt and its off-shoots, and the various **jihad** movements and radical **Shia** factions allied to the **Hezbollah**.

ISLAMIZATION

A process peculiar to Muslim countries which seeks to implement Koranic or **sharia law** with a view to the creation of an Islamic state. While sometimes pursued by governments, as in Iran, Sudan and **Pakistan** in the 1980s, it has most vigorously been advocated by **Islamist** groups. Its common features have included the introduction of **interest-free banking**; canonical punishments (**hudood**); and rigid dress codes for women, especially the wearing of the veil, *hijab*.

ISRAEL

The Jewish state. Israel's history prior to 1948 is that of **Palestine**, within which **Zionists** had pressed for the creation of a Jewish state since the late nineteenth century. The Second World War led to an increase in Jewish migration to British-mandated **Palestine**, which in turn increased tension between Jewish settlers and Arabs. **Partition** into Jewish and Arab states was proposed, but was rejected by Palestinian Arabs. As details of the **Holocaust** emerged, Zionist leaders, impatient with the mandate, resorted to violence before proclaiming on 14 May 1948 an independent state of Israel within the **UN** partition boundaries. The neighbouring Arab states immediately invaded, but by early 1949 Israeli forces had not only repulsed the Arabs but had added territory to the land granted by the UN, thereby gaining control of some 75 per cent of Palestine. In subsequent Arab-Israeli wars (1956, 1967 and 1973) Israel occupied more Arab territory.

ISRAELI-OCCUPIED TERRITORIES

The Arab territory captured by **Israel** during the 1967 **Six-Day War** and subsequently occupied. The territories consisted of the (Egyptian) **Gaza Strip** and **Sinai** peninsula, the (Jordanian) **West Bank** and East **Jerusalem** and the (Syrian) **Golan Heights**. Successive Israeli governments have encouraged the expansion of Jewish **settlements** in the territories. The Sinai was returned to Egypt in the early 1980s under the terms of an Israeli-Egyptian peace accord. In September 1993 Israel and the **PLO** signed the so-called **Gaza-Jericho First** agreement under the terms of which Israel withdrew from the Gaza Strip and the West Bank town of Jericho in May 1994 and handed control of the area to a Palestinian authority.

ITAIPÚ DAM

The largest hydro-electric dam in the world. A joint project by Brazil and Paraguay on the river Paraná, costing an estimated of US$15,000 million, it is intended to generate 12.6 million kilowatts per hour when fully operational. Its construction led to a rapid influx of foreign investment into Paraguay and fuelled rapid economic growth between 1970 and 1980 which was localized in character and did not sustain the wider modernization of the economy. The majority of the finance, engineering expertise and construction came from Brazil; Paraguay, which lacked the capacity to use the energy generated by just one of the 18 turbines, was to sell the surplus energy to Brazil.

ITT SCANDAL

A scandal involving the activities of ITT (International Telephone and Telegraph) in the USA and overseas. The scandal broke in 1972 when a leaked memo from an ITT lobbyist indicated that the corporation had agreed to pay $400,000 towards the cost of that year's Republican convention in exchange for the settling of several outstanding anti-trust law suits against ITT. The corporation also funnelled funds through the **CIA** to the **right-wing** opposition in Chile in order to undermine the elected Marxist government of Salvador Allende, who was planning to nationalize the Chilean telephone company (Chitelco) in which ITT owned a 70 per cent share. Following the nationalization ITT pursued a relentless campaign which aimed to create chaos in Chile, and which culminated in the 1973 coup which overthrew the Allende government.

ITU

The International Telecommunications Union. A **UN** specialized agency since 1947, the ITU, based in Geneva, was originally founded in 1932 to promote international co-operation in telecommunications. It has over 160 member countries.

IUCN

The International Union for the Conservation of Nature and Natural Resources, also called the World Conservation Union, is based in Gland, Switzerland. Founded in 1948, the IUCN comprises representatives of government agencies and conservation organizations from over 100 countries. It is noted for the Red Data Books, produced by its Survival Service Commission, which give information on endangered and rare species of plants and animals. Five other IUCN commissions cover ecology, education, legislation, landscape planning and national parks.

IVF

In vitro fertilization, the medical technique in which an egg (ovum) is fertilized outside the body and the embryo is transferred to the uterus. The procedure involves mixing the ovum with sperm in a glass receptacle, hence *in vitro* as well as the colloquial expression 'test tube babies'. The procedure was perfected by Patrick Steptoe and Robert Edwards who achieved the first successful human pregnancy by IVF, resulting in the birth of Louise Brown on 26 July 1978 in Oldham, UK. The technique has raised a number of **bio-ethics** questions.

IVORY COAST *see* CÔTE D'IVOIRE

IWC

The International Whaling Commission, an intergovernmental association originally representing countries involved in whaling, and set up in 1946 to manage that industry; it has grown to become a 40-member body (including many countries opposed to whaling), but has no powers to enforce its resolutions. By 1970 eight species of whales had been hunted to near extinction; after years of pressure from environmental groups, the IWC in 1982 announced a moratorium on commercial whaling, which took effect from 1986. However, some commercial whaling continued (as well as whaling under the provision for 'scientific study'), carried out largely by Japan, Norway and Iceland, which either announced that they would not apply the (voluntary) moratorium, or resigned from the IWC. Although the pro-whaling countries failed in a bid to have the moratorium lifted at the annual conference in May 1993, in the following year the IWC agreed to a change of approach, replacing the moratorium with a permanent sanctuary for whales in the southern oceans. It had meanwhile been revealed in February 1994 that the **Soviet Union** had regularly under-reported its catches to the IWC over 40 years, which cast doubt on the IWC's current calculations of the world's whale stocks.

IZVESTIYA

(Russian, 'news') The influential Russian daily newspaper, founded in 1917, which under the Soviet system was the organ of the Presidium of the Supreme Soviet (the legislature), while **Pravda** was the organ of the party. Following the failed **August coup** in 1991, *Izvestiya* was transferred to its staff, who voted to appoint the reformist Igor Golembyovsky as editor-in-chief. In 1992, the paper was supported by Russian President Boris Yeltsin in its ownership dispute with the Russian Supreme Soviet, since when it has been one of the President's strongest advocates.

JACKAL

The popular nickname for Illich Ramirez Sanchez, the notorious terrorist, also known as Carlos. The name derives from Frederick Forsyth's 1970 novel *The Day of the Jackal*. Sanchez, a Venezuelan, worked for various groups allegedly from bases in Hungary, Iraq, South **Yemen** and **Yugoslavia**. His work reportedly included the kidnapping in 1975 of 11 oil ministers during an **OPEC** meeting. Following the end of the **Cold War** he is said to have gone into retirement in Syria.

JACKSON/VANIK AMENDMENT

The legislative basis for the USA to withhold trade concessions (e.g. **MFN** treatment and the granting of export credits) to countries which do not allow free emigration. The amendment, sponsored by Democratic Senator Henry Jackson and Democratic Representative Charles Vanik, was attached to the wide-ranging Trade Act 1975, and was initially aimed especially at the **Soviet Union** and certain east European countries which placed barriers on the emigration of their Jewish citizens.

JAL AIR DISASTER

The world's worst air crash involving a single aircraft, a Boeing 747 on a Japan Air Lines (JAL) flight from Tokyo to Osaka, which crashed in mountainous terrain on 12 August 1985 and killed 520 of the 524 passengers and crew. The accident was thought to be due to metal fatigue in one of the rear internal pressure bulkheads. Although an investigation conducted by the Japanese Transport Ministry failed to provide conclusive proof of this, in its final report on the crash the ministry criticized inadequate maintenance.

JAMAHARIYAH

(Arabic, 'state of the masses') A term coined by the Libyan regime of Col. Moamer al Kadhafi which in 1977 changed the official name of the country from 'Libyan Arab People's Republic' to 'Socialist People's Libyan Arab Jamahariyah'. The decision was one of several reached at a session of the General People's Congress (the Libyan equivalent of parliament) to proclaim officially 'the installation of people's power'.

JAMAICA AGREEMENT

An agreement reached in Kingston (Jamaica) in January 1976 by the Interim Committee of the **IMF** on major amendments to the Fund's Articles of Agreement. In particular, the decisions reached at Kingston covered the sale of some of the IMF's holdings of gold, and the 'restitution' of some to Fund members; the effective legalization of the floating system of currencies which already existed de facto; a redefinition of the valuation of the IMF's 'currency', the **SDR** (special drawing right); improved international surveillance of members' exchange rate policies; and an increase of members' quotas in the Fund by about a third.

JAMES BAY POWER PROJECT

A controversial hydroelectric project proposed by the Canadian state-owned Hydro Quebec company, involving the flooding of 10,000 square miles (26,000 sq km) in the James Bay area of Hudson Bay, which was strongly resisted by native Cree and Inuit populations. In February 1992 the International Water Tribunal, invited by Hydro Quebec to assess the project, recommended that it be halted for an **environmental impact assessment**. Cancellations of contracts to buy electricity also threaten the plan, which was originally scheduled for completion in 2006.

JAMMAAT AL-MUSLIMEEN

(Arabic, 'Society of Muslims') A black Muslim **fundamentalist** group in Trinidad and Tobago. The group staged an attempted coup in late July 1990, during which they held the Prime Minister and several cabinet ministers captive; their demands included the Prime Minister's resignation, elections within 90 days, the formation of a coalition government which would include the rebels, and an amnesty to be granted to all participants in the coup. In the face of the loyalty to the government of the security forces they surrendered on 1 August, having obtained a pardon in exchange for the Prime Minister's release. The 114 members of the group were imprisoned until July 1992 when the High Court, following a ruling by the Privy Council in London in November 1991, upheld the pardon and ordered their release and compensation for wrongful arrest. The government launched an appeal in May 1993.

JANATHA VIMUKTI PERAMUNA *see* JVP

JERUSALEM

The ancient and bitterly contested **Middle Eastern** city which is one of the primary holy sites of all three great monotheistic world religions (Judaism, Christianity and Islam). Jerusalem (and Bethlehem) were envisaged as 'international zones' under the **UN** partition of **Palestine**, but after the 1948 Arab-Israeli War the city was divided between **Israel**, which held the West, and Transjordan, which annexed the East. East Jerusalem was captured by Israel during the 1967 **Six-Day War**. In 1980 Israel adopted legislation strengthening the status of Jerusalem as the 'indivisible' capital of Israel. The international community refused, however, to recognize Jerusalem as Israel's capital and the few countries with embassies in the city shifted them to Tel Aviv.

JEWISH AGENCY

Quasi-governmental body which has organized the immigration of Jews to **Israel** since its establishment in 1929 under the terms of the British Palestine Mandate, and set in motion Israel's independence in 1948. Reconstituted in 1971, it remains, despite recent corruption scandals, one of the holy cows of **Zionism**. The agency is largely funded by the Jewish community of the **diaspora**.

JEWISH LOBBY

Collective term for the powerful US Jewish pressure groups such as the **AIPAC** and **B'nai B'rith**. The Jewish lobby is particularly influential within the Democratic Party and is especially active in promoting support for **Israel**.

JHARKAND MUKTI MORCHA

(Bihari, 'Jharkand People's Party') A separatist movement based in the north-east Indian state of Bihar. It was founded in 1980 and is committed to a separate state for the Jharkand tribespeople. In September 1992 it was responsible for a two-week economic blockade of the state in an attempt to force the central government to concede its demands. Its leader, Asim Mahato, was assassinated by unknown gunmen near the Bihar town of Jamshedpur in May 1993.

JIHAD

(Arabic, 'effort') A term commonly signifying 'holy war', a divine institution enjoined upon Muslims to extend Islam or to defend it from danger. In colonial times the concept inspired Muslims to resist European occupation; more recently it has been espoused by a network of radical Muslim groups, particularly in the **Middle East**, which are committed to the overthrow of allegedly corrupt Muslim leaders. In Egypt the *al-Jihad* group uncovered in 1979 claimed responsibility for the assassination of President Anwar el Sadat in October 1981. Since the mid-1980s the group has been associated with a variety of terrorist attacks against government leaders and the Christian minority in Upper Egypt.

JIU VALLEY MINERS

The coal miners of Romania's Jiu Valley area, who have played a decisive role in postcommunist politics. Anti-government demonstrations by students and others in the capital Bucharest in April–June 1990 were brutally dispersed by a force of 10,000 miners, allegedly transported to Bucharest at the government's behest. The miners returned in September 1991, to protest at government economic policy, and fought police during three days of riots which forced Prime Minister Petre Roman from office. Hundreds of people were injured in each incident.

JOHN BIRCH SOCIETY

An extreme **right-wing** group founded in the USA in 1958 by Robert H. W. Welch. It derived its name from Capt. John M. Birch who had conducted behind-the-lines intelligence work in China until being killed by the Chinese **communists** in 1945. In addition to advocating traditional right-wing values, the aim of the society was to expose a 'communist conspiracy' which, it alleged, was operating through a series of front organizations. Among the more preposterous of the society's claims was that Republican President Dwight D. Eisenhower and Secretary of State John Foster Dulles were communists. In 1968 the group claimed to have 100,000 members.

JOINT DECLARATION

The 1984 Sino-British agreement which enshrined the British acceptance that Hong Kong should revert to Chinese sovereignty on 1 July 1997. The declaration provided that at that date not only the New Territories should revert to China (having hitherto been held on a 99-year lease) but also Hong Kong Island, which had been ceded to Britain in 1842. The whole territory would comprise a Chinese 'special administrative region' which would have a high degree of autonomy and in which Hong Kong's **capitalist** system and lifestyle should remain unchanged for 50 years from 1997.

JOINT LIAISON GROUP

The joint Sino-British liaison group set up to discuss matters arising from the planned transition of Hong Kong to Chinese sovereignty in 1997 under the 1984 **Joint Declaration**. The work of the Joint Liaison Group was thrown into some disarray by Governor Chris Patten's announcement in November 1992 of proposed moves towards democracy in Hong Kong in advance of the 1997 handover.

JOINT VENTURE

An economic undertaking entered into jointly by a government, or commercial interests within a country, and outside investors. Typically, joint ventures have been between developing countries and outside investors from the developed world; since the late 1980s they have also been seen increasingly in former **communist** countries. Such ventures are seen by the local party as an opportunity to secure much-needed external investment, and by the outside investor as an opportunity to gain a toe-hold for spreading their interests in the country concerned, whose markets may hitherto have been strictly controlled.

JONESTOWN MASSACRE

The mass deaths at Jonestown, an agricultural commune in the Guyana jungle. The Rev. Jim Jones, founder in 1957 of a US religious cult, the People's Temple, moved 1,000 of his followers to Guyana in 1976 to set up the Jonestown commune. In November 1978 the members of a delegation investigating the sect – led by US Congressman Leo Ryan – were murdered while visiting Jonestown. Following the incident Jones ordered his followers to take poison. He then shot himself. A total of 913 bodies, including that of Jones, were discovered at the commune on 29 November.

JONGLEI CANAL

A major Sudanese development and irrigation scheme along the White Nile, Bahr al-Zeraf and Sobat Rivers. Construction began in 1970s although it had been proposed as early as 1948. The main goals were to keep 11,500 million cubic yards (15,000 million cubic metres) of water from being lost annually through evaporation in the swamp or *sudd* regions, as well as to establish flood control, improve river navigation and develop an extensive agricultural scheme. The conserved water was to be shared by Sudan and Egypt. However, construction was halted in 1984 as a result of the conflict between the government in Khartoum and the rebel **SPLA**.

JORDAN

The name taken by Transjordan (in effect the east bank of the Jordan) in 1949 after the acquisition in 1948 of some 2,300 square miles (5,900 sq km) of **Palestine**, the remainder of which had become the state of **Israel** following the termination of the British mandate. Transjordan had become fully independent in 1946 following the termination of its British mandate.

JOYRIDER

A person who steals a car to drive it fast and recklessly for pleasure. In the UK the Aggravated Vehicle-Taking Act passed on 6 March 1992 increased the maximum penalty for joyriding to five years' imprisonment.

JUCHE

(Korean, translated as 'self-reliance', 'self-image' or 'self-independence') The prevailing ideology of North Korea. Formulated in the mid-1950s by the country's **Great Leader**, Kim Il Sung, *Juche* gradually came to replace Marxist-Leninism as the ideology of the ruling Korean Worker's Party (KWP). Its four principles are (i) the primacy of the ruling party; (ii) equality of status for all parties of the international **communist** movement; (iii) **autarchy** and the construction of a socialist economy from native resources; and (iv) national security through the maintenance of a powerful army. In addition to cementing the basis of Kim's extravagant personality cult, Juchism also gave North Korea a unique ideological identity and allowed the leadership to circumvent many of the problems arising from the **Sino-Soviet split**.

JUDEA AND SAMARIA *see* WEST BANK

JUNK BONDS

High-risk, high-yield bonds, not secured by tangible assets, which were symbolic of the financial risks and massive profits associated with the US stock market in the late 1980s. A leading player in the junk bond market was Michael Milken, of Drexel, Burnham, Lambert Inc., a major Wall Street investment house. In 1990 Milken was sentenced to 10 years' in prison for fraud, although the sentence was reduced in 1992 in recognition of his co-operation with the authorities.

JUNTA

(from Spanish, 'committee', 'council') A political term for a ruling body formed by a small group, normally after a **coup d'état**. First occurring in nineteenth century **Latin America**, their membership can be a combination of civilians and military, as was the case in El Salvador between 1979 and 1982. However, since the 1950s most juntas have been solely military, consisting of the chiefs of the various military services and military police, typified by the four-member junta in Chile between 1973 and 1989 and the three-member junta ruling Argentina from 1976 to 1983.

JVP

(Sinhala acronym for *Janatha Vimukti Peramuna* – National Liberation Front) A Sinhalese insurgent group founded in 1967 by Rohana Wijeweere which sought to combine Marxist ideals with a brand of Buddhist fundamentalism that evoked the glories of **Sri Lanka**'s Buddhist past. After gaining formal recognition as a political party in 1982, the group was proscribed in 1983 for its open espousal of violence. It re-emerged in 1987 in response to radical Tamil **nationalism** and became responsible for a brutal assassination campaign against its opponents. Most of the JVP's leadership and effectively the JVP itself were wiped out during a fierce counteroffensive launched by the Sri Lankan Army during late 1989 and early 1990.

KABAKA OF BUGANDA

The King of the Buganda, an ancient kingdom in Uganda. Ronald Muwenda Mutebi, was crowned the 36th Kabaka in a ceremony restoring the kingdom on 31 July 1993. The revival of the kingdom had the blessing of the government, and President Yoweri Museveni's presence at the ceremony was regarded as a gesture to repay the Baganda people for their support during the 1981–6 civil war. The previous Kabaka, Mutebi's father, was Sir Edward Frederick Mutesa – 'King Freddy'. In 1963 he had become the first federal President of Uganda but was overthrown in 1966 by Milton Obote.

KACH

(Hebrew, 'thus') An ultra-militant Zionist group which has defined the outer boundary of the far right in **Israel** since the early 1970s. Founded by Rabbi Meyer Kahane (the group's leader until his assassination in New York in 1990), Kach advocates 'transfer' or the physical removal of all Arabs from Israel and from the **Israeli-occupied territories**. The Israeli government declared it an illegal terrorist organization in March 1994 after Baruch Goldstein, perpetrator of the February 1994 **Hebron mosque massacre** of Palestinian worshippers, was reported to have links with the group.

KACHIN INDEPENDENCE ORGANIZATION *see* KIO

KAL-007

The identification number of the Korean Airlines Boeing 747 airliner which was shot down by a Soviet fighter aircraft over Sakhalin Island, off Siberia, in September 1983. All 269 passengers and crew on the scheduled flight from New York City to Seoul were killed in the incident, and there was widespread international condemnation of the **Soviet Union** for having ordered the attack. Precisely why the airliner had strayed so far from its prescribed route, and why it failed to respond to Soviet challenges prior to its destruction, remain unresolved.

KALASHNIKOV *see* AK-47

KAMPUCHEA

Cambodia. The names Cambodia and Kampuchea are both transliterations of the country's traditional name in the Khmer language, which is sometimes rendered phonetically as 'Kambuja'. Cambodia was adopted as the English spelling for the French transliteration 'Cambodge'. After independence the country was known as the Kingdom of Cambodia. Under Lon Nol's Khmer Republic (1970–5) official use of the transliteration Cambodia (but not Kampuchea) was discouraged, possibly because of its colonial connotations. The **Khmer Rouge** regime (1975–9) changed the country's title to Democratic Kampuchea and it was at this time that 'Kampuchea' began to appear as the country's name in the Western media.

KANAKS

The native Melanesian population of the French overseas territory of New Caledonia. A minority in the population as a whole, the Kanaks are in the majority in two of the country's three provinces: the North and the Loyalty Islands. Kanak demands for independence, voiced largely through the coalition Kanak Socialist National Liberation Front, conflicted with the wishes of the white community to remain attached to France. This led to political violence in the 1980s. Tensions between the Kanaks and the settlers escalated into political violence in the 1980s, until a new constitutional structure was implemented under the 1988 **Matignon Accord**.

KAREN NATIONAL UNION *see* KNU

KASHMIR

The territory in the north-west of the **Indian sub-continent** which has been the subject of rival claims by India and **Pakistan** and the cause of two wars between them, in 1948 and 1965. The conflict centres on the controversial accession to India in 1947 of the Hindu ruler of this predominantly Muslim kingdom in apparent defiance of an agreement by all parties to hold a plebiscite. The accession was challenged by Pakistan which, in September 1947, lent its support to a Muslim-led rebellion in Kashmir. The war between India and Pakistan in 1948 resulted in the containment of the Muslim rebels in the northern half of the territory. The 1965 conflict changed little, but further fighting in 1971 resulted in the de facto border being somewhat modified. India and Pakistan agreed at Simla in 1972 to respect the new **line of control**. The Muslim-held area had been designated **Azad Kashmir**, while the state of Jammu and Kashmir is constitutionally a part of India. The Kashmir crisis has been marked by continuing violence between the Indian security forces and militant Muslim groups and by several thousand civilian deaths.

KASSINGA MASSACRE

The killing of more than 700 Namibians on 4 May 1978 during an airborne attack by South African troops on a **SWAPO** refugee camp in Kassinga, Angola. Between 200 and 300 refugees were abducted and detained in **Namibia**, although for five years the South African government consistently denied that it was holding prisoners from Kassinga. In 1980 the International Committee of the Red Cross (**ICRC**) reported that at least 118 Kassinga survivors remained in detention; 137 people were eventually released, the final group in September 1984.

KATA'IB *see* PHALANGE

KATYN

The site near the Russian city of Smolensk where some 15,000 captive Polish Army officers were massacred in 1940. The Poles had been deported to camps in the **Soviet Union** following the Soviet occupation of eastern Poland in 1939. For decades the official Soviet accounts blamed German troops for carrying out the Katyn killings after they invaded the area in 1941, but in April 1990 the Soviet Union officially admitted responsibility.

KAZAKHSTAN

The largest although not the most populous of the newly independent **Central Asian** republics, Kazakhstan was until 1991 one of the 15 constituent republics of the **Soviet Union**.

KEATING FIVE

The US Senators linked with Charles Keating, the owner of the failed Lincoln savings and loan, who had accepted a total of $1.3 million in campaign contributions from him in the mid-1980s, and were alleged to have intervened on his behalf when he was investigated for criminal fraud. The five were Democrats Alan Cranston, majority whip in the upper chamber, John Glenn, Dennis De Concini, and Donald Riegel, and Republican John McCain. The Senate Ethics Committee investigated the matter between November 1990 and February 1991. It found that four had displayed poor judgment, but that there was substantial evidence of misconduct against only Alan Cranston, who had accepted by far the largest share of the contributions. Cranston – who had announced his intention not to seek re-election in 1992 on the grounds of ill health – was rebuked by the committee on 20 November 1991, for 'improper conduct'.

KENNEBUNKPORT

A coastal town in the US state of Maine where President George Bush owned a holiday home in which he spent his summer vacations.

KENNEDY DOCTRINE *see* FREEDOM DOCTRINE

KENNEDY DYNASTY

Prominent US political family from the state of Massachusetts. Of Irish-Catholic descent, the family's political tradition began with Joseph Kennedy, a multi-millionaire and ambassador to the UK in 1938–40, whose sympathy towards **fascism** was the cause of considerable controversy. Three sons of this domineering father went on to achieve high office. John F. Kennedy was elected President in 1960, but was assassinated in Dallas in 1963. Robert Kennedy, who had served as Attorney General in his elder brother's administration, was assassinated in California in June 1968 when he was poised to be chosen as the Democratic Party's presidential candidate. Edward Kennedy has served as a member of the Senate since 1962; his ambition for higher office was terminally damaged by the **Chappaquiddick** incident of 1969, and after an unsuccessful attempt to win the Democratic Party nomination in 1980, he effectively renounced his presidential ambitions. The first of the third generation of Kennedys emerged into mainstream politics in 1986 with the election to the House of Representatives of Joseph Kennedy III, one of the children of Robert.

KENNEDY ROUND

The **GATT** round of multilateral trade negotiations held in 1964–7, covering, for the first time, various non-tariff measures and also agriculture. It resulted in a number of agreements of particular interest to the large number of newly independent countries, as well as to the traditional developed trading nations, but made only limited progress on agriculture.

KENT STATE

Kent State University, in the US state of Ohio, where the Ohio National Guard opened fire on demonstrating students on 4 May 1970, killing four people and wounding nine. The demonstration followed the announcement on 30 April by President Richard Nixon that he had ordered an military incursion into Cambodia, thereby formally extending the parameters of the **Vietnam War**. The announcement unleashed a wave of student protests which caused the National Guard to be deployed in 16 states. In addition to the incident at Kent State, two people were shot at Jackson State College, a black campus in Mississippi, and students at some 350 colleges staged strikes.

KEYNESIAN

An exponent of the highly influential branch of economic theory developed by John Maynard Keynes (1883–1946), which challenged the classical economic assumption that **capitalism** inevitably involved a cycle of booms and slumps. Keynes argued in his *General Theory of Employment, Interest and Money* (1936) that the level of employment was determined by demand, rather than by wages. Therefore, non-inflationary growth could be achieved and full employment maintained by increasing aggregate demand, particularly through government intervention in the form of public works programmes, even at the risk of running a budget deficit. Keynesian theory was first applied in the USA as the basis for F. D. Roosevelt's New Deal, and became the prevailing economic orthodoxy in both the USA and Western Europe in the post-War period. However, in the face of **stagflation** in the 1970s, it was challenged by **monetarism**, an economic theory advanced by the **Chicago Boys** and adopted by the **New Right** which focused on policies to affect the supply side rather than the demand side.

KGB

(Russian acronym for *Komitet Gosudarstvennoy Bezopasnosti* – 'Committee on State Security') The **Soviet Union's** security police, established in 1954. The KGB structure bound together 17 separate agencies, employing an estimated 100,000 staff, whose responsibilities spanned domestic and foreign intelligence-gathering, the supervision of censorship and of travel to and from the Soviet Union, and control of a force of some 300,000 border guards. The KGB was scrapped after the **August coup** of 1991 and replaced in Russia in January 1994 by the Federal Counterintelligence Service.

KHALISTAN

(Punjabi, 'land of the pure') The name of the independent Sikh state, conforming to the present boundaries of the Indian state of Punjab, demanded by Sikh extremists. It gained prominence in 1982 as the object of a 'holy struggle' (*dharmyudha*) launched by the main Sikh political organization, the **Akali Dal**, under the control of militant factions. The storming by Indian troops of the **Golden Temple** in Amritsar in June 1984, which resulted in the deaths of several hundred Sikh militants, hardened the demand for a Sikh homeland and unleashed a wave of violence that continues to dominate political life in Punjab.

KHE SANH

One of the bloodiest and most protracted battles of the **Vietnam War**. The siege of the US Marine base at Khe Sanh, situated close to the border with Laos and just south of the **DMZ**, lasted from mid-January to early April 1968. The North Vietnamese and their southern allies launched the siege as a strategy to divert US resources and attention to the remote north away from the southern urban targets of February's **Tet offensive**. In the USA the siege represented a turning point in the war. Daily media reports of the plight of the besieged marines aroused feelings of despair among the US public which quickly turned to anger at the Johnson adminstration and its Vietnam policy. For President Lyndon Johnson the siege became a personal obsession and he ordered one of the most concentrated bombing missions ever made in order to relieve the marines. The North Vietnamese lost some 10,000 men at Khe Sanh, mostly as a result of the bombing; fewer than 500 marines died during the siege.

KHMERS ROUGES

The term coined by Cambodian leader Prince Norodom Sihanouk for the Chinese-backed Cambodian **communists** who came to power in 1975. Led by Pol Pot, the *Khmer Rouge* regime embarked on a disastrous pre-planned economic and social experiment, based to a large extent on China's **Great Leap Forward** of the late 1950s. By the time the regime was toppled by Vietnam in late 1978, many hundreds of thousands of Cambodians had died from brutal treatment, starvation and disease. The ousted *Khmers Rouges* took up arms against the new pro-Vietnamese government (the backbone of which was a group of mutinous *Khmer Rouge* cadres), joining Sihanouk in the Western-backed **CGDK**. The *Khmers Rouges* refused to accept the terms of a peace accord signed in 1991 and boycotted **UN**-supervised elections held two years later. The new coalition government formed in 1993 has pursued an aggressive military policy against the *Khmers Rouges*, which has nevertheless maintained control of large sections of western and northern Cambodia.

KIBBUTZ

(Hebrew, 'gathering' or 'collective') An Israeli collective settlement, typically agriculturally based, in which all wealth is held in common. The first kibbutz was organized at Deganya in **Palestine** in 1909. In subsequent years kibbutzim played an important role in the pioneering of new Jewish settlements in Palestine. Following the creation of **Israel** in 1948, the democratic and egalitarian nature of the kibbutz exercised a forceful influence on Israeli politics and society in general.

KILLING FIELDS

Areas of rural Cambodia used by the **Khmers Rouges** during their period in power (1975–9) to execute their opponents and critics and hide their remains. Since the release in 1984 of the British film *The Killing Fields* the term has often been employed in a wider sense to symbolize the all-pervading brutality of the *Khmer Rouge* regime.

KING DAVID HOTEL

The site in **Jerusalem** of a notorious bomb attack carried out in July 1946 against British soldiers and officials by the Jewish **guerrilla** group **Irgun**.

KIO

The Kachin Independence Organization, a separatist group which, until it signed a ceasefire with the ruling **SLORC** in February 1994, had been regarded as the most effective and best organized of the myriad insurgent groups operating in Burma.

KIRGHIZIA *see* KIRGIZSTAN

KIRGIZSTAN

A republic in **Central Asia**, one of the successor states of the former **Soviet Union**. Previously the Soviet republic of Kirgizia, it declared independence after the failed **August coup** of 1991. Some 40 per cent of the population of 4.5 million is composed of the Turkic-speaking, moderately Islamic Kirgiz community, originally a nomadic and pastoral people. The considerable community of ethnic Russians and Ukrainians settled in Kirgizstan in the nineteenth and twentieth centuries.

KIRIBATI

The Micronesian territory composed of 33 atolls within an area of 2 million square miles (5 million sq km). A former British colony, when it was known as the Gilbert Islands, Kiribati achieved independence on 12 July 1979. The Gilbert Islands were administered jointly with the Ellice Islands as the Gilbert and Ellice Islands Colony until 1 October 1975, when the Ellice Islands were allowed to secede to form a separate territory, **Tuvalu**.

KITH AND KIN

A slogan adopted by British supporters of Ian Smith's declaration of **UDI** in **Rhodesia** in 1965. The slogan was based on the belief that the British government would have neither the political will nor the desire to act against 'white Rhodesians' because of their kinship ties with people in the UK.

KLEPTOCRACY

The term used to describe the corrupt and authoritarian rule of Ferdinand and Imelda Marcos in the Philippines between November 1965 and February 1986. They, together with almost 300 of their 'cronies', were accused by a government commission in 1987 of having defrauded the state of some

US$90,000 million. The term has subsequently been applied to other regimes guilty of massive embezzlement of state funds.

KMT

(Chinese abbreviation of *Kuomintang*, 'Nationalist Party of China') The ruling party of **Taiwan**, which still claims to be the legitimate government of mainland China (the **PRC**). Founded in 1894 by Sun Yat-sen, the KMT gained its current name in October 1919. Its ideology is based on Sun Yat-sen's Three Principles of the People: **nationalism**, democracy, and social wellbeing.

Having come to power following the overthrow of the Manchu imperial dynasty, the party governed China in the inter-war period, during which time it was engaged in conflict with the Chinese **Communist** Party (CCP) and local warlords. During its period in office the party was associated with massive corruption and inefficiency, and the government was defeated by Communist forces in 1949, whereupon it fled to Taiwan. Here, under the leadership of Gen. Chiang Kai-shek, the KMT presided over a highly centralized system, effectively a **one-party state**. However, under increasing pressure for democratization, it gradually relaxed control from the 1970s onwards, allowing other political parties to function from 1987.

KNEECAPPING

A form of punishment carried out particularly by the **IRA** and other paramilitary organizations in **Northern Ireland**. Kneecapping – crippling victims by shooting them in the knee – has generally been performed less on political opponents than upon those who have brought the organization into disrepute, frequently supporters or former supporters whose behaviour has been condemned by the leaders. More recently those deemed to have committed 'anti-social' crimes such as mugging or drug dealing have also been kneecapped.

KNESSET

(Hebrew, 'assembly') The **Israeli** unicameral 120-member legislature located in **Jerusalem**. Israel has never adopted a formal, written constitution, but among several constitutional laws the Basic Law (The Knesset) was passed in 1958.

KNU

The Karen National Union, a **guerrilla** organization in Burma which has fought for a separate Karen state since the late 1940s. Reports in early 1994 indicated that the KNU was engaged in preliminary peace talks with members of the ruling **SLORC**.

KOEVOET

(Afrikaans, 'crowbar') The paramilitary **counterinsurgency** unit which operated in **Namibia** during the period of South African rule. The unit comprised more than 1,000 mostly black members commanded by white South African police officers or mercenaries, including former members of the Rhodesian **Selous Scouts**. It was used exclusively to combat the activities of **SWAPO guerrillas**, concentrating its operations in the north of the country where its use of terror and intimidation were widely feared. *Koevoet* members allegedly received *kopgeld* or'head money' for each person they killed.

KOMSOMOL

The youth movement of the **CPSU**.

KONFRONTASI

(Indonesian, 'confrontation') The low-level military conflict launched by Indonesia in 1963 against the newly formed Federation of **Malaysia**. Indonesian President Sukarno perceived the formation of the Federation (comprising the Malay peninsular, Singapore, and neighbouring Sarawak and Sabah on the island of Borneo) as a base of neo-colonialism intent on subverting his **Guided Democracy** experiment. With the backing of China and the **Soviet Union**, Sukarno initiated military action along the border with Sarawak and Sabah and in mid-1964 Indonesian military forces were sent into the Malay Peninsula. Malaysian and Commonwealth troops contained the Indonesian challenge and, following Sukarno's downfall in 1966, the new regime ended *konfrontasi*.

KOR

(Polish acronym for *Komitet Obrony Robotnikow*, 'Committee for the Defence of Workers') A group founded by dissident intellectuals and professionals in Warsaw in September 1976 to assist workers and students arrested for protesting against the economic reforms originally mooted by the **communist** government in June 1976. The KOR offered legal assistance, gave financial assistance to families, and also publicised many cases.

KOREAGATE

The US scandal in 1977 involving Park Tong Sun , a South Korean rice broker. In the nine years following his appointment as his country's exclusive rice-purchasing agent in 1968, Park claimed to have given cash and gifts worth US$850,000 to 31 Democratic members of **Congress** in an effort to buy influence. Indicted on 36 criminal charges, Park was given immunity in return for co-operating with the authorities. In the subsequent investigation, three Congressman were reprimanded, and one, Richard T. Hanna, served a year in prison for fraud.

KOREAN WAR

The war in 1950–3 between **communist** North Korea (supported by the **Soviet Union** and China) and South Korea (supported by the USA and the **UN**). With each claiming to be the legitimate government of the entire peninsula, a series of military provocations by both sides culminated on 25 June 1950 with a full-scale invasion by the North across the **38th parallel**. After quickly occupying much of the South, the North was itself overrun on the intervention of UN (largely US) forces, before the tide was turned once again by the intervention in November of huge numbers of Chinese 'volunteers'. From early 1951 onwards the war became a static attritional conflict which ended with the signing of an armistice agreement on 27 July 1953. The agreement meant that the ceasefire line (which straddled the 38th parallel) became a Demilitarized Zone (**DMZ**), and came to constitute the de facto border between the two Korean states. Total UN casualties (those killed, wounded, captured or missing) in the conflict were estimated at 160,000, of whom 142,000 were from the USA. South Korean casualties were estimated at 1,113,000, while Chinese and North Korean losses were generally thought to have exceeded 900,000 and 520,000 respectively. The North also suffered civilian casualties in excess of 1 million as a result of US bombing.

KOSOVAR ALBANIANS

The Albanian-speaking community which forms some 85 per cent of the population of the Serbian province of Kosovo-Metohija (Kosovo). Their numerical dominance upsets Serbian nationalists, for whom Kosovo has a special significance within **Yugoslavia** as the historical cradle of Serbian culture. Alleged discrimination by Kosovar Albanians against local Serbs formed the pretext for a Serbian crackdown in June 1990, the imposition of direct rule from Belgrade, arrests of Albanian nationalists and the closure of Albanian-language schools. The Kosovar Albanians responded by proclaiming Kosovo an independent republic after holding illegal elections to a Kosovar assembly in May 1992. Ibrahim Rugova, an activist advocating passive resistance to Serbian rule, was elected (again illegally) as Kosovo's President.

KRAJINA

(Serbo-Croat, 'borderlands') Several pockets of territory within the present and historic borders of **Croatia**, whose total population of some 300,000 is mainly Serb and which have been under Serb control since the Croatian war of 1991–2. The Yugoslav civil war arguably began in Krajina: local Serbs, apprehensive about rising Croatian **nationalism**, voted overwhelmingly in a referendum on 12 May 1991 'to remain part of **Yugoslavia** with Serbia and **Montenegro**'. This vote contrasted with a Croatian referendum on 19 May, effectively calling for independence. A civil war in Croatia began with armed clashes between Krajina Serbs and Croatian police in

May and June 1991. The Republic of Serbian Krajina, under a Serbian nationalist President, Milan Babic, was proclaimed in December 1991, with the clear aim of eventual unification with a **Greater Serbia**. The Krajina comprise a strip of land in eastern Slavonia conquered in 1991 by the Yugoslav People's Army (JNA), including the town of **Vukovar**; and a belt of land extending from the Banija, south of the Croatian capital Zagreb, to northern Dalmatia.

KREMLIN

A walled complex of buildings in central Moscow, the seat of the government of the **Soviet Union** and a term often used as synonymous with the Soviet leadership. In February 1994, in a symbolic gesture, the Russian government and presidency transferred their headquarters to the **White House**, formerly the seat of the Russian Parliament.

KREMLIN COUP *see* AUGUST COUP

KREMLINOLOGY

The close study of political machinations within the **Kremlin**. During the years of **Cold War** the highly secretive and centralized party machine of the **CPSU** revealed little of its internal politics. However, Western journalists and academics schooled in Kremlinology were sometimes able to draw far-reaching inferences from the most apparently mundane government statements, and from such signs as changes in personnel or status as revealed by public protocol.

KU KLUX KLAN

A US white **racist** paramilitary organization with a long history of acts of violence against blacks and those associated with the liberal-left or the **civil rights movement**. Established in Tennessee at the end of the Civil War in 1865, the Klan rapidly spread throughout the defeated states of the **South**, terrorizing the newly emancipated black population. It was banned in 1871, but re-emerged in Georgia in 1915 and by the mid-1920s had spread beyond the boundaries of the old Confederacy and was estimated to have 5 million members. When the USA entered the war against Nazi Germany, the Klan was discredited and it was disbanded in 1944. It re-emerged once more in the 1960s, particularly in the South, as a reaction against the civil rights movement. Despite harassment by the federal authorities, the Klan remains active, although it appears to be once again in a period of decline.

KUNG FU RIOTS

Serious disturbances in Madagascar in response to the August 1984 banning of the martial art of kung fu. King fu clubs had attracted 10,000 members, mainly urban youths, and were held responsible for a rise in crime. Rioting in December 1984, which resulted in the death of at least 50 people, was followed by the dismissal of senior security personnel. On 1 August 1985 the security forces attempted to take the headquarters of the clubs, whose members they accused of seeking a 'state within a state' and of planning to seize political power. In the subsequent clashes at least 20 were killed, including Pierre Mizael Andrianarijaona, the grand master of kung fu on the island, who had denounced the 'godless' nature of the Ratsiraka regime.

KUOMINTANG *see* KMT

KURDISTAN

The land of the Kurds, a Muslim people, whose numbers were estimated in 1990 at some 18–20 million. Kurds live in the mainly mountainous region of eastern and southeastern Turkey, northern Iraq, parts of north-western Iran, and a slice of north-eastern Syria. Since the early thirteenth century much of this area has been called Kurdistan, although it was not until the sixteenth century that the term came into common usage. The existence of Kurdistan is officially denied by Turkey while Iraq and Iran are reluctant to acknowledge that it is as extensive as the Kurds claim.

KURILES (NORTHERN TERRITORIES)

The four islands (or groups of islands) whose disputed ownership has been the main obstacle to good relations between Japan and Russia. Etorofu, Kunashiri, Shikotan and the Habomai group, lying off the north-western coast of Japan, were occupied by the Soviet Army after the **Soviet Union** declared war on Japan on 8 August 1945. The emotive dispute centres on whether these islands are to be considered among those which the **Allies** agreed would be handed to the Soviet Union when it entered the war against Japan. In 1956 a Soviet-Japanese declaration stated that Shikotan and the Habomai islets would be returned to Japan on the conclusion of a peace treaty, but this was repudiated by successive Soviet and Russian governments. Japanese insistence on the return of all four islands impeded the signing of a peace treaty between Japan and the Soviet Union, and held up any Japanese offer of significant economic aid to Russia. Boris Yeltsin's first visit to Japan as Russian President took place only on 11–13 October 1993, after public cancellations of two earlier scheduled visits, and failed to produce significant progress on the issue.

KYRGYZIA, KYRGYZSTAN *see* KIRGIZSTAN

LAKE NYOS DISASTER

The escape of toxic gas from Lake Nyos, a remote volcanic lake in north-east Cameroon, which killed up to 2,000 people. It began on the night of 26 August 1986, when a dense cloud of carbon dioxide mixed with hydrogen sulphur erupted through a fissure in the lake bottom, killing around 90 per cent of the inhabitants of the villages around the lake as they slept. A further 20,000 people living further away were seriously affected.

LAME DUCK PRESIDENT

An outgoing US President, in the period of over two-and-a-half months between the presidential elections (in early November) and the beginning of the new president's term on 20 January of the following year. The term applies particularly to incumbents who have been defeated in a bid for re-election, but also to those not seeking re-election, or not able to do so because of the constitutional bar on serving more than two terms. Although specific to the USA, the common usage of the term has meant that in recent years it has also come to be applied to leaders in other countries who face imminent and certain departure from office.

LANCASTER HOUSE AGREEMENT

The agreement brokered by UK Foreign and Commonwealth Secretary Lord Carrington, ending **UDI** and heralding the independence of **Zimbabwe**. After months of tense negotiations at Lancaster House in London, the agreement was signed on 21 December 1979 by former Rhodesian leader Ian Smith, the then Prime Minister Bishop Abel Muzorewa, Robert Mugabe and Joshua Nkomo, the two main nationalist leaders, and Lord Carrington and Sir Ian Gilmour, representing the British delegation. It provided for a new constitution, under which white minority rights were safeguarded, and instituted special legislative representation for whites for seven years. It also specified a short transition period, during which British sovereignty over the country would be re-established and would be exercised by a Governor (Lord Soames). During the transition the opposing forces were demobilized and a Commonwealth peacekeeping force was deployed. Democratic elections under the new Constitution were held on 27–29 February 1980 and independence was declared on 18 April 1980.

LAND FOR PEACE

The diplomatic formula in **Middle East** peace negotiations whereby **Israel** relinquishes territory captured from the Arab states in return for recognition and peace. The formula was used in the 1979 Israeli-Egyptian peace agreement, wherein the Israeli-occupied **Sinai** peninsula was returned to Egypt, which in turn established full diplomatic relations with the Jewish state. In 1994 negotiations have been under way on a 'land for peace' deal covering an Israeli withdrawal from the **Golan Heights** in return for Syrian recognition.

LÄNDER

(German, 'lands') The 16 states of Germany which exercise competence in all matters not devolved to the federal government. The *Länder* have exclusive responsibility for culture, education, environment, local government and planning, police, and broadcasting, while the federal government is responsible for currency, defence, foreign policy, and posts and telecommunications. Each *Land* has its own constitution, elected legislature, and government, whose members send delegates to fill the 69-seat *Bundesrat* (the federal legislature's upper chamber).

LATIFUNDIO

(Spanish, 'large estate') A large tract of land generally worked by landless peasants or holders of *minifundios* in a semi-feudal relationship with the *latifundista* or landowner. Spain and Portugal awarded *latifundios* throughout most of **Latin America** to servants of the crown during the colonial period. The power of the *latifundistas* grew after the granting of independence to the colonies during the nineteenth century, leading to the phenomenon of **caudillismo** which hindered national political development and provoked periodic peasant uprisings. Most valuable agricultural land in Latin America remains in the hands of a few *latifundistas*, a situation highlighted by the January 1994 uprising in Mexico by the **EZLN**, whose demands include that of land reform.

LATIN AMERICA

A term used to describe the Spanish-speaking countries of **Central America, South America** and the **Caribbean**, as well as Portuguese-speaking Brazil. A region of dramatically contrasting geography, it nevertheless retains the imprint of Iberian **colonialism**, a legacy denounced by the indigenous population during the 1992 **Columbus Quincentenary**. Other persistent themes include the frailty of democratic government in the face of the military, who in the majority of countries have yet to relinquish their considerable power, and the fragility of economic development, which remains dependent on the export of raw materials.

LATVIA

One of the three **Baltic states**, with a population of 2.7 million, whose territory historically formed part of the Russian empire. The first independent Latvian state was proclaimed in 1918 in the wake of the First World War, but it was annexed in 1940 by the **Soviet Union**, to become one of the its 15 constituent republics. Latvia declared independence in May 1990 and was admitted to the **UN** in September 1991. The Soviet authorities encouraged Russian emigration to Latvia, and as a result some 40 per cent of the population today is ethnically Russian; Lats barely form a majority.

LAW OF THE PARTIES

A **Latin American** electoral system used particularly in Uruguay, where it was formally introduced in 1910. It allows several candidates from each party (usually belonging to different factions) to stand in presidential elections. The winner is the most popular candidate within the party which obtains the highest vote. The system thus combines both **primaries** and the presidential election into one process. In congressional elections the electorate votes for the preferred party but also for a preferred slate of candidates within that party.

LAW OF RETURN

Israeli legislation which allows any Jew to settle in **Israel**. As of the early 1990s some 20 per cent of world Jewry were Israeli.

LAW OF THE SEA *see* UNCLOS

LDC

Least Developed Country, a category used by the **UN** to describe (currently) 47 of its poorest member states. According to UN estimates, over 500 million people lived in LDCs in 1990.

The acronym 'LLDC' was sometimes used for Least Developed Country in the 1980s, in an unsuccessful attempt to avoid confusion, since 'LDC' had once stood for 'less developed country', an obsolete term now discarded in favour of 'developing country'. The current meaning of LDC dates from the UN Conference on the Least Developed Countries held in Paris in September 1981. The conference adopted, but failed to do much about implementing, a New Sustainable Programme of Action to assist 31 countries then classified as LDCs. Since that time there have been repeated calls for special treatment to ease the debt burden of LDCs and to improve trading relations. In February 1992 **UNCTAD** reported that 80 per cent of the world's estimated 17 million refugees were concentrated in the 47 LDCs.

LEASEBACK

An arrangement under which one country may administer and govern a territory while another country holds sovereignty. A leaseback arrangement for the Falkland/Malvinas islands, whereby the islands would continue to be under UK government but with a transfer of sovereignty to Argentina, was one of various formulas put forward prior to the 1982 **Falklands War** to settle the long-running dispute between the UK and Argentina. It was rejected by the islanders, who wanted a 25-year freeze on sovereignty negotiations.

LEFT-WING

An umbrella term describing **communist**, **socialist** or **social democratic** ideologies or their adherents. The use of 'left-wing' and '**right-wing**' to describe political ideologies dates back to the National Assembly of Revolutionary France, in which the delegates seated on the left were the most radical, and those on the right the more **conservative**.

LENINISM

The ideology derived from the writings of Vladimir Ilyich Lenin (1870–1924), a key interpreter of the thought of Karl Marx and the architect of Soviet **communism**. Adapting Marxist theory to the backward, largely agrarian conditions in his native Russia, Lenin advocated revolution through the leadership of a vanguard party, operating according to the principles of **democratic centralism**. As head of the Bolshevik Party, he was instrumental in engineering the seizure of power in October 1917, and established the Soviet state before his death from a stroke in 1924.

While successful in defending the revolution from outside attack, Lenin employed methods of terror and allowed the dictatorship of the proletariat to become the dictatorship of the party, resulting in the creation of a monolithic bureaucracy. However, his strategy for accelerating the process of revolution, and his application of Marxism to a backward economy, have been the inspiration of communist parties throughout the world.

LESOTHO

A former British colony known as Basutoland until its independence in October 1966. The territory, under British control from 1868, had been annexed to the Cape Colony in 1871, but in 1883 the British government resumed control. Basutoland was subsequently administered as one of the British 'High Commission Territories' (together with **Botswana** and Swaziland).

LESOTHO LIBERATION ARMY *see* LLA

LETTER OF INTENT

An undertaking given by a country to the **IMF** as to its future economic and monetary policies. Such undertakings are generally demanded by the Fund before approval is given to the release of financial resources. Requirements tend to be rigorous; the publication of their details sometimes occasions considerable political disquiet and may give rise to serious industrial and social unrest.

LEVANT

A term deriving from the French *lever*, 'to rise', as in sunrise, therefore denoting 'the east', and historically referring to the countries along the eastern shores of the Mediterranean. The name Levant States was used to describe Syria and Lebanon in a 1920 League of Nations mandate under which they were occupied by France. The term Levant is sometimes still used for those two states, of which Lebanon gained full independence from France in 1944 and Syria in 1946.

LIB-LAB PACT

The parliamentary agreement between the UK Labour and Liberal parties in 1977–8. The Labour Party's narrow parliamentary majority following the October 1974 general election was whittled away through by-election losses and defections, so that by March 1977 there was an effective majority against the government in the House of Commons. Agreement was reached in that month between Labour and the Liberal Party whereby the latter would support the government 'in the pursuit of economic recovery'. This pact was continued until the end of the 1977–8 parliamentary session. The Labour Party then experienced the **winter of discontent**, involving serious industrial unrest, and was defeated at the general election in May 1979, when the Liberal Party also lost ground.

LIBERAL INTERNATIONAL

A UK-based international organization founded in 1947 in Oxford, with a permanent secretariat in London, which holds annual conferences involving liberal parties from approximately 25 countries worldwide.

LIBERALISM

A broad ideology which emerged from the Enlightenment of the eighteenth century, and challenged traditions of obedience and hierarchy by advocating a state based on reason and individual rights. At the heart of classical liberalism lay the revolutionary belief that individuals possessed natural rights which should not be abrogated by government. This was epitomized in the American Declaration of Independence (1776), which stated the 'self-evident truths' that 'all men are created equal; and they are endowed by their Creator with inherent and inalienable rights; that among these are life, liberty and the pursuit of happiness'. Liberal thinkers such as John Locke and Baron de Montesquieu advocated minimal government (including the separation of powers and the rule of law) together with laissez faire economic development.

Faced with an increasing challenge from **socialism**, this essentially negative definition of rights (stressing the freedom from constraint) was revised in the late nineteenth century to include a definition of the state as the guarantor of a minimal standard of living. Thus, while modern liberal parties chart a **centrist** course between **conservatism** and socialism, some of them also advocate the importance of a welfare state, and most support a degree of government intervention in the economy.

LIBERATION THEOLOGY

Theological teachings developed in **Latin America** in the late 1960s urging the Catholic Church to translate its spiritual mission into one of practical solidarity with the poor and with the struggle against oppression. It challenged the Catholic Church's historical identification with the region's strict social hierarchies and took its inspiration from the liberal rule of Pope John XXIII and the social radicalism identified with the conferences of Latin American Bishops in Medellín, Colombia (1968), and in Puebla, Mexico (1979). In Nicaragua adherents of liberation theology in 1979 supported revolutionary change and accepted posts in the government of the **left-wing Sandinistas**. Its embrace by the region's grassroots clergy, many of whom were also influenced by **Marxism**, led to the widespread establishment of **CEBs** (Christian Base Communities) despite the disapproval of the conservative papacies of Pope Paul VI and, especially, Pope John Paul II, who stressed that the Church's role was not to encourage social activism but spiritual work.

LIBERTARIANISM

A vague twentieth century ideology, mainly confined to the USA and UK, which advocates individualism, spontaneous, non-coercive social structures, and a reduction in the functions of the state. At its most extreme, it has similarities with **anarchism**. Libertarianism also tends to support an extreme form of free market economy, and is opposed to government intervention. Accordingly, while being similar to modern

conservatism and classical **liberalism** in its emphasis on laissez faire economics, libertarianism differs from them in advocating the lifting of all controls on individual behaviour.

LIBOR

The London inter-bank offered rate, a rate of interest paid by commercial banks in London for loans between themselves. Libor is generally used as a benchmark for rates charged on other loans, often quoted as a given percentage over (above) Libor.

LIBYAN EMBASSY SIEGE

The events surrounding the shooting of a British police officer outside the Libyan embassy in London in April 1984. Relations between Libya and the UK were tense during early 1984 as a result of a series of bomb attacks aimed at exiled Libyan opponents of the regime of Col. Moamer al Kadhafi. The attacks culminated on 17 April in a gun attack on a demonstration being staged by anti-Kadhafi activists outside the Libyan People's Bureau (embassy) in London. A British police officer, WPC Yvonne Fletcher, was killed in the shooting, which was apparently directed from inside the bureau. After the failure of negotiations aimed at finding a mutually acceptable solution to the resulting crisis, the UK announced on 22 April its decision to sever diplomatic relations.

LIMA GROUP

A coalition of Peru, Brazil, Argentina and Uruguay with the aim of supporting the **Contadora** group in the latter's peace efforts for **Central America**. Set up on the initiative of Peru's President Alan García Pérez, the group was launched at his inauguration in Lima on 29 July 1985. The first joint effort with the Contadora group was the 1986 'Caraballeda Message', which included demands for the withdrawal of foreign advisers and the cessation of support for insurgent groups in Central America. As the co-operation between the two groups grew closer, they together became known as the **Group of Rio** which continued to operate after the Contadora group was officially disbanded in April 1990.

LIMEHOUSE DECLARATION

The political statement issued on 25 January 1981 by four senior members of the British Labour Party, Roy Jenkins, David Owen, William Rodgers and Shirley Williams, who became popularly known as the **Gang of Four**, effectively launching the Social Democratic Party (SDP). The declaration, made outside Owen's east London home, was a response to the perceived leftwards move of Labour Party, and over the succeeding months the SDP gained the allegiance of increasing numbers of disaffected Labour MPs. The SDP subsequently merged with the Liberal Party to form the Liberal Democrats.

LIMITS TO GROWTH

A study published in 1972 which predicted a global crisis if current trends in economic and population growth continued unchanged. The study was undertaken by the Massachusetts Institute of Technology, having been commissioned by the **Club of Rome**. Complex mathematical models which were employed in the study produced a prediction that the current world order would collapse within 100 years unless rectifying measures were taken. The report's recommendations for action included **zero population growth**, pollution control and recycling.

LINE OF ACTUAL CONTROL

The de facto border separating Indian and Pakistani-controlled areas of **Kashmir**. The line refers to the position of troops on the ground in Kashmir at the end of the 1971 Indo-**Pakistan** War. Leaders of the two countries meeting in Simla in 1972 agreed that the line of control resulting from the ceasefire would be 'respected by both sides without prejudice to the recognized position of either side'.

LISBON PROTOCOL

A protocol signed in May 1992 defining the way in which those successor states of the **Soviet Union** in possession of nuclear weapons would implement the **START** I treaty on arms reduction. Signatories of the protocol were Russia, **Byelarus**,

Kazakhstan and **Ukraine**, all of which had inherited Soviet **nuclear weapons**. They undertook to regard Russia as the successor state of the Soviet Union in respect of **START** I. Byelarus, Kazakhstan and Ukraine would cease to have nuclear weapons by the end of the decade, either transferring them to Russia or destroying them, and would formalize their non-nuclear status by adhering to the non-proliferation treaty (**NPT**). START I was subsequently ratified by Kazakhstan (July 1992), Russia (November 1992) and Byelarus (February 1993), while Ukraine announced in February 1994 that it would lift its remaining objections to ratification. Byelarus acceded to the NPT in July 1993 and Kazakhstan in December 1993.

LITHUANIA

The largest of the **Baltic states**, with a population of 3.7 million, only 20 per cent of whom are non-Lithuanian. Lithuania came under Russian rule in 1795. It declared independence in 1918, but was annexed by the **Soviet Union** in 1939, and was one of the 15 Soviet republics until, under the nationalist leadership of **Sajudis**, it declared independence in March 1990. Lithuania was admitted to the **UN** in September 1991. It has enjoyed since then a relatively friendly relationship with Russia, which withdrew the last of its troops in August 1993.

LITTLE BOY

The nickname of the atomic bomb (containing uranium-235) which was dropped by the USA on **Hiroshima** on 6 August 1945. Of the 245,000 people then living in the city, at least 140,000 had died by the end of 1945.

LITTLE RED BOOK

A collection of quotations from the writings of Chinese **Communist** Party (CCP) leader Mao Zedong, which was the principal propaganda document during the **Cultural Revolution**. The pocket-sized volume, bound in red plastic, intended as a popular introduction to 'Mao Zedong thought', was issued by Defence Minister Lin Biao to reverse Mao's declining influence in the CCP after the failure of the **Great Leap Forward**. From mid-1966 to October 1968 – the height of the Cultural Revolution – 740 million copies were issued in various languages.

LIVE AID

The pop concerts organized by the **Band Aid** charity and held simultaneously in venues throughout the world on 13 July 1984. The two main events were in Wembley Stadium in London and JFK Stadium in Philadelphia, where a host of musicians performed, donating their services free, as did everyone else involved in the event. The concerts were televised and broadcast worldwide. All proceeds from the concerts (including ticket receipts, record sales and television fees) went to Band Aid to support its relief work in Ethiopia. By 17 July £50 million (US$75 million) had been raised.

LLA

The **Lesotho** Liberation Army, the armed wing of the Basotho Congress Party (BCP). Opposed to the authoritarian government of Chief Leabua Jonathan and subsequent military regimes, the LLA was most active in the early and mid-1980s. When the BCP won a landslide victory in democratic elections in March 1993, the new government then tried to integrate the LLA into the Royal Lesotho Defence Force (RLDF). Junior RLDF officers resisted this move, which was an important factor in the violent clashes between sections of the RLDF in January 1994.

LLDC *see* LDC

LOBBY SYSTEM

The system in the UK whereby journalists and others are enabled to meet members of either house of parliament on an informal basis. The phrase derives from the physical layout of certain lobbies in the Houses of Parliament which are accessible (subject to limitations) by outsiders. Information given on lobby terms is generally not attributable to an identified source. Delegations and others are also enabled to 'lobby' MPs at parliament in order to present petitions or grievances on a more public basis.

LOCKERBIE

The Scottish town on which a Pan Am airliner – flight PA103, en route from London to New York – crashed after an explosion on board in December 1988. All 259 passengers and crew were killed, as well as 11 people in the town. Mandatory air, arms and diplomatic sanctions were imposed by the **UN** against Libya in April 1992 when the Libyan authorities refused to extradite to the UK or the USA two Libyans (Abdelbaset Ali Mohamed al-Megrahi and Al-Amin Khalifa Fhimah) accused of organizing the bombing of the airliner. In November 1993 the UN approved a stricter package of sanctions against Libya, but stopped short of banning the sale of Libyan oil exports. Despite the imposition of the new sanctions, doubts were widely expressed over the attachment of sole blame to Libya. Some reports proclaimed the involvement of Iran and radical Palestinian factions in the bombing.

LOCKHEED SCANDAL

The political scandal which emerged in Japan in 1976, and involving the acceptance of bribes by Kakuei Tanaka, Prime Minister in 1972–4, from the US Lockheed Aircraft Corporation. The scandal epitomized the system of **money politics** which reached its height under Tanaka. In October 1983 a Tokyo court found Tanaka guilty of accepting bribes, a verdict upheld by the Tokyo High Court in July 1987. He was sentenced to four years imprisonment, but remained free while appeals were filed, and the case remained under consideration by the Japanese Supreme Court at the time of his death in December 1993. Despite his conviction he continued to sit in the **Diet** and to exercise enormous influence within the ruling Liberal Democratic Party (LDP) until forced to retire after a stroke in 1985. His powerful LDP faction fell under the dominance of Noboru Takeshita and Shin Kanemaru, who were subsequently implicated in, respectively, the **Recruit-Cosmos scandal** and the **Sagawa Kyubin scandal**.

LOK SABHA

(Hindi, 'People's Assembly') The lower house of the Indian parliament, the upper chamber being the **Rajya Sabah**. It has 545 members, of whom 543 are chosen by direct election through a simple majority system in single-member constituencies. The remaining two members are appointed by the President to represent the Anglo-Indian community.

LOMÉ CONVENTION

The agreement which regulates the various aid and trading relationships between the **EU** and the **ACP** group of developing countries. There have been four Lomé Conventions to date, from Lomé I in 1975 to Lomé IV, signed in 1989, which for the first time maps out a 10-year rather than a five-year programme. Finance under Lomé comes mainly through the European Development Fund (EDF), worth 10,000 million **ECU** in 1990–5. About half of EDF money goes in grants for projects, and the rest is divided mainly between a structural adjustment facility, the **Stabex** and Sysmin schemes to smooth out fluctuations in ACP country earnings from primary products, and emergency relief.

LONDON CLUB

The informal grouping of commercial external creditors from developed countries. The London Club meets frequently to discuss commercial debts outstanding to its members from developing countries which are experiencing severe repayment problems. Its role has been to arrange consolidation and **debt rescheduling** as appropriate in such cases. The corresponding grouping of official creditors is the **Paris Club**.

LONDON DUMPING CONVENTION

The Convention on the Prevention of Marine Pollution by Dumping of Wastes and Other Matter, adopted at a conference in London in December 1972 and in force since 30 August 1975. The convention aims to control the discharging of hazardous waste into the world's oceans from ships and aircraft. Among the substances considered most damaging are mercury, cadmium, plastics, oils, and materials produced for chemical and **biological warfare**. In November 1993 parties to the convention agreed a definitive ban on the dumping of nuclear waste at sea, replacing the moratorium in force since 1983.

LONG MARCH

The 6,000-mile (nearly 10,000 km) journey undertaken in 1934–5 by the Chinese **Communist** Party to avoid encirclement by the forces of the nationalist **KMT**. In October 1934 the communists left the Jianxi region, where they had established a Chinese Soviet Republic, for the north-west, arriving one year later in Shaanxi. Only 4,000 people of the 86,000 who had embarked on the journey reached their destination. During the Long March, Mao Zedong's position as party leader was confirmed by his election, in January 1935, as chairman of the Military Affairs Committee. Following the victory of the communists in 1949, the Long March became a symbol both of the sacrifices made in the cause of the revolution and of the durability of the communist cause.

LONG TELEGRAM

The document written by George Kennan when he was US chargé d'affaires in Moscow in February 1946, in response to a request for an 'interpretive analysis' of Soviet intentions, in which he expounded **containment** as the proper US response to Soviet foreign policy.

LOOSE CANNON

A term (derived from the danger involved in the recoil of unsecured naval guns) used to describe a person whose unauthorized actions represent a danger for the organization of which he is a part. It is particularly associated with Lt.-Col. Oliver North, a member of the US **NSC** and a key participant in the **Iran-contra affair**. In accordance with the administration's official view that the Iran-Contra affair was the result of North's personal initiative, he was described by Secretary of State George Shultz as having been 'a loose cannon on the gun deck of state at the NSC'. However, in his testimony before the Congressional committee of inquiry into the affair on 7–14 July 1987, North disputed this interpretation of his role and asserted that he had acted with the approval of his superiors.

LOS ANGELES RIOTS

Major disturbances which occurred in Los Angeles between 29 April and 4 May 1992, involving widespread destruction and ethnic violence. The riots were sparked off when an all-white jury acquitted four white police officers who had been filmed beating black motorist Rodney King in 1991. More than 50 people were killed, and the damage to property was estimated at US$1,000 million. The disturbances also highlighted the tensions between the black and white communities, and the hostility which had developed between African Americans and recent Asian immigrants. Two of the police officers at the centre of the case were later convicted on federal charges of having violated King's **civil rights**.

LOUVRE ACCORD

An agreement designed to reduce monetary and economic instability, reached on 21 February 1987 in Paris by finance ministers and central bank governors of Canada, France, West Germany, Japan, the UK and the USA. The meeting was held amidst some turmoil in the exchange markets. The participants undertook to intensify their efforts to co-ordinate economic policy, so as to promote more balanced economic growth and to reduce existing imbalances. The countries running big surpluses on their balance of payments undertook to strengthen domestic demand and to reduce external surpluses while maintaining price stability. Countries with balance-of-payments deficits undertook, conversely, to encourage steady, low-inflation growth while reducing their domestic imbalances and external deficits. On exchange rates, the participants expressed their intention of fostering stability around the levels which were then current – a substantial realignment having already taken place since the **Plaza Accord** of January 1985.

LOVE CANAL

A school and housing estate in Niagara City, New York State, which was the first place to be declared a US Federal Disaster Area as a result of chemical pollution. Love Canal was built in the late 1950s on a landfill site where chemical waste had been dumped by Hooker Chemical some ten years previously. In 1977, as the drums containing the waste corroded, **dioxin** and other toxic gases penetrated into homes. Only 12 years later was the site considered to be free from contamination. Occidental Petroleum, which had acquired Hooker, was found liable for clean-up costs of $325 million, but in March 1993 a court rejected New York State's potentially precedent-setting claim for punitive damages.

LOYALISTS

Supporters of the closest of links between **Northern Ireland** and the **United Kingdom** as a whole. The term has a more intense meaning than **Unionist**. It is frequently used to denote the most fervent supporters of the union among the Protestant majority population. Some of the more militant groups of loyalists – such as the **UDA**, the **UFF** and the **UVF** are banned in Northern Ireland. The 'loyalist' strike of 1974 was instrumental in causing the collapse of the short-lived **power-sharing** Northern Ireland assembly and executive.

LSD

The abbreviation by which the drug lysergic acid became widely known. Discovered by a Swiss chemist in the early 1940s, LSD, also called simply 'acid', was used in the treatment of psychiatric patients and widely experimented with by the **CIA**. It became popular within the youth culture of the USA and Europe in the 1960s and, despite its illegality, remains in widespread use. When taken it produces a hallucinogenic 'trip' in the user, involving heightened and altered awareness.

LTTE *see* TAMIL TIGERS

LUSTRATION

Postcommunist **Czechoslovakia's** controversial process of identifying and purging those found to have collaborated in the past with the **StB** (the secret police) under the **communist** regime. Lustration (or 'purification') was regarded by some as a key part of the **decommunization** process. The first significant act of lustration took place in March 1991, when several parliamentary deputies were publicly denounced as former collaborators by a parliamentary commission on the basis of evidence in the StB archive. In June 1991 a screening law was passed, allowing the dismissal of state employees found to have collaborated with the StB. Critics of lustration argued that the StB archive was unreliable and incomplete; that although many had been forced to collaborate under duress, there was no formal legal means of refuting allegations; and that the process would be manipulated by unscrupulous politicians keen to discredit their rivals.

LUXEMBOURG COMPROMISE

An agreement among **EC** leaders reached informally in 1966, providing guidelines on the vexed question of whether a member country could veto a decision by the **Council of Ministers**. It became the working practice that unanimity was required, despite the formal rules allowing decisions by **qualified majority voting**, if a member country considered that its vital interests were at stake.

M-19

(Spanish abbreviation of *Movimiento 19 de Abril* – '19 April Movement') The former Colombian **guerrilla** group named in memory of disputed elections held on 19 April 1970, which set them on the course of armed struggle from 1974 until 1990. In 1989 it called a unilateral ceasefire, signed a peace agreement and constituted itself as a political party. Following the May 1990 presidential elections in which it participated as the Democratic Alliance M-19, it was represented in the Cabinet and subsequently helped formulate a new Constitution which came into effect in July 1991.

MAASTRICHT

The Netherlands town where the 12 **EU** member states met in December 1991 for the summit which concluded the Treaty on European Union. They returned on 7 February 1992 for the formal signing of the treaty, which, as a result, is commonly called the Maastricht Treaty. Eventually ratified by all 12 member states (after an initial rejection by referendum in

Denmark), the Maastricht Treaty came into force in November 1993. Integral parts of the Treaty are the agreements on **European political union** and on **EMU**. Beyond these, the Treaty commits the member states to implement two 'intergovernmental pillars' of co-operation outside the Community's decision-making machinery. The first of these covers common foreign and security policy, including the eventual framing of a common defence policy, with the **WEU** becoming the 'defence component of the Union'. A review conference on this 'pillar' is scheduled for 1996. The second 'intergovernmental pillar' is co-operation on judicial and home affairs. The Maastricht Treaty also creates the **cohesion** fund and a Committee of the Regions.

McCARTHYISM

The anti-**communist** hysteria prominent in the USA in the early 1950s, built upon a foundation established by the House Committee on **Un-American Activities**. Senator Joseph R. McCarthy of Wisconsin was catapulted to national prominence after making a speech in Wheeling, West Virginia, in February 1952, in which he accused the US establishment of being riddled with subversives. For over two years, until his censure by the Senate in late 1954, McCarthy became the personification of an anti-communist 'witch hunt' which relied upon unsubstantiated allegations, innuendo, and guilt by association. Those whom McCarthy particularly targeted for public denunciation were the 'communists and queers' within the **State Department**, and figures associated with the presidency of Harry S. Truman, whom McCarthy held responsible for having failed to defend US interests in Asia. McCarthy's period of influence coincided largely with the **Korean War**, and exploited widespread public frustration over the unsuccessful nature of the limited conflict.

MACEDONIA

A small landlocked republic, which declared independence from **Yugoslavia** in 1991. Macedonia has exceptionally difficult relations with all its neighbours, even by **Balkan** standards. Albania is sensitive over Macedonia's considerable Albanian community; Serbs have historically regarded Macedonian territory as their own; Bulgaria regards Macedonian nationality as a fiction; and Greece has refused to recognize Macedonia, claiming that its very name implies a historic insult and a territorial claim on the northern Greek province of the same name (Greece refers to Macedonia by the name of its capital, Skopje). In a compromise move Macedonia won widespread international recognition in late 1993 and early 1994 under the name Former Yugoslav Republic of Macedonia (FYROM).

MAD

The mutually assured destruction which would result from a full-scale nuclear war between the **superpowers**, according to theorists of the 'balance of terror'. The MAD theory dominated strategic thinking from the 1960s until the 1980s, when ideas of **flexible response** and limited nuclear war began to take hold. MAD was based on the perception that both superpowers possessed an offensive weapons capability which could destroy the other, and that there was no effective defence – hence the concern about controlling **ABM** defences, to prevent them upsetting this assumption. **Deterrence** was based upon this grim certainty, and on demonstrating the resolve to retaliate if attacked. In its simplest form, MAD assumed **massive retaliation** once an attack had been detected, and before the incoming missiles actually struck. It could also encompass the more complex scenario of the superpowers having a 'second strike capability' – the ability to hit back with weapons protected against the initial assault, either in deep underground hardened silos, on submarines, or constantly on the move.

MAD COW DISEASE *see* BSE

MAFIA

In Italy, the network of clandestine, family-based groups extensively involved in organized crime which have become entwined with the functioning of the state. Used loosely the term may include not only the original Sicilian Mafia (first mentioned in an official document in 1865) but also its Neapolitan and Calabrian counterparts, the **Camorra** and **'Ndrangheta**. Offshoots in the USA extended their control over rackets such as protection, extortion, prostitution, gambling and illegal liquor, to the extent that the word mafia became synonymous with organized crime, and in this sense it is now used internationally with no suggestion of an Italian connection, as applied for example to the 'Russian mafia'.

The Sicilian Mafia began as an association offering protection and a means of self-advancement in a region where the state exercised little control. Its involvement in criminal activity grew gradually, but with a rapid shift into new areas including narcotics when its original rural base was disrupted in the chaotic economic development of the 1960s and 1970s. Latterly the judicial authorities have scored some notable successes against the Mafia, including the arrest in January 1993 of Salvatore Riina, the informal head of the Sicilian Mafia, and the application of new measures introduced in August 1992 in a climate of public outrage over the assassinations of senior judges Giovanni Falcone and Paolo Borsellino. However, it is estimated that Sicily's 150 Mafia families are still able to influence some 10 per cent of the electorate on the island. Moreover, the Mafia infiltration of top-level national political structures has begun to be revealed in the **Operation Clean Hands** corruption investigations, uncovering allegations of links with senior Christian Democratic Party figures including former Prime Minister Giulio Andreotti.

MAGHREB

(Arabic, 'west') The region of North Africa bordering the Mediterranean. The Maghreb comprises the countries of Morocco, Algeria, Tunisia and Libya. The Arab Maghreb Union (**AMU**), established in 1989 to foster economic and defence cooperation between the Maghreb states, also includes Mauritania as a member.

MAGIC BULLET

A widely used term which generally suggests scepticism over the **Warren Commission's** conclusions regarding one of the three bullets which, according to its findings, were fired by Lee Harvey Oswald during the assassination of President John F. Kennedy in Dallas, on 22 November 1963. Film of the shooting showed that Kennedy and Governor John B. Connally (who was sitting directly in front of the President) reacted to wounds inflicted in a shorter time interval than that in which Oswald's bolt-action rifle could be aimed and fired. Therefore it was possible to conclude that there had been a single assassin only by interpreting what appeared to be separate wounds as having been inflicted by a single shot. Thus, the magic bullet is alleged to have made seven wounds in two people: having struck Kennedy in the back it exited from his throat, entered Connally's back, shattered his fifth rib, exited from his chest, entered his right forearm (splintering the radius bone), before exiting and entering his thigh. The bizarre (and, many have argued, impossible) path of the magic bullet is widely seen as one of the most implausible elements of the official version of Kennedy's assassination. Its plausibility was further undermined by the recovery of the alleged bullet (commission exhibit 399), found lying on Connally's hospital stretcher. The bullet showed no sign of the damage which would have been expected had it caused the wounds ascribed to it.

MAGIC CIRCLE

The nickname for the former 'inner circle' of the Conservative Party. This grouping, comprising certain members of the Cabinet (or shadow cabinet) together with influential 'elder statesmen', held supreme sway over the party. In particular, it was instrumental in securing the emergence – until the later 1960s – of a leader who it was deemed could be relied upon to uphold the party's traditions. After the Conservatives' loss of office in 1964 the power of this circle was effectively broken, as rules were adopted for the first time for formal leadership contests. The term was coined in 1963 by Iain Macleod.

MAGNOX

A type of gas-cooled nuclear reactor in which a magnesium alloy called Magnox shields the uranium fuel rods. Magnox reactors were built in the UK as the generation of nuclear plant preceding the **AGR**, and are now at the end of their planned life-span. The problem of the immense and imminent cost of decommissioning them was a key element in the UK government's decision that nuclear power generation could not be privatized along with the rest of the electricity supply industry.

MAGYAR

The Hungarian language, or a person of Hungarian descent, whether resident inside the borders of modern Hungary (established by the Treaty of Trianon in 1920) or in Hungarian communities beyond (in neighbouring Romania, Slovakia or Serbia). The Magyars are descended from a tribe of Asiatic people who settled in historic Hungary (the land flanked by the Carpathian mountains) in the tenth century. Magyar is a Finno-Ugric language, unrelated to the German and **Slavonic** languages of their neighbours.

MAJLIS ASH-SHURA

(Arabic, 'session') The name given to a body approximating a consultative or parliamentary assembly in some Muslim countries in the **Middle East**. Said to derive from a traditional gathering of notables in a Bedouin tent, it is deemed by some Muslims to represent the basis of Muslim democratic politics. In practice its evolution has varied across the Muslim world. In Jordan and Iran it is an elected body with substantial powers to make and amend laws; in other countries, such as Saudi Arabia where a *Majlis* was inaugurated only as recently as December 1993, it is a non-elected council whose functions are restricted to an advisory role.

MALAWI

A landlocked country in southern Africa with a population of 10.4 million, which was known as Nyasaland while under British rule and became independent in July 1964. The territory had first been declared a British protectorate in 1891. In 1953 it became part of the **Central African Federation**, with **Zimbabwe** (then called Southern Rhodesia) and **Zambia** (then called Northern Rhodesia), but this unsuccessful federal experiment was abandoned in 1963.

MALAYASIA

A south-east Asian country with a population of more than 18.8 million by 1992. The Federation of Malaysia was established in September 1963 through the union of the Federation of Malaya (11 peninsular states which had secured independence from the UK in August 1957), the internally self-governing state of Singapore, and the former British colonies of Sarawak and North Borneo (Sabah). Singapore seceded from the Malaysian Federation in August 1965.

MALI

A country of 9.8 million people in west Africa. Formerly French Soudan, it achieved independence in September 1960 following the failure of the **Federation of Mali** in which it was joined with Senegal.

MALVINAS

The alternative name for the Falkland Islands, the UK dependent territory off the coast of southern Argentina. Argentinian claims to the islands led to their occupation in 1982 by Argentinian troops and the subsequent **Falklands War**.

MANDARINS

The informal description used in the UK to denote the most senior civil servants (by analogy with the members of the mandarin class in imperial China and the influence which they exercised). The term, which reflects the belief that they are able to manipulate the working of government, refers specifically to the Heads of the Home Civil Service and of the Diplomatic Service, together with the permanent secretaries (or permanent under-secretaries) heading the main government departments and their immediate deputies.

MAOISM

The doctrine associated with the Chinese revolutionary leader and later Chairman of the Chinese **Communist** Party (CCP), Mao Zedong. Defined largely by its departure from the **Marxism-Leninism** of the **Soviet Union**, Maoism saw the vanguard of the revolution as being the peasantry rather than the industrial proletariat, largely because China's economy was still primarily agricultural and the urban CCP had been destroyed by Chiang Kai-Shek's **KMT** in 1927. Maoism placed the peasantry above even the communist party as a revolutionary vanguard: the **Cultural Revolution** was intended to revitalize the party and prevent it from becoming overly bureaucratic, as had happened in the Soviet Union. Maoism also declared that the historical stages of traditional Marxism could be accelerated by a conscious effort of popular will. This belief led to the disastrous **Great Leap Forward**. Maoism's reliance on the peasantry, however, made it an important model for communist revolutions in other underdeveloped countries.

MAORIS

The indigenous Polynesian people of New Zealand, constituting some 13 per cent of the current population of 3.3 million, who were deemed to have ceded sovereignty to the British crown in the 1840 Treaty of **Waitangi**.

MARCHING SEASON

In **Northern Ireland**, the period in the summer when the main sectarian demonstrations have traditionally taken place. Marches by the majority **loyalist** organizations such as the Protestant **Orange Order** culminate in the commemoration of the 1690 Battle of the Boyne on 12 July and the 1689 relief of Londonderry on 12 August. They have frequently been marked by clashes between the loyalist and republican communities.

MARIELITOS

The 125,000 disaffected Cubans boatlifted from the Cuban port of Mariel to Miami, USA, between April and June 1980. The exodus was officially sanctioned by the Cuban government following the occupation in April of the Peruvian embassy in Havana by a large number of dissidents. Cuba granted leaving permits particularly to 'undesirables', including drug addicts and criminals, who unlike other refugees, were given a cool reception. In December 1984 Cuba and the USA signed an agreement in which Cuba agreed to accept back alleged criminals among the Mariel exiles in exchange for Cuban political prisoners, but the launch of the Florida-based **Radio Martí** in May 1985 caused a sharp deterioration in Cuban-US relations and Cuba's immediate abrogation of the immigration agreement. As of mid-1994 some 1,600 Mariel Cubans were being held in US prisons.

MARKOV AFFAIR

The controversy associated with the death in London on 11 September 1978 of Georgi Markov, a Bulgarian journalist employed by the BBC World Service. In an apparent accident on a London street four days earlier, a Bulgarian secret service agent posing as a passer-by allegedly injected with Markov with a poison pellet, using a specially adapted umbrella. For the public, the Markov Affair seemed to typify the subterfuge and skullduggery of **Cold War** undercover operations.

MARONITES

A Christian sect derived from refugee Monothelites (Christian heretics) of the seventh century. Maronites are widely associated with Lebanon, where, until the late 1980s, the **Phalange** and other Maronite parties and **militias** constituted the most powerful political force. As dictated by custom a Maronite is still to hold the Lebanese presidency, but Syrian domination of Lebanon has led to a shift in the balance of power in recent years. While Maronites still hold effective control of their Kesrouan heartland, on a national scale they are on the political periphery.

MARSHALL PLAN

A plan to assist the economic recovery of post-war Europe, proposed by US

Secretary of State George Marshall in June 1947. The scheme offered US funding to European countries if they co-operated with each other in drafting recovery programmes. It was intended to pre-empt **communist** influence in **Western Europe**, and interim aid to France and Italy in late 1947 helped these countries overcome communist-led strikes. Because of opposition to its conditions from the **Soviet Union**, the Marshall Plan was confined to the 16 countries of Western Europe which met in Paris from July to September 1947 to draft a recovery programme, and which then formed the **OEEC**. Between 1948 and 1952 the Marshall Plan was responsible for the provision of aid worth US$17,000 million.

MARSH ARABS

The inhabitants of the southern marshes of Iraq which cover some 6,000 square miles (15,500 sq km) of the country around Garna, where the Tigris and the Euphrates rivers meet above Basra to form the Shatt al-Arab. Also known as the Madan, they are almost entirely of **Shia** Muslim origin. They follow a centuries-old tradition of living in small clusters of two or three houses kept above water by rushes that are constantly replenished. Since an abortive Shia uprising in March 1991 they have been the subject of repeated attacks by Iraqi military forces and the victims of a government programme to drain the marshes in an attempt to resettle and thereby fragment the population.

MARTIAL LAW

A body of emergency laws administered by military personnel, generally (although not always) following the assumption of power by members of the armed forces. Government is conducted by decrees or ordinances. The chief characteristic of martial law has been the restriction of civil liberties and the curtailment of political participation by parties and interest groups. It has been imposed frequently in the newly independent states of Africa and Asia, is common throughout the **Middle East**, and was until the 1980s the shared experience of most **Latin American** countries; martial law was also notoriously used in 1981–3 in Poland, in an attempt to crush **Solidarity**, and from 1980 in Turkey, where it was lifted by the mid-1980s except in the Kurdish-inhabited provinces.

MARXISM-LENINISM

A polemical term used by regimes which claim to be the valid interpreters of true **communism**. The term combines the words Marxism and **Leninism** to stress its lineage from the two greatest theorists of communism, Karl Marx and Vladimir Ilyich Lenin. The **Soviet Union** under Joseph Stalin claimed a monopoly on Marxism-Leninism. Other regimes have also claimed that true Marxism-Leninism is expressed exclusively through their ideologies, such as **Maoism** in China, Castroism in Cuba and **Juchism** in North Korea. Deviation from Marxism-Leninism, as officially defined, also serves to brand internal opponents of the regime.

MASERU RAID

The South African raid on alleged **ANC** targets in Maseru, the capital of **Lesotho**, on 9 December 1982. This was the biggest South African invasion of any country other than Angola and **Namibia**. It was carried out by 100 commandos of the South African Defence Force **(SADF)**, who attacked a dozen homes in the city after nightfall, killing 30 South Africans and 12 Lesotho nationals. Some of the victims were members of the ANC, but there was no evidence that the targets were 'terrorist' bases. South Africa's use of troops – against a non-Marxist Commonwealth country – was a response to the growing strength of the ANC inside South Africa and a means of reassuring the increasingly nervous white population that the government was capable of dealing with the threat from external agitation.

MASHRIQ

The geographical region ranging from the western border of Egypt to the western border of Iran and including the modern states of Egypt, Sudan, Saudi Arabia, **Yemen**, **Oman**, Kuwait, **UEA**, **Israel**, **Jordan**, Lebanon, Syria and Iraq.

MASON-DIXON LINE

The boundary between the US states of Maryland and Pennsylvania, which marks the border between the former slave states of the **South** and the northern states where slavery was illegal. During the period of **segregation** the Mason-Dixon Line similarly marked the border between the segregationist south and non-segregationist north.

MASSIVE RETALIATION

The threat to launch full-scale nuclear war if provoked. The policy of massive retaliation was not only part of nuclear deterrence and the **MAD** theory, but was also used earlier, under President Dwight Eisenhower and Secretary of State John Foster Dulles in the 1950s, the period of a clear US nuclear weapons ascendancy. In the aftermath of the **Korean War**, they used the threat of nuclear force to counter the danger of the **Soviet Union** promoting other limited peripheral wars elsewhere. Any new local aggression, they made clear, could expect to meet not just local defence, but massive retaliation at a time and place of the USA's choosing. The Soviet development of **ICBMs** made this a highly risky threat, and in the 1960s US policymakers went over to the idea of using 'graduated **deterrence**' instead, matching the level of retaliation to the level of force used in the aggression.

MATIGNON ACCORD

The tripartite agreement negotiated in 1988 between parties representing the native **Kanak** population in the French overseas territory of New Caledonia, the white community, and the French government. Signed at the Hotel Matignon (the official residence since 1958 of the French prime minister) in Paris on 26 June 1988, the accord returned administrative control of New Caledonia to France for one year prior to the introduction of local rule on 14 July 1989. The accord envisaged a 1998 independence referendum, in which the franchise would be restricted to residents of New Caledonia at the time of signing and their descendants. The Matignon Accord, (also known as the Rocard Plan after French Prime Minister Michel Rocard who chaired the talks), was approved in a French national referendum in November 1988.

MATRIX CHURCHILL

The UK machine tool company at the centre of the events leading to the **Scott inquiry** into defence-related exports to Iraq. Paul Henderson, Trevor Abrahams and Peter Allen, executives of Matrix Churchill (then Iraqi-owned), were arrested in October 1990 shortly after the Iraqi invasion of Kuwait and charged with illegally exporting machine tools and computer equipment to Iraq. Their trial was halted after a month and all three were acquitted on 9 November 1992, after Alan Clark, Minister of Trade in 1986–9 and Minister of State for Defence Procurement in 1989–92, retracted evidence given to customs investigators, and the judge found that documents suppressed by ministerial **gagging orders** established that the defendants that been acting with the support of the government. It also emerged that Henderson had acted as an **MI6** agent.

MAU MAU

The secret political society in Kenya which developed into a violent anti-colonial rebellion in the early 1950s. The term first appeared in the late 1940s; its exact meaning, and the origins of the movement, remain controversial. Mau Mau was confined almost entirely to the Kikuyu, the dominant ethnic group in Kenya, and its aims were to drive out the European settlers. The clandestine nature and violent methods of the militant movement attracted much attention. A full-scale rebellion broke out in October 1952 with a series of terrible killings, and the colonial authorities in the same month declared a state of emergency. More than 100 leading nationalist figures were arrested, including Jomo Kenyatta, who was sentenced to seven years' imprisonment as a Mau Mau leader in 1954. The colonial government also launched military operations against Mau Mau; reinforcements from neighbouring colonies were brought in and at the height of the rebellion some 10,000 British troops were deployed. Increasingly tough security measures halted most Mau Mau activity and by 1956 the emergency was ended, although isolated incidents were reported until 1959. By the end of the conflict Mau Mau had killed 100 Europeans and 2,000 Africans and had suffered over loses of over 11,500. When Kenya obtained independence in December 1963, Kenyatta was its first President.

MAXWELL MILLIONS

A popular term for the scandal surrounding the conduct and death of UK media magnate Robert Maxwell in 1991, and the collapse of companies controlled by him. Maxwell, who had suffered business setbacks in the late 1960s, had recovered to create a vast network of media and financial interests. However, in the course of 1991 rumours began circulating which cast doubt upon the viability of his empire, and in November of that year he fell overboard to his death from his yacht near the Canary Islands. Immediately after his death, facts emerged of massive fraud, involving in particular the use of pension funds under his control to bolster up his private and public companies; two of his sons were subsequently charged with complicity in their father's frauds. One repercussion of the affair was a close review of the whole framework of the law and regulations within which occupational pensions schemes operate in the UK.

MAYOTTE

An island in the Indian Ocean. Part of the Comoro archipelago, Mayotte is administered by France and has been a *collectivité territoriale* since December 1976, sending one deputy to the French National Assembly and one member to the Senate. However, the island is claimed by Comoros, which officially represents it at the **UN**. A UN-supervised referendum to determine the future of the island has been postponed indefinitely.

MAZE BREAKOUT

A breakout of republican inmates from the Maze prison near Belfast in **Northern Ireland**. On 25 September 1983 a total of 38 prisoners, serving lengthy terms, escaped from the prison; one prison officer was stabbed and killed. Half of the prisoners were recaptured within a matter of days, some others were arrested either in Northern Ireland, in Ireland or elsewhere over the succeeding years, and at least three were killed by the security forces, but a number remained at liberty.

MDF

(Hungarian acronym for *Magyar Demokrata Forum* – 'Hungarian Democratic Forum') The Christian democratic party formed during the communist era in September 1988 which governed Hungary in 1990–4 following the collapse of **communism** in **1989**. Its policy of moderate economic reform successfully attracted foreign investment, but unemployment rose and living standards stagnated. In elections in May 1994 the MDF lost badly to the revived, formerly communist, Hungarian Socialist Party, which had campaigned on a technocratic ticket.

MÉDECINS SANS FRONTIÈRES

(French, 'doctors without frontiers') An **NGO** founded in Paris by a group of French doctors in 1971 to provide emergency medical aid worldwide. It has six operational sections in Europe (including France, Belgium and the Netherlands), and 12 branch offices in the UK, Europe, North America, Japan and Hong Kong. It is funded largely by individuals, whose contributions cover 50 per cent of its US$180 million budget, while its relief staff are mostly volunteers. In 1993 it sent out 2,500 medical personnel to 65 countries affected by war, famine and natural disaster, in some cases without government consent.

MEDELLÍN CARTEL

A **Latin American** drug cartel based in the northern city of Medellín, Colombia. Its origins lay in the 1970s marijuana boom, but its leaders, Pablo Escobar Gaviria and Gonzalo Rodríguez Gacha, switched to the processing of Bolivian and Peruvian coca when they realized the potential market for cocaine, especially in the USA. In the 1980s they amassed vast fortunes and, through a combination of corruption and terror, including the assassination of two presidential candidates, distorted the functioning of state bodies, particularly the judiciary, and the political process. International and domestic pressure led to an all-out war on the cartel in the late 1980s, moderated in the 1990s by offers of leniency and assurances of non-extradition to the USA on drug trafficking charges for those who surrendered. Although many cartel leaders accepted the offers, others were shot by anti-drug police, including Gacha, and in December 1993, after the largest manhunt in the country's history, Escobar was finally killed.

MEDICAID

The US system whereby the state provides assistance to the poor in meeting the cost of medical treatment.

MEDICARE

The US system whereby the state provides the bulk of the medical costs incurred by those over 65 years of age.

MEDIUM-RANGE BALLISTIC MISSILE *see* IRBM

MEECH LAKE ACCORD

A constitutional agreement negotiated between the Canadian federal government and the country's provincial Premiers at Meech Lake in 1987 which was never implemented. The accord devolved considerable powers to provincial governments and sought to negate separatist pressure in the province of Quebec. A predominantly French-speaking province, Quebec was induced to sign the 1982 constitution in return for greater autonomy and the recognition of its status as a 'distinct society'. The package was approved by the federal parliament on 22 June 1988, but to become operational it required ratification by all of the provincial legislatures within two years. The 1990 deadline expired with neither Manitoba not Newfoundland having ratified the agreement (Newfoundland had initially approved it but, after a change of government, rescinded its ratification in April 1990), and the Meech Lake Accord collapsed. Elements within it were retained in the **Charlottetown accord**.

MELANESIAN SOCIALISM

A type of **socialism** associated with the former ruling party of **Vanuatu**, the *Vanua'aku Pati*, and its leader, Fr Walter Lini, in the 1980s. Melanesian socialism was notable for its non-aligned foreign policy.

MERCOSUR

(Spanish, 'southern market') A **common market** formally announced in March 1991 by the governments of Argentina, Brazil, Paraguay and Uruguay to come into operation by 1 January 1995. Subsequent failure to agree on common tariffs raised doubts that the deadline could be met. In March 1994 Brazil won support for the creation of a South American Free Trade Association to be negotiated once final arrangements on Mercosur were agreed. It was also agreed that an established Mercosur should, as a bloc, seek membership of **NAFTA**.

MESSINA CONFERENCE

The June 1955 meeting between the Foreign Ministers of Belgium, France, Italy, Luxembourg, the Netherlands and West Germany, at which they agreed to pursue European economic integration by creating 'a common European market' alongside the European Coal and Steel Community (**ECSC**, established by the **Schuman Plan**). The proposals discussed at Messina, based on an initiative from the **Benelux** countries, reached fruition in the **Rome Treaty** of March 1957.

MFA

The Multi-Fibre Arrangement, a textile trade regime agreed within the framework of **GATT**, to which 44 countries now subscribe. It covers about one-third of the world's entire trade in textiles (especially cotton and man-made fibres) and clothing. First concluded in 1974, it has been extended repeatedly. It was designed to bring order into the international textile and clothing trade to take account of the increasing switch of production to the developing countries and the corresponding decline in manufacture in the traditional developed countries. In December 1993 the MFA was extended for one further year, so as to bring its currency into line with that of the **Uruguay Round** agreements; thereafter the MFA's provisions were to be phased out over a 10-year period.

MFN

Most-favoured-nation treatment. This is supposed to be a cardinal principle of international trade as enshrined in Article I of the **GATT**. In according MFN treatment to another state, one country undertakes unconditionally to grant terms to it, on tariffs and related matters, which are no less favourable than the terms granted to other trading partners (i.e. other non-preferential partners). Even under the original Article I definition, however, there were a number of conditions under which the application of MFN status could be diluted. The growth of regional free trade areas and the introduction of the **GSP** scheme in the 1970s created more preferential trading arrangements, and MFN status now means little more than that no special discrimination will be applied. Some countries (notably the USA under the **Jackson/Vanik amendment** and in respect of China) have linked the granting or renewal of MFN status at various times to aspects of human rights.

MI5

The UK Security Service. The counterintelligence service was originally established in 1909, and its current role is to assess threats to the security of the UK. In the post-1945 era, and until the end of the **Cold War**, its attention was directed particularly towards the **Soviet Union** and its allies. In 1992 it was given responsibility for leading the offensive against **IRA** activity on the British mainland (i.e. excluding **Northern Ireland** itself). MI5 was placed on a statutory basis in 1989, and the name of its director general was first officially acknowledged in December 1991. Details purporting to describe some of MI5's operations were published in the controversial book **Spycatcher** in 1987.

MI6

The UK's Secret Intelligence Service (SIS). MI6 was originally formed in 1909 (together with the counterintelligence service which evolved into **MI5**); its present role is to produce secret intelligence in support of the government's security, defence, foreign and economic policies. The existence of MI6 in peacetime was traditionally not acknowledged by the government, and the name of its chief was officially disclosed only in May 1992. Legislation to place MI6 on a statutory basis for the first time was enacted in 1994.

MIA

Missing In Action, a term describing servicemen or servicewomen whose bodies have never been recovered after disappearing during a military operation. After the **Vietnam War** some veterans and politicians alleged that a number of the 1,600 US servicemen listed as MIA in **Indo-China** were being held in camps by the Vietnamese government to be used as bargaining chips in future negotiations. Although no concrete evidence has been discovered to support such claims, the MIA issue has been a sensitive domestic concern for post-War US administrations and has undoubtedly delayed the normalization of relations between the USA and Vietnam. At the time of the lifting of US trade sanctions against Vietnam in February 1994, US President Bill Clinton insisted that a full restoration of diplomatic relations would require further progress on the MIA issue. In 1988 the USA and Vietnam started joint MIA searches; as of early 1994 teams had recovered some 280 sets of remains.

MICRONESIA

The Federated States of Micronesia (FSM), a Pacific country comprising more than 600 islands spread 1,800 miles (2,900 km) across the archipelago of the Caroline Islands. Having been a constituent element of the UN **Trust Territory** of the Pacific Islands created in 1947, the FSM signed a Compact of Free Association with the USA in 1982 which gave the country internal self-government and US economic aid in return for continuing US control of its defence and foreign policies. With the termination of the Trust Territory in 1990, the FSM became an independent state, and joined the **UN** in September 1991.

MIDDLE AMERICA

The notional constituency of middle-class, middle-aged, small town US citizens who espouse moderate views and traditional values, and who constitute the **silent majority** of the population.

MIDDLE EAST

A geographical term denoting lands around the southern and eastern coast of the Mediterranean, stretching from Morocco to the Arabian peninsula and Iran, and sometimes beyond. With an inner core including the Muslim Arab states, **Israel** and Iran, more peripheral countries such as Turkey, Afghanistan, **Pakistan**, Cyprus and even Greece are often included within the compass of the Middle East.

MIDDLE EAST WATCH *see* HUMAN RIGHTS WATCH

MIDWEST

A geographical term for a region of the USA which lies between the East and the West. It is usually taken to include the industrial states clustered around the Great Lakes – Ohio, Indiana, Illinois, Wisconsin, Michigan, and Minnesota – together with the **Farm Belt** states of North Dakota, South Dakota, Nebraska, Kansas, Iowa and Missouri. Politically the region is important as it contains several key **battleground states**. Since the 1970s the Midwest has been afflicted by economic decline in both its industry and agriculture, and a steady migration of population towards the **Sun Belt** states of the South and West.

MIGA *see* IFC

MILITANT

The far-left **Trotskyist** group, associated with the *Militant Tendency* newspaper, which formed a faction within the UK Labour Party until the late 1980s. Militant activists stirred controversy by allegedly using ruthless tactics to ensure that allies were nominated as prospective parliamentary candidates, sometimes at the expense of incumbent Labour MPs. Under the leadership of Neil Kinnock Labour began to expel Militant members in 1983, and by the early 1990s Militant influence had declined.

MILITARY-INDUSTRIAL COMPLEX

A phrase first used by US President Dwight D. Eisenhower in January 1961 when he warned 'against the acquisition of unwarranted influence, whether sought or unsought, by the military-industrial complex'. Since then the term has come to signify the symbiotic relationship between the military establishment and industrial corporations, which service each other's mutual needs as mediated by elected political officials. While this relationship has been most fully developed in the USA, it has also been important in France, the UK and the former **Soviet Union**.

MILITIAS

A military force, often civilian-based and auxiliary to the regular army. Militia forces have exerted varying degrees of military and political power in a number of states. In Lebanon tension between religious and ethnic communities resulted in civil war between opposing militias in 1975–91. During this period the strongest militias included **Amal** and the Iranian-backed **Hezbollah** (both **Shia**), the **Maronite** Christian Lebanese Forces, the **Druse** Progressive Socialist Party and the **Israeli**-backed **South Lebanon Army**.

MINERS' STRIKE

The year-long strike by members of the UK National Union of Mineworkers (NUM) in 1984–5. While there had been a history of industrial conflict in the coal mining industry in the UK (for instance leading to the imposition of the **three-day week** in 1973–4), the situation was intensified in the early years of the 1979 Conservative government when it was characterized by the contrasting personalities of the NUM president Arthur Scargill and the National Coal Board chair Sir Ian MacGregor who had the full support of the Prime Minister Margaret Thatcher. At issue were not only pay claims but plans for a drastic reduction in the size of the industry, while accusations were made against Scargill and his supporters as representing the **enemy within**. The strike, which started in March 1984, was not based on a national ballot of NUM members, and this feature continued to be a point of controversy and led to a number of complicated legal cases. The strikers, who enjoyed considerable popular support, came frequently into sharp confrontation with the police, notably through the action of pickets at Orgreave coking plant and other sites. Limited mining continued, especially by members of the breakaway Union of Democratic Mineworkers, and the existence of large stocks of coal at pitheads and power stations reduced the effect of the restriction of coal production. The strike was eventually called off in March 1985. Over the succeeding years the role of coal in the economy was further reduced, with the number of miners falling from around 200,000 to about 10,000 and the number of deep-mined pits from around 170 to under 20. Legislation was passed in 1993–4 for the **privatization** of the coal industry.

MINISTRY OF INTERNATIONAL TRADE AND INDUSTRY *see* MITI

MINURSO

The small **UN** Mission for the Referendum in **Western Sahara**, which began work in September 1991. Its efforts to prepare a referendum on the future of the territory were impeded by shortage of personnel, and by the absence of the minimum necessary level of agreement between Morocco and the independence movement, the **Polisario Front**.

MINUTEMAN

A US land-based long-range nuclear missile, which like **Polaris** was one of the new generation of **ICBMs** introduced from 1960. Together they ended US nuclear reliance on long-range bombers, and banished the myth of the **missile gap**.

MIR

(Russian, 'peace' and also 'world') An advanced type of space station first launched by the **Soviet Union** in 1986. A modern version of the *Salyut* series, Mir was designed to be upgradable by the addition of extra modules dedicated to specific scientific purposes. Permanently manned, it has been visited by several paying foreign cosmonauts to compensate for a lack of space funding. It is now ageing, and a new generation *Mir-2* is scheduled to replace it in 1996.

MIRV

A multiple independently targeted re-entry vehicle, as fitted on missiles from the late 1960s, first by the USA and then by the **Soviet Union**, so that one missile could carry several warheads. Whereas **arms control** discussions had previously focused on missile numbers, the introduction of MIRVs led to much more complex arguments about warhead numbers, which bedevilled negotiations up to the conclusion of the **START** II agreement in 1992.

MISSILE GAP

The alarmist view which took hold in the USA in 1959 and 1960 that the **Soviet Union**, having achieved a breakthrough in space with the launching of **Sputnik**, was also producing nuclear missiles so fast that it was about to establish a dangerous superiority in the **arms race**. Publicized in Gen. Maxwell Taylor's bestselling book *The Uncertain Trumpet*, the issue was exploited by John F. Kennedy, who repeated throughout his successful presidential campaign in 1960 his determination that the USA should be in first place. The **Polaris** and **Minuteman** programmes were doubled as a result. In fact the belief in Soviet strength was largely the result of Soviet bluffing, and Kennedy himself, from his briefings from the outgoing Eisenhower administration, knew that there was no real missile gap.

MISSING IN ACTION *see* MIA

MITI

The Ministry of International Trade and Industry, the Japanese government agency which directs economic strategy. Within the environment of **money politics**, MITI has successfully overseen the rational evolution and spectacular growth of the Japanese economy since the Second World War.

MK

Umkhonto we Sizwe (Xhosa / Zulu, 'Spear of the Nation'), the armed wing of South Africa's main anti-**apartheid** movement, the **ANC**. MK was founded in 1960 in the wake of the **Sharpeville** massacre and the banning of the ANC and **PAC**. Its campaign began on 16 December 1961 with a series of dramatic explosions, and over the next 18 months it launched more than 200 attacks on government installations. It was formally banned on 10 May 1963. The organization suffered a major setback in July 1963 when the police discovered its headquarters, and eight senior MK leaders, including Nelson Mandela, were given life sentences in the subsequent **Rivonia trial**. For the next decade MK operations tended to be conducted from bases outside South Africa by volunteers who had received military training in Angola, Mozambique, Tanzania and Libya. With the rapid increase in mass popular protest in South Africa accompanying the 1976 **Soweto riots**, MK underground cells were successfully established within the country, allowing for more frequent attacks. In August 1990 the ANC, having been unbanned six months earlier, suspended the armed struggle and all MK activities ceased. An agreement in November 1993 between the South African government, the ANC and 18 other parties provided for the incorporation of MK into a new National Defence Force.

MNLF

The Moro National Liberation Front – a militant Muslim organization demanding independence or autonomy for the mainly Muslim southern Philippines. The MNLF, led by Nur Misuari, has waged a **guerrilla** war against the government since its foundation in 1968. Following talks in Tripoli in December 1976, the MNLF appeared ready to accept autonomy for the 13 provinces in the southern islands of Mindanao, Palawan and the Sulu Archipelago, but the deal collapsed amidst controversy surrounding a terms of an accompanying referendum. The MNLF's influence declined markedly after limited autonomy was granted to four provinces in 1989–90 by the government of President Corazon Aquino. Although the guerrilla war continues, it is much reduced in scale since the 1970s.

MNR

The Mozambique National Resistance, also known as Renamo, the rebel **guerrilla** movement which conducted a brutal war against the government from 1976 until 1992. The early history of the organization is disputed, although it is likely that it was established by the intelligence service in **Rhodesia** in an effort to halt the Marxist-Leninist Frelimo government's support for Zimbabwean national liberation organizations. On Zimbabwean independence in 1980, South African military intelligence took control of the MNR and increased its support (which the organization always categorically denied receiving, despite South African admissions).

By mid-1982 the MNR claimed to be active in half the country's provinces. However, there was considerable evidence to suggest that its guerrillas operated only in thinly populatedareas, that it had very little genuine grassroots support, and that many of its fighters, some of whom were children, had been pressganged into service. In 1984 South Africa undertook under the **Nkomati Accord** to halt all aid to the MNR, but it nevertheless continued to provide substantial covert military and financial aid. From early 1986 the MNR stepped up its campaign, attacking infrastructure. The installations at **Cabora Bassa** and along the **Beira Corridor** were favourite targets.

Direct talks between the MNR and the government finally began in July 1990 and culminated in a peace treaty on 4 October 1992 to end the 16-year civil war. MNR troops were to be demobilized and the MNR transformed into a political party which would contest multiparty elections scheduled for October 1994.

MOBUTUISM

A political ideology built, sometimes incoherently, around the thoughts, policies and whims of President Mobutu Sese Seko of Zaïre. Mobutuism advocated a policy of authenticity and Zaïrean **nationalism**, under which in 1971 the country's name was changed from Congo-Kinshasa to Zaïre and the people were exhorted to drop their Christian (mission) names in favour of African ones. In 1973 private companies were nationalized under the ideology, only to be denationalized the following year. In 1974 Mobutuism was adopted as the official policy of the Popular Movement for the Revolution (MPR), the sole legal party from 1969 until the reluctant acceptance of a multiparty system in 1991.

MOHAJIR QAUMI MAHAZ

(Urdu, 'Migrants' National Party') A Pakistani political party founded in 1986 to represent the interests of Urdu-speaking minority Muslim migrants from India (*mohajirs*), and to win recognition of the group as the country's fifth nationality (in addition to the Baluchis, Pathans, Punjabis and Sindhis). Its power base lies in urban centres of the southern province of Sind, home to the majority of *mohajirs*, where its strong performance in the general elections of 1988 and 1990 enabled it to command important ministerial positions in the provincial government. The party's alleged involvement in corruption and political thuggery led in early 1992 to military action against its supporters, forcing its leader, Altaf Hussain, to flee the country. Since then the party has suffered divisions which contributed to its poor showing in the October 1993 general election.

MOJAHEDIN*see* MUJAHEDDIN

MOLDOVA

One of the successor states of the **Soviet Union**, and a member of the **CIS**. Moldova declared independence in 1991 after the failed **August coup** attempt. A majority of Moldova's population of 4.4 million speaks Romanian; the **Slavonic** minority in its **Dnestr** region rebelled in 1991-2, fearing that a newly independent Moldova would seek unification with Romania.

MOLES

A term used to describe individuals who penetrate an organization in order to acquire sensitive information. It is most often applied to infiltrators into the security services – for example agents or recruits of the Soviet and east European intelligence services who fed back to those countries secret defence and associated material of Western nations. By extension, it is also used to describe employees of government and similar bodies who 'whistle blow' by leaking information, generally to the media, in order to expose what they see as illegal or unethical conduct in those organizations.

MONCADA BARRACKS

The scene of a daring rebel attack on 26 July 1953 in Santiago de Cuba which marked the transition from peaceful to armed struggle in an effort to overthrow the dictatorship of Fulgencio Batista. It brought to national prominence Fidel Castro, a young lawyer and member of the reformist Ortodoxo party who nevertheless led a splinter group that favoured insurrection. The attack was a military failure, with the death of three rebels, summary execution of 68 more and the capture of 42, including Castro, who were imprisoned and later amnestied. However, it captured the public imagination and Castro's *History Will Absolve Me!*, a reconstruction of his defence analyzing the reasons for the attack, was the first important document of the Cuban Revolution. Before leaving for exile in Mexico, Castro established in 1955 the 26 July Movement (M–26–7), open to all Cubans opposed to the dictatorship.

MONDAY CLUB

A **right-wing** grouping of the UK Conservative Party, formed in 1960. Established in reaction to Harold Macmillan's **wind of change** speech, the Club was characterized by support for the South African regime, and subsequently the Rhodesian **UDI** regime, by advocacy of voluntary repatriation of black **Commonwealth** immigrants, and by opposition to anti-**apartheid** activities such as sporting boycotts. It had a revival in 1968 at the time of tension over increased Commonwealth immigration and Enoch Powell's **rivers of blood** speech. It has numbered several Conservative MPs among its membership.

MONETARISM

The branch of economics which argues that control of the money supply is the key to ensuring a stable economy. The theory of monetarism was formulated by the **Friedmanite** economists of the Chicago school as a challenge to standard **Keynesian** theories, which had failed to explain the emergence of sustained high inflation and unemployment in the **stagflation** of the 1970s. It was a key component of the economic policies associated with the **New Right** in the 1980s.

MONEY POLITICS

A descriptive term for the Japanese political system which evolved under the 1946 constitution. Based on a triangular relationship between the ruling Liberal Democratic Party (LDP), which held office from 1955 to 1993, the civil service, and big business interests, the system involved bribery and patronage, and led to the periodic eruption of corruption scandals. The development of well-defined factions within the ruling party, each of which required lavish campaign funds for its members to compete for election to the **Diet** within the country's multi-member constituencies, exacerbated the tendency towards corruption. The system of money politics reached its apogee under the premiership of Kakuei Tanaka who came to power in 1972, was forced from office by corruption allegations in 1974, and in 1983 was convicted of accepting bribes in the **Lockheed scandal**. Other major scandals thereafter included the **Recruit-Cosmos scandal** and the **Sagawa Kyubin scandal**. In 1993 the LDP was ejected from office largely because of its unwillingness to reform the system of money politics. It was succeeded by a coalition which has gone some way towards securing reform through the abolition of the multi-member electoral system and more stringent laws governing the receipt of political donations.

MONKEY BUSINESS

The name of a yacht on which the candidate for the 1988 Democratic presidential nomination, Gary Hart, 50, took a cruise to the island of Bimini, in March 1987, in the company of model and actress Donna Rice, 29. Hart, a former Senator from Colorado, had been runner-up to Walter Mondale in the 1984 nomination contest, and was an early front-runner for the 1988 nomination. In response to allegations concerning his marital infidelity, Hart had challenged reporters to 'follow me around'. Almost immediately it was reported that he had spent the night with Rice, and that they had taken the Bimini cruise together. On 8 May, within days of the revelation, Hart withdrew from the nomination contest.

MONTENEGRO

The small republic which, with the much larger Serbia, makes up the Federal Republic of **Yugoslavia** (FRY) declared on 27 April 1992. Montenegro was a republic of the former Socialist Yugoslavia, with Montenegrins comprising 2.6 per cent of Yugoslavia's population according to the 1981 census. Like Serbs, Montenegrins are mainly Orthodox Christians and speak Serbo-Croat, and some Serbs claim that they are not a distinct group. However, there have been recent indications of resistance to Serb domination in the FRY structure. Montenegro has 30 members in the federal Chamber of Citizens, whereas Serbia has 108; each has 20 members in the 40-seat Chamber of the Republics.

MONTGOMERY BUS BOYCOTT

A year-long boycott of the public transport system in Montgomery, Alabama, which provided a key early victory for the US **civil rights movement**. The boycott began on 5 December 1955, after a black woman, Rosa Parks, had been arrested for refusing to give up her seat on a bus to a white passenger. On 23 April 1956 the Supreme Court ruled (in relation to a separate case) that segregation on buses was unconstitutional. Further rulings overturned the Montgomery city ordinances which had allowed segregation, and the policy was finally abandoned on 21 December 1956. The boycott was important in stimulating similar actions elsewhere in the **South**, and also demonstrated that non-violent mass protests in the cause of **civil rights** could be sustained. The Montgomery action also saw the rise to national prominence of Martin Luther King Jr, the most charismatic black leader to advocate non-violent resistance.

MONTONEROS

An Argentine **guerrilla** group composed of students and former Catholic activists, drawing its ideology from **Peronism, socialism** and **nationalism**. The Montoneros began armed action in 1970 against military personnel and **right-wing** Peronists and trade union leaders. Following the 1976 military coup they engaged in open warfare with security forces and **death squads**, providing the justification for the junta's dirty war.

MONTREAL PROTOCOL

An agreement signed in 1987 by 24 countries which undertook to halve their **CFC** production by 1999. The protocol aims to reduce damage to the **ozone layer** and to contain the **greenhouse effect**, both of which are affected by the presence of CFCs in the atmosphere. The protocol was strengthened when ministers from 91 countries agreed at a conference in Copenhagen on 23–5 November 1992 to advance the target date for halving CFC production by four years to 1996. At this meeting, industrialized countries pledged an additional US$500 million on top of the US$240 million already offered to help developing countries meet the protocol's targets. For their part, developing countries agreed to bring the fumigant methyl bromide under the terms of the protocol. However, environmental groups claimed that the measures undertaken to limit production of methyl bromide were insufficient.

MORAL MAJORITY

A large US organization of evangelical Christians, under the leadership of Jerry Falwell, which constitutes a powerful pressure group in support of **family values**. The group was particularly influential on the right of the Republican Party, and strongly supported the values associated with the Presidency of Ronald Reagan (1981–9).

MORAL REARMAMENT

A revivalist movement established in the UK in 1938 by the US-born Lutheran pastor Frank Buchman. MRA, which succeeded Buchman's previous Oxford Movement, based its teaching on the four 'absolutes' of purity, unselfishness, honesty and love, and on the importance of 'life-change'. While expounding political and social concerns in a rejection of both **capitalism** and **communism**, it came to be perceived as stridently anti-Marxist. It reached its peak in the late 1950s, but lost much of its influence after the death of Buchman in 1961 and of his successor Peter Howard in 1965.

MORO AFFAIR

The kidnapping in 1978 of Aldo Moro, president of the Italian Christian Democratic Party (DC), by the **left-wing Brigate Rosse**, and his assassination after the government refused to meet the kidnappers' demands. Moro was abducted on 16 March, on his way to the parliament where DC Prime Minister Giulio Andreotti was due to present a government with which the Italian **Communist** Party (PCI) would co-operate for the first time. The kidnappers threatened to kill Moro unless the government met certain conditions, including the release of some 'communist' detainees. The Italian state was plunged into crisis as the parties debated the proper response. The DC eventually decided against any concessions, and Moro was killed on 9 May; his body was found in a car parked midway between the headquarters of the PCI and the DC. In 1993, Andreotti was accused of having approved a Mafia killing of two people who were in possession of sensitive information about Moro's assassination.

MORO NATIONAL LIBERATION FRONT *see* MNLF

MOSCOW REBELLION

The October 1993 rebellion of a **red-brown** coalition against Russian President Boris

Yeltsin's suspension on 21 September of the Russian parliament. Yeltsin's move was a response to months of deadlock between the parliament and the presidency. The rebel alliance of **communists**, nationalists and conservatives was led by Vice-President Aleksandr Rutskoi and Supreme Soviet Chair Ruslan Khasbulatov. Denouncing the suspension of parliament as unconstitutional, they declared Rutskoi the legal President. An armed rebel attempt to seize a television centre in Moscow on 3 October prompted some military units to intervene on behalf of Yeltsin on the following day. They stormed the **White House** and arrested the rebels, who were subsequently released in February 1994 under the terms of an amnesty passed by the new parliament.

MOSSAD

(Hebrew, from *Mossad Merkazi Le-Modiin U-Letafkidim Meyuhadim* – 'Central Institute for Intelligence and Security') The most important, powerful and prominent of the Israeli intelligence agencies. Mossad, founded in 1951 by Isser Harel, who served as its director until 1963, concerns itself with matters of espionage, intelligence gathering and covert political operations in foreign countries. Major operations carried out by the organization include the kidnapping of the Nazi Adolf Eichmann from Argentina in 1961 and bringing him to **Israel** to stand trial for war crimes, and the rescue of hostages from a hijacked Israeli airliner being held at **Entebbe**, Uganda, in 1976. Mossad has also been linked with the assassination of several prominent Palestinians in various Arab, African and European countries.

MOST-FAVOURED-NATION *see* MFN

MOSTAR BRIDGE

The *Stari Most* ('old bridge'), a narrow, single-span stone bridge constructed in 1566 over the river Neretva in **Bosnia-Hercegovina**, which was destroyed by Croat bombardment in November 1993 during the fighting in Bosnia. The bridge was one of the former **Yugoslavia's** most celebrated historic monuments, in a town which featured a mixed community of **Bosnian Muslims**, Croats, Serbs and Jews. Its destruction, after months of brutal fighting between local Muslims and Croats, was a heavy symbolic blow to the ideal of inter-ethnic harmony.

MOTHER OF BATTLES

The retaliation threatened by President Saddam Hussein as a response to any invasion of Iraq. Throughout the latter part of 1990, as the allied force assembled in the **Gulf** in response to the Iraqi invasion of Kuwait, he declared that if Iraq were in turn to be attacked this would result in the 'mother of battles'. In the event, little effective Iraqi opposition was shown during the **Gulf War**, either to the allied air operations in January 1991 or to the land battle which ensued in February of that year.

MOTHERS OF THE PLAZA DE MAYO

A group of Argentinian mothers campaigning for information on the whereabouts of **disappeared** relatives kidnapped during the **dirty war** (1976–83). Their silent demonstrations, denoted by the wearing of white headscarves, on the Plaza de Mayo in the capital Buenos Aires, began in April 1977 and continued thereafter every Thursday despite death and abduction threats. A sister organization, the Grandmothers of the Plaza de Mayo, emerged in 1979 to trace children of the disappeared who had been illegally placed for adoption by the authorities. The Mothers gained world renown and inspired similar organizations in Chile, El Salvador, Guatemala, Peru and the Philippines. They vigorously opposed the law of **Due Obedience** and the **Full Stop Law**, both of which exempted the military from prosecution over human rights abuses, and the pardons conferred on the military by President Carlos Menem. In 1985 a small group, including some of the founding members, who believed in a more conciliatory approach to an elected government, left and formed a new organization.

MOUNT PINATUBO

A volcano in the Philippines, dormant for 600 years before it began to erupt in June

1991. More serious than the damage which the eruption caused to the nearby US **Clark Field air base** was its environmental impact, demonstrating the global climate's sensitivity to changes in the atmosphere. The ash and sulphur dioxide which the volcano spewed out impeded solar radiation from reaching the earth, thereby contributing to a deceleration in **global warming** over 1991–2.

MOUNT ST HELENS

A volcano in Washington State, north-west USA, whose eruption in May 1986 (like that of **Mount Pinatubo** in the Philippines in 1991) was traced as the cause of climate changes world wide, in particular contributing to a reduction in **global warming**.

MSA

The Mutual Security Act, the US legislation, originally passed in 1951, under which economic and military aid was provided to friendly countries to maintain the defences of the non-**communist** world. It included arrangements for disposing of agricultural surpluses, which grew to become the US **food aid** programme.

MUJAHEDDIN

(Arabic, 'holy warriers') A term which gained wide currency following its adoption by the Iranian **Mujaheddin-i-Khalq** and by armed Islamic radicals and tribal leaders in Afghanistan who claimed to be engaged in a **jihad** against the Soviet presence there in 1979–89. Since then it has been used by insurgent Muslim groups in areas as diverse as Kashmir and the Philippines, who justify their involvement in violent conflict by reference to their religious obligation to extend Islam and seek its fulfilment in the creation of an Islamic state.

MUJAHEDDIN-I-KHALQ

(Persian, 'Holy Warriors of the People') A lay guerrilla organization representing left-wing Muslim groups in Iran. Founded in the early 1970s, it was banned after the **Islamic Revolution** for its espousal of a variant of **Islamic socialism** and its criticism of the regime of Ayatollah Khomeini. Its violent confrontation with the **Pasdaran** (Islamic Revolutionary Guards) led to thousands of its supporters being arrested, tortured and summarily executed. It currently operates from Iraq where its bases have been subjected to repeated attacks by the Iranian air force. In early 1994 the group was implicated in a number of bomb attacks staged against targets inside Iran.

MUKHABARRAT

(Arabic, 'Party Intelligence') The most powerful and feared of the three Iraqi security agencies, independently responsible to the **Revolutionary Command Council**. (The other two are the *Amn* or State Security and the *Etikhbarrat* or Military Intelligence.) It is believed to have developed directly out of the *Jihaz Haneen* ('instrument of yearning') – a special unit of the Iraqi branch of the Arab **Ba'ath** Socialist Party dating from the mid-1960s. It is a distinctly political body charged with the surveillance of state and corporate institutions as well as of mass organizations.

MULDERGATE *see* INFORMATION SCANDAL

MULTI-FIBRE ARRANGEMENT *see* MFA

MULTILATERAL INVESTMENT GUARANTEE AGENCY *see* IFC

MULTILATERALISM

The concept of operating at the international level through international organizations and by seeking agreements with several countries. In taking a multilateralist approach, countries may also intend to help strengthen international organizations, particularly the **UN**. A choice between multilateralism and bilateralism is evident in such areas as **aid, arms control** and trade policy.

MULTINATIONAL CORPORATION

A large company operating in more than one country. Multinationals may be said to differ from transnational corporations, whose interests lie principally in the home country. Both are accused of furthering **neocolonialism** by exploiting cheap labour in the host country and extracting more from the host economy than they invest.

MUNICH OLYMPICS MASSACRE

The massacre which arose from a failed attempt to rescue nine **Israeli** athletes taken hostage during the 1972 Munich Olympic Games. The Arab '**Black September**' organization, protesting at the expulsion of Palestinian organizations from Jordan, had seized the hostages and shot dead two other Israeli athletes in a pre-dawn raid on the Olympic village on 5 September. In the face of a threat to execute one hostage every two hours, the German authorities promised to meet the captors' demand for safe passage out of Germany, and took them late the same evening to a nearby military airfield. However, they then mounted a rescue attempt in which all nine Israeli hostages, five of the eight Arab captors and one German policeman died.

MUSCAT AND OMAN *see* OMAN

MUSLIM BROTHERHOOD

The most prominent **Sunni** Muslim fundamentalist movement currently active in Egypt which has inspired several offshoots in other parts of the **Middle East**. Founded in 1928 by Hassan al-Banna, it gained notoriety as a vehement advocate of an Islamic state and one of the bitterest critics of Egypt's secular politics. It was banned in 1954, and is still technically illegal, but has enjoyed de facto recognition since entering into coalition politics under the regime of President Hosni Mubarak. In general elections held in 1984 it emerged as the major parliamentary opposition and in 1987, along with two smaller parties, succeeded in winning the second largest number of parliamentary seats after the ruling National Democratic Party.

MUSLIM PARLIAMENT

An assembly of (self-appointed) representatives of the British Muslim community which held its first session on 4–5 January 1992. It was first proposed in July 1990 by the UK-based Muslim Institute which played a leading role in mobilizing Muslim public opinion against the publication of **The Satanic Verses**. Formally committed to acknowledging the supremacy of British law, the parliament nevertheless seeks to protect Muslim interests in the UK somewhat along the lines of the **Board of Deputies of British Jews**.

MUSLIM WORLD LEAGUE

The international Muslim body, also known as *Rabitat al Alam al Islami*, founded in 1962 with its headquarters in Mecca, Saudi Arabia. It has some 30 offices worldwide with several European branches concentrating on mosque-building. Originally created to advance Islamic unity through financial assistance for education, medical care and relief work with an annual estimated budget of around £2 million (US$3 million), it has recently been reported to act as a financial pipeline for Saudi-backed radical **Sunni** Muslim groups in Asia, Africa and the **Middle East**.

MUTUAL SECURITY ACT *see* MSA

MUTUALLY ASSURED DESTRUCTION *see* MAD

MY LAI

A hamlet in the central Vietnamese province of Quang Ngai where US soldiers carried out an infamous massacre of South Vietnamese civilians on 16 March 1968. A platoon commanded by Lt. William Calley had entered the hamlet, which, according to inaccurate intelligence reports, was the headquarters of a crack **Viet Cong** battalion. Although the platoon met with no resistance, they embarked on an orgy of nauseating violence killing as many as 350 of My Lai's inhabitants, including women, babies and children. The US army launched a secret investigation into the massacre in April 1969, details of which were first revealed in November 1970. The revelation served to heighten significantly anti-war sentiment in the USA. Paradoxically, the sentencing of Calley to life imprisonment in March 1971 for his part in the massacre also intensified anti-war feeling in the USA, particularly among **right-wingers** who argued that Calley and others had been made scapegoats for those directing the war. The national outrage over the verdict led the army to reduce Calley's sentence significantly.

MYANMA NAINGNAN

(Burmese, 'Union of Myanma') The official name of Burma since the country was renamed by the ruling military junta (**SLORC**) in June 1988. The SLORC explained that the previous English name, Union of Burma, implied that the population were all Burmans, whereas the new name stressed the importance of embracing all ethnic minority groups in the country.

NAACP

The National Association for the Advancement of Colored People. Founded in 1909, the NAACP was one of the key organizations in the US **civil rights movement**. Advocating non-violent resistance, during the 1960s it supported the **sit-in** demonstrations and **freedom rides** which were used to challenge **segregation** and institutionalized **racism**.

NAC

The North Atlantic Council, the highest executive body of **NATO**, which normally meets twice a year at ministerial level, and is in permanent session in Brussels as a meeting of the ambassadors of member countries.

NACC

The North Atlantic Co-operation Council, the forum set up in 1991 by **NATO** to cope with the pressures for it to broaden its role as a regional security organization, and to embrace countries in central and eastern Europe and the former **Soviet Union** which had been NATO's adversaries in the **Cold War**. The NACC held its first meeting, between foreign ministers, in December 1991 in Brussels. By the December 1992 meeting it had grown to 36 participants and was proposing joint planning and training and possibly joint peacekeeping missions – an idea which NACC defence ministers endorsed the following March. By early 1994, however, the NACC forum had been sidelined by the launching of the **partnerships for peace** programme.

NADER'S RAIDERS

The professional associates of US consumer advocate Ralph Nader. From the 1960s Nader's Raiders undertook studies on the safety and reliability of consumer products, ranging from automobiles to baby food to banking. In some cases, this resulted in the introduction of stricter legislation. Nader's fame as an advocate of consumer issues began with the publication in 1965 of *Unsafe at Any Speed*, an exposé of the US motor industry.

NAFTA

The North American Free Trade Agreement, which became operational on 1 January 1994. Its origins lay in the Free Trade Agreement (FTA) between Canada and the USA which came into effect in January 1989. Despite Canadian charges of unfair competition, the prosect of an extended market and dramatically reduced labour costs (especially for US companies) led to the addition of Mexico and the formal signing of NAFTA in December 1992. The trilateral signing of labour and environmental side agreements in August 1993 enabled NAFTA's passage through a divided US Congress in November. Canada continued to express a determination to renegotiate certain sections of the treaty, which was welcomed by the Mexican government, if not the bulk of the population, and regarded enthusiastically or as inevitable by other governments in **Latin America** and the **Caribbean**.

NAGORNY KARABAKH

A mountainous enclave in the Muslim and Turkic-speaking former Soviet republic of **Azerbaijan**, where the community of Christian Armenian-speakers is engaged in a war of independence. The conflict began in 1988 when intercommunal violence broke out in Nagorny Karabakh. In

November 1989 the neighbouring republic of Armenia claimed sovereignty over the area (a move it subsequently repudiated), prompting a bloody pogrom by Azeris against ethnic Armenians elsewhere in Azerbaijan. Although Armenia has consistently denied providing military support to its ethnically kindred allies in Nagorny Karabakh, forces from the enclave have scored a remarkable series of victories. They captured and held some 20 per cent of Azerbaijani territory despite a bloody Azeri counter-offensive in early 1994. As of February 1994, some 18,000 people had been killed in the conflict and 1 million made homeless.

NAGYMAROS *see* GABCIKOVO

NAKHICHEVAN

An enclave with a mainly Azeri population, under the sovereignty of **Azerbaijan**, which is located between **Armenia**, Turkey and Iran. Nakhichevan looked vulnerable as ethnic Armenian forces from **Nagorny Karabakh** seized Azerbaijani territory to the east of it in the early 1990s, but Turkey has effectively guaranteed the enclave's security.

NAMIBIA

A country with an area of over 300,000 square miles (824,000 sq km), but with a population of only about 1.5 million which lies between Angola and South Africa on the coast of south-west Africa. Namibia achieved independence only in March 1990. It had been a German colony from 1884 until 1915, when it came under South African rule with the name South West Africa. In 1920 a League of Nations mandate provided for a further period of South African administration. The **UN** terminated the mandate in 1966, but South Africa, in defiance of the UN, continued to run the country, and applied its **apartheid** system there. South Africa's continuing presence was ruled illegal by the **ICJ** in June 1971, and was contested in a protracted liberation struggle led by **SWAPO**. Implementation of a UN-sponsored independence plan based on the 1978 UN Security Council **Resolution 435** was finally agreed in December 1988, and completed in March 1990, when SWAPO formed the first democratically elected government.

NANNY STATE

The pejorative term employed in the UK to denote what is perceived as over-involvement of government (especially central government) in the day-to-day decisions of individuals and industry. Those using the phrase are normally on the right of the political spectrum, and regard the excessive powers of government as undermining self-reliance and as stifling enterprise and initiative.

NAPALM

A substance developed by US scientists during the Second World War to thicken gasoline for its use as an incendiary in flame throwers or fire bombs. It has been employed in many conflicts since 1945, most notably during the **Vietnam War** when its use by the US air force against civilians generated some of the most potent images of that war.

NARMADA DAM

A controversial Indian dam project, also known as the Sardar Sarovar dam project, encompassing a network of about 30 dams to harness the waters of the Narmada River which flows through the states of Gujarat, Madhya Pradesh and Maharashtra. Costing an estimated US$5,500 million, it aroused fierce opposition among environmentalists in India and abroad for its planned displacement of some 300,000 tribal people settled in the affected areas as well as the adverse effects on flora and fauna. The project was suspended in August 1993 after a mass rally by environmental activists belonging to the *Narmada Bachao Andolan* ('Save the Narmada Movement') forced the Indian government to order a review of the scheme. In March of that year the dam's main backer, the **World Bank**, had cancelled all loans in response to environmental groups.

NASA

The National Aeronautics and Space Administration, the US government agency created in 1958 to co-ordinate civilian activities in space. Tensions in its original charter centred on its civilian role while sharing underlying technologies and contractors with the military, and its international brief to co-operate on space technology and science, whereas the military emphasized the need for US hegemony in space. It also had to set the political benefits of manned flight against the scientific advantages of less costly unmanned missions.

NASA's manned programmes were Mercury and Gemini (1959–66), the lunar landing **Apollo Project** (1966–72), SkyLab (1973–4), and the **space shuttle** flights from 1981. The shuttle programme was marred by the 1986 **Challenger disaster**, but prestige was recovered by the successful December 1993 **Hubble Space Telescope** repair mission, while NASA's funding crisis was eased by a November 1993 agreement on a joint US-Russian space station.

NASSAU CONFERENCE

The December 1962 meeting in the capital of the Bahamas between UK Prime Minister Harold Macmillan and US President John F. Kennedy, where Kennedy offered the **Polaris** missile as the means of modernizing the UK's nuclear weapons capability. The meeting had been made necessary when the US side decided to scrap development of the **Skybolt** air-to-ground missile unless the UK was willing to meet significant development costs.

NASSERISM

The political programme and ideology of Egyptian and Arab leader Gamal Abdel Nasser. Nasserism, which held sway in Egypt and the Arab world during the 1950s and 1960s, incorporated a number of elements, including an appeal to Arab **nationalism** and unity, Arab socialism and reformist Islam. The personality of Nasser and the success of his regime – the political victory of the **Suez crisis** in 1956, the building of the **Aswan High Dam** and the introduction of fundamental social reforms in Egypt – ensured that Nasserism embodied itself in wide-ranging Arab political movements, even after the disaster of the Arab defeat at the hands of **Israel** in the 1967 **Six-Day War**.

NATION OF ISLAM

The most influential of US **Black Muslim** groups, founded in 1930 by Master Farad Muhammad and currently led by Louis Farrakhan. From 1934 it was led by Elijah Muhammad and preached separate black development, suggesting that self-reliance and self-assertion were the only legitimate black response to the **segregation** imposed by the white majority. Combined with a rigorous code of personal morality, the message had a significant impact upon those in the vanguard of the **civil rights movement**. Among the most prominent of the Nation's members was Malcolm X, a dynamic figure whose charisma and oratory saw him rise from the slums of the Bronx, via criminality and imprisonment, to become one of Elijah Muhammad's most trusted lieutenants. Malcolm broke with Elijah in 1963 and was assassinated in New York on 21 February 1965. In the 1970s the Nation began making a greater appeal to the growing black middle class, and there was a significant reduction in the movement's anti-white **racism**. By the time of Elijah's death in 1975 it had spawned a multi-million dollar commercial empire. Under Farrakhan's leadership the Nation has returned to many of its most basic, anti-white, beliefs, and has frequently been accused of **anti-Semitism**. The Nation continues to reject attempts to integrate with the white community, and demands a separate land, rich in minerals, for black people, as a form of compensation for the centuries of slavery.

NATIONAL DEBT

A country's accumulated government debt, financed through borrowing either domestically or externally. Interest payments on the national debt are a call upon current revenue, and generally any reduction in the principal of the national debt must also be met from revenue. Since the mid-1980s, however, the international community has not only devised various **debt rescheduling** schemes for specified groups of developing countries, but has also actually written down (or written off) certain of these debts, for example under arrangements covered by the **Trinidad terms**.

NATIONAL FRONT

In the UK, a fringe nationalist and **racist** party founded in 1967 from small neo-**fascist** groups, including the League of Empire Loyalists, the British National Party, and the Racial Preservation Society. The NF opposed non-white immigration into Britain, and also had strong **anti-Semitic** leanings. It fought national elections during the 1970s and received some 3 per cent of the vote, but was hampered by organized opposition, such as the **Anti-Nazi League**. It fragmented in the 1980s after its leading figure, John Tyndall, left to found a new British National Party.

The term 'National Front' is sometimes adopted by broad coalition governments. In France, however,as in the UK, it has been hijacked by the extreme right. The *Front national*, founded in 1972 and led by Jean-Marie Le Pen, became in the mid-1980s the most successful party of its kind in **Western Europe**. Although unrepresented in the National Assembly since 1993, in the elections to the **European Parliament** in June 1994 it won 11 seats.

NATIONAL HEALTH SERVICE *see* NHS

NATIONAL LIBERATION FRONT *see* FLN

NATIONAL MOVEMENT OF STREET CHILDREN

A Brazilian **NGO** to protect, organize and empower street children. Founded in 1985 it currently incorporates 3,000 'street educators' in 25 states who operate in local commissions and reach tens of thousands of children and adolescents in streets and public parks. These organize children into *núcleos* defined by their lifestyles, common location or street trade, which meet regularly, and send delegates to a national conference every three years. The group fights to create and preserve effective municipal and state councils on children's rights and brings human rights violations and assassinations of street children to international attention.

NATIONAL PATRIOTIC FRONT OF LIBERIA *see* NPFL

NATIONAL RIFLE ASSOCIATION *see* NRA

NATIONAL SECURITY ADVISER

One of the most important non-Cabinet figures within the US executive branch, whose function is to advise the president on domestic, foreign and military matters relating to national security. The National Security Adviser works closely with the National Security Council (**NSC**). Henry Kissinger, as National Security Adviser under President Nixon from 1969, overshadowed the Secretary of State on major foreign policy matters, although Kissinger himself subsequently became Secretary of State and restored the pre-eminence of that Cabinet-rank office.

NATIONAL SECURITY COUNCIL *see* NSC

NATIONAL SERVICE

The system of compulsory conscription of men (and in some cases women) for the armed forces. In the USA, compulsory military service arrangements were introduced in 1940, lifted in 1947, and then reintroduced in 1948, but the (selective) compulsory service system was finally discontinued in 1973. In the UK national service was introduced in 1939, and the last recruits were called up for their two-year period of service in 1960. Compulsory national service remains in all other **NATO** countries except Belgium, Canada, Iceland and Luxembourg. It is an ingrained part of the political ethos in Switzerland, where the armed forces are seen as properly consisting of the country's citizens collectively bearing arms. **Israel** has compulsory national service for women as well as men.

NATIONALISM

The concept that every nation should find expression in an individual state. Nationalism implies a consciousness of language, culture and national identity differentiating one people from another, but it does not necessarily involve a claim to national superiority. Since the rise of the nation state in the early modern period, nationalism has fuelled political movements of both right and left. It has represented a key element of **conservative** and **fascist** ideologies, while also serving as a dynamic for struggles of national liberation against colonial powers. This latter role has been particularly evident since 1945 in Africa and many parts of Asia, where the rise of nationalism has been an important precursor to the achievement of independence. The collapse of the former Soviet bloc has seen the re-emergence of old nationalist suspicions between former ideological allies.

NATIONALIST CHINA *see* TAIWAN

NATIONALIZATION

Taking privately owned industries or other activities into public ownership, normally by acquiring their assets (with or without compensation), and usually to create state-owned monopolies. Nationalization is generally undertaken by **left-wing** governments; however, it may sometimes also be carried out by **right-wing** and essentially nationalistic regimes, especially in respect of foreign-owned undertakings. Massive nationalization took place in the countries of eastern Europe after the end of the Second World War, while in the UK the 1945–51 Labour government acquired large sections of productive industry and of services. The process of reversing nationalization may take the form of **privatization** as such, other methods of introducing competition, or 'hiving off' of services while retaining state ownership and ultimate control.

NATO

The Brussels-based North Atlantic Treaty Organization, formed in April 1949 and the basic Western alliance in the subsequent four decades of the **Cold War**. NATO came into being during the Soviet blockade of Berlin, reflecting fears of Communist aggression and taking as its basic tenet that an armed attack on any NATO country would be seen as an attack on them all. The concept of the '**nuclear umbrella**' rapidly assumed, and retained, a central role in the identity of the NATO alliance, with Western Europe unable to match the Russians for strength in conventional forces. The Soviet bloc in turn saw NATO as its principal threat, and the **Warsaw Pact** of 1955 was formed in a sense as its mirror image. NATO grew from the original 12 members of the Atlantic Alliance to include Greece and Turkey (1952), Germany (1955) and Spain (1982), but France withdrew in 1966 from NATO military structures, as President Charles de Gaulle took his stand against the dominant influence of the USA.

Rooted in the geopolitics of the Cold War, NATO faced an identity crisis in the 1990s. Following the collapse of communism several former Warsaw Pact countries from central and eastern Europe began pressing to be allowed to join, and the **partnerships for peace** programme was introduced in early 1994 in response to this pressure. Almost simultaneously, NATO forces became involved in the first-ever direct military action in NATO's own name, to enforce a **UN**-backed **no-fly zone** over Bosnia.

NAURU

A Pacific island originally colonized by Germany, and later administered jointly by the UK, Australia and New Zealand before becoming an independent republic in January 1968. Nauru has amassed a considerable amount of wealth from the royalties derived from phosphate-mining, although this activity has left 80 per cent of the island uninhabitable.

NAXALITE

A supporter of the violent extreme **left-wing** Indian movement which developed in the late 1960s as an off-shoot of the **Communist** Party of India (Marxist). Aimed against landlords in possession of large illegal landholdings, the movement derived its name from its first major campaign, launched in 1967, in Naxalbari, a sub-division of the Darjeeling district of West Bengal. While the movement itself was shortlived and the popularity of its programme of violence restricted to young radicals from the Indian middle classes, its appeal was wide enough to spawn a period of Naxalite politics in other states, including Bihar and Andhra Pradesh.

'NDRANGHETA

The network of clandestine groups involved in organized crime in Italy's southernmost region, Calabria. The 'Ndrangheta is often grouped together with the Sicilian **Mafia** and the Neapolitan **Camorra**.

NEA

The Nuclear Energy Agency. Set up within the **OECD** in 1958 to promote co-operation on nuclear power, the NEA has latterly concerned itself with safety issues. South Korea, although not an OECD member, joined the NEA in 1993.

NEAR ABROAD

A phrase used in Russia to denote neighbouring states of the former **Soviet Union** in which Russia retains a special interest (for economic, military-strategic or nationalistic reasons). The phrase has been criticized as implying that these states are somehow less than fully sovereign and are liable to be included within a newly imposed Russian sphere of influence, particularly through the institution of the **CIS**.

NEAR EAST

An outmoded term denoting lands around the eastern shore of the Mediterranean Sea, including north-western Africa, south-western Asia and, often, the Balkan peninsula. In recent times it has been largely supplanted by the term **Middle East**.

NEC

In the UK, the Labour Party's national executive committee. The NEC is the key policy-making and administrative organ of the Labour Party between annual conferences. Its composition, reflecting the nature and history of the party, includes the leader and deputy leader of the party (both directly elected by the entire party under special **OMOV** arrangements), the treasurer (elected by the whole annual conference), one youth member elected at the national youth conference, one member elected by the Black and Asian Socialist Society, and representatives of various divisions (12 elected by trade union delegates, one elected by socialist, co-operative and other organizations, seven nominated by constituency parties and elected by individual members under a system of OMOV, and five women members elected by annual conference as a whole). By 1995 a given proportion of NEC trade union and constituency members must be women.

NECKLACING

Killing someone by placing a petrol-filled tyre around their neck, then setting fire to it. The practice emerged in the mid-1980s in South Africa's **townships** where extreme black militants 'necklaced' other blacks suspected of collaborating with the authorities, including members of the police, local councillors and informers.

NEGRITUDE

(French, 'blackness') The concept that Black Africans by virtue of their race have wholly different experiences and values from other people. The concept, developed in the French colonies as a response to the French policy of assimilation, is ambiguous and difficult to define. It is a conservative doctrine whose exponents rejected the notion of class struggle, the focus of their concern being the removal of colonial domination rather than social change. Moreover, with its assertion that Africans are innately different from other people, it is an essentially **racist** concept. However, one positive aspect of Negritude was its emphasis on African history and culture and its attack on cultural imperialism. Key figures in the Negritude movement include **Caribbean** writer Aimé Césaire, who popularized the concept through his journal *Tropique,* and former President of Senegal Léopold Senghor. Although Negritude contributed to uniting some Africans behind the anti-colonial movement, it never really spread beyond French-speaking Africa.

NEM

The New Economic Mechanism, a package of economic reforms introduced in January 1968 by the **communist** regime of Janos Kadar in Hungary, over a decade after the brutal suppression of the **Hungarian Uprising**. The NEM sought to decentralize economic decision-making, to introduce market structures and to stimulate private entrepreneurship. It was widely regarded as the most radical package of reforms introduced by a communist state in **Eastern Europe**. Hungary achieved a degree of prosperity seldom seen elsewhere in the region and its political creed was dubbed **goulash socialism**.

NEOCOLONIALISM

The indirect domination of the developing world by the economically advanced nations through **economic imperialism**. Colonial rule declined sharply between the end of the Second World War and the mid-1960s, and was replaced by neocolonialism, maintained by the economic power of the **First World** and **multinational corporations**.

NEO-NAZIS

Active supporters of movements similar to inter-war German National Socialism, who admire the **fascist** ideology of their forebears, particularly its **racist** and **anti-Semitic** elements. Fringe neo-Nazi groups are active in Germany, where support for Nazism is illegal, as well as in other European countries (including Russia) and the USA. Attacks on Jewish targets, **Gastarbeiter** and asylum seekers in Germany during the 1990s led to the imposition of harsher sentences on those convicted of such attacks, and the banning of several neo-Nazi organizations.

NEUTRON BOMB

A **nuclear weapon** developed by the USA, the proposed deployment of which by **NATO** forces in Europe in the late 1970s caused such a public outcry that the Carter administration backtracked. The purpose of the bomb was to reduce the destruction of property which might be caused if nuclear weapons were used in Europe (and particularly in West Germany) against a tank attack under the **flexible response** doctrine. Its peculiarity was that it caused relatively little blast damage, but released enough neutron and gamma-ray radiation to kill soldiers in tanks (or anyone else) for miles around.

NEW CLASS

The theory that any political party or **bureaucracy** with a monopoly of power will become a self-perpetuating oligarchy, peopled by corrupt officials whose primary interest is the accumulation of power. This theory was expounded from 1950 by the Yugoslav **communist** party official Milovan Djilas, particularly in his book *The New Class*. Djilas's controversial theory was a direct attack on the **CPSU** and widened the split between **Yugoslavia** and the **Soviet Union**. Djilas was expelled from the party in 1954 amid efforts to effect a Soviet-Yugoslav rapprochement.

NEW COMMONWEALTH

A term applied to former British colonies in Asia, Africa and the **Caribbean** which became members of the **Commonwealth** on independence in the years following the Second World War. It was used to distinguish these countries from the 'old Commonwealth' or **White Commonwealth** representing the 'white' dominions (Australia, Canada, New Zealand and South Africa), whose sovereignty was confirmed under the 1931 Statute of Westminster.

NEW COURSE

Policies within the **communist bloc** associated with the early period of **de-Stalinization**, especially Soviet Prime Minister Giorgi Malenkov's July 1953 call for a switch of resources from the military to the provision of consumer goods, and the Hungarian reform programme of 1953–5. The Hungarian New Course, drawn up by Prime Minister Imre Nagy who was later a key figure in the **Hungarian uprising**, resembled Malenkov's approach except that it envisaged the mobilization of the masses through a Patriotic **Popular Front**.

NEW ECONOMIC MECHANISM *see* NEM

NEW HEBRIDES *see* VANUATU

NEW JEWEL MOVEMENT

A **left-wing** party founded in Grenada in 1973 which in 1979 overthrew the repressive government of Sir Eric Gairy in an almost bloodless coup and established a People's Revolutionary Government under Prime Minister Maurice Bishop. The new government was noted for wide-ranging social and welfare reforms but its close ties with Cuba alienated the USA and more conservative **Caribbean** countries. The NJM itself was split, and a pro-Soviet faction, led by Deputy Prime Minister Bernard Coard, overthrew the more moderate Bishop on 13 October 1983, ordering his execution, along with that of three others, six days later. This provided sufficient excuse for the US military invasion on 25 October which was supported by six Caribbean countries. Coard and 13 others were subsequently charged with Bishop's murder and received death sentences in 1986. These were postponed on appeal and finally commuted to life imprisonment in August 1991.

NEW LEFT

A group of radical thinkers and activists in Europe and the USA which emerged in the 1950s, and was given impetus by disenchantment with the **Soviet Union** following the suppression of the 1956 **Hungarian uprising**. The New Left differed from the 'old left' by expanding traditional interpretations of Marxism. It moved away from rigid economic determinism, and instead emphasized hitherto marginalized aspects of Marxism such as cultural hegemony and the alienation implicit within the **capitalist** system. In Europe, the New Left was a key factor in the events of **1968**. In the USA, it was in the forefront of the campaign against the **Vietnam War**, distrusted conventional politics, and extolled participatory democracy as expressed in the **Port Huron Statement**. Many New Left activists turned eventually to traditional **left-wing** parties, or to the single-issue politics embodied in **feminism** or the **green** movement.

NEW ORDER

Gen. Suharto's military-backed regime in Indonesia, as distinct from his predecessor Sukarno's 'old order' dominated by the **communist PKI**. Under Suharto's New Order regime, which came to power following the destruction of Sukarno's leftist power-base in 1965–6, the Indonesian armed forces emerged as the country's dominant political institution. The military's often brutal suppression of political dissent has provided sufficient stability for the implementation of liberal economic strategies and pro-Western foreign policies.

NEW PEOPLE'S ARMY

The military wing of the **Communist** Party of the Philippines—Marxist-Leninist (CPP-ML), which split from the pro-Soviet Communist Party of the Philippines (PKP) in 1968. Since its inception the NPA has waged a **guerrilla** war against the Philippine government, often in loose alliance with Muslim insurrectionists of the **MNLF** in Mindanao and the southern islands. Having initially adopted an exclusively rural revolutionary strategy, the NPA began waging war in the cities in the 1980s with the formation of squads of urban guerrillas known as **Sparrow Units**. At the height of its influence, in the mid-1980s, the NPA was thought to number around 20,000 fighters and was widely regarded as the most dangerous communist insurgency movement in Asia. Since the return of civilian rule which accompanied the fall of the Marcos regime in 1986, however, the movement has suffered a significant decline in size and influence.

NEW RIGHT

The group of Western European and US theorists who, in the 1970s and 1980s, propounded a political agenda founded on laissez faire and **monetarist** economic policies and a reduced role for the state in both economic and social life. The New Right's emphasis on individualism sets it apart from traditional **conservative** paternalism (the 'old right'), but part of its political dynamism stems from its advocacy of moral conservatism and its criticism of the permissive society of the 1960s as the root of contemporary social ills. Unlike the **New Left** two decades earlier, the New Right attained political power with the election of Margaret Thatcher in the UK in 1979 and Ronald Reagan in the USA in 1980.

NEW WORLD INFORMATION AND COMMUNICATION ORDER *see* NWICO

NEW WORLD ORDER

The phrase used by US President George Bush in an address to **Congress** on 11 September 1990 to describe the new era of great power co-operation and effective international organizations which he saw emerging with the end of the **Cold War**. The phrase was repeated in Bush's State of the Union message of 29 January 1991. In the context of the US-led **Gulf War** against Iraq and the new atmosphere of co-operation with the **Soviet Union**, Bush appealed for support for the US stance by saying: 'What is at stake is more than one small country; it is a big idea; a new world order – where diverse nations are drawn together in common cause to achieve the universal aspirations of mankind'.

NEWLY INDUSTRIALIZED COUNTRIES *see* NICs

NGO

A non-governmental organization – a body (national or international) which is outside the framework of any national government. NGOs may frequently be involved in international relations not only through their own activities but also especially through full or observer status with specific international organizations (especially those concerned with developmental, social, humanitarian and cultural matters, such as **Amnesty International**, **Médecins sans frontières** and **Oxfam**.

NHS

The National Health Service, the UK's state health care system. The architect of the service was Aneurin Bevan, health minister in the Labour government of Clement Attlee, drawing from the **Beveridge Report** of 1942 on the **welfare state**. The 1946 National Health Service Act aimed to institute universally available, free or inexpensive health care, funded by national insurance payments and other taxation. The NHS was officially inaugurated on 5 July 1948.

In the 1980s the Conservative government of Margaret Thatcher imposed strict curbs on the escalating cost of health care. A series of Conservative reforms in the 1980s and 1990s, including the establishment of NHS trusts, was designed to improve the efficiency of the NHS but provoked criticism that the quality of aspects of NHS treatment had declined.

NICs

Newly Industrialized Countries, a category used increasingly in international organizations to group highly competitive economies such as South Korea and **Taiwan** which have clearly outgrown the label 'developing country'.

NIEO

The new international economic order, launched at the sixth special session of the **UN General Assembly** on raw materials and development in April–May 1974. The session, which was called in the wake of the 1973 world oil price explosion, issued a declaration on the establishment of an NIEO 'based on equity, sovereign equality, interdependence, common interest and co-operation among all states, irrespective of their economic and social systems', and setting out a 'programme of action on the establishment of an NIEO'. This programme involved arrangements for international trade under which commercial policies would be designed to encourage developing countries' exports of manufactures as well as of primary commodities. It also involved an increasing flow of capital to developing countries.

NIKKEI INDEX *see* DOW JONES INDEX

1922 COMMITTEE

A body consisting of all Conservative backbench MPs in the UK House of Commons. The name commemorates the decision in 1922, forced on the party leadership by Conservative backbenchers, to bring down Lloyd George's coalition government. Elections to the 1922 Committee's 12-member executive, held at the beginning of a parliamentary session, serve as a barometer for the mood of the party. Chaired in recent years by deceptively bluff Yorkshireman Sir Marcus Fox, the 1922 Committee prides itself on being able to keep its finger on the pulse of the party and as such plays a pivotal political role.

1968

A year of unrest throughout **Western Europe** and the USA, when young radicals in particular were inspired by the ideas of the **New Left** to challenge the old order but, ultimately, failed to overturn it. Student demonstrations in Western Europe demanded reform of the antiquated and overcrowded university systems; in the USA, they opposed the **Vietnam War**. All were marked by admiration for **communist** revolutions in the **Third World**. The failure of these movements to secure the changes they promised, however, was epitomized by the **Gaullist** government's deflection of workers' revolutionary demands during the May **évènements** in France. Later that same summer came the crushing of the **Prague Spring** by **Warsaw Pact** tanks in **Czechoslovakia**.

1984

A date with a unique resonance, evoking the nightmare **totalitarian** future. It was George Orwell, writing in 1948 at the onset of the Cold War, who gave the year 1984 this special significance by using it as the title of his most famous political novel. *1984,* first published in 1949, depicted a world dominated by three **superpowers** in a state of permanent conflict. Each superpower strongly resembled its rivals, being run strictly according to a state ideology which borrowed from the extreme right and left, and which aimed at the total subordination of the individual to the state. Social conformity was ensured by a comprehensive system of surveillance. The state was dominated by a party elite, supported by a **propaganda** machine that promoted a **cult of personality** surrounding the state's leader, **Big Brother**. A counterpart to this bleak vision was Aldous Huxley's ironically titled view of a future *Brave New World,* where social control was effected through the distribution of synthetic pleasure.

1989

The year of popular revolutions against the **communist** regimes in the countries of **Eastern Europe**. A crucial factor was the perception that, under Mikhail Gorbachev, the **Soviet Union** would no longer invoke the **Brezhnev doctrine** and intervene to halt deviations from the Soviet line. Beginning with the opening of the Hungarian-Austrian border in May, and accelerating after the formation of a **Solidarity**-led government in Poland in August, the revolutions culminated in November and December with the demolition of the **Berlin Wall**, the fall of Todor Zhivkov in Bulgaria, the election of **Charter 77** leader Vaclav Havel as President in **Czechoslovakia**, and the violent overthrow and execution of dictator Nicolae Ceausescu in Romania. The euphoria of the revolutions of 1989, however, soon gave way to the realization that economic and democratic reconstruction would be painful and protracted.

1992

The year in which the **EU** completed the preparation of the **single market**, as defined in the **Single European Act**. Publicity was generated in member states to alert businesses in particular to the challenges and opportunities that this created. The key date was 31 December 1992, and the publicity campaign in the UK fastened on 1992, whereas in France the slogans all referred to 1993, the year when the single market would come into being.

NIXON DOCTRINE

The defence and foreign policy doctrine formulated by Richard Nixon, US President in 1969–74; it was also known as the Guam Doctrine as it was first stated during a presidential visit to the island in 1969. Whilst upholding US treaty commitments – including the continued provision of a nuclear shield and of economic and military assistance to threatened allies – the doctrine required those allies to 'bear the manpower burden of their own defence'. The policy was a reaction to the deployment of a vast number of US troops in the **Vietnam War**, and sought to maintain the country's global military role whilst avoiding involvement in localized conflicts.

NKOMATI ACCORD

A mutual non-aggression pact between the governments of Mozambique and South Africa signed on 16 March 1984. Under its terms, all members of the South African liberation movement, the **ANC**, were expelled from Mozambique and the South African government undertook to halt all aid to the **MNR**, the Mozambican rebel group. However, it quickly became clear that South Africa was not abiding by the agreement; documents recovered from MNR headquarters in August 1985 proved that the rebels were still receiving substantial South African assistance.

NKOSI SIKELEL'I AFRIKA

(Xhosa / Zulu, 'God bless Africa') The traditional African hymn adopted by the **ANC** in South Africa as its anthem and frequently sung at anti-apartheid gatherings. It was agreed in March 1994 that in the spirit of national reconciliation it would be one of the country's two national anthems, at least until a new constitution is adopted. The other anthem is the Afrikaans *Die Stem* ('The Voice'), which had been the official national anthem under the **apartheid** regime, having been adopted by the then Union of South Africa in 1957 to replace *God Save the Queen.*

NMP

Net material product, a measure of the size of a (**communist**) centrally planned command economy, corresponding to **GNP** but not an identical measure. NMP is the total net value of goods and 'productive' services, including turnover taxes, produced by the economy. It excludes economic activities not contributing directly to material production, such as public administration, defence, and personal and professional services.

NO FIRST USE

The proposition that the **superpowers** should each pledge not to be the first to use **nuclear weapons**. Superficially straightforward, it was popular with peace campaigners in the 1980s. It was anathema, however, to **NATO** strategists, who regarded the nuclear components of **flexible response** as a necessary part of any European defence equation in the face of Soviet tank superiority. The **Soviet Union** accordingly made political capital out of the idea, calling repeatedly for the USA to sign a joint declaration on no first use. NATO in turn tried to deflect the argument by declaring at its July 1990 summit a commitment to no first use of any military force.

NO-FLY ZONE

A prohibited area for fixed-wing aircraft or helicopter flight. In August 1992 France, Russia, the UK and the USA proclaimed a 'no-fly zone' over southern Iraq (south of the 32nd parallel), aimed at protecting the **Shia** Marsh Arab population from Iraqi forces. In the first incident of its kind, a US aircraft in December 1992 shot down an Iraqi fighter plane within this zone. In October 1992 the **UN** imposed a no-fly zone in Bosnian airspace as part of efforts to contain the conflict there.

NOBEL PRIZES

Prestigious prizes, carrying large monetary rewards, awarded annually since 1901 to individuals or institutions pre-eminent in their field. The prizes are financed from a trust established by the Swedish scientist and engineer Alfred Nobel (the inventor of dynamite) who died in 1896. Originally there were five such prizes (physics, chemistry, physiology or medicine, and literature, awarded by the relevant Swedish academies, and peace, awarded by a committee elected by the Norwegian parliament). In 1969 a sixth annual prize was instituted, for economic sciences.

NOIRISME

(from French, literally 'blackism') A word coined to define a Haitian brand of black supremacy originating in the 1920s and 1930s as a reaction to US occupation and the oppression of the black majority by a mulatto (mixed race) ruling class. The emergence of *noirisme* coincided with the **Black Power** movement in the USA and black **nationalism** in Jamaica, but went further, claiming superiority over non-blacks. President François 'Papa Doc' Duvalier used *noirisme* to justify the persecution of mulatto opponents (although black opponents were also killed) by the **Tontons Macoutes** under the pretext of destroying the mulatto grip on power.

NOMENKLATURA

(Russian, 'list of names and offices') The system of appointments in the **Soviet Union**, co-ordinated by the security police (the **KGB** or its precursor the NKVD) and the Cadres Department of the **CPSU** Central Committee, which together assigned 'suitable' candidates to a range of state offices. The nomenklatura system ensured discipline and deference to the party. Those rewarded by the nomenklatura came to be regarded as an elite and were treated preferentially in the distribution of resources such as apartments, cars and holidays. In the early post-communist period, well-placed officials were sometimes able to re-invent themselves as business leaders and secure the choicest assets when state industries were being sold – a process described derisively as 'nomenklatura privatization'.

NON-ALIGNED MOVEMENT

The grouping of states declaring themselves not to be aligned with either **superpower** in the **Cold War**. The movement was inspired by the **Bandung conference** of 1955 and, in organizational terms, founded in 1961 by the leaders of 25 states meeting in Belgrade, **Yugoslavia**. Despite a substantial rise in membership, which stood at 108 in September 1992, the movement has suffered from a perceptible loss of influence resulting from the gradual waning in East-West tension. Since the early 1990s the movement has sought to respond to the changing international scene by redefining its role less in terms of its commitment to disarmament and **decolonization** than in terms of its concern with 'equitable international economic relations'.

NON-PERMANENT MEMBER *see* UN SECURITY COUNCIL

NON-PROLIFERATION *see* NPT

NOPEC

A journalists' term coined in the 1970s to describe oil producing countries outside **OPEC**, including the USA, the **Soviet Union** (and now several of its successor states), the UK and Norway, several Gulf states, Mexico and (since 1993) Ecuador. In early 1994 some NOPEC countries were reported to be involved in informal negotiations with OPEC, mediated by Oman, aimed at a joint strategy to reduce oil output and boost world oil prices which had fallen to around US$14 a barrel, their lowest level in five years.

NORAD

The North American Aerospace Defence Command, established jointly by the USA and Canada in August 1957 to integrate their defence against bomber and ballistic missile attack. NORAD's headquarters is at Colorado Springs.

NORAID

An organization in the USA whose role is to raise funds to support the republican cause in **Northern Ireland**.

NORDIC COUNCIL

A regional advisory body of parliamentarians from Denmark, Finland, Iceland, Norway and Sweden, established on 13 February 1953. The 87-seat council, whose members are elected by and from the national parliaments, meets annually. It aims to further the co-ordination of legislation and administrative practice between its member countries. Although its decisions are non-binding, they are generally implemented since they reflect the views of the national parliaments.

NORMALIZATION

The sinister name for the programme aimed at stabilizing **communist** rule in **Czechoslovakia** after the suppression of the 1968 **Prague Spring**. Normalization, under Communist Party leader Gustav Husak, featured a purge of tens of thousands of politically unreliable professionals and communist party members; an end to freedom of speech, and new curbs on press freedom; and a deliberate show of strength by the state, including a return to the rhetoric and style of the era of **Stalinism**.

NORTH

The countries with developed (industrialized) economies, as differentiated from the **South**, the developing countries. Geographically this term is a very broad generalization with numerous exceptions, but it has been used increasingly since the 1970s. It avoids the implication either of a necessary progression from developing to developed, or of a hierarchy from the **First World** down to the **Third World** or **Fourth World**. In the 1990s, since the abandonment of **communism** by the countries of **Eastern Europe** and the former **Soviet Union**, it has become plausible to abandon the always shaky assumption that these **Second World** countries belonged automatically to the North category; the less developed former Soviet republics, particularly those in **Central Asia**, would more usefully be categorized as part of the South.

NORTH AMERICAN FREE TRADE AGREEMENT *see* NAFTA

NORTH ATLANTIC COUNCIL *see* NAC

NORTH SEA OIL

The petroleum reserves found in the North Sea in the late 1960s and exploited from the early 1970s. The term is generally used to cover also natural gas deposits, whose discovery predates those of oil by some years. Oil and gas have been brought ashore by tanker or piped to land in the UK, Norway, the Netherlands and Germany. Development was given a sharp impetus by the temporary Arab oil sanctions of 1973 and the subsequent longer-term oil price increases instigated by **OPEC**, although North Sea oil prices are in line with those charged on the international markets both by OPEC and by other producers. In the main, countries with North Sea oil and gas have failed to use the revenue for major investment purposes.

NORTH-SOUTH

Relations between the developed **North** and the **South** or developing countries. The global debate on economic issues became increasingly polarized as a North-South debate in the 1970s, expressly so in the **CIEC** dialogue which began in 1975, and increasingly also in international organizations such as **UNCTAD**.

NORTHERN IRELAND

The north-eastern part of the island of Ireland forming a component of the **United Kingdom** of Great Britain and Northern Ireland. Under the Government of Ireland Act 1920 a legislature was set up for the **six counties** forming a part of the province of Ulster, while in 1922 the Irish Free State was established covering the other **26 counties** which now comprise the Republic of Ireland. About 58 per cent of the population of Northern Ireland are Protestant and largely **Unionist**, and have traditionally been the dominant community; the remaining 42 per cent are Catholic and include a major republican element spearheaded on the political front by **Sinn Féin** and in the military field by the **IRA**. Since the late 1960s there has been a state of civil unrest in Northern Ireland which has caused the loss of more than 3,000 lives. Not only has there been sectarian violence between members of the two communities, but also attacks particularly by the IRA and other republican organizations against the Royal Ulster Constabulary and the large British Army presence. Ireland's constitutional claim to the whole island has proved a stumbling block in discussions over the future of Northern Ireland, but the **Downing Street Declaration** of December 1993 by the British and Irish Prime Ministers was widely seen as a breakthrough in this respect.

NORTHERN RHODESIA *see* ZAMBIA

NOW

The National Organization for Women, the largest US campaigning feminist organization. NOW has some 150,000 members, both men and women, and fights for equal rights for women, particularly in employment. Founded in 1966, it came to prominence in the 1970s during the unsuccessful campaign to ratify the **ERA**, the Equal Rights Amendment to the US Constitution. NOW was more effective, however, in obtaining the passage of equal rights legislation on a state level.

NPFL

The National Patriotic Front of Liberia, one of the three main factions in the Liberian civil war. The war began in early 1990 when the NPFL launched its rebellion against President Samuel Doe, led by Charles Taylor, a former member of Doe's regime. Doe was killed in September 1990, but the country became embroiled in a more protracted civil war as the NPFL engaged in fierce fighting against Doe loyalists, known as Ulimo, and against **ECOMOG**, the regional peacekeeping force deployed to defend the interim government of Amos Sawyer. A peace agreement between the three factions was eventually agreed in July 1993. After a series of delays, a transitional government was installed in May 1994, in which the NPFL held seven portfolios.

NPT

The Non-Proliferation Treaty, an **arms control** agreement approved by the **UN** in June 1968, opened for signature in July, and effective from March 1970; its formal title is the Treaty on the Non-Proliferation of **Nuclear Weapons**. The NPT was concluded when five countries had nuclear weapons (China, France, the **Soviet Union**, the UK and the USA), and specified rules and procedures to prevent the spread of the technology to other countries, involving the **IAEA** in the inspection of nuclear power installations, and holding review conferences every five years. France and China refused to sign it, however (although both effectively observed its provisions). After the Soviet Union broke up in 1991, the four nuclear-weapons successor states were brought into the NPT (albeit with considerable difficulty and protracted negotiation until 1994 in the case of Ukraine), with all save Russia giving up nuclear weapons. The NPT's controls may have restricted proliferation, but have proven insufficient to prevent the spread of nuclear weapons entirely; some 16 countries were believed to have the technology by 1993. A major crisis erupted in that year over inspections in North Korea, which threatened to leave the NPT.

NRA

The National Rifle Association, one of the wealthiest and most powerful pressure groups in the USA. A consistent opponent of any moves toward tighter **gun control**, the NRA enjoys the support of numerous US politicians, including former Presidents Ronald Reagan and George Bush.

NSC

The National Security Council, a US executive body established in 1947 to advise the president on domestic, foreign and military matters relating to national security. The way in which the NSC functions varies according to individual presidents, although its evolution has been marked by a steady increase in size and influence. The **National Security Adviser**, a post currently held by Anthony Lake, is one of the most powerful non-Cabinet figures within the US government.

NUCLEAR ENERGY

The energy – also called atomic energy – which is released during the fission or fusion of atomic nuclei. When a neutron strikes the nucleus of an atom of a fissile substance, for example uranium-235 or plutonium, the nucleus splits, releasing energy and producing more neutrons, which in turn strike other atoms to produce a chain reaction. In a nuclear reactor, energy is produced in a controlled process; in **nuclear weapons** (or an accident such as that at **Chernobyl**) this release of energy is uncontrolled and destructive.

NUCLEAR ENERGY AGENCY *see* NEA

NUCLEAR-FREE ZONE

A zone or region where there are either no **nuclear weapons** (more precisely termed a nuclear weapons-free zone), or no nuclear installations of any kind. Declaration of nuclear weapons-free zones was one route pursued in **arms control**, in the **Antarctic Treaty**, the **Outer Space Treaty**, the **Seabed Treaty**, the **Tlatelolco Treaty** in **Latin America**, and the **Rarotonga Treaty**. With the growth in the 1970s and 1980s of opposition to **nuclear power**, some local communities began to want to identify themselves as nuclear-free in the wider sense, an idea adopted in the UK for instance by some local councils. Such declarations indicated a political stance, but lacked the legal force to prevent for example the transit of nuclear waste material.

NUCLEAR FUEL CYCLE

The stages through which nuclear fuel passes from the mining of uranium ore, through the production of fuel, both uranium and plutonium, to reprocessing and the disposal of nuclear wastes. Refined uranium from uranium ore must be enriched to increase the proportion of fissile uranium-235, and can then be used in nuclear reactors. Metal rods of enriched uranium are bombarded by neutrons in a nuclear reactor, producing **nuclear energy**. In addition, a small quantity of plutonium is produced which may be extracted from the spent uranium fuel by **nuclear reprocessing** and used in nuclear weapons. The difficulty of ensuring safe disposal of radioactive residues from nuclear reactors is one of the principal themes of the environmentalist movement.

NUCLEAR NON-PROLIFERATION *see* NPT

NUCLEAR REPROCESSING

The extraction of unused uranium and newly formed plutonium from spent uranium fuel rods in nuclear reactors. One third of the fuel rods in a reactor must be replaced annually. The spent fuel rods are transported to nuclear reprocessing sites where they are dissolved in nitric acid to produce uranium nitrate, plutonium nitrate, and other salts. The uranium and plutonium are then recovered, but in the process highly radioactive wastes are generated. Nuclear reprocessing is highly controversial because of the potential dangers, and the difficulty of disposing of the nuclear wastes safely. Plants such as **Thorp** at **Sellafield** are therefore opposed by environmentalists.

NUCLEAR TEST BAN TREATY

The first specific treaty on nuclear **arms control**, signed by the **Soviet Union**, the USA and the UK in Moscow on 5 August 1963 after five years of talks. A partial ban only, it prohibited atmospheric tests, underwater tests and testing in space, but allowed underground tests provided that they caused no radiation damage outside the testing state's territory. Most countries joined the treaty, but not the other two nuclear weapons states, France and China, although both stopped atmospheric testing eventually (in 1974 and 1980 respectively). A Threshold Nuclear Test Ban signed by the **superpowers** at the **SALT** talks in 1974 (but not ratified by the USA) limited testing to devices under 150 kilotons. Pressure for a comprehensive test ban treaty led to the reopening of talks in 1977, despite serious problems with verification. These talks stopped and started, and had still not produced any agreement as of 1994, although real discussion was under way and moratoriums had been declared by Russia in October 1991 and by France and the USA the following year. China continued testing underground; the UK opposed a formal moratorium, but, lacking test sites, has in practice conducted no tests since 1962 apart from joint tests with the USA in Nevada.

NUCLEAR UMBRELLA

Originally a Soviet proposal made at the **UN** in 1963, that both **superpowers** should retain a limited number of missiles armed with **nuclear weapons**, until the completion of a three-stage 'programme of general and complete disarmament'. At the UN Disarmament Conference in 1964, the **Soviet Union** insisted that this nuclear umbrella idea should be the sole basis for discussion. The USA wanted more open terms of reference, and the ensuing deadlock effectively blocked the discussion of any proposals on complete disarmament. The term nuclear umbrella was later used loosely to refer to an overt or implicit defence commitment by a nuclear power to a non-nuclear ally; for example, the USA was represented as providing a nuclear umbrella in **Western Europe**.

NUCLEAR WEAPONS

The generic term for the weapons technology whose unprecedented power has dominated global military-strategic calculations since 1945, when the USA dropped a single atomic bomb on **Hiroshima**, followed by a second on Nagasaki. The power of nuclear weapons comes from the energy within atoms. This power is released, together with radioactive contamination, either by fission (splitting the atom, as in the first atomic bombs), or by fusion, a more sophisticated technology using an initial fission reaction which creates sufficient heat to set off the fusion of atomic nuclei in a chain reaction. The **H-bomb** was a fusion device, first tested by the USA in 1952. Military strategy in the nuclear age has placed great emphasis on **deterrence**, since both superpowers had a nuclear capability from the 1950s which could make nuclear war unwinnable. Restricting the circle of countries with nuclear weapons was also a major concern, underlying the conclusion of the **Nuclear Test-Ban Treaty** and the **NPT**.

Nuclear weapons are not only more destructive, but also much smaller and lighter than conventional bombs, and the nuclear **arms race** was accompanied by the rapid development of missiles, including **ICBMs**, which were capable of delivering nuclear warheads on distant targets. Modern battlefield weapons, including artillery shells and mines, may also have nuclear devices; this has raised fears that their use, however localized, would mean crossing the nuclear threshold and setting off an escalation to all-out global war.

NUCLEAR WINTER

The predicted climatic effect of the immense amount of smoke and dust which would be created in a large-scale nuclear war. The hypothesis, first advanced in 1983, is that this would screen out sunlight for weeks, and cause temperatures to fall to levels at which plants and animals would be wiped out and human life would be unsustainable.

NUNAVUT

(Inuit, 'Our Land') A 770,000 square mile (2,000,000 sq km) region in the eastern portion of Canada's Northwest Territories which, under the terms of an agreement reached on 16 December 1991 and confirmed by referendum on 3–5 November 1992, became a semi-autonomous Inuit territory. Nunavut, which covers some 20 per cent of Canadian land and is home to 17,000 Inuit, constituted Canada's largest aboriginal land claim. Under the agreement, the Inuit were granted outright ownership of 135,000 square miles (350,000 sq km) of land, thereby becoming the world's largest private landowners.

NUREMBERG WAR CRIMES TRIBUNAL

The 1945–6 trial of the surviving leaders of Nazi Germany, conducted by a four-member tribunal drawn from the USA, the **Soviet Union**, the UK and France. The Nuremberg proceedings, the most prominent of the numerous war crimes trials which were held throughout Europe, included conventional war crimes charges, together with two new categories of offence. These were 'crimes against peace' (the planning and waging of wars of aggression), and 'crimes against humanity' (atrocities committed against civilians before or during the war), both of which had a dubious basis in international law. Also, by seeking to hold the Nazi leaders responsible for the course of events which had led to the war, the Nuremberg proceedings were marred by an appearance of seeking to vindicate Allied policy during the same period. Furthermore, by confining the accused to those of the defeated enemy, the trial did not acknowledge the existence of war crimes committed by the Allied powers.

In total 24 men were indicted for trial at Nuremberg, including Hermann Goering, the most senior surviving Nazi. One committed suicide; one was found unfit to plead; three were acquitted (including Hans Fritsche, a Propaganda Ministry official whose selection for trial appeared to have been an error); seven received prison sentences; and 12 were sentenced to death, including Goering and Martin Bormann, the only one of the 24 who was tried in absentia. Goering committed suicide within hours of his scheduled execution; the other 10 were hanged in the early hours of 16 October 1946.

NWICO

The New World Information and Communication Order. Introduced in 1980 after being adopted by the General Conference of **UNESCO** in 1978, the NWICO was an attempt to formulate a response to **Third World** concerns regarding US hegemony over the global news media. During the first part of the 1980s this was the battleground for an international confrontation which was largely manifested within UNESCO and which was one of the main factors in the eventual US and UK withdrawals from that organization. In the battle over the 'information order' the USA, with support from some of the Western European countries, maintained that its dominant role in integrating the mass media was a consequence of the natural workings of the international market for information.

NYASALAND *see* MALAWI

OAPEC

The Organization of Arab Petroleum Exporting Countries, established in 1968 to safeguard the interests of, and promote co-operation among, Arab oil-producing countries, most of which are also members of **OPEC**. Its member states – accounting for more than 25 per cent of world oil output – are Algeria, Bahrain, Egypt, Iraq, Kuwait, Libya, Qatar, Saudi Arabia, Syria and the **UAE**; Egypt's membership was suspended in 1979 but restored in 1989; Tunisia ceased to be a member in 1987. The Council's headquarters were temporarily relocated from Kuwait to Cairo in December 1990 following the Iraqi occupation of Kuwait, but were expected to return to Kuwait in mid-1994.

OAS

1. (French, abbreviation of *Organization de l'Armée Secrète* – 'Secret Army Organization') A group dominated by extremist European settlers in Algeria, hostile to de Gaulle's policy of negotiating Algerian independence from France. Led by renegade army officers, the OAS espoused **Algérie française**, fought the pro-independence **FLN** in Algeria itself, and waged a terrorist campaign both there and in metropolitan France. On 22 April 1961, four French generals – Challe, Jouhaud, Salan and Zeller – led a coup attempt against de Gaulle, but failed to win the backing of the bulk of the French army; some 200 rebel officers were arrested.

2. The Organization of American States, an inter-American regional organization founded in 1948 to foster peace, security, mutual understanding and co-operation. It is made up of 35 countries from northern, central and southern America and the **Caribbean**; Cuba's membership was suspended in 1962. In the **Cold War** period the OAS was viewed as a US proxy organization, notably during the 1962 **Cuban missile crisis**, in 1964 when it voted for sanctions against Cuba and in 1965 when it supported the US invasion of the Dominican Republic. However, in 1979 it disregarded US hostility to **left-wing Sandinistas** and demanded the removal of the Somoza dictatorship in Nicaragua, and in 1982 it tried to broker an end to the

Falklands War. In the late 1980s it supported the **Arias Plan** for peace in **Central America** and condemned the US invasion of Panama. It opposed the **autogolpe** in Peru in 1992 and since 1993 has played a major role with the **UN** in attempting to restore democracy in Haiti.

OAU

The Organization of African Unity, established in 1963 to promote continental unity and solidarity. With 53 members it is the most important and comprehensive of all African political organizations. Its other aims are to improve living conditions, to defend the sovereignty and territorial integrity of African states, to eradicate all forms of colonialism and to promote international co-operation. It has also sought to mediate in disputes between member states and in 1993 established structures for the prevention, management and resolution of continental crises. Policy is co-ordinated at the annual assembly of the heads of state of member countries.

OCCUPIED TERRITORIES *see* ISRAELI-OCCUPIED TERRITORIES

OCEANIA

The Pacific island regions of Polynesia, Micronesia and Melanesia. Oceania is sometimes considered also to include **Australasia**.

OCTOBER SURPRISE

A persistent but unsubstantiated allegation that the 1980 campaign team of Ronald Reagan and George Bush conspired with representatives of the government of Iran in order to reap electoral advantage by delaying the resolution of the **hostage crisis**. The Republican campaign was concerned that beleaguered presidential incumbent Jimmy Carter might boost his popularity shortly before the November election by securing the release of the 52 hostages being held in the US embassy in Tehran. Negotiations were alleged to have been conducted by Bush in order to prevent this so-called 'October surprise', and to promise in return that when the Reagan administration was in government it would supply arms to Iran. Despite circumstantial evidence – including the release of the hostages on the day of Reagan's inauguration, and the later uncovering of the **Iran-contra affair** – a Congressional inquiry failed to find any firm proof of such a deal.

ODA

Official development assistance, the classification of **foreign aid** which excludes certain forms of loans, **tied aid** and military assistance, and which is used to measure whether donor countries are meeting (as few do) the **UN** aid target of 0.7 per cent of **GNP**.

ODENDAAL REPORT

The report of the Commission of Inquiry into South-West Africa, chaired by F. H. Odendaal, which laid the foundations for the full implementation of **apartheid** in **Namibia**. Published in 1964, the report divided the country into 11 sections. One was reserved for the white population (which then constituted less than 7 per cent of the total population) and consisted of 60 per cent of the territory, including the commercial farming and mining areas. The remaining 40 per cent of the land, mainly large tracts of sandy desert or barren mountains, was allocated to 10 **bantustans**, the black population having been divided along apartheid lines into 10 groups. This division was made mainly on the basis of language, whereas the white population, with distinct Afrikaans-, German- and English-speaking communities, was regarded as a homogenous group.

ODER-NEISSE LINE

The border, marked by the rivers Oder and Neisse (Odra and Nysa in Polish), between postwar Germany and Poland. The border was settled at the conferences of **Yalta** and **Potsdam** in the summer of 1945. Germany lost its prewar eastern territories of Posnania and (northern) Silesia, whose considerable German-speaking population was transferred westwards over the Oder-Neisse line. The border was accepted by west Germany in 1970 under the **Ostpolitik**, and confirmed by the 1990 **two-plus-four talks**.

OECD

The Organization for Economic Co-operation and Development, formed in 1961 (on the basis of the **OEEC**) to co-ordinate policies in these areas among the industrialized market economies (initially 20 Western countries, plus Japan from 1964, Finland from 1969, Australia from 1971 and New Zealand from 1973; Mexico joined these 24 in 1994, and South Korea and Hungary are also on the threshold). The OECD council meets annually at ministerial level at its Paris headquarters, usually in June, with the secretariat ensuring policy implementation and continuity; by convention the secretary-general is always a European. Influential OECD studies assess the economic performance and policies of individual member countries, while there are global assessments, forecasts and recommendations twice a year in the *OECD Economic Outlook* and *OECD Employment Outlook*, other studies on specific issues and economic sectors, and an annual review of **foreign aid** by the most important of the OECD subsidiary committees, the **DAC**.

OECS

The Organization of Eastern Caribbean States, an associate institution of the **OAS** established in 1981 by seven small eastern **Caribbean** islands. Set up originally to give these countries a higher profile in the region, in 1983 the OAS supported **Operation Urgent Fury**, the US invasion of Grenada. Defence was then its principal preoccupation, but since the late 1980s political unity among member countries has been a central issue. Latterly it has also fought to preserve the volume of banana exports to the **EU** in the face of stiff competition from producers in **Central America**.

OEEC

The now defunct Organization for European Economic Co-operation, precursor of the OECD. Set up with 16 member countries in 1948, its function was to co-ordinate economic policies, initially on the postwar reconstruction which the USA was helping to finance through the **Marshall Plan**. The emphasis of its work changed in the 1950s to the co-ordination of economic expansion, and it became more appropriate for the USA and Canada to participate as full (rather than associate) members; the OEEC thus gave up its European regional identity and was transformed in 1961 into the OECD.

OFFICIAL DEVELOPMENT ASSISTANCE *see* ODA

OFFSHORE FUNDS

Financial resources not 'domiciled' in the main countries in which they are used. Although the development of so-called **Eurodollars** began during the 1960s, the gradual abolition of currency restrictions in that decade facilitated the establishment of key financial markets in new areas, such as some countries or territories in the **Caribbean**, which adopted favourable taxation and other treatment of such services. While offshore funds are generally used for legitimate commercial purposes, their very fluidity and ease of transfer can make them susceptible to diversion for money-laundering and for the concealment of the proceeds of drug trafficking.

OIC

The Jeddah-based Organization of the Islamic Conference. Formed in May 1971, the OIC engages in the promotion of Islamic solidarity and co-ordinates the policies of its 48 member countries. Originally envisaged as a Muslim commonwealth, its supreme policy making body is the Conference of Heads of State which meets every three years and is aided by a Secretariat, headed by a Secretary-General, which acts as its executive organ. The OIC's economic, political and cultural activities are conducted through a wide range of subsidiary and affiliated organizations, including the **Islamic Development Bank**, the Islamic Educational, Scientific and Cultural Organization (ISESCO) and the Islamic Solidarity Fund. It has also attempted to set the moral agenda, as in March 1989 when at the height of the Rushdie affair, its Conference of Foreign Ministers called on member states to boycott the controversial novel, **The Satanic Verses**.

OIREACHTAS

(Gaelic, 'assembly') The bicameral legislature of the Republic of Ireland, comprising the 166-seat lower house, the **Dáil Éireann**, and the 60-seat upper house or Senate, the *Seanad Éireann*.

OKINAWA

A island in southern Japan which, in 1945, was the scene of the most ferocious land battle in the Pacific War. After being administered by the USA until 1972, the island reverted to Japanese control, although more than one-fifth of its total area is taken up by US military bases. The crucial point in the 1969 reversion agreement, signed between President Richard Nixon and Eisaku Sato, was the latter's insistence that all US nuclear weapons be withdrawn from Okinawa in accordance with Japan's anti-nuclear principles which prohibit the possession, introduction or development of nuclear arms on its soil. The US government agreed, and it was publicly stated that such weapons would not be re-introduced under any circumstances. However, according to reputable but unsubstantiated claims in May 1994, the two sides signed a secret agreement which allowed US forces to re-introduce nuclear weapons to Okinawa at a time of crisis.

OLD COMMONWEALTH *see* WHITE COMMONWEALTH

OMAN

The **Gulf** Sultanate known as Muscat and Oman until 1970. Muscat and Oman gained independence from the UK in 1951.

OMARSKA

The site of an alleged concentration camp in **Bosnia-Hercegovina**, where it was claimed that inmates were systematically tortured, starved and murdered by their Bosnian Serb guards. Omarska was exposed by British television reporters in mid-1992, and television pictures of its emaciated inmates appeared to bear out the allegations of genocide and **ethnic cleansing** made by the majority-Muslim government of Bosnia-Hercegovina; a **UN** war crimes tribunal was established in May 1993 to verify these claims.

OMB

The Office of Management and Budget, created in 1970 by US President Richard Nixon from the Bureau of the Budget. The main function of the OMB is to prepare the federal budget for submission to **Congress**. It also attempts to reconcile budget disputes between government departments and agencies, all of which submit their appropriations requests to the OMB. The Director of the OMB (currently Alice Rivling) is one of the president's principal economic advisers, and the office is one of the few executive branch positions for which the appointee requires Senate approval.

OMBUDSMAN

A term of Swedish origin, indicating a commissioner appointed by a parliament, whose role it is to investigate and report on complaints against government and its officials. The post of ombudsman has been created in a number of countries.

OMON *see* BLACK BERETS

OMOV

One-member-one-vote, the controversial package of reforms of the UK Labour Party, passed at its conference in September 1993, which reduced the voting power of the trade unions in three key aspects of party affairs: the nomination of parliamentary candidates was to be made by a poll of constituency party members alone; the bloc vote at the party conference was reformed to give trade unions a reduced, fixed 70 per cent share of the vote; and elections to the party leadership were to be organized on the basis of an electoral college awarding only one-third of the votes to levy-paying union members. The adoption of OMOV was regarded as a victory for the party's then leader, John Smith, and for the party's 'modernizers'.

100 FLOWERS BLOOM

A political slogan coined by Mao Zedong. It has come to denote a brief period in the first half of 1957 when the **communist** government of China encouraged an unprecedented degree of free speech and public criticism. Mao first suggested in 1956 that the government should 'let 100 flowers bloom, and diverse schools of thought contend'. He launched the 100 Flowers movement in February 1957, and by April it had begun to take hold of the public imagination. The government was shocked by the scale of the strikes, demonstrations and public denunciations which followed. The dissent was increasingly stifled from June onwards, and in later years Mao suggested that the entire campaign had been no more than a means of identifying and destroying reactionary elements.

ONE-PARTY STATE

A country where only one political organization is permitted to function legally, or where one party remains in total control. The party maintains power by controlling the coercive apparatus of the state, and through a network of patronage, particularly concerning appointments. While claiming to represent the will of the people, such ruling parties are often slow to react to social change, although their monolithic structure usually conceals a mosaic of competing interest groups.

ONE OF US

The tacit description of Conservatives who belonged to the circle in favour with Margaret Thatcher while UK Prime Minister in 1979–90. While her first Cabinet formed in May 1979 was representative of a relatively wide spectrum of Conservative thought and ideology, most of those ministers who did not share her particular political outlook were gradually excluded from positions of influence as being 'not one of us' and therefore of suspect loyalty.

ONUC

The **UN** Operation in the Congo, originally created on 14 July 1960 by **UN Security Council** Resolution 143. It was at this point supposedly mandated to assist the government of the Congo in restoring order. The conditions of civil war made this an impossible mandate to interpret without controversy, which provoked serious division within the UN. The extension of the ONUC mandate in February 1961 empowered it to use force in the last resort because the Katanga secession was identified as a serious civil war situation and a threat to international peace and security. ONUC did use force to end the Katanga secession, and thereafter remained in place until 1964, its role in restoring order having been clarified in August 1961 by the formation of a recognizable central government.

OPEC

The Organization of Petroleum Exporting Countries. Established in September 1960 by Iran, Iraq, Kuwait, Saudi Arabia and Venezuela, it was subsequently enlarged to include Qatar (1961), Indonesia and Libya (1962), Abu Dhabi (1967, later transferred to the **UAE**, 1974), Algeria (1969), Nigeria (1971), Ecuador (1973), and Gabon (1975). It aims to co-ordinate and unify petroleum policies among member countries in order to ensure stable prices for petroleum producers, and succeeded in securing a dramatic price increase in 1973. Since 1982, however, its efforts to maintain price levels by setting production quotas have intensified the divisions among members with diverse economic and political interests. Ecuador, in January 1993, became the first OPEC member to leave the organization. The fall in oil prices – to well below OPEC's reference price of US$21 a barrel – has aggravated tensions, especially between Iran and Saudi Arabia, the organization's largest producers.

OPEN GOVERNMENT

The ideal of 'transparency' in the making and implementation of government policy. In the UK, this concept was brought to the fore particularly in 1993 with the issue of a document setting out a code of practice on access to information held by central government, to be independently policed by the **ombudsman** (although falling short of proposals for any US-type **freedom of information** legislation). The code also covered a new statutory right of access for subjects to see personal information held about them by government, access to health and safety information held by public authorities, and new provisions relating to the **30-year rule**.

OPEN SKIES

Mutual surveillance by unarmed military or civilian aircraft over the territories of the member states of **NATO** and the former **Warsaw Pact**. First put forward by US President Dwight Eisenhower in 1955 but rejected at that time by the **Soviet Union**, the Open Skies plan was adopted in February 1990 in Ottawa, Canada, by the 16 NATO and seven Warsaw Pact countries. A treaty was subsequently negotiated under the auspices of the **CSCE** and was formally endorsed by 51 member states of the CSCE in March 1992.

OPERATION BOOTSTRAP

A post-Second World War US programme to promote industrialization in Puerto Rico. Comparable with the **Alliance for Progress** and **Caribbean Basin Initiative**, it drew substantial foreign investment attracted by low labour costs, lack of trade barriers and generous tax incentives.

OPERATION CLEAN HANDS

The operation launched by Milan magistrates in February 1992 in response to accusations of corruption in the city's Socialist Party. The wave of scandals spread to engulf virtually every political party in Italy as the extent of corruption, mostly involving bribes from business to influential local politicians and their parties, was revealed. By the end of 1993, Operation Clean Hands (*mani pulite*) had led to the arrest of over 1,500 members of the business community, civil servants and local politicians, with 3,000 more under investigation. Those under suspicion included 250 parliamentary deputies and four former heads of government; 10 people had committed suicide. The investigations stemming from Operation Clean Hands also uncovered suspected collusion between the **Mafia** and the Christian Democratic Party.

OPERATION IRMA

A media term for the airlift of some 40 people seriously injured in the war in **Bosnia-Hercegovina** to hospitals in the UK, Sweden and Italy in August 1993. The operation was named after Irma Hadzimuratovic, a wounded five-year-old girl whose plight was given extensive coverage by the Western media, and who was flown out of Sarajevo on the personal initiative of UK Prime Minister John Major. Bosnian doctors pointed out that the high cost of the airlift would have been more effectively spent on improving medical facilities within Bosnia.

OPERATION JUST CAUSE

The code name for the US military invasion of Panama between 20 December 1989 and 13 February 1990. It was the largest US airlift since the **Vietnam War** involving 26,000 troops, including 3,000 parachutists, and saw the first operational use of the **stealth bomber**. The stated objectives of the operation were to restore democracy, protect US residents, combat drug trafficking and safeguard 1977 treaties covering the operation of the **Panama Canal**. US policy focused on the arrest of dictator Gen. Manuel Noriega Morena and his extradition to the USA on drug trafficking charges. Noriega gained asylum in the papal nunciature until a negotiated settlement resulted in his surrender and transfer to Miami, Florida, in early January. The invasion was widely condemned in **Latin America**, notably by the **OAS**, and several governments called for fresh elections after the USA installed Guillermo Endara as President. Later its justification was further questioned when it became clear that Noriega had previously co-operated with the **CIA** and that drug-trafficking and money-laundering continued unabated. Equally, the Endara government, whose free-market economic policies were deeply unpopular, was accused of corruption.

According to official US figures, 23 US troops were killed and 324 wounded and, on the Panamanian side, 202 civilians and 300 (later revised to 51) members of Noriega's Panama Defence Forces (FDP) were killed. Non-government US sources estimated civilian deaths at over 300 while

Panamanian sources put them as high as 7,000. Thousands were left homeless.

OPERATION MAGIC CARPET

The airlift of some 50,000 Jews from **Yemen** to **Israel** in the late 1940s and early 1950s.

OPERATION MOSES

The secret airlift of Ethiopian Jews, or **Falashas**, to **Israel** from refugee camps in Sudan. Between September 1984 and March 1985 some 7,000 Ethiopian Jews who had fled to Sudan to avoid the Ethiopian famine were evacuated in this operation, which was sponsored jointly by the Israeli government and the non-governmental **Jewish Agency**. It later emerged that the **CIA** had been involved in the operation. Although apparently undertaken with the tacit agreement of the Ethiopian and Sudanese governments, the airlift caused a major controversy in both countries, neither of which had diplomatic relations with Israel.

OPERATION PEACE FOR GALILEE

The codename for **Israel's** full-scale invasion of Lebanon in June 1982, launched with the aim of eradicating the **PLO** from Lebanon. After heavy Israeli bombardment of Beirut, in August PLO forces withdrew to other Arab countries under the supervision of US and other Western troops. Despite the PLO withdrawal, the Israeli operation was not regarded as a success. The **Sabra and Chatila** massacre caused international outrage; Israel's chief ally, **Phalangist** leader Bashir Gemayel, was assassinated; and, by the time of Israel's final withdrawal to its newly established **security zone** in the south in mid-1985, PLO fighters had returned.

OPERATION PROVIDE ASSISTANCE

The codename for the US relief operation launched on 23 July 1994 to deliver humanitarian relief to Rwandan refugees in Zaïre. The US$175 million operation, which included food drops and the despatch of food and medical supplies, was prompted by an outbreak of cholera in the massive camps which had sprung up virtually overnight, filled with mainly **Hutu** refugees who fled Rwanda as the rebel **RPF** took control of the country.

OPERATION PROVIDE COMFORT

The code-name for an emergency relief programme announced by Western allied forces on 16 April 1991, for the besieged Kurdish population of northern Iraq. Also known as Operation Provide Relief, it followed the creation by the **EC** and the USA of Kurdish 'safe havens' north of the 36th parallel, aimed at protecting rebel-held Kurdish areas which became the target of a major Iraqi military offensive in the aftermath of the **Gulf War**. The operation continues despite the formation in July 1992 of a partially autonomous Kurdish government in northern Iraq.

OPERATION RESCUE

The most prominent of the many US anti-abortionist groups, and a key component of the **Right to Life** lobby. The group has been responsible for a nationwide campaign against abortion clinics which has been characterized by mass picketing, the harassment of those seeking abortions and acts of violence against medical staff. The campaign led to the enactment of the Freedom of Access bill in May 1994 which made it a federal offence to block access to clinics, damage their property, or injure or intimidate patients or staff. In the same month a state court in Texas ordered Operation Rescue (together with another anti-abortionist group, Rescue America-National) to pay more than $1,000,000 in punitive damages to a clinic which had been blockaded during the 1992 Republican National Convention in Houston, in the largest award ever made against the anti-abortion lobby.

OPERATION RESTORE HOPE

The codename given to the December 1992 deployment of a US-led 35,000-strong multinational force in **Somalia**. Initiated by the USA with the support of the **UN**, this operation was to ensure the safe delivery of international aid to Somalis who were starving as a result of the year-long civil war, and to assist an existing UN operation (**UNOSOM**). The first members arrived in Mogadishu on 9 December 1992 and the operation formally ended on 4 May 1993, when responsibility for relief efforts was assumed by an expanded UNOSOM force.

OPERATION ROLLING THUNDER

A programme of sustained US bombing of North Vietnam launched by the administration of President Lyndon Johnson in March 1965. The campaign continued, with occasional breaks, until late 1968. Although it was soon apparent that Rolling Thunder had failed in its objective of subduing the Hanoi government and forcing it into accepting a negotiated settlement, Johnson would not halt the bombing because to have done so would have been seen as a sign of weakness.

OPERATION SHEEPSKIN

The invasion of Anguilla in March 1969 by 300 British troops and 50 police to restore British rule. The **Caribbean** island had long resented rule by St Kitts-Nevis and in May 1967 seized control by forcibly expelling the Kittitian police. A declaration of independence in February 1969 provoked the British intervention, and British police remained until 1972. The UK administered the island directly from 1971 until it formally assumed the status of a British Dependent Territory, separate from St Kitts-Nevis, in 1980.

OPERATION TURQUOISE

The codename for the French military operation in **Rwanda** launched on 23 June 1994 in the wake of the terrible violence which followed the death of President Juvénal Habyarimana. The humanitarian mission, sanctioned by the **UN Security Council**, was to protect civilians. The rebel **RPF** opposed the operation, arguing that previous French support for the Habyarimana regime demonstrated that the mission could not be conducted without bias. The operation also received lukewarm support from the international community. Under the **UN** mandate the operation was authorized until 21 August. Almost from the outset, the French government made it clear that it would like to see the bulk of its 2,500 troops out of Rwanda by the end of July, when it was hoped that an expanded UN force (**UNAMIR**) would take over. However, as July came to an end it seemed unlikely that the UN force would be in a position to relieve the French in the very near future.

OPERATION URGENT FURY

The codename for the military invasion of the **Caribbean** island of Grenada in October 1983. Some 7,000 US Marines, backed by 400 **OECS** Caribbean troops, took part in the three-day operation which was preceded by a secret commando operation. The latter was marred by bad planning and faulty intelligence and resulted in the deaths of several US troops, 45 Grenadians and 24 Cuban construction workers. The pretext for the US invasion was the rescue of US medical students embroiled in political chaos following the murder of popular **left-wing New Jewel Movement** Prime Minister Maurice Bishop by hardline **Stalinists**. The invasion was widely questioned internationally, but initially received local support which dissipated as US development aid dwindled.

OPM

(Indonesian acronym for *Organizasi Papua Merdaka*, 'Papua Independent Organization') A small secessionist **guerrilla** movement which has unsuccessfully fought for independence for the Indonesian province of **Irian Jaya**.

OPTING OUT

The term used loosely in the UK from the late 1980s in relation variously to schools, **NHS** units, the **Social Chapter** of the **Maastricht** Treaty and the treaty's provisions on **EMU**. For schools, opting out implies the achievement of grant-maintained status outside the control of local education authorities, under the terms of the Education Reform Act 1988 (**GERBIL**). For hospitals, other health care units and general medical practices, the expression is less accurately used to indicate the acquisition of the status of **NHS** trusts and fundholding practices, with their own financial accountability but still as integral components of the NHS itself. As regards the 1991 Maastricht agreement, the UK 'opted out' of the application of the provisions of the Social Chapter and of EMU.

OPUS DEI

(Latin, 'the work of God') A unique and relatively recent organization within the Catholic Church, founded by the Aragonese priest José Maria Escriva de Balaguer who died in 1975 (and was subsequently beatified). Opus Dei is associated with the political right in Spain and was particularly influential at the end of the Franco period. Pope John Paul II gave the organization the status of a personal prelature, outside the ordinary church hierarchy. Although it is not a religious order as such, and its members hold ordinary jobs, full members do live in Opus Dei residences and make a commitment to celibacy.

ORANGE ORDER

A Protestant organization in **Northern Ireland**. Its members (**loyalists** and **Unionists**) support the retention of Northern Ireland within the **United Kingdom**. Its name derives from King William III, Prince of Orange, who defeated the Catholic James II in 1689–90. Many of the order's annual demonstrations, during the **marching season**, commemorate battles and other events of that period.

ORGANIZATION OF AFRICAN UNITY *see* OAU

ORGANIZATION OF AMERICAN STATES *see* OAS

ORGANIZATION OF ARAB PETROLEUM EXPORTING COUNTRIES *see* OAPEC

ORGANIZATION OF EASTERN CARIBBEAN STATES *see* OECS

ORGANIZATION FOR ECONOMIC CO-OPERATION AND DEVELOPMENT *see* OECD

ORGANIZATION FOR EUROPEAN ECONOMIC CO-OPERATION *see* OEEC

ORGANIZATION OF PETROLEUM EXPORTING COUNTRIES *see* OPEC

ORIENTAL DESPOTISM

A concept expounded by Karl A. Wittfogel in his 1957 study *Oriental Despotism: A Comparative Study of Total Power*, which argued that the rulers of modern **communist** states, especially China, were a throwback to historical counterparts who had maintained their power by a form of oriental tyranny. This notion was later extended to explain the development of **fascism** in Japan, and to account for the fragility of some Asian democracies in the postwar period. Wittfogel's thesis has since been regarded by its critics as an expression of **orientalism**.

ORIENTALISM

A term made famous by the Palestinian-born US academic Edward Said in his 1977 book *Orientalism*. Said sought to reveal the assumptions underlying nineteenth and twentieth century Western attitudes to the 'Orient', defined mainly as the Near East, Islam and the Arabs. Foremost among these assumptions, developed in learned treatises and in travelogues alike, was a view of the Orient as essentially irrational and exotic. This fuelled a complex array of 'orientalist' ideas (**oriental despotism**, oriental splendour, cruelty and sensuality), which, Said argued, provided the rationale for European **racism**, and subsequently, the force for European colonial expansion.

OSS

The Office for Strategic Services, the US intelligence organization which was the predecessor of the **CIA**. Established in June 1942 during the Second World War, the OSS combined intelligence-gathering and analysis with **covert operations** including sabotage, the rescue of Allied servicemen from behind enemy lines and the co-ordination of native resistance movements in occupied countries.

OSSIES

Slang for the former East Germans, so dubbed after the unification of Germany in 1990 by the West Germans who, in turn, were nicknamed Wessies. The terms persisted as the differences between the citizens of former East and West Germany were revealed and, to an extent, developed into mutual resentment fuelled particularly by economic disparity.

OSTPOLITIK

(German, 'Eastern policy') The approach of West Germany (the **BRD**) in the late 1960s towards improving relations with **Eastern Europe** and particularly with East Germany (the **DDR**). It was associated especially with Willy Brandt, who was Foreign Minister from 1966 and became Chancellor in 1969 in a coalition government led by his Social Democrats. *Ostpolitik* involved a gradual policy of **detente**, abandoning the **Hallstein Doctrine** and concluding a series of treaties, the most important of which were the August 1970 treaty with the **Soviet Union** renouncing the use of force, and the treaty with Poland of November 1970 recognizing existing state borders. These treaties led to the September 1971 **Four-Power Agreement** on West Berlin and the 1972 Basic Agreement between the BRD and the DDR, which set out the notion of 'two states, one nation' to describe the relations between East and West Germany. Brandt was awarded the Nobel Peace Prize in 1971 for his work on *Ostpolitik*.

OUKO MURDER

The killing of the Kenyan Foreign Minister in 1990, apparently in an attempt to silence critics of corruption within the government. Robert Ouko was taken from his home on 13 February; his partially burnt body was found three days later nearly 4 miles (6 km) away. At the request of President Daniel arap Moi, John Troon, a UK Scotland Yard detective, investigated the murder. In evidence to a judicial inquiry in November 1991 Troon named Kiprono Nicholas K. Biwott, a Cabinet minister and close political ally of Moi, as a 'prime suspect' in the murder. Biwott was dismissed from the Cabinet and subsequently arrested along with Hezekiah Oyungi, hitherto a Permanent Secretary at the presidency and chief of state security. However, they were both released within two weeks because of an apparent lack of evidence.

OUTER SPACE TREATY

Essentially an **arms control** agreement, reached at the **UN** in late 1966, which entered into force with 84 signatory countries in October 1967. The treaty defined acceptable space exploration activity and forbade the claiming of sovereignty in space. It extended the concept of **nuclear-free zones** by prohibiting the placing in orbit (or on the moon or other celestial bodies) of **nuclear weapons** and other weapons of mass destruction. It banned military bases on the moon or planets, but did not explicitly cover the deployment in space of **ABM** systems, a factor which became relevant in connection with the US **Star Wars** programme in the 1980s.

OUTING

The public declaration by militant homosexual campaigners that a prominent person is gay (homosexual). The outing movement began in the late 1980s, especially in the USA. Its premise was that homosexuals who concealed their sexuality were adding to the prevailing climate of shame and prejudice, which had been aggravated as a result of **AIDS**. The term derives from the expression 'to come out (of the closet)', describing the voluntary acknowledgement by an individual that s/he is homosexual.

OVAL OFFICE

The US president's office within the **White House** and a key site of executive meetings and historic decisions. The term has become synonymous.with the locus of presidential power.

OVERKILL

A military capability beyond that which would be sufficient to destroy an adversary totally. **Superpower** stocks of **nuclear weapons** were built up in the **arms race** to the point that they had a massive overkill capability. The term has since been borrowed from the chilling vocabulary of military planning, and debased by its use for any mismatch between power and purpose.

OXFAM

A UK-based charity which funds both disaster relief and long-term aid in the fields of health (particularly clean water), agriculture and training in some 70 underdeveloped countries. Oxfam, based in Oxford, was founded in 1942 to help women and children in Nazi-occupied Greece; it now has some 40 overseas field offices. It is funded by donations and by trade with overseas producers and disadvantaged groups in the UK.

OZONE LAYER

A stratum of the atmosphere, 10–20 miles (15–30 km) above the earth, which is rich in ozone, a form of oxygen which protects the earth from the most harmful effects of ultraviolet radiation from the sun. The reduction in the concentration of ozone in the ozone layer resulting from environmental pollution, particularly **CFCs,** has become one of the principal concerns of the environmental movement since a 'hole in the ozone layer' over Antarctica was first discovered in the early 1980s. The consequences of the thinning of the ozone layer include increasing occurrence of skin cancers, and damage to plants and crops. The depletion of ozone is most serious over Antarctica, but the concentration of ozone in the northern hemisphere has been estimated to have declined by 14 per cent since 1969. The **Montreal Protocol** attempted to limit the use of CFCs in an attempt to reduce damage to the ozone layer.

P-2

The clandestine Italian Masonic lodge *Propaganda Due,* whose members included some of the most prominent figures in the armed forces, business and politics, and whose head, Licio Gelli, appears to have attempted to use the lodge to construct an anti-**communist** network at the summit of the state. The existence of P-2 was revealed in May 1981, and revelations of its alleged membership created a scandal which brought down the government. In March 1986, the Chamber of Deputies accepted the report of a parliamentary commission which had concluded in 1984 that the list of alleged members of P-2 was largely genuine. A total of 22 members of P-2 were charged with political conspiracy and activities against the state, and Gelli, who had been charged in absentia, was eventually extradited to Italy from Switzerland in 1988. He was tried and convicted on charges relating to the **Bologna bombing** and also for fraudulent bankruptcy linked to the **Banco Ambrosiano** scandal.

PAC

1. The Pan-Africanist Congress, a South African liberation organization which operated in exile and underground until 1990 in the struggle against the **apartheid** regime, but which has latterly transformed itself into a political party. The PAC was founded in 1959 by former members of the **ANC** under the influence of **pan-Africanism**. It was banned in 1960 following the **Sharpeville** massacre. In contrast to the ANC (which it failed to challenge as the main liberation movement), the PAC has from the outset rejected multiracial co-operation on the grounds that it safeguards 'white interests'. It refused to participate in the multiparty constitutional talks which preceded the 1994 democratic non-racial elections. However, it did contest the elections. Claiming to be the authentic voice of the black population, it called for the radical redistribution of wealth (including the land) from the 'settlers' (i.e. the white population) to the black majority. It won five seats in the National Assembly. The armed wing of the PAC, the Azanian People's Liberation Army (APLA), carried out a number of armed attacks on the white community in 1993.

2. The political action committee, a phenomenon of the US political system. PACs are established by pressure groups in order to raise campaign funds for candidates who support their particular cause. PACs provide an important source of funding, but have also been widely criticized for exerting an unhealthy influence on the political process.

PACIFIC RIM

The region bordering the Pacific Ocean, including the West Coast of the Americas, and the countries of East Asia and **Australasia**, which have experienced massive economic growth since the Second World War. The main dynamism for growth came from the countries of East Asia, whose production in 1990 equalled that of North America, having been one-quarter that of North America in 1960. These changing economic realities have forced a shift in global geopolitical attention from Europe to the Pacific region.

PAIRING

The convention in the UK Parliament whereby pairs of MPs, one each from the government and opposition sides, agree that if one is unable to be present to vote the other will abstain. This convention is generally arranged by the relevant whips, and in particular it enables ministers to be absent on government business without risking the reduction of the government's majority. The arrangement may on occasion be suspended by the opposition as a means of bringing pressure to bear upon the government. The system also operates in the US **Congress**, where pairs are listed in the Congressional Record after the names of the members not voting.

PAKISTAN

The country created as an explicitly Muslim homeland which gained independence in 1947 with the **partition** of the **Indian subcontinent**. A geographical anomaly at inception, its two parts, East Pakistan and West Pakistan, were separated by over 900 miles (1,500 km) of Indian territory. East Pakistan seceded in 1971 (as **Bangladesh**).

PALAU *see* BELAU

PALESTINE

An historic region of the **Middle East**, comprising parts of the states of **Israel** and **Jordan**. During the twentieth century the region has been the object of conflicting claims between Jewish and Arab nationalist movements. In 1988 the **PLO** proclaimed the establishment of an independent Palestinian state. While this existed in name only (since the territory of Palestine – the **West Bank** and **Gaza Strip** – remained under Israeli occupation), up to 100 nations recognized the new state. More significantly, the PLO at the same time recognized Israel's right to exist. The PLO's acceptance of a 'two-state solution' eventually resulted in its signing of the **Gaza-Jericho First** peace accord with Israel in 1993.

PALESTINE LIBERATION ORGANIZATION *see* PLO

PALESTINE NATIONAL COUNCIL *see* PNC

PALESTINIAN ECONOMIC COUNCIL FOR DEVELOPMENT AND RECONSTRUCTION *see* PECDAR

PALME COMMISSION

The Independent Commission on Disarmament and Security Issues, headed by the Swedish statesman Olof Palme. The Commission sought to stimulate a broader perception of the concept of global security in an era when **arms control** talks were dominated by the opposing **superpowers**. It produced the *Common Security* report in April 1982 and continued work thereafter although Palme had been returned to office as Swedish Prime Minister. Palme was assassinated in February 1986.

PAN-AFRICANISM

The political philosophy which calls for the merger of existing African states into a single state, based on the belief that the multiplicity of African societies share sufficient common characteristics to justify such a union. However, there is no consensus as to how the goal is to be achieved: some proponents argue for the immediate establishment of a single state (a tendency associated with the first President of Ghana, Kwame Nkrumah); some advocate a two-phase process beginning with the unification of regions; and others envisage nothing more than a confederation of sovereign states. Pan-Africanism was most influential in the colonial period, and by the mid-1960s regional and ethnic interests within the newly independent states as well as conflict between states effectively dashed any hopes for the success of Pan-Africanism.

PANAMA CANAL

The waterway connecting the Atlantic and Pacific oceans since 1914. A 1903 treaty, giving the USA the right to build the canal and to hold it in 'perpetuity' in return for a modest annual fee, remained fundamentally unchanged until the 1978, when the USA and Panama concluded a new Panama Canal Treaty and a Treaty of Neutrality. Effective from 1 October 1979, the new Canal Treaty recognized Panamanian sovereignty over the Canal Zone and specified that US troops stationed there (the headquarters of the US Southern Command) should be withdrawn by the year 2000. Panama was to receive a greater share in shipping toll revenues, a fixed annuity, and an additional annual fee for services to the newly formed Panama Canal Commission. This commission, composed of US and Panamanian directors, would run the canal. Panama subsequently claimed that the USA had failed to honour all its financial commitments under the treaties. A **right-wing** US congressional lobby campaigned, meanwhile, for the renegotiation or annulment of the 1978 treaties.

PANCASILA

(Indonesian, 'five principles') The Indonesian secularist state ideology, first put forward by Gen. Sukarno in 1945 as the philosophical foundation of the Indonesian revolution. The five principles of *pancasila* are: (i) belief in the one supreme god; (ii) just and civilized humanity; (iii) the unity of Indonesia; (iv) democracy led by the wisdom of deliberations (*musyawarah*) among representatives; and (v) social justice for all the people of Indonesia. Legislation passed by the Indonesian government in the mid-1980s required all mass social and political organizations to redraft their constitutions so as to accept *pancasila* as their 'sole ideological foundation'. Although largely accepted, the move met with some opposition, notably from the 'Petition of 50' opposition grouping which had been formed in 1980 and comprised generals, academics and former politicians dissatisfied with President Suharto's **New Order** regime.

PANCHAYAT

(Hindi, 'council' or 'assembly') A feature of traditional Hindu systems of government. It was generally composed of local elders drawn from a particular village or caste who were entrusted with the resolution of disputes. A modern variation of the system was attempted by King Mahendra of Nepal under the country's 1962 Constitution which sought to fashion a multi-tiered non-party state, presided over by the monarch, where class organizations and *panchayats* reaching all the way from village to national level acted as forums of political consultation.

PAN-SLAVISM

The idea that all or some **Slavonic** peoples share aspects of the same national identity. Pan-Slavists have emphasized linguistic and cultural similarities between nominally different Slavic peoples and point to historic common interests. Croatian pan-Slavist intellectuals lobbying for the unification of 'South Slavs' were the inspiration for the creation of **Yugoslavia** in 1918. Pan-Slavism has foundered on the problem that culturally similar Slav groups, as for instance Serbs and Croats, have been capable of mutual antagonism.

PAPER TIGER

Something which appears to offer a threat, but which in reality poses no danger. The term originated in nineteenth century China and entered the Western vocabulary as a result of its use by Mao Zedong.

PAPUA INDEPENDENT ORGANIZATION *see* OPM

PARIAH STATE

A regime widely reviled and shunned by a majority of other states because of the extreme nature of its policies and actions. The term reflects Western standards and aspirations and therefore some regimes labelled as pariah states enjoy full and close relations with many countries. Iran, for example, while frequently referred to as a pariah state, has managed to develop good links with generally pro-Western Islamic nations including Indonesia and Malaysia.

Col. Moamer al Kadhafi's Libya and Saddam Hussein's Iraq are classic current examples of the pariah state. Kadhafi's alleged involvement in the 1988 **Lockerbie** disaster and Saddam's 1990 invasion of Kuwait led to the imposition of **UN** sanctions aimed at forcing a reversal of policy (in the case of Libya) or a change of leadership (in the case of Iraq). Other regimes currently on the threshold of pariah statehood include Serbia and North Korea, while South Africa, having abandoned **apartheid**, has rid itself of the appellation.

PARIS CLUB

The informal grouping of industrialized countries which deals with debts owed to its member countries by developing countries and by severely indebted middle-income countries. In the 1990s much of its attention has been focused on the deferment of repayment of the huge debts of the former **Soviet Union**. The Paris Club was first created by the main west European countries in the context of dealing with Argentina's debt problems in 1957, building on arrangements initiated earlier in the decade. It grew to become the principal international forum for considering arrangements for renegotiation, consolidation and **debt rescheduling**. It deals with debts arising from loans made or guaranteed by official bilateral creditors, as distinct from purely commercial bilateral debts which are covered by the **London Club**.

PARIS CONVENTION ON THE PROTECTION OF INDUSTRIAL PROPERTY *see* WIPO

PARTIAL TEST BAN TREATY *see* NUCLEAR TEST BAN TREATY

PARTITION

The division of a country into separate parts. In modern politics the term is sometimes used of Ireland, but more often identified with the partition of India. This desperate expedient was adopted by the departing British imperial power in 1947 after the failure of efforts to reconcile Muslim leaders to a 'one India' solution. The creation of a separate Muslim state of **Pakistan** proved notably unsuccessful in preventing large-scale and widespread **communal violence**.

PARTNERSHIPS FOR PEACE

A programme drawn up on the initiative of US President Bill Clinton, and launched formally at the **NATO** summit in January 1994. As NATO's 'partners for peace', the former member countries of the **Warsaw Pact** and the successor states of the former **Soviet Union** could be involved in military co-operation beyond the scope of the **NACC** forum, but short of full membership of NATO. By May 1994, 18 countries had signed up for the programme; Russia eventually decided to do so in June, having held out unsuccessfully for several months for special status and for some form of veto over NATO action within areas of potential Russian interest.

PASDARAN

(Persian acronym for *Pasdaran-e-Inqilab* – 'revolutionary guards') The popular militia established by the late Iranian leader, Ayatollah Ruhollah Khomeini, in May 1979. Designed as a force under the direct command of clerics, it played a key role in consolidating the **Islamic revolution** by disciplining the armed retainers of revolutionary committees and acting as a counterweight to the regular army. However, its emergence as an independent power that assumed the right to make arrests, run prisons and monitor the work of government officials became, in time, a focal point of issue between the government and radical clerics.

PASS LAWS

Regulations in South Africa which restricted the free movement of the majority African population, and which were a key feature of the **apartheid** regime. The pass laws stipulated that Africans could only work outside the **bantustans** as contract workers; workers who left the bantustans without first registering as contract workers were only permitted to remain in another area for periods of 72 hours at a time. Workers resident outside the bantustans (and their spouses and children) were only permitted to remain if born where they were resident or if they had worked there continuously for 10 years for the same employer. The controls were enforced by the compulsory carrying of 'passes', documents listing their status in the area which had to be shown to the police or local government officials on demand. The first passes were carried by slaves in the Cape colony as early as 1760, and most African men had long been forced to carry passes; all African women had to carry passes from 1 February 1963. Between 1916 and 1984, an estimated 17 million were prosecuted, imprisoned or evicted under various pass laws, with arrests and prosecutions peaking in the period 1975–6, when they totalled 381,858. The regulations were the source of considerable resentment and sparked numerous protests including the 1960 demonstration at **Sharpeville**. The pass laws themselves were scrapped on 1 July 1986 when passes were replaced by 'identity documents' which did not have to be carried at all times.

PASSIVE RESISTANCE

A form of non-violent civil disobedience in which protestors refuse to co-operate with the authorities but stop short of actual obstruction. Also known as *Satyagraha*, the policy was pioneered by Mahatma Gandhi who first encouraged its use by the Indian community in South Africa in 1907 and whose campaigns of passive resistance to British rule in India beginning in 1919 did much to bring about Indian independence in 1947.

PATHET LAO

(Lao, 'Land of the Lao') The term used since 1954 by Western commentators to refer to the Lao **communist** movement as a whole.

PATRIOT MISSILE

The US anti-aircraft and anti-missile missile which proved generally effective against Iraq's **Scud** missiles during the **Gulf War** at the beginning of 1991.

PATRIOTIC FRONT

The alliance established in October 1976 between the two main liberation movements opposed to **UDI** in Rhodesia. The PF brought together Robert Mugabe's ZANU (Zimbabwe African National Union) and ZAPU (Zimbabwe African People's Union) led by Joshua Nkomo, with the objective of achieving genuine black majority rule. In practice ZANU and ZAPU and their respective military wings remained separate organizations. Nevertheless, at subsequent constitutional negotiations the nationalist side was represented by a joint PF delegation, and it was the PF (rather than ZANU or ZAPU) which was recognized by the **UN General Assembly**, **OAU** and Rhodesia's independent neighbours as the 'sole legitimate representative of the Zimbabwean people'. After the **Lancaster House Agreement** 'ZANU-PF' and 'PF-ZAPU' campaigned separately in the first democratic elections, and remained separate following the independence of **Zimbabwe** in April 1980, with ZANU in the ascendant and with tensions between them, particularly in Matebeleland. However, official merger negotiations began in September 1985, and a formal unity agreement was signed on 22 December 1987. The merged party kept the name ZANU-PF, with Mugabe as its president and first secretary and Nkomo as a vice-president and second secretary.

PAX AMERICANA

(Derived from the classical *Pax Romana*) Peace imposed by America. The term is used to characterize the hegemony of the

USA in the post-war period. Economically dominant, in 1945 the USA was also the world's foremost military power and the sole possessor of the atomic bomb. The bipolar military configuration of the **Cold War** established limits to Pax Americana, however, by recognizing the existence of separate **superpower** spheres of influence. The limits of US military power were exposed by the **Korean War** and the **Vietnam War**, and US economic dominance was eroded in the 1960s and 1970s. These changes ensured that, although the Cold War ended in 1989, there was no return to US global hegemony.

PC

Political correctness. The PC doctrine, which originated among US academics in the 1980s, involves the proscription of language – particularly that relating to gender and race – to ensure that it is acceptable to the self-appointed representatives of minority groups. It rapidly developed beyond the elimination of terms likely to cause offence, and became susceptible to caricature with the coining of expressions – such as 'terminally challenged' to describe the dead – which are widely considered absurd. The authoritarian fashion with which it has been pursued on campuses, together with the tendency of many of its adherents to denigrate the works of 'dead white males' in favour of studying the cultural products of minorities, regardless of their merit, have led many to criticize PC as a form of intellectual **fascism**. While PC poses a threat to academic freedom and independence, its impact outside academic, media and liberal-left circles remains extremely limited.

PCBs

Polychlorinated biphenyls, a class of chemicals, some highly toxic, which are found in common use in such things as refrigerator coolants, jet engine lubricants and electrical insulating materials. PCBs have the potential to cause cancer once they enter the atmosphere, and to damage the immune system of animals.

PEACE CORPS

The organization of US volunteers established by President John F. Kennedy in 1961 as a means of extending assistance to developing countries. Living in conditions similar to those prevailing in the host country, Peace Corps workers were paid subsistence wages to assist in skilled tasks such as construction or irrigation projects. In addition to providing much-needed skills, the organization – which at its peak involved 16,000 people – was also conceived as a means of projecting US values, and as the embodiment of the youthful idealism of the Kennedy era epitomized in the term **Camelot**. In March 1993 President Bill Clinton outlined a national service programme whereby young people could have college loans offset by voluntary service. Although domestic in orientation, this scheme was perceived as a successor to the Peace Corps.

PEACE DIVIDEND

The savings from military budgets which were widely expected, and to a lesser extent actually realized, because of reductions in the **arms race** with the ending of the **Cold War**. The 1992 US presidential election campaign was replete with suggestions as to how the peace dividend could be spent. The **UNDP** estimated in mid-1994 that declining world military spending since 1987 meant an aggregate peace dividend of $935,000 million, but pointed out that this had not been harnessed to meet basic human needs.

PEACE PEOPLE

Members of a movement for reconciliation between the Protestant and Catholic communities in **Northern Ireland**. The Peace Movement, later renamed the Community of the Peace People, was formed in August 1976 by two Catholics – Betty Williams and Mairead Corrigan – who were subsequently jointly awarded the 1976 **Nobel** Peace Prize. The Peace People's Movement in Britain was established in 1977 by Jane Ewart-Biggs, whose husband, the UK ambassador to Ireland, had been assassinated the previous year.

PEACE PROCESS

A general term for the full range of diplomatic efforts undertaken in an attempt to resolve a particular regional or bilateral conflict. The term '**Middle East** peace process' has been widely used in connection with the Arab-**Israeli** dispute.

PEACEFUL CO-EXISTENCE

The aim of the two **superpowers** during the era of **detente** in the 1970s. The USA and the **Soviet Union** tacitly agreed not to disturb the balance of power and avoided engaging in proxy conflict in the **Third World**. Trade between the **communist bloc** and the West increased and the Soviet Union borrowed heavily from Western banks. The **Afghan War** of 1979 marked the decisive end of peaceful co-existence and a renewed phase of **Cold War**.

PEACENIKS

Opponents of the **Vietnam War**. This colloquial and generally derisive term, widely used in the USA, echoed words like 'beatnik' in the use of the Russian suffix 'nik', meaning 'a person who'. This had entered the international vocabulary following the **Soviet Union's** October 1957 launch of **Sputnik** (meaning 'fellow traveller'), the world's first artificial space satellite.

PEACOCK THRONE

A metaphor for the pre-1979 Iranian monarchy and a reference to the throne used by the two Pahlavi shahs at their coronations. The original Peacock Throne was seized by the Iranian conqueror, Nadir Shah, during a raid on the Mughal bastion, the Red Fort, in Delhi, India, in 1793. The existing throne displayed at the Museum of the Crown Jewels in the Golestan Palace in Tehran, the Iranian capital, is believed to be a reproduction of the original.

PEARCE COMMISSION

The UK government body established in November 1971 to investigate whether proposals to settle the dispute with **Rhodesia** over **UDI** were acceptable to the whole Rhodesian population. After the failed **Tiger Talks** of December 1966 (and the subsequent unsuccessful *Fearless* talks of October 1968) there had been an interval in negotiations until early 1971. Eventually in mid-November Sir Alec Douglas Home, the UK Foreign and Commonwealth Secretary, signed the Anglo-Rhodesian Settlement with Rhodesian leader Ian Smith. The settlement provided for the gradual but slow increase in black political power, leading to majority rule by the beginning of the next century. The Pearce Commission's report published on 23 May 1972 revealed that 97 per cent of Africans questioned were strongly opposed to the Settlement. Thus rejected, the proposals were officially abandoned by UK government.

PEARSON COMMISSION

The Pearson Commission on International Development, named after its chair, the former Canadian Prime Minister Lester Pearson. Set up in 1968, it published in October 1969 the influential report *Partners in Development*. It was this report which formulated the proposition that developed countries should be devoting 0.7 per cent of **GNP** to official development assistance by 1975. This target was widely endorsed but generally not met, and continues to be monitored by the main aid donors in the **DAC**.

PECDAR

The Palestinian Economic Council for Development and Reconstruction, the Palestinian body established to deal with economic issues in the 'self rule' area created by the 1993 '**Gaza-Jericho First**' peace agreement.

PENTAGON

The location of the US Defence Department and the Departments of the Army, Navy and Air Force. The name is derived from the building's five-sided design, and has come to be used as a term to describe both the Defence Department and the heart of the country's military establishment.

PENTAGON PAPERS

The name acquired by those sections of a secret, government-produced 47-volume study of the **Vietnam War** which were leaked by one of its authors, Daniel Ellsberg (with the assistance of others whom he did not identify), and published by the US press, initially by the *New York Times* on 13 June 1971. Attempts by the administration to suppress publication of the material on the grounds of national security were defeated by the judiciary; the matter was decided ultimately by the Supreme Court, which ruled on 30 June by six votes to three to uphold the rights guaranteed by the First Amendment of the **Bill of Rights**.

PENTAGONALE

The grouping of five central European states founded in August 1990 and later expanded into the **Hexagonale** and the **CEI** (Central European Initiative). Austria, the then **Czechoslovakia**, Hungary, Italy and **Yugoslavia** attended the inaugural summit of the Pentagonale in Venice on 31 July–1 August 1990. Initially intended to promote European economic and cultural links, the Pentagonale acquired more political salience as a forum for co-operation between Eastern and Western Europe after the revolutions in Eastern Europe in 1989. In Italy, in particular, it was seen as a means of counterbalancing a newly united Germany.

PEOPLE POWER

The popular support in the Philippines for Corazon Aquino, leader of the opposition to President Ferdinand Marcos, which helped to bring down the Marcos regime. In response to massive fraud in the elections of 7 February 1986, which Marcos claimed to have won, Defence Minister Juan Ponce Enrile and Deputy Chief of Staff Lt.-Gen. Fidel Ramos defected to Aquino. Thousands of people, heeding a call from Cardinal Jaime Sin to protect the rebels from troops loyal to Marcos, formed a human shield around the rebel headquarters. Further popular demonstrations convinced the US government to withdraw its support for Marcos, forcing him to resign on 25 February, whereupon Aquino assumed the presidency.

PEOPLE'S REPUBLIC OF CHINA *see* PRC

PERESTROIKA

(Russian, 'restructuring') The slogan adopted by Soviet leader Mikhail Gorbachev in late 1986 to denote his policies of pragmatic reform, particularly in the economic sphere. *Perestroika's* themes were efficiency (as reflected in decentralization, the limited introduction of market mechanisms, and campaigns against alcohol abuse) and equality of opportunity (an emphasis on ending corruption, nepotism and excessive party privilege). *Perestroika*, however, failed to galvanize a moribund **command economy**, and Gorbachev's liberal critics attacked it as timid and directionless.

PERIOD OF COMMUNIST REBELLION

The **KMT's** term for the **communist** revolution of 1949 in mainland China, which resulted in the proclamation of the People's Republic of China (**PRC**) and the KMT's flight to **Taiwan**. There, the KMT announced '**Temporary Provisions** effective during the period of Communist Rebellion', which was formally declared at an end on 30 April 1991. During this period, the KMT continued to proclaim itself as the only legitimate government of China, and the provisions provided the justification for the maintenance of a **one-party state** in Taiwan.

PERMANENT MEMBER *see* UN SECURITY COUNCIL

PERMANENT REPRESENTATIVE

At the **UN**, the emissary of a member state (often termed its ambassador to the UN), who represents its interests at UN headquarters in New York. The representative's permanent status is emphasized in contradistinction to specially appointed delegates who may be chosen from time to time to express a member state's opinion on specific issues under consideration by the UN.

PERMANENT REVOLUTION

A theory expounded by Leon Trotsky which suggested that the stages of revolution posited by Karl Marx could be telescoped in backward countries (such as Russia). Supported by international revolution, **socialism** could thus be established directly without societies having to pass first through the stage of bourgeois democracy. The failure of socialist revolution to occur in Western Europe (particularly Germany) in the immediate aftermath of the First World War, and the triumph of Joseph Stalin's alternative vision of socialism in one country, resulted in the marginalization of **Trotskyists** within the international socialist movement during the inter-war period and their eventual resort to creating an alternative **Fourth International**. However, the ideology of permanent revolution enjoyed a revival in the 1960s, as its critique of the **Soviet Union** as a 'deformed' or 'degenerate' workers' state corresponded to the **New Left's** disenchantment with orthodox **communism**. With its emphasis on international revolution, the theory differs from Mao Zedong's concept of **continuing revolution**.

PERONISM

An Argentinian political tradition represented by the Justicialist Party founded in 1945. Originally it was a populist movement uniting trade unionists, Catholics, nationalists, dissident radicals and conservatives behind Lt.-Gen. Juan Perón, President in 1946–55 and 1973–74, a charismatic authoritarian greatly assisted by the popularity of his first wife, Evita; both entered folklore as defenders of the working class and social justice. Unlike other regional movements based on personality cults, Peronism remained a strong political force, surviving Perón's exile during the military dictatorship of 1955–73 and his death in 1974 as a result of its highly organized trade union sections, a powerful bulwark of Peronism. Under the leadership and control of President Menem, however, the Justicialist Party has shifted to the right at the expense of the predominantly state-sector unions, the victims of neo-liberal privatization policies.

PERSHING

Two generations of US intermediate-range missiles based in Europe during the **Cold War**, the Pershing 1A in the 1960s and the faster, more accurate, Pershing II, capable of reaching Soviet territory. The deployment of 108 Pershing IIs in **West Germany**, as a reinforcement of the **nuclear umbrella** and under sole US control, was part of the controversial 1979 **twin-track decision**. Along with **cruise** missiles, they started arriving in 1983 despite the bitter hostility of peace protestors. Their removal, under the **INF Treaty** of 1987, was completed on 13 March 1991 and the last missile was destroyed in the USA on 6 May 1991.

PETRODOLLARS

The term used to indicate the dollar-denominated funds which flooded into international circulation following the massive increase in oil prices in 1973–4. This flow of financial resources was generally to **OPEC** countries which were not able immediately to use them for domestic investment purposes. Accordingly, the funds were generally 'recycled' to oil-importing countries (both developed and developing) which faced large increases in their energy costs. The **IMF's** special oil facilities were one vehicle for this recycling of petrodollars.

PHALANGE

The main **right-wing Maronite** Christian movement in Lebanon. The Phalangist Party and its militias (the *Kata'ib* or Lebanese Forces) spearheaded the Christian side in the Lebanese civil war (1975–91) during which they were allied with **Israel**. The Phalange boycotted the 1992 general election in protest at what it regarded as Syrian domination of Lebanon. In early 1994 the Lebanese government launched a crackdown on Phalangist militants; among those arrested was the leader of the Lebanese Forces militia, Samir Geagea.

PHARE

(French, 'lighthouse' and French acronym for 'Poland and Hungary; economic reconstruction assistance') The **EU's** programme in the early 1990s for aid initially to Poland and Hungary, and thereafter extended to the rest of **Central** and **Eastern Europe**.

PIDE

(Portuguese acronym for *Polícia Internacional de Defesa de Estado* – 'International Police for the Defence of the State') The repressive secret police under the authoritarian **Estado Novo** of António de Oliveira Salazar. The PIDE was established in 1945 on the basis of an earlier secret police force, with headquarters in Lisbon, Oporto, and Coimbra. It relied on informers (thought to number one person in every 90), torture and interrogation, and its powers were extended in March 1956 to allow it to hold suspected subversives in prison without charge for renewable periods of three years. Its efficiency in suppressing dissent gave rise to the witticism that 'in Portugal nothing works except the PIDE'. The PIDE was abolished following the **Carnation Revolution** of 1974.

PIEDS NOIRS

(French, 'black feet') A term used to describe White French settlers who were resident in France's North African colonies, especially Algeria, and who returned to France after the decolonization of these territories in the 1960s. Their name is believed to derive either from their long association with Africa, hence the reference to 'black', or from the impoverished background of the large majority which was supposed to account for their 'dirty', or 'black' feet.

PII *see* GAGGING ORDER

PING-PONG DIPLOMACY

The process which led to the renewal of links between China and the USA, marked by the Sino-US summit of 22-28 February 1972 and the full normalization of relations in 1978. The first breakthrough after two decades of antagonism was the official invitation extended by China to a US table tennis team in April 1971.

PINKO

Pejorative US term for liberals or those on the political left. First used in a *Time* magazine article in 1926, the term found a wider postwar usage and was frequently used by Republicans to smear their Democratic opponents.

PIPER ALPHA

An offshore oil platform located some 125 miles (200 km) north-east of Aberdeen, Scotland, on which in 1988 an explosion and fire caused 167 deaths. The disaster, on the night of 6 July 1988, was the worst in the history of **North Sea oil** exploration and exploitation.

PKI

The **Communist** Party of Indonesia, founded in 1920 and proscribed in 1966. Support for the PKI grew rapidly during the post-colonial Sukarno years; President Sukarno's increasing support for the PKI, and the PKI's growing influence within sections of the army, meant that by 1965 the delicate balance of power between the party and the military was disintegrating. In October a group of pro-Communist officers, believing a **right-wing** coup to be imminent, themselves carried out a coup in which six generals were killed. The revolt, for which the PKI had declared its support, was immediately crushed, and a massacre followed in which at least 500,000 known or suspected PKI members or sympathizers were murdered. With the quelling of the unrest, an army-backed **New Order** regime took power and the PKI was banned. A few members of the party remained in prison as of 1994, others having been executed during the 1970s and 1980s.

PL480

The legislative basis of US **food aid** programmes, originally passed as Public Law number 480 of the US **Congress** in 1954. Despite the government's preference for more resounding names such as Food for Freedom or **Food for Peace,** the programme continued to be known as PL480 through the succeeding decades.

PLA

The People's Liberation Army, the armed forces (including navy and air force) of China (**PRC**), numbering some 3 million in 1993. The PLA, a largely peasant army distinguished by its ideological commitment and discipline, ensured the success of the **communist** Revolution in 1949. It played an important role in restraining the excesses of the **Cultural Revolution** in 1969, and later in suppressing the 1989 pro-democracy movement at **Tiananmen Square**.

PLANNED ECONOMY *see* COMMAND ECONOMY

PLAZA ACCORD

An agreement reached on 17 January 1985 in New York by finance ministers and central bank governors of the **G-5** countries (France, West Germany, Japan, the UK and the USA). The meeting was held in the context of the persistent strength of the US dollar and weak international oil prices. In their communiqué the participants reaffirmed their commitment to pursue monetary and fiscal policies which promoted convergence of economic performance at non-inflationary, steady growth. They stressed the importance of removing structural barriers to growth, and reaffirmed their previous commitments to undertake co-ordinated intervention in the foreign exchange markets as necessary.

PLO

The Palestine Liberation Organization, founded in 1964 as 'the only legitimate spokesman for all matters concerning the Palestinian people'. The PLO's supreme organ is the Palestine National Council (**PNC**) which elects a central council and an executive committee. Yassir Arafat, leader of **al-Fatah**, the main component of the PLO, has led the organization since 1969. The other main PLO factions include the Popular Front for the Liberation of Palestine, the Democratic Front for the Liberation of Palestine and the Palestinian Liberation Front. In September 1993 the PLO signed a historic peace agreement (**Gaza-Jericho First**) with **Israel**.

PNC

The Palestine National Council, the supreme organ of the **PLO** and the Palestinian 'parliament in exile'.

POCKET VETO

The practice whereby a US president kills legislation after **Congress** has been adjourned, by refusing to give it his assent. Under normal circumstances a president either vetoes legislation, signs it into law, or else refuses to sign it (thereby expressing a degree of disapproval of its content) after which it becomes law following the elapse of 10 working days. If he receives a bill less than 10 days prior to a congressional adjournment, however, a refusal to sign it results in the death of the bill. Unlike the exercise of a normal presidential veto, the pocket version does not require the president to give a written explanation of his action to Congress, nor is it subject to being overridden by a two-thirds vote of the legislature.

POLARIS

A submarine-launched nuclear missile, the most significant of a new generation of US **ICBMs** which banished the myth of the **missile gap**, and which the US Navy began using from 1960. Polaris was also offered to the UK, and became the basis of the UK independent nuclear capability. This aspect of the UK-US **special relationship**, agreed at the December 1962 **Nassau conference** between UK Prime Minister Harold Macmillan and US President John F. Kennedy, precipitated French President Charles de Gaulle's famous '*non*' to UK membership of the **EC**.

POLICE STATE

A regime in which government is largely dominated by the forces of coercion. The term, a translation of the German *Polizeistaat*, became popular in the 1930s as a description of Nazism. Its current usage describes any system in which the use of coercion by the state is not under social control, and in which the police, or their equivalent, have broad powers to suppress political opposition in order to maintain the ruling elite in power.

POLISARIO FRONT

(Spanish acronym for the *Frente Popular para la Liberacion de Saguia el Hamra y Rio de Oro* – 'Popular Front for the Liberation of Saguia el Hamra and Rio de Oro') A liberation movement which fights for the independence of Moroccan-controlled **Western Sahara**. It was originally established in Mauritania in 1973 to fight against Spanish control of the Western Sahara. After Spain withdrew and Morocco and Mauritania partitioned the region between them in 1975, Polisario relocated to Algeria which equipped it with arms and bases. In 1976 the group proclaimed an independent Saharan Arab Democratic Republic (**SADR**). Polisario signed a peace deal with Mauritania in 1979, but Morocco then unilaterally annexed Mauritania's portion of Western Sahara. During the 1980s Polisario sustained a dual military and diplomatic campaign, but in September 1991 the group signed a ceasefire agreement to facilitate a **UN** plan to hold a referendum on the status of the Western Sahara.

POLITBURO

A key committee in the leadership structures of most **communist** parties, elected in the case of the **Soviet Union** by the **central committee** of the **CPSU**. Politburo membership was divided between permanent members and candidate members without voting rights, with the total reaching up to 40 members in the CPSU.

POLITICAL CORRECTNESS *see* PC

POLL TAX *see* COMMUNITY CHARGE

POLLUTER PAYS

The principle which states that those who cause industrial pollution should offset its effects by compensating for the damage incurred or by implementing measures to avoid the pollution being caused in the first place. The policy is difficult to enforce, mainly because atmospheric **transboundary pollution** can be hard to trace to its source. More localized pollution, such as oil spillage from a tanker, is more easily identifiable. The principle of polluter pays was endorsed in the Rio Declaration signed at the 1992 **Earth Summit**.

PONTING AFFAIR

The trial and acquittal of Clive Ponting in the UK in 1985 under the 1911 Official Secrets Act. Ponting, a high-flying civil servant in the Ministry of Defence, was accused of leaking classified information to Labour MP Tam Dalyell, relating to the sinking of the Argentinian cruiser **Belgrano** during the 1982 **Falklands War**. His motive had been to make public what he considered to be attempts by the government to avoid acknowledgment of changes in the rules of engagement prior to the sinking of the cruiser. Ponting's acquittal, although generally unexpected, was widely acclaimed in 'right-to-know' circles.

POPULISM

A broad ideology which claims to defend the interests of 'the people' against those of entrenched bureaucracy, big business and other manifestations of the modern, urban state. Populist leaders tend to be demagogues, and to blame current economic and social problems on conspiracy or corruption among specific groups engaged in the pursuit of their own interests.

PORT HURON STATEMENT

The founding policy statement of the **SDS**, a radical US student movement created in 1960. The Port Huron statement was issued at the movement's first convention in June 1962. An embodiment of the central ideas of the **New Left**, the statement condemned nuclear weapons, **capitalism**, the **military-industrial complex**, US foreign policy, the authoritarianism of the **Soviet Union**, and the paternalism of the welfare state.

POSITIVE DISCRIMINATION *see* AFFIRMATIVE ACTION

POST-INDUSTRIAL SOCIETY

A view of contemporary society posited on the notion of a science-based and technocentric future. This view assumes, controversially, that the constraints of industrial toil have been replaced by leisure, and that the concerns of the traditional working class with the production and distribution of material goods have been superseded by the production and distribution of information technology. Other definitions include the importance of service employment; the pre-eminence accorded to the professional, scientific and technical strata; and the aspiration towards quality of life, rather than quantity of goods.

POTSDAM

The conference held from 17 July to 1 August 1945 between the **Soviet Union**, UK and USA, the **Big Three** allied powers of the Second World War, to decide the treatment of defeated Germany. The **Yalta** Conference in February 1945 had divided Germany into four occupation zones, allotted to France, the Soviet Union, the UK and the USA, and the Potsdam agreement aimed to ensure 'that Germany will never again threaten her neighbours or the peace of the world'. It made provisions for demilitarization and **denazification** under allied occupation; for economic restructuring which would treat Germany as a whole; for reparations to the allies, particularly the Soviet Union; and for territorial revisions, including ceding Königsberg to the Soviet Union and provisionally fixing Poland's western frontier with Germany along the **Oder-Neisse line** (thereby allowing the Soviet Union to compensate Poland with German territory in the west for land it had itself seized in eastern Poland). The Potsdam agreement was suspended only in 1990, on the signing of the final settlement treaty between the wartime allies and the **DDR** and **BRD** (East and West Germany) after the **two-plus-four talks**.

POUJADIST

The **populist** French movement of shopkeepers led by Pierre Poujade in the 1950s. Threatened by modernization and expanding large-scale commerce, the Poujadistes protested against the 1953 turnover tax on small shopkeepers, and won 12 per cent of the vote and 51 seats in the 1956 National Assembly elections, standing as the extreme **right-wing** *Union de défense des commerçants et artisans* and the *Union et fraternité française*. Passing into more general usage, the term poujadist is applied to populist protests, particularly of the lower-middle class, which feels its interests disregarded by both organized labour and the elite.

POULSON AFFAIR

The affair leading to the resignation in 1972 of Reginald Maudling as Home Secretary in the UK Conservative Cabinet. John Poulson was an architect who built up a major international practice in the 1960s. He became also involved in construction work, and increased his standing through contacts with influential politicians. By the early 1970s Poulson's business concerns encountered grave financial difficulties, and as a result of disclosures made during his bankruptcy examination he was charged with corruption relating to bribes given to national and local politicians aimed at winning contracts. In February–March 1974 he was sentenced to seven years' imprisonment; T. Dan Smith, a Newcastle Labour councillor, was given a six-year sentence. Maudling, who resigned from the Cabinet over gifts Poulson had made to a theatre supported by his wife, was not charged with any criminal offence.

POVERTY TRAP

A term used to describe the situation when people taking up low-paid employment are then in a worse financial position than when they were unemployed, because they lose welfare benefit and incur costs for travelling, meals and, often, childcare. Unemployed people who are poorly skilled and ill-educated and unable to find well-paid work may thus be trapped in the benefits system as victims of the **dependency culture**.

POWER SHARING

The sharing of political power, particularly between majority and minority communities, in order to allow the minority community a part in the political process which it has otherwise been denied. The term has been applied to **Northern Ireland**, where in 1974 a short-lived power sharing executive was established. It collapsed in the face of a **loyalist** strike, and **direct rule** was reimposed.

PR

Proportional representation. A broad category of electoral systems having in common one main feature – the intention that the political parties in parliament should be represented in proportion to their overall percentage support among the electorate. This is not the result achieved by the **single-member constituency** system, as is frequently argued in the UK by advocates of PR, who include Liberal Democrats and an element in the Labour Party. Opponents of PR point to Western Europe for examples of weak and volatile coalition governments, with parliamentary support fragmented among numerous parties. In some cases, however, the impact of small parties is counteracted by allocating no representation to parties whose support is below a certain threshold (5 per cent in the example of Germany).

PR systems are broadly divisible into those where voters choose a party list, and (less commonly) those like the Hare system where they can rank individuals on those lists in their own order of preference. They may vote for a single national list, or for lists in regional multi-member constituencies, or, often, for a combination of these. Some systems also include provision for a number of seats elected in single-member constituencies. Political scientists have developed versions of PR to respond to many differing sets of priorities in terms of the balancing of local representation with overall proportionality; among those in current use are the D'Hondt system, the Droop quota system and the Hagenbach-Bischoff system.

PRAGUE SPRING

Communist Czechoslovakia's brief experiment in 1968 with **socialism with a human face**. An 'action programme' in April set out plans to extend democracy and **civil rights**, and the newly freed press radicalized the political climate, although communist party leader Alexander Dubcek never questioned the leading role of the communist party while in office. The Prague Spring was crushed by an invasion by **Warsaw Pact** tanks and troops in September 1968, a reimposition of Soviet regional might which laid the ground for the **Brezhnev doctrine**.

PRAVDA

(Russian, 'Truth') The official newspaper of the **CPSU** and part of the Soviet establishment, co-operating with state censors and receiving official blessing in return; its editor regularly attended meetings of the **politburo**. It had a huge circulation, which dropped rapidly after the collapse of the **Soviet Union** in 1991. *Pravda* was briefly banned following the **Moscow rebellion** of 1993.

PRC

The People's Republic of China, the official name of mainland China, which was declared on 1 October 1949 after the **communist** revolution and the **PLA's** defeat of the nationalist **KMT**. The Republic of China, proclaimed in 1911, was abolished and replaced with a 'people's republic'. The PRC is the world's third largest state in area, and also its most populous: the population is projected to rise to 1,300 million by 2000.

PREFERENTIAL TRADE AREA OF EASTERN AND SOUTHERN AFRICA

see PTA

PRESSLER AMENDMENT

An amendment to the Foreign Assistance Act in 1985, barring US military and economic aid to Pakistan unless the president certified that the country did not possess a nuclear weapon. The amendment was moved by, and named after, Democratic Senator Larry Pressler. The Act, as amended, was approved by President Ronald Reagan on 8 August 1985. The Pressler amendment was invoked in October 1990, when the US **Congress** suspended aid after failing to receive a presidential certification testifying that Pakistan's nuclear programme was being designed exclusively for peaceful purposes.

PRIMARIES

Ballots held in US states in the early part of a presidential election year to choose delegates for the nominating conventions of the Democratic and Republican parties. Although not mandatory in every state, the practice of holding primaries or **caucuses** has become very widespread over the last century. The ballot is open to all members of the electorate unless it is a 'closed primary' in which case it is restricted to party members. By tradition, the first primary of the presidential campaign is held in New Hampshire.

PRIVATIZATION

The dismantling of government ownership of industries and services, and the sale or disposal either of these enterprises or of their assets. In some cases the enterprises may have been established by the state or lower tiers of government directly; alternatively they may originally have been brought into public ownership through **nationalization**, confiscation or other methods. The privatization of public corporations and services in the UK, spearheaded by the Thatcher government in the 1980s (on both ideological and economic grounds) and carried on into the 1990s, was emulated in many other countries, in both the developed and the developing world. Moreover, the collapse of the **communist** regimes in the **Soviet Union** and **eastern Europe** in 1989–91 led to massive sales of state assets in those countries. In the UK in particular many privatizations have been effected in such a way as to spread ownership of shares widely among the population in general in a 'property-owning democracy'.

PRODUCTION RESPONSIBILITY SYSTEM

A feature of economic reforms in China (**PRC**), whereby the responsibility for agricultural production was gradually transferred from the communes to individual peasant households. By the mid-1980s, most land had been subcontracted to the peasants, who were obliged to sell a certain share of produce to the state at state-imposed prices, but were permitted to sell any surplus on the open market.

PROFUMO AFFAIR

The scandal leading to the resignation in 1963 of John Profumo as Secretary of State for War in the UK Conservative Cabinet. The affair was seen by many as being indicative of a perceived lack of direction and leadership in Harold Macmillan's government. Profumo had become involved in a relationship with a young woman called Christine Keeler, and alarm was caused by the fact that she also had a simultaneous relationship with Eugene Ivanov, a Soviet naval attaché in London. In the House of Commons Profumo denied any impropriety, but as increasingly lurid details emerged he was forced to resign. The security aspects of the affair were the subject of an exhaustive inquiry by senior judge Lord Denning.

PROPAGANDA

(Latin, 'that which is to be spread') The distribution of information calculated to change public opinion in a specific direction. In the **West**, it is a negative term because it implies the distortion of truth for political ends. In the **Soviet Union**, however, there was a distinction between propaganda, the reasoned argument of complex issues, and agitation, the emotional stirring of the masses. All states engage in propaganda activity, particularly during wartime.

PROPORTIONAL REPRESENTATION *see* PR

PROTECTED VILLAGES *see* STRATEGIC HAMLETS

PROVISIONAL IRA *see* IRA

PROXIMITY TALKS

A device used in international diplomacy where a mediator is seeking to bring opposing sides towards negotiation but the protagonists refuse to meet face to face.

Proximity talks involve meetings between the mediator and the protagonists, usually in the same location and in rapid succession. One example concerns the dispute over the division of Cyprus since 1974; the **UN** Secretary-General has sometimes appeared to make progress at proximity talks in New York with the (Greek) Cypriot government and with Turkish Cypriot (**TRNC**) representatives, but eventual face-to-face meetings have done little more than dramatize disagreements over the proposals elaborated in this way.

PSBR

The public-sector borrowing requirement. A country's PSBR for a given period of time (usually a year) is the measure of how much must be borrowed by the public sector if expenditure and revenue are to be balanced. Conversely, if revenue exceeds expenditure, there is a public-sector debt repayment (PSDR). The UK government defines the PSBR as comprising the borrowing requirement of central government, of local authorities and of public corporations, while the overall figure is deemed to be reduced by net **privatization** proceeds. The measure of PSBR has become increasingly central to economic strategy in the UK in particular since the 1980s, as the government has sought to control the growth in the money supply. The pursuit of reductions in the PSBR has in turn encouraged the government to work towards removing large portions of public expenditure to the non-governmental sector.

PTA

The Preferential Trade Area for Eastern and Southern Africa, a grouping founded in 1981 to improve regional commercial and economic co-operation. As of July 1994 it had 22 members; South Africa was expected to be invited to join following the successful holding of non-racial democratic elections in April 1994. In November 1993, the PTA established a free trade area (**COMESA**).

PUBLIC AGAINST VIOLENCE

Slovakia's sister party to the Czech **Civic Forum**, founded in November 1989 during the **Velvet Revolution**. Public Against Violence was a popular front drawing together various disparate political forces in opposition to the **communist** regime, to demand free elections. It fragmented after elections in 1990.

PUBLIC INTEREST IMMUNITY CERTIFICATE *see* GAGGING ORDER

PUGWASH

An international organization of scientists which takes its name from the venue of the first annual conference, held in 1957 in Pugwash in eastern Canada. It focused initially on ways in which the scientific community, transcending the **Cold War**, could contribute to **arms control** and the eventual elimination of **nuclear weapons**. Latterly it has expanded its concept of global security to embrace environmental issues and **sustainable development**.

PWR

Pressurized water reactor – a type of nuclear reactor which uses water as a moderator in the chain reaction and as a coolant of the fuel rods. Water under high pressure transmits heat from the core of the reactor to steam generators which drive electricity turbines. The PWR's design is controversial because of the possibility that a sudden accidental loss of the coolant may rapidly lead to a meltdown of the nuclear core (as threatened in the **Three Mile Island** accident of 1979) leading to an extremely dangerous release of radiation.

PY NANDÍ

(Guaraní, 'barefoot ones') Paraguayan peasant militias and violent supporters of the **right-wing** Colorado Party. The *Py Nandí* were essential to the Colorados' victory in the 1947 civil war. In 1954, following the coup of Gen. Alfredo Stroessner, the *Py Nandí* were organized into a military-sponsored surveillance and counterinsurgency service, and played an important role in the defeat of **left-wing guerrillas** in 1960.

Dominating mass rallies in his support during periods of crisis, they also contributed to Stroessner's long-unchallenged dictatorship (1954–89).

QUAI D'ORSAY

A term used for the French Ministry of Foreign Affairs, whose headquarters are located in this street alongside the river Seine in Paris. Also on the Quai d'Orsay is the Bourbon palace, where the Council of the Five Hundred met during th the French Revolution and where the National Assembly now meets.

QUALIFIED MAJORITY VOTING

Within the **EU**, a formula for determining whether there is sufficient approval for a decision by the **Council of Ministers** and the **European Council** (except where unanimity is required). To prevent a decision being taken, opponents must mobilize enough votes for the specified 'blocking minority'. The scope for decision-making by qualified majority vote was extended under the **Single European Act** in 1987 and is to be further discussed in 1996 under the **Maastricht** Treaty framework. In the 12-member EU the weighted allocation of votes between states gave the largest member countries 10 each, falling to two for Luxembourg; 23 votes out of the total of 76 were sufficient to block decisions. The **Ioannina compromise** in March 1994 specified that the blocking minority would be 27 votes out of 90 in an enlarged 16-member EU.

QUANGO

A quasi-autonomous non-governmental organization. The description is used especially in the UK to indicate bodies set up by the government (through statute or otherwise), which have duties and responsibilities almost akin to government organs but which are nevertheless at arm's length from government. The term more recently favoured by the government for such organizations is 'non-departmental public bodies'. In May 1994 an independent report estimated that there were 5,521 quangos in the UK with over 70,000 non-elected 'quangocrats' controlling £46,600 million (US$70,200 million) – nearly one-third of all public expenditure.

QUEMOY AND MATSU

Two small islands between the west coast of **Taiwan** and mainland China (**PRC**), which are a constituent part of Taiwan. Following the **KMT's** flight to Taiwan in 1949, China bombarded Quemoy (also known as Chinmen) and Matsu in 1954, and again in 1958, in order to 'liberate' Taiwan. It appeared that US support for the KMT might precipitate a Sino-US conflict, but on each occasion the crisis subsided with no further aggression.

RACISM

The belief in the innate superiority of a particular race and the consequent practice of discrimination on the grounds of race. Although it is most often used to describe the experiences of black people subject to attack from racist groups like the **Ku Klux Klan** in the USA or living under **segregation** or **apartheid** in South Africa, it is appropriate to use the term to describe **anti-Semitism** and the experiences of other groups, and to apply it to Nazi and **neo-Nazi** thought.

RADICAL CHIC

A somewhat derogatory term for the fashionable advocacy of radical causes, particularly those associated with the **Black Power** movement, by rich, white liberals. The term was derived from an essay of the same name by Tom Wolfe, published in 1971, in which he lambasted a group of privileged white New Yorkers for their support for the **Black Panthers**. By welding together a political concept and an element of style, Wolfe's term perfectly captured the process through which serious political movements and ideas were stripped of ideological content and turned into fashion accessories by those who held positions of privilege within the very structures which those movements and ideas sought to destroy.

RADIO FREE EUROPE

A radio broadcasting operation covering the countries of **Eastern** and **Central Europe**, funded by the US government and operating from Munich under US management. Founded in 1949, it was originally funded through the CIA until connections with the security service were severed in 1971. On 1 October 1976, it merged with its sister organization, Radio Liberty, which broadcasts to the countries of the former **Soviet Union**, to become RFE/RL Inc., a non-profit, private corporation funded by grants from the US Congress. The stated aims of RFE/RL are to provide 'a non-partisan perspective on domestic affairs' in the region; 'to encourage further peaceful evolution of democracy'; and 'to compensate for the continued weakness of domestic media'. RFE's operations have been reduced following budget cuts announced in October 1993.

RADIO MARTÍ

A Florida-based Spanish-language radio station run by **anti-Castroites** directing propaganda at Cuba. The station, named somewhat incongruously after the Cuban independence hero and poet José Martí, was launched in May 1985 by the US Information Agency (USIA) and led to a breakdown in US-Cuban relations. The USIA also set up the television station TV Martí in March 1990. Radio Martí is regularly jammed by the Cuban authorities and TV Martí is seen by only a tiny minority of Cubans. Despite international criticism, as of mid-1994 the US government appears committed to continue funding the two stations, at an estimated cost of US$21 million per annum.

RAF *see* ROTE ARMEE FRACTION

RAINBOW COALITION

A description of the supporters of the charismatic black leader, the Rev. Jesse Jackson, who unsuccessfully sought the US Democratic Party presidential nomination in 1984 and 1988. Jackson's radicalism mobilized support from all races (hence the term 'rainbow') among the poor and the dispossessed, and drew into the political process many who had been hitherto excluded. Nevertheless, when the Democrats did succeed in winning a presidential election, in 1992, it was by choosing white, Southern presidential and vice-presidential candidates and recapturing the support of white voters in the **South**, rather than through the support of Jackson's rainbow coalition.

RAINBOW WARRIOR

The ship owned by the environmentalist protest group **Greenpeace** which was preparing to lead protest action against French **nuclear tests** in the Pacific, when it was sunk in Auckland harbour by French secret agents from **DGSE** on 10 July 1985. This attack, which killed one crew member, soured relations between France and New Zealand for years. The New Zealand authorities arrested two French agents who were convicted and sentenced to 10-year prison terms for manslaughter and sabotage. In an accord whereby France paid US$7 million in compensation to New Zealand, the agents were later transferred for three years' confinement at a French military base on Hao atoll; New Zealand protested when they were allowed home early (ostensibly for medical reasons), and in May 1990 a **UN** arbitration panel ruled that France had violated the accord. Eventually, during a visit to New Zealand in April 1991, French Prime Minister Michel Rocard admitted French blame for the Rainbow Warrior affair and declared the matter closed.

RAJYA SABHA

(Hindi, 'Assembly of the State') The upper house of the Indian legislature, the lower chamber being the **Lok Sabha**. It consists of 245 members, mostly indirectly elected by state assemblies, of whom one-third are elected every two years. The President nominates 12 members on the strength of achievement in culture, science or social service.

RAMADAN

(Arabic, 'great heat') The ninth month of the Islamic lunar calendar. Fasting during this 'holy' month, known as *sawm*, constitutes one of the five 'pillars' of Islam, in addition to the *shahadah* (affirming the unity of God); *salah* (the five daily ritual prayers); **zakat** (almsgiving); and **haj** (the pilgrimage to Mecca).

RAMSAR CONVENTION

The Convention on Wetlands of International Importance, Especially as Waterfowl Habitat, a unique international environmental convention, in force since 1975, which designates over 500 wetland sites worldwide for protection. About 50 countries participate, each pledging to protect at least one wetland site, or replace it with one of equal importance. The convention is named after the Iranian town, now called Sakht-Sar, where it was signed in 1971. Ramsar listings cover only 3 per cent of the world's wetlands.

RAND CORPORATION

A **right-wing** US **think tank** established at the end of the Second World War. It was initially the propaganda agency of the US Air Force, established under the guise of a scientific institute attached to the Douglas Aircraft Corporation in Santa Monica, California. The name was derived from the term 'R and D', a commonly used abbreviation of 'research and development'. Composed largely of economists, the Rand became a leading source of advice to the US military establishment on **Cold War** strategy.

RANGOON BOMBING

An attack on a South Korean government delegation at Rangoon, Burma, on 9 October 1983, which killed 17 people, including four members of the Cabinet. The bombing was carried out by North Korean agents and was believed to have been aimed at assassinating South Korean President Chun Doo Hwan.

RANN OF KUTCH

(Hindi, 'salt marsh wilderness') The disputed border, also known as the Great Rann of Kutch, between India and **Pakistan** which lies adjacent to the southern Pakistani province of Sind. The boundaries, last demarcated in 1923–4, were not properly defined on the **partition** of the **Indian subcontinent** in 1947, mainly because the area was flooded for the much of the year. At independence Pakistan contested the original border which led to military skirmishes with India in April–June 1965. A ceasefire agreement was followed in February 1968 by a **UN** boundary tribunal award, which granted Pakistan 300 square miles (780 sq km) which had hitherto been Indian territory. Beyond the area of the tribunal's award lies the final stretch, about 50 miles (80 km) in length, known as the Sir Creek area which remains unresolved and the subject of continuing bilateral talks between the two countries.

RAROTONGA DECLARATION

The South Pacific Declaration on Natural Resources and the Environment, adopted at a conference held in Rarotonga, Cook Islands, in March 1982 on the South Pacific's human environment. In addition to guidelines on the sustainable management of the natural resources of the region, the declaration stated that 'the storage and release of nuclear wastes in the Pacific regional environment shall be prevented', and that 'the testing of nuclear devices against the wishes of the people shall not be permitted'. These anti-nuclear sentiments were embodied in the 1986 **Rarotonga Treaty**.

RAROTONGA TREATY

The South Pacific **Nuclear-free zone** Treaty which prohibits its signatories from acquiring, manufacturing, storing, stationing or testing nuclear explosive devices and from dumping radioactive waste in their territories. The treaty was signed by Australia, Cook Islands, Fiji, **Kiribati**, New Zealand, Niue, **Tuvalu**, and Western Samoa at the 16th annual conference of the **South Pacific Forum** on 4–6 August 1985; Papua New Guinea signed in September 1985, **Nauru** in July 1986, and Solomon Islands in May 1987. The treaty came into force on 11 December 1986. Subsequently, protocols to the treaty concerning the world's nuclear-armed powers were signed by China and the **Soviet Union**, but not by those with dependencies in the region – France, the UK, and the USA.

RASTAFARIANISM

A predominantly **Caribbean** religious cult originating in the 1930s in the slums of Kingston, Jamaica, and strongly influenced by the ideas of Marcus Garvey. Rastafarians look to Ethiopia as their spiritual home and worship the late Ethiopian Emperor Haile Selassie, (known before his accession as Prince Ras Tafari), as the god-king of all Africans. They suffered systematic persecution due to their distinctive hairstyle and dress, rejection of material possessions, refusal to participate in elections and habit of smoking ganja (a type of cannabis), an integral part of their religion. In Jamaica they were victimized until the mid-1960s, and in Dominica a **Dread Law** criminalized Rastafarianism. The cult influenced the Caribbean **Black Power** movement and from the mid-1970s was popularized through reggae music, chiefly that of Bob Marley, when Black Power was on the wane. Since then Rastafarianism has spread to the USA, Europe and parts of Africa.

REAGANOMICS

A popular term for the economic policies pursued by US President Ronald Reagan (1981–9). Reaganomics involved a shift away from the demand management associated with **Keynesianism**, in favour of the supply-side theories of **monetarism**. The core elements of the policy were cuts in direct taxation, to be paid for by reductions in public expenditure; a cut in the rate of inflation through the exercise of tight monetary control; a reduction in the size of the budget deficit; economic and financial deregulation; and the release of funds into private, productive channels through increased savings. After suffering the deepest post-war recession in 1981–2, Reagan then presided over the strongest post-war period of recovery. However, while tax cuts were successfully implemented, the administration failed to achieve its desired targets in reducing non-defence public expenditure. Furthermore, Reagan's **Cold War** rhetoric was accompanied by a massive increase in US military expenditure, with the result that the budget deficit increased greatly during his period in office.

REAPPORTIONMENT

The US term for the redrawing of electoral districts and redistribution of legislative seats to take account of population shifts.

RE-COMPAS

(from Spanish *compañeros*, 'comrades') Rearmed **left-wing Sandinistas** in Nicaragua who emerged in 1991 to fight **right-wing re-contras** in order to preserve the social achievements of their 1979 revolution. However, in 1992 they joined up with *re-contras* as *revueltos* ('mixed together'), demanding that the right-wing National Opposition Union government of President Violeta Barrios de Chamorro should honour 1990 peace pledges on land, credits and housing. The army, although still dominated by Sandinistas, was accused of using excessive force to crush a *re-compa* rebellion in July 1993. Small bands, described by the government as 'bandits', remain active in border regions with Honduras.

RE-CONTRAS

(from Spanish *contra*, 'against') Former members of the Nicaraguan **right-wing contras** who resumed fighting in 1991 accusing the National Opposition Union government of President Violeta Barrios de Chamorro of failing to honour peace pledges of land, credits, and security and colluding with **left-wing Sandinistas** who they demanded should be purged from the state security forces. The 2,000 strong-group also fought against left-wing **re-compas** until May 1992 when, as *revueltos* ('mixed together'), they temporarily joined together to struggle for agrarian reform and other common aims. Many surrendered in 1992–3, but a complete ceasefire had yet to be achieved by July 1994.

RECRUIT-COSMOS SCANDAL

The Japanese political scandal which brought down the government in 1989. The Recruit business information and employment company had between 1984 and 1986 sold pre-flotation shares in its Cosmos real estate subsidiary at preferential rates to politicians and civil servants. These shares then increased greatly in value when the stock was floated in late 1986. The scandal over this device, which constituted a form of bribery, broke in late 1988 and led, on 25 April 1989, to the resignation of Prime Minister Noboru Takeshita.

RED ARMY

The Russian (and later Soviet) army, formed in 1917–18 by the Bolsheviks and organized by Leon Trotsky to fight the anti-**communist** 'White' armies. The military, with the Red Army as its linchpin, assumed an increasingly central role in the politics, economy and society of the **Soviet Union**, particularly with the outbreak of the Second World War and the subsequent onset of the **Cold War**. Abroad the Red Army represented the might of the Soviet **superpower**.

RED BRIGADES *see* BRIGATE ROSSE

RED-BROWN

An alliance of the far left (red) and far right (brown), born out of political expediency, but which can reflect similarities in political outlook. On the level of ideology, red-brown alliances share a totalitarian emphasis on state power. Other common features are the **cult of personality**, and an emphasis on peasant values including an antipathy toward ethnic minorities, intellectuals and **capitalists**. A red-brown coalition of Russian neo-**fascists**, extreme nationalists and **communists** rallied in the **Moscow Rebellion** of October 1993.

RED CRESCENT *see* IFRC

RED CROSS *see* IFRC

RED DATA BOOKS *see* IUCN

RED-GREEN ALLIANCE

A term in German politics to describe a governing coalition, as formed in several **Länder** but never yet at federal level, between the 'red' Social Democrats and the ecologist **Greens**.

RED GUARDS

Groups composed mainly of students and schoolchildren who, as 'Red Guards of the **Cultural Revolution**', had the task of unmasking revisionists and enthusiastically promoting **Maoism**. The Red Guards emerged in the summer of 1966; the 1966–7 academic year was cancelled, enabling them to devote themselves full time to political activity and a series of mass rallies in Beijing between 18 August and 26 November which were addressed by Mao Zedong. The Red Guards' attempts to purge and replace the Chinese Communist Party apparatus throughout the country led to widespread chaos, and in 1967–8 the People's Liberation Army began to restore order. By autumn 1968 the Red Guards had been largely suppressed.

REDS UNDER THE BED

A **Cold War** satirical phrase denoting Western paranoia, particularly in **conservative** political circles, that a secret conspiracy of 'red' or **communist** activists was preparing to weaken and destabilize the state and society, in order to serve the imperialist ends of an inexorably expanding communist bloc. Such sentiments contributed to **McCarthyism** in the USA.

RE-EDUCATION CAMPS

Prisons in which high-ranking military and civilian leaders of a defeated regime are held by their revolutionary conquerors supposedly for purposes of 're-education'. After the **Vietnam War**, the **communist** victors in Vietnam dispatched hundreds of thousands of former South Vietnamese officials to camps. It was only in mid-1992 that the Vietnamese government announced the closure of its last camp.

REFUSENIK

A name coined in the 1970s for Jews seeking permission to emigrate from the **Soviet Union**, many of whose applications were refused. They were subject to discrimination, including dismissal from their jobs and police harassment, in the lengthy period while their applications were processed. A prominent organizer of refuseniks, Anatoly Shcharansky, was jailed in July 1978 for treason, in connection with links to Western journalists. He was released in February 1986, and emigrated to **Israel**.

REJECTIONISTS

A term employed to describe the radical Palestinian factions which oppose mainstream **PLO** policies, particularly negotiation with **Israel**. In January 1994 the 10 main 'rejectionist' groups formed a Syrian-based alliance to oppose the Israeli-PLO **Gaza-Jericho First** deal. The principal members of the alliance included **Hamas**, the Popular Front for the Liberation of Palestine and the Democratic Front for the Liberation of Palestine.

RENAMO *see* MNR

REPUBLIC OF CHINA *see* TAIWAN

RESOLUTION 242

A key resolution on the Arab-**Israeli** conflict adopted unanimously by the **UN Security Council** in November 1967 shortly after Israel's victory in the **Six-Day War**. The resolution, proposed by the UK, called for the 'withdrawal of Israeli armed forces from territories occupied in the recent conflict' and also said that all states in the region had the right to live within secure and recognized boundaries.

The resolution was accepted by Israel and by the front-line Arab states except Syria, but on the basis of differing interpretations of the key phrase calling for an Israeli withdrawal. The resolution included no specific reference to Palestinian rights, but merely called for a 'just settlement' of the refugee problem. It was this omission, together with the implied recognition of Israel, which led the **PLO** to reject the resolution until 1988.

RESOLUTION 348

The **UN Security Council** resolution adopted in October 1973 which called for the implementation of a ceasefire between Arabs and **Israel**is engaged in the **Yom Kippur War**. The resolution, which received the support of 14 of the Council's 15 member states, with China refraining from voting, urged the parties concerned to 'start immediately . . . the implementation of **Resolution 242** [of November 1967] in all of its parts' and decided that immediate negotiations should be initiated 'aimed at establishing a just and durable peace in the **Middle East**'.

RESOLUTION 435

The **UN Security Council** Resolution passed on 29 September 1978 which laid the basis for the independence of **Namibia**. It provided for a ceasefire, the partial demobilization of South African forces and the confinement to base of both **SWAPO** and South African military forces; the abolition of all discriminatory legislation and the release of all political prisoners; and the democratic election of a Constituent Assembly and the adoption of an independence constitution. The year-long process was to be supervised by a UN monitoring force (**UNTAG**). As a result of the imposition of successive preconditions by the South African government, the implementation of Resolution 435 only began on 1 April 1989. Namibian independence was declared on 21 March 1990.

RETTIG REPORT

A major human rights report by the Truth and Reconciliation Commission (CVR) to the Chilean government in March 1991 and named after CVR chair Raúl Rettig. Covering human rights violations between September 1973 and March 1990 under the **right-wing** military regime of Gen. Augusto Pinochet Ugarte, it detailed 2,279 deaths, including 1,068 executions or deaths under torture, 957 **disappeared** persons and 90 security force members killed by the regime's opponents. Those guilty were not named, the report's remit being to document repression rather than carry out a judicial investigation.

REVOLUTION OF THE FLOWERS *see* CARNATION REVOLUTION

REVOLUTIONARY BOLIVARIST MOVEMENT

Venezuelan military rebels who staged abortive military coups in February and November 1992. Strongly nationalist, they sought to establish a **junta** of national reconstruction to deal with economic problems, social disparity and official corruption taking advantage of the low popularity of the social democratic government of President Carlos Andrés Pérez. Most of the imprisoned ringleaders, including the rebels' popular leader Lt. Col Hugo Chávez Frías, were pardoned by March 1994. The rebellions hastened the fall of Pérez, whose suspension from office was made permanent in August 1993 and who was imprisoned on corruption charges in May 1994.

REVOLUTIONARY COMMAND COUNCIL

An unelected body which acts as the effective locus of power in some countries which have experienced a military takeover. The most prominent current example is in Iraq where it has been acknowledged as the supreme ruling body since a military coup in 1968. Led by President Saddam Hussein, its members also occupy key posts in the Cabinet. Its decrees, which overrule laws passed by the Iraqi parliament, remain the ultimate authority for all changes affecting government, political affairs and the economy. An identically named body established in Sudan after a military coup in 1989 was dissolved in October 1993 as part of a package of political reforms.

REVOLUTIONARY FRONT OF EAST TIMOR *see* FRETILIN

REVOLUTIONARY GUARDS *see* PASDARAN

REVOLVING DOOR

A US term denoting rapid movement between public office and involvement in the private sector, with former office-holders able to command high fees as business consultants, and then, often, re-entering government. The practice has raised criticisms concerning its potential for ethical violations.

REYKJAVIK SUMMIT

The meeting in the Icelandic capital in October 1986 at which Soviet leader Mikhail Gorbachev and US President Ronald Reagan appeared to move rapidly towards, and even reach agreement on, an extraordinary proposal to eliminate half their strategic weapons within five years and to abolish all **nuclear weapons** (strategic, intermediate, and battlefield) within 10 years. In preparations for Reykjavik (a follow-up to the 1985 **Geneva summit**), Gorbachev had stressed opposition to the US **Star Wars** project and Reagan had emphasized the demand for the elimination of Soviet intermediate-range missiles (INFs, of which SS-20s were the most important) in Asia and Europe. The temporary euphoria of Reykjavik evaporated as it became evident that any Soviet INF offer was conditional on the scrapping of Star Wars, that Reagan would not abandon his pet project, and that less misty-eyed **hawks** within **NATO** were horrified by the implications for **flexible response** if battlefield nuclear weapons were foregone. Gorbachev retreated to the offer of eliminating INF missiles from Europe but keeping 100 in Asia, and an **INF Treaty** took another year to agree.

RHODESIA

The name used for **Zimbabwe** by the white minority government from the declaration of **UDI** in November 1965 to independence following the **Lancaster House Agreement** in April 1980. While under British rule the territory was known as Southern Rhodesia.

RIGHT TO CHOOSE

The US pressure group dedicated to preserving the availability of legal abortions. A loose coalition of liberals and feminists, the movement has campaigned in support of the landmark **Roe v. Wade** 1973 Supreme Court decision which provides the basis for legal abortion in the USA, and has opposed the anti-abortionist **Right to Life** movement.

RIGHT TO LIFE

The powerful US anti-abortionist pressure group with strong links to the Christian right and the Republican Party. The movement is composed of a coalition of anti-abortionists, the most militant of whom have used tactics of violence and intimidation in an attempt to prevent clinics from performing legal abortions. The movement has also campaigned for a revision of the landmark **Roe v. Wade** 1973 Supreme Court decision which provided the basis for legal abortion in the USA. In the forefront of the Republican campaign of **family values** in 1992, the movement suffered a serious setback with the subsequent defeat of the party in the presidential elections.

RIGHT-WING

A general term for ideologies or political standpoints including **conservatism**, the **New Right** and, in some interpretations, **fascism**. The term originates from the National Assembly of Revolutionary France in which more conservative elements (the nobility and clergy) sat on the right, and more radical elements on the left (hence **left-wing**). Some of the key characteristics associated with the right are a defence of **capitalism** and private property, respect for authority, whether of the state or of tradition, and opposition to **socialism** and **communism**.

RIO GROUP *see* GROUP OF RIO

RIO SUMMIT *see* EARTH SUMMIT

RIO TREATY

An inter-American defence pact. Officially named the Inter-American Treaty on Reciprocal Assistance, it was signed in 1947 by all American states except Nicaragua and Ecuador (who acceded in 1948 and 1950 respectively). Cuba left in 1960, while Trinidad and Tobago joined in 1967 and the Bahamas in 1982. It is based on the mutual defence principle of the **Act of Chapultepec** and states that members should not resort to force and that any disputes should only be referred to the **UN** if they cannot be settled within the organization. Further terms provide for mutual assistance in the case of armed attack within the region, and consultation if the attack were outside the region or in the case of aggression other than armed attack within the region. In 1975 a protocol was approved which extends the Treaty's terms to **OAS** member countries. The treaty has been applied most notably in territorial disputes between neighbouring countries, in civil wars (Guatemala in 1954 and Dominican Republic in 1965) and the attempted invasion of Panama in 1959.

RIVERS OF BLOOD

The controversial speech made by UK Conservative MP Enoch Powell on 20 April 1968 in which he warned of what he saw as the social and economic consequences of continued immigration into the UK of black people from the Commonwealth. The speech was made shortly after the rapid enactment of the Commonwealth Immigrants Act 1968 and also as the Race Relations Bill 1968 was about to be considered in Parliament. Urging drastic limitation of black Commonwealth immigration and the encouragement of voluntary repatriation, Powell said that as he looked ahead he was filled with foreboding, and that like the Roman, he seemed to see 'the River Tiber foaming with much blood'. As a result of this cataclysmic speech Powell was dismissed from the Conservative Party's shadow cabinet.

RIVONIA TRIAL

The trial in South Africa in 1963–4 at which Nelson Mandela and seven others were sentenced to life imprisonment. Liliesleaf Farm in Rivonia, near Johannesburg, was where police had discovered the headquarters of **MK**, the **ANC's** armed wing. Mandela (who was already serving a five-year prison term), Walter Sisulu, Govan Mbeki, Raymond Mhlaba, Ahmed Kathrada, Elias Motsoaledi, Andrew Mlangeni and two whites, Lionel Bernstein and Denis Goldberg, were charged with sabotage and conspiring to cause violent revolution – capital offences. The trial lasted from October 1963 until June 1964, capturing worldwide attention and prompting the **UN Security Council** to urge its abandonment. The accused did not so much deny the charges as explain that they had been forced to resort to violent means of change since peaceful protest had proved fruitless. Mandela made his now famous address from the dock in which he said: 'I have cherished the ideal of a democratic and free society in which all persons live together in harmony and with equal opportunities. It is an ideal which I hope to live for and to achieve. But, if needs be, it is an ideal for which I am prepared to die.' All the defendants except Bernstein were found guilty, and all but Goldberg were sent to **Robben Island**.

ROBBEN ISLAND

A bleak, rocky outcrop off the coast of South Africa, within sight of Cape Town, the site of the notorious maximum security prison where opponents of the **apartheid** regime were imprisoned. **ANC** leader Nelson Mandela and others convicted in the **Rivonia trial** were sent to the Island in 1964. Hundreds of other political and criminal offenders from South Africa and **Namibia** were also held there in extremely harsh conditions, forced to work in lime quarries or gather and process seaweed from the surrounding icy waters. Robben Island is also an important environmental site, with distinctive marine life, bird colonies and vegetation. There are plans to close the prison by 1995–6 and develop the island as a tourist attraction, including the conversion of the prison into a museum.

ROE v. WADE

The landmark 1973 Supreme Court decision which made abortion legal in the USA. The case arose from a challenge by Jane Roe (a Texan woman whose true name was withheld) to a state law which made abortion a crime except in the case of needing to save the potential mother's life. The Court supported the challenge, judging that the law constituted an interference with the right to privacy as guaranteed by the Constitution. Although not specifically guaranteed, the right to privacy was inferred by the Court as a result of the 'zones of privacy' guaranteed within the **Bill of Rights**. The ruling had the effect of overturning abortion laws throughout the country. Although partially undermined in the 1980s and early 1990s as a result of the Court becoming more conservative, the ruling has continued to provide the basis for legal abortions in the USA.

ROGERNOMICS

A derogatory term for the economic strategy implemented in New Zealand under Labour governments in the 1980s, named after Roger Douglas who was Finance Minister in 1984–8. Rogernomics was based on extensive deregulation and privatization policies accompanied by the removal of money supply controls, and won praise internationally for achieving spectacular growth in the mid-1980s. By the end of the decade, however, the growth boom had ended and New Zealand was left with a legacy of stagnation, inflation, high interest rates, and a widening gap between rich and poor. Rogernomics opened the way in the early 1990s for the Nationalist Party's Ruth Richardson to pursue even more ruthlessly the dismantling of New Zealand's **welfare state**, once a pioneer of its type in the world.

ROMANIES OF EASTERN EUROPE

The (Gypsy) community spread throughout **Central Europe**, **Eastern Europe** and the **Balkans**, and particularly Romania. Nomadic Romanies are descended from Indian tribes who migrated to Europe in about AD 1300. Many have retained their nomadic existence and speak a dialect derived in part from sanskrit. There is a history of mutual antagonism between Romanies and various majority communities; an estimated 400,000 Romanies were killed in the Nazi **genocide**, and discrimination and prejudice continues. Figures are unreliable, but the Romany parliament, established in 1992 has claimed that there are some 10 million Romanies in Europe. Unemployment and poverty are high in the Romany community, and rates of literacy generally low.

ROME TREATY

The Treaty of Rome signed on 25 March 1957 by Belgium, France, Italy, Luxembourg, the Netherlands and West Germany, which created the European Economic Community (**EEC**), the forerunner of the **EC** and **EU**. The Treaty of Rome was the culmination of ideas discussed at the **Messina Conference**. It established a common external tariff, abolished internal trade tariffs, and created an internal free market in labour, capital, goods and services. Strictly speaking there were two treaties signed at the same time in Rome, the EEC Treaty and a separate **Euratom** Treaty which set up the European Atomic Energy Community.

RONDAS CAMPESINAS

(Spanish, 'peasant patrols') Peruvian peasant self-defence patrols used in a **counter-insurgency** drive against **left-wing guerrillas**. The first *rondas* sprang up in the 1970s in the northern Andes with the aim of halting cattle thefts. In the early 1980s the army promoted similar patrols in the southern Ayacucho area in order to create the impression that there was a popular drive against **Sendero Luminoso** guerrillas. Atrocities by the guerrillas against peasant communities, especially in the late 1980s, forced villages throughout zones of conflict to form their own independent *rondas*.

THE ROSENBERGS

A US couple, Julius and Ethel, who were executed for having allegedly supplied the **Soviet Union** with atom bomb secrets. The couple were arrested in 1950, largely upon the testimony of self-confessed Soviet agents who co-operated with the authorities in return for leniency. Although there was little firm evidence against the couple, their trial was held at the height of the **Cold War** and the anti-**communist** paranoia associated with **McCarthyism**. Marred by bias, the trial ended with the couple being condemned to death in March 1951. Despite a series of appeals, stays of execution, pleas for mercy and public demonstrations, they were electrocuted in Sing Sing prison on 19 June 1953.

ROSTOCK RIOTS

The disturbances in the eastern German town of Rostock in August 1992, directed against foreign nationals seeking asylum in Germany. Hundreds of **right-wing** youths attacked a reception centre for asylum-seekers, stoning it on successive nights and setting fire to it on 25 August. Some local German residents applauded the rioters; the State Interior Minister expressed 'a certain understanding' for them, and local police were criticized afterwards for showing insufficient resolve in confronting them. Although 15,000 people rallied in Rostock on 29 August to protest at the riots, the incident dramatically illustrated both the rise of right-wing extremism and violence and the scale of social problems confronted by eastern Germany.

ROTE ARMEE FRAKTION

(German, 'Red Army Faction') A **left-wing** German revolutionary group most active in the 1970s, effectively as the continuation of the **Baader-Meinhof** group. The RAF was noted for the murder of industrialists, bank raids to fund its operations and attacks on military installations. The West German government responded with increased security measures and surveillance, including the notorious **Berufsverbot** policy. Many RAF members were arrested, but sporadic attacks continued in the 1980s. In June 1990 the arrest of nine RAF suspects in East Germany brought to public attention the involvement of the East German **Stasi** police in helping them to evade capture.

ROUND TABLE AGREEMENT

An agreement following multi-party talks, and particularly the agreement struck in Poland in April 1989 by the **communist** government of Gen. Wojciech Jaruzelski and the 'constructive opposition'. Key elements in this were re-legalization of the opposition **Solidarity** movement, and the calling of partially free elections (in which the opposition was entitled to compete for 35 per cent of seats). The Round Table agreement marked the end of the Communist Party's monopoly on power in Poland and was the first evidence of the dramatic collapse of communism in **Eastern Europe**.

RPF

Rwandan Patriotic Front – the **Tutsi**-dominated rebel group which launched a civil war against the government of President Juvénal Habyarimana in October 1990. A peace agreement between the two sides signed in August 1993 provided for the establishment of a multiparty transitional government and legislature in the period leading to multiparty democratic elections. However, little progress had been made in the implementation of this agreement by April 1994, when Habyarimana was killed in a plane crash. His death unleashed terrible violence as supporters of his military regime, unhappy at the prospect of sharing power with the RPF, sought to eliminate all opponents to their hold on power. In mid-April the RPF announced the resumption of its military activity to stop the killings of innocent people and to restore peace to the country. Having made steady advances, on 18 July the RPF claimed victory after taking the last government stronghold. It declared a ceasefire as the remnants of the government army fled to Zaïre. The following day a RPF-dominated coalition government was sworn in.

RSS

(Hindi acronym for *Rashtriya Swayemsevak Sangh* – 'National Union of Selfless Servants') An extremist Hindu organization founded in 1925 in Nagpur, India, by Keshar Baliram Hedgewar. It concentrates on recruiting young men and women as volunteers (*swayemsevaks*) dedicated to the creation of a Hindu nation (*Hindu rashtra*). Banned in 1948 after its involvement in the assassination of Mahatma Gandhi, it resurfaced as a political force in alliance with **right-wing** parties in the 1950s. Its profile in recent years has been raised through co-operation with the pro-Hindu **BJP**, along with which it was implicated in the destruction of the **Ayodhya mosque** in December 1992.

RUBICON SPEECH

The speech given by South African State President P. W. Botha to the Natal congress of the ruling National Party on 15 August 1985, three weeks after an indefinite state of emergency had been declared in the most populous areas of the country. It was widely expected that Botha would announce genuine reform of the **apartheid** system. However, refusing to 'cross the Rubicon' and enter a new phase in the country's history, he merely reiterated reform plans which were already discredited, and rejected demands for universal suffrage, maintaining that it would lead to the domination of one group by another. With no prospects of change, those demanding **sanctions** stepped up their campaign.

RUKH

(Ukrainian, 'movement') **Ukraine's** moderate nationalist opposition movement, formally established in September 1989, when Ukraine was still one of the **Soviet Union's** 15 constituent republics. *Rukh* rapidly attracted a membership of at least 300,000 by calling for the restoration of Ukrainian linguistic and cultural traditions. In elections in March 1990 it was by far the largest of the non-**communist** parties. Since Ukraine's independence in late 1991, *Rukh* has campaigned against membership of the **CIS**, but in elections in April 1994 it performed poorly outside western Ukraine.

RUN-OFF

The final (second or subsequent) round of an election, used where no candidate has achieved an absolute majority in the previous round. In the run-off, the electorate is required to choose between the two highest-placed contestants.

RUSHDIE AFFAIR *see* SATANIC VERSES

RUSSIAN FEDERATION (RUSSIA)

Russia's official name (including the parenthesis) since December 1991, when it replaced the Russian Soviet Federated Socialist Republic, which had been the largest republic of the **Soviet Union**. Russia has assumed the Soviet mantle as a regional **superpower**, applying pressure through the **CIS** to re-create a sphere of influence in the **near abroad**, which is home to an estimated 20 million ethnic Russians.

RUST BELT

A term used to refer to areas of industrial decline, particularly the industrial states of the US **Midwest** which have experienced a steady erosion in their heavy manufacturing base in recent years.

RWANDA

A central Africa country which gained independence in July 1962. In the late nineteenth century Rwanda, with **Burundi**, fell under German control when they were known as Ruanda-Urundi. During the First World War, the Germans were driven out by Belgian forces and in 1919 the two territories were mandated to Belgium by the League of Nations.

The death of President Juvénal Habyarimana on 6 April 1994 unleashed genocidal levels of violence in Rwanda with up to 1 million people killed and 2.5 million displaced within three months. Although generally presented as a tribal conflict, with the majority **Hutu** inflicting mindless violence on the minority **Tutsi**, the violence was essentially politically motivated; supporters of Habyarimana's military regime were seeking to eliminate all opposition to its hold on power.

RWANDAN PATRIOTIC FRONT *see* RPF

S&L SCANDAL

The US scandal arising from the devastating collapse in the late 1980s of many Savings and Loans (also known as Thrifts), the main US mechanism for funding home mortgages. The regulations which restricted the investment activities of S&Ls were largely removed during the administration of President Ronald Reagan. Many people then made imprudent loans and investments, or were fraudulently looted by their own executives, with the result that hundreds became insolvent. The full extent of the scandal began to emerge in 1989, and the Resolution Trust Corporation was established as a mechanism for the federal government to rescue ailing and bankrupt S&Ls. In December 1992 the total cost of the bailout was estimated at $130,000 million by outgoing Treasury Secretary Nicholas F. Brady.

SAARC

The South Asian Association for Regional Co-Operation. An economic alliance founded in 1985 to promote economic cooperation between the seven independent states of South Asia, namely **Bangladesh**, Bhutan, India, Maldives, Nepal, **Pakistan** and **Sri Lanka**. Its most notable economic achievements to date have been the conclusion of a **South Asian Preferential Trade Agreement** and successful mediation in the conflict between Nepal and Bhutan over the issue of Bhutanese refugees in Nepal. However, the organization remains vulnerable to latent tensions arising from members' misgivings over India's dominant role in the region.

SABRA AND CHATILA

Refugee camps in West Beirut where up to 1,000 Palestinian civilians were massacred by gunmen on 16 September 1982 during **Israel's** invasion of Lebanon. While no group claimed responsibility for the massacre, blame has been widely attributed to **Phalange** militiamen controlled by Elie Hubayqah (Lebanese Minister of State for Social Affairs and the Handicapped since October 1992) and members of the Haddad militia (precursor of the **SLA**) led by Maj. Saad Haddad. However, in the immediate aftermath debate focused on the possibility of Israeli collusion in, or responsibility for, the atrocity. An official Israeli inquiry into the massacre (the Kahan inquiry) placed direct responsibility for the actual massacre on the Lebanese Phalangists. At the same time, the report found that certain Israeli political and military leaders bore varying degrees of indirect responsibility for its occurrence. Particular criticism was directed at the Defence Minister, Ariel Sharon, for having taken the decision to allow the Phalangists to enter the camps without direct Israeli supervision, in the light of which Sharon resigned from the Cabinet.

SACEUR

The Supreme Allied Commander Europe, designated by the USA to head the NATO forces in Europe, who also serves concurrently as Commander-in-Chief of US forces in Europe.

SADC

The Southern African Development Community, a grouping of states to harmonize economic policy and regional trade liberalization. Its members are Angola, **Botswana**, **Lesotho**, **Malawi**, Mozambique, **Namibia**, Swaziland, **Tanzania**, **Zambia** and **Zimbabwe**. It was founded in August 1992 when it replaced the Southern African Development Co-ordination Conference (SADCC). Leaders of the member states, recognizing the changed regional political situation, indicated that South Africa would be invited to join once a democratically elected government was in place. However, they acknowledged the need to safeguard against South African economic domination. Officials envisaged the eventual creation of a regional parliament and a peacekeeping force, and hoped that member states would ultimately adopt unified defence and foreign policies.

SADF

The South African Defence Force, the collective name of the armed forces during the **apartheid** period. It consisted of a core of permanent personnel, who represented about 10 per cent of the total force, plus white conscripts, and a number of black volunteers. All white males over the age of 18 were subject to conscription, and having completed their initial service were subject to recall at any time until the age of 55. Despite being termed a 'defence' force, the SADF was habitually used to invade and destabilize the **frontline states**. As part of the transition to democracy the SADF has been replaced by the South Africa National Defence Force (SANDF), drawing its personnel from the SADF, the armed forces of the 'independent' **bantustans**, the **MK** – the armed wing of the **ANC** – and other similar groups. It is expected that the integration process will take three years.

SADR

The Saharan Arab Democratic Republic, the independent state proclaimed in the disputed **Western Sahara** by the **Polisario Front** in February 1976. By the time that the SADR was admitted to the **OAU** in 1982 it had been recognized by over 70 countries.

SAF

The structural adjustment facility, an **IMF** facility – financed from special funds – which was introduced in 1986 to provide balance of payments assistance on concessional terms to low-income developing countries. SAF loans are provided to support medium-term (generally three-year) structural adjustment programmes, which are supposed to help members to establish the conditions for sustainable growth, to strengthen their balance of payments positions, and to facilitate relations with creditors and a reduction in trade and payments restrictions. The enhanced structural adjustment facility (ESAF) was introduced in 1987, with a larger pool of resources and designed to cover more ambitious programmes. The life of the ESAF was renewed in December 1993, and in early 1994 the number of countries eligible for ESAF assistance was increased to 78.

SAFE HAVEN

A zone declared inviolable by the **UN** to protect civilians in a war situation. In the wake of the **Gulf War** and the ensuing Iraqi offensive against **Kurdish guerrillas** in northern Iraq, a safe haven defended by allied troops was declared there in April 1991. Six 'safe areas' were also declared in **Bosnia-Hercegovina** in May 1993 to protect **Bosnian Muslim** civilians encircled by Serb forces, but the UN policy was humiliated by continued Serb bombardment of the safe areas and by the invasion of one of them, Gorazde, in April 1994.

SAGAWA KYUBIN SCANDAL

A Japanese political scandal which became public in 1992, involving huge payments to Japanese politicians by a transport firm which also had links with the organized criminal syndicates of the **Yakuza**. The firm at the centre of the scandal was Tokyo Sagawa Kyubin, the largest regional affiliate in the Kyoto-based Sagawa Kyubin group, Japan's second-largest parcel delivery firm. The most prominent victim of the scandal was Shin Kanemaru, who was forced to resign as vice-president of the Liberal Democratic Party (LDP) in August 1992, and who was arrested on charges of evading tax payments on illicit political donations in March of the following year. The scandal, one of a series involving the **money politics** system associated with the LDP, intensified the pressure for wholesale political reform. The ruling party's failure to deliver this led to a series of splits in June 1993, and to a general election in July when it was ejected from office for the first time since its formation in 1955.

SAHEL

(Arabic, 'edge', 'border' or 'coast') The belt of land 120 to 180 miles (190 to 290 km) wide between the Sahara Desert and the savannah to the south, stretching across North Africa from Mauritania in the west to Ethiopia in the east. It has intermittent rainfall and contains low scrub and grasses. Its thinly scattered population of nomadic people have in recent years been joined by herdspeople and farmers (who cultivate areas with higher than average rainfall), resulting in the overgrazing and overfarming of the area and making the population susceptible to famine as a result of drought.

SAIRI

The Supreme Assembly of the **Islamic revolution** in Iraq – the most important Iraqi **Shia** opposition party, led by Ayatollah Sayyid Muhammad Baqer al-Hakim, which was established in exile in Tehran on 7 November 1982. Dominated by pro-Iranian Islamic clerics (*ulama*), it is committed to the creation of an Islamic state in Iraq and acts as an umbrella for several similarly oriented dissident Iraqi Shia groups operating from Iran, Syria and Lebanon. In March 1991 it led a massive Shia rebellion in southern Iraq which was crushed by the Iraqi regime.

SAJUDIS

The Lithuanian Restructuring Movement, a conservative-**nationalist** party, formally founded in October 1988. *Sajudis* Chair Vytautas Landsbergis was elected as Supreme Council Chair (ex officio President of **Lithuania**) in March 1990 and guided his country to independence in September 1991. *Sajudis* was, however, defeated by the former **communist** Democratic Party of Labour in legislative elections in November 1992.

SALAMI TACTICS

The postwar strategy of the Hungarian **communist** party under Matyas Rakosi. Formally part of a broad coalition government from 1945, the communists eliminated their rivals one by one, like slicing down a salami sausage. Smallholders' leader Bela Kovacs was arrested in February 1947; Prime Minister Ferenc Nagy was driven into exile in May 1947; weaker parties were dissolved, including the Social Democrats in June 1948; the Smallholders president Zoltan Tildy was replaced in July 1948; the Democratic Populists were dissolved in December 1948; and rigged elections in May 1949 returned a communist-dominated parliament. Amid a climate of terror, Rakosi's potential rival for the communist leadership, Laszlo Rajk, was executed in October 1949 after a **show trial**.

SALT

The Strategic Arms Limitation Talks, held between the two **superpowers** between 1969 and 1979. The first round, SALT I, in 1969–72, produced the important 1972 treaty limiting **ABM** systems, and another accord on limiting each side's overall number of ballistic missiles (both **ICBMs** and **SLBMs**), but without agreement on how to account for multiple warheads (**MIRVs**). The second phase, SALT II, began with the Washington summit of 1973. At this meeting Richard Nixon and Leonid Brezhnev set out an agenda for moving from **arms control** – the stage involving weapons classifications and ceilings – on to the actual **START** arms reduction process. Although the talks became bogged down in the complexities of the MIRV issue, the climate of

detente was restored by the new US President Jimmy Carter (1977–81) and his decision to halt development of the **neutron bomb** and long-range B-1 bomber. A SALT II treaty was concluded and signed by Carter and Brezhnev in Vienna on 18 June 1979 (after which the SALT talks were renamed START), but the Soviet intervention in the **Afghan War** destroyed any prospect of its being ratified by the US Senate. Carter's successor Ronald Reagan never resubmitted it for ratification, although both the USA and the **Soviet Union** agreed informally to conform to its provisions. (These involved limiting missile launchers to 2,400 each, of which 1,320 could be fitted with MIRVs up to a specified number of warheads. The modernisation of missiles was constrained by limiting each side to one new light ICBM.)

SAM

A surface-to-air missile, a general term encompassing such weapons as **NATO's** Hawk and **Sidewinder**, the **Patriot** missile used against Iraqi **Scud** missiles in the **Gulf War**, and any missile, whether heat-seeking or otherwise guided, which is fired from ground to air; the smaller SAMs include a variety of hand-held weapons such as may be used by **guerrillas** against aircraft.

SAMIZDAT

(Russian, 'self-publishing') The illegal publication of 'subversive' literature, the origins of which lay in the activities of a group of Moscow poets in the early 1960s.

SAN FRANCISCO CONFERENCE

The international conference held in San Francisco, USA, in April–June 1945, at the end of which participants signed the **UN** Charter. The conference was attended by delegates from 51 countries, comprising 47 fully independent states, **Byelarus** (then Byelorussia) and **Ukraine** (which were constituent republics of the **Soviet Union**), and India and the Philippines (which had not at that stage achieved full independence from Britain and the USA respectively).

SAN JOSÉ GROUP

A loose organization of Central American countries, whose aim is to restore stability and economic prosperity in the region. It originated in the January 1988 Central American summit in San José and was updated in October 1993 when the presidents of Costa Rica, El Salvador, Guatemala, Honduras, Nicaragua and Panama signed the Guatemala protocol forming an economic union which was to be 'voluntary, complementary and gradual'. The San José Group has been receiving development aid, US$25 million in 1993, from the **EC** in return for closer co-operation and the consolidation of human rights and democracy.

SANCTIONS

Measures taken by one country, or by groups of countries, to put pressure on an illegal regime or on another country deemed guilty of unacceptable behaviour. The term was first introduced in 1919 in the constitution of the League of Nations (the precursor of the **UN**). The League instituted, but could not enforce, sanctions against Italy in 1936 following its invasion of Abyssinia. More recent examples of sanctions include those levied by the USA against Cuba (from 1960), Nicaragua (in 1985–90), and the military regime in Haiti (since 1991). UN mandatory sanctions include trade restrictions placed on Rhodesia in 1966 in the wake of **UDI**, oil and arms embargoes on **apartheid** South Africa, comprehensive sanctions placed on Iraq after its 1990 invasion of Kuwait and maintained after the **Gulf War**, and sanctions against **Yugoslavia**. The effectiveness of sanctions may be undermined by lack of commitment in carrying them out, by weaknesses in their enforcement, and by **sanctions-busting** such as that exposed by the **Bingham report** in the case of Rhodesia.

SANCTIONS-BUSTING

Covert evasion of trade restrictions, both by a country subject to **sanctions**, and by its suppliers. Evidence of sanctions-busting operations to supply the **UDI** government of Rhodesia was revealed by the 1978 **Bingham report**. It is widely assumed that similar operations supplied the **apartheid** regime in South Africa. Sanctions-busting has latterly detracted from the effectiveness of sanctions against **Yugoslavia** and Haiti.

SANDINISTAS

Members of the **left-wing** Nicaraguan Sandinista National Liberation Front (FSLN) named in honour of Augusto César Sandino, the leader of a small peasant army that waged a **guerrilla** campaign (1926–33) against the US occupation of Nicaragua. The FSLN, founded in 1961, combined radical Christian, Marxist and **nationalist** currents into a popular movement enjoying widespread support which triumphed in the civil war (1978–79) to overthrew the US-backed Somoza dictatorship. In power the FSLN encouraged popular participation in the construction of a new society and faced US sanctions and US-backed **right-wing contras** despite holding free elections in 1984 and promoting a mixed economy. Economic crisis and shock stabilization programmes in the late 1980s made the FSLN government of President Daniel Ortega unpopular, and it lost the 1990 elections. A subsequent split, setting hardliners, critical of political support for the right-wing UNO government, against a social democratic wing, remains to be healed.

SANDZAK

A region of the Yugoslav Republic of Serbia with a considerable Muslim community. Sandzak, which is located at the conjunction of the Bosnian, Serbian and Montenegrin borders, was the site of bitter inter-ethnic conflict during the Second World War, and is a potential location for renewed intercommunal violence in the former **Yugoslavia**. The stability of the region depends in part on whether Sandzak Muslims press to join the planned Muslim-Croat Bosnian Federation and on the nature of any plan for a **Greater Serbia**.

SANROC

The South African Non-Racial Olympic Committee, the organization established in the early 1960s with the aim of ensuring the isolation of **apartheid** South Africa in the sports arena – a mission it accomplished, with other anti-apartheid groups, with almost total effectiveness. SANROC was replaced by the South African Olympic Committee in July 1991 when, following political developments in South Africa, the country was readmitted to the International Olympic Committee.

SANTO REBELLION

The secession attempt in February 1980 by Espirito Santo, the main island of **Vanuatu**, on the granting of independence to Vanuatu. The rebellion, led by Jimmy Stevens, was supported by the country's minority francophone population, but was suppressed in August by troops sent from Papua New Guinea at the request of Vanuatu's government.

SARAJEVO SIEGE

The encirclement and bombardment of Sarajevo, the capital of **Bosnia-Hercegovina**, by Bosnian Serb forces in 1992–4. The siege, which began in May 1992, was one of the first acts of the war in Bosnia-Hercegovina; it followed a March 1992 referendum which had overwhelmingly endorsed Bosnian independence. During the siege the Bosnian Serb Army used sniper fire and indiscriminate shelling in a bid to terrorize Sarajevo's citizens and to apply pressure to the (majority-**Muslim**) Bosnian government. As the siege progressed, conditions in the city worsened, with shortages of electricity, food, water and medical supplies. **UN** aid flights, which began in July 1992, and the arrival of 6,000 UN peacekeepers in Bosnia-Hercegovina in autumn 1992 alleviated conditions. The siege continued despite the designation of Sarajevo in May 1993 as one of six UN **safe areas**. Only in February 1994 did the international community take decisive action, prompted by outrage over a mortar attack which killed up to 68 civilians in a market place. The situation dramatically improved when Bosnian Serb forces were threatened with massive air strikes if they failed to withdraw from a 20-km exclusion zone around Sarajevo.

SARVODYA MOVEMENT

(Hindi, 'welfare for all') An Indian variant of traditional agrarian socialism inspired by the Indian nationalist leader Mahatma Gandhi. It was developed in the 1960s by Gandhi's follower Vinoba Bhave, regarded by many as Gandhi's spiritual heir. Renouncing a life of personal comfort in favour of selflessness, service and spiritual purity, Bhave journeyed throughout India persuading landowners, and sometimes whole villages, to donate land for the landless and give themselves to co-operative community service. After his death, Bhave's mission was continued by his disciple, Jayaprakash Narayan.

THE SATANIC VERSES

The novel by the Muslim-born British author, Salman Rushdie, published in September 1988. Variously regarded as a tale of migration and religious mythology, it became the subject of a worldwide controversy after Muslims claimed that it had blasphemed the Prophet Muhammad. The allegation triggered violent protests across the Muslim world where governments ordered the book to be banned. Muslims in North America and Europe, notably the UK, also agitated, unsuccessfully, for the book to be banned.

The novel's symbolic status as the embodiment of free speech against the tyranny of religious doctrine was finally enshrined in February 1989 when the Ayatollah Ruhollah Khomeini of Iran pronounced a **fatwa** which judged the book blasphemous and sentenced Rushdie to death for apostasy. The Iranian government was reported shortly afterwards to have despatched assassination squads abroad to implement the verdict. Rushdie obtained the official protection of the British government and has lived in hiding since February 1989. His efforts and those of his supporters to persuade world governments to impose sanctions on Iran to force it to rescind the *fatwa* have so far met with little success.

SATELLITE STATES *see* CLIENT STATES

SATURDAY NIGHT MASSACRE

One of the key events in the **Watergate** scandal, and the catalyst for Congress to begin considering the impeachment proceedings against US President Richard Nixon which led to his resignation in 1974. On Saturday 20 October 1973, Nixon ordered Attorney General Elliot Richardson to dismiss the Watergate special prosecutor Archibald Cox because of his insistence on access to key tapes of Nixon's **White House** conversations. Richardson, who refused on the grounds that such a move was inconsistent with his pledge to the Senate of an independent investigation, resigned. Deputy Attorney General William Ruckelshaus, who also refused to execute the command, was dismissed, and Nixon then promoted Solicitor General Robert Bork to the position of acting Attorney General. Although Bork dismissed Cox, the incident terminally damaged Nixon both in the eyes of Congress and the press.

SAVAK

(Persian acronym for *Sazman-e-Ettelat 'at va Amniyat-e-Keshvar* 'Security and Information Organization') The now defunct Iranian security service established in 1957 with the assistance of the USA and **Israeli** intelligence services. Used to crush political opposition to Mohammad Reza Shah Pahlavi, it was said at the height of its power in the mid-1970s to employ some 20,000 people and rely on a further 18,000 to act as informers. It was dismantled by the Shah's government in December 1979 as a final desperate move to halt the advance of the Islamic revolution.

SAVE THE CHILDREN

The largest international voluntary agency in the UK, which works with deprived children both in the UK and in some 50 underdeveloped countries. It engages both in disaster relief and in long-term development projects, focusing on children's rights.

SCANDINAVIA

The peninsula in north-western Europe, divided between Norway in the western part and Sweden in the east. In an historical sense, the term also applies to Denmark and Iceland. These four countries, with Finland, comprise the **Nordic Countries**.

SCARMAN REPORT

The report of a public inquiry into the April 1981 **Brixton riots** in the UK. Lord Scarman, a law lord, was appointed to carry out the public inquiry into the disorders. His report was published in November 1981. Scarman identified the causes of the riots as a breakdown in relations between the police and the community, unemployment and social deprivation, racial disadvantage, and a rising level of street crime. His recommendations covered not only direct matters (such as police accountability and the law on **racist** marches) but also more general aspects of the problems facing inner-city areas, including housing and education, with special reference to the needs of ethnic minorities.

SCHENGEN GROUP

The nine countries within the **EU** which are party to the Schengen Agreement on abolishing border controls between their territories while improving police co-operation. The original group which met in Schengen in Luxembourg in June 1985 consisted of the **Benelux** countries, France and West Germany. Their draft agreement was held up in 1989, but signed in June 1990 when the Germans had persuaded the others that it should incorporate East Germany. The other EU members joined the agreement with the exception of Denmark, Ireland and the UK (which remained concerned about removing checks against terrorists, weapons, drug traffickers and animals with rabies). The agreement was finally ratified to take effect from December 1993, but removal of passport controls was further delayed, with France still worried that the liberal Dutch attitude on drugs would provide a weak link for dealers to penetrate the whole region.

SCHUMAN PLAN

The idea advanced on 9 May 1950 which, in expanded form, lay at the origin of the **ECSC**. French Foreign Minister Robert Schuman's proposal envisaged that a supranational body to control coal and steel production in France and Germany would promote European integration while making conflict between France and Germany 'materially impossible'.

SCORCHED EARTH

A **counterinsurgency** operation in which crops are burned, villages destroyed and the local population forced to flee. An example of the implementation of a scorched earth policy was that ordered in highland Guatemala during 1982–3 by Gen. Efraín Ríos Montt, a born again **fundamentalist** Protestant Christian and head of a three-man military **junta**. Unbridled savagery was used to clear the mainly Indian population out of areas where **URNG guerrillas** received widespread support.

SCOTT AFFAIR *see* THORPE CASE

SCOTT INQUIRY

The 1993–4 inquiry into UK defence-related exports to Iraq. The inquiry under Lord Justice Scott was set up following the collapse of the **Matrix Churchill** trial, although the inquiry's terms of reference included the **supergun** and other defence and dual-use sales. Much of the inquiry focused on whether the government had relaxed the arms embargo on Iraq without informing Parliament, and on the controversial use of **gagging orders** designed to prevent confidential information being revealed in court. Prime Minister John Major was called to give evidence, as were his predecessor Baroness Thatcher and various senior Cabinet ministers and civil servants. The main public hearings of the inquiry formally ended on 30 March 1994.

SCUD

The surface-to-surface missile latterly notorious for its use by Iraq during the **Gulf War**, when a few dozen were fired at **Israel** and a similar number at allied forces in Saudi Arabia. The Scud was originally a Soviet-made missile derived from German wartime V-2 technology. Iraq used two modified versions, reducing the size of the warhead but doubling and even tripling the original range up to a maximum of nearly 550 miles (900 km). The damage they caused was very limited; many fell short or off-target, or were destroyed by **Patriot** anti-aircraft missiles; but the psychological impact in Israel was considerable, and allied aircraft had great difficulty in locating and destroying mobile Iraqi scud launchers.

SDECE *see* DGSE

SDI *see* STAR WARS

SDR

The special drawing right, the international reserve asset created by the **IMF** and allocated to members to supplement their existing reserve assets. SDRs were established under amendments to the IMF Articles of Agreement effective 1969, and by 1993 amounted to 2 per cent of members' total non-gold reserves. The SDR is also the unit of account of the IMF. It was originally valued in relation to the US dollar but is now determined daily on the basis of a basket of the US, German, French, Japanese and UK currencies. The IMF has the authority to create unconditional liquidity by allocating SDRs to members and other participants. The last such general allocation took place in 1981.

SDS

Students for a Democratic Society, the radical US group founded in 1960 from the student section of the League of Industrial Democracy. The SDS was committed to challenging the US state through non-violent but not necessarily legal means. An integral part of the **New Left**, and in the forefront of the student protest movement against the **Vietnam War**, it reached the peak of its strength in 1968–9 when it was estimated to have between 60,000 and 100,000 members and a local chapter on almost every US campus. Thereafter, riven by ideological feuds and fissures, the movement declined rapidly.

SEABED TREATY

An **arms control** agreement opened for signature at the **UN** in 1971 banning the placement of **nuclear weapons** and other weapons of mass destruction on the seabed outside a coastal state's **territorial waters**, which it specified as being up to 12 nautical miles offshore. It was signed and ratified by the USA and the **Soviet Union** (neither **superpower** was planning to place weapons on the seabed), by the UK and by most non-nuclear weapons states, but not by China or France.

SEATO

South-East Asia Treaty Organization. A pro-Western military alliance established in 1955 by the signatories of the South East Asia Collective Defence Treaty, which included Australia, France, New Zealand, **Pakistan**, the Philippines, Thailand, the UK and the USA. Designed as an instrument of the **Cold War** to contain the influence of **communism** in **south-east Asia**, the alliance fell into gradual disarray amid disagreement over the merits of US involvement in **Indo-China** in the 1960s. SEATO was formally dissolved on 30 June 1977; the Defence Treaty remained in force until at least January 1980.

SECOND WORLD

The formerly **socialist** countries of Central and **Eastern Europe** and the **Soviet Union**. The term was a construct of the **Cold War**, and the disintegration of the Soviet bloc since **1989** has somewhat altered its meaning. The countries of the Second World, however, remain less prosperous than those of the **First World**.

SECONDARY PICKETING

Industrial action taking the form of picketing at a workplace not directly involved with a trade dispute in order to encourage its workers to strike, as well as to disrupt work and increase pressure on employers to settle the dispute. In the UK secondary picketing was largely banned under the Employment Act 1980 (which also effectively placed limits on the number of people allowed on any one picket) and under subsequent legislation. During the 1984–5 **miners' strike** the use of '**flying pickets**' and secondary action became a major issue between the National Union of Mineworkers and the government.

SECRET SPEECH

Soviet leader Nikita Khrushchev's seminal speech to a closed session of the 20th party congress of the **CPSU** in February 1956, attacking Stalin's legacy. Khrushchev argued that the **'cult of personality'** attached to Stalin had given rise to 'grave perversions of party principles, of party democracy, of revolutionary legality'. The Secret Speech began a process of **de-Stalinization**, which was delayed in **Eastern Europe**, however, by the **Hungarian uprising** later in the year.

SECURITATE

Communist Romania's security police, which mounted a brutal defence of the regime of Nicolae Ceausescu during the December 1989 revolution. The Securitate was an elite organization which offered significant privileges to its agents in an impoverished society. Under Ceausescu the Securitate supervised a network of tens of thousands of paid informants in all walks of life, and effectively prevented open dissent.

SECURITY ZONE

The **Israeli**-controlled belt of southern Lebanon which forms a physical and military hurdle between Lebanon and northern Israel. Israel announced the creation of the zone in June 1985, almost three years after Israeli troops had launched a mass invasion of Lebanon in implementation of the so-called **Operation Peace for Galilee**. Since its creation the 6–12 mile (10–20 km) 'security zone' has been patrolled jointly by the Israeli army and its proxy militia, the South Lebanon Army (**SLA**). Lebanese-based Palestinian and Lebanese **guerrillas** have fought constantly with Israeli and SLA forces both in and around the edges of the zone. In recent years **Hezbollah** has emerged as the most potent of the anti-Israeli forces operating in the area. All Arab parties involved in the **Middle East** peace process, and particularly Syria, have maintained that an Israeli-Lebanese peace accord would not be feasible without an Israeli withdrawal from the zone.

SEGREGATION

A policy pursued in the US **South** whereby blacks were denied access to a wide range of facilities reserved for whites. Although the different provision for the two races was notionally 'separate but equal', in reality the facilities open to black citizens were of inferior standard. Segregation covered most aspects of everyday life, including public transport, housing, education and recreational facilities, and was applied in the US armed forces until the 1950s. Together with measures to prevent most blacks from exercising the right to vote, the system of segregation ensured that blacks were treated as second-class citizens for 100 year after the abolition of slavery in the USA. The dismantling of segregation in the 1950s and 1960s followed legal challenges and direct action by the **civil rights movement**, and was reflected in legislation passed by the federal government.

SEJM

The lower house of the Polish National Assembly comprising 460 directly elected members. The term was also used to describe Poland's unicameral legislature during the **Communist** period.

SELA

The Latin American Economic System, a consulting and co-ordinating body founded in October 1975 by **Latin American** and **Caribbean** countries with the aim of accelerating joint economic and social development. Spain joined in 1979. The Latin American Council, SELA's main decision-making body, meets annually and dominant issues include economic relations with the USA, Latin American debt and joint marketing of regional commodities. SELA obtained **UN** observer status in 1980.

SELF-IMMOLATION

A method of political protest in which protestor burns him- or herself to death in public. One of the most famous examples occurred in June 1963 when Thich Quang Duc, a 73-year-old Vietnamese Buddhist monk, burned himself to death in a public square in **Saigon** in protest at the South Vietnamese government's refusal to meet the demands of Buddhist demonstrators. Although during the years that followed many more monks and nuns burned themselves to death, the photographs of Thich Quang Duc's self-immolation were those which provided one of the most potent images of the **Vietnam War**. The **Czechoslovak** student Jan Palach also became an icon of protest by his self-immolation in **Wenceslas Square** in 1969.

SELLAFIELD

A **nuclear reprocessing** and waste management site in Cumbria, UK, known until 1971 as **Windscale**, which includes Calder Hall power plant. Opponents of the Sellafield plant claim that radiation from it has caused cancers among the workforce, health problems in the surrounding area, and leukaemia in the children of men who work at Sellafield. A new type of reprocessing plant at Sellafield, known as **Thorp**, was finally approved and began functioning in March 1994 having been delayed for many years by protests from environmental groups.

SELOUS SCOUTS

The elite Rhodesian army unit which specialized in counterinsurgency operations against the liberation movements fighting for black majority rule during the period of **UDI**. The unit was responsible for raids on the refugee camps in Chimoio in Mozambique in November 1977 in which 1,000 Zimbabwean refugees were killed; it was officially disbanded in 1980 when **Zimbabwe** gained independence.

SEMTEX

A malleable, odourless plastic explosive, widely used by terrorist organizations. Its name is derived from Semtin, the town in the **Czech Republic** where it was manufactured, and 'explosive'. In March 1991, the Czechoslovak President Vaclav Havel revealed that over 1,000 tonnes of Semtex had been exported from **Czechoslovakia** to Libya by the previous regime – sufficient explosive to supply 'world terrorism' for '150 years'. Havel hinted that the exports had been made not for profit, but on the orders of the Soviet government.

SENDERO LUMINOSO

(Spanish, 'Shining Path') A Peruvian **Maoist guerrilla** group founded in 1970 as a result of a split in the Peruvian **Communist** Party. Led by Abimael Guzmán Reynoso, a professor of philosophy, the group favours a return to the Inca system of co-operative agriculture, an aim which it maintains can be achieved by a prolonged **people's war** for the control of the countryside followed by the capitulation of urban centres of power. After years of preparations, *Sendero Luminoso* initiated an armed struggle in May 1980 in the southern Andes, carrying out kidnappings and sabotage and attacks on security forces and **rondas campesinas**. Their actions spread to bombings in the capital Lima and activity in central jungle areas where they raised funds by offering protection to drug traffickers. Guzmán was captured in September 1992 and sentenced to death; this sentence was later commuted to life imprisonment. Since then he has sent three letters of surrender to the government. By 1993–4 the group was divided between those in prison (Black Sendero) and those still active (Red Sendero), thought to be incapable of large scale co-ordinated actions.

SENEGAMBIA

The shortlived confederation between Senegal and The Gambia. Plans for the Confederation were announced on 19 August 1981 in the wake of an armed rising in The Gambia, which raised Senegalese fears of instability in its neighbour. The Confederation was founded on 1 February 1982 and provided for a supranational parliament and executive, joint military forces, and an eventual economic union. The President of Senegal was named as Confederation President, with the Gambian Head of State as Vice-President. By the late 1980s there were signs of deteriorating relations between two countries. In August 1989 President Abdou Diouf of Senegal withdrew troops from The Gambia without consultation, and in the following month he declared that the Confederation had failed and was not worth continuing. It was formally dissolved at the end of September 1989.

SEPARATE DEVELOPMENT

A euphemism for **apartheid** adopted by advocates of the system, although the term pre-dates apartheid. As early as 1913 separate development was used as a justification for the imposition of the Native Land Act, which enforced the territorial marginalization of the black majority.

SERETSE KHAMA AFFAIR

The connivance of the British colonial authorities and the white minority regimes in South Africa and **Rhodesia** to deny Seretse Khama the chieftainship of the Bamangwato tribe in **Botswana** (then the British protectorate of Bechualand). In 1948 Seretse Khama had married a white woman (Ruth Williams) while pursuing his legal career in London. The marriage was opposed by his uncle and regent, Tshekedi Khama, as well as by the South African and Rhodesian governments, which feared the political consequences of a mixed marriage on their borders. Under considerable pressure, in 1950 the British decided to exile Seretse Khama. He was allowed to return in 1956 after he renounced the chieftainship. However, he had widespread popular support among the Bamangwato and no other chief was appointed. Seretse Khama thus enjoyed all the traditional power of a chief while being free to act within the modern political system. In 1965 his Botswana Democratic Party won the pre-independence elections and at independence in 1966 he became President, a position he held until his death in 1980.

SETTLEMENTS

Jewish communities established in the **Israeli-occupied territories**. Jewish settlers, *yishuv*, built the base on which the state of Israel was constructed in 1948. After the 1967 **Six-Day War** successive Israeli governments viewed the captured Arab land as a legitimate extension of the state of Israel and as part of the creation of the wider biblical state of **Eretz Israel**. Hence, during the 1970s and 1980s, Israel initiated a massive drive to establish civilian and military settlements throughout the territories. In the late 1980s, the drive to settle large numbers of Russian immigrants checked progress towards a Middle East peace conference. The new Labour government which came to power in 1992 froze new settlement, but existing ones remained in place even under the terms of the 1993 **Gaza-Jericho First** peace deal between Israel and the **PLO**.

17TH PARALLEL

The demarcation line between North and South Vietnam. The **Geneva Agreements** of July 1954, which followed the French defeat by North Vietnam at **Dien Bien Phu** some two months earlier, temporarily divided Vietnam at the 17th parallel into two zones. The Agreements provided that the country should be reunited following a general election in July 1956. However, all North Vietnamese proposals for the holding of elections were rejected by the South, and the country remained divided into a **communist** North and a US-sponsored South until the fall of the southern regime in 1975. Formal reunification, under the name of the Socialist Republic of Vietnam, was proclaimed in July 1976.

SEVESO

A town north of Milan, Italy, the scene in 1976 of one of Europe's worst industrial pollution disasters, which then gave rise to a waste disposal scandal. An explosion on 10 July 1976 at the Icmesa chemical plant, owned by the Swiss company Hoffman LaRoche, released a cloud of **dioxin** with the immediate consequence that 193 cases of severe chloracne were registered, and with unknown wider and longer-term health implications. The accident led in 1982 to the **EC** Seveso Directive, intended to prevent such disasters in future, and in September 1983 five executives of the company were sentenced to between two and a half and five years' imprisonment for violating safety regulations. Most of the residue from the accident was buried on the site of the dismantled factory, but reports persisted about secret waste disposal deals. In November 1993 the German government agreed to support efforts to trace 41 canisters of waste from Seveso which were allegedly buried secretly by the East German government in return for payment from Hoffman LaRoche.

SEXISM

Discrimination on the grounds of gender, with women almost invariably losing out to men. Sexism is based on the assumption, sometimes unconscious, that one sex is superior to another. It is vehemently challenged by **feminism**. Sexists also insist on conformity with the traditional stereotyping of social roles on the basis of gender. Attempts to counter sexism have included **affirmative action**.

SEXUAL HARASSMENT

Unwanted sexual advances, usually, but not exclusively, made by men to women. Those in the workplace tend to involve a relationship of unequal status between the parties, for example, sexual favours demanded in return for pro- motion. The US Equal Employment Opportunities Commission issued figures indicating that charges of sexual harassment in the USA almost doubled between 1981 and 1989.

SEXUAL REVOLUTION

The liberalization of established social and moral attitudes to sex which began in the **West** at least in the mid- to late-1960s. During this period the impact of **women's lib**, the increasing number of economically independent women and the general introduction of the oral contraceptive pill combined to allow women in particular to reassess their attitudes to sex and marriage.

SEZ

Special economic zones, the regions established in China in which special tax, import and export conditions apply. The establishment of the SEZs was intended to encourage foreign investment by overseas Chinese, and they have tended to be located on the south-east coast. The establishment of the first three SEZs in Guangdong province was approved by the National People's Congress in August 1980, since when they have proliferated.

SHAH BANO CASE

The legal case giving rise to a landmark Indian Supreme Court judgment in April 1986 which appeared to overrule **sharia law** (Islamic law) by granting maintenance rights to a divorced Muslim woman, Begum Shah Bano, under the Indian Criminal Procedure Code. The verdict triggered fierce opposition from traditional Muslims who regarded it as an attempt to abolish currently enforced Islamic principles in the domain of Muslim personal law. The protest led the government in May 1986 to approve the Muslim Women (Protection of Rights on Divorce) Act, allowing Muslim women to appeal to the Muslim religious endowment, or **waqf**, for compensation equal to the sum received by a Hindu woman.

SHANGHAI COMMUNIQUE

The document issued jointly by the USA and China in Shanghai following talks between Chinese Premier Zhou Enlai and US President Richard Nixon at the conclusion of the latter's historic visit to China in February 1972. In the communiqué, which served as the basis for the establishment of formal diplomatic relations between the two countries in 1979, China and the USA recognized 'essential differences' in their social and political systems while agreeing to conduct future relations on the basis of the **Five Principles of Coexistence**. On the **Taiwan** question, China reaffirmed its position that Taiwan was a province of China, that its 'liberation' was an internal affair and that therefore all US forces and military installations should be withdrawn from Taiwan. The USA acknowledged the oneness of China, reaffirmed its interest in a peaceful settlement of the Taiwan question and affirmed its 'ultimate objective' of the withdrawal of all its forces and military installations from Taiwan.

SHAPE

The Supreme Headquarters Allied Powers Europe, the **NATO** military headquarters of Allied Command Europe (one of the three NATO allied commands, the others being Allied Command Channel, with its HQ in Northwood near London, and Allied Command Atlantic, with its HQ in Norfolk, Virginia). SHAPE was moved from Paris to near Mons in Belgium in 1967, after de Gaulle's decision to withdraw

France from the NATO military command structure.

SHARIA LAW

The canonical law of Islam as prescribed in the Koran and the *Sunnah* (the spoken and acted example of the Prophet Muhammad). Derived from the Arabic *shara'a* (to enact or prescribe), its interpretation has been the subject of numerous schools of law acknowledged variously by the **Shia** and **Sunni** sects of Islam. The application of sharia law is the main objective of **Islamization** programmes currently pursued by some Muslim governments. It is the dominant legal system in Saudi Arabia and some **Gulf** states; a Sharia Bill enforcing Islamic law was passed in Pakistan in May 1991. Its application in many Muslim countries remains uneven, with some forcing it to co-exist with European legal codes, and others choosing to relegate it to the domain of family and religious law. The application of sharia law in Sudan in 1983 was a major factor in the start of rebel activities by the **SPLA**. The Sudanese government has since exempted the southern states, where most of the Christian population live, from sharia law.

SHARPEVILLE

A South African **township** 50 miles (80 km) from Johannesburg, where on 21 March 1960 the police killed 69 demonstrators protesting peacefully against the hated **pass laws**; most were shot in the back as they tried to flee. A further 180 people were injured. A state of emergency was declared, mass arrests were made and on 5 April the **ANC** and **PAC**, the two main anti-apartheid organizations, were declared unlawful. The international community condemned the shootings and the **UN Security Council** called for the abandonment of **apartheid**.

SHATALIN PLAN *see* 500 DAYS PLAN

SHERPAS

A fanciful usage derived from the use of 'summit' to denote a top-level international meeting. The 'sherpas' are the senior officials whose support work makes the achievement of the summit possible, but who, like the real sherpas (skilled Nepalese guides in the Himalayas), leave the limelight to others.

SHIA

(Arabic, 'faction' or 'party') Members of the minority sect of Islam. Also known as the Shi'ites, they make up some 10 per cent of all Muslims. Their forerunners broke away from the majority **Sunni** branch immediately after the death of the Prophet Muhammad in 632 AD. The Shia themselves are divided into three major different branches, the **Twelvers** which has the largest number of adherents; the Zaydis; and the Ismailis. Shi'ism is professed by a majority of the population in Iran, where the Twelver branch has been the official religion since the sixteenth century. A majority of Iraqis also adhere to Shi'ism, as do small minorities in several Muslim countries in Asia and the **Middle East**.

SHIN BET

The **Israeli** internal security agency, also known as the General Security Service.

SHINING PATH *see* SENDERO LUMINOSO

SHOCK THERAPY

A policy of rapid transition from a **command economy** to a market-based economy, which in the short term imposes economic and social hardship in pursuit of medium- to long-term gains. Poland's **Balcerowicz plan** is a noted example of shock therapy.

SHOOT TO KILL

The pejorative term used to describe a policy that undercover and other security forces in **Northern Ireland** were accused of pursuing, especially in the early 1980s. The allegation was that they would deliberately seek to shoot **IRA** members and other republican sympathizers dead rather than aiming to maim. In 1988 the UK government decided not to take any further action on the allegations of a shoot to kill policy, which were being investigated by the Stalker inquiry. In the same year, similar accusations were made over the 'Death on the Rock' incident, when three IRA members were killed by the security forces in Gibraltar, although a subsequent inquest returned a verdict of lawful killing.

SHORT SHARP SHOCK

A system designed to discourage criminal behaviour, especially among persistent juvenile offenders, through a harsh regime at special detention centres. In the UK the scheme was tried for a while in the early 1980s, and following examination of 'shock incarceration' 'boot camps' in the USA the reintroduction of a parallel scheme as part of the UK government's plans to deter young non-violent offenders is scheduled under the Criminal Justice and Public Order Act 1994.

SHOW TRIAL

Prosecutions for political reasons, with ritual humiliation of the accused and their conviction on spurious charges, often based on false confessions. Show trials serve as an instrument of state terror designed to discourage dissent and to discredit the opposition. Show trials played a significant role in the **Stalinist** regimes of Eastern Europe in the early 1950s, where they were used to discredit **communist** party officials with any suspect associations, as well as democrats and nationalists.

SIBERIA

The vast and sparsely populated region of Russia east of the Urals, rich in minerals and natural resources but with an inhospitable climate, where many of the **gulags** of the **Soviet Union** were located.

SICARIOS

(Spanish, 'paid killers') Teenage male assassins from poor neighbourhoods in Colombia. The first *sicarios* appeared in the late 1970s in confrontations between rival drug clans, but as the state cracked down on drugs they graduated to assassinating policemen and judges. They also targeted newspaper editors, trade union leaders and politicians, and were responsible for the assassination in April 1990 of **M-19** presidential candidate Carlos Pizarro Léongómez. Most of the new breed were hired by the **Medellín cartel** from youth gangs in the city where the fantasy of wealth from drugs, mingled with the daily routine of drug-related killings, made them particularly fearless.

SIDESHOW

The term often used to describe the locality and predicament of Cambodia during the **Vietnam War**. The expression refers to the fact that during the 1960s and early 1970s US military involvement in Cambodia was a largely secret adjunct to the greater conflict under way in Vietnam. William Shawcross, in his book on US policy towards Cambodia in the 1960s and 1970s, *Sideshow*, says of the term: 'Journalists who covered the war there used the term with irony; in Washington DC some officials employed it almost as a matter of policy.'

SIDS

Small Island Developing States, seen as particularly vulnerable on environmental issues. The first international conference on SIDS, in Barbados in April–May 1994, lobbied for the fulfilment of promises made at the 1992 **Earth Summit**; the SIDS can also deploy 20 per cent of the vote in the **UN General Assembly**. Among their acute environmental problems are species loss, pollution from toxic waste, and depletion of fishing grounds, while several of them face complete obliteration if **global warming** causes ocean levels to rise.

SIERRA CLUB

Probably the world's first environmental pressure group, formed in 1892 in the USA by naturalist John Muir. The club took its name from Muir's book *My First Summer in the Sierra*, which described a camping trip in 1869 and elaborated such concepts as environmental conservation and the importance of ecosystems. These ideas were later taken up by environmental pressure groups such as **Friends of the Earth** and **Greenpeace**. The Sierra Club currently has some 600,000 members, campaigning for the preservation of the North American Sierras and of comparable regions worldwide.

SILENT MAJORITY

A phrase used to denote those who are neither vocal nor politically active, who are regarded by adherents of **conservatism** as a repository of moderate, sober values. It is argued that the silent majority is invariably overshadowed by vociferous extremists. The phrase, whose original poetic meaning was the dead as opposed to the living, was used by US President Richard Nixon on 3 November 1969, in an attack upon opponents of the **Vietnam War**. 'If a vocal minority, however fervent its cause, prevails over reason, this nation has no future as a free society . . . . And so tonight to you, the great silent majority of my fellow Americans, I ask for your support'.

SILENT SPRING

A key text in the development of the environmental movement, published in 1962 by US biologist and ecologist Rachel Carson, which described the harmful effects of synthetic pesticides on ecosystems. *Silent Spring* cited over 600 research papers to back its indictment of 23 pesticides widely used in agriculture. The use of all but nine of these substances, the best-known of which was **DDT**, has since been banned in industrialized countries.

SIMÓN BOLIVAR NATIONAL GUERRILLA CO-ORDINATING BOARD

A **left-wing** alliance of **guerrilla** groups in Colombia, founded in 1987 and bringing together the **FARC** guerrillas, **M-19**, the National Liberation Army (ELN) and the Popular Liberation Army (EPL).

SIMONSTOWN AGREEMENT

The agreement made in 1955 between South Africa and the UK under which the Royal Navy relinquished control of the Simonstown naval base, near Cape Town, to the South African Navy but was allowed to continue using its facilities and maintain a headquarters there. The agreement preserved and enhanced the Royal Navy's position in the South Atlantic and Indian Ocean, but was a target of anti-**apartheid** campaigns against military contact with the South African regime. The agreement was terminated by the UK Labour Government in 1975.

SINAI

The Egyptian desert peninsular and point of Arab-**Israeli** conflict. The Sinai was occupied by Israel in 1956–57 and again in 1967 after its triumph in the **Six-Day War**. Following the 1973 **Yom Kippur War**, new Egyptian and Israeli lines were established on either side of a **UN** buffer zone. Under the terms of the 1979 Israeli-Egyptian peace accord a large proportion of the Sinai was returned to Egypt by 1982.

SINATRA DOCTRINE

A colloquial name for the policy which allowed **Warsaw Pact** countries to determine their own course of development, as the hard-line **communist** regimes in eastern Europe began collapsing in late **1989**. Soviet Foreign Ministry spokesman Gennady Gerasimov, speaking in October 1989 on US television, evoked it in the words of the song made famous by the US singer Frank Sinatra, *My Way*. The 'Sinatra doctrine' recognized the absolute right of each state to determine its own socio-political development. It represented the antithesis of the **Brezhnev doctrine** under which the **Soviet Union** had previously reserved the right to intervene militarily in any allied country where **socialism** was perceived to be under threat of being overturned.

SINGLE EUROPEAN ACT

A package of revisions to the **EC** treaties, worked out in the mid-1980s, signed in February 1986, and implemented, once all the member states had ratified it, from July 1987. Setting out the objective of making 'concrete progress towards European unity', it introduced institutional changes, with more qualified majority voting in place of a requirement for unanimity in the **Council of Ministers** and more involvement for the **European Parliament**. It also set out specific policies, with commitments on creating the **single market**, on 'economic and social cohesion', on research and technology, on environmental protection, and, most controversially, on **EMU** or economic and monetary union. A separate section (Title III) contained an intergovernmental agreement on European political co-operation, to encourage cohesive foreign policies among member states and to promote consultation and joint policy-making and implementation.

SINGLE MARKET

A term widely used in the **EU** in the run-up to **1992**, after which there were to be no physical, technical or fiscal barriers to the free movement of goods, services, capital and labour among the 12 member states, creating a single internal market of over 320 million people. The single market programme, implemented under the **Single European Act**, also included a **Social Charter** with guarantees on workers' rights.

SINGLE-MEMBER CONSTITUENCY

The basic unit of an electoral system on the UK or US model. The candidate may be elected by **simple plurality** under the **first past the post** system, or an absolute majority may be required. In the latter case, an initial round of voting with several candidates may have to be followed by a **run-off**. The single-member constituency system is linked with the doctrine that parliamentarians are accountable to the particular interests of the local electorate. This view has been eroded, however, by the development of the party system, and the importance of national rather than individual constituency campaigns in the age of the mass media. The proponents of **PR** stigmatize the single-member constituency system as unfair in that the composition of the resulting parliament will not reflect the proportion of the vote cast nationwide, often to the disadvantage of smaller parties.

SINGLE TRANSFERABLE VOTE

A voting mechanism (sometimes abbreviated to stv) which takes account not only of voters' first choices, but also of their preferences as between less attractive options. The voter chooses options in order of preference. Instead of allocating points to each option, and adopting the option with the best score, the stv process involves a laborious count, concentrating initially on totalling the first preference votes. Thereafter, the procedure varies in different versions of stv. In one version, the option with the fewest first preference votes is eliminated; those ballot papers are then attributed to their second choice; the votes are recounted, and this process is repeated until one option has an overall majority. The variant used in **Northern Ireland** for elections to the **European Parliament** applies stv in one three-member constituency, reallocating the 'surplus votes' for successful candidates rather than reattributing the votes for the least successful.

SINN FÉIN

(Gaelic, 'Ourselves alone') One of the most prominent revolutionary parties fighting initially for the republican independence of Ireland, and, since partition, for the reunification of the country, north and south of the border. *Sinn Féin* was represented in the Irish **Dáil** in 1957–61. In 1969 *Sinn Féin* split, as did its military wing, the **IRA**. One part became *Sinn Féin*-The Workers' Party (later just Workers' Party), which had representation in the Irish **Dáil** between 1981 and 1992, while the other retained the name *Sinn Féin*. The latter had representation in the UK House of Commons from 1981 to 1992, Owen Carron being first elected as anti-**H Block** and Gerry Adams, *Sinn Féin* president, being elected in 1983 and 1987 but not taking up his seat). The organization is also represented on a number of local councils in **Northern Ireland**. Although not proscribed either in the UK or Ireland, *Sinn Féin* has because of its association with the IRA experienced a number of sanctions against its participation in public life. In 1993 its leadership entered into partly clandestine discussions with the UK government, but as of July 1994 had held back from endorsement of the Anglo-Irish **Downing Street Declaration** of December 1993.

SINO-SOVIET SPLIT

The rift between the two largest powers in the **communist** world from 1960 onwards. Its origins lay in the emergence of differences between the Chinese and Soviet Communist Parties (the CCP and **CPSU**), and Chinese criticism of Soviet rapprochement with the **Western** powers, which Mao Zedong regarded as a 'revisionist' policy towards 'imperialism'. The **Soviet Union** reacted to this criticism by halting aid to China. The Soviet signature of the 1963 nuclear test ban treaty caused a further deterioration in Sino-Soviet relations, as did the Chinese **Cultural Revolution** of 1966–9. The split culminated in armed clashes between guards along the eastern part of the Sino-Soviet border in 1969. A formal end to hostility came only in May 1989, when Mikhail Gorbachev became the first Soviet leader to visit Beijing since Nikita Khrushchev in September–October 1959. State and party relations were normalized on 16 May in talks between Gorbachev and Deng Xiaoping which addressed the 'three obstacles' (the Soviet Union's support for Vietnamese troops in Kampuchea in December 1978, the Soviet invasion of Afghanistan a year later, and the presence of Soviet troops in Mongolia). Gorbachev's visit, however, was overshadowed by the student pro-democracy demonstrations in **Tiananmen Square**.

SIPRI

The Stockholm International Peace Research Institute, an independent research institute, founded in 1966 to celebrate 150 years of Sweden's being at peace, and funded principally by the Swedish government. SIPRI produces research on the **arms race**, the arms trade, disarmament and **arms control**. By working only with published data, it avoids the restrictions imposed by considerations of security and confidentiality.

SIS *see* MI6

SIT-IN

A form of mass protest used in the US **civil rights movement**. The term originated as a description of a protest launched in February 1960 against **segregation** in the **South**, whereby blacks sat at lunch-counters reserved for white customers and demanded to be served. The scope of the protest was later expanded to cover other segregated facilities including libraries, beaches, and public transport. Many of those arrested for participating in sit-ins accepted prison sentences rather than pay fines. Supported in the northern states by economic boycotts of those commercial organizations which maintained segregated facilities, the sit-in movement was effective in forcing desegregation in many areas. The term sit-in later came to denote the occupation of any site as a form of protest, and was particularly associated with student radicalism from the 1960s onwards.

SITUATION ROOM

A room in the basement of the **White House** used by **NSC** personnel and others during international crises.

THE SIX

In the jargon of European integration, the original six members of the **ECSC** in 1952 and the **EEC** in 1958, namely France, West Germany, Italy and the **Benelux** countries. Progressive enlargement of the European Communities (**EC**) had taken it from the Six to the Twelve by 1986.

SIX COUNTIES

The six counties comprising **Northern Ireland** and forming part of the **United Kingdom**. At the time of partition of Ireland the Irish Free State, created in 1922, consisted of **26 counties** and Northern Ireland (under the Government of Ireland Act 1920) the remaining six (Antrim, Armagh, Down, Fermanagh, Londonderry and Tyrone). Although the term **Ulster** is commonly used to denote Northern Ireland, three of the counties of the province of Ulster (Cavan, Donegal and Monaghan) remained within the Free State (and now in the Republic of Ireland).

SIX-DAY WAR

The June 1967 Arab-**Israeli** war. Following months of rising tension in the region and with Arab forces mobilizing their armies, Israel carried out a series of devastating pre-emptive air strikes against Egypt, Jordan, Syria and Iraq early on 5 June. With the benefit of complete air supremacy, Israeli forces achieved a swift and complete victory. By the time hostilities ended in a ceasefire on 10 June Israel had captured the **Sinai** peninsular and **Gaza Strip** from Egypt, the Old City of **Jerusalem** and the **West Bank** from Jordan and the **Golan Heights** from Syria. As a result of the Six-Day War, Israel almost tripled the land under its control and increased the number of Palestinian Arabs under its rule from 300,000 to around 1.2 million.

SIZEWELL

The site in Suffolk on the east coast of England where the UK's first **PWR**-type nuclear power station has been built, known as Sizewell B (Sizewell A is a **Magnox** reactor). Due to reach full operating capacity in February 1995, in April 1994 its opening was delayed to allow studies balancing the need for the plant with the danger of pollution from its routine radioactive discharges. The controversial Sizewell B project, originally intended as the first in a new generation of UK nuclear power stations, had been approved after a protracted public inquiry which ended in 1988. Plans for Sizewell C, which would double the capacity of Sizewell B and replace six existing ageing nuclear power stations, were submitted to the government by Nuclear Electric in October 1993.

SKOPJE *see* MACEDONIA

SKYBOLT

A long-range airborne ballistic missile which the UK ordered from the USA following the collapse of its own **Blue Streak** project in 1960. In early 1963 the USA itself cancelled the Skybolt project after disappointing performances in initial test flights. At their **Nassau conference** in the Bahamas in December 1962 Prime Minister Harold Macmillan and President John Kennedy agreed that in place of Skybolt the UK should purchase the submarine-launched **Polaris** missile to which it would attach its own nuclear warheads.

SKYTRAIN

An innovative low-cost transatlantic air service operated by Laker Airways in the late 1970s and early 1980s. Freddie Laker applied in the early 1970s for a licence to operate a scheduled service for which advance reservation would not be necessary, and in the face of considerable UK government opposition the airline was eventually in 1977 allowed 'dual designation' under the **Bermuda Convention**. Flights started in September of that year, but Laker Airways subsequently ran into financial difficulties and collapsed in 1982.

SLAVONIC

Pertaining to the language or culture of Slavs. Most. but not all, of the peoples of **Central Europe** and **Eastern Europe** are Slav-speakers; they include Poles, Czechs, Slovaks, Slovenes, Croats, Serbs, Macedonians (of the former **Yugoslavia**), Bulgarians, Russians, Ukrainians, and Byelarussians. Some Slavonic languages are closely related, as for instance Bulgarian and Serb; linguistic differences have sometimes been exaggerated for political reasons, in order more emphatically to assert the distinct nationhood of one group in relation to another. Non-Slav ethnic groups in central and eastern Europe and the former **Soviet Union** include Lithuanians, Latvians, Estonians, Hungarians, Romanians, and Albanians; the peoples of the **Transcaucasus** and **Central Asia**; and various minority groups including the **Romanies of Eastern Europe** and the Crimean Tatars.

SLBM

Submarine-launched ballistic missile. SLBMs with nuclear warheads, starting with the **Polaris** missiles deployed by the USA from 1960, were the third and easiest to protect in the 'triad' of strategic or intercontinental weapons, together with long-range bombers and **ICBMs**.

SLEAZE FACTOR

A term dramatizing criticism of ethical standards during the administration of US President Ronald Reagan, 1981–9. 'The sleaze factor' was a chapter title in L. Barret's 1983 book *Gambling with History*, and the sentiment it evoked was widely used against Reagan in the 1984 election campaign.

SLORC

The State Law and Order Restoration Council – the ruling military junta in Burma. The SLORC took power in September 1988 after a long period of anti-government protests had rendered the country virtually ungovernable. Since then the SLORC has maintained a firm grip on the levers of power and has refused to relinquish authority despite the overwhelming victory in elections held in 1990 of Aung San Suu Kyi's mainly civilian National League for Democracy. In the past few years Gen. Khin Nyunt, the country's intelligence chief and a protegé of ageing strongman Ne Win, has emerged as the most prominent member of the SLORC.

SLOVAKIA

The **Central European** republic which became an independent state with the division of **Czechoslovakia** in the **velvet divorce** of January 1992. It is confronted with the problem of its ethnic minorities, including a restive, 500,000-strong community of Hungarians (some 10 per cent of the population) in the south.

SLOVENIA

A small mountainous state in **Central Europe**. Slovenia was part of **Yugoslavia**, and one of its most prosperous and Westernized republics, until June 1991, when it declared independence. There was fierce fighting in June–July 1991, as units of the Yugoslav National Army (JNA) entered Slovenia from bases in neighbouring Croatia, but Slovene units successfully resisted this invasion. International recognition came in January 1992, and Slovenia has taken no further military part in the Yugoslav civil war.

SMALL IS BEAUTIFUL

The title of a book published in 1973 by Ernst Schumacher, which became a slogan of environmentalists in their campaign against the mass industrial society and its wasteful use of resources. The book, subtitled '*A Study of Economics as if People Mattered*', criticized industrialism for losing sight of the spiritual aspect in human lives.

SMALL ISLAND DEVELOPING STATES *see* SIDS

SMART WEAPONS

Weapons which use 'intelligent' guidance systems, including laser technology, to avoid interception and home in on targets. This expression caught the imagination of weapons enthusiasts in early 1991, when the **Gulf War** gave the US-led allies an opportunity to demonstrate the sophistication of their equipment. However, initial reports seem to have over-estimated their hit-rate rather badly on this occasion.

SMITHSONIAN AGREEMENT

An agreement reached in New York on 17–18 December 1971 by the finance ministers and central bank governors of the **G-10** countries, which signalled the beginning of the break-up of the international monetary conventions in operation since the end of the Second World War. In the months before the Smithsonian meeting, foreign exchange markets had suffered serious disruption, and in August 1971 the USA had suspended the convertibility of the US dollar for gold, a serious blow to the **gold standard**. The meeting reached agreement on three main points. The US dollar was to be devalued against gold (from $35 to $38 per ounce). Wider exchange rate fluctuations were to be allowed for G-10 country currencies, up to 2.25 per cent above or below par rather than just 1.0 per cent. Finally, discussions should begin promptly, especially within the **IMF** framework, to consider reform of the international monetary system over the longer term.

SMOKING GUN

An incriminating piece of evidence which ties a person (usually a senior politician) to a crime, often one actually committed by underlings. The term arose from the

Watergate scandal where it was used to identify one of the subpoenaed **White House** tapes. On this smoking gun tape, of 23 June 1972, President Richard Nixon was heard directing his aides to demand that the **CIA** intervene to impede the **FBI** investigation of Watergate. Since then it has been applied to other scandals involving US presidents, most notably to the **Iran-contra affair**, where the absence of a smoking gun ensured the political survival of Ronald Reagan.

SNAKE IN THE TUNNEL

The **EC** currency arrangement adopted in 1972, following the **Smithsonian agreement** of December 1971. The Smithsonian agreement had established 2.25 per cent margins of fluctuation above and below fixed exchange rates. The EC countries (i.e. the **Six**) agreed in March 1972 that within this 'tunnel' or framework, the maximum permitted gap between the currencies of any two EC member states should not exceed 2.25 per cent, thus creating a form of joint community float, or 'snake'. Moreover, the three **Benelux** countries operated a 'worm within the snake' of a maximum mutual divergence of 1.5 per cent. The four countries which were at that time applicants to join the EC (Denmark, Ireland, Norway and the UK) associated themselves with the 'snake'. A few months later, however, the UK was forced to withdraw from the arrangement, and sterling floated independently, together with the Irish punt. The French franc was withdrawn from the snake arrangements in March 1976. The snake was more formally superseded by the **EMS** effective March 1979.

SOCIAL CHAPTER

The section in the original draft of the **Maastricht** treaty which covered social rights (and particularly workers' rights), intended to be applied across the **EU**. The UK Conservative government strongly resisted the inclusion of the social chapter, having already made its position clear by **opting out** over the 1989 **Social Charter** which embodied essentially the same ideas. In the eventual denouement, at the Maastricht summit on the night of 10–11 December 1991, the other 11 member countries agreed to omit the social chapter from the treaty itself. Instead they confirmed their 'desire to continue down the path indicated by the Social Charter', and added a social policy annex to the treaty which would enable them to do this through Community institutions for application in their respective countries.

SOCIAL CHARTER

The 'Community charter of fundamental social rights', approved by the **EU** at a **European Council** meeting in December 1989, but with the UK **opting out**. The charter, drafted by the **Commission** under the presidency of Jacques Delors, was regarded by UK Prime Minister Margaret Thatcher as a '**socialist** charter'. Its proposals included guarantees on workers' rights to union membership, to information and consultation, and to decent wages and health and safety standards at work – much of which was carried forward into the **Social Chapter** of the **Maastricht** Treaty.

SOCIAL CLEANSING *see* DISPOSABLES

SOCIAL CONTRACT

An agreement between the UK Labour government and the **TUC** in the mid-1970s concerning social and economic policy. The concept had its origins in a document agreed between the TUC and the Labour Party (then in opposition) in January 1973, which set out the economic policy to be followed by a future Labour government. It was then embodied in a set of TUC guidelines in June 1974 describing the factors which were expected to be taken into account in wage negotiations. This 'contract', involving voluntary wage restraint within a form of **incomes policy**, was extended with certain adjustments in successive years, but collapsed in 1978 in the context of the approaching **winter of discontent** with its serious industrial conflict.

SOCIAL CREDIT

An economic idea, and a political force strongest in western Canada. Social credit is based on the underconsumptionist economic analysis of British engineer Maj. C.

H. Douglas (1879–1952), who advocated the periodic distribution of money or 'social credit' to increase public purchasing power. This simple but coherent idea was well received in many **capitalist** countries during the severe economic depression of the 1930s. In Canada, the Social Credit Party came to power in Alberta in 1935 and remained in government until 1971, while in British Columbia it governed in 1952–72 and 1975–91. In both provinces, however, there was little attempt to implement the fundamentals of the Social Credit doctrine, as in practice the party tended to pursue a course of fiscal conservatism combined with provincial development schemes.

SOCIAL DEMOCRACY

A strand of evolutionary **socialism**, which found full expression in **Western European** countries in the post-war period. Social democratic parties emerged in the late nineteenth century, pursuing power through constitutional means with the object of enacting reforms to ameliorate the worst excesses of **capitalism**. This approach was strengthened by a widening of the franchise, and by revulsion from the violence of revolutionary socialism as exemplified by the Bolshevik Revolution in Russia.

In government, the policies of social democratic parties have included the creation of an extensive welfare state, the pursuit of full employment through **Keynesian** economics, the nationalization of key industries, and the erosion of class privileges through progressive taxation and educational reform. While it became the political orthodoxy of many Western European countries, in the 1970s social democracy became associated with **stagflation** and lack of political vision, and in the 1980s was largely eclipsed by the **New Right**.

SOCIALISM

A broad ideology whose principal feature is opposition to private ownership of the means of production on the grounds that it leads to the exploitation of labour by capital. In order to overcome this, socialism posits the public or state ownership of the means of production. Originating in the nineteenth century, the ideology had roots in preindustrial experiments in communal ownership and social reorganization, philosophically derived from New Testament Christianity. Modern socialism evolved, like **liberalism**, from the humanist values of the Enlightenment of the eighteenth century, and grew in response to the massive social dislocation and emergence of an impoverished working class associated with the Industrial Revolution.

There developed two distinct strands of socialism, which may be distinguished as evolutionary and revolutionary in their approach to overcoming the evils of **capitalism**. The evolutionary approach, attacked by Marxists as 'revisionist', ranged from experiments in benign paternalism to the advocacy of reformist legislation by **social democratic** parties. In the post-war period, this led to the creation throughout **Western Europe** of extensive **welfare state** systems, and the widespread nationalization of industries.

The tradition of revolutionary socialism was dominated by the thinking of Karl Marx. For Marx, socialism was a transitional stage between capitalism and full **communism**, and was characterized by social ownership of the means of production. This was seen as a necessary step prior to the withering away of the state and complete common ownership. Political parties claiming adherence to this tradition, however, and often called communist rather than socialist, have been associated when in power with a highly developed system of state and party control in the **command economies** of countries such as the **Soviet Union** and, after 1945, **Eastern Europe** and the **PRC**.

SOCIALISM WITH A HUMAN FACE

A slogan associated especially with Alexander Dubcek and the reformist leadership of the **Communist** Party of **Czechoslovakia** in the **Prague Spring** of 1968. Without challenging the leading role of the communist party, socialism with a human face broke with the authoritarianism of the **Stalinist** era and sought to mobilize society in support of its aims. It espoused greater freedom of speech, democratization of the party, and a form of pluralism, insofar as groups were encouraged to promote the interests of their members.

SOCIALIST INTERNATIONAL

An organization uniting over 60 major **socialist** and **social democratic** parties worldwide, founded in mid-1951 at a congress in Frankfurt. Its precursors were the Second International (1889–1914) and the Labour and Socialist International (1923–40), the non-**communist** alternative to the Third International. The Socialist International, commonly abbreviated to SI, has recently attempted to expand its non-European membership, particularly under the presidency (from 1976) of former West German Chancellor Willy Brandt. Former French Prime Minister Pierre Mauroy took over the SI presidency from the ailing Brandt at the 19th SI congress in Berlin on 15–17 September 1992.

SOCIETY OF COMBATANT CLERGY

An informal Iranian pressure group representing 'pragmatist' clerical factions loyal to current Iranian President Ali Akbar Hashemi Rafsanjani. Candidates endorsed by the group claimed to have won more than 70 per cent of the seats in the country's fourth **majlis ash shura**, elected in April and May 1992.

SOLEDAD BROTHER

The title of a prison diary written in Soledad prison by self-taught **Black Power** activist George Jackson, and published in 1971. Jackson, having served 11 years for petty theft, was then accused of killing a prison warder; his case, taken up by Angela Davis, became a cause célèbre for US liberals and radicals when, on 28 August 1971, he was shot while trying to escape from San Quentin prison in California. It was widely believed that the escape attempt had been encouraged by the authorities to provide a pretext for the shooting.

SOLIDARITY

The Polish trade union and opposition movement, founded in 1980 by striking workers at the **Gdansk shipyard**. Solidarity's leaders included the future President, Lech Walesa. Officially recognized in November 1980, Solidarity grew rapidly, attracting some 9 million members – workers and intellectuals alike – and advocating a radical reduction of the **Communist** Party's power. After initially advocating co-operation with Solidarity, the Polish government succumbed to Soviet pressure and introduced **martial law** in December 1981. Solidarity was formally banned the following autumn and forced underground, but was re-legalized under the **Round Table agreement** which resulted from talks in February–April 1989 between the 'constructive opposition' and the government. After the first round of partially free elections in June 1989, a Solidarity candidate, Tadeusz Mazowiecki, became Prime Minister. Political divisions, particularly over the **shock therapy** of the **Balcerowicz plan**, split Solidarity in the run-up to presidential elections in November 1990, in which Mazowiecki stood – unsuccessfully – against Walesa.

SOMALIA

A country in the **Horn of Africa**, formed in July 1960 by the merger of the British **Somaliland** Protectorate and the **UN Trust Territory** of Somalia (an Italian colony before the Second World War). The country descended into civil war in the 1990s. Fighting broke out in November 1991 between factions of the United Somali Congress, the coalition which had led a rebellion to overthrow the dictator Mohammed Siyad Barre. In December 1992, with Somalia in the grip of famine, the UN sanctioned **Operation Restore Hope** to restore order and protect aid shipments.

SOMALILAND

The area of northern **Somalia** which, prior to Somali independence in 1960, constituted the British Somaliland Protectorate, and which was proclaimed independent in May 1991 by the Somali National Movement. As of August 1994, the territory had not been recognized as an independent state by the **UN** or any other international bodies.

SONS OF GLYNDWR

A group of ardent Welsh nationalists. In 1982–3 it claimed responsibility for a number of fire-bomb attacks on English-owned second homes in Wales.

SOROS FOUNDATION

A philanthropic organization established by billionaire fund manager and currency speculator George Soros, a Hungarian based in the USA, with the aim of raising educational standards in Central and **Eastern Europe**. Soros's specific goal was to improve understanding of free market economies and democracy; to this end he created a series of Open Society Foundations in Eastern Europe and beyond from the late 1970s. Since the outbreak of war in **Bosnia-Hercegovina** in 1992, the Soros Foundation has also disbursed considerable funds for humanitarian purposes.

SOUND BITE

A short phrase or sentence, designed for maximum impact, which is extracted for use in broadcast news reports from a recorded speech by a political leader. The practice of writing speeches to include sound bites developed in the 1970s and 1980s, bringing with it the criticism that complex issues are being reduced to catch-phrases.

SOUTH

1. The developing countries, as differentiated from the developed **North**. Geographically this term is a very broad generalization with numerous exceptions, but it has been used increasingly since the 1970s. It avoids the implication of a necessary progression from developing to developed, and offers a less hierarchical equivalent to **Third World** (while also covering the less commonly used category **Fourth World**).

2. A geo-political term which describes the southern states of the USA, particularly the 11 states of the old Confederacy – Alabama, Arkansas, Florida, Georgia, Louisiana, Mississippi, North Carolina, South Carolina, Tennessee, Texas, and Virginia – which fought an unsuccessful war of secession in 1861–5, together with West Virginia and Oklahoma. The Confederate States were slave-owning and had a clear cultural and economic identity which was increasingly divergent from that of the rest of the USA. Despite the defeat of the Confederacy, the South retained its homogeneity: it remained economically backward, culturally distinct, and practised **segregation** towards blacks, who were denied many of the most basic **civil rights**. The South displayed unswerving support for the Democratic Party (a phenomenon known as the 'Solid South') until the 1960s, when the Democratic Party supported the **civil rights movement** which dismantled institutionalized segregation. This shattered the allegiance of the South, with the result that, since 1968, most Southern states have tended to vote Republican in presidential elections. In recent years the region has seen high investment, economic growth and immigration from the North and **Midwest**, particularly by those seeking to retire in the **Sun Belt**. The belief that the Democratic Party could only recapture the **White House** by regaining its popularity in the South was borne out by the 1976 election of Jimmy Carter (Georgia) and the 1992 victory of Bill Clinton (Arkansas).

SOUTH AFRICAN DEFENCE FORCE

see SADF

SOUTH AMERICA

The continent bounded by the Caribbean Sea to the north, the Pacific and Atlantic oceans to the west and east, and Antarctica to the south. A major part of **Latin America,** it comprises 12 countries and one French department, all to varying degrees characterized by debt, dependency on raw material exports and large-scale migration from rural to urban areas. The North (Guyana, **Surinam**, French Guiana and the economically dominant Venezuela and Colombia) has mixed populations, cultures and languages. The northern Andean region (Ecuador, Peru and Bolivia) has largely Indian populations clustered around barren sierras or in groing cities. To the east, Brazil, its northern half embracing the Amazon basin, is marked out from the rest by sheer size and by its Portuguese heritage in language and culture (as opposed to the Spanish heritage of the majority of its neighbours). Finally in the southern cone region Argentina, Chile, Paraguay and Uruguay have retained a strong European influence, most evident in their populous capital cities.

SOUTH ASIAN ASSOCIATION FOR REGIONAL CO-OPERATION *see* SAARC

SOUTH ASIAN PREFERENTIAL TRADE AGREEMENT

A general tariff framework adopted in principle by **SAARC** leaders meeting in Dhaka, Bangladesh, in April 1993. The arrangement, aimed at lowering or abolishing tariffs on intra-regional trade, was first mooted during ministerial-level SAARC trade liberalization talks in May 1992; details of the agreement are expected to be negotiated over the next three years before formal ratification by SAARC.

SOUTH LEBANON ARMY

Israeli-backed militia force established in southern Lebanon in the late 1970s by Maj. Saad Haddad. Currently led by Maj.-Gen. Antoine Lahad, the SLA operates against **Hezbollah** and radical Palestinian factions alongside its Israeli paymasters in Israel's self-declared **security zone** in southern Lebanon.

SOUTH MOLUCCANS

A group active in Holland in the 1970s which sought the return of independence to the South Moluccas (forcibly incorporated into Indonesia in 1950). There were some 35,000 South Moluccans resident in Holland, including their President-in-Exile, Dr Jan Manusama. In December 1975, South Moluccan activists attacked a train and the Indonesian Consulate General in Amsterdam; in May 1977, they captured another train and took over a school and briefly held hostages.

SOUTH PACIFIC COMMISSION

A forum for dialogue between Pacific countries and those countries which administer Pacific territories. The SPC is non-political, confining itself to initiatives in the social, economic and cultural fields. Founded on 6 February 1947 under the Canberra Agreement signed by the governments of Australia, France, the Netherlands (which withdrew in 1962), New Zealand, the UK and the USA, the SPC has 27 members. Independent and self-governing states – Cook Islands, Fiji, **Nauru**, Niue, Papua New Guinea, Solomon Islands, **Tuvalu**, and Western Samoa – joined between 1965 and 1980. In 1983 American Samoa, the Federated States of **Micronesia**, French Polynesia, Guam, **Kiribati**, the Marshall Islands, New Caledonia, the Northern Mariana Islands, **Belau** (also known as Palau), Pitcairn, Tokelau, Tonga, **Vanuatu**, and Wallis and Futuna were admitted to full membership.

SOUTH PACIFIC FORUM

An organization of the independent and self-governing territories of the South Pacific. The forum was established at a meeting in Wellington, New Zealand, in August 1971, with the aim of offering newly independent countries of the South Pacific a representative regional organization. It grew out of a commercial pressure group, the Pacific Islands Producers' Association. The original members – Australia, the Cook Islands, Fiji, **Nauru**, New Zealand, Tonga and Western Samoa – have since been joined by **Kiribati**, the Marshall Islands, the Federated States of Micronesia, Niue, Papua New Guinea, the Solomon Islands, **Tuvalu** and **Vanuatu**.

SOUTH WEST AFRICA *see* NAMIBIA

SOUTH-EAST ASIA

The geographical region lying between the Indian and the Pacific oceans and between the Asian land mass and the Indonesian archipelago. According to a strict definition the region comprises the modern states of Thailand, Malaysia and Singapore as well as the three states of **Indo-China** – Cambodia, Laos and Vietnam. However, Burma, Brunei, Indonesia and the Philippines are also usually considered part of the region.

SOUTH-EAST ASIA TREATY ORGANIZATION *see* SEATO

SOUTHERN AFRICAN DEVELOPMENT COMMUNITY *see* SADC

SOUTHERN RHODESIA *see* ZIMBABWE

SOUTHERN AFRICAN DEVELOPMENT CO-ORDINATION CONFERENCE *see* SADCC

SOUTH-SOUTH

Relations between the **South** or developing countries. It is an expression used mainly by those seeking to foster direct and co-operative links. A South-South emphasis, in debates such as those on the **NIEO** and **NWICO**, addresses the post-colonial problem of a world economy and global information system which are structured to link the South countries on the 'periphery' not with each other but to the 'centre' (the **North** countries).

SOVIET BLOC *see* COMMUNIST BLOC

SOVIET UNION

The Union of Soviet Socialist Republics (USSR), founded on 30 December 1922 and dissolved on 25 December 1991. The Soviet Union's vast territory occupied some 20 per cent of the Eurasian land mass. Its 15 republics were the **Russian Federation** (RSFSR – by far the largest), **Armenia**, **Azerbaijan**, Byelorussia (now **Byelarus**), **Georgia**, **Kazakhstan**, Kirghizia (now **Kirgizstan**), Moldavia (now **Moldova**), **Tajikistan**, Turkmenia (now **Turkmenistan**), **Ukraine**, **Uzbekistan**, and the three **Baltic states** annexed in 1940 – **Estonia**, **Latvia** and **Lithuania**.

SOWETO RIOTS

The uprising in June 1976 in the South African **township** of Soweto. The protests began when African schoolchildren rejected the use of Afrikaans as a medium of instruction, regarding it as a language of oppression. Up to 10,000 children were confronted by police who fired tear gas as they marched through Soweto on 16 June. The children responded by throwing stones. The police then fired into the crowd, killing at least one person, Hector Pieterson. A photograph of a distraught youth carrying Pieterson's body, accompanied by Pieterson's sobbing sister, became a potent symbol of the riot and of the children's courage. Over the following days pupils and students across the country began to riot, attacking police patrols and government buildings. On 26 June the government relented, dropping the requirement for Afrikaans to be used, but the country's schools remained closed until the end of the year. The official death toll from the uprising was 575, with 2,389 wounded. The riots led to a rapid increase in mass popular protests and provided a pattern of urban protests which persisted until the unbanning of the **ANC** in 1990.

SPACE SHUTTLE

The generic name for the US retrievable space craft operated by **NASA**. The original development cost of four shuttles was an estimated $15,000 million and the first test flight, under the name STS-1, was in 1981. Early confidence was shattered by the 1986 **Challenger disaster**, from which the programme was slow to recover. However the success of the Endeavour mission in December 1993, which successfully repaired the **Hubble Space Telescope**, restored public and political confidence in the US manned space programme, but doubts remained about the viability of the shuttle as a transportation system to construct and service the planned Space Station.

SPARROW UNITS

Small groups of urban **guerrillas** formed in the 1980s by the **New People's Army** (NPA), the **communist** insurgency movement in the Philippines. While the NPA had traditionally pursued a rural revolutionary strategy, the Sparrow Units were designed to operate within cities, and specialized in assassinations.

SPEARHEAD GROUP

An association founded in 1986 between Papua New Guinea, the Solomon Islands and **Vanuatu**, the three predominantly Melanesian member countries of the **South Pacific Forum**, which aims to promote Melanesian interests in the region, focusing initially on the issue of independence for the (Melanesian) French-administered territory of New Caledonia.

SPECIAL DRAWING RIGHT *see* SDR

SPECIAL ECONOMIC ZONE *see* SEZ

SPECIAL RELATIONSHIP

The close relationship between the UK and the USA which developed from their alliance during the Second World War and which emphasized their shared cultural heritage. The relationship was based on the personal friendship of US President Franklin D. Roosevelt and British Prime Minister Winston Churchill, and their shared determination to defeat Nazi Germany. Although increasingly one-sided – the UK's subordination was demonstrated by the **Suez crisis** of 1956 – the relationship continued during the **Cold War** period, with the UK providing support for US foreign policy and serving as an unsinkable 'aircraft carrier' for the US Air Force. Although sometimes still invoked by politicians on both sides of the Atlantic, in recent years the term has become something of an anachronism as Britain's membership of the **EU**, the ending of the Cold War, and changing US perceptions of the nature of its strategic interests, have all served to undermine the relationship. Remarks by President Bill Clinton in Berlin in July 1994 suggested that his administration saw Germany as a better partner than the UK for a special relationship.

SPIEGEL AFFAIR

The confrontation in 1962 over press freedom and ministerial authoritarianism in West Germany, which led to the resignation of Defence Minister Franz Josef Strauss and continued to dog his image in subsequent decades. The German weekly magazine *Der Spiegel* in October 1962 published a critique of West German defence policy, claiming that the previous month's **NATO** exercise 'Fallex 62' had demonstrated the inappropriateness of relying on NATO nuclear forces against a putative attack by the **Soviet Union**. On publication of the article, federal police raided the offices of the magazine, and its publisher and founder Rudolf Augstein was arrested together with other members of staff. In the resulting furore Strauss admitted having ordered the action against *Der Spiegel*, and he was forced to resign on 30 November.

SPIN DOCTOR

A member of an election candidate's campaign team who interprets for the media, as favourably as possible, the candidate's performance in a particular event. The term first became part of the political vocabulary during the 1988 US presidential campaign. At that time it was used specifically with reference to the set-piece debates which are a traditional aspect of US presidential contests, and after which the spin doctors attempted to influence the media in assessing the performance of candidates.

SPLA

The Sudan People's Liberation Army, the main rebel movement in southern Sudan, founded in March 1984 and in revolt ever since against the Khartoum-based government. It rejects the increasing **Islamization** of the country, and in particular the application of **sharia law** in the predominantly non-Muslim south. The SPLA was weakened by splits which resulted in 1993 in the emergence of two main factions, one led by Torit leader Col. John Garang and another, SPLA-United headed by Riek Machar, which brought together three hitherto separate groups. In early 1994 the Khartoum government launched a major offensive against the rebels, while at the same time welcoming the mediatory efforts of neighbouring countries which sought to resolve the conflict through negotiation.

SPRATLY ISLANDS

A group of disputed islets, coral reefs and sandbars in the South China Sea, claimed, either in whole or in part, by Brunei, China, **Malaysia**, the Philippines, **Taiwan** and Vietnam. The dispute came to a head in 1992 after China and Vietnam awarded contracts separately to Western companies to drill for oil in the waters of the disputed archipelago.

SPRINGER AFFAIR

The shooting and serious wounding of German student leader Rudi Dutschke on 11 April 1968 by Josef Bachmann, a reader of the mass-circulation **right-wing** *Bild Zeitung* newspaper which was owned by media magnate Axel Springer. The Springer newspapers, which at that time accounted for some 70 per cent of daily sales in Berlin and Hamburg, had called for harsh measures against the student radicals of **1968** and encouraged their readers to take the law into their own hands. The shooting provoked large-scale demonstrations throughout Germany and made Springer a principal target of the *Ausserparlamentärische opposition* (**APO**).

SPUTNIK

(Russian, 'fellow traveller') The first artificial satellite. The launch of Sputnik 1 by the **Soviet Union** on 4 October 1957 caused an international sensation in the midst of the **Cold War**. It raised fears in the USA that the country was strategically at risk from outer space and had lost its position of scientific and technological pre-eminence. An undeclared space race developed as the USA resolved to reverse this presumed Soviet technological superiority, which was also assumed to extend to military prowess and to mean a **missile gap**. From Sputnik to the first (US) moon walk took less than 12 years.

SPYCATCHER AFFAIR

The controversy in the UK over the memoirs of retired **MI5** agent Peter Wright. In the early 1980s Wright wrote his memoirs, *Spycatcher*, which were to be published in Australia where he was then living. The book itself was critical of many aspects of the nature and conduct of MI5, and contained a number of lurid allegations concerning the service's activities. The UK authorities were granted an interim injunction in the Australian courts in September 1985 preventing publication, having argued that the memoirs represented a breach of official secrets legislation and of Wright's duty to the British Crown. However, they were subsequently refused a permanent injunction. There then followed a series of court actions, not only in Australia and the UK but also in other countries, to prevent publication of the book's contents in newspapers. As details came increasingly into circulation, the House of Lords ruled in October 1988 against a ban on publication, although it upheld the duty of members of the security services not to disclose information about their work.

SRI LANKA

The island state off the south-east coast of India. It adopted its present name in 1972, when it became a republic within the **Commonwealth**. Under the former name, Ceylon, it had been a British colony and gained independence in 1948. Since the early 1980s Sri Lanka, with a majority Sinhalese population, has been riven by conflict with the secessionist **Tamil Tigers** in the north and east.

STABEX

The European scheme for helping to stabilize the export earnings of developing countries. Stabex was introduced in the 1970s and developed under the successive **Lomé Conventions** – the agreements regulating the relationship between the European Union (**EU**) and the African, **Caribbean** and Pacific (**ACP**) countries. It involved payments to producers of primary commodities such as coffee, cocoa and groundnuts when they were particularly severely hit by year-on-year fluctuations in prices and production levels. The system, geared more directly to individual commodities than the IMF's **compensatory financing**, was an influential model for the much-discussed idea of a global **Common Fund** for commodity stabilization, an issue which dominated the **UN** Conference on Trade and Development (**UNCTAD**) in the 1970s and early 1980s. Stabex also has a 'little brother', the Sysmin scheme, introduced under the third Lomé

Convention to cover minerals such as iron and copper.

STAGFLATION

A portmanteau term describing the economic situation in which stagnant levels of growth and employment coincide with rising inflation. The term was coined in the UK by **Tory** MP Iain Macleod in November 1965, since when it has entered the wider political vocabulary and has become an accepted term among economists. A politically destabilizing phenomenon, its prevalence in the **West** in the 1970s led to the rise of the **New Right**.

STAKHANOVITE

A term for an exceptionally productive worker, deriving from the legendary exploits of Soviet coal miner Alexei Stakhanov, who was lionized by the Soviet propaganda machine for successfully extracting 102 tonnes of coal in one shift in 1935, during the second **five-year plan**. Stakhanovites were rewarded with bonuses, superior apartments, and holidays.

STALINGRAD

The city located on the Volga river in southern Russia, known under the Tsars as Tsaritsyn, whose name was changed to Volgograd after the 1917 revolution, and changed again to Stalingrad in 1925 in honour of the Soviet leader Joseph Stalin, who had organized its defences against the 'White Russians' during the civil war. The city's name reverted to Volgograd in 1961 as part of the **de-Stalinization** campaign.

STALINISM

Totalitarian policies developed under Soviet leader Joseph Stalin, characterized by a hierarchical party with a monopoly on power; a **cult of personality** and a sophisticated **propaganda** machine; a **police state** and policy of terror; and an emphasis on patriotic 'war socialism', with the goal of rapid industrialization. Stalin's successor Nikita Khrushchev initiated **de-Stalinization** with his **secret speech** of 1956.

STALKER INQUIRY

The inquiry into alleged **shoot to kill** operations by the security forces in **Northern Ireland** in late 1982. The inquiry, under the deputy chief constable of Greater Manchester John Stalker, was set up in 1984 to examine such allegations. Stalker's report was submitted to the chief constable of the Royal Ulster Constabulary in September 1985 and to the Northern Ireland Director of Public Prosecutions in February 1986. However, in May 1986 Stalker was removed from the inquiry team in controversial circumstances involving alleged unrelated misconduct, and was replaced by the chief constable of West Yorkshire Colin Sampson. No criminal proceedings were taken as a result of the Stalker-Sampson inquiry, although some members of the RUC were disciplined.

STANDBY ARRANGEMENT

The arrangement whereby **IMF** member countries borrow from the Fund (or, more precisely, purchase reserves on credit). The borrowing member country gets an assurance that it will be able to make drawings on the Fund up to a specified amount during a given period, without further review of its performance and policies, so long as it has observed the performance criteria and other terms included in the arrangement (and set out in the **letter of intent**).

STAR CHAMBER

The UK Cabinet committee established in the 1980s by Prime Minister Margaret Thatcher to determine public spending programmes for the forthcoming year. Nicknamed after the powerful Star Chamber of the fourteenth–seventeenth centuries, the discussions were frequently heated as ministers defended their budgets in the light of the financial and economic constraints of the time. In 1993 the process was largely replaced by a procedure whereby the Chief Secretary to the Treasury, responsible for expenditure, carries out in-depth discussions with individual ministers; in addition new and more sophisticated measures of spending projections have been also developed.

STAR WARS

The US Strategic Defence Initiative (SDI), a plan for a ground- and space-based system which would use (as yet unproven) laser technology to bring down any ballistic missiles launched against the USA. The project was particularly dear to the heart of President Ronald Reagan, who first announced it in March 1983. It was instantly dubbed Star Wars, the name of a hugely successful science fiction film.

The USA's **NATO** partners showed no enthusiasm, since it was in essence an effort to make the USA invulnerable, and thus failed to address any of the problems of the 'European theatre of war'. The **Soviet Union** opposed it bitterly, arguing that it profoundly destabilized the nuclear balance, and that its development (let alone its testing or implementation) contravened US treaty commitments on **ABMs** and the non-militarization of space. Soviet hostility, and Reagan's unwillingness to abandon SDI, proved a stumbling block for arms reduction proposals at the **Reykjavik summit** in 1986.

By 1987, however, the US **Congress** was losing faith in the technology, which remained unconvincing despite the huge finances channelled into it; funding was cut, and tests in space were prohibited. The SDI programme continued, but the altered superpower relationship by the end of the decade changed the emphasis of US policy decisively towards arms control. Despite the efforts of the US administration under President George Bush (1989–93) to preserve the 'missile umbrella' concept in modified form, as **Brilliant Pebbles** or **GPALS**, in May 1993 the new Clinton administration announced the 'end of the Star Wars era' and the scrapping of the programme.

START

The Strategic Arms Reduction Talks between the **superpowers**, which began in June 1982 despite the deadlock over **SALT** II. The US side began by pressing for major **ICBM** cuts (land-based strategic missiles being much less significant in the US arsenal than in the Soviet one). The **NATO** decision, however, to go ahead with deployment of **cruise** and **Pershing** II missiles in Europe, prompted a Soviet walkout from the START talks in November 1982, and when they reconvened in 1985 it was under an 'umbrella' framework linking strategic, intermediate and space-based systems, with the Soviet side focusing on demanding a halt to **Star Wars**. After the 1987 **INF Treaty** the START talks in Geneva moved towards separating the agenda on strategic weapons, creating a potential START I agreement and deferring more complex areas to START II. In the event, whereas START I took nearly a decade (and was signed in Moscow in July 1991 between the **Soviet Union** and the USA), START II was agreed in principle in Washington in a completely different global context in June 1992, and signed only six months later by Russia and the USA in January 1993. START II went far beyond the 25–35 per cent cuts in missile numbers and **MIRV** ceilings agreed in START I, committing both sides to cut two-thirds of their strategic arsenals and to eliminate all MIRVs by the year 2003.

The collapse of the **Soviet Union** created complexities in the START I ratification process, particularly with **Ukraine**, but the promise of large-scale US aid eventually cleared the way for the accession by early 1994 of all four post-Soviet nuclear weapons states. (The agreement involved three of them, **Byelarus**, **Kazakhstan** and Ukraine, transferring ownership of all remaining weapons to the fourth, Russia.)

STASI

The Ministry of State Security of **communist** East Germany (the **DDR**). The Stasi police force co-ordinated a network of agents and informants in all walks of life. After the dissolution of the DDR, German citizens were permitted access to the Stasi files on themselves. This helped to reveal the extent of the Stasi monitoring system, which had often involved using a subject's friends or relatives as informants.

STATE DEPARTMENT

The name for the US government department handling foreign affairs, headed by the Secretary of State and located at **Foggy Bottom**. As the right to negotiate with foreign states is the sole prerogative of the executive (although tangible diplomatic results tend to be subject to ratification by **Congress**), the Secretary of State wields enormous authority. While this varies in accordance with the style and inclinations of individual presidents, the head of the State Department is one of the key positions in any US administration and is a core member of the **NSC**.

STATE OF EMERGENCY

Government in which the executive power has declared itself not to be subject to the usual restraints on its exercise of authority, for example by the legislature or the judiciary. Rights and freedoms normally guaranteed under the constitution may be held in abeyance. Many countries' constitutions lay down the circumstances when a state of emergency may be declared (either nationwide or in specified areas), defining the special powers which will then be in operation, how long this can continue, and how (or whether) a state of emergency may be prolonged. In practice this has often been irrelevant, with a state of emergency being imposed after a military coup and the suspension of the constitution.

STATE FARM

The large collective farms (in Russian, *kolkhoz*) created by **collectivization**, which pooled land, personnel and equipment in state-run agricultural enterprises.

StB

(Czechoslovak, *Statni Bezpecnost*, 'state security police') **Communist Czechoslovakia's** security police, whose main function was to identify opponents of the regime and to dissuade them, sometimes ruthlessly, from open dissent. Following the abolition of the StB in February 1990, controversy over claims about past collaboration led to the **lustration** legislation.

STEALTH BOMBER

A US bomber built largely from carbon composites. Formally known as the B-2, the aircraft's texture, smooth-contoured shape and concealed heat sources were designed to reflect only a minimal radar image, thereby rendering it almost invisible to traditional air defence systems. The four-engined aircraft was bizarrely shaped, with a wingspan of 172 feet (52.4 metres), a length of 69 feet (21 metres) and no tail. The most costly aircraft ever built, it made its maiden flight at Edwards Air Force Base in southern California on 17 July 1989. Originally devised to replace the country's aging fleet of **B-52** bombers, the B-2 was seen as a means of destroying Soviet command systems in the initial stage of a **superpower** conflict. The revision of strategic requirements following the end of the **Cold War**, together with the huge cost of the aircraft, however, has led to a persistent downward revision of the number to be produced.

DIE STEM *see* NKOSI SIKELEL'I AFRIKA

STERLING AREA

Traditionally those countries, principally British dependent territories or independent members of the **Commonwealth**, which held their reserves in the form of sterling balances rather than in gold or other foreign currencies. There were over 60 countries in the sterling area. From the mid-1960s, as the UK began experiencing severe balance of payments problems, arrangements were concluded to protect those countries against potential losses arising from fluctuations in the external value of sterling. These arrangements were successively extended until, following the 1973–4 oil price rises and the emergence of massive flows of **petrodollars**, they were terminated at the end of 1974. Meanwhile, increasing numbers of countries had broken their link with sterling in the aftermath of the **Smithsonian agreement** and subsequent upheavals in the exchange markets.

STERN GANG

a Jewish **guerrilla** group founded in **Palestine** in 1940. Named after an early leader Abraham Stern, who was killed during a clash with British police, the group carried out a number of attacks on British personnel in Palestine. The group assassinated Lord Moyne, UK Minister of State for Middle Eastern Affairs, in Cairo in late 1944. From 1945 the group collaborated with

Irgun and **Haganah** in a guerrilla campaign which, in part, led to the establishment of a Jewish state, **Israel**, in 1948. One of the leading members of the Stern Gang was Itzhak Shamir who went on to serve as Prime Minister of Israel during the 1980s and early 1990s.

STOCKHOLM SYNDROME

A psychological condition in which hostages grow to empathize with their captors' political or personal convictions and aspirations. One celebrated instance was Patty Hearst, the US heiress kidnapped in 1974 by the **Symbionese Liberation Army**. The term derives from a 1973 bank robbery in Stockholm during the course of which several people taken as hostages lent their support to the robbers.

STONEHOUSE AFFAIR

The circumstances surrounding the disappearance of UK Labour MP John Stonehouse in 1974. Stonehouse was a middle-ranking minister in 1967–70. After Labour went into opposition in 1970 he sought to develop wide-ranging business interests. However, for a variety of reasons these combined to put him in a desperate financial situation, and in November 1974 he faked his suicide off the Miami coast. Shortly afterwards he was arrested in Australia and was extradited to the UK. In August 1976 he was convicted in the UK of fraud, theft and forgery; he was sentenced to seven years' imprisonment and only then resigned as an MP.

STONEWALL

An organization formed in the USA in the wake of the 1969 **Stonewall Riot**, which lobbies and campaigns for the legal and social equality of homosexual men and women. A branch of the organization was founded in 1988 in the UK in response to anti-homosexual measures contained in **Clause 28** of the 1988 Local Government Act. In the UK the group lobbies vigorously for equality in the age of consent for homosexuals and heterosexuals, and rejected the 'compromise' reduction of the age of consent for homosexuals from 21 to 18, which was adopted in February 1994 as a clause in the Criminal Justice and Public Order Bill.

STONEWALL RIOT

The serious street disturbances in New York on 26 June 1969 which followed a police raid on the Stonewall Inn, then the largest gathering place for the city's homosexual community at a time when homosexuality was outlawed and lesbian and gay bars and clubs were prohibited. The raid provoked the first violent reaction from homosexuals and marked the beginning of a new era of gay activism. The lesbian and gay community was galvanized and organizations demanding gay rights sprang up virtually overnight. In June 1994 the 25th anniversary of the riot was marked in New York by a week of events including a demonstration outside the **UN** building in which hundreds of thousands of people from across the world demanded the extension of the **Universal Declaration of Human Rights** to include homosexuals.

STOP-GO

A pejorative description of a self-generated economic cycle dictated by political expediency. Faced with rapid economic growth and the possibility of 'overheating', measures are taken to suppress domestic demand, to curb inflation and to deal with balance-of-payments problems. When such measures precipitate a rise in unemployment, attempts are made to try to reflate the economy. 'Stop-go' mechanisms have been a feature of UK economic policy since 1945, particularly in the 1980s and 1990s.

STORMONT

The government and parliament buildings of **Northern Ireland** in Belfast. Stormont was the seat of the Northern Ireland parliament from 1932 until the introduction of **direct rule** in 1972, and this term denoted both the legislative and the executive identities of Northern Ireland, and Northern Ireland's limited form of self-government.

STRATEGIC ARMS LIMITATION TALKS *see* SALT

STRATEGIC ARMS REDUCTION TALKS *see* START

STRATEGIC DEFENCE INTITIATIVE *see* STAR WARS

STRATEGIC HAMLETS

A method of **counterinsurgency**, sometimes known as 'protected villages', which was used to great effect by British forces during the fight against **communist guerrillas** in Malaya during the **Emergency** of the early 1950s. Devised by British counterinsurgency expert Robert Thompson, the strategy aimed to corral peasants into armed stockades, thereby depriving guerrillas of their grass-roots support. Encouraged by Thompson, South Vietnam launched a vast and expensive 'strategic hamlet' campaign in 1962 aimed at depriving the **Viet Cong** of rural support. However, Vietnam was not Malaya, and the strategy not only failed to produce the desired results, but served to strengthen peasant resentment against the southern regime and increase support for the Viet Cong.

STRUCTURAL ADJUSTMENT FACILITY *see* SAF

STRUCTURAL FUNDS

The financial instruments used by the **EU** to support projects and programmes in member states which further (i) social goals such as combating unemployment (through the **ESF**); (ii) development in disadvantaged areas (through the European Regional Development Fund set up in 1975); or (iii) the overall cohesion of the EU, particularly since the poorer Mediterranean countries became members in the 1980s.

SUBIC BAY

The 60,000-acre (24,000-hectare) US naval base in the Philippines which served as the main supply and repair centre for the US Seventh Fleet until it was decommissioned in September 1992. Like the other major US base in the Philippines, the **Clark Field air base**, Subic Bay had been first leased to the USA in 1947. Growing Filipino **nationalism** prevented the USA from being able to renew its lease, which expired in September 1991, and the last military personnel were withdrawn on 24 November 1992.

SUBSIDIARITY

The resolution of problems at the lowest appropriate level. Although not specific to the **EU** – the word was used, for example, in the Vatican's 1985 review of **Vatican II** – references to subsidiarity have become almost obligatory since the late 1980s in statements on the EU's future. The concept is given particular emphasis in the **Maastricht** documents on **European political union**, and goes together with the idea of promoting 'a union closer to its citizens'. It is seen as the governing principle to be applied in determining whether decisions should be handled at the local, regional, national or Community level. **Eurosceptics** see federalism as the real antithesis of subsidiarity.

SUDAN PEOPLE'S LIBERATION ARMY *see* SPLA

SUEZ CRISIS

The **Middle East** crisis precipitated by the nationalization of the Suez Canal by Egyptian President Gamal Abdel Nasser in July 1956. Nasser had acted after the USA had reneged on a commitment to help finance the construction of the **Aswan High Dam**. His action angered France and the UK, who feared for the stability of Middle Eastern oil supplies to Europe. With diplomatic efforts to solve the crisis under way, France and the UK, with the assistance of **Israel**, formulated plans for the military seizure of the Canal. Israeli forces invaded Egypt on 29 October 1956; French and British troops followed (on the pretext of supporting a **UN** ceasefire call) and occupied the canal zone. However, the combined opposition expressed by the USA and the **Soviet Union** to the invasion brought a swift end to the Anglo-French action, principally because of political and economic pressure which the US administration was able to exert on the British government. The Europeans withdrew in December 1956 and the Israelis withdrew from the **Sinai** and **Gaza Strip** in March 1957. While the episode served to underline Britain's decline as an imperial power, it also advanced Nasser's Arab nationalist credentials.

SULLIVAN CODE

A set of employment principles drawn up in March 1977 by Rev. Leon Sullivan, a board member of IBM, to be followed by US companies operating in South Africa and designed to eliminate workplace **apartheid**. The principles were: desegregation of all facilities; equal and fair employment practices for all employees; equal pay for all those doing equal and comparable work for the same period; initiation of a development training programme to prepare substantial numbers of blacks for supervisory, administrative, clerical and technical jobs; increasing the number of blacks in management and supervisory roles; and improving the quality of employees' lives outside the work environment. Originally endorsed by 12 major US companies, the Code was subsequently adopted by a number of other foreign companies. However, it was criticized as a means of forestalling economic **sanctions** rather than promoting real change. In the late 1980s Sullivan himself conceded that the Code had done little to bring about genuine improvements, and he called for sanctions.

SUN BELT

A geographical term in the USA used to describe the 'sunshine states' of the **South** and West, particularly Florida and California, which in recent years have been a magnet for migration from the recession-hit North East and **Midwest**.

SUNNI

(FromArabic *sunnah* – 'custom of the Prophet Muhammad') The majority Muslim sect, the minority sect being the **Shia** or Shi'ite. Sometimes known as the 'orthodox', Sunnis follow one of the four Sunni Schools of Law – the Hanafi, the Hanbali, the Maliki or the Shafi.

SUNNINGDALE AGREEMENT

The abortive December 1973 agreement on the future of **Northern Ireland**. The agreement was the result of a tripartite conference between representatives of the Irish and UK governments and of the short-lived **power-sharing** Northern Ireland executive-designate. It envisaged the establishment of a joint Council of Ireland, and changes in the relationship between Northern Ireland and the Republic of Ireland. Although all three sides approved implementation of the agreement, there was strong opposition from **loyalist** workers, who staged a widely observed strike. In the face of this resistance, the power-sharing executive collapsed in May 1974 and **direct rule** was reimposed.

SUPER 301

A US trade weapon designed to pry open overseas markets. Passed by **Congress** in 1988, the measure was bolted on to Section 301 of the 1974 Trade Act. It empowered the government – in the face of the failure of negotiations to remove tariffs deemed to be unfair – to impose punitive tariffs of up to 100 per cent against exports from those countries which had been cited as unfair traders. The legislation was used in 1989–90, with Japan, India and Brazil being singled out as unfair traders. In the event, however, the disputes with all three countries were resolved without recourse to sanctions. The measure expired in 1990, but in March 1994 President Bill Clinton reactivated it through an executive order as part of an escalating trade dispute with Japan.

SUPER TUESDAY

The **primary** elections for several states in the US **South** which take place on the second Tuesday in March in presidential election years. Candidates seeking the presidential nomination of either the Republican or Democratic Party compete to win delegates to their party's nominating convention in a series of primaries and **caucuses** held in every state between February and June. A strong early performance is seen as vital to a candidate's public profile and ability to raise campaign funds for the contest. Accordingly, a number of Southern states have, since 1984, chosen to hold their elections on Super Tuesday, in order to maximize their influence on the campaign.

SUPERGUN

An enormous cannon which was reportedly in the process of development by Iraq. Details of the weapon first emerged in April 1990 when it became the focus of international attention after British customs officials seized a consignment of steel cylinders manufactured by two UK-based companies and bound for Iraq. It was alleged at the time that the cylinders were to be fitted together to form the barrel of a giant 40-metre 'super-gun', possibly with the intention of launching missiles or satellites. Iraq maintained that the cylinders were for use in its petro-chemical industry.

SUPERPOWER

A country which is not only a great power but also has global responsibilities and capabilities. As used by US political scientist W. T. R. Fox in the title of his 1944 book *The Superpowers*, this applied to the UK, the USA and the **Soviet Union**. During the **Cold War** period, the term 'superpower' designated the two global military powers, the USA and Soviet Union. Since the demise of the Soviet Union and the collapse of **communism** in December 1991, the USA is generally recognized to be the world's sole superpower.

SUPPLY SIDE ECONOMICS

A body of economic theory which first gained wide currency in the 1970s, based on the proposition that an economy is driven primarily through the efficiency of markets, at the micro level, rather than through management of demand at the macro level. An essential element of the application of supply side economic policy is a reduction in marginal income tax rates in order to improve incentives – a course followed by the UK Conservative government since 1979, and by the USA in the 1980s in the form of **Reaganomics**.

SUPREME ALLIED COMMANDER EUROPE *see* SACEUR

SURINAM

A country on the north-east coast of **South America**. Hitherto named Dutch Guiana, Surinam attained autonomy within the Kingdom of the Netherlands in 1954 and became independent in 1975.

SUSTAINABLE DEVELOPMENT

Development within the limits of the earth's resources. The concept implies accepting that continued economic growth is necessary, to meet the needs of the world's population particularly in the developing world, but at the same time resisting further damage to the ecology of the planet which would compromise future generations. It emphasizes better management of finite resources, particularly energy, and the increased use of renewable resources. The 1992 **Earth Summit** focused on the ideal of sustainable development, formulating goals and targets in **Agenda 21**.

SWADESHI

(Hindi, 'pertaining to one's region or country', 'traditional way of life') A Hindu concept with a long history which was revived by the Indian nationalist leader, Mahatma Gandhi in the 1920s. It was predicated on the belief that Indian regeneration depended upon forging closer links between the individual and his / her native land, culture and community. Designed to develop an attitude of cultural self-respect and independence from European ideas and institutions, it was to become one of the most important strands in the ideology of Indian **nationalism**.

SWAPO

The South West Africa People's Organization of **Namibia**, the liberation movement and since 1990 the ruling party in Namibia. Founded in 1958, SWAPO sought the liberation from South Africa of the territory then called South West Africa. Its independence proposals from 1978 onwards were based on a **UN** plan, **Resolution 435**. Although SWAPO was never banned, its members were restricted, its leaders imprisoned or restricted and its offices attacked. Initially a non-violent organization, it faced growing repression by the South African authorities and became increasingly frustrated by the failure of the efforts of international institutions to act against the Pretoria regime. In August 1966 SWAPO proclaimed an armed struggle, supervised by its external wing which had bases in Zambia and (after 1974) in Angola. **guerrilla** activity was conducted by SWAPO's military wing, the People's Liberation Army of Namibia (PLAN) which received assistance from the **Soviet Union**. By the late 1980s, South Africa was finally persuaded to accept Namibian independence, under a formula which linked Resolution 435 with a withdrawal of Cuban forces from neighbouring Angola. SWAPO won the pre-independence elections in November 1989, despite a dirty tricks campaign by the South African government, and on 21 March 1990 the SWAPO leader, Sam Nujoma, became the first President of independent Namibia.

SYMBIONESE LIBERATION ARMY

A US **guerrilla** movement founded in 1973 by black radical Donald De Freeze. Its name was derived from its view that the dynamic for social change lay in oppressed minorities working together in a symbiotic relationship with each other. The group never numbered more than around 20 members, but achieved a disproportionate degree of publicity through its campaign of violence against the state. In 1974 it kidnapped heiress Patty Hearst (who then joined the group in what was seen as an instance of the **Stockholm syndrome**) and extorted $2 million from her father, Randolph Hearst, in the form of food distributed to the poor. De Freeze and several of his followers were killed by Los Angeles police on 17 May 1974, and on 18 September 1975 Hearst and three others were captured while robbing a bank. At her subsequent trial Hearst claimed that she had been coerced into joining the SLA.

SYSTEMIC TRANSFORMATION FACILITY

A temporary **IMF** facility introduced in April 1993 to help promote the transition to market-based economic systems, which was being attempted by many of the formerly centrally planned economies. Prospective beneficiaries were not only the countries of **eastern Europe** and of the former **Soviet Union** but also countries in the transformation process elsewhere, notably in Asia. A country would qualify to use the facility if its traditional trade and payment arrangements were disrupted, and if it had a substantial and permanent increase in net import costs, owing to a shift towards world market pricing, especially for energy products.

TAFT-HARTLEY ACT

US legislation passed in 1947 which severely limited the rights of organized labour to pursue industrial disputes and political goals. Championed by Senator Robert Taft and Representative Fred Hartley, the measure outlawed strikes by government employees, prohibited compulsory union membership at a place of work, made unions liable for breaches of contract, prevented them from making financial contributions to political campaigns and gave the government the power to impose an 80-day 'cooling off period' in any dispute. President Harry S. Truman denounced the legislation as 'a slave labour law' and vetoed it, but his veto was overturned by Congress.

TAIWAN

An island off the coast of the People's Republic of China (**PRC**), formerly known as Formosa. The present government is derived from the **KMT** government, which fled the mainland in 1949 after the **communist** victory there. It continues to claim to legal jurisdiction of this 'lost' territory (the whole of mainland China) and designates itself as the Republic of China.

TAJIKISTAN

A state in **Central Asia**, independent since 1991, and formerly one of the **Soviet Union's** 15 constituent republics. Tajikistan is ethnically heterogeneous, its population of 5.6 million people including Pamirs, Uzbeks, Russians and others. Since September 1992 there has been civil war between **communists** and an alliance of democrats and supporters of the Islamic Renaissance Party. Tajikistan occupies a strategically sensitive mountainous region at the southern extreme of former Soviet Central Asia bordering Afghanistan. Russia has been anxious to reassert control over the region and has found a vulnerable government compliant. **CIS** border troops patrol the Tajik frontier, which is regarded by Russia as a bastion against militant Islam.

TAKING THE FIFTH *see* FIFTH AMENDMENT

TAKRITI CLAN

The blood-related group native to the small Iraqi town of Takrit on the river Tigris, about 100 miles (160 km) from Baghdad. Part of the so-called 'Sunni triangle' bounded by Baghdad, Mosul and the mid-Euphrates towns of Ana, Rawa and Falluja, it represents the heart of the country's dominant **Sunni** minority and is the mainstay of the leadership of the Iraqi Ba'ath Party as well as the birthplace of President Saddam Hussein. Since the Ba'ath military coup in 1968 until recently, Takriti origin was considered to be the sole criterion for entry into the innermost political circles.

TAMIL TIGERS

The popular name of the Liberation Tigers of Tamil Eelam (LTTE), the main Tamil separatist **guerrilla** group in **Sri Lanka**, which seeks the creation of an independent Tamil homeland, Eelam, in the north-east of the country. It emerged in 1983 after the outbreak of anti-Tamil riots in the majority-Sinhalese areas and has waged a violent campaign in pursuit of its demands, despite Indian attempts at mediation between 1987–90. Since then the LTTE has continued its war against the Sinhalese-dominated government and has claimed responsibility for the deaths of thousands of other Sri Lankans, including Muslims and Tamils of Indian origin.

TAMMANY HALL

A colloquial term for the machinery of the dominant Democratic Party in New York City; Tammany Hall was the headquarters of the Tammany Society, a political organization which controlled New York in the years immediately after the civil war. The term acquired a wider usage and came to denote **cronyism** and the politics of patronage, whereby party machines used local administrations to provide welfare services such as jobs and housing in return for electoral support. It was common in many US eastern cities, but the Tammany Hall system of local government has broken down since the 1970s. The death of Mayor Richard Daley of Chicago, in 1976, saw the passing of the last of the old-style city bosses.

TANDONA

(Spanish, 'the big class') An elite El Salvadorean officer group. Its 45 members were graduates of the class of 1966 at the military academy who rose rapidly through the ranks thanks to the *tanda* system of mutual protection and support, and who became infamous for their fierce direction of **counterinsurgency** operations in the 1980s. Prominent members included Maj. Roberto D'Aubuisson Arrieta (founder of the ruling ARENA party and closely associated with the **death squads** and the assassination of Archbishop Oscar Romero) and Gen. René Emilio Ponce, the Defence Minister until compulsorily retired with other *Tandona* members in the wake of the 1993 **Truth Commission** human rights report.

TANZANIA

The east African country of 27.8 million people formed in 1964 and comprising mainland Tanganyika and the Indian Ocean islands of Zanzibar and Pemba. The term is often used inaccurately to describe the mainland part of the country only.

TAOISEACH

(Gaelic, 'leader') The Prime Minister of the Republic of Ireland, who holds executive authority under the Irish parliamentary republican system.

TASK FORCE

A common military term which was given a special resonance in the UK at the time of the 1982 **Falklands War**, when a hurriedly assembled task force sailed 8,000 miles (13,000 km) south-west to the South Atlantic and joined battle with Argentina. It consisted of 30 warships, supporting aircraft and auxiliary vessels, with its operational nerve centre aboard the aircraft carrier *Hermes*. The passenger liner *Canberra* and the container ship *Atlantic Conveyor* were among the vessels requisitioned as troop and arms ships. Argentine naval forces in the same conflict operated under the overall designation Task Force 79, headed by the aircraft carrier *Veinticinco de Mayo*.

TASS

The **Soviet Union's** state news agency. The **CPSU** frequently made policy announcements through TASS. After the collapse of the union in 1991, the agency was renamed ITAR-TASS and awarded a measure of independence, but remained under (Russian) state ownership.

TATARS

A Muslim, Turkic-speaking ethnic minority of the **Russian Federation**, numbering at least 5 million and based mainly in the Volga region of southern Russia. The Tatars, descendants of the Mongols of the Golden Horde, were a great power in the mediaeval era, sweeping west from the Asian steppes as far as central Europe. In the eighteenth and nineteenth centuries the Tatars were absorbed into the Russian empire. In November 1992 the **Russian Federation's** Tatar Autonomous Republic proclaimed its own constitution, including the right to veto Russian legislation. In a landmark arrangement in February 1994 the Russian government agreed to respect the Tatarstan constitution in return for guarantees on the Tatar contribution to the central exchequer.

TD

(Gaelic, *Teachta Dáila*) A member of the Irish **Dáil** or lower house of parliament.

TEAM SPIRIT

The name given to the large, joint military exercise held annually by the armed forces of South Korea and the USA. Usually held early in the year, the exercise is seen as a powerful symbol of the determination of the USA (which continues to have some 18,000 troops stationed permanently in South Korea) to protect its ally against possible attack from **communist** North Korea.

TEAMSTERS

The widely used abbreviation of the International Brotherhood of Teamsters, Chauffeurs, Warehousemen and Helpers of America. The Teamsters is the largest and, through its control of the trucking industry, the most powerful single trade union in US history. However, its persistent criminal connections have also made it a byword for corruption in organized labour. The deregulation of the trucking industry in the 1980s considerably weakened the influence of the union.

TELSTAR

The US communications satellite launched on 10 July 1962. Telstar was the first satellite to be paid for by a private company, the US telecommunications giant AT&T. Telstar 1, unlike **Echo 1**, did more than passively reflect signals from earth; it received and amplified them and sent them on immediately, i.e. in 'real time'.

TEMPORARY PROVISIONS

Measures announced by the **KMT** in **Taiwan** in April 1948, which extended the mandate of delegates elected in November 1947 to the National Assembly in mainland China until 'free and fair' elections could be held there. After the KMT's flight to Taiwan in 1949, following the **Communist** victory on the mainland, the 'Temporary Provisions effective during the **Period of Communist Rebellion**' became a characteristic feature of Taiwanese politics. Following a 1966 constitutional amendment permitting the holding of supplementary elections to Taiwan's main legislative bodies, the ageing National Assembly delegates have been gradually replaced.

TERAI REGION

(Nepali, 'land at the foot of the mountains') The flat plains territory at the northern fringe of the Gangetic plain which constitutes some 15 per cent of the land area of Nepal. Bordering the Indian states of West Bengal, Bihar and Uttar Pradesh, the area is geographically and culturally distinct from the hills region. Its population, amounting to some 30 per cent of Nepal's total population, is mainly Indian in origin. In the early 1990s the area was the stage for anti-government activity led by dissident groups of Nepalis operating from areas across the border in India.

TERRITORIAL WATERS

The offshore area in which a coastal state claims sovereign jurisdiction, save for the customary rights of freedom of navigation for merchant shipping. A limit of three nautical miles was generally applied until the 1940s, when contested claims were made by coastal states for jurisdiction up to 200 nautical miles. An intermediate position, that territorial waters should be extended to 12 miles offshore, had gained widespread acceptance by 1982, when the **UNCLOS** agreement effectively coupled this with a 200-mile **EEZ**.

TEST BAN TREATY *see* NUCLEAR TEST BAN TREATY

TET OFFENSIVE

Probably the single most important event in the **Vietnam War**. During the Tet (lunar new year) holiday in late January 1968 the **Viet Cong** launched a massive offensive throughout South Vietna, aiming to deliver a crippling blow to the Saigon regime by generating a mass uprising and decimating the **ARVN**, the southern army. In the event the offensive failed in its military objectives and the Viet Cong suffered such huge losses that it never really fully recovered and as a consequence became increasingly dependent on its North Vietnamese allies. However, the offensive was a major political success, effectively forcing the US government to reconsider its Vietnam policy. After years of positive assessments of the war by politicians and reporters alike, the US public was stunned and depressed by television pictures of Viet Cong **guerrillas** attacking the US embassy in Saigon, and a mass reassessment of the conflict followed.

THALIDOMIDE

The drug which as a side effect caused grievous physical disabilities to unborn children. It became widely available in 1960 as a remedy for pregnant women suffering morning sickness. In November 1961 the drug's manufacturers, Chemie Grunenathal, withdrew thalidomide after doctors traced a link with the birth in 46 countries of thousands of children with a variety of abnormalities. Many were born with stunted limbs and misshapen hands and feet. The scandal drew attention to the procedures for testing drugs. The UK *Sunday Times* led a campaign in 1972–3 for adequate compensation payments to people affected by thalidomide. It emerged in 1994 that the drug was being successfully used for the treatment of leprosy.

THATCHERISM

The political philosophy of Margaret Thatcher, UK Prime Minister from 1979 to 1990. This was typified by the pursuit of **conviction politics**, and its economic basis was largely founded on **monetarist** theories. It stressed the role of the individual and the importance of personal incentives, and spearheaded the process of **privatization**. The period of Thatcherism was, however, accompanied by generally rising unemployment and the effective deindustrialization of the UK economy. Thatcher's lengthy term of office was characterized by the dominance of the Prime Minister within the Cabinet, in contrast with the less confrontational attitude of her successor, John Major.

THAW

A relaxation of **superpower** tension in the **Cold War**, such as occurred during the **detente perio**d of the 1970s. The term was also used in the **Soviet Union** to describe the loosening of cultural restrictions under Nikita Khrushchev after 1953, as part of the process of **de-Stalinization**.

THINK TANK

A colloquial term used to describe a group of experts who gather to consider particular issues (generally social, political and economic) with a view to providing possible solutions and/or new directions. The **Brookings Institution** and the **Rand Corporation** are among the most famous US think tanks, while in the UK a notable example is the Centre for Policy Studies, an independent **right-wing** group launched in 1974 and associated with **Thatcherism**.

THIRD MAN

Kim Philby, a former UK diplomat who defected to the **Soviet Union** in January 1963. After the defection of diplomats Guy Burgess and Donald Maclean in 1951 a prolonged investigation was held to identify the person, the 'third man', who had warned them of their imminent discovery. Philby, like Burgess a member of the pre-war Cambridge **apostles**, was interrogated, but no proof could be found. He was required, however, to leave the diplomatic service and he subsequently worked as a journalist in the Lebanon, from where he flew to Moscow after being confronted by the UK intelligence services. In 1979 Anthony Blunt was revealed to have been the 'fourth man' who had acted as a talent-spotter for the Soviet Union and had passed secret information to that country while working for the UK counter-intelligence Security Service **MI5**.

THIRD PATH

A Jamaican experiment in democratic **socialism** in 1974–80. Proposed by Prime Minister Michael Manley of the People's National Party (PNP), it promised a middle way between **capitalism** and communism as a route for **Third World** countries to achieve economic and political self-sufficiency. The nationalization of important parts of the economy was balanced by partial land reform and the encouragement of agricultural co-operatives. Increased export taxes on foreign-owned bauxite companies financed the introduction of welfare benefits, a minimum wage and higher spending on health and education. The US government interpreted the process as **communist**, especially after closer ties with Cuba were established, and mounted a propaganda campaign which deterred US investment and tourism. Transnational corporations also began looking for cheaper bauxite supplies. In the ensuing economic crisis, the **IMF** made aid conditional on the reversal of the policy, which led to austerity, social unrest and the PNP's defeat in the 1980 election.

THIRD WINDOW

The **World Bank** intermediate financing facility established with effect from July 1975. The aim of this facility was to provide loans to developing countries which had a particularly low average per capita income. Loans were made with extended repayment terms, and at concessional rates of interest (below the Bank's current normal rate for loans, but higher than the nil interest charged by the **IDA**) The difference from the normal rate was met from a special fund to which certain industrialized and oil-exporting countries contributed. In 1975–6 the World Bank made some $700 million of loans under the third window arrangements.

THIRD WORLD

An expression (*tiers monde*) coined by the French writer Georges Balandier to describe the countries of Africa, Asia and Latin America which are, to a varying degree, economically underdeveloped by comparison with those of the **First World** and the **Second World**. China is usually excluded from the term as are **Israel** and South Africa. Most Third World countries are former colonies, and the term may, therefore, also signify the oppressed or exploited nations of the world. Some observers argue that the **North-South** distinction is more accurate than the terms First or Third World.

30-YEAR RULE

The practice in the UK whereby most public records are only released for general access 30 years after their date of origin. Certain exceptions are made even to this rule in respect of issues thought to be particularly sensitive, especially those relating to the royal family and to intelligence matters, to which a longer period may apply. Some relaxation was promised in July 1993 within the context of the government's policy of **open government**.

38TH PARALLEL

The demarcation line between North and South Korea, one of the most tense and heavily fortified borders in the world.

The Korean peninsula, annexed by Japan in 1910, was liberated in August–September 1945 to the north of the 38th parallel of latitude by Soviet troops, and to the south by US forces. Korea was thus divided into two roughly equal halves, damaging the country's infrastructure and transport system, and leaving the bulk of the country's industry and natural resources in the northern sector, whilst most of the population and agricultural land were in the south. As the two spheres of occupation solidified into separate Korean states in 1948, each reflecting the ideological disposition of its **superpower** sponsor, the 38th parallel became one of the front lines of the **Cold War**.

On 25 June 1950 North Korean forces invaded the South. In the ensuing **Korean War** the South was supported by **UN** (largely US) forces whilst the North was assisted by Chinese troops. When an armistice agreement halted the fighting in 1953, the front line, still called the 38th parallel, actually straddled the 38th line of latitude, with Southern forces holding territory to the north of 38°N in the central and eastern sectors of the front, and Northern troops holding ground further south in the western sector. This front line has remained the de facto border between the two Korean states since that time.

THORP

Thermal oxide reprocessing plant – the highly controversial **nuclear reprocessing** plant which started operations in March 1994 after British Nuclear Fuels finally obtained the go-ahead. Spent nuclear fuel rods from nuclear power stations in the UK and abroad, particularly Germany and Japan, will be brought to Thorp, which is situated at **Sellafield** in Cumbria, in order to have the plutonium extracted from them. Politicians and environmentalists worldwide have raised objections on the grounds that it is not economically viable and will produce quantities of plutonium which could encourage nuclear proliferation. There are also complaints of inadequate public consultation. The original plan to build Thorp prompted a campaign of protest by environmental pressure groups led by **Friends of the Earth**, and culminating in the 1977 **Windscale** enquiry – the UK's first public enquiry into a nuclear power development. The project was approved, but when construction was completed in 1992 commissioning was delayed because the British Nuclear Installation Inspectorate insisted on a reduction in proposed levels of radioactive emissions.

THORPE CASE

The 1979 court case which spelt the end of the political career of Jeremy Thorpe, the former leader of the UK Liberal Party. Thorpe had resigned as party leader in May 1976, five months after a statement in court (in an unrelated case) by Norman Scott that he and Thorpe had some years previously had a homosexual relationship. Thorpe, who denied the allegation, was subsequently charged with conspiracy and incitement to kill Scott, but was acquitted in June 1979.

THOUSAND DAYS

A description of the term of office of US President John F. Kennedy (20 January 1961–22 November 1963) which was ended prematurely by his assassination in Dallas, Texas. Like **Camelot**, the term tends to romanticize Kennedy, and suggests an administration cruelly cut short before being able to fulfil its early promise.

300 GROUP

A British all-party campaign launched in the 1970s to get more women into parliament, local government and other areas of public life. Of the 651 MPs elected in April 1992, 60 were women, compared with 44 in the outgoing parliament.

THREE-DAY WEEK

The period of restricted economic activity resulting from the 1973–4 **miners' strike** and other industrial action in the UK. In November 1973 the National Union of Mineworkers began an overtime ban in support of a wage claim in breach of the current **incomes policy**, and this developed into a full stoppage of work in February-March 1974. The economic position was also gravely affected by the embargo imposed by **OPEC** oil producing countries in October-November 1973 and the simultaneous oil price explosion, and by industrial action on the part of power engineers, railway employees and other workers. Meanwhile, a state of emergency was proclaimed in mid-November, under which in mid-December a package of measures was introduced limiting electricity supplies by a third and effectively imposing three-day working. In the context of this situation, the Conservative Prime Minister Edward Heath called a premature general election for 28 February 1974 on the issue of 'Who governs Britain?'. The election was lost by the Conservatives and resulted in the formation of a (minority) Labour government.

THREE GORGES DAM

A massive hydroelectric project to create a reservoir on the upper reaches of the Yangtze River in China. Although under attack for the environmental damage which it is claimed will result, Chinese officials maintain that the dam will improve water quality in the lower reaches of the Yangtze.

THREE MILE ISLAND

The nuclear reactor at Harrisburg in Pennsylvania, USA, where a large-scale nuclear accident occurred on 28 March 1979 and the nuclear core of the reactor came within an hour of melting down. Some 190,000 people were evacuated from the area. The Three Mile Island accident highlighted environmentalists' fears about **PWRs**. There were no direct casualties, but a report concluded that meltdown of the nuclear core was only avoided by good fortune, and the release of low-level radiation in the accident has been blamed for above average death rates among the elderly in the affected area. The Three Mile Island incident prompted the US government to cancel all nuclear reactors ordered in the five years prior to the accident.

THREE WORLDS THEORY

The doctrine adopted by the Chinese **Communist** Party (CCP) in 1974 which redefined the terms First, Second and **Third World**. The CCP division of the world placed the USA and the **Soviet Union** (regarded as the more aggressive of the two) in the First World; developed countries attempting to liberate themselves from influence of the two **superpowers** in the **Second World**; and Africa, Asia (including China), and Latin America in the **Third World**. In the context of the **Sino-Soviet split**, the CCP advocated the alliance of the Second and Third Worlds against the First.

TIANANMEN SQUARE

The central square in Beijing, China, and the site of the mass student demonstrations in April–June 1989 which were brutally suppressed on 3–4 June by units of the People's Liberation Army with the death of up to 5,000 people, according to Western estimates.

Pro-democracy demonstrations by students began throughout China after the death of Hu Yaobang on 15 April 1989 and continued despite a warning in an editorial in the *People's Daily* of 26 April apparently endorsed by Deng Xiaoping. Over 1,000 students occupying Tiananmen Square began a hunger strike on 13 May, exciting sympathy among workers. The leadership of the Chinese Communist Party (CCP) was at first divided over the correct response to the students' demands, which included further democratization, 'genuine dialogue' with the country's leaders and an end to corruption, but conservative elements in the leadership gained the upper hand. **Martial law** was declared in Beijing on 20 May, but the scale of the demonstrations prevented troops from entering Tiananmen Square, until, on 4 June, they began firing on demonstrators. Order was forcibly reimposed in Beijing and throughout the country.

The Tiananmen Square events brought conservative figures in the Chinese leadership into the ascendancy, including Jiang

Zemin who at a party central committee plenum on 23–24 June became CCP General Secretary. He replaced Zhao Ziyang, who had been dismissed from his post after he had called for moderation and had met students on 19 May.

TIED AID

Aid which is conditional upon the recipient using the money to buy goods from the donor country, or, more recently, using it in some other way specified by the donor.

TIGER TALKS

The negotiations held aboard HMS *Tiger* off Gibraltar on 2–4 December 1966 between UK Prime Minister Harold Wilson and Rhodesian leader Ian Smith, which failed to end Rhodesian **UDI**. Although Wilson virtually conceded independence to Smith's government in return for a commitment to make progress towards black majority rule, the deal was rejected by Smith's obdurate Rhodesian Front. Wilson responded by calling on the **UN** to impose mandatory economic **sanctions**. The next official round of talks, which took place on HMS *Fearless* on 9–13 October 1968, also proved unsuccessful. The next attempt to resolve the situation was the 1971 **Pearce Commission**.

TIGERS

An army of Serb irregulars notorious for their alleged war crimes during the Yugoslav civil war. Led by Zeljko Raznjatovic (under the nom de guerre 'Arkan') the Tigers were said to have murdered civilians and prisoners of war during fighting in 1991–3 in the Croatian town of **Vukovar** and in **Bosnia-Hercegovina**. Raznjatovic subsequently turned to politics, leading a Serbian Unity Party which performed poorly in Serbian legislative elections in December 1993 despite his reputation in Serbia as a war hero and the tacit support of Serbian President Slobodan Milosevic.

TITOISM

The political creed of Josip Broz Tito, **Yugoslavia's communist** leader from 1945 until his death in 1980, which was contrived above all to secure stability. Titoism was a pragmatic blend of elements: (i) a refusal to accept the **Stalinist** model, permitting greater adaptability; (ii) authoritarian leadership allied to a **cult of personality**; (iii) a repressive policy towards **nationalism**; (iv) an emphasis on economic prosperity; and (v) workers' self-management.

TLATELOLCO TREATY

A treaty banning **nuclear weapons** in **Latin America** and the **Caribbean**, signed on 14 February 1967. The ban did not extend to nuclear energy, and nuclear tests for peaceful purposes were allowed as was the presence in the region of foreign nuclear powers with territorial interests which pledged not to use nuclear weapons against Latin American countries. All countries of the region were signatories except Cuba, which objected to the nuclear weapons in US bases in the region. The treaty was not ratified by Argentina and Brazil, who complained that it discriminated against developing countries; Chile suspended its implementation in 1974, charging that some Latin American countries with nuclear programmes were not full members. The treaty was amended in August 1992, paving the way for its ratification by Argentina in November 1993, Chile in January 1994 and Brazil in May 1994.

TOKYO ROUND

The **GATT** round of multilateral trade negotiations held in 1973–9. This round, with the widest ever participation, was designed to be of special benefit to the developing countries, as well as to promote the general expansion of world trade. The round resulted in agreements to cut a wide range of industrial and agricultural tariffs by about one-third over an eight-year period. Although most concessions were negotiated bilaterally, the benefits were extended to all GATT countries under the **MFN** (most-favoured-nation) rules. Moreover, notwithstanding the MFN regime, the Tokyo Round encouraged GATT members to grant preferential and more favourable treatment to developing countries.

TOKYO WAR CRIMES TRIBUNAL

The trial of wartime Japanese leaders, on the same model as the **Nuremberg War Crimes Tribunal**. The proceedings in Tokyo, organized by the International Military Tribunal for the Far East, were the most highly publicized of the many war crimes trials which took place following the Pacific War. Among the 28 defendants was Hideki Tojo, the Japanese Prime Minister and Minister of War at the time of the attack on Pearl Harbour in December 1941. As at Nuremberg, the defendants were accused of crimes against humanity and crimes against peace, the latter category including the conspiracy to wage an aggressive war. The trial began on 3 May 1946, and the 11-member panel of judges delivered its verdicts on 4 November 1948. As at Nuremberg, the proceedings were judicially flawed and, unlike Nuremberg, were marked by serious instances of bias. Seven of the accused (including Tojo) were sentenced to death, and were hanged on 23 December 1948. Of the remainder, 18 received prison sentences, two died during the proceedings and one was deemed unfit to stand trial. Six of those imprisoned died while in custody, and the others were released on parole after serving a portion of their sentences. The last to be released were freed on 7 April 1958.

TONTONS MACOUTES

(Creole, plural form of 'Uncle Knapsack' – a bogeyman) The notorious Haitian **right-wing** secret police and paramilitary force set up in 1958 by President François 'Papa Doc' Duvalier to quash opposition to his regime. Its members were black and recruited chiefly from shanty towns and the rural destitute, and their reign of terror ensured the survival of **Duvalierism** into its second generation. After the September 1991 coup their role was largely taken over by the **attachés**.

TORREY CANYON

A Liberian-registered oil tanker which ran aground off the south-west English coast on 18 March 1967. The vessel was owned by a subsidiary of the Union Oil Company of California and was on charter to BP. Most of its cargo of 117,000 tonnes of crude oil was spilt into the sea, outside British territorial waters, and thick oil was washed up on the holiday beaches of Cornwall, necessitating a massive clear-up operation.

TORRICELLI LAW

The name given to the legislation passed by the US **Congress** in October 1992 tightening the trade embargo on Cuba ostensibly to force the government of President Fidel Castro to hold free and fair elections. Sponsored by Robert J. Torricelli, a Democratic member of the House of Representatives with close links with Miami **anti-Castroites**, it made it illegal for subsidiaries of US companies anywhere in the world to trade with Cuba and closed US ports to any ship which had put into Cuba within the previous six months. It was condemned by the **UN General Assembly** as counter-productive, an affront to human rights and contrary to the spirit of international co-operation.

TORY

A colloquial term for the UK **Conservative** Party which has acquired such wide usage that the two names are now interchangeable. It derives from a sixteenth century Irish word used abusively of Catholic outlaws.

TOTAL WAR

War which involves civilians as well as the military, and in which all national production is channelled towards the war effort. The concept of total war first became a reality during the Second World War, as air power allowed the combatants to attack civilians, and the economies of the participants were geared completely towards military production.

TOTALITARIANISM

A term coined by US social scientists in the 1950s, and influenced by the **Cold War**, which arose from the perceived similarities between the political systems of Nazi Germany and the **Soviet Union**. The term was intended to describe a political system which subjected all aspects of life to control by the state, itself legitimized by an all-pervasive ideology. Totalitarianism was considered to differ from more traditional forms of dictatorship in that it required the active participation of the whole population.

Although Nazi Germany and the Soviet Union maintained their regimes by similar means (for example, a **police state**, control of the media, and **propaganda**), the declared aims of these states – respectively to establish a racially pure state, and to construct **socialism** – differed fundamentally. The regimes also diverged in other basic ways, for example in their attitude to private property, in their interpretation of **nationalism**, and in the importance they attached to race. Although frequently used in polemical argument, the term was never fully accepted among political scientists and remained essentially a pejorative description of the Soviet system.

TOTTENHAM RIOTS *see* BROADWATER FARM

TOWER COMMISSION

A commission under the chairmanship of former Republican Senator John G. Tower, established by President Ronald Reagan to inquire into the role of the National Security Council (**NSC**) in the **Iran-contra affair**. The three-member panel, established on 27 November 1986, also included Edmund S. Muskie (Democratic Secretary of State under President Jimmy Carter), and Lt.-Gen. Brent Scowcroft (NSC Adviser under President Gerald Ford. The report of the commission, issued on 26 February 1987, was critical of some senior members of the Reagan administration (particularly White House Chief of Staff Donald Regan, who immediately resigned), but found no evidence that the President or Vice-President George Bush had known of the Iran-contra affair.

TOWNSHIPS

Urban areas in South Africa inhabited by the country's black population. Established during the era of **apartheid**, townships were the only urban areas where members of the African community could legally reside; the centres of towns and cities were reserved for white residents, and in rural areas Africans were expected to live in **bantustans**. Although generally associated with the African community, townships were also established for the Asian and **Coloured** communities. Townships were the focus of anti-apartheid struggle, particularly from the mid-1970s onwards. The largest and most famous township is Soweto, in Johannesburg, scene of the 1976 **Soweto riots**.

TRABANT

The small car manufactured in millions by **communist** East Germany (the **DDR**). Built to the same basic specification for decades, and notorious for its unreliability, poor performance and high pollution, the Trabant came to embody the DDR's failure to keep pace with the economic advance of the West.

TRANSBOUNDARY POLLUTION

The spread of airborne or waterborne pollutants, often in the form of **acid rain**, from the country where they are generated to another country. The dumping of chemicals into rivers can pollute areas downstream; the tall chimneys of some power stations, built in preference to installing equipment to clean flues, cause pollutants to be released into the upper atmosphere where they may be carried great distances before being washed back to earth as acid rain. The phenomenon has caused friction between Canada and the USA, for example, and between **Scandinavia** and the UK. The 1979 Geneva Convention on Long-Range Transboundary Air Pollution has been in effect since 1983.

TRANSCAUCASUS

The region between the Caspian and Black Seas to the south of the Caucasus mountains which was formerly part of the **Soviet Union** but now comprises the independent states of **Georgia**, **Azerbaijan** and **Armenia**. Russia has been anxious to retain influence in the Transcaucasus, which it regards as a barrier to Turkish and Iranian interests in **Central Asia**. There have been allegations of Russian military support for the **Abkhaz** rebels in Georgia and for Armenian rebels in the Azerbaijani enclave of **Nagorny Karabakh**, as part of a deliberate policy to destabilize Transcaucasian republics and allow Russia to reassert its regional pre-eminence. As a result, Turkey's foothold in Turkic-speaking Azerbaijan, which it regarded as a gateway to **Central Asia**, has appeared to slip since the demise of the pro-Turkish regime there in June 1993. Georgia reluctantly agreed to join the Russian-dominated **CIS** in December 1993.

TRANSJORDAN *see* JORDAN

TRANSKEI *see* BANTUSTANS

TRANSNATIONAL CORPORATION *see* MULTINATIONAL CORPORATION

TRANSPARENCY

Openness in the operation of rules or institutions. In the **GATT** talks on world trade, demands for increased transparency are made for example about certain countries' import regimes, or about how intellectual property rules are applied. In the **EU** context, transparency is one of the buzzwords of the 1990s. Thus pledges of increased transparency in EU decision-making were made to encourage the Danish people to reverse their referendum vote against the ratification of the **Maastricht** treaty in 1992.

TREASON TRIAL

The marathon South African trial of 156 anti-**apartheid** activists arrested on 5 December 1956, including the current President of South Africa, Nelson Mandela, which ended on 29 March 1961 with all the defendants being found not guilty (although Mandela was among those subsequently sentenced to life imprisonment at the **Rivonia trial**). The preparatory examination of the case began in December 1956 and was completed in September 1957, when the magistrate concluded that there was 'sufficient reason' to try them on charges of treason. The trial proper began in 1958 and over the ensuing years the prosecution argued that the **ANC** and its allies sought the violent overthrow of the government and the establishment of a **communist** state. The treason trial led to the establishment of a London-based support fund which evolved into **IDAF**.

TREATY ON EUROPEAN UNION *see* MAASTRICHT

TREUHANDANSTALT

(German, 'trust agency'). The privatization agency established in March 1990 by the **DDR** government in preparation for the unification of East and West Germany on 3 October 1990. Its task was to oversee the transfer to private ownership of East Germany's 8,000 state-owned enterprises. In view of the problems of determining ownership of property, and the risks of investing in firms previously functioning under a **command economy**, privatization proceeded slowly, and only 1,000 firms had been sold by April 1991. A further 330, employing 80,000 people, had been closed down as too unprofitable to sell, and the resulting unemployment provoked criticism of the *Treuhandanstalt*.

TREVI GROUP

The group of Justice and Interior Ministers within the **EU**, set up in 1976, and concerned with such issues as asylum policy and setting up a joint police database to combat drug trafficking and terrorism.

TRIAD

The powerful Chinese criminal syndicate, active in Hong Kong, mainland China, Singapore, **Taiwan**, Europe and North America. Triad fraternities, based on ritualized sworn brotherhood, first made their mark on the underworld in south-east China in the late eighteenth century. In recent years the Triad network has been heavily involved in international drug trafficking.

TRIBUNE GROUP

The UK Labour Party's leading 'soft left' faction, particularly influential in the 1960s, which took its name from the *Tribune* newspaper first published in 1937. The Group has historically supported further nationalization and a withdrawal from the **EC**. Its most prominent supporters have (at one time or another) included Aneurin Bevan, former party leaders Michael Foot and Neil Kinnock, and latterly Gordon Brown and John Prescott, the deputy leader from July 1994.

TRIDENT

A US-made multiple-warhead submarine-launched nuclear missile, introduced by the US Navy in refitted Poseidon submarines, and in the larger Trident-class submarines first delivered in 1981. A more powerful Trident II missile was first introduced in 1990. Plans for major cuts in the Trident programme were announced in 1992 by US President George Bush in line with the emphasis on arms reduction in the **START** treaties. In the UK the Conservative government, despite escalating costs, stood by its 1982 decision to replace **Polaris** missiles (and the **Chevaline** upgrade) with Trident II, but finally conceded in November 1993 that the number of warheads would be less than originally planned.

TRILATERAL COMMISSION

An influential organization of elite and establishment figures from Japan, North America, and the countries of the **EU**, which attempts to influence world economic policy and particularly to encourage a more unified economic system among the industrialized countries. Its 350 members are top politicians, businessmen and bankers, trades unionists, and media and intelligentsia figures. Founded in 1972–3 by US banker David Rockefeller, it first achieved notoriety in 1976 when US President Jimmy Carter admitted that senior posts in his administration were overwhelmingly staffed by its members. The Trilateral Commission is opposed by socialist and nationalist ideologies; by the developing world, which sees in it the 'rich man's club'; and by those defending perceived interests of national security.

TRINIDAD TERMS

An official debt reduction scheme launched by John Major, then UK Chancellor of the Exchequer, in 1990. Under this scheme, it was proposed, some 20 extremely poor countries (especially in sub-Saharan Africa) would see two-thirds of their aggregate government-to-government debt written off, provided they had an active economic programme agreed with the **IMF**. They would also be granted a five-year 'interest holiday' on their remaining debt, whose repayment would be rescheduled over up to 25 years. By early 1994 a total of 22 countries had benefited under these arrangements.

TRNC

The Turkish Republic of Northern Cyprus, proclaimed as a separate republic in November 1983, in the area north of the **Green Line** which has been occupied by Turkish troops since July 1974. The TRNC's territory comprises about 40 per cent of the island of Cyprus, but the regime (headed by a directly elected executive president, Rauf Denktash, and with a 50-member parliament) has received no international recognition except that of Turkey.

TROIKA

(Russian, 'three-horse carriage') A term loosely meaning three leaders, or the representatives of three countries. In the **EU** the Foreign Ministers of the member states which last held, currently holds, and will next hold, the rotating presidency of the European **Council of Ministers** work together as a troika for the sake of continuity. In the **Soviet Union** on the death of Joseph Stalin in 1953, a 'collective leadership' centred on the troika of Georgi Malenkov, Lazar Kaganovich and Vyacheslav Molotov, until the emergence of Nikita Khrushchev as leader in 1954–5.

TROOPS OUT!

The slogan used from the 1970s to encapsulate the call for the unilateral and unconditional withdrawal of the British army from **Northern Ireland**. A Troops Out movement campaigns on this issue.

TROTSKYIST

An adherent of the political thought of Leon Trotsky (Lev Bronstein, 1879–1940). Trotskyist groups have been on the fringe of the **Communist** movement since Trotsky was defeated by Joseph Stalin in 1924 as leader of the Soviet Communist party. In 1938, they formed the **Fourth International** to oppose the Stalinist leadership of the international Communist movement. Adhering to the theories of **permanent revolution**, Trotskyists criticized the **Soviet Union** for having degenerated into a bureaucratic state, or even reverted to **capitalism**.

TRUCIAL STATES *see* UAE

TRUMAN DOCTRINE

The US foreign policy principle of declaring US support for governments on the grounds of their opposition to **communism**. US President Harry Truman proposed to Congress on 12 March 1947 that the USA should intervene on behalf of 'free peoples who are resisting attempted subjection by armed minorities or by outside pressure'. Regarded as a declaration of US participation in the **Cold War**, the doctrine was formulated when the UK withdrew from actively supporting the Greek government against communist insurgents, and from helping Turkey to resist pressure from the **Soviet Union** – tasks which were assumed by the USA.

TRUST TERRITORY

A former colonial territory which the **UN** held in trust while fostering the conditions which would allow it to become a fully sovereign state. Eleven trust territories were created after the end of the Second World War, each of which was administered through another state, itself accountable to the UN. Of the 11, only the UN Trust Territory of the Pacific Islands was designated a 'strategic area'. Its status was partially terminated in 1986, to be replaced by 'compacts of free association' between its four individual members and the USA. The last such compact (with **Belau**) was concluded in November 1993.

TRUSTEESHIP COUNCIL

The **UN** body established under Chapter XIII of the UN Charter as one of the organization's six 'principal organs', and charged with overseeing the transition of **trust territories** to self-government. The UN's involvement in these territories, however, was generally effected through other bodies such as the Special Committee on **Decolonization**, set up by the **UN General Assembly** in 1961.

TRUTH COMMISSION

A **UN**-sponsored commission investigating human rights abuses during the 1980–91 civil war in El Salvador. Its report, *From Madness to Hope*, published in March 1993, found the army and army-linked paramilitary groups guilty of atrocities against some 75,000 people, mostly civilians, as a result of the government's **counterinsurgency** strategy. The **FMLN guerrillas** were held responsible for 300 **disappeared** and 400 murders. The report also revealed US complicity in covering-up the mass-killings. It called for a special investigation into **death squads** and listed 103 members of the military to be purged, recommending that all those named in the report be banned from public office for at least 10 years. The UN stressed that the recommendations were mandatory under the peace accord, but both government and army rejected the report as biased. The US suspension of military aid in March 1993, however, forced the government to retire the 103 named military personnel, including **Tandona** officers.

TUAREGS

A nomadic people living in the **Sahel** areas of **Mali** and Niger. Their demands for autonomy have brought them into conflict with the governments of both countries, and years of tension escalated into a full-scale rebellion in the early 1990s. As a result Tuareg areas in Mali and Niger were heavily militarized and some 100,000 Tuaregs went into exile in neighbouring Algeria, **Burkina Faso** and Mauritania. In April 1992 the government of Mali concluded a peace agreement with the rebels in its territory, although details were only finalized in May 1994. Peace talks in Niger began in February 1994.

TUC

The Trades Union Congress, the key umbrella employees' organization in the UK, originally founded in 1868. In mid-1994 a total of 68 individual trade unions were affiliated to the TUC, with an affiliated membership of just over 7.5 million; comparative figures for 1979 were 109 and about 12 million. Over this period the decline in individual unions largely reflected mergers, while the drop in membership was affected by the increase in unemployment – particularly in the traditionally highly-unionized heavy industries – and by the growth in self-employment. In the late 1970s the TUC still had a major role in consultation with government on a wide range of economic and social matters. However, its influence in these areas was restricted under the succeeding Conservative governments which introduced a series of legislative measures on industrial relations and on trade union regulation. In 1994 the TUC sought to 'relaunch' itself around a tightly defined set of priorities.

TUNA WAR

The name given to a joint Ecuadorean and Peruvian policy in the late 1960s and early 1970s to seize and fine US boats fishing in their territorial waters. The conflict arose out of a 1950s treaty between Chile, Ecuador and Peru in which a 200-mile territorial limit was claimed in order to regulate tuna fishing off their coasts. This measure to safeguard an important resource and source of income was claimed to be in breach of international law by the US government which encouraged its fishing fleet to ignore the limit.

TUPAMAROS

A former Uruguayan **guerrilla** group named after the eighteenth century Peruvian Indian leader Tupac Amarú, and founded in 1962 by Raúl Sendic Antonaccio, an activist in sugarcane cutters' strikes. After four years of robberies in aid of the rural poor, the group turned to the cities and, in the crisis years of the late 1960s, increasingly to violence. The group came to international attention over the killing of a **CIA** agent in 1970, and over a series of kidnappings, including that of the British ambassador. The group was defeated and survivors captured in a major **counterinsurgency** offensive in 1972. The prisoners were amnestied in 1985 on the return of democratic rule, and Sendic pledged his co-operation with the government, reorganizing the *Tupamaros* into a political party, the National Liberation Movement (MLN).

TUPOLEV

Soviet aircraft named after their designer, Andrey Tupolev, including the first supersonic passenger plane, the TU-144 (also known by its **NATO** code-name 'Charger'). The TU-144 was test flown in 1968 and publicly shown in Moscow in 1970, antedating the Anglo-French **Concorde** project. It therefore presented the Soviet authorities with a **propaganda** coup at the time, but subsequently proved unreliable in service.

TURKISH REPUBLIC OF NORTHERN CYPRUS *see* TRNC

TURKMENISTAN

An independent state in **Central Asia** since 1991, and formerly, as Turkmenia, the southernmost of the **Soviet Union's** 15 constituent republics. The Turkic-speaking, moderately Islamic and clan-oriented Turkmens form the predominant ethnic group; others, in a population of 3.9 million, include Russians, Kazakhs and Uzbeks. Turkmenistan is rich in oil and natural gas and has been comparatively successful in attracting foreign investment. It is ruled by an authoritarian regime with a **cult of personality** attached to President Saparmurad Niyazov.

TUTSI

A people of central Africa. They constitute a minority of the population in **Burundi** and in **Rwanda**; the **Hutu** are in the majority in both countries.

TUVALU

The Polynesian islands formerly known as the Ellice Islands, which achieved independence from the UK on 1 October 1978. Until 1 October 1975, when they became a separate dependency under the name of Tuvalu, the islands were jointly administered with the Gilbert Islands, which later became **Kiribati**. The change in status followed a 1974 referendum in which the islanders voted overwhelmingly for separate status. Tuvalu is a 'special member' of the **Commonwealth**.

TWA HIJACK

The infamous 1985 hijacking of a US airliner by Lebanese **guerrillas**. The US Trans World Airlines (TWA) aircraft carrying 145 passengers and eight crew was hijacked on 14 June en route from Athens to Rome by gunmen who forced it to land at Beirut. The hijackers demanded the release from **Israel**'s Atlit detention camp of 766 Lebanese **Shia** and Palestinian detainees. The identity of the hijackers remained unclear, although it was claimed that they were in some way linked to **Hezbollah**. During the early stages of the drama, the hijackers shot dead a US Navy diver but released other passengers. The plane made a series of flights between Algiers and Beirut before the remaining hostages were taken off the plane and into Beirut under the supervision of Shia **Amal** officials. In what it insisted was an unrelated move, the Israeli government on 24 June released a small number of the Atlit detainees. The final hostages were freed by **Amal** on June 30, and by early September Israel had freed the remainder of the Atlit detainees.

TWELVERS *see* SHIA

26 COUNTIES

A term for the Republic of Ireland, used with the connotation that the division of the island of Ireland, into the 26 counties of the South and the **six counties** of the North, is temporary and undesirable. The division dates from 1922, when the 26 counties became the Irish Free State. This included three of Ireland's four historic provinces – Leinster, Munster and Connacht – and three of the nine counties of **Ulster**. The 1937 Constitution establishing an independent Ireland nominally applies to the whole of the island of Ireland (Eire); however, pending the 'reintegration of the national territory' the laws enacted by the Irish Parliament (**Oireachtas**) apply only in the 26 counties. Ireland's constitutional claim to the whole island has proved a stumbling block in discussions over Northern Ireland, particularly among **Unionist** politicians, despite efforts to find a reassuring formulation, most recently in the 1993 **Downing Street Declaration**.

TWIN-TRACK DECISION

The decision by **NATO** in December 1979 to modernize its **nuclear weapons** deployed in Europe, in particular by introducing new intermediate-range forces (INF), **cruise** and **Pershing** II missiles. Ostensibly this was one 'track' in the response to Soviet deployment of SS-20 missiles targeting **Western Europe**; the other was to negotiate for their removal. In practice the Soviet side refused to negotiate under the threat of cruise and Pershing, and the apparently greatly increased danger of a nuclear war in Europe galvanized European peace movements against the NATO missiles on an unprecedented scale.

TWO-PLUS-FOUR TALKS

The negotiations in 1990 between the four **Allies** of the Second World War – France, the **Soviet Union**, the UK and the USA – and the two German states (**DDR** and **BRD**) over the security implications of impending German unification. The first round of talks was held on 5 May, followed by meetings on 22 June, 17 July and 7 September. Before the third round the Soviet Union implicitly gave its acquiescence to a united Germany's membership of **NATO**, thus opening the way for the treaty to be signed on 12 September in Moscow. Its provisions confirmed the borders of united Germany, and envisaged the withdrawal of Soviet troops from former East German territory by the end of 1994. The treaty ceded to Germany full sovereignty over its affairs, ending the 'rights and responsibilities' of the Allies towards Berlin and

Germany and thereby terminating the 1945 **Potsdam** agreement.

TWO-SPEED EUROPE

An idea floated by French President François Mitterrand in a speech to the European Parliament in 1984, that the relaunched process of European integration in the **EC** (later the **EU**) could proceed faster for certain countries, with the remaining members possibly taking the same steps at a later date. The result, he suggested, could be 'a Europe of **variable geometry**'. The suggestion was highly controversial, implying that the EU would be shaped by 'core' countries (particularly France and Germany) which provided the 'motor' for integration. The two-speed idea, however, resurfaced in the 1990s both with regard to **EMU** (when **Bundesbank** president Karl Otto Pohl in June 1990 put forward the idea of France, Germany and the **Benelux** countries entering a European central banking system first), and with regard to the enlargement of the EU.

TWYFORD DOWN

An area containing two SSSIs (Sites of Special Scientific Interest) and an SAM (Scheduled Ancient Monument) which in the early 1990s became the focus of a fierce contest over the extension of the M3 motorway in southern England. In a test case for **EC** environmental law, the EC **Commission** threatened the UK government with legal action for allegedly pressing ahead with construction without conducting an **environmental impact assessment** as required by EC law. However, the EC dropped the case in July 1992, claiming that it was satisfied that the UK government's environmental studies satisfied the spirit of EC directives.

TYNWALD

The parliament of the Isle of Man, a UK Crown Dependency. The principal chamber of Tynwald is the 24-member directly elected House of Keys; the Legislative Council has four ex officio members, and eight elected by and from the House of Keys. Tynwald celebrated its millennium in 1979; only the Althing of Iceland claims to be older (dating back to at least 930), but its existence has not been uninterrupted.

U-2

The high-flying reconnaissance aircraft which were used secretly by the USA in the late 1950s to fly missions between Norway and **Pakistan**, gathering military information as they crossed Soviet territory. In a major blow to **detente**, a planned summit conference in Paris between the USA, the **Soviet Union**, the UK and France in May 1960 was aborted when Soviet air defences shot down a U-2 near Sverdlovsk, captured its pilot and exposed the existence of these spying missions. Khrushchev took a particularly strong line both in condemning the US action, and in threatening action against countries providing facilities for US reconnaissance of this kind. The captured pilot, Francis Gary Powers, was put on trial in Moscow and sentenced to 10 years' imprisonment, but was returned to the USA in a February 1962 spy swap.

UAE

The United Arab Emirates, a union of seven oil-rich emirates – Abu Dhabi, Dubai, Sharjah, Ras al-Khaimah, Fujairah, Umm al-Qaiwain and Ajman – situated along the eastern coast of the Arabian peninsular. The UAE's petroleum and natural gas reserves are among the world's largest. Formerly known as the Trucial States, the seven emirates were administered by the UK in 1971. The UK had favoured, on independence, the creation of a federation which would include the seven emirates plus Qatar and Bahrain. However, Qatar and Bahrain withdrew.

UAR

The United Arab Republic, the political union of Egypt and Syria proclaimed in 1958. The differing interests of the two countries led, in 1961, to a military coup in Syria and the dissolution of the union. Despite the dissolution, Egypt retained the title of UAR until 1971 when it took the name Arab Republic of Egypt. The attempt at union, one of a number of such pan-Arabist efforts, was a manifestation of **Nasserism** and **Ba'athism**, the two most important movements in the Arab world during the 1950s and 1960s.

UB40

The document issued by the UK government Employment Service to people claiming unemployment benefit or income support.

UDA

The Ulster Defence Association, the dominant paramilitary Protestant organization in **Northern Ireland**. The UDA came to the fore in the early 1970s and has been blamed – either directly or indirectly – for about a third of civilian killings in Northern Ireland since the outbreak of major disturbances in 1969. Most, but not all, of its victims have been Catholics. However, it was only in August 1992 that it was officially proscribed. The **UFF** is associated with the UDA.

UDF

The United Democratic Front, the South African anti-**apartheid** umbrella organization founded in May 1983 and disbanded in August 1991. The UDF shared the aims of the **ANC**, but was committed to achieving an end to apartheid by peaceful means. It organized non-violent resistance to apartheid ranging from residents' committees to mass demonstrations. In Natal supporters of the UDF came into conflict with supporters of **Inkatha**. In February 1988 the organization was restricted, effectively prohibiting it from pursuing political activities. The ban was lifted on 2 February 1990, when restrictions on the ANC were also lifted. The UDF was disbanded in August 1991 and control of its activities was taken over by the ANC.

UDI

The Unilateral Declaration of Independence, the proclamation by Prime Minister Ian Smith on 11 November 1965 that Southern **Rhodesia** was rejecting its status as a self-governing colony and would henceforth be an independent monarchy within the **Commonwealth**. The declaration was signed by Smith, leader of the Rhodesian Front Party, and by all 15 members of his Cabinet, who rejected British government insistence that they should accept black majority rule. UDI met international condemnation. No country formally recognized the Smith regime, although the **apartheid** regime in South Africa was sympathetic to it. Britain declared the regime 'illegal' and imposed unilateral **sanctions** which were soon given international application through the **UN**. Despite negotiations beginning with the **Tiger Talks**, UDI continued until 12 December 1979. It ended with the (temporary) resumption of British sovereignty under the **Lancaster House Agreement**, with Lord Soames as Governor.

UFF

The Ulster Freedom Fighters, a paramilitary Protestant organization in **Northern Ireland**. Since the early 1970s the UFF has carried out large numbers of killings, especially of Catholics. It is widely considered to be the main military wing of the **UDA**. The organization was proscribed in November 1973.

UGANDAN ASIANS

A term used to describe the 80,000 Ugandans of Asian (predominantly Indian) descent who were expelled from Uganda in 1972; they were given 90 days to leave by Idi Amin. The Asian community was identified in the mind of many Ugandans with British colonialism, and the move was widely supported. By December 1972, 90 per cent of the Asians had left, the majority, as British passport holders, going to the UK and others to India. They left behind assets worth an estimated £500 million (US$750 million).

In October 1992 Ugandan President Yoweri Museveni asked for the forgiveness of the Ugandan Asians and invited all of them to return, promising that they would be able to recover their property or seek compensation for their losses. The first property was returned in February 1993.

UHURU

(Swahili, 'freedom') The slogan adopted by many African independence movements in the 1950s and 1960s and most frequently associated with Kenya.

UJAMAA

(Swahili 'familyhood') A word adopted as the name of the brand of **African socialism** developed by President Julius Nyerere of Tanzania. He first used the term in a 1962 pamphlet in which he argued that socialism was a matter of distribution and an 'attitude of mind'. '*Ujamaa*', he wrote, 'describes our socialism. It is opposed to **capitalism** . . . and it is equally opposed to doctrinaire socialism.' In 1967 he combined *Ujamaa* with the concept of **villagization** leading to the creation of *ujamaa* villages in which small groups of farmers would work together on communal farms and pool their resources.

UKRAINE

Formerly the second largest of the **Soviet Union's** 15 constituent republics, and since 1991 an independent state (and founder member of the **CIS**), with a population of some 52.2 million, and chronic economic difficulties.

ULSTER

One of the four historic provinces of Ireland, comprising the island's nine north-eastern counties. Ulster had the largest concentration of Protestants in the island, and showed the strongest determination to remain within the **United Kingdom**. At the time of partition in 1922 most of Ulster – the **six counties** (Antrim, Armagh, Down, Fermanagh, Londonderry and Tyrone) – became **Northern Ireland** as part of the UK, whereas the counties of Cavan, Donegal and Monaghan were among the **26 counties** included within the Irish Free State. 'Ulster' is commonly if inaccurately used by Unionists as synonymous with Northern Ireland.

ULSTER DEFENCE ASSOCIATION *see* UDA

ULSTER FREEDOM FIGHTERS *see* UFF

ULSTER VOLUNTEER FORCE *see* UVF

UMKHONTO WE SIZWE *see* MK

UMOA

The West African Monetary Union. An umbrella monetary union formed in November 1973, it was designed to preserve the **franc zone** system and the **CFA franc** established by the French colonial authorities in West Africa. UMOA's seven members (Benin, Burkina, Côte d'Ivoire, Mali, Niger, Senegal and Togo) use the franc of the *Communauté financière africaine*. The central issuing bank of the UMOA is the Central Bank of West African States, in Dakar, Senegal.

UN

The United Nations, the most significant international organization in the period since the Second World War. The UN emerged originally from wartime co-ordination among the **Allies** and their declarations, in particular the Atlantic Charter of August 1941, the Washington Declaration by 26 Allied countries on 1 January 1942, the Dumbarton Oaks conference of the **Big Four** in 1944, the **Yalta** conference of the **Big Three** in February 1945, and the **San Francisco Conference** from 25 April to 25 June 1945, formally entitled the United Nations Conference on International Organization. The UN Charter was signed at the end of this meeting, on 26 June, and entered into force on 24 October 1945, when the UN was formally established, with its headquarters in New York.

Replacing the unsuccessful inter-war League of Nations, the UN rapidly evolved to become the centre of a wide-ranging network of globally oriented specialized agencies. The UN's objectives are enshrined in the 111 articles of the Charter, the most important of them being the maintenance of world peace and the development of economic, social, cultural and humanitarian co-operation on an international basis. The Charter also defines the UN's structures, finances and procedures and establishes its six 'principal organs', namely the **UN General Assembly**, the **UN Security Council**, the Economic and Social Council (**ECOSOC**), the **Trusteeship Council**, the International Court of Justice

(**ICJ**) and the **UN Secretariat** headed by the secretary-general. The UN system consists additionally of numerous subsidiary bodies and a number of specialized agencies (now 16 in all) each with its own constitution, membership and budget.

Membership of the UN is confined to states, as distinct from non-governmental or international entities. Membership has risen from 51 at inception to 184 as of early 1994. No member state has ever been expelled from the UN although some, notably South Africa and the former Socialist Federal Republic of **Yugoslavia**, have had their memberships suspended. Indonesia temporarily withdrew its membership in 1965–6, and China was represented in 1949–71 only by the Nationalist government based in **Taiwan**.

UN ECONOMIC COMMISSION *see* ECONOMIC COMMISSION

UN ECONOMIC AND SOCIAL COMMISSION *see* ECONOMIC COMMISSION

UN GENERAL ASSEMBLY

One of the six principal organs of the **UN**, established under Chapter IV of the UN Charter to act as the organization's plenary body, representing all 184 of its member states, and meeting in regular session for the last quarter of every year. Its chief functions include the approval of the budget and the adoption of resolutions on a wide range of issues. In addition, it sets the UN's priorities, calls international conferences and oversees the work of the UN's numerous subsidiary bodies.

UN SECRETARIAT

One of the six 'principal organs' of the **UN** listed in Chapter III of its Charter. The Secretariat, and the functions of the Secretary-General, are covered in detail in Chapter XV of the Charter. In practice its structure has evolved over time; sweeping changes were announced in February 1992 by Secretary-General Boutros Boutros-Ghali, cutting down the number of top departments to eight, each headed by an Under-Secretary-General. The Secretary-General is elected by the **UN Security Council**, subject to approval by the **UN General Assembly**. The election is normally for a five-year term, but in 48 years there have been only six holders of this office. The first, Trygve Lie of Norway, took office in February 1946. His five-year term was extended for a further three years in controversial circumstances in 1950, when the General Assembly overrode a Soviet veto in the Security Council, but, with the **Soviet Union** continuing to regard him as illegally elected, he announced in November 1952 that he would resign. Subsequent holders of the office have been Dag Hammarskjöld of Sweden (from April 1953 until his death in the Congo in September 1961), U Thant of Burma (1961–71), Kurt Waldheim of Austria (1972–81), Javier Pérez de Cuéllar of Peru (1982–91), and the incumbent since 1 January 1992, Boutros Boutros-Ghali of Egypt.

UN SECURITY COUNCIL

One of the six principal organs of the , established under Chapter V of the **UN** Charter. The Security Council has 'primary responsibility for the maintenance of international peace and security'. Its original composition provided for a total of 11 members – five permanent members (China – **Taiwan** until 1971 when it was replaced by the **PRC**, France, the former **Soviet Union**, the UK and the USA), and six non-permanent members to be elected for two-year terms by the **UN General Assembly**. The growth of UN membership led in 1965 to the enlargement of the Council to 15 members (the original five permanent members plus 10 non-permanent members). In December 1991 Russia became a permanent member following the dissolution of the Soviet Union in that month. Each of the five permanent members has the power of veto; all decisions also require an affirmative vote by nine members. The Council meets frequently during the year and is empowered to take decisions that are binding on all UN members.

UN SPECIAL FUND *see* UNDP

UN-AMERICAN ACTIVITIES

The Committee on Un-American Activities was established by the US House of Representatives in 1938 to investigate anti-democratic movements. In addition to calling individuals to testify before it, the Committee launched an investigation of the film industry in 1947. This initiative led studios to promise not to employ communists, and to draw up a blacklist of actors, writers, directors and technicians who were considered politically suspect or who had refused to co-operate with the investigation. The Committee reached the height of its influence in the 1950s when anti-**communist** hysteria provided a fertile ground for **McCarthyism**.

UNAMIR

The **UN** Assistance Mission to **Rwanda** established in October 1993 to assist in the implementation of the peace agreement signed in August 1993 by the government of President Juvénal Habyarimana and the rebel **RPF**. Little progress in the implementation of the agreement had been made by the time of the death of Habyarimana in April 1994. The UNAMIR force, with just 2,500 military members, then found itself unable to cope with the terrible violence unleashed by his death. Faced with the choice of greatly reinforcing UNAMIR, withdrawing it completely, or reducing its size, the **UN Security Council** on 22 April ordered the scaling down of the operation to just 270 members. This decision was heavily condemned by African governments and **NGOs**, which accused the UN of applying double standards to Africa and Europe (the Security Council vote having coincided with a decision to dispatch 6,500 extra troops to **Bosnia-Hercegovina**). As the full horror of the conflict became increasingly apparent, on 17 May the Security Council agreed in principle to expand UNAMIR to 5,500 troops from African countries. However, it was agreed initially to send only 150 unarmed observers and an 800-strong Ghanian battalion to secure Kigali airport. As it became clear that the bulk of the force would not be deployed before the end of July the French launched **Operation Turquoise** in June to provide humanitarian assistance in the interim.

UNCED *see* EARTH SUMMIT

UNCHR

The **UN** Commission on Human Rights, a Geneva-based organization founded in 1946 as an intergovernmental body and subsidiary of the **ECOSOC** within the UN system. Composed of 43 members, it aims to promote and protect human rights. The UNCHR is authorized to appoint human rights rapporteurs to investigate alleged human rights abuses in UN member states; it is presented with their findings during its annual meeting, held usually in the first quarter of the year.

UNCLOS

The **UN** Conference on the Law of the Sea. There have been three such conferences, in 1958, in 1960, and an epic 11-session UNCLOS III conference in 1973–82. A draft treaty was eventually approved by 130 participating countries in April 1982, but the USA was one of four countries voting against it, and refused to pay its assessed contribution towards setting up a Preparatory Commission. The Convention opened for signature in December 1992, and had been signed by 159 countries in all by the deadline of end-1984, but not by the USA and other industrialized countries such as the UK, West Germany, Italy, Belgium and Spain. Considerable consensus had been achieved at UNCLOS III on **territorial waters** and **contiguous zones**, on **EEZs** and **continental shelf** jurisdiction, and on rights of passage through straits. These elements of the UNCLOS III convention were soon being widely treated as having legal force, although as of 1994 the convention had yet to achieve the 60 ratifications which were needed for its formal entry into force. The main controversial issue, and the reason for US rejection, was the proposed creation of an International Seabed Authority. This was conceived as a supranational body which would give real force to the notion of the ocean floor as part of the global commons. It would control and license companies engaging in seabed mining, and thus derive, and distribute, revenue from the exploitation of mineral and other resources. By 1994, there were signs of US willingness to sign the Convention.

UNCTAD

The **UN** Conference on Trade and Development, a Geneva-based body established by the **UN General Assembly** in 1964 as one of its permanent organs. This status entitles it to be financed by the UN's regular budget, instead of by voluntary contributions as is the case for UN specialized agencies. It currently has 187 members, including 184 members of the UN. Policy-making is entrusted to a Conference of Ministers which meets every four years, while a Trade and Development Board, meeting annually, is responsible for providing direction and implementation. UNCTAD played a major role in promoting debate on a New International Economic Order (**NIEO**) and in the 1970s it was the principal vehicle enabling **Third World** countries to press for structural changes in world trading arrangements, notably a **Common Fund** to stabilize commodity markets. However, some major industrialized countries have shown a marked reluctance to dealing with such issues at UNCTAD, where the Third World countries are perceived as having more opportunity to press their cause than within the **GATT**, the **IMF** and the **World Bank**.

UNDERCLASS

A socio-political term for the most disadvantaged within a society. In addition to being poor, those within the underclass are usually unemployed, badly educated, inadequately housed, and disproportionately drawn from ethnic minority backgrounds. The underclass is deeply alienated from its host society in general, and from the political process in particular, and tends to be largely impervious to attempts to improve its position through increased welfare provision.

UNDOF

The UN Disengagement Observer Force set up in May 1974 by **UN Security Council** Resolution 350, to supervise the ceasefire agreed between **Israel** and Syria following the 1973 **Yom Kippur war**. It was credited with helping to preserve stability on the **Golan Heights**, despite tension particularly at the time of the two Israeli invasions of neighbouring Lebanon (in 1978 and 1982), and has had its mandate renewed every six months, most recently in May 1994.

UNDP

The **UN** Development Programme, established by the **UN General Assembly** on 22 November 1965 when the UN Expanded Programme of Technical Assistance (UNEPTA) and the UN Special Fund (UNSF) were combined. The UNDP works with over 150 governments and over 30 **NGOs** to promote more rapid economic growth and improved living standards throughout Africa, **Latin America**, the **Middle East** and parts of Europe. It supports projects in five main areas: (i) surveying and assessing natural resources; (ii) stimulating capital investments; (iii) vocational and professional training; (iv) transferring technology and stimulating local technological skill; and (v) aiding economic and social planning. The UNDP publishes an annual Human Development Report, which in recent years has featured the ranking of countries in the Human Development Index (**HDI**).

UNEF

The **UN** Emergency Force in the **Middle East**. UNEF I was set up in 1956 under **UN General Assembly** Resolution 998, and with Egypt's consent, to secure and supervise a ceasefire in the **Suez crisis**. Having overseen the withdrawal of foreign forces, UNEF I patrolled the armistice lines between Egypt and **Israel** until 1967, when it was withdrawn at the request of Egyptian President Nasser. UNEF II was set up in October 1973 by **UN Security Council** Resolution 340, and interposed between Israel and Egypt in **Sinai** to observe and supervise the ceasefire following the **Yom Kippur war**. It was withdrawn after the 1979 **Camp David agreement** (since the **Soviet Union** opposed altering its role to one of supervising a US-backed treaty) and replaced by a Western and US-backed Multinational Force.

UNEP

The **UN** Environment Programme, based in Nairobi, Kenya, and appointed by and accountable to the **UN General Assembly**. UNEP was created in 1972 as the major institutional outcome of the UN Conference on the Human Environment (**Habitat**), held in Stockholm in June that year. Its objectives include promoting international environmental co-operation, recommending appropriate global environment strategies, and reviewing the progress of environmental programmes by UN-appointed bodies. It is administered by a Governing Council composed of representatives of 58 countries elected by the UN General Assembly on a rotating basis.

UNESCO

The Paris-based **UN** Educational, Scientific and Cultural Organization. A UN specialized agency, it was founded in 1946 to promote international collaboration in education, science and culture. The field of communication and the flow of information have been particularly controversial issues for UNESCO, with an impassioned debate about a New World Information and Communication Order (**NWICO**) dominating its proceedings in the early 1980s. Current UNESCO membership consists of 181 states; the USA withdrew in 1984, as did the UK and Singapore in 1985, after alleging financial and administrative mismanagement. The supreme policy-making body is the General Conference which meets once every two years; policy is implemented by a 51-member Executive Board. As Director-General, the controversial Amadou M'Bow of Senegal was succeeded in 1987 by the more conciliatory Federico Mayor Zaragoza of Spain. The Forum for Reflection, UNESCO's **think tank**, was established in November 1992 to discuss the future direction of the organization.

UNFICYP

The **UN** Peacekeeping Force in Cyprus, originally created in March 1964 by **UN Security Council** Resolution 186, and used with the consent of the government of Cyprus in 1964–74 as a kind of police force, to prevent fighting between the majority Greek Cypriot and minority Turkish Cypriot (**TRNC**) communities. Since the 1974 Turkish invasion and the de facto division of the island along the **Green Line**, UNFICYP's role has changed to that of a buffer force.

UNFPA

The **UN** Fund for Population Activities. This body, based in New York, was created in 1967 as a subsidiary organ of the **UN General Assembly**, until 1969 with the title Trust Fund for Population Activities. It is charged with the co-ordination of population policy in the developing world with the aim of reducing fertility through the promotion of family planning and modern forms of contraception. Since the mid-1980s it has been engulfed in controversy, and suffered the withdrawal of US funding from 1985 to 1993 over allegations that its population control programmes actively encourage abortion.

UNHCR

The **UN** High Commissioner for Refugees. The Office of the High Commissioner was established in 1951 to provide international protection for refugees, arrange emergency relief and find permanent solutions for the resettlement of refugees. The High Commissioner, currently Sadako Ogata, is directly elected by the **UN General Assembly** and is responsible to the General Assembly and to **ECOSOC**; the Executive Committee of the High Commissioner's Programme, established by ECOSOC, includes representatives of 46 states, both members and non-members of the UN, and meets annually in Geneva. The UNHCR also seeks to maximise the number of countries party to the 1951 UN Convention and the 1971 Protocol Relating to the Status of Refugees, both of which are currently endorsed by 106 countries.

UNICEF

The **UN** Children's Emergency Fund. A semi-autonomous agency of the UN, financed entirely by voluntary contributions, UNICEF is based in New York. It was established in 1946 to improve the situation of children, particularly in developing countries. One of its greatest achievements was the organization of the first World Summit for Children held in New York in

September 1989 which resulted in the Convention on the Rights of the Child, currently endorsed by 148 countries. The organization is administered by a 41-member Executive Board which is headed by the Executive Director, and whose members are elected by the UN body **ECOSOC**.

UNIDO

The **UN** Industrial Development Organization. A specialized agency of the UN since 1986, UNIDO was originally established in 1967. It aims to promote industrial development, especially in the least developed countries (**LDCs**). Its policy-making organ, the General Conference, which represents its total membership, currently 161, meets biennially to approve the budget and, if necessary, to elect a Director-General for four-year term. A 53-member Industrial Development Board acts as the organization's executive body.

UNIFIL

The **UN** Interim Force for Southern Lebanon, the UN peacekeeping force deployed in southern Lebanon since 1978. The first UNIFIL troops were dispatched to the area following a large-scale **Israeli** invasion of Lebanon in March 1978 designed to secure Israel's northern border against Palestinian incursions. Despite the deaths of some 200 troops, the UNIFIL mandate has been routinely renewed. However, since 1991 the UNIFIL presence in the south has been reduced in line with attempts by the Lebanese government to increase its presence in the area.

UNIKOM

The **UN** Iraq-Kuwait Observer Mission, approved under **UN Security Council** Resolution 689 passed on 9 April 1991, at the end of the **Gulf War** which ousted Iraqi forces from Kuwait. The 300-strong unarmed mission was entrusted with the establishment of a demilitarized zone between Iraq and Kuwait, extending 10 km into Iraq and 5 km into Kuwait. In November 1992 the UN decided that a new border should take effect from 15 January 1993, running slightly north of the demilitarized zone set by 1991 ceasefire terms, giving Kuwait control over the former Iraqi naval base at Umm al Qasr.

UNILATERAL DECLARATION OF INDEPENDENCE *see* UDI

UNILATERALISM

The belief that individual states should independently renounce the use of nuclear weapons. Unilateral nuclear disarmament was advocated in Britain from the mid-1950s by the anti-nuclear campaigning group **CND** and by more radical sections of the Labour Party, briefly becoming official party policy in 1960 and again in the early 1980s.

UNION TREATY

In the **Soviet Union**, a package of measures revising the relationship between the central executive institutions and the 15 constituent republics, whose planned signature (by nine republics) in 1991 prompted the **August coup** attempt by conservative **communists**. The Union Treaty, which had been agreed only after months of negotiations between federal and republican officials, recognized republican sovereignty and granted republics control over their own resources, effectively ceding considerable powers from the centre. It became irrelevant after the coup, as the republics successively seceded from the Soviet Union.

UNIONISTS

Members of political parties and other organizations in **Northern Ireland** committed to the maintenance of the union between Northern Ireland and the rest of the **United Kingdom**. Traditionally, the unionist movement was closely identified with the Conservative Party. The majority of Northern Ireland members of the UK parliament from 1921 were unionist supporters of the Conservatives, while Unionists also dominated the Northern Ireland parliament at **Stormont**. However, in 1969 the Democratic Unionists (DUP) formed a dissident **'loyalist'** Protestant grouping, and in 1972, with the imposition of **direct rule** in Northern Ireland, MPs of the Ulster Unionist Council (now commonly referred to as the official Ulster Unionists – OUP) ceased to take the Conservative whip in the UK House of Commons.

UNITA

(Portuguese acronym for *União Nacional para a Independência Total de Angola*, 'National Union for the Total Independence of Angola') The Angolan rebel organization led by Jonas Savimbi. UNITA fought alongside the Popular Movement for the Liberation of Angola (MPLA) during the struggle against colonial rule, but following the Portuguese withdrawal in 1975 it turned its attention to rivalry with the MPLA. Backed by the USA and South Africa, who opposed the Marxist and Cuban-backed MPLA government, it fought a prolonged war. It came under increasing pressure to negotiate with the Angolan government after the abortive UNITA-South African attack in 1988 on **Cuito Cuanavale** in which both UNITA and South Africa sustained considerable losses. Repeated peace initiatives finally resulted in May 1991 in the Bicesse Peace Accord, which provided for the demobilization of both sides, for the establishment of a new integrated national army and for multi-party democratic elections. The elections to the legislature were held in September 1992, when UNITA came a poor second to the MPLA. Savimbi secured 40.07 per cent of the vote in the simultaneous presidential elections, just denying incumbent President José Eduardo dos Santos an outright first-round victory. However, the results were rejected by UNITA. Its **guerrilla** activities were resumed and quickly escalated into a full-scale civil war. Talks to end the conflict finally began in November 1993; topics covered included the composition of the security forces, national reconciliation, allocation of Cabinet posts to UNITA and the organization of the second round of presidential elections. Talks were still continuing in June 1994.

UNITED ARAB EMIRATES *see* UAE

UNITED ARAB REPUBLIC *see* UAR

UNITED KINGDOM

The official title of the country often loosely referred to as **Britain**. **Great Britain** and Ireland were unified as the United Kingdom of Great Britain and Ireland under the 1800 Act of Union. The creation of the Irish Free State in 1922 made it necessary to amend the full title of the UK to the United Kingdom of Great Britain and **Northern Ireland**.

UNITED NATIONS *see* UN

UNITING FOR PEACE

A resolution passed by the **UN General Assembly** in July 1950, enabling it to decide on action against breaches of the peace and acts of aggression in cases where the **UN Security Council** was hamstrung by the veto of one of its five **permanent members**. The **Soviet Union** never accepted the legality of the procedure, which was devised by the USA to circumvent the Soviet veto (although, in June 1956, the absence of the Soviet representative had in fact made it possible for the USA to get action approved through the Security Council when North Korea invaded South Korea). Invoked to condemn Chinese aggression in Korea, the Uniting for Peace resolution was used again at the time of the **Suez crisis** in 1956, this time to raise a UN force, when two of its original sponsors – France and the UK – vetoed a Security Council motion demanding a ceasefire and the immediate withdrawal of their forces from the Suez Canal. Similar procedures were invoked, but ignored, to call for the withdrawal of Soviet troops from Hungary in the same year.

UNIVERSAL DECLARATION OF HUMAN RIGHTS

A declaration adopted without dissent by **UN** member states in 1948, although with abstentions by the **communist bloc** countries, South Africa and Saudi Arabia. Hailed as the first ever international **Bill of Rights**, it established the principle that the practices of governments, and their treatment of their citizens, were a matter for international concern. The UN Charter, adopted in 1945, had reaffirmed the UN's commitment to 'promote universal respect for, and observance of human rights for all', and required its members to 'pledge themselves to take joint and separate action in co-operation with the Organization' to achieve these ends.

UNIVERSAL POSTAL UNION *see* UPU

UNOSOM

The **UN** Operation in **Somalia**. The first UNOSOM force, consisting of 500 armed troops, was deployed in September 1992 to protect emergency relief supplies to Somalis who were starving as a result of the civil war which had broken out in November 1991. However, the force was largely ineffective and was superseded in December 1992 by the US-led **Operation Restore Hope**. This was in turn replaced on 4 May 1993 by an expanded 30,000-strong UN force, UNOSOM II. The **UN Security Council's** Resolution 813 on the formation of UNOSOM II, passed unanimously on 26 March 1993, gave it unprecedented authority to do whatever was necessary to maintain peace, disarm warring factions and protect relief workers.

In June 1993 the focus of the operation shifted when the Security Council ordered the arrest and punishment of those responsible for the killing of 24 Pakistani UNOSOM members. Efforts were then concentrated on the capture of Gen. Mohammed Farah Aydid and other members of his Somali National Alliance. This change of emphasis entailed the loss of considerable local support and created tensions within UNOSOM, with the Italian government expressing the strongest misgivings. In November the hunt for Aydid was abandoned and the role of the force was reappraised, the US government, under increasing domestic pressure, announcing the withdrawal of 8,100 troops by 31 March 1994. By April 1994 all Western countries had withdrawn from UNOSOM. The scaled-down operation had been given a new mandate by the Security Council on 4 February 1994 which placed the emphasis on peace-making and reconstruction, and which set March 1995 as the date for the completion of the UNOSOM mission.

UNPO

The Unrepresented Nations' and Peoples' Organization. Founded in The Hague, Netherlands, on 11 February 1991, to defend 'the right of self-determination of oppressed peoples around the world', UNPO is currently composed of representatives from 51 ethnic and minority groups worldwide. It has three subsidiary bodies – a general assembly, a court and a legal council charged with advising members on the judicial aspects of self-determination.

UNPROFOR

The **UN** Protection Force, whose establishment was authorized by the **UN Security Council** in January 1992. A 14,000-strong force, drawn from 30 countries, including France, Russia and the UK, was dispatched to **Croatia** in March 1992 to monitor a ceasefire between Croatia and the **Krajina** Serbs. UNPROFOR's mandate was enlarged in June 1992, when troops were also deployed in **Bosnia-Hercegovina** (with the principal object of protecting the means of aid distribution) and, in smaller numbers, in **Macedonia**. UNPROFOR troops have been subject to persistent harassment by all parties in the war.

UNRWA

The **UN** Relief and Works Agency for Palestine Refugees. The UNRWA was created by the **UN General Assembly** in 1949 as a temporary agency to provide relief for the estimated 750,000 Palestinian Arabs displaced from their homes and lands as a result of the 1948–9 Arab-**Israeli** War and the establishment of the state of Israel. The UNRWA was subsequently called upon to assist Palestinians displaced as a result of renewed hostilities in the **Middle East**. The agency has generally operated with the consent of the Israeli government.

UNSCOM

The **UN** Special Commission on Iraq, consisting of weapons experts from the UN and the **IAEA**, which aims to secure the nuclear and chemical disarmament of Iraq by gaining information on its nuclear and chemical stockpiles, conducting on-site weapons inspections and destroying all non-conventional and ballistics missiles with a range above 150 km. It was formally established under **UN Security Council** Resolution 687 passed on 3 April 1991, which set the terms of a ceasefire following Iraq's defeat in the **Gulf War**. It has been led since its inception by Rolf Ekeus (Sweden).

UNTAC

The **UN** Transitional Authority in Cambodia. UNTAC was established as part of a UN peace deal for Cambodia signed by the warring factions and regional and international powers in October 1991. Its civilian and military components began arriving in Cambodia in late 1991 to enforce a ceasefire, supervise demobilization and effectively administer the country ahead of general elections. The operation was the UN's most substantial peacekeeping operation to date. Despite numerous political and military obstacles, UNTAC managed to supervise peaceful general elections in May 1993 (albeit without the participation of the **Khmers Rouges**) which paved the way for the creation of a new coalition government. The final elements of the massive UNTAC presence withdrew at the end of 1993 despite the continuation of hostilities between the new government and the *Khmers Rouges*.

UNTAG

The **UN** Transitional Assistance Group, deployed in **Namibia** under the terms of UN Security Council **Resolution 435** in April 1989 in the run-up to independence. A multinational force, comprising 4,000 infantry and a 300-member military observer unit, it was charged with supervising the demobilization of South African and **SWAPO** forces, creating and maintaining an atmosphere conducive to the holding of free elections, and supervising the independence process. The UN had never before mounted such an expensive and complex peacekeeping operation and UNTAG's role received worldwide approval.

UPPER VOLTA *see* BURKINA FASO

UPU

The Universal Postal Union, a **UN** specialized agency since 1948, charged with promoting and developing international collaboration in postal services. The UPU is based in Berne, Switzerland, and dates originally from 1874, and from 1878 under its present name.

URNG

The Guatemalan National Revolutionary Unity – the unified command of Guatemalan **guerrilla** groups. Formed in 1982, the URNG's programme centres on an end to repression and on human rights guarantees, land reform, equality for Indian and mestizo populations, popular representation in government and non-alignment. More recently its efforts have been largely confined to the diplomatic front and aimed at achieving ceasefires and negotiations with civilian governments. Meanwhile its three armed factions – the Rebel Armed forces, the Guerrilla Army of the Poor and the Organization of the People in Arms – operated autonomously in the 1980s and are still active in 12 of the country's 22 departments.

URUGUAY ROUND

The latest **GATT** round of multilateral trade negotiations, launched at Punta del Este in Uruguay in September 1986. Its timetable had to be extended several times, but an overall agreement was finally signed in Geneva in December 1993. By the conclusion of the negotiations a total of 125 countries were participating, although many of the final deals were settled between the **EC**, the USA and Japan, and only 111 countries actually signed the Final Act in Marrakesh in April 1994. Once ratified, the agreements are to become effective at the beginning of 1995. The Uruguay Final Act includes provision for the establishment of a World Trade Organization. It also extends the coverage of GATT in the fields of agriculture, textiles and clothing, services, and industrial property rights. Binding commitments have been given by individual countries to reduce or eliminate specific tariffs and non-tariff barriers to merchandise trade, with average tariff reductions of over one-third.

USTASA

(Serbo-Croat, 'insurgent') The Croatian **fascist** movement which ruled a Nazi puppet state (comprising most of present-day **Croatia** and **Bosnia-Hercegovina**) during the Second World War. The Ustasa had strong links with the Roman Catholic Church and pursued a policy against the mainly Orthodox Serbs of forcible conversion, expulsion and genocide. Including the many Jews and **Romanies** also massacred, hundreds of thousands are thought to have died. Despite the Ustasa's brutal record and its subordination to Nazi Germany, its term in power is celebrated by some Croatian nationalists as Croatia's first experience of independence.

UVF

The Ulster Volunteer Force, a paramilitary Protestant organization in **Northern Ireland**. The UVF is one of the oldest such organizations, having been formed in 1912. It was banned in 1966 (before the outbreak of major disturbances in Northern Ireland in 1969) but its proscription was lifted in May 1974; however, it was once again proscribed in November 1975 after it had been involved in various acts of violence.

UZBEKISTAN

The most populous of the republics of **Central Asia**, formerly one of the **Soviet Union's** 15 constituent republics, and independent since 1991. The largest ethnic group among its 21 million population are Turkic-speaking, moderately Islamic and clan-oriented Uzbeks.

VANUATU

(Bislama, 'Our Land') The Melanesian archipelago, formerly known as the New Hebrides, jointly administered as a condominium by France and the UK from 1906 until its independence on 30 July 1980. Attempts at secession by the main, northern island of Espiritu Santo and the southern island of Tanna shortly before independence were crushed by troops from Papua New Guinea called in by the new Vanuatan government, and the rebels, including their leader, Jimmy Stevens, were imprisoned. The name Vanuatu was bestowed by the *Vanua'aku Pati* (Our Land Party), which formed the government upon independence and ruled until December 1991.

VANUNU AFFAIR

The case of Mordechai Vanunu, an **Israeli** technician employed at the Dimona nuclear research plant in the Negev desert of southern Israel. Vanunu was sentenced to 18 years' imprisonment in March 1988 following his conviction on charges of divulging official secrets concerning Israel's nuclear research programme. The charges had arisen after the British *Sunday Times* had published an article based on information supplied by Vanunu which suggested that Dimona was being used to manufacture components for **nuclear weapons**. Following publication of the article Vanunu was kidnapped by the Israeli secret service (**Mossad**) while in Rome and was brought back to Israel to stand trial.

VARIABLE GEOMETRY, EUROPE OF

The situation envisaged by French President Mitterrand, when he proposed a possible **two-speed Europe** in 1984. Countries would participate to different degrees in the various elements of European integration, both inside and outside the **EU**, and the shape of institutions would therefore take on a variable geometry.

VAT

Value added tax, a form of indirect taxation. VAT was first implemented (in France) in 1954. It involves taxing each stage of production or provision through which goods or services pass. The tax is levied on the basis of 'value added' during that stage. It is collected by requiring traders to charge the required percentage VAT on their output sales (sales of goods which leave them after being processed), and then to pay the money over to the government, after subtracting their input tax, i.e. the VAT which they paid to the traders from whom they received goods prior to processing. Specific goods and services may be either exempt or zero-rated. The UK

Conservative government severely dented its popular support when it announced in March 1993 that domestic fuel and power would cease to be zero-rated. The **EC** (now **EU**) decided in 1992 that there should be a minimum standard rate of VAT of 15 per cent throughout the Community, within the framework of the **single internal market**. A portion of the VAT receipts of the individual member states is allocated to the EU, and this provides around half of the EU's 'own resources' for its general budget.

VATICAN II

The Second Vatican Council (the first was in 1869–70), which met in four sessions between 11 October 1962 and 8 December 1965. It was the 21st Ecumenical Council in the history of the Roman Catholic Church and by far the largest, with 2,692 members of the episcopate participating, and was launched by Pope John XXIII although its later stages were presided over by his successor Pope Paul VI. The Council adopted a Constitution on the Church in the Modern World which was regarded as a landmark in adapting doctrine to contemporary circumstances. It took steps in a liberal direction (even on 'natural' birth control) which Pope John Paul II has in some respects reversed since 1978. Other key documents of Vatican II included Declarations (statements of principles) on religious liberty and on relations with non-Christian faiths, emphasizing that there were elements of truth in Hinduism, Buddhism and Islam, condemning anti-Semitism, and formally exonerating the Jewish people of responsibility for the crucifixion of Christ.

VELASQUISMO

A political trend in Peru inspired by Gen. Juan Velasco Alvarado, President 1968–75, whose leftist-sounding state-initiated reforms, initially supported by the centre-right Christian Democrats as well as the **Communist** Party, delivered far less than promised, most critically in the area of land distribution to peasants. In Ecuador, *Velasquismo* was the product of a populist movement surrounding the charismatic but at times authoritarian José María Velasco Ibarra (President on five occasions between 1933 and 1972), which appealed mainly to non-unionized workers and virtually disappeared after Velasco's death in 1979.

VELVET DIVORCE

Czechoslovakia's relatively amicable dissolution and division into the **Czech Rebublic** and **Slovakia**, which was formally implemented on 1 January 1992. Czechs and Slovaks speak similar languages, but had distinct historical and social backgrounds prior to the creation of Czechoslovakia in 1918 from territories of the former Austro-Hungarian Empire. Despite economic growth and educational improvements, many Slovaks regarded the union as advantageous only to the more numerous Czechs. With the collapse of **communism** after the **Velvet Revolution** of 1989, Slovak **nationalism** revived. Elections in June 1992 revealed the extent of political polarization between the two republics; the Czechs elected the neo-liberal Civic Democratic party led by Vaclav Klaus, while the Slovaks elected the populist, social-democratic Movement for a Democratic Slovakia (HZDS) led by Vladimir Meciar. Although the HZDS had sought no specific mandate for independence, the Slovak National Council declared its sovereignty in July 1992, and the same month negotiations on the dissolution of the federation began. The Czechs perceived that a 'velvet divorce' would deliver them political and economic stability, and so acquiesced in the dissolution.

VELVET REVOLUTION

The near-bloodless overthrow of **Czechoslovakia's communist** regime in November-December 1989. Despite moderate reforms in the **Soviet Union** and elsewhere in **Eastern Europe**, the Czechoslovak communist party had remained highly orthodox. Tens of thousands of anti-government demonstrators were prompted to rally in the capital Prague on 17 November 1989 by the collapse of hardline communist regimes in Bulgaria and the **DDR** in the preceding few weeks. Violent clashes with riot police at the demonstration left 140 demonstrators injured, spurring ever greater numbers of protestors to rally on Prague's streets over the next few days. Amid the tumult, opposition forces combined to form the Czech **Civic Forum** and the Slovak **Public Against Violence**. On 24 November communist leader Milos Jakes resigned; a demoralized communist party agreed to the appointment on 10 December of a government with a non-communist majority. On 29 December 1989, the former dissident playwright Vaclav Havel became interim President.

VENDA *see* BANTUSTANS

VERKRAMPTE

(Afrikaans, 'narrow') A term used to describe ultra-conservative South African whites who resisted bids to reform **apartheid**. Originally applied to those on the far right of the National Party, the adjective is employed now to describe even further to the right, such as members of the Conservative Party, who have denounced the multi-racial Interim Constitution.

VERLIGTE

(Afrikaans, 'enlightened') A term used to describe liberal members of the South African National Party and other members of the **Afrikaner** community who were prepared to countenance reform of the **apartheid** system.

VIENNA CONVENTION 1961

The international agreement under which all signatories guarantee the immunity, rights and privileges of diplomatic staff and the integrity of embassies within their countries. The convention formalized a longstanding recognition of the need for immunity in the conduct of diplomatic relations.

VIET CONG

(Vietnamese, 'Vietnamese communists') Members of the pro-**communist** National Front for the Liberation of South Vietnam (NFL), founded in 1960 to fight against South Vietnamese and US forces. The name was coined by the South Vietnamese regime to differentiate the NFL from the **Viet Minh**.

VIET MINH

(Vietnamese, abbreviation of *Viet Nam Doc Lap Dong Minh Hoi*, 'Vietnamese Independence League') The Vietnamese **communist**-led national front organization founded by Ho Chi Minh in 1941 to oppose the Japanese occupation of **Indo-China**, and later directed against the French colonial power. In 1954 the Viet Minh achieved victory over the French at the battle of **Dien Bien Phu**.

VIETNAM WAR

The 1954–75 war between North and South Vietnam, the latter assisted from 1961 by the USA. The longest revolutionary effort in modern times and one of the watersheds of twentieth century history, the war resulted in victory for the North and the union of the two Vietnams in 1976. Some 900,000 **Viet Cong** and North Vietnamese, 400,000 South Vietnamese and 50,000 US troops died in the war. The conflict also had a profound effect on US politics and society.

VIETNAMIZATION

President Richard Nixon's programme for the US withdrawal 'with honour' from Vietnam. Launched in June 1969 when Nixon announced the first major withdrawal of US troops from Vietnam, the programme culminated in the 1973 Paris Agreements which provided for the US to withdrew all remaining troops from Vietnam. In theory, the central thrust of the strategy was to improve the capabilities of the US-backed South Vietnamese forces (**ARVN**) and strengthen the control of the government of South Vietnam over the population so that it could eventually oppose North Vietnam unsupported. In reality, Vietnamization was essentially a 'cut and run' strategy, designed by and for the USA. It was dictated by the collapse of the will to support the war among the decision-making elite in the USA. The strategy did very little to improve the morale or fighting ability of the ARVN soldiers, who were expected to fight on alone against an army which had defeated the armed forces of the most powerful country in the world. The final irony of the Vietnamization programme was that it served to unite the opposing Vietnamese regimes on at least one issue – complete distrust of the USA.

VIETVETS

A term used to describe US veterans of the **Vietnam War**. As many as 300,000 US servicemen were wounded during the war and while a further 2 million returned physically intact, many shoulder enormous psychological scars, as do thousands more Vietnamese, Cambodian and Lao civilians and soldiers. On their return to the USA, many servicemen joined veteran organizations which lobbied on their behalf. In the 1980s some veteran groups became involved in the campaign to persuade the government to investigate alleged sightings in **Indo-China** of US servicemen listed as **MIA**.

VILLAGIZATION

A concept advocated by President Julius Nyerere of **Tanzania**. It was based on the belief that the country's economy and the welfare of the rural population could be improved if people abandoned living in widely dispersed small holdings and gathered in large villages, which could give them access to modern equipment and better services. The village settlement policy was abandoned in 1966 when it became apparent that only a few highly motivated and politicized villages were benefiting from the system. The following year it was combined with **Ujamaa**, Nyerere's version of **African socialism**. *Ujamaa* villages were established in which small groups worked on communal farms and the prevailing atmosphere was intended to replicate that of the African extended family. However, the policy failed to increase production and often caused hardship and resentment.

LA VIOLENCIA

(Spanish, 'The Violence') The period of bloody conflict which swept Colombia in 1948–65, leaving up to 200,000 people dead. Although precipitated by the **Bogatazo** rioting in the capital, it was a primarily rural occurrence, in which Liberal party supporters fought against Conservatives. However, political motives were often used as a screen to justify banditry, the settling of scores, and the seizure of land, while large landowners used it as a cover for large-scale evictions. Most of the violence involved Liberal peasants fighting Conservative peasants for small spoils, sustained by intense partisan rivalries and fuelled by vendettas which were passed from one generation to the next.

VIRGIN LANDS

Former Soviet leader Nikita Khrushchev's grandiose 1954 policy to convert millions of acres of open plains in Soviet **Kazakhstan** into arable farming land. The project served a valuable **propaganda** purpose in promoting Soviet self-sufficiency in food, but drew much-needed investment away from the **Soviet Union's** existing agricultural land. Despite initial high yields in the mid-1950s, the project failed when soil erosion destroyed the agricultural potential of the land.

VISEGRAD TRIANGLE / VISEGRAD FOUR

The organization of states in **Central Europe**, initially Poland, Hungary and **Czechoslovakia** (later the **Czech Republic** and **Slovakia**), founded in the Hungarian town of Visegrad in February 1991. The group's initial purpose was to persuade the West that Central Europe was better qualified for foreign investment and rapid accession to European institutions, including the **EU**, than were the former **communist** states of **Eastern Europe**. Its member countries also share anxiety over rising Russian **nationalism**.

VISHWA HINDU PARISHAD

(Hindi, 'World Hindu Party') An affiliate of the **RSS** and founded in 1964 by Madhav Sadashiv Gowalkar. Working mainly through educational and missionary channels, its followers aim to create a unified Hindu society, purge India of 'foreign' ideologies and reverse non-Hindu influences in India, especially Islam. The movement played a key role in the campaign, politically spearheaded by the **BJP**, to transform the **Ayodhya mosque** into a Hindu temple, and was subsequently implicated in the destruction of the mosque in December 1992.

VOEREN / FOURONS

The Flemish and French names for a group of mainly francophone villages in Belgium's Flemish-speaking **Flanders** region, whose election of francophone José Happart as Mayor in 1986 brought down the government of Prime Minister Wilfried Martens. Happart refused to take a language test in Flemish, the official language of the region, thus placing himself outside the criteria for office, but his repeated election as Mayor forced Martens to negotiate concessions. Eventually, in January 1989, Happart's bilingual deputy Nico Droeven became mayor; Happart entered the Socialist Party list for the June 1989 European elections; and Martens returned to lead a new government.

VOICE OF AMERICA

An external broadcasting service owned by the USA and based in Washington DC, which disseminates the government's views and policy via radio broadcasting in 42 languages worldwide, and also operates a limited television service.

VOJVODINA

A province of Serbia, adjacent to the Croatian and Hungarian borders, 22 per cent of whose population of some 2 million is ethnically Hungarian. In the turmoil accompanying the break-up of **Yugoslavia** Vojvodina has remained free of serious violence, despite the inter-ethnic conflict in neighbouring **Bosnia-Hercegovina** and **Croatia**, reports of discrimination against Hungarians, and the controversial removal of the province's autonomous status in March 1989.

VOLK

(Afrikaans / German, 'people' or 'nation') A notion entrenched in the concept of **nationalism** and essentially **racist**. The word is used exclusively to describe white communities and conveys the idea that these communities must be kept pure. The word gained prevalence during the Nazi period and is now used by **neo-Nazis** as well as by members of the **Afrikaner** community in South Africa to describe themselves. In South Africa, Afrikaner extremists have been demanding the establishment of a *volkstaat*, or homeland, where they can enjoy autonomy and maintain their way of life in the post-**apartheid** period.

VOODOO ECONOMICS

A pejorative term for **Reaganomics**, the economic strategy propounded by US President Ronald Reagan. The term was used by George Bush in his 1980 campaign against Reagan for the Republican presidential nomination. Prior to the nomination convention, however, Bush withdrew from the contest to become Reagan's running-mate and, as Vice-President, later gave his support to Reaganomics.

VOSTOK

(Russian, meaning 'east' and also 'upward flow') The craft in which Yuri Gagarin undertook the first space flight by a human, on 12 April 1961. This 108-minute flight, which involved one complete orbit of the earth, grabbed headlines all over the world. It reasserted Soviet space supremacy in a period of **Cold War**, eclipsing the much shorter US Mercury space hop a few weeks later. The last Vostok flight was on 16 June 1963, when Valentina Tereshkova became the first woman in space. Later Soviet flights were by Voskhod and Soyuz spacecraft.

VTOL

Vertical take-off and landing, a term used to describe fixed-wing aircraft which do not require a runway and which can thus be used in confined areas including on seaborne aircraft carriers. Extensive research into the design of such craft began in the 1950s; the first successful VTOL was the SC1 built in 1960 by Shorts Brothers of Belfast, Northern Ireland. However, the first VTOL to go into operational use as a combat jet was the Harrier Jump Jet. The

Royal Air Force took delivery of the first Jump Jet on 18 April 1969.

VUKOVAR

A town on the river Danube in the eastern Slavonia region of **Croatia**, which fell to the Yugoslav People's Army (JNA) and Serb irregulars in November 1991 after a three-month siege. Serb tactics at Vukovar – which was heavily bombarded, causing massive **collateral damage** – were subsequently repeated throughout the war in former **Yugoslavia**. Vukovar had an ethnically mixed pre-war population; its capture, in which Serb irregulars – including the notorious **Tigers** – allegedly committed war crimes, was the first major instance of **ethnic cleansing**.

WACO SIEGE

A 51-day siege of the headquarters of the Branch Davidian religious cult near Waco, Texas, which began on 28 February 1993, after a bungled raid by agents from the federal Bureau of Alcohol, Tobacco and Firearms had been repulsed by heavily armed cult members. The siege ended on 19 April when the compound was consumed by fire following an assault by **FBI** units. The cult's leader, David Koresh, and more than 70 of his followers, including a number of children, died in the blaze. A handful of cult members survived, and several of them claimed that the fire had been started by the assaulting forces, whereas the authorities maintained that it had been an act of arson by those within the compound.

WAFD

(Arabic, 'delegation') An Egyptian party formed in 1919 as the main liberal-nationalist movement in the pre-Nasser period. It was dissolved in 1952 following the imposition of one-party rule under the Arab Socialist Union (ASU). In 1983 it was reorganized as the centre-left New Wafd Party which had been briefly active in 1978. In 1984 it worked closely with religious parties, notably the **Muslim Brotherhood**, and emerged as the second largest opposition party after the Brotherhood in parliamentary elections held that year.

WAITANGI

The Treaty of Waitangi in 1840, under which the **Maoris** of New Zealand ceded sovereignty to the British crown, and were in return granted possession of their 'lands and estates, forests, fisheries'; since 1867 four seats in the parliament have been reserved for Maori members. The provisions of the Treaty of Waitangi were largely ignored by European settlers, until attempts to make more equitable arrangements were made in the 1970s.

WALK IN THE WOODS FORMULA

The closest thing to a real breakthrough in US-Soviet arms control negotiations in the early 1980s. Negotiations were under way in Geneva, as **NATO** was pressing ahead with modernization of its intermediate-range nuclear weapons (INF), using **cruise** and **Pershing** II missiles. On 16 July 1982 the two chief negotiators – Paul Nitze and Yuli Kvitsinsky – took their 'walk in the woods'. They drafted plans for the **Soviet Union** to keep only 75 SS-20 missiles, rather than 350, while the US would abandon Pershing and deploy only 75 (rather than 464) cruise missiles in **Western Europe**. However, they failed to persuade their governments. Kvitsinsky told Nitze in September 1982 that the formula had been rejected by the Soviet side, and Nitze thus had no need to disclose that it had also been rejected by the USA.

WALLONIA

The largely francophone southern region of Belgium. A process of devolution of power to the regions (Wallonia, **Flanders** and **Brussels**) began in 1970, and was crowned with parliamentary approval on 14 July 1993. The strength of persisting linguistic and cultural divisions, illustrated in the 1980s by the **Voeren/Fourons** controversy, still poses a real threat to the future unity of Belgium. Although Wallonia experienced early industrialization, it has not matched the post-war economic growth of Flanders.

WALVIS BAY

The only deep-water port on the coast of **Namibia**. The question of sovereignty over Walvis Bay and the Penguin Islands, the dozen off-shore islands to the south of the port, was unresolved when Namibia gained its independence from South Africa in March 1990. The enclave remained under South African control until August 1992, when a joint administration was instituted. In August 1993 South Africa formally agreed to relinquish its claims, which it did with effect from 1 March 1994.

WAPPING DISPUTE

A bitter industrial dispute in the UK newspaper industry lasting just over a year in 1986–7. The dispute was centred around the relocation of the editorial offices and printing works of News International, the publishers of *The Times*, the *Sunday Times* and other newspapers, from the **Fleet Street** area of London to a new site at Wapping further east – the move being associated with radical changes in technology and working practices. The course of the dispute was widely seen as clear evidence of the determination of management to break free from hardened and entrenched industrial practices.

WAQF

(Arabic, 'stopping', hence a 'perpetuity'; plural *awqaf*) The giving of property by will or by gift in perpetuity to the Islamic authorities for pious works or for the public good. The proceeds pay for the upkeep of mosques and charities, and the endowment once made cannot normally be regained by the original owners. In modern times the accumulation in Muslim countries of *waqf* property administered by the state, in the form of a ministry of *awqaf*, has amounted to a substantial proportion of public land.

WAR POWERS ACT

A measure passed by US **Congress** in 1973, over a presidential veto, in the wake of the **Vietnam War**. It aimed to curb the ability of the executive to commit forces to a foreign combat zone for more than 90 days.

WARNOCK REPORT

A UK report, published in July 1984, on **bio-ethics** as well as the social and legal implications of recent and potential developments in the field of human-assisted reproduction. Chaired by Dame Mary (Baroness) Warnock, the committee recommended in particular that certain forms of infertility treatment such as artificial insemination by donor and **IVF** (in vitro fertilization) were ethically acceptable; that 'surrogate' motherhood was open to strong moral objections and that the provision of surrogacy services should be banned; and that research on human embryos should be permitted only up to the fourteenth day after fertilization. Most of the report's conclusions were incorporated in the Human Fertilization and Embryology Act 1990.

WARREN COMMISSION

The commission of inquiry chaired by the head of the US Supreme Court, Chief Justice Earl Warren, which investigated the circumstances of the assassination of President John F. Kennedy in Dallas on 22 November 1963. Established in the immediate aftermath of the shooting, the Commission held hearings and examined evidence before producing the Warren Report on 24 September 1964. The Report confirmed the conclusions of the Dallas police and the **FBI** by finding that the assassination had been the work of a single man, Lee Harvey Oswald, and that there was no evidence of a wider conspiracy, thus giving no credence to the **grassy knoll** theory of a second gunman. To sustain the single-assassin theory, the Commission was forced to conclude that only three shots were fired in all, which in turn entailed a belief that seemingly separate wounds had been inflicted by a single shot, a theory which became known as that of the **magic bullet**. The thoroughness of the Commission's investigation has been widely and consistently criticized, while its Report has been condemned as politically expedient and inconsistent with both the facts of the case and with the 26 volumes of hearings, exhibits and evidence published by the Commission itself.

WARSAW PACT

The title commonly used for the Warsaw Treaty Organization, which was in effect the **communist** counterpart to **NATO** in the **Cold War**. Albania, Bulgaria, **Czechoslovakia**, East Germany (the **DDR**), Hungary, Poland, Romania, and the **Soviet Union** were the original signatories, in May 1955, of the Warsaw Treaty of Friendship, Co-operation and Mutual Assistance. Albania played no real part and withdrew formally in 1968. Following the collapse of **communism** in central and Eastern Europe, the Warsaw Pact was dissolved in February 1991.

WASP

White Anglo-Saxon Protestant. The settlers of the 13 British colonies which later constituted themselves into the USA were WASPs. Although subsequent waves of US immigrations came from diverse sources, WASPs have continued to constitute the majority of the US establishment. In its purest application the term WASP implies membership of a prosperous family in one of the 13 original states, particularly those constituting New England.

WATERGATE

The scandal which forced the 37th president of the USA, Richard Milhous Nixon, to resign from office on 9 August 1974, the only US president ever to have done so. On 17 June 1972, four months before Nixon's landslide re-election, five men employed by the Committee to Re-elect the President (**CREEP**) were arrested, having broken into the headquarters of the Democratic National Convention in the Watergate building in Washington DC. The subsequent investigation, pursued doggedly by *Washington Post* reporters Bob Woodward and Carl Bernstein revealed a catalogue of dirty tricks perpetrated by the Nixon campaign against the Democrats. Among those implicated by one of the burglars was John Dean, the White House counsel, whose televised testimony before the Senate in mid-1973 incriminated Nixon in the attempt to cover up White House involvement in the Watergate burglary. The revelation that Nixon had routinely taped White House conversations throughout his presidency led to a protracted struggle between independent counsel (special prosecutor) Archibald Cox and the President for control of the tapes. Despite dismissing Cox, Nixon was finally forced to release some of the subpoenaed tapes. Although incomplete, the material showed his involvement in the cover-up, and confirmed the impression of a president who had acted with scant regard for the Constitution. In late July the House judiciary committee voted to impeach Nixon for having violated his duty to uphold the law, and for having 'prevented, obstructed, and impeded the administration of justice'. In the face of almost certain impeachment by the whole House, and likely conviction by the Senate, Nixon announced his resignation in a televised address to the nation on the evening of 8 August. On 8 September he was pardoned for all crimes by his successor, Gerald Ford, but several of his closest White House aides served prison terms for their role in the Watergate affair.

WATTS

The black ghetto of Los Angeles where severe rioting broke out on 11–16 August 1965. The riot was triggered by allegations of police brutality towards a group of black motorists, but was underpinned by the endemic problems of racism, poverty, unemployment and deprivation, and fuelled by a heat wave. The riot saw widespread destruction and looting, the deployment of the National Guard, and the imposition of a curfew. A total of 34 people died and more than 1,000 were injured, while damage to property was estimated at $100 million. Until surpassed by the 1992 **Los Angeles riots**, the Watts unrest was the worst civil disturbance in a US city in the twentieth century, and was later seen as the beginning of a series of ghetto riots which scarred the USA in the mid-1960s.

WCC

The World Council of Churches, formally constituted in 1948. The WCC's chief denominations – Anglican, Baptist, Congregational, Lutheran, Methodist, Moravian, Old Catholic, Orthodox, Presbyterian, Reformed and Society of Friends (the Roman Catholic Church is not a member but sends official observers to meetings) – number some 320 from over 100 countries. The WCC Assembly (the governing body) meets every seven to eight years to frame policy and consider a main theme. The most recent Assembly, the seventh, was held in Canberra, Australia, in 1991.

WEATHERMEN

An urban **guerrilla** force founded in the USA in June 1969 with the declared aim of launching violent attacks upon the state in order to provoke an authoritarian response which would encourage popular revolution. The group was an offshoot of the **SDS** and the opposition to the **Vietnam War**. Its name was derived from a line in Bob Dylan's song *Subterranean Homesick Blues*: 'You don't need a weatherman to know which way the wind blows.' Organized in cells of four or five members, the Weathermen were responsible for many bombings and robberies, and a number were killed in gun battles with the police. In the 1970s the group changed its name to the Weatherpeople and, eventually, to Weather Underground; although its activities decreased in scope, it remained active into the 1980s.

WELFARE STATE

A state social security system, particularly in the UK, designed to provide basic means to all, and incorporating benefit payments to the unemployed, the sick, the elderly and the disabled, and free or inexpensive health care.

The welfare state in the UK was rooted in the radical **Beveridge Report** of 1942, which recommended the establishment of (i) a comprehensive system of social insurance; and (ii) a national health service. Although accepted in principle by the wartime coalition government of Winston Churchill, the institution of the welfare state was the accomplishment of the postwar Labour government of Clement Attlee.

WENCESLAS SQUARE

The area in central Prague which was the focal point for popular unrest in 1968, when **Warsaw Pact** troops invaded **Czechoslovakia** to suppress the **Prague Spring**. The student Jan Palach became an icon of resistance when he burned himself to death in 1969 in Wenceslas Square; commemorations at the site of this protest were later a feature of dissident action, culminating in the **Velvet Revolution** of **1989** which brought down the **communist** regime.

WESSIES *see* OSSIES

WEST

A misleading term in a variety of usages in international affairs. Never strictly geographical even when applied to Europe and North America, it was extended in its **Cold War** usage to include Australia and New Zealand, in contradistinction to 'East', a similarly inaccurate synonym for the **communist bloc**. In the categorization of the world according to types of economic system, West also loosely corresponds to countries with developed market economies, leading to its use sometimes to include Japan. In the language of world development the **North-South** distinction, which has gained general acceptance, places the West and much of the East in the same category, the **North**.

WEST AFRICAN MONETARY UNION *see* UMOA

WEST BANK

The territory of **Palestine** west of the River Jordan, claimed from 1949 to 1988 as part of Jordan, but occupied by **Israel** since the 1967 **Six-Day War**. The territory, excluding East **Jerusalem**, is widely referred to within Israel by its biblical names, **Judaea and Samaria**, and is considered as part of **Eretz Israel**. The West Bank has an area of some 2,269 sqare miles (5,879 sq km) and a Palestinian population of close to 1 million. In addition, there are a large number of Israeli settlements throughout the territory. Under the terms of the **Gaza-Jericho First** peace deal signed by Israel and the **PLO** in September 1993, Israeli forces withdrew from the West Bank town of Jericho and handed control to a Palestinian authority in May 1994. The withdrawal was the first stage of a plan which provided for a full Israeli withdrawal from the West Bank which would become an autonomous Palestinian entity.

WEST GERMANY *see* BRD

WEST INDIES FEDERATION

A political grouping of British colonies in the **Caribbean**. It was established, together with a federal parliament, by the UK government in 1958 to ease administration in the colonies in preparation for their ultimate independence. It was immediately unpopular, being widely seen as reinforcing colonialist ties, and was effectively undermined by the wealthier islands of Jamaica and Trinidad who feared that they would have to support the smaller and poorer islands. The resulting weak federal government could not avert a final rupture in 1961 when Jamaica opted for independence and left, quickly followed by Trinidad. The Federation was disbanded in 1962. However, the term West Indies is still widely used in the UK to describe the English-speaking Caribbean.

WEST NEW GUINEA *see* IRIAN JAYA

WESTERN ALLIES

The USA, the UK and France in the period after 1945 when, with the onset of the **Cold War**, the **Soviet Union** became estranged from its wartime allies and there was no longer a common purpose uniting the **Big Three** or the **Big Four**.

WESTERN AUSTRALIA INC

The scandal involving corrupt links between the ruling Australian Labour Party (ALP) and entrepreneurs in the state of Western Australia in the 1980s. Brian Burke, ALP Premier of Western Australia between 1983 and 1988, was arrested in June 1992 for his part in the scandal. A Royal Commission report, released on 20 October 1992, revealed that more than A$1,000 million in public money had been wasted on a series of unsuccessful ventures by local entrepreneurs. The ALP lost the state elections in February 1993.

WESTERN EUROPE

A geographically inaccurate and politically imprecise description, used in the **Cold War** to mean non-**communist** Europe, just as **Eastern Europe** was used to describe countries behind the **iron curtain**. 'Western Europe' generally included the eastern Mediterranean countries of Greece, Cyprus, Malta and also Turkey, which stretched the meaning of Western and even of Europe. Conversely, it excluded Finland, for geostrategic reasons, and Austria was a marginal case, but it did not correspond exactly to European members of the Western Alliance, as **NATO** was often described, or of the **WEU**, since Western Europe included the neutral Sweden, Ireland and Switzerland. Nor could it be identified as countries with pluralist democracies, so long as Spain and Portugal were dictatorships. The collapse of **communism** in **1989**, and the break-up of **Yugoslavia**, have made it even less convincing to view Europe in bipolar terms. The revival of the concept of **Central Europe** may, in turn, give Western Europe a clearer meaning.

WESTERN EUROPEAN UNION *see* WEU

WESTERN HOSTAGES

Westerners kidnapped and held by various groups in Lebanon during the 1980s and 1990s. Although it has denied involvement, the radical Shi'ite **Hezbollah** movement was widely believed to have been the organizing force behind most of the kidnappings. Between 1982 and 1992, a total of 92 foreigners were held hostage in Lebanon of whom at least 10 died in captivity. Perhaps the most famous of the Western hostages was Terry Waite, the Archbishop of Canterbury's special envoy, who was held from 1987 to 1991.

WESTERN SAHARA

The disputed territory divided between Morocco and Mauritania under a 1975 treaty following Spain's withdrawal from the region which it had controlled since the nineteenth century. The treaty was opposed by the Algerian-backed **Polisario**

Front, which in 1976 proclaimed an independent Saharan Arab Democratic Republic (**SADR**). While Mauritania withdrew its troops from the region after concluding a peace treaty with Polisario in 1979, Morocco refused to withdraw its claim and waged war on the Front. **UN** efforts to broker a peace in the territory by organizing a referendum to allow the inhabitants to choose independence or integration into Morocco were frustrated in 1992–3. A fresh UN diplomatic drive in early 1994 raised hopes of a referendum being held before the year-end.

WESTLAND AFFAIR

The UK cabinet crisis in 1985–6 over the future of the sole remaining British helicopter manufacturer. Westland, which had been experiencing financial difficulties, was the subject of rival bids, principally from the US Sikorsky's parent company UTC together with the Italian Fiat, and from a European consortium. The Defence Secretary Michael Heseltine, who favoured the European solution, perceived a bias on the part of his cabinet colleagues in favour of the Sikorsky/UTC bid, and resigned over the Cabinet's handling of the matter. The Trade and Industry Secretary Leon Brittan also resigned after it emerged that he had sanctioned the leaking to the press of a confidential letter written to Heseltine by the Attorney General, Sir Patrick Mayhew. In the event, UTC/Fiat took a substantial minority holding in Westland, while after further problems Westland was acquired in early 1994 by the UK engineering and defence group GKN, which already held a considerable minority stake.

WESTMINSTER

The central political decision-making institutions in the UK. The term derives from the area (and borough) in which the Houses of Parliament are situated, and is used in contradistinction to **Whitehall**, the adjacent area housing the offices of many of the most important government departments, which indicates the bureaucratic and administrative structure of government. Westminster also signifies central as distinct from local, regional (or **Northern Ireland**) government, and increasingly indicates political powers exercised on a national as opposed to European level.

WET

A liberal member of the UK Conservative Party. Particularly during the period of Margaret Thatcher's premiership in 1979–90, the term was used somewhat pejoratively, indicating that the person concerned did not share the Prime Minister's **conviction politics** and was possibly not really **one of us**. While Thatcher's first Cabinet, formed in May 1979, included a number of 'wets', their number gradually fell and their influence diminished.

WETBACK

A colloquial term for an illegal immigrant to the USA. The term is applied particularly to Hispanics, especially the many Mexicans who have crossed illegally into the USA in recent years, traditionally by swimming the Rio Grande.

WEU

The Western European Union, set up in 1954 by the enlargement of the **Brussels Treaty** as a forum for European military co-operation. The WEU was sidelined in the **Cold War** period by the existence of the wider **NATO** alliance, but it proclaimed its 'reactivation' in 1984 as the voice of Western Europe on defence issues. In the early 1990s it presented itself as one answer to the question of how European integration might proceed on the security front, finding favour with those who resisted the 'federalist' implications of expanding the **EU's** sphere of activity. WEU members at the outset were Belgium, France, Germany, Luxembourg, Italy, the Netherlands and the UK; Spain and Portugal joined in 1988, and Greece in 1992, when Denmark and Ireland were given observer status. The WEU Council and secretariat moved to Brussels (from Paris and London respectively) in January 1993.

WFC

The World Food Council, a subsidiary organ of the **UN General Assembly** created in 1974 and based in New York. Set up on the specific recommendation of the 1974 World Food Conference, its responsibilities include reviewing the world food situation and the proposals advanced by governments to alleviate world hunger. Since 1992 its mandate and functions have been under review by the General Assembly. Its Secretariat ceased to exist in May 1993, when its functions and activities were transferred to the new UN Department for Policy Co-ordination and Sustainable Development.

WFP

The World Food Programme, set up in 1963 under the joint authority of the **UN**'s **ECOSOC** and **FAO**, and effectively the UN's operational arm for multilateral **food aid**. Its governing body and main policy-making organ is the Committee on Food Aid Policies and Programmes. The focus of WFP work has shifted in line with the growing perception that the main use of food aid should be confined to emergency relief.

WFTU

The World Federation of Trade Unions. Formed in 1945, it was the successor to the International Federation of Trade Unions dating from 1901. In 1949 the WFTU suffered its first major split when pro-Western trade unions broke away to form the **ICFTU**, in protest against the domination of WFTU by **left-wing** and pro-Soviet trade unions. The organization's headquarters were in Prague until 1990, when the Czechoslovak government withdrew its permission for the WFTU's secretariat to operate, and it claimed to have more than 2 million members representing national and international trade unions, but the collapse of **communism** across Eastern Europe from 1989 placed its future, and even its existence, in serious doubt.

WHITE AUSTRALIA POLICY

Restrictions on immigration to Australia which aimed to keep out black, especially Asian, immigrants. The policy was dismantled at the end of the 1960s and its last remnants swept away in 1975 when assisted passages were made available to non-European immigrants. The official policy of assimilating immigrants into Anglo-Australian culture was replaced by a policy of multiculturalism. Immigration was partly responsible for the surge in Australia's population from 7.5 million in 1947 to 17 million in 1990.

WHITE COMMONWEALTH

A popular term used to describe the former British dominions of Australia, Canada, New Zealand and South Africa, colonized by European settlers, which gained independence as members of the **Commonwealth** under the 1931 Statute of Westminster. It was synonymous with 'old Commonwealth', while British colonies in Asia, Africa and the **Caribbean** which became independent after the Second World War acquired the label '**New Commonwealth**'.

WHITE FLIGHT

A reference to the increasing tendency of affluent, white, families to relocate to suburbs and rural areas in response to rising level of crime and deteriorating infrastructure in US cities. The effect of this white flight has been to accelerate the growth of non-white ghettos, thereby exacerbating inner-city problems.

WHITE HOUSE

1. The official residence and office of the president of the USA, located in the country's federal capital, Washington DC. It was under construction during the administration of George Washington (1789–97), and the first President to live in the White House was John Adams (1797–1801) who took up residence on 1 November 1800. The building acquired its name when it was refurbished after Washington had been burnt by occupying British troops during the War of 1812 (1812–14).

2. The building in central Moscow which housed the Russian Congress of People's Deputies (legislature) until its dissolution in September 1993. The White House was the centre of resistance to the **August coup** in 1991, and the scene of heavy fighting as pro-Yeltsin troops bombarded the building to end the **Moscow rebellion** of October 1993. In February 1994 the White House became the seat of the Russian government and presidency, which made a symbolic transfer from the **Kremlin**.

WHITE PAPER

A document issued by the UK government containing policy and/or legislative decisions. A White Paper may or may not be preceded by a consultative **Green Paper**. The contents of important White Papers are themselves often debated in Parliament, prior to the introduction of legislation implementing the detail of the broad policy conclusions.

WHITE REVOLUTION

A programme of social and economic reform initiated in 1962 by Mohammad Reza Pahlavi, Shah of Iran in 1941–79, and endorsed by a popular referendum in 1963. Its main points were the abolition of the landlord-serf relationship; the nationalization of forests; the sale of government factories to pay for land reform; the amendment of the election law to allow the enfranchisement of women; the sharing of company profits by workers; and the establishment of a literacy corps to facilitate compulsory education. The undermining of traditional religious observance was a factor in the alienation of Muslim clerics.

WHITEHALL

The machinery of central government in the UK. The term derives from the street of that name in London, just east of the Houses of Parliament, in which the offices of some of the most important government departments have traditionally been sited. It is used to denote the **bureaucracy**, while political decision-making lies with **Westminster**. It also signifies central as distinct from local or regional administration.

WHITEWATER

The name of a small Arkansas development corporation which lay at the heart of a scandal involving US President Bill Clinton and First Lady Hillary Rodham Clinton. The affair, sometimes referred to as 'Whitewatergate', became public in late 1993 when it was alleged that Clinton, who invested in Whitewater in 1978, might have acted improperly in supporting the company while serving as Governor of Arkansas. In 1982 Clinton's partner in Whitewater, James McDougal, bought the Madison Guaranty Savings, a savings and loan company (**S&L**)which went bankrupt in 1989. The third partner in Whitewater, Hillary Clinton, was also its lawyer, and she too faced conflict-of-interest allegations in connection with the affair, as well as claims that she had filed inaccurate tax returns on behalf of herself and her husband. The affair was given a further dimension by the apparent suicide in July 1993 of Vince Foster, the White House's counsel – and a partner in Hillary's Arkansas law firm – who was working to sort out Whitewater's back taxes. The Whitewater allegations were dismissed by supporters of the Clintons as arising from events which had occurred many years ago and in a state where business and political matters were notoriously interwoven. More damaging than the precise allegations themselves, however, was the growing belief that there had been a White House cover-up of the affair. In the face of growing public pressure, an independent counsel (special prosecutor), Robert Fiske, was appointed to investigate the matter in January 1994.

WHITLAM AFFAIR

The controversial dismissal in November 1975 of Prime Minister Gough Whitlam by the Governor-General of Australia, Sir John Kerr. Whitlam, leader of the Australian Labor Party (ALP), had come to power in December 1972 after 23 years of conservative rule. In October 1975, however, the opposition Liberal Party leader Malcolm Fraser precipitated a constitutional crisis by threatening to use his majority in the Senate to block the budget. Kerr dismissed Whitlam on 11 November, appointing Fraser as Prime Minister, and then calling fresh elections when Fraser proved unable to command sufficient support in the legislature. The result of the elections, on 13 December, was a heavy defeat for the ALP.

WHO

The World Health Organization, a **UN** specialized agency based in Geneva, founded in 1948 with the aim of attaining the highest possible level of health for all peoples through technical collaboration with its members in the areas of disease eradication, nutrition, environmental hygiene, and health service administration. Its 187 member states are represented in the World Health Assembly which meets annually to decide policy and approve the budget, while general guidance on policy and its implementation are left to a smaller Executive Board and the Secretariat. Among the organization's greatest achievements was the eradication of smallpox; it has recently been stretched by the demands placed upon its Global Programme on **AIDS**, while also pursuing the objectives in its programme of Health for All by the Year 2000.

WIND OF CHANGE

The resounding phrase used by UK Prime Minister Harold Macmillan in a speech to the South African parliament on 3 February 1960. Macmillan told the white minority legislature: 'The wind of change is blowing through this continent, and whether we like it or not, this growth of national consciousness is a political fact. We must all accept it as a fact, and our national policies must take account of it.' He made it clear that the South African government's policy of **apartheid** would not be supported by his government, and called for a greater share in political power for the black population. The speech highlighted the growing rift between the UK and South African governments, marked by the departure of South Africa from the **Commonwealth** the following year.

WINDSCALE

The site of a nuclear reactor in Cumbria, UK, built to provide plutonium for military purposes, which was the site of one of the world's first nuclear accidents, a serious fire on 8 October 1957. The overheating of graphite bricks which encased the uranium fuel rods in the reactor, caused 11 tons of uranium to oxidise, releasing radioactive materials into the atmosphere and igniting a fire in the reactor core. The fire burned for 16 hours before it was extinguished. The UK government sought to minimise publicity, and did little to acknowledge the scale of the accident, beyond ordering the destruction of milk from an area of land seven miles long by two miles wide close to the site. No records were kept on people living near Windscale at the time, and therefore it is impossible to quantify the incidence of cancers attributable to exposure to radiation released in the accident. Windscale was renamed **Sellafield** in 1971 under a reorganization of the UK's nuclear agencies.

WINTER OF DISCONTENT

The time of industrial unrest in the UK over the winter of 1978–9. Within the framework of the lengthy period of **incomes policy** which had continued almost unabated since 1972, in August 1978 the Labour government introduced a strict 5 per cent guideline for pay increases in the coming pay round. This policy was rejected by the **TUC** and by the Labour Party itself, and sparked off a series of stoppages of work, especially in transport and the public services, gravely damaging the image of the Labour Party as the 1979 general election approached.

WIPO

The World Intellectual Property Organization, established by a convention in July 1967, which became a **UN** specialized agency on 17 December 1974. The WIPO administers more than 15 treaties relating to the two principal categories of intellectual property: copyright (ie written work, film, recording and other works of art) and industrial property (industrial designs, inventions, patents and trademarks). The primary treaty in the first category is the Berne Convention for the Protection of Literary and Artistic Works first signed in 1886 and repeatedly amended. It requires its 90-odd members to give copyright protection to works originating in member states and establishes minimum standards for such protection. The WIPO also administers the Paris Convention on the Protection of Industrial Property, whose 100-plus signatories are obliged to give the same protection to nationals of other member states as they give their own. Dating from 1883 and frequently revised, the Paris Convention has provoked discord as developing countries have lobbied for shorter protection periods in order to ease the transfer of technology.

WIRTSCHAFTSWUNDER *see* ECONOMIC MIRACLE

WMO

The World Meteorological Organization, a specialized agency of the **UN** based in Geneva and established on 4 April 1951 to co-ordinate, standardize and improve world meteorological activities and encourage an efficient exchange of meteorological information between states. The WMO has been increasingly concerned with the assessment of global climate change. In 1988 it organized an International Panel on Climate Change which made recommendations on the problem of **global warming** to the Second World Climate Conference held in Geneva in November 1990 and to the June 1992 **Earth Summit** in Rio.

WOLFENDEN REPORT

The report of a UK committee chaired by Sir John Wolfenden, which recommended in particular the decriminalization of homosexual acts between males and an increase in penalties for soliciting by prostitutes. The landmark report, published on 4 September 1957, led to the Street Offences Act 1959 (introduced by the government) and to the Sexual Offences Act 1967, which permitted homosexual acts in private between consenting male adults (in England and Wales).

WOMEN'S LIB

The informal women's liberation movement based on **feminism** which emerged in the **West** in the late 1960s. It coincided with the entry of greater numbers of women into the workforce and the consequent increase in the number of economically independent women. Although the movement covered a broad spectrum of views, its basic aim was to challenge **sexism**. All so-called 'women's libbers' argued that women should have equal rights with men, enjoy equal access to education and employment, and receive equal pay for equal work. Other issues on which they campaigned included abortion rights. By questioning traditional social mores, Women's Lib also played a major role in the **sexual revolution**.

WOODSTOCK

An open-air rock music festival held in upstate New York in mid-August 1969, characterized by spontaneity and ingenuity in accommodating the unexpectedly large number of young people who gathered for the event. The 'spirit of Woodstock' was evoked, if not always recreated, at various other festival venues the following year. In some ways it represented the high-water mark of mass participation in the 'sixties' youth counter-culture, and gave rise to the label 'Woodstock generation'.

WORKFARE

A concept developed in the USA in the 1980s, but as yet largely untried, whereby recipients of welfare are required to work in return for assistance which they receive from the state. The aim of the policy – which is particularly popular with, but by no means confined to, the **right-wing** of the Republican Party – is to break a perceived pattern of welfare-dependency by re-establishing a degree of individual responsibility in welfare matters.

WORLD BANK *see* IBRD

WORLD CLIMATE CONVENTION

The **UN** Framework Convention on Climate Change, adopted at the 1992 **Earth Summit**, which bound signatory states to limit their emissions of **greenhouse gases** in order to combat the **greenhouse effect**, but failed to set specific targets for such reductions. The convention merely recommended that signatory countries revert to the 1990 level of emissions of greenhouse gases by the end of the decade, and was criticized by environmentalists as insufficiently stringent.

WORLD CONFERENCE ON HUMAN RIGHTS

The first meeting of its kind, held in Vienna on 14–25 June 1993, under the auspices of the **UNCHR**. Its 'Declaration and Programme of Action', adopted by consensus by delegates from around 180 countries, stated that human rights were 'universal, indivisible and interdependent', and that their protection was the legitimate concern of the international community. Some 1,500 **NGOs** working in the field of human rights attended the conference but were denied participation in the drafting of the final declaration, at the insistence of a number of countries including China and Japan.

WORLD CONSERVATION STRATEGY

A policy document first published in 1980 (with a revised version in 1991) warning of profound dangers to the earth's life-support systems, and synthesizing a global approach to overcoming these dangers. Sponsored by the **FAO**, the **IUCN**, **UNESCO** and the **WWF**, it emphasizes the importance of **biological diversity**, and the risks inherent in the continued use of **fossil fuels**.

WORLD CONSERVATION UNION *see* IUCN

WORLD COUNCIL OF CHURCHES *see* WCC

WORLD ECONOMIC FORUM

A gathering of leading politicians, bankers and businesspeople, convened annually since 1970, and largely concerned with global economic and monetary matters.

WORLD FEDERATION OF TRADE UNIONS *see* WFTU

WORLD FOOD COUNCIL *see* WFC

WORLD FOOD PROGRAMME *see* WFP

WORLD HEALTH ORGANIZATION *see* WHO

WORLD HERITAGE SITE

An area of natural or historic significance as designated by **UNESCO** under the 1972 World Heritage UNESCO Convention. Lists of such sites, drawn up by participating states, are published biennially, but the scheme has no statutory powers to protect them.

WORLD INTELLECTUAL PROPERTY ORGANIZATION *see* WIPO

WORLD METEOROLOGICAL ORGANIZATION *see* WMO

WORLD PEACE COUNCIL

An international organization which promoted international **communism** and campaigned for an end to war. It was relatively successful in attracting non-communist members and had over 2,500 affiliates in 142 countries. The Council was founded in November 1950 in Warsaw, and stemmed from the World Congress of Intellectuals for Peace held in Wroclaw, also in Poland, in August 1948. Before moving to its current location in Helsinki, it was expelled from both Paris and Vienna.

WORLD TRADE CENTRE BOMBING

The World Trade Centre, one of New York City's most famous landmarks, was badly damaged on 26 February 1993, when a van packed with explosives was detonated in its underground car park. Six people were killed and more than 1,000 were injured in the blast. After a trial lasting five months, four Muslim fundamentalists – followers of a blind Egyptian cleric, Shaikh Abdul Rahman, who was resident in the USA – were convicted on 4 March 1994 on charges arising from the bombing. A fifth man is still to be tried, while two other suspects remain at large; rewards of $2 million were offered for information leading to their arrest. In a related case, a further 15 men, including Shaikh Rahman, were due to be tried in September 1994, having been arrested in the aftermath of the Trade Centre bombing on charges of plotting to attack further targets in New York City.

WORLD TRADE ORGANIZATION

see GATT

WORLDWATCH INSTITUTE

An independent not-for-profit research organization founded by Lester Brown and based in Washington DC. Worldwatch aims to increase public awareness of threats to the environment and thereby to stimulate an appropriate response among policy-makers. It publishes, among other things, the bi-monthly journal *World Watch*, the annual *State of the World* survey, and a recently initiated series, *Vital Signs*.

WWF

The World Wide Fund for Nature, known until 1988 as the World Wildlife Fund. One of the largest international conservation organizations, it was formed in 1961, and raises funds on the basis of voluntary public donations, for a variety of conservation projects. Together with **UNEP** and the **IUCN**, the WWF was involved in drawing up the **World Conservation Strategy**.

XINHUA

The abbreviation of Xinhua She, the state-owned New China News Agency. Xinhua carries services in several languages. Founded in 1931, it has bureaux in all of China's 30 provincial and regional capitals and about 95 foreign bureaux.

YAKUZA

Japanese criminal syndicates which control activities such as prostitution and gambling. Officially tolerated by the authorities, they were required by a law which came into force on 1 March 1992 to register with the local authorities. In practice, the measure accelerated a process whereby the Yakuza were transforming themselves into legitimate limited companies.

YALTA

The summit meeting between the **Big Three** wartime **Allies** – the **Soviet Union**, the UK and the USA – held on 4–12 February 1945 in the Crimean resort of Yalta. The summit achieved Soviet agreement to join the war against Japan three months after victory in Europe, in return for concessions in the **Far East**; the admission of France as a joint occupier of soon-to-be defeated Germany; Soviet participation in the **UN**; and the extension of the Soviet border into eastern Poland, which would itself be compensated by territory from Germany. The participants also signed the 'Declaration on Liberated Europe', which promised the restoration of sovereignty in all European countries, free elections and economic reconstruction. Thus, although it became a cliché to identify the Yalta summit with the West's 'betrayal' of **Eastern Europe**, it did not, in fact, enshrine the division of the region into spheres of influence.

YAOUNDÉ CONVENTION

The name of two successive agreements in the 1960s which catered for France's relationship with its former colonies once it had joined the **EEC**. In the mid-1970s the Yaoundé Convention was succeeded by the broader **Lomé Convention**.

YEAR ZERO

A slogan adopted by the **Khmer Rouge** to denote the start of their almost four-year period of government in Cambodia in April 1975. Although the term signified a revolutionary renunciation of former ideological, political, social and economic systems, the policies instigated at the start of Year Zero were based, to a large extent, on the Chinese **Great Leap Forward** of the late 1950s. In the West, the phrase, along with other terms such as the **Killing Fields**, came to symbolize the terrible cost in human lives of the implementation of radical *Khmer Rouge* policies.

YELLOW RAIN

The chemical weapon allegedly used by Vietnamese forces in **south-east Asia**. In the early 1980s the USA claimed that

Vietnamese troops had been using non-indigenous 'potent mycotoxins' ('yellow rain') against their enemies in Cambodia and Laos. However, a number of scientific reports released in the mid-1980s rejected the US allegations. One study found that samples of 'yellow rain' usually contained a proportion of pollen and that in all likelihood the substance was in fact pollen-laden bee faeces.

YEMEN

The state situated on the south-western tip of the Arabian peninsula. The Republic of Yemen was founded in May 1990 by the unification of the Yemen Arab Republic (North Yemen) and the People's Democratic Republic of Yemen (South Yemen). After months of rising tension, civil war erupted between the North and the South in May 1994. The South, based in **Aden**, attempted to secede shortly after the onset of fighting.

YIPPIES

Members of the Youth International Party, a loosely organized radical group founded in 1968 by Jerry Rubin and Abbie Hoffman. The Yippies became an important part of the US youth movement and opposition to the **Vietnam War**. They were key participants in the 1968 Chicago demonstrations associated with the Democratic convention, and both Rubin and Hoffman were tried among the **Chicago Eight**. The Yippies were determinedly anti-bureaucratic, and eschewed much orthodox political activity. Instead they stressed the importance of spontaneity, drugs, music, and a willingness to outrage **Middle America** in creating political change.

YOM KIPPUR WAR

The October 1973 Arab-Israeli War. Syrian and Egyptian forces launched an attack on **Israel** on 6 October as it observed *Yom Kippur* (the Jewish Day of Atonement). The declared aims of Syria and Egypt were to recover the Arab territories lost to Israel during the 1967 **Six-Day War**. Caught off guard, Israel lost ground at first but fought back to regain its position by the ceasefire of 24 October. During the next two years, the USA (which had intervened decisively in the war by airlifting arms to Israel) managed to mediate military disengagement agreements between Israel on the one hand and Egypt and Syria on the other. Part of the reason for the diplomatic intervention of the USA was the use by the Arab states of their strongest weapon – the power to impose an embargo on the export of oil.

YOUNG TURKS

A term used to describe individuals or groups who, while lacking experience, are deemed to posses the energy and ambition needed to push for political power. An example of its usage can be found in Thailand, where a group of nationalist and vaguely socialist 'Young Turk' officers led two unsuccessful coups in the 1980s. The term is derived from the secret society of officers responsible for the Turkish revolution of 1908.

YUGOSLAVIA

The country in the **Balkans** which was effectively dissolved in April 1992 in a state of civil war, although a rump Federal Republic of Yugoslavia (**FRY**) was then created by two of the six former Yugoslav republics (Serbia and **Montenegro**). As an independent country, Yugoslavia dated back to 1918 and the Kingdom of Serbs, Croats and Slovenes, renamed in 1929 as the Kingdom of Yugoslavia. It was ethnically and culturally diverse, with Serbs and Croats forming some 60 per cent of the population, and the remainder made up of Slovenes, **Bosnian Muslims**, Albanians, Macedonians and Jews. The ethnic rivalries of the inter-war period laid the ground for extreme brutality after the German invasion in the Second World War; hundreds of thousands were killed by the **Chetniks** and particularly the Nazi puppet **Ustasa** regime. Only the **communist** Partisans led by Josip Broz Tito championed the ideal of a unified Yugoslavia. Their victory in 1945 led to the establishment of a socialist state, whose six constituent republics were **Bosnia-Hercegovina, Croatia, Macedonia,** Montenegro, Serbia and **Slovenia**. Tito's death in 1980 marked a new era of uncertainty, growing **nationalism** and economic decline. By 1991 the **Titoist** ideal of a unified Yugoslavia was in disgrace and Yugoslavia's constituent republics, with the exception of Serbia and Montenegro, declared independence. Fighting broke out as Serb nationalists attempted to achieve their goal of a **Greater Serbia**.

YUPPIE

A Young Urban Professional Person – a term which first surfaced in the USA in 1983 to identify a new generation of young, ambitious, hard-working high fliers, generally in the finance, advertising and hitech industries. In the UK yuppies were often also described as 'Thatcher's children', as they appeared to embody the aspirations of **Thatcherism**. The term (which spawned numerous more or less humorous variants) is still in common usage, but yuppies were really a phenomenon of the boom years of the mid- to late 1980s.

ZAÏRE

A central African country with a population of around 39.9 million. Formerly a Belgian colony (known as Belgian Congo), it gained independence in June 1960 as the Republic of Congo, although to differentiate it from its smaller northern neighbour it was known as Congo-Kinshasa. The adoption of the name Zaïre in 1971 was part of the implementation of **Mobutuism**, the political ideology of President Mobutu Sese Seko.

ZAKAT

(Arabic,'purification') One of the five fundamental 'pillars' of Islam. It pertains to the giving of alms to the poor (who must be Muslim) on a stipulated scale in order to legitimize or 'purify' what is retained. The other four requirements of Islam (accepted by all branches) are *shahadah* (the affirmation of Divine unity); *salah* (the five daily ritual prayers); *sawm* (fasting in the month of **Ramadan**); and **haj** (the pilgrimage to Mecca). **Jihad** (holy war), though sometimes regarded as a sixth pillar, is not universally obligatory. *Zakat* has attracted notice when incorporated within a larger programme of **Islamization** as in **Pakistan** under the regime of President Mohammed Zia ul-Haq (1979–88).

ZAMBIA

A landlocked country of 8.6 million people in southern Africa. Known as Northern Rhodesia until independence in October 1964, it had been declared a British protectorate in 1911 and came under direct British Colonial Office control in 1924. In 1953 it became part of the **Central African Federation**, with **Zimbabwe** (then called Southern Rhodesia) and **Malawi** (then called Nyasaland), but this unsuccessful federal experiment was abandoned in 1963.

ZANU *see* PATRIOTIC FRONT

ZAPATISTA NATIONAL LIBERATION ARMY *see* EZLN

ZAPU *see* PATRIOTIC FRONT

ZEEBRUGGE DISASTER *see* HERALD OF FREE ENTERPRISE

ZERO GROWTH

An attempt to emphasize an ecological perspective, and to challenge the standard assumption in economic planning worldwide that growth rates are a measure of success. The thesis was advanced in the influential report *Limits to Growth*, published in 1972 by the **Club of Rome**, that growth increasingly entailed overstretching the finite resources of the planet. Zero growth and even negative growth became an element in **green** political programmes in the 1970s, but the implication that greens were against higher living standards made these ideas as difficult to popularize in the **North** as they were resented in the **South**. As a buzzword, '**sustainable development**' has proven much more palatable.

ZERO OPTION

US President Ronald Reagan's proposal in 1981 on intermediate nuclear weapons (INF), that the Soviet side should scrap the SS-20 missile entirely, in return for **NATO** cancellation of the decision to modernize its arsenal by deploying **cruise** and **Pershing** missiles in Europe. The zero option had more rhetorical than actual impact, and was fatally flawed in Soviet eyes in that it said nothing about any corresponding cuts in independent French and UK nuclear weapons.

ZERO POPULATION GROWTH

A demographic situation in which the number of births is equalled by the number of deaths, thus balancing the level of population. The world's population increased by about 1.7 per cent annually between 1980 and 1990 and, although the rate of population growth is slowing, the world's increasing population strains its resources. ZPG was one of the recommendations in the 1972 report **Limits to Growth**.

ZIL

The large black limousines built specially for high-ranking **Communist** Party leaders in the **Soviet Union** and its **client states**.

ZIMBABWE

A landlocked country in southern Africa with a population of some 10.6 million, which became independent in April 1980 after a long struggle by nationalist liberation movements and as a result of the **Lancaster House Agreement**. The country's turbulent history had seen it accorded the status of a self-governing British Colony in 1923 under the name Southern Rhodesia, and then, in 1953, brought into the **Central African Federation** with **Zambia** (then called Northern Rhodesia) and **Malawi** (then called Nyasaland). The Federation was dissolved in December 1963, and the white settler Rhodesian Front party declared **UDI** in Southern Rhodesia in November 1965, taking the name **Rhodesia**. Under a short-lived 'internal settlement' attempted as a compromise by the white regime, the name Zimbabwe-Rhodesia was used in 1979–80.

ZIMBABWE AFRICAN NATIONAL UNION *see* PATRIOTIC FRONT

ZIMBABWE AFRICAN PEOPLE'S UNION *see* PATRIOTIC FRONT

ZIONISM

The Jewish nationalist movement for the creation of a national home in the predominantly Arab state of **Palestine**. Zionism takes its name from the hill in Jerusalem on which the ancient palace of King David, and later the temple, were built. It was propounded in the late nineteenth century by Theodore Herzl and others who called for the preservation of the Jewish people by national reunion. The Balfour Declaration of 1917 first recognized Zionist aspirations and lent the movement political weight. The **Holocaust** provided Zionism with a seemingly unanswerable case and the independent state of **Israel** was established in 1948. Since the formation of Israel, Zionism has been supported by the majority of the world's Jewish communities and has been an active international force.

ZIRCON AFFAIR

The controversy over a British space satellite, whose purpose was reported to be surveillance of civilian and military radio communications. A reporter, Duncan Campbell, had prepared a BBC television programme, one of a series entitled 'Secret Service', on the circumstances surrounding the Zircon satellite project. However, just before the programme was to have been transmitted in January 1987 the BBC's managing director, Alasdair Milne, withdrew it on the grounds of national security. Nevertheless the contents of the programme became widely known. Further controversy arose over the actions of the police in obtaining warrants to search premises for documents and film relating to the series.

ZVIADISTS

The supporters of Zviad Gamsakhurdia, who was deposed as President of **Georgia** in January 1992. The Zviadists opposed the new regime of former Soviet Foreign Minister Eduard Shevardnadze, but Zviadist resistance in the west of the country, centring around the town of Zugdidi, was finally crushed in November 1993 after Georgian forces had received reinforcements from Russia. Gamsakhurdia himself died at the end of 1993.

BIOGRAPHICAL INDEX

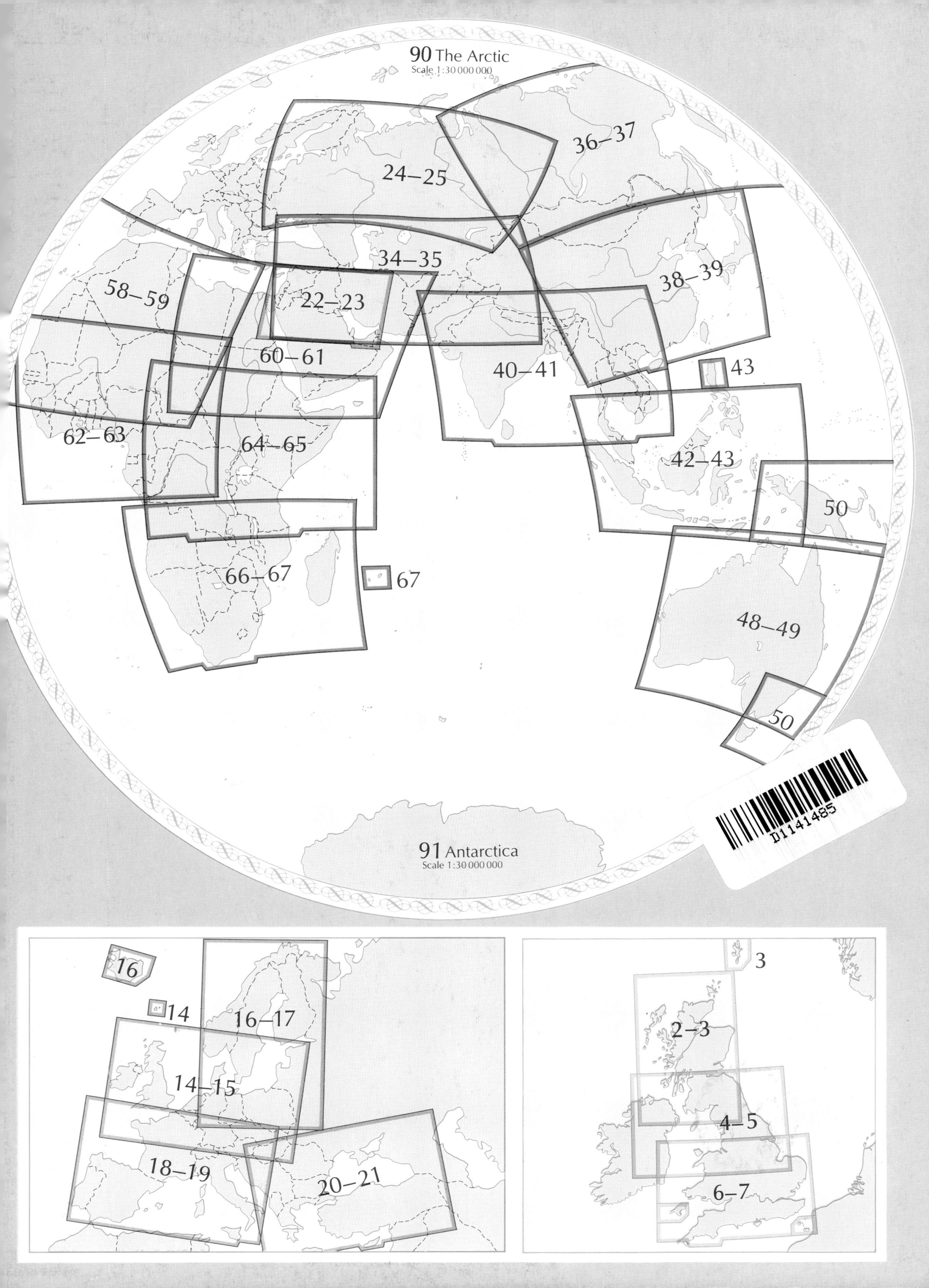
90 The Arctic
Scale 1:30 000 000
36–37
24–25
34–35
38–39
58–59
22–23
60–61
40–41
43
62–63
64–65
42–43
50
66–67
67
48–49
50
91 Antarctica
Scale 1:30 000 000
16
14
16–17
14–15
18–19
20–21
3
2–3
4–5
6–7

The Daily Telegraph

WORLD ATLAS

Published by Telegraph Publications,
Peterborough Court, At South Quay,
181 Marsh Wall, London E14 9SR

First published 1988

Designed, edited, drawn and reproduced
by cartographers, geographers, artists
and technicians at ESSELTE MAP SERVICE.

British Library Cataloguing in Publication Data
The Daily Telegraph World Atlas.
1. World Atlases
912

ISBN 0-86367-241-8

Printed in Sweden

FOREWORD

In recent decades, the World appears to have become smaller and in many ways less mysterious. Air travel has brought different parts of the globe effectively closer. International telephone dialling provides instant long-distance communications, and television, radio and newspapers provide snapshots of events worldwide as they happen. An earthquake in Mexico, a drought in Ethiopia, a nuclear accident in Chernobyl – the day-to-day life of faraway places is brought vividly into our living rooms.

Our perception of the World is therefore conditioned largely by what we see. And it is in this context that a high-calibre atlas provides the essential overview, the framework on which a fuller understanding of the World around us can be based. We believe that by using a new, revolutionary approach to cartography, *The Daily Telegraph World Atlas* gives an insight into the life of the planet that today's readers require.

We have taken advantage of the great strides made in space technology and in particular the incredible detail supplied by satellite imagery and satellite photography to compile maps which relate the physical variations of the Earth's surface to the type of landscape and land-use found there. This exciting technique – often referred to as environmental mapping – surpasses traditional mapping by presenting more information at a glance with far greater clarity. One has only to compare this atlas with any other traditional physical atlas to see that we are now at the start of a new era in atlas publishing.

Christopher Milsome
Publishing Director

THE WORLD IN MAPS

UNITED KINGDOM

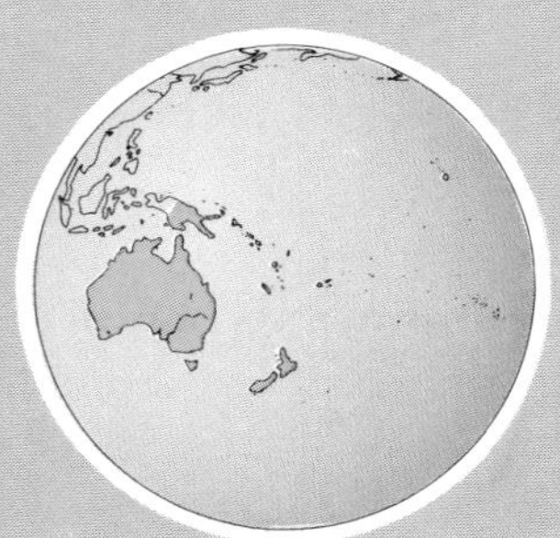

EUROPE

ASIA

AUSTRALIA

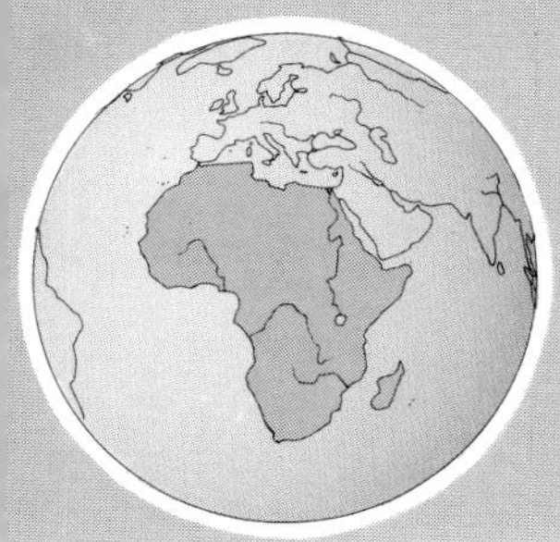

AFRICA

NORTH AMERICA

SOUTH AMERICA

THE ARCTIC AND ANTARCTIC

THE WORLD

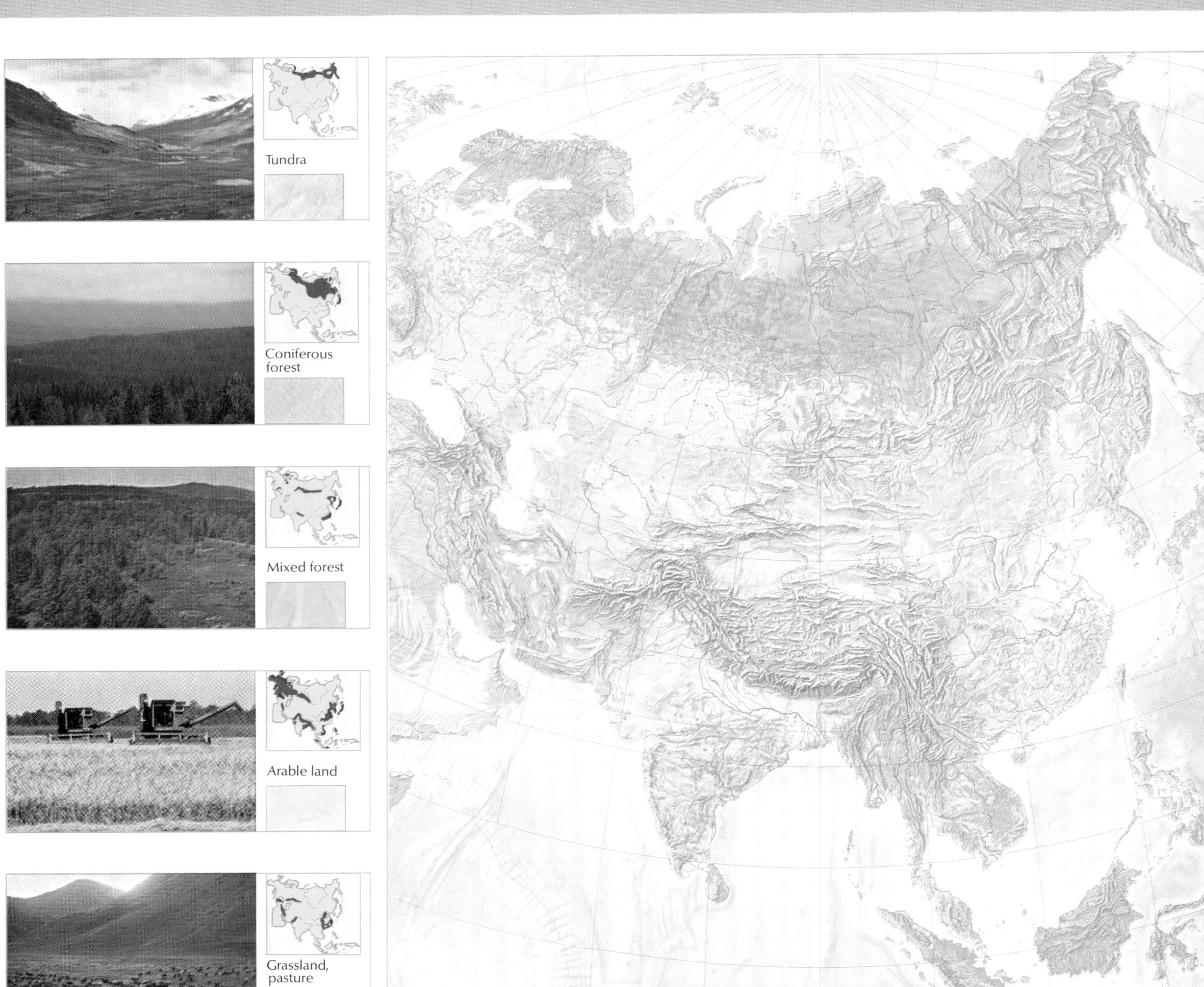
Tundra
Coniferous forest
Mixed forest
Arable land
Grassland, pasture

THE WORLD in maps

A map is a representation of the face of the Earth. It lacks, however, the realism of an aerial photograph: mountains, rivers, seas and cities are indicated by signs and colours. The Earth's surface, in all its endless variety, has to be sorted and arranged so that it may be presented in a form that is easily understood. In the past, cartography has perhaps been a little too abstract; most people will recall the traditional school atlas where the lowland Sahara was shown in lush green, while upland Africa's rich vegetation was represented in parched brown; the map gave no intimation of the specific characteristics of the landscape with its forests and grasslands, its deserts and cultivated plains.

Satellite imagery and photographs of the Earth taken from space have inspired a new era in cartography. Now the surface of the Earth can be shown as a series of interrelated environments. Each type of environment is represented by a particular colour which allows the reader to see land-use at a glance. Hill shading reveals the undulations of upland and mountainous areas. Settlement patterns, communications and administrative divisions are overprinted to give the user as clear a picture of our planet as is possible in two dimensions. The colour is superb – not only are these maps easy to read, they are also beautiful to behold.

Semi-desert, Steppe

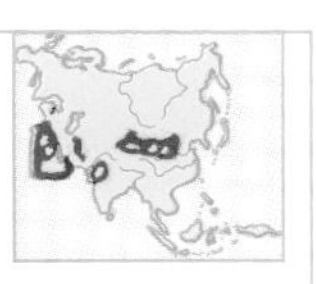

Other desert

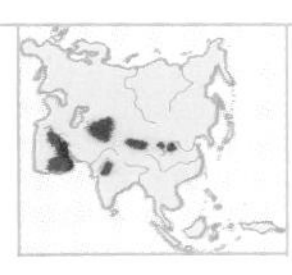

Sand desert

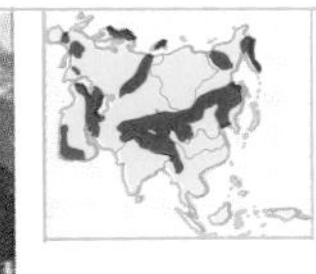

Mountain

Tropical rain forest

The key on the left indicates the main classes into which different environments have been grouped. Certain specific environments not shown here have their own unique colour classification. A complete display of all the classes can be found inside the back cover. It should be noted that the British Isles has a separate series of colour classifications which is also displayed inside the back cover.

NORTH SEA
Orkney Islands
Shetland Islands
Mainland
Westray
Papa Westray
Sanday
Stronsay
North Ronaldsay
Shapinsay
Rousay
Eday
Hoy
Flotta
Burray
South Ronaldsay
Scapa Flow
Pentland Firth
Stromness
Kirkwall
Dunnet Head
Duncansby Head
Sinclairs' Bay
Wick
Thurso
Fair Isle
Foula
Papa Stour
Yell
Unst
Fetlar
Whalsay
Bressay
West Burra
Yell Sound
Herma Ness
Sumburgh Head
Fitful Head
Lerwick
St. Magnus Bay
to Aberdeen
to Lerwick
Sule Skerry
Stack Skerry
North Rona
Sula Sgeir
Cape Wrath
Strathy Point
Point of Stoer
Butt of Lewis
Lewis
Harris
Eye Peninsula
Stornoway
Broad Bay
North Minch
Little Minch
Shiant Isles
Flannan Isles
Gallan Head
Scarp
Taransay
North Uist
Benbecula
South Uist
Outer Hebrides
Western Isles
Monach Isles
Skye
Raasay
Scalpay
Rona
Inner Sound
Sound of Raasay
Cuillin Hills
Trotternish
Loch Snizort
Dunvegan Head
Idrigill Point
Wester Ross
Easter Ross
Black Isle
Moray Firth
Dornoch Firth
Tarbat Ness
Loch Shin
Loch Broom
Loch Maree
Loch Torridon
Loch Ness
Inverness
Beauly Firth
Highland
Grampian
Strathbogie
Buchan
Buchan Ness
Kinnaird's Head
Fraserburgh
Peterhead
Aberdeen
Elgin
Banff
Huntly
Keith
R. Spey
R. Deveron
R. Findhorn
R. Don
Ben Hope
Ben Klibreck
Ben Wyvis
Beinn Dearg
Ben More Assynt
Beinn Dhorain
Ullapool
Lochinver
Kyle of Lochalsh
© ESSELTE MAP SERVICE

Scale 1:1 250 000

0 10 20 30 40 50 km
0 10 20 30 miles

© ESSELTE MAP SERVICE

Scale 1:1250000 — 0 10 20 30 50 km; 0 10 20 30 miles

Scale 1:1250000

Humberside
R. Humber
Spurn Head
Cleethorpes
Grimsby
Scunthorpe
Doncaster
Goole
Thorne
Pontefract
Wakefield
West Yorkshire
Halifax
Huddersfield
Barnsley
South Yorkshire
Sheffield
Rotherham
Peak District
Gainsborough
East Retford
Worksop
Lincoln
R. Witham
Lincolnshire
Lincoln Wolds
Louth
Mablethorpe
Sutton-on-Sea
Skegness
Boston
The Wash
Chesterfield
Mansfield
Derbyshire
Nottinghamshire
Nottingham
Derby
Stoke-on-Trent
Newark-on-Trent
Grantham
Sleaford
Spalding
King's Lynn
Hunstanton
Cromer
Norfolk
Norwich
Great Yarmouth
Lowestoft
Thetford
Grime's Graves
Wisbech
Peterborough
Stamford
The Fens
March
Ely
Leicestershire
Leicester
Loughborough
Melton Mowbray
Burton upon Trent
Tamworth
Lichfield
Rugeley
West Midlands
Birmingham
Coventry
Wolverhampton
Nuneaton
Hinckley
Rugby
Warwickshire
Warwick
Royal Leamington Spa
Stratford-upon-Avon
Vale of Evesham
Evesham
Worcester
Kettering
Corby
Wellingborough
Northamptonshire
Northampton
Cambridgeshire
Huntingdon
Cambridge
St. Neots
Bedford
Bedfordshire
Milton Keynes
Bletchley
Suffolk
Bury St. Edmunds
Ipswich
Felixstowe
Harwich
Colchester
Clacton-on-Sea
to Rotterdam
to Gothenburg
to Esbjerg
to Hook of Holland
to Zeebrugge
Hertfordshire
Luton
Stevenage
Hitchin
St. Albans
Hemel Hempstead
Watford
Harlow
Chelmsford
Essex
Southend-on-Sea
Foulness
Buckinghamshire
Aylesbury
High Wycombe
Oxfordshire
Oxford
Witney
Banbury
Cheltenham
Gloucestershire
Cirencester
Swindon
Greater London
LONDON
R. Thames
Slough
Windsor
Reading
Berkshire
Newbury
Maidenhead
Henley-on-Thames
Gravesend
Isle of Sheppey
Sheerness
Margate
North Foreland
Ramsgate
Canterbury
Deal
Dover
Folkestone
Kent
Maidstone
North Downs
Tonbridge
Royal Tunbridge Wells
Sevenoaks
to Vlissingen
to Ostend
to Dunkirk
Wiltshire
Salisbury Plain
Salisbury
Chippenham
Devizes
Trowbridge
Andover
Basingstoke
Hampshire
Winchester
Southampton
Portsmouth
New Forest
Bournemouth
Poole
Guildford
Woking
Crawley
Horsham
West Sussex
South Downs
East Sussex
The Weald
Brighton
Worthing
Chichester
Lewes
Eastbourne
Beachy Head
Hastings
Dungeness
Isle of Wight
Newport
Cowes
Ryde
The Needles
St. Catherine's Point
Selsey Bill
Lulworth Cove
ENGLISH CHANNEL
to Cherbourg
to St. Malo
to Caen
to le Havre
to Dieppe
to Boulogne
Calais
FRANCE
Same scale as main map
C de la Hague
Alderney
to Weymouth
Guernsey
St. Peter Port
Herm
Sark
Channel Islands
Jersey
St. Helier

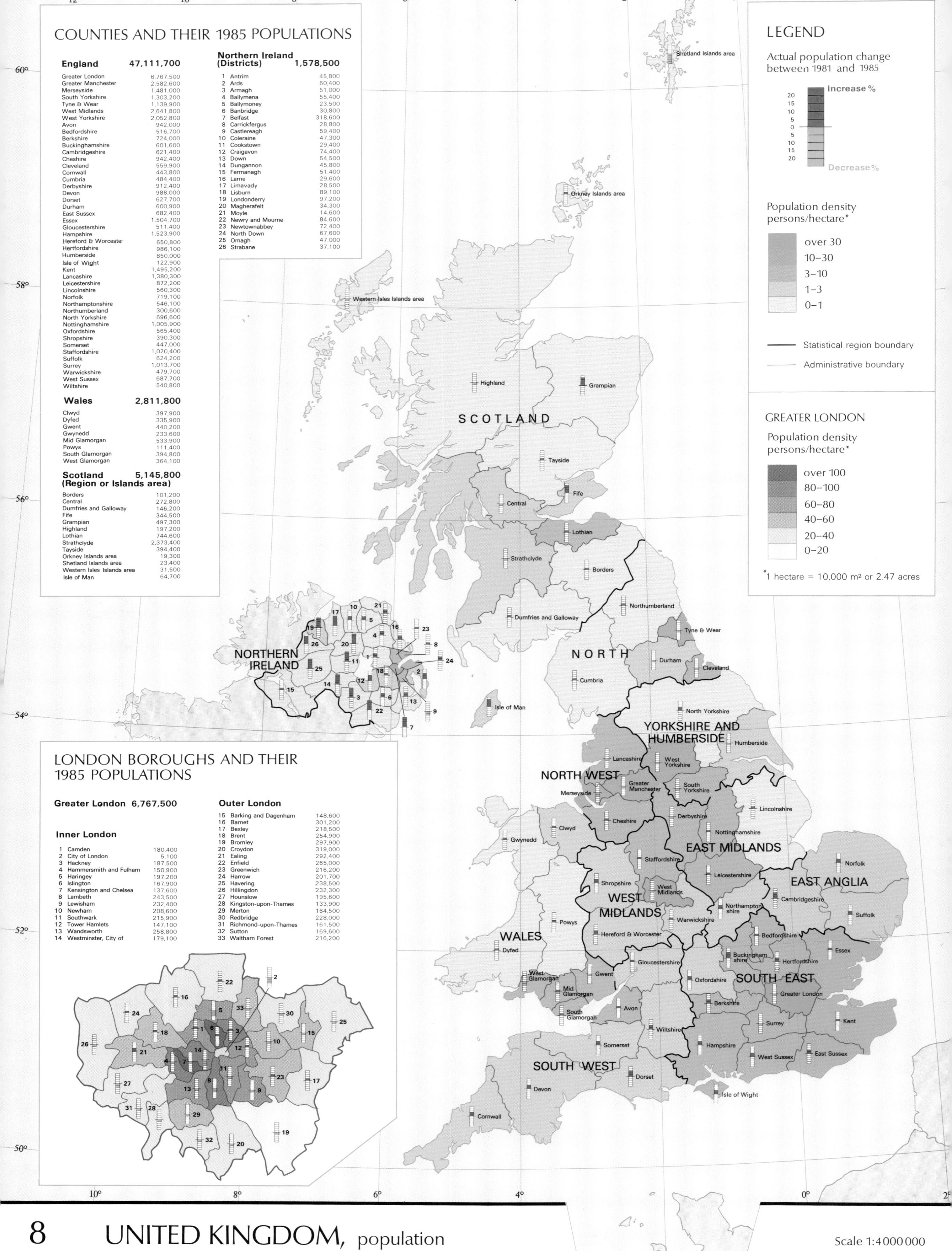

COUNTIES AND THEIR 1985 POPULATIONS

England	47,111,700
Greater London	6,767,500
Greater Manchester	2,582,600
Merseyside	1,481,000
South Yorkshire	1,303,200
Tyne & Wear	1,139,900
West Midlands	2,641,800
West Yorkshire	2,052,800
Avon	942,000
Bedfordshire	516,700
Berkshire	724,000
Buckinghamshire	601,600
Cambridgeshire	621,400
Cheshire	942,400
Cleveland	559,900
Cornwall	443,800
Cumbria	484,400
Derbyshire	912,400
Devon	988,000
Dorset	627,700
Durham	600,900
East Sussex	682,400
Essex	1,504,700
Gloucestershire	511,400
Hampshire	1,523,900
Hereford & Worcester	650,800
Hertfordshire	986,100
Humberside	850,000
Isle of Wight	122,900
Kent	1,495,200
Lancashire	1,380,300
Leicestershire	872,200
Lincolnshire	560,300
Norfolk	719,100
Northamptonshire	546,100
Northumberland	300,600
North Yorkshire	696,600
Nottinghamshire	1,005,900
Oxfordshire	565,400
Shropshire	390,300
Somerset	447,000
Staffordshire	1,020,400
Suffolk	624,200
Surrey	1,013,700
Warwickshire	479,700
West Sussex	687,700
Wiltshire	540,800

Wales	2,811,800
Clwyd	397,900
Dyfed	335,900
Gwent	440,200
Gwynedd	233,600
Mid Glamorgan	533,900
Powys	111,400
South Glamorgan	394,800
West Glamorgan	364,100

Scotland (Region or Islands area)	5,145,800
Borders	101,200
Central	272,800
Dumfries and Galloway	146,200
Fife	344,500
Grampian	497,300
Highland	197,200
Lothian	744,600
Strathclyde	2,373,400
Tayside	394,400
Orkney Islands area	19,300
Shetland Islands area	23,400
Western Isles Islands area	31,500
Isle of Man	64,700

Northern Ireland (Districts)		1,578,500
1	Antrim	45,800
2	Ards	60,400
3	Armagh	51,000
4	Ballymena	55,400
5	Ballymoney	23,500
6	Banbridge	30,800
7	Belfast	318,600
8	Carrickfergus	28,800
9	Castlereagh	59,400
10	Coleraine	47,300
11	Cookstown	29,400
12	Craigavon	74,400
13	Down	54,500
14	Dungannon	45,800
15	Fermanagh	51,400
16	Larne	29,600
17	Limavady	28,500
18	Lisburn	89,100
19	Londonderry	97,200
20	Magherafelt	34,300
21	Moyle	14,600
22	Newry and Mourne	84,600
23	Newtownabbey	72,400
24	North Down	67,600
25	Omagh	47,000
26	Strabane	37,100

LONDON BOROUGHS AND THEIR 1985 POPULATIONS

Greater London 6,767,500

Inner London		
1	Camden	180,400
2	City of London	5,100
3	Hackney	187,500
4	Hammersmith and Fulham	150,900
5	Haringey	197,200
6	Islington	167,900
7	Kensington and Chelsea	137,600
8	Lambeth	243,500
9	Lewisham	232,400
10	Newham	208,600
11	Southwark	215,900
12	Tower Hamlets	147,100
13	Wandsworth	258,800
14	Westminster, City of	179,100

Outer London		
15	Barking and Dagenham	148,600
16	Barnet	301,200
17	Bexley	218,500
18	Brent	254,900
19	Bromley	297,900
20	Croydon	319,000
21	Ealing	292,400
22	Enfield	265,000
23	Greenwich	216,200
24	Harrow	201,700
25	Havering	238,500
26	Hillingdon	232,300
27	Hounslow	195,600
28	Kingston-upon-Thames	133,900
29	Merton	164,500
30	Redbridge	228,000
31	Richmond-upon-Thames	161,500
32	Sutton	169,600
33	Waltham Forest	216,200

UNITED KINGDOM, population

Scale 1:4 000 000

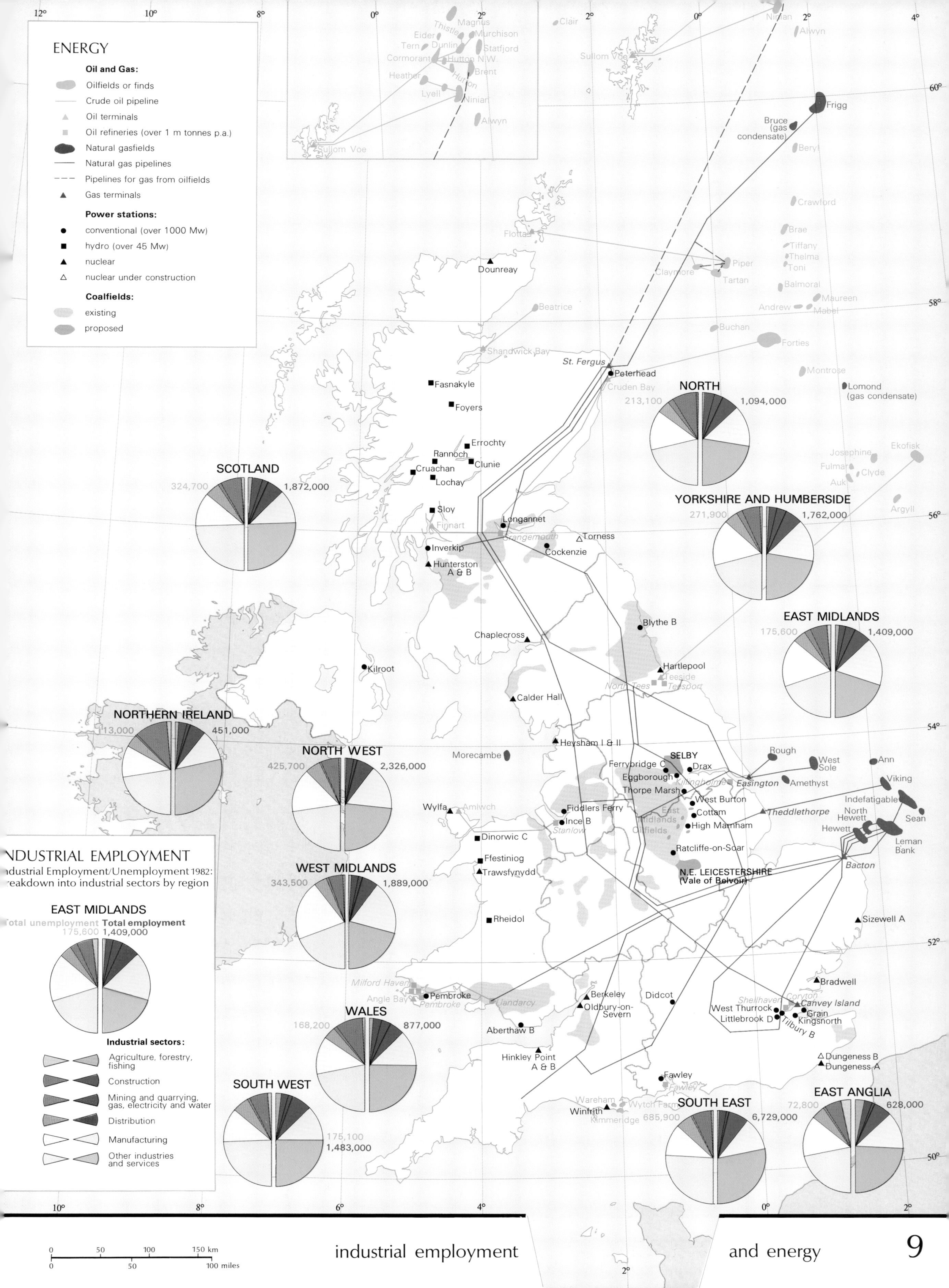

industrial employment and energy

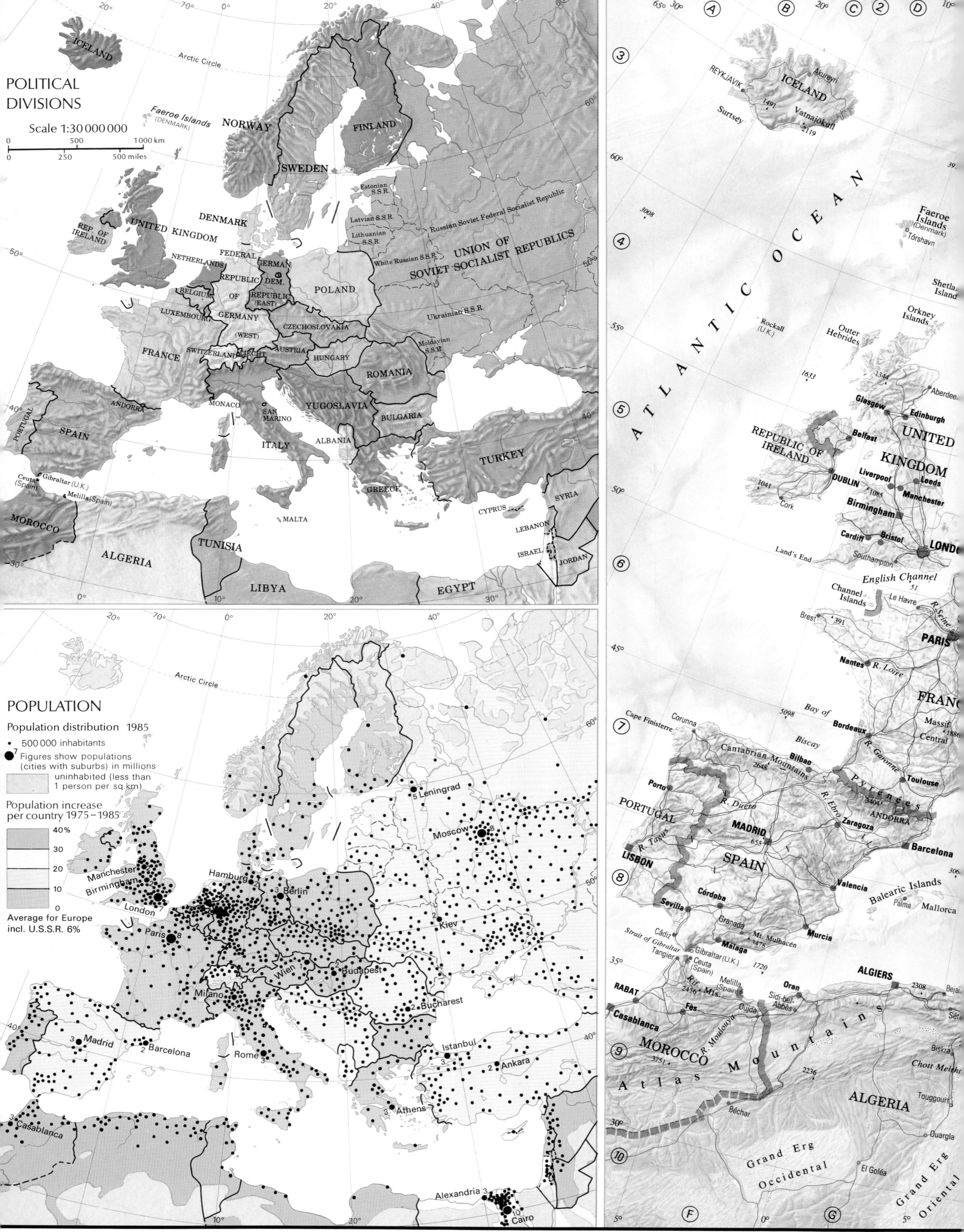
POLITICAL DIVISIONS
Scale 1:30 000 000
0 500 1000 km
0 250 500 miles
Arctic Circle
ICELAND
Faeroe Islands (DENMARK)
NORWAY
SWEDEN
FINLAND
Estonian S.S.R.
Latvian S.S.R.
Lithuanian S.S.R.
Russian Soviet Federal Socialist Republic
UNION OF SOVIET SOCIALIST REPUBLICS
White Russian S.S.R.
Ukrainian S.S.R.
Moldavian S.S.R.
DENMARK
UNITED KINGDOM
REP. OF IRELAND
NETHERLANDS
BELGIUM
LUXEMBOURG
FEDERAL REPUBLIC OF GERMANY (WEST)
GERMAN DEM. REPUBLIC (EAST)
POLAND
CZECHOSLOVAKIA
AUSTRIA
HUNGARY
ROMANIA
SWITZERLAND
FRANCE
ANDORRA
MONACO
SAN MARINO
PORTUGAL
SPAIN
ITALY
YUGOSLAVIA
BULGARIA
ALBANIA
GREECE
TURKEY
MALTA
CYPRUS
SYRIA
LEBANON
ISRAEL
JORDAN
Ceuta (Spain)
Gibraltar (U.K.)
Melilla (Spain)
MOROCCO
ALGERIA
TUNISIA
LIBYA
EGYPT
POPULATION
Population distribution 1985
500 000 inhabitants
Figures show populations (cities with suburbs) in millions
uninhabited (less than 1 person per sq.km)
Population increase per country 1975–1985
40%
30
20
10
0
Average for Europe incl. U.S.S.R. 6%
Leningrad
Moscow
Hamburg
Berlin
Manchester
Birmingham
London
Paris
Kiev
Wien
Budapest
Milano
Bucharest
Madrid
Barcelona
Rome
Istanbul
Ankara
Athens
Casablanca
Alexandria
Cairo
ATLANTIC OCEAN
REYKJAVIK
Akureyri
Vatnajökull
Surtsey
Faeroe Islands (Denmark)
Tórshavn
Shetland Islands
Orkney Islands
Outer Hebrides
Rockall (U.K.)
Aberdeen
Glasgow
Edinburgh
Belfast
UNITED KINGDOM
REPUBLIC OF IRELAND
DUBLIN
Cork
Liverpool
Leeds
Manchester
Birmingham
Cardiff
Bristol
Land's End
Southampton
English Channel
Channel Islands
Le Havre
R. Seine
Brest
PARIS
Nantes
R. Loire
Bay of Biscay
Bordeaux
Massif Central
R. Garonne
Toulouse
Cape Finisterre
Corunna
Cantabrian Mountains
Bilbao
Pyrenees
ANDORRA
Porto
PORTUGAL
R. Duero
R. Ebro
Zaragoza
MADRID
R. Tagus
LISBON
SPAIN
Barcelona
Valencia
Balearic Islands
Palma
Mallorca
Córdoba
Sevilla
Granada
Mt. Mulhacén
Murcia
Cádiz
Málaga
Strait of Gibraltar
Tangier
Gibraltar (U.K.)
Ceuta (Spain)
Melilla (Spain)
Rif Mts.
RABAT
Fès
Oujda
Oran
Sidi-bel-Abbès
ALGIERS
Casablanca
MOROCCO
R. Moulouya
Atlas Mountains
Biskra
Chott Melrhir
Touggourt
ALGERIA
Béchar
Ouargla
Grand Erg Occidental
El Goléa
Grand Erg Oriental

LAMBERT'S CONFORMAL CONIC PROJECTION

Scale 1:15 000 000 — 0, 200, 400, 600 km; 0, 200, 300, 400 miles

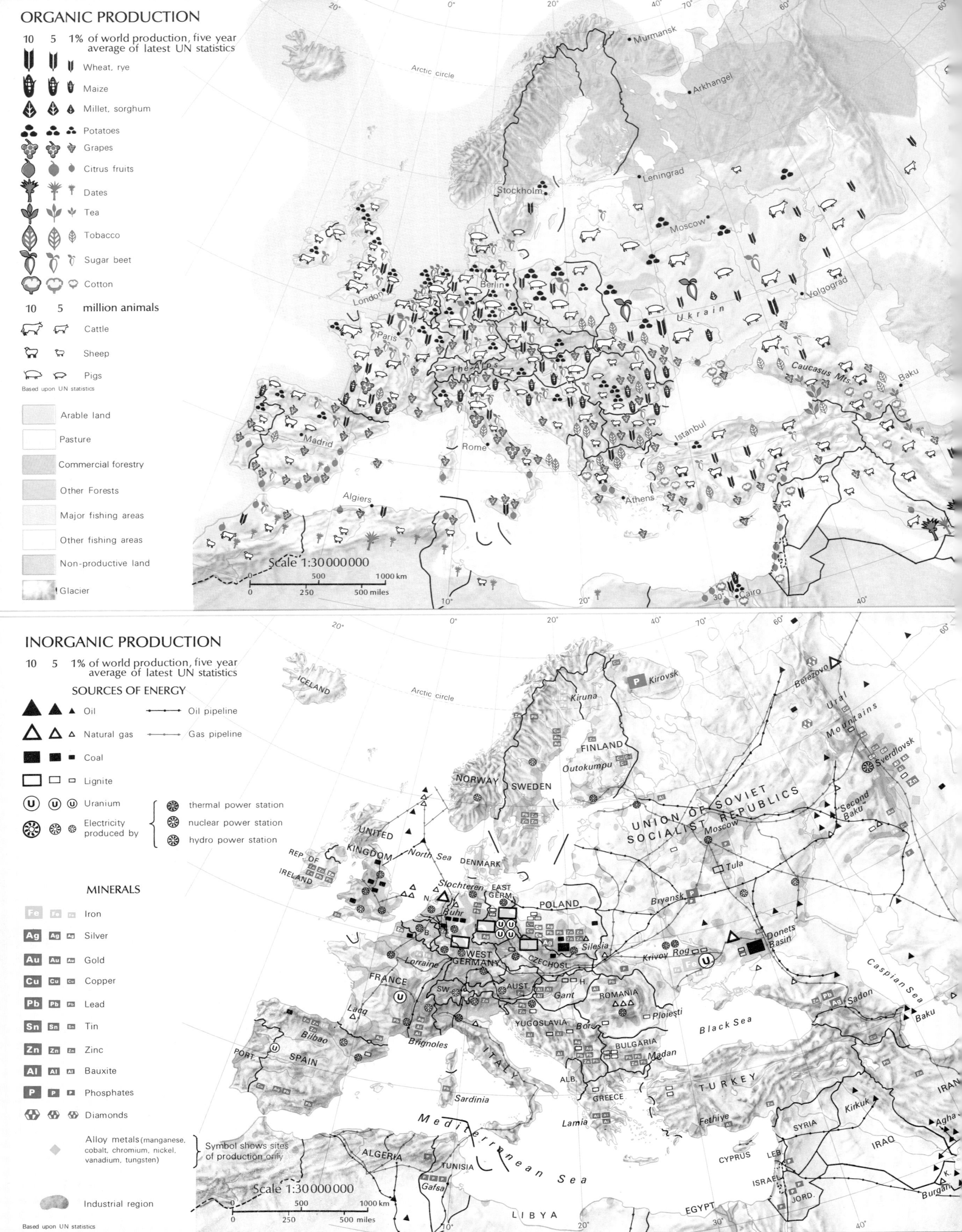

© ESSELTE MAP SERVICE

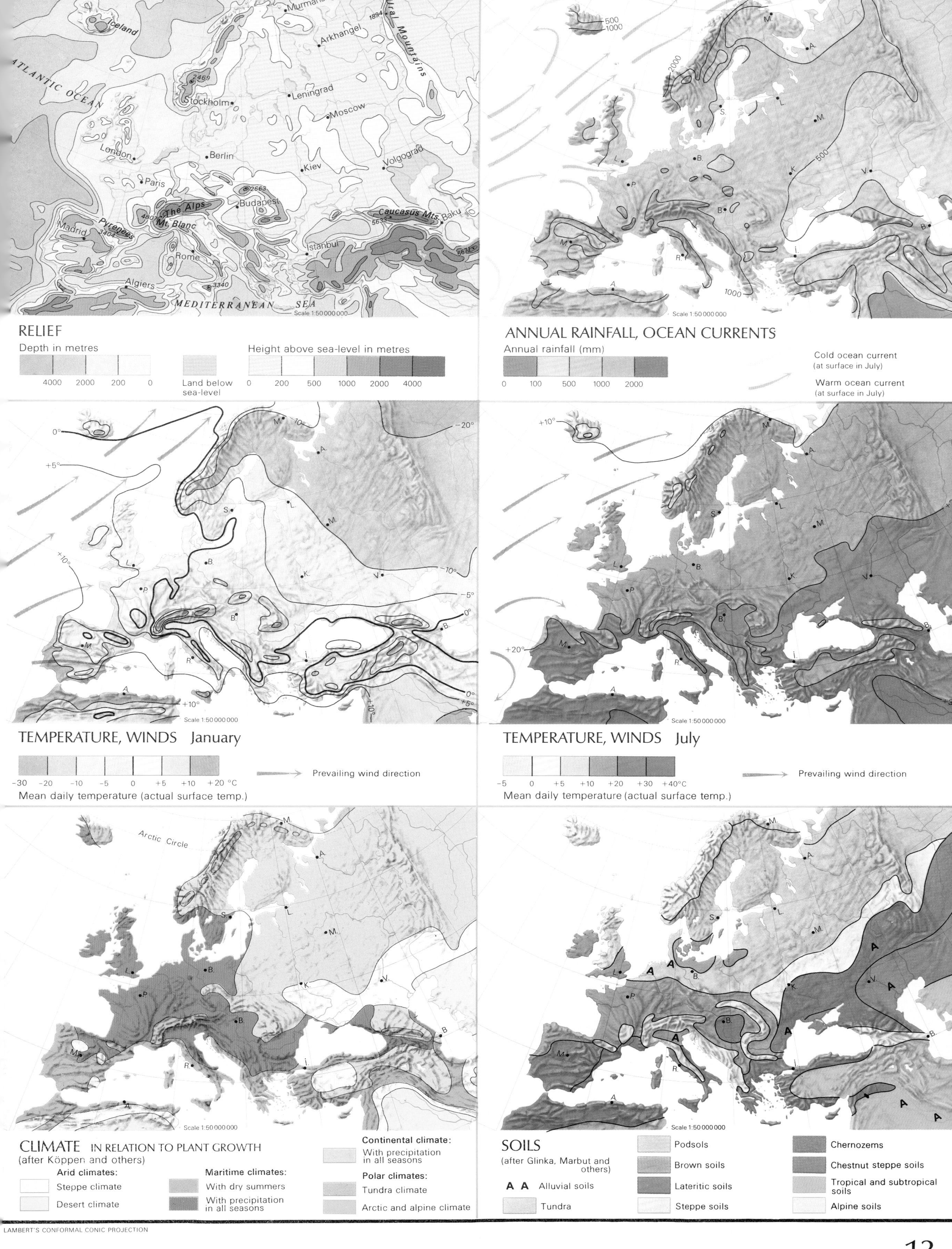

Iceland
Murmansk
Arkhangel
Ural Mountains
1894
ATLANTIC OCEAN
2469
Stockholm
Leningrad
Moscow
London
Berlin
Kiev
Volgograd
Paris
2663
The Alps
Budapest
4807
Mt. Blanc
Caucasus Mts.
Baku
5633
5674
Madrid
Pyrenees
3404
Rome
Istanbul
Algiers
3340
MEDITERRANEAN SEA
Scale 1:50 000 000
RELIEF
Depth in metres
4000 2000 200 0
Land below sea-level
Height above sea-level in metres
0 200 500 1000 2000 4000
500
1000
2000
500
1000
ANNUAL RAINFALL, OCEAN CURRENTS
Annual rainfall (mm)
0 100 500 1000 2000
Cold ocean current (at surface in July)
Warm ocean current (at surface in July)
0°
+5°
+10°
-10°
-20°
-5°
+10°
+5°
TEMPERATURE, WINDS January
-30 -20 -10 -5 0 +5 +10 +20 °C
Mean daily temperature (actual surface temp.)
Prevailing wind direction
+10°
+20°
+30
TEMPERATURE, WINDS July
-5 0 +5 +10 +20 +30 +40°C
Mean daily temperature (actual surface temp.)
Prevailing wind direction
Arctic Circle
CLIMATE IN RELATION TO PLANT GROWTH
(after Köppen and others)
Arid climates:
Steppe climate
Desert climate
Maritime climates:
With dry summers
With precipitation in all seasons
Continental climate:
With precipitation in all seasons
Polar climates:
Tundra climate
Arctic and alpine climate
SOILS
(after Glinka, Marbut and others)
A A Alluvial soils
Tundra
Podsols
Brown soils
Lateritic soils
Steppe soils
Chernozems
Chestnut steppe soils
Tropical and subtropical soils
Alpine soils
LAMBERT'S CONFORMAL CONIC PROJECTION

Föroyar
(Faeroe Islands)
(Denmark)
Norðoyar
Streymoy
Vágar
Eysturoy
Tórshavn
Sandoy
Suðuroy
Shetland Islands
(U.K.)
Mainland
Orkney
Islands
Fair Isle
Outer Hebrides
Inner Hebrides
North West Highlands
Grampian Mountains
Scotland
Aberdeen
Dundee
Glasgow
Edinburgh
Southern Uplands
Northern Ireland
Belfast
Londonderry
Newcastle-upon-Tyne
UNITED
KINGDOM
North Sea
Great
Fisher Bank
Dogger Bank
NORWAY
Bergen
Stavanger
Irish Sea
Isle of Man
REPUBLIC OF IRELAND
(EIRE)
DUBLIN
(BAILE ATHA CLIATH)
Galway
Limerick
Cork
Connaught
Leinster
Munster
Ulster
Liverpool
Manchester
Leeds
Sheffield
Bradford
Kingston-upon-Hull
Nottingham
Leicester
Birmingham
Coventry
Wolverhampton
Wales
Cardiff
Swansea
Bristol
England
LONDON
Cambridge
Norwich
Southampton
Portsmouth
Brighton
Plymouth
Exeter
Celtic Sea
Saint George's Channel
Bristol Channel
English Channel
(La Manche)
Strait of Dover
(Pas de Calais)
ATLANTIC OCEAN
Channel Islands
(U.K.)
Guernsey
Jersey
NETHERLANDS
AMSTERDAM
'S-GRAVENHAGE
(THE HAGUE)
Rotterdam
Utrecht
BELGIUM
BRUXELLES
(BRUSSELS)
Antwerpen
Gent
LUXEMBOURG
FRANCE
PARIS
Normandie
Picardie
Bretagne
Ile de France
Le Havre
Rouen
Caen
Brest
Rennes
Nantes
Le Mans
Orléans
Tours
Reims
Lille
Frisian Islands

Scale 1:5 000 000

0 100 200 km

0 50 100 miles

ICELAND
(ÍSLAND)
Greenland Sea
Arctic Circle
Vatnajökull
REYKJAVÍK
Hekla
ATLANTIC
OCEAN
Norwegian Sea
NORWAY
(NORGE)
SWEDEN
(SVERIGE)
FINLAND
(SUOMI)
Lappland
Norrland
Gulf of Bothnia
Trondheim
Murmansk
Poluostrov Kol'skiy
(Kola Peninsula)
Beloye More
(White Sea)
Barents Sea

Scale 1:5 000 000
0 100 200 km
0 50 100 miles

A
B
C
D
1
2
3
4
10°
45°
40°
5°
0°
ATLANTIC
OCEAN
Bay of Biscay
La Manche
(English Channel)
UNITED
KINGDOM
Dartmoor
Torbay
Plymouth
Bournemouth
Weymouth
Isle of Wight
Worthing
Eastbourne
Newhaven
Portland Bill
Start Point
St. Austell
Newquay
Redruth
Penzance
Falmouth
Lizard
Cape Cornwall
Land's End
Bishop Rock
Isles of Scilly
Pas de Calais
Cape Gris-Nez
Boulogne-sur-Mer
Saint-Omer
Tourcoing
Roubaix
Lille
Béthune
Bruay-en-Artois
Douai
Arras
Denain
Cambrai
Berck
Collines de l'Artois
Abbeville
Le Tréport
Dieppe
Fécamp
Amiens
Saint-Quentin
Picardie
Channel Islands
(U.K.)
Alderney
Guernsey
St. Peter Port
Sark
Jersey
St. Helier
Cap de la Hague
Pointe de Barfleur
Cherbourg
Cotentin
Baie de la Seine
Cap d'Antifer
Le Havre
Lillebonne
Rouen
Beauvais
Creil
Compiègne
Soissons
Reims
Aisne
Oise
Ile de France
Caen
Lisieux
Bayeux
Saint-Lô
Coutances
Granville
Normandie
Golfe de Saint-Malo
Baie de Lannion
Perros-Guirec
Paimpol
Roscoff
Morlaix
Guingamp
Lannion
Ile d'Ouessant
Brest
Landerneau
Plouguerneau
Pointe de Saint-Mathieu
Monts d'Arrée
Iroise
Crozon
Ménez Hom
Pointe du Raz
Baie d'Audierne
Quimper
Pont-l'Abbé
Pointe de Penmarch
Concarneau
Lorient
Ile de Groix
Carnac
Quiberon
Vannes
Belle-Ile
Le Palais
Bretagne
Saint-Brieuc
Lamballe
Cap Fréhel
Saint-Malo
Dinard
Dinan
Le Mont-Saint-Michel
Avranches
Fougères
Rennes
Bassin de Rennes
Vitré
Laval
Mayenne
Alençon
Mancelles
Alpes Mancelles
Les Coëvrons
Le Mans
Forêt d'Ecouves
Mont Pinçon
Flers
Argentan
Evreux
Mantes-la-Jolie
Saint-Denis
Versailles
PARIS
Meaux
Coulommiers
Dreux
Chartres
Melun
Fontainebleau
Etampes
Sens
Troyes
Pithiviers
Orléans
Montargis
Collines du Perche
Nogent-le-Rotrou
Châteaudun
Vendôme
Blois
Tours
Amboise
Saumur
Angers
Chinon
Loudun
Cholet
Nantes
Saint-Nazaire
Guérande
Pointe du Croisic
Pointe de Saint-Gildas
Noirmoutier
Pornic
Rezé
Lac de Grand Lieu
Redon
Châteaubriant
Ancenis
Loire
Sarthe
Loir
Anjou
Vierzon
Bourges
Berry
Nevers
Châteauroux
Issoudun
Touraine
Châtellerault
Poitiers
Plaines et Seuil du Poitou
Parthenay
Bocage Vendéen
La Roche-sur-Yon
Les Sables-d'Olonne
Luçon
Niort
Fontenay-le-Comte
Marais Breton
Saint-Jean-de-Monts
Ile d'Yeu
Pertuis Breton
Ile de Ré
Pertuis d'Antioche
La Rochelle
Rochefort
Saint-Denis-d'Oléron
Ile d'Oléron
Marennes
Saintes
Cognac
Angoulême
Limoges
Limousin
Pointe de la Coubre
Pointe de Grave
Le Verdon-sur-Mer
Royan
Gironde
Lesparre-Médoc
Étang d'Hourtin
Carcans-Plage
Lacanau
Mérignac
Pessac
Bordeaux
Bègles
Libourne
Bergerac
Périgueux
Sarlat-la-Canéda
Brive
Tulle
Dordogne
Cap Ferret
Arcachon
Étang de Cazaux
Étang de Biscarrosse
Mimizan
Les Landes
Côte d'Argent
Mont-de-Marsan
Dax
Adour
Biarritz
Bayonne
Gascogne
Agen
Montauban
Toulouse
Auch
Tarbes
Lourdes
Pau
Saint-Gaudens
Muret
Castres
Albi
Rodez
Millau
Aurillac
Massif Central
Clermont-Ferrand
Puy de Dôme
Vichy
Moulins
Montluçon
Plateau de Millevaches
Monts Dore
Monts du Cantal
Plomb du Cantal
Causse de Gramat
Causses
Montpellier
Sète
Béziers
Narbonne
Carcassonne
Perpignan
Étang de Leucate
Languedoc
Petites Pyrénées
Pyrénées
ANDORRA
Pic d'Estats
Pico de Aneto
Puerto de Somport
FRANCE
Rías Altas
Cabo Ortegal
Ría de Santa Marta
El Ferrol del Caudillo
La Coruña
(Corunna)
Carballo
Camariñas
Cabo Touriñán
Cabo de Finisterre
Ría de Muros y Noya
Santiago de Compostela
Villagarcía de Arosa
Rías Bajas
Pontevedra
Ría de Vigo
Vigo
Lugo
Galicia
Orense
Ponferrada
Costa Verde
Cabo de Peñas
Avilés
Gijón
Oviedo
Asturias
Picos de Europa
Santander
Torrelavega
Cordillera Cantábrica
(Cantabrian Mts.)
León
Bilbao
Baracaldo
Portugalete
San Sebastián
Irún
Provincias Vascongadas
Vitoria
Pamplona
Navarra
Burgos
Miranda de Ebro
Logroño
La Rioja
Castilla la Vieja
Palencia
Valladolid
Zamora
Salamanca
Segovia
Ávila
Soria
Zaragoza
Aragón
Huesca
Lérida
Cataluña
Barcelona
Hospitalet
Badalona
Sabadell
Tarrasa
Manresa
Mataró
Gerona
Figueras
Golfo de Rosas
Cabo de Creus
Costa Brava
Tarragona
Reus
Tortosa
Costa Dorada
Delta del Ebro
Golfo de San Jorge
Cabo de Tortosa
Ebro
Sistema Ibérico
Duero
Sierra de Guadarrama
Sierra de Gredos
MADRID
Alcalá
Getafe
Leganés
Aranjuez
Guadalajara
Toledo
Talavera de la Reina
Cuenca
Teruel
Castellón
Sagunto
Valencia
Golfo de Valencia
Costa del Azahar
Castilla la Nueva
La Mancha
Ciudad Real
Puertollano
Albacete
Alicante
Elche
Murcia
Cartagena
Cabo de Palos
Mar Menor
Costa Blanca
Cabo de la Nao
Sierra Morena
Córdoba
Jaén
Linares
Úbeda
Sistemas Béticos
Sierra Nevada
Mulhacén
Granada
Málaga
Almería
Cabo de Gata
Golfo de Almería
Costa del Sol
Marbella
Algeciras
Gibraltar (U.K.)
La Línea
Punta de Europa
Tarifa
Estrecho de Gibraltar
(Str. of Gibraltar)
Cabo Trafalgar
Cádiz
Jerez de la Frontera
Sevilla
Huelva
Golfo de Cadiz
Las Marismas
Andalucía
Guadalquivir
Extremadura
Badajoz
Mérida
Cáceres
Plasencia
SPAIN
(ESPAÑA)
Islas Baleares
(Balearic Islands) (Spain)
Mallorca
Palma
Ibiza
Formentera
Cabrera
Menorca
PORTUGAL
Braga
Porto
(Oporto)
Vila Nova de Gaia
Matosinhos
Póvoa de Varzim
Viana do Castelo
Aveiro
Coimbra
Cabo Mondego
Figueira da Foz
Serra da Estrela
Nazaré
Estremadura
Tejo (Tagus)
Santarém
LISBOA (LISBON)
Sintra
Setúbal
Cabo Espichel
Baía de Setúbal
Évora
Alentejo
Beja
Cabo de Sines
Algarve
Faro
Lagos
Cabo de São Vicente
Sagres
Douro
Tânger
MOROCCO
Ceuta (Sp.)
Punta Almina
Alborán (Sp.)
MEDITER
AL JAZĀ'IR
(ALGIERS)
ALGE
Blida
Médéa
Ech Cheliff
Miliana
Ténès
Cherchell
Dahra

FEDERAL REP. OF GERMANY
(BUNDESREPUBLIK DEUTSCHLAND)
LUXEMBOURG
SWITZERLAND
LIECHTENSTEIN
AUSTRIA
ČESKOSLOVAKIA
CZECHOSLOVAKIA
HUNGARY
(MAGYARORSZÁG)
YUGOSLAVIA
ITALY
(ITALIA)
SAN MARINO
VATICAN STATE
(CITTA DEL VATICANO)
MONACO
TUNISIA
MALTA
Praha
(Prague)
Wien
(Vienna)
Budapest
München
(Munich)
Zürich
Bern
(Berne)
Milano (Milan)
Torino
(Turin)
Genova
(Genoa)
Venezia
(Venice)
Firenze
(Florence)
Bologna
Roma
(Rome)
Napoli (Naples)
Bari
Palermo
Messina
Catania
Cagliari
Ljubljana
Zagreb
Sarajevo
Lyon
Marseille
Nice
Tunis
Alpi
Bayern
(Bavaria)
Corse
(Corsica)
(Fr.)
Sardegna
(Sardinia)
(Italy)
Sicilia
(Sicily)
Ligurian Sea
Tyrrhenian Sea
Adriatic Sea
Ionian Sea
Gulf of Venice
Golfo di Genova
Golfo di Taranto
Canale di Sicilia
Canale di Malta
Strait of Bonifacio
Pantelleria
(Italy)
Elba
Montecristo
Stromboli
Isole Eolie o Lipari
Ustica
ANEAN SEA
3000
3500

WIEN (VIENNA)
Bratislava
BUDAPEST
HUNGARY (MAGYARORSZÁG)
ROMANIA
Transilvania
Carpathian Mts.
Cluj-Napoca
Iaşi
Kishinev
Odessa
BUCUREŞTI (BUCHAREST)
Constanţa
Delta Dunării (Mouths of the Danube)
BEOGRAD (BELGRADE)
YUGOSLAVIA
Sarajevo
Novi Sad
Timişoara
BULGARIA
SOFIYA (SOFIA)
Plovdiv
Varna
Burgas
Stara Planina (Balkan Mts.)
Rodopi (Rhodope Mts.)
Skopje
ALBANIA (SHQIPERIA)
TIRANA
ITALY
Adriatic Sea
GREECE (HELLAS)
Thessaloniki (Salonica)
ATHÍNAI (ATHENS)
Piraiévs
Pelopónnisos (Peloponnese)
Kríti (Crete)
Kritikón Pélagos (Sea of Crete)
Aiyaíon Pélagos (Aegean Sea)
Ionion Pélagos (Ionian Sea)
Iónioi Nísoi (Ionian Islands)
Kikládhes (Cyclades)
Nótioi Sporádhes (Dodecanese)
Ródhos (Rhodes)
MEDITERRANEAN SEA
İstanbul
İstanbul Boğazi (Bosporus)
Marmara Denizi (Sea of Marmara)
Çanakkale Boğazi (Dardanelles)
Bursa
İzmir
Eskişehir
Antalya
Anadolu

UNION OF SOVIET SOCIALIST REPUBLICS
Black Sea
Azovskoye More
(Sea of Azov)
Krym
(Crimea)
Dnepropetrovsk
Donetsk
Makeyevka
Voroshilovgrad
Zaporozh'ye
Krivoy Rog
Rostov-na-Donu
Taganrog
Zhdanov
Melitopol'
Berdyansk
Kerch'
Simferopol'
Sevastopol'
Yalta
Krasnodar
Novorossiysk
Maykop
Armavir
Stavropol'
Pyatigorsk
Nal'chik
Ordzhonikidze
Groznyy
Sochi
Sukhumi
Kutaisi
Batumi
Tbilisi
Rustavi
Yerevan
Leninakan
Kirovakan
Bol'shoy Kavkaz
(Caucasus Mts.)
Elbrus
5633
Kazbek
5047
Gruziya
Georgia
Armeniya
Ozero Sevan
Prikaspiyskaya Nizmennost' (Caspian Depression)
Stavropol'skaya Vozvyshennost'
Nogayskiye Step'
TURKEY
(TÜRKIYE)
ANKARA
Samsun
Trabzon
Erzurum
Kayseri
Sivas
Malatya
Elâzığ
Diyarbakır
Konya
Adana
Mersin
Tarsus
Gaziantep
Kahramanmaraş
İskenderun
Urfa
Van Gölü
Doğu Karadeniz Dağları (Pontine Mts.)
Toros Dağları
Güneydoğu Toroslar
Büyük Ağrı Dağı
(Mount Ararat)
5165
Tuz Gölü
SYRIA
(SŪRIYAH)
Halab (Aleppo)
Al Lādhiqīyah
(Latakia)
Ḥamāh
Ar Raqqah
Dayr az Zawr
IRAQ
Al Mawşil
(Mosul)
Kirkūk
Erbil
Mesopotamia
IRAN
Orūmīyeh
CYPRUS
NICOSIA
Limassol
Larnaca
Famagusta
Troodos
1952
Scale 1:5 000 000
0
100
200 km
0
50
100 miles

TURKEY
Adana
Tarsus
Mersin
Gaziantep
Urfa
Iskenderun
Antakya
Halab (Aleppo)
Al Mawsil (Mosul)
CYPRUS
Limassol
Mediterranean Sea
Al Lādhiqīyah (Latakia)
Hamāh
Hims
Ţarābulus (Tripoli)
BAYRŪT (BEIRUT)
LEBANON
Saydā (Sidon)
Şūr (Tyre)
DIMASHQ (DAMASCUS)
SYRIA (SŪRĪYAH)
Ar Raqqah
Dayr az Zawr
Al Ḩasakah
Al Furāt
(Euphrates)
Dijlah (Tigris)
IRAQ (AL 'IRAQ)
BAGHDĀ
Karbalā'
An Najaf
Bādiyat ash Shām
(Syrian Desert)
Al Ḩamād
Tel Aviv-Yafo
ISRAEL
Hefa (Haifa)
YERUSHALAYIM (JERUSALEM)
'AMMĀN
Az Zarqā'
Irbid
Gaza Strip
Ghazzah
Be'er Sheva
Bahr al Mayyit (Dead Sea)
JORDAN (AL URDUN)
Būr Sa'īd (Port Said)
Al Ismā'īlīyah
As Suways (Suez)
Sīnā' (Sinai)
EGYPT (MISR)
Qinā
Al Uqşur (Luxor)
Aswān
Birkat Nasser (Lake Nasser)
Aş Şaḩrā' ash Sharqīyah
Red Sea
An Nafūd
SAUDI ARABIA
(AL 'ARABĪYAH AS SU'ŪDĪYAH)
Al Ḩijāz (Hejaz)
Najd (Nejd)
Tabūk
Taymā'
Ḩā'il
Buraydah
Al Madīnah (Medina)
Yanbu'
Tropic of Cancer

Caspian Sea
TEHRĀN
Rey
Tajrīsh
Rasht
Qazvīn
Zanjān
Hamadān
Qom
Arāk
Kāshān
Esfahan
Shīrāz
Yazd
Semnān
Gorgān
Sārī
Bābol
Āmol
Qahremānshahr (Kermānshāh)
Sanandaj
Ahvāz
Dezfūl
Shūshtar
Behbehān
Būshehr
Kāzerūn
Bandar Abbas
Qeshm
Khorramshahr (Khurramshahr)
Ābādān
Al Başrah (Basra)
Al 'Amārah
An Nāşiriyah
Al Kūt
Qasr-e Shīrīn
Sulaimāniya
Mahābād
K h a m s e h
K o r d e s t ā n
L o r e s t ā n
K h ū z e s t ā n
F ā r s
L ā r e s t ā n
Reshteh-ye Kūhhā-ye Alborz (Elburz Mts.)
Kūh-e Damāvand 5671 (Mt Demavend)
Dasht-e Kavīr
Dasht-e Lūt
I R A N (P E R S I A)
K ū h h ā - y e Z a g r o s (Z a g r o s M t s.)
Kūh-e Dinār
Zard Kūh
Kūh-e Kharānaq
Kūh-e Hormoz
Darÿācheh-ye Ürūmīyeh
Darÿācheh-ye Namak
Darÿācheh-ye Bakhtegān
Darÿācheh-ye Mahārlū
Bātlāq-e Gavkhūnī
Hawr al Hammār
Hawr as Suwayqiyah
Shaţţ al 'Arab
KUWAIT
AL KUWAYT (KUWAIT)
Al Jahrah
Faylakah
Būbiyān
BAHRAIN
AL MANĀMAH (MANAMA)
QATAR
AD DAWḤAH (DOHA)
UNITED ARAB EMIRATES
ABŪ ZABY (ABU DHABI)
Dubayy (Dubai)
AR RIYĀD (RIYADH)
Ad Dammām
Al Khubar
Aẓ Ẓahrān (Dhahran)
Al Hufūf
Al Mubarraz
Al Qaţīf
Al Jubayl
Ra's Tannūrah
Al Khafjī
Ḥafar al Bāţin
Al Kharj
Ad Dahnā'
Al Ḥasā
Aş Şummān
Ad Dibdibah
Al Jiwā'
Aḑ Ḑafrah
OMAN
Musandam Pen.
Strait of Hormuz
The Gulf (Persian Gulf)
Tropic of Cancer
Scale 1:5 000 000
0 100 200 km
0 50 100 miles

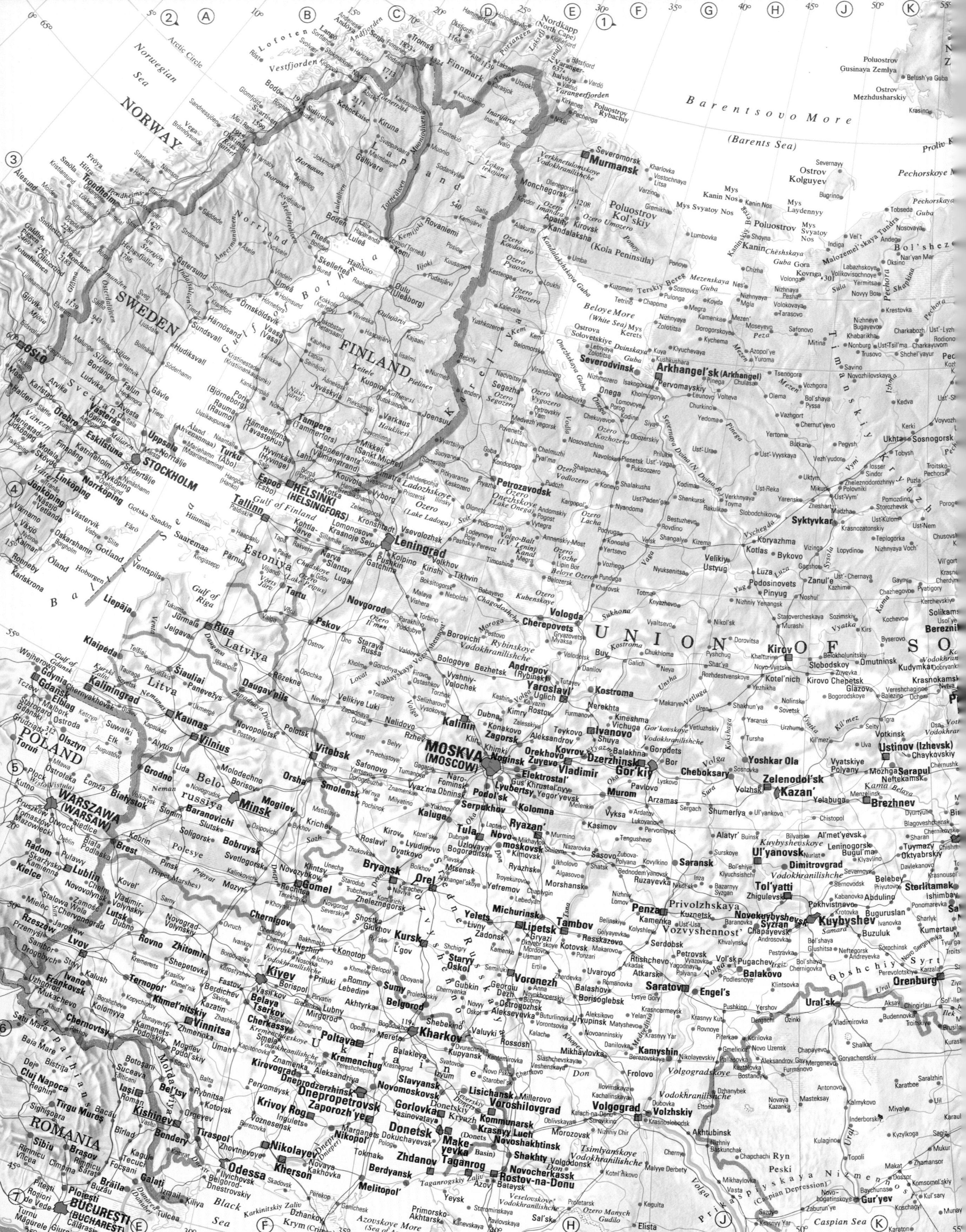

Norwegian Sea
NORWAY
SWEDEN
FINLAND
Barentsovo More
(Barents Sea)
Poluostrov Kol'skiy
(Kola Peninsula)
Beloye More
(White Sea)
Gulf of Bothnia
Gulf of Finland
Baltic Sea
Estoniya
Latviya
Litva
POLAND
Belorussiya
Ukraina
ROMANIA
Black Sea
Azovskoye More
(Sea of Azov)
Caspian Sea
UNION OF SOVIET
OSLO
STOCKHOLM
HELSINKI
(HELSINGFORS)
Tallinn
Riga
Vilnius
Minsk
WARSZAWA
(WARSAW)
BUCUREŞTI
(BUCHAREST)
MOSKVA
(MOSCOW)
Leningrad
Murmansk
Arkhangel'sk
Kiyev
Kharkov
Odessa
Donetsk
Dnepropetrovsk
Gor'kiy
Kazan'
Kuybyshev
Saratov
Volgograd
Rostov-na-Donu
Orenburg
Kirov
Vologda
Yaroslavl'
Smolensk
Bryansk
Voronezh
Lvov
Kishinev
Gomel
Tula
Ryazan'
Penza
Syktyvkar
Petrozavodsk
Novgorod
Pskov
Kaliningrad
Vilnius
Gdańsk
Lublin
Kraków
Astrakhan'
Gur'yev
Ural'sk

Scale 1:10 000 000

0 100 200 300 400 km
0 100 200 miles

ATLANTIC OCEAN
Greenland Sea
Jan Mayen I. (Nor.)
Faeroe Is. (Denmark)
Norwegian Sea
West Spitsbergen
Svalbard (Nor.)
Bear I. (Nor.)
Franz Josef Land (U.S.S.R.)
Barents Sea
Novaya Zemlya
Kara Sea
North Sea
Bay of Biscay
REP. OF IRELAND
DUBLIN
Glasgow
Birmingham
LONDON
UNITED KINGDOM
AMSTERDAM
NETHERLANDS
BRUSSELS
PARIS
FRANCE
SPAIN
MADRID
Barcelona
Valencia
Bilbao
Bordeaux
Nantes
Pyrenees
ANDORRA
Marseille
Lyon
Turin
Genoa
Milan
Corsica
Sardinia
ITALY
ROME
Naples
Palermo
Sicily
Catania
MALTA
TUNIS
Adriatic Sea
NORWAY
OSLO
Bergen
Trondheim
Tromsø
North Cape
SWEDEN
STOCKHOLM
Gothenburg
DENMARK
COPENHAGEN
Hamburg
BERLIN
Munich
Frankfurt
Cologne
BONN
FINLAND
HELSINKI
Murmansk
Kola Peninsula
White Sea
Baltic Sea
POLAND
WARSAW
Gdansk
Kaliningrad
Cracow
PRAGUE
CZECHOSLOVAKIA
VIENNA
AUSTRIA
HUNGARY
BUDAPEST
YUGOSLAVIA
BELGRADE
ROMANIA
BUCHAREST
BULGARIA
SOFIA
ALBANIA
TIRANA
GREECE
ATHENS
Thessaloniki
Aegean Sea
Crete
Istanbul
Bosporus
Bursa
Izmir
ANKARA
TURKEY
Anatolia
Konya
Adana
NICOSIA
CYPRUS
Mediterranean Sea
Black Sea
Crimea
Sea of Azov
Sevastopol
Simferopol
Odessa
Nikolayev
Zhdanov
Donetsk
Dnepropetrovsk
Kharkov
Kiyev
Ukrainian S.S.R.
Moldavian S.S.R.
Lvov
Minsk
White Russian S.S.R.
Vilnius
Lithuanian S.S.R.
Riga
Latvian S.S.R.
Tallinn
Estonian S.S.R.
Leningrad
L. Ladoga
L. Onega
Petrozavodsk
Arkhangel
Novgorod
Kalinin
MOSCOW
Bryansk
Gomel
Kursk
Tula
Voronezh
Voroshilovgrad
Rostov-na-Donu
Krasnodar
Stavropol
Sochi
Caucasus Mts.
Mt. Elbrus
Georgian S.S.R.
Tbilisi
Yerevan
Mt. Ararat
Azerbaydzhan S.S.R.
Baku
Grozny
Astrakhan
Volgograd
R. Volga
R. Don
Saratov
Penza
Kuybyshev
Tolyatti
Ulyanovsk
Kazan
Gorkiy
Yaroslavl
Ivanovo
Kirov
Kotlas
Ukhta
Vorkuta
Perm
Ustinov (Izhevsk)
R. Kama
Ufa
Magnitogorsk
Orenburg
Uralsk
Ural Mountains
Serov
Nizhniy Tagil
Sverdlovsk
Chelyabinsk
Tyumen
Tobolsk
Petropavlovsk
Omsk
Novosibirsk
Tomsk
Kemerovo
Prokopyevsk
Barnaul
Biysk
Pavlodar
Semipalatinsk
Ust-Kamenogorsk
Karaganda
Tselinograd
Aktyubinsk
Guryev
R. Ural
Kirghiz Steppe
Kazakh S.S.R.
UNION OF SOVIET
Russian Soviet Feder
West Siberian Plain
Khanty-Mansiysk
R. Ob
R. Irtysh
Sergin
Berezniki
Gulf of Ob
Yamal Peninsula
Dikson
Dudinka
Igarka
Arctic Circle
Caspian Sea
Shevchenko
Ust-Urt
Aral Sea
Syr Darya
Kzyl-Orda
Kyzyl-Kum
Uzbekistan S.S.R.
Urgench
Krasnovodsk
Kara-Kum
Turkmenistan S.S.R.
Ashkhabad
Bukhara
Samarkand
Tashkent
Chimkent
Turkistan
Dushanbe
Tadzhikistan S.S.R.
Frunze
Kirghiz S.S.R.
Alma-Ata
Balkhash
Lake Balkhash
L. Zaysan
Dzungar
Tian Shan
Yining
Urumqi
Kashi
East Turkistan
Tarim Basin
Shache
Sinkiang
Kunlun
Plateau of Tibet
Tibet
Pamir
Karakoram
Kashmir
Hindu Kush
Himalayas
LEBANON
BEIRUT
SYRIA
Aleppo
DAMASCUS
ISRAEL
Haifa
Tel Aviv-Yafo
JERUSALEM
JORDAN
AMMAN
Mosul
BAGHDAD
IRAQ
Mesopotamia
R. Tigris
R. Euphrates
Basra
KUWAIT
Tabriz
Rasht
TEHRAN
Elburz Mts.
Mt. Demavend
Dasht-i Kavir
IRAN
Esfahan
Zagros Mountains
Abadan
Shiraz
Kerman
Mashhad
Zahedan
Bandar Abbas
Persian Gulf
BAHRAIN
QATAR
UNITED ARAB EMIRATES
ABU DHABI
Dubayy
Gulf of Oman
MUSCAT
OMAN
SAUDI ARABIA
RIYADH
Nafud
Hejaz
Nejd
Medina
Mecca
Jiddah
Tropic of Cancer
Rub al Khali
YEMEN
SAN'A'
SOUTH YEMEN
ADEN
Hadramawt
Red Sea
Port Sudan
LIBYA
Cyrenaica
Benghazi
Tobruk
EGYPT
Alexandria
CAIRO
Port Said
Suez
R. Nile
L. Nasser
Aswan
Luxor
Nubian Desert
SUDAN
KHARTOUM
Omdurman
Kassala
Eritrea
Asmara
Massawa
ETHIOPIA
ADDIS ABABA
L. Tana
Blue Nile
DJIBOUTI
AFGHANISTAN
KABUL
Herat
Kandahar
Mazar-i-Sharif
PAKISTAN
ISLAMABAD
Peshawar
Rawalpindi
Lahore
Faisalabad
Multan
Quetta
Karachi
Hyderabad
R. Indus
Punjab
Srinagar
Amritsar
Ludhiana
Chandigarh
Thar Desert
DELHI
Meerut
Moradabad
Bareilly
Agra
Jaipur
Jodhpur
Ajmer
Gwalior
Kanpur
Lucknow
Gorakhpur
Allahabad
Varanasi
Patna
NEPAL
KATHMANDU
Mt. Everest
Mt. Dhaulagiri
Sikkim
INDIA
Hindustan
Ahmadabad
Kutch
Rajkot
Indore
Bhopal
Jabalpur
R. Narmada
Vadodara
Surat
Nagpur
Raipur
Jamshedpur
Calcutta
Arabian Sea

LAMBERT'S AZIMUTHAL EQUAL-AREA PROJECTION

Scale 1:25 000 000

0 500 1000 km
0 200 400 600 miles

UNION OF SOVIET
Mediterranean Sea
Black Sea
Caspian Sea
Aral Sea
Red Sea
Persian Gulf
Gulf of Oman
Gulf of Aden
Arabian Sea
Bay
INDIAN OC
Mozambique Channel
GREECE
ATHENS
TURKEY
ANKARA
Istanbul
CYPRUS
NICOSIA
LEBANON
BEIRUT
SYRIA
DAMASCUS
ISRAEL
JORDAN
AMMAN
JERUSALEM
IRAQ
BAGHDAD
IRAN
TEHRAN
KUWAIT
SAUDI ARABIA
RIYADH
Nafud
Nejd
Rub al Khali
BAHRAIN
QATAR
UNITED ARAB EMIRATES
OMAN
MUSCAT
YEMEN
SAN'A'
SOUTH YEMEN
ADEN
Hadramawt
Socotra
(S.Yemen)
LIBYA
EGYPT
CAIRO
Alexandria
SUDAN
KHARTOUM
Omdurman
Nubian Desert
Eritrea
ETHIOPIA
ADDIS ABABA
Ethiopian Plateau
DJIBOUTI
SOMALIA
MOGADISHU
Ogaden
KENYA
Mombasa
DAR ES SALAAM
Zanzibar
Pemba I.
SEYCHELLES
VICTORIA
Amirante Is.
(Sey.)
Aldabra Is.
(Sey.)
COMOROS
MORONI
Mayotte
(Fr.)
MADAGASCAR
ANTANANARIVO
Kazakh S.S.R.
Kirghiz Steppe
Kyzyl-Kum
Kara-Kum
Uzbekistan S.S.R.
Turkmenistan S.S.R.
Tadzhikistan S.S.R.
Kirghiz S.S.R.
Tashkent
Alma-Ata
Tian Shan
East Turkistan
Tarim Basin
Kunlun
Plateau of Tibet
AFGHANISTAN
KABUL
Hindu Kush
Pamir
Karakoram
Kashmir
PAKISTAN
Karachi
Lahore
Rawalpindi
Faisalabad
Thar Desert
INDIA
DELHI
Bombay
Calcutta
Madras
Bangalore
Hyderabad
Deccan
Western Ghats
Eastern Ghats
Malabar Coast
Coromandel Coast
Himalaya
NEPAL
KATHMANDU
Mt. Everest
Laccadive Is.
(India)
MALDIVES
MALÉ
SRI LANKA
COLOMBO
Chagos Archipelago
(U.K.)
Equator
Tropic of Cancer
20°
30°
40°
50°
60°
70°
80°

LAMBERT'S AZIMUTHAL EQUAL-AREA PROJECTION

Scale 1:25 000 000

0 500 1000 km
0 200 400 600 miles

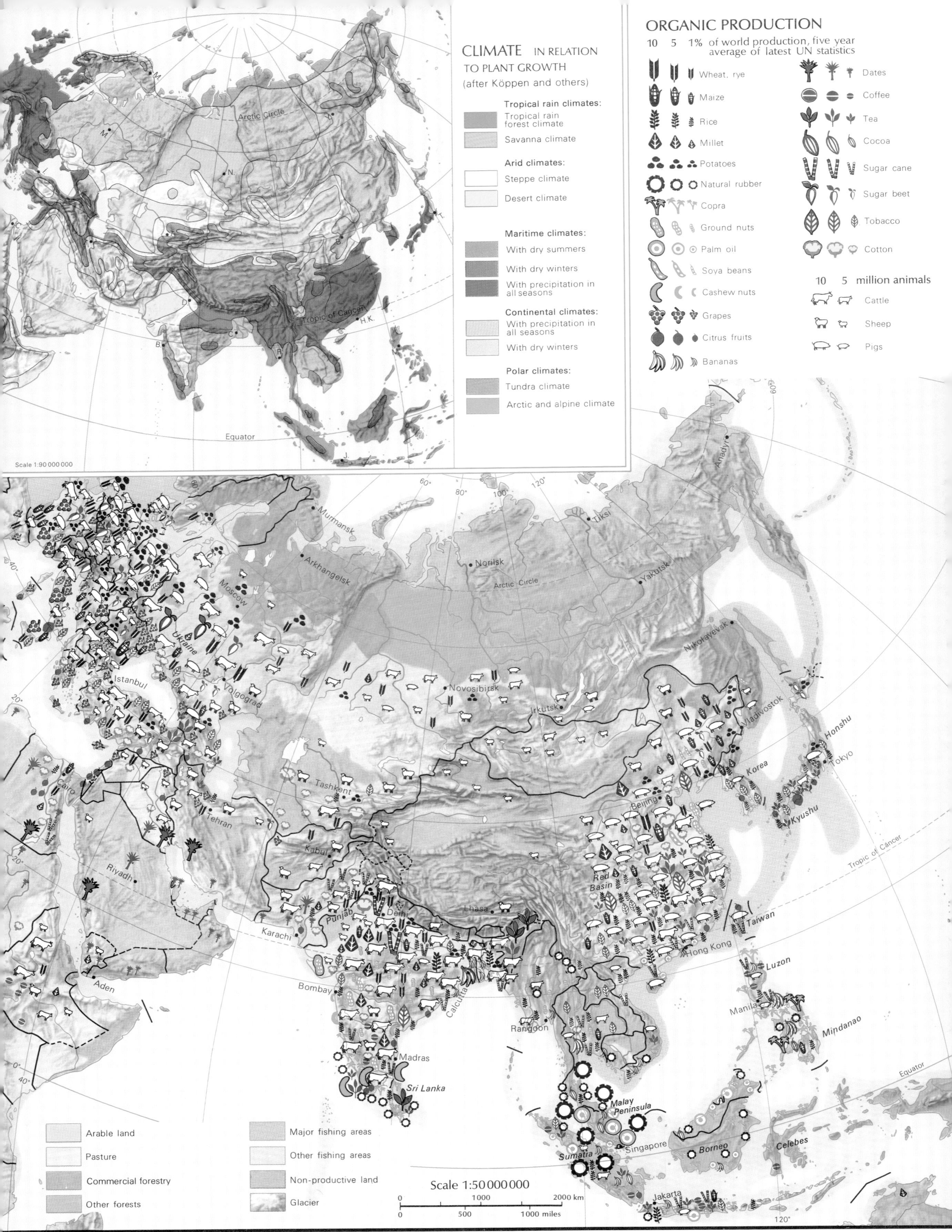

CLIMATE IN RELATION TO PLANT GROWTH
(after Köppen and others)
Tropical rain climates:
Tropical rain forest climate
Savanna climate
Arid climates:
Steppe climate
Desert climate
Maritime climates:
With dry summers
With dry winters
With precipitation in all seasons
Continental climates:
With precipitation in all seasons
With dry winters
Polar climates:
Tundra climate
Arctic and alpine climate
Arctic Circle
Tropic of Cancer
Equator
H.K.
Scale 1:90 000 000
ORGANIC PRODUCTION
10 5 1% of world production, five year average of latest UN statistics
Wheat, rye
Maize
Rice
Millet
Potatoes
Natural rubber
Copra
Ground nuts
Palm oil
Soya beans
Cashew nuts
Grapes
Citrus fruits
Bananas
Dates
Coffee
Tea
Cocoa
Sugar cane
Sugar beet
Tobacco
Cotton
10 5 million animals
Cattle
Sheep
Pigs
Murmansk
Arkhangelsk
Norilsk
Tiksi
Anadyr
Yakutsk
Arctic Circle
Moscow
Ukraine
Nikolayevsk
Istanbul
Volgograd
Novosibirsk
Irkutsk
Vladivostok
Honshu
Tokyo
Korea
Kyushu
Cairo
Tashkent
Beijing
Tehran
Kabul
Riyadh
Red Basin
Tropic of Cancer
Lhasa
Punjab
Delhi
Karachi
Taiwan
Hong Kong
Luzon
Aden
Bombay
Calcutta
Manila
Rangoon
Mindanao
Madras
Sri Lanka
Equator
Malay Peninsula
Singapore
Celebes
Sumatra
Borneo
Jakarta
Arable land
Pasture
Commercial forestry
Other forests
Major fishing areas
Other fishing areas
Non-productive land
Glacier
Scale 1:50 000 000
0 1000 2000 km
0 500 1000 miles

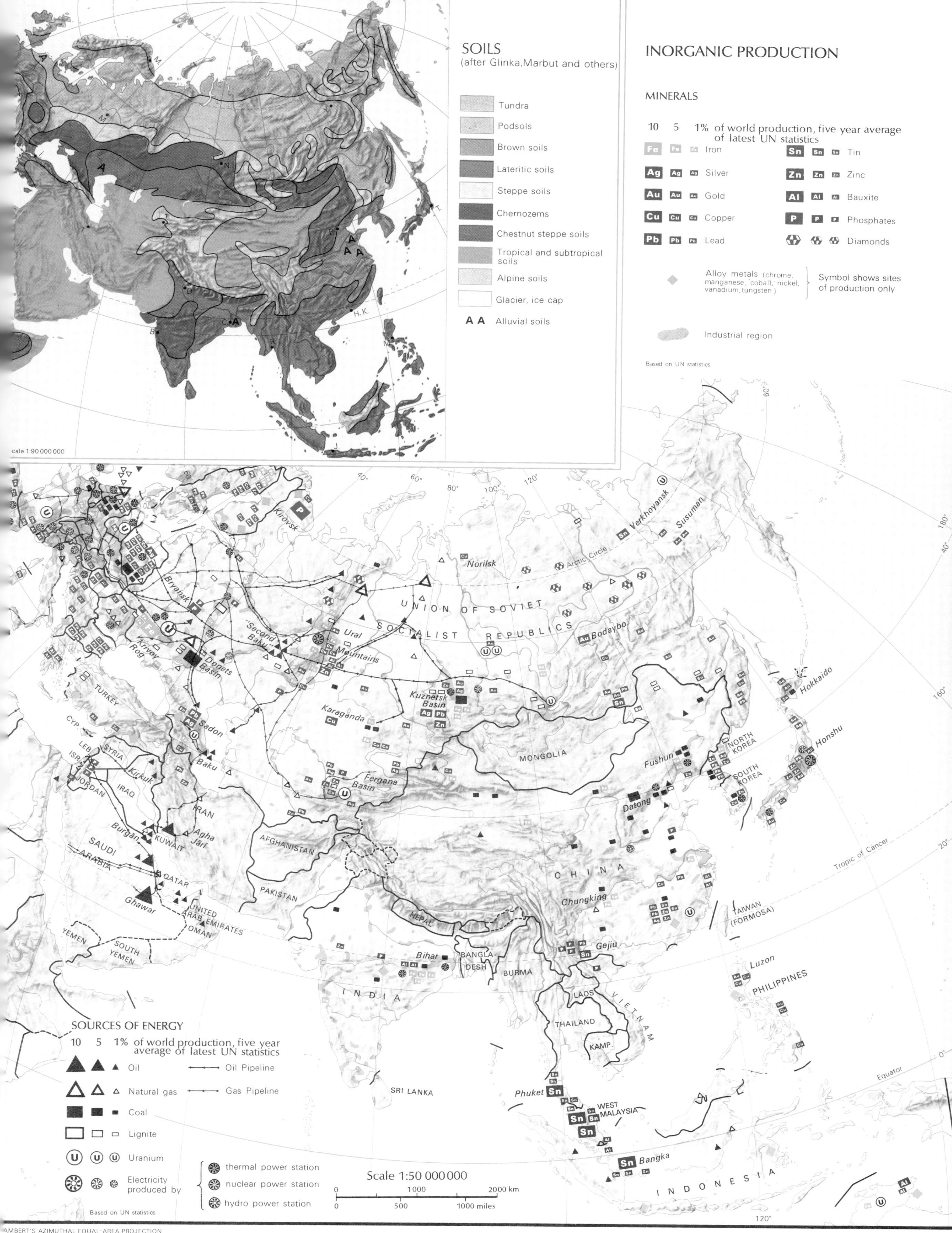

SOILS
(after Glinka, Marbut and others)
Tundra
Podsols
Brown soils
Lateritic soils
Steppe soils
Chernozems
Chestnut steppe soils
Tropical and subtropical soils
Alpine soils
Glacier, ice cap
A A Alluvial soils
cale 1:90 000 000
INORGANIC PRODUCTION
MINERALS
10 5 1% of world production, five year average of latest UN statistics
Fe Iron
Ag Silver
Au Gold
Cu Copper
Pb Lead
Sn Tin
Zn Zinc
Al Bauxite
P Phosphates
Diamonds
Alloy metals (chrome, manganese, cobalt, nickel, vanadium, tungsten)
Symbol shows sites of production only
Industrial region
Based on UN statistics
SOURCES OF ENERGY
10 5 1% of world production, five year average of latest UN statistics
Oil
Oil Pipeline
Natural gas
Gas Pipeline
Coal
Lignite
Uranium
Electricity produced by
thermal power station
nuclear power station
hydro power station
Based on UN statistics
Scale 1:50 000 000
0 1000 2000 km
0 500 1000 miles
UNION OF SOVIET SOCIALIST REPUBLICS
Norilsk
Verkhoyansk
Susuman
Arctic Circle
Kirovsk
Bryansk
Krivoy Rog
Donets Basin
'Second Baku'
Ural Mountains
Bodaybo
Kuznetsk Basin
Karaganda
Sadon
Baku
Fergana Basin
MONGOLIA
Fushun
NORTH KOREA
SOUTH KOREA
Hokkaido
Honshu
Datong
TURKEY
CYP.
SYRIA
LEB.
ISR.
JORDAN
IRAQ
Kirkuk
IRAN
Agha Jari
Burgan
KUWAIT
SAUDI ARABIA
QATAR
Ghawar
UNITED ARAB EMIRATES
OMAN
YEMEN
SOUTH YEMEN
AFGHANISTAN
PAKISTAN
NEPAL
C H I N A
Chungking
TAIWAN (FORMOSA)
Tropic of Cancer
Bihar
BANGLA-DESH
BURMA
Gejiu
I N D I A
LAOS
VIETNAM
THAILAND
KAMP.
Luzon
PHILIPPINES
SRI LANKA
Phuket
WEST MALAYSIA
Bangka
I N D O N E S I A
Equator
LAMBERT'S AZIMUTHAL EQUAL-AREA PROJECTION

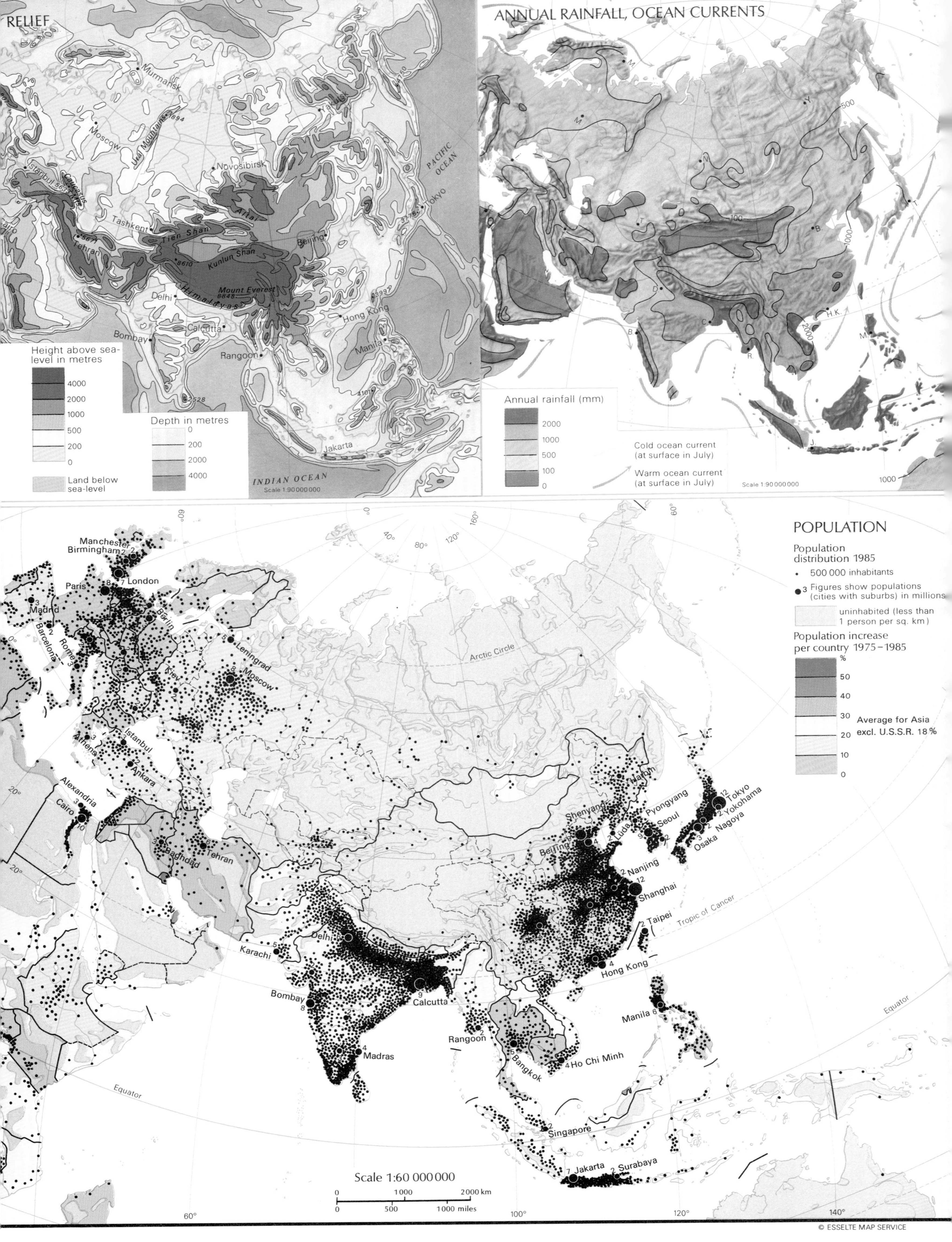
RELIEF
Height above sea-level in metres
4000
2000
1000
500
200
0
Land below sea-level
Depth in metres
0
200
2000
4000
Murmansk
Moscow
Ural Mountains
Novosibirsk
Caucasus
Istanbul
Tashkent
Tien Shan
Altai
Tehran
Kunlun Shan
Mount Everest 8848
Himalayas
Delhi
Calcutta
Bombay
Rangoon
Hong Kong
Manila
Beijing
Tokyo
Yakutsk
PACIFIC OCEAN
INDIAN OCEAN
Jakarta
Scale 1:90 000 000
ANNUAL RAINFALL, OCEAN CURRENTS
Annual rainfall (mm)
2000
1000
500
100
0
Cold ocean current (at surface in July)
Warm ocean current (at surface in July)
Scale 1:90 000 000
POPULATION
Population distribution 1985
500 000 inhabitants
Figures show populations (cities with suburbs) in millions
uninhabited (less than 1 person per sq. km)
Population increase per country 1975–1985
%
50
40
30
20
10
0
Average for Asia excl. U.S.S.R. 18 %
Manchester
Birmingham
London
Paris
Madrid
Barcelona
Rome
Berlin
Kiev
Leningrad
Moscow
Istanbul
Athens
Ankara
Alexandria
Cairo
Baghdad
Tehran
Karachi
Delhi
Bombay
Calcutta
Madras
Rangoon
Bangkok
Ho Chi Minh
Singapore
Jakarta
Surabaya
Manila
Hong Kong
Taipei
Shanghai
Nanjing
Beijing
Shenyang
Harbin
Lüda
Pyongyang
Seoul
Tokyo
Yokohama
Nagoya
Osaka
Arctic Circle
Tropic of Cancer
Equator
Scale 1:60 000 000
1000
2000 km
500
1000 miles
© ESSELTE MAP SERVICE

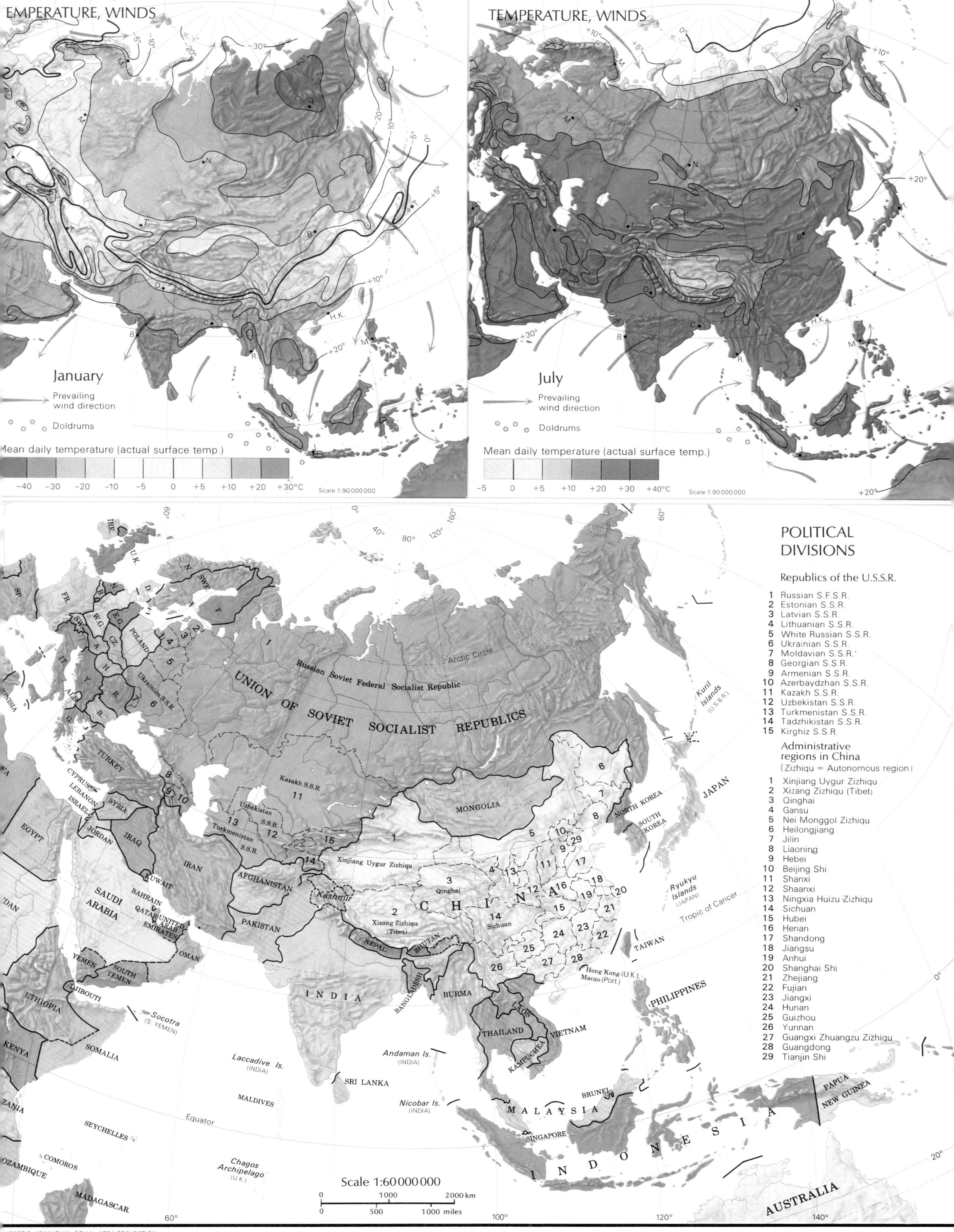

TEMPERATURE, WINDS
January
Prevailing wind direction
Doldrums
Mean daily temperature (actual surface temp.)
-40 -30 -20 -10 -5 0 +5 +10 +20 +30°C
Scale 1:90 000 000
TEMPERATURE, WINDS
July
Prevailing wind direction
Doldrums
Mean daily temperature (actual surface temp.)
-5 0 +5 +10 +20 +30 +40°C
Scale 1:90 000 000
POLITICAL DIVISIONS
Republics of the U.S.S.R.
1 Russian S.F.S.R.
2 Estonian S.S.R.
3 Latvian S.S.R.
4 Lithuanian S.S.R.
5 White Russian S.S.R.
6 Ukrainian S.S.R.
7 Moldavian S.S.R.
8 Georgian S.S.R.
9 Armenian S.S.R.
10 Azerbaydzhan S.S.R.
11 Kazakh S.S.R.
12 Uzbekistan S.S.R.
13 Turkmenistan S.S.R.
14 Tadzhikistan S.S.R.
15 Kirghiz S.S.R.
Administrative regions in China
(Zizhiqu = Autonomous region)
1 Xinjiang Uygur Zizhiqu
2 Xizang Zizhiqu (Tibet)
3 Qinghai
4 Gansu
5 Nei Monggol Zizhiqu
6 Heilongjiang
7 Jilin
8 Liaoning
9 Hebei
10 Beijing Shi
11 Shanxi
12 Shaanxi
13 Ningxia Huizu Zizhiqu
14 Sichuan
15 Hubei
16 Henan
17 Shandong
18 Jiangsu
19 Anhui
20 Shanghai Shi
21 Zhejiang
22 Fujian
23 Jiangxi
24 Hunan
25 Guizhou
26 Yunnan
27 Guangxi Zhuangzu Zizhiqu
28 Guangdong
29 Tianjin Shi
UNION OF SOVIET SOCIALIST REPUBLICS
Russian Soviet Federal Socialist Republic
Arctic Circle
Kuril Islands (U.S.S.R.)
Kazakh S.S.R.
Uzbekistan S.S.R.
Turkmenistan S.S.R.
Ukrainian S.S.R.
MONGOLIA
NORTH KOREA
SOUTH KOREA
JAPAN
Xinjiang Uygur Zizhiqu
Qinghai
Xizang Zizhiqu (Tibet)
Sichuan
C H I N A
Ryukyu Islands (JAPAN)
Tropic of Cancer
TAIWAN
Hong Kong (U.K.)
Macao (Port.)
PHILIPPINES
TURKEY
CYPRUS
LEBANON
ISRAEL
SYRIA
JORDAN
IRAQ
IRAN
EGYPT
KUWAIT
BAHRAIN
QATAR
UNITED ARAB EMIRATES
SAUDI ARABIA
OMAN
YEMEN
SOUTH YEMEN
DJIBOUTI
ETHIOPIA
SOMALIA
KENYA
Socotra (S. YEMEN)
AFGHANISTAN
Kashmir
PAKISTAN
NEPAL
BHUTAN
BANGLADESH
I N D I A
BURMA
LAOS
THAILAND
VIETNAM
KAMPUCHEA
Laccadive Is. (INDIA)
Andaman Is. (INDIA)
SRI LANKA
MALDIVES
Nicobar Is. (INDIA)
SEYCHELLES
Equator
COMOROS
Chagos Archipelago (U.K.)
MADAGASCAR
BRUNEI
M A L A Y S I A
SINGAPORE
I N D O N E S I A
PAPUA NEW GUINEA
AUSTRALIA
IRE.
U.K.
FR.
SP.
N.
SWE.
F.
D.
POLAND
E.G.
W.G.
CZ.
SW.
A.
H.
R.
B.
Y.
IT.
ALB.
G.
Scale 1:60 000 000
0 1000 2000 km
0 500 1000 miles
LAMBERT'S AZIMUTHAL EQUAL-AREA PROJECTION

© ESSELTE MAP SERVICE

Scale 1:10 000 000

0 100 200 300 400 km
0 100 200 miles

Poluostrov Yamal
(Yamal Peninsula)
Obskaya Guba (Gulf of Ob')
Gydanskiy Poluostrov
Tazovskaya Guba
Arctic Circle
Gory Byrranga
Poluostrov Taymyr
(Taymyr Peninsula)
Ozero Taymyr
Severo Sibirskaya Nizmennost'
More Laptevykh
Ostrov Bol'shoy Begichev
Ostrov Peschanyy
Anabarskiy Zaliv
Olenëkskiy Zaliv
Khatangskiy Zaliv
Noril'sk
Dudinka
Gory Putorana
Anabarskoye Ploskogor'ye
Zapadno Sibirskoye Nizmennost'
(West Siberian Plain)
Nizhnevartovskoye
Vilyuyskoye Plato
Sredne Sibirskoye Ploskogor'ye
(Central Siberian Plateau)
Plato Syverma
Tsentralno Tungusskoye Plato
Vilyuyskoye Vodokhranilishche
UNION OF SOVIET SOCIALIST
Tomsk
Novosibirsk
Kemerovo
Anzhero-Sudzhensk
Achinsk
Krasnoyarsk
Kansk
Divnogorsk
Zaozernyy
Bratsk
Bratskoye Vodokhranilishche
Ust'-Ilimsk
Ust'-Kut
Belovo
Kiselevsk
Prokop'yevsk
Novokuznetsk
Leninsk-Kuznetskiy
Biysk
Abakan
Minusinsk
Tayshet
Nizhneudinsk
Tulun
Zima
Cheremkhovo
Usol'ye-Sibirskoye
Angarsk
Irkutsk
Shelekhov
Ulan-Ude
Chita
Borzya
Ozero Baykal
(Lake Baikal)
Severo Baykal'skoye Nagor'ye
Patomskoye Nagor'ye
Stanovoye Nagor'ye
Vitimskoye Ploskogor'ye
Yablonovyy Khrebet
(Yablonovyy Range)
Khrebet Khamar Daban
Vostochnyy Sayan
Zapadnyy Sayan
Tannu Ola
Altay
MONGOLIA
(MONGOL ARD ULS)
Hangayn Nuruu
Gichgeniyn Nuruu
Govi Altay
Hövsgöl Nuur
Uvs Nuur
Hyargas Nuur
Har Us Nuur
Ulaanbaatar
(Ulan Bator)
Hulun Nur
Manzhouli
Hailar
Hulun Buir Meng

Vostochno Sibirskoye More
(East Siberian Sea)
Ostrov Kotel'nyy
O.Stolbovoy
Lyakhovskiye Ostrova
Ostrov Semenovskiy
Proliv Dmitriya Lapteva
Mys Svatoy Nos
Poluostrov Shirokostan
Yanskiy Zaliv
Tiksi Guba Buorkhaya
Yano-Indigirskaya Nizmennost'
Kolymskaya Nizmennost'
Severnyy Anyuyskiy Khrebet
Yuzhnyy Anyuyskiy Khrebet
Anadyrskoye Ploskogor'ye
Anadyrskaya Nizmennost'
Anadyrskiy Zaliv
Chaunskaya Guba
Arctic Circle
Oloyskiye Gory
Gory Ushurakchan
Chuvanskiye Gory
Yukagirskoye Ploskogor'ye
Khrebet Cherskogo (Cherskiy Range)
Momskiy Khrebet
Verkhoyanskiy Khrebet (Verkhoyansk Range)
Khrebet Orulgan
Khrebet Suntar Khayata
Khrebet Kolymskiy (Kolyma Range)
Khrebet Ulakhan-Chistay
Khrebet Tas-Kystabyt
Oymyakonskoye Ploskogor'ye
Khrebet Sette-Daban
Yudomo Mayskoye Nagor'ye
Khrebet Dzhugdzhur (Dzhugdzhur Range)
Aldanskoye Nagor'ye
Stanovoy Khrebet (Stanovoy Range)
Khrebet Tukuringra
Khrebet Dzhagdy
Khrebet Bureinskiy
Khrebet Turana
Sikhote Alin
Xiao Hinggan Ling (Lesser Khingan Mts.)
Yilehuli Shan
Koryakskiy Khrebet (Koryak Range)
Penzhinskiy Khrebet
Sredinnyy Khrebet
Poluostrov Kamchatka
Poluostrov Taygonos
Zaliv Shelikhova
Gizhiginskaya Guba
Penzhinskaya Guba
Okhotskoye More
(Sea of Okhotsk)
Bering Sea
Karaginskiy Zaliv
Ostrov Karaginskiy
Kamchatskiy Zaliv
Kronotskiy Zaliv
Avachinskiy Zaliv
Petropavlovsk-Kamchatskiy
Sopka Klyuchevskaya 4750
Kuril'skiye Ostrova (Kuril Islands)
Ostrov Paramushir
Ostrov Simushir
Ostrov Urup
Ostrov Iturup
Proliv Bussol'
Proliv Kruzenshterna
Sakhalin
Sakhalinskiy Zaliv
Zaliv Terpeniya
Zaliv Aniva
Tatarskiy Proliv
Yuzhno-Sakhalinsk
Kholmsk
Okha
Shantarskiye Ostrova
Tauyskaya Guba
Udskaya Guba
Magadan
Yakutsk
Khabarovsk
Komsomol'sk-na-Amure
Nikolayevsk-na-Amure
Blagoveshchensk
Birobidzhan
Svobodnyy
Tynda
Ayan
Okhotsk
Qiqihar
Heilong Jiang
Amur
Lena
Aldan
Kolyma
Indigirka
Yana
Zeya
Bureya
Zeya Vodokhranilishche
REPUBLICS
CHINA
Mys Lopatka
Mys Terpeniya
Mys Aniva
Mys Kril'on

MONGOLIA
(MONGOL ARD ULS)
Gobi
Dundgovĭ
Dornogovĭ
Ömnögovĭ
Xinjiang Uygur Zizhiqu
(Sinkiang Uighur)
Ürümqi (Urumchi)
Bogda Shan
Turpan
Turpan Pendi (Turfan Depr.)
Hami
Karlik Shan
Lop Nur
Altun Shan
Kunlun Shan
Qaidam Pendi (Tsaidam Basin)
Qinghai (Tsinghai)
Qinghai Hu (Koko Nor)
Xining
Qilian Shan
Badain Jaran Shamo
Nei Mongol Zizhiqu (Inner Mongolia)
Hohhot
Baotou
Yin Shan
Mu Us Shamo (Ordos Plateau)
Ningxia Huizu Zizhiqu
Yinchuan
Lanzhou
Tengger Shamo
Datong
Shanxi
Taiyuan
Shijiazhuang
Handan
Shaanxi
Xi'an
Xianyang
Baoji
Qin Ling
Luoyang
Zhengzhou
Kaifeng
Henan
Xizang Zizhiqu (Tibet)
Nyainqentanglha Shan
Yarlung Zangbo Jiang (Tsangpo)
Tanggula Shan
Bayan Har Shan
Hengduan Shan
Sichuan Pendi (Red Basin)
Sichuan (Szechwan)
Chengdu
Nanchong
Chongqing
Zigong
Neijiang
Wutunghliao
Gongga Shan
Hubei
Wuhan
Yichang
Shashi
Chang Jiang (Yangtze Kiang)
Hunan
Changsha
Zhuzhou
Xiangtan
Hengyang
Guizhou
Guiyang
Zunyi
Yunnan
Kunming
Dukou
Guangxi Zhuangzu Zizhiqu (Kwangsi Chuang)
Nanning
Liuzhou
Guilin
Guangzhou (Canton)
Foshan
Kowloon
Victoria
Hong Kong
Macao (Port.)
Zhanjiang
Haikou
Hainan Dao
Beibu Wan (Gulf of Tonkin)
Nan Hai (South China Sea)
VIETNAM
HA NOI
Hai Phong
LAOS
THAILAND
BURMA
Mandalay
RANGOON
INDIA
Arunachal Pradesh
Nagaland
Imphal
Irrawaddy
Salween
Mekong
CHINESE WALL
© ESSELTE MAP SERVICE

Scale 1:10 000 000
0 100 200 300 400 km
0 100 200 miles

AFGHANISTAN
PAKISTAN
INDIA
NEPAL
Sikkim
SRI LANKA
(CEYLON)
MALDIVES
Arabian Sea
Bay of
INDIAN OCEAN
Qing Zang Gaoyuan
(Plateau of Tibet)
Xizang Zizhiqu
(Tibet)
Gangdisê Shan
Himalaya
Thar Desert
(Great Indian Desert)
Rajasthan
Punjab
Haryana
Himachal Pradesh
Jammu and Kashmir
Uttar Pradesh
Bihar
West Bengal
Orissa
Madhya Pradesh
Gujarat
Maharashtra
Karnataka
Andhra Pradesh
Tamil Nadu
Kerala
Malabar Coast
Coromandel Coast
Western Ghats
Eastern Ghats
Deccan
Vindhya Range
Satpura Range
Rann of Kutch
Gulf of Kutch
Gulf of Khambhat
Gulf of Mannar
Palk Strait
Nine Degree Channel
Eight Degree Channel
Lakshadweep
(Laccadive Islands)
(India)
Amindivi Islands
Kandahar
Quetta
Karachi
Hyderabad
Sukkur
Multan
Lahore
Faisalabad
Rawalpindi
ISLAMABAD
Peshawar
Srinagar
Amritsar
Jullundur
Ludhiana
Chandigarh
DELHI
Jaipur
Agra
Kanpur
Lucknow
Allahabad
Varanasi
(Benares)
Patna
KATMANDU
Mt. Everest
DAKHA
Calcutta
Jamshedpur
Ahmadabad
Vadodara
Indore
Bhopal
Jabalpur
Nagpur
Surat
Bombay
Pune
(Poona)
Nasik
Aurangabad
Sholapur
Hyderabad
Vishakhapatnam
Vijayawada
Cuttack
Bhubaneswar
Hubli
Bangalore
Mysore
Madras
Calicut
Coimbatore
Madurai
Cochin
Trivandrum
Tiruchirappalli
Colombo
Jaffna
Kandy
Trincomalee
Cape Comorin
Dondra Head

BURMA
THAILAND
(SIAM)
LAOS
KAMPUCHEA
(CAMBODIA)
VIETNAM
BANGLA DESH
MALAYSIA
CHINA
Arunachal Pradesh
Meghalaya
Assam
Nagaland
Manipur
Mizoram
Tripura
Sichuan Pendi
(Red Basin)
Sichuan
(Szechwan)
Yunnan
Guizhou
Hunan
Hubei
Guangxi Zhuangzu Zizhiqu
(Kwangsi Chuang)
Qinghai
(Tsinghai)
Hainan Dao
Chengdu
Chongqing
Kunming
Guiyang
Nanning
Guilin
Wuhan
Changsha
Hengyang
Zhanjiang
Haikou
Mandalay
RANGOON
Bassein
Moulmein
Pegu
Prome
Sittwe
(Akyab)
Chittagong
Gauhati
Shillong
Imphal
HA NOI
Hai Phong
Hue
Da Nang
Qui Nhon
Nha Trang
Da Lat
Ho Chi Minh (Saigon)
PHNOM PENH
VIANG CHAN
(Vientiane)
Luang Prabang
KRUNG THEP (BANGKOK)
Thon Buri
Chiang Mai
Nakhon Sawan
Nakhon Ratchasima
Ubon Ratchathani
Khon Kaen
Udon Thani
Surat Thani
Nakhon Si Thammarat
Songkhla
Hat Yai
Phuket
Mergui
Tavoy
Andaman Islands
(India)
North Andaman
Middle Andaman
South Andaman
Port Blair
Little Andaman
Nicobar Islands
(India)
Car Nicobar
Great Nicobar
Little Nicobar
Ten Degree Channel
Preparis North Channel
Preparis South Channel
Coco Islands
(Burma)
Mergui Archipelago
Andaman Sea
Gulf of Martaban
Gulf of Thailand
Bight of Bangkok
South China Sea
Beibu Wan
(Gulf of Tonkin)
Paracel Islands
(China)
Bay of Bengal
Mouths of the Irrawaddy
Mouths of the Mekong
Mekong
Irrawaddy
Salween
Chindwin
Chang Jiang (Yangtze Kiang)
Jinsha Jiang
(Yangtze Kiang)
Lancang Jiang
(Mekong)
Nu Jiang (Salween)
Brahmaputra
Ganges
Hengduan Shan
Daxue Shan
Bayan Har Shan
Nyainqentanglha Shan
Qinling Shan
Arakan Yoma
Pegu Yoma
Chin Hills
Naga Hills
Shan Plateau
Khorat Plateau
Tenasserim
Isthmus of Kra
Wuling Shan
Tonle Sap
Gongga Shan
(Minya Konka)
Namjagbarwa Feng
Hkakabo Razi
Fan si Pan
Doi Inthanon
Three Pagodas Pass
Scale 1:10 000 000

BURMA
THAILAND
KAMPUCHEA
VIETNAM
MALAYSIA
BRUNEI
KRUNG THEP (BANGKOK)
Thon Buri
PHNOM PENH
Ho Chi Minh (Saigon)
Qui Nhon
Nha Trang
Da Lat
Cam Ranh
Gulf of Thailand
Andaman Sea
Mergui Archipelago
South China Sea
Nansha Qundao
(Nanshan Islands)
(claimed by China, Vietnam and Philippines)
Zhongye Qundao (Zhongye Is.)
Nanwei Dao (Spratly I.)
Con Son
Mouths of the Mekong
Ko Phuket
Songkhla
Hat Yai
George Town
Ipoh
KUALA LUMPUR
Kota Baharu
Kuala Terengganu
Kuantan
Melaka
Johor Baharu
SINGAPORE
Strait of Malacca
Kepulauan Natuna
Natuna Besar
Kepulauan Anambas
Kepulauan Riau
Kepulauan Lingga
Kepulauan Tambelan
Kota Kinabalu
BANDAR SERI BEGAWAN
Sabah
Sarawak
Kuching
Kalimantan (Borneo)
Pontianak
Banjarmasin
Balikpapan
Banda Aceh
Medan
Pekanbaru
Padang
Jambi
Palembang
Bengkulu
Sumatera
Pulau Simeulue
Pulau Nias
Pulau Siberut
Kepulauan Mentawai
Pulau Enggano
Pulau Bangka
Pulau Belitung
Bandarlampung
Selat Sunda (Sunda Strait)
Pulau Rakata (Krakatau)
JAKARTA
Bogor
Bandung
Cirebon
Semarang
Yogyakarta
Surakarta
Surabaya
Malang
Madura
Bali
Lombok
Laut Jawa (Java Sea)
Jawa (Java)
INDONESIA
Equator
INDIAN OCEAN
Christmas Island (Austr.)

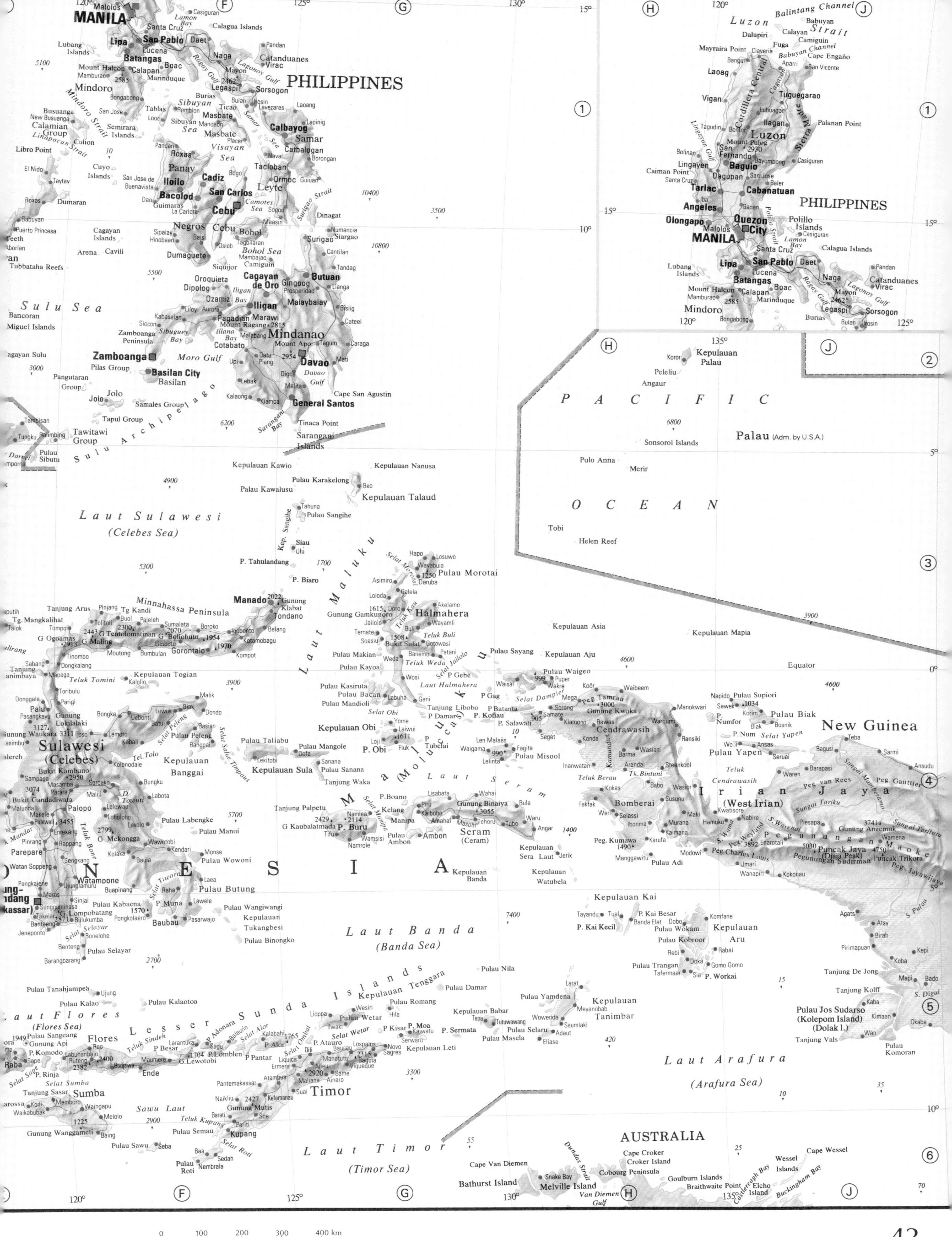

Scale 1:10 000 000

0 100 200 300 400 km

0 100 200 miles

PHILIPPINES
Northern Mariana Is.
Mariana Is.
Guam I.
(U.S.A.)
Marshall Islands
Trust Territory of the Pacific Islands
(Adm. by U.S.A.)
Palau
Caroline Islands
Federated States of Micronesia
Equator
NAURU
KIRIBATI
INDONESIA
PAPUA NEW GUINEA
SOLOMON ISLANDS
TUVALU
(N.Z.)
WESTERN SAMOA
(FR.)
VANUATU
FIJI
TONGA
New Caledonia
(Fr.)
Tropic of Capricorn
Northern Territory
Queensland
Western Australia
AUSTRALIA
South Australia
New South Wales
Victoria
NEW ZEALAND
Tasmania
POLITICAL DIVISIONS
Scale 1:60 000 000
0
1000
2000 km
500
1000 miles
Manila
Sydney
Melbourne
POPULATION
Population distribution 1985
500 000 inhabitants
Figures show populations (cities with suburbs) in millions
uninhabited (less than 1 person per sq. km)
Population increase per country 1975 – 1985
0
10
20
30
40
50 %
Average for Oceania 17%
Luzon Strait
Paracel Is.
(China)
South China Sea
Laoag
Ilagan
Luzon
Angeles
Cabanatuan
MANILA
Quezon City
San Pablo
Legaspi
Mindoro
PHILIPPINES
Samar
Tacloban
Panay
Roxas
Iloilo
Cebu
Leyte
Palawan
Negros
Philippine Trench
Butuan
Sulu Sea
Cagayan de Oro
Mindanao
Zamboanga
Davao
Basilan
Kota Kinabalu
Mt. Kinabalu
Sandakan
Sabah
BANDAR SERI BEGAWAN
BRUNEI
MALAYSIA
Sulu Archipelago
City
Celebes Sea
Sarawak
Manado
Ternate
Halmahera
Moluccas
Borneo
Samarinda
Balikpapan
Strait of Makassar
Celebes
INDONESIA
Banjarmasin
Kendari
Buru
Ceram
Ambon
Ujungpandang (Makassar)
Banda Sea
Surabaya
Flores Sea
Jawa
Singaraja
Lombok
Bali
Mataram
Sumbawa
Flores
Ende
Dili
Lesser Sunda Islands
Timor
Sumba
Kupang
Timor Sea
Tanimbar
Darwin
Cape Londonderry
Wyndham
Ord R.
Daly Waters
Derby
Kimberley Plateau
Broome
Tennant C
Port Hedland
Dampier
Great Sandy Desert
North West Cape
Hamersley Range
Lake Mackay
Tropic of Capricorn
Gibson Desert
AUST
Carnarvon
Western Australia
Meekatharra
Mount Woodroffe
Great Victoria Desert
Leonora
Geraldton
Lake Barlee
Kalgoorlie
Boulder
Nullarbor Plain
Perth
Northam
Norseman
Great Australian Bi
Fremantle
Narrogin
Bunbury
Esperance
Cape Leeuwin
Albany

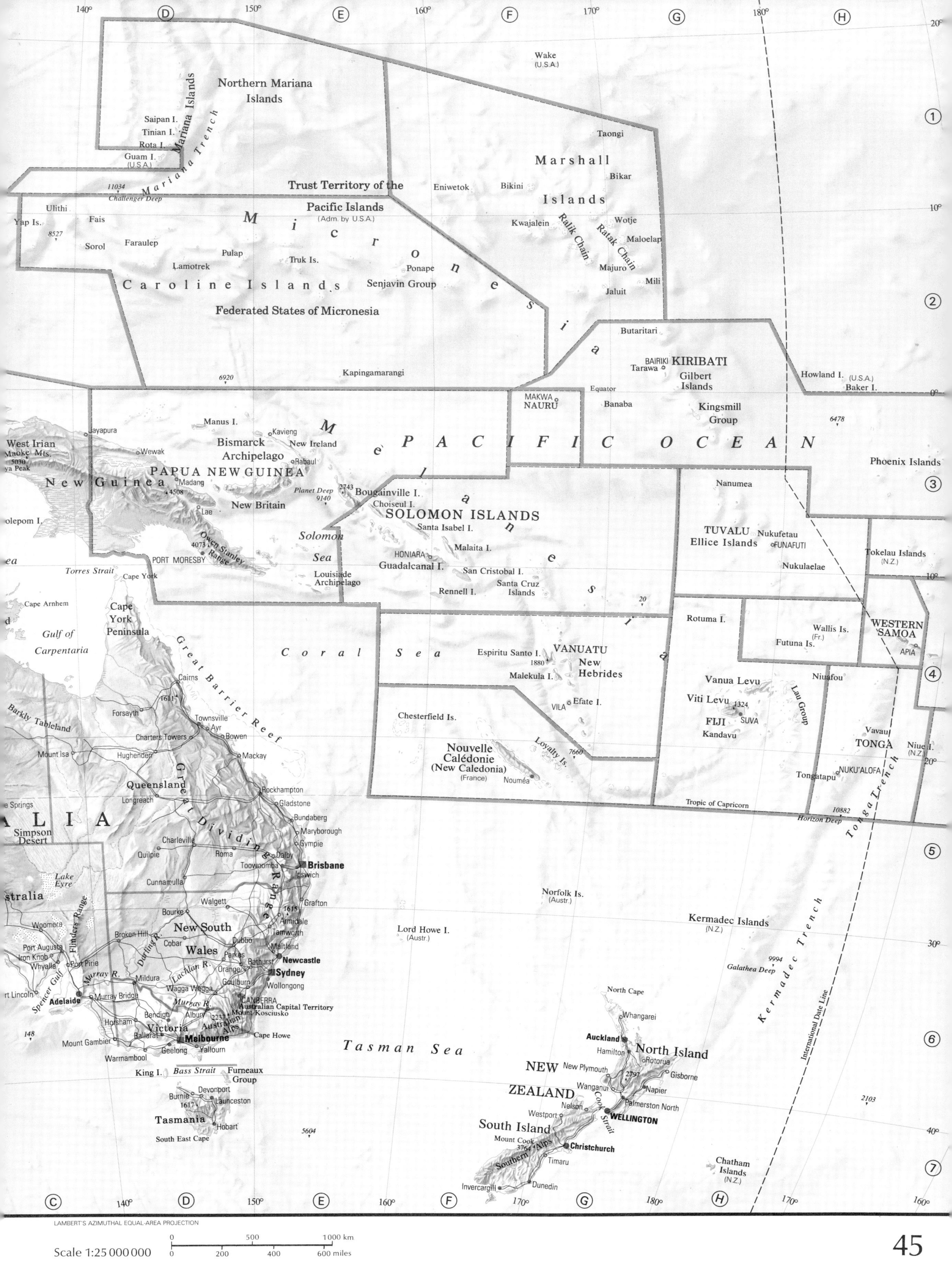

Northern Mariana Islands
Mariana Islands
Saipan I.
Tinian I.
Rota I.
Guam I. (U.S.A.)
Mariana Trench
11034 Challenger Deep
Wake (U.S.A.)
Taongi
Marshall Islands
Bikar
Eniwetok
Bikini
Trust Territory of the Pacific Islands (Adm. by U.S.A.)
Kwajalein
Ralik Chain
Ratak Chain
Wotje
Maloelap
Majuro
Mili
Jaluit
Ulithi
Yap Is.
Fais
8527
Sorol
Faraulep
Pulap
Lamotrek
Truk Is.
Ponape
Senjavin Group
Micronesia
Caroline Islands
Federated States of Micronesia
Butaritari
BAIRIKI KIRIBATI
Tarawa
Gilbert Islands
Kapingamarangi
6920
Howland I. (U.S.A.)
Baker I.
Equator
MAKWA NAURU
Banaba
Kingsmill Group
6478
Manus I.
Kavieng
New Ireland
Jayapura
Wewak
West Irian
Maoke Mts.
Bismarck Archipelago
Rabaul
PAPUA NEW GUINEA
New Guinea
Madang
4508
PACIFIC OCEAN
Phoenix Islands
Melanesia
Planet Deep 9140
2743
Bougainville I.
Choiseul I.
Lae
New Britain
SOLOMON ISLANDS
Santa Isabel I.
Nanumea
TUVALU Ellice Islands
Nukufetau
FUNAFUTI
Nukulaelae
Tokelau Islands (N.Z.)
Solomon Sea
4073
Owen Stanley Range
PORT MORESBY
HONIARA
Guadalcanal I.
Malaita I.
San Cristobal I.
Torres Strait
Cape York
Louisiade Archipelago
Rennell I.
Santa Cruz Islands
20
Rotuma I.
Cape Arnhem
Gulf of Carpentaria
Cape York Peninsula
Wallis Is. (Fr.)
Futuna Is.
WESTERN SAMOA
APIA
Coral Sea
Espiritu Santo I.
1880
VANUATU New Hebrides
Malekula I.
Niuafou
Great Barrier Reef
Cairns
1611
Barkly Tableland
Forsayth
Townsville
Ayr
Bowen
Charters Towers
Mount Isa
Hughenden
Mackay
VILA
Efate I.
Vanua Levu
Viti Levu
1324
SUVA
FIJI
Kandavu
Lau Group
Chesterfield Is.
Nouvelle Calédonie (New Caledonia) (France)
Nouméa
Loyalty Is.
7660
Vavau
TONGA
Niue I. (N.Z.)
NUKU'ALOFA
Tongatapu
Tonga Trench
Queensland
Longreach
Great Dividing Range
Rockhampton
Gladstone
Bundaberg
Maryborough
Gympie
Tropic of Capricorn
10882 Horizon Deep
Simpson Desert
Charleville
Quilpie
Roma
Dalby
Toowoomba
Brisbane
Ipswich
Lake Eyre
Cunnamulla
Norfolk Is. (Austr.)
Walgett
Grafton
Bourke
1615
Armidale
Tamworth
Flinders Range
Woomera
New South Wales
Broken Hill
Darling R.
Cobar
Dubbo
Maitland
Newcastle
Lord Howe I. (Austr.)
Kermadec Islands (N.Z.)
Kermadec Trench
Port Augusta
Iron Knob
Whyalla
Port Pirie
Murray R.
Mildura
Lachlan R.
Parkes
Bathurst
Orange
Sydney
Wollongong
Galathea Deep
9994
Spencer Gulf
Adelaide
Murray Bridge
Wagga Wagga
Goulburn
Murray R.
CANBERRA
Australian Capital Territory
Mount Kosciusko
Australian Alps
2237
Albury
Bendigo
Horsham
Victoria
Ballarat
Melbourne
Cape Howe
148
Mount Gambier
Geelong
Yallourn
Warrnambool
Tasman Sea
King I.
Bass Strait
Furneaux Group
Devonport
Burnie
1617
Launceston
Tasmania
Hobart
South East Cape
5604
North Cape
Whangarei
Auckland
Hamilton
Rotorua
North Island
NEW ZEALAND
New Plymouth
2797
Gisborne
Wanganui
Napier
Nelson
Cook Strait
Palmerston North
WELLINGTON
Westport
South Island
Mount Cook
3764
Southern Alps
Christchurch
Timaru
Dunedin
Invercargill
Chatham Islands (N.Z.)
International Date Line
2103
LAMBERT'S AZIMUTHAL EQUAL-AREA PROJECTION
Scale 1:25 000 000
0 500 1000 km
0 200 400 600 miles

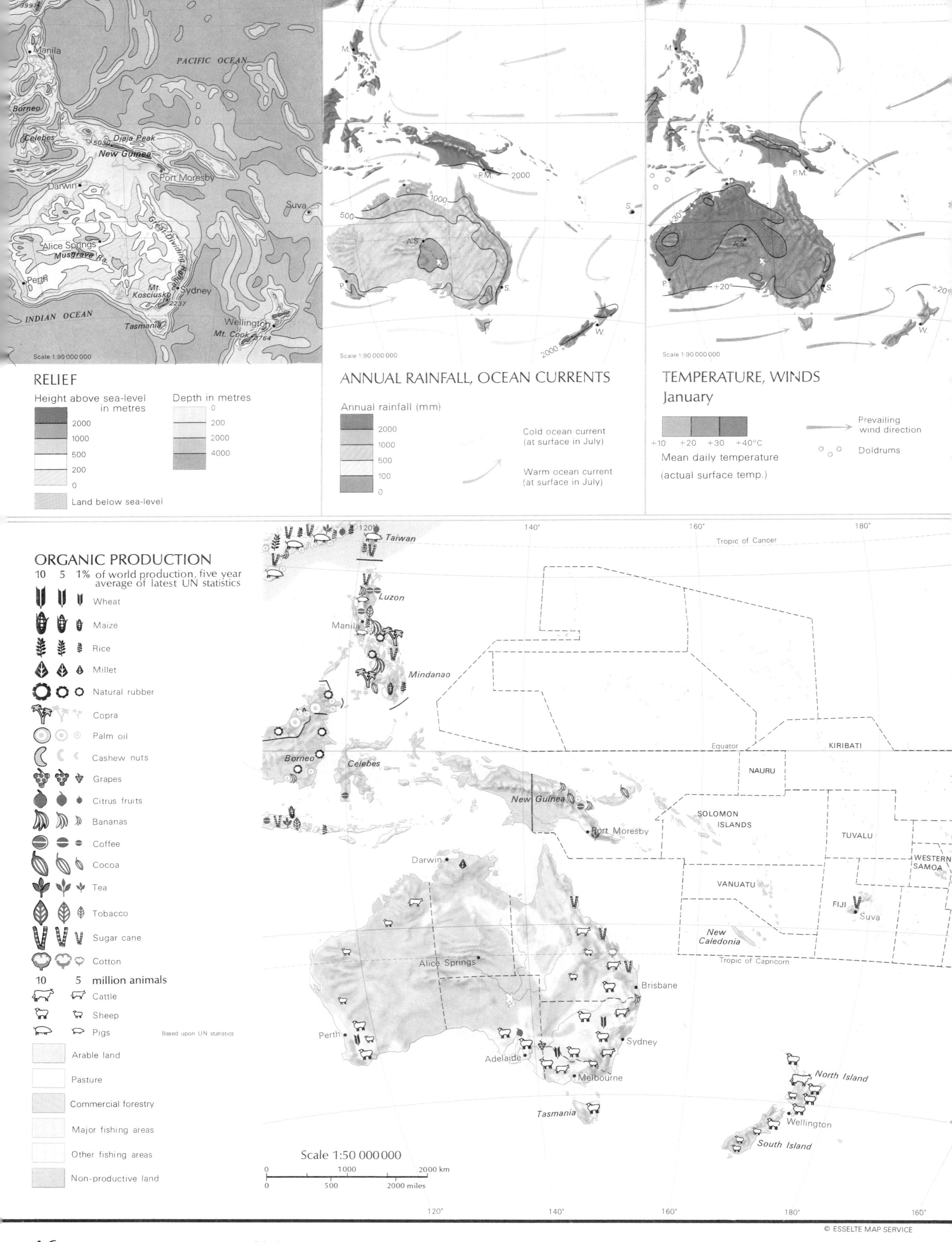
Manila
PACIFIC OCEAN
Borneo
Celebes
Djaja Peak
5030
New Guinea
Port Moresby
Darwin
Suva
Alice Springs
Musgrave Ra.
Great Dividing Range
Perth
Mt. Kosciusko
2237
Sydney
INDIAN OCEAN
Tasmania
Wellington
Mt. Cook
3764
Scale 1:90 000 000
RELIEF
Height above sea-level in metres
2000
1000
500
200
0
Land below sea-level
Depth in metres
0
200
2000
4000
ANNUAL RAINFALL, OCEAN CURRENTS
Annual rainfall (mm)
2000
1000
500
100
0
Cold ocean current (at surface in July)
Warm ocean current (at surface in July)
TEMPERATURE, WINDS
January
+10 +20 +30 +40°C
Mean daily temperature
(actual surface temp.)
Prevailing wind direction
Doldrums
ORGANIC PRODUCTION
10 5 1% of world production, five year average of latest UN statistics
Wheat
Maize
Rice
Millet
Natural rubber
Copra
Palm oil
Cashew nuts
Grapes
Citrus fruits
Bananas
Coffee
Cocoa
Tea
Tobacco
Sugar cane
Cotton
10 5 million animals
Cattle
Sheep
Pigs
Based upon UN statistics
Arable land
Pasture
Commercial forestry
Major fishing areas
Other fishing areas
Non-productive land
Taiwan
Tropic of Cancer
Luzon
Manila
Mindanao
Borneo
Celebes
Equator
KIRIBATI
NAURU
New Guinea
Port Moresby
SOLOMON ISLANDS
TUVALU
WESTERN SAMOA
Darwin
VANUATU
FIJI
Suva
New Caledonia
Tropic of Capricorn
Alice Springs
Brisbane
Perth
Sydney
Adelaide
Melbourne
Tasmania
North Island
Wellington
South Island
Scale 1:50 000 000
1000 2000 km
500 2000 miles
© ESSELTE MAP SERVICE

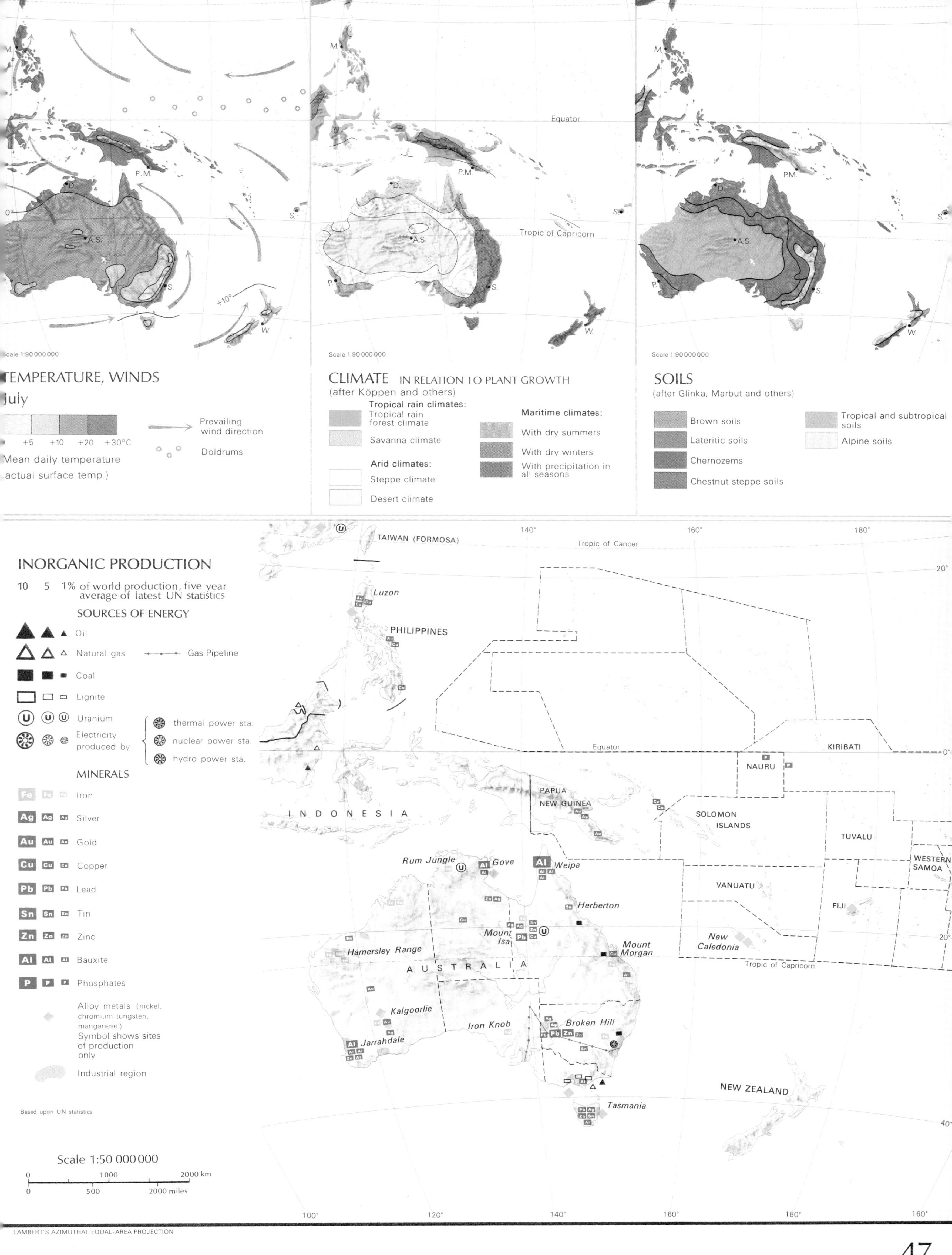

TEMPERATURE, WINDS
July
+5 +10 +20 +30°C
Mean daily temperature
actual surface temp.)
Prevailing wind direction
Doldrums
Scale 1:90 000 000
CLIMATE IN RELATION TO PLANT GROWTH
(after Köppen and others)
Tropical rain climates:
Tropical rain forest climate
Savanna climate
Arid climates:
Steppe climate
Desert climate
Maritime climates:
With dry summers
With dry winters
With precipitation in all seasons
SOILS
(after Glinka, Marbut and others)
Brown soils
Lateritic soils
Chernozems
Chestnut steppe soils
Tropical and subtropical soils
Alpine soils
Equator
Tropic of Capricorn
INORGANIC PRODUCTION
10 5 1% of world production, five year average of latest UN statistics
SOURCES OF ENERGY
Oil
Natural gas
Gas Pipeline
Coal
Lignite
Uranium
Electricity produced by
thermal power sta.
nuclear power sta.
hydro power sta.
MINERALS
Iron
Silver
Gold
Copper
Lead
Tin
Zinc
Bauxite
Phosphates
Alloy metals (nickel, chromium, tungsten, manganese)
Symbol shows sites of production only
Industrial region
Based upon UN statistics
Scale 1:50 000 000
0 1000 2000 km
0 500 2000 miles
TAIWAN (FORMOSA)
Tropic of Cancer
Luzon
PHILIPPINES
INDONESIA
PAPUA NEW GUINEA
NAURU
KIRIBATI
SOLOMON ISLANDS
TUVALU
WESTERN SAMOA
VANUATU
FIJI
New Caledonia
Rum Jungle
Gove
Weipa
Herberton
Mount Isa
Mount Morgan
Hamersley Range
AUSTRALIA
Kalgoorlie
Iron Knob
Broken Hill
Jarrahdale
Tasmania
NEW ZEALAND
LAMBERT'S AZIMUTHAL EQUAL-AREA PROJECTION

Scale 1:10 000 000

PAPUA-NEW GUINEA
Coral Sea
PACIFIC
OCEAN
Coral Sea Islands Territory (Austr.)
Great Barrier Reef
Gulf of Carpentaria
Cape York Peninsula
Queensland
Great Artesian Basin
Great Dividing Range
New South Wales
Victoria
Tasman Sea
Torres Strait
Louisiade Archipelago
Tropic of Capricorn
Capricorn Channel
Curtis Channel
Bass Strait
Simpson Desert
Sturt Desert
Lake Eyre Basin
Lake Eyre
Lake Torrens
Lake Frome
Flinders Ranges
Mount Lofty Ranges
Brisbane
Sydney
Newcastle
Wollongong
CANBERRA
Australian Capital Territory
Melbourne
Geelong
Adelaide
Rockhampton
Mackay
Townsville
Cairns
Mount Isa
Cape Melville
Cape Flattery
Cape York
Cape Grenville
Cape Byron
Cape Howe
Wilsons Promontory
King Island
Flinders Island
Kangaroo Island
Fraser or Great Sandy Island
Moreton Island
Lord Howe Island
Balls Pyramid
Murray R.
Darling R.
Murrumbidgee R.
Lachlan River
Mount Kosciusko 2237
Mount Bimberi 1912
Mount Bartle Frere 1611
Groote Eylandt
Wellesley Islands
Mornington Island
Cape Arnhem
Gove Peninsula
Eyre Peninsula
Yorke Peninsula
Spencer Gulf
Gulf St. Vincent
Port Phillip Bay
Willis Group
Holmes Reefs
Flinders Reefs
Marion Reef
Lihou Reef and Cays
Mellish Reef
Frederick Reef
Kenn Reef
Saumarez Reef
Wreck Reef
Cato Island and Bank
Récifs et Iles Chesterfield (Fr.)
Pocklington Reef
Rossel Island
Tagula Island
Misima Island
Normanby Island
Deboyne Island
10°
15°
20°
25°
30°
35°
135°
140°
145°
150°
155°
F
G
H
J
K
1
2
3
4
5
6
0 100 200 300 400 km
0 100 200 miles

Halmahera
Kepulauan Asia
Kepulauan Mapia
Equator
Pulau Sayang
Kepulauan Aju
Pulau Waigeo
New Guinea
Pulau Biak
Numfor
Pulau Yapen
Selat Yapen
Teluk Cendrawasih
Cendrawasih
P. Obi
Pulau Misool
Laut Seram
Gunung Kwoka
Irian Jaya
(West Irian)
Bomberai
Seram
(Ceram)
Ambon
Gunung Binaiya
Kepulauan Sera Laut
Kepulauan Banda
Kepulauan Watubela
Pulau Adi
INDONESIA
Kepulauan Kai
P. Kai Besar
P. Kai Kecil
Kepulauan Aru
(Aru Islands)
Pulau Wokam
Pulau Kobroor
Pulau Trangan
P. Workai
Pulau Nila
Pulau Damar
Pulau Yamdena
Kepulauan Tanimbar
(Tanimbar Islands)
Kepulauan Babar
P. Moa
P. Sermata
Pulau Selaru
Pulau Masela
Kepulauan Leti
Laut Arafura
(Arafura Sea)
Pegunungan Maoke (Maoke Mts.)
Puncak Jaya
(Jaya Peak)
Pegunungan Sudirman
Puncak Trikora
Peg. Jayawijaya
Gunung Angemuk
Peg. van Rees
Peg. Gauttier
Sungai Mamberamo
Jayapura
Vanimo
Mount Sulen
Central Range
Bismarck Range
Sepik River
Ramu River
Mount Wilhelm
Mt. Giluwe
Doma Peaks
Lake Murray
Strickland River
Fly River
S. Digul
Tanjung De Jong
Tanjung Kolff
Pulau Jos Sodarso
(Kolepom I.)
(Dolak I.)
Tanjung Vals
Pulau Komoran
Merauke
Daru
Gulf of Papua
Great North East Channel
Kaniet Islands
Ninigo Islands
Aua
Wuvulu
Hermit Islands
Admiralty Islands
Manus
Lorengau
Rambutyo
Lou
Bismarck
Purdy Islands
Schouten Islands
Manam
PAPUA
Karkar
Long Island
Umboi
Vitiaz Strait
Dampier Strait
Madang
Mount Bangeta
Huon Peninsula
Huon Gulf
Cape Cretin
Lae
NEW GUINEA
(NIUGINI)
PORT MORESBY
Owen Stanley
Mount Victoria
Murray Islands
Mulgrave Island
Banks Island
Torres Strait
Prince of Wales Island
Cape York
Endeavour Strait
JARDINE RIVER NATIONAL PARK
Cape York Peninsula
Cape Grenville
Coral Sea
AUSTRALIA
Cape Van Diemen
Bathurst Island
Melville Island
Dundas Strait
Van Diemen Gulf
Cape Croker
Croker Island
Cobourg Peninsula
Goulburn Islands
Braithwaite Point
Castlereagh Bay
Elcho Island
Buckingham Bay
Wessel Islands
Cape Wessel
Sydney
Wollongong
Shellharbour
Beecroft Head
Jervis Bay
CANBERRA
Australian Capital Territory
Mount Bimberi
Lake Cowal
KANANGRA BOYD N.P.
BLUE MOUNTAINS N.P.
Wagga Wagga
Lachlan River
Murrumbidgee R.
Riverina
Murray River
Loddon River
Albury
Shepparton
Bendigo
Mount Kosciusko
Snowy Mountains
Australian Alps
Mount Feathertop
AUSTRALIA
Cape Howe
Mallacoota
Melbourne
Geelong
Port Phillip Bay
Western Port
Ninety Mile Beach
Lakes Entrance
Wilsons Promontory
WILSON'S PROMONTORY N.P.
South East Point
Venus Bay
Waratah Bay
Tasman Sea
King I.
Cape Wickham
Bass Strait
Three Hummock Island
Hunter Island
Cape Grim
Flinders Island
Furneaux Group
Cape Barren Island
Clarke
Banks Strait
Cape Portland
Tasmania
Launceston
Legges Tor
Macquarie Harbour
Freycinet Peninsula
Tasman Peninsula
Hobart
Storm Bay
HARTZ MOUNTAINS NATIONAL PARK
Port Davey
Bruny
South East Cape
South Island
Jackson Head
Mount Aspiring
FIORDLAND NATIONAL PARK
Doubtful Sound
Lake Wakatipu
Lake Te Anau
Resolution
Cape Providence
Invercargill
Foveaux Strait
Stewart Island
Mount Anglem
Ruapuke
Southwest Cape
Port Pegasus

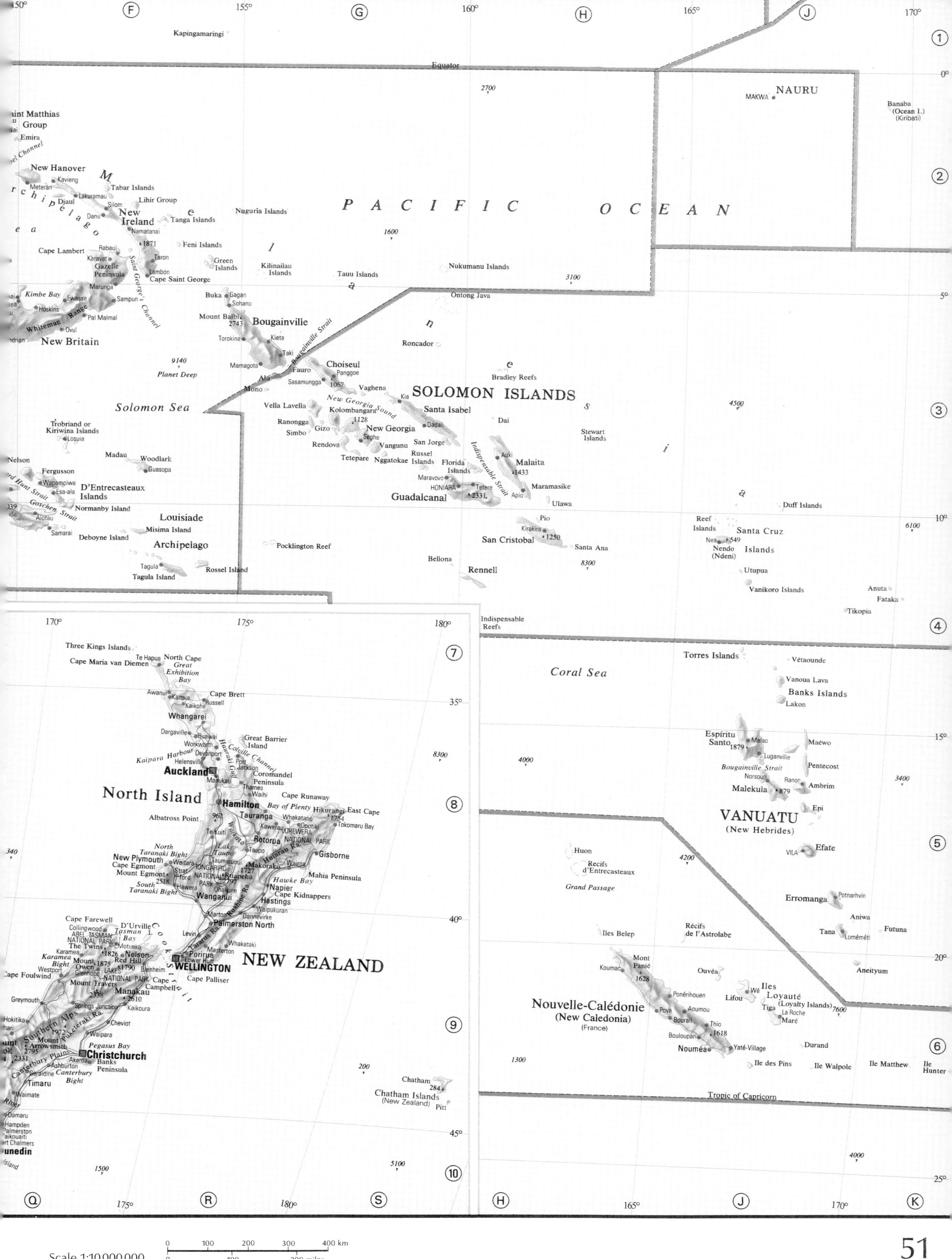

0 100 200 300 400 km
0 100 200 miles

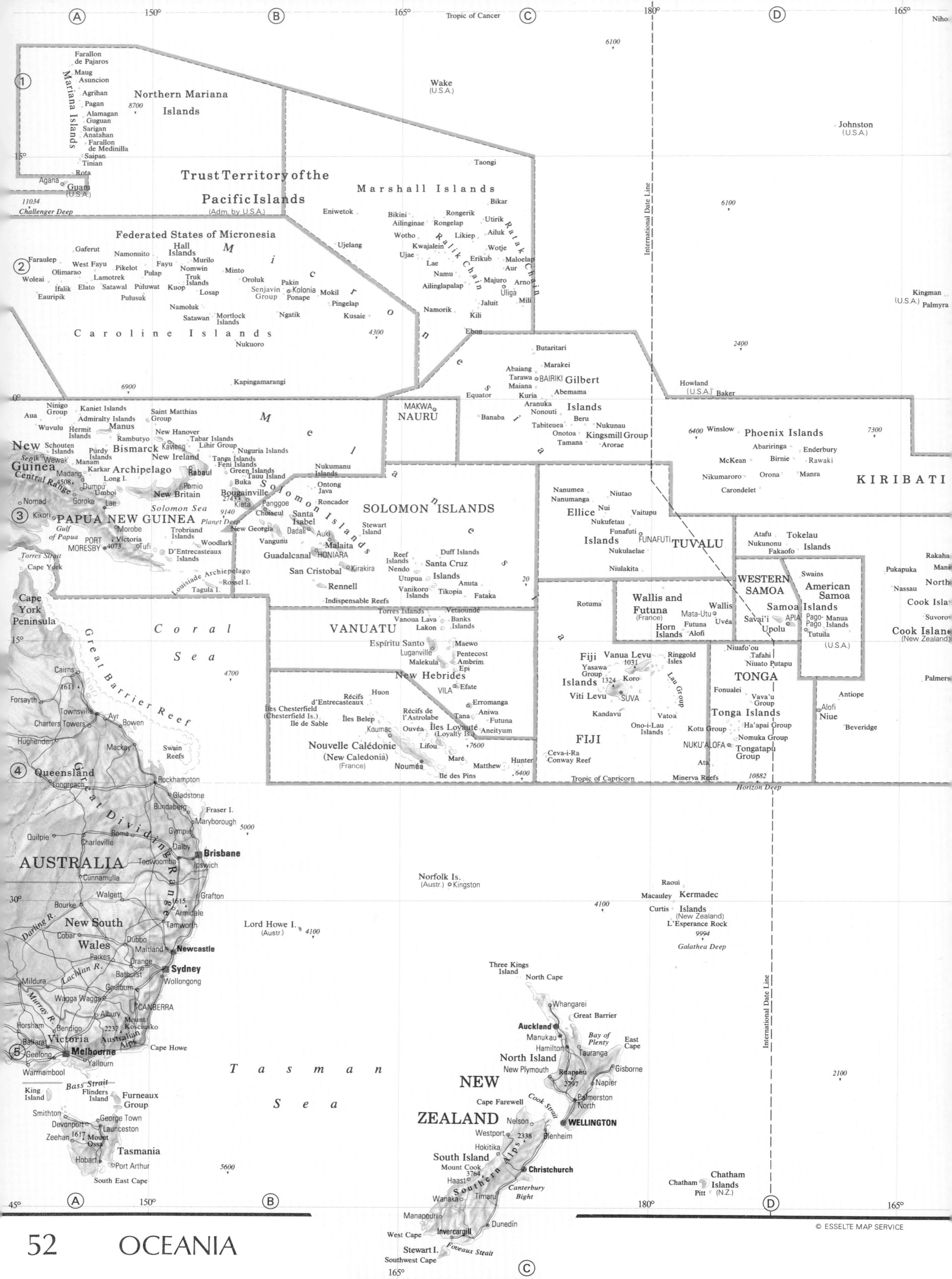

Tropic of Cancer
150°
165°
180°
Northern Mariana Islands
Mariana Islands
Farallon de Pajaros
Maug
Asuncion
Agrihan
Pagan
Alamagan
Guguan
Sarigan
Anatahan
Farallon de Medinilla
Saipan
Tinian
Rota
Agana
Guam (U.S.A.)
11034 Challenger Deep
Wake (U.S.A.)
Johnston (U.S.A.)
Trust Territory of the Pacific Islands (Adm. by U.S.A.)
Marshall Islands
Taongi
Bikar
Eniwetok
Bikini
Ailinginae
Rongerik
Rongelap
Utirik
Ailuk
Wotho
Likiep
Kwajalein
Ujae
Ujelang
Wotje
Maloelap
Lae
Erikub
Aur
Namu
Majuro
Arno
Ailinglapalap
Uliga
Mili
Jaluit
Namorik
Kili
Ebon
Ralik Chain
Ratak Chain
International Date Line
Federated States of Micronesia
Micronesia
Gaferut
Namonuito
Hall Islands
Murilo
Faraulep
West Fayu
Pikelot
Fayu
Nomwin
Minto
Olimarao
Lamotrek
Pulap
Truk Islands
Oroluk
Woleai
Ifalik
Elato
Satawal
Puluwat
Kuop
Losap
Senjavin Group
Pakin
Kolonia
Ponape
Mokil
Eauripik
Pulusuk
Pingelap
Namoluk
Kusaie
Satawan
Mortlock Islands
Ngatik
Caroline Islands
Nukuoro
Kapingamarangi
Kingman (U.S.A.)
Palmyra
Butaritari
Marakei
Abaiang
Tarawa
BAIRIKI
Gilbert Islands
Maiana
Abemama
Kuria
Aranuka
Equator
Nonouti
Banaba
Beru
Tabiteuea
Nukunau
Onotoa
Kingsmill Group
Tamana
Arorae
Howland (U.S.A.)
Baker
Phoenix Islands
Winslow
Abariringa
Enderbury
McKean
Birnie
Rawaki
Nikumaroro
Orona
Manra
Carondelet
KIRIBATI
MAKWA
NAURU
Melanesia
Ninigo Group
Kaniet Islands
Saint Matthias Group
Aua
Admiralty Islands
Manus
Wuvulu
Hermit Islands
New Hanover
Rambutyo
Tabar Islands
Lihir Group
New Guinea
Schouten Islands
Kavieng
Sepik
Wewak
Purdy Islands
Bismarck Archipelago
Nuguria Islands
Manam
New Ireland
Tanga Islands
Feni Islands
Green Islands
Tauu Island
Madang
Karkar
Rabaul
Nukumanu Islands
Central Range
4508
Long I.
Dumpu
Pomio
Ontong Java
Umboi
New Britain
Buka
Goroka
Lae
Bougainville
Roncador
Nomad
Solomon Sea
2743
Kieta
Solomon Islands
Panggoe
Choiseul
Santa Isabel
Kikori
PAPUA NEW GUINEA
Planet Deep
9140
New Georgia
Stewart Island
SOLOMON ISLANDS
Gulf of Papua
Morobe
Trobriand Islands
Vangunu
Dadali
Auki
Malaita
PORT MORESBY
Victoria 4073
Tufi
Woodlark
Guadalcanal
HONIARA
Torres Strait
D'Entrecasteaux Islands
Reef Islands
Duff Islands
Cape York
Louisiade Archipelago
San Cristobal
Kirakira
Nendo
Santa Cruz Islands
Rossel I.
Rennell
Utupua
Anuta
Tagula I.
Vanikoro Islands
Tikopia
Fataka
Indispensable Reefs
Cape York Peninsula
Torres Islands
Vetaounde
Vanoua Lava
Banks Islands
Lakon
VANUATU
Coral Sea
Espíritu Santo
Maewo
Luganville
Pentecost
Malekula
Ambrim
Epi
New Hebrides
VILA
Efate
Erromanga
Aniwa
Tana
Futuna
Aneityum
Huon
Récifs d'Entrecasteaux
Îles Chesterfield (Chesterfield Is.)
Île de Sable
Îles Belep
Récifs de l'Astrolabe
Koumac
Ouvéa
Îles Loyauté (Loyalty Is.)
Lifou
Nouvelle Calédonie (New Caledonia) (France)
Maré
Nouméa
Matthew
Hunter
Île des Pins
7600
6400
Great Barrier Reef
Cairns
1611
Forsayth
Townsville
Ayr
Charters Towers
Bowen
Hughenden
Mackay
Swain Reefs
Queensland
Longreach
Rockhampton
Gladstone
Bundaberg
Fraser I.
Maryborough
Gympie
Great Dividing Range
Quilpie
Roma
Charleville
Dalby
AUSTRALIA
Toowoomba
Brisbane
Ipswich
Cunnamulla
Walgett
Grafton
Bourke
1615
Armidale
Darling R.
New South Wales
Tamworth
Cobar
Dubbo
Maitland
Newcastle
Parkes
Orange
Lachlan R.
Bathurst
Sydney
Mildura
Goulburn
Wollongong
Murray R.
Wagga Wagga
CANBERRA
Albury
Horsham
Bendigo
2237
Mount Kosciusko
Australian Alps
Ballarat
Victoria
Geelong
Melbourne
Cape Howe
Yallourn
Warrnambool
Bass Strait
King Island
Flinders Island
Furneaux Group
Smithton
George Town
Devonport
Launceston
Zeehan
1617
Mount Ossa
Tasmania
Hobart
Port Arthur
South East Cape
Nanumea
Nanumanga
Niutao
Nui
Ellice Islands
Vaitupu
Nukufetau
Funafuti
FUNAFUTI
TUVALU
Nukulaelae
Niulakita
Atafu
Nukunonu
Fakaofo
Tokelau Islands
Rotuma
Wallis and Futuna (France)
Mata-Utu
Wallis
Uvéa
Futuna
Horn Islands
Alofi
WESTERN SAMOA
Swains
American Samoa
Samoa Islands
Savai'i
APIA
Upolu
Pago-Pago
Manua Islands
Tutuila
(U.S.A.)
Fiji Islands
Vanua Levu
Ringgold Isles
1031
Yasawa Group
1324
Koro
Lau Group
Viti Levu
SUVA
Kandavu
Vatoa
Ono-i-Lau Islands
FIJI
Ceva-i-Ra
Conway Reef
Niuafo'ou
Tafahi
Niuato Putapu
TONGA
Fonualei
Vava'u Group
Tonga Islands
Ha'apai Group
Kotu Group
Nomuka Group
NUKU'ALOFA
Tongatapu Group
Ata
Minerva Reefs
Tropic of Capricorn
10882 Horizon Deep
Alofi
Niue
Antiope
Beveridge
Pukapuka
Rakahanga
Manihiki
Nassau
Northern
Cook Islands
Suvorov
Cook Islands (New Zealand)
Palmerston
Norfolk Is. (Austr.)
Kingston
Raoul
Macauley
Kermadec Islands (New Zealand)
Curtis
L'Esperance Rock
9994 Galathea Deep
Lord Howe I. (Austr.)
Tasman Sea
Three Kings Island
North Cape
Whangarei
Great Barrier
Auckland
Manukau
Bay of Plenty
East Cape
Hamilton
Tauranga
North Island
Gisborne
New Plymouth
Ruapehu
2797
Napier
NEW ZEALAND
Cape Farewell
Cook Strait
Palmerston North
Nelson
WELLINGTON
Westport
2338
Blenheim
Hokitika
South Island
Mount Cook 3764
Christchurch
Southern Alps
Haast
Canterbury Bight
Wanaka
Timaru
Manapouri
Dunedin
West Cape
Invercargill
Stewart I.
Foveaux Strait
Southwest Cape
Chatham Islands (N.Z.)
Chatham
Pitt
6100
8700
6900
4300
2400
7300
20
4700
5000
4100
5600
2100
15°
30°
45°
© ESSELTE MAP SERVICE

PACIFIC OCEAN
Hawaiian Islands
Honolulu
Oahu
Molokai
Maui
Lanai
Kahoolawe
Hawi
Mauna Kea
Hilo
Mauna Loa
Hawaii
Hawaii (U.S.A.)
Tropic of Cancer
Cape San Lucas
Tepic
Guadalajara
MEXICO
Manzanillo
Revilla Gigedo Islands (Mexico)
Clipperton (Fr.)
Equator
Tabuaeran
Kirimati (Kiritimati) (Christmas I.)
Malden
Starbuck
Vostok
Caroline
Flint
Polynesia
Marquesas Islands (France)
Eiao
Hatutu
Nuku Hiva
Ua Huka
Ua Pou
Fatu Hutu
Hiva Oa
Tahuata
Rocher Thomasset
Fatu Hiva
Îles du Désappointement
Napuka
Pukapuka
Manihi
Ahe
Rangiroa
Îles du Roi Georges
Mataiva
Îles Palliser
Apataki
Aratika
Takume
Raroia
Angatau
Fakahina
Makatea
Kaukura
Niau
Fakarava
Raraka
Makemo
Nihiru
Tuamotu Archipelago
Tahanea
Motutunga
Marutea
Tehuata
Amanu
Haraiki
Reitoru
Ravahere
Tauere
Hao
Nengonengo
Manuangi
Paraoa
Pinaki
Vahitahi
Pukaruha
Reao
Tatakoto
Ahunui
Vairaatea
Vanavana
Tureia
Îles du Duc de Gloucester
Tematangi
Group Actaeon
Marutea
Mururoa
Maria
Fangataufa
Morane
Mangareva
Temoe
Gambier Islands
Motu One
Manuae
Maupiti
Maupihaa
Leeward Islands
Bora-Bora
Huahine
Raiatea
Moorea
Maiao
Tetiaroa
Papeete
Tahiti
Windward Islands
Society Islands
Hereheretue
French Polynesia
Maria
Rimatara
Rurutu
Tubuai
Tubuai Islands
Raevavae
Rapa
Ilots de Bass
Oeno
Henderson
Ducie
Adamstown
Pitcairn
(U.K.)
Tropic of Capricorn
Sala y Gómes (Chile)
Easter Island (Rapa Nui) (Chile)
Cook Islands
Aitutaki
Manuae
Mitiaro
Atiu
Mauke
Rarotonga
Mangaia
Ernest Legouvé
Maria Theresa
MERCATOR'S PROJECTION
Scale 1:27 000 000
0 500 1000 km
0 200 400 600 miles

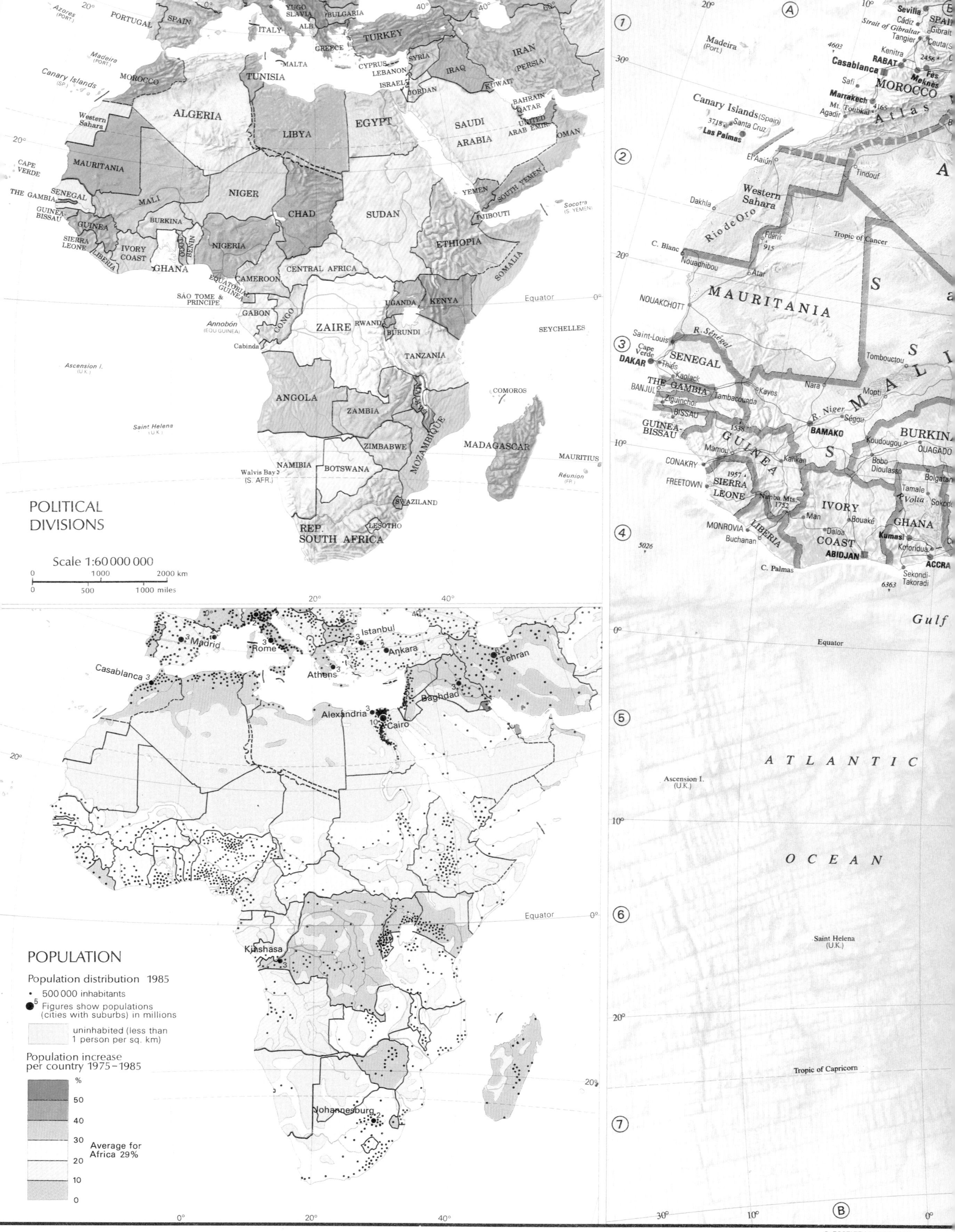

POLITICAL DIVISIONS
Scale 1:60 000 000
0 1000 2000 km
0 500 1000 miles
Azores (PORT.)
PORTUGAL
SPAIN
YUGOSLAVIA
BULGARIA
ITALY
ALB.
TURKEY
GREECE
MALTA
CYPRUS
LEBANON
SYRIA
IRAQ
IRAN (PERSIA)
ISRAEL
JORDAN
KUWAIT
Madeira (PORT.)
Canary Islands (SP.)
MOROCCO
TUNISIA
ALGERIA
LIBYA
EGYPT
SAUDI ARABIA
BAHRAIN
QATAR
UNITED ARAB EMIR.
OMAN
Western Sahara
CAPE VERDE
MAURITANIA
THE GAMBIA
SENEGAL
GUINEA-BISSAU
GUINEA
SIERRA LEONE
LIBERIA
MALI
NIGER
CHAD
SUDAN
YEMEN
SOUTH YEMEN
Socotra (S. YEMEN)
DJIBOUTI
BURKINA
IVORY COAST
GHANA
TOGO
BENIN
NIGERIA
ETHIOPIA
SOMALIA
CENTRAL AFRICA
CAMEROON
EQUATORIAL GUINEA
SÃO TOME & PRINCIPE
GABON
CONGO
ZAIRE
UGANDA
KENYA
RWANDA
BURUNDI
Equator
Annobón (EQU.GUINEA)
Cabinda
SEYCHELLES
TANZANIA
Ascension I. (U.K.)
ANGOLA
ZAMBIA
MALAWI
COMOROS
Saint Helena (U.K.)
ZIMBABWE
MOZAMBIQUE
MADAGASCAR
MAURITIUS
Réunion (FR.)
NAMIBIA
Walvis Bay (S. AFR.)
BOTSWANA
SWAZILAND
LESOTHO
REP. SOUTH AFRICA
POPULATION
Population distribution 1985
500 000 inhabitants
Figures show populations (cities with suburbs) in millions
uninhabited (less than 1 person per sq. km)
Population increase per country 1975–1985
%
50
40
30
Average for Africa 29%
20
10
0
Madrid
Rome
Istanbul
Ankara
Tehran
Casablanca
Athens
Baghdad
Alexandria
Cairo
Kinshasa
Johannesburg
Sevilla
Cádiz
Strait of Gibraltar
Gibraltar
Tangier
Ceuta
Kenitra
RABAT
Casablanca
Fes
Meknès
Safi
MOROCCO
Marrakech
Mt. Toubkal
4165
Agadir
Atlas
Madeira (Port.)
Canary Islands (Spain)
3718
Santa Cruz
Las Palmas
El Aaiún
Tindouf
Western Sahara
Dakhla
Rio de Oro
Tropic of Cancer
Fdérik
915
C. Blanc
Nouadhibou
Atar
MAURITANIA
NOUAKCHOTT
Saint-Louis
R. Sénégal
Cape Verde
DAKAR
Thiès
SENEGAL
Kaolack
THE GAMBIA
BANJUL
Tambacounda
Kayes
Nara
Tombouctou
Mopti
Ziguinchor
BISSAU
GUINEA-BISSAU
R. Niger
Ségou
BAMAKO
MALI
GUINEA
Mamou
Kankan
Koudougou
OUAGADOUGOU
BURKINA
CONAKRY
FREETOWN
SIERRA LEONE
1957
Nimba Mts.
1752
Man
Bobo Dioulasso
Tamale
Volta
Bolgatanga
Sokodé
IVORY COAST
Bouaké
Daloa
GHANA
Kumasi
Koforidua
MONROVIA
LIBERIA
Buchanan
ABIDJAN
ACCRA
C. Palmas
Sekondi-Takoradi
5026
6363
Gulf
Equator
ATLANTIC
Ascension I. (U.K.)
OCEAN
Saint Helena (U.K.)
Tropic of Capricorn

Cagliari
Sardinia
ITALY
Palermo
Mt. Etna
Sicily
Catania
VALLETTA
MALTA
ALGIERS
Bejaïa
Constantine
Skikda
Annaba
Bizerta
TUNIS
Sousse
Sfax
Gabès
Sétif
Biskra
Djelfa
TUNISIA
Ghardaïa
Touggourt
Hassi Messaoud
Ouargla
Grand Erg Oriental
Goléa
In Salah
Ahaggar
Tamanrasset
ATHENS
GREECE
Crete
Izmir
ANKARA
TURKEY
Antalya
Adana
Aleppo
Mosul
Nineveh
Kirkuk
R. Tigris
TEHRĀN
IRAN
Qom
Esfahan
Yazd
Kermān
Zāhedān
Zagros Mountains
NICOSIA
CYPRUS
LEBANON
BEIRUT
Latakia
SYRIA
DAMASCUS
BAGHDĀD
IRAQ
An Najaf
R. Euphrates
Ahvāz
Khorramshahr
Ābādān
Persepolis
Shīrāz
Basra
KUWAIT
Bandar Abbās
Mediterranean Sea
TRIPOLI
Zuara
Misrātah
Tripolitania
Benghazi
Beida
Tubruq
Sirte
Ajdābiyā
Cyrenaica
Alexandria
Haifa
ISRAEL
Tel Aviv-Yafo
Port Said
AMMĀN
JORDAN
JERUSALEM
Tanta
Suez Canal
Suez
Sinai Pen.
Giza
CAIRO
Matrūh
Qattara Depr.
Siwah
Banī Suwayf
Al Minyā
Asyūt
Qina
Luxor
Thebes
Idfū
Aswān
Al Khārijah
EGYPT
R. Nile
LIBYA
Libyan Desert
Fezzan
Sabhā
Awbārī
Kufra Oases
Al Kufrah
L. Nasser
Wādī Halfā
Nubian Desert
Port Sudan
Red Sea
Hejaz
Nafud
Persian Gulf
BAHRAIN
AL MANĀMAH
DOHA
QATAR
Dubayy
UNITED ARAB EMIRATES
Gulf of Oman
MUSCAT
Az Zahrān
Buraydah
'Unayzah
Al Hufūf
RIYADH
SAUDI ARABIA
Nejd
Medina
Yanbu
Jiddah
Mecca
Al Qunfudhah
Rub al Khali
OMAN
Tropic of Cancer
Salālah
Sahara
Air
Tibesti
Mt. Emi Koussi
Bilma
Agadez
Faya-Largeau
NIGER
CHAD
Tahoua
Maradi
Zinder
Sokoto
Kano
Zaria
Kaduna
Jos
Bauchi
Abuja
Maiduguri
N'DJAMENA
L. Chad
Abéché
NIGERIA
R. Niger
R. Benue
Ogbomosho
Ibadan
LAGOS
Enugu
Onitsha
Aba
Port Harcourt
Calabar
Mt. Cameroon
Adamaoua Mts.
CAMEROON
Nkongsamba
Douala
YAOUNDÉ
Bioko
MALABO
Garoua
Moundou
Sarh
R. Chari
Oubangui-Chari
CENTRAL AFRICAN REPUBLIC
Bouar
Berbérati
BANGUI
Bangassou
Nubia
Atbarah
R. Atbarah
Omdurman
KHARTOUM
Kassala
Wad Medanī
El Fasher
El Obeid
Marra Mts.
Nyala
SUDAN
Malakāl
Wau
White Nile
Blue Nile
Juba
Massawa
Eritrea
Asmara
YEMEN
SAN'Ā
Hodeida
Ta'izz
SOUTH YEMEN
Hadramawt
Al Mukallā
ADEN
Gulf of Aden
Socotra (S.Yemen)
C. Guardafui
Ras Dashan
Gondar
L. Tana
Dessye
DJIBOUTI
Berbera
Hargeysa
Diredawa
Harer
ADDIS ABABA
ETHIOPIA
Ogaden
Jimma
Virga Alam
R. Juba
SOMALIA
L. Turkana
Isha Baydabo
MOGADISHU
Kismayu
Equator
Equatorial Guinea
Bata
SÃO TOMÉ AND PRÍNCIPE
São Tomé
Príncipe
LIBREVILLE
C. Lopez
GABON
CONGO
R. Oubangui
R. Congo
R. Zaire
Mbandaka
R. Uele
Aketi
Buta
Isiro
Kabarega Falls
L. Albert
UGANDA
Mount Elgon
Tororo
Jinja
KAMPALA
Entebbe
Lake Victoria
KENYA
Nanyuki
Kisumu
Nakuru
Mount Kenya
NAIROBI
Kisangani
Boyoma Falls
Mt. Ruwenzori
L. Rutanzige (L. Edward)
Ubundi
L. Mai-Ndombe
ZAIRE
Lake Kivu
Bukavu
KIGALI
RWANDA
BUJUMBURA
BURUNDI
Mwanza
SERENGETI NAT. PARK
Mt. Kilimanjaro
Arusha
Voi
Mombasa
Pemba I.
Masai Steppe
Tanga
Zanzibar
DAR ES SALAAM
Loubomo
BRAZZAVILLE
KINSHASA
Pointe Noire
Cabinda (Angola)
Livingstone Falls
Boma
Matadi
Bandundu
R. Kasai
Ilebo
Kindu
Kongolo
Kigoma
Tabora
Kananga
Mbuji-Mayi
R. Kwango
Kabalo
Kalemie
L. Tanganyika
TANZANIA
Dodoma
Kilosa
Iringa
Rift Valley
R. Lualaba
Kamina
Shaba
Mbeya
L. Mweru
Kasama
L. Bangweulu
L. Malawi
R. Ruvuma
Mtwara
LUANDA
Malanje
R. Cuanza
ANGOLA
Luena
Kolwezi
Likasi
Lubumbashi
Kitwe
Ndola
Luanshya
Lobito
Benguela
Huambo
R. Zambezi
ZAMBIA
Kabwe
Mongu
LUSAKA
R. Kafue
MALAWI
Mzuzu
LILONGWE
Lichinga
Blantyre
Zomba
Tete
Namibe
Lubango
Menongue
R. Cunene
R. Cubango
Ovambo
Caprivi Strip
Livingstone
Victoria Falls
Wankie
L. Kariba
HARARE
Kadoma
Que Que
Gweru
ZIMBABWE
Mutare
Beira
Quelimane
Moçambique
MOZAMBIQUE
Grootfontein
Okavango Swamp
Makgadikgadi Pans
Bulawayo
Zimbabwe
NAMIBIA
Namib Desert
Swakopmund
Walvis Bay (S. Africa)
WINDHOEK
Gobabis
BOTSWANA
Serowe
Kalahari Desert
R. Limpopo
KRUGER NAT. PARK
Pietersburg
GABORONE
Krugersdorp
PRETORIA
Johannesburg
Klerksdorp
MAPUTO
MBABANE
SWAZILAND
Inhambane
Lüderitz
Keetmanshoop
Hotazel
R. Vaal
Vereeniging
Upington
Welkom
Kimberley
Bloemfontein
MASERU
LESOTHO
R. Orange
Drakensberg
Richards Bay
Pietermaritzburg
Durban
Bitterfontein
REP. SOUTH AFRICA
Calvinia
Graaff Reinet
Queenstown
Umtata
East London
Saldanha
CAPE TOWN
Paarl
Karroo
Worcester
Uitenhage
Grahamstown
Port Elizabeth
Cape of Good Hope
C. Agulhas
INDIAN OCEAN
SEYCHELLES
VICTORIA
Amirante Is. (Sey.)
Aldabra Is. (Sey.)
MORONI
COMOROS
Mayotte (France)
Cap Bobraomby
Antsiranana
Mt. Tsaratanana
Mahajanga
Mozambique Channel
Tromelin (Fr.)
ANTANANARIVO
Toamasina
Antsirabe
MADAGASCAR
Fianarantsoa
Toliara
Tropic of Capricorn
Taolanaro
Cap Vohimena
PORT LOUIS
MAURITIUS
St. Denis
Réunion (France)
MILLER'S STEREOGRAPHIC PROJECTION
Scale 1:25 000 000
0 500 1000 km
0 200 400 600 miles

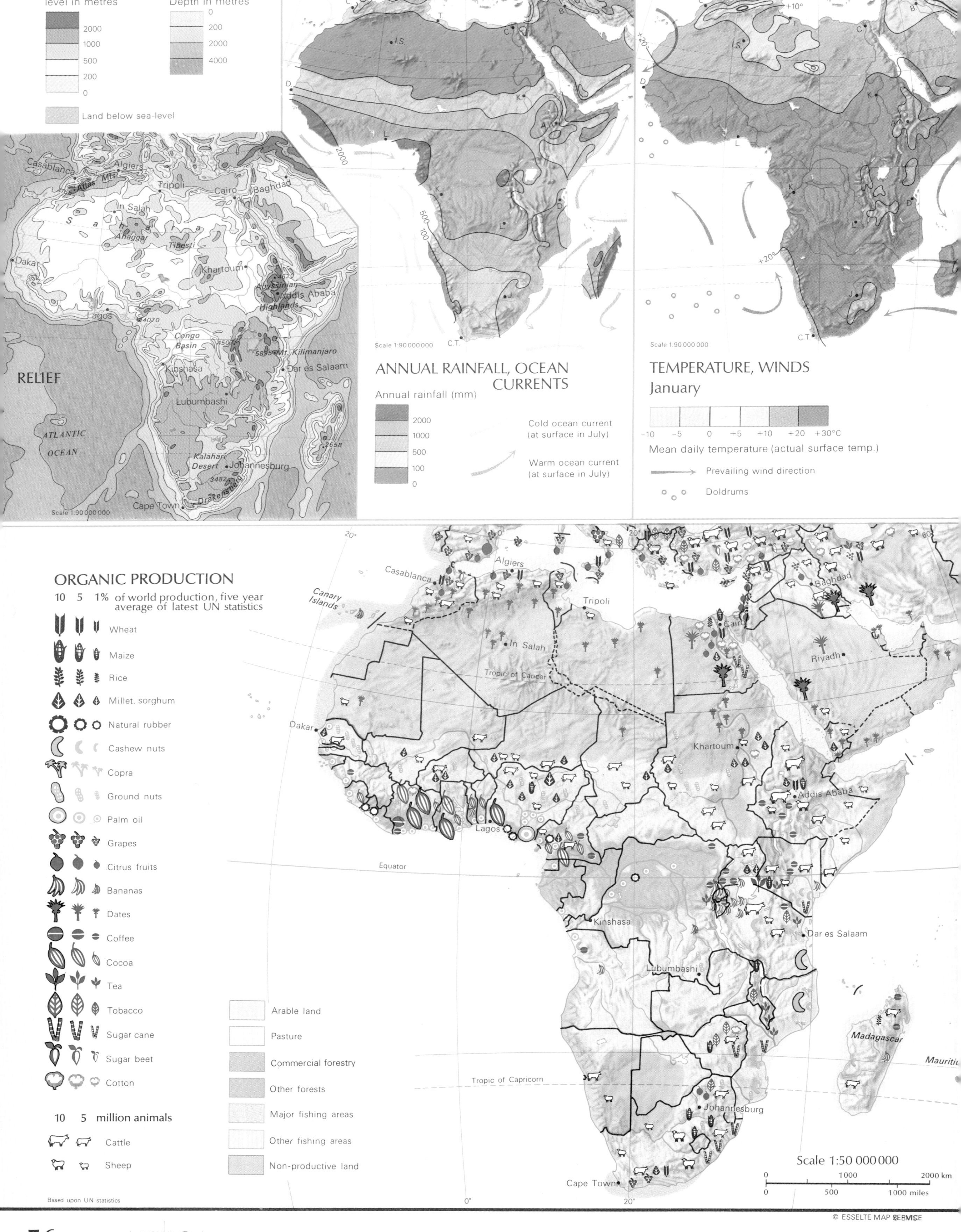
Height above sea-level in metres
2000
1000
500
200
0
Depth in metres
0
200
2000
4000
Land below sea-level
RELIEF
Casablanca
Algiers
Atlas Mts.
Tripoli
Cairo
Baghdad
In Salah
Sahara
Ahaggar
Tibesti
Dakar
Khartoum
Abyssinian Highlands
Addis Ababa
Lagos
Congo Basin
Mt. Kilimanjaro
Kinshasa
Dar es Salaam
Lubumbashi
ATLANTIC OCEAN
Kalahari Desert
Johannesburg
Drakensberg
Cape Town
Scale 1:90 000 000
ANNUAL RAINFALL, OCEAN CURRENTS
Annual rainfall (mm)
2000
1000
500
100
0
Cold ocean current (at surface in July)
Warm ocean current (at surface in July)
TEMPERATURE, WINDS
January
-10 -5 0 +5 +10 +20 +30°C
Mean daily temperature (actual surface temp.)
Prevailing wind direction
Doldrums
ORGANIC PRODUCTION
10 5 1% of world production, five year average of latest UN statistics
Wheat
Maize
Rice
Millet, sorghum
Natural rubber
Cashew nuts
Copra
Ground nuts
Palm oil
Grapes
Citrus fruits
Bananas
Dates
Coffee
Cocoa
Tea
Tobacco
Sugar cane
Sugar beet
Cotton
10 5 million animals
Cattle
Sheep
Arable land
Pasture
Commercial forestry
Other forests
Major fishing areas
Other fishing areas
Non-productive land
Canary Islands
Riyadh
Tropic of Cancer
Equator
Tropic of Capricorn
Madagascar
Mauritius
Scale 1:50 000 000
0 1000 2000 km
0 500 1000 miles
Based upon UN statistics
© ESSELTE MAP SERVICE

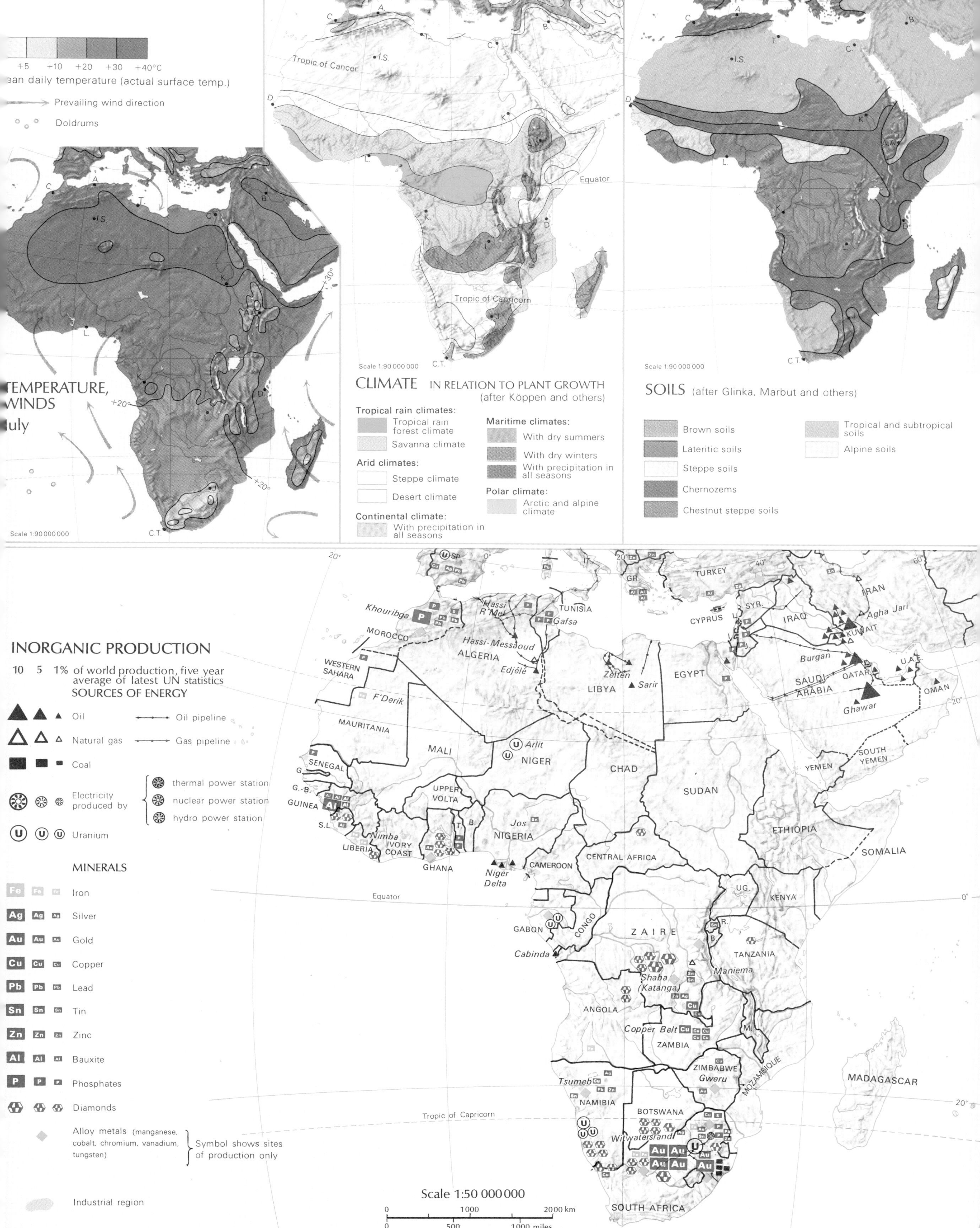
+5 +10 +20 +30 +40°C
ean daily temperature (actual surface temp.)
Prevailing wind direction
Doldrums
TEMPERATURE,
WINDS
July
Scale 1:90 000 000
CLIMATE IN RELATION TO PLANT GROWTH
(after Köppen and others)
Tropical rain climates:
Tropical rain forest climate
Savanna climate
Arid climates:
Steppe climate
Desert climate
Continental climate:
With precipitation in all seasons
Maritime climates:
With dry summers
With dry winters
With precipitation in all seasons
Polar climate:
Arctic and alpine climate
Tropic of Cancer
Equator
Tropic of Capricorn
Scale 1:90 000 000
SOILS (after Glinka, Marbut and others)
Brown soils
Lateritic soils
Steppe soils
Chernozems
Chestnut steppe soils
Tropical and subtropical soils
Alpine soils
Scale 1:90 000 000
INORGANIC PRODUCTION
10 5 1% of world production, five year average of latest UN statistics
SOURCES OF ENERGY
Oil
Oil pipeline
Natural gas
Gas pipeline
Coal
Electricity produced by
thermal power station
nuclear power station
hydro power station
Uranium
MINERALS
Iron
Silver
Gold
Copper
Lead
Tin
Zinc
Bauxite
Phosphates
Diamonds
Alloy metals (manganese, cobalt, chromium, vanadium, tungsten)
Symbol shows sites of production only
Industrial region
Based upon UN statistics
MOROCCO
Khouribga
Hassi R'Mel
Hassi-Messaoud
ALGERIA
Edjélé
TUNISIA
Gafsa
WESTERN SAHARA
F'Derik
MAURITANIA
MALI
Arlit
NIGER
LIBYA
Zelten
Sarir
EGYPT
CHAD
SUDAN
TURKEY
CYPRUS
SYR.
IRAQ
IRAN
Agha Jari
KUWAIT
Burgan
QATAR
U.A.E.
SAUDI ARABIA
Ghawar
OMAN
YEMEN
SOUTH YEMEN
ETHIOPIA
SOMALIA
SENEGAL
G.-B.
GUINEA
S.L.
LIBERIA
Nimba
IVORY COAST
GHANA
UPPER VOLTA
NIGERIA
Jos
Niger Delta
CAMEROON
CENTRAL AFRICA
GABON
CONGO
Cabinda
ZAIRE
Shaba (Katanga)
Maniema
UG.
KENYA
TANZANIA
ANGOLA
Copper Belt
ZAMBIA
ZIMBABWE
Gweru
MOZAMBIQUE
MADAGASCAR
Tsumeb
NAMIBIA
BOTSWANA
Witwatersrand
SOUTH AFRICA
Equator
Tropic of Capricorn
Scale 1:50 000 000
0 1000 2000 km
0 500 1000 miles
MILLER'S STEREOGRAPHIC PROJECTION

Scale 1:10 000 000

ITALY
Sardinia
Sicily
Palermo
Messina
Reggio di Calabria
Catania
Siracusa
Ionian Sea
GREECE
Peleponnese
Cyclades
Rhodes
Sea of Crete
Crete
Iraklion
Khánia
MALTA
VALLETTA
Mediterranean Sea
AL JAZĀ'IR (ALGIERS)
Blida
Ech Cheliff
Skikda
Annaba
Constantine
Sétif
Batna
Biskra
TUNIS
TUNISIA
Safāqis (Sfax)
Qābis (Gabès)
Khalīj Qābis
Jarbah
TARĀBULUS (TRIPOLI)
Misrātah
Jabal Nafūsah
Tripolitania
Khalīj Sirt (Gulf of Sirt)
Benghazi
Al Bayḑā' (Beida)
Darnah
Tubruq
Cyrenaica
Al Jabal al Akhḑar
Ouargla
Touggourt
Ghardaïa
Laghouat
Grand Erg Oriental
Al Ḩamādah al Ḩamrā'
Ghadāmis
Sabhā
Fezzan
Idhān Murzuq
Ghāt
Tassili N-Ajjer
Ahaggar
Hoggar
Tamanrasset
Plateau du Tademaït
LIBYA
Libyan Desert
EGYPT
Sarīr Kalanshiyū
Ramlat Rabyānah
Wāḩāt al Kufrah (Kufra Oases)
Tropic of Cancer
Sahara
Tibesti
Emi Koussi
Plateau du Djado
Ténéré du Tafassasset
Aïr
Agadez
Erg de Ténéré
Grand Erg de Bilma
Bilma
NIGER
Talak
Tagama
Kaouar
Borkou
Ennedi
Bodélé
CHAD
Kanem
Lake Chad
N'DJAMENA
Abéché
Ouaddaï
SUDAN
Al Junaynah
Batha
Guéra
Baguirmi
Salamat
Sarh
CENTRAL AFRICAN REPUBLIC
CAMEROON
Maroua
Garoua
Maiduguri
Bornu
Kano
Katsina
Sokoto
Zaria
Kaduna
Bauchi
Jos
Jos Plateau
NIGERIA
NIAMEY
Zinder
Maradi
BENIN
Niger
Benue
Ilorin
Adrar des Iforas
59

Mediterranean Sea
Ionian Sea
Sicily
Siracusa
MALTA
GREECE
ATHINAI (ATHENS)
Peloponnese
Sea of Crete
Crete
Iraklion
Rhodes
Cyclades
T U R K
Konya
Adana
Antalya
Taurus Mountains
CYPRUS
NICOSIA
Limassol
LEBANON
BAYRŪT (BEIRUT)
DIMASHQ (DAMASCUS)
ISRAEL
Tel Aviv-Yafo
YERUSHALAYIM (JERUSALEM)
'AMMAN
JORDAN (AL URDUN)
TRIPOLI (TARĀBULUS)
Benghazi
Khalīj Sirt (Gulf of Sirt)
Cyrenaica
Tripolitania
L I B Y A
Fezzan
Sabhā
Libyan Desert
Ramlat Rabyānah
Wāḥāt al Kufrah (Kufra Oases)
Sarīr Kalanshiyū
As Sarīr
Baḥr ar Rimāl al 'Aẓīm
Al Iskandarīyah (Alexandria)
AL QAHIRAH (CAIRO)
Al Jīzah (Giza)
Būr Sa'īd (Port Said)
As Suways (Suez)
Munkhafaḍ al Qaṭṭārah (Qattara Depression)
Sīnā' (Sinai)
E G Y P T (MISR)
Aṣ Ṣaḥrā' al Gharbīyah
Aṣ Ṣaḥrā' ash Sharqīyah
Aṣ Ṣaḥrā' al Janūbīyah
Asyūṭ
Al Uqṣur (Luxor)
Aswān
ASWAN HIGH DAM
Birkat Nasser (Lake Nasser)
Tropic of Cancer
S a h a r a
Tibesti
Emi Koussi
Sarīr Tibistī
Borkou
Ennedi
Erg du Djourab
C H A D
Abéché
Ouaddaï
Sahel
Wādī Ḥalfā'
Aṣ Ṣaḥrā' an Nūbiyah (Nubian Desert)
Baḥr an Nīl (Nile)
S U D A N
Nūbiyah (Nubia)
Umm Durmān (Omdurman)
AL KHARTŪM (KHARTOUM)
Kassalā
Būr Sūdān
Wad Madanī
Kurdufān
Dārfūr
Marra Mountains
Al Fāshir (El Fasher)
Baḥr al Ghazāl
Bahr al Azraq (Blue Nile)
Bahr al Abyad (White Nile)
Lake Tana
CENTRAL AFRICAN REPUBLIC
© ESSELTE MAP SERVICE

Scale 1:10 000 000

0 100 200 300 400 km

0 100 200 miles

MAURITANIA
NOUAKCHOTT
Nouadhibou
Cap Blanc
Ile Tidra
Cap Timiris
Atar
Akjoujt
Adrar
Tagant
Kiffa
Néma
Oualata
Aoukâr
Hodh
El Mreyer
Taoudenni
El Djouf
Erg Atouila
Erg in Sakkane
Tanezrouft
Adrar des Iforas
Kidal
MALI
BAMAKO
Tombouctou
Gao
Mopti
Ségou
Kayes
Sikasso
Niger
Lac Faguibine
Hombori
SENEGAL
DAKAR
Cap Vert
Thiès
Saint-Louis
Kaolack
Ziguinchor
Sénégal
THE GAMBIA
BANJUL
Gambia
GUINEA-BISSAU
BISSAU
Arquipélago dos Bijagós
GUINEA
CONAKRY
Fouta Djallon
Kankan
SIERRA LEONE
FREETOWN
LIBERIA
MONROVIA
IVORY COAST
ABIDJAN
Bouaké
BURKINA
OUAGADOUGOU
Bobo Dioulasso
GHANA
ACCRA
Kumasi
Tamale
Lake Volta
TOGO
LOMÉ
BENIN
PORTO-NOVO
Cotonou
NIAMEY
Gulf of Guinea
Bight of Benin
Grain Coast
Ivory Coast
Gold Coast
Cape Palmas
Cape Three Points
ATLANTIC OCEAN
Equator
CAPE VERDE
(CABO VERDE)
Santo Antão
São Vicente
Mindelo
Santa Luzia
São Nicolau
Sal
Boa Vista
Maio
São Tiago
Fogo
Brava
PRAIA

Scale 1:10 000 000

0 100 200 300 400 km
0 100 200 miles

CHAD
SUDAN
CENTRAL AFRICAN REPUBLIC
ZAÏRE
CONGO
UGANDA
RWANDA
BURUNDI
ANGOLA
ZAMBIA
TANZA
N'DJAMENA
AL KHARTUM (KHARTOUM)
Al Khartum Bahri
Umm Durmān
BANGUI
KINSHASA
BRAZZAVILLE
LUANDA
KAMPALA
KIGALI
BUJUMBURA
Kisangani
Mbandaka
Kananga
Mbuji-Mayi
Lubumbashi
Likasi
Kolwezi
Matadi
Kikwit
Bandundu
Ilebo
Bukavu
Goma
Kigoma
Tabora
Mwanza
Jinja
Entebbe
Gulu
Juba
Wad Madanī
Al Ubayyid (El Obeid)
Al Fāshir (El Fasher)
Nyala
Abéché
Sarh
Moundou
Garoua
Maroua
Berbérati
Bangassou
Bambari
Lake Chad
Lake Victoria
Lake Tanganyika
Lake Kyoga
Lake Albert
Lake Edward
Lake Kivu
Lake Rukwa
Lac Mai-Ndombe
Lac Tumba
Lac Moero (Lake Mweru)
Lake Bangweulu
Sahel
Kanem
Bodélé
Borkou
Ennedi
Baguirmi
Batha
Guéra
Salamat
Ouaddaï
Dar Sila
Kurdufān
Dar Hamar
Dar Nūbah
Nūbiyah
Al Iglīm al Janūbīyah
Jonglei
Sudd
Equateur
Haut-Zaïre
Kivu
Kasai Occidental
Kasai Oriental
Shaba
Bandundu
Cuvette
Plateaux
Pool
Sangha
Likouala
Cuanza Norte
Lunda Norte
Zaire
Jabal Marrah 3088
Ruwenzori 5119
Chutes de Livingstone (Livingstone Falls)
Chutes Ngaliema (Stanley Falls)
Kabarega Falls (Murchison Falls)
Portes d'Enfer
Chutes de Katende (Katende Falls)
Chutes Tembo (Tembo Falls)
Chutes de la Lufira (Lufira Falls)
Kalambo Falls
Ash Shallāl as Sablūkah (Sixth Cataract)
Bahr al Ghazal
Bahr al Abyad (White Nile)
Bahr al Azraq (Blue Nile)
Ubangi
Congo
Kasai
Lualaba
Chari
Logone
Salonga National Park
Garamba National Park
Virunga
Monts Mitumba
© ESSELTE MAP SERVICE

Red Sea
Dahlak Archipelago
Jaza'ir Farasān
Kamarān
Y E M E N
SAN'Ā'
Hadramawt
SOUTH YEMEN
Quayti
Ramlat as Sab'atayn
Al Mukallā
Ra's Fartak
Wādī al Masīlah
Suquṭrā (Socotra)
(S.Yemen)
Jabal Hajhir
'Abd al Kūrī
Al Ikhwān
Ra's Asir (Cape Guardafui)
Al Hudaydah (Hodeida)
Ta'izz
Bāb al Mandab
Barim (S.Yemen)
Shaykh 'Uthmān
BALADIYAT 'ADAN (ADEN)
Little Aden
Gulf of Aden
Asmara
Massawa
Keren
Eritrea
Adwa
Makale
Ras Dashan
Danakil Plain
Lake Afrēra
Assab
DJIBOUTI
Golfe de Tadjourah
Zeila
Berbera
Hargeysa
Dessye
Lake Tana
Awash
Diredawa
Harar
Jijiga
ADDIS ABABA
Shoa
E T H I O P I A
Ethiopian Plateau
Adama
Lake Zwai
Lake Shala
Jimma
Webbe Shibeli
Bale
Sidamo
L. Abaya
Lake Chamo
Lake Stefanie
Lake Turkana (Lake Rudolf)
Haud
Ogaden
Hararge
Nugāl
Migiurtinia
Ras Hāfūn
Hāfūn (Dante)
Ras el Cheil
Mudug
Beled Weyne
Hobyā (Obbia)
Mahadday Weyne
S O M A L I A
Benadir
MUQDISHO (MOGADISHU)
Marka
Baraawe
Baydabo
Juba
Kismāyu
Bajun Islands
Ra's Chiamboni
Chalbi Desert
Marsabit
Mount Nyiru
K E N Y A
Nanyuki
Mount Kenya
Meru
Lake Rudolf
Garissa
Tana
Lamu
Pate Island
Manda Island
Malindi
Ras Ngomeni
NAIROBI
Kilimanjaro
Arusha
Moshi
Tsavo N.P.
Mombasa
Kilindini
Tanga
Masai Steppe
Pemba Island
Chake Chake
Zanzibar
Zanzibar Island
DAR ES SALAAM
Morogoro
Mafia Island
Selous Game Reserve
Rufiji
Kilwa Kivinje
Kilwa Masoko
Kilwa Kisiwani
Lindi
Mtwara
Mikindani
Cabo Delgado
Ruvuma
Mocímboa da Praia
I N D I A N
O C E A N
Equator
SEYCHELLES
Praslin
Silhouette
La Digue
VICTORIA
African Is.
Eagle
Saint Joseph
Amirante Islands (Sey.)
Poivre Is.
Île Desrouches
Platte
Ile des Noefs
Alphonse
Bijoutier
St. Francois
Coetivy (Sey.)
Providence
Saint Pierre
Cerf
Aldabra Islands (Sey.)
Cosmoledo Group
Assumption
Astove
Farquhar Group
Scale 1:10 000 000
0 100 200 300 400 km
0 100 200 miles

ATLANTIC OCEAN
ANGOLA
NAMIBIA
BOTSWANA
SOUTH AFRICA
ZAIRE
ZAMBI
ZIMB
LESOTHO
Tropic of Capricorn
Namib Desert
Kalahari
Cape Province
Orange Free State
Transvaal
Shaba
Lunda Norte
Lunda Sul
Cuanza Norte
Cuanza Sul
Huambo
Bié
Moxico
Huíla
Cunene
Cuando Cubango
Ovamboland
Damaraland
Namaland
Ngamiland
Barotseland
Copperbelt
LUANDA
Malanje
Lobito
Benguela
Lubango
Namibe
WINDHOEK
Walvis Bay
(S. Africa)
Swakopmund
Lüderitz
GABORONE
LUSAKA
Livingstone
(Maramba)
Lubumbashi
Bulawayo
PRETORIA
Johannesburg
Kimberley
Bloemfontein
MASERU
Pietermaritzburg
Port Elizabeth
East London
CAPE TOWN
Cape of Good Hope
Cape Agulhas
Okavango Swamp
Etosha Pan
Makgadikgadi Pan
(Makarikari)
Lake Ngami
Victoria Falls
Kalahari Gemsbok N.P.
Great Karroo
Drakensberg
10°
15°
20°
25°
30°
A
B
C
D
1
2
3
4
5
6

Scale 1:10 000 000

POLITICAL DIVISIONS
Names of the American states, with their standard abbreviations
AL. Alabama
AK. Alaska
AZ. Arizona
AR. Arkansas
CA. California
CO. Colorado
CT. Connecticut
DE. Delaware
FL. Florida
GA. Georgia
HI. Hawaii
ID. Idaho
IL. Illinois
IN. Indiana
IA. Iowa
KS. Kansas
KY. Kentucky
LA. Louisiana
ME. Maine
MD. Maryland
MA. Massachusetts
MI. Michigan
MN. Minnesota
MS. Mississippi
MO. Missouri
MT. Montana
NE. Nebraska
NV. Nevada
N.H. New Hampshire
N.J. New Jersey
N.M. New Mexico
N.Y. New York
N.C. North Carolina
N.D. North Dakota
OH. Ohio
OK. Oklahoma
OR. Oregon
PA. Pennsylvania
R.I. Rhode Island
S.C. South Carolina
S.D. South Dakota
TN. Tennessee
TX. Texas
UT. Utah
VT. Vermont
VA. Virginia
WA. Washington
W.V. West Virginia
WI. Wisconsin
WY. Wyoming
D.C. District of Columbia (Federal)
CANADA
UNITED STATES
MEXICO
Greenland (DENMARK)
ICELAND
Northwest Territories
Yukon
British Columbia
Alberta
Saskatchewan
Manitoba
Ontario
Québec
Newfoundland and Labrador
New Br.
Prince Edw. I.
Nova Scotia
Bermuda (U.K.)
THE BAHAMAS
CUBA
HAITI
DOMINICAN REPUBLIC
Puerto Rico (U.S.A.)
JAMAICA
BELIZE
HONDURAS
GUATEMALA
EL SALVADOR
NICARAGUA
COSTA RICA
PANAMA
VENEZUELA
COLOMBIA
POPULATION
Population distribution 1985
• 500 000 inhabitants
●3 Figures show populations (cities with suburbs) in millions
uninhabited (less than 1 person per sq.km)
Population increase per country 1975–1985
50%
40
30
20 Average for North and Central America 10%
10
0
Scale 1:60 000 000
0 1000 2000 km
0 500 1000 miles
San Francisco 5
Los Angeles 12
Minneapolis 2
Chicago
Toronto 3
Montreal 3
Boston 4
New York 18
Philadelphia 6
Baltimore
Washington
Saint Louis 2
Dallas 3
Houston 3
Miami 3
Havana 2
Guadalajara 3
Mexico City 15
Caracas 3
Bogotá 4
Bering Sea
Bering Strait
Saint Lawrence I.
Nome
Yukon R.
Mount McKinley
Anchorage
Seward
Aleutian Islands
Aleutian Trench
Pribilof Islands
Bristol Bay
Dutch Harbor
Unalaska I.
Unimak I.
Alaska Peninsula
Kodiak Island
Gulf of Alaska
PACIFIC OCEAN
Tropic of Cancer

Greenland
(Denmark)
Baffin Bay
Davis Strait
Ellesmere Island
Axel Heiberg Island
Sverdrup Islands
Queen Elizabeth Islands
Magnetic Nort Pole (1980)
Geomagnetic North Pole
Thule
Prince Patrick Island
Parry Islands
Melville Island
Devon Island
Beaufort Sea
M'Clure Strait
Banks Island
Somerset Island
Prince of Wales Island
Victoria Island
Boothia Pen.
Baffin Island
Melville Peninsula
Upernavik
Umanak
Jakobshavn
Disko
Egedesminde
Angmagssalik
Godthåb
Frederikshåb
Julianehåb
C. Farewell
Barrow
Brooks Range
Prudhoe Bay
Alaska
(USA)
Aklavik
Inuvik
Fairbanks
Yukon R.
Dawson
Mackenzie Mountains
Mackenzie River
Great Bear Lake
Port Radium (Echo Bay)
Northwest Territories
Arctic Circle
Foxe Basin
Back R.
Yukon
Mount Logan
Whitehorse
Skagway
Juneau
Southampton Island
Hudson Strait
Cape Chidley
Labrador Sea
Yellowknife
Kazan R.
Great Slave Lake
Hay River
Liard R.
Coast Mountains
Rocky Mountains
Ungava Peninsula
Ungava Bay
Hudson Bay
Newfoundland and Labrador
Peace R.
Lake Athabasca
Churchill
CANADA
Schefferville
Goose Bay
Labrador
British Columbia
Prince George
Dawson Creek
Mc Murray
Reindeer Lake
Lynn Lake
Port Nelson
Nelson R.
Belcher Islands
Gagnon
Corner Brook
St. John's
Newfoundland
Alberta
Saskatchewan
Manitoba
Severn R.
James Bay
Anticosti I.
Sept-Îles
Port Cartier
Québec
Gulf of Saint Lawrence
St. Pierre and Miquelon (Fr.)
Edmonton
North Saskatchewan R.
Lake Winnipeg
Albany R.
Moosonee
Prince Edward Island
Sydney
Cape Breton Island
Vancouver Island
Fraser R.
Kamloops
Calgary
South Saskatchewan R.
Saskatoon
Victoria
Vancouver
Regina
Lake Manitoba
Winnipeg
Brandon
Ontario
New Brunswick
Nova Scotia
Halifax
Saint John
Seattle
Tacoma
Mount Rainier
Cascade Range
Spokane
Missouri R.
Red River
Thunder Bay
Lake Superior
Québec
Trois-Rivières
St. Lawrence River
Portland
Columbia River
Salem
Helena
Yellowstone R.
Bismarck
Duluth
Sault Sainte Marie
Sudbury
Montreal
OTTAWA
Portland
Columbia Plateau
Billings
Great Plains
Lake Huron
Lake Michigan
Lake Ontario
Hudson R.
Boston
Cape Cod
Boise
Snake R.
Minneapolis
St. Paul
Pierre
Toronto
Hamilton
Rochester
Niagara Falls
Buffalo
Sioux Falls
Mississippi R.
Milwaukee
Madison
Great Salt Lake
Coast Ranges
Reno
Salt Lake City
Cheyenne
North Platte R.
Omaha
Des Moines
Detroit
Toledo
Lake Erie
Cleveland
Newark
New York
Sacramento
Oakland
San José
Great Basin
Sierra Nevada
Lincoln
Chicago
Gary
Pittsburgh
Philadelphia
Columbus
Baltimore
WASHINGTON
Mount Elbert
Denver
Indianapolis
UNITED STATES (USA)
Cincinnati
Mount Whitney
Death Valley
Colorado Springs
Kansas City
St. Louis
Ohio R.
Louisville
Richmond
Norfolk
Appalachian Mountains
Colorado R.
Las Vegas
Colorado Plateau
Grand Canyon
Wichita
Nashville
Mount Mitchell
Cape Hatteras
Los Angeles
Long Beach
San Bernardino
San Diego
Santa Fe
Albuquerque
Rio Grande
Tulsa
Arkansas R.
Oklahoma City
Memphis
Charlotte
Bermuda Islands (U.K.)
Phoenix
Tucson
Tijuana
Mexicali
Lubbock
Red River
Little Rock
Birmingham
Atlanta
Charleston
Savannah
Fort Worth
Dallas
Brazos R.
Jackson
El Paso
Ciudad Juárez
Pecos R.
Baton Rouge
Mobile
New Orleans
Jacksonville
ATLANTIC OCEAN
Guadalupe I. (Mexico)
Hermosillo
Austin
Beaumont
Houston
Galveston
San Antonio
Cape Canaveral
Florida
Tampa
St. Petersburg
Lower California
Gulf of California
Western Sierra Madre
Chihuahua
Eastern Sierra Madre
Rio Bravo del Norte
Corpus Christi
Miami
NASSAU
THE BAHAMAS
Tropic of Cancer
Gulf of Mexico
Key West
Straits of Florida
Torreón
Saltillo
Monterrey
Matamoros
Culiacán
HAVANA
Santa Clara
Camagüey
West Indies
Puerto Rico Trench
MEXICO
Hispaniola
DOMINICAN REPUBLIC
San Juan
C. San Lucas
Mazatlán
Tampico
Yucatán Channel
CUBA
Santiago de Cuba
Guantánamo
HAITI
PORT-AU-PRINCE
SANTO DOMINGO
Puerto Rico (U.S.A.)
San Luis Potosí
Aguascalientes
León
Mérida
Chichén Itzá
Greater Antilles
Bay of Campeche
Yucatan
JAMAICA
KINGSTON
Revilla Gigedo Is. (Mexico)
Guadalajara
Morelia
MEXICO CITY
Veracruz
Mt. Popocatepetl
Puebla
Mt. Citlaltepetl
BELIZE
BELMOPAN
Caribbean Sea
Aruba I. (Neth.)
Curaçao I. (Neth.)
Bonaire I. (Neth.)
Acapulco
Southern Sierra Madre
Isthmus of Tehuantepec
GUATEMALA
San Pedro Sula
HONDURAS
TEGUCIGALPA
P. Gallinas
Maracaibo
Barquisimeto
CARACAS
Valencia
Middle America Trench
Mt. Tajamulco
Quezaltenango
SAN SALVADOR
EL SALVADOR
NICARAGUA
Santa Marta
Barranquilla
Cartagena
VENEZUELA
León
MANAGUA
Lake Nicaragua
Panama Canal (Pan./U.S.A.)
Colón
PANAMA
Magdalena R.
San Cristóbal
Bucaramanga
Orinoco R.
COSTA RICA
SAN JOSÉ
Medellín
Manizales
COLOMBIA
BOGOTÁ
MILLER'S BIPOLAR PROJECTION
Scale 1:25 000 000
0 500 1000 km
0 200 400 600 miles

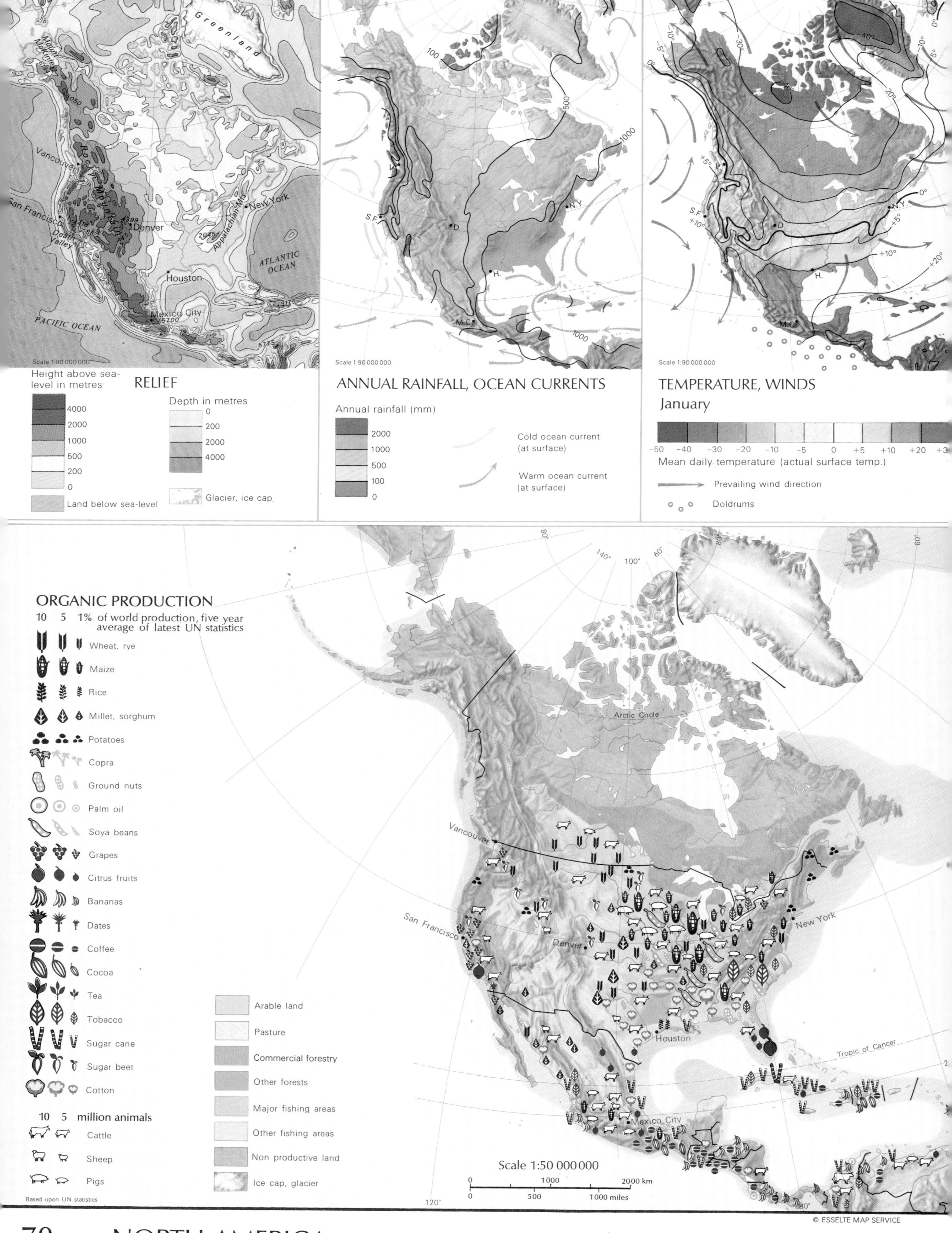
RELIEF
Height above sea-level in metres
4000
2000
1000
500
200
0
Land below sea-level
Depth in metres
0
200
2000
4000
Glacier, ice cap
Greenland
Vancouver
San Francisco
Death Valley
Denver
Houston
Mexico City
New York
Rocky Mountains
Appalachian Mts
ATLANTIC OCEAN
PACIFIC OCEAN
Scale 1:90 000 000
ANNUAL RAINFALL, OCEAN CURRENTS
Annual rainfall (mm)
2000
1000
500
100
0
Cold ocean current (at surface)
Warm ocean current (at surface)
Scale 1:90 000 000
TEMPERATURE, WINDS
January
-50 -40 -30 -20 -10 -5 0 +5 +10 +20
Mean daily temperature (actual surface temp.)
Prevailing wind direction
Doldrums
Scale 1:90 000 000
ORGANIC PRODUCTION
10 5 1% of world production, five year average of latest UN statistics
Wheat, rye
Maize
Rice
Millet, sorghum
Potatoes
Copra
Ground nuts
Palm oil
Soya beans
Grapes
Citrus fruits
Bananas
Dates
Coffee
Cocoa
Tea
Tobacco
Sugar cane
Sugar beet
Cotton
10 5 million animals
Cattle
Sheep
Pigs
Based upon UN statistics
Arable land
Pasture
Commercial forestry
Other forests
Major fishing areas
Other fishing areas
Non productive land
Ice cap, glacier
Arctic Circle
Tropic of Cancer
Vancouver
San Francisco
Denver
Houston
New York
Mexico City
Scale 1:50 000 000
0 1000 2000 km
0 500 1000 miles

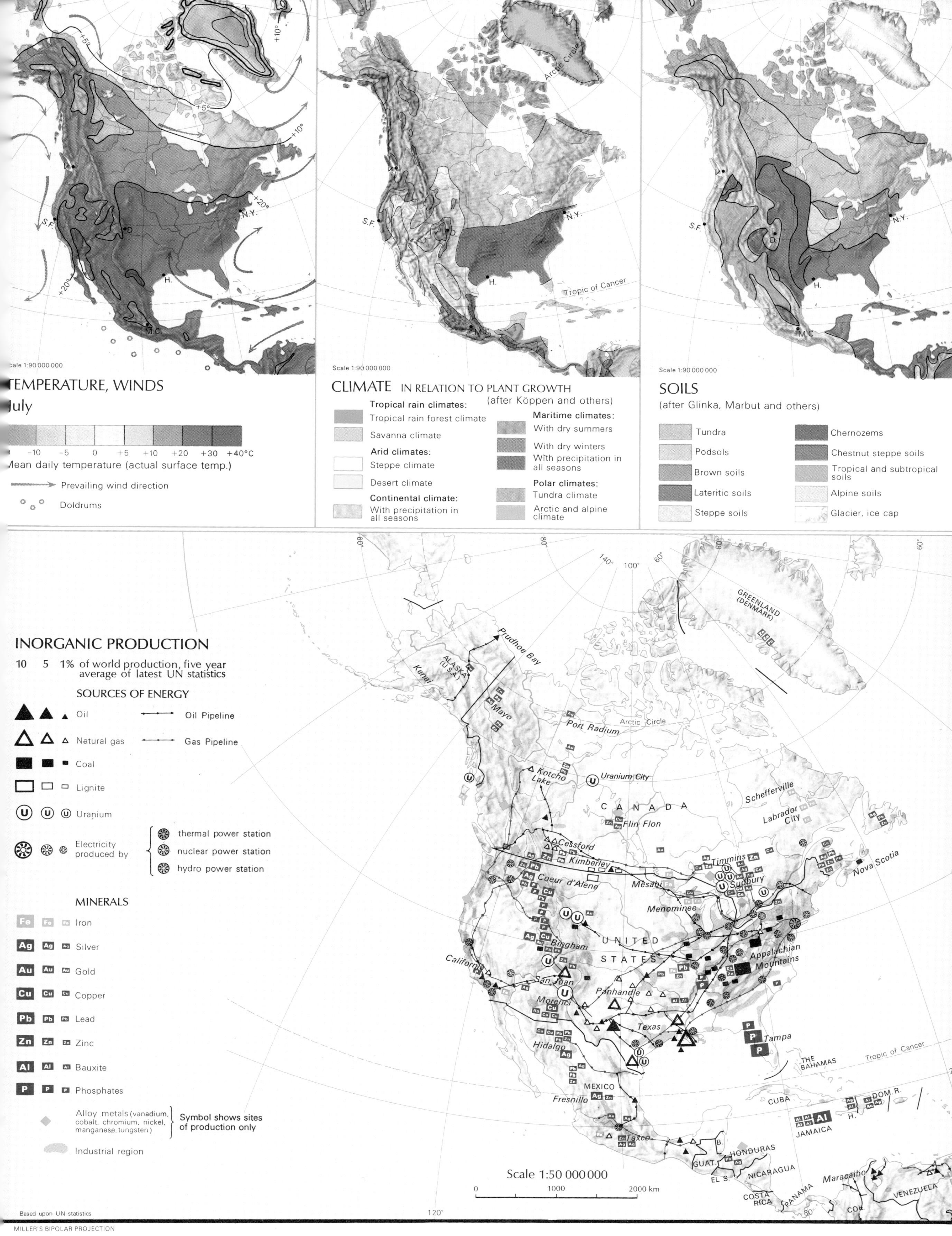

Scale 1:90 000 000
TEMPERATURE, WINDS
July
-10 -5 0 +5 +10 +20 +30 +40°C
Mean daily temperature (actual surface temp.)
Prevailing wind direction
Doldrums
CLIMATE IN RELATION TO PLANT GROWTH
(after Köppen and others)
Tropical rain climates:
Tropical rain forest climate
Savanna climate
Arid climates:
Steppe climate
Desert climate
Continental climate:
With precipitation in all seasons
Maritime climates:
With dry summers
With dry winters
With precipitation in all seasons
Polar climates:
Tundra climate
Arctic and alpine climate
Arctic Circle
Tropic of Cancer
SOILS
(after Glinka, Marbut and others)
Tundra
Podsols
Brown soils
Lateritic soils
Steppe soils
Chernozems
Chestnut steppe soils
Tropical and subtropical soils
Alpine soils
Glacier, ice cap
INORGANIC PRODUCTION
10 5 1% of world production, five year average of latest UN statistics
SOURCES OF ENERGY
Oil
Oil Pipeline
Natural gas
Gas Pipeline
Coal
Lignite
Uranium
Electricity produced by
thermal power station
nuclear power station
hydro power station
MINERALS
Iron
Silver
Gold
Copper
Lead
Zinc
Bauxite
Phosphates
Alloy metals (vanadium, cobalt, chromium, nickel, manganese, tungsten)
Symbol shows sites of production only
Industrial region
GREENLAND (DENMARK)
Prudhoe Bay
ALASKA (U.S.A.)
Kenai
Mayo
Port Radium
Kotcho Lake
Uranium City
CANADA
Flin Flon
Schefferville
Labrador City
Cessford
Kimberley
Coeur d'Alene
Mesabi
Timmins
Sudbury
Nova Scotia
Menominee
UNITED STATES
Bingham
California
San Juan
Panhandle
Appalachian Mountains
Morenci
Texas
Tampa
Hidalgo
THE BAHAMAS
MEXICO
Fresnillo
CUBA
DOM. R.
JAMAICA
Taxco
HONDURAS
GUAT.
EL S.
NICARAGUA
COSTA RICA
PANAMA
Maracaibo
VENEZUELA
Scale 1:50 000 000
0 1000 2000 km
Based upon UN statistics
MILLER'S BIPOLAR PROJECTION

ARCTIC OCEAN
Chukchi Sea
Beaufort Sea
Bering Sea
Gulf of Alaska
PACIFIC OCEAN
U. S. S. R.
Chukotskiy Poluostrov
Anadyrskiy Zaliv
Bering Strait
Mys Dezhneva
Mys Chukotskiy
Saint Lawrence Island
Gambell
Cape Lisburne
Point Hope
Icy Cape
Wainwright
Point Lay
Barrow
Point Barrow
Smith Bay
Cape Halkett
Harrison Bay
Teshekpuk Lake
Prudhoe Bay
Deadhorse
Camden Bay
Kaktovik
De Long Mountains
Brooks Range
Baird Mountains
NOATAK NATIONAL PRESERVE
KOBUK VALLEY N.P.
GATES OF THE ARCTIC N.P. AND PRES.
Endicott Mountains
Philip Smith Mountains
Mount Michelson
Mount Isto
Romanzof Mountains
Lookout Ridge
Colville
Umiat
Anaktuvuk Pass
Kotzebue
Kotzebue Sound
Cape Prince of Wales
Wales
Cape Rodney
Seward Peninsula
BERING LAND BRIDGE NAT PRES
Nome
Norton Sound
Norton Bay
Stuart
Unalakleet
Saint Michael
Cape Romanzof
Hooper Bay
Saint Matthew
Hall
Nelson Island
Nunivak Island
Cape Mohican
Etolin Strait
Bethel
Kuskokwim
Kuskokwim Bay
Kuskokwim Mountains
Cape Newenham
Hagemeister
Bristol Bay
Walrus Islands
Cape Constantine
Dillingham
Yukon
Galena
Ruby
Tanana
Kaiyuh Mountains
Koyukuk
Hughes
Allakaket
Alaska (UNITED STATES)
Yukon Flats
YUKON FLATS NATIONAL MONUMENT
Fort Yukon
Birch Creek
Circle
White Mountains
Arctic Village
Chandalar
Venetie
Porcupine
Fairbanks
College
Nenana
Manley Hot Springs
Eagle Summit
YUKON-CHARLEY RIVERS NAT. PRES
Eagle
Chicken
Big Delta
Delta Junction
Mount Hayes
Mount Harper
McGrath
Mount McKinley 6194
DENALI NAT. PARK AND PRES.
Alaska Range
Mount Foraker
Talkeetna Mts.
Mount Sanford
Mount Blackburn
Mount Marcus Baker
WRANGELL-SAINT ELIAS N.P. AND PRES.
Wrangell Mountains
Mount Bona
Mount Lucania
Chugach Mountains
Valdez
Cordova
Prince William Sound
Hinchinbrook
Anchorage
Cook Inlet
Kenai
Kenai Mts.
Kenai Peninsula
KENAI FJORDS N.P.
Seward
Homer
Seldovia
Barren Islands
Stevenson Entrance
Shuyak
Afognak
Kodiak
Kodiak Island
Shelikof Strait
Trinity Islands
Chirikof
Iliamna L.
LAKE CLARK NAT. PARK AND PRES.
Redoubt Volcano
Aleutian Range
KATMAI NAT. PARK AND PRES.
Mount Katmai
BECHAROF NAT. MON.
Becharof Lake
ANIAKCHAK NAT. MON. AND PRES.
Alaska Peninsula
Mount Veniaminof
Port Heiden
Port Moller
Pavlof Volcano
Cold Bay
Shishaldin Volcano
Unimak
Unimak Pass
Sanak Islands
Shumagin Islands
Sand Point
Chignik
Perryville
Sutwik
Kayak
Cape Yakataga
Bering Glacier
Malaspina Glacier
Mount Saint Elias
Mount Logan
Yakutat Bay
Yakutat
Mount Fairweather
GLACIER BAY N.P. AND PRES.
Cross Sound
Chichagof
Juneau
Haines
Skagway
Lynn Canal
Chatham Strait
ADMIRALTY NAT. MON.
Stephens Passage
Alexander Archipelago
Baranof
Sitka
Kruzof
Kuiu
Petersburg
Wrangell
Etolin
Christian Sound
Prince of Wales I.
Craig
Ketchikan
MISTY FJORDS NAT. MON.
Revilla Gigedo
Metlakatla
Dall
Dixon Entrance
Cape Knox
Graham
Masset
Prince Rupert
Hecate Strait
Queen Charlotte Islands
Moresby
Cape Saint James
Queen Charlotte Sound
Yukon Territory
Whitehorse
Dawson
Klondike Plateau
Mayo
Ogilvie Mts.
Mount Klotz
Old Crow
Porcupine Plain
British Mountains
Richardson Mountains
Herschel
Mackenzie Bay
Kugmallit Bay
Tuktoyaktuk
Inuvik
Aklavik
Fort McPherson
Arctic Red River
Eskimo Lakes
District of Inuvik
Cape Bathurst
Cape Dalhousie
Liverpool Bay
Fort Good Hope
Mackenzie Mountains
Selwyn Mountains
Keele Peak
Macmillan Pass
Pelly Mountains
Ross River
Faro
Carmacks
Pelly Crossing
Stewart Crossing
Kluane Lake
KLUANE N.P.
Haines Junction
Destruction Bay
Lake Laberge
Carcross
Teslin
Teslin Lake
Atlin
Atlin Lake
Watson Lake
Swift River
Johnsons Crossing
Cassiar
Dease Lake
Stikine Ranges
Telegraph Creek
Coast Mountains
Mount Ratz
Mount Fatullo
Stewart
Skeena Mountains
Pribilof Islands
Saint Paul
Saint George
Fox Islands
Unimak
Akun
Akutan
Tigalda
Unalaska
Dutch Harbor
Makushin Volcano
Sedanka
Umnak
Mount Vsevidof
Nikolski
Islands of Four Mountains
Chuginadak
Yunaska
Amukta Pass
Samalga Pass
Seguam
Amlia
Atka
Korovin Volcano
Great Sitkin
Andreanof Islands
Adak
Kanaga
Tanaga
Little Tanaga
Kagalaska
Delarof Islands
Gareloi
Amchitka Pass
Amchitka
Rat Islands
Semisopochnoi
Little Sitkin
Segula
Kiska
Kiska Volcano
Buldir
Near Islands
Semichi Islands
Attu
Agattu
Aleutian Islands (U.S.A.)

Scale 1:10 000 000

0 100 200 300 400 km
0 100 200 miles

Northwest Territories
District of Fort Smith
District of Keewatin
Great Bear Lake
Great Slave Lake
Lake Athabasca
Coronation Gulf
Boothia Peninsula
Gulf of Boothia
Queen Maud Gulf
King William Island
Victoria Strait
Arctic Circle
Hudson Bay
Cape Churchill
Mackenzie Mountains
Rocky Mountains
British Columbia
Alberta
Saskatchewan
Manitoba
Ontario
CANADA
Edmonton
Calgary
Saskatoon
Regina
Winnipeg
Thunder Bay
Lake Winnipeg
Lake Winnipegosis
Lake Manitoba
Reindeer Lake
Wollaston Lake
Cree Lake
Lake Superior
Lake of the Woods
Red Lake
Lac Seul
Lake Nipigon
Churchill
Port Nelson
York Factory
Chesterfield Inlet
Montana
Wyoming
North Dakota
South Dakota
Minnesota
Wisconsin
Nebraska
UNITED STATES
Minneapolis
Saint Paul
Duluth
Milwaukee
Chicago
Madison
Bismarck
Fargo
Missoula
Great Falls
Cheyenne
Sioux Falls
Black Hills
Sand Hills
Moose Jaw
Medicine Hat
Lethbridge
Prince Albert
Brandon
Minot
Rapid City

Scale 1:10 000 000

0 100 200 300 400 km

0 100 200 miles

British Columbia
Alberta
Saskatchewan
Manitoba
Vancouver
Victoria
Washington
Seattle
Tacoma
Spokane
Medicine Hat
Regina
Moose Jaw
Brandon
Portland
Salem
Oregon
Eugene
Idaho
Boise
Montana
Great Falls
Missoula
Billings
Rocky Mountains
North Dakota
Bismarck
South Dakota
Rapid City
Wyoming
Casper
Cheyenne
Nebraska
Great Basin
Nevada
Reno
Las Vegas
Utah
Salt Lake City
Ogden
Provo
Colorado
Denver
Aurora
Lakewood
Colorado Springs
Pueblo
Kansas
California
Sacramento
San Francisco
Oakland
San Jose
Fresno
Los Angeles
Long Beach
Pasadena
San Bernardino
Riverside
Santa Ana
San Diego
Mojave Desert
Arizona
Phoenix
Tucson
Scottsdale
Tempe
Glendale
Flagstaff
Colorado Plateau
New Mexico
Albuquerque
Santa Fe
Roswell
Texas
Amarillo
Lubbock
El Paso
San Antonio
Stockton Plateau
UNITED
Tijuana
Mexicali
Ciudad Juárez
Chihuahua
Hermosillo
Sonora
Coahuila
Monterrey
Saltillo
Torreón
Durango
Culiacán
Sinaloa
Sierra Madre Occidental
MEXICO
Baja California Norte
Baja California Sur
Golfo de California
La Paz
Cabo San Lucas
Isla de Guadalupe (Mexico)
Tropic of Cancer
PACIFIC OCEAN

ATLANTIC OCEAN
Gulf of Mexico
Gulf of Maine
THE BAHAMAS
CUBA
LA HABANA (HAVANA)
Ontario
Québec
Minnesota
Wisconsin
Michigan
Iowa
Illinois
Indiana
Ohio
Missouri
Kentucky
Tennessee
Arkansas
Mississippi
Alabama
Georgia
Florida
Louisiana
South Carolina
North Carolina
Virginia
West Virginia
Pennsylvania
New York
Maryland
New Jersey
Delaware
Connecticut
Massachusetts
Vermont
New Hampshire
Maine
New Brunswick
OTTAWA
Montréal
Toronto
Chicago
Detroit
New York
Philadelphia
WASHINGTON
Boston
Atlanta
Memphis
Houston
Dallas
New Orleans
Miami
Jacksonville
Tampa
Nashville
Louisville
Saint Louis
Kansas City
Minneapolis
Saint Paul
Milwaukee
Cleveland
Pittsburgh
Baltimore
Buffalo
Charlotte
Birmingham
NASSAU
Florida Keys
Straits of Florida
Tropic of Cancer
© ESSELTE MAP SERVICE
Scale 1:10 000 000
0 100 200 300 400 km
0 100 200 miles

UNITED STATES
Texas
Louisiana
Mississippi
Alabama
Gulf of Mexico
MEXICO
MEXICO CITY
PACIFIC OCEAN
GUATEMALA
BELIZE
HONDURAS
EL SALVADOR
NICARAGUA
COSTA RICA
TEGUCIGALPA
SAN SALVADOR
MANAGUA
SAN JOSÉ
Bahía de Campeche
Yucatán Peninsula
Golfo de Tehuantepec
Tropic of Cancer
Houston
San Antonio
Austin
Corpus Christi
Shreveport
Jackson
Montgomery
Birmingham
Atlanta
Mobile
New Orleans
Baton Rouge
Beaumont
Chihuahua
Torreón
Saltillo
Monterrey
Matamoros
Tampico
Guadalajara
Aguascalientes
San Luis Potosí
León
Querétaro
Puebla
Veracruz
Acapulco
Oaxaca de Juárez
Mérida
Campeche
Villahermosa
Coatzacoalcos
Tuxtla Gutiérrez
Chetumal
Tapachula
Mazatlán
Victoria de Durango
Tepic
Zacatecas
Morelia
Cuernavaca
Toluca
Guatemala
San Pedro Sula
Santa Ana
Managua
Granada
León
Puntarenas
Cartago
Limón
Sierra Madre Oriental
Sierra Madre Occidental
Sierra Madre del Sur
Golfo de Fonseca
Lago de Nicaragua
Golfo de Honduras
Canal de Yucatán

A T L A N T I C
O C E A N
Sargasso Sea
Bermuda Islands (U.K.)
Hamilton
Tropic of Cancer
THE BAHAMAS
Bahama Islands
West Indies
(Indias Occidentales)
NASSAU
Grand Bahama Island
Little Abaco Island
Great Abaco Island
Eleuthera Island
Andros Island
Cat Island
San Salvador (Watling I.)
Great Exuma Island
Long Island
Acklins Island
Crooked Island
Mayaguana Island
Great Inagua Island
Little Inagua Island
Turks and Caicos Islands (U.K.)
Caicos Islands
Turks Islands
Grand Turk
CUBA
HABANA (HAVANA)
Santa Clara
Camagüey
Holguín
Santiago de Cuba
Guantánamo
Cayman Islands (U.K.)
JAMAICA
KINGSTON
Montego Bay
HAITI
PORT-AU-PRINCE
Hispaniola
DOMINICAN REPUBLIC
SANTO DOMINGO
Santiago
Puerto Rico (U.S.A.)
San Juan
Ponce
Mayagüez
Virgin Islands (U.K.)
Virgin Islands (U.S.A.)
Greater Antilles (Antillas Mayores)
Lesser Antilles (Antillas Menores)
Islas de Barlovento
Leeward Islands
Windward Is.
Islas de Sotavento
ST. KITTS AND NEVIS
ANTIGUA AND BARBUDA
SAINT JOHN'S
Montserrat (U.K.)
Guadeloupe (Fr.)
DOMINICA
ROSEAU
Martinique (Fr.)
Fort-de-France
SAINT LUCIA
CASTRIES
SAINT VINCENT
KINGSTOWN
BARBADOS
BRIDGETOWN
GRENADA
SAINT GEORGE'S
Tobago
TRINIDAD AND TOBAGO
PORT OF SPAIN
Netherlands Antilles
Aruba
Curaçao
Bonaire
Willemstad
Isla de Margarita
Caribbean Sea
VENEZUELA
CARACAS
Maracaibo
Valencia
Barquisimeto
Maracay
Barcelona
Cumaná
Maturín
Ciudad Bolívar
Ciudad Guayana
COLOMBIA
Barranquilla
Cartagena
Santa Marta
Cúcuta
Bucaramanga
Medellín
PANAMÁ
PANAMA
Colón
Istmo de Panamá
Golfo de Panamá
Golfo de Venezuela
Lago de Maracaibo
Orinoco
South Carolina
Columbia
Charleston
Savannah
Jacksonville
Florida
Orlando
Tampa
Miami
Fort Lauderdale
Florida Keys
Straits of Florida
Cape Canaveral
© ESSELTE MAP SERVICE

Scale 1:25 000 0

JAMAICA
Puerto Rico (U.S.A.)
ST. KITTS AND NEVIS
ANTIGUA AND BARBUDA
Guadeloupe (France)
Pointe-à-Pitre
DOMINICA
Martinique (France)
Fort-de-France
ST. LUCIA
BARBADOS
BRIDGETOWN
ST. VINCENT
GRENADA
Lesser Antilles
Caribbean Sea
Aruba I.
Curaçao I. (Neth.)
P. Gallinas
Santa Marta
Barranquilla
Cartagena
Maracaibo
Barquisimeto
Maracay
CARACAS
Valencia
Cumaná
Barcelona
TRINIDAD AND TOBAGO
PORT OF SPAIN
Colón
PANAMÁ
Cúcuta
San Cristóbal
Ciudad Bolívar
Ciudad Guayana
Cerro Bolívar
R. Orinoco
VENEZUELA
Angel Falls
Kaieteur Falls
Mt. Roraima
GEORGETOWN
PARAMARIBO
Cayenne
GUYANA
SURINAM
French Guiana
Guiana Highlands
Medellín
Bucaramanga
Manizales
Mt. Tolima
BOGOTÁ
Buenaventura
Ibagué
Cali
Meta R.
Llanos
Guaviare R.
Orinoco R.
Boa Vista
Roraima
Amapá
Macapá
COLOMBIA
Pasto
QUITO
Mt. Cotopaxi
Ambato
Guayaquil
Cuenca
Tumbes
Putumayo R.
Amazon R.
R. Negro
Branco R.
Manaus
Amazon R.
Xingu R.
Marajó I.
Belém
São Luís
Santarém
Fonte Boa
Iquitos
Leticia
Marañón R.
Amazonas
Pará
R. Tocantins
Parnaíba
Fortaleza
Sobral
Teresina
Maranhão
Ceará
Mossoró
Rio Grande do Norte
C. São Roque
Natal
Fernando de Noronha I. (Braz.)
St. Peter and St. Paul Rocks (Braz.)
Equator
ATLANTIC OCEAN
Selvas
Juruá R.
Purus R.
Madeira R.
Tapajós R.
Ucayali R.
Cajamarca
Trujillo
Chimbote
Mt. Huascarán
Huánuco
Cerro de Pasco
PERU
Acre
Pôrto Velho
BRAZIL
Caatingas
Piauí
Juàzeiro do Norte
Paraíba
João Pessoa
Campina Grande
Pernambuco
Caruaru
Recife
Garanhuns
Alagoas
Maceió
Sergipe
Aracaju
Juàzeiro
Campos
Barreiras
Bahia
Feira
Alagoinhas
Salvador
Rio Branco
Guajará Mirim
Rondônia
Cobija
LIMA
Callao
La Oroya
Huancayo
Huancavelica
Ayacucho
Cuzco
Pisco
Ica
MACHU PICCHU
Guaporé R.
Beni R.
Mato Grosso
Goiás
Xingu R.
Araguaia R.
Lake Titicaca
Mt. Ancohuma
Trinidad
Mt. Coropuna
Puno
Arequipa
LA PAZ
Mt. Illimani
BOLIVIA
Cuiabá
Distrito Federal
BRASÍLIA
Anápolis
Goiânia
S. Francisco R.
Vitória
Jequié
Itabuna
Ilhéus
Mollendo
Tacna
Arica
Oruro
Cochabamba
Santa Cruz
Llallagua
Lake Poopó
SUCRE
Potosí
Montes Claros
Brazilian Highlands
Minas Gerais
Teófilo Otoni
Governador Valadares
Paranaíba R.
Mato Grosso do Sul
Uberlândia
Belo Horizonte
Uberaba
Itabira
Espírito Santo
Vitória
Iquique
Tarija
Chaco
Paraguay R.
Campo Grande
Presidente Prudente
São José
São Paulo
Ribeirão Prêto
Juiz de Fora
Mt. Bandeira
Rio de Janeiro
Campos
Tocopilla
Pilcomayo R.
PARAGUAY
Ponta Porã
Bauru
Campinas
Volta Redonda
Niterói
C. Frio
Trindade I. (Braz.)
Martin Vaz Is. (Braz.)
Antofagasta
Jujuy
Bermejo R.
Gran Chaco
ASUNCIÓN
Paraná R.
Londrina
Paraná
Sorocaba
São Paulo
Santos
Rio de Janeiro
Tropic of Capricorn
Mt. Llullaillaco
Salta
Mt. Galán
Tucumán
Ponta Grossa
Iguaçu Falls
Curitiba
Formosa
Joinvile
Santa Catarina
Blumenau
Florianópolis
S. Félix I.
S. Ambrosio I. (Chile)
Copiapó
Mt. Ojos del Salado
Atacama Desert
Andes
Resistencia
Corrientes
Posadas
Santiago del Estero
Salado R.
Catamarca
Uruguay R.
Passo Fundo
Río Grande do Sul
Caxias do Sul
La Serena
La Rioja
Salinas Grandes
Uruguaiana
Santa Maria
Pôrto Alegre
L. dos Patos
CHILE
San Juan
Santa Fe
Paraná
Salto
Paysandú
Pelotas
Río Grande
Mt. Aconcagua
Córdoba
Rosario
Mendoza
San Luis
Río Cuarto
URUGUAY
Lake Mirim
Viña del Mar
Valparaíso
SANTIAGO
Zárate
Junín
River Plate
MONTEVIDEO
BUENOS AIRES
La Plata
Pampas
Juan Fernández Islands (Chile)
Rancagua
Talca
ARGENTINA
Santa Rosa
Azul
Tandil
Mar del Plata
Talcahuano
Concepción
Chillán
Colorado R.
Bahía Blanca
Temuco
Neuquén
Plaza Huincul
Valdivia
Osorno
Viedma
Gulf of San Matías
Puerto Montt
San Carlos de Bariloche
Chiloé I.
Rawson
Patagonia
Puerto Aisén
Comodoro Rivadavia
Gulf of San Jorge
Cerro San Valentín
Puerto Deseado
Falkland Islands (U.K.)
Stanley
Río Gallegos
Strait of Magellan
Tierra del Fuego
Punta Arenas
Ushuaia
Cape Horn
South Georgia (U.K.)
Peru-Chile Trench
BIPOLAR PROJECTION
500 1000 km
200 400 600 miles

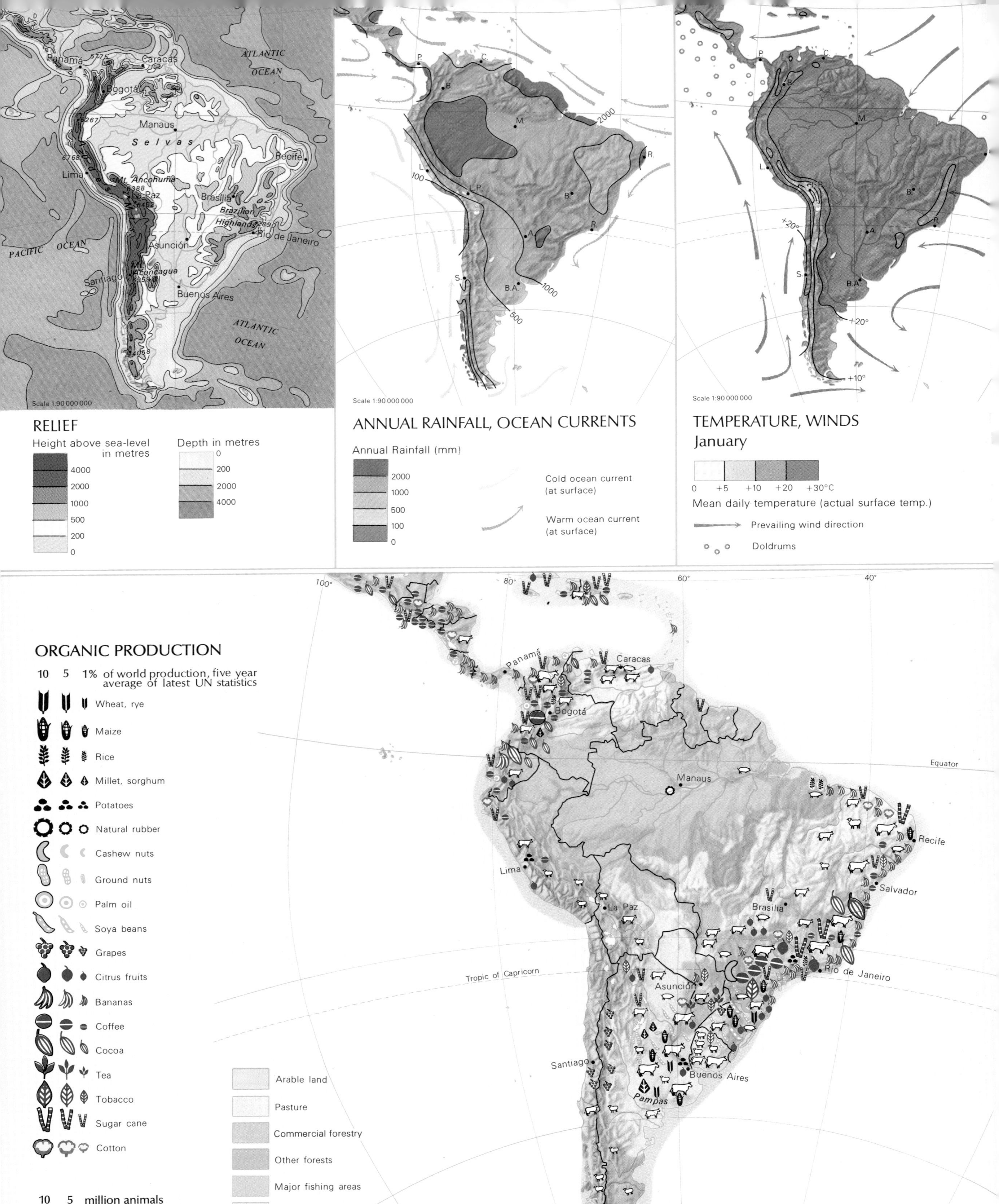

RELIEF
Height above sea-level in metres
4000
2000
1000
500
200
0
Depth in metres
0
200
2000
4000
Scale 1:90 000 000
Panamá
Caracas
Bogotá
Manaus
Selvas
Recife
Lima
Mt. Ancohuma
La Paz
Brasília
Brazilian Highlands
Rio de Janeiro
Asunción
Mt. Aconcagua
Santiago
Buenos Aires
ATLANTIC OCEAN
PACIFIC OCEAN
ANNUAL RAINFALL, OCEAN CURRENTS
Annual Rainfall (mm)
2000
1000
500
100
0
Cold ocean current (at surface)
Warm ocean current (at surface)
TEMPERATURE, WINDS
January
0
+5
+10
+20
+30°C
Mean daily temperature (actual surface temp.)
Prevailing wind direction
Doldrums
ORGANIC PRODUCTION
10 5 1% of world production, five year average of latest UN statistics
Wheat, rye
Maize
Rice
Millet, sorghum
Potatoes
Natural rubber
Cashew nuts
Ground nuts
Palm oil
Soya beans
Grapes
Citrus fruits
Bananas
Coffee
Cocoa
Tea
Tobacco
Sugar cane
Cotton
10 5 million animals
Cattle
Sheep
Pigs
Based upon UN statistics
Arable land
Pasture
Commercial forestry
Other forests
Major fishing areas
Other fishing areas
Non-productive land
Glacier
Equator
Tropic of Capricorn
Salvador
Pampas
Scale 1:50 000 000
0
1000
2000 km
500
1000 miles

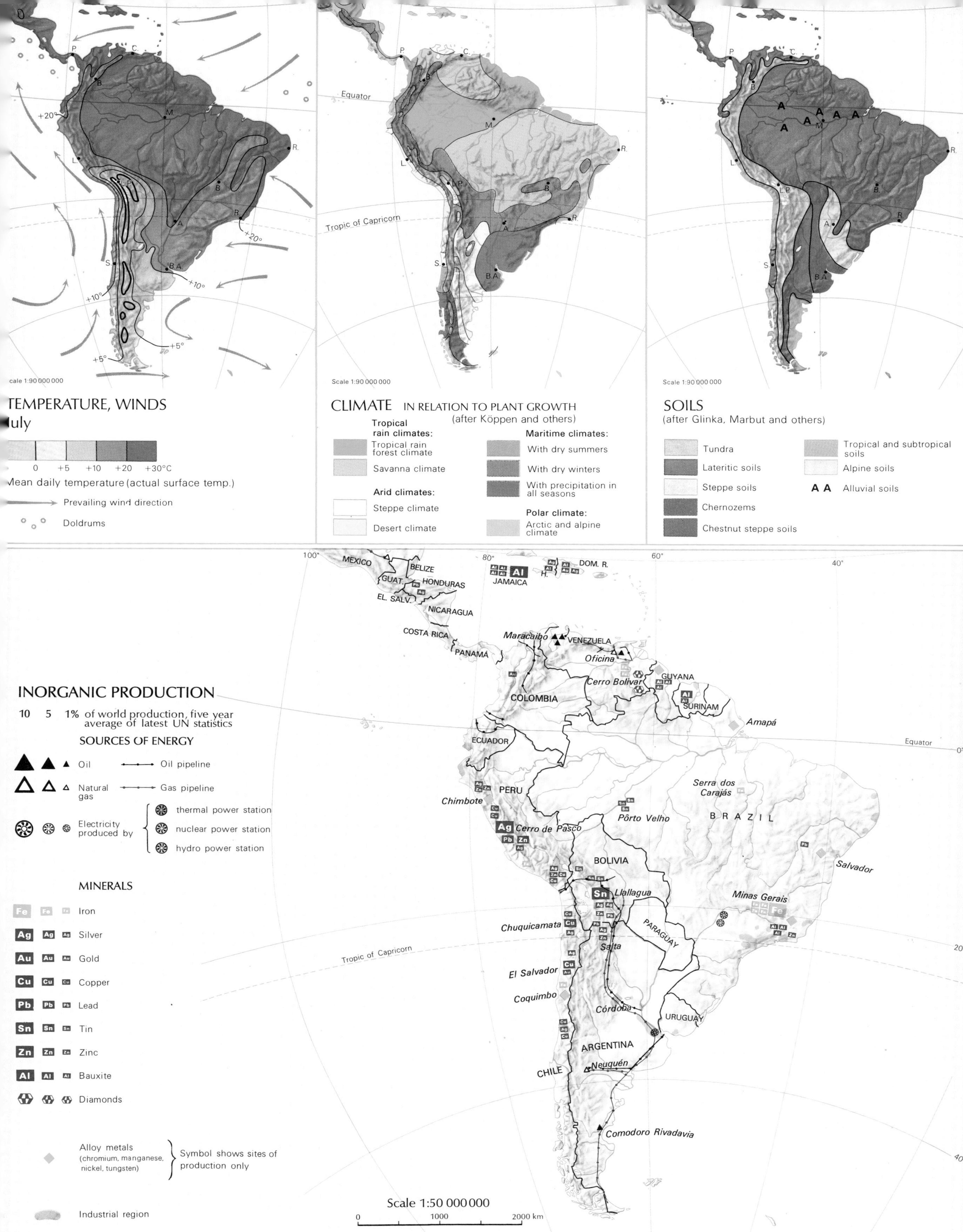
cale 1:90 000 000
TEMPERATURE, WINDS
July
0 +5 +10 +20 +30°C
Mean daily temperature (actual surface temp.)
Prevailing wind direction
Doldrums
Scale 1:90 000 000
CLIMATE IN RELATION TO PLANT GROWTH
(after Köppen and others)
Tropical rain climates:
Tropical rain forest climate
Savanna climate
Arid climates:
Steppe climate
Desert climate
Maritime climates:
With dry summers
With dry winters
With precipitation in all seasons
Polar climate:
Arctic and alpine climate
Scale 1:90 000 000
SOILS
(after Glinka, Marbut and others)
Tundra
Lateritic soils
Steppe soils
Chernozems
Chestnut steppe soils
Tropical and subtropical soils
Alpine soils
A A Alluvial soils
INORGANIC PRODUCTION
10 5 1% of world production, five year average of latest UN statistics
SOURCES OF ENERGY
Oil
Oil pipeline
Natural gas
Gas pipeline
Electricity produced by
thermal power station
nuclear power station
hydro power station
MINERALS
Iron
Silver
Gold
Copper
Lead
Tin
Zinc
Bauxite
Diamonds
Alloy metals (chromium, manganese, nickel, tungsten)
Symbol shows sites of production only
Industrial region
Based upon UN statistics
MEXICO
BELIZE
GUAT.
HONDURAS
EL SALV.
NICARAGUA
COSTA RICA
PANAMÁ
JAMAICA
DOM. R.
H.
Maracaibo
VENEZUELA
Oficina
Cerro Bolívar
GUYANA
SURINAM
COLOMBIA
Amapá
ECUADOR
Equator
PERU
Chimbote
Serra dos Carajás
Pôrto Velho
BRAZIL
Cerro de Pasco
BOLIVIA
Salvador
Llallagua
Minas Gerais
Chuquicamata
PARAGUAY
Salta
Tropic of Capricorn
El Salvador
Coquimbo
Córdoba
URUGUAY
ARGENTINA
Neuquén
CHILE
Comodoro Rivadavia
Scale 1:50 000 000
0 1000 2000 km
MILLER'S BIPOLAR PROJECTION

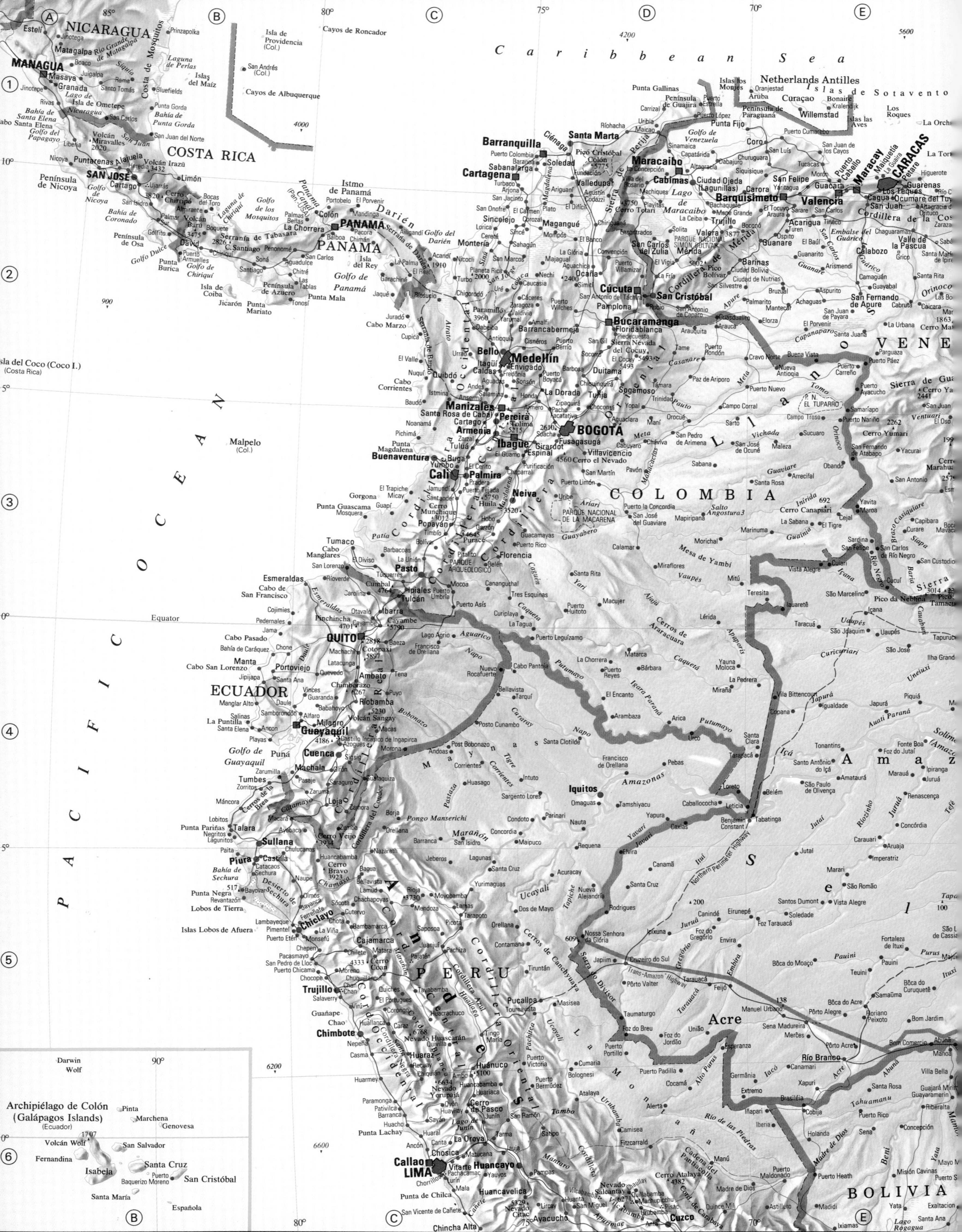
Caribbean Sea
PACIFIC OCEAN
NICARAGUA
COSTA RICA
PANAMA
COLOMBIA
ECUADOR
PERU
BOLIVIA
Netherlands Antilles
Islas de Sotavento
Managua
Granada
Lago de Nicaragua
San José
Limón
Panamá
Golfo de Panamá
Golfo de Darién
Istmo de Panamá
Isla de Coiba
Barranquilla
Cartagena
Santa Marta
Maracaibo
Lago de Maracaibo
Golfo de Venezuela
Península de Guajira
Curaçao
Aruba
Bonaire
Willemstad
Caracas
Valencia
Barquisimeto
Mérida
Cúcuta
San Cristóbal
Bucaramanga
Medellín
Manizales
Pereira
Armenia
Ibagué
Bogotá
Buenaventura
Cali
Palmira
Neiva
Popayán
Pasto
Tumaco
Esmeraldas
Ibarra
Tulcán
Quito
Equator
Cotopaxi 5897
Chimborazo 6267
Ambato
Riobamba
Guayaquil
Golfo de Guayaquil
Cuenca
Machala
Loja
Tumbes
Talara
Sullana
Piura
Chiclayo
Cajamarca
Trujillo
Chimbote
Nevado Huascarán 6768
Huánuco
Cerro de Pasco
Callao
LIMA
Huancayo
Huancavelica
Ayacucho
Cuzco
Iquitos
Leticia
Pucallpa
Acre
Rio Branco
Malpelo (Col.)
Isla del Coco (Coco I.) (Costa Rica)
Archipiélago de Colón (Galápagos Islands) (Ecuador)
Isabela
Fernandina
Santa Cruz
San Cristóbal
Amazonas
Putumayo
Caquetá
Orinoco
Llanos
Cordillera Occidental
Cordillera Central
Cordillera Oriental
Andes
Selvas
Montaña
Trans-Amazon Highway
Northern Perimeter Highway

Scale 1:10 000 000

0 100 200 300 400 km
0 100 200 miles

PACIFIC OCEAN
PERU
BOLIVIA
CHILE
PARAGUAY
ARGENTINA
Amazonas
Acre
Rondônia
Chaco Boreal
Gran Chaco
Chaco Central
Chaco Austral
Llanos de Moxos
Llanos de Chiquitos
Tropic of Capricorn
LIMA
Callao
Iquitos
Manaus
Pucallpa
Huancayo
Huancavelica
Ayacucho
Cuzco
Arequipa
Puno
Nazca
Ica
Pisco
Tacna
Arica
Iquique
Antofagasta
Calama
Copiapó
Vallenar
La Serena
LA PAZ
Oruro
Cochabamba
Santa Cruz
SUCRE
Potosí
Tarija
Trinidad
Riberalta
Cobija
Pôrto Velho
Rio Branco
Corumbá
ASUNCIÓN
Concepción
Salta
San Salvador de Jujuy
San Miguel de Tucumán
Santiago del Estero
Catamarca
La Rioja
Resistencia
Corrientes
Posadas
Formosa
Goya
Reconquista
Lago Titicaca
Lago de Poopó
Salar de Uyuni
Salar de Atacama
Desierto de Atacama
Isla Independencia
Punta Carreta
Cordillera Oriental
Cordillera Occidental
Cordillera Real
Cordillera Central
Serra dos Parecis
Serra do Tombador
Serra dos Pacaás Novos
Amazonas
Madeira
Mamoré
Guaporé
Beni
Ucayali
Marañón
Pilcomayo
Bermejo
Paraguai
Paraná
Salado
Dulce
6800
4000
7500
5000
8000
7900
2900
6200
15°
20°
25°
70°
65°
60°
75°
A
B
C
D
E
1
2
3
4
5
6

Scale 1:10 000 000

0 100 200 300 400 km

0 100 200 miles

BRAZIL
PARAGUAY
URUGUAY
BOLIVIA
PERU
CHILE
Planalto do Mato Grosso
Gran Chaco
Chaco Boreal
São Paulo
Paraná
Santa Catarina
Rio Grande do Sul
BRASÍLIA
Goiânia
Uberlândia
Campinas
Santos
Curitiba
Florianópolis
Pôrto Alegre
Campo Grande
Corumbá
ASUNCIÓN
Encarnación
Posadas
Corrientes
Resistencia
Santa Fé
Paraná
Rosario
Córdoba
BUENOS AIRES
La Plata
MONTEVIDEO
Santiago del Estero
San Miguel de Tucumán
Salta
San Salvador de Jujuy
Mendoza
San Juan
La Rioja
Catamarca
SANTIAGO
Valparaíso
Viña del Mar
La Serena
Coquimbo
Copiapó
Antofagasta
Iquique
Arica
Tacna
Arequipa
Cuzco
LA PAZ
Oruro
Cochabamba
SUCRE
Potosí
Tarija
Santa Cruz
Trinidad
Lago Titicaca
Salar de Uyuni
Desierto de Atacama
Sierra de Famatina
Sierras de Córdoba
Llanos de Chiquitos
Pantanal de São Lourenço
P A C I

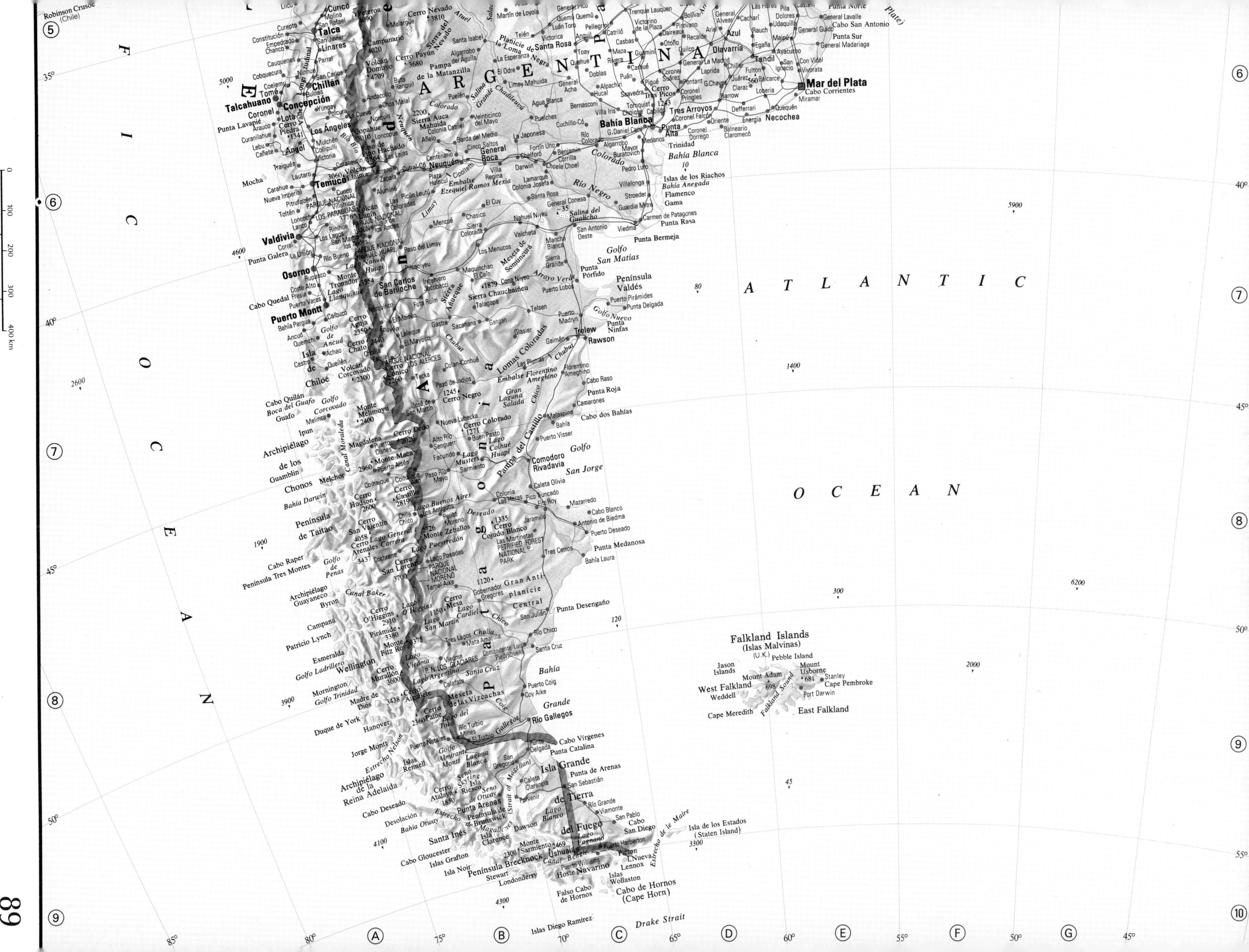

Scale 1:10 000 000
0 100 200 300 400 km
0 100 200 miles

Scale 1:30 000 000

0 500 1000 km
0 250 500 miles

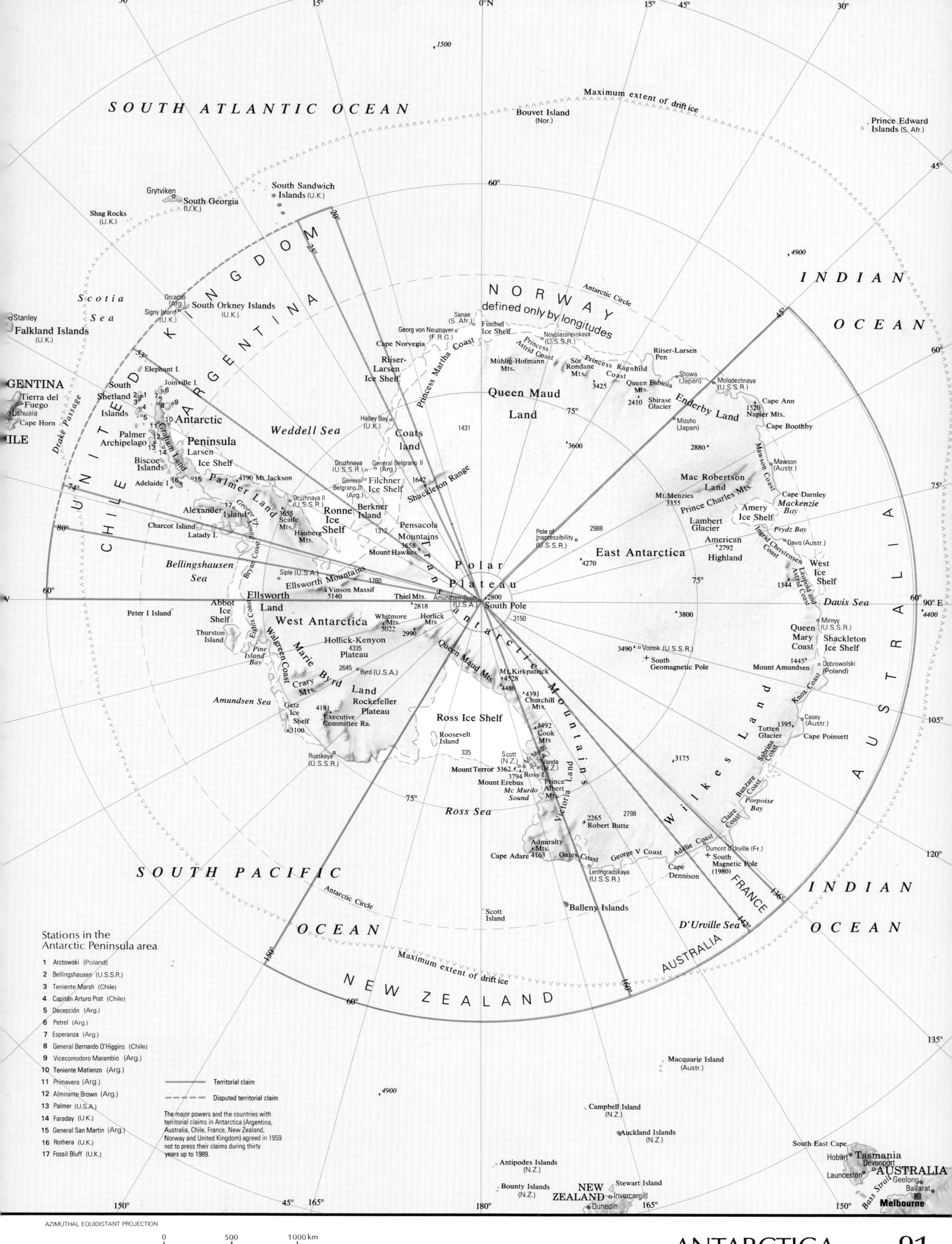

AZIMUTHAL EQUIDISTANT PROJECTION

Scale 1:30 000 000 — 0, 500, 1000 km; 0, 250, 500 miles

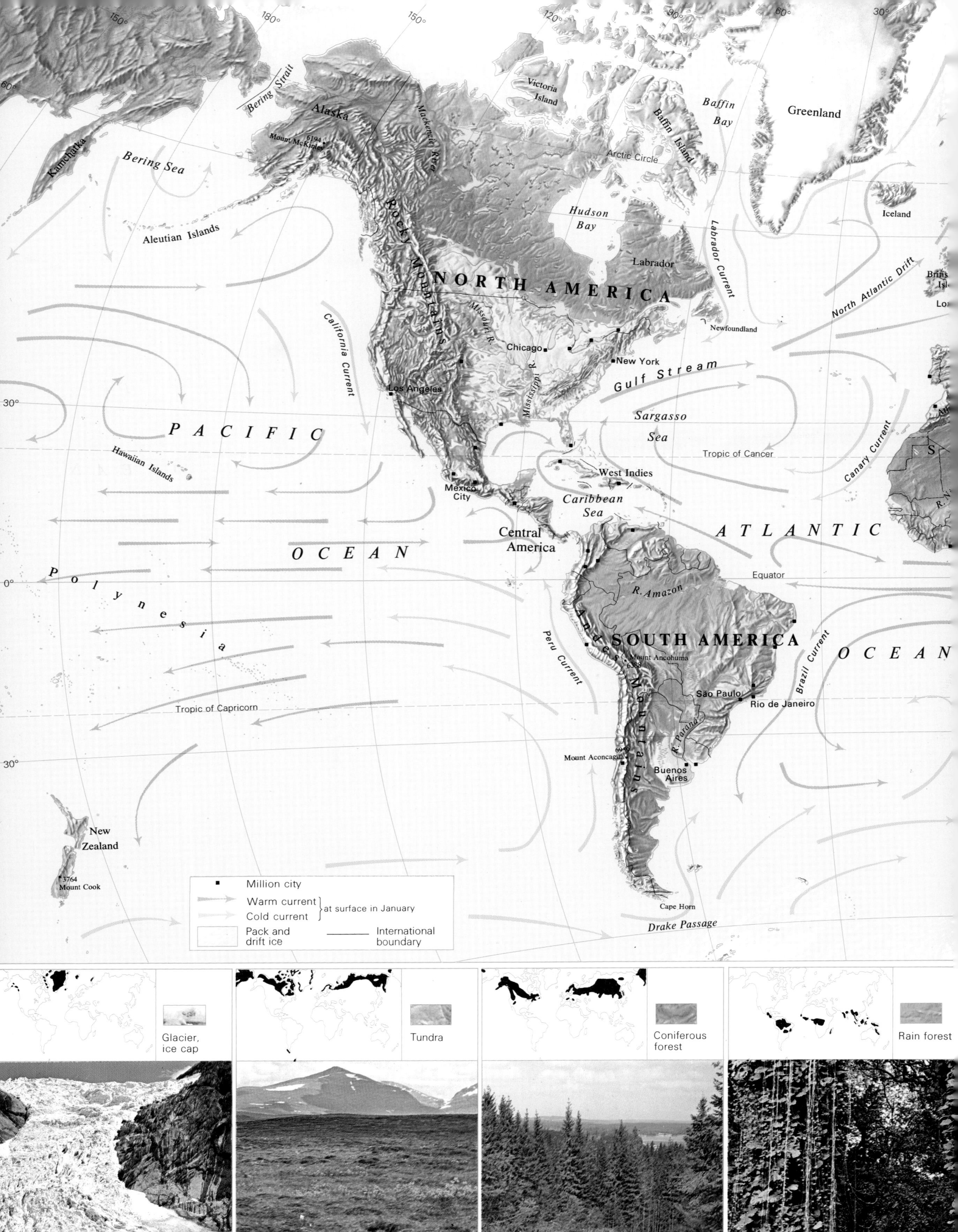
Bering Strait
Alaska
Mount McKinley
6194
Kamchatka
Bering Sea
Aleutian Islands
Victoria Island
Baffin Bay
Baffin Island
Greenland
Arctic Circle
Hudson Bay
Labrador
Labrador Current
Iceland
North Atlantic Drift
Mackenzie River
Rocky Mountains
NORTH AMERICA
Missouri R.
California Current
Chicago
New York
Newfoundland
Mississippi R.
Gulf Stream
Los Angeles
PACIFIC
Sargasso Sea
Tropic of Cancer
Canary Current
Hawaiian Islands
West Indies
Mexico City
Caribbean Sea
Central America
ATLANTIC
OCEAN
Polynesia
Equator
R. Amazon
SOUTH AMERICA
Andes Mountains
Mount Ancohuma
6388
Peru Current
Brazil Current
OCEAN
São Paulo
Rio de Janeiro
Tropic of Capricorn
R. Paraná
Mount Aconcagua
6959
Buenos Aires
New Zealand
3764
Mount Cook
Cape Horn
Drake Passage
Million city
Warm current
Cold current
at surface in January
Pack and drift ice
International boundary
Glacier, ice cap
Tundra
Coniferous forest
Rain forest

VAN DER GRINTEN'S PROJECTION

Scale 1:90 000 000 at the equator

0° 0 400 800 km; 30°; 60° 200 600 1000 km

0° 0 200 400 600 miles; 30°; 60° 100 300 500 miles

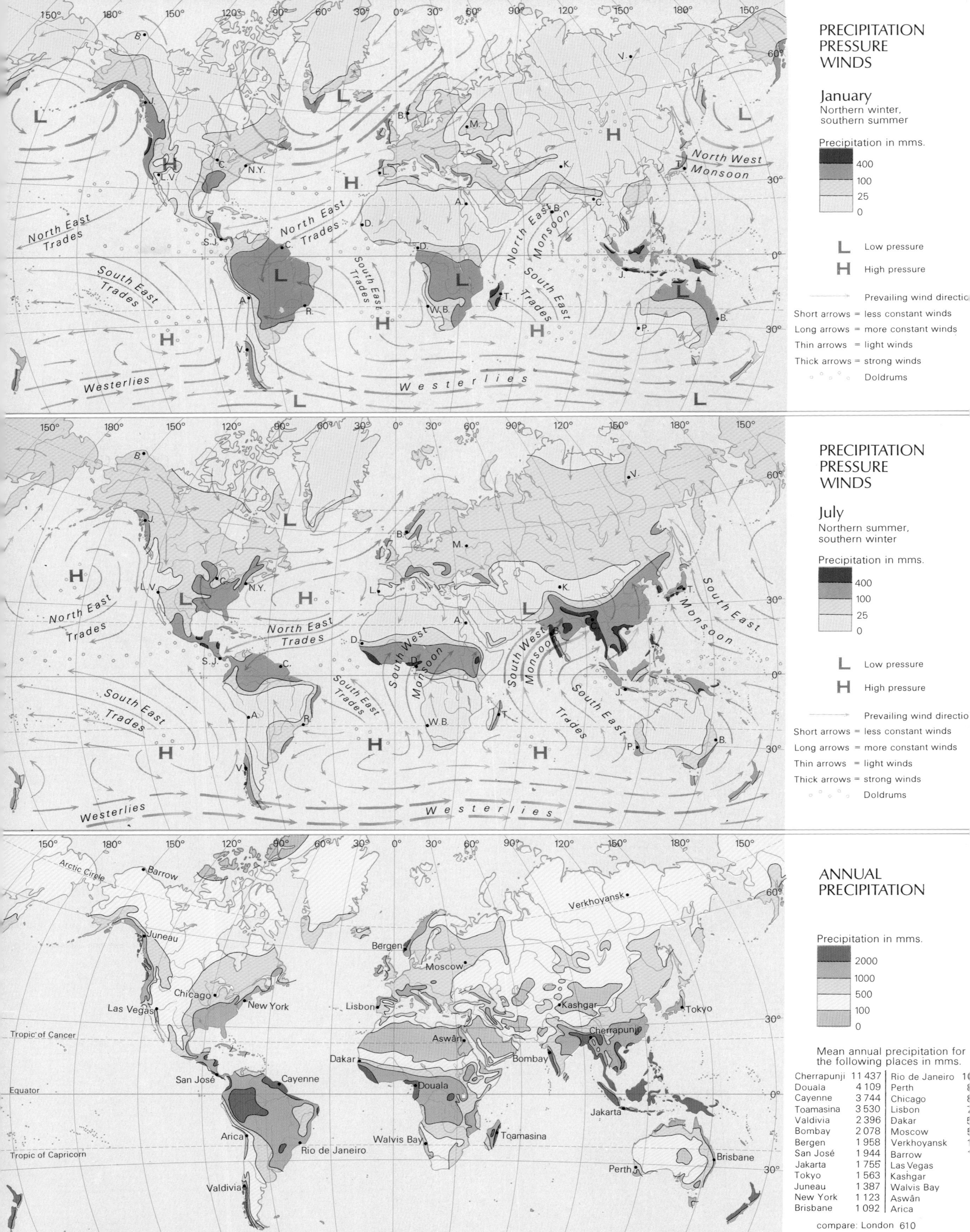

Mean annual precipitation for the following places in mms.

Cherrapunji	11 437	Rio de Janeiro	[illegible]
Douala	4 109	Perth	[illegible]
Cayenne	3 744	Chicago	[illegible]
Toamasina	3 530	Lisbon	[illegible]
Valdivia	2 396	Dakar	[illegible]
Bombay	2 078	Moscow	[illegible]
Bergen	1 958	Verkhoyansk	[illegible]
San José	1 944	Barrow	[illegible]
Jakarta	1 755	Las Vegas	[illegible]
Tokyo	1 563	Kashgar	[illegible]
Juneau	1 387	Walvis Bay	[illegible]
New York	1 123	Aswân	[illegible]
Brisbane	1 092	Arica	[illegible]

compare: London 610

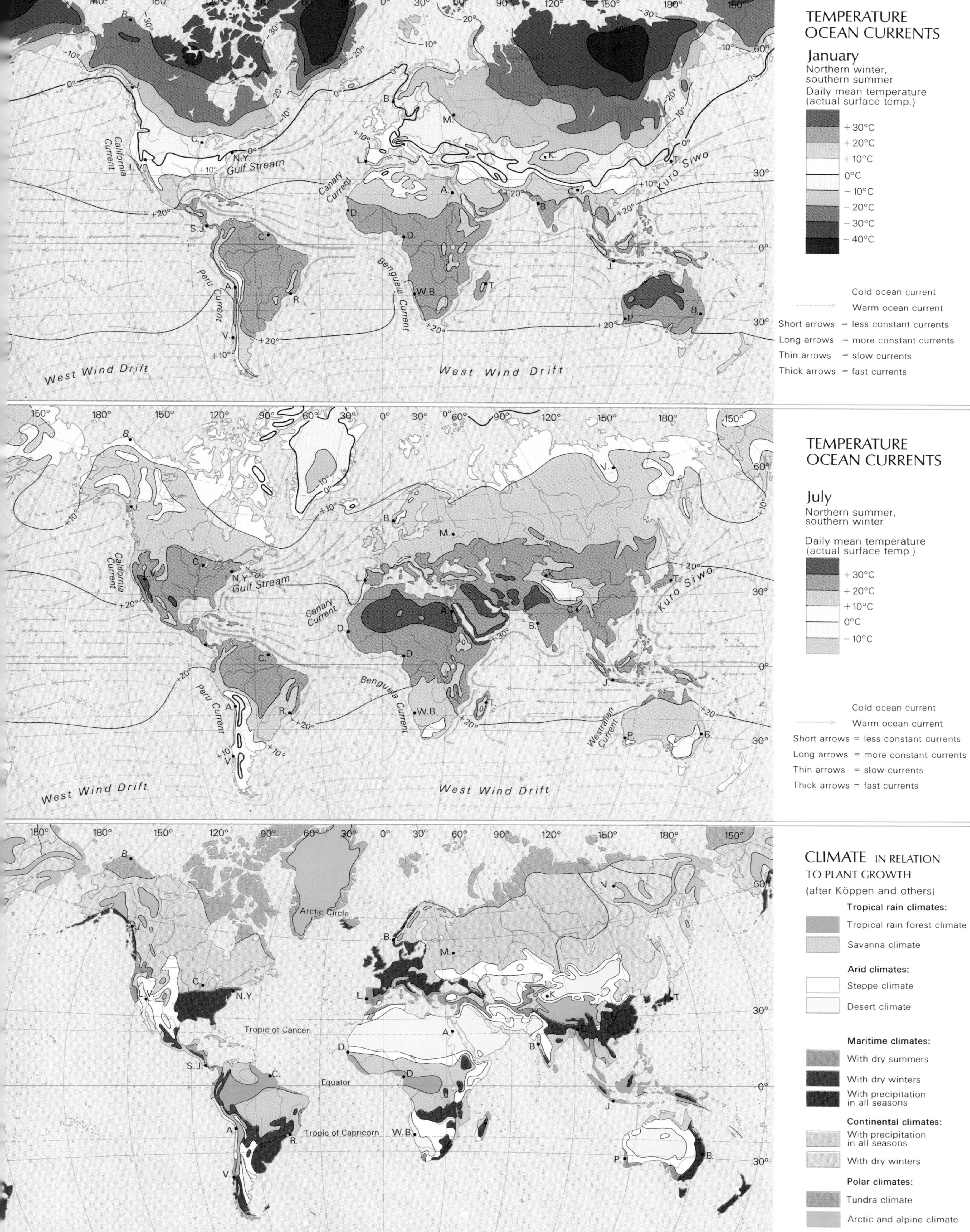

VAN DER GRINTEN'S PROJECTION

Scale 1:220 000 000
at the equator

Arctic Circle
Beaufort Sea
Bering Strait
Greenland
Baffin Bay
Alaska
Mackenzie River
Kamchatka
Bering Sea
Jan Mayen I.
Canadian
Iceland
Aleutian Islands
Hudson Bay
Shield
Labrador
British Isles
Great Lakes
St. Lawrence R.
Newfoundland
Iberian Peninsula
Mississippi R.
Azores
Lower California
Tropic of Cancer
Hawaiian Islands
Gulf of Mexico
Canary Islands
Antilles
Caribbean Sea
Cape Verde Islands
Marshall Islands
PACIFIC
ATLANTIC
Equator
Galápagos Islands
R. Amazon
OCEAN
OCEAN
Fiji
Tuamotu Archipelago
Tropic of Capricorn
Easter Island
R. Paraná
New Zealand
Ice cap
Continental shelf
The earth was formed several billion years ago – equivalent to more than four feet on the scale used here to show the last 600 million years.
PROTEROZOIC
PRE-CAMBRIAN
CAMBRIAN
The oldest rocks known date back 3.9 billion years
Life in sea onl
Worms
Jellyfish
Trilobites
5000–4000 mill.years ago
600
Pre-Cambrian folding
Great extent of shallow
PERMIAN/TRIASSIC
200 million years ago
Panthalassa
JURASSIC/CRETACEOUS
135 million years ago
LAURASIA
Panthalassa
Tethys Sea
GONDWANALAND
TERTIARY
65 million years ago
QUATERNARY
Present day
NORTH AMERICA
EURASIA
AFRICA
SOUTH AMERICA
AUSTRALIA
ANTARCTICA
CONTINENTAL DRIFT
Boundary between plates
Canadian Shield
Baltic Shield
EURASIAN PLATE
AMERICAN PLATE
PACIFIC PLATE
AFRICAN PLATE
INDIAN PLATE
NAZCA PLATE
ANTARCTIC PLATE
PLATE TECTONICS
Plate boundaries
Active ocean ridge
Ocean trench
Fracture zone
Direction of movement
Pre-Cambrian folding (later partly overlaid through sedimentation and younger folding)

Franz Josef Land
Barents Sea
Novaya Zemlya
Norwegian Sea
Fennoscandia
West Siberian Plain
R. Ob
R. Yenisei
R. Lena
L. Baykal
R. Amur
Arctic Circle
Bering Strait
Bering Sea
Sea of Okhotsk
Kamchatka
Aleutian Islands
Sakhalin
Kuril Islands
Honshu
R. Danube
Black Sea
Caspian Sea
Mediterranean Sea
Persian Gulf
R. Nile
R. Indus
R. Ganges
Hwang Ho
Yangtze Kiang
PACIFIC OCEAN
Tropic of Cancer
Mariana Islands
Marshall Islands
Caroline Islands
Philippine Islands
South China Sea
Bay of Bengal
Sri Lanka
Arabian Sea
Borneo
Sumatra
Sunda Islands
Java
New Guinea
Equator
INDIAN OCEAN
R. Congo
Madagascar
Coral Sea
New Hebrides
Fiji
Australia
Tropic of Capricorn
Tasman Sea
New Zealand
PRIMARY (Palaeozoic)
ORDOVICIAN SILURIAN DEVONIAN
Upper Palaeozoic
CARBONIFEROUS PERMIAN
SECONDARY (Mesozoic)
TRIASSIC JURASSIC CRETACEOUS
TERTIARY (Caenozoic)
QUATERNARY
Graptolites
Nautiloids
Shellfish
Sea lilies
Bony fishes
Primitive amphibians
Giant insects
Ichthyosaurs
Primitive birds
First Mammals
Giant reptiles
Mammals
Birds
Man
440 400 350 300 270 225 200 180 136 100 65
Present day
Volcanic activity
Caledonian folding
Great swamps
Hercynian folding
Great lava flows
Extensive swamps and shallow seas
Alpine folding
Scale 1:90 000 000
MOUNTAIN BUILDING
Main trend lines
Main fault zones
Sediment overlaid plateau
Pre-Cambrian folding (stable shields)
Caledonian folding
Hercynian folding
Alpine folding
EARTHQUAKES AND VOLCANOES
Jan Mayen I.
Surtsey
Aleutian Is.
Azores
Mt. Etna
Mt. Klyuchevskaya Sopka
Mariana Is.
Mt. Cotopaxi
Mt. Kilimanjaro
Sunda Islands
New Hebrides
Tristan da Cunha
Zone of strong seismic activity (frequent earthquakes)
Zones of less frequent seismic activity (earthquakes can occasionally occur even in other areas)
Active volcano or zone of volcanic activity (several minor volcanoes)
VAN DER GRINTEN'S PROJECTION

90°
A
0°
B
90°
1
2
3
4
5
Baffin Bay
Greenland
Mohns Ridge
Novaya Zemlja
Barents Sea
Norwegian Sea
Jan Mayen Ridge
Norwegian Basin
Arctic Circle
Iceland
Scandinavia
Ural Mountains
A S I
Hudson Bay
Labrador Basin
Irminger Basin
Mid-Atlantic Ridge
Hatton Bank
Rockall Bank
North Sea
Celtic Shelf
EUROPE
NORTH AMERICA
NORTH ATLANTIC OCEAN
Mt. Blanc 4807
The Alps
5633 Caucasus
Caspian Sea
Tien Shan
Pamir
Appalachians
Sohm Abyssal Plain
Azores
Mediterranean Sea
Atlas Mountains
Sargasso Sea
Canary Islands
Himalayas
Mt. Everest 8848
Kane Fracture Zone
Tropic of Cancer
Red Sea
Puerto Rico Trench 9219
Antilles
Indus Cone
Cape Verde Islands
AFRICA
Arabian Basin
Ganges Cone
Ceara Abyssal Plain
Carlsberg Ridge
Cameroon Mountains
Romanche Fracture Zone
Guinea Basin
Equator
Somali Basin
Great Indian Basin
0°
5895
Mt. Kilimanjaro
Seychelles Bank
Andes
SOUTH AMERICA
Mid-Indian Ridge
INDIAN OCEAN
Ninety East Ridge
Peru-Chile Trench
Brazil Basin
Angola Basin
Madagascar
Wharton Basin
Tropic of Capricorn
7975
SOUTH ATLANTIC OCEAN
Walvis Ridge
Rio Grande Fracture Zone
Grande Ridge
Mt. Aconcagua 6959
Mocambique Basin
Southwest Indian Ridge
Cape Abyssal Plain
Cape Agulhas
Cape Basin
Marion Fracture Zone
Argentine Basin
Conrad Rise
Southeast Indian Ridge
Atlantic-Indian Rise
Falkland Islands
Kerguelen Gaussberg Ridge
Australian-Antarctic Basin
Enderby Abyssal Plain
Meteor Depth 8264
Scotia Ridge
Cape Horn
90°
0°
90°
FISHING
Density of animal plankton
Over 500 milligrams per cubic metre water
200–500 ›› ›› ››
50–200 ›› ›› ››
under 50 ›› ›› ››
Important catch of:
whale
herring, cod and similar fish
tuna
crab, prawn and other shellfish
© EMS

MERCATOR'S PROJECTION

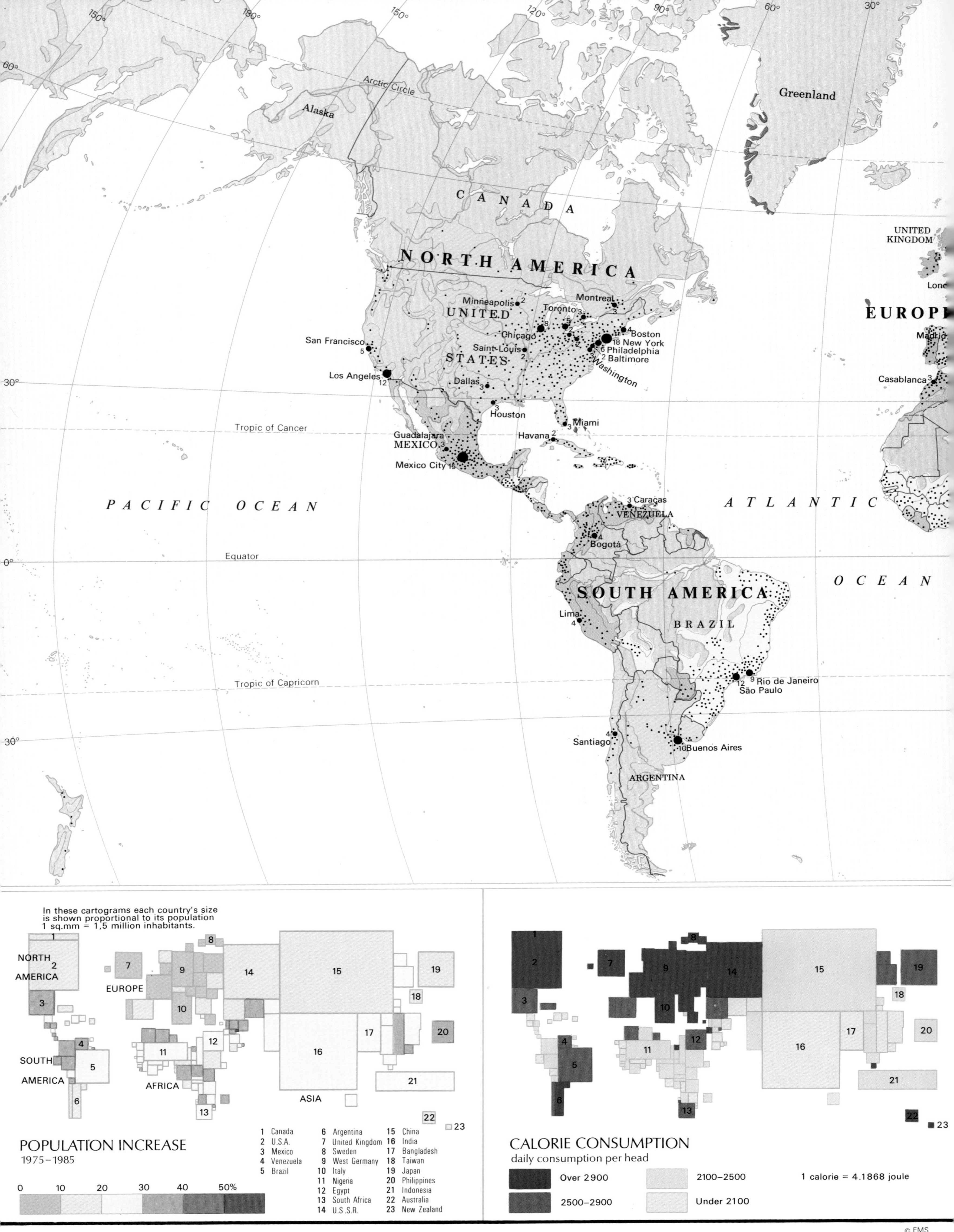

Greenland
Alaska
Arctic Circle
CANADA
NORTH AMERICA
UNITED STATES
UNITED KINGDOM
EUROPE
Minneapolis 2
Montreal 3
Toronto 3
Chicago 8
Boston 4
New York 18
Philadelphia 6
Baltimore 2
Washington
San Francisco 5
Saint Louis 2
Los Angeles 12
Dallas 3
Houston 3
Miami 3
Havana 2
Madrid
Casablanca 3
Tropic of Cancer
Guadalajara 3
MEXICO
Mexico City 15
PACIFIC OCEAN
ATLANTIC OCEAN
Caracas 3
VENEZUELA
Bogotá 4
Equator
SOUTH AMERICA
Lima 4
BRAZIL
Tropic of Capricorn
Rio de Janeiro 9
São Paulo 12
Santiago 4
Buenos Aires 10
ARGENTINA
In these cartograms each country's size is shown proportional to its population 1 sq.mm = 1,5 million inhabitants.
NORTH AMERICA
EUROPE
SOUTH AMERICA
AFRICA
ASIA
POPULATION INCREASE
1975–1985
0 10 20 30 40 50%
1 Canada
2 U.S.A.
3 Mexico
4 Venezuela
5 Brazil
6 Argentina
7 United Kingdom
8 Sweden
9 West Germany
10 Italy
11 Nigeria
12 Egypt
13 South Africa
14 U.S.S.R.
15 China
16 India
17 Bangladesh
18 Taiwan
19 Japan
20 Philippines
21 Indonesia
22 Australia
23 New Zealand
CALORIE CONSUMPTION
daily consumption per head
Over 2900
2500–2900
2100–2500
Under 2100
1 calorie = 4.1868 joule

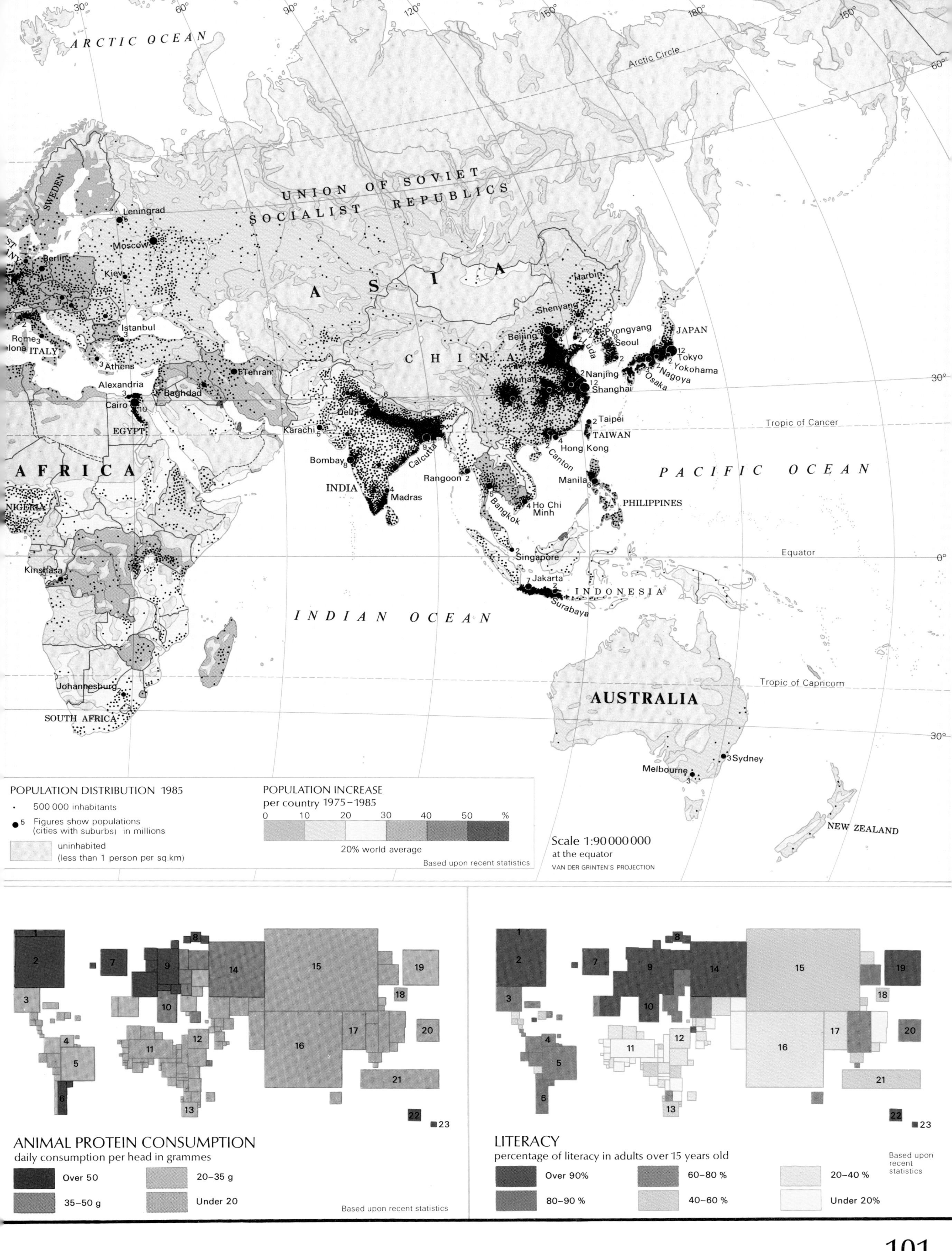
ARCTIC OCEAN
Arctic Circle
UNION OF SOVIET SOCIALIST REPUBLICS
ASIA
CHINA
SWEDEN
Leningrad
Moscow
Berlin
Kiev
Istanbul
Rome
ITALY
Athens
Alexandria
Cairo
EGYPT
Baghdad
Tehran
Karachi
Delhi
Bombay
INDIA
Madras
Calcutta
Rangoon
Bangkok
Ho Chi Minh
Singapore
Jakarta
Surabaya
INDONESIA
Manila
PHILIPPINES
Hong Kong
Canton
Taipei
TAIWAN
Shanghai
Nanjing
Wuhan
Beijing
Shenyang
Harbin
Luda
Pyongyang
Seoul
JAPAN
Tokyo
Yokohama
Nagoya
Osaka
Tropic of Cancer
PACIFIC OCEAN
Equator
INDIAN OCEAN
AFRICA
NIGERIA
Kinshasa
Johannesburg
SOUTH AFRICA
Tropic of Capricorn
AUSTRALIA
Sydney
Melbourne
NEW ZEALAND
POPULATION DISTRIBUTION 1985
500 000 inhabitants
Figures show populations (cities with suburbs) in millions
uninhabited (less than 1 person per sq.km)
POPULATION INCREASE per country 1975–1985
0 10 20 30 40 50 %
20% world average
Based upon recent statistics
Scale 1:90 000 000 at the equator
VAN DER GRINTEN'S PROJECTION
ANIMAL PROTEIN CONSUMPTION
daily consumption per head in grammes
Over 50
35–50 g
20–35 g
Under 20
Based upon recent statistics
LITERACY
percentage of literacy in adults over 15 years old
Over 90%
80–90 %
60–80 %
40–60 %
20–40 %
Under 20%
Based upon recent statistics

U.S.S.R.
Kamchatka
Arctic Circle
Bering Strait
Bering Sea
Aleutian Islands
Alaska (U.S.A.)
Beaufort Sea
Victoria Island
Mackenzie River
Baffin Bay
Baffin Island
Greenland (DENMARK)
Jan Mayen I. (NORWAY)
Reykjavik
ICELAND
Faeroe Islands (DENMARK)
UNITED KINGDOM
REP. OF IRELAND
Dublin
Hudson Bay
CANADA
Labrador
Newfoundland
St. Pierre & Miquelon (FR.)
Ottawa
UNITED STATES
Washington
Mississippi R.
International Date Line
Monday
Sunday
Midway I. (U.S.A.)
Hawaiian Islands
Hawaii (U.S.A.)
Tropic of Cancer
Lower California
Gulf of Mexico
Florida
Nassau
THE BAHAMAS
Bermuda (U.K.)
Azores (PORT.)
PORTUGAL
Lisbon
Gibraltar (U.K.)
Rabat
MOROCCO
Madeira (PORT.)
Canary Islands (SP.)
Western Sahara
MAURITANIA
Nouakchott
ATLANTIC
MEXICO
Mexico City
Havana
CUBA
Kingston
HAITI
DOMINICAN REP.
Puerto Rico (U.S.A.)
ST. KITTS-NEVIS
ANTIGUA & BARBUDA
DOMINICA
ST. LUCIA
ST. VINCENT
BARBADOS
GRENADA
TRINIDAD & TOBAGO
Port of Spain
JAMAICA
Port-au-Prince
Santo Domingo
BELIZE
Belmopan
HONDURAS
Tegucigalpa
Guatemala
GUATEMALA
EL SALVADOR
San Salvador
NICARAGUA
Managua
San José
COSTA RICA
PANAMA
Panamá
Caracas
VENEZUELA
GUYANA
Georgetown
SURINAM
Paramaribo
French Guiana
Bogotá
COLOMBIA
Quito
ECUADOR
Galápagos Islands (ECU.)
Clipperton I. (FR.)
CAPE VERDE ISLANDS
Praia
SENEGAL
Dakar
THE GAMBIA
Banjul
Bissau
GUINEA-BISSAU
GUINEA
Conakry
Freetown
SIERRA LEONE
Monrovia
LIBERIA
IVORY COAST
Bamako
PACIFIC
OCEAN
Palmyra I. (U.S.A.)
Kiritimati
Bairiki
Equator
KIRIBATI
Phoenix Islands
TUVALU
Funafuti
Tokelau Islands (N.Z.)
Wallis & Futuna Is. (FR.)
WESTERN SAMOA
Apia
Samoa (U.S.A.)
FIJI
Suva
TONGA
Nukualofa
Cook Islands (N.Z.)
Society Islands
Tahiti
French Polynesia
Marquesas Islands
Tuamotu Archipelago
Mururoa
Tubuai Islands
Pitcairn I. (U.K.)
Tropic of Capricorn
Easter Island (CHILE)
R. Amazon
BRAZIL
Brasília
PERU
Lima
La Paz
BOLIVIA
Sucre
PARAGUAY
Asunción
CHILE
R. Paraná
Santiago
Buenos Aires
URUGUAY
Montevideo
ARGENTINA
Kermadec Islands (N.Z.)
Wellington
NEW ZEALAND
Falkland Islands (U.K.)
Tierra del Fuego
South Georgia (U.K.)
Ascension I. (U.K.)
Saint Helena (U.K.)
Trindade I. (BRAZ.)
Tristan da Cunha (U.K.)
AMERICAN ASPECT
centre Chicago
EUROPEAN ASPECT
centre London
EAST ASIATIC ASPECT
centre Peking
MILITARY POLITICS
N.A.T.O., A.N.Z.U.S.
Warsaw Pact
Other communist states
Arab League
Other states
W. William-Olsson projection

TRADE POLITICS

E.E.C. | E.E.C. associated, Commonwealth | E.F.T.A. | L.A.I.A. | Comecon | Other countries | O.P.E.C.

A
B
C
D
E
F
G
1
2
3
4
5
150°
180°
120°
90°
60°
30°
0°
Beaufort Sea
Prudhoe Bay
Bering Strait
Alaska
Mackenzie River
Kamchatka
Bering Sea
Aleutian Islands
Baffin Bay
Greenland
Baffin Island
Arctic Circle
Uranium City
Hudson Bay
Godthåb
Iceland
Labrador
British Isles
Kemano
Alberta
NORTH AMERICA
Saskatchewan
Grand Coulee
Columbia River
Wyoming
Fremont Co.
North Dakota
Elliott Lake
Great Lakes
Montreal
St. Lawrence R.
Newfoundland
Utah
Kansas
Illinois
Pennsylvania
West Virginia
Kentucky
California
Hoover
Panhandle
Tennessee
Valencia
Texas
Louisiana
Gulf of Mexico
Tampico
PACIFIC
Hawaiian Islands
Tropic of Cancer
West Indies
Caribbean Sea
Maracaibo
ATLANTIC
OCEAN
Equator
Orito
R. Amazon
SOUTH AMERICA
OCEAN
Santa Cruz
Minas Gerais
Tropic of Capricorn
Don Otto
R. Paraná
Malargüe
New Zealand
Comodoro Rivadavia
Tierra del Fuego
CANADA
63
81
U.S.A.
615
422
WESTERN EUROPE
562
133
727
COMMUNIST COUNTRIES INCL. CHINA
687
JAPAN
196
MEXICO
115
55
NORTH AFRICA
132
31
71
11
779
115
MIDDLE EAST
17
REST OF ASIA
63
85
NORTHERN SOUTH AMERICA
129
WEST AFRICA
50
101
SOUTH EAST ASIA
59
98
SOUTHERN SOUTH AMERICA
19
27
REST OF AFRICA
20
OCEANIA
32
NORTH AMERICA
784
699
WESTERN EUROPE
496
583
1925
COMMUNIST COUNTRIES INCL. CHINA
2009
JAPAN
18
97
185
190
SOUTHERN ASIA
21
LATIN AMERICA
26
137
AFRICA
104
OCEANIA
115
68
OIL: production, consumption, sea transport (metric tons)
139
production (million tons/year)
83
consumption (million tons/year)
transport of crude oil (million tons/year)
less than 20
20–100
100–200
200–400
400–800
over 800
COAL: production, consumption (metric tons)
330
production (million tons/year)
394
consumption (million tons/year)
coal and lignite expressed in comparable values (coal equivalent)

ARCTIC OCEAN
Svalbard
Novaya Zemlya
Barents Sea
Vorkuta
R. Ob
Siberia
R. Lena
R. Yenisei
Bratsk
Lake Baikal
"Third Baku"
Kuznetsk Basin
Arctic Circle
Bering Strait
Alaska
Bering Sea
Kamchatka
Sea of Okhotsk
Aleutian Islands
Sakhalin
Kuril Islands
Hokkaido
Honshu
Sakuma
Kyushu
R. Amur
Manchuria
Billingen
R. Volga
Second Baku
EUROPE
Donets Basin
R. Ural
Volgograd
Ploiesti
Black Sea
Caspian Sea
Baku
ASIA
Dzungaria
Fergana Basin
Mediterranean Sea
Hassi-Messaoud
Zaltan
Kirkuk
Aghā Jarī
Burgān (Kuwait)
Persian Gulf
Abu Dhabi
Ghawar
Aswān Sadd el Aali
R. Nile
Red Sea
Arlit
AFRICA
Bakouma
Moanda
R. Congo
Kariba
Cabora Bassa
Madagascar
Rössing
Witwatersrand
Bhakra
R. Indus
R. Ganges
Assam
Bihar
Szechwan (Red Basin)
Hwang Ho
Yangtze Kiang
PACIFIC OCEAN
Tropic of Cancer
Gulf of Bengal
Arabian Sea
Sri Lanka
Equator
South China Sea
Philippine Islands
Brunei
Borneo
Sumatra
Sunda Islands
New Guinea
INDIAN OCEAN
Rum Jungle
Coral Sea
Tropic of Capricorn
AUSTRALIA
Snowy Mts
Gippsland Shelf
Tasman Sea
New Zealand
LAND
sedimentary basin (partly oil-bearing)
bedrock without thick sediment cover
hydro electric power > 500 Mw
deposits of:
uranium
crude oil
tar sands or oil shales
natural gas
coal
lignite
SEA
sedimentary basin (partly oil-bearing)
shallow seabed without thick sediment cover
shallow sea (continental shelf)
200 m
2000 m
deep sea
Scale 1:90 000 000 at the equator
NORTH AMERICA 2359 1533
WESTERN EUROPE 832 572
COMMUNIST COUNTRIES INCL. CHINA 3089 1349
CENTRAL AMERICA (INCL. VENEZUELA AND COLOMBIA) 428 285
AFRICA 500 99
MIDDLE EAST 1193 408
REST OF ASIA 365 186
SOUTH AMERICA 133 46
OCEANIA 128 34
Hydro-electric & nuclear power 3,6%
Natural gas 21,4%
Coal, lignite 29,4%
Crude oil 45,6%
THE WORLD'S SOURCES OF ENERGY
PRODUCTION OF ENERGY
Total annual production of primary energy (crude oil, natural gas, coal, lignite, peat, hydro-electric and nuclear power)
primary energy expressed in million tons coal
537 AFRICA 99 1981 1962
CONSUMPTION OF ENERGY
Total annual consumption of primary energy per person by country (expressed in kilograms of coal)
100 1000 3000 6000 kilograms per person
VAN DER GRINTEN'S PROJECTION

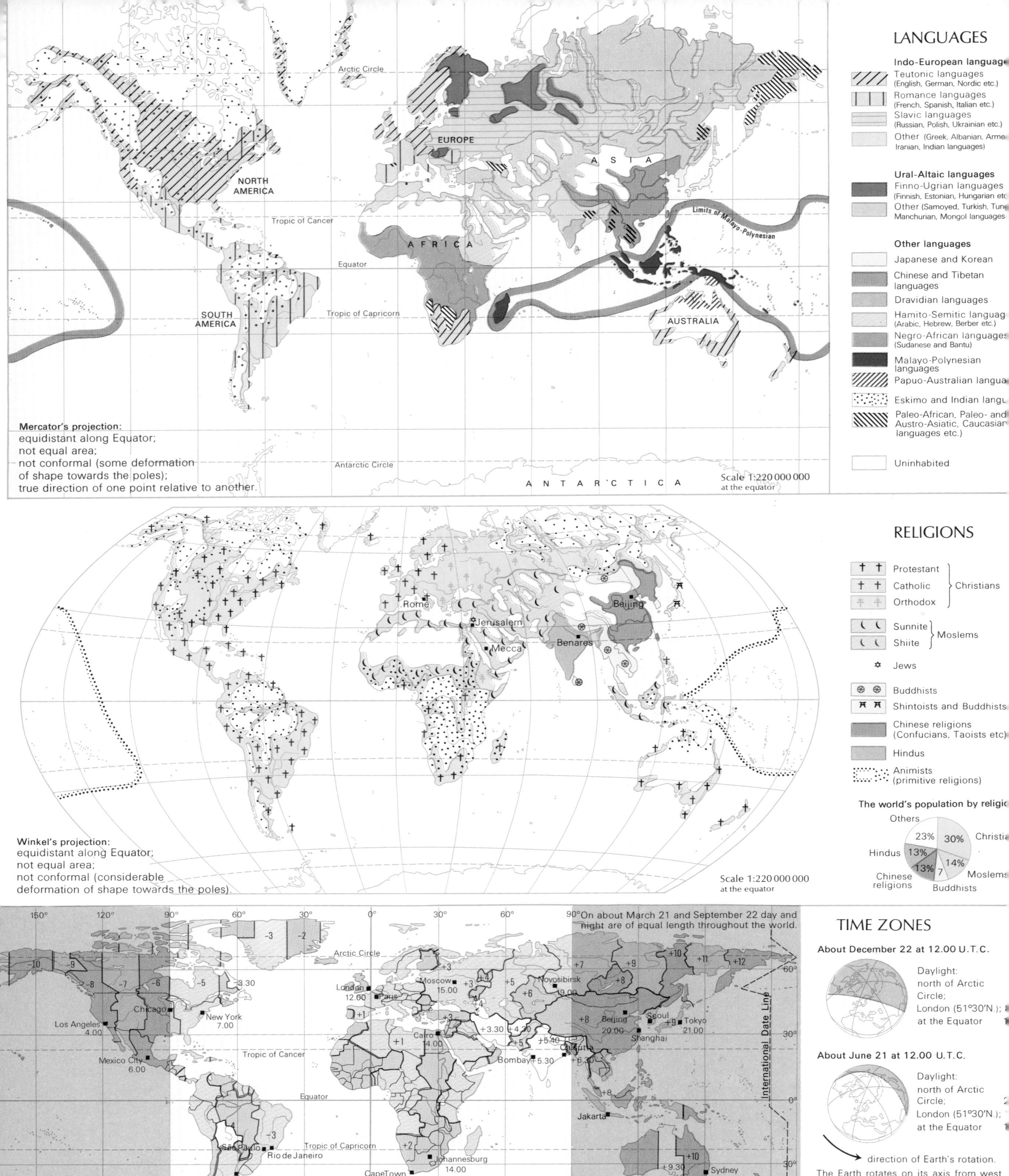
LANGUAGES
Indo-European languages
Teutonic languages (English, German, Nordic etc.)
Romance languages (French, Spanish, Italian etc.)
Slavic languages (Russian, Polish, Ukrainian etc.)
Other (Greek, Albanian, Armenian, Iranian, Indian languages)
Ural-Altaic languages
Finno-Ugrian languages (Finnish, Estonian, Hungarian etc.)
Other (Samoyed, Turkish, Tungus, Manchurian, Mongol languages)
Other languages
Japanese and Korean
Chinese and Tibetan languages
Dravidian languages
Hamito-Semitic languages (Arabic, Hebrew, Berber etc.)
Negro-African languages (Sudanese and Bantu)
Malayo-Polynesian languages
Papuo-Australian languages
Eskimo and Indian languages
Paleo-African, Paleo- and Austro-Asiatic, Caucasian languages etc.)
Uninhabited
Arctic Circle
EUROPE
ASIA
NORTH AMERICA
Tropic of Cancer
Limits of Malayo-Polynesian
AFRICA
Equator
SOUTH AMERICA
Tropic of Capricorn
AUSTRALIA
Mercator's projection:
equidistant along Equator;
not equal area;
not conformal (some deformation of shape towards the poles);
true direction of one point relative to another.
Antarctic Circle
ANTARCTICA
Scale 1:220 000 000 at the equator
RELIGIONS
Protestant
Catholic
Orthodox
Christians
Sunnite
Shiite
Moslems
Jews
Buddhists
Shintoists and Buddhists
Chinese religions (Confucians, Taoists etc.)
Hindus
Animists (primitive religions)
The world's population by religion
Others 23%
Christians 30%
Hindus 13%
Chinese religions 13%
Buddhists 7
Moslems 14%
Rome
Jerusalem
Mecca
Beijing
Benares
Winkel's projection:
equidistant along Equator;
not equal area;
not conformal (considerable deformation of shape towards the poles).
Scale 1:220 000 000 at the equator
TIME ZONES
About December 22 at 12.00 U.T.C.
Daylight: north of Arctic Circle; London (51°30′N.); at the Equator
About June 21 at 12.00 U.T.C.
Daylight: north of Arctic Circle; London (51°30′N.); at the Equator
direction of Earth's rotation.
The Earth rotates on its axis from west to east and completes one rotation in about 24 hours. The Earth has been divided into 24 Standard Time Zones. The lines separating these Zones on land mostly follow country or province boundaries. Many countries however use a different standard, eg. British Summer Time.
On about March 21 and September 22 day and night are of equal length throughout the world.
Arctic Circle
Los Angeles 4.00
Chicago
New York 7.00
Mexico City 6.00
London 12.00
Paris
Moscow 15.00
Cairo 14.00
Novosibirsk 19.00
Bombay 5.30
Calcutta
Beijing 20.00
Seoul
Tokyo 21.00
Shanghai
Jakarta
Tropic of Cancer
Equator
International Date Line
São Paulo
Rio de Janeiro
Tropic of Capricorn
Buenos Aires 9.00
Cape Town
Johannesburg 14.00
Sydney 22.00
Universal Time Coordinated
Plate Carrée projection:
equidistant along Equator and along meridians;
not equal area;
not conformal (deformation of shape towards the poles).
Scale 1:220 000 000 at the equator
Antarctic Circle
6.00 U.T.C.
12.00 U.T.C.
18.00 U.T.C.
24.00 U.T.C.
−10 −9 −8 −7 −6 −5 −4 −3 −2 −1 0 +1 +2 +3 +4 +5 +6 +7 +8 +9 +10 +11 +12−

GLOSSARY and INDEX

The **GLOSSARY**, p. 107–109, provides an English translation of those geographical names and words which are presented on the maps in the languge of the area concerned. For languages using non-Latin alphabets, official transcriptions have been used throughout the entire atlas—in maps, glossary and index.

The words in the glossary are mostly single words, but some prefixes and suffixes are also translated into English. In some cases the name on the map is abbreviated, for instance **Khr**. for the Russian **Khrebet** (mountain chain or range). In the glossary both the full name and its abbreviation is given.

The **INDEX**, p. 111–202, contains about 47.000 names found in the map section. As a general rule each entry is referred to the map page where the place or feature is shown at the largest scale and where it is best seen in its national and environmental context. The oceans and some oceanic islands are referred to small-scale maps to show the extent of the oceans and, for the islands, their correct location.

Each name in the index is located by a map page number and an index square on that particular page. The locational reference is to the name and not, for instance, the extent of country or the position of the town. The squares are defined by letters and figures. For example the town Nyeri in Kenya is found in the index with the reference 65 F 5 which means that Nyeri is found on page 65 in index square F (marked at the top and at the bottom of the map spread) and 5 (marked at the sides of the spread).

Some names are given only a page number as reference. Some of these names appear on the maps of the Polar regions, where an index with letters and figures would be confusing. Other entries refer to names on the thematical maps of the continents which do not have index squares.

GLOSSARY

A

- **å** *Dan., Nor., Swe.* river
- **açude** *Portugese* reservoir
- **adrar** *Berber* mountains
- **ákra, akrotition** *Greek* cape
- **Alb, Alp** *German* mountains, peak
- **alpes** *French* mountains
- **alpi** *Italian* mountains
- **-älv, -älven** *Swedish* river
- **ao** *Thai* bay
- **archipiélago** *Spanish* archipelago
- **arquipélago** *Portugese* archipelago
- **arrecife** *Spanish* reef
- **arroyo** *Spanish* brook
- **-ås, -åsen** *Swedish* hills
- **atol** *Portugese* atoll
- **aïn** *Arabic* spring

B

- **bab** *Arabic* strait
- **bælt** *Danish* strait
- **bahia** *Spanish* bay
- **bahr, baḥr** *Arabic* river, sea
- **baia** *Portugese* bay
- **baie** *French* bay
- **ballon** *French* mountain
- **balta** *Romanian* marsh
- **bañados** *Spanish* marsh
- **-bandao** *Chinese* peninsula
- **barrage** *French* dam
- **baraji** *Turkish* reservoir
- **batang** *Indonesian* river
- **batu** *Malay* mountain
- **Becken** *German* basin
- **ben** *Gaelic* mountain
- **Berg** *German* mountain, hill
- **berg** *Afrikaan, Dutch* mountains
- **-berg** *Swedish* mountain, hill
- **Berge** *German* mountains
- **-bergen** *Swedish* mountains
- **-berget** *Swedish* mountain, hill
- **bi'r** *Arabic* well
- **birkat** *Arabic* lake
- **boca** *Spanish* river mouth
- **boğazi** *Turkish* strait
- **bogd** *Mongolian* range
- **bol'shoy** *Russian* big
- **bong** *Korean* mountain
- **-breen** *Norwegian* glacier
- **Bucht** *German* bay
- **bugt** *Danish* bay
- **buḥayrah** *Arabic* lake
- **buḥayrat** *Arabic* lake, lagoon
- **bukit** *Indon., Malay* mountain
- **-bukten** *Swedish* bay
- **burnu, burun** *Turkish* cape

C

- **c., cabo** *Spanish* cape
- **c., cabo** *Port.* cape
- **cachoeira** *Portugese* waterfall
- **canal** *Fr., Port., Sp.* canal, channel
- **canale** *Italian* canal, channel, strait
- **cao nguyen** *Vietnamese* plateau
- **c., cap** *French* cape
- **capo** *Italian* cape
- **causse** *French* upland
- **c., co., cerro** *Spanish* mountain
- **c., co., cerros** *Spanish* mountains
- **chapada** *Portugese* hills
- **chott** *Arabic* intermittent lake, salt marsh
- **chuŏr phnum** *Cambod.* mountains
- **ciudad** *Spanish* city
- **co** *Chinese* lake
- **col** *French* pass
- **colina** *Spanish* hill
- **colinas** *Spanish* hills
- **colli** *Italian* hills
- **collines** *French* hills
- **con** *Vietnamese* islands
- **cord., cordillera** *Sp.* mountains
- **corno** *Italian* mountain
- **costa** *Spanish* coast
- **côte** *French* coast, hills
- **crêt** *French* peak
- **cuevas** *Spanish* caves

D

- **dağ, daği** *Turkish* mountain
- **dāgh** *Persian* mountains
- **dağlar, dağlan** *Turkish* mountains
- **dahr** *Arabic* hill
- **-dal, -dalen** *Nor., Swe.* valley
- **danau** *Indonesian* lake
- **-dao** *Chinese, Vietnam.* island
- **daryācheh** *Persian* lake
- **dasht** *Persian* desert
- **deniz, denizi** *Turkish* sea
- **desierto** *Spanish* desert
- **détroit** *French* strait
- **dhar** *Arabic* escarpment
- **-dian** *Chinese* lake
- **dijk** *Dutch* dike
- **djebel** *Arabic* mountain, mountains
- **-djupet** *Swedish* deep
- **-do** *Korean* island
- **doi** *Thai* mountain
- **dolina** *Russian* valley
- **dolok** *Indonesian* mountain

E

- **-egga** *Norwegian* mountain
- **-elv, -elva** *Nor.* river
- **embalse** *Spanish* reservoir
- **erg** *Arabic* desert
- **espigão** *Portugese* highland
- **estero** *Spanish* estuary
- **estrecho** *Spanish* strait
- **étang** *French* pond
- **-ey** *Icelandic* island

F

- **falaise** *French* cliff
- **farsh** *Arabic* upland
- **-fell** *Icelandic* mountain
- **-feng** *Chinese* mountain
- **firth** *Gaelic* estuary, strait
- **-fjäll** *Swedish* hill, mountain
- **-fjällen** *Swedish* mountain, mountains
- **-fjället** *Swedish* mountain
- **-fjell, -fjellet** *Norwegian* mountain
- **-fjöll** *Icelandic* mountain
- **-fjord** *Norwegian* fjord
- **-fjorden** *Nor., Swe.* fjord, lake
- **-fjördur** *Icelandic* fjord, bay
- **-flói** *Icelandic* bay
- **foci** *Italian* river mouths
- **-fonni** *Norwegian* glacier
- **fontaine** *French* spring
- **-foss** *Icelandic* waterfall

G

- **g., gora** *Russian* mountain, hill
- **G., gunung** *Malay* mountain
- **G., gunung** *Indonesian* mountain
- **gebergte** *Dutch* mountains
- **Gebirge** *German* mountains
- **greçidi** *Turkish* pass
- **ghubbat** *Arabic* bay
- **Gipfel** *German* peak
- **gji** *Albanian* bay
- **gol** *Mongol* river
- **göl, gölü** *Turkish* lake
- **golfe** *French* gulf
- **golfo** *It., Sp.* gulf
- **gora** *Serbo-Croathian* mountains

góra *Polish*	mountain
gorje *Serbo-Croathian*	mountains, hills
gory *Russian*	mountains, hills
góry *Polish*	mountains
grotte *French*	grotto
gryada *Russian*	mountain
guba *Russian*	bay
guelb *Arabic*	mountain
-guntō *Japanese*	islands

H

Haff *German*	lagoon
-hai *Chinese*	sea, lake
-haixia *Chinese*	strait
-halvøya *Norwegian*	peninsula
-hama *Japanese*	beach
hamada *Arabic*	desert
hammādat *Arabic*	plateau
hāmūn *Persian*	lake, marsch
harrat *Arabic*	lava flow
-hav *Swedish*	sea, bay
havre *French*	harbor
hawr *Arabic*	lake
-he *Chinese*	river
Heide *German*	heath
hka *Burmese*	river
-holm *Danish*	island
horn *German*	cape, mountain
hory *Czech., Slovenian*	mountains
-hu *Chinese*	lake

I

i., isla *Spanish*	island
idhan *Arabic*	dunes
île *French*	island
îles *French*	islands
ilha *Portugese*	islands
Insel *German*	island
Inseln *German*	islands
Insulá *Romanian*	island
'irq *Arabic*	dunes
islas *Spanish*	islands
isola *Italian*	island
isole *Italian*	islands
istmo *Spanish*	isthmus

J

jabal *Arabic*	mountain, mountains
järv *Estonian*	lake
-järvi *Finnish*	lake
-jaur *Lappish*	lake
-javre *Lappish*	lake
jazā'ir *Arabic*	islands
jazīrat *Arabic*	island
jazīreh *Persian*	island
jebel *Arabic*	mountain
jezero *Serbo-Croathian, Albanian*	lake
jezioro *Polish*	lake, lagoon
-jiang *Chinese*	river
jibāl *Arabic*	mountains
-jima *Japanese*	island
-joki *Finnish*	river
-jøkulen *Norwegian*	glacier
-jökull *Icelandic*	glacier

K

kabīr *Persian*	mountains
-kaikuō *Japanese*	strait
-kaise *Lappish*	mountain
kalns *Latvian*	mountain
Kamm *German*	ridge
kanaal *Dutch*	canal
kanal *Rus., S. C., Swe., Ger.*	canal, channel
kanava *Finnish*	canal, channel
Kap *German*	cape
-kapp *Norwegian*	cape
kas *Cambodian*	island
kavīr *Persian*	desert
kep *Albanian*	cape
k., kep., kepulauan *Indon.*	islands
khalīj *Arabic*	gulf
khashm *Arabic*	mountain
Khr., Khrebet *Russian*	mountain range
ko *Thai.*	island
-ko *Japanese*	lake, lagoon
koh *Afgan.*	mountains
kólpos *Greek*	bay
körfezi *Turkish*	gulf, bay
Kórgustik *Estonian*	mountain
kosa *Russian*	spit
kotlina *Polish*	basin
-kou *Chinese*	bay, pass
krueng *Indonesian*	river
kryazh *Russian*	mountains
kuala *Malay*	bay
kūh *Persian*	mountain
kūhha *Persian*	mountains
-kulle *Swedish*	hill
kyun *Burmese*	island

L

l., lac *French*	lake
la *Tibethan*	pass
lacs *French*	lakes
lacul *Bulgarian*	lake
lago *It., Sp. Port.*	lake
L., lagoa *Portugese*	lake, lagoon
lagos *Port., Sp.*	lakes
lag., laguna *Spanish*	lagoon, lake
l., laut *Indonesian*	sea
les *Czechoslovakian*	mountains, forest
liman *Russian*	estuary, bay
limni *Greek*	lake
-ling *Chinese*	peak
llano *Spanish, Port.*	plain
llanos *Spanish, Port.*	plains
loch *Gaelic*	lake, inlet
lough *Gaelic*	lake

M

m., munţii *Romanian*	mountains
mae *Thai*	river
-mak *Turkish*	river
-man *Korean*	bay
mar *Spanish*	sea
marais *French*	marsch
mare *Italian*	sea
massif *French*	mountain, mountains
Meer *German*	sea, lake
meer *Afrikaans, Dutch*	sea, lake
mer *French*	sea
mesa *Spanish*	mesa
meseta *Spanish*	plateau
mierzeja *Polish*	spit
-misaki *Japanese*	cape
mont *French*	mount
montagna *Italian*	mountain
montagne *French*	mountain
montagnes *French*	mountains
montaña *Spanish*	mountain
montañas *Spanish*	mountains
monte *It., Port., Sp.*	mount
montes *Port., Sp.*	mountains
monti *Italian*	mountains
monts *French*	mountains
more *Russian*	sea
morro *Port., Sp.*	hill, mountain
motu *Polynesian*	island, rock
mui *Vietnamese*	point
munkhafad *Arabic*	depression
munţii *Romanian*	mountains
mys *Russian*	cape

N

nafūd *Arabic*	desert
najor'ye *Russian*	plateau, mountains
namakzār *Persian*	salt flat
-näs *Swedish*	peninsula
nasjonal park *Nor.*	national park
neem *Estonian*	cape
-nes *Ice., Nor.*	peninsula, point
ness *Gaelic*	promontory
nev., nevado *Spanish*	mountain
ngoc *Vietnamese*	mountain
niso *Greek*	islands
nizmennost' *Russian*	plain
nunatakk *Eskimoo*	peak
nuruu *Mongol*	mountains
nuur *Mongol*	lake

O

-ö *Swe., Dan., Nor.*	island
o., ostrov *Russian*	island
-öarna *Swedish*	islands
-ön *Swedish*	island
óri *Greek*	mountains
óros *Greek*	mountain, mountains
ostrov *Russian*	island
ostrova *Russian*	islands
ostrovul *Romanian*	island
otok *Serbo-croathian*	island
-øy, -øya *Norwegian*	island
oz., ozero *Russian*	lake
ozera *Russian*	lakes

P

pahorkatina *Czech.*	hills
palla *Italian*	peak
pampa *Spanish*	plain
pantanal *Port., Sp.*	swamp
parc national *French*	national park
parq. nac., parque nacional *Port., Sp.*	national park
pas *French*	strait
paso *Spanish*	pass
Pass *German*	pass
passe *French*	passage
passo *Italian*	pass
pasul *Romanian*	pass
peg., pegunungan *Indonesian*	mountains
pélagos *Greek*	sea
peña *Spanish*	peak, rock
-pendi *Chinese*	basin
peninsula *Spanish*	peninsula
pereval *Russian*	pass
pertuis *French*	strait
peski *Russian*	desert
phnum *Cambodian*	mountain
pic *French*	peak
pico *Port., Sp.*	peak
picos *Port., Sp.*	peaks
-piggen *Norwegian*	mountains
pik *Russian*	peak
plaine *French*	plain
planalto *Portugese*	plateau
planina *Serbo-Croathian*	mountain
plato *Bulgarian, Russian*	plateau
playa *Spanish*	beach
ploskogorje *Russian*	plateau
pointe *French*	point
poluostrov *Russian*	peninsula
ponta *Portugese*	point
porog *Russian*	waterfall
presa *Spanish*	reservoir, dam
prohod *Bulgarian*	pass
proliv *Russian*	strait
promontorio *It., Sp.*	promonotyr
puerto *Spanish*	pass
puig *Catalonian*	peak
pulau *Indon., Malay*	island
puna *Spanish*	upland
punta *It., Sp.*	point, peak
puncak *Indonesian*	peak
puo *Laotian, Thai*	mountain
puy *French*	peak

Q

qanāt *Arabic*	canal
-quando *Chinese*	islands
qurnat *Arabic*	mountains

R

r. *Port., Sp.*	river
rags *Latvian*	cape
ramlat *Arabic*	dunes
rās, ra's *Arabic*	cape
rās *Persian*	cape
ravnina *Russian*	plain
récif *French*	reef
récifs *French*	reefs
R., reprêsa *Portugese*	dam, reservoir
-retto *Japanese*	islands
ria *Spanish*	estuary
rio *Portugese*	river
río *Spanish*	river
riviera *Italian*	coast
rivière *French*	river
rt *Serbo-Croathian*	cape
Ruck *German*	mountain

S

sa. *Portugese*	mountains
saar *Estonian*	island
sabkhat *Arabic*	lagoon, salt marsh
sadd *Arabic*	dam
saguia *Arabic*	wadi
şsahrā' *Arabic*	desert
salar *Spanish*	salt flat
salina, salinas *Spanish*	salt marsh, salt flat
-sälkä *Finnish*	ridge
-sanmyaku *Japanese*	range
-san *Jap., Korean*	mountain
-sanchi *Japanese*	mountains
-sanmaek *Korean*	mountains
sarīr *Arabic*	desert
Sattel *German*	pass
saurums *Latvian*	strait
sebkha *Arabic*	salt flat
sebkra *Arabic*	intermittent lake
See *German*	lake
Seen *German*	lakes
selat *Indonesian*	strait
serra *Portugese, Sp.*	mountains, mountain
serania, serranias *Sp.*	mountains
shamo *Chinese*	desert
-shan *Chinese*	mountains, mountain, island
-shankou *Chinese*	pass
sharm *Arabic*	bay
-shima *Japanese*	island
-shotō *Japanese*	islands
-shuiku *Chinese*	reservoir
sierra *Spanish*	mountains

silsilesi *Turkish*	mountains
-sjö *Norwegian*	lake
-sjön *Swedish*	lake, bay
serrania *Spanish*	mountains
sopka *Russian*	mountain
Spitze *German*	peak
sierra *Spanish*	mountains
step' *Russian*	plain
štit *Slovenian*	peak
stretto *Italian*	strait
-suidō *Japanese*	channel
-sund *Swedish*	sound
s., sungai *Indonesian*	river

T

tg., tanjung *Indones.*	cape
-tangar-, tangi *Icelandic*	point
tassili *Berber*	plateau
taung *Burmese*	mountain
teluk *Indonesian*	bay
ténéré *Berber*	desert
tepe, tepesi *Turkish*	peak, hill
thiu khao *Thai.*	mountains
-tind, -tindane *Nor.*	mountain
-tō *Japanese*	island
tónlé *Cambodian*	lake
-top *Dutch*	peak
-träsk *Swedish*	lake
-tunturi *Finnish*	mountain

U–V

uul *Mongol*	mountain, mountains
-vaara *Finnish*	hill
val *French, Italian*	valley
valle *Italian, Spanish*	valley
vallée *French*	valley
-vatn *Ice., Nor.*	lake
-vesi *Finnish*	lake
-vidda *Norwegian*	plateau
-viken *Swedish*	gulf
Virful *Romanian*	mountain
vodokhranilishche *Russian*	reservoir
vol., volcán *Spanish*	volcano
vozvyshennost *Russian*	upland
vrh., vrchovina *Czech., Slo.*	mountains
-väin *Estonian*	strait
-vötn *Icelandic*	lake

W–Z

wādi *Arabic*	wadi
wāhat *Arabic*	oasis
Wald *German*	forest, mountains
-wan *Ch., Jap.*	bay
-xan *Chinese*	strait
-yama *Japanese*	mountain
y., yarimadasi *Turkish*	peninsula
yoma *Burmese*	mountains
-zaki *Japanese*	point
zalew *Polish*	lagoon
zaliv *Russian*	gulf, bay
zatoka *Polish*	gulf
zee *Dutch*	sea, lake

INDEX

A

Almalyk 35 H 2
Almansa 18 C 4
Almazán 18 C 3
Almaznyy 36 K 3
Almeirim 85 H 4
Almelo 14 E 4
Almenara 87 H 4
Almenara, Sierra de la 18 C 4
Almendra, Embalse de 18 B 3
Almendralejo 18 B 4
Almería 18 C 4
Almería, Golfo de 18 C 4
Al'met'yevsk 24 K 5
Älmhult 17 F 4
Almina, Punta 58 D 1
Almirante 84 B 2
Almirante Brown 91
Almirante Montt, Golfo 89 B 9
Almirós 20 B 3
Almodôvar 18 B 4
Almogasta 88 C 4
Almonte 18 B 4
Almora 40 CD 2
Almoustarat 62 D 2
Almuñécár 18 C 4
Almus 21 E 2
Alness 2 B 3
Alney, Gora 37 TU 4
Alnmouth 5 E 2
Alnön 16 G 3
Alnwick 5 E 2
Alo 63 J 3
Alofi (Cook Is.) 52 D 4
Alofi (Wallis and Futuna) 52 D 3
Alomata 65 F 2
Along 41 F 2
Alongshan 37 M 5
Alónnisos 20 B 3
Alor, Pulau 43 F 5
Alor, Selat 43 F 5
Alor Setar 42 B 2
Álora 18 C 4
Alotau 49 J 1
Alotau 51 F 4
Alpachiri 89 D 6
Alpena 77 K 2
Alpercatas, Serra das 85 JK 5
Alpes Mancelles 18 C 2
Alpha 49 H 3
Alpha River 49 H 3
Alphonse 65 J 6
Alpi Carniche 19 F 2
Alpi Dolomitiche 19 F 2
Alpi Marittime 19 E 3
Alpi Orobie 19 EF 2
Alpine (TX, U.S.A.) 76 F 5
Alpine (WY, U.S.A.) 76 D 3
Alqueva, Barragem de 18 B 4
Als 17 EF 5
Alsask 73 Q 5
Alsasua 18 C 3
Alsfeld 15 E 4
Alsh, Lake 2 B 3
Al'skiy Khrebet 37 P 5
Alsten 16 F 2
Alston 5 D 2
Alta 16 H 2
Alta Gracia 88 D 5
Altaelva 16 H 2
Altafjorden 16 H 1
Altagracia de Orituco 84 E 2
Altai 36 EF 6
Altamachi 86 C 4
Altamaha River 77 K 5
Altamira 85 H 4
Altamont 76 B 3
Altamura 19 G 3
Altan 36 J 6
Altanbulag 36 J 5
Altaqracia 84 D 1
Altar 76 D 5
Altas, Rías 18 B 3
Altat 36 F 4
Altata 76 E 7
Altatump 25 M 3
Altay (China) 35 M 1
Altay (Mongolia) 36 G 6
Altay (U.S.S.R.) 25 N 3
Altay (U.S.S.R.) 25 R 5
Altay Shan 35 M 1
Altayskiy 25 QR 5
Altdorf 19 E 2
Altenburg 15 F 4
Altevatnet 16 G 2
Altıntaş 20 D 3
Altiplanicie Mexicana 78 B 2
Altiplano 86 C 4
Altkirch 19 E 2
Altmark 15 F 4
Altmühl 15 F 5
Altnaharra 2 B 2
Alto Araguaia 87 F 4
Alto Chicapa 66 B 2
Alto Garças 87 F 4
Alto Molócuè 67 F 3
Alto Paraguai 86 E 3
Alto Parnaíba 87 G 2
Alto Purus 86 B 2–3
Alto Río Senguerr 89 B 8
Alto Sucuriú 87 F 4
Alto Turi 87 G 1
Alto Zaza 66 B 1
Alto-Alentejo 18 B 4
Alton (IL, U.S.A.) 77 H 4
Alton (U.K.) 7 D 2
Alton Downs 49 F 4
Altoona 77 L 3
Altrincham 5 D 3
Altun Ha 78 E 4
Āltūn Kūprī (Iraq) 22 D 2
Altun Shan 38 AB 3
Alturas 76 B 3
Altus 76 G 5
Altynasar 35 G 1
Alu 51 G 3
Alucra 21 E 2
Aluk 64 D 3
'Alūla 65 J 2
Alūm (Iran) 23 E 2
Aluminé 89 B 6
Alupka 21 D 2
Alur 40 C 4
'Ālūs (Iraq) 22 D 2
Alushta 21 D 2
Al'Uyūn (Saudi Arabia) 22 D 4
Alva (OK, U.S.A.) 76 G 4
Alva (U.K.) 3 C 3
Alvano, Kūh-e (Iran) 23 E 2
Alvarães 85 F 4
Alvdal 16 F 3
Älvdalen 16 F 3
Älvdalen 17 F 3
Alvear 88 E 4
Alvelos, Serra de 18 B 4
Alvesta 17 F 4
Alvid 2 C 3
Ålvik 17 E 3
Älvkarleby 17 G 3
Alvorado 87 G 3
Alvord Valley 76 C 3
Älvsbyn 16 H 2
Alwar 40 C 2
Alxa Youqi 38 D 3
Alxa Zuoqi 38 DE 3
Alyangula 49 F 1
Alyaskitovyy 37 Q 3
Alygdzher 36 G 5
Alys-Khaya 37 P 2
Alysy-Garakh 37 Q 2
Alytus 17 H 5
Alzamay 36 G 4
Am Dam 63 J 3
Am Djéména 63 H 3
Am Guereda 63 J 3
Am Raya 63 H 3
Am Timan 63 J 3
Am Zoer 63 J 3
Amada 60 E 4
Amada Gaza 64 B 4
Amadeus, Lake 48 E 3
Amadi 64 E 3
Amadjuak Lake 75 N 2–3
Amahai 43 G 4
Amain, Monts d' 18 D 2
Amakinskiy 36 K 1
Åmål 59 K 3
Åmål 17 F 4
Amalfi (Colombia) 84 D 2
Amalfi (Italy) 19 F 3
Amalias 20 B 3
Amambaí 87 EF 5
Amami-ō-shima 39 J 5
Amanã, Lago 85 F 4
Amangel'dy 25 N 5
Amanino 37 T 4
Amanotkel' 35 G 1
Amanu 53 F 4
Amanzimtoti 67 E 6
Amapá 85 H 3
Amapá 85 H 3
Amar 63 FG 4
'Amara 60 E 4
Amarante 87 H 2
Amārat Abū Sinn 60 EF 5
Amarillo 76 F 4
Amaro Leite 87 G 3
Amarti 65 G 2
Amasra 21 D 2
Amasya 21 E 2
Amataurá 84 E 4
Amazar 36 M 5
Amazon 85 H 4
Amazonas 84–85 EF 4
Amazonas 85 H 4
Amba Farit 65 F 2
Ambala 40 C 1
Ambalavao 67 H 4
Ambam 63 G 5
Ambanja 67 H 2
Ambar 36 EF 2
Ambarchik 36 G 4
Ambarchik 37 U 2
Ambardakh 37 P 1
Ambarnyy 16 K 2
Ambato 84 C 4
Ambato Boény 67 H 3
Ambatofinandrahana 67 H 4
Ambatolampy 67 H 3
Ambatondrazaka 67 H 3
Ambatosoratra 67 H 3
Ambatry 67 G 4
Ambelos, Ákra 20 B 3
Amberg 15 F 5
Ambérieu-en-Bugey 19 E 2
Ambgaon 40 D 3
Ambidédi 62 B 3
Ambikapur 40 D 3
Ambilobe 67 H 2
Amble-by-the-Sea 5 E 2
Ambleside 5 D 2
Ambo 86 A 3
Amboasary 67 H 4
Ambodifototra 67 HJ 3
Ambohibe 67 G 4
Ambohimahasoa 67 H 4
Ambohitralanana 67 J 3
Ambon 43 G 4
Ambon, Pulau 43 G 4
Ambositra 67 H 4
Ambovombe 67 H 5
Ambre, Cap d' 67 H 2
Ambre, Montange d' 67 H 2
Ambrim 51 J 5
Ambriz 66 A 1
Ambur 40 C 5
Amchitka 72 A 5
Amchitka Pass 72 AB 5
'Amd 61 H 5
Amderma 25 M 2
Amdo 38 B 4
Ameca 78 B 3
Amendolara 19 G 3–4
'Āmeri (Iran) 23 F 3
American Falls Reservoir 76 D 3
American Highland 91
American Samoa 52 D 3
Americus 77 K 5
Amersham 7 D 2
Amery Ice Shelf 91
Ames 77 H 3
Amesbury 7 D 2
Amet 40 B 2
Ametlla de Mar 18 D 3
Amfilokhia 20 B 3
Amfissa 20 B 3
Amga 37 O 3
Amgu 39 L 1
Amguema 72 B 2
Amguid 59 G 3
Amgun' 37 P 5
Amhara 65 F 2
Amherst 75 P 6
Amherst Island 77 L 3
Amiata 19 F 3
Amiens 18 D 2
Amik Gölü 21 E 3
Amili 41 G 2
'Amīnābād (Iran) 23 F 3
Amindivi Islands 40 B 5
Aminuis 66 B 4
Amirante Islands 65 J 6
Amisk Lake 73 R 5
Amka 37 Q 4
Amlia 72 C 5
Amlwch 6 B 1
'Amm Adām 60 F 5
'Ammān (Jordan) 22 B 3
Ammanford 6 B 2
Ammarfjället 16 G 2
Ammarnäs 16 G 2
Ammokhostos → Famagusta 21 D 3
Amo 36 H 3
Āmol (Iran) 23 F 1
Amolar 86 E 4
Amorgós 20 C 3
Amos 75 M 6
Åmot 17 E 4
Amour, Djebel 59 F 2
Amourj 58 D 5
Amoy 39 G 6
Ampanihy 67 G 4
Amparafaravola 67 H 3
Ampitsikanana 67 H 2
Amposta 18 D 3
Ampthill 7 D 1
'Amrān 61 G 5
Amravati 40 C 3
Amri 35 H 5
'Amrit (Syria) 22 B 2
Amritsar 40 C 1
Amroha 40 C 2
Amsā'ad 59 K 2
Amsterdam (Netherlands) 14 DE 4
Amsterdam (N.Y., U.S.A.) 77 M 3
Amstetten 19 F 2
Amtkeli 21 F 2
Āmūda (Syria) 22 C 1
Amu-Dar'ya 35 G 2
Amudat 64 E 4
Amukta Pass 72 C 5
Amulrea 3 C 3
Amundsen Gulf 73 N 1
Amundsen Sea 91
Amundsen-Scott 91
Amungen 16 G 3
Amuntai 42 E 4
Amur 37 P 5
Amursk 37 P 5
Amvrakikos Kólpos 20 B 3
Amysakh 36 L 2
An Nabatīyah at Tahta (Lebanon) 22 B 2
An Nabk (Syria) 22 B 2
An Nabk Abū Qasr (Saudi Arabia) 22 C 3
An Nafidah 19 F 4
An Nafūd (Saudi Arabia) 22 CD 3
An Nāfūrah 59 K 3
An Nāhiyah (Iraq) 22 C 2
An Najaf (Iraq) 22 D 2–3
An' Nakhl (Egypt) 22 AB 3
An Nāmūs, Jabal 59 J 3–4
An Nashshāsh (United Arab Emirates) 23 FG 5
An Nashwawh (Iraq) 23 E 3
An Nāsirīyah (Iraq) 23 E 3
An Nhon 41 J 5
An Nu'ayrīyah (Saudi Arabia) 23 E 4
An Nuhūd 60 D 6
An Nu'mān (Saudi Arabia) 22 B 4
An Nu'mānīyah (Iraq) 23 D 2
An Nuqayr (Saudi Arabia) 23 E 4
An Nūwfalīyah 59 J 2
An Tuc 41 J 5
An Uaimh Navan 4 B 3
An Xian 38 D 4
Ana Maria, Golfo de 79 G 3
Anabar 36 K 1
Anabarskiy Zaliv 36 KL 1
Anabarskoye Ploskogor'ye 36 J 1–2
Anaco 85 F 2
Anaconda 76 D 2
Anadoli 20–21 CD 3
Anadyr' 37 X 3
Anadyr' 37 X 3
Anadyrskaja Nizmennost' 37 X 2
Anadyrskiy Liman 37 X 3
Anadyrskiy Zaliv 37 Y 3
Anadyrskiy Zaliv 72 B 3
Anadyrskoye Ploskogor'ye 37 VW 2
Anáfi 20 C 3
Anåfjället 16 F 3
Anaghit 65 F 1
Anagni 19 F 3
'Ānah (Iraq) 22 C 2
Anáhuac 78 C 2
Anaï 59 H 4
Anaimalai Hills 40 C 5
Anajás 85 J 4
Anajatuba 87 H 1
Anakapalle 40 D 4
Anaklia 21 F 2
Anaktuvuk Pass 72 G 2
Analalava 67 H 2
Anamá 85 F 4
Anambas, Kepulauan 42 C 3
Anamur 21 D 3
Anamur Burnu 21 D 3
Anamur Burum (Turkey) 22 A 2
Anamuryum 21 D 3
Anangravnen, Sopka 37 U 4
Anantapur 40 C 5
Anantnag 35 K 4
Anan'yev 20 C 1
Anapa 21 E 2
Anapka 37 U 3
Anápolis 87 G 4
Anapu 85 H 4
Anār (Iran) 23 G 3
Anārak (Iran) 23 F 2
Anarisfjällen 16 F 3
Anatahan 52 A 1
Anatolia 20–21 D 3
Añatuya 88 D 4
Anauá 85 F 3
Anavarza 21 E 3
Anavelona 67 G 4
Anavilhanas, Arquipélago das 85 F 4
'Anazah, Jabal (Iraq) 22 C 2
Anbyŏn 39 J 3
Ancares, Sierra de 18 B 3
Ancasti, Sierra de 88 C 4
Ancenis 18 C 2
Ancha 37 P 3
Anchor Bay 76 B 4
Anchorage 72 H 3
Anci 39 G 3
Ancohuma 86 C 4
Ancon (Ecuador) 84 B 4
Ancón (Peru) 86 A 3
Ancona 19 F 3
Ancuabe 67 F 2
Ancud 89 B 7
Ancud, Golfo de 89 B 7
Anda 39 J 1
Andacollo (Argentina) 89 B 6
Andacollo (Chile) 88 B 5
Andahuaylas 86 B 3
Andalgala 88 C 4
Åndalsnes 16 E 3
Andalucía 18 BC 4
Andaman Islands 41 F 5
Andaman Sea 41 G 5–6
Andamooka 49 F 5
Andapa 67 H 2
Andara 66 C 3
Andarab 35 H 3
Andaraí 87 H 3
Andeg 24 K 2
Andenes 16 G 2
Andéranboukane 62 E 2
Anderson (IN, U.S.A.) 77 J 3–4
Anderson (N.W.T., Can.) 72 M 2
Anderson (S.C., U.S.A.) 77 K 5
Anderstorp 17 F 4
Andes (Colombia) 84 C 2
Andes Mountains 81 C 2–6
Andevoranto 67 H 3
Andfjorden 16 G 2
Andhra Pradesh 40 C 4
Andikira 20 B 3
Andikíthira 20 B 3
Andilamena 67 H 3
Andilanatoby 67 H 3
Andīmeshk 34 D 4
Andīmeshk (Iran) 23 E 2
Andípaxoi 20 AB 3
Andiria Burun 21 D 3
Andiria burun (Cyprus) 22 B 2
Andırın 21 E 3
Andirlangar 35 L 3
Andiyskiy Khrebet 21 G 2
Andizhan 35 J 2
Andkhui 35 H 3
Andoas 84 C 4
Andomskiy Pogost 24 G 3
Andong 39 J 3
Andorra 18 D 3
Andorra la Vella 18 D 3
Andover 7 D 2
Andöya 16 G 2
Andradina 87 F 5
Andraitx 18 D 4
Andranopasy 67 G 4
André Félix National Park 64 C 3
Andreanof Islands 72 BC 5
Andreas 4 C 2
Andrepatsy 67 H 3
Andrews 76 F 5
Andreyevka 21 E 1
Andreyevka 24 K 5
Andreyevka 25 Q 6
Andreyevo-Ivanovka 20 D 1
Andreyevsk 36 KL 4
Andreyevskiy 36 KL 4
Andria 19 G 3
Andriamena 67 H 3
Andriba 67 H 3
Andringitra 67 H 4
Androka 67 G 5
Androna, Plateau de l' 67 H 3
Andropov 24 G 4
Ándros 20 B 3
Ándros 20 C 3
Andros Island 79 G 3
Androsovka 24 J 5
Androth 40 B 5
Andrushevka 17 J 5
Andryushka 37 S 2
Andselv 16 G 2
Andu Tan 42 D 2
Andudu 64 D 4
Andújar 18 C 4
Andulo 66 B 2
Andyngda 36 L 2
Aneby 17 FG 4
Anécho 62 E 4
Anéfis 62 E 2
Anegada, Bahía 89 D 7
Anegada Passage 79 K 4
Aneityum 51 JK 6
Añelo 89 C 6
Aneroft 5 D 2
Aneto, Pico de 18 D 3
Aney 63 G 2
Ang Thong 41 H 5
Angamos, Punta 86 B 5
Ang'angxi 39 H 1
Angar 43 H 4
Angara 36 F 4
Angarsk 36 H 5
Angas Downs 48 E 4
Angatau 53 F 4
Angaul 36 H 5
Angaur 43 H 2

Boulder (Australia) 48 C 5
Boulder (U.S.A.) 76 F 3
Boulia 49 F 3
Boulogne-sur-Mer 18 D 1
Boulouli 62 C 2
Bouloupari 51 J 6
Boulsa 62 D 3
Boultoum 63 G 3
Bouly 58 C 5
Boumdeïd 58 C 5
Boun Neua 41 H 3
Bouna 62 D 4
Boundiali 62 C 4
Boundji 63 GH 6
Boundou 62 B 3
Boundoukou 62 D 4
Bounoum 62 A 2
Bountiful 76 D 3
Bounty Islands 91
Bourail 51 J 6
Bourem 62 D 2
Bouressa 62 E 1
Bourg 19 E 2
Bourganeuf 18 D 2
Bourges 18 D 2
Bourget, Lac du 19 E 2
Bourgogne 19 DE 2
Bourgogne, Canal de 18 D 2
Bourgoin-Jallieu 19 E 2
Bourke 49 H 5
Bourne 7 D 1
Bournemouth 7 D 2
Bournemouth (Airport) 7 D 2
Bouroum 62 D 3
Bourton-on-the-Water 7 D 2
Bourtoutou 63 J 3
Boussens 18 D 3
Bousso 63 H 3
Bouvet Island 91
Bouza 63 F 3
Bovril 88 E 5
Bow 73 P 5
Bowen (Argentina) 88 C 5
Bowen (Australia) 49 H 2
Bowes 5 C 2
Bowkan (Iran) 23 E 1
Bowland Forest 5 D 2–3
Bowling Green 77 J 4
Bowling Green, Cape 49 H 2
Bowman 76 F 2
Bowman Bay 75 MN 2
Bowmore 3 A 4
Bowral 49 J 5
Boxholm 17 G 4
Boxing 39 G 3
Boyabat 21 D 2
Boyabo 64 B 4
Boyang 39 G 5
Boyang Hu 38 G 5
Boyarka 36 G 1
Boyarsk 36 J 4
Boyle 14 B 4
Boyne, River 4 B 3
Boyuibe 86 D 5
Boz Dağı 20 C 3
Bozcaada 20 C 3
Bozdağ 21 D 3
Bozdoğan 20 C 3
Bozeman 76 D 2
Bozene 64 B 4
Bozkır 21 D 3
Bozok Platosu 21 DE 3
Bozouls 18 D 3
Bozoum 64 B 3
Bozova 21 E 3
Bozshakul' 25 OP 5
Bozüyük 20 D 3
Bra 19 E 3
Brač 19 G 3
Bracadale 2 A 3
Bracciano, Lago di 19 F 3
Bräcke 16 G 3
Bracki Kanal 19 G 3
Brackley 7 D 1
Bracknell 7 D 2
Bracora 3 B 3
Brad 20 B 1
Bradano 19 G 3
Bradda Head 4 C 2
Bradenton 77 K 6
Bradford (PA, U.S.A.) 77 L 3
Bradford (U.K.) 5 E 3
Bradford-on-Avon 7 C 2
Bradley Reefs 51 H 3
Bradshaw 48 E 2
Brady 76 G 5
Brady Mountains 76 G 5
Brae 2 D 1
Braemar 3 C 3
Braga 18 B 3
Bragado 88 D 6
Bragança 18 B 3
Bragança 85 J 4
Bragina 37 X 3
Brahman Baria 41 F 3
Brahmaputra 41 F 2
Brăila 20 C 1
Brailsford 7 D 1
Brainerd 77 H 2
Braintree 7 E 2
Braithwaite Point 48 E 1
Brăk 59 H 3
Brakna 58 C 5
Brålanda 17 F 4
Bramdean 7 D 2
Bramhapuri 40 C 3
Brämön 16 G 3
Brampton 75 L 7
Brampton (U.K.) 5 D 2
Brancaster 7 E 1
Brandberg 66 A 4
Brandberg West Mine 66 A 4
Brande 17 E 4
Brandenburg 15 F 4
Brandon 5 E 2
Brandon 7 E 1
Brandon 73 S 6
Brandsby 5 E 2
Brandvlei 66 C 6
Braniewo 15 GH 4
Branston 7 D 1
Brantford 75 L 7
Brás 85 G 4
Bras d'Or Lake 75 PQ 6
Brasil, Planalto do 87 H 4
Brasiléia 86 C 3
Brasília 87 G 4
Brasília Legal 85 G 4
Brasília, Parque Nacional do 87 G 4
Braslav 17 J 4
Braşov 20 C 1
Brass 63 F 5
Brassey, Mount 48 E 3
Bratca 20 B 1
Bratislava 15 G 5
Bratsk 36 H 4
Bratskoye Vodokhranilishche 36 H 4
Bratslav 20 C 1
Brattleboro 77 M 3
Brattvåg 16 E 3
Braţul Borcea 20 C 2
Bratul Chilia 20 C 1
Braţul Cremenea 20 C 2
Bratul Sfintu Gheorghe 20 C 1–2
Braunau am Inn 19 F 2
Braunschweig 15 F 4
Braunton 6 B 2
Brava 62 AB 7
Bråviken 17 G 4
Bravo, Cerro 84 C 5
Brawley 76 C 5
Bray 75 M 2
Bray (South Africa) 66 C 5
Bray (U.K.) 4 B 3
Brazil 86–87 EG 3
Brazil Basin 98 A 4
Brazil Current 92
Brazo Casiquiare 84 E 3
Brazos River 77 G 5
Brazzaville 63 GH 6
Brčko 19 G 3
Brda 15 G 4
Brdy 15 F 5
Brea, Cerros de la 84 B 4
Breadalbane 3 B 3
Breaden, Lake 48 D 4
Bready 4 B 2
Breaza 20 C 1
Brebes 42 C 5
Brechin 3 C 3
Breckenridge 76 G 5
Brecknock, Península 89 B 9
Breclav 15 G 5
Brecon 6 C 2
Breda 14 D 4
Bredasdorp 66 C 6
Bredbyn 16 G 3
Brede 7 E 2
Bredy 25 M 5
Bregenz 19 E 2
Breiðafjörður 16 A 2
Breiðdalur 16 C 3
Breivikbotn 16 H 1
Brejo (Maranhão, Brazil) 87 H 1
Brejo (Piauí, Brazil) 87 H 2
Brekken 16 F 3
Brekstad 16 EF 3
Bremangerlandet 16 D 3
Bremen 15 E 4
Bremer Bay 48 B 5
Bremer Bay 48 B 5
Bremerhaven 15 E 4
Bremerton 76 B 2
Brenner 19 F 2
Brenta, Gruppo di 19 F 2
Brentwood 7 E 2
Brescia 19 F 2
Bressanone 19 F 2
Bressay 2 D 1
Brest (France) 18 C 2
Brest (U.S.S.R.) 17 H 5
Brestova 19 F 2
Bretagne 18 C 2
Breteuil 18 D 2
Breton, Pertuis 18 C 2
Brett, Cape 51 Q 8
Breueh, Pulau 42 A 2
Breves 85 H 4
Brevik 17 E 4
Brevoort Island 75 P 3
Brewarrina 49 H 4–5
Brewerville 62 B 4
Brewster, Kap 90
Brewton 77 J 5
Brezhnev 24 K 4
Brežice 19 G 2
Brézina 59 F 2
Bria 64 C 3
Briançon 19 E 3
Briare, Canal de 18 D 2
Brichany 20 C 1
Bride 4 C 2
Bridestowe 6 B 2
Bridge of Earn 3 C 3
Bridge of Gaur 3 B 3
Bridge of Orhy 3 B 3
Bridgend 2 C 3
Bridgend 3 A 4
Bridgend (Mid-Glamorgan) 6 C 2
Bridgend (Rep. of Ireland) 4 B 2
Bridgeport (CA, U.S.A.) 76 C 4
Bridgeport (CT, U.S.A.) 77 M 3
Bridger Peak 76 E 3
Bridgetown (Australia) 48 B 5
Bridgetown (Barbados) 79 KL 5
Bridgewater 75 P 7
Bridgnorth 6 C 1
Bridgwater 6 C 2
Bridgwater Bay 6 C 2
Bridlington 5 E 2
Bridlington Bay 5 E 2
Bridport 6 C 2
Brig 19 E 2
Brigg 5 E 3
Brigham City 76 D 3
Brighouse 5 E 3
Bright 49 H 6
Brightlingsea 7 E 2
Brighton 7 D 2
Brignoles 12
Brigstock 7 D 1
Brijuni 19 F 3
Brikama 62 A 3
Brindisi 19 G 3
Brinkene 58 E 3
Brinklow 7 D 1
Brisbane 49 J 4
Bristol 6 C 2
Bristol (Airport) 6 C 2
Bristol (TN, U.S.A.) 77 K 4
Bristol Bay 72 EF 4
Bristol Channel 6 C 2
Britânia 87 F 4
British Columbia 73 MN 4–5
British Isles 92
British Mountains 72 JK 2
Brits 66 D 5
Britstown 66 C 6
Brive 18 D 2
Briviesca 18 C 3
Brixham 6 C 2
Brixton 6 C 3
Brno 15 G 5
Broad Bay 2 A 2
Broad Sound 49 H 3
Broadback 75 M 5
Broadclyst 6 C 3
Broadford 2 B 3
Broadstairs 7 E 2
Broadus 76 EF 2
Broadview 73 R 5
Broadway 6 C 3
Broadway 7 D 1
Broadwey 6 C 2
Broadwindsor 6 C 3
Brochet 73 R 4
Brochet, Lake 73 R 4
Brocken 15 F 4
Brockenhurst 7 D 2
Brockman, Mount 48 B 3
Brock's Creek 48 E 1
Brockville 75 M 7
Brod 20 B 2
Broderick Falls 64 EF 4
Brodick 3 B 4
Brodnica 15 G 4
Brody 17 J 5
Broken Hill 49 G 5
Brokhovo 37 ST 4
Brokopondo 85 G 3
Bromölla 17 F 4
Bromyard 6 C 1
Brönderslev 17 F 4
Bronnikovo 25 N 4
Brönnöysund 16 F 2
Bronte 19 F 4
Brooke's Point 42 E 2
Brookfield 77 H 4
Brookhaven 77 H 5
Brookings (CA, U.S.A.) 76 B 3
Brookings (S.D., U.S.A.) 77 G 3
Brookland 7 E 2
Brooks 73 P 5
Brooks Range 72 FH 2
Brookston 77 H 2
Brookton 48 B 5
Brookville 49 H 3
Broom, Loch 2 B 3
Broome 48 C 2
Broome, Mount 48 D 2
Brora 2 C 2
Brora, River 2 B 2
Brough 5 D 2
Brough Head 2 C 2
Broughshane 4 B 2
Broughton 5 D 3
Broughton 7 D 1
Broughton in Furness 5 D 2
Broughton Island 75 P 2
Broughtown 2 C 2
Broutona, Ostrov 37 S 6
Brovst 17 E 4
Brown Lake 73 T 2
Brown River (Queensland, Austr.) 49 G 2
Browne Range Nature Reserve 48 CD 3–4
Brownfield 76 F 5
Brownhills 7 D 1
Browning 76 D 2
Brownsville 77 G 6
Brownwood 76 G 5
Browse Island 48 C 1
Broxburn 3 C 4
Bruay-en-Artois 18 D 1
Bruce Crossing 77 J 2
Bruce, Mount 48 B 3
Bruce Peninsula 75 L 7
Bruchsal 15 E 5
Bruck 19 G 2
Brückenau 15 EF 4
Brugge 14 D 4
Brumado 87 H 3
Bruncio 19 F 2
Bruneau 76 C 3
Brunei 42 D 2
Brunflo 16 FG 3
Brunsbüttel 15 E 4
Brunswick 77 K 5
Brunswick Bay 48 C 2
Brunswick, Peninsula de 89 B 9
Bruny 50 L 9
Brus, Laguna de 78 F 4
Brusilovka 24 KL 5
Brusovo 25 R 3
Brusque 88 G 4
Brussels 14 DE 4
Brusset, Erg 63 FG 2
Bruxelles 14 DE 4
Bruzual 84 E 2
Bryan 77 G 5
Bryan Coast 91
Bryanka 36 F 4
Bryansk 24 F 5
Bryanskoye 21 G 2
Brydekirk 3 C 4
Bryne 17 E 4
Bryn'kovskaya 21 E 1
Bryukhovetskaya 21 E 1
Bryungyadinskiye Gory 37 PQ 3
Brza Palanka 20 B 2
Brzeg 15 G 4
Bu Craa 58 C 3
Bū Ḥasā' (United Arab Emirates) 23 F 5
Bu Khanum 41 H 5
Bu Tu Suay 41 J 5
Bua Yai 41 H 4
Buandougou 62 C 4
Buapinang 43 F 4
Buba 62 A 3
Bubanza 64 D 5
Bubaque 62 A 3
Būbīyān (Kuwait) 23 E 3
Bucak 20 D 3
Bucaramanga 84 D 2
Buccaneer Archipelago 48 C 2
Buchan 2 C 3
Buchan Ness 2 D 3
Buchanan 62 B 4
Buchanan, Lake (Queensland, Austr.) 49 H 3
Buchanan, Lake (TX, U.S.A.) 76 G 5
Buchanan, Lake (Western Australia) 48 C 4
Buchardo 88 D 5
Bucharest 20 C 2
Bucharest → Bucureşti 20 C 2
Buchlyvrie 3 B 3
Buchs 19 E 2
Buck, Lake 48 E 2
Buckeye 76 D 5
Buckfastleigh 6 C 2
Buckhaven 3 C 3
Buckie 2 C 3
Buckingham 7 D 2
Buckingham Bay 49 F 1
Buckinghamshire 7 D 2
Buckland 7 E 1
Buckland 72 E 2
Buckland Tableland 49 H 3
Buckley 6 C 1
Buckley 6 C 1
Bucknall 7 D 1
Buco Zau 63 G 6
Bucureşti 20 C 2
Bucyrus 77 K 3
Bud Bud 65 H 4
Budacu, Virful 20 C 1
Budapest 20 A 1
Budaun 40 C 2
Bude 6 B 2
Bude Bay 6 B 2
Budennovka 24 K 5
Budennovsk 21 F 2
Búðardalur 16 A 2
Buðir 16 C 3
Budjala 64 B 4
Budleigh Salterton 6 C 2
Buea 63 F 5
Buen Pasto 89 C 8
Buena Vista 84 E 2
Buenaventura (Colombia) 84 C 3
Buenaventura (Mexico) 76 E 6
Buenavista 76 E 7
Buendia, Embalse de 18 C 3
Buengas 66 B 1
Buenópolis 87 H 4
Buenos Aires 88 DE 5
Buenos Aires, Lago 89 B 8
Buffalo (N.W.T., Can.) 73 P 3
Buffalo (N.Y., U.S.A.) 77 L 3
Buffalo (OK, U.S.A.) 76 G 4
Buffalo (S.D., U.S.A.) 76 F 2
Buffalo (WY, U.S.A.) 76 E 3
Buffalo Lake 73 OP 3
Buffalo Narrows 73 Q 4
Buftea 20 C 2
Bug 15 H 4
Buga 84 C 3
Bugala Island 64 E 5
Bugarach, Pech de 18 D 3
Bugarikhta 36 KL 5
Bugat 36 H 6
Bugel, Tanjung 42 D 5
Bugene 64 E 5
Bugojno 19 G 3
Bugorkan 36 J 3
Bugöynes 16 J 2
Bugrino 24 J 2
Bugsuk 42 E 2
Bugt 37 M 6
Bugul'deyka 36 J 5
Bugul'ma 24 K 5
Buguruslan 24 K 5
Buh He 38 C 3
Buhayrat al Asad (Syria) 22 C 1–2
Buhayrat Shārī (Iraq) 22 D 2
Buhera 67 E 3
Būhōdle 65 H 3
Bui Dam 62 D 4
Builth Wells 6 C 1
Buinsk 24 J 5
Buir Nur 36 L 6
Buitepos 66 B 4
Buítrago del Lozoya 18 C 3
Bujaraloz 18 CD 3
Bujaru 85 J 4
Buje 19 F 2
Bujumbura 64 D 5
Buka 51 F 3
Bukachacha 36 L 5
Bukadaban Feng 38 B 3
Bukakata 64 E 5
Bukama 64 D 6
Bukanskoye 25 Q 5
Bukantau, Gory 35 G 2
Bukavu 64 D 5
Bukene 64 E 5
Bukhara 35 G 3
Bukit Gandadiwata 43 EF 4
Bukit Harun 42 E 3
Bukit Kambuno 43 EF 4
Bukit Masurai 42 B 4
Bukit Mawa 42 D 3
Bukit Raya 42 D 4
Bukit Sulat 43 G 3
Bukittinggi 42 B 4
Bukoba 64 E 5
Bukukun 36 K 6
Bukuru 63 F 4
Bukwimba 64 E 5
Būl, Kūh-e (Iran) 23 F 3
Bula 43 H 4
Bulambuk 36 G 5
Bulan 43 F 1
Bulancak 21 E 2

C

Coppermine **73** OP 2
Copplestone **6** C 3
Coqên **40** E 1
Coquet, River **5** E 2
Coquimbo **88** B 4
Corabia **20** B 2
Coral Harbour **73** UV 3
Coral Sea **52** B 3–4
Coral Sea Islands Territory **49** HJ 1–2
Corantijn **85** G 3
Corato **19** G 3
Corbridge **5** DE 2
Corby **7** D 1
Corcaigh **14** B 4
Corcovado, Golfo **89** B 7
Corcovado, Volcán **89** B 7
Cordele **77** K 5
Cordilheiras, Serra das **85** J 5
Cordillera Azul **84** C 5
Cordillera Blanca **84** C 5
Cordillera Cantábrica **18** BC 3
Cordillera Central (Colombia) **84** C 2–3
Cordillera Central (Dominican Rep.) **79** H 4
Cordillera Central (Peru) **84** C 5
Cordillera Central (Philippines) **43** J 1
Cordillera, Costa de la **84** E 2
Cordillera de Carabaya **86** B 3
Cordillera de Chichas **86** C 4–5
Cordillera de Chilca **86** B 4
Cordillera de Huanzo **86** B 3
Cordillera de la Costa **84** E 2
Cordillera de Lípez **86** C 5
Cordillera de Mérida **84** D 2
Cordillera del Condor **84** C 4
Cordillera Domeyko **86** C 5
Cordillera Isabella **78** EF 5
Cordillera Negra **84** C 5
Cordillera Occidental **86** BC 3–4
Cordillera Occidental (Colombia) **84** C 2–3
Cordillera Oriental **86** BC 3–5
Cordillera Oriental (Colombia) **84** CD 2–3
Cordillera Real (Bolivia) **86** C 4
Cordillera Real (Ecuador) **84** C 4
Cordillera Vilcabamba **86** B 3
Córdoba (Argentina) **88** D 5
Córdoba (Mexico) **78** C 4
Córdoba (Spain) **18** BC 4
Córdoba, Sierra de **88** D 5
Cordova (AK, U.S.A.) **72** H 3
Córdova (Peru) **86** A 3
Corfe Castle **7** C 2
Corfu **20** A 3
Corguinno **87** E 4
Coria **18** B 4
Corigliano Calabro **19** G 4
Corinda (Queensland, Austr.) **49** F 2
Coringa Islands **49** J 2
Corinth (Greece) **20** B 3
Corinth (MS, U.S.A.) **77** J 5
Corinto **87** H 4
Corisco, Baie de **63** F 5
Corisco Island **63** F 5
Cork (Queensland, Austr.) **49** G 3
Cork (Rep. of Ireland) **14** B 4
Corleone **19** F 4
Çorlu **20** C 2
Cornafulla **4** AB 3
Cornelio **76** D 6
Cornélio Procópio **87** F 5
Cornelius Grinnel Bay **75** P 3
Corner Brook **75** Q 6
Cornhill **2** C 3
Corno Grande **19** F 3
Cornwall (Ontario, Can.) **75** MN 6
Cornwall (U.K.) **6** B 2
Coro **84** E 1
Coroatá **87** H 1
Corocoro **86** C 4
Coroico **86** C 4
Coromandel Coast **40** D 5
Coromandel Peninsula **51** R 8
Coronado, Bahía de **78** F 6
Coronation **73** P 5
Coronation Gulf **73** P 2
Corondo **88** D 5
Coronel **89** B 6
Coronel Dorrego **89** D 6
Coronel Fabriciano **87** H 4
Coronel Falcón **89** D 6
Coronel Oviedo **88** E 4
Coronel Pringles **89** D 6
Coronel Suárez **89** D 6
Corongo **84** C 5
Coropuna, Nevado **86** B 4
Corozal **78** E 4
Corozal **84** CD 2
Corpus **88** E 4
Corpus Christi **77** G 6
Corque **86** C 4
Corquin **78** E 5
Corral **89** B 6
Corrales **88** E 5
Corran **3** B 3
Corrente (Bahía, Brazil) **87** H 3
Corrente (Piauí, Brazil) **87** G 3
Correntes **87** F 4
Correntes, Cabo das **67** F 4
Correntina **87** GH 3
Corrib, Lough **14** B 4
Corrientes **84** C 4
Corrientes (Argentina) **88** E 4
Corrientes (Argentina) **88** E 4
Corrientes (Peru) **84** C 4
Corrientes, Cabo (Argentina) **89** E 6
Corrientes, Cabo (Colombia) **84** C 2
Corrigin **48** B 5
Corryong **49** H 6
Corse **19** E 3
Corse, Cap **19** E 3
Corsica **19** E 3
Corsicana **77** G 5
Corte **19** E 3
Corte Alto **89** B 7
Cortegana **18** B 4
Cortez (Spain) **18** C 3
Cortez (U.S.A.) **76** E 4
Cortona **19** F 3
Corubal **62** B 3
Coruche **18** B 4
Çoruh **21** F 2
Çoruh Dağları **21** F 2
Çorum **21** D 2
Corumba (Goiás, Brazil) **87** G 4
Corumbá (Mato Grosso do Sul, Brazil) **86** E 4
Corumbá de Goiás **87** G 4
Corunna **18** B 3
Coruripe **87** J 3
Corvallis **76** B 3
Corvo **58** A 1
Corwen **6** C 1
Corwen **6** C 1
Cosamaloapan **78** C 4
Cosenza **19** G 4
Coshocton **77** K 3
Cosmoledo Group **65** H 6
Cosne-sur-Loire **18** D 2
Costa Blanca **18** C 4
Costa Blanca **18** C 4
Costa Brava **18** D 3
Costa de la Luz **18** B 4
Costa de Mosquitos **78** F 5
Costa del Azahar **18** D 3–4
Costa del Sol **18** C 4
Costa Dorada **18** D 3
Costa Rica **78** EF 6
Costa Verde **18** B 3
Cotabato **43** F 2
Cotagaita **86** C 5
Cotahuasi **86** B 4
Côte d'Argent **18** C 3
Côte d'Azur **19** E 3
Côte de l'Ile de France **18** D 2
Côte d'Ivoire → Ivory Coast **62** CD 4
Côte d'Or **19** D 2
Coteau du Missouri **76** FG 2
Cotentin **18** C 2
Cotherstone **49** H 3
Cotonou **62** E 4
Cotopaxi **84** C 4
Cotswold Hills **7** C 2
Cottbus **15** F 4
Cottica **85** H 3
Cottingham **5** E 3
Cotulla **76** G 6
Coubre, Pointe de la **18** C 2
Couhé **18** CD 2
Čoukkarašša **16** H 2
Coulommiers **18** D 2
Council **72** E 3
Council Bluffs **77** GH 3
Coupar Angus **3** C 3
Courantyne **85** G 3
Courland **17** H 4
Courmayeur **19** E 2
Courtenai **73** M 6
Courtown **6** A 1
Coutances **18** C 2
Coutras **18** CD 2
Couvin **14** D 4
Cove **2** B 3
Coventry **7** D 1
Coverack **6** B 2
Covilhã **18** B 3
Covington (GA, U.S.A.) **77** K 5
Covington (KY, U.S.A.) **77** K 4
Covington (TN, U.S.A.) **77** J 4
Covington (VA, U.S.A.) **77** L 4
Cowal **3** B 3
Cowal, Lake **49** H 5
Cowan, Lake **48** C 5
Cowargarze **38** C 4
Cowbridge **6** C 2
Cowdenbeath **3** C 3
Cowell **49** F 5
Cowes **7** D 2
Cowfold **7** D 2
Cowra **49** H 5
Coxim **87** F 4
Cox's Bazar **41** F 3
Coy Aike **89** C 9
Coyame **76** E 6
Coyle → Coig **89** B 9
Coylton **3** B 4
Coyotitan **76** E 7
Cracow **15** H 4
Cracow **49** J 4
Cradock **66** D 6
Crai **6** C 3
Craig (AK, U.S.A.) **72** L 4
Craig (CO, U.S.A.) **76** E 3
Craigavon **4** B 2
Craigavon **4** B 2
Craighouse **3** B 4
Craigie **3** B 4
Craignure **3** B 3
Craigs Range **49** J 4
Crail **3** C 3
Craiova **20** B 2
Cramlington **5** E 2
Crampel **58** E 2
Crampel → Kaga Bandoro **64** B 3
Cranbrook **73** O 6
Cranbrook (Western Australia) **48** B 5
Cranford **4** B 2
Cranleigh **7** D 2
Craolândia **85** J 5
Crary Mountains **91**
Crasna **20** B 1
Crater Lake **76** B 3
Cratère du Nouveau-Québec **75** N 3
Cratéus **87** H 2
Crathie **3** D 3
Crato (Amazonas, Brazil) **85** F 5
Crato (Ceará, Brazil) **87** J 2
Cravo Norte **84** E 2
Crawford **76** F 3
Crawfordjohn **3** C 4
Crawfordsville **77** J 3
Crawley **7** D 2
Crazy Peak **76** D 2
Creaggan **3** B 3
Creagorry **2** A 3
Crediton **6** C 2
Cree **73** Q 4
Cree Lake **73** Q 4
Creel **76** E 6
Creetown **3** B 4
Creggan **4** B 2
Creggans **3** B 3
Creil **18** D 2
Cremona **19** F 2
Crepori **85** G 5
Cres **19** F 3
Crescent City **76** B 3
Cressage **6** C 1
Crest **19** DE 3
Creston **77** H 3
Crestview **77** J 5
Crêt de la Neige **19** E 2
Crete **20** BC 3
Cretin, Cape **50** E 3
Creus, Cabo de **18** D 3
Creuse **18** D 2
Crevillente **18** C 4
Crewe **5** D 3
Crewkerne **6** C 2
Crianlarich **3** B 3
Cribyn **6** B 1
Criccieth **6** B 1
Criciúma **88** G 4
Crickhowell **6** C 3
Cricklade **7** D 2
Crieff **3** C 3
Crimea **21** D 1
Crimond **2** D 3
Crinan **3** B 3
Crinan Canal **3** B 3
Cristal, Monts de **63** G 5
Cristalândia **87** G 3
Cristino Castro **87** H 2
Cristmas Island **53** E 2
Cristóbal, Colón Pico **84** D 1
Crişul Alb **20** B 1
Crişul Repede **20** B 1
Crkvena Planina **20** B 2
Crna Gora **20** A 2
Crna Gora **20** B 2
Crna Reka **20** B 2
Crni Drim **20** B 2
Črni Vrh (Yugoslavia) **19** G 2
Crni Vrh (Yugoslavia) **19** G 3
Croatia **19** G 2
Crockett **77** G 5
Croft-on-Tees **5** E 2
Croissette, Cap **19** DE 3
Croker, Cape **48** E 1
Croker Island **48** E 1
Cromarty **2** BC 3
Cromarty Firth **2** B 3
Cromer **7** E 1
Crook **5** E 2
Crooked Creek **72** F 3
Crooked Island **79** H 3
Crooked Island Passage **79** GH 3
Crookham **5** D 2
Crookham Hill **7** E 2
Crookston **77** G 2
Crosby **4** C 2
Crosby (N.D., U.S.A.) **76** F 2
Crosby (U.K.) **5** D 3
Cross (Nigeria) **63** F 4
Cross, Cape **66** A 4
Cross City **77** K 6
Cross Fell **5** D 2
Cross Lake **73** S 5
Cross Sound **72** K 4
Crossett **77** H 5
Crossgar **4** C 2
Crossgates **3** C 3
Crosshill **3** B 4
Crossmaglen **4** B 2
Crotone **19** G 4
Crow Agency **76** E 2
Crow Lake **74** J 6
Crowell **76** G 5
Crowland **7** D 1
Crowley **77** H 5
Crowley Ridge **77** H 4
Crowling **5** D 3
Crown Prince Frederik Island **73** U 2
Crows Nest **49** J 4
Crowsnest Pass **73** OP 6
Croxton **7** D 1
Croyde **6** B 2
Croydon **7** D 2
Croydon **49** G 2
Crozon **18** C 2
Cruden Bay **2** D 3
Crudgington **6** C 1
Crumlin **4** B 2
Cruz Alta **88** F 4
Cruz Alta (Argentina) **88** D 5
Cruz, Cabo **79** G 4
Cruz del Eje **88** CD 5
Cruz Grande (Chile) **88** B 4
Cruz Grande (Mexico) **78** C 4
Cruzeiro **87** G 5
Cruzeiro do Oeste **87** F 5
Cruzeiro do Sul **84** D 5
Crymych **6** B 2
Crynant **6** C 3
Crystal Brook **49** F 5
Ctesiphon (Iraq) **23** D 2
Cu Lao Cham **41** J 4
Cu Lao Hon **41** J 5
Cu Lao Re **41** J 4
Cua Rao **41** H 4
Cuale **66** B 1
Cuamba **67** F 2
Cuando Cubango **66** BC 3
Cuangar **66** B 3
Cuango **66** B 1
Cuango **66** B 1
Cuanza **66** B 1
Cuanza Norte **66** AB 1
Cuanza Sul **66** AB 2
Cuareim **88** E 4
Cuarteron Reef **42** D 2
Cuarto **88** D 5
Cuauhtémoc **76** E 6
Cuba **79** F 3
Cubal **66** A 2
Cubango **66** B 3
Cubati **66** B 3
Cubuk **21** D 2
Cuchi **66** B 2
Cuchi **66** B 2
Cuchilla de Santa Ana **88** EF 5
Cuchilla Grande **88** EF 5
Cuchillo-Có **89** D 6
Cuchumatanes, Sierra de los **78** D 4
Cuckfield **7** D 2
Cucuí **84** E 3
Cucumbi **66** B 2
Cucurpe **76** D 5
Cúcuta **84** D 2
Cuddalore **40** CD 5
Cuddapah **40** C 5
Cudi Dağı **21** F 3
Cue **48** B 4
Cuéllar **18** C 3
Cuemba **66** B 2
Cuenca (Ecuador) **84** C 4
Cuenca (Spain) **18** C 3
Cuencamé de Ceniceros **78** B 3
Cuerda del Pozo, Embalse de la **18** C 3
Cuernavaca **78** BC 4
Cuero **77** G 6
Cuevas de Artá **18** D 4
Cuevo **86** D 5
Cufra Oasis → Wāhāt al Kufrah **59** K 4
Cuiabá **86** E 4
Cuiabá **86** E 4
Cuiari **84** E 3
Cuilapa **78** D 5
Cuillin Hills **2** A 3
Cuillin Sound **3** A 3
Cuilo **66** B 1
Cuilo **66** B 1
Cuima **66** B 2
Cuito Cuanavale **66** B 3
Cuiuni **85** F 4
Cujmir **20** B 2
Cukurca **21** F 3
Cukurca (Turkey) **22** D 1
Culan **18** D 2
Culbokie **2** B 3
Culcairn **49** H 6
Culdaff **4** B 2
Culgoa River **49** H 4
Culiacán **76** E 7
Culion **43** F 1
Cullen **2** C 3
Cullera **18** C 4
Cullman **77** J 5
Cullompton **6** C 2
Cullybackey **4** B 2
Culrain **2** B 3
Culswick **2** D 1
Cultowa **49** G 5
Cults **2** C 3
Culuene **87** F 3
Culver, Point **48** C 5
Cumaná **85** F 1
Cumaria **84** D 5
Cumbal **84** C 3
Cumberland **77** L 4
Cumberland Islands **49** H 3
Cumberland, Lake (KY, U.S.A.) **77** J 4
Cumberland Lake (Sask., Can.) **73** R 5
Cumberland Peninsula **75** OP 2
Cumberland Plateau **77** JK 4
Cumberland River **77** J 4
Cumberland Sound **75** O 2
Cumbernauld **3** B 4
Cumbrian Mountains **5** D 2
Cûmina **85** G 4
Cuminapanema **85** GH 4
Cuminestown **2** C 3
Cummins **49** F 5
Cumnock **3** B 4
Çumra **21** D 3
Cunani **85** H 3
Cunco **89** B 6
Cunene **66** A 3
Cunene **66** B 3
Cuneo **19** E 3
Cungena **48** E 5
Cunnamulla **49** H 4
Cunningham **3** B 4
Cupar **3** C 3
Cupica **84** C 2
Cuprija **20** B 2
Curaçao, Isla **84** E 1
Curacautin **89** B 6
Curanilahue **89** B 6
Curaray **84** CD 4
Curare **84** E 3
Curcubata, Virful **20** B 1
Curdimurka **49** F 4
Curepipe **67** K 6
Curepto **89** B 6
Curiapo **85** F 2
Curicó **89** B 5–6
Curicuriari **84** E 4
Curimatá **87** H 2–3
Curious, Mount **48** A 4
Curiplaya **84** C 3
Curitiba **88** FG 4
Curnamona **49** F 5
Curoca **66** A 3
Currais Novos **87** J 2
Curralinho **85** J 4
Currie **49** G 6
Currie **50** K 8
Curtea de Argeş **20** BC 1
Curtici **20** B 1
Curtina **88** E 5
Curtis **52** D 5
Curtis Channel **49** J 3
Curtis Island **49** J 3
Curuá **85** H 5
Curuá (Pará, Brazil) **85** H 4
Curuá, Ilha **85** J 3
Curuá Una **85** H 4
Curuaí **85** G 4
Curuçá **85** J 4
Curuçambaba **85** J 4
Curuguaty **86** E 5
Curumu **85** H 4
Curupá **85** J 5

Djafou 59 F 3
Djaja Peak 43 J 4
Djaja Peak 50 C 2
Djako 64 C 3
Djamaa 59 G 2
Djambala 63 G 6
Djanet 59 G 4
Djaret 59 F 3
Djaul 51 F 2
Djebel Aïssa 58 E 2
Djebel Amour 59 F 2
Djebel Chélia 59 G 1
Djebel Edough 19 E 4
Djebel Onk 59 G 2
Djebel Ounane 59 G 3
Djebel Telerhteba 59 G 4
Djebobo 62 E 4
Djédaa 63 H 3
Djedi 59 F 2
Djelfa 59 F 2
Djéma 64 D 3
Djemila 59 G 1
Djenienbou Rezg 58 E 2
Djénné 62 D 3
Djerba → Jarbah 59 H 2
Djerem 63 G 4
Djéroual 63 H 3
Djibo 62 D 3
Djibouti 65 G 2
Djibouti 65 G 2
Djiguéni 58 D 5
Djikdjik 63 J 2
Djilbabo Plain 65 F 4
Djokupunda 64 C 6
Djolu 64 C 4
Djombo 64 C 4
Djougou 62 E 4
Djoum 63 G 5
Djourab, Erg du 63 H 2
Djugu 64 E 4
Djúpivogur 16 C 3
Dmanisi 21 F 2
Dnepr 24 F 6
Dneprodzerzhinsk 21 D 1
Dnepropetrovsk 21 E 1
Dneprovskiy Liman 20 D 1
Dneprovsko-Bugskiy Kanal 17 HJ 5
Dnestr 20 C 1
Dnestrovskiy Liman 20 D 1
Dno 17 K 4
Dô, Lac 62 D 2
Doa 67 E 3
Doany 67 H 2
Doba (Chad) 63 H 4
Doba (China) 40 E 1
Dobbiaco 19 F 2
Dobel 65 F 4
Dobele 17 H 4
Döbeln 15 F 4
Doblas 89 D 6
Dobo 43 H 5
Doboj 19 G 3
Dobreta Turnu Severin 20 B 2
Dobrogea 20 C 2
Dobrowolski 91
Dobroye 37 R 7
Dobrudzhanska Plato 20 C 2
Dobruja 20 C 2
Dobryanka 24 L 4
Doce 87 H 4
Docking 7 E 1
Docksta 16 G 3
Doctor Arroyo 78 B 3
Dod Ballapur 40 C 5
Doda Betta 40 C 5
Dodecanese 20 C 3
Dodge City 76 F 4
Dodman Point 6 B 2
Dodoma 65 F 6
Dofa 43 G 4
Dog Creek 73 N 5
Dogai Coring 40 E 1
Doğankent 21 E 3
Dogger Bank 14 D 4
Doghārūn 35 G 4
Dōgo 39 K 3
Dogonbadān (Iran) 23 F 3
Dogondoutchi 63 E 3
Doğu Karadeniz Dağlari 21 EF 2
Doğubayazıt 21 F 3
Doguéraoua 63 F 3
Dogwaya 60 EF 5
Do'gyaling 40 E 1
Doha (Qatar) 23 F 4
Dohad 40 B 3
Dohazan 41 F 3
Dōhō Nugālēd 65 H 3
Doi Inthanon 41 G 4
Doilungdêqen 41 F 2
Dois de Novembro, Cachoeira 85 F 5
Dois Irmãos 85 J 5
Dois Irmãos, Serra 87 H 2
Doka (Indonesia) 43 H 5
Doka (Sudan) 60 F 6
Dokka 17 F 3
Doko 64 D 4
Dokshitsy 17 J 5
Dokuchayevsk 21 E 1
Dolak Island 50 C 3
Dolanog 6 C 1
Dolbeau 75 N 6
Dôle 19 E 2
Doleib Hill 64 E 3
Dolgellau 6 C 1
Dolgiy, Ostrov 25 LM 2
Dolgiy-Most 36 G 4
Dolinsk 37 Q 6
Dolinskaya 21 D 1
Dolni Dŭbnik 20 B 2
Dolo 65 G 4
Dolon, Pereval 35 K 2
Dolores (Argentina) 89 E 6
Dolores (Uruguay) 88 E 5
Dolphin and Union Strait 73 OP 2
Dolphinton 3 C 4
Dolwyddelan 6 C 1
Dolzhanskaya 21 E 1
Dom Aquino 87 F 4
Dom Cavati 87 H 4
Dom, Kūh-e (Iran) 23 F 2
Dom Pedrito 88 F 5
Doma Peaks 50 D 3
Domadare 65 G 4
Domaniç 20 C 3
Domažlice 15 F 5
Domba 38 C 4
Dombarovskiy 25 L 5
Dombås 16 E 3
Dombovár 20 A 1
Domeyko 86 C 5
Domeyko, Cordillera 86 C 5
Dominica 79 K 4
Dominica Passage 79 K 4
Dominican Republic 79 J 3–4
Dominion, Cape 75 M 2
Domino 75 Q 5
Domiongo 64 C 5
Domo → Damot 65 H 3
Domodossola 19 E 2
Dompierre 18 D 2
Dompu 43 E 5
Domuyo, Volcán 89 BC 6
Don (Mexico) 76 E 6
Don (U.S.S.R.) 24 H 6
Don Benito 18 B 4
Don Khi 41 H 4
Don, River (Grampian) 2 C 3
Don, River (S. Yorkshire) 5 E 3
Donadeu 88 D 4
Donaghadee 4 C 2
Donald 49 G 6
Donau 15 E 5
Donauwörth 15 F 5
Doncaster 5 E 3
Dondo (Angola) 66 A 1
Dondo (Indonesia) 43 F 4
Dondo (Mozambique) 67 E 3
Dondra Head 40 D 6
Donegal 4 AB 2
Donegal Bay 14 B 4
Donegal Mountains 14 B 4
Donets Basin 12
Donets Basin 21 E 1
Donets, Severskiy 21 F 1
Donetsk 21 E 1
Donetskiy Kryazh 21 E 1
Donetskiy Kryazh 21 EF 1
Donfeng 39 J 2
Dong Ha 41 J 4
Dong Hai 39 HJ 5
Dong He 38 D 2
Dong Hoi 41 J 4
Dong Jiang 38 FG 6
Dong Khe 41 J 3
Dong Nai 41 J 5
Dong Taijnar Hu 38 B 3
Dong Ujimqin Qi 39 G 1
Donga 63 G 4
Dong'an 38 F 5
Dongara 48 AB 4
Dongargarh 40 D 3
Dongchuan 38 D 5
Donges 18 C 2
Dongfang 38 E 7
Donggala 43 E 4
Donggi Cona 38 C 3
Donggou 39 H 3
Donghai 39 G 4
Donghai Dao 38 F 6
Dongkalang 43 F 3
Donglan 38 E 6
Donglük 38 A 3
Dongning 39 K 2
Dongo (Angola) 66 B 2
Dongo (Zaire) 64 B 4
Dongo (Zaire) 64 B 6
Dongou 63 H 5
Dongoura 62 C 3
Dongping 39 G 3
Dongshan 39 G 6
Dongshan Dao 39 G 6
Dongsheng 38 EF 3
Dongtai 39 H 4
Dongting Hu 38 F 5
Dongtou 39 H 5
Dongwe 66 C 2
Dongxiang 38 G 5
Dongying 39 G 3
Dongzhen 38 D 3
Dongzhi 39 G 4
Donington 5 E 3
Donja Brela 19 G 3
Donjek 72 K 3
Donji Miholjac 19 G 2
Donji Vakuf 19 G 3
Dönna 16 F 2
Donnybrook 48 B 5
Donskoye 21 F 1
Donuzlav, Ozero 21 D 1
Doocharry 4 A 2
Doonerak, Mount 72 H 2
Door Peninsula 77 J 3
Dora Baltea 19 E 2
Dora, Lake 48 C 3
Doramarkog 38 C 4
Dorbod 39 H 1
Dorchester 6 C 2
Dorchester, Cape 75 M 2
Dordogne 18 D 3
Dordrecht 14 D 4
Dore Lake 73 Q 5
Dore, Monts 18 D 2
Dores do Indaiá 87 G 4
Dori 62 D 3
Doring 66 B 6
Dorking 7 D 2
Dormidontovka 37 P 6
Dornbin 19 E 2
Dornoch 2 B 3
Dornoch Firth 2 B 3
Dornod 36 K 6
Dornogovĭ 38 EF 2
Doro (Indonesia) 43 G 3
Doro (Mali) 62 D 2
Dorogobuzh 24 F 5
Dorogorskoye 24 H 2
Dorohoi 20 C 1
Döröö Nuur 36 F 6
Dorotea 16 G 3
Dorovitsa 24 J 4
Dorra (Saudi Arabia) 23 E 3
Dorre Island 48 A 4
Dorrigo 49 J 5
Dorset 6–7 C 2
Dortmund 15 E 4
Dörtyol 21 E 3
Dörtyol (Turkey) 22 B 1
Doruma 64 D 4
Doruokha 36 K 1
Dos de Mayo 84 D 5
Dosatuy 36 L 5
Doshi 35 H 3
Dosso 62 E 3
Dossor 34 E 1
Dothan 77 J 5
Douai 18 D 1
Douala 63 FG 5
Douandago 64 B 3
Doubs 19 E 2
Doubtful Sound 50 P 10
Douentza 62 D 3
Dougga 59 G 1
Douglas (AK, U.S.A.) 72 L 4
Douglas (AZ, U.S.A.) 76 E 5
Douglas (South Africa) 66 C 5
Douglas (U.K.) 4 C 2
Douglas (WY, U.S.A.) 76 EF 3
Doumbouene 63 J 3
Doumé 63 G 5
Douna 62 D 3
Doune 3 B 3
Dounreay 2 C 2
Dourada, Serra 87 G 3
Dourado, Monte 85 H 4
Dourados 87 F 5
Dourbali 63 H 3
Douro 18 B 3
Dove, River 7 D 1
Dover (DE, U.S.A.) 77 L 4
Dover (U.K.) 7 E 2
Dover, Strait of 14 D 4
Dovre 16 E 3
Dovrefjell 16 E 3
Dow Dehak (Iran) 23 F 2
Dow Rūd (Iran) 23 E 2
Dow Sar 34 D 3
Dow Sar (Iran) 23 E 2
Dowa 67 E 2
Dowlatābād 34 F 5
Dowlatābād (Iran) 23 G 3
Downham Market 7 E 1
Downhill 4 B 2
Downpatrick 4 C 2
Downtown 7 D 2
Dowra 4 B 2
Dozois, Réservoir 75 M 6
Drâa, Cap 58 C 3
Drâa, Hamada du 58 D 3
Drâa, Wadi 58 D 3
Drabat 'Ali, Ra's 61 J 5
Drac 19 E 3
Dragan 16 FG 3
Drăgăşani 20 B 2
Dragonera 18 D 4
Dragör 17 F 4
Draguignan 19 E 3
Drain 76 B 3
Drake 49 J 4
Drake Passage 91
Drake Strait 89 CD 10
Drakensberg 66 DE 4
Drakensberg 66 D 5
Drakensberg (Lesotho) 66 D 5–6
Dráma 20 B 2
Drammen 17 F 4
Drangajökull 16 A 2
Drangedal 17 E 4
Drangsnes 16 A 2
Dranka 37 U 4
Draperstown 4 B 2
Dras 35 K 4
Drau 19 F 2
Drava 19 G 2
Dráva 20 A 1
Dravograd 19 G 2
Drawa 15 G 4
Drawsko, Jezioro 15 G 4
Drayton 49 J 4
Drayton Valley 73 O 5
Drean 19 E 4
Dresden 15 F 4
Dreux 18 D 2
Drevsjö 16 F 3
Drina 19 G 3
Drini 20 B 2
Driva 16 E 3
Drniš 19 G 3
Dröbak 17 F 4
Drogheda 4 B 3
Drogobych 15 H 5
Droichead Nua 4 B 3
Droitwich 7 C 1
Drokiya 20 C 1
Drôme 19 DE 3
Dromore 4 B 2
Dronfield 5 E 3
Drosh 35 J 3
Drumbeg 2 B 2
Drumclog 3 B 4
Drumfree 4 B 2
Drumheller 73 P 5
Drumlithe 3 D 3
Drummnod 76 D 2
Drummond Range 49 H 3
Drummondville 75 N 6
Drummore 4 C 2
Drumnadrochit 2 B 3
Drumod 4 B 3
Drumshanbo 4 A 2
Druskininkai 17 H 5
Druzhba 20 C 2
Druzhbovka 21 D 1
Druzhina 37 R 2
Druzhkovka 21 E 1
Druzhnaya 91
Druzhnaya II 91
Drvar 19 G 3
Drvenik 19 G 3
Drweca 15 G 4
Dry River 48 E 2
Dry Tortugas 77 K 7
Dryanovo 20 C 2
Dryden 74 J 6
Drymen 3 B 3
Drysdale River 48 D 1–2
Drysdale River National Park 48 D 2
Dschang 63 F 4
Du Bois 77 L 3
du Couedic, Cape 49 F 6
Duaringa 49 H 3
Dubai → Dubayy 61 JK 3
Dubawnt 73 R 3
Dubawnt Lake 73 R 3
Dubayy (United Arab Emirates) 23 G 4
Dubbo 49 H 5
Dubenskiy 24 L 5
Dubica 19 G 2
Dublin (Airport) 4 B 3
Dublin (GA, U.S.A.) 77 K 5
Dublin (Rep. of Ireland) 4 B 3
Dubna 24 G 4
Dubna 24 G 5
Dubno 17 J 5
Dubossary 20 C 1
Dubovka 24 J 6
Dubovskoye 21 F 1
Dubreka 62 B 4
Dubrovitsa 17 J 5
Dubrovnik 19 G 3
Dubrovnoye 25 NO 4
Dubuque 77 H 3
Duc de Gloucester, Îles du 53 F 4
Duchesne 76 D 3
Duchess 49 F 3
Ducie 53 G 4
Dudhi 40 D 3
Dudinka 25 R 2
Dudley 7 C 1
Dūdo 65 J 3
Dudub 65 H 3
Dudypta 36 F 1
Duékoué 62 C 4
Dueré 87 G 3
Duero 18 C 3
Duff Islands 51 J 3
Dufftown 2 C 3
Duga-Zapadnaya, Mys 37 R 4
Dugi Otok 19 F 3
Dugo Selo 19 G 2
Duhūn Tarsū 59 J 4
Duifken Point 49 G 1
Duirinish 2 A 3
Duisburg 14 E 4
Duitama 84 D 2
Dujūma 65 G 4
Duk Fadiat 64 E 3
Duk Faiwil 64 E 3
Dukagjini 20 A 2
Dukān (Iraq) 23 D 2
Dukana 65 F 4
Duke of York Bay 73 UV 2
Dukhān (Qatar) 23 F 4
Duki (Pakistan) 35 H 4
Duki (U.S.S.R.) 37 P 5
Dukou 38 D 5
Duku 63 G 3
Dukwe 66 D 4
Dulan 38 C 3
Dulce 88 D 4
Dulce, Bahia 78 C 4
Dulce, Golfo 78 F 6
Dul'durga 36 K 5
Duleek 4 B 3
Dulga-Kyuyel' 36 K 3
Dulgalakh 37 O 2
Dulla 65 F 3
Duluth 77 H 2
Dūmā 60 F 2
Dumaguete 43 F 2
Dumai 42 B 3
Dumanlı Dağı 21 F 3
Dumaran 43 EF 1
Dumaring 42 E 3
Dumayr (Syria) 22 B 2
Dumbarton 3 B 4
Dumboa 63 G 3
Dumfries 3 C 4
Dumfries and Galloway 3 BC 4
Dumont d'Urville 91
Dumpu 50 E 3
Dumraon 40 D 2
Dumyāt 60 E 2
Dun Laoghaire 4 B 3
Duna 20 A 1
Dunaföldvár 20 A 1
Dunajec 15 GH 5
Dunan 2 B 3
Dunántúl 20 A 1
Dunărea 20 C 1
Dunaujváros 20 A 1
Dunav 20 B 2
Dunay 36 M 1
Dunay 39 K 2
Dunayevtsy 24 E 6
Dunbar (Australia) 49 G 2
Dunbar (U.K.) 3 C 3
Dunbeath 2 C 2
Dunblane 3 C 3
Dunboyne 4 B 3
Duncan 76 G 5
Duncan Passage 41 F 5
Duncansby Head 2 C 2
Dunchurch 7 D 1
Duncow 3 C 4
Dundalk 4 B 2
Dundalk Bay 4 B 3
Dundas, Lake 48 C 5
Dundas Strait 48 E 1
Dundee (Airport) 3 C 3
Dundee (South Africa) 66 E 5
Dundee (U.K.) 3 C 3
Dundgovĭ 38 E 1
Dundonald 4 C 2
Dundonnell 2 B 3
Dundrennan 3 C 4
Dundwa Range 40 D 2
Dunecht 2 C 3
Dunedin 51 Q 10
Dunes de l'Akchar 58 C 4
Dunes de l'Azéffal 58 BC 4
Dunfanaghy 4 B 2
Dunfermline 3 C 3
Dungannon 4 B 2
Dungarpur 40 B 3
Dungas 63 F 3
Dungeness 7 E 2

E

Furmanovo 24 JK 6
Furnas Dam 87 G 5
Furnas, Represa de 87 G 5
Furneaux Group 50 L 9
Furneaux Group 52 A 5
Furqlus (Syria) 22 B 2
Fürstenfeld 19 G 2
Fürstenfeldbrück 15 F 5
Fürstenwalde 15 F 4
Fürth 15 F 5
Furth im Wald 15 F 5
Furudal 16 G 3
Furukawa 39 M 3
Fury and Hecla Strait 74 L 1–2
Fusagasugá 84 D 3
Fushë-Lura 20 B 2
Fushun 39 H 2
Fusong 39 J 2
Fusui 38 E 6
Futa, Passo della 19 F 3
Futa Ruím 89 BC 7
Futuna (Vanuatu) 51 K 5
Futuna (Wallis and Futuna) 52 D 3
Fuwaris (Saudi Arabia) 23 E 3
Fuxian Hu 38 D 6
Fuxin 39 H 2
Fuyang 38 G 4
Fuyu 37 M 6
Fuyu 39 H 1
Fuyuan (China) 38 D 5
Fuyuan (U.S.S.R.) 37 O 6
Fuyun 35 M 1
Fuzhou 38 G 5
Fyn 17 F 4
Fyne, Loch 3 B 3
Fyresvatn 17 E 4
Fyrsjön 16 G 3
Fyvie 2 C 3

G

Gabba' 65 J 3
Gabbs 76 C 4
Gabela 66 A 2
Gabès 59 H 2
Gabon 63 F 5
Gabon 63 G 6
Gaborone 66 D 4
Gaboto 88 D 5
Gabras 60 D 6
Gabredarre 65 G 3
Gabrey, Vozvyshennost' 36 F 1
Gabriel Strait 75 O 3
Gabriel y Galan, Embalse de 18 B 3
Gabrovo 20 C 2
Gacé 18 D 2
Gach Sārān (Iran) 23 F 3
Gacko 19 G 3
Gada 63 F 3
Gadag 40 C 4
Gadamai 60 F 5
Gadame 64 E 3
Gäddede 16 F 3
Gadê 38 C 4
Gadhap 35 H 5
Gadsden 77 J 5
Gadūk, Gardaneh-ye (Iran) 23 F 2
Gadwal 40 C 4
Gaeta 19 F 3
Gaeta, Golfo di 19 F 3
Gaferut 52 A 2
Gaffney 77 K 4
Gafsa 57
Gafsa → Qafsah 59 G 2
Gag, Pulau 43 G 4
Gagan 51 F 3
Gagarin 24 F 4
Gagere 63 F 3
Gagnoa 62 C 4
Gagnon 75 O 5
Gagra 21 F 2
Gagshor 24 JK 3
Gahkom 23 G 3
Gai Xian 39 H 2
Gaibanda 40 E 2
Gaillac 18 D 3
Gaillimh 14 B 4
Gaimán 89 C 7
Gainesville (FL, U.S.A.) 77 K 6
Gainesville (GA, U.S.A.) 77 K 5
Gainesville (TX, U.S.A.) 77 G 5
Gainsborough 7 D 1
Gairdner, Lake 49 F 5
Gairloch 2 B 3
Gaizina Kalns 17 J 4
Gakankoy 37 T 4
Gakarosa 66 C 5
Gakona 72 H 3
Gal Tardo 65 H 4
Gala (Greece) 20 C 2
Gala (Tibet, China) 40 E 2
Galadi (Ethiopia) 65 H 3
Galadi (Nigeria) 63 F 3
Galán, Cerro 88 C 4
Galana 65 F 5
Galanino 36 F 4
Galápagos Islands 84 B 6
Galashiels 3 C 4
Galathea Deep 52 D 5
Galați 20 C 1
Galatina 19 G 3
Galbraith 49 G 2
Galdhöpiggen 16 E 3
Galeana 76 E 5
Galeana (Mexico) 78 C 3
Galeh Dār (Iran) 23 F 4
Galela 43 G 3
Galena 72 F 3
Galera, Punta 89 B 7
Galesburg 77 H 3
Gali 21 F 2
Galich 24 H 4
Galicia (Poland) 15 H 5
Galicia (Spain) 18 B 3
Galilee, Lake 49 H 3
Galiléia 87 H 4
Galimyy 37 T 3
Gälka'yo 65 H 3
Gallan Head 2 A 2
Gallarate 19 E 2
Galle 40 D 6
Gallego 18 C 3
Gallegos 89 B 9
Gallinas, Punta 84 D 1
Gallipoli 19 G 3
Gällivare 16 H 2
Gallo 18 C 3
Gallo, Capo 19 F 4
Gallo Mountains 76 E 5
Galloway 3 B 4
Gallup 76 E 4
Galole 65 F 5
Galty Mountains 14 B 4
Galveston 77 H 6
Galveston Bay 77 H 6
Gálvez 88 D 5
Galway 14 B 4
Galway Bay 14 B 4
Gam 66 C 4
Gama 89 D 7
Gama, Isla 89 D 7
Gamarri, Lake 65 G 2
Gamba (Gabon) 63 F 6
Gamba (Tibet, China) 40 E 2
Gambaga 62 D 3
Gambeila 64 E 3
Gambell 72 C 3
Gambia 62 A 3
Gambie 62 B 3
Gambier Islands 53 FG 4
Gamboma 63 H 6
Gamboola 49 G 2
Gamboula 64 B 4
Gamkunoro, Gunung 43 G 3
Gamleby 17 G 4
Gamlingay 7 D 1
Gammelstad 16 H 2
Gamo Gofa 65 F 3
Gamud 65 F 4
Gamvik 16 J 1
Gan Jiang 38 G 5
Ganale 65 G 3
Ganaly 37 T 5
Ganāveh (Iran) 23 F 3
Ganda 66 A 2
Gandadiwata, Bukit 43 EF 4
Gandajika 64 C 6
Gandak 40 D 2
Gandaua 35 H 5
Gander 75 R 6
Gandesa 18 D 3
Gandhi Sagar Dam 40 C 3
Gandhinagar 40 B 3
Gandi 63 F 3
Gandía 18 C 4
Gand-i-Zirreh 35 G 5
Gandu 87 J 3
Ganeb 58 C 5
Ganetti 60 E 5
Ganga 40 E 2
Ganga, Mont de 63 G 4
Ganga, Mouths of the 40–41 EF 3
Gangakher 40 C 4
Gangan 89 C 7
Ganganagar 40 B 2
Gangapur 40 C 2
Gangara 63 F 3
Gangaw 41 F 3
Gangawati 40 C 4
Gangca 38 D 3
Gangdisê Shan 40 DE 1
Ganges 40 E 3
Ganges Cone 98 B 3
Ganghar 40 C 3
Gangmar Co 40 D 1
Gangotri 40 C 1
Gangtok 40 E 2
Gangu 38 E 4
Gani 43 G 4
Ganina Gar' 36 F 4
Gannan 37 M 6
Gannat 18 D 2
Gannett Peak 76 DE 3
Ganquan 38 E 3
Gansu 38 DE 3
Gant 12
Ganta 62 C 4
Gantang 38 D 3
Ganyesa 66 C 5
Ganzhou 38 F 5
Ganzurino 36 J 5
Gao 62 D 2
Gao Xian 38 D 5
Gao'an 38 G 5
Gaohe 38 F 6
Gaolan 38 D 3
Gaoligong Shan 38 C 5
Gaolou Ling 38 E 5–6
Gaomi 39 GH 3
Gaona 88 D 4
Gaoping 38 F 3
Gaotai 38 C 3
Gaotang 39 G 3
Gaoua 62 D 3
Gaoual 62 B 3
Gaoyi 38 F 3
Gaoyou 39 G 4
Gaoyou Hu 39 G 4
Gaozhou 38 F 6
Gap 19 E 3
Gapan 43 J 1
Gar 40 C 1
Gara'ad 65 H 3
Garachiné 84 C 2
Garai 35 J 3
Garaina 50 E 3
Garamba National Park 64 D 4
Garangan (Iran) 23 F 3
Garanhuns 87 J 2
Garantah 42 E 5
Garar, Plaine de 63 J 3
Garara 50 E 3
Garba Hārrey 65 G 4
Garberville 76 B 3
Garbokaray 36 G 5
Garboldisham 7 E 1
Garbosh, Kūh-e (Iran) 23 EF 2
Garco 40 E 1
Garda, Lago di 19 F 2
Gardaneh-ye Āvej 34 D 3
Gardaneh-ye Āvej (Iran) 23 E 2
Gardaneh-ye Gadūk (Iran) 23 F 2
Gardaneh-ye Kandovān (Iran) 23 F 1
Gardaneh-ye Khāneh Sorkh (Iran) 23 G 3
Gardaneh-ye Kowlī Kosh (Iran) 23 F 3
Garden City 76 F 4
Gardermoen 17 F 3
Gardez 35 H 4
Gardiner 76 D 2
Gardo → Qardo 65 H 3
Gardula 65 F 3
Garelochhead 3 B 3
Gareloi 72 B 5
Garet el Djenoun 59 G 3
Gargano, Promontorio del 19 G 3
Gargnäs 16 G 2
Gargouna 62 DE 2
Gari 25 M 4
Garies 66 B 6
Garissa 65 FG 5
Garkida 63 G 3
Garlieston 3 B 4
Garmal 65 J 3
Garmdasht (Iran) 23 E 3
Garmisch-Partenkirchen 15 F 5
Garmsar 34 E 3
Garmsar (Iran) 23 F 2
Garnett 77 G 4
Garonne 18 D 3
Garoua (Cameroon) 63 G 4
Garoua (Niger) 63 G 3
Garoua Boulai 63 G 4
Garōwe 65 H 3
Garphyttan 17 G 4
Garri, Kūh-e (Iran) 23 E 2
Garrison 4 A 2
Garrison Dam 76 F 2
Garry Bay 73 U 2
Garry Lake 73 R 2
Garsen 65 F 5
Garsila 60 C 6
Garstang 5 D 3
Garth 6 C 1
Garut 42 C 5
Garvagh 4 B 2
Garvagh 4 B 3
Garvald 3 C 4
Garve 2 B 3
Garwa 40 D 3
Garwolin 15 H 4
Gary 77 J 3
Garyn' 36 J 4
Garza 88 D 4
Garze 38 C 4
Garzón 84 C 3
Gas Hu 38 B 3
Gasan-Kuli 34 E 3
Gascogne 18 CD 3
Gascoyne Junction 48 B 4
Gascoyne River 48 A 3
Gashagar 63 G 3
Gashaka 63 G 4
Gasht 35 G 5
Gashua 63 G 3
Gashun 21 F 1
Gaspar, Selat 42 C 4
Gaspé 75 P 6
Gaspé, Cap de 75 P 6
Gaspé, Péninsule de 75 O 6
Gassi Touil 59 G 2
Gassol 63 G 4
Gastello, Iméni 37 R 3
Gastonia 77 K 4
Gastre 89 C 7
Gästrikland 17 G 3
Gata, Akra (Cyprus) 22 A 2
Gata, Cabo de 18 C 4
Gata, Sierra de 18 B 3
Gatamaran 50 L 9
Gatchina 17 K 4
Gatehouse of Fleet 3 B 4
Gates of the Arctic National Park and Preserve 72 G 2
Gateshead (N.W.T., Can.) 73 S 1
Gateshead (U.K.) 5 E 2
Gatineau Park 75 M 6
Gatooma → Kadoma 66 D 3
Gattinara 19 E 2
Gatton 49 J 4
Gatvand (Iran) 23 E 2
Gatwick (Airport) 7 D 2
Gauani 65 G 2
Gauhati 41 F 2
Gauja 17 H 4
Gaula 16 E 3
Gauldalen 16 F 3
Gaurdak 35 H 3
Gaurihar 40 CD 2
Gausta 17 E 4
Gauttier, Pegunungan 43 J 4
Gāv Kosh (Iran) 23 E 2
Gavanka 37 T 4
Gavāter 35 G 5
Gāvbandi (Iran) 23 F 4
Gavbūs, Kūh-e (Iran) 23 FG 4
Gávdhos 20 B 4
Gave de Pau 18 C 3
Gävle 17 G 3
Gävlebukten 17 G 3
Gawler 49 F 5
Gawler Ranges 49 F 5
Gaxun Nur 38 D 2
Gaya (India) 40 E 3
Gaya (Niger) 62 E 3
Gaya (Nigeria) 63 F 3
Gaydon 7 D 1
Gaylord 77 K 2
Gayndah 49 J 4
Gayny 24 K 3
Gaysin 20 C 1
Gayvoron 20 D 1
Gaz (Iran) 23 F 2
Gaz, Bandare-e (Iran) 23 F 1
Gaza → Ghazzah 60 E 2
Gaza Strip 22 AB 3
Gazammi 63 G 3
Gazaoua 63 F 3
Gazelle Peninsula 51 F 2
Gaziantep 21 E 3
Gaziantep (Turkey) 22 B 1
Gaziantep Yaylası 21 E 3
Gazimur 36 L 5
Gazimurskiy Zavod 36 L 5
Gazipaşa 21 D 3
Gazli 35 G 2
Gbarnga 62 C 4
Gboko 63 F 4
Gcoverega 66 C 3
Gdańsk 15 G 4
Gdansk, Gulf of 15 G 4
Gdov 17 J 4
Gdynia 15 G 4
Gearhart Mountain 76 B 3
Gebe, Pulau 43 G 4
Gebze 20 C 2
Gechia 64 F 3
Gedi 65 F 5
Gediz 20 C 3
Gediz 20 C 3
Gedser 17 F 5
Geelong 49 G 6
Geelvink Channel 48 A 4
Gefara Plain → Jifārah Plain 59 H 2
Gegamskiy Khrebet 21 G 2–3
Gê'gyai 40 D 1
Geidam 63 G 3
Geigar 60 E 6
Geikie 73 R 4
Geilo 17 E 3
Geiranger 16 E 3
Geita 64 E 5
Gejiu 31
Gejiu 38 D 6
Gel 64 D 3
Gela 19 F 4
Gelai 65 F 5
Gelendzhik 21 E 2
Gelibolu 20 C 2
Gelibolu Yarimadasi 20 C 2
Gellinsör 65 H 3
Gelsenkirchen 15 E 4
Gemena 64 B 4
Gemerek 21 E 3
Gemlik 20 C 2
Gemlik Körfezi 20 C 2
Gemona 19 F 2
Gemsbok National Park 66 C 4–5
Gemuru 42 E 4
Genç 21 F 3
Gencek 20 D 3
Geneina → Al Junaynah 60 C 6
General Acha 89 D 6
General Alvear (Argentina) 89 C 5–6
General Alvear (Argentina) 89 DE 6
General Belgrano 89 E 6
General Belgrano II 91
General Belgrano III 91
General Bernardo O'Higgins 91
General Bravo 78 C 2
General Carrera, Lago 89 B 8
General Chaves 89 D 6
General Conesa 89 CD 7
General Daniel Cerri 89 D 6
General Guido 89 E 6
General La Madrid 89 D 6
General Lavalle 89 E 6
General Madariaga 89 E 6
General Martín Miguel de Güemes 86 D 5
General Paz 88 E 4
General Pico 89 D 6
General Pinedo 88 D 4
General Pinto 88 D 5
General Roca 89 C 6
General San Martin 91
General Santos 43 G 2
General Treviñe 78 C 2
General Trias 76 E 6
General Vargas 88 F 4
General Villegas 88 D 6
Geneva (N.Y., U.S.A.) 77 L 3
Genève 19 E 2
Gengma 38 C 6
Genichesk 21 DE 1
Genil 18 C 4
Genoa 19 E 3
Genova 19 E 3
Genova, Golfo di 19 E 3
Genovesa Isla 84 B 6
Gent 14 D 4
Genteng 42 C 5
Genyem 50 CD 2
Geographe Bay 48 B 5
Geographe Channel 48 A 3
Geok-Tepe 34 F 3
Georg von Neumayer 91
George (Quebec, Can.) 75 O 4
George (South Africa) 66 C 6
George, Lake (FL, U.S.A.) 77 K 6
George, Lake (N.Y., U.S.A.) 77 M 3
George, Lake (Uganda) 64 E 5
George, Lake (Western Australia) 48 C 3
George Town (Malaysia) 42 AB 2
George Town (Tasmania, Austr.) 50 L 9
George V Coast 91
George VI Sound 91
George West 76 G 6
Georgetown (Cayman Is.) 79 F 4
Georgetown (Gambia) 62 B 3
Georgetown (Guyana) 85 G 2
Georgetown (Queensland, Austr.) 49 G 2
Georgetown (S.C., U.S.A.) 77 L 5
Georgetown (The Bahamas) 79 G 3
Georgetown (TX, U.S.A.) 76 G 5
Georgia (U.S.A.) 77 K 5
Georgia (U.S.S.R.) 21 F 2
Georgian Bay 75 L 6
Georgina River 49 F 3
Georgiu-Dezh 24 G 5
Georgiyevka 25 Q 6
Georgiyevka 35 K 2
Georgiyevsk 21 F 2
Gera 15 F 4
Gerais, Chapadão dos 87 G 4
Geral de Goiás, Serra 87 G 3
Geral do Paraná, Serra 87 G 3
Geral ou Grande, Serra 87 G 3
Geral, Serra 88 F 4

H

I

J

Kheri 40 D 2
Kherpuchi 37 P 5
Khersan (Iran) 23 F 3
Kherson 21 D 1
Khesh 35 H 4
Kheta 25 Q 2
Kheta 36 G 1
Kheta 36 H 1
Khetta, Levaya 25 O 3
Kheyrābād 34 F 5
Kheyrābād (Iran) 23 E 3
Kheyrābād (Iran) 23 G 3
Khibiny 16 K 2
Khilchipur 40 C 3
Khil'mi, Gora 37 S 1
Khilok 36 J 5
Khilok 36 K 5
Khimki 24 G 4
Khíos 20 C 3
Khíos 20 C 3
Khirbat Isrīyah (Syria) 22 BC 2
Khlong Makham 41 H 5
Khmelev 24 F 5
Khmel'nik 24 E 6
Khmel'nitskiy 24 E 6
Khobol'chan 37 Q 2
Khodzha Mubarek 35 H 3
Khodzheyli 34 F 2
Khoe 37 Q 5
Khogali 64 D 3
Khok Kloi 41 G 6
Khokhropar 35 J 5
Khokiley 25 Q 2
Kholm (Afghanistan) 35 H 3
Kholm (U.S.S.R.) 17 K 4
Kholmogory 24 H 3
Kholmsk 37 Q 6
Kholodnoye 25 M 3
Kholzun, Khrebet 25 Q 5
Khomān 34 DE 3
Khomas Highland 66 B 4
Khomeyn (Iran) 23 F 2
Khomeyni, Bandar-e (Iran) 23 E 3
Khomokashevo 36 HJ 3
Khon Kaen 41 H 4
Khong 41 J 5
Khong Sedone 41 J 4
Khongkhoyuku 37 O 3
Khongo 37 S 3
Khonj (Iran) 23 F 4
Khonsār (Iran) 23 F 2
Khonu 37 O 2
Khonu 37 Q 2
Khoper 24 H 5
Khoppuruo 36 L 4
Khor 37 P 6
Khor 37 P 6
Khor Anghar 65 G 2
Khora 20 B 3
Khorāsān 34 F 4
Khorat Plateau 41 H 4
Khorb el Ethel 58 D 3
Khordogoy 36 L 3
Khorgo 36 K 1
Khorinsk 36 J 5
Khorintsy 36 M 3
Khorixas 66 A 4
Khorog 35 J 3
Khoronkhu 37 O 3
Khoronnokh 36 LM 2
Khorram (Iran) 23 E 1
Khorramābād (Iran) 23 E 2
Khorramshahr (Iran) 23 E 3
Khorsābād (Iraq) 22 D 1
Khosheutovo 21 G 1
Khoshyeylaq (Iran) 23 G 1
Khosrowābād (Iran) 23 E 3
Khosta 21 EF 2
Khotin 20 C 1
Khouribga 58 D 2
Khovu-Aksy 36 F 5
Khowrjān (Iran) 23 F 3
Khowst 35 H 4
Khoydype, Gora 25 N 2
Khoyniki 24 F 5
Khrami 21 F 2
Khrebet Bol'shoy Balkhan 34 EF 3
Khrebet Borong 37 P 2
Khrebet Bureinskiy 37 O 5
Khrebet Chayatyn 37 P 5
Khrebet Cherskogo 36 KL 5
Khrebet Cherskogo 37 P 1–2
Khrebet Chingiz-Tau 25 P 6
Khrebet Dygdy-Sise 37 O 4
Khrebet Dzhagdy 37 O 5
Khrebet Dzhaki-Unakhta Yakbyyana 37 OP 5–6
Khrebet Dzhugdzhur 37 OP 4
Khrebet Dzhungarskiy Alatau 25 PQ 6–7
Khrebet Iskaten' 72 B 2
Khrebet Kadyr-Egi-Tayga 36 G 5
Khrebet Kamennyy 37 UV 3
Khrebet Karatau 35 H 2
Khrebet, Katunski 25 R 5–6
Khrebet Ket-Kap 37 O 4
Khrebet Ketmen' 35 KL 2
Khrebet Khamar Daban 36 HJ 5
Khrebet Kholzun 25 Q 5
Khrebet Khugdyungda 36 G 2
Khrebet Kivun 37 P 5
Khrebet Kodar 36 L 4
Khrebet Kolymskiy 37 SU 3
Khrebet Kopet-Dag 34 F 3
Khrebet Koryakskiy 37 VW 3
Khrebet Kungey Alatau 35 K 2
Khrebet Mayskiy 37 O 4–5
Khrebet Narymskiy 25 QR 6
Khrebet Nuratau 35 H 2
Khrebet Orulgan 37 N 2
Khrebet Pay-Khoy 25 M 2
Khrebet Pekul'ney 37 WX 2
Khrebet Pribrezhnyy 37 P 4
Khrebet Rarytkin 37 WX 2
Khrebet Rarytkin 37 WX 3
Khrebet Saur 25 QR 6
Khrebet Semme-Dahan 37 P 3
Khrebet Sette-Daban 37 P 3
Khrebet Suntar Khayata 37 PQ 3
Khrebet Taaga 37 N 4
Khrebet Talasskiy Alatau 35 J 2
Khrebet Tarbagatay 25 Q 6
Khrebet Taskyl 36 G 5
Khrebet Tas-Kystabys 37 QR 3
Khrebet Terskey Alatau 35 K 2
Khrebet Tukuringra 37 N 5
Khrebet Turana 37 O 5
Khrebet Udokan 36 L 4
Khrebet Ulakhan-Chistay 37 QR 2–3
Khrebet Ulan-Burgasy 36 J 5
Khrebet Umnyn Syverma 36 GH 2
Khrebet Verkhoyanskiy 37 N 2–3
Khrebet Yam-Alin' 37 OP 5
Khrebet Yankan 36 L 4
Khrebet Yuzhno Chuyskiy 25 R 6
Khroma 37 Q 1
Khromskaya Guba 37 R 1
Khrom-Tau 25 L 5
Khrustal'nyy 39 KL 2
Khudoseya 25 Q 2–3
Khudumelapye 66 C 4
Khudzhakh 37 R 3
Khuff 59 J 3
Khuff (Saudi Arabia) 22 B 4
Khugdyungda, Khrebet 36 G 2
Khugiani 35 H 4
Khuis 66 C 5
Khulga 25 M 3
Khulkhuta 21 G 1
Khulna 40 E 3
Khulo 21 F 2
Khummi, Ozero 37 P 5
Khūrab (Iran) 23 F 3
Khurai 40 C 3
Khūran (Iran) 23 G 4
Khurays (Saudi Arabia) 23 E 4
Khurayt 60 D 6
Khurchan 37 S 4
Khurda 40 E 3
Khurīyā Murīya, Jazā' ir 61 K 5
Khurja 40 C 2
Khurmalik 35 G 4
Khurr, Wādī al (Saudi Arabia) 22 C 3
Khurramshahr (Iran) 23 E 3
Khursanīyah (Saudi Arabia) 23 E 4
Khushab 35 J 4
Khust 20 B 1
Khutse 66 C 4
Khuwayy 60 D 6
Khuzdar 35 H 5
Khūzestān (Iran) 23 E 3
Khuzhir 36 J 5
Khvāf 34 FG 4
Khvāf 34 G 4
Khvalynsk 24 J 5
Khvojeh, Kūh-e (Iran) 23 E 2
Khvor (Iran) 23 G 2
Khvormūj (Iran) 23 F 3
Khvormūj, Kūh-e (Iran) 23 F 3
Khvoy 34 D 3
Khwaja Amran 35 H 4
Khyber Pass 35 J 4
Kia 51 G 3
Kiama 64 B 6
Kiamba 43 F 2
Kiambi 64 D 6
Kiana 72 E 2
Kiantajärvi 16 J 2
Kiapulka 64 D 6
Kiāseh (Iran) 23 F 1
Kibaha 65 F 6
Kibamba 64 D 5
Kibangou 63 G 6
Kibau 64 F 6
Kibaya 65 F 6
Kiberege 65 F 6
Kiberg 16 K 1
Kiboko 65 F 5
Kibombo 64 D 5
Kibondo 64 E 5
Kibre Mengist 65 F 3
Kibris → Cyprus 21 D 3
Kibungu 64 E 5
Kibuye 64 D 5
Kibwezi 65 F 5
Kibworth Harcourt 7 D 1
Kicevo 20 B 2
Kichi Kichi 63 H 2
Kichiga 37 U 4
Kicking Horse Pass 73 O 5
Kidal 62 E 2
Kidatu 65 F 6
Kidderminster 7 C 1
Kidepo National Park 64 E 4
Kidira 62 B 3
Kidnappers, Cape 51 R 8
Kidsgrove 7 C 1
Kidwelly 6 B 2
Kiel 15 F 4
Kielce 15 H 4
Kielder 5 D 2
Kieler Bucht 15 F 4
Kienge 66 D 2
Kieta 51 G 3
Kiffa 58 C 5
Kifissós 20 B 3
Kifrī (Iraq) 22 D 2
Kifri (Iraq) 23 D 2
Kigali 64 E 5
Kiğı 21 F 3
Kigille 64 E 3
Kigilyakh 37 Q 1
Kignan 62 C 3
Kigoma 64 D 5
Kihelkonna 17 H 4
Kihnu 17 H 4
Kii-hantō 39 L 4
Kiik 25 O 6
Kiiminki 16 J 2
Kii-suidō 39 KL 4
Kikai-jima 39 JK 5
Kikiakki 25 Q 3
Kikinda 20 B 1
Kikládhes 20 C 3
Kikori 50 D 3
Kikwit 64 B 6
Kil 17 F 4
Kilafors 16 G 3
Kilakkarai 40 C 6
Kilambé 78 E 5
Kīlan (Iran) 23 F 2
Kilberry 3 B 4
Kilberry 4 B 3
Kilbirnie 3 B 4
Kilbrannan Sound 3 B 4
Kilbride 2 A 3
Kilbride 3 B 3
Kilbride 4 B 3
Kilbuck Mountains 72 F 3
Kilchoan 3 A 3
Kilchu 39 J 2
Kilcogy 4 B 3
Kilcormac 4 B 3
Kilcoy 49 J 4
Kilcreggan 3 B 4
Kilcullen 4 B 3
Kildare 4 B 3
Kil'din, Ostrov 16 K 2
Kildrummy 2 C 3
Kilembe 64 C 6
Kili 52 C 2
Kilibo 62 E 4
Kılıç Dağları 20 C 3
Kilifi 65 F 5
Kilimanjaro 65 F 5
Kilimanjaro National Park 65 F 5
Kilinailau Islands 51 G 2
Kilindini 65 F 5
Kilindoni 65 F 6
Kilis (Turkey) 22 B 1
Kilitbahir 20 C 2
Kiliya 20 C 1
Kilkampton 6 B 2
Kilkee 14 B 4
Kilkeel 4 C 2
Kilkenny 4 B 3
Kilkis 20 B 2
Killarney 14 B 4
Killashandra 4 B 2
Killeen 76 G 5
Killelu 65 G 2
Killin 3 B 3
Killinek 75 O 3
Kíllini Óros 20 B 3
Killmacrenan 4 B 2
Killough 4 C 2
Kilmaluag 2 A 3
Kilmarnock 3 B 4
Kilmartin 3 B 3
Kilmelford 3 B 3
Kil'mez' 24 K 4
Kil'mez 24 K 4
Kilmore 49 H 6
Kilombero 65 F 6
Kilosa 65 F 6
Kilpisjärvi 16 H 2
Kilp-Javr 16 K 2
Kilrea 4 B 2
Kiltan 40 B 5
Kiltoom 4 B 3
Kilur Karim (Iran) 23 F 3
Kilwa 64 D 6
Kilwa Kisiwani 65 F 6
Kilwa Kivinje 65 F 6
Kilwa Masoko 65 F 6
Kilwaughter 4 B 2
Kilwinning 3 B 4
Kilyos 20 C 2
Kimaan 43 J 5
Kimba 49 F 5
Kimball 76 G 3
Kimball, Mount 72 J 3
Kimbe Bay 51 F 3
Kimberley 73 O 6
Kimberley (South Africa) 66 CD 5
Kimberley (Western Australia) 48 D 2
Kimberley Downs 48 C 2
Kimberley Plateau 48 D 2
Kimbolton 7 D 1
Kimch'aek 39 J 2
Kimch'on 39 J 3
Kimhandu 65 F 6
Kimi (Cameroon) 63 G 4
Kimi (Greece) 20 B 3
Kimito 17 H 3
Kimongo 63 G 6
Kimovsk 24 G 5
Kimparana 62 BC 3
Kimpese 64 A 6
Kimry 24 G 4
Kimvula 64 B 6
Kinabalu, Gunung 42 E 2
Kinabatangan 42 E 2
Kinawley 4 B 2
Kinbrace 2 C 2
Kincardine 2 B 3
Kinchang 41 G 2
Kinchega National Park 49 G 5
Kinda (Sweden) 17 G 4
Kinda (Zaire) 64 C 6
Kindamba 63 G 6
Kindambi 64 C 6
Kindat 41 F 3
Kinder 77 H 5
Kindersley 73 Q 5
Kindia 62 B 4
Kindu 64 D 5
Kineshma 24 H 4
King 50 K 8
King Christian IX Land 90
King Christian X Land 90
King City 76 B 4
King Edward VII Falls 85 G 3
King Frederik VIII Land 90
King George Islands 75 M 4
King George Sound 48 B 6
King Island 49 G 6
King Leopold Ranges 48 CD 2
King Sound 48 C 2
King William Island 73 S 2
King Williams Town 66 D 6
Kingaroy 49 J 4
Kingarth 3 B 4
Kinghorn 3 C 3
Kingisepp (U.S.S.R.) 17 J 4
Kingissepp (Estoniya, U.S.S.R.) 17 H 4
Kingman (AZ, U.S.A.) 76 D 4
Kingman (Pacific Ocean, U.S.A.) 52 E 2
Kingombe 64 D 5
Kingombe 64 D 5
Kingoonya 49 F 5
King's Lynn 7 E 1
Kings Peak (CA, U.S.A.) 76 B 3
Kings Peak (UT, U.S.A.) 76 DE 3
King's Somborne 7 D 2
Kingsbridge 6 C 2
Kingsclere 7 D 2
Kingscote 49 F 6
Kingscourt 4 B 3
Kingskerswell 6 C 3
Kingsmill Group 52 C 3
Kingsport 77 K 4
Kingsteignton 6 C 2
Kingston 75 M 7
Kingston (Jamaica) 79 G 4
Kingston (Norfolk Is., Austr.) 52 C 4
Kingston (N.Y., U.S.A.) 77 M 3
Kingston (South Australia) 49 F 6
Kingston Peak 76 C 4
Kingston upon Hull 5 E 3
Kingston Upon Thames 7 D 2
Kingstown 79 K 5
Kingsville 76 G 6
Kingswood 6 C 3
Kington 6 C 1
Kinguji 64 B 6
Kingussie 3 BC 3
Kiniama 66 D 2
Kinkala 63 G 6
Kinlochewe 2 B 3
Kinlochleven 3 B 3
Kinmaw 41 F 4
Kinna 17 F 4
Kinnaird's Head 2 D 3
Kinnegad 4 B 3
Kinnekulle 17 F 4
Kinoosao 73 R 4
Kinross 3 C 3
Kinsale 14 B 4
Kinsarvik 17 E 3
Kinshasa 64 B 5
Kinston 77 L 4
Kintampo 62 D 4
Kintap 42 E 4
Kintinku 64 EF 6
Kintyre 3 B 4
Kinyangiri 64 E 5
Kinyeti, Jabal 64 E 4
Kinzia 64 B 5
Kipaka 64 D 5
Kiparissiakós Kolpós 20 B 3
Kipawa, Lac 75 M 6
Kipembawe 64 E 6
Kipengere Range 64 E 6
Kipili 64 E 6
Kipini 65 G 5
Kipnuk 72 E 4
Kippen 3 B 3
Kipushi 66 D 2
Kirakira 51 H 4
Kirané 62 B 2
Kiraz 20 C 3
Kirbey 36 H 2
Kirbey 36 K 2
Kircubbin 4 C 2
Kirdimi 63 H 2
Kirenga 36 J 4
Kirensk 36 J 4
Kirghiz Steppe 34–35 FG 1
Kirgiz Step' 34–35 FH 1
Kirgiziya 35 JK 2
Kirgizskiy Khrebet 35 J 2
Kiri 64 B 5
Kiribati 52 DE 3
Kırıkhan 21 E 3
Kırıkhan (Turkey) 22 B 1
Kırıkkale 21 D 3
Kirikos, Ayios 20 C 3
Kirillovka 21 E 1
Kirimati 53 E 2
Kirishi 17 K 4
Kiritimati 53 E 2
Kiritimati 53 E 2
Kirk Michael 4 C 2
Kırkağaç 20 C 3
Kirkbampton 5 D 2
Kirkbean 3 C 4
Kirkby 5 D 3
Kirkby in Ashfield 7 D 1
Kirkby Lonsdale 5 D 2
Kirkby Stephen 5 C 2
Kirkby Thore 5 D 2
Kirkbymoorside 5 E 2
Kirkcaldy 3 C 3
Kirkcolm 3 B 4
Kirkconnel 3 B 4
Kirkcudbright 3 BC 4
Kirkee → Khadki 40 B 4
Kirkenes 16 K 2
Kirkham 5 D 3
Kirkhill 2 B 3
Kirkintilloch 3 B 4
Kirkjubæjarklaustur 16 B 3
Kirkland 3 C 4
Kirkland Lake 75 L 6
Kırklareli 20 C 2
Kirkmichael 3 D 3
Kirkpatrick, Mount 91
Kirksville 77 H 3
Kirktown of Auchterless 2 C 3
Kirktown of Culsalmond 2 C 3
Kirkūk (Iraq) 22 D 2
Kirkwall 2 C 2
Kirkwall (Airport) 2 C 2
Kirkwhelpington 5 E 2
Kirkwood (MO, U.S.A.) 77 H 4
Kirkwood (South Africa) 66 D 6
Kırlangıç Burnu 20 D 3
Kirov 24 F 5
Kirov 24 J 4
Kirovabad 34 D 2
Kirovakan 21 F 2
Kirovo Chepetsk 24 K 4
Kirovograd 21 D 1
Kirovsk 16 K 2
Kirovsk 17 K 4
Kirovsk 34 G 3
Kirovskiy 35 K 2
Kirovskiy 37 T 5
Kirovskiy 39 K 1
Kirriemuir 3 C 3
Kirs 24 K 4
Kırşehir 21 D 3

Kirtachi 62 E 3
Kirthar Range 35 H 5
Kirtlebridge 3 C 4
Kirton 7 D 1
Kiruna 16 H 2
Kirundu 64 D 5
Kir'yanovskaya Kontora 36 H 4
Kisa 17 G 4
Kisabi 64 D 6
Kisaki 65 F 6
Kisalföld 20 A 1
Kisambo 64 B 6
Kisangani 64 D 4
Kisangire 65 F 6
Kisar, Pulau 43 G 5
Kiselevsk 25 R 5
Kishagarh 40 B 2
Kishangarh 40 BC 2
Kishb, Harrat al 61 G 4
Kishi 62 E 4
Kishinev 20 C 1
Kishorgani 41 F 3
Kishtwar 35 K 4
Kisii 64 E 5
Kisiju 65 F 6
Kısılırmak 21 D 2
Kısır Dağı 21 F 2
Kiska 72 A 5
Kiska Volcano 72 A 5
Kiskőei Viztároló 20 B 1
Kiskőrös 20 A 1
Kiskunfélegyháza 20 A 1
Kiskunhalas 20 AB 1
Kislovodsk 21 F 2
Kismāyu 65 G 5
Kisoro 64 DE 5
Kissidougou 62 B 4
Kissū, Jabal 60 D 4
Kisumu 64 E 5
Kisvárda 20 B 1
Kita 62 C 3
Kitab 35 H 3
Kita-daitō-jima 39 K 5
Kitai, Ozero 20 C 1
Kitakyushū 39 JK 4
Kitale 64 F 4
Kitami 39 M 2
Kitami-sanchi 39 M 2
Kitanda 64 D 6
Kitangari 67 F 2
Kitangiri, Lake 64 E 5
Kitchener 75 L 7
Kitee 16 K 3
Kiteiyab 60 E 4
Kitete 64 E 6
Kitgum 64 E 4
Kíthira 20 B 3
Kíthira 20 B 3
Kithnos 20 B 3
Kitimat 72 M 5
Kitimat Ranges 72–73 M 5
Kitinen 16 J 2
Kitoboynyy 37 S 6
Kitoy 36 H 5
Kit's Coty House 7 E 2
Kitsman 20 C 1
Kittanning 77 KL 3
Kittilä 16 H 2
Kitui 65 F 5
Kitunda 64 E 6
Kitwe 66 D 2
Kitzbühel 19 F 2
Kitzbüheler Alpen 19 F 2
Kiunga (Kenya) 65 G 5
Kiunga (Papua New Guinea) 50 D 3
Kiuruvesi 16 J 3
Kivak 72 C 3
Kivalina 72 E 2
Kivijärvi 16 HJ 3
Kivik 17 F 4
Kiviõli 17 J 4
Kivu 64 D 5
Kivu, Lake 64 D 5
Kivun, Khrebet 37 P 5
Kiwaba N'zogi 66 B 1
Kiya 25 R 4
Kīyāmakī Dāgh 34 D 3
Kiyeng-Kyuyel' 37 S 2
Kiyeng-Kyuyel', Ozero 36 JK 1
Kiyev 24 F 5
Kiyevka 25 O 5
Kiyevka 39 K 2
Kiyevskoye Vodokhranilishche 24 F 5
Kıyıköy 20 C 2
Kiyma 25 N 5
Kizel 25 L 4
Kizema 24 H 3
Kizha 36 J 5
Kizhinga 36 J 5
Kızıl Dağ 21 D 3
Kızıl Tepe 20 D 2
Kızılcahamam 21 D 2
Kızılırmak 21 E 2
Kizilirmak 21 E 3
Kizil'skoye 25 L 5
Kızıltepe 21 F 3
Kızıltepe (Turkey) 22 C 1
Kizimen, Sopka 37 U 4
Kizimi 63 H 2
Kizlyar 21 G 2
Kizlyarskiy Zaliv 21 G 2
Kizyl-Arvat 34 F 3
Kizyl-Atrek 34 E 3
Kizyl-Su 34 E 3
Kjöllefjord 16 J 1
Kjölur 16 B 3
Kjöpsvik 16 G 2
Klabat, Gunung 43 G 3
Kladanj 19 G 3
Kladno 15 F 4
Klagan 42 E 2
Klagenfurt 19 F 2
Klaipėda 17 H 4
Klamath Falls 76 B 3
Klamath Mountains 76 B 3
Klamath River 76 B 3
Klamono 43 H 4
Klarälven 17 F 3
Klatovy 15 F 5
Klawer 66 B 6
Klea → Abū Tulayh 60 E 5
Klein Aub 66 B 4
Kleinsee 66 B 5
Klerksdorp 66 D 5
Klevan' 17 J 5
Klichka 36 L 5
Klin 24 G 4
Klina 20 B 2
Klintehamn 17 G 4
Klintsovka 24 J 5
Klintsy 24 F 5
Klipgat 66 C 4
Klippan 17 F 4
Klit 17 E 4
Kłodzko 15 G 4
Kłomnice 15 G 4
Klondike Plateau 72 K 3
Klosi 20 B 2
Klotz, Lac 75 N 3
Klotz, Mount 72 K 2
Kluane Lake 72 K 3
Kluane National Park 72 K 3
Kluczbork 15 G 4
Klukhorskiy Pereval 21 F 2
Klyavlino 24 K 5
Klyazma 24 H 4
Klyuchevaya 24 H 2
Klyuchevskaya Sopka 37 U 4
Klyuchi 36 K 5
Klyuchr 37 U 4
Knack 2 A 2
Knaresborough 5 E 2
Knarsdale 5 D 2
Kneža 20 B 2
Knighton 6 C 1
Knin 19 G 3
Knittelfeld 19 FG 2
Knjaževac 20 B 2
Knock 2 C 3
Knösen 17 EF 4
Knosós 20 C 3
Knottingley 5 E 3
Knowle 7 D 1
Knox, Cape 72 L 5
Knox Coast 91
Knoxville (IA, U.S.A.) 77 H 3
Knoxville (TN, U.S.A.) 77 K 4
Knoydart 3 B 3
Knud Rasmussen Land 90
Knutsford 5 D 3
Knutsford 6 C 1
Knyazhevo 24 H 4
Knysna 66 C 6
Ko Chan 41 G 6
Ko Chang 41 H 5
Ko Kut 41 H 5
Ko Lanta 41 G 6
Ko Phangan 41 H 6
Ko Phuket 41 G 6
Ko Samui 41 G 6
Ko Samui 41 H 6
Ko Tao 41 GH 5
Ko Tarutao 41 G 6
Ko Way 41 H 6
Koal 63 H 3
Koartac 75 N 3
Koba 42 C 4
Koba 43 J 5
Kobar Sink 65 G 2
Kobbo 65 F 2
Kobdo → Hovd 36 F 6
Kōbe 39 KL 4
København 17 F 4
Kobenni 58 D 5
Koblenz 15 E 4
Koboldo 37 O 5
Kobrin 17 H 5
Kobroor, Pulau 43 H 5
Kobuk 72 EF 2
Kobuk 72 F 2
Kobuk Valley National Park 72 F 2
Kobuleti 21 F 2
Kobyai 37 N 3
Koca Çal 21 D 3
Koca Çay 20 C 3
Kocaeli 20 CD 2
Kočani 20 B 2
Kocasu 20 C 3
Koch 75 M 2
Kochechum 36 G 2
Kochegarovo 36 L 4
Kochenga 36 H 4
Kochevo 24 K 4
Kōchi 39 K 4
Kochikha 36 G 1
Koçhisar Ovası 21 D 3
Kochkorka 35 K 2
Kočhmar 20 C 2
Kochmes 25 M 2
Kochubey 21 G 2
Kock 15 H 4
Kodar, Khrebet 36 L 4
Kodar, Khrebet 36 L 4
Kodi 43 E 5
Kodiak 72 G 4
Kodiak Island 72 G 4
Kodima 24 H 3
Kodino 24 GH 3
Kodok 64 E 3
Kodori, Mys 21 F 2
Kodyma 20 D 1
Kodžha Balkan 20 C 2
Koel 40 D 3
Kōes 66 B 5
Kofçaz 20 C 2
Koffiefontein 66 C 5
Kofiau, Pulau 43 GH 4
Köflach 19 G 2
Koforidua 62 D 4
Koggala 40 D 6
Kogil'nik 20 C 1
Kogon 62 B 3
Koh i Qaisar 35 G 4
Kohat 35 J 4
Koh-Hisar 35 H 3–4
Koh-i-Baba 35 H 4
Kohima 41 F 2
Koh-i-Mazar 35 H 4
Koh-i-Pantar 35 H 5
Koh-i-Sangan 35 GH 4
Kohistan 35 J 3
Kohlu 35 H 5
Kohtla-Järve 17 J 4
Kohunlich 78 E 4
Koitere 16 K 3
Kojonup 48 B 5
Kojūr (Iran) 23 F 1
Kokalaat 35 G 1
Kokand 35 J 2
Kökar 17 H 4
Kokaral, Ostrov 34 FG 1
Kokas 43 H 4
Kokcha 35 H 3
Kokchetav 25 N 5
Kokemäenjoki 16 H 3
Kokemäki 16 H 3
Kokkola 16 H 3
Koko 64 F 2
Koko Nor 38 D 3
Kokoda 50 E 3
Kokomo 77 J 3
Kokonau 43 J 4
Kokong 66 C 4
Kokora, Ozero 36 H 1
Kokpekty 25 Q 6
Koksaray 35 H 2
Kokshaga 24 J 4
Koksoak 75 O 4
Kokstad 66 D 6
Koktuma 25 Q 6
Kokuora 37 Q 1
Kok-Yangak 35 J 2
Kola 16 K 2
Kola 16 K 2
Kola Peninsula 24 G 2
Kolahun 62 BC 4
Kolai 35 J 3
Kolaka 43 F 4
Kolar 40 C 5
Kolar Gold Fields 40 C 5
Kolari 16 H 2
Kolbachi 37 M 5
Kolbio 65 G 5
Kolda 62 B 3
Kolding 17 E 4
Kole 64 C 5
Kole 64 D 4
Koléa 18 D 4
Kolepom Island 43 J 5
Kolesnoye 20 D 1
Kolesovo 37 S 1
Kolff, Tanjung 43 J 5
Kolguyev, Ostrov 24 J 2
Kolhapur 40 B 4
Koli 16 J 3
Koliganek 72 F 4
Kolka 17 H 4
Kolkasrags 17 H 4
Kollegal 40 C 5
Kollumúli 16 C 2
Kolmanskop 66 AB 5
Kolmården 17 G 4
Kolmogorovo 36 F 4
Köln 15 E 4
Kolo 15 G 4
Kołobrzeg 15 G 4
Kologi 60 E 6
Kolokani 62 C 3
Koloko 62 C 3
Kololo 65 G 3
Kolombangara 51 G 3
Kolomna 24 G 4
Kolomyya 20 C 1
Kolondieba 62 C 3
Kolonia 52 E 1
Kolonodale 43 F 4
Kolosovka 25 O 4
Kolozero, Ozero 16 K 2
Kolpakovo 37 T 5
Kolpashevo 25 Q 4
Kolpino 17 K 4
Kólpos Ierisou 20 B 2
Kólpos Kallonis 20 C 3
Kólpos Kassándras 20 B 2–3
Kólpos Khanion 20 B 3
Kol'skiy, Poluostrov 24 G 2
Koluton 25 N 5
Kolva 24 L 2
Kolvitskoye, Ozero 16 K 2
Kolwa 35 G 5
Kolwezi 66 D 2
Kolyma 37 T 2
Kolyma Range 37 U 3
Kolymskaya 37 T 2
Kolymskaya 37 V 2
Kolymskaya Nizmennost' 37 ST 2
Kolymskiy, Khrebet 37 SU 3
Kolymskoye Nagor'ye 37 S 3
Kolyshley 24 H 5
Kolyuchinskaya Guba 72 C 2
Kolyvan' 25 Q 5
Koma 65 F 3
Komadugu Gana 63 G 3
Komadugu Yobe 63 G 3
Komandorski Islands 27 TU 4
Komandorskije Ostrova 27 TU 4
Komarichi 24 F 5
Komárno 15 G 5
Komarom 20 A 1
Komati Poort 67 E 5
Komatsu 39 L 3
Komba 64 C 4
Kombat 66 B 3
Kombissiguiri 62 D 3
Kombolchia 65 FG 2
Komdi 41 G 2
Kome 64 E 5
Kome Island 64 E 5
Komelek 37 O 3
Komfane 43 HJ 5
Komló 20 A 1
Kommunarka 25 R 2
Kommunarsk 21 E 1
Kommunist 37 X 3
Kommunizma, Pik 35 J 3
Komodo, Pulau 43 E 5
Komoé 62 D 4
Komoé, Parc National de la 62 D 4
Komono 63 G 6
Komoran, Pulau 43 J 5
Komotiní 20 C 2
Kompas Berg 66 C 6
Kompong Cham 41 J 5
Kompong Chhnang 41 H 5
Kompong Som 41 H 5
Kompong Speu 41 H 5
Kompong Sralao 41 J 5
Kompong Thom 41 J 5
Kompot 43 F 3
Komrat 20 C 1
Komsa 25 R 3
Komsomolets 25 M 5
Komsomol'sk 35 G 3
Komsomol'skiy 25 M 2
Komsomol'skiy 34 E 1
Komsomolskiy 21 G 1
Komsomol'sk-na-Amure 37 P 5
Komusan 39 JK 2
Kon Plong 41 J 5
Kona 62 D 3
Konakovo 24 G 4
Konarak 40 E 4
Konda 25 M 3
Konda 43 H 4
Kondagaon 40 D 4
Kondakova 37 T 2
Kondakovo 37 S 2
Kondinin 48 B 5
Kondoa 65 F 5
Kondon 37 P 5
Kondopoga 24 F 3
Kondor 34 F 3
Kondut 48 B 5
Konetsbor 24 L 3
Konevits, Ostrov 16 K 3
Konevo 24 G 3
Kong 62 D 4
Kong Frederik VI-Kyst 75 T 3
Konginskiye Gory 37 T 3
Kongkemul, Gunung 42 E 3
Kongola 66 C 3
Kongolo 64 D 6
Kongor 64 E 3
Kongsberg 17 EF 4
Kongsvinger 17 F 3
Kongur Shan 35 K 3
Kongwa 65 F 6
Koni, Poluostrov 37 S 4
Koni, Poluostrov 37 S 4
Koniakar 62 B 3
Konin 15 G 4
Konitsa 20 B 2
Konjed Jān (Iran) 23 F 2
Könkämä älv 16 H 2
Konkan 40 B 4
Konko 66 D 2
Konkouré 62 B 3
Konkudera 36 K 4
Konosha 24 H 3
Konoshchel'ye 25 R 2
Konotop 24 F 5
Konqi He 38 A 2
Końskie 15 H 4
Konstantinovka 21 E 1
Konstantinovskiy 21 F 1
Konstanz 15 E 5
Kontagora 63 F 3
Kontcha 63 G 4
Kontiomäki 16 J 3
Kontum 41 J 5
Konus, Gora 37 O 4
Konya 21 D 3
Konya Ovası 21 D 3
Konza 65 F 5
Konzaboy 37 T 2
Konzhakovskiy Kamen', Gora 25 LM 4
Kookynie 48 C 4
Kooline 48 B 3
Koolivoo, Lake 49 F 3
Koonalda 48 D 5
Koör 43 H 4
Koorda 48 B 5
Kootenay 73 O 5–6
Kootenay National Park 73 O 5
Kooussa 62 C 4
Kop Geçidi 21 F 2
Kopanovka 21 G 1
Kópasker 16 B 2
Kópavogur 16 A 3
Koper 19 F 2
Kopervik 17 DE 4
Kopet-Dag, Khrebet 34 F 3
Kopeysk 25 M 5
Köping 17 G 4
Koplik 20 A 2
Köpmanholmen 16 G 3
Koppang 16 F 3
Kopparberg 17 FG 4
Koprivniča 19 G 2
Kopychintsy 24 E 6
Kop'yevo 25 R 5
Kopylovka 25 Q 4
Kor (Iran) 23 F 3
Koralpe 19 FG 2
Koramlik 35 M 3
Korangi 35 H 6
Koraput 40 D 4
Korarou, Lac 62 D 2
Korba 40 D 3
Korbach 15 E 4
Korbol 63 H 3
Korça 20 B 2
Korchino 25 Q 5
Korčula 19 G 3
Korčulanski Kanal 19 G 3
Kord Küy 34 E 3
Kord Küy (Iran) 23 G 1
Kord Sheykh (Iran) 23 F 3
Kordān (Iran) 23 F 2
Kordestān 34 D 3
Kordestān (Iran) 23 E 2
Kordofan → Kurdufān 60 DE 6
Kords 34 FG 5
Korea Strait 39 J 4
Korelaksha 16 K 2
Korennoye 36 J 1
Korenovsk 21 E 1
Korenshty 20 C 1
Korets 17 J 5
Korf 37 V 3
Korfa, Zaliv 37 V 3–4
Korfovskiy 37 P 6
Korgen 16 F 2
Korhogo 62 C 4
Korienza 62 D 2
Korim 43 J 4

L

Lobva **25** M 4
Locarno **19** E 2
Loch Arkaig **3** B 3
Loch Awe **3** B 3
Loch Broom **2** B 3
Loch Carron **2** B 3
Loch Doon **3** B 4
Loch Earn **3** B 3
Loch Eriboll **2** B 2
Loch Ericht **3** B 3
Loch Etive **3** B 3
Loch Ewe **2** B 3
Loch Fyne **3** B 3
Loch Hourn **3** B 3
Loch Katrine **3** B 3
Loch Laggan **3** B 3
Loch Leven **3** C 3
Loch Linnhe **3** B 3
Loch Lochy **3** B 3
Loch Lomond **3** B 3
Loch Long **3** B 3
Loch Maree **2** B 3
Loch Morar **3** B 3
Loch Ness **2** B 3
Loch Nevis **3** B 3
Loch Rannoch **3** B 3
Loch Shiel **3** B 3
Loch Shin **2** B 2
Loch Snizort **2** A 3
Loch Sunart **3** B 3
Loch Tay **3** B 3
Loch Torridon **2** B 3
Lochaber **3** B 3
Lochailort **3** B 3
Lochaline **3** B 3
Lochboisdale **2** A 3
Lochdon **3** B 3
Lochearnhead **3** B 3
Locheport **2** A 3
Locherben **3** C 4
Lochgair **3** B 3
Lochgilphead **3** B 3
Lochinver **2** B 2
Lochmaddy **2** A 3
Lochnagar **3** C 3
Lochranza **3** B 4
Lochy, Loch **3** B 3
Lock **49** F 5
Lockerbie **3** C 4
Lockhart River Mission **49** G 1
Lockton **5** E 2
Locminé **18** C 2
Locri **19** G 4
Lod (Israel) **22** B 3
Loddon River **49** G 6
Lodève **18** D 3
Lodeynoye Pole **24** F 3
Lodi **19** E 2
Lödingen **16** G 2
Lodja **64** C 5
Lödöse **17** F 4
Lodwar **64** F 4
Łodz **15** G 4
Loelli **64** E 3
Loeriesfontein **66** B 6
Lofa **62** B 4
Lofoten **16** F 2
Lofsdalen **16** F 3
Loftus **5** E 2
Lofty Ranges, Mount **49** F 5
Loga **62** E 3
Logan **76** D 3
Logan, Mount **72** J 3
Logan Mountains **72** M 3
Logansport **77** J 3
Logg **3** B 4
Logone **63** H 3–4
Logone Birni **63** G 3
Logoualé **62** C 4
Logroño **18** C 3
Logrosán **18** B 4
Lögstör **17** E 4
Lögumkloster **17** E 4
Lögurinn **16** C 2
Lohardaga **40** D 3
Lohit **41** G 2
Lohja **17** H 3
Lohjanjärvi **17** H 3
Lohjanselkä **17** H 3
Loholoho **43** F 4
Loikaw **41** G 4
Loimaa **17** H 3
Loimijoki **17** H 3
Loir **18** C 2
Loir, Vaux du **18** D 2
Loire **18** C 2
Loire, Val de **18** D 2
Loja **18** C 4
Loja **84** C 4
Loji **43** G 4
Lojo **17** H 3
Loka (Sudan) **64** E 4
Loka (Zaire) **64** B 4
Lokan tekojärvi **16** J 2
Lokandu **64** D 5
Lokaw **64** C 5
Löken **17** F 4
Lokgwabe **66** C 4
Lokhpodgort **25** N 2
Lokichar **65** F 4
Lokichokio **64** E 4
Lokilalaki, Gunung **43** F 4
Lokka **16** J 2
Lökken (Denmark) **17** E 4
Lökken (Norway) **16** E 3
Loknya **17** K 4
Loko (Burkina) **64** B 4
Loko (Nigeria) **63** F 4
Lokoja **63** F 4
Lokomo **63** H 5
Lokoro **64** C 5
Lokosovo **25** O 3
Loks Land **75** P 3
Loksa **17** J 4
Lokshak **37** O 5
Lokwa-Kangole **65** F 4
Lol **64** D 3
Lola **62** C 4
Loliondo **65** F 5
Lolland **17** F 5
Lolo **64** C 4
Loloda **43** G 3
Lolodorf **63** G 5
Lolowau **42** A 3
Lom (Bulgaria) **20** B 2
Lom (Cameroon) **63** G 4
Lom Sak **41** H 4
Loma Bonita **78** C 4
Loma Mountains **62** B 4
Loma Negra, Planicie de la **89** C 6
Lomami **64** C 4
Lomas **86** B 4
Lomas Colorados **89** C 7
Lomas de Zamora **88** E 6
Lombarda, Serra **85** H 3
Lombarton **4** C 2
Lomblen, Pulau **43** F 5
Lombok **42** E 5
Lombok, Selat **42** E 5
Lomé **62** E 4
Lomela **64** C 5
Lomela **64** C 5
Loméméti **51** J 5
Lomié **63** G 5
Lomond, Loch **3** B 3
Lomonosov **17** J 4
Lomonosovka **25** N 5
Lomovoye **24** GH 3
Lomphat **41** J 5
Lompobatang, Gunung **43** F 5
Lompoc **76** B 5
Łomża **15** H 4
Loncoche **89** B 6
Loncopue **89** B 6
Londiani **64** F 5
London **75** L 7
London (U.K.) **7** DE 2
Londonderry **4** B 2
Londonderry **89** B 10
Londonderry, Cape **48** D 1
Londonderry, Isla (Chile) **89** B 9
Londrina **87** F 5
Lone Pine **76** C 4
Long Akah **42** DE 3
Long Bay **77** L 5
Long Beach (CA, U.S.A.) **76** C 5
Long Beach (N.Y., U.S.A.) **77** M 3
Long Beach (WA, U.S.A.) **76** B 2
Long Eaton **7** D 1
Long Island (Papua New Guinea) **50** E 3
Long Island (Quebec, Can.) **75** M 5
Long Island (The Bahamas) **79** G 3
Long Lake **74** K 6
Long, Loch **3** B 3
Long Marston **5** E 3
Long Melford **7** E 1
Long Range Mountaines **75** Q 6
Long Stratton **7** E 1
Long Valley **76** D 5
Long Xian **38** E 4
Long Xuyen **41** J 5
Longa (Angola) **66** A 2
Longa (Angola) **66** B 2
Longa (Brazil) **87** H 1
Longbleh **42** E 3
Longchuan **38** C 6
Longde **38** E 3
Longford (Tasmania, Austr.) **50** L 9
Longford (U.K.) **4** B 3
Longformacus **3** C 4
Longframlington **5** E 2
Longhai **39** G 6
Longhoughton **5** E 2
Longhua **39** G 2
Longhui **38** F 5
Longitudinal, Valle **89** B 6
Longjiang **37** M 6
Longkou **39** GH 3
Longlac **74** K 6
Longleju **42** E 3
Longlin **38** E 6
Longling **38** C 6
Longmanhill **2** C 3
Longmen **38** F 6
Longmont **76** F 3
Longmorn **2** C 3
Longnan **38** FG 6
Longnor **7** D 1
Longquan **39** G 5
Longreach **49** G 3
Longridge **5** D 3
Longs Peak **76** E 3
Longsegah **42** E 3
Longshan **38** E 5
Longsheng **38** F 5
Longshou Shan **38** D 3
Longside **2** D 3
Longtoft **5** E 2
Longtown **3** C 4
Longview (TX, U.S.A.) **77** GH 5
Longview (WA, U.S.A.) **76** B 2
Longwy **19** E 2
Longxi **38** D 3
Longyan **38** G 5
Longyao **38** G 3
Longzhou **38** E 6
Lonkin **41** G 2
Lons-le-Saunier **19** E 2
Lonton **41** G 2
Lontra **85** H 4
Loo **21** E 2
Looc **43** F 1
Looe **6** B 2
Lookout, Cape **77** L 5
Lookout Ridge **72** F 2
Loolmalasin **65** F 5
Loongana **48** D 5
Loop Head **14** AB 4
Lop **35** L 3
Lop Buri **41** H 5
Lop Nur **38** B 2
Lopari **64** C 4
Lopatin **34** D 2
Lopatina, Gora **37** Q 5
Lopatka **37** T 5
Lopatka, Mys **37** T 5
Lopatki **25** N 5
Lopcha **37** M 4
Lopez, Cap **63** F 6
Lopphavet **16** H 1
Loppi **17** H 3
Lopud **19** G 3
Lopydino **24** K 3
Lora **35** H 4
Lora del Río **18** B 4
Loralai **35** H 4
Lorca **18** C 4
Lord Howe Island **49** K 5
Lord Mayor Bay **73** TU 2
Lordegān (Iran) **23** F 3
Lordsburg **76** E 5
Lorengau **50** E 2
Lorestān (Iran) **23** E 2
Loreto **76** D 6
Loreto **84** D 4
Loreto (Maranhão, Brazil) **85** JK 5
Loreto (Mexico) **78** B 3
Lorica **84** C 2
Lorient **18** C 2
Lorn **3** B 3
Lörrach **15** E 5
Lorraine **19** E 2
Lorraine (Queensland, Austr.) **49** F 2
Lorton **5** E 2
Lorugumu **64** F 4
Los **16** G 3
Los Alamos **76** E 4
Los Alerges, Parque Nacional **89** B 6
Los Andes **88** B 5
Los Ángeles (Chile) **89** B 6
Los Angeles **76** BC 5
Los Antiguos **89** B 8
Los Blancos **86** D 5
Los Frentones **88** D 4
Los Gatos **76** B 4
Los, Îles de **62** B 4
Los Juríes **88** D 4
Los Lagos **89** B 6
Los Lavaderos **78** C 3
Los Menucos **89** C 7
Los Mochis **76** E 6
Los Monegros **18** C 3
Los Palacios **78** F 3
Los Paraguas, Parque Nacional **89** B 6
Los Pozos **88** BC 4
Los Reyes de Salgado **78** B 4
Los Roques, Islas **84** E 1
Los Teques **84** E 1
Los Vilos **88** B 5
Losap **52** B 2
Lošinj **19** F 3
Losinoborskaya **25** R 4
Lospalos **43** G 5
Lossiemouth **2** C 3
Lost Trail Pass **76** D 2
Lostwithiel **6** B 2
Losuia **51** F 3
Losuwo **43** G 3
Lot **18** D 3
Lota **89** B 6
Lothian **3** C 4
Loto **64** C 5
Lotta **16** J 2
Lotuke, Jabal **64** E 4
Lou **50** E 2
Loubomo **63** G 6
Loubuzhuang **38** A 3
Loudéac **18** C 2
Loudun **18** D 2
Loué **18** C 2
Louga **62** A 2
Lough Allen **4** A 2
Lough Conn **14** B 4
Lough Foyle **4** B 2
Lough Neagh **4** B 2
Lough Ree **4** B 3
Lough Sheelin **4** B 3
Lough Swilly **4** B 2
Loughborough **7** D 1
Loughton **7** E 2
Louhans **19** E 2
Louis Trichardt **66** DE 4
Louisa **77** K 4
Louisa Reef **42** D 2
Louisiade Archipelago **49** J 1
Louisiade Archipelago **51** F 4
Louisiana **77** H 5
Louisville **77** J 4
Loukhi **16** K 2
Loukolela **63** H 6
Loulan Yiji **38** A 2
Loum **63** FG 5
Loup **76** G 3
Loups Marins, Lacs des **75** N 4
Lourdes **18** C 3
Louśtin **15** F 4
Louth (Australia) **49** H 5
Louth (Lincolnshire U.K.) **5** EF 3
Louth (Rep. of Ireland) **4** B 3
Loutrá Killinis **20** B 3
Louviers **18** D 2
Louwater **66** B 4
Lövånger **16** H 3
Lovat **17** K 4
Lovech **20** B 2
Loveland **76** E 3
Lovell **76** E 3
Lovelock **76** C 3
Loviisa **17** J 3
Lovington **76** F 5
Lovisa **17** J 3
Lovozero **16** L 2
Lovozero, Ozero **16** L 2
Lóvua **66** C 1
Lóvua **66** C 2
Low, Cape **73** UV 3
Lowa **64** D 5
Lowa **64** D 5
Lowell **77** M 3
Lower California **76** D 6
Lower Hutt **51** R 9
Lower Lough Erne **4** B 2
Lower Post **72** M 4
Lower Red Lake **77** H 2
Lower Tunguska River **36** F 3
Lowestoft **7** E 1
Lowicz **15** G 4
Lowshān (Iran) **23** E 1
Loxton (South Africa) **66** C 6
Loxton (South Australia) **49** G 5
Loyalty Islands **51** J 6
Loyauté, Iles **51** J 6
Loyoro **64** E 4
Lozére, Mont **18** D 3
Loznica **20** A 2
Lozovaya **25** P 5
Loz'va **25** M 4
Lu Tao **39** H 6
Lua **64** B 4
Luacano **66** C 2
Luahasibuka **42** A 4
Luala **67** F 3
Lualaba **64** D 5
Luama **64** D 6
Lu'an **39** G 4
Luan He **39** G 2
Luán Toro **89** D 6
Luan Xian **39** G 3
Luanda **66** A 1
Luando **66** B 2
Luando **66** B 2
Luando Reserve **66** B 2
Luang Prabang **41** H 4
Luanginga **66** C 2
Luangue **66** B 1
Luangwa **67** E 2
Luangwa Valley Game Reserve **67** E 2
Luanping **39** G 2
Luanshya **66** D 2
Luanza **64** D 6
Luapala **66** D 2
Luarca **18** B 3
Luashi **66** C 2
Luau **66** C 2
Luba **63** F 5
Lubalo **66** B 1
Luban **15** G 4
Lubānas Ezers **17** J 4
Lubang Islands **43** EF 1
Lubango **66** A 2
Lubao **64** D 6
Lubartów **15** H 4
Lübbenau **15** F 4
Lubbock **76** F 5
Lübeck **15** F 4
Lubefu **64** C 5
Lubefu **64** C 5
Lubero **64** D 5
Lubika **64** D 6
Lubilash **64** C 6
Lubin **15** G 4
Lublin **15** H 4
Lubnān, Jabal (Lebanon) **22** B 2
Lubny **24** F 5
Luboń **15** G 4
Lubondaie **64** D 6
Lubuagan **43** J 1
Lubudi **64** D 6
Lubue **64** B 5
Lubuklinggau **42** B 4
Lubumbashi **66** D 2
Lubutu **64** D 5
Lubwe **66** D 2
Lucala **66** B 1
Lucala **66** B 1
Lucan **4** B 3
Lucania, Mount **72** J 3
Lucano, Appenino **19** G 3
Lucapa **66** C 1
Lucas **86** E 3
Lucas, Lake **48** D 3
Lucca **19** F 3
Luce Bay **4** C 2
Lucea **79** G 4
Lucena (Philippines) **43** F 1
Lucena (Spain) **18** C 4
Lučenec **15** G 5
Lucera **19** G 3
Lucero **76** E 5
Luchulingo **67** F 2
Lüchun **38** D 6
Lucira **66** A 2
Luckenwalde **15** F 4
Lucker **5** E 2
Lucknow **40** D 2
Lucksta **16** G 3
Lucon **18** C 2
Lucusse **66** C 2
Lucy Creek **49** F 3
Lüda **39** H 3
Ludborough **5** EF 3
Ludbreg **19** G 2
Lüderitz **66** AB 5
Lüderitz Bay **66** AB 5
Ludgavan **6** B 2
Ludgershall **7** D 2
Ludgorsko Plato **20** C 2
Ludhiana **40** C 1
Ludian **38** D 5
Ludington **77** J 3
Ludlow **6** C 1
Ludogorie **20** C 2
Luduş **20** B 1
Ludvika **17** G 3
Ludwigsburg **15** E 5
Ludwigshafen **15** E 5
Ludwigslust **15** F 4
Ludza **17** J 4
Luebo **64** C 6
Lueki **64** D 5
Luena (Angola) **66** B 2
Luena (Angola) **66** C 2
Luena (Zaire) **64** D 6
Luena (Zambia) **67** E 2
Luena Flats **66** C 2
Luengue **66** C 3
Luepa **85** F 2
Lüeyang **38** E 4
Lufeng **38** D 5
Lufeng **38** G 6
Lufico **66** A 1
Lufira **64** D 6
Lufira, Chutes de la **64** D 6
Lufira Falls **64** D 6
Luga **17** J 4
Luga **17** J 4
Lugano **19** E 2
Lugansk → Voroshilovgrad **21** E 1
Luganville **51** J 5
Lugards Falls **65** F 5
Lugela **67** F 3

M

Miyaly 34 E 1
Miyazaki 39 K 4
Miyi 38 D 5
Miyun 39 G 2
Mizan Teferi 64 F 3
Mizdah 59 H 2
Mizen Head 14 AB 4
Mizhi 38 F 3
Mizil 20 C 2
Mizoram 41 F 3
Mizque 86 D 4
Mizuho 91
Mizusawa 39 M 3
Mjölby 17 G 4
Mjöndalen 17 E 4
Mjösa 17 F 3
Mkangira 65 F 6
Mkasu 65 F 6
Mkata 65 F 6
Mkoani 65 F 6
Mkokotoni 65 F 6
Mkomazi 65 F 5
Mkomazi Game Reserve 65 F 5
Mkuku 66 D 2
Mkulwe 64 E 6
Mkushi 66 D 2
Mladá Boleslav 15 F 4
Mladenovac 20 B 2
Mlala Hills 64 E 6
Mława 15 H 4
Mleihas 58 D 4
Mleti 21 F 2
Mljet 19 G 3
Mljetski kanal 19 G 3
Mlnta 63 G 5
Mmadinare 66 D 4
Mmbatho 66 D 5
Mo i Rana 16 F 2
Moa 62 B 4
Moab 76 E 4
Moabi 63 G 6
Moʻalla (Iran) 23 F 2
Moamba 67 E 5
Moanda (Gabon) 63 G 6
Moanda (Zaire) 63 G 7
Moate 4 B 3
Moatize 67 E 3
Moba 64 D 6
Mobārakeh (Iran) 23 F 2
Mobaye 64 C 4
Mobayi-Mbongo 64 C 4
Mobeka 64 B 4
Moberly 77 H 4
Mobile 77 J 5
Mobile Bay 77 J 5
Mobridge 76 F 2
Mocajuba 85 J 4
Moçambique 67 G 3
Mocambique Basin 98 B 5
Mocha → Al Mukhā 61 G 6
Mocha, Isla 89 B 6
Mochudi 66 D 4
Mocímboa da Praia 67 G 2
Mockfjärd 17 FG 3
Môco, Morro de 66 AB 2
Mocoa 84 C 3
Mococa 87 G 5
Moctezuma 76 E 6
Moctezuma 78 B 3
Mocuba 67 F 3
Modane 19 E 2
Model Town 35 J 4
Modena (Italy) 19 F 3
Modena (U.S.A.) 76 D 4
Modesto 76 B 4
Modica 19 F 4
Modjamboli 64 C 4
Modowi 43 H 4
Modra 63 H 1
Modriča 19 G 3
Modur Dağı 21 F 3
Moe 49 H 6
Moelfre 5 B 1
Moelv 16 F 3
Moengo 85 H 2
Moero, Lac 64 D 6
Moffat 3 C 4
Moga 64 D 5
Mogadiscio → Muqdisho 65 H 4
Mogadishu 65 H 4
Mogadouro, Serra do 18 B 3
Mogāl (Iran) 23 F 1
Mogaung 41 G 2
Mogdy 37 O 5
Mogi das Cruzes 87 G 5
Mogilev 17 JK 5
Mogilev Podol'skiy 20 C 1
Mogil-Mogil 49 H 4
Mogi-Mirim 87 G 5
Mogincual 67 G 3
Mogocha 36 LM 5
Mogochin 25 Q 4
Mogogh 64 E 3
Mogok 41 G 3
Mogotoyevo, Ozero 37 R 1
Mogoyn 36 G 6
Mogoytui 36 KL 5
Mogu 65 G 4
Moguqi 37 M 6
Mogzon 36 K 5
Mohács 20 A 1
Mohall 76 F 2
Moḩammadābād (Iran) 23 G 3
Mohammedia 58 D 2
Mohe 37 M 5
Moheda 17 F 4
Moheli 67 G 2
Mohenjo Daro 35 H 5
Mohican, Cape 72 D 3
Mohill 4 B 3
Mohnyin 41 G 3
Mohon Peak 76 D 5
Mohona 40 C 2
Mohoro 65 F 6
Moidart 3 B 3
Mointy 25 O 6
Moise 75 O 5
Moisie 75 O 5
Moissac 18 D 3
Moïssala 63 H 4
Moitaco 85 F 2
Mojácar 18 C 4
Mojave 76 C 4
Mojave Desert 76 C 4
Mojiang 38 D 6
Mojjo 65 F 3
Moju 85 J 4
Mokambo 66 D 2
Mokhotlong 66 D 5
Mokhovaya 37 T 5
Mokil 52 B 2
Moklakan 36 L 4
Mokokchung 41 F 2
Mokolo 63 G 3
Mokp'o 39 J 4
Mokra Gora 20 B 2
Mokwa 63 E 4
Mol 14 E 4
Mola di Bari 19 G 3
Molagno 78 C 3
Molat 19 F 3
Molchanovo 25 Q 4
Mold 6 C 1
Moldava 20 C 1
Moldaviya 20 C 1
Molde 16 E 3
Moldefjorden 16 E 3
Moldes 88 D 5
Moldova Nouă 20 B 2
Moldoveanu, Virful 20 B 1
Mole Game Reserve 62 D 4
Molegbe 64 C 4
Moleke 64 B 5
Molepolole 66 D 4
Molfetta 19 G 3
Molina (Argentina) 88 C 5
Molina (Chile) 89 B 6
Molina de Aragón 18 C 3
Molina de Segura 18 C 4
Moline 77 H 3
Moling 41 F 2
Moliro 64 E 6
Molkābād (Iran) 23 F 2
Molkom 17 F 4
Mollendo 86 B 4
Molochansk 21 E 1
Molochnyy Liman 21 E 1
Molodechno 17 J 5
Molodezhnaya 91
Molodo 36 M 2
Molodogvardeyskaya 25 O 5
Molokai 53 E 1
Molokai Fracture Zone 99 D 2
Molong 49 H 5
Molopo 66 C 5
Molotovo 21 F 2
Moloundou 63 H 5
Molteno 66 D 6
Moluccas 43 G 4
Molus Ridge 98 A 1
Moma (Mozambique) 67 F 3
Moma (U.S.S.R.) 37 QR 2
Mombaça 87 J 2
Mombasa 65 FG 5
Mombetsu 39 M 2
Mombi New 41 F 3
Mombo 65 F 5
Mombotuta Falls 66 D 2
Momboyo 64 B 5
Momi 64 D 5
Mompono 64 C 4
Mompós 84 D 2
Momskiy Khrebet 37 QR 1–2
Momskiy Khrebet 37 QR 2
Mön 17 F 5
Mon 41 G 4–5
Mon Yul 41 F 2
Mona, Canal de la 79 J 4
Mona, Isla 79 J 4
Mona Quimbundo 66 B 1
Monach Isles 2 A 3
Monaco 19 E 3
Monaghan 4 B 2
Monahans 76 F 5
Monapo 67 G 2
Monarch Mountain 73 M 5
Monashee Mountains 73 O 5
Monasterevin 4 B 3
Monastery of Saint Catherine (Egypt) 22 AB 3
Monatélé 63 G 5
Monbetsu 39 M 2
Moncalieri 19 E 2–3
Moncayo, Sierra del 18 C 3
Monchegorsk 16 K 2
Mönchen-Gladbach 14 E 4
Monclova 78 B 2
Moncton 75 O 6
Mondego 18 B 3
Mondego, Cabo 18 B 3
Mondjuko 64 C 5
Mondo 63 H 3
Mondoñedo 18 B 3
Mondovi 19 E 3
Mondragone 19 F 3
Mondy 36 H 5
Money 41 K 4
Moneygall 4 B 3
Moneymore 4 B 2
Moneyslane 4 B 2
Monfalcone 19 F 2
Monforte 18 B 4
Mong Cai 41 J 3
Mong Hang 41 G 3
Mong Hpayak 41 G 3
Mong La 41 G 3
Mong Lin 41 H 3
Mong Loi 41 H 3
Mong Yai 41 G 3
Monga 64 C 4
Mongala 64 C 4
Mongalla 64 E 3
Mongbwalu 64 D 4
Monger, Lake (Western Australia) 48 B 4
Monghyr 40 E 2
Mongo (Chad) 63 H 3
Mongo (Sierra Leone) 62 B 4
Mongol Ard Uls 36 GH 6
Mongolia 36 GH 6
Mongolo 36 J 2
Mongono 63 G 5
Mongonu 63 G 3
Mongororo 63 J 3
Mongu 66 C 3
Mônguà 66 B 3
Monguel 58 C 5
Mönhhaan 38 F 1
Monichkirchen 19 G 2
Monigotes 88 D 5
Monjes, Islas los 84 D 1
Monkey Bay 67 EF 2
Monkey River 78 E 4
Monkira 49 G 3
Monkoto 64 C 5
Monmouth 6 C 2
Mono (Solomon Is.) 51 G 3
Mono (Togo) 62 E 4
Mono Lake 76 C 4
Monolithos 20 C 3
Monong 66 C 4
Monopoli 19 G 3
Monor 20 A 1
Monou 63 J 2
Monreal del Campo 18 C 3
Monreale 19 F 4
Monroe (LA, U.S.A.) 77 H 5
Monroe (MI, U.S.A.) 77 K 3
Monroe (N.C., U.S.A.) 77 K 5
Monrovia 62 B 4
Mons 14 D 4
Monsanto 18 B 3
Monse 43 F 4
Monsefú 84 C 5
Mönsterås 17 G 4
Mont Afao 59 G 3
Mont Aigoual 18 D 3
Mont Ajir 63 F 2
Mont aux Sources 66 D 5
Mont Blanc 19 E 2
Mont Cameroon 63 F 5
Mont de Ganga 63 G 4
Mont Deingueri 64 D 3
Mont du Metal 59 G 4
Mont Ei Loutone 63 G 1
Mont Gréboun 63 F 1
Mont Iboundji 63 G 6
Mont Jacques-Cartier 75 OP 6
Mont Joli 75 O 6
Mont Kavendou 62 B 3
Mont Lozére 18 D 3
Mont Mézenc 18 D 3
Mont Mina 62 C 3
Mont Mpelé 63 G 6
Mont Ngoua 64 C 3
Mont Niéndkoué 62 C 4
Mont Panié 51 H 6
Mont Pelat 19 E 3
Mont Pinçon 18 C 2
Mont Tahat 59 G 4
Mont Tembo 63 G 5
Mont Tonkou 62 C 4
Mont Ventoux 19 E 3
Mont Zedness 58 C 4
Montagne d'Ambre 67 H 2
Montagne de Lure 19 E 3
Montagne Pelée 79 K 5
Montague 72 H 4
Montague, Isla 76 D 5
Montalbán 18 C 3
Montalegre 18 B 3
Montana 76 DE 2
Montargis 18 D 2
Montauban 18 C 2
Montauban 18 D 3
Montbard 19 D 2
Montbeliard 19 E 2
Montbrison 18 D 2
Montceau-les-Mines 18 D 2
Mont-de-Marsan 18 C 3
Monte Pascoal, Parque Nacional de 87 J 4
Monte Alban 78 C 4
Monte Alegre 85 H 4
Monte Azul 87 H 4
Monte Bello Islands 48 AB 3
Monte Binga 67 E 3
Monte Carlo 19 E 3
Monte Carmelo 87 G 4
Monte Caseros 88 E 5
Monte Cinto 19 E 3
Monte Claros 87 H 4
Monte Comán 88 C 5
Monte Cristo 86 D 3
Monte d'Oro 19 E 3
Monte Dourado 85 H 4
Monte Fitz Roy 89 B 8
Monte Lindo 86 E 5
Monte Maca 89 B 8
Monte Melimoyo 89 B 7
Monte Negro Falls 66 A 3
Monte Quemado 88 D 4
Monte Rosa 19 E 2
Monte Santo 85 J 5
Monte Sarmiento 89 B 9
Monte Tronador 89 B 7
Monte Zeballos 89 B 8
Montech 18 D 3
Montecristi 79 H 4
Montecristo 19 F 3
Montego Bay 79 G 4
Montejinnie 48 E 2
Montelimar 19 D 3
Montemoreos 78 C 2
Montemor-o-Novo 18 B 4
Montenegro 88 F 4
Montepuez 67 F 2
Montepulciano 19 F 3
Monterado 42 C 3
Monterey 76 B 4
Monterey Bay 76 B 4
Montería 84 C 2
Montero 86 D 4
Monterotondo 19 F 3
Monterrey 78 BC 2
Montes Altos 85 J 5
Montes de Leon 18 B 3
Montes de Toledo 18 C 4
Montes Universales 18 C 3
Montes Vasços 18 C 3
Montesilvano 19 F 3
Montevideo 88 EF 5–6
Montgomery 6 C 1
Montgomery 77 J 5
Monthey 19 E 2
Monti Aurunci 19 F 3
Monti dei Frentani 19 FG 3
Monti di Ala 19 E 3
Monti Iblei 19 F 4
Monti Lepini 19 F 3
Monti Peloritani 19 FG 4
Monti Sabini 19 F 3
Monti Volsini 19 F 3
Monticello 76 E 4
Montiel, Campo de 18 C 4
Montigny-le-Roi 19 E 2
Montigny-les-Metz 19 E 2
Montijo, Golfo de 79 F 6
Montilla 18 C 4
Mont-Louis 18 D 3
Montluçon 18 D 2
Montmagny 75 NO 6
Monto 49 J 3
Montoro 18 C 4
Montpelier (ID, U.S.A.) 76 D 3
Montpelier (VT, U.S.A.) 77 M 3
Montpéllier 18 D 3
Montréal 75 N 6
Montreal Lake 73 QR 5
Montréjeau 18 D 3
Montreux 19 E 2
Montrose (U.K.) 3 C 3
Montrose (U.S.A.) 76 E 4
Monts Bagzane 63 F 2
Monts Bambouto 63 G 4
Monts Bleus 64 E 4
Monts Chic-Chocs 75 O 6
Monts d'Amain 18 D 2
Monts d'Arrée 18 C 2
Monts d'Aubrac 18 D 3
Monts de Cristal 63 G 5
Monts de la Medjerda 59 G 1
Monts de Lacaune 18 D 3
Monts de Toura 62 C 4
Monts des Ksour (Algeria) 58 EF 2
Monts des Ksour (Tunisia) 59 GH 2
Monts des Oulad Naïl 59 F 2
Monts Dore 18 D 2
Monts du Beaujolais 19 D 2
Monts du Hodna 59 FG 1
Monts du Hombori 62 D 2
Monts du Livradois 18 D 2
Monts du Lyonnais 19 D 2
Monts Koungou 63 G 6
Monts Kundelungu 64 D 6–7
Monts Malimba 64 D 6
Monts Mandingues 62 B 3
Monts Marungu 64 D 6
Monts Mbang 63 G 4
Monts Mitumba 64 D 5–6
Monts Moukandé 63 G 6
Monts Mugila 64 D 6
Monts Nimba 62 C 4
Monts Notre-Dame 75 O 6
Monts Otish 75 N 5
Monts Tamgak 63 F 2
Monts Tarouadji 63 F 2
Monts Timétrine 62 D 2
Montsalvy 18 D 3
Montsant, Sierra de 18 D 3
Montseck, Sierra del 18 D 3
Montseny, Sierra de 18 D 3
Montserrat 79 K 4
Monveda 64 C 4
Monviso 19 E 3
Monywa 41 G 3
Monza 19 E 2
Monze 66 D 3
Monzón 18 D 3
Moonie 49 J 4
Moonie River 49 H 4
Moonta 49 F 5
Moor of Rannoch 3 B 3
Moora 48 B 5
Mooraberree 49 G 4
Moore, Lake 48 B 4
Moorea 53 EF 4
Moorfoot Hills 3 C 4
Moorhead 77 G 2
Moorlands 49 F 6
Moorreesburg 66 B 6
Moose 75 L 5
Moose Jaw 73 Q 5
Moose Pass 72 H 3
Moosehead Lake 77 N 2
Moosomin 73 R 5
Moosonee 75 L 5
Mopeia 67 F 3
Mopipi 66 CD 4
Mopti 62 D 3
Moqokorei 65 H 4
Moquegua 86 B 4
Mora (Cameroon) 63 G 3
Mora (Spain) 18 C 4
Mora (Sweden) 17 F 3
Mora de Ebro 18 D 3
Moraca 20 A 2
Moradabad 40 C 2
Morado, Cerro 86 CD 5
Morafenobe 67 G 3
Morąg 15 G 4
Moraleda, Canal 89 B 7
Moraleya 18 B 3
Moramanga 67 H 3
Moran 76 D 3
Morane 53 F 4
Morant Cays 79 G 4
Morar, Loch 3 B 3
Morata, Puerto de 18 C 3
Moratuwa 40 C 6
Morava (Czechoslovakia) 15 G 5
Morava (Western Australia) 48 B 4
Morava (Yugoslavia) 20 B 2
Moravița 20 B 1
Morawhanna 85 G 2
Moray Firth 2 C 3
Morbi 40 B 3
Mordaga 36 M 5
Morden 73 S 6
Mordovo 24 H 5
Möre 17 G 4
More Laptevykh 36 MN 1
Möre og Romsdal 16 E 3
Morebath 6 C 3
Morecambe 5 D 2
Morecambe Bay 5 D 2
Moree 49 H 4
Morehead 50 D 3
Morehead City 77 L 5

N

Nakfa **65** F 1
Nakhichevan' **21** FG 3
Nakhichevan' **34** CD 3
Nakhodka **25** O 2
Nakhodka **25** P 2
Nakhodka **39** K 2
Nakhon Nayok **41** H 5
Nakhon Pathom **41** G 5
Nakhon Phanom **41** H 4
Nakhon Ratchasima **41** H 5
Nakhon Sawan **41** GH 4
Nakhon Si Thammarat **41** G 6
Nakina **74** K 5
Nakło **15** G 4
Naknek **72** F 4
Nako **62** D 3
Nakonde **67** E 1
Nakop **66** B 5
Nakskov **17** F 5
Näkten **16** F 3
Näkten **16** F 3
Nakuru **65** F 5
Nalayh **36** J 6
Nalázi **67** E 4
Nal'chik **21** F 2
Näldsjön **16** F 3
Näldsjön **16** F 3
Nalgimskaya **37** VW 3
Nalgonda **40** C 4
Nallamala Range **40** C 4
Nallıhan **20** D 2
Nālūt **59** H 2
Nam Ca Dinh **41** H 4
Nam Can **41** J 6
Nam Co **41** F 1
Nam Dinh **41** J 3
Nam Ou **41** H 3
Nam Phang **41** H 4
Nam Phong **41** H 4
Nam Teng **41** G 3
Namaacha **67** E 5
Namacunde **66** B 3
Namacurra **67** F 3
Namak, Daracheh-ye (Iran) **23** F 2
Namak, Kavir-e (Iran) **23** G 1
Namaki (Iran) **23** G 3
Namakzar-e Shadad **34** F 4
Namaland **66** B 5
Namanga **65** F 5
Namangan **35** J 2
Namanyere **64** E 6
Namapa **67** G 2
Namaponda **67** G 3
Namaqualand **66** B 5
Namarrói **67** F 3
Namasagali **64** E 4
Namatanai **51** F 2
Nambour **49** J 4
Namche Bazar **40** E 2
Namdalen **16** F 3
Nametil **67** F 3
Namib Desert **66** AB 3–5
Namib Desert Park **66** AB 4
Namibe **66** A 3
Namibe Reserve **66** A 3
Namibia **66** B 4
Namiquipa **76** E 6
Namjagbarwa Feng **38** C 5
Namkham **41** G 3
Namlan Pan **41** G 3
Namlea **43** G 4
Namling **40** E 2
Namoi River **49** H 5
Namoluk **52** B 2
Namonuito **52** A 2
Namorik **52** C 2
Namoya **64** D 5
Nampa **76** C 3
Nampala **62** C 2
Namp'o **39** HJ 3
Nampula **67** F 3
Namrole **43** G 4
Namru **40** D 1
Namsang **41** G 3
Namsê La **40** D 2
Namsen **16** F 2–3
Namsos **16** F 3
Namsvattnet **16** F 2
Namton **41** G 3
Namtsy **37** N 3
Namtu **41** G 3
Namu **52** C 2
Namuli **67** F 3
Namuno **67** F 2
Namur **14** DE 4
Namutoni **66** B 3
Namwala **66** D 3
Namwŏn **39** J 3
Namy **37** O 2
Namya Ra **41** G 2
Namyit Island **42** D 1
Nan Hulsan Hu **38** C 3
Nan Ling **38** EF 5
Nana Kru **62** C 5
Nanaimo **73** N 6
Nanam **39** JK 2
Nanambinia **48** C 5
Nanao **39** L 3
Nancha **37** N 6
Nanchang **38** G 5
Nancheng **38** G 5
Nanchong **38** E 4
Nanchuan **38** E 5
Nancowry **41** F 6
Nancy **19** E 2
Nanda Devi **40** D 1
Nandan **38** E 6
Nander **40** C 4
Nandod **40** B 3
Nandu Jiang **38** E 7
Nandurbar **40** B 3
Nandyal **40** C 4
Nanfeng **38** G 5
Nang Xian **38** B 5
Nanga Emboko **63** G 5
Nanga Parbat **35** J 3
Nangakelawit **42** D 3
Nangapinoh **42** D 4
Nangatayap **42** D 4
Nangin **41** G 5
Nangnim-sanmaek **39** J 2
Nangong **38** G 3
Nangqên **38** C 4
Nanguneri **40** C 6
Nanhua **38** D 5
Nanhui **39** H 4
Nanjian **38** D 5
Nanjiang **38** E 4
Nanjing **39** G 4
Nankang **38** F 5
Nanking → Nanjing **39** G 4
Nankova **66** B 3
Nanle **38** G 3
Nannine **48** B 4
Nanning **38** E 6
Nannup **48** B 5
Nanortalik **75** S 3
Nanpan Jiang **38** D 6
Nanpara **40** D 2
Nanpi **39** G 3
Nanping **38** D 4
Nanping **39** G 5
Nansei-shotō **39** J 5
Nansha Qundao **42** D 2
Nanshan Islands **42** D 2
Nansikan, Ostrov **37** PQ 4
Nansio **64** E 5
Nantais, Lac **75** N 3
Nantes **18** C 2
Nanton **73** P 5
Nantong **39** H 4
Nantou **39** H 6
Nantucket Island **77** N 3
Nantucket Sound **77** MN 3
Nantulo **67** F 2
Nantwich **5** D 3
Nantwich **6** C 1
Nantyffyllon **6** C 3
Nantyglow **6** C 2
Nanumanga **52** C 3
Nanumea **52** C 3
Nanuque **87** HJ 4
Nanusa, Kepulauan **43** G 3
Nanwei Dao **42** D 2
Nanxiong **38** F 5
Nanyang **38** F 4
Nanyuki **65** F 4
Nanzhang **38** F 4
Nanzhao **38** F 4
Nanzhil **66** D 3
Nao, Cabo de la **18** D 4
Naococane, Lac **75** N 5
Naoli He **37** O 6
Náousa **20** B 2
Napaku **42** E 3
Napalkovo **25** OP 1
Napana **37** T 4
Napas **25** Q 4
Napassoq **75** R 2
Napata **60** E 5
Nape **41** J 4
Napido **43** J 4
Napier **51** R 8
Napier Mountains **91**
Naples (FL, U.S.A.) **77** K 6
Naples (Italy) **19** F 3
Napo **38** E 6
Napo (Peru) **84** D 4
Napoli **19** F 3
Napperby **48** E 3
Napuka **53** F 3
Naqa **60** E 5
Naqadeh (Iran) **23** D 1
Naqb, Ra's an (Jordan) **22** B 3
Naqsh-e Rostam (Iran) **23** F 3
Nara (Japan) **39** L 4
Nara (Mali) **62** C 2
Nara (Pakistan) **35** H 6
Naracoorte **49** G 6
Naran **36** G 6
Naran **38** F 1
Naranjos **78** C 3
Narasapur **40** D 4
Narasun **36** K 5
Narathiwat **41** H 6
Narayanganj **41** F 3
Narberth **6** B 2
Nærbö **17** E 4
Nærbö **17** E 4
Narbonne **18** D 3
Narborough **7** E 1
Nares Strait **90**
Naretha **48** C 5
Narew **15** H 4
Narlı **21** E 3
Narmada **40** B 3
Narman **21** F 2
Narnaul **40** C 2
Naroch **17** J 5
Narodnaya, Gora **25** LM 2
Naro-Fominsk **24** G 4
Narok **65** F 5
Narooma **49** J 6
Narowal **35** J 4
Närpes **16** H 3
Närpiö **16** H 3
Narrabri **49** HJ 5
Narrandera **49** H 5
Narrogin **48** B 5
Narromine **49** H 5
Narsimhapur **40** C 3
Narsinghgarh **40** C 3
Narsinghpur **40** E 3
Narssalik **75** S 3
Narssaq **75** R 3
Narssaq **75** S 3
Narssarssuaq **75** ST 3
Năruja **20** C 1
Narungombe **65** F 6
Narva **17** J 4
Narvik **16** G 2
Narvski Zaliv **17** J 4
Narwietooma **48** E 3
Nar'yan Mar **24** K 2
Narym **25** Q 4
Narymskiy, Khrebet **25** QR 6
Naryn **35** JK 2
Naryn **35** K 2
Naryn **36** G 5
Narynkol' **35** KL 2
Nås **17** F 3
Nås **17** F 3
Näsåker **16** G 3
Näsåker **16** G 3
Nasarawa **63** F 4
Năsăud **20** B 1
Nashtarūd (Iran) **23** F 1
Nashville **77** J 4
Našice **19** G 2
Näsijärvi **16** H 3
Näsijärvi **16** H 3
Nasik **40** B 3
Nāsir **64** E 3
Nasirabad (India) **40** B 2
Nasirabad (Pakistan) **35** H 5
Naskaupi **75** P 5
Nasmah **59** H 2
Nasmgani **40** D 3
Nasrābād (Iran) **23** F 2
Nass **72** M 4
Nassau (Cook Is.) **52** D 3
Nassau (The Bahamas) **79** G 2
Nasser, Birkat (Egypt) **22** A 5
Nasser, Lake (Egypt) **22** A 5
Nassian **62** D 4
Nässjö **17** FG 4
Nastapoka Islands **75** M 4
Næstved **17** F 4
Nasva **17** K 4
Nata **66** D 4
Nata **66** D 4
Natal **87** JK 2
Natal (Amazonas, Brazil) **85** F 5
Natal (Indonesia) **42** A 3
Natal (South Africa) **66–67** E 5
Natara **37** MN 2
Natashquan **75** P 5
Natashquan **75** QR 5
Natchez **77** H 5
Natchitoches **77** H 5
Nathdwara **40** B 3
Natīh **61** K 4
Natitingou **62** E 3
Natityāy, Jabal **60** E 4
Natividade **87** G 3
Natkyizin **41** G 5
Natron, Lake **65** F 5
Natrūn, Wādī an **60** DE 2
Nattaung **41** G 4
Nattavaara **16** H 2
Natuna Besar **42** C 3
Natuna, Kepulauan **42** C 3
Natuna Utara **42** C 3
Naturaliste, Cape **48** A 5
Naturaliste Channel **48** A 4
Naturno **19** F 2
Nauchas **66** B 4
Nauja Bay **75** M 2
Naujoji-Akmene **17** H 4
Naukluft **66** B 4
Naul **4** B 3
Naumburg **15** F 4
Naungpale **41** G 4
Naupe **84** C 5
Nā'ūr (Jordan) **22** B 3
Naurskaya **21** G 2
Nauru **51** J 2
Naurzum **25** M 5
Naushahro Firoz **35** H 5
Naushki **36** J 5
Nauta **84** D 4
Nautanwa **40** D 2
Nava **78** B 2
Navahermosa **18** C 4
Navajo Reservoir **76** E 4
Naval **43** F 1
Navalmoral de la Mata **18** B 4
Navarino **89** C 10
Navarra **18** C 3
Navassa **79** G 4
Navia (Argentina) **88** C 5
Navia (Spain) **18** B 3
Navidad **88** B 5
Naviraí **87** F 5
Navlya **24** F 5
Năvodari **20** C 2
Navoi **35** H 2
Navojoa **76** E 6
Navolato **76** E 7
Navolok **24** G 3
Navplion **20** B 3
Navrongo **62** D 3
Navsari **40** B 3
Navtlug **21** G 2
Nawabganj **40** D 2
Nawabshah **35** H 5
Nāwah **35** H 4
Nawalgarh **40** C 2
Nawāṣīf, Ḥarrat **61** G 4
Naws, Ra's **61** K 5
Náxos **20** C 3
Nāy Band (Iran) **23** F 4
Nāy Band, Ra's-e (Iran) **23** F 4
Nayakhan **37** T 3
Nayarit **78** B 3
Nayarit, Sierra **78** B 3
Nayland **7** E 2
Nayoro **39** M 2
Naystenyarvi **16** K 3
Nazaré **18** B 4
Nazaré (Bahía, Brazil) **87** J 3
Nazaré (Goiás, Brazil) **85** J 5
Nazareth (Peru) **84** C 5
Nazarovka **24** H 5
Nazarovo **36** F 4
Nazas **78** B 2
Nazca **86** B 3
Nazca Ridge **99** E 4
Naze **39** J 5
Nazerat (Israel) **22** B 2
Nazilli **20** C 3
Nazimovo **36** F 4
Nazina **25** P 3
Nazira **41** F 2
Nazmiye **21** EF 3
Nazran' **21** F 2
Nazwa **61** K 4
Nchelenge **66** D 1
Ncheu **67** E 2
Ndala **64** E 5
N'dalatando **66** A 1
Ndali **62** E 4
Ndandawala **65** F 6
Ndélé **64** C 3
Ndélélé **63** G 5
Ndendé **63** G 6
Ndeni **51** J 4
Ndindi **63** G 6
N'Djamena **63** H 3
Ndjolé **63** G 6
Ndogo, Lagune **63** G 6
Ndola **66** D 2
Ndoro **63** G 6
Ndrhamcha, Sebkha de **58** BC 5
Ndu **64** C 4
Nea (Norway) **16** F 3
Nea (Solomon Is.) **51** J 4
Nea Filippías **20** B 3
Néa Zíkhni **20** B 2
Neagh, Lough **4** B 2
Neagh, Lough **14** B 4
Neale, Lake **48** E 3
Neápolis **20** B 2
Néapolis **20** B 3
Near Islands **72** A 5
Neath **6** C 2
Nebbou **62** D 3
Nebine River **49** H 4
Nebit-Dag **34** E 3
Neblina, Pico da **84** E 3
Nebo **49** H 3
Nebolchi **24** F 4
Nebraska **76** FG 3
Nebraska City **77** G 3
Nechako **73** N 5
Nechako Plateau **73** N 5
Nechako Reservoir **73** M 5
Nechi **84** D 2
Neckar **15** E 5
Necochea **89** E 6
Nédéley **63** H 2
Nedong **41** F 2
Needles **76** CD 5
Nefedovo **25** O 4
Neftah **59** G 2
Neftegorsk **21** EF 2
Neftegorsk **24** K 5
Neftekamsk **24** K 4
Neftekumsk **21** F 2
Neftelensk **36** J 4
Nefteyugansk **25** O 3
Nefyn **5** B 1
Negage **66** B 1
Negala **62** C 3
Negelli **65** F 3
Negomano **67** F 2
Negombo **40** C 6
Negotin **20** B 2
Negotka **25** Q 4
Negra, Cordillera **84** C 5
Negra, Punta **84** B 5
Negra, Serra **85** J 5
Negrais, Cape **41** F 4
Négrine **59** G 2
Negritos **84** B 4
Negro, Cerro **89** C 7
Negro, Río (Brazil) **85** F 4
Negro, Río (Uruguay) **88** EF 5
Negros **43** F 2
Negru Vodă **20** C 2
Nehāvand **34** D 3
Nehāvand (Iran) **23** E 2
Nehbandan **34** FG 4
Nehe **37** MN 6
Nehoiu **20** C 1
Nehone **66** B 3
Nei Monggol Zizhiqu **38** DG 2
Neige, Crêt de la **19** E 2
Neijiang **38** E 5
Neilton **76** B 2
Neiqiu **38** F 3
Neiva **84** CD 3
Nejanilini Lake **73** S 4
Nejd (Saudi Arabia) **22** CD 5
Nejo **64** F 3
Neka (Iran) **23** F 1
Nekemt **65** F 3
Nekrasovka **39** L 2
Neksikan **37** R 3
Neksö **17** G 4
Nelemnoye **37** S 2
Nel'gese **37** O 2
Nelichu **64** E 3
Nelidovo **24** F 4
Nel'kan **37** P 4
Nel'keskan **36** M 2
Nelkuchan, Gora **37** P 3
Nellore **40** CD 5
Nel'ma **37** P 6
Nelson (Br. Col., Can.) **73** O 6
Nelson (Man., Can.) **73** S 5
Nelson (New Zealand) **51** Q 9
Nelson (U.K.) **5** D 3
Nelson, Cape **49** G 6
Nelson, Estrecho **89** AB 9
Nelson Head **73** N 1
Nelson Island **72** D 3
Nelspruit **67** E 5
Nelyaty **36** L 4
Néma **58** D 5
Neman **17** HJ 5
Nembrala **43** F 6
Nemira, Virful **20** C 1
Némiscau **75** M 5
Nemours → Ghazaouet **58** E 1
Nemrutdağı **21** E 3
Nemunas **17** H 4
Nemuro **39** N 2
Nemuy **37** P 4
Nen Jiang **39** H 1
Nenana **72** H 3
Nenana **72** H 3
Nendo **51** J 4
Nene, River **7** E 1
Nengonengo **53** F 4
Nenjiang **37** N 6
Nenthead **5** D 2
Néon Karlovásion **20** C 3
Nepa **36** J 4
Nepa **36** J 4
Nepal **40** D 2
Nepalganj **40** D 2
Nepeña **84** C 5
Nephi **76** D 4
Nepoko **64** D 4
Nera **37** Q 3
Nérac **18** D 3
Nercha **36** L 5
Nerchinsk **36** L 5
Nerchinskiy Khrebet **36** L 5

Onilahy **67** G 4
Onitsha **63** F 4
Onk,Djebel **59** G 2
Onkuchakh **36** KL 2
Ono-i-Lau Islands **52** CD 4
Onomichi **39** K 4
Onon **36** L 5
Onon Gol **36** K 6
Onotoa **52** C 3
Onovgay **37** T 4
Onsala **17** F 4
Onseepkans **66** B 5
Onslow **48** B 3
Onslow Bay **77** L 5
Ontario (Canada) **74** JL 5
Ontario (OR, U.S.A.) **76** C 3
Ontario, Lake **77** L 3
Onteniente **18** C 4
Ontojärvi **16** J 3
Ontong Java **51** G 3
Oodnadatta **49** F 4
Ookiep **66** B 5
Ooldea **48** E 5
Oologah Lake **77** G 4
Oorindi **49** G 3
Oostende **14** D 4
Ootacamund **40** C 5
Opala (U.S.S.R.) **37** T 5
Opala (Zaire) **64** C 5
Opanake **40** D 6
Opari **64** E 4
Opasatika **74** L 6
Opatija **19** F 2
Opava **15** G 5
Opelousas **77** H 5
Ophir **72** F 3
Opienge **64** D 4
Opis (Iraq) **22** D 2
Opiscotéo, Lac **75** O 5
Opobo **63** F 5
Opochka **17** J 4
Opoczno **15** GH 4
Opole **15** G 4
Oporto **18** B 3
Oposhnya **24** F 6
Opotiki **51** R 8
Opp **77** J 5
Oppdal **16** EF 3
Oppland **16** E 3
Opportunity **76** C 2
Oputo **76** E 5
Or, Côte d' **19** D 2
Oradea **20** B 1
Öræfajókull **16** B 3
Orah **59** J 3
Orahovica **19** G 2
Orai **40** C 2
Oran **58** E 1
Orange (Australia) **49** H 5
Orange (France) **19** D 3
Orange (Namibia) **66** B 5
Orange (TX, U.S.A.) **77** H 5
Orange, Cabo **85** H 3
Orange Free State **66** D 5
Orange Park **77** K 5
Orange Walk **78** E 4
Orango, Ilha de **62** A 3
Oranienburg **15** F 4
Oranje **66** B 5
Oranje Gebergte **85** GH 3
Oranjemund **66** B 5
Oranjestad **84** E 1
Oranzherei **21** G 1
Orapa **66** D 4
Orbetello **19** F 3
Orbigo **18** B 3
Orbost **49** H 6
Orcadas **91**
Ord, Mount **48** D 2
Ord River **48** D 2
Ord River Dam **48** D 2
Ordenes **18** B 3
Ordoquí **89** D 6
Ordos Plateau **38** E 3
Ordu **21** E 2
Ordynskoye **25** Q 5
Ordzhonikidze **21** E 2
Ordzhonikidze **21** FG 2
Ordzhonikidzeabad **35** HJ 3
Orealla **85** G 2
Orebić **19** G 3
Örebro **17** G 4
Oregon **76** BC 3
Oregon Inlet **77** LM 4
Öregrund **17** G 3
Orekhov **21** E 1
Orekhovo **20** B 2
Orekhovo Zuyevo **24** G 4
Orel' **21** D 1
Orel **24** G 5
Orel', Ozero **37** P 5
Orellana (Peru) **84** C 4
Orellana (Peru) **84** C 5
Orem **76** D 3
Oren **20** C 3
Orenburg **24** K 5
Orense **18** B 3
Orestiás **20** C 2
Öresund **17** F 4
Orford **7** E 1
Organ Peak **76** E 5
Organ Pipe Cactus National Monument **76** D 5
Orgañá **18** D 3
Orgeyev **20** C 1
Órgiva **18** C 4
Orhaneli **20** C 3
Orhangazi **20** C 2
Orhon Gol **36** H 6
Ori **87** J 2
Orick **76** B 3
Oriental, Cordillera **86** BC 3–5
Oriental, Cordillera (Colombia) **84** CD 2–3
Oriente **89** D 6
Orihuela **18** C 4
Orillia **75** M 7
Orimattila **17** J 3
Orinduik **85** F 3
Orinoco (Colombia) **84** E 2
Orissa **40** DE 3
Orissaare **17** H 4
Oristano **19** E 4
Orivesi **16** H 3
Orivesi **16** J 3
Oriximiná **85** G 4
Orizaba **78** C 4
Orjen **20** A 2
Orkadalen **16** EF 3
Orkanger **16** E 3
Örkelljunga **17** F 4
Orkla **16** E 3
Orkney (South Africa) **66** D 5
Orkney Islands **2** C 2
Orlando **77** K 6
Orléans **18** D 2
Orlik **36** G 5
Orlovskaya **37** V 3
Orlu **63** F 4
Ormara **35** G 5
Ormoc **43** F 1
Órmos Almiroú **20** B 3
Ormskirk **5** D 3
Orne **18** C 2
Ornö **17** G 4
Örnsköldsvik **16** G 3
Oro, Monte d' **19** E 3
Orobie, Alpi **19** EF 2
Orocué **84** D 3
Orodara **62** CD 3
Orofino **76** C 2
Örög Nuur **36** F 5
Orog Nuur **38** D 1
Orogrande **76** E 5
Oroluk **52** B 2
Oromocto **75** O 6
Oron (Nigeria) **63** F 5
Oron (U.S.S.R.) **36** L 4
Orona **52** D 3
Oropesa **18** B 4
Oropesa **18** CD 3
Oroqen Zizhiqi **37** M 5
Oroquieta **43** F 2
Óros Ossa **20** B 3
Orosei **19** E 3
Oroszlány **20** A 1
Orotukan **37** S 3
Oroville (CA, U.S.A.) **76** B 4
Oroville (WA, U.S.A.) **76** C 2
Oroyëk **37** S 3
Orphir **2** C 2
Orpington **7** E 2
Orqohan **37** M 6
Orr **77** H 2
Orrefors **17** G 4
Orroroo **49** F 5
Orsa **16** F 3
Orsa Finnmark **16** F 3
Orsasjön **16** F 3
Orsha **17** K 5
Orsk **25** L 5
Orşova **20** B 2
Ørsta **16** E 3
Orta **21** D 2
Ortà, Lago d' **19** E 2
Ortaca **20** C 3
Ortegal, Cabo **18** B 3
Orthez **18** C 3
Ortigueira **18** B 3
Ortiz **76** D 6
Ortles **19** F 2
Orto-Ayan **37** NO 1
Orton **5** C 2
Ortona **19** F 3
Ortonville **77** G 2
Oruhito **66** A 3
Orulgan, Khrebet **37** N 2
Orūmīyeh **34** D 3
Orūmīyeh, Daryācheh-ye (Iran) **23** D 1
Orungo **64** E 4
Oruro **86** C 4
Orust **17** F 4
Orvault **18** C 2
Orvieto **19** F 3
Osa **24** L 4
Osa **36** H 5
Osa, Península de **78** F 6
Ōsaka **39** L 4
Osakarovka **25** O 5
Ōsaka-wan **39** L 4
Osam **20** B 2
Osborne **76** G 4
Osby **17** F 4
Osceola **77** H 3
Oschiri **19** E 3
Osen **16** F 3
Osensjöen **16** F 3
Osh **35** J 2
Osha **25** O 4
Oshakati **66** B 3
Oshawa **75** M 7
Oshikango **66** B 3
Ō-shima **39** L 2
Oshivelo **66** B 3
Oshkosh **77** J 3
Oshmarino **36** D 1
Oshmyany **17** J 5
Oshnavīyeh (Iran) **23** D 1
Oshogbo **63** EF 4
Oshtoran Kūh (Iran) **23** E 2
Oshtorīnān (Iran) **23** E 2
Oshwe **64** B 5
Osijek **19** G 2
Osimo **19** F 3
Osinniki **25** R 5
Osinovka **25** Q 6
Osinovo **25** R 3
Osipovichi **17** J 5
Osire **66** B 4
Oskaloosa **77** H 3
Oskamull **3** A 3
Oskarshamn **17** G 4
Oskarström **17** F 4
Oskino **36** J 3
Öskjuuvatn **16** B 2
Oskoba **36** H 3
Oslo **17** F 4
Oslob **43** F 2
Oslofjorden **17** F 4
Osmanabad **40** C 4
Osmancık **21** DE 2
Osmaneli **20** D 2
Osmaniye **21** E 3
Osmaniye (Turkey) **22** B 1
Os'mino **17** J 4
Osmotherley **5** E 2
Osmyanskaya Vozvyshennost' **17** J 5
Osnabrück **15** E 4
Osor **19** F 3
Osorno **89** B 7
Osoyoos **73** NO 6
Osöyra **17** E 3
Ospito **84** E 2
Osprey Reef (Queensland, Austr.) **49** H 1
Ossa, Mount **50** L 9
Ossa, Mount **52** A 5
Ossa, Óros **20** B 3
Osse **63** F 4
Ossora **37** U 4
Ostashkov **24** F 4
Östavall **16** G 3
Österdalälven **16** F 3
Österdalen **16** F 3
Östergötland **17** G 4
Östersund **16** FG 3
Ostfriesische Inseln **14–15** E 4
Östhammar **17** G 3
Östhavet **16** JK 1
Östmark **17** F 3
Ostrava **15** G 5
Ostroda **15** GH 4
Ostrogozhsk **24** GH 5
Ostrołeka **15** H 4
Ostroshitski Gorodok **17** J 5
Ostrov (Czechoslovakia) **15** F 4
Ostrov (Romania) **20** C 2
Ostrov (Russia, U.S.S.R.) **17** J 4
Ostrov Atlasova **37** ST 5
Ostrov Barsa-Kel'mes **34** F 1
Ostrov Beringa **27** T 4
Ostrov Bol'shoy Begichev **36** KL 1
Ostrov Bol'shoy Berezovy **17** J 3
Ostrov Bol'shoy Lyakhovskiy **37** Q 1
Ostrov Bol'shoy Shantar **37** P 4–5
Ostrov Broutona **37** S 6
Ostrov Chirinkotan **37** S 6
Ostrov Dolgiy **25** LM 2
Ostrov Ekarma **37** S 6
Ostrov Feklistova **37** P 4–5
Ostrov Gogland **17** J 3
Ostrov Gusmp **37** U 1–2
Ostrov Iony **37** Q 4
Ostrov Iturup **37** R 6–7
Ostrov Karaginskiy **37** U 4
Ostrov Ketoy **37** S 6
Ostrov Kharimkotan **37** ST 6
Ostrov Kil'din **16** KL 2
Ostrov Kokaral **34** FG 1
Ostrov Kolguyev **24** J 2
Ostrov Konevits **16** K 3
Ostrov Kotel'nyy **37** P 1
Ostrov Krestovskiy **37** U 1
Ostrov Makanrushi **37** S 6
Ostrov Malyy Lyakhovskiy **37** Q 1
Ostrov Matua **37** S 6
Ostrov Mednyy **27** TU 4
Ostrov Men'shikova **37** PQ 5
Ostrov Mezhdusharskiy **24** K 1
Ostrov Moshchnyy **17** J 4
Ostrov Nansikan **37** Q 4
Ostrov Ogurchinskiy **34** E 3
Ostrov Onekotan **37** ST 6
Ostrov Paramushir **37** T 5
Ostrov Peschanyy **36** L 1
Ostrov Rasshua **37** S 6
Ostrov Raykoke **37** S 6
Ostrov Semenovskiy **37** O 1
Ostrov Shiashkotan **37** S 6
Ostrov Shumshu **37** T 5
Ostrov Simushir **37** S 6
Ostrov Stolbovoy **37** P 1
Ostrov Urup **37** S 6
Ostrov Valaam **16** K 3
Ostrov Vaygach **25** L 1
Ostrov Vozrozhdeniya **34** F 1
Ostrov Zav'yalova **37** RS 4
Ostrova Chernyye Brat'ya **37** S 6
Ostrova Diomida **72** D 2
Ostrova Medvezh'i **37** U 1
Ostrova Solovetskiye **24** G 2
Ostrova Srednego **37** S 6
Ostrova Tyulen'i **34** E 1–2
Ostrovnoy **37** U 4
Ostrovnoy, Mys **37** T 3
Ostrovnoye **37** TU 5
Ostrovnoye **37** U 2
Ostrovul Letea **20** C 1
Ostrovul Sfîntu Gheorghe **20** C 1–2
Ostrow Mazowiecka **15** H 4
Ostrow Wielkopolski **15** G 4
Ostrowiec Świetokrzyski **15** H 4
Ostryak, Gora **37** W 3
Ostrzeszow **15** G 4
Ostuni **19** G 3
Ōsumi-shotō **39** JK 4
Osuna **18** BC 4
Os'van' **24** L 2
Osvejskoje, Ozero **17** J 4
Oswego **77** L 3
Oswestry **6** C 1
Otar **35** K 2
Otaru **39** M 2
Otautau **50** P 10
Otava **15** F 5
Otavalo **84** C 3
Otavi **66** B 3
Otchinjau **66** A 3
Otepää Kõrgustik **17** J 4
Otgon **36** G 6
Othonoí **20** A 3
Oti **62** E 4
Oti-daitō-jima **39** K 6
Otish, Monts **75** N 5
Otjiha'vara **66** B 4
Otjikondo **66** B 3
Otjimbingwe **66** B 4
Otjinene **66** B 4
Otjinoko **66** B 4
Otjipatera Mountains **66** B 4
Otjitambi **66** AB 3
Otjituuo **66** B 3
Otjiwarongo **66** B 4
Otjovazandu **66** AB 3
Otjozondjou **66** B 4
Otjozondu **66** B 4
Otkrytyy **37** M 4
Otley **5** E 3
Otočac **19** G 3
Otog Qi **38** E 3
Otoño **89** D 6
Otoskwin **74** JK 5
Otra **17** E 4
Otradnaya **21** F 2
Otradnoye **37** T 5
Otranto **20** A 2
Otshandi **66** A 3
Otshikuku **66** B 3
Ot-Siyen **36** M 1
Otsu **39** L 4
Otta **16** E 3
Ottadalen **16** E 3
Ottawa **75** M 6
Ottawa **75** MN 6
Ottawa (KS, U.S.A.) **77** G 4
Ottawa Islands **75** L 4
Ottenby **17** G 4
Otter Creek **77** K 6
Otterburn **5** D 2
Ottery St. Mary **6** C 2
Ottumwa **77** H 3
Oturkpo **63** F 4
Otuwe **66** B 4
Otway, Bahía **89** B 9
Otway, Cape **49** G 6
Otwock **15** H 4
Ötz **19** F 2
Ou Neua **41** H 3
Ouachita Mountains **77** GH 5
Ouad Naga **58** B 5
Ouadane **58** C 4
Ouadda **64** C 3
Ouaddaï **63** J 3
Ouagadougou **62** D 3
Ouahigouya **62** D 3
Ouahran → Oran **58** E 1
Ouaka **64** C 3
Oualam **62** E 3
Oualata **58** D 5
Oualidia **58** D 2
Ouallene Bordj **59** F 4
Ouan Taredert **59** G 3
Ouanary **85** H 3
Ouanda-Djallé **64** C 3
Ouando **64** D 3
Ouango **64** C 4
Ouangolodougou **62** CD 4
Ouani **63** H 2
Ouaqui **85** H 3
Ouarane **58** CD 4
Ouargaye **62** DE 3
Ouargla **59** G 2
Ouarkziz, Jbel **58** D 3
Ouarra **64** D 3
Ouarsenis, Massif de l' **59** F 1
Ouarzazate **58** D 2
Ouassou **62** B 3
Ouatcha **63** F 3
Oubangui **63** H 5
Oudeïka **62** D 2
Oudje **59** G 2
Oudong **41** H 5
Oudtshoorn **66** C 6
Oued Rhiou **59** F 1
Oued Zem **58** D 2
Oueïta **63** J 2
Ouéllé **62** D 4
Ouémé **62** E 4
Ouessant, Ile de **18** B 2
Ouesso **63** H 5
Ouezzane **58** D 2
Ougarou **62** E 3
Ouham **63** H 4
Ouidah **62** E 4
Ouiriguó **78** E 4
Ouistreham **18** C 2
Oujaf **58** D 5
Oujda **58** E 2
Oujeft **58** C 4
Oulad Naïl, Monts des **59** F 2
Oulainen **16** HJ 3
Oulankajoki **16** J 2
Ould Yenjé **58** C 5
Ouled Djellal **59** G 2
Oulossébougou **62** C 3
Oulu **16** J 2
Oulujärvi **16** J 3
Oulujoki **16** J 3
Oum Chalouba **63** J 2
Oum el Asell **58** E 4
Oum el Bouaghi **59** G 1
Oum er Rbia **58** D 2
Oum Hadjer **63** H 3
Oumé **62** C 4
Oumm ed Droûs Guebli, Sebkhet **58** C 4
Oumm ed Droûs Telli, Sebkha **58** C 4
Ounane, Djebel **59** G 3
Ounasjoki **16** H 2
Oundle **7** D 1
Ounianga **63** J 2
Ounianga Kebir **63** J 2
Ounianga Serir **63** J 2
Ounissoui Baba **63** G 2
Ouricuri **87** HJ 2
Ourinhos **87** G 5
Ouro Prêto **87** H 5
Ourthe **14** E 4
Ōu-sanmyaku **39** M 2–3
Ouse, River (N. Yorkshire) **5** E 3
Ouse, River (Norfolk) **7** E 1
Oust **18** C 2
Outagouna **62** E 2
Outaouais **75** M 6
Outapi **66** A 3
Outardes, Rivière aux **75** O 5–6
Outat Oulad el Haj **58** E 2
Outer Hebrides **2** A 3
Outjo **66** B 4
Outlook **73** Q 5
Outokumpu **16** J 3
Outwell **7** E 1
Ouvéa **51** J 6
Ouyen **49** G 5–6
Ovacık **21** D 3

Pulau Kofiau **43** GH 4
Pulau Komodo **43** E 5
Pulau Komoran **43** J 5
Pulau Komoran **50** C 3
Pulau Kundur **42** B 3
Pulau Labengke **43** F 4
Pulau Lasia **42** A 3
Pulau Laut **42** E 4
Pulau Lepar **42** C 4
Pulau Lingga **42** B 4
Pulau Lomblen **43** F 5
Pulau Madura **42** D 5
Pulau Makian **43** G 3
Pulau Mandioli **43** G 4
Pulau Mangole **43** G 4
Pulau Manipa **43** G 4
Pulau Manui **43** F 4
Pulau Mao **43** G 5
Pulau Masalembo **42** D 5
Pulau Masela **43** GH 5
Pulau Maya **42** C 4
Pulau Mega **42** B 4
Pulau Midai **42** C 3
Pulau Misool **43** H 4
Pulau Morotai **43** G 3
Pulau Moyo **42** E 5
Pulau Muna **43** F 5
Pulau Mursala **42** A 3
Pulau Nias **42** A 3
Pulau Nila **43** G 5
Pulau Num **43** J 4
Pulau Numfor **43** H 4
Pulau Obi **43** G 4
Pulau Padang **42** B 3
Pulau Panaitan **42** B 5
Pulau Pantar **43** F 5
Pulau Pejantan **42** C 3
Pulau Peleng **43** F 4
Pulau Pemarung **42** E 4
Pulau Penida **42** E 5
Pulau Pinang **42** B 2
Pulau Pini **42** A 3
Pulau Rakata **42** C 5
Pulau Rangsang **42** B 3
Pulau Rinja **43** E 5
Pulau Romang **43** G 5
Pulau Roti **43** F 6
Pulau Rupat **42** B 3
Pulau Salawati **43** H 4
Pulau Samosir **42** A 3
Pulau Sanana **43** G 4
Pulau Sanding **42** B 4
Pulau Sangeang **43** E 5
Pulau Sangihe **43** G 3
Pulau Sawu **43** F 6
Pulau Sayang **43** G 3
Pulau Sebanka **42** BC 3
Pulau Sebatik **42–43** E 3
Pulau Sebuku **42** E 4
Pulau Selaru **43** H 5
Pulau Selatan **42** B 4
Pulau Selayar **43** F 5
Pulau Semau **43** F 6
Pulau Sepanjang **42** E 5
Pulau Serasan **42** C 3
Pulau Sermata **43** G 5
Pulau Siberut **42** A 4
Pulau Sibutu **43** E 3
Pulau Simeulue **42** A 3
Pulau Simuk **42** A 3
Pulau Singkep **42** B 4
Pulau Sipora **42** A 4
Pulau Subi **42** C 3
Pulau, Sungai **43** J 5
Pulau Supiori **43** J 4
Pulau Tahulandang **43** FG 3
Pulau Taliabu **43** FG 4
Pulau Tanahbala **42** A 4
Pulau Tanahjampea **43** F 5
Pulau Tanahmasa **42** A 4
Pulau Tebingtinggi **42** B 3
Pulau Terentang **42** E 4
Pulau Trangan **43** H 5
Pulau Tuangku **42** A 3
Pulau Tubelai **43** G 4
Pulau Utara **42** B 4
Pulau Waigeo **43** H 4
Pulau Wangiwangi **43** F 5
Pulau Weh **42** A 2
Pulau Wetar **43** G 5
Pulau Wokam **43** H 5
Pulau Workai **43** HJ 5
Pulau Wowoni **43** F 4
Pulau Yamdena **43** H 5
Pulau Yapen **43** J 4
Puławy **15** H 4
Pulicat **40** D 5
Pulkkila **16** J 3
Pullman **76** C 2
Pulo Anna **43** H 3
Pulog, Mount **43** J 1
Pulonga **24** H 2
Pulozero **16** K 2
Pulton-Le-Fylde **5** D 3
Pułtusk **15** H 4
Pulusuk **52** A 2
Puluwat **52** A 2
Puma Yumco **41** F 2
Pumpsaint **6** C 1
Puna de Atacama **86** C 5–6
Puná, Isla **84** B 4
Punakha **40** E 2
Puncak Jaya **43** J 4
Puncak Trikora **43** J 4
Punda Milia **67** E 4
Punduga **24** H 3
Pune **40** B 4
Punia **64** D 5
Puning **38** G 6
Punjab **40** BC 1
Punkaharju **16** J 3
Puno **86** B 4
Punta Alegre **79** G 3
Punta Almina **58** D 1
Punta Alta **89** D 6
Punta Angamos **86** B 5
Punta Arenas **89** B 9
Punta Ballenita **88** B 4
Punta Bermeja **89** D 7
Punta Burica **78** F 6
Punta Cachos **88** B 4
Punta Carreta **86** A 3
Punta Catalina **89** C 9
Punta, Cerro de **79** J 4
Punta Colorada **88** B 4
Punta de Arenas **89** C 9
Punta de Chilca **86** A 3
Punta de Europa **18** BC 4
Punta de Mata **85** F 2
Punta del Diamante **78** BC 4
Punta Delgada **89** D 7
Punta Delgado **89** C 9
Punta dell' Alice **19** G 4
Punta Desengaño **89** C 8
Punta Eugenia **76** C 6
Punta Falcone **19** E 3
Punta Fijo **84** D 1
Punta Galera **89** B 7
Punta Gallinas **84** D 1
Punta Gorda (Belize) **78** E 4
Punta Gorda (Nicaragua) **78** F 5
Punta Gorda, Bàhía de **78** F 5
Punta Gruesa **86** B 5
Punta Guascama **84** C 3
Punta Lachay **84** C 6
Punta Lavapié **89** B 6
Punta Lengua de Vaca **88** B 5
Punta Licosa **19** F 3
Punta Magdalena **84** C 3
Punta Maisí **79** H 3
Punta Mala **84** C 2
Punta Mariato **84** B 2
Punta Medanosa **89** CD 8
Punta Morro **88** B 4
Punta Negra **84** B 5
Punta, Ninfas **89** D 7
Punta Norte **89** E 6
Punta Palazzo **19** E 3
Punta Pariñas **84** B 4
Punta Pórfido **89** D 7
Punta Poro **88** E 4
Punta Prieta **76** D 6
Punta Rasa **89** D 7
Punta Rieles **86** E 5
Punta Roja **89** CD 7
Punta Rotja **18** D 4
Punta Sarga **58** B 4
Punta Stilo **19** G 4
Punta Sur **89** E 6
Punta Topocalma **88** B 5
Punta Verde **78** F 5
Puntarenas **78** EF 6
Puolanka **16** J 3
Puper **43** H 4
Puqi **38** F 5
Puquio **86** B 3
Puquios **88** C 4
Pur **25** P 2
Pura **36** E 1
Pura **36** E 1
Puracé **84** C 3
Purcell Mountains **73** O 5
Purdy Islands **50** E 2
Puri **40** E 4
Puri **60** B 1
Purificación **84** D 3
Purikari Neem **17** J 4
Purinskoye, Ozero **36** E 1
Purna **40** C 3
Purnea **40** E 2
Pursat **41** H 5
Purton **7** D 2
Purtuniq **75** N 3
Purukcahu **42** D 4
Purulia **40** E 3
Purus **85** F 4
Puruvesi **16** J 3
Purwakarta **42** C 5
Pusan **39** J 3
Pushchino **37** T 5
Pushkin **17** K 4
Pushkino **24** J 5
Pusht-i-Rud **35** G 4
Pusteci **20** B 2
Pustoretsk **37** U 3
Pustoshka **17** J 4
Puszcza Notecka **15** G 4
Putao **41** G 2
Putian **39** G 5
Putina **86** C 3
Puting, Tanjung **42** D 4
Putla de Guerrero **78** C 4
Putnok **20** B 1
Putorana, Gory **36** FH 2
Puttalam **40** C 6
Puttenham **7** D 2
Puttgarden **15** F 4
Putumayo **84** D 4
Putussibau **42** D 3
Puulavesi **16** J 3
Puy Crapaud **18** C 2
Puy de Dôme **18** D 2
Puy de Sancy **18** D 2
Puyang **38** G 3
Puyo **84** C 4
Puzla **24** K 3
Pwani **65** F 6
Pweto **64** D 6
Pwllheli **6** B 1
Pyagina, Poluostrov **37** S 4
Pyakupur **25** P 2–3
Pyal'ma **24** G 3
Pyandzh **35** H 3
Pyaozero, Ozero **16** K 2
Pyapon **41** G 4
Pyasina **36** E 1
Pyasino, Ozero **25** R 2
Pyatigorsk **21** F 2
Pyatigory **24** KL 3
Pyatikhatki **21** D 1
Pyatistennoy **37** TU 2
Pyat'kovende, Gora **37** T 2
Pyawbwe **41** G 3
Pygmalion Point **41** F 6
Pyhäjärvi **16** J 3
Pyhäjärvi **17** H 3
Pyhäjoki **16** HJ 3
Pyhäntä **16** J 3
Pyhäselkä **16** JK 3
Pyhätunturi **16** J 2
Pyinmana **41** G 4
Pyl'karamo **25** Q 3
Pym **25** O 3
Pymta **37** T 5
P'yŏnggang **39** J 3
P'yŏngyang **39** HJ 3
Pyramid Lake **76** C 3–4
Pyramids **60** E 3
Pyrénées **18** CD 3
Pyshchug **24** J 4
Pytalovo **17** J 4
Pyu **41** G 4

Q

Qābis **59** H 2
Qābis, Khalīj **59** H 2
Qabr Hūd **61** H 5
Qaderābād (Iran) **23** F 3
Qādir Karam (Iraq) **23** D 2
Qādub **65** J 2
Qā'emshahr (Iran) **23** F 1
Qafsah **59** G 2
Qagan (Nei Monggul Zizhiqu, China) **36** L 6
Qagan Nur (Nei Monggul Zizhiqu, China) **38** F 2
Qagan Nur (Qinghai, China) **38** C 3
Qagan Tohoi **38** B 3
Qagcaka **40** D 1
Qahar Youyi Houqi **38** F 2
Qahar Youyi Qianqi **38** F 2
Qahremānshahr (Iran) **23** E 2
Qaidam He **38** C 3
Qaidam Pendi **38** BC 3
Qal 'at al Husn (Syria) **22** B 2
Qal 'at al Marqab (Syria) **22** B 2
Qal' at Dīzah (Iraq) **23** D 1
Qal' at Sukkar (Iraq) **23** E 3
Qala'an Nahl **60** E 6
Qala-Nau **35** G 4
Qālat **35** H 4
Qal'at Abū Ghār (Iraq) **23** DE 3
Qal'at al Akhdar (Saudi Arabia) **22** B 4
Qal'at al Mu'azam (Saudi Arabia) **22** BC 4
Qal'at Bīshah **61** G 4
Qal'at Sālih (Iraq) **23** E 3
Qal'eh (Iran) **23** G 1
Qal'eh Asgar (Iran) **23** G 3
Qal'eh-ye Now (Iran) **23** E 2
Qalīb ash Shuyūkh (Kuwait) **23** E 3
Qallābāt **60** F 6
Qamalung **38** C 4
Qamar, Ghubbat al **61** J 5
Qamata **66** D 6
Qamdo **38** C 4
Qamīnis **59** JK 2
Qamsar (Iran) **23** F 2
Qanāt as Suways (Egypt) **22** A 3
Qandala **65** H 2
Qapqal **35** L 2
Qaqortog **75** S 3
Qar Wagēr **65** H 2
Qarā Dāgh **34** D 3
Qarā', Jabal **61** J 5
Qara Tarai **35** H 4
Qārah **40** C 6
Qarah Dāgh (Iraq) **22** D 1
Qarānqū **34** D 3
Qar'at al Ashkal **19** E 4
Qārat Dalmā' **59** K 3
Qārawah (Saudi Arabia) **23** E 3
Qardo **65** H 3
Qareh Āghāj (Iran) **23** E 1
Qareh Sū **34** DE 4
Qareh Sū (Iran) **23** G 1
Qarhan **38** B 3
Qarnayn (United Arab Emirates) **23** F 4
Qarqan He **35** M 3
Qarqannah, Juzur **59** H 2
Qarqi **35** M 2
Qārūn, Birkat **60** E 3
Qaryat al Gharab (Iraq) **23** D 3
Qaryat al 'Ulyā (Saudi Arabia) **23** E 4
Qasa Murg **35** G 4
Qasr Ahmād **59** J 2
Qasr al Azraq (Jordan) **22** B 3
Qasr al Hayr (Syria) **22** BC 2
Qasr al Khūbbaz (Iraq) **22** D 2
Qasr Āmij (Iraq) **22** C 2
Qasr as Sabīyah (Kuwait) **23** E 3
Qasr bū Hādī **59** J 2
Qasr Burqu' (Jordan) **22** BC 2
Qasr Farāfirah **60** D 3
Qasr Hamām **61** H 4
Qasr-e Qand **35** G 5
Qasr-e Shīrīn (Iran) **23** DE 2
Qatar **23** F 4
Qatif (Saudi Arabia) **23** E 4
Qatlīsh **34** F 3
Qatrūyeh (Iran) **23** G 3
Qattara Depression **60** D 3
Qawām al Hamzah (Iraq) **23** D 3
Qawz Abū ulū' **60** E 5
Qawz Rajab **60** F 5
Qāyen **34** F 4
Qaysān **60** E 6
Qayyārah (Iraq) **22** D 2
Qazvīn (Iran) **23** F 1
Qeshm **34** F 5
Qeshm **34** F 5
Qeshm [ö] (Iran) **23** G 4
Qeshm [ort] (Iran) **23** G 4
Qeydār (Iran) **23** E 1
Qeydū (Iran) **23** F 2
Qeys (Iran) **23** F 4
Qezel Owzan (Iran) **23** E 1
Qezi'ot (Israel) **22** B 3
Qian Gorlos **39** H 2
Qian Shan **39** H 2–3
Qian'an **39** H 1
Qianjiang **38** E 5
Qianning **38** D 4
Qianwei **38** D 5
Qianxi **38** E 5
Qianyang **38** F 5
Qiaojia **38** D 5
Qiaowan **38** C 2
Qichun **38** G 4
Qidong **39** H 4
Qiemo **35** M 3
Qift (Egypt) **22** A 4
Qijiang **38** E 5
Qijiaojing **38** B 2
Qila Ladgasht **35** G 5
Qila Saifullah **35** H 4
Qilian **38** D 3
Qilian Shan **38** CD 3
Qimantag **38** B 3
Qimen **39** G 5
Qin Xian **38** F 3
Qinā (Egypt) **22** A 4
Qina, Wādī (Egypt) **22** A 4
Qin'an **38** E 4
Qing He **38** E 3
Qing Jiang **38** F 4
Qing Zang Gaoyuan **40** DE 1
Qingchuan **38** E 4
Qingdao **39** H 3
Qinggang **39** J 1
Qinghai **38** C 3
Qinghai Hu **38** D 3
Qinghe **35** N 1
Qingjiang (Jiangsu, China) **39** G 4
Qingjiang (Jiangxi, China) **38** G 5
Qinglong **38** DE 5
Qinglong (Hebei, China) **39** G 2
Qingshen **38** D 5
Qingshuihe **38** F 3
Qingxu **38** F 3
Qingyang **38** E 3
Qingyuan **39** H 2
Qinhuangdao **39** GH 3
Qinling Shan **38** EF 4
Qinqliu **38** G 5
Qinzhou **38** E 6
Qionghai **38** F 7
Qionglai **38** D 4
Qionglai Shan **38** D 4
Qiongshan **38** F 7
Qiongzhou Haixia **38** EF 6
Qiqiar **36** M 5
Qiqihar **37** M 6
Qir (Iran) **23** F 3
Qira **35** L 3
Qirdi (Saudi Arabia) **23** E 4
Qirjat Shemona (Israel) **22** B 2
Qirjat Yam (Israel) **22** B 2
Qiryat Gat (Israel) **22** B 3
Qirzah **59** H 2
Qishn **61** J 5
Qishrān **61** FG 4
Qitai **35** M 2
Qitaihe **39** K 1
Qitbīt, Wādī **61** J 5
Qiyang **38** F 5
Qog Qi **38** E 2
Qog Ul **39** G 2
Qogir Feng **35** K 3
Qolleh-ye Damāvand **34** E 3
Qolleh-ye Damāvand (Iran) **23** F 2
Qoltag **38** A 2
Qom (Iran) **23** F 2
Qom (Iran) **23** F 2
Qomdo **38** C 4
Qomolangma Feng **40** E 2
Qomrūd (Iran) **23** F 2
Qomsheh **34** E 4
Qomsheh (Iran) **23** F 2–3
Qonggyai **41** F 2
Qôrnoq **75** R 3
Qorveh **34** D 3
Qorveh (Iran) **23** E 2
Qosbeh-ye Nassār (Iran) **23** E 3
Qotbābād (Iran) **23** F 3
Qotbābād **34** F 5
Qotbābād (Iran) **23** G 4
Qotur **34** C 3
Qu Xian **39** G 5
Quairading **48** B 5
Quajará **85** G 5
Quan Dao Nam Du **41** H 6
Quan Long **41** J 6
Quan Phu Quoc **41** H 5
Quang Ngai **41** J 4
Quang Tri **41** J 4
Quang Yen **41** J 3
Quanshuigou **35** K 3
Quanzhou (Fujian, China) **39** G 6
Quanzhou (Guangxi Zhuangzu Zizhiqu, China) **38** F 5
Qu'Appelle **73** R 5
Quaraí **88** E 5
Quartu Sant' Elena **19** E 4
Quartz Mountain **76** B 3
Quartzsite **76** D 5
Quatro Ciénegas **78** B 2
Quayti **61** H 5
Qūchān **34** F 3
Queanbeyan **49** H 6
Québec **75** N 5
Québec **75** N 6
Quebracho **88** E 5
Quebracho Coto **88** D 4
Quedal, Cabo **89** B 7
Queen Bess, Mount **73** N 5
Queen, Cape **75** M 3
Queen Charlotte Islands **72** KL 5
Queen Charlotte Sound **72** LM 5
Queen Charlotte Strait **72–73** M 5
Queen Elizabeth Islands **90**
Queen Fabiola Mountains **91**
Queen Mary Coast **91**
Queen Maud Gulf **73** R 2
Queen Maud Land **91**
Queen Maud Mountains **91**
Queens Channel **48** D 1
Queensferry **3** C 4
Queensland **49** GH 3
Queenstown (New Zealand) **50** P 9
Queenstown (South Africa) **66** D 6
Queenstown (Tasmania, Austr.) **50** L 9
Quehue **89** D 6
Queimada, Ilha **87** G 5
Queimadas **87** HJ 3
Quela **66** B 1
Quelimane **67** F 3
Quellén **89** B 7
Quelpart **39** J 4
Quemado **76** E 5
Quembo **66** B 2
Quemchi **89** B 7
Quemoy **39** G 6

R

S

Saale 15 F 4
Saalfeld 15 F 4
Saanen 19 E 2
Saarbrücken 15 E 5
Sääre 17 H 4
Saaremaa 17 H 4
Saarijärvi 16 J 3
Saariselkä 16 J 2
Saarlouis 14 E 5
Saavedra 89 D 6
Šabac 20 A 2
Sabadell 18 D 3
Sabah 42 E 2
Sabak 42 B 3
Sabán 84 E 2
Sabana 84 D 3
Sabanalarga 84 C 1
Sabang 42 A 2
Sabang 43 E 3
Sabanözü 21 D 2
Săbăoani 20 C 1
Sabará 87 H 4
Sabari 40 D 4
Şabāyā 61 G 5
Sabaya 86 C 4
Sabderat 64 F 1
Şabḥā' (Saudi Arabia) 61 G 4
Şabḥa (Jordan) 22 B 2
Sabhā (Libya) 59 H 3
Sabhā, Wāhāt 59 H 3
Sabidana, Jabal 60 F 5
Sabina Shoal 42 E 2
Sabinas 78 B 2
Sabinas Hidalgo 78 B 2
Sabine 77 H 5
Sabini, Monti 19 F 3
Şabīr, Jabal 61 G 6
Şābirīyah (Kuwait) 23 E 3
Sabkhat al Bardawīl (Egypt) 22 A 3
Sabkhat Albū Gharz (Iraq) 22 C 2
Sabkhat Maṭṭi (United Arab Emirates) 23 F 5
Sable, Cape 75 O 7
Sable, Cape 77 K 6
Sable, Île de 52 B 4
Sable Island 75 P 7
Sablinskoye 21 F 2
Sæböl 16 A 2
Sabonkafi 63 F 3
Sábor 18 B 3
Sabou 62 D 3
Sabozo 63 G 1
Sabrātah 59 H 2
Sabres 18 C 3
Sabrina Coast 91
Sabun 25 Q 3
Sæby 17 F 4
Şabyā' 61 G 5
Sabyndy 25 O 5
Sabzevār (Iran) 23 G 1
Saca, Vîrful 20 C 1
Sacajawea Peak 76 C 2
Sacanana 89 C 7
Sacavém 18 B 4
Sacco 19 F 3
Sacedón 18 C 3
Săcele 20 C 1
Sachkhere 21 F 2
Sachs Harbour 73 N 1
Sachsen 15 F 4
Saco 76 E 2
Sacramento 76 B 4
Sacramento Mountains 76 E 5
Sacramento Valley 76 B 3–4
Sacuriuiná 86 E 3
Sad ad Darbandī Khān (Iraq) 23 D 2
Sad ad Dūkān (Iraq) 23 D 1–2
Sad Bi'Ar (Syria) 22 B 2
Sad Kharv (Iran) 23 G 1
Sadabá 18 C 3
Sa'dah 61 G 5
Sadani 65 F 6
Sadberge 5 E 2
Sadd al Aswān (Egypt) 22 A 4
Saddajaure 16 G 2
Saddell 3 B 4
Saddle Peak 41 F 5
Sadiya 41 G 2
S'adīyah, Hawr as (Iraq) 23 E 2
Sado 18 B 4
Sadochye, Ozero 34 F 2
Sadon 21 F 2
Sado-shima 39 L 3
Sadovoye 21 F 1
Safané 62 D 3
Şafāqis 59 H 2
Safed Khirs 35 J 3
Safed Koh 35 GH 4
Saffānīyah, Ra's as (Saudi Arabia) 23 E 3
Säffle 17 F 4
Safford 76 E 5
Saffron Walden 7 E 1
Safi 58 D 2
Safīd Dasht (Iran) 23 E 2
Safīd, Kūh-e (Iran) 23 E 2
Safīd Rūd (Iran) 23 E 1
Safonovo 24 F 4
Safonovo 24 J 2
Safonovo 37 X 3
Safrā' al Asyāh (Saudi Arabia) 22 D 4
Safrā' as Sark (Saudi Arabia) 22 D 4
Safranbolu 21 D 2
Şafwān (Iraq) 23 E 3
Saga (China) 40 E 2
Saga (Japan) 39 K 4
Saga (U.S.S.R.) 25 M 5
Sagaing 41 G 3
Sagala 62 C 3
Sagan 35 K 3
Sagar 40 C 3
Sagar 40 E 3
Sagastyr 37 N 1
Sagavanirktok 72 H 2
Sage 76 D 3
Saggart 4 B 3
Saghād (Iran) 23 F 3
Saginaw 77 K 3
Saginaw Bay 77 K 3
Sagiz 34 E 1
Sagleipie 62 C 4
Saglek Bay 75 P 4
Saglouc 75 M 3
Sagres 18 B 4
Sagu (Indonesia) 43 F 5
Sagu (Romania) 20 B 1
Sagua de Tánamo 79 H 3
Sagua la Grande 79 G 3
Saguache 76 E 4
Saguenay 75 NO 6
Saguia el Hamra 58 C 3
Saguia el Hamra 58 C 3
Sagunto 18 C 4
Sagwon 72 H 2
Sahagún (Colombia) 84 C 2
Sahagún (Spain) 18 B 3
Sahara 58–59 EG 4
Saharanpur 40 C 2
Saharsa 40 E 2
Sahiwal 35 J 4
Sahl Rakbah 61 G 4
Sahlābad 34 F 4
Şahneh (Iran) 23 E 2
Sahrā' al Hajārah (Iraq) 22–23 D 3
Şaḥrā' Bayyūḍah 60 E 5
Sahuaripa 76 E 6
Sahuayo de Diaz 78 B 4
Sahul Shelf 99 C 4
Sai Yok 41 G 5
Saiapoun 41 H 4
Saibai 50 D 3
Said Bundas 64 C 3
Saïda 58 F 2
Sa'īdābād (Iran) 23 G 3
Sa'īdīyeh (Iran) 23 E 1
Saidor 50 E 3
Saidpur 40 E 2
Saigon 41 J 5
Saihan Toroi 38 D 2
Saiki 39 K 4
Saimaa 16 J 3
Saimaan kanava 16 J 3
Sain Alto 78 B 3
Sā'īn Dezh (Iran) 23 E 1
Saindak 35 G 5
Saint Alban's (Newfoundl., Can.) 75 Q 6
St. Albans (U.K.) 7 D 2
Saint Albans (VT, U.S.A.) 77 M 3
Saint Albert 73 P 5
St. Andrews 3 C 3
Saint Ann's Bay 79 G 4
Saint Anthony 75 QR 5
Saint Arnaud 49 G 6
St. Asaph 6 C 1
Saint Augustin Saguenay 75 Q 5
Saint Augustine 77 K 6
St. Austell 6 B 2
St. Austell Bay 6 B 2
St. Blazey 6 B 2
St. Brides Bay 6 B 2
St. Bride's Major 6 C 3
St. Buryan 6 B 2
Saint Catherine, Monastery of 60 E 3
St. Catherine's Point 7 D 2
Saint Christopher 79 K 4
Saint Clair River 77 K 3
St. Clears 6 B 2
Saint Cloud 77 H 2
St. Columb Major 6 B 2
Saint Croix 79 JK 4
St. David's 6 B 2
St. David's Head 6 B 2
St. Dennis 6 B 2
St. Dogmaels 6 B 1
Saint Elias, Mount 72 J 3
Saint Elias Mountains 72 K 3
Saint Félicien 75 N 6
Saint Flores National Park 64 C 3
Saint Francis 76 F 4
Saint Francis Bay 66 A 5
Saint Francis, Cape 66 CD 6
Saint Francois 65 J 6
Saint Francois Mountains 77 H 4
St. Gallen 19 E 2
Saint George (AK, U.S.A.) 72 D 4
Saint George (Queensland, Austr.) 49 H 4
Saint George (UT, U.S.A.) 76 D 4
Saint George, Cape 75 PQ 6
Saint George, Cape (Papua New Guinea) 51 F 2
Saint George's 79 K 5
Saint Georges 85 H 3
Saint George's Bay 75 Q 6
St. George's Channel 6 B 1
Saint George's Channel 51 F 2–3
St. Germans 6 B 2
Saint Helena 54 B 6
Saint Helena Bay 66 B 6
St. Helens 5 D 3
Saint Helens, Mount 76 B 2
St. Helier 7 C 3
St. Helier 14 C 5
Saint Ignace 77 K 2
Saint Ignace Island 74 K 6
St. Issey 6 B 2
St. Ives (Cambridgeshire) 7 D 1
St. Ives (Cornwall) 6 B 2
St. Ives Bay 6 B 2
Saint James, Cape 72 L 5
Saint Jérôme 75 N 6
Saint John (Canada) 75 O 6
Saint John (Liberia) 62 C 4
Saint John River 75 O 6
Saint John's (Antigua) 79 K 4
Saint John's (Canada) 75 R 6
Saint Johns (AZ, U.S.A.) 76 E 5
St. John's Chapel 5 D 2
Saint Johns River (FL, U.S.A.) 77 K 5–6
Saint Johnsbury 77 M 3
St. Johnstown 4 B 2
Saint Joseph (MI, U.S.A.) 77 J 3
Saint Joseph (MO, U.S.A.) 77 H 4
Saint Joseph (Seychelles) 65 J 6
Saint Joseph, Lake 74 J 5
St. Just 6 B 2
Saint Kitts and Nevis 79 K 4
Saint Kitts [Saint Christopher] 79 K 4
Saint Laurent 85 H 2
Saint Lawrence 49 H 3
Saint Lawrence, Gulf of 75 P 6
Saint Lawrence Island 72 C 3
Saint Lawrence River 75 O 6
Saint Léonard 75 O 6
Saint Louis (MO, U.S.A.) 77 H 4
Saint Lucia 79 K 5
Saint Lucia, Cape 67 E 5
Saint Lucia, Lake 67 E 5
St. Magnus Bay 2 D 1
St. Margaret's at Cliffe 7 E 2
St. Margaret's Hope 2 C 2
St. Marks 77 K 5
Saint Mary Peak 49 F 5
St. Mary's (U.K.) 6 A 3
St Marys 2 C 2
Saint Marys 50 L 9
St. Marys (AK, U.S.A.) 72 E 3
Saint Mary's Bay 75 R 6
Saint Matthew 72 C 3
Saint Matthias Group 51 E 2
Saint Maurice 75 N 6
St. Mawes 6 B 2
Saint Michael 72 E 3
Saint Michaels 76 E 4
St Moritz 19 E 2
St. Neots 7 D 1
St. Niklaas 14 D 4
Saint Paul (AK, U.S.A.) 72 D 4
Saint Paul (Alb., Can.) 73 P 5
Saint Paul (Liberia) 62 B 4
Saint Paul (MN, U.S.A.) 77 H 3
St. Peter and St. Paul Rocks 81 G 2
St. Peter Port 7 C 3
St. Peter Port 14 C 5
Saint Petersburg 77 K 6
Saint Pierre 75 Q 6
Saint Pierre (Seychelles) 65 J 6
Saint Pierre et Miquelon 75 Q 6
St. Roch Basin 73 ST 2
Saint Stephen 75 O 6
Saint Thomas (Ontario, Can.) 75 L 7
Saint Vincent 79 K 5
Saint Vincent, Gulf 49 F 6
Saint Vincent Passage 79 K 5
St. Walburg 73 Q 5
St. Weonards 6 C 3
Saint-Amand-Mont-Rond 18 D 2
Saint-André, Cap 67 G 3
Saint-Avold 19 E 2
Saint-Barthélemy 79 K 4
Saint-Brieuc 18 C 2
Saint-Calais 18 D 2
Saint-Chamond 19 D 2
Saint-Claude 19 E 2
Saint-Cyr-sur-Loire 18 D 2
Saint-Denis (France) 18 D 2
Saint-Denis (Réunion) 67 K 6
Saint-Denis-d'Oléron 18 C 2
Saint-Dié 19 E 2
Saint-Dizier 19 DE 2
Sainte Genevieve 77 H 4
Sainte Lucie, Canal de 79 K 5
Saint-Elie 85 H 3
Saintes 18 C 2
Saintes-Maries-de-la Mer 19 D 3
Sainte-Thérèse 75 MN 6
Sainte-Étienne 18 D 2
Saintfield 4 C 2
Saint-Florent, Golfe de 19 E 3
Saint-Flour 18 D 2
Saint-Gaudens 18 D 3
Saint-Georges 75 NO 6
Saint-Gildas, Pointe de 18 C 2
Saint-Jean 75 N 6
Saint-Jean, Lake 75 N 6
Saint-Jean-d'Angély 18 C 2
Saint-Jean-de-Luz 18 C 3
Saint-Jean-de-Monts 18 C 2
Saint-Junien 18 D 2
Saint-Lô 18 C 2
Saint-Louis (Senegal) 62 A 2
Saint-Malo 18 C 2
Saint-Marc 79 H 4
Saint-Martin 79 K 4
Saint-Martin-Vésubie 19 E 3
Saint-Nazaire 18 C 2
Saint-Omer 18 D 1
Saint-Paul (Réunion) 67 K 6
Saint-Péray 19 D 3
Saint-Pierre (Réunion) 67 K 6
Saint-Pons 18 D 3
Saint-Quentin 18 D 2
Saint-Savin 18 D 2
Saint-Seine-l'Abbaye 19 DE 2
Saint-Thomas (Puerto Rico) 79 JK 4
Saint-Tropez 19 E 3
Saint-Yrieix-la-Perche 18 D 2
Saipal 40 D 2
Saipan 52 A 1
Sajama 86 C 4
Sajama, Nevado 86 C 4
Sajānan 19 E 4
Sajīd 61 G 5
Sajó 20 B 1
Sajzī (Iran) 23 F 2
Saka 65 F 5
Sakabinda 66 CD 2
Sakai 39 L 4
Sakākah (Saudi Arabia) 22 C 3
Sakakawea, Lake 76 F 2
Sakala Kõrgustik 17 J 4
Sakami 75 M 5
Sakami, Lac 75 M 5
Sakami River 75 N 5
Sakania 66 D 2
Sakar 20 C 2
Sakaraha 67 G 4
Sakarat Dağı 21 E 2
Sakaraya 20 D 3
Sakarya 20 D 2
Sakashima-guntō 39 HJ 6
Sakata 39 L 3
Sakçağöz 21 E 3
Sakchu 39 J 2
Sakété 62 E 4
Såkevare 16 G 2
Sakhalin 37 Q 5
Sakhalinskiy Zaliv 37 Q 5
Sakhandzha 37 N 2
Sakht Sar (Iran) 23 F 1
Saki 21 D 1
Sakoli 40 D 3
Sakon Nakhon 41 H 4
Sakrivier 66 C 6
Saksaul'skiy 35 G 1
Sakti 40 D 3
Säkylä 16 H 3
Sal 21 F 1
Sal (Cape Verde) 62 B 6
Sala 17 G 4
Sala Andong Tuk 41 H 5
Sala Consilina 19 G 3
Sala y Gómes 53 H 4
Salaca 17 H 4
Salacgrīva 17 H 4
Salada 78 B 2
Salada, Gran Laguna 89 C 7
Saladillo 89 E 6
Salado 88 D 4
Salado 89 C 6
Salaga 62 D 4
Salagle 65 G 4
Salair 25 R 5
Salairskiy Kryazh 25 R 5
Salal 63 H 3
Salālah (Oman) 61 J 5
Salālah (Sudan) 60 F 4
Salamá 78 D 4
Salamanca (Mexico) 78 B 3
Salamanca (Spain) 18 B 3
Salamat 63 J 3
Salamina 84 C 2
Salamis (Cyprus) 21 D 3
Salamis (Cyprus) 22 AB 2
Salamis (Greece) 20 B 3
Salar de Antofalla 88 C 4
Salar de Arizaro 86 C 5
Salar de Atacama 86 C 5
Salar de Coipasa 86 C 4
Salar de Hombre Muerto 88 C 4
Salar de Uyuni 86 C 5
Salas 18 B 3
Salatiga 42 D 5
Salavat 24 L 5
Salaverry 84 C 5
Salavina 88 D 4
Salawati, Pulau 43 H 4
Salbris 18 D 2
Salcantay, Nevado 86 B 3
Salchininkai 17 J 5
Salcombe 6 C 2
Saldanha 66 B 6
Saldus 17 H 4
Sale (Australia) 49 H 6
Salé (Morocco) 58 D 2
Sale (U.K.) 5 D 3
Şālehābād (Iran) 23 E 2
Salekhard 25 N 2
Salem (IL, U.S.A.) 77 J 4
Salem (India) 40 C 5
Salem (OR, U.S.A.) 76 B 3
Salemi 19 F 4
Salen 3 B 3
Sälen 16 F 3
Salentina, Penisola 19 G 3–4
Salerno 19 FG 3
Salerno, Golfo di 19 F 3
Sales 85 H 5
Saletekri 40 D 3
Salford 5 D 3
Salgótarján 20 AB 1
Salgueiro 87 J 2
Salhus 17 E 3
Sali (Algeria) 58 E 3
Sali (Argentina) 88 C 4
Sali (Yugoslavia) 19 FG 3
Salida 76 E 4
Salihli 20 C 3
Salima 67 E 2
Salīmah, Wāhāt 60 D 4
Salin 41 F 3
Salina (Italy) 19 F 4
Salina (KS, U.S.A.) 76 G 4
Salina (UT, U.S.A.) 76 D 4
Salina del Gualicho 89 D 7
Salina Grande 89 C 6
Salinas 76 B 4
Salinas (Ecuador) 84 B 4
Salinas (Minas Gerais, Brazil) 87 H 4
Salinas, Cabo de 18 D 4
Salinas de Hidalgo 78 B 3
Salinas Grandes 88 CD 4–5
Salinas Peak 76 E 5
Salinas, Ponta das 66 A 2
Salinitas 86 B 5
Salinópolis 85 J 4
Salisbury (Canada) 75 M 3
Salisbury (MD, U.S.A.) 77 L 4
Salisbury (U.K.) 7 D 2
Salisbury → Harare 67 E 3
Salisbury Plain 7 CD 2
Şalkhad (Syria) 22 B 2
Salla 16 J 2
Salling 17 E 4
Salloway 2 D 1
Sallūm 60 F 5
Salluyo, Nevado 86 C 3
Sallyana 40 D 2
Salmās 34 C 3
Salmi 16 K 3
Salmon 76 D 2
Salmon Arm 73 O 5
Salmon Mountains 76 B 3
Salmon River 76 CD 2
Salmon River Mountains 76 CD 2–3
Salo (Burkina) 64 B 4
Salo (Finland) 17 H 3
Saló (Italy) 19 F 2
Salon-de-Provence 19 E 3
Salong, Tünel-e- 35 H 3
Salonga National Park 64 C 5
Salonica 20 B 2
Salonta 20 B 1
Salop 6 C 1
Salor 18 B 4
Salou 18 D 3
Saloum 62 A 3

Sawtayr 60 E 5
Sawtooth Mountains 77 H 2
Sawu Laut 43 F 5
Sawu, Pulau 43 F 6
Ṣawwān, Ard aṣ 60 F 2
Saxby 7 D 1
Saxmundham 7 E 1
Saxton 5 E 3
Say 62 E 3
Sayaboury 41 H 4
Sayak 25 P 6
Sayakskaya Pristan' 25 P 6
Sayán 86 A 3
Sayan Vostochnyy 36 G 5
Sayan, Zapadnyy 36 F 5
Sayang, Pulau 43 GH 3
Sayat 35 G 3
Saydā (Lebanon) 22 B 2
Saydy 37 O 2
Sayhūt 61 J 5
Saynshand 38 F 2
Sayram Hu 35 L 2
Saywūn 61 H 5
Sázava 15 F 5
Sazdy 34 D 1
Sazin 35 J 3
Sbaa 58 E 3
Scaër 18 C 2
Scafell Pike 5 D 2
Scaife Mountains 91
Scalasaig 3 A 3
Scalea 19 G 4
Scalone, Passo dello 19 G 4
Scalpay 2 B 3
Scammon Bay 72 D 3
Scandinavia 93
Scapa Flow 2 C 2
Ščara 15 H 4
Scaramia, Capo 19 F 4
Scarba 3 B 3
Scarborough (Trinidad and Tobago) 85 F 1
Scarborough (U.K.) 5 E 2
Scarp 2 A 2
Schaffhausen 15 E 5
Schärding 19 F 2
Schefferville 75 O 5
Scheibbs 19 FG 2
Schelde 14 D 4
Schenectady 77 M 3
Schiltigheim 19 E 2
Schio 19 F 2
Schklov 17 K 5
Schladming 19 F 2
Schleswig 15 E 4
Schleswig-Holstein 15 E 4
Schneeberg 15 F 4
Schönebeck 15 F 4
Schouten Islands 50 D 2
Schuls → Scoul 19 F 2
Schultz Lake 73 S 3
Schurz 76 C 4
Schwabach 15 F 5
Schwäbisch Hall 15 EF 5
Schwaner, Pegunungan 42 D 4
Schwarzwald 15 E 5
Schwatka Mountains 72 F 2
Schwaz 19 F 2
Schwedt 15 F 4
Schweinfurt 15 F 4
Schweizer Reneke 66 CD 5
Schwenningen 15 E 5
Schwerin 15 F 4
Schwyz 19 E 2
Sciacca 19 F 4
Scicli 19 F 4
Scioto River 77 K 4
Scoresby Sound 90
Scoresbysund 90
Scotia Ridge 98 A 5
Scotia Sea 91
Scotlandville 77 H 5
Scott 73 Q 5
Scott (Antarctica) 91
Scott, Cape 72 M 5
Scott, Cape (N.T., Austr.) 48 D 1
Scott City 76 F 4
Scott Island 91
Scott Reef 48 C 1
Scottburgh 67 E 6
Scottsbluff 76 F 3
Scottsdale 76 D 5
Scottsdale (Tasmania, Austr.) 50 L 9
Scottsville 77 J 4
Scourie 2 B 2
Scrabster 2 C 2
Scranton 77 L 3
Scugog, Lake 75 M 7
Scunthorpe 5 E 3
Scuol 19 F 2
Scutari, Lake → Skardarsko Jezero 20 A 2
Se Kong 41 J 4
Sea Islands 77 K 5
Sea of Azov 21 E 1
Sea of Crete 20 BC 3
Sea of Japan 39 KL 3
Sea of Marmara → Marmara Denizi 20 C 2
Sea of Okhotsk 37 R 4
Sea of the Hebrides 2–3 A 3
Seabra 87 H 3
Seabrook, Lake 48 B 5
Seaford 7 E 2
Seaforde 4 C 2
Seahorse Point 73 V 3
Seahouses 5 E 2
Seal 73 S 4
Seamer 5 E 2
Seaside 76 B 2
Seaton 6 C 2
Seaton Delaval 5 E 2
Seattle 76 B 2
Seba 43 F 6
Sebanka, Pulau 42 BC 3
Sebastián Vizcaino, Bahía 76 D 6
Sebatik, Pulau 42 E 3
Sebatik, Pulau 42 E 3
Sebba 62 E 3
Sébékoro 62 C 3
Sebeş 20 B 1
Sebewaing 77 K 3
Sebezh 17 J 4
Sebha → Sabhā 59 H 3
Sebha Oasis → Wāhāt Sabhā 59 H 3
Şebinkarahisar 21 E 2
Sebjet Agsumal 58 C 4
Sebjet Aridal 58 C 3
Sebkha Azzel Matti 58 F 3
Sebkha de Ndrhamcha 58 B 5
Sebkha de Rhallamane 58 D 4
Sebkha de Timimoun 58–59 F 3
Sebkha de Tindouf 58 D 3
Sebkha Iguetti 58 D 3
Sebkha Mekerrhane 59 F 3
Sebkha Oumm ed Droûs Telli 58 C 4
Sebkha Tah 58 C 3
Sebkhet Oumm ed Droûs Guebli 58 C 4
Sebou 58 D 2
Sebring 77 K 6
Sebuku, Pulau 42 E 4
Secchia 19 F 3
Sechura 84 B 5
Sechura, Bahía de 84 B 5
Sechura, Desierto de 84 B 5
Second Baku 12
Secunderabad 40 C 4
Seda 18 B 4
Sedah 43 F 6
Sedalia 77 H 4
Sedan 19 DE 2
Sedanka 72 D 5
Sedano 18 C 3
Sedbergh 5 D 2
Seddenga 60 DE 4
Sededema 37 S 2
Sedel'nikovo 25 P 4
Sédhiou 62 A 3
Sedom (Israel) 22 B 3
Sedona 76 D 5
Seeheim 66 B 5
Seend 7 C 2
Sées 18 D 2
Seesen 15 F 4
Şefaatli 21 D 3
Sefadu 62 B 4
Sefīd Dasht (Iran) 23 F 2
Sefrou 58 E 2
Segag 65 G 3
Segamat 42 B 3
Segantur 42 E 3
Segbana 62 E 3
Segesta 19 F 4
Seget 43 H 4
Segezha 16 K 3
Seghe 51 G 3
Seghnān 35 J 3
Segine I-yy 37 P 3
Segorbe 18 C 4
Ségou 62 C 3
Segovia 18 C 3
Segozero, Ozero 16 K 3
Segré (France) 18 C 2
Segre (Spain) 18 D 3
Seguam 72 C 5
Séguédine 63 G 1
Séguéla 62 C 4
Seguin 76 G 6
Segula 72 A 5
Segura 18 C 4
Segura, Sierra de 18 C 4
Sehithwa 66 C 4
Sehore 40 C 3
Sehwan 35 H 5
Seil 3 B 3
Seiland 16 H 1
Seinäjoki 16 H 3
Seine 18 D 2
Seine, Baie de la 18 C 2
Sekayu 42 B 4
Seke 64 E 5
Sekena 20 B 3
Sekenke 64 E 5
Seki 20 C 3
Sekkemo 16 H 2
Sekoma 66 C 4
Sekondi-Takoradi 62 D 5
Sekondya 37 MN 2
Selaru, Pulau 43 H 5
Selassi 43 H 4
Selat Alas 42 E 5
Selat Alor 43 F 5
Selat Bangka 42 C 4
Selat Berhala 42 B 4
Selat Dampier 43 H 4
Selat Gaspar 42 C 4
Selat Jailolo 43 G 3–4
Selat Karimata 42 C 4
Selat Laut 42 E 4
Selat Lombok 42 E 5
Selat Madura 42 D 5
Selat Makassar 42 E 4
Selat Manipa 43 G 4
Selat Mentawai 42 A 4
Selat Morotai 43 G 3
Selat Obi 43 G 4
Selat Ombai 43 G 5
Selat Peleng 43 F 4
Selat Roti 43 F 6
Selat Salue Timpaus 43 F 4
Selat Sape 43 E 5
Selat Selayar 43 F 5
Selat Serasan 42 C 3
Selat Sumba 43 F 5
Selat Sunda → Sunda Strait 42 BC 5
Selat Tiworo 43 F 4
Selat Wetar 43 G 5
Selat Yapen 43 J 4
Selatan, Pulau 42 B 4
Selatan, Tanjung 42 D 4
Selawik 72 F 2
Selawik Lake 72 F 2
Selayar, Pulau 43 F 5
Selayar, Selat 43 F 5
Selbu 16 F 3
Selbusjöen 16 F 3
Selby 76 G 2
Selby (U.K.) 5 E 3
Selçuk 20 C 3
Seldovia 72 G 4
Selebi-Pikwe 66 D 4
Selebir 37 O 2
Selemdzha 37 O 5
Selemdzhinsk 37 O 5
Selendi 20 C 3
Selenduma 36 J 5
Selenge 36 H 6
Selenge (Mongolia) 36 J 6
Selenge (Zaire) 64 B 5
Selennyakh 37 Q 2
Sélestat 19 E 2
Selety 25 O 5
Seletyteniz, Ozero 25 O 5
Selfjord 17 E 4
Selfoss 16 A 3
Selgon 37 P 6
Sélibaby 58 C 5
Selim 21 F 2
Selima Oasis → Wāhāt Salīmah 60 D 4
Selinunte 19 F 4
Seliyarovo 25 O 3
Selizharovo 24 F 4
Selkirk 3 C 4
Selkirk Mountains 73 O 5
Sella di Conza 19 G 3
Sellafirth 2 D 1
Selle, Pic de la 79 H 4
Sellyakhskaya Guba 37 P 1
Selma (AL, U.S.A.) 77 J 5
Selma (CA, U.S.A.) 76 C 4
Selong 42 E 5
Selous Game Reserve 65 F 6
Selsey 7 D 2
Selsey Bill 7 D 2
Selty 24 K 4
Selukwe → Shurugwi 66 DE 3
Selva 88 D 4
Selvagens, Ilhas 58 B 2
Selvānā 34 C 3
Selvas 84–85 EF 5
Selwyn 49 G 3
Selwyn Lake 73 R 3–4
Selwyn Mountains 72 LM 3
Sem Tripa 85 H 4
Semani 20 A 2
Semara 58 C 3
Semarang 42 D 5
Sematan 42 C 3
Semau, Pulau 43 F 6
Sembakung, Sungai 42 E 3
Sembé 63 G 5
Şemdinli 21 F 3
Semenovskiy, Ostrov 37 O 1
Semichi Islands 72 A 5
Semikarakorskiy 21 F 1
Semiluki 24 G 5
Semiozernoye 25 M 5
Semipalatinsk 25 Q 5
Semirara Islands 43 F 1
Semīrom (Iran) 23 F 3
Semisopochnoi 72 AB 5
Semitau 42 D 3
Semium 42 C 3
Semiyarka 25 P 5
Semiz-Bugu 25 OP 5
Semliki 64 DE 4
Semme Dahan, Khrebet 37 P 3
Semmering 19 G 2
Semnān 34 E 3
Semnān (Iran) 23 F 2
Semporna 43 E 3
Semuda 42 D 4
Sena (Bolivia) 86 C 3
Sena (Mozambique) 67 E 3
Sena Madureira 84 E 5
Senador Canedo 87 G 4
Senador Pompeu 87 J 2
Senaja 42 E 2
Senanga 66 C 3
Sendai 39 JK 4
Sendai 39 M 3
Sendai-wan 39 M 3
Sendelingsdrif 66 B 5
Sêndo 38 C 4
Senegal 62 AB 3
Sénégal (River) 62 B 2
Senekal 66 D 5
Seney 77 J 2
Senftenberg 15 F 4
Sênggê Zangbo 40 D 1
Sengiri, Mys 34 E 2
Sengkang 43 F 4
Senhor do Bonfim 87 H 3
Senigallia 19 F 3
Senja 16 G 2
Senjavin Group 52 B 2
Senkaku-shotō 39 H 5
Şenkaya 21 F 2
Senkyabasa 36 K 2
Sennaya 21 E 1
Senneterre 75 M 6
Senno 17 J 5
Sennybridge 6 C 2
Seno de Otway 89 B 9
Seno Skyring 89 B 9
Senorbi 19 E 4
Sens 18 D 2
Senta 20 B 1
Sentani 50 D 2
Sentinel Peak 73 N 5
Şenyurt 21 F 3
Şenyurt (Turkey) 22 C 1
Seo de Urgel 18 D 3
Seoni 40 C 3
Seoul 39 J 3
Sepanjang, Pulau 42 E 5
Separation Point 75 Q 5
Sepasu 42 E 3
Sepik River 50 D 2
Sepone 41 J 4
Sept-Îles 75 O 5
Sequillo 18 B 3
Sequoia National Park 76 C 4
Şerafettin Dağları 21 F 3
Seraing 14 E 4
Serakhs 35 G 3
Seram 43 G 4
Seram, Laut 43 GH 4
Seram Laut, Kepulauan 43 H 4
Serang 42 C 5
Serasan, Pulau 42 C 3
Serasan, Selat 42 C 3
Serbia 20 B 2
Serdo 65 G 2
Serdobsk 24 HJ 5
Serebryansk 25 Q 6
Serebryanskiy 16 L 2
Sered 15 G 5
Seredka 17 J 4
Şereflikoçhisar 21 D 3
Seremban 42 B 3
Serengeti National Park 64 EF 5
Serengeti Plain 64 EF 5
Serenje 67 E 2
Sergach 24 J 4
Sergelen 36 J 6
Sergeyevo 25 R 4
Sergino 25 N 3
Sergipe 87 J 3
Sergiyevka 21 F 2
Seria 42 D 3
Serian 42 D 3
Sérifos 20 B 3
Serifou, Sténon 20 B 3
Serik 20 D 3
Seringa, Serra da 85 H 5
Seringapatam Reef 48 C 1
Serkovo 25 R 2
Sermata, Pulau 43 G 5
Sernovodsk 24 K 5
Sernyy-Zavod 34 F 2
Séro 62 B 3
Seroglazovka 21 G 1
Serov 25 M 4
Serowe 66 D 4
Serpa 18 B 4
Serpentine Lakes 48 D 4
Serpiente, Boca de la 85 F 2
Serpukhov 24 G 5
Serra Acarai 85 G 3
Serra Bom Jesus da Gurguéia 87 H 2
Serra Bonita 87 G 4
Serra da Bodoquena 86 E 5
Serra da Canastra 87 G 4
Serra da Chela 66 A 3
Serra da Estrela (Mato Grosso, Brazil) 87 F 4
Serra da Estrêla (Portugal) 18 B 3
Serra da Gorongosa 67 E 3
Serra da Ibiapaba 87 H 1–2
Serra da Mantiqueira 87 GH 5
Serra da Neve 66 A 2
Serra da Providência 86 D 3
Serra da Seringa 85 H 5
Serra da Tabatinga 87 H 3
Serra das Alpercatas 85 JK 5
Serra das Araras 87 F 4
Serra das Cordilheiras 85 J 5
Serra de Alvelos 18 B 4
Serra de Caldeirão 18 B 4
Serra de Grândola 18 B 4
Serra de Itiúba 87 HJ 3
Serra de Maracaju 86–87 EF 5
Serra de Nogueira 18 B 3
Serra de São Jerônimo 87 EF 4
Serra de São Mamede 18 B 4
Serra do Aguapeí 86 E 4
Serra do Apiaú 85 F 3
Serra do Cachimbo 85 G 5
Serra do Caiapó 87 F 4
Serra do Caramulo 18 B 3
Serra do Chifre 87 H 4
Serra do Divisor 84 D 5
Serra do Escorial 87 H 3
Serra do Espinhaço 87 H 4
Serra do Estrondo 85 J 5
Serra do Gerês 18 B 3
Serra do Gurupi 85 J 4–5
Serra do Jibão 87 G 4
Serra do Mar 88 G 4
Serra do Marão 18 B 3
Serra do Matão 85 H 5
Serra do Mogadouro 18 B 3
Serra do Navio 85 H 3
Serra do Paraiso 87 F 3–4
Serra do Paranapiacaba 87 G 5
Serra do Penitente 85 J 5
Serra do Ramalho 87 H 3
Serra do Roncador 87 F 3
Serra do Sargento Paixão 86 DE 3
Serra do Tiracambu 87 G 1
Serra do Tombador 86 E 3
Serra do Uruçui 87 H 2
Serra Dois Irmãos 87 H 2
Serra dos Aimorés 87 HJ 4
Serra dos Apiacás 86 E 2–3
Serra dos Caiabis 86 E 3
Serra dos Carajás 85 H 4–5
Serra dos Gradaús 85 H 5
Serra dos Pacaás Novos 86 D 3
Serra dos Parecis 86 D 3
Serra dos Xavantes 87 G 3
Serra Dourada 87 G 3
Serra Formosa 87 E 3
Serra Geral 88 F 4
Serra Geral de Goiás 87 G 3
Serra Geral do Paranã 87 G 3
Serra Geral ou Grande 87 G 3
Serra Grande 87 H 2
Serra Lombarda 85 H 3
Serra Negra 85 J 5
Serra Nova 85 F 5
Serra Talhada 87 J 2
Serra Tumucumaque 85 H 3
Serra Urubuquara 85 H 4
Sérrai 20 B 2
Serrana, Banco de 79 G 5
Serranía de Baudó 84 C 2
Serranía de Huanchaca 86 D 3
Serranía de Imataca 85 F 2
Serranía de Santiago 86 DE 4
Serranía de Tabasara 84 B 2
Serranía del Darién 84 C 2
Serranías Turagua 85 F 2
Serranilla, Banco 79 G 4
Serres 19 E 3
Serrezuela 88 C 5
Serrinha 87 J 3
Serrota 18 BC 3
Sertã 18 B 4
Sêrtar 38 D 4
Sertavul Geçidi 21 D 3
Seruai 43 J 4

Skaliskaya, Gora **36** D 1
Skanderborg **17** E 4
Skåne **17** F 4
Skanör **17** F 4
Skara **17** F 4
Skara Brae **2** C 2
Skærbæck **17** E 4
Skärblacka **17** G 4
Skardu **35** K 3
Skärhamn **17** F 4
Skarsöy **16** E 3
Skarstind **16** E 3
Skarsvåg **16** J 1
Skarżysko-Kamienna **15** H 4
Skeena **72** M 5
Skeena Mountains **72** M 4
Skeggöxl **16** A 2
Skegness **7** E 1
Skeiðárarsandur **16** B 3
Skeldon **85** G 2
Skeleton Coast Park **66** A 3
Skellefteå **16** H 3
Skellefteälven **16** G 2
Skelleftehamn **16** H 3
Skelmersdale **5** D 3
Skerries **4** B 3
Ski **17** F 4
Skíathos **20** B 3
Skibbereen **14** B 4
Skibotn **16** H 2
Skiddaw **5** D 2
Skidegate **72** L 5
Skidel' **17** H 5
Skien **17** E 4
Skierniewice **15** H 4
Skiftet **17** H 3
Skigersta **2** A 2
Skíros **20** B 3
Skikda **59** G 1
Skipton **5** D 3
Skíros **20** B 3
Skive **17** E 4
Skjálfandafljót **16** B 2
Skjálfandi **16** B 2
Skjern **17** E 4
Skjervöy **16** H 1
Skjoldungen **75** T 3
Sklad **36** M 1
Škofja Loka **19** F 2
Skoghall **17** F 4
Skokholm **6** B 2
Skomer **6** B 2
Skópelos **20** B 3
Skopi **20** C 3
Skopje **20** B 2
Skorodum **25** O 4
Skorovatn **16** F 3
Skörping **17** EF 4
Skövde **17** F 4
Skovorodino **37** M 5
Skowhegan **77** M 3
Skradin **19** G 3
Skrekken **17** E 3
Skudeneshavn **17** DE 4
Skurup **17** F 4
Skutskär **17** G 3
Skvira **24** E 6
Skwentna **72** G 3
Skye **2** A 3
Slagnäs **16** G 2
Slamannan **3** C 4
Slamet, Gunung **42** C 5
Slane **4** B 3
Slaney, River **4** B 3
Slannik **20** C 2
Slano **19** G 3
Slantsy **17** J 4
Slashchevskaya **24** H 6
Śląsk **15** G 4
Slatina **20** B 2
Slautnoye **37** V 3
Slave Coast **62** E 4
Slave Lake **73** O 4
Slave River **73** P 3–4
Slavgorod **21** E 1
Slavgorod **25** P 5
Slavnoye **37** R 6
Slavonska Požega **19** G 2
Slavonski Brod **19** G 2
Slavuta **17** J 5
Slavyanka **39** K 2
Slavyansk **24** G 6
Slavyansk-na-Kubani **21** E 1
Sławno **15** G 4
Sleaford **7** D 1
Sleat **3** B 3
Sleat, Sound of **2–3** B 3
Sleeper Islands **75** L 4
Slettuheiði **16** B 2
Slieve Bloom Mountains **4** B 3
Slieve Donard **4** C 2
Sligo **14** B 4
Slite **17** G 4
Sliven **20** C 2
Slobodchikovo **24** J 3
Slobodka **20** C 1
Slobodskoy **24** K 4
Slobodzeya **20** C 1
Slobozia **20** C 2
Slochteren **12**
Slocum Mountain **76** C 4
Slonim **17** J 5
Slough **7** D 2
Slovakia **15** H 5
Slovechno **17** J 5
Slovenija **19** FG 2
Slovenske Gorice **19** G 2
Slovensko **15** GH 5
Sluch' **17** J 5
Slŭnchev Bryag **20** C 2
Slunj **19** G 2
Słupia **15** G 4
Słupsk **15** G 4
Slutsk **17** J 5
Slyudyanka **36** H 5
Småland **17** G 4
Smålandsstenar **17** F 4
Smallwood Réservoir **75** P 5
Smedervo **20** B 2
Smedjebacken **17** G 3
Smela **24** F 6
Smidovich **37** O 6
Smidovich **90**
Smirnovskiy **25** N 5
Smirnykh **37** Q 6
Smith **73** P 4
Smith Arm **73** N 2
Smith Bay **72** G 1
Smith Falls **75** M 7
Smithers **73** M 5
Smithfield **5** D 2
Smithsborough **4** B 2
Smithton **50** L 9
Smithtown-Gladstone **49** J 5
Smjörfjöll **16** C 2
Smögen **17** F 4
Smokey Dome **76** CD 3
Smoky Cape **49** J 5
Smoky Falls **74** L 5
Smoky Hill **76** F 4
Smoky Hills **76** G 4
Smoky River **73** O 5
Smöla **16** E 3
Smolensk **24** F 5
Smólikas Óros **20** B 2
Smolyan **20** B 2
Smooth Rock Falls **75** L 6
Smorgon' **17** J 5
Smygehamn **17** F 4
Smyrna → İzmir **20** C 3
Smythe, Mount **73** MN 4
Snaefell **4** C 2
Snæfell **16** B 3
Snæfellsjökull **16** A 3
Snæfellsnes **16** A 3
Snag **72** J 3
Snake **76** C 2
Snake Bay **48** E 1
Snake River Plain **76** D 3
Snare **73** O 3
Snåsa **16** F 3
Snåsvattnet **16** F 3
Snezhnogorsk **25** R 2
Snezhnoye **37** W 2
Sněžnik **19** F 2
Śnieżka **15** G 4
Śnieżnik **15** G 4
Snigirevka **21** D 1
Snizort, Loch **2** A 3
Snöhetta **16** E 3
Snoul **41** J 5
Snow Lake **73** R 5
Snow Mountain **76** B 4
Snowbird Lake **73** R 3
Snowdon **6** B 1
Snowdrift **73** P 3
Snowville **76** D 3
Snowy Mountains **49** H 6
Snowy River **49** H 6
Snyatyn **20** C 1
Snyder **76** F 5
Soacha **84** D 3
Soahanina **67** G 3
Soalala **67** H 3
Soanierana-Ivongo **67** H 3
Soasiu **43** G 3
Soavinandriana **67** H 3
Soay **2** A 3
Soba **63** F 3
Sobat → Sawbā **64** E 3
Sobolevo **37** T 5
Sobolokh Mayan **37** MN 2
Sobopol **37** N 2
Sobradinho, Barragem de **87** H 3
Sobral **87** H 1
Socaire **86** C 5
Sochaczew **15** GH 4
Sochi **21** E 2
Society Islands **53** EF 4
Socorro (Colombia) **84** D 2
Socorro (N.M., U.S.A.) **76** E 5
Sócota **84** C 5
Socotra **65** J 2
Soda Plains **35** K 3
Sodankylä **16** J 2
Soddu **65** F 3
Söderhamn **16** G 3
Söderköping **17** G 4
Södermanland **17** G 4
Södertälje **17** G 4
Södra Kvarken **17** G 3
Soe **43** F 5
Soela Väin **17** H 4
Soest **15** E 4
Sofádhes **20** B 3
Sofala, Baía de **67** EF 4
Sofia (Madagascar) **67** H 3
Sofia → Sofiya **20** B 2
Sofiya **20** B 2
Sofiyevka **21** D 1
Sofiysk **37** O 5
Sofiysk **37** PQ 5
Sofporog **16** K 2
Sōfu-gan **39** LM 5
Sog Xian **38** B 4
Sogamoso **84** D 2
Soğanlı **21** D 2
Sogda **37** O 5
Sogeri **50** E 3
Sogn og Fjordane **16** E 3
Sogndalsfjöra **16** E 3
Sognefjorden **16** E 3
Sognesjöen **16** D 3
Sogo Hills **65** F 4
Sogo Nur **38** D 2
Sogod **43** F 1
Sogolle **63** H 2
Sogom **25** N 3
Söğüt **20** D 2
Söğüt Gölü **20** CD 3
Sohag → Sawhāj **60** E 3
Soham **7** E 1
Sohano **51** FG 3
Sohm Abyssal Plain **98** A 2
Sohŭksan-do **39** J 4
Soila **38** C 4
Soissons **18** D 2
Sojat **40** B 2
Sŏjosŏn-man **39** H 3
Sokal' **17** H 5
Sokch'o **39** J 3
Söke **20** C 3
Sokele **64** C 6
Sokhondo, Gora **36** K 6
Sokhor, Gora **36** J 5
Sokna **17** E 3
Sokodé **62** E 4
Sokol **20** A 2
Sokółka **15** H 4
Sokolo **62** C 3
Sokolov **15** F 4
Sokolozero **16** K 2
Sokone **62** A 3
Sokosti **16** J 2
Sokota **65** F 2
Sokoto **63** EF 3
Söl **65** H 3
Sola **17** E 4
Solai **65** F 4
Solbad Hall **19** F 2
Solberg **16** G 3
Soldatovo **37** V 3
Sölden **19** F 2
Soldotna **72** G 3
Soledad (Colombia) **84** D 1
Soledad (Venezuela) **85** F 2
Soledade (Amazonas, Brazil) **84** E 5
Soledade (Río Grande do Sul, Brazil) **88** F 4
Solenoye (Russia, U.S.S.R.) **21** F 1
Solenoye (Ukraine, U.S.S.R.) **21** D 1
Solenzara **19** E 3
Solferino **19** F 2
Solhan **21** F 3
Soligorsk **17** J 5
Solikamsk **24** L 4
Sol'-Iletsk **24** L 5
Soliman **19** F 4
Solimões **84** E 4
Solingen **15** E 4
Solita **84** D 2
Solitaire **66** B 4
Sollas **2** A 3
Sollefteå **16** G 3
Sollerön **17** FG 3
Solling **15** E 4
Sologne Bourbonnais **18** D 2
Solok **42** B 4
Solomon Islands **51** GH 3
Solomon Sea **51** F 3
Solon **39** H 1
Solontsovo **36** KL 5
Solör **17** F 3
Solothurn **19** E 2
Solovetskiye, Ostrova **24** G 2
Solov'yevsk **36** L 5
Solov'yevsk **37** MN 5
Solta **19** G 3
Soltānābād (Iran) **23** E 3
Soltānābād **34** F 3
Soltau **15** E 4
Sol'tsy **17** K 4
Solva **6** B 2
Sölvesborg **17** FG 4
Solway Firth **3** C 4
Solwezi **66** D 2
Solyanka **36** M 3
Soma **20** C 3
Somabula **66** D 3
Somali Basin **98** B 3
Somalia **65** GH 3–4
Sombang, Gunung **42** E 3
Sombo **66** C 1
Sombor **20** A 1
Sombrerete **78** B 3
Sombrero Channel **41** F 6
Somcuța Mare **20** B 1
Somero **17** H 3
Somerset (Australia) **49** G 1
Somerset (KY, U.S.A.) **77** K 4
Somerset (U.K.) **6** C 2
Somerset East **66** CD 6
Somersham **7** E 1
Somerton **6** C 2
Someș **20** B 1
Someșu Mare **20** B 1
Somme **18** D 1
Sommen **17** G 4
Somnath **40** B 3
Somnitel'nyy **37** P 5
Somontano **18** C 3
Somoto **78** E 5
Somport, Puerto **18** C 3
Somuncurá, Meseta de **89** C 7
Son **40** D 3
Son **40** D 3
Son Ha **41** J 4
Son La **41** H 3
Soná **84** B 2
Sonakh **37** P 5
Sonaly **25** O 6
Sönch'ŏn **39** H 3
Sönderborg **17** EF 5
Sondershausen **15** F 4
Söndre Strömfjord **75** R 2
Söndre Strömfjord **75** RS 2
Sondrio **19** E 2
Sonepur **40** D 3
Sonequera **86** C 5
Song **63** G 4
Song Cau **41** J 5
Song Da **41** H 3
Song Hong **41** H 3
Song Ma **41** H 3
Songea **67** F 2
Songhua Hu **39** J 2
Songhua Jiang **39** J 1
Songjiang **39** H 4
Songkhla **41** H 6
Songling **37** M 6
Songnim **39** J 3
Songo **67** E 3
Songolo **64** A 6
Songpan **38** D 4
Songwe **64** E 6
Songxi **39** G 5
Sonid Youqi **38** F 2
Sonid Zuoqi **38** F 2
Sonipat **40** C 2
Sonkel', Ozero **35** K 2
Sonmiani **35** H 5
Sonmiani Bay **35** H 5
Sonneberg **15** F 4
Sono **85** J 5
Sonoita **76** D 5
Sonoma Peak **76** C 3
Sonora (Mexico) **76** D 6
Sonora (TX, U.S.A.) **76** F 5
Sonora, Rio **76** D 6
Sonoran Desert **76** D 5
Sonqor (Iran) **23** E 2
Sonsón **84** CD 2
Sonsonate **78** DE 5
Sonsorol Islands **43** H 2
Sop Bau **41** H 3
Sopka Anangravnen **37** U 4
Sopka Kizimen **37** U 4
Sopka Shiveluch **37** U 4
Sopochnaya Karga **36** DE 1
Sopochnoye **37** T 4
Sopot **15** G 4
Sopron **20** A 1
Sopur **35** J 4
Sor **18** B 4
Sor Kaydak **34** E 1–2
Sor Mertvyy Kultuk **34** E 1
Sör Rondane Mountains **91**
Sora **19** F 3
Sorada **40** D 4
Söråker **16** G 3
Sorata **86** C 4
Sordoginskiy Khrebet **37** OP 3
Sorel **75** N 6
Sorell **50** L 9
Sörfold **16** G 2
Sorgues **19** D 3
Sorgun **21** E 3
Soria **18** C 3
Soriano **88** E 5
Sorikmerapi, Gunung **42** A 3
Sorkh, Kūh-e (Iran) **23** G 2
Sorkheh **34** E 3
Sorkheh (Iran) **23** F 2
Sorn **3** B 4
Sorocaba **87** G 5
Sorochinsk **24** K 5
Sorok **36** H 5
Soroki **20** C 1
Sorolen **25** P 6
Sorong **43** H 4
Soroti **64** E 4
Söröya **16** H 1
Söröyane **16** E 3
Sorraia **18** B 4
Sörreisa **16** G 2
Sorrento **19** F 3
Sorsatunturi **16** J 2
Sorsele **16** G 2
Sorso **19** E 3
Sorsogon **43** F 1
Sort **18** D 3
Sortavala **16** K 3
Sortland **16** FG 2
Sör-Tröndelag **16** F 3
Sörvagur **14** A 1
Sörværöy **16** F 2
Sŏsan **39** J 3
Sosna **36** J 3
Sosnogorsk **24** KL 3
Sosnovka **24** H 2
Sosnovka **24** J 4
Sosnovka **36** J 5
Sosnovo-Ozerskoye **36** K 5
Sosnovy Bor **17** J 4
Sosnovyy Bor **25** Q 3
Sosnovyy Mys **25** N 3
Sosnowiec **15** G 4
Sosumav **67** H 2
Sos'va **25** M 4
Sos'va, Malaya **25** MN 3
Sos'va, Severnaya **25** MN 3
Sos'vinskaya Kul'tbaza **25** M 3
Sosyka **21** EF 1
Sotavento, Islas de **84** E 1
Sotik **64** F 5
Sotkamo **16** J 3
Sotnikovskoye **21** F 1
Sotonera, Embalse de la **18** C 3
Sotouboua **62** E 4
Sotra **17** D 3
Sotsial **25** P 6
Souanké **63** G 5
Soubré **62** C 4
Soudan **49** F 3
Souf **59** G 2
Souflíon **20** C 2
Soufrière (Guadeloupe) **79** K 4
Soufrière (St. Vincent) **79** K 5
Souillac **18** D 3
Souilly **19** E 2
Souk Ahras **59** G 1
Souk el Arbaa du Rharb **58** D 2
Soukourালla **62** C 4
Sŏul **39** HJ 3
Soumenselkä **16** H 3
Sound of Arisaig **3** B 3
Sound of Harris **2** A 3
Sound of Jura **3** B 3–4
Sound of Mull **3** B 3
Sound of Raasay **2** A 3
Sound of Sleat **2–3** B 3
Sound of Sleat **2–3** B 3
Sounfat **62** E 1
Soúnion, Ákra **20** B 3
Sountellane **63** G 2
Soure **85** J 4
Souris **73** R 6
Souris **75** P 6
Souris River **73** R 6
Sous **58** D 2
Sousa **87** J 2
Sousel **85** H 4
Sousse (Tunisia) **59** H 1
Soutergate **5** D 2
South Africa **66** CD 6
South Alligator River **48** E 1
South Andaman **41** F 5
South Atlantic Ocean **91**
South Aulatsivik **75** P 4
South Australia **48–49** EF 4
South Australian Basin **99** C 5
South Bay **73** V 3
South Bend (IN, U.S.A.) **77** J 3
South Bend (WA, U.S.A.) **76** B 2
South Benfleet **7** E 2
South Brent **6** C 3
South Carolina **77** K 5

Thai Nguyen 41 J 3
Thailand 41 GH 4
Thailand, Gulf of 41 H 5
Thakhek 41 HJ 4
Thal 35 J 4
Thal Desert 35 J 4
Thalabarivat 41 J 5
Thale Luang 41 H 6
Thallon 49 H 4
Tham Khae 41 J 4
Thamad Bū Ḥashishah 59 J 3
Thamarīd 61 J 5
Thame 7 D 2
Thames (New Zealand) 51 R 8
Thames, River 7 E 2
Thāmir, Jabal 61 H 6
Thamūd 61 H 5
Thana 40 B 4
Thangoo 48 C 2
Thangool 49 J 3
Thanh Hoa 41 J 4
Thanīyah, Jabal 61 H 5
Thanjavur 40 C 5
Thann 19 E 2
Thano Bula Khan 35 H 5
Thap Sakae 41 GH 5
Thapston 7 D 1
Thar Desert 40 B 2
Tharad 40 B 3
Thargomindah 49 G 4
Tharrawaddy 41 G 4
Tharrawaw 41 G 4
Tharthār, Bahr ath (Iraq) 22 D 2
Tharthār, Wādī ath (Iraq) 22 D 2
Thásos 20 B 2
Thásos 20 B 2
Thásos 20 B 2
Thateng 41 J 4
Thaton 41 G 4
Thau, Bassin de 18 D 3
Thaungdut 41 FG 3
Thayetchaung 41 G 5
Thayetmyo 41 G 4
Thazi 41 F 4
The Alps 19 EF 2
The Bahamas 79 GH 2
The Brothers → Al Ikhwān 65 J 2
The Bush 4 B 3
The Cheviot 3 C 4
The Dalles 76 B 2
The Everglades 77 K 6
The Fens 7 DE 1
The Gambia 62 A 3
The Granites 48 E 3
The Granites 48 E 3
The Great Oasis → Wāhāt al Khārijah 60 E 3–4
The Gulf 23 EF 3–4
The Hague 14 D 4
The Johnston Lakes 48 C 5
The Lizard 6 B 2
The Mearns 3 C 3
The Merse 3 C 4
The Monument 49 G 3
The Mumbles 6 B 2
The Needles 7 D 2
The North Sound 2 C 2
The Pas 73 R 5
The Solent 7 D 2
The Teeth 43 E 2
The Trossachs 3 B 3
The Twins 51 Q 9
The Valley 79 K 4
The Wash 7 E 1
The Weald 7 E 2
Thebes 20 B 3
Thebes (Egypt) 22 A 4
Theddlethorpe 7 E 1
Thedford 76 F 3
Theinkun 41 G 5
Thelon 73 S 3
Thénia 18 D 4
Theologos 20 B 2
Thermaïkos Kólpos 20 B 2–3
Thermopílai 20 B 3
Thermopolis 76 E 3
Theronsvalley 66 BC 4
Thesiger Bay 73 MN 1
Thessalía 20 B 3
Thessaloníki 20 B 2
Thetford 7 E 1
Thetford Mines 75 N 6
Thief River Falls 77 G 2
Thiel Mts. 91
Thiers 18 D 2
Thiès 62 A 3
Thiesi 19 E 3
Thika 65 F 5
Thiladummathi Atoll 40 B 6
Thimphu 40 E 2
Þingvallavatn 16 A 3
Þingvellir 16 A 3
Thio (Ethiopia) 65 G 2
Thio (New Caledonia) 51 J 6
Thionville 19 E 2
Thiou 62 D 3
Thira 20 B 3
Thíra 20 C 3
Third Cataract → Ash Shallāl ath Thālith 60 E 5
Thirsk 5 E 2
Thisted 17 E 4
Thitu Island 42 D 1
Thivai 20 B 3
Thiviers 18 D 2
Þjórsá 16 B 3
Thlewiaza 73 S 3
Thoen 41 G 4
Thoeng 41 H 4
Thohoyandou 67 E 4
Thomas Shoal 42 E 2
Thomastown 4 B 3
Thomasville (AL, U.S.A.) 77 J 5
Thomasville (GA, U.S.A.) 77 K 5
Thompson 73 S 4
Thompson Falls 76 C 2
Thomson River 49 G 3
Thon Buri 41 GH 5
Thongwa 41 G 4
Thonon 19 E 2
Þórisvatn 16 B 3
Þorlákshöfn 16 A 3
Thornaby-on-Tees 5 E 2
Thornby 7 D 1
Thorne 5 E 3
Thorney 7 D 1
Thornton Cleveleys 5 D 3
Thornton Dale 5 E 2
Þórshöfn 16 B 2
Thowa 65 F 5
Thráki 20 C 2
Thrakikón Pélagos 20 BC 2
Three Forks 76 D 2
Three Hummock Island 50 L 9
Three Kings Islands 51 Q 7
Three Pagodas Pass 41 G 4
Three Points, Cape 62 D 5
Three Springs 48 B 4
Throssel, Lake 48 C 4
Thruxton 7 D 2
Thuillier, Mount 41 F 6
Thule 90
Thun 19 E 2
Thundelarra 48 B 4
Thunder Bay (Canada) 74 K 6
Thunder Bay (MI, U.S.A.) 77 K 3
Thung Luang 41 G 5
Thung Song 41 G 6
Thung Wa 41 G 6
Thüringen 15 F 4
Thüringer Wald 15 F 4
Thurles 4 B 3
Thursby 5 D 2
Thurso 2 C 2
Thurston Island 91
Thusis 19 E 2
Thwaite 5 C 2
Thy 17 E 4
Thylungra 49 G 4
Tíago 85 G 4
Tian Shan 35 KM 2
Tianchang 39 G 4
Tiandong 38 E 6
Tian'e 38 E 6
Tiangua 87 H 1
Tianjin 39 G 3
Tianjin Xingang 39 G 3
Tianjun 38 C 3
Tianlin 38 E 6
Tianmen 38 F 4
Tianmu Shan 39 G 4
Tianshifu 39 H 2
Tianshui 38 E 4
Tiantai 39 H 5
Tianyang 38 E 6
Tianzhu 38 D 3
Tiaret 59 F 1
Tiassalé 62 D 4
Tibaradine 59 F 3
Tibati 63 G 4
Tiber 19 F 3
Tiberias → Teverya 60 F 2
Tibesti 63 H 1
Tibet 40 E 1
Tibet, Plateau of 40 DE 1
Tibiri 63 E 3
Tibiri 63 E 3
Tibistī, Sarīr 59 J 4
Tibnah (Syria) 22 B 2
Tibni (Syria) 22 C 2
Tibro 17 F 4
Tiburon, Isla 76 D 6
Ticao 43 F 1
Tichit 58 D 5
Tichla 58 B 4
Ticino 19 E 2
Ticul 78 E 3
Tidaholm 17 F 4
Tiddim 41 F 3
Tideswell 7 D 1
Tidikelt Oases 59 F 3
Tidirhine, Jbel 58 E 2
Tidjettaouine 59 F 4
Tidjikdja 58 C 5
Tidra, Ile 58 B 5
Tiebissou 62 CD 4
Tiel 62 A 3
Tieli 39 J 1
Tieling 39 H 2
Tielongtan 35 K 3
Tiéme 62 C 4
Tienba 62 C 4
Tientsin 39 G 3
Tierp 17 G 3
Tierra Blanca 78 C 4
Tierra Colorada 78 C 4
Tierra de Barros 18 B 4
Tierra de Campos 18 BC 3
Tierra del Fuego, Isla Grande de 89 C 9
Tierra del Pan 18 B 3
Tierra del Vino 18 B 3
Tieté 87 F 5
Tifariti 58 C 3
Tiflis → Tbilisi 21 F 2
Tifton 77 K 5
Tifu 43 G 4
Tiga 51 J 6
Tigalda 72 E 5
Tigil' 37 T 4
Tigil' 37 T 4
Tignère 63 G 4
Tigre 84 C 4
Tigres, Baía dos 66 A 3
Tigris (Iraq) 23 D 2
Tiguent 58 B 5
Tiguentourine 59 G 3
Tigui 63 H 2
Tiguidit, Falaise de 63 F 2
Tihāmat 61 G 5
Tījī 59 H 2
Tijuana 76 C 5
Tijucas 88 G 4
Tikal 78 E 4
Tikamgarh 40 C 3
Tikanlik 38 A 2
Tikaré 62 D 3
Tikchik Lakes 72 F 3
Tikhoretsk 21 F 1
Tikhtoozero, Ozero 16 K 2
Tikhvin 24 F 4
Tikkakoski 16 J 3
Tikopia 51 J 4
Tikrīt 61 G 2
Tiksha 16 K 3
Tikshozero, Ozero 16 K 2
Tiksi 37 N 1
Tilaiya Reservoir 40 E 3
Tilbeşar Ovası 21 E 3
Tilbooroo 49 H 4
Tilburg 14 E 4
Tilbury 7 E 2
Tilbury 14 E 4
Tilcara 86 C 5
Tilemsi el Fasi 58 E 3
Tilemsi, Vallée du 62 E 2
Tilia 58 F 3
Tilichiki 37 V 3
Tilin 41 F 3
Tillabéri 62 E 3
Tillamook 76 B 2
Tillanchong 41 F 6
Tillia 63 E 2
Tiloa 62 E 2
Tilogne 62 B 2
Tílos 20 C 3
Tilpa 49 G 5
Til'tim 25 M 2
Ti-m Missao 59 F 4
Timā 60 E 3
Timagami, Lake 75 L 6
Timanskiy Kryazh 24 JL 2–3
Timar 21 F 3
Timaru 51 Q 9
Timashevskaya 21 E 1
Timbákion 20 B 3
Timbauba 87 J 2
Timbédra 58 D 5
Timberscombe 6 C 3
Timbio 84 C 3
Timbo 62 BC 4
Timbuktu → Tombouctou 62 D 2
Timeiaouine 59 F 4
Timétrine 62 D 2
Timétrine, Monts 62 D 2
Timfi Óros 20 B 3
Timg'aouine 59 F 4
Timia 63 F 2
Timimoun 58 F 3
Timimoun, Sebkha de 58–59 F 3
Timir-Atakh-Tas 37 S 2
Timiris, Cap 58 B 5
Timiş 20 B 1
Timiskaming, Lake 75 M 6
Timişoara 20 B 1
Timkapaul' 25 M 3
Timmins 75 L 6
Timmoudi 58 E 3
Timon 87 H 2
Timor 43 G 5
Timor, Laut 43 G 6
Timor Sea 43 G 6
Timoshino 24 G 3
Timote 88 D 6
Timpton 37 N 4
Timrå 16 G 3
Timsgorry 2 A 2
Timur 35 H 2
Ti-n Amzi 59 F 4
Tin Asaguid 62 E 2
Tin City 72 D 2
Tin Ethisane 62 D 2
Tin Fouye 59 G 3
Ti-n Rerhoh 59 F 4
Ti-n Taoundi 59 G 4
Ti-n Tarabine 59 G 4
Tin Tounannt 62 D 1
Ti-n Zaouâtene 59 F 4
Tinaca Point 43 G 2
Tinaco 84 E 2
Tindalo 64 E 3
Tindivanam 40 CD 5
Tindouf 58 D 3
Tindouf, Hamada de 58 D 3
Tindouf, Sebkha de 58 D 3
Tinef 59 F 4
Tineldjame 59 F 3
Tineo 18 B 3
Tinerhir 58 D 2
Tinfouchy 58 D 3
Tingharat, Ḥamādat 59 H 3
Tingkawk Sakan 41 G 2
Tingmiarmiut 75 T 3
Tingo María 84 C 5
Tingréla 62 C 3
Tingri 40 E 2
Tingsryd 17 FG 4
Tinguiririca 89 BC 5
Tingvoll 16 E 3
Tinh Gia 41 J 4
Tinharé, Ilha de 87 J 3
Tini Wells 60 C 6
Tinian 52 A 2
Tinkisso 62 BC 3
Tinnsjö 17 E 4
Tinogasta 88 C 4
Tinombo 43 F 3
Tínos 20 C 3
Tinrhert, Hamada de 59 G 3
Tinsukia 41 G 2
Tintagel 6 B 2
Tintagel Head 6 B 2
Tintane 58 C 5
Tintina 88 D 4
Ti-n-Toumma 63 G 2
Tio, Pico de 62 C 4
Tioman 42 B 3
Tione di Trento 19 F 2
Tiongui 62 C 3
Tiouardiouine Aguelman 59 G 4
Tiouilit Anagoum 58 B 5
Tipperary 4 B 3
Tipperary 14 B 4
Tipton, Mount 76 D 4
Tiptree 7 E 2
Tiquisate 78 D 5
Tiracambu, Serra do 87 G 1
Tirah 35 J 4
Tirān (Egypt) 22 B 4
Tirān (Iran) 23 F 2
Tirana 20 AB 2
Tirano 19 F 2
Tiras Mountains 66 B 5
Tiraspol' 20 C 1
Tirat Karmel (Israel) 22 B 2
Tire 20 C 3
Tirebolu 21 E 2
Tiree 3 A 3
Tiree (Airport) 3 A 3
Tirgelir 37 Q 3
Tîrgi Frumos 20 C 1
Tîrgovişte 20 C 2
Tîrgu Bujor 20 C 1
Tîrgu Cărbuneşti 20 B 2
Tîrgu Jiu 20 B 1
Tîrgu Mureş 20 BC 1–2
Tîrgu Neamţ 20 C 1
Tîrgu Ocna 20 C 1
Tîrgu Secuiesc 20 C 1
Tirich Mir 35 J 3
Tiririne 59 G 4
Tiris 58 C 4
Tîrnăveni 20 B 1
Tirnavos 20 B 3
Tiro 62 B 4
Tirol 19 F 2
Tirso 19 E 3
Tiruchchirappalli 40 C 5
Tiruchendur 40 C 6
Tirunelveli 40 C 6
Tiruntán 84 D 5
Tirupati 40 C 5
Tiruppur 40 C 5
Tiruvannamalai 40 C 5
Tisa 20 A 1
Tisdale 73 R 5
Tisisat Falls 65 F 2
Tissemsilt 59 F 1
Tista 40 E 2
Tisul' 25 R 4
Tisza 20 B 1
Tiszafüred 20 B 1
Tiszántúl 20 B 1
Tit 59 F 3
Titaf 58 E 3
Tit-Ary 37 N 1
Titchfield 7 D 2
Titicaca, Lago 86 C 4
Titlagarh 40 D 3
Titograd 20 A 2
Titov Veles 20 B 2
Titov vrh 20 B 2
Titova Korenica 19 G 3
Titovo Užice 20 A 2
Titran 16 E 3
Titule 64 D 4
Titusville 77 K 6
Tiui 85 GH 3
Tivaouane 62 A 3
Tiveden 17 F 4
Tiverton 6 C 2
Tiwī 61 K 4
Tiworo, Selat 43 F 4
Tizatlan 78 C 4
Tizi n'Test 58 D 2
Tizi Ouzou 59 F 1
Tizimín 78 E 3
Tiznit 58 D 3
Tjåhumas 16 G 2
Tjeggelvas 16 G 2
Tjidtjak 16 G 2
Tjörn 17 F 4
Tjotta 16 F 2
Tjust 17 G 4
Tkhach 21 F 2
Tkibuli 21 F 2
Tkvarcheli 21 F 2
Tlalnepantla 78 C 4
Tlapa de Comonfort 78 C 4
Tlaxcala 78 C 4
Tlemcen 58 E 2
Tlemcès 63 E 2
Tlētē Ouate Gharbi, Jabal 22 C 2
Tlyarata 21 G 2
Tmassah 59 J 3
Tni Haïa 58 E 4
Toaca, Virful 20 C 1
Toamasina 67 H 3
Toay 89 D 6
Toba & Kakar Ranges 35 H 4
Toba, Danau 42 A 3
Tobago, Isla 85 F 1
Tobarra 18 C 4
Tobermore 4 B 2
Tobermorey 49 F 3
Tobermory 75 L 6
Tobermory (U.K.) 3 A 3
Tobi 43 H 3
Tobin, Lake 48 D 3
Tobo 43 H 4
Toboali 42 C 4
Tobol 25 M 5
Tobol 25 N 4
Tobol'sk 25 N 4
Tobruk → Ṭubruq 59 K 2
Tobseda 24 K 2
Tobysh 24 K 3
Tocantinia 85 J 5
Tocantinópolis 85 J 5
Tocantins 85 J 4
Tocapilla 86 B 5
Töcksfors 17 F 4
Toco 86 C 5
Toconao 86 C 5
Tocorpuri, Cerro de 86 C 5
Todenyang 65 F 4
Todi 19 F 3
Todmorden 5 D 3
Todos os Santos, Baia de 87 J 3
Todos Santos 76 D 7
Tofino 73 M 6
Tofte 17 F 4
Togatax 35 L 3
Togher (Roundwood) 4 B 3
Togiak 72 E 4
Togian, Kepulauan 43 F 4
Togni 60 F 5
Togo 62 E 4
Togqên 40 D 1
Togtoh 38 F 2
Toguchin 25 Q 4
Togur 25 Q 4
Togyz 35 G 1
Tohen 65 J 2
Tohma 21 E 3
Toibalewe 41 F 5
Toijala 16 H 3
Toista 2 A 2
Toisvesi 16 J 3
Tok (AK, U.S.A.) 72 J 3

U

Uglovoya 37 NO 5
Ugol'naya 37 X 3
Ugoyan 37 N 4
Ugulan 37 T 3
Ugumun 36 L 2
Ugun 37 N 4
Ugut 25 O 3
Uherské Hradiště 15 G 5
Uig 2 A 3
Uíge 66 B 1
Uil 34 E 1
Uilpata 21 F 2
Uiñaimarca, Lago 86 C 4
Uinta Mountains 76 DE 3
Uis Mine 66 AB 4
Uitenhage 66 D 6
Ujae 52 C 2
Ujarrás 78 F 6
Ujelang 52 B 2
Ujiji 64 D 6
Ujjain 40 C 3
Ujung 43 F 5
Ujung Pandang 43 E 4–5
Ujunglamuru 43 F 4
Uk 36 G 4
Uka 37 U 4
Ukara 64 E 5
Ukelayat 37 W 3
Ukerewe 64 E 5
Ukhaydir (Iraq) 22 D 2
Ukholovo 24 H 5
Ukhta 24 K 3
Ukiah (CA, U.S.A.) 76 B 4
Ukiah (OR, U.S.A.) 76 C 2
Ukmergė 17 HJ 4
Ukraina 24 FG 6
Ukrainka 25 P 4
Uktym 24 J 3
Uku 66 A 2
Ukuma 66 B 2
Ukwaa 64 E 3
Ula 20 C 3
Ulaanbaatar 36 J 6
Ulaangom 36 F 6
Ulaanhus 36 E 6
Ulaga 37 O 2
Ulakhan Botuobuya 36 K 3
Ulakhan-Cistay, Khrebet 37 QR 2–3
Ulakhan-Kyugel' 36 KL 3
Ulakhan-Sis, Kryazh 37 S 1–2
Ulakhe 39 K 2
Ulamba 64 C 6
Ulan 38 C 3
Ulan Bator 36 J 6
Ulan Ul Hu 38 B 4
Ulanbel 35 J 2
Ulan-Burgasy, Khrebet 36 J 5
Ulan-Khol 21 G 1
Ulansuhai Nur 38 E 2
Ulan-Ude 36 J 5
Ularunda 49 H 4
Ulaş 21 E 3
Ulastay 35 M 2
Ulawa 51 H 3
Ul'ba 25 Q 5
Ul'beya 37 Q 3
Ulbeya 37 Q 4
Ulbster 2 C 2
Ulchin 39 J 3
Ulcinj 20 A 2
Ule Träsk 16 J 3
Uleåborg 16 HJ 3
Ulefoss 17 E 4
Ulety 36 K 5
Ulhasnagar 40 B 4
Uliastay 36 G 6
Uliga 52 C 2
Ulindi 64 D 5
Ullapool 2 B 3
Ullared 17 F 4
Ullatti 16 H 2
Ulldecona 18 D 3
Ullsfjorden 16 G 2
Ullswater 5 D 2
Ullŭng-do 39 K 3
Ulm 15 E 5
Ulmeni 20 C 1
Ulongué 67 E 2
Ulovo 37 S 1
Ulricehamn 17 F 4
Ulsan 39 J 3
Ulsta 2 D 1
Ulsteinvik 16 E 3
Ultevis 16 G 2
Ulu 43 G 3
Ulu 60 E 6
Ulubat Gölü 20 C 2
Uludağ 20 C 2–3
Ulugqat 35 J 3
Ulukışla 21 D 3
Ulunga 37 P 6
Ulungur He 35 M 1
Ulungur Hu 35 M 1
Ulunkhan 36 K 5
Uluru (Ayers Rock - Mount Olga) National Park 48 E 4
Ulus 21 D 2
Ulutau, Gory 35 H 1
Ulva 3 A 3
Ulverston 5 D 2
Ulvön 16 G 3
Ul'ya 37 Q 4
Ulya 37 Q 4
Ul'yankovo 24 J 4
Ul'yanovsk 24 J 5
Ul'yanovskoye 25 O 5
Uma 36 M 5
Uman' 20 D 1
Umanak 90
Umánaq 75 T 3
Umari 43 J 4
Umarkot 35 HJ 5
Umba 16 K 2
Umboi 50 E 3
Umbozero, Ozero 16 KL 2
Umbria 19 F 3
Umeå 16 H 3
Umeälven 16 G 3
Umiat 72 G 2
Umm al 'Abīd 59 J 3
Umm al Arānib 59 H 3
'Umm al Armad (Qatar) 23 F 4
Umm al Birak (Saudi Arabia) 22 C 5
Umm al Ḥayt, Wādī 61 J 5
Umm al Jamājim (Saudi Arabia) 23 D 4
Umm al Qaywayn (United Arab Emirates) 23 G 4
'Umm al Sheif (United Arab Emirates) 23 F 4
Umm as Samīm 61 K 4
'Umm at Ṭūz (Iraq) 22 D 2
Umm az Zumūl 61 K 4
Umm az Zumūl (United Arab Emirates) 23 G 5
Umm Bāb (Qatar) 23 F 4
Umm Badr 60 D 6
Umm Bel 60 D 6
Umm Buru 60 C 5
Umm Dafok 60 C 6
Umm Dhibbān 60 DE 6
Umm Durmān 60 E 5
Umm Hagar 65 F 2
Umm Haraz 60 C 6
Umm Inderaba 60 E 5
Umm Kaddādah 60 D 6
Umm Lahai 60 D 5
Umm Lajj (Saudi Arabia) 22 B 4
'Umm Qam'ul (United Arab Emirates) 23 G 4
Umm Qawzayn 60 D 6
Umm Rumaylah 60 E 5
Umm Ruwābah 60 E 6
'Umm Saīd (Qatar) 23 F 4
Umm Sa'id → Musay'īd 61 J 4
Umm Sayyālah 60 E 6
Umm Urūmah (Saudi Arabia) 22 B 4
Umma (Iraq) 23 D 3
Umnak 72 D 5
Umnyn Syverma, Khrebet 36 GH 2
Umpilua 67 F 2
Umpulo 66 B 2
Umraniye 20 D 3
Ums 66 B 4
Umtali → Mutare 67 E 3
Umtata 66 D 6
Umuarama 87 F 5
Umvuma 67 E 3
Una 87 J 4
Una (Yugoslavia) 19 G 2
Unadilla 77 K 5
Unaí 87 G 4
Unai Pass 35 H 4
Unalakleet 72 E 3
Unalaska 72 D 5
Unapoo 2 B 2
Unari 16 J 2
'Unayzah (Jordan) 22 B 3
'Unayzah (Saudi Arabia) 22 D 4
Underberg 66 D 5
Undva Neem 17 H 4
Undyulyung 37 N 2
Unecha 24 F 5
Uneiuxi 84 E 4
Ung, Jabal al 19 E 4
Unga 72 E 4
Ungava Bay 75 O 4
Ungava, Peninsule d' 75 MN 4
Ungwatiri 60 F 5
Uniabmund 66 A 4
União (Acre, Brazil) 84 D 5
União (Maranhão, Brazil) 87 H 1
União do Vitória 88 F 4
União dos Palmares 87 J 2
Unije 19 F 3
Unimak 72 E 5
Unimak Pass 72 E 5
Unini 85 F 4
Unión 89 C 6
Union City 77 J 4
Union of Soviet Socialist Republics 24–37
Uniondale 66 C 6
United Arab Emirates 23 FG 5
United Kingdom 14 CD 3–4
United States 76–77
Unitsa 24 FG 3
Unity 73 Q 5
Universales, Montes 18 C 3
University City 77 H 4
Unkyur 37 O 2
'Unnab, Wādi al (Jordan) 22 B 3
Unnao 40 D 2
Unst 2 D 1
Unuli Horog 38 B 3
Ünye 21 E 2
Unzba 24 H 4
Unzha 24 H 4
Uoyan 36 K 4
Upanu 37 X 3
Upar Ghat 40 D 3
Upata 85 F 2
Upavon 7 D 2
Upemba, Lac 64 D 6
Upemba National Park 64 D 6
Upernavik 90
Upi 43 F 2
Upington 66 C 5
Upolu 52 D 3
Upper Arlington 77 K 3
Upper Broughton 7 D 1
Upper Klamath Lake 76 B 3
Upper Lough Erne 4 B 2
Upper Red Lake 77 H 2
Upper Tean 7 D 1
Upperlands 4 B 2
Uppingham 7 D 1
Uppland 17 G 3
Uppsala 17 G 4
Upshi 35 K 4
Upwey 6 C 2
'Uqlat as Ṣuqūr (Saudi Arabia) 22 C 4
Ur 61 H 2
Ur Suq ash Shuyūkh (Iraq) 23 DE 3
Ura Guba 16 K 2
Uracoa 85 F 2
Urad Qianqi 38 E 2
Urad Zhonghou Lianheqi 38 E 2
Urak 37 Q 4
Ural 34 E 1
Ural Mountains 25 LM 2–4
Uralovka 37 N 5
Ural'sk 24 K 5
Urambo 64 E 6
Urandangie 49 F 3
Urandi 87 H 3
Urangan 49 J 4
Uranium City 73 Q 4
Uraricoera 85 F 3
Uraricoera 85 F 3
Ura-Tyube 35 H 3
'Uray'irah (Saudi Arabia) 23 E 4
'Urayq, Nafūd al 61 G 3–4
Urbandale 77 H 3
Urbano Santos 87 H 1
Urbino 19 F 3
Urco 84 D 4
Urcos 86 B 3
Urdzhar 25 Q 6
Uré 84 C 2
Ure, River 5 E 2
Ureki 21 F 2
Uren 24 J 4
Urengoy 25 P 2
Urewera National Park 51 R 8
Urez 25 P 4
'Urf, Jabal al (Egypt) 22 A 4
Urfa 21 E 3
Urfa (Turkey) 22 C 1
Urfa Platosu 21 E 3
Urgamal 36 F 6
Urgel, Llano de 18 D 3
Urgench 34 FG 2
Ürgüp 21 D 3
Urgut 35 H 3
Urho 35 M 1
Ūrī 59 J 4
Uribe 84 D 3
Uribia 84 D 1
Urimán 85 F 2
Uritskoye 25 N 5
Uritskoye 37 M 3
Urjala 16 H 3
Urkan 37 N 5
Urla 20 C 3
Urlu Dağ 21 D 2
Uruk 36 J 5
Urmannyy 25 N 3
Urmi 37 O 5
Urmia, Lake → Daryācheh-ye Orūmīyeh 34 D 3
Urninskoye Boloto 25 O 4
Uromi 63 F 4
Uroševac 20 B 2
Urrao 84 C 2
Urshult 17 FG 4
Ursus 15 H 4
Uruaçu 87 G 3
Uruana 87 FG 4
Uruapan 78 B 4
Urubamba 86 B 3
Urubamba 86 B 3
Urubu 85 G 4
Urubupunga Dam 87 F 5
Urubuquara, Serra 85 H 4
Urucará 85 G 4
Urucu 85 F 4
Uruçuca 87 J 3
Uruçuí 87 H 2
Uruçui Prêto 87 GH 2
Uruçui, Serra do 87 H 2
Urucuia 87 G 4
Urucurituba 85 G 4
Uruguaiana 88 E 4
Uruguay 88 E 5
Uruguay 88 E 5
Uruk (Iraq) 23 D 3
Urul'ga 36 KL 5
Urumchi 35 M 2
Ürümqi 35 M 2
Urup 21 F 2
Urup, Ostrov 37 S 6
'Uruq ar Rumaylah 61 H 4
'Urūq as Subay' 61 G 4
Urusha 37 M 5
Urutágua 87 G 3
Uruwira 64 E 6
Uruzgan 35 H 4
Uryung-Khaya 36 KL 1
Uryupinsk 24 H 5
Urzhum 24 J 4
Urziceni 20 C 2
Usa 25 M 2
Uşak 20 C 3
Usakos 66 B 4
Usal'gin 37 P 5
Usambara Mountains 65 F 5
Usborne, Mount 89 E 9
Ušće 20 B 2
Usedom 15 F 4
'Usfān 61 F 4
'Ushayrah (Saudi Arabia) 23 DE 4
Ushirombo 64 E 5
Ushkan'iy, Gory 37 X 2
Ushki 37 U 4
Ushki, Zaliv 37 R 4
Ush-Tobe 25 P 6
Ushuaia 89 C 9
Ushumun 37 N 5
Ushurakchan, Gory 37 U 2
Usina 85 H 5
Usinge 64 E 6
Usk 6 C 2
Uska 40 D 2
Üsküdar 20 C 2
Usman 24 GH 5
Usmas ezers 17 H 4
Usoke 64 E 6
Usol'ye 24 L 4
Usol'ye-Sibirskoye 36 H 5
Uspenka 25 P 5
Uspenskiy 25 O 6
Uspenskoye 21 F 2
U.S.S.R. 21 F 1
Ussuri 37 O 6
Ussuriysk 39 K 2
Ust Usa 24 J 5
Ust'-Allakh 37 O 3
Ust'-Amginskoye 37 O 3
Ust'-Barguzin 36 JK 5
Ust'-Bokhapcha 37 S 3
Ust'-Bol'sheretsk 37 ST 5
Ust'-Charky 37 P 2
Ust'-Chayka 36 J 3
Ust'-Chernaya 24 K 3
Ust'-Chona 36 K 3
Ust'-Dzhegutinskaya 21 F 2
Uster 19 E 2
Usti 15 F 4
Ustica 19 F 4
Ust'-Ilimpeya 36 HJ 3
Ust'-Ilimsk 36 H 4
Ust'-Ilimskiy Vodokhranilishche 36 H 4
Ustinov 24 K 4
Ustinovka 21 D 1
Ust'-Ishim 25 O 4
Ustka 15 G 4
Ust-Kada 36 H 5
Ust'-Kamchatsk 37 U 4
Ust'-Kamenogorsk 25 Q 6
Ust'-Kamo 36 G 3
Ust'-Kan 36 F 4
Ust'-Karabula 36 G 4
Ust'-Karenga 36 L 5
Ust'-Karsk 36 L 5
Ust'-Katav 25 L 5
Ust'-Khayryuzovo 37 T 4
Ust'-Koksa 25 R 5
Ust'-Kolik'yegan 25 P 3
Ust'-Kulom 24 K 3
Ust'-Kut 36 J 4
Ust'-Kuyga 37 P 2
Ust-Labinsk 21 EF 1
Ust'-Luga 17 J 4
Ust'-Lyzha 24 L 2
Ust'-Maya 37 O 3
Ust'-Mayn 37 W 3
Ust'-Mil' 37 O 4
Ust'-Nem 24 K 3
Ust'-Nera 37 Q 3
Ust'-Olenëk 36 L 1
Ust'-Omchug 37 R 3
Ust'-Ordynskiy 36 HJ 5
Ust'-Ozernoye 25 R 4
Ust'-Paden'ga 24 H 3
Ust'-Penzhino 37 V 3
Ust'-Pit 36 F 4
Ust'-Port 25 Q 2
Ust'-Reka 24 J 3
Ustrem 25 N 3
Ust'-Shchugor 24 L 3
Ust'-Sopochnoye 37 T 4
Ust'-Sugoy 37 S 3
Ust'-Tatta 37 O 3
Ust'-Tigil 37 T 4
Ust'-Tsil'ma 24 K 2
Ust'-Tym 25 Q 4
Ust'-Ulagan 25 R 5
Ust'-Umal'ta 37 O 5
Ust'-Un'ya 37 N 5
Ust'-Ura 24 H 3
Ust'-Urgal 37 O 5
Ust'Urov 36 M 5
Ust'-Us 36 F 5
Ust'-Usa 24 L 2
Ust'-Uyskoye 25 M 5
Ustyurt, Plato 34 F 2
Ust'-Vaga 24 H 3
Ust'-Voyampolka 37 T 4
Ust'-Vym' 24 K 3
Ust'-Vyyskaya 24 J 3
Ust'-Yudoma 37 P 4
Ust'-Yuribey 25 N 2
Usu 35 L 2
Usulután 78 E 5
Usumacinta 78 D 4
Utah 76 D 4
Utah Lake 76 D 3
Utajärvi 16 J 3
Utara, Pulau 42 B 4
Utata 36 H 5
Utena 17 J 4
Utës 25 P 5
Utesiki 37 W 2
Utete 65 F 6
Uthai Thani 41 H 4
Uthal 35 H 5
Uthumphon Phisai 41 H 5
Utiariti 86 E 3
Utica 77 M 3
Utiel 18 C 4
Utique 19 F 4
Utirik 52 C 2
Utkholok 37 T 4
Utlängan 17 G 4
Utopia 48 E 3
Utorgosh 17 K 4
Utrecht 14 E 4
Utrera 18 B 4
Utsjoki 16 J 2
Utsunomiya 39 L 3
Utta 21 G 1
Uttar Pradesh 40 D 2
Uttaradit 41 H 4
Uttoxeter 7 D 1
Uttyakh 37 O 2
Utukok 72 E 2
Utulik 36 H 5
Utupua 51 J 4
Uulbayan 38 F 1
Uuldza 36 K 6
Uuldza Gol 36 K 6
Uusikaarlepyy 16 H 3
Uusikaupunki 17 H 3
Uusimaa 17 H 3
Uva 24 K 4
Uvá (Goiás, Brazil) 87 F 4
Uvalde 76 G 6
Uvarovo 24 H 5
Uvdal 17 E 3
Uvéa 52 D 3
Uvinza 64 E 6
Uvira 64 D 5
Uvs Nuur 36 F 5
Uwajima 39 K 4
Uwayl 64 D 3
'Uwaynāt, Jabal al 60 D 4
'Uwaynāt, Tall (Iraq) 22 D 1
'Uwayrid, Ḥarrat al 60 F 3
Uxin Qi 38 E 3
Uxituba 85 G 4
Uxmal 78 E 3

W

X

Z

MAP SYMBOLS

Symbols

Scale 1:5 000 000, 1:10 000 000

Bombay	More than 5 000 000 inhabitants
Milano	1 000 000 – 5 000 000 inhabitants
Zürich	250 000 – 1 000 000 inhabitants
Dijon	100 000 – 250 000 inhabitants
Dover	25 000 – 100 000 inhabitants
Torquay	Less than 25 000 inhabitants
Tachiumet	Small sites
WIEN	National capital
Atlanta	State capital

Major road

Other road

Road under construction

Railway

Railway under construction

Train ferry

National boundary

Disputed national boundary

State boundary

Disputed state boundary

Undefined boundary in the sea

4807	Height above sea-level in metres
3068	Depth in metres
	National park
Niniveh	Ruin
	Pass
KAINJI DAM	Dam
	Wadi
	Canal
	Waterfall
	Reef

Symbols

Scale 1:15 000 000, 1:25 000 000, 1:27 000 000, 1:30 000 000

Shanghai	More than 5 000 000 inhabitants
Barcelona	1 000 000 – 5 000 000 inhabitants
Venice	250 000 – 1 000 000 inhabitants
Aberdeen	50 000 – 250 000 inhabitants
Beida	Less than 50 000 inhabitants
Mawson	Scientific station
CAIRO	National capital

Major road

Railway

Railway under construction

National boundary

Disputed national boundary

State boundary

Disputed state boundary

Undefined boundary in the sea

8848	Height above sea-level in metres
11034	Depth in metres
2645	Thickness of ice cap
	Dam
Thebes	Ruin
	Wadi
	Canal
	Waterfall
	Reef